Gravel Edition / Pentagon Papers / Volume II

The Senator Gravel Edition

The Pentagon Papers

*The Defense Department
History of United States
Decisionmaking on Vietnam*

Volume II

Beacon Press *Boston*

The contents of this volume are drawn from the
official record of the U.S. Senate Subcommittee
on Public Buildings and Grounds. No copyright is claimed
in the text of this official Government document.

Library of Congress catalog card number: 75–178049

International Standard Book Number: 0–8070–0526–6 (hardcover)
0–8070–0527–4 (paperback)

Beacon Press books are published under the
auspices of the Unitarian Universalist Association

Printed in the United States of America

EXPLANATORY NOTE

The preparation of the subcommittee record was performed under the direction of Senator Gravel. No material was added to or changed in the study or appended documents and statements. In some cases, material was illegible or missing. If this occurred within a direct quotation, the omission was indicated with a bracketed statement. If it occurred in narrative text, it was bridged by removing the entire sentence in which it appeared, when it was evident that no substantive material would be lost by this procedure; otherwise, the omission was indicated by a bracketed statement. All other bracketed insertions appear in the original study.

Contents

[*At the end of each volume is a collection of documents, a section entitled "Justification of the War—Public Statements," and a Glossary*]

Contents of Volume II

Gravel Edition / Pentagon Papers / Volume II

1.   The Kennedy Commitments and Programs, 1961

Summary and Analysis

When Kennedy took office, the prospect of an eventual crisis in Vietnam had been widely recognized in the government, although nothing much had yet been done about it. Our Ambassador in Saigon had been sending worried cables for a year, and twice in recent months [in September 1960 and again in December] had ended an appraisal of the situation by cautiously raising the question of whether the U.S. would not sooner or later have to move to replace Diem. Barely a week after taking office, Kennedy received and approved a Counter-Insurgency Plan (CIP) which, at what seems to have been a rather leisurely pace, had been going through drafting and staffing for the previous eight months.

The CIP was a most modest program by the standard we have become accustomed to in Vietnam. It offered Diem financial support for a 20,000 man increase in his army, which then stood at 150,000; plus support for about half of the counter-guerrilla auxiliary force known as the Civil Guard. In return, it asked Diem for a number of reforms which appeared to the American side as merely common sense—such as straightening out command arrangements for the army under which 42 different officials directly responsible to Diem (38 province chiefs, 3 regional commanders, and a Chief of Staff) shared operational command.

The CIP was superseded in May by an enlarged version of the same program, and the only longer term significance the original program held was that it presumably offered the Administration a lesson in dealing with Diem (and perhaps, although it was not foreseen then, a lesson in dealing with Vietnamese governments generally). The negotiations dragged on and on; the U.S. military and eventually most of the civilians both in Saigon and Washington grew impatient for getting on with the war; Diem promised action on some of the American points, and finally even issued some decrees, none of which were really followed up. For practical purposes, the list of "essential reforms" proposed as part of the CIP, including those Diem had given the impression he agreed to, could have been substituted unchanged for the list of reforms the U.S. requested at the end of the year, with equal effect, as the quid pro quo demanded for the much enlarged U.S. aid offer that followed the Taylor Mission.

Negotiations with Diem came to an end in May, not because the issues had been resolved, but because the U.S. decided to forget trying to pressure Diem for a while and instead try to coax him into reforming by winning his confidence. Partly, no doubt, this reflected the view that pressure was getting nowhere and the alternative approach might do better. Mainly, however, the changed policy, and the somewhat enlarged aid program that accompanied it, reflected the pressures created by the situation in neighboring Laos. (We will see that there is a strong case to be made that even the Fall, post-Taylor Mission, decisions were essentially dominated by the impact of Laos. But in May the situation was unambiguous. Laos, not anything happening in Vietnam, was the driving force.)

A preliminary step came April 20. Immediately following the Bay of Pigs disaster, and with the prospect of a disaster in Laos on the very near horizon, Kennedy asked Deputy Secretary of Defense Gilpatric to work up a program for saving Vietnam. The program was delivered, as requested, a week later. It was a somewhat enlarged version of the CIP, with the implication, not spelled out in the paper, that the new effort would be put into effect without making any demands on Diem. (Simultaneously, Ambassador Durbow, who had been in Vietnam for four years, was being replaced by Nolting, and this added to the hope that a new start might be made with Diem.) There is nothing to suggest that anything more was expected of Gilpatric's program, and indeed all the evidence suggests that the main point of the exercise was to work General Lansdale into the role of government-wide coordinator and manager of the country's first major test in the new art of counter-insurgency. Lansdale served as Executive Officer of the Task Force which Gilpatric organized and which he proposed should be given a continuing, dominant role in managing the Vietnamese enterprise.

By the time the report was submitted on April 27 when the Laos crisis was reaching its peak, a new Geneva conference had been agreed upon. But there were serious doubts that the pro-western side in Laos would be left with anything to negotiate about by the time the conference opened. Even the U.S.-favored settlement (a coalition government) represented a major, if prudent, retreat from the previous U.S. position taken during the closing months of the Eisenhower Administration.) So the situation in Laos was bad, if unavoidable; and it followed right on the heels of the Bay of Pigs, and at a time when the Soviets were threatening to move against Berlin. The emphasis of the Gilpatric Task Force shifted from shaping up the counter-insurgency aid program for Vietnam, to finding ways to demonstrate to the South Vietnamese (and others) that a further retreat in Laos would not foreshadow an imminent retreat in Vietnam.

On April 28, an annex to the Task Force report proposed to counter the impact of Laos with U.S. support for an increase in South Vietnamese forces (the original report had proposed only more generous financial support for forces already planned under the CIP) and, further, a modest commitment of U.S. ground combat units in South Vietnam, with the nominal mission of establishing two training centers. On April 29, Kennedy endorsed the proposals of the original draft, but took no action on the far more significant proposals in the annex. On May 1, a revised Task Force draft came out, incorporating the Laos Annex proposals, and adding a recommendation that the U.S. make clear an intent to intervene in Vietnam to the extent needed to prevent a Viet Cong victory. At this point, practical control of the Task Force appears to have shifted out of Gilpatric's (and Defense's) hands to State (and, apparently, George Ball.) A State redraft of the report came out May 3, which eliminated the special role laid out for Lansdale, shifted the chairmanship of the continuing Task Force to State, and blurred, without wholly eliminating, the Defense-drafted recommendations for sending U.S. combat units to Vietnam and for public U.S. commitments to save South Vietnam from Communism. But even the State re-draft recommended consideration of stationing American troops in Vietnam, for missions not involving combat with the Viet Cong, and a bilateral U.S.-SVN security treaty. On May 4 and 5, still acting under the pressure of the Laos crisis, the Administration implied (through a statement by Senator Fulbright at the White House following a meeting with Kennedy, and at Kennedy's press conference the next day) that it was considering stationing American forces in Vietnam. On May 6, a final draft of the Task Force report came out, essentially following the State draft of May 3. On May 8, Kennedy signed a letter to Diem, to be delivered by Vice President Johnson the next week, which promised Diem strong U.S. support, but did not go beyond the program out-lined in the original Task Force report; it offered neither to finance expanded South Vietnamese forces, nor to station American troops in Vietnam. On May 11, the recommendations of the final, essentially State-drafted, report were formalized. But by now, the hoped for cease-fire in Laos had come off. Vice President Johnson in Saigon on the 12th of May followed through on his in-structions to proclaim strong U.S. support for and confidence in Diem. When Diem talked of his worries about U.S. policy in Laos, Johnson, obviously acting on instructions, raised the possibility of stationing American troops in Vietnam or of a bilateral treaty. But Diem wanted neither at that time. Johnson's in-structions were not available to this study, so we do not know how he would have responded if Diem had asked for either troops or a treaty, although the language of the Task Force report implies he would only have indicated a U.S. willingness to talk about these things. With Johnson, came the new Ambassador, Fritz Nolting, whose principal instruction was to "get on Diem's wavelength" in contrast to the pressure tactics of his predecessor.

A few weeks later, in June, Diem, responding to an invitation Kennedy had sent through Johnson, dispatched an aide to Washington with a letter outlining Saigon's "essential military needs." It asked for a large increase in U.S. support for Vietnamese forces (sufficient to raise ARVN strength from 170,000 to 270,000 men), and also for the dispatch of "selected elements of the American Armed Forces", both to establish training centers for the Vietnamese and as a symbol of American commitment to Vietnam. The proposal, Diem said, had been worked out with the advice of MAAG Saigon, whose chief, along with the JCS and at least some civilian officials, strongly favored getting American troops into Vietnam.

The question of increased support for Vietnamese forces was resolved through the use of the Staley Mission. This was normally a group of economic experts intended to work with a Vietnamese group on questions of economic policy. Particularly at issue was whether the Vietnamese could not be financing a larger share of their own defenses. But the economic proposals and programs, all of which turned out to be pretty general and fuzzy, comprised a less impor-tant part of the report than the discussion of Vietnamese military requirements. Here the study group reflected the instructions of the two governments. On the basis of the Staley Report, the U.S. agreed to support a further increase of 30,000 in the RVNAF, but deferred a decision on the balance of the South Vietnamese request on the grounds that the question might not have to be faced since by the time the RVNAF reached 200,000 men, sometime late in 1962, the Viet Cong might already be on the run. The Staley Report also contained what by now had already become the usual sorts of nice words about the importance of social, political, and administrative reforms, which turned out to have the usual relevance to reality. The U.S. was still sticking to the May formula of try-ing to coax Diem to reform, instead of the equally unsuccessful January formula of trying to pressure him to reform.

The other issue—the request for "elements of the American Armed Forces" —was left completely obscure. From the record available, we are not sure that Diem really wanted the troops then, or whether Kennedy really was willing to send them if they were wanted. All we know is that Diem included some language in his letter that made the request a little ambiguous, and that Washington—either on the basis of clarification from Diem's aide who delivered the letter, or on its own initiative, or some combination of both—interpreted the letter as not asking for troops, and nothing came of the apparent request.

A new, and much more serious sense of crisis developed in September. This time the problem was not directly Laos, but strong indications of moderate deterioration of Diem's military position and very substantial deterioration of morale in Saigon. There was a sharp upswing in Viet Cong attacks in September, including a spectacular raid on a province capital 55 miles from Saigon during which the province chief was publicly beheaded by the insurgents. At the end of September, Diem surprised Nolting by asking the U.S. for a U.S.-GVN defense treaty. By Diem's account the loss of morale in Saigon was due to worries about U.S. policy growing out of the Laos situation. Both U.S. officials in Washington and South Vietnamese other than those closest to Diem, though, put most of the blame on deterioration within South Vietnam, although the demoralizing effect of Viet Cong successes was unquestionably magnified by uncertainties about the U.S. commitment to Vietnam. In response, President Kennedy sent General Taylor and Walt Rostow, then both on the White House staff, to Vietnam, accompanied by some less prominent officials from State and Defense.

What Taylor and Rostow reported was that Saigon faced a dual crisis of confidence, compounded out of doubts arising from Laos that the U.S. would stick by South Vietnam, and doubts arising from the Viet Cong successes that Diem's unpopular and inefficient regime could beat the Viet Cong anyway. The report said that a U.S. military commitment in Vietnam was needed to meet the first difficulty; and that the second could best be met by supplying a generous infusion of American personnel to all levels of the Vietnamese government and army, who could, it was hoped, instill the Vietnamese with the right kind of winning spirit, and reform the regime "from the bottom up" despite Diem's weaknesses. The report recommended the dispatch of helicopter companies and other forms of combat support, but without great emphasis on these units. Probably, although the record does not specifically say so, there was a general understanding that such units would be sent even before the report was submitted, and that is why there is relatively little emphasis on the need for them.

The crucial issue was what form the American military commitment had to take to be effective. Taylor, in an eyes only cable to the President, argued strongly for a task force in the delta, consisting mainly of army engineers to work where there had been a major flood. The *delta* was also where the VC were strongest, and Taylor warned the President that the force would have to conduct some combat operations and expect to take casualties. But Taylor argued that the balance of the program, less this task force, would be insufficient, for we had to "convince Diem that we are willing to join him in a showdown with the Viet Cong . . ."

We do not know what advice President Kennedy received from State: Sorenson claims all the President's advisors on Vietnam favored sending the ground force; but George Ball, at least, who may not have been part of the formal decision group, is widely reported to have opposed such a move; so did Galbraith, then Ambassador to India, who happened to be in Washington; and perhaps some others. From Defense, the President received a memo from McNamara for himself, Gilpatric, and the JCS, stating that they were "inclined to recommend" the Taylor program, but only on the understanding that it would be followed up with more troops as needed, and with a willingness to attack North Vietnam. (The JCS estimated that 40,000 American troops would be needed to "clean up" the Viet Cong.) The Taylor Mission Report, and Taylor's own cables, had also stressed a probable need to attack, or at least threaten to attack, North Vietnam.

The McNamara memo was sent November 8. But on November 11, Rusk and McNamara signed a joint memo that reversed McNamara's earlier position: it recommended deferring, at least for the time being, the dispatch of combat units. This obviously suited Kennedy perfectly, and the NSAM embodying the decisions was taken essentially verbatim from the recommendations of the Rusk/McNamara paper, except that a recommendation that the U.S. was commiting itself to prevent the loss of Vietnam was deleted.

But where the Taylor Report had implied a continuation of the May policy of trying to coax Diem into cooperating with the U.S., the new program was made contingent on Diem's acceptance of a list of reforms; further Diem was to be informed that if he accepted the program the U.S. would expect to "share in decision-making" . . . rather than "advise only." Thus, the effect of the decision was to give Diem less than he was expecting (no symbolic commitment of ground forces) but to accompany this limited offer with demands for which Diem was obviously both unprepared and unwilling to accede to. On top of this, there was the enormous (and not always recognized) extent to which U.S. policy was driven by the unthinkability of avoidably risking another defeat in Southeast Asia hard on the heels of the Laos retreat.

Consequently, the U.S. bargaining position was feeble. Further, Galbraith at least, and probably others, advised Kennedy that there was not much point to bargaining with Diem anyway, since he would never follow through on any promises he made. (Galbraith favored promoting an anti-Diem military coup at the earliest convenient moment.) Kennedy ended up settling for a set of promises that fell well short of any serious effort to make the aid program really contingent on reforms by Diem. Since the war soon thereafter began to look better, Kennedy never had any occasion to reconsider his decision on combat troops; and no urgent reason to consider Galbraith's advice on getting rid of Diem until late 1963.

End of Summary and Analysis

CHRONOLOGY

1960–1961   *Situation in Vietnam*
According to Ambassador Durbrow there was widespread popular dissatisfaction with the Diem Government and a growing guerrilla threat. At the same time, there had been a very gradual growth of U.S. involvement in assisting the GVN to counter the VC.
In the U.S. two questions influenced decisions about Vietnam: first, what should the U.S. give Diem to counter the communists; secondly, what—if any—demands should be posed as a *quid pro quo* for assistance?

US–Soviet Relations
The problems of dealing with Moscow were far more pressing than those related to Vietnam. A feeling that America's position

in the world had been eroded by the USSR prevailed; Kennedy was particularly determined to regain American strength, prestige and influence. Anything which could be construed as American weakness *vis-a-vis* the USSR was to be avoided. This affected policy toward Vietnam.

Situation in Laos

The US-backed, pro-American faction under Phoumi Nosavan was losing to the pro-Communist/neutralist faction supported by the Soviet Union.

Commitment of U.S. forces was rejected and on May 2, 1961 a cease-fire was declared. President Kennedy decided to support a coalition solution, even though the odds on coalition leader Souvanna Phouma's staying in power were very low. As a consequence of this decision, Washington believed that Southeast Asian leaders doubted the sincerity of the U.S. commitment to the area, and the U.S. felt compelled to do something to restore confidence, demonstrate U.S. resolve and dispel any idea Moscow might have that the U.S. intended to withdraw from Southeast Asia. Laos was thus particularly influential in development of policy toward Vietnam.

20 Jan 1961   *President Kennedy Inaugurated*

28 Jan 1961   *Kennedy Approves the Counterinsurgency Plan (CIP) for Vietnam*
Gradually developed during 1961, the CIP was to be the basis for expanded U.S. assistance to Vietnam. Kennedy automatically approved its main provisions; negotiations with Diem about the CIP began 13 February and continued through May of 1961. The U.S. offered $28.4 million to support a 20,000-man increase in the ARVN (for a new total of 170,000); to train, equip and supply a 32,000-man Civil Guard at $12.7 million. The full package added less than $42 million to the current $220 million aid program.

The CIP called for consolidation of the RVNAF chain of command (never fully accomplished under Diem.) No agreement was reached on the question of strategy during this period. (Diem wanted "strategic" outposts, Agrovilles, lines of strength throughout the country; the MAAG favored a "net and spear" concept— small units operating out of pacified areas to find the enemy, call in reserve forces, gradually extend security to all of Vietnam.) Civil reforms included urging Diem to broaden his government, include opposition political leaders in the cabinet, give the National Assembly some power, institute civic action to win hearts, minds and loyalty of the peasants.

The CIP assumed the GVN had the potential to cope with the VC if necessary corrective measures were taken and if adequate forces were provided. The implicit bargain of the plan: the U.S. would support "adequate forces" *if* Diem would institute "necessary corrective measures." Again, although sociopolitical reforms were sought through the CIP and other plans, they were not realized during the early Kennedy years.

Mid-Jan 1961 *A Lansdale Report on Vietnam*
Following a trip to Vietnam, Major General E. G. Lansdale called for strong support for Diem and recommended the U.S. demonstrate that support immediately. Only if Diem's confidence in the U.S. were restored would U.S. influence be effective, said Lansdale. He recommended the immediate transfer of Durbrow (he was "too close to the forest" and was not trusted by the GVN) and immediate adoption of social, economic, political and military programs to prove U.S. backing for Diem as well as help Diem stabilize the countryside.

February– *Durbrow Negotiations with Diem on the CIP*
May 1961 Diem stalled the implementation of his "major promises" (to establish a central intelligence organization, put operational control for counterinsurgency operations under the military command system, reform the cabinet and governmental administration). Washington held up the "green light" on aid as long as Diem stalled—although the JCS and MAAG in Saigon were impatient to get on with the war and were annoyed by the delay. Finally, in mid-May (after Durbrow had ended his four-year tour in Vietnam) Diem implemented some "major promises" by decree. But nothing changed.

12 Apr 1961 *Rostow Memorandum for President Kennedy*
W. W. Rostow suggested several ways for "gearing-up the whole Vietnam operation." These included: assigning a first-rate, full-time backstop man in Washington to Vietnam affairs (Lansdale); a Vice Presidential visist in Southeast Asia; exploring ways to use new American techniques and gadgets in the fight against the VC; replacing the ICA (AID) chief; high-level discussion of tactics for persuading Diem to broaden his government; a Presidential letter to Diem in which Kennedy would reaffirm support for him but express the urgency attached to finding a "more effective political and morale setting" for military operations.

20 Apr 1961 *The Presidential Program for Vietnam*
Deputy Secretary of Defense Gilpatric was directed to appraise the current status and future prospects of the VC drive in South Vietnam, then recommend a series of actions to prevent communist domination of the GVN.
(At this same time: the Bay of Pigs invasion force surrendered and the Laos crisis was coming to a head.)
Gilpatric and Lansdale headed a Task Force established immediately to carry out these instructions.

27 Apr 1961 *Gilpatric Task Force Report Submitted; the NSC Meets*
This first Task Force draft called for a moderate acceleration of the CIP program approved in January, with stress on vigor, enthusiasm and strong leadership. The report recommended building on present US-GVN programs, infusing them with a new sense of urgency and creating action programs in almost every field to create a viable and increasingly democratic government in SVN to prevent communist domination. No ARVN increase beyond the already-authorized 20,000-man addition was recommended; a

modest MAAG increase was proposed. The US would support the Civil Guard and Self-Defense Corps. Emphasis was on stabilizing the countryside, not on pressing Diem for political or administrative reforms. (Gilpatric wanted Lansdale to go to Vietnam immediately after the program was approved to consult with Vietnamese and US leaders and make further recommendations for action; but McNamara made Lansdale's mission contingent upon an invitation from the US Ambassador in Saigon—an invitation that never came.)

The NSC was to discuss this report but the 27 April meeting was dominated by the acute Laotian crisis.

28 Apr 1961   *Laos Annex to (first) Task Force Report*
A report—a response, really—concerning the critical situation in Laos and its effect on Vietnam was prepared for the NSC on 28 April. It recommended a two-division ARVN increase and deployment of 3600 US troops to Vietnam (two 1600-man teams to train each new division; 400 Special Forces troops to speed overall ARVN counterinsurgency training). Rationale: to enable ARVN to guard against conventional invasion of South Vietnam. (Both the increased forces and their justification were different from two earlier reports. Lansdale had advocated no ARVN increase but felt some US force build-up was called for as a demonstration of American support for the GVN. Gilpatric's military aide, Colonel E. F. Black, wrote the other report which saw no need for more US troops but recommended expansion of ARVN to meet the threat of increased infiltration. These views were rejected in favor of Black's second paper which advocated more ARVN troops—to counter overt aggression, not increased infiltration—and commitment of US troops for training purposes —not for political reassurance or demonstration of US resolve. Black's second paper was sent to the NSC.)

29 Apr 1961   *Kennedy Decisions on the Draft Report*
Kennedy did not act on the Laos Annex. He approved only the limited military proposals contained in the first Gilpatric Task Force report. The 685-man MAAG would be increased to 785 to enable it to train the approved 20,000 new ARVN troops. Kennedy also authorized the MAAG to support and advise the Self Defense Corps (40,000 men); authorized MAP support for the entire Civil Guard of 68,000 (*vice* 32,000 previously supported); ordered installation of radar surveillance equipment and okayed MAP support and training for the Vietnamese Junk Force.

1 May 1961   *NSC Meets; New Draft of the Task Force Report Issued*
Kennedy again deferred decision on sending troops into Laos apparently because the feeling that the US would not make such a move was now firm.

The 1 May draft report was little different from the 28 April version. The Laos Annex was incorporated into the main paper; the US was to make known its readiness to "intervene unilaterally" in Southeast Asia to fulfill SEATO commitments (*vice* intervene in conjunction with SEATO forces). ARVN increases were now justified by the threat of overt aggression as well as increased infiltration.

3 May 1961   *State (George Ball) Revision of Task Force Report*
This draft was very different from the original. Lansdale's role was eliminated; the Gilpatric-Lansdale Task Force was to be replaced by a new group chaired by Ball, then Undersecretary of State. (Lansdale reacted with a "strong recommendation" that Defense stay out of the directorship proposed by State and said the "US past performance and theory of action, which State apparently desires to continue, simply offers no sound basis for winning. . .") In State's rewritten political section of the report, the Defense recommendation to make clear US determination to intervene unilaterally if necessary to save South Vietnam from communism was replaced by a proposal to explore new bilateral treaty arrangements with Diem (arrangements which might mean intervention against the guerrillas but might mean intervention only against DRV attack). The need for new arrangements was tied to the "loss" of Laos. State incorporated unchanged the Defense draft as the military section of its revised report, but implied "further study" would be given to some Defense recommendations. Overall, the State revision tried to tone down commitments to Vietnam suggested in the Defense version. It left the President a great deal of room to maneuver without explicitly overruling recommendations presented him.

5 May 1961   *NSC Meeting*
Again, Laos was the main subject. Most agreed the chance for salvaging anything out of the cease-fire and coalition government was slim indeed. Ways in which to reassure Vietnam and Thailand were sought. The Vice President's trip to Southeast Asia was announced after the meeting.

6 May 1961   *Second State Re-Draft of the Task Force Report*
Here, military actions were contained in an annex; the political section reflected less panic over the loss of Laos; deployment of US troops was less definite—called something which "might result from an NSC decision following discussions between Vice President Johnson and President Diem." The matter is being studied, said the draft. The report said: Diem "is not now fully confident of US support," that it is "essential (his) full confidence in and communication with the United States be restored promptly." (Lansdale's recommendations of January, April, etc.) The report called for a "major alteration in the present government structure," "believed" a combination of inducements plus discreet pressures might work, but it was unenthusiastic both about Diem, and his chances of success. The Diem-is-the-only-available-leader syndrome is evident here.

10 May 1961   *JCSM 320–61*
"Assuming the political decision is to hold Southeast Asia outside the communist sphere," the JCS emphatically recommended deployment of sufficient US forces to provide a visible deterrent to potential DRV/CHICOM action, release ARVN from static to active counterinsurgency operations, assist training and indicate

US firmness. (In JCSM 311–61 of 9 May, the Chiefs recommended deployment of US forces to Thailand also.)

11 May 1961 *NSAM 52*

Directed "full examination" by DOD of a study on the size and composition of forces which might comprise a possible commitment of troops to Southeast Asia. In effect, Kennedy "took note" of the study but made no decision on the issue of troop commitment. The Ambassador in Saigon was empowered to open negotiations about a bilateral treaty but was directed to make no commitments without further review by the President. These recommendations from the May 6 Task Force report were approved: help the GVN increase border patrol and counterinsurgency capability through aerial surveillance and new technological devices; help set up a center to test new weapons and techniques; help ARVN implement health, welfare and public work projects; deploy a 400-man special forces group to Nha Trang to accelerate ARVN training; instruct JCS, CINCPAC, MAAG to assess the military utility of an increase in ARVN from 170,000 to 200,000 (the two-division increase recommended previously).

9–15 May *Vice President Johnson Visits Southeast Asia*
1961

Purpose: to reassure Asian leaders that despite Laos, the United States could be counted on to support them. Johnson reported the mission had halted the decline of confidence in the United States, but did not restore confidence already lost. Johnson strongly believed that faith must be restored, the "battle against communism must be joined in Southeast Asia with strength and determination" (or the US would be reduced to a fortress America with defenses pulled back to California's shores); he believed there was no alternative to US leadership in Southeast Asia but that any help extended—military, economic, social—must be part of a mutual effort and contingent upon Asian willingness to "take the necessary measures to make our aid effective." He reported that American troops were neither required nor desired by Asian leaders at this time.

Calling Thailand and Vietnam the most immediate, most immediate, most important trouble spots, the Vice President said the US "must decide whether to support Diem—or let Vietnam fall," opted for supporting Diem, said "the most important thing is imaginative, creative, American management of our military aid program," and reported $50 million in military and economic assistance "will be needed if we decide to support Vietnam." The same amount was recommended for Thailand.

The Vice President concluded by posing this as the fundamental decision: "whether . . . to meet the challenge of Communist expansion now in Southeast Asia or throw in the towel." Cautioning that "heavy and continuing costs" would be required, that sometime the US "may be faced with the further decision of whether we commit major United States forces to the area or cut our losses and withdraw should our other efforts fail," Johnson recommended "we proceed with a clear-cut and strong program of action."

18 May 1961   *Lansdale Memorandum for Gilpatric*
Landsdale noted Diem's rejection of US combat forces *per se* at this time but pointed out Diem seemed willing to accept troops for training purposes only. At this same time, MAAG Chief McGarr requested 16,000 US troops (combat units) be sent, nominally to establish centers to train RVNAF divisions. If Diem would not accept 16,000, McGarr would settle for 10,000 men.

5 June 1961   *Rostow Note to McNamara*
Saying "we must think of the kind of forces for Thailand now, Vietnam later," Rostow suggested "aircraft, helicopters, communications, men, Special Forces, militia teachers, etc." would be needed to support a "counter-guerrilla war in Vietnam." Rostow does not mention combat units.

9 June 1961   *Diem Letter to Kennedy*
Here, in response to Vice President Johnson's request that he outline military needs, Diem did request US troops explicitly for training RVNAF "officers and technical specialists"—not entire divisions. He proposed ARVN be increased from 170,000 to 270,000 to "counter the ominous threat of communist domination"—a threat he documented by inflated infiltration figures and words about the "perilous" situation created by the Laos solution. To train these 100,000 new ARVN troops Diem asked for "considerable expansion" of the MAAG in the form of "selected elements of the American Armed Forces."

Mid-June to   *The Staley Mission*
July 1961   A team headed by Eugene Staley (Stanford Research Insitute) was to work with Vietnamese officials in an effort to resolve the continuing problem of how Vietnam was to finance its own war effort (deficit financing, inflation, the commodity import program, piaster/dollar exchange rates, all presented difficulties). But the Staley group became the vehicle for force level discussions and economic issues were treated rather perfunctorily. The group "does not consider itself competent to make specific recommendations as to desired force levels" but adopted two alternative levels for "economic planning purposes": 200,000 if the insurgency in Vietnam remains at present levels, if Laos does not fall; 270,000 if the Vietcong significantly increase the insurgency and if the communists win *de facto* control of Laos.

11 Aug 1961   *Kennedy Decision NSAM 65*
President Kennedy agreed with the Staley Report (of 4 August) that security requirements demanded first priority, that economic and social programs had to be accelerated, that it was in the US interest to promote a viable Vietnam. He agreed to support an ARVN increase to 200,000 if Diem in turn agreed to a plan for using these forces. The 270,000 level was thus disapproved. But the plan for using ARVN forces had not yet been drawn. Diem had not yet designed—much less implemented—social reforms supposedly required in return for US assistance.

15 Aug 1961   *NIE 14–3/53.61*
Although collapse of the Saigon regime might come by a coup or

from Diem's death, its fall because of a "prolonged and difficult" struggle was not predicted.

Late Aug   *Theodore White Reports*
1961   "The situation gets worse almost week by week . . ." particularly the military situation in the delta. If the U.S. decides it must intervene, White asked if we had the people, instruments or clear objectives to make it successful.

1 Sep 1961   *General McGarr Reports*
The ARVN has displayed increased efficiency, a spirit of renewed confidence is "beginning to permeate the people, the GVN and the Armed Forces."

27 Sep 1961   *Nolting Reports*
Nolting was "unable report . . . progress toward attaining task force goals of creating viable and increasingly democratic society," called the government and civil situation unchanged from early September. A series of large scale VC attacks in central Vietnam, the day-long VC seizure of Phuoc Vinh, capital of [former] Phuoc Thanh Province—55 miles from Saigon—in which the VC publicly beheaded Diem's province chief and escaped before government troops arrived and increased infiltration through Laos demonstrated "that the tide has not yet turned" militarily.

1 Oct 1961   *Diem Request*
Diem requested a bilateral treaty with the U.S. This surprised Nolting but probably did not surprise the White House, already warned by White of the grave military situation.

1 Oct 1961   *State "First 12-Month Report"*
This political assessment mirrored Nolting's "no progress" report but State found the military situation more serious than Embassy reports had indicated.

5 Oct 1961   *The "Rostow Proposal"*
Suggested a 25,000-man SEATO force be put into Vietnam to guard the Vietnam/Laos border between the DMZ and Cambodia. (The Pathet Lao had gained during September, as had VC infiltration through Laos to the GVN. This prompted plans for U.S. action.)

9 Oct 1961   *JCSM 717–61*
The JCS rejected the Rostow proposal: forces would be stretched thin, they could not stop infiltration, and would be at the worst place to oppose potential DRV/CHICOM invasion. The Chiefs wanted to make a "concentrated effort in Laos where a firm stand can be taken saving all or substantially all of Laos which would, at the same time, protect Thailand and protect the borders of South Vietnam." But if this were "politically unacceptable" the Chiefs "provided . . . a possible limited interim course of action": deployment of about 20,000 troops to the central highlands near Pleiku to assist the GVN and free certain GVN forces for offensive action against the VC.

10 Oct 1961   *"Concept of Intervention in Vietnam"*
Drafted by Alexis Johnson, the paper blended Rostow's border control proposal with the JCS win-control-of-the-highlands counter-proposal for the initial mission of U.S. forces in Vietnam. "The real and ultimate objective" of U.S. troops was also addressed. To defeat the Vietcong and render Vietnam secure under a non-Communist government, Johnson "guessed" three divisions would be the ultimate force required in support of the "real objective." The paper estimated a satisfactory settlement in Laos would reduce but not eliminate infiltration into South Vietnam, that even if infiltration were cut down, there was no assurance that the GVN could "in the foreseeable future be able to defeat the Viet Cong." Unilateral U.S. action would probably be necessary. The plan's viability was dependent on the degree in which the GVN accelerated "political and military action in its own defense."

11 Oct 1961   NSC Meeting on Vietnam
The NSC considered four papers: the Alexis Johnson draft; an NIE estimate that SEATO action would be opposed by the DRV, Viet Cong and the Soviet Union (airlift), that these forces stood a good chance of thwarting the SEATO intervention; third, a JCS estimate that 40,000 U.S. troops would be required to "clean up the Viet Cong threat" and another 128,000 men would be needed to oppose DRV/CHICOM intervention (draining 3 to 4 reserve divisions). Finally, a memorandum from William Bundy to McNamara which said "it *is* really now or never if we are to arrest the gains being made by the Viet Cong," and gave "an early and hard-hitting operation" a 70 percent chance of doing that. Bundy added, the chance of cleaning up the situation "depends on Diem's effectiveness, which is very problematical," favored going in with 70–30 odds but figured the odds would slide down if the U.S. "let, say, a month go by" before moving.

13 Oct 1961   Saigon Message 488
Reversing his previous position, Diem requested an additional fighter-bomber squadron, civilian pilots for helicopters and C-47 transports and U.S. combat units for a "combat-training" mission near the DMZ, possibly also in the highlands. He asked consideration be given a possible request for a division of Chiang Kai-shek's troops to support the GVN. Nolting recommended "serious and prompt" attention for the requests.

14 Oct 1961   New York Times
In an article leaked by the government—perhaps by Kennedy himself—leaders were called reluctant to send U.S. combat units into Southeast Asia. Obviously untrue, the leak was probably designed to end speculation about troop deployment and guard Kennedy's freedom of action.

20 Oct 1961   CINCPAC Recommendation
Admiral Felt felt the pros and cons of U.S. troop deployment added up in favor of *no* deployment until other means of helping Diem had been exhausted.

18–24 Oct   *Taylor Mission to Vietnam*
1961   On the 18th, Diem said he wanted no U.S. combat troops for any
                 mission. He repeated his request for a bilateral defense treaty,
                 more support for ARVN and combat-support equipment (heli-
                 copters, aircraft, etc.).

23 Oct 1961   *Ch MAAG Message*
                 General McGarr suggested that the serious Mekong River flood
                 could provide a cover for U.S. troop deployment: combat units
                 could be disguised as humanitarian relief forces and be dispatched
                 to the delta.

25 Oct 1961   *Saigon Message 536*
                 Taylor reported the pervasive crisis of confidence and serious loss
                 in Vietnamese national morale created by Laos and the flood,
                 weakened the war effort. To cope with this Taylor recommended:
                 Improvement of intelligence on the VC; building ARVN mobility;
                 blocking infiltration into the highlands by organizing a border
                 ranger force; introduction of U.S. forces either for emergency,
                 short-term assistance, or for more substantial, long-term support
                 (a flood relief plus military reserve task force). Diem had reacted
                 favorably "on all points."

1 Nov 1961   *BAGUIO Message 0005*
                 Taylor told the President, Rusk and McNamara "we should put
                 in a task force (6–8,000 men) consisting largely of logistical troops
                 for the purpose of participating in flood relief and at the same time
                 of providing a U.S. military presence in Vietnam capable of as-
                 suring Diem of our readiness to join him in a military showdown
                 with the Viet Cong . . ."

1 Nov 1961   *BAGUIO 0006* EYES ONLY *FOR THE PRESIDENT*
                 Taylor concluded that the communist strategy of taking over
                 Southeast Asia by guerrilla warfare was "well on the way to suc-
                 cess in Vietnam"; he said the GVN was caught in "interlocking
                 circles" of bad tactics and bad administrative arrangements which
                 allow VC gains and invite a political crisis. He recommended
                 more U.S. support for paramilitary groups and ARVN mobility;
                 the MAAG should be reorganized and increased and the task force
                 introduced to "conduct such combat operations as are necessary
                 for self-defense and for the security of the area in which (it) is
                 stationed," among other things. Taylor felt the disadvantages of
                 deployment were outweighted by gains, said SVN is "not an ex-
                 cessively difficult or unpleasant place to operate" and the "risks of
                 backing into a major Asian war by way of SVN" are not impres-
                 sive: North Vietnam "is extremely vulnerable to conventional
                 bombing . . . there is no case for fearing a mass onslaught of
                 communist manpower . . . particularly if our air power is al-
                 lowed a free hand against logistical targets . . ."

3 Nov 1961   *Taylor Report*
                 The "Evaluation and Summary" section suggested urgency and
                 optimism: SVN is in trouble, major U.S. interests are at stake;
                 prompt and energetic U.S. action—military, economic, political—

can lead to victory without a U.S. take-over of the war, can cure weaknesses in the Diem regime. That the Vietnamese must win the war was a unanimous view—but most mission participants believed all Vietnamese operations could be substantially improved by America's "limited partnership" with the GVN. The GVN is cast in the best possible light; any suggestion that the U.S. should limit rather than expand its commitment—or face the need to enter the battle in full force at this time—is avoided. Underlying the summary was the notion that "graduated measures on the DRV (applied) with weapons of our own choosing" could reverse any adverse trend in the South. And ground troops were always possible. The Taylor Report recommended the U.S. make obvious its readiness to act, develop reserve strength in the U.S "to cover action in Southeast Asia up to the nuclear threshold in that area" and thereby sober the enemy and discourage escalation. However, bombing was a more likely Vietnam contingency than was use of ground troops; the latter option was tied to a U.S. response to renewed fighting in Laos and/or overt invasion of South Vietnam. But Taylor suggested troops be sent to Diem; the Taylor Report and cables recommend combat troop deployment to Vietnam. (A message from Nolting summarizing the Diem-Taylor meeting on which the recommendations apparently rest [Saigon message 541, 25 Oct 61] does *not* indicate any enthusiasm on Diem's part to deployment of troops, however. He hinted U.S. troops for training *might* be requested, then dropped the subject.)

Appendices to the Taylor Report written by members of the group give a slightly different picture. There is less optimism about the GVN's chances of success, less optimism about chances of U.S action—political or military—tipping the balance. For example: William Jordan (State) said almost all Vietnamese interviewed had emphasized the gravity of the situation, growing VC successes and loss of confidence in Diem. The ARVN lacked aggressiveness, was devoid of any sense of urgency, short of able leaders. Sterling Cottrell (State) said: It is an open question whether the GVN can succeed even with U.S. assistance. Thus it would be a mistake to make an irrevocable U.S. commitment to defeat communists in South Vietnam. Foreign military forces cannot win the battle at the village level—where it must be joined; the primary responsibility for saving Vietnam must rest with the GVN. For these reasons Cottrell argued against a treaty which would either shift ultimate responsibility to the U.S. or engage a full U.S. commitment to defeat the Vietcong.

5 Nov 1961   *SNIE 10-4-61*

This estimated the DRV would respond to an increased U.S troop commitment by increasing support to the Vietcong. If U.S. commitment to the GVN grew, so would DRV support to the VC. Four possible U.S. courses were given: airlift plus more help for ARVN; deployment of 8–10,000 troops as a flood relief task force; deployment of 25–40,000 combat troops; with each course, warn Hanoi of U.S. determination to hold SVN and U.S. intention to bomb the DRV if its support for the VC did not cease. The SNIE estimated air attacks against the North would not cause its VC support to stop and figured Moscow and Peking would react strongly to air attacks.

8 Nov 1961   *McNamara Memorandum for the President*
Secretary McNamara, Gilpatric and the JCS were "inclined to recommend that we do commit the U.S. to the clear objective of preventing the fall of South Vietnam to communism and that we support this commitment by the necessary military actions." The memorandum said the fall of Vietnam would create "extremely serious" strategic implications worldwide, that chances were "probably sharply against" preventing that fall without a U.S. troop commitment but that even with major-troop deployment (205,000 was the maximum number of ground forces estimated necessary to deal with a large overt invasion from the DRV and/or China) the U.S. would still be at the mercy of external forces—Diem, Laos, domestic political problems, etc.—and thus success could not be guaranteed. McNamara recommended against deployment of a task force (the 8,000-man group mentioned in the Taylor Report) "unless we are willing to make an affirmative decision" to fully support a commiment to save South Vietnam.

11 Nov 1961   *Rusk/McNamara Memorandum for the President*
This may have been prepared at Kennedy's specific instruction; it recommended what Kennedy wanted to hear: that the decision to commit major ground forces could be deferred. In this paper, rhetoric is escalated from that of McNamara's 8 November memorandum but U.S. actions recommended are far less significant, less committing. Military courses are divided into two phrases: first, promptly deploy support troops and equipment (helicopters, transport aircraft, maritime equipment and trainers, special intelligence and air reconnaissance groups, other men and materiel to improve training, logistics, economic and other assistance programs). Then study and *possibly* deploy major ground combat forces at a later date. Despite the clear warning that even deployment of major U.S. units could not assure success against communism, the memorandum's initial recommendation was that the U.S. "commit itself to the clear objective of preventing the fall of South Vietnam to Communism," be prepared to send troops and to "strike at the source of aggression in North Vietnam." A number of diplomatic moves (in the U.N., in NATO and SEATO councils, etc.) are suggested to signal U.S. determination; economic, social and other programs designed to help South Vietnam are suggested; ways to elicit improvements from Diem are recommended.

14 Nov 1961   *DEPTEL 619 to Saigon*
This was Nolting's guidance, based on the Rusk/McNamara memorandum. Nolting was told the anti-guerrilla effort "must essentially be a GVN task . . . No amount of extra aid can be substituted for GVN taking measures to permit [it] to assume offensive and strengthen the administrative and political bases of government . . . Do not propose to introduce into GVN the U.S. combat troops now but propose a phase of intense public and diplomatic

activity to focus on infiltration from North. Shall decide later on course of action should infiltration not be radically reduced." Diem's taking necessary measures—political, military, economic —to improve his government and relations with the people were a prerequisite to further U.S. assistance: "Package should be presented as first steps in a partnership in which the U.S. is prepared to do more as joint study of facts and GVN performance makes increased U.S. aid possible and productive." Strictly for his own information, Nolting was told Defense was "preparing plans for the use of U.S. combat forces in SVN under various contingencies, including stepped up infiltration as well as organized . . . (military) intervention. However, objective of our policy is to do all possible to accomplish purpose without use of U.S. combat forces." And, Nolting was to tell Diem: "We would expect to share in the decision-making process in the political, economic and military fields as they affect the security situation."

22 Nov 1961   **NSAM 111**
Called the "First Phase of Vietnam Program" this NSAM approved all Rusk/McNamara recommendations of 11 November except the first one: their initial recommendation that the U.S. commit itself to saving South Vietnam was omitted.

7 Dec 1961   *Alexis Johnson/Rostow Redraft ("Clarification") of Nolting's 14 November Guidance*
"What we have in mind is that in operations directly related to the security situation, partnership will be so close that one party will not take decisions or actions affecting the other without full and frank prior consultation." This is different from the idea that American involvement should be so intimate that the GVN would be reformed "from the bottom up"—despite Diem.
(Although Washington gave in—or gave up—on the kind and degree of pressure to exert on Diem, Washington did not soften on Lansdale. Despite four requests from Diem and the recommendations from Cottrell, the Taylor Report and William Bundy that Lansdale be sent to Saigon, he did not get there until late 1965.)

11 Dec 1961   New York Times
Two U.S. helicopter companies (33 H–21Cs, 400 men) arrived in Vietnam, the first direct U.S. military support for the GVN.
ICC reaction: shall we continue functioning here in the face of U.S. assistance (increase barred by the Geneva Accords)?

15 Dec 1961   New York Times
Reported the formal exchange of letters between Kennedy and Diem announcing a stepped-up aid program for Vietnam.

I. BACKGROUND

A. INTRODUCTION

In the summer of 1959, it was hard to find an American official worried about Vietnam. This was not because things were going well. They were not.

A National Intelligence Estimate published in August portrayed Diem as unpopular, his economy as developing less rapidly than its rival in the North, and his government under pressure from guerrillas encouraged and in part supported from the North. Nevertheless, the NIE suggested no crisis then or for the foreseeable future. What the NIE called "harassment" (i.e., support for the VC) from the North would continue, but overt invasion seemed most unlikely. Neither communist nor anti-communist enemies within South Vietnam were seen as an immediate threat. Diem would remain as President, said the NIE, "for many years." In sum, the NIE saw the situation in Vietnam as unhappy, but not unstable. That was to be about as close to good news as we would hear from South Vietnam for a long time.

From then on, the classified record through the end of 1961 shows a succession of bleak appraisals of the regime's support in the cities, and among the military, almost always accompanied by increasingly bleak estimates of increased VC strength and activity in the countryside. A dispatch from our Embassy in Saigon in March, 1960, described the situation in grave terms, but ended on the hopeful note that as of January Diem was recognizing his problems and promising to do something about them. In August, an NIE analysis reported a "marked deterioration since January." In November, a military coup barely failed to overthrow Diem.

In January, 1961 an old counterinsurgency hand, General Edward Lansdale, went to Vietnam to look things over for the Secretary of Defense. He returned with a report that "the Viet Cong hope to win back Vietnam south of the 17th parallel this year, if at all possible, and are much further along towards accomplishing this goal than I had realized from reading the reports received in Washington."

Nevertheless, the situation was never seen as nearly so grave as these reports, read years later, might suggest. We will see that at least up until the fall of 1961, while appraisals of the situation sometimes suggested imminent crisis, the recommendations made to the President (by the authors of these frightening appraisals) always implied a less pessimistic view.

The top levels of the Kennedy Administration dealt only intermittently with the problem of Vietnam during 1961. There was a flurry of activity in late April and early May, which we will see was essentially an offshoot of the Laos crisis which had come to a head at that time. A much more thorough review was undertaken in the fall, following General Taylor's mission to Saigon, which then led to an important expansion of the American effort in Vietnam.

No fundamental new American decisions on Vietnam were made until the Buddhist unrest in the last half of 1963, and no major new military decisions were made until 1965. Consequently, the decisions in the fall of 1961 (essentially, to provide combat support—for example, helicopter companies—but to defer any decision on direct combat troops) have come to seem very important. This paper tries to describe what led up to those decisions, what alternatives were available and what the implications of the choices were.

The story is a fairly complicated one. For although it is hard to recall that context today, Vietnam in 1961 was a peripheral crisis. Even within Southeast Asia it received far less of the Administration's and the world's attention than did Laos. The *New York Times Index for 1961* has eight columns of Vietnam, twenty-six on Laos. Decisions about Vietnam were greatly influenced by what was happening elsewhere. In the narrow Vietnamese context, the weaknesses and peculiarities of the Diem government had a substantial, if not always obvious, impact on the behavior of both the Vietnamese officials seeking American aid and the American decision-makers pondering the nature and terms of the aid they would offer.

As it happens, the Eisenhower Administration was never faced with a need for high-level decisions affecting the crisis developing in Vietnam during 1960. A formal Counterinsurgency Plan, intended to be the basis of an expanded program of assistance to Vietnam, was being worked on through most of that year, but (presumably reflecting a subdued sense of urgency), it took eight months to reach the White House. By that time, a new Administration had just taken office. President Kennedy promptly approved the plan, but this merely set off lengthy negotiations with the Vietnamese about whether and when they would do their share of the CIP. In April, though, a crisis atmosphere developed, not because of anything fresh out of Vietnam, but because of a need to shore up the Vietnamese and others in Southeast Asia in the face of a likely collapse of the U.S. position in Laos. This led to a U.S. offer to discuss putting American troops into Vietnam, or perhaps negotiate a bilateral security treaty with the Vietnamese. When, however, Vice President Johnson mentioned the possibility of troops to Diem in May, Diem said he wanted no troops yet. The idea of a bilateral treaty similarly slipped out of sight. Consequently, although the United States had itself indicated a willingness in May to discuss a deeper commitment, the South Vietnamese did not take up the opportunity, and the Administration had no occasion to face up to really hard decisions.

But by October, the situation in Vietnam had worsened. The VC were becoming disturbingly aggressive. Now, Diem did raise the question of a treaty. This request, coming after the American offer in May to consider such steps and in the context of a worsening situation in Vietnam, could hardly be ignored. The Taylor Mission and the Presidential review and decisions of November followed.

The present paper is organized around these natural climaxes in the policy process. The balance of Part I describes the situation inherited by the new Administration. Part II covers the period through the May peak. Part III covers the fall crisis.

B. THE CONTEXT

In January, 1961, there were five issues that were going to affect American policy toward Vietnam. They turned on:

1. *The VC Insurgency Itself*

An illustration of the growth of the insurgency, but also of the limits of U.S. concern can be seen in the 1960 CINCPAC Command History. For several years prior to 1960, CINCPAC histories do not mention the VC insurgency at all. In 1960, the development of a counterinsurgency plan for Vietnam (and simultaneously one for Laos) received a fair amount of attention. But when, in April, MAAG in Saigon asked for additional transports and helicopters for the counterinsurgency effort, CINCPAC turned down the requests for transports, and OSD overruled the recommendation CINCPAC forwarded for 6 helicopters. By December, OSD was willing to approve sending 11 helicopters (of 16 newly requested) on an "emergency" basis. But the emergency was partly a matter of reassuring Diem after the November coup, and the degree of emergency is suggested by the rate of delivery: 4 in December, and the balance over the next three months.

The record, in general, indicates a level of concern such as that illustrated by the helicopter decisions: growing gradually through 1960, but still pretty much of a back-burner issue so far as the attention and sense of urgency it commanded among policy-level officials. As we will see, the new Kennedy Administration gave it more attention, as the Eisenhower Administration undoubtedly would have had it remained in office. But it is important (though hard, now that Vietnam has loomed so large) to keep in mind how secondary an issue the VC threat to Vietnam seemed to be in early 1961.

2. Problems with the Diem Government

Yet, although the VC gains were not seen—even in the dispatches from Saigon—as serious enough to threaten the immediate collapse of the Diem government, those gains did have the effect of raising difficult questions about our relations with Diem that we had never had to face before. For by late 1960, it was a quite widely held view that the Diem government was probably going to be overthrown sooner or later, barring major changes from within. In contrast to the May 1959 NIE's confident statement that Diem "almost certainly" would remain president "for many years," we find the August 1960 NIE predicting that the recent "adverse trends," if continued, would "almost certainly in time cause the collapse of Diem's regime."

The simple, unhappy fact was that whatever his triumphs in 1955 and 1956, by the end of the 1950s the feeling was growing that the best thing that could be said for Diem was that he was holding the country together and keeping it from succumbing to the communists. Once even this came into doubt, talk among Vietnamese and eventually among Americans of whether it might be better to look for alternative leadership became inevitable.

The sense of trouble shows through even among the optimists. We find Kenneth Young, U.S. Ambassador to Thailand and a strong believer in Diem, warning him in October, 1960 that "there seems to be somewhat of a crisis of confidence in Vietnam."

But the long list of measures Young suggested were all tactical in nature, and required no basic changes in the regime.

Our Ambassador in Saigon (Eldridge Durbrow) was more pessimistic:

> . . . situation in Viet-Nam [December, 1960] is highly dangerous to US interests. Communists are engaged in large-scale guerrilla effort to take over countryside and oust Diem's Government. Their activities have steadily increased in intensity throughout this year. In addition, Diem is faced with widespread popular dissatisfaction with his government's inability to stem the communist tide and its own heavy-handed methods of operation. It seems clear that if he is to remain in power he must meet these two challenges by improvements in his methods of conducting war against communists and in vigorous action to build greater popular support. We should help and encourage him to take effective action. Should he not do so, we may well be forced, in not too distant future, to undertake difficult task of identifying and supporting alternate leadership.

But the difficulties (and risks) of that task looked forbidding. During the November, 1960 coup attempt the U.S. had apparently used its influence to get the coup leaders to negotiate with Diem for reforms, allowing Diem to retain his position with reduced powers. Whether because of their own indecision or U.S. pressure, the coup leaders allowed a delay that let Diem bring loyalist troops in to regain control. (Three years later, a leader of the November, 1963 coup "somewhat emphatically" told an American agent that "it would do no good to send anyone around to attempt to stop things, as happened in November, 1960.")

The situation that was left—with a number of American officials unhappy with Diem and doubtful that he was capable of winning the war, yet unwilling to risk a coup—produced strains within the American government. Short of encouraging a coup, we seemed to have two alternatives: attempt to pressure Diem or attempt to so win his confidence that he would accept our advice willingly. The only effective form of U.S. pressure, however, was to withhold aid, and doing so would sooner or later weaken the war effort.

Consequently a division developed, mainly (but not purely) along the lines of Defense against State, about the advisability of using pressure. The division was particularly sharp since Diem seemed willing to go part way, at least, in meeting our military suggestions, so that the Defense view tended to be that the U.S. would be weakening the war effort if aid were withheld to seek to gain civil reforms that not many people in Defense regarded as crucial. Besides, it was argued, Diem would not succumb to pressure anyway. We would just encourage another coup, and the communists would exploit it.

Given this sort of argument, there would always (at least through 1961) be at least two layers to decisions about aid to Vietnam: What should the U.S. be willing to give? and What, if any, demands should be made on Diem in return for the aid?

3. Problems with the Soviets

But from Washington, both problems within Vietnam—how to deal with the Viet Cong, and how to deal with Diem—seemed quite inconsequential compared to the problems of dealing with the Soviets. There were two elements to the Soviet problem. The first, which only indirectly affected Vietnam, was the generally aggressive and confident posture of the Russians at that time, and the generally defensive position of the Americans. To use W.W. Rostow's terminology, the Soviets were then entering the third year of their "post-sputnik" offensive, and their aggressiveness would continue through the Cuban missile crisis. On the U.S. side there was dismay even among Republicans (openly, for example, by Rockefeller; necessarily subdued by Nixon, but reported by any number of journalists on the basis of private conversations) at what seemed to be an erosion of the American position in the world. The Coolidge Commission, appointed by the President, warned him in January, 1960, to, among other steps, "close the missile gap" and generally strengthen our defenses. Kennedy, of course, made erosion of our position in the world a major campaign issue. All of this made 1961 a peculiarly difficult year for Americans to make concessions, or give ground to the Soviets when it could be avoided, or even postponed. That was clear in January, and everything thereafter that was, or could be interpreted to be a weak U.S. response, only strengthened the pressure to hold on in Vietnam.

A further element of the Soviet problem impinged directly on Vietnam. The new Administration, even before taking office, was inclined to believe that unconventional warfare was likely to be terrifically important in the 1960s. In January 1961, Krushchev seconded that view with his speech pledging Soviet support to "wars of national liberation." Vietnam was where such a war was actually going on. Indeed, since the war in Laos had moved far beyond the insurgency stage, Vietnam was the only place in the world where the Administration faced a well-developed Communist effort to topple a pro-Western government with an externally-aided pro-communist insurgency. It was a challenge that could hardly be ignored.

4.   *The Situation in Laos*

Meanwhile, within Southeast Asia itself there was the peculiar problem of Laos, where the Western position was in the process of falling apart as Kennedy took office. The Eisenhower Administration had been giving strong support to a pro-American faction in Laos. As a consequence, the neutralist faction had joined in an alliance with the pro-communist faction. The Soviets were sending aid to the neutralist/communist alliance, which they recognized as the legitimate government in Laos; the U.S. recognized and aided the pro-western faction. Unfortunately, it turned out that the neutralist/communist forces were far more effective than those favored by the U.S., and so it became clear that only by putting an American army into Laos could the pro-Western faction be kept in power. Indeed, it was doubtful that even a coalition government headed by the neutralists (the choice the U.S. adopted) could be salvaged. The coalition government solution would raise problems for other countries in Southeast Asia: there would be doubts about U.S. commitments in that part of the world, and (since it was obvious that the communist forces would be left with de facto control of eastern Laos), the settlement would create direct security threats for Thailand and Vietnam. These problems would accompany a "good" outcome in Laos (the coalition government); if the Pathet Lao chose to simply overrun the country outright (as, short of direct American intervention, they had the power to do), the problem elsewhere in Southeast Asia would be so much the worse. Consequently, throughout 1961, we find the effects of the Laos situation spilling over onto Vietnam.

5.   *The Special American Commitment to Vietnam*

Finally, in this review of factors that would affect policy-making on Vietnam, we must note that South Vietnam, (unlike any of the other countries in Southeast Asia) was essentially the creation of the United States.

Without U.S. support Diem almost certainly could not have consolidated his hold on the South during 1955 and 1956.

Without the threat of U.S. intervention, South Vietnam could not have refused to even discuss the elections called for in 1956 under the Geneva settlement without being immediately overrun by the Viet Minh armies.

Without U.S. aid in the years following, the Diem regime certainly, and an independent South Vietnam almost as certainly, could not have survived.

Further, from 1954 on there had been repeated statements of U.S. support for South Vietnam of a sort that we would not find in our dealings with other countries in this part of the world. It is true there was nothing unqualified about this support: it was always economic, and occasionally accompanied by statements suggesting that the Diem regime had incurred an obligation to undertake reforms in return for our assistance. But then, until 1961, there was no occasion to consider any assistance that went beyond economic support and the usual sort of military equipment and advice, and no suggestion that our continued support was in doubt.

Consequently, the U.S. had gradually developed a special commitment in South Vietnam. It was certainly not absolutely binding, even at the level of assistance existing at the start of 1961, much less at any higher level the South Vietnamese might come to need or request. But the commitment was there; to let it slip would be awkward, at the least. Whether it really had any impact on later decisions is hard to say. Given the other factors already discussed, it is not hard to believe that in its absence, U.S. policy might have followed exactly the same course it has followed. On the other hand, in the absence of a pre-existing special relation with South Vietnam, the U.S. in 1961 possibly would have at least considered a coalition government for Vietnam as well as Laos, and chosen to limit direct U.S. involvement to Thailand and other countries in the area historically independent of both Hanoi and Peking. But that is the mootest sort of question. For if there had been no pre-existing commitment to South Vietnam in 1961, there would not have been a South Vietnam to worry about anyway.

C. SUMMARY

Looking over the context we have been reviewing, it seems like a situation in which mistakes would be easy to make. The Viet Cong threat was serious enough to demand action; but not serious enough to compete with other crises and problems for the attention of senior decision-makers. A sound decision on tactics and levels of commitment to deal with the Viet Cong involved as much a judgment on the internal politics of non-communists in Vietnam as it did a judgment of the guerrillas' strength, and character, and relation with Hanoi. (Even a judgement that the war could be treated as a strictly military problem after all, involved at least an implicit judgement, and a controversial one, about Vietnamese politics.) Even if Diem looked not worth supporting it would be painful to make a decision to let him sink, and especially so in the world context of 1961. Faced with a challenge to deal with wars of national liberation, it would be hard to decide that the first one we happened to meet was "not our style." And after the U.S. stepped back in Laos, it might be hard to persuade the Russians that we intended to stand firm anywhere if we then gave up on Vietnam. Finally, if the U.S. suspected that the best course in Vietnam was to seek immediately an alternative to Diem, no one knew who the alternative might be, or whether getting rid of Diem would really make things better.

Such was the prospect of Vietnam as 1961 began, and a new Administration took office.

II. THE COUNTERINSURGENCY PLAN

A. WINTER, 1961

The Vietnam Counter-Insurgency Plan which was being worked on through most of 1960 finally reached the White House in late January, apparently just after Kennedy took office. We do not have a document showing the exact date, but we know that Kennedy approved the main provisions of the Plan after a meeting on January 28th, and negotiations with Diem began February 13.

The provisions of the CIP tell a good deal about how the Viet Cong threat looked to American and Vietnamese officials at the beginning of 1961, for there is nothing in the record to suggest that anyone—either in Saigon or Washington, Vietnamese or American—judged the CIP to be an inadequate response to the VC threat.

The U.S. offered Diem equipment and supplies to outfit a 20,000 man increase in his army. The cost was estimated at $28.4 million. The U.S. also offered to train, outfit and supply 32,000 men of the Civil Guard (a counterguerrilla auxiliary) at a cost of $12.7 million. These two moves would help Diem expand the RVNAF to a total of 170,000 men, and expand the Civil Guard to a total of 68,000 men. There were some further odds and ends totalling less than another million. The full package added up to less than $42 million, which was a substantial but not enormous increment to on-going U.S. aid to Vietnam of about $220 million a year. (Since most of these costs were for initial outfitting for new forces, the package was mainly a one-time shot in the arm.)

For their part, the Vietnamese were supposed to pay the local currency costs of the new forces, and carry out a number of military and civil reforms.

The key military reforms were to straighten out the chain of command, and to develop an agreed overall plan of operations.

> The chain of command problem was that control of the counterinsurgency effort in the provinces was divided between the local military commander and the Province Chief, a personal appointee of Diem, and reporting directly to Diem. Even at a higher level, 3 regional field commands reported directly to Diem, by-passing the Chief of Staff. So a total of 42 officials with some substantial (and overlapping) control of the war effort reported directly to Diem: 38 Province Chiefs, 3 regional commanders, and the Chief of Staff. The "reform" eventually gotten from Diem put the regional commanders under the Chief of Staff, and combined the office of Province Chief (usually a military man in any event) and local field commander. But the Province Chiefs still were personally responsible to Diem, and could appeal directly to him outside the nominal chain of command. Diem's reform, consequently, turned out to be essentially meaningless. His reluctance to move on this issue was not surprising. After all, the division and confusion of military authority served a real purpose for a ruler like Diem, with no broad base of support: it lessened the chance of a coup that would throw him out.

> The overall plan issue, on which not even a paper agreement was reached during the period covered by this account, was really an argument over strategy. It has a familiar ring.

> Diem seemed oriented very much towards maintaining at least the pretense of control over all of South Vietnam. Consequently, he favored maintaining military outposts (and concentrating the population in Agrovilles, the predecessors of the strategic hamlets) along "lines of strength" (generally main roads) which stretched throughout the country. To assert at least nominal control over the countryside between these lines of strength, the military forces would periodically organize a sweep. In contrast to this, the American plan stressed what MAAG called a "net and spear" concept. Small units would scour the jungles beyond the pacified area. When this "net" found an enemy unit, they would call in reserves (the spear) for a concentrated attempt to destroy the unit. As new areas were thus cleared, the net would be pushed further out into previously uncontested areas. It is not clear how well refined either concept was, or (with

hindsight) whether the American plan was really a great deal more realistic than Diem's. But the American interest is getting Diem to agree to a plan does seem to have been primarily oriented to getting him to agree to some systematic procedure for using forces to clear areas of VC control, instead of tying up most of his forces defending fixed installations, with periodic uneventful sweeps through the hinterland.

On the civil side, the stress in the CIP was on trying to shore up the regime's support within the cities by such steps as bringing opposition leaders into the government, and giving the National Assembly the power to investigate charges of mismanagement and corruption in the executive.

The Plan also called for "civic action" and other steps to increase the change of winning positive loyalty from the peasants.

A good deal of bureaucratic compromise had gone into the CIP. Ambassador Durbrow only reluctantly conceded any real need for the 20,000 man force increase. The stress on civil reforms, in particular on civil reforms as part of a *quid pro quo,* came into the plan only after the Saigon Embassy became involved, although there were general allusions to such things even in the original military draft of the CIP.

Nevertheless, there was at least a paper agreement, and so far as the record shows, substantial real agreement as well. No one complained the plan was inadequate. It would, "if properly implemented," "turn the tide." And, by implication, it would do so without any major increase in American personnel in Vietnam, and indeed, aside from the one-shot outfitting of the new units, without even any major increase in American aid.

None of this meant that the warnings that we have seen in the Saigon Embassy's dispatches or in the August SNIE were not seriously intended. What it did mean was that, as of early 1961, the view that was presented to senior officials in Washington essentially showed the VC threat as a problem which could be pretty confidently handled, given a little more muscle for the army and some shaping up by the Vietnamese administration. Any doubts expressed went to the will and comptence of the Diem regime, not to the strength of the VC, the role of Hanoi, or the adequacy of U.S. aid.

Consequently, among the assumptions listed as underlying the CIP, we find (with emphasis added):

> That the Government of Viet-Nam has the basic potential to cope with the Viet Cong guerrilla threat *if necessary corrective measures are taken and adequate forces are provided.*

That of course was the heart of the CIP bargain: the U.S. would provide support for the "adequate forces" if Diem would take the "necessary corrective steps." The hinted corollary was that our commitment to Diem should be contingent on his performance:

> That *at the present time* the Diem government offers the best hope for defeating the Viet Cong.

B. LANSDALE'S REPORT

Running against these suggestions (of a firm bargaining position contingent on Diem's performance), was concern that if Diem were overthrown his successors might be no better; and that the VC might exploit the confusion and perhaps even civil war following a coup. Further, there was an argument that part of Diem's reluctance to move on reforms was that he was afraid to make any concession that might weaken his grip: consequently the U.S. needed to reassure him that he could count on our firm support to him personally.

A strong statement of this point of view is contained in a report submitted in January by Brig. General Edward Lansdale, then the Assistant to the Secretary of Defense for Special Operations. Lansdale had become famous for his work in the Philippines advising on the successful campaign against the Huk insurgents. In 1955 and 1956, he was a key figure in installing and establishing Diem as President of South Vietnam. As mentioned in the Introduction, Lansdale visited Vietnam in early January. Here, from his report, are a few extracts on Diem and how Lansdale felt he should be handled:

> . . . We must support Ngo Dinh Diem until another strong executive can replace him legally. President Diem feels that Americans have attacked him almost as viciously as the Communists, and he has withdrawn into a shell for self-protection. We have to show him by deeds, not words alone, that we are his friend. This will make our influence effective again.
>
> . . . If the next American official to talk to President Diem would have the good sense to see him as a human being who has been through a lot of hell for years—and not as an opponent to be beaten to his knees—we would start regaining our influence with him in a healthy way. Whatever else we might think of him, he has been unselfish in devoting his life to his country and has little in personal belongings to show for it. If we don't like the heavy influence of Brother Nhu, then let's move someone of ours in close. This someone, however, must be able to look at problems with understanding, suggest better solutions than does Nhu, earn a position of influence. . . .
>
> Ambassador Durbrow should be transferred in the immediate future. He has been in the "forest of tigers" which is Vietnam for nearly four years now and I doubt that he himself realizes how tired he has become or how close he is to the individual trees in this big woods. Correctly or not, the recognized government of Vietnam does not look upon him as a friend, believing he sympathized strongly with the coup leaders of 11 November.
>
> . . . Ngo Dinh Diem is still the only Vietnamese with executive ability and the required determination to be an effective President. I believe there will be another attempt to get rid of him soon, unless the U.S. makes it clear that we are backing him as the elected top man. If the 11 November coup had been successful, I believe that a number of highly selfish and mediocre people would be squabbling among themselves for power while the Communists took over. The Communists will be more alert to exploit the next coup attempt. . . .

Lansdale's view was not immediately taken up, even though Hilsman reports that his presentation impressed Kennedy enough to start the President thinking about sending the General to Saigon as our next Ambassador. Instead, Kennedy made what was under the circumstances the easiest, least time-consuming decision, which was simply to let the Ambassador he had inherited from the Eisenhower Administration go forward and make a try with the plan and negotiating tactics already prepared.

Durbrow's guidance specifically tells him (in instructions he certainly found suited his own view perfectly):

. . . considered U.S. view (is) that success requires implementation entire plan . . . If Ambassador considers GVN does not provide necessary cooperation, he should inform Washington with recommendations which may include suspension U.S. contribution.

C. NEGOTIATING THE CIP

Kennedy's approval of the CIP apparently was seen as quite a routine action. None of the memoirs of the period give it any particular attention. And, although both Schlesinger and Hilsman refer to General Lansdale's report as shocking the President about the state of things in Vietnam, that report itself does not criticize the CIP, or the adequacy of its programs.

The guidance to Durbrow assumed agreement could be reached "within two weeks." This choice of language in the guidance cable implies that we believed Diem would quickly agree on the terms of the CIP, and the question of using pressure against him ("suspension of U.S. contribution") would only arise later, should he fail to follow through on his part of the agreement.

As it turned out, Durbrow's efforts took a more complicated form. Even reaching a nominal agreement on the Cip took about 6 weeks. Then, Durbrow recommended holding up what is constantly referred to as "the green light" on increased aid until Diem had actually signed decrees implementing his major promises.

On March 8 (in response to a Washington suggestion for stepping up some aid prior to agreement on the CIP), Saigon cabled that:

. . . despite pressure of Embassy and MAAG, GVN has not decreed the required measures and will continue to delay unless highly pressured to act.

But by the 16th both the MAAG Chief and the Ambassador were taking a gentler line. Durbrow's cable of that date reports that agreement on military reforms had reached a point "which MAAG considers it can live with provided GVN follows through with proper implementation." He was more concerned about the civil reforms, but nevertheless concluded the cable with:

Comments: Diem was most affable, exuded confidence and for first time expressed some gratitude our CIP efforts which he promised implement as best he could. Again before giving full green light believe we should await outcome detail discussion by GVN-US officials. In meantime MAAG quietly ordering some equipment for 20,000 increase.

And a week later, Washington replied, agreeing that the "green light" should be held up until the CIP was approved, but also noting that since success depended on the willing cooperation of the Vietnamese, the Embassy ought not to push Diem too hard in the negotiations.

Following this, the CIP negotiations dragged on inconclusively, and there is a ghostly quality to it all. There are cables giving encouraging progress reports which, in fact, seem limited to vague promises which, with hindsight, we know to have been quite meaningless, MAAG (and eventually the JCS in Washington) grew increasingly impatient with Durbrow's insistence on further holding up the "green light." They wanted to get on with the war.

By the end, Durbrow was simply holding out for Diem to actually complete the paperwork on some steps he had long ago said he intended to take. His very last cable (May 3) gives a good feeling for the flavor of the negotiations that had been going on between Diem and Durbrow for the nearly 3 months since the CIP talks began (and indeed it gives the flavor of Durbrow's relations with Diem at least since the previous October).

During the inauguration reception at Palace April 29, Diem took me aside and asked if I had given green light for US implementation of our part of counter insurgency plan (CIP). I replied frankly that I had not and noted that as stated in my letter of February 13 certain minimum actions must be taken by the GVN first if CIP is to produce results. I listed following actions: (1) Establishment of a central intelligence organization; (2) assignment of operational control for counter insurgency operations within military chain of command; and (3) implementation of reforms announced by Diem on February 6. Diem replied that he would do all these things, but that time was required to work out details. He said various GVN Cabinet members and Joint General Staff studying proposals and have different ideas. Since he wants to be sure that whatever done is well thought out, will be successful and not have to be changed in future he letting responsible officials thoroughly consider proposals. Diem stated that Secretary Thuan working on detailed statute for central intelligence organization, but it required more work and needs to be polished up. I replied that frankly time was slipping by and as yet there no action on these three points, which essential before I can give "green light" on equipment for 20,000 increase in armed forces.

In connection Diem remarks, Vice President Tho told me April 28 that he had not seen CIP, although he had heard of its existence, and he does not believe other Ministers have seen it either. Question thus arises as to whether Diem's statement that various Cabinet members studying CIP refers only to Thuan. I gave Tho fairly detailed fill-in on CIP contents. Tho said action now by President, at least implementation of reforms, needed in order capitalize on present upswing in popular feeling about situation following GVN success in carrying out elections despite VC efforts to disrupt. Stating he did not know when if ever reforms will be implemented, he commented that failure take such action after so many promises would lose all momentum gained from elections. Tho added that, aside from psychological impact, reforms likely take (*sic;* make) little change unless Diem himself changes his methods of operating. He noticed that if "super ministers" without real authority they likely become just additional level in bureaucracy without making GVN more effective.

On May 2 in course my formal farewell call I asked Diem if decrees yet signed on intelligence organization, chain of command and reforms. Diem stated he working on these matters but went through usual citation of difficulties including problem of convincing available personnel that they capable and qualified carry out responsibilities. He stated he already named Colonel Nguyen Van Yankee to head intelligence organization, Colonel Yankee has selected building for his headquarters and in process recruiting staff, while Secretary Thuan working on statute for organization. Re chain of command, I strongly emphasized that this one of most important factors in CIP, GVN must organize itself to follow national plan with one man in charge operational control and not waste time chasing will of wisps. Diem replied that he not feeling well (he has cold) and with inauguration he has not had time focus on this question but he will do it. He stated that he realizes only effective way is to place counter insurgency operations under Joint General Staff, but that his generals disagreed as to exactly how this should be done.

Diem, referring Sihanouk's Vietiane press conference (Vientiane's 1979), stated he did not believe there would be 14-nation conference and he afraid Laos almost lost already. Diem argued that since PL occupy almost all of southern Laos, we must agree increase in RVNAF to provide additional personnel to train self defense corps which in very bad shape.

Comment: Although Thuan has indicated to (MAAG Chief) General McGarr decree designating single officer to conduct counter insurgency operations being signed imminently, I asked him morning May 3 when seeing off Harriman and Lemnitzer whether I would receive before departure "present" he has long promised me. He replied presents often come when least expected, which apparently means Diem not yet ready sign decree.

While we should proceed with procurement equipment for 20,000 increase as recommended my 1606, I do not believe GVN should be informed of this green light, particularly until above decree signed. Durbrow.

The February 6 reforms referred to involved a cabinet re-organization Diem had announced before the start of the CIP negotiations. The intelligence re-organization was to consolidate the 7 existing services. The chain of command problem has been discussed above. Diem finally issued decrees on all these points a few days after Durbrow went home. The decrees were essentially meaningless: exactly these same issues remained high on the list of "necessary reforms" called for after the Taylor Mission, and indeed throughout the rest of Diem's life.

D. DURBROW'S TACTICS

Did Durbrow's tactics make sense? There is an argument to be made both ways. Certainly if Durbrow's focus was on the *pro forma* paperwork, then they did not. Mere formal organizational re-arrangements (unifying the then 7 intelligence services into 1, setting up at least a nominal chain of command for the war) often change very little even when they are seriously intended. To the extent they are not seriously intended, they are almost certain to be meaningless. Vice President Tho, of course, is cited in the cable as making exactly that point. The very fact that Durbrow chose to include this remark in the cable (without questioning it) suggests he agreed. But if squeezing the formal decrees out of Diem really did not mean much, then what was the point of exacerbating relations with Diem (not to mention relations with the military members of the U.S. mission) to get them? In hindsight, we can say there was none, unless the U.S. really meant what it had said about making U.S. support for Diem contingent on his taking "corrective measures." Then the function of those tactics would not have been to squeeze a probably meaningless concession from Diem; for the cable quoted alone makes it pretty clear that it would have been naive to expect much follow-through from Diem. The purpose would have been to begin the process of separating U.S. support for Vietnam from support for the Diem regime, and to lay the basis for stronger such signals in the future unless Diem underwent some miraculous reformation. That, of course, is exactly the tack the U.S. followed in the fall of 1963, once the Administration had really decided that we could not go on with the Diem regime as it then existed.

All this can be said with hindsight. It is not clear how much of this line of thinking should be attributed to American officials in Washington or Saigon at the time. There is no hint in the cables we have that Durbrow was thinking this way. Rather he seems to have felt that the concessions he was wringing from Diem represented real progress, but that we would have to keep up the pressure (presumably with threats to suspend aid—as his guidance considered—even after the "green light" was given) to keep goading Diem in the right direction. Meanwhile, the predominant view (pushed most strongly, but hardly exclusively by the military) was that we should, and could effectively get on with the war with as much cooperation as we could get from Diem short of interfering with the war effort: it was all right to try for a *quid pro quo* on aid, but not very hard. The Lansdale view went even further, stressing the need for a demonstration of positive, essentially unqualified support for Diem if only to discourage a further coup attempt, which Lansdale saw as the main short-run danger.

In a significant way, Lansdale's view was not very different in its analysis of tactics from the view that Diem was hopeless. Both Lansdale, with his strong pro-Diem view, and men like Galbraith with a strong anti-Diem view, agreed that Diem could not be pressured into reforming this regime. ("He won't change, because he can't change," wrote Galbraith in a cable we will quote in more detail later.)

Where the Lansdale and Galbraith views differed—a fundamental difference, of course,—was in their estimate of the balance of risks of a coup. Lansdale, and obviously his view carried the day, believed that a coup was much more likely to make things worse than make things better. This must have been an especially hard view to argue against in 1961, when Diem did not look as hopeless as he would later, and when a strong argument could be made that the U.S. just could not afford at that time to risk the collapse of a pro-Western government in Vietnam. It must have seemed essentially irresistible to take the route or at least postponing, as seemed quite feasible, a decision on such a tough and risky course as holding back on support for Diem. The President, after all, could remember the charges that the Truman Administration had given away China by holding back on aid to Chiang to try to pressure him toward reform. As a young Congressman, he had even joined the chorus.

Meanwhile Durbrow was about to come home (he had been in Vietnam for 4 years); security problems in Vietnam were, at best, not improving; and the repercussions of Laos were spilling over and would make further moves on Vietnam an urgent matter. By the middle of April, the Administration was undertaking its first close look at the problem in Vietnam (in contrast to the almost automatic approval of the CIP during the opening days of the new Administration).

III.   THE SPRING DECISIONS—I

A.   THE "PRESIDENTIAL PROGRAM"

The development of what eventually came to be called "The Presidential Program for Vietnam" formally began with this memorandum from McNamara to Gilpatric:

20 April 1961

MEMORANDUM FOR THE DEPUTY SECRETARY OF DEFENSE

This will confirm our discussion of this morning during which I stated that the President has asked that you:

a. Appraise the current status and future prospects of the Communist drive to dominate South Viet-Nam.

b. Recommend a series of actions (military, political and/or economic, overt and/or covert) which, in your opinion, will prevent Communist domination of that country.

The President would like to receive your report on or before Thursday, April 27.

During the course of your study, you should draw, to the extent you believe necessary, upon the views and resources of the State Γ partment and CIA. Mr. Chester Bowles was present when the President discussed the matter with me, and I have reviewed the project with Mr. Allen Dulles. Further, the President stated that Mr. Walt Rostow would be available to counsel with you.

Gilpatric, although obviously given a completely free hand under the terms of the memo, nevertheless set up an interagency task force to work on the report. A draft was ready April 26, and Gilpatric sent it to the President the following day. But this turned out to be only the first, and relatively unimportant phase of the effort. For the Laos crisis came to a boil just as the first Gilpatric report was finished, and the Task Force was continued with the essentially new mission of a recommending additional measure to keep our position from falling apart in the wake of what was happening in Laos. Consequently, to understand these late-April, early-May decisions, we have to treat separately the initial Gilpatric effort and the later, primarily State-drafted revision, dated May 6. The same general factors were in the background of both efforts, although Laos was only one of the things that influenced the April 26 effort, while it became the overwhelming element in the May 6 effort. It is worth setting out these influencing factors, specifically:

1. The security situation in Vietnam.
2. The Administration's special interest in counter-insurgency.
3. The apparent futility and divisiveness of the Durbrow (pressure) tactics for dealing with Diem.
4. Eventually most important, and substantially narrowing the range of options realistically open to the Administration, the weakness of US policy in Laos, and the consequent strongly felt need for a signal of firm policy in Vietnam.

1. *The Security Situation in Vietnam*

The VC threat in Vietnam looked worse in April than it had in January. We will see that Gilpatric's report painted a bleak picture. Yet, there is no hint in the record that concern about the immediate situation in Vietnam was a major factor in the decision to formulate a new program.

VC strength was estimated at 3-15,000 in Lansdale's January memorandum; 8-10,000 in a March NIE; 10,000 in an April briefing paper (apparently by Landsdale) immediately preceding—and recommending—the Gilpatric Task Force; then 12,000 one week later in the Gilpatric report proper. VC incidents were reported high for April (according to the Task Force report, 650 per month, 4 times higher than January), but an upsurge in activity had long been predicted to coincide with the Vietnamese elections. As would happen in the future, the failure of the VC to prevent the elections was considered a sign of government strength.

On the basis of the Task Force statistics, we could assume that the situation was deteriorating rapidly: taken literally, they indicate an increase in VC strength of 20 percent in about a week, plus the large increase in incidents. But neither cables from the field, nor the Washington files show any sense of a sharply deteriorating situation. And, as we will see, the initial Task Force Report, despite its crisis tone, recommended no increase in miltary strength for the Vietnamese, only more generous US financial aid to forces already planned under the CIP.

2.   The Administration's Special Interest in Counter-insurgency

A more important impetus to the Gilpatric effort than any sense of deterioration in Vietnam seems to have been the Administration's general interest in doing something about counter-insurgency warfare, combined with an interest in finding more informal and more efficient means of supervising policy than the Eisenhower Administration's elaborate National Security structure. The effort in Vietnam obviously required some coordination of separate efforts by at least State, Defense, CIA, and ICA (a predecessor of AID). Further, once a coordinated program was worked out, the idea appears to have been to focus responsibility for seeing to it that the program was carried out on some clearly identified individual. This search for a better way to organize Gilpatric effort, although it became inconsequential after the original submission.

3.   The Apparent Futility and Divisiveness of the Durbrow (Pressure) Tactics for Dealing With Diem

Late April was a peculiarly appropriate time to undertake the sort of sharpening up of policy and its organization just described. It was probably clear by then that Durbrow's pressure tactics were not really accomplishing much with Diem. Besides, Durbrow had been in Vietnam for four years by April, and a new Ambassador would normally have been sent in any event. Fritz Nolting had been chosen by early April, and he was scheduled to take over in early May. Further, Diem had just been reelected, an essentially meaningless formality to be sure, but still one more thing that helped make late April a logical time for taking a fresh look at US relations with Diem. And even to people who believed that a continuation of Durbrow's pressure tactics might be the best approach to Diem, events elsewhere and especially in Laos must have raised questions about whether it was a politic time to be threatening to withhold aid.

4.   The Weakness of US Policy in Laos, and the Need for a Signal of Firm Policy in Vietnam

The situation in the world that April seemed to create an urgent requirement for the US to do something to demonstrate firmness, and especially so in Southeast Asia. The Task Force was set up the day after the Bay of Pigs invasion force surrendered, and at a time when the Laos crisis was obviously coming to head. There had been implicit agreement in principle between the US and the Soviets to seek a cease fire in Laos and to organize a neutral coalition government. But it was not clear at all that the cease-fire would come while there was anything left worth arguing about in the hands of the pro-Western faction. Gilpatric's initial Task Force report reached the President the day of a crisis meeting in Laos, and the more important second phase of the effort began then, in an atmosphere wholly dominated by Laos.

But even before the Laos crisis reached its peak, there was a sense in Washington and generally in the world that put strong pressures on the Administration to look for ways to take a firm stand somewhere; and if it was not to be in Laos, then Vietnam was next under the gun.

Something of the mood of the time can be sensed in these quotes, one from a March 28 NIE on Southeast Asia, another from Lansdale's notes, and finally a significant question from a Kennedy press conference:

From the NIE:

There is a deep awareness among the countries of Southeast Asia that developments in the Laotian crisis, and its outcome, have a profound impact on their future. The governments of the area tend to regard the Laotian crisis as a symbolic test of strengths between the major powers of the West and the Communist bloc.

From Lansdale's notes (about April 21):

1. Psychological—VN believed always they main target. Now it comes— "when our turn comes, will we be treated the same as Laos?" Main task GVN confidence in US.

And suggesting the more general tone of the time (even a week before the Bay of Pigs, prompted by the Soviet orbiting of a man in space) this question at Kennedy's April 12 news conference:

Mr. President, this question might better be asked at a history class than at a news conference, but here it is anyway. The Communists seem to be putting us on the defensive on a number of fronts—now, again, in space. Wars aside, do you think there is a danger that their system is going to prove more durable than ours.

The President answered with cautious reassurance. Eight days later, after the Bay of Pigs, and the day he ordered the Task Force to go ahead, he told the Association of Newspaper Editors:

. . . . it is clearer than ever that we face a relentless struggle in every corner of the globe that goes far beyond the clash of armies, or even nuclear armaments. The armies are there. But they serve primarily as the shield behind which subversion, infiltration, and a host of other tactics steadily advance, picking off vulnerable areas one by one in situations that do not permit our own armed intervention. . . . We dare not fail to see the insidious nature of this new and deeper struggle. We dare not fail to grasp the new concepts, the new tools, the new sense of urgency we will need to combat it—whether in Cuba or South Vietnam. (Notice Kennedy's explicit assumption about US armed intervention as a means of dealing with insurgencies. Not too much can be read into his remark, for it probably was inspired primarily by criticism of his refusal to try to save the Bay of Pigs contingent. But the balance of the record adds significance to the comment.)

B. THE APRIL 26 REPORT

The available Gilpatric file consists mostly of drafts of the report and memos from Lansdale. It contains a memorandum dated April 13, in which Lansdale advised Gilpatric of a meeting with Rostow, at which Rostow showed Lansdale a copy of a memorandum to Kennedy recommending a fresh crack at the Vietnam situation. Here is Rostow's memorandum:

'   April 12, 1961

MEMORANDUM TO THE PRESIDENT

FROM: WWR

Now that the Viet-Nam election is over, I believe we must turn to gearing up the whole Viet-Nam operation. Among the possible lines of action that might be considered at an early high level meeting are the following:

1.   The appointment of a full time first-rate back-stop man in Washington. McNamara, as well as your staff, believes this to be essential.

2.   The briefing of our new Ambassador, Fritz Nolting, including sufficient talk with yourself so that he fully understands the priority you attach to the Viet-Nam problem.

3.   A possible visit to Viet-Nam in the near future by the Vice President.

4.   A possible visit to the United States of Mr. Thuan, acting Defense Minister, and one of the few men around Diem with operational capacity and vigor.

5.   The sending to Viet-Nam of a research and development and military hardware team which would explore with General McGarr which of the various techniques and gadgets now available or being explored might be relevant and useful in the Viet-Nam operation.

6.   The raising of the MAAG ceiling, which involves some diplomacy, unless we can find an alternative way of introducing into the Viet-Nam operation a substantial number of Special Forces types.

7.   The question of replacing the present ICA Chief in Viet-Nam, who, by all accounts, has expended his capital. We need a vigorous man who can work well with the military, since some of the rural development problems relate closely to guerrilla operations.

8.   Settling the question of the extra funds for Diem.

9.   The tactics of persuading Diem to move more rapidly to broaden the base of his government, as well as to decrease its centralization and improve its efficiency.

Against the background of decisions we should urgently take on these matters, you may wish to prepare a letter to Diem which would not only congratulate him, reaffirm our support, and specify new initiatives we are prepared to take, but would make clear to him the urgency you attach to a more effective political and morale setting for his military operation, now that the elections are successfully behind him.

Neither this memo, nor other available papers, give us a basis for judging how far the stress on the importance of Vietnam was already influenced by developments in Laos, and how much it reflects a separable interest in taking on the challenge of "wars of liberation." Both were undoubtedly important. But this Rostow memo turned out to be pretty close to an agenda for the initial Task Force report. It seems very safe to assume that the "full-time, first-rate, backstop man in Washington" Rostow had in mind was Lansdale. (Gilpatric himself obviously could not be expected to spend full-time on Vietnam.) Presumably the President's request for the Gilpatric report was intended as either a method of easing Lansdale into that role, or at least of trying him out in it.

Following the description of the Rostow memo, Gilpatric's file contains several carbon copies of a long paper, unsigned but certainly by Lansdale, which among other things recommends that the President set up a Task Force for Vietnam which would lay out a detailed program of action and go on to supervise the implementation of that program. The date on the paper is April 19, but a draft must have been prepared some days earlier, probably about the time of Lansdale's discussion with Rostow on the 13th, since the available copies recommended that the Task Force submit its report to the President by April 21. The paper explicitly foresaw a major role for General Lansdale both in the Task Force, and thereafter in supervising the implementation of the report.

This Task Force was apparently intended to supersede what the paper refers to as "one of the customary working groups in Washington" which was "being called together next week by John Steeves, Acting Assistant Secretary of State for Far Eastern Affairs."

In view of all this, it is not surprising to find that the first phase of the Task Force effort appears, from the record, to have been very much a Gilpatric-Lansdale show. The first meeting of the group (which included State and CIA representatives) was apparently held April 24, four days after Gilpatric was told to go ahead. Present files do not show whether there was another full meeting of the group before the first version of the report (dated April 26) was sent to the President on the 27th.

Here are the opening sections, which introduce the list of proposed actions which make up the program.

A PROGRAM OF ACTION TO PREVENT COMMUNIST
DOMINATION OF SOUTH VIETNAM
APPRAISAL OF THE SITUATION

After meeting in Hanoi on 13 May 1959, the Central Committee of the North Vietnamese Communist Party publicly announced its intention "to smash" the government of President Diem. Following this decision, the Viet Cong have significantly increased their program of infiltration, subversion, sabotage and assassination designed to achieve this end.

At the North Vietnamese Communist Party Congress in September 1960, the earlier declaration of underground war by the Party's Control

Committee was reaffirmed. This action by the Party Congress took place only a month after Kong Le's coup in Laos. Scarcely two months later there was a military uprising in Saigon. The turmoil created throughout the area by this rapid succession of events provides an ideal environment for the Communist "master plan" to take over all of Southeast Asia.

Since that time, as can be seen from the attached map, the internal security situation in South Vietnam has become critical. What amounts to a state of active guerrilla warfare now exists throughout the country. The number of Viet Cong hard-core Communists has increased from 4400 in early 1960 to an estimated 12,000 today. The number of violent incidents per month now averages 650. Casualties on both sides totaled more than 4500 during the first three months of this year. Fifty-eight percent of the country is under some degree of Communist control, ranging from harassment and night raids to almost complete administrative jurisdiction in the Communist "secure areas."

The Viet Cong over the past two years have succeeded in stepping up the pace and intensity of their attacks to the point where South Vietnam is nearing the decisive phase in its battle for survival. If the situation continues to deteriorate, the Communists will be able to press on to their strategic goal of establishing a rival "National Liberation Front" government in one of these "secure areas" thereby plunging the nation into open civil war. They have publicly announced that they will "take over the country before the end of 1961."

This situation is thus critical, but is not hopeless. The Vietnamese Government, with American aid, has increased its capabilities to fight its attackers, and provides a base upon which the necessary additional effort can be founded to defeat the Communist attack. Should the Communist effort increase, either directly or as a result of a collapse of Laos, additional measures beyond those proposed herein would be necessary.

In short, the situation in South Vietnam has reached the point where, at least for the time being, primary emphasis should be placed on providing a solution to the internal security problem.

The US Objective: To create a viable and increasingly democratic society in South Vietnam and to prevent Communist domination of the country.

Concept of Operations: To initiate on an accelerated basis, a series of mutually supporting actions of a military, political, economic, psychological and covert character designed to achieve this objective. In so doing, it is intended to use, and where appropriate extend, expedite or build upon the existing US and Government of Vietnam [GVN] programs already underway in South Vietnam. There is neither the time available nor any sound justification for "starting from scratch." Rather the need is to focus the US effort in South Vietnam on the immediate internal security problem; to infuse it with a sense of urgency and a dedication to the overall US objective; to achieve, through cooperative inter-departmental support both in the field and in Washington, the operational flexibility needed to apply the available US assets in a manner best calculated to achieve our objective in Vietnam; and, finally, to impress on our friends, the Vietnamese, and on our foes, the Viet Cong, that come what may, the US intends to *win* this battle.

The program that followed this strongly worded introduction was very modest, not merely compared to current US involvement, but to the effort the US undertook following the Taylor Mission in the fall. The program is essentially simply a moderate acceleration of the CIP program approved in January, with a great deal of stress on vigor, enthusiasm, and strong leadership in carrying out the program.

In particular, the program proposes no increase in the Vietnamese army, and only a moderate (in hindsight, inconsequential) increase in the size of our MAAG mission. The main military measures were for the US to provide financial support for the 20,000-man increase in the RVNAF and to provide support for the full complement of counter-insurgency auxiliary forces (Civil Guard and Self-Defense Corps) planned by Diem. Both were modest steps. For under the CIP we were already planning to pay support costs for 150,000 men of the RVNAF and 32,000 men of the Civil Guard. This Task Force proposal, which had been urged for some weeks by MAAG in Saigon, simply said that we would provide the same support for all the Vietnamese forces that we had already planned to provide for most of them.

For the rest, the Presidential Program in its final form, issued May 19, turned out (after a great deal of stirring around) to be close to that proposed in the April 26 draft.

Two comments are needed on this material. First, the program Lansdale and Gilpatric proposed was not so narrowly military as the repeated emphasis on priority for the internal security problem might suggest. Rather, the emphasis was on stabilizing the countryside, in contrast to pressing Diem on political and administrative reforms mainly of interest to Diem's urban critics. This reflected both Lansdale's judgments on counter-insurgency, which look good in hindsight, and his strongly pro-Diem orientation, which looks much less good.

Second, the reference to a communist "master plan" for Southeast Asia (and similar language is found in a number of other staff papers through the balance of 1961) suggests a view of the situation which has been much criticized recently by men like Galbraith and Kennan. Public comments by those who were closely involved (both those critical of policy since 1965, such as Sorenson and Hilsman, and those supporting the Administration, such as William Bundy) suggest a more sophisticated view of the problem. Here we simply note that the formal staff work available strongly supports Galbraith and Kennan, although this does not necessarily imply that the senior members of the Administration shared the view that North Vietnam was operating (in the words of another staff paper) as the "implementing agent of Bloc policy" rather than in fairly conventional, mainly non-ideological pursuit of its own national interest.

C. LANSDALE'S ROLE

In his April 27 memorandum transmitting the Report to the President, Gilpatric noted that:

> . . . in the short time available to the Task Force it was not possible to develop the program in complete detail. However, there has been prepared a plan for mutually supporting actions of a political, military, economic, psychological, and covert character which can be refined periodically on the basis of further recommendations from the field.

Toward this end, Brigadier General E.G. Lansdale, USAF, who has been designated Operations Officer for the Task Force, will proceed to Vietnam immediately after the program receives Presidential approval. Following on the spot discussions with US and Vietnamese officials, he will forward to the Director of the Task Force specific recommendations for action in support of the attached program.

This appears to have been the high point of Lansdale's role in Vietnam policy. Lansdal by this time had already sent (with Gilpatric's approval) messages requesting various people to meet him in Saigon, May 5. This is from a memorandum he sent to Richard Bissell, then still a Deputy Director of the CIA, requesting the services of one of his colleagues from the 1955–1956 experience in Vietnam:

> I realize Redick is committed to an important job in Laos and that this is a difficult time in that trouble spot. I do feel, however, that we may yet save Vietnam and that our best effort should be put into it.
> Redick, in my opinion, is now so much a part of the uninhibited communications between President Diem and myself that it goes far beyond the question of having an interpreter. His particular facility for appreciating my meaning in words and the thoughts of Diem in return is practically indispensable to me in the role I am assigned in seeking President Kennedy's goal for Vietnam.

But none of this was to be. Present files contain a thermofax of McNamara's copy of the memorandum Gilpatric sent to the President. In McNamara's handwriting the words (Lansdale) "will proceed to Vietnam immediately" are changed to "will proceed to Vietnam when requested by the Ambassador." As we will see below, when the Task Force Report was redrafted the next week, Lansdale's key role disappeard entirely, at the request of the State Department, but presumably with the concurrence of the White House.

D.   KENNEDY'S APRIL 29 DECISIONS

Although our record is not clear, it appears that the cover memorandum was sent to the President as Gilpatric had signed it, and that McNamara's correction reflected a decision made after the paper went to the President, rather than a change in the language of the memo. In any event, at a meeting on April 29, President Kennedy approved only the quite limited military proposals of the draft report it transmitted. Decisions were deferred on the balance of the paper, which now included an annex issued April 28 on much more substantial additional military aid believed required by the situation in Laos. The military measures approved during this first go-around were:

> (1) Increase the MAAG as necessary to insure the effective implemention of the military portion of the program including the training of a 20,000-man addition to the present GVN armed forces of 150,000. Initial appaisal of new tasks assigned CHMAAG indicates that approximately 100 additional military personnel will be required immediately in addition to the present complement of 685.
> (2) Expand MAAG responsibilities to include authority to provide support and advice to the Self Defense Corps with a strength of approximately 40,000.

(3) Authority MAP support for the entire Civil Guard Forces of 68,000 MAP support is now authoritized for 32,000; the remaining 36,000 are not now adequately trained and equipped.

(4) Install as a matter of priority a radar surveillance capability which will enable the GVN to obtain warning of Communist over-flights being conducted for intelligence or clandestine air supply purposes. Initially, this capability should be provided from US mobile radar capability.

(5) Provide MAP support for the Vietnamese Junk Force as a means of preventing Viet Cong clandestine supply and infiltration into South Vietnam by water. MAP support, which was not provided in the Counterinsurgency Plan, will include training of junk crews in Vietnam or at US bases by US Navy Personnel.

The only substantial significance that can be read into these April 29 decisions is that they signalled a willingness to go beyond the 685-man limit on the size of the US military mission in Saigon, which, *if* it were done openly, would be the first formal breech of the Geneva Agreements. For the rest, we were providing somewhat more generous support to the Vietnamese than proposed in the CIP. But the overall size of the Vietnamese forces would be no higher than those already approved. (The 20,000-man increase was already part of the CIP.) No one proposed in this initial draft that the Administration even consider sending American troops (other than the 100-odd additional advisors). It was not, by any interpretation, a crisis response.

Indeed, even if Kennedy had approved the whole April 26 program, it would have seemed (in hindsight) most notable for the "come what may, we intend to win" rhetoric in its introduction and for the supreme role granted to Task Force (and indirectly to Lansdale as its operations officer) in control of Vietnam policy. Lansdale's memoranda leave no real doubt that he saw the Report exactly that way—which presumably was why he made no effort to risk stirring up trouble by putting his more controversial views into the paper. For example, although Lansdale believed the key new item in Vietnam policy was a need for emphatic support for Diem, only the barest hint of this view appears in the paper (and it is not even hinted at in Lansdale's preliminary draft of the report distributed at the April 24th meeting of the Task Force).

That is when this opening phase of the Task Force effort has to be separated from what followed. As just noted, it was remarkable mainly for the strength of the commitment implied to South Vietnam, which the President never did unambiguously endorse, and for the organizational arrangement it proposed, with the key role for Lansdale and Gilpatric, which was eliminated from the later drafts. All of the factors behind the May reappraisal (cited at the beginning of this chapter) undoubtedly contributed to the decision to set up the Task Force. But Rostow's memorandum and the modest dimensions of the resulting proposals suggest the main idea really was to sharpen up existing policy and its administration, rather than to work out a new policy on the assumption that the existing program had become substantially obsolete. Immediately after April 27, this changes. Although Gilpatric and Lansdale continued to head up the Task Force through the Presidential decisions of May 11, their personal role became increasingly unimportant. The significance no longer was in putting new people in charge of a new style for running the program, but in developing a new program that would offset the impact of Laos.

E. THE LAOS ANNEX

On April 28, an annex had been issued to the basic report which went far beyond the modest military proposals in the original. The most reasonable assumption is that the annex was drawn up in response to comments at the April 27 NSC meeting at which the Report was to have been considered, but which turned out to be devoted to the by-then acute state of the crisis in Laos. On the grounds that the neutralization of Laos would solidify communists *de facto* control of eastern Laos (including the mountain passes which were the historic invasion route to southern Vietnam), the annex advocated U.S. support for a two-division increase in the RVNAF. To rapidly train these forces, there was now a recommendation on U.S. manpower commitments that dwarted the previous recommendation for a MAAG increase: specifically, a 1600-man training team for each of the two new divisions, plus a 400-man special forces contingent to speed up counter-insurgency training fot the South Vietnamese forces: a total of 3600 men, not counting the MAAG increase already authorized.

It is interesting that in the annex this force increase (and the bulk of the U.S. troop commitment) was specifically justified as insurance against a conventional invasion of South Vietnam. Some earlier drafts show the evolution of this concept. There is an alternate draft, apparently by Lansdale, which was not used but which recommended a U.S. troop commitment as reassurance to the Vietnamese of U.S. determination to stand by them. It did not recommend any increase in South Vietnamese forces. Instead, it stressed very heavily the damage to U.S. prestige and the credibility of our guarantees to other countries in Southeast Asia should we go through with the Laos settlement without taking some strong action to demonstrate that we were finally drawing a line in Southeast Asia.

Contrasting sharply with Lansdale's draft was the first draft of the paper that was finally issued. This was by Gilpatric's military aide, Col. E.F. Black. It concludes that South Vietnamese forces would have to be increased by two divisions, mainly to deal with threat of increased infiltration. Black stressed that the President would have to decide that the US would no longer be bound by the limitations of the 1954 Geneva Agreements (which Defense had long been lobbying against). But his paper recommends no substantial troop commitment. The reference to the Geneva Agreements apparently referred to a relatively modest increase in manpower beyond the 685-man ceiling, and to the introduction of new types of equipment not in Vietnam in 1954.

So the record contains three versions of the Annex—Black's first draft, Lansdale's alternate draft, and then Black's revised paper, which was finally issure as the annex to the Report. The effect of considering them all is an odd one. The initial Black paper recommends an increase in Vietnamese forces to deal with the infiltration problem, but no substantial US troop commitment. The Lansdale alternative recommends a substantial US troop commitment, but no increase in Vietnamese forces. The final paper recommends both the RVNAF increase and the US troop commitments, but changes the reason for each: the reason for the RVNAF increase became a need for better protection against overt invasion, not an increased infiltration threat. And the reason for the US troop commitment became a desire to rapidly train the new Vietnamese troops, not for political reassurance.

If taken literally, all of this implies an extraordinarily rapid series of reappraisals and reversals of judgment. But surely, the only realistic interpretation is that in this case (because a series of rough drafts happens to be included in the available file) we are getting a glimpse at the way such staff paperwork really gets drafted, as opposed to the much more orderly impression that is given if we saw only the finished products. Gilpatric (undoubtedly in consultation with at least McNamara, although the files do not show any record of this) was presumably interested primarily in what recommendations to make to the President, and secondarily in providing a bureaucratically suitable rationale for those recommendations. This rationale may, or may not, have coincided with whatever more private explanation of the recommendations that McNamara or Gilpatric may have conveyed to the President or people like McGeorge Bundy and Rostow on the White House staff. The lesson in this, which will not come as a surprise to anyone who has ever had contact with the policy-making process, is that the rationales given in such pieces of paper (intended for fairly wide circulation among the bureaucracy, as opposed to tightly held memoranda limited to those closest to the decision-maker) do not reliably indicate why recommendations were made the way they were.

F. THE MAY 1 REVIEW

Meanwhile, Kennedy, as noted earlier, did not act on the annex at the April 29 meeting when he approved the much more modest military proposals of the basic Report. But on that day, there was a cable alerting CINCPAC to be ready to move 5000-men task forces to Udorn, Thailand, and to Touraine, (Da Nang), South Vietnam. Classified records available for this study do not explain this alert. But the public memoirs indirectly refer to it, and as would be expected, the alert was intended as a threat to intervene in Laos if the communists failed to go through with the cease fire which was to precede the Geneva Conference. Here is the cable:

From: JCS
TO: CINCPAC
INFO: CHMAAG VIENTIANE
         CHJUSMAAG BANGKOK THAILAND
         CHMAAG SAIGON VIETNAM

JCS DA 995131   From JCS.

1. Request you prepare plans to move brigade size forces of approximately 5,000 each into Udorn or vicinity and into Tourane or vicinity. Forces should include all arms and appropriate air elements. Plans should be based solely on US forces at this time.
2. Decision to make these deployments not firm. It is expected that decision as to Thailand will be made at meeting tentatively scheduled here on Monday. Decision regarding Vietnam will be even later due to consideration of Geneva Accords.
3. It is hoped that these movements can be given SEATO cover but such possibility must be explored before becoming a firm element of your planning. State is taking action to explore this aspect.
4. Decision was not repeat not reached today concerning implementation of SEATO Plan 5/60.

The crisis in Laos was now at its peak. According to Schlesinger's account, reports reached Washington April 26 that the Pathet Lao were attacking strongly, with the apparent intention of grabbing most of the country before the cease-fire went into effect. At 10 p.m. that night, the JCS sent out a "general advisory" to major commands around the world, and specifically alerted CINC-PAC to be prepared to undertake airstrikes against North Vietnam, and possibly southern China.

The next day—the day the Task Force Report came to the President—there were prolonged crisis meetings in the White House. The President later called in Congressional leaders, who advised against putting troops into Laos. Schlesinger quotes Rostow as telling him the NSC meeting that day was "the worst White House meeting he had ever attended in the entire Kennedy administration."

The Laos annex to the Gilpatric Report was issued on the 28th, in an atmosphere wholly dominated by the crisis in Laos. On the 29th, Kennedy's go-ahead on the Task Force's original military recommendations was squeezed into a day overwhelmingly devoted to Laos. This was the day of the cable, just cited, alerting CINCPAC for troop movements to Thailand and possibly Vietnam. The "SEATO Plan 5/60" referred to in the closing paragraph of the cable was the plan for moving major units into Laos.

On May 1 (the Monday meeting referred to in the cable), Kennedy again deferred any decision on putting troops into Laos. According to available accounts, there is a strong sense by now (although no formal decision) that the U.S. would not go into Laos: that if the cease-fire failed, we would make a strong stand, instead, in Thailand and Vietnam. (On the 28th, in a speech to a Democratic dinner in Chicago, the President had hinted at this:

> We are prepared to meet our obligations, but we can only defend the freedom of those who are determined to be free themselves. We can assist them—we will bear more than our share of the burden, but we can only help those who are ready to bear their share of the burden themselves.

Reasonable qualifications, undoubtedly, but ones that seemed to suggest that intervention in Laos would be futile. On Sunday (the 30th), another hint came in remarks by Senator Fulbright on a TV interview show: he opposed intervention in Laos, and said he was confident the government was seeking "another solution."

So the decision anticipated Monday, May 1, in the JCS cable to CINCPAC was not made that day after all. But that day a new draft of the Task Force Report was issued. It contained only the significant change (other than blending the April 28 annex into the basic paper). The original draft contained a paragraph (under "political objectives") recommending we "obtain the political agreement [presumably from the SEATO membership] needed to permit the prompt implementation of SEATO contingency plans providing for military intervention in South Vietnam should this become necessary to prevent the loss of the country to Communism."

In the May 1 revision, the following sentence was added to the paragraph: "The United States should be prepared to intervene unilaterally in fulfillment of its commitment under Article IV, 2. of Manila Pact, and should make its determination to do so clear through appropriate public statements, diplomatic discussions, troop deployments, or other means." (The cited clause in the Manila (SEATO) Pact, which the paper did not quote,

If, in the opinion of any of the Parties, the inviolability or the integrity of the territory or the sovereignty or political independence of any Party in the treaty area or of any other State or territory to which the provisions of paragraph 1 of this Article from time to time apply is threatened in any way other than by armed attack or is affected or threatened by any fact or situation which might endanger the peace of the area, the Parties shall consult immediately in order to agree on the measures which should be taken for the common defense.)

The May 1 draft also cleared up, or papered over, part of the confusion described earlier regarding the rationale for the military measures recommended in the Laos annex: the increased RVNAF force levels were attributed now both to concern over increased infiltration and to concern over overt invasion. But the US troop commitments are still described solely as for training, with no mention of the original political rationale.

G. STATE'S REDRAFT

Lansdale circulated the May 1 draft among the Task Force, with a note that comments should be in May 2, with a final Task Force review scheduled the morning of May 3, all in anticipation of an NSC meeting on the paper May 4.

George Ball, then Deputy Under Secretary of State, asked to postpone the meeting for a day. Lansdale sent Gilpatric a memorandum opposing the postponement. "It seems to me that George Ball could appoint someone to represent him at the meeting, and if he has personal or further comments they could come to us later in the day at his convenience." But Gilpatric delayed the meeting a day, and State produced a drastic revision of the paper.

On the organizational issues, the State draft was brutally clearcut. It proposed a new version of the Gilpatric memorandum transmtiting the Report, in which:

1. The paragraph (quoted earlier) describing Lansdale's special role is deleted.
2. A new paragraph is added to the end of the memorandum, in which Gilpatric is made to say: "Having completed its assignment . . . I recommend that the present Task Force be now dissolved."

Later sections of the paper were revised accordingly, giving responsibility for coordinating Vietnam policy to a new Task Force with George Ball as chairman. (In the final version, the Task Force has a State Department director, but no longer included Presidential appointees representing their departments. The whole Task Force idea had been downgraded to a conventional interagency working group. Although it continued to function for several years, there will be little occasion to mention it again in this paper.)

State's proposal on organization prevailed. From the record available, the only thing that can be said definitely is that State objected, successfully, to having an Ambassador report to a Task Force chaired by the Deputy Secretary of Defense, and with a second defense official (Lansdale) as executive officer. There may have been more to it. We know Lansdale's experience and his approach to guerrilla warfare initially won him a good deal of favor at the White House. But his memorandum suggest that his ideas on a number of issues (support for Phoumi in Laos, liberation of North Vietnam, essentially unqualified support for Diem in South Vietnam) went well beyond what the Administration judged reasonable. So it is quite possible that the President would have had second thoughts on Lansdale, aside from State's objections on bureaucratic grounds.

In any event, Lansdale's reaction to State's proposal on organization was to advise McNamara and Gilpatric that:

> My strong recommendation is that Defense stay completely out of the Task Force directorship as now proposed by State . . . Having a Defense officer, myself or someone else, placed in a position of only partial influence and of no decision permissibility would be only to provide State with a scapegoat to share the blame when we have a flop . . . The US past performance and theory of action, which State apparently desires to continue, simply offers no sound basis for winning, as desired by President Kennedy.

But the final version of the Task Force Report, dated May 6, followed very closely the State revision submitted May 3, including the shift in control of the Task Force. [see also Doc. 87]

H.   WIDENING THE OPTIONS

What is most striking about the revised drafts is that they excluded a tone of almost unqualified commitment to Vietnam, yet on the really important issues included qualifications which left the President a great deal of freedom to decide whatever he pleased without having to formally overrule the Task Force Report.

For example, the assertion (from the April draft) that the US should impress on friend and foe that "come what may, we intend to win" remained in the final paper. But this hortatory language is from the introduction; it described one of the effects the program in the balance of the paper was supposed to achieve, but did not ask the President to do or say anything not spelled out in the body of the paper. (We will see, when we come to the fall decisions, that the wisdom of an unqualified commitment to save Vietnam from Communism is treated afresh, with no suggestion that any such decision had already been made in May.)

On the other hand, the explicit recommendation in the Defense draft that we make clear our "determination . . . to intervene unilaterally . . . should this become necessary to save the country from communism . . ." was dropped. Instead, there is a recommendation for exploring a "new bilateral arrangement" which might (the text is not explicit) extend to fighting the guerrillas, if that should become necessary to save the country, but also might only cover overt North Vietnamese invasion.

Further, the need for these arrangements was now tied to the "loss" of Laos. The May 3 draft suggests we "undertake military security arrangements which establish beyond doubt our intention to stand behind Vietnam's resistance to Communism . . ." since "it is doubtful whether the Vietnamese Government can weather the pressures which are certain to be generated from the loss of Laos without prompt, and dramatic support for its security from the U.S."

In the May 6 final draft, "establish beyond doubt" was toned down to "emphasize" and the flat reference to the loss of Laos was changed to "if Laos were lost."

Similarly, the recommendations on the two new South Vietnamese divisions, and the two 1600-man US combat units to train them was described as a firm recommendation in the military section of the May 3 draft (which State left untouched from the Defense version), but were indirectly referred to as something for study in State's re-drafted political section. In the final paper, they were still firm recommendations in a military annex, but not in the main paper, where Defense was only described as studying this and other uses for US troops short of direct commitment against the guerrillas. US troop commitments were no longer recommended, only referred to as something "which might result from an NSC decision following discussions between Vice President Johnson [whose mission to Asia had been announced May 5] and President Diem."

Yet an interesting aspect of the State redraft is that, although its main impact was to soften the commitments implied in the Defense draft, a quick reading might give the contrary impression. We will see this same effect in the political sections to be discussed below. What seems to happen is that the very detail of the State treatment creates a strong impression, even though the actual proposals are less drastic and more qualified than those proposed by Defense. The contrast is all the sharper because the Defense draft leaned the other way. For example, the profoundly significant recommendation that the US commit itself to intervene unilaterally, if necessary, to prevent a Viet Cong victory in South Vietnam, is tossed into the Defense version most casually, with a reference to the Manila Treaty that makes it sound as if such a commitment, in fact, already existed.

In contrast, here is the State language referring to the proposed bilateral treaty (which in effect is a substitute for the Defense proposed unlimited unilateral commitment):

> The Geneva Accords have been totally inadequate in protecting South Vietnam against Communist infiltration and insurgency. Moreover, with increased Communist success in Laos dramatic US actions in stiffening up its physical support of Vietnam and the remainder of Southeast Asia may be needed to bolster the will to continue to resist the Communists. The inhibitions imposed on such action by certain parts of the Geneva Accords, which have been violated with impunity by the Communists, should not prevent our action. We should consider joining with the Vietnamese in a clearcut defensive alliance which might include stationing of US forces on Vietnamese soil. As a variant of this arrangement certain SEATO troops might also be employed.
>
> Bilateral military assistance by the United States pursuant to a request by South Vietnam along the lines of that undertaken during 1958 in response to the request by Lebanon for military assistance, would be in keeping with international law and treaty provisions. The provisions of the Geneva Accords of 1954, which prohibited the introduction of additional military arms and personnel into Vietnam, would not be a bar to the measures contemplated. The obvious, large-scale and continuous violation of these provisions of the Geneva Accords by North Vietnam in introducing large numbers of armed guerrillas into South Vietnam would justify the corresponding non-observance of these provisions by South Vietnam. Indeed, authorization for changing PEO Laos into an ordinary MAAG was justified on this legal theory. It should be recognized that the foregoing proposals require careful and detailed consideration and preparation particularly with regard to the precise mission of US forces used.

In addition to the previously cited advantages such an action might have at least two other important political and military advantages:

(a) It could release a portion of the ARVN from relatively static military functions to pursue the war against the insurgents and

(b) It would place the Sino-Soviet Bloc in the position of risking direct intervention in a situation where US forces were already in place, accepting the consequence of such action. This is in direct contrast to the current situation in Laos.

Alternatively, there are several potential political and military disadvantages to such an action, principal among these being:

(a) Some of the neutrals, notably India, might well be opposed, and the attitude of the UK and France is uncertain.

(b) This would provide the Communists with a major propaganda opportunity.

(c) The danger that a troop contribution would provoke a DRV/CHICOM reaction with the risk of involving a significant commitment of US force in the Pacific to the Asian mainland. The French tied up some 200,000 troops during the unsuccessful Indo-China effort.

This might significantly weaken the Diem regime in the long run, having in mind the parallel of Rhee in Korea.

This language is not solely the State Department's. In a Gilpatric memo to be cited shortly, we will see that the JCS, for example, had a hand in describing the role for US troops. Even so, the overall effect of the draft, as already noted, tones down very drastically the commitment implied by the May 1 Defense version:

1. The proposal is no longer for a unilateral, unlimited commitment to save Vietnam from communism. It only proposes consideration of a new treaty with South Vietnam (unlike the Defense draft which proposed reading a unilateral commitment into the existing Manila Treaty); and its purpose is to "bolster the will" of the South Vietnamese to resist the communists, not (as the Defense draft apparently meant) to guarantee that the US would join the war should the South Vietnamese effort prove inadequate.

2. It gives pro and con arguments for sending US troops, in contrast to the Defense draft which included a flat recommendation to send at least the 3600 men of the two division training teams and the special forces training team.

A reasonable judgment, consequently, is that State thought the Defense draft went too far in committing the US on Vietnam. (And in view of the positions he would take in 1965, George Ball's role as senior State representative on the Task Force obviously further encourages that interpretation.) But that is only a judgment. It is also possible to argue, in contrast, that perhaps State (or State plus whatever White House influence may have gone into the draft) simply was tidying up the Defense proposals: for example, that the redrafters felt that a new bilateral treaty would be a firmer basis for a commitment to save Vietnam than would reliance on a reinterpretation of the SEATO Treaty. Similar arguments can be made on the other points noted above.

Consequently, on any question about the *intent* of the redrafters, only a judgment and not a statement of fact can be provided.

But on the question of the *effect* of the redraft, a stronger statement can be made: for whatever the intent of the redrafters, the effect certainly was to weaken the commitments implied by the Defense draft, and leave the President a great deal of room for maneuver without having to explicitly overrule the recommendations presented to him.

I. THE TROOP ISSUE

To return to a question of judgement, it is difficult to assess how far this gradual hedging of proposals for very strong commitments to Vietnam simply reflected a desire (very probably encouraged by the White House) to leave the President freedom of action. To some extent it surely reflects a growing hope that perhaps the Laos cease-fire would come off; the country would not be flatly lost; and consequently, that the May 1 Defense draft, and even the May 3 State draft, reflected a somewhat panicky overestimate of how far we needed to go to keep Southeast Asia from falling apart. The two motives obviously overlapped.

There are indications that, as late as May 5, the estimate for saving something out of Laos remained bleak. On May 4, after a visit to the President, Senator Fullbright (who had opposed intervention in Laos along with other Congressional leaders) announced from the steps of the White House that he would support troop commitments to Thailand and Vietnam. An NSC meeting the following day (May 5) was devoted to discussing steps to reassure Vietnam and Thailand. Then in the afternoon, the President announced Vice President Johnson's visit to Asia at a press conference, which included this garbled exchange:

> *Q.* Mr. President, there have been reports that you would be prepared to send American forces into South Vietnam if that became necessary to prevent Communist domination of that country. Could you tell us whether that is correct, and also anything else you have regarding plans for that country?
>
> *A.* Well, we have had a group working in the government and we have had a Security Council meeting about the problems which are faced in Vietnam by the guerrillas and by the barrage which the present government is being subjected to. The problem of troops is a matter—the matter of what we are going to do to assist Vietnam to obtain [retain?] its independence is a matter under consideration. There are a good many [issues?] which I think can most usefully wait until we have had consultations with the government, which up to the present time—which will be one of the matters which Vice President Johnson will deal with; the problem of consultations with the Government of Vietnam as to what further steps could most usefully be taken.

On May 8, the reconstituted International Control Commission (established by the Geneva Agreement of 1954) arrived in Laos, hoping to supervise a cease-fire. The cease-fire had been agreed to in principle by both sides as early as May 1. The question was whether the Pathet Lao would really stop advancing. Aside from American intervention, a cease-fire was the only hope of the larger, but less effective, pro-Western forces led by Phoumi. Certainly hopes were higher by the 8th than they were a week earlier, but this might not be saying much. The documentary record is ambiguous. The final draft of the letter Vice President Johnson would deliver to Diem was dated May 8, and in this letter

Kennedy did not go much beyond the proposals in the April 27 version of the task force report. There was no mention of U.S. troop commitments, nor of a bilateral treaty. Even on the question of a further increase (beyond 170,000) in the RVNAF, Kennedy promised Diem only that this will be "considered carefully with you, if developments should so warrant."

But the same day, Gilpatric sent a memo to the JCS asking their views on U.S. troops in Vietnam:

> . . . In preparation for the possible commitment of U.S. forces to Vietnam, it is desired that you give further review and study of the military advisability of such action, as well as to the size and composition of such U.S. forces. Your views, which I hope could include some expression from CINCPAC, would be valuable for consideration prior to the NSC meeting this week (currently scheduled for Friday, May 12).

This in turn was based on a statement in the May 6 Task Force draft, which said that such a study was being carried out, with particular consideration being given to deploying to South Vietnam

> . . . two U.S. battle groups (with necessary command and logistics units), plus an engineer (construction-combat) battalion. These units would be located in the "high plateau" region, remote from the major population center of Saigon-Cholon, under the command of the Chief, MAAG. To help accelerate the training of the G.V.N. army, they would establish two divisional field training areas. The engineer battalion would undertake construction of roads, air-landing strips and other facilities essential to the logistical support of the U.S. and Vietnamese forces there.

The purpose of these forces (again, from the May 6 draft) would be to

> . . . provide maximum psychological impact in deterrence of further Communist aggression from North Vietnam, China, or the Soviet Union, while rallying the morale of the Vietnamese and encouraging the support of SEATO and neutral nations for Vietnam's defense;
> —release Vietnamese forces from advanced and static defense positions to permit their fuller commitment to counterinsurgency actions;
> —provide maximum training to approved Vietnamese forces; and
> —provide significant military resistance to potential North Vietnam Communist and/or Chinese Communist action.

The JCS reply, dated May 10, deferred details on the composition of U.S. forces, but quite emphatically recommended that we do send them, "assuming the political decision is to hold Southeast Asia outside the communist sphere." Here is the JCS memo:

> In considering the possible commitment of U.S. forces to South Vietnam, the Joint Chiefs of Staff have reviewed the overall critical situation in Southeast Asia with particular emphasis upon the present highly flammable situation in South Vietnam. In this connection the question, however, of South Vietnam should not be considered in isolation but rather in conjunction with Thailand and their overall relationship to the security of Southeast Asia. The views of the Joint Chiefs of Staff on the question re-

garding the development of U.S. forces into Thailand were provided to you BY JCSM-311-61, dated 9 May 1961. The current potentially dangerous military and political situation in Laos, of course, is the focal point in this area. Assuming that the political decision is to hold Southeast Asia outside the Communist sphere, the Joint Chiefs of Staff are of the opinion that U.S. forces should be deployed immediately to South Vietnam; such action should be taken primarily to prevent the Vietnamese from being subjected to the same situation as presently exists in Laos, which would then required deployment of U.S. forces into an already existing combat situation.

In view of the foregoing, the Joint Chiefs of Staff recommend that the decision be made to deploy suitable U.S. forces to South Vietnam. Sufficient forces should be deployed to accomplish the following purposes:

Provide a visible deterrent to potential North Vietnam and/or Chinese Communist action;

Release Vietnamese forces from advanced and static defense positions to permit their fuller commitment to counterinsurgency actions;

Assist in training the Vietnamese forces to the maximum extent possible consistent with their mission;

Provide a nucleus for the support of any additional U.S. or SEATO military operation in Southeast Asia; and

Indicate the firmness of our intent to all Asian nations.

In order to maintain U.S. flexibility in the Pacific, it is envisioned that some or all of the forces deployed to South Vietnam would come from the United States. The movement of these troops could be accomplished in an administrative manner and thus not tax the limited lift capabilities of CINCPAC.

In order to accomplish the foregoing the Joint Chiefs of Staff recommend that:

President Diem be encouraged to request that the United States fulfill its SEATO obligation, in view of the new threat now posed by the Laotian situation, by the immediate deployment of appropriate U.S forces to South Vietnam;

Upon receipt of this request, suitable forces could be immediately deployed to South Vietnam in order to accomplish the above-mentioned purpose. Details of size and composition of these forces must include the views of both CINCPAC and CHMAAG which are not yet available.

The NSC meeting that dealt with the Task Force Report was held the next day (the 11th, rather than the 12th as originally anticipated). The President avoided committing himself on the troop issue any further than he had already been committed by the time of his May 5 press conference. The resulting NSAM 52 [Doc. 88] (signed by McGeorge Bundy) states only that:

The President directs full examination by the Defense Department under the guidance of the Director of the continuing Task Force on Vietnam, of the size and composition of forces which would be desirable in the case of a possible commitment of U.S. forces to Vietnam." (The Task Force Director at this point referred to Sterling Cottrell, a Foreign Service Officer, rather than to Gilpatric.)

So the President went no further, really, than to take note of a study that was already well underway. The record does not help us judge what significance to attach to the qualification that the study be done under the guidance of the State Department officer now heading the Task Force.

On other issues relating to our military commitments the President again, with minor alterations, endorsed the proposals of the May 6 draft. On the question of a formal alliance with South Vietnam NSAM 52 reports that:

> The Ambassador is authorized to begin negotiations looking toward a new bilateral arrangement with Vietnam, but no firm commitment will be made to such an arrangement without further review by the President.

The President also "confirmed" the decisions quoted earlier accepting the April 27 military recommendations, and accepted the following further recommendations (all from the May 6 report) "with the objective of meeting the increased security threat resulting from the new situation along the frontier between Laos and Vietnam."

> 1. Assist the G.V.N. armed forces to increase their border patrol and insurgency suppression capabilities by establishing an effective border intelligence and patrol system, by instituting regular aerial surveillance over the entire frontier area, and by applying modern technological area-denial techniques to control the roads and trails along Vietnam's borders. A special staff element (approximately 6 U.S. personnel), to concentrate upon solutions to the unique problems of Vietnam's borders, will be activated in MAAG, Vietnam, to assist a similar special unit in the RVNAF which the G.V.N. will be encouraged to establish; these two elements working as an integrated team will help the G.V.N. gain the support of nomadic tribes and other border inhabitants, as well as introduce advanced techniques and equipment to strengthen the security of South Vietnam's frontiers.
>
> 2. Assist the G.V.N. to establish a Combat Development and Test Center in South Vietnam to develop, with the help of modern technology, new techniques for use against the Viet Cong forces (approximately 4 U.S. personnel).
>
> 3. Assist the G.V.N. forces with health, welfare and public work projects by providing U.S. Army civic action mobile training teams, coordinated with the similar civilian effort (approximately 14 U.S. personnel).
>
> 4. Deploy a Special Forces Group (approximately 400 personnel) to Nha Trang in order to accelerate G.V.N. Special Forces training. The first increment, for immediate deployment to Vietnam, should be a Special Forces company (52 personnel).
>
> 5. Instruct JCS, CINCPAC, and MAAG to undertake an assessment of the military utility of a further increase in the G.V.N. forces from 170,000 to 200,000 in order to create two new division equivalents for deployment to the northeast border region. The parallel political and fiscal implications should be assessed.

In general Kennedy did not seem to have *committed* the U.S., by these decisions, significantly further than the U.S. had already been committed by the President's public speeches and remarks at press conferences. In the expanded military aid program approved by the President, there was no item that committed the U.S. any further than we had gone in the case of Laos (that is, beyond providing advisors, materiel, and some *covert* combat assistance).

A debatable exception was the decision to send 400 special forces troops to speed training of their South Vietnamese counterparts. The idea of sending some Green Berets antedates the Task Force effort. Rostow mentioned it in his April 12 memo, quoted above. It can be argued whether it was really prudent to view this decision as separable from the "combat troops" issue (which also were being considered nominally, at least, for training, not necessarily combat). But obviously the President was sold on their going, and since the Vietnamese Special Forces were themselves supported by CIA rather than the regular military aid program, it was possible to handle these troops covertly. In any event, althought there would eventually be 1200 Green Berets in Vietnam (before the first commitment of U.S. combat units) they were apparently never cited as a precedent for or a commitment to a more overt role in the war.

These, then, were the measures relating to military commitments undertaken as a result of the April/May review. The principle *objective* of these measures (together with the non-military elements of the program) as stated in the Task Force report, and formally adopted in the NSAM, was "to prevent Communist domination of Vietnam." There was no uncertainty about why these steps were taken: quite aside from the Administration's strong feelings that we had to deal with the challenge of wars of national liberation, the program adopted seems quite minimal as a response to what was—even after the cease-fire was confirmed—a serious setback in Laos. No one in the government, and no one of substantial influence outside it, questioned the need for some action to hold things together in Southeast Asia.

For the fact was that our stake in Vietnam had increased because of what had been happening in Laos, quite aside from anything that we did or said. Collapse in Vietnam would be worse after Laos than it might have seemed before. And to do nothing after Laos would not really have made the U.S. look better if Vietnam fell; it would only have increased the likelihood both that that would happen, and greatly increased the extent to which the U.S. (and within U.S. politics, the Kennedy Administration) would be blamed for the collapse.

The Laotian situation did not even provide, then, a precedent for seeking to settle the Vietnamese situation through the same coalition government route. For in Laos, the pro-U.S. faction was plainly being defeated militarily in open battle despite a good deal of U.S. aid. The only U.S. alternative to accepting the coalition solution was to take over the war ourselves. Further, there was a strong neutralist faction in Laos, which could provide a premier for the government and at least a veneer of hope that the settlement might be something more than a face-saving way of handing the country over to the communist faction.

Neither of these conditions held for Vietnam, aside from all the other factors reviewed in the introduction to this paper which left the Administration no realistic option in the neutralist direction, even assuming that there was any temptation at that time to move in that direction. To have simply given up on Vietnam at that point, before any major effort had been attempted to at least see if the situation could be saved at reasonable cost, seems to have been, even with the hindsight we now have, essentially out of the question.

That is why, in the context of the time, the commitments Kennedy actually made seem like a near-minimal response which avoided any real deepening of our stake in Vietnam.

There is far more of a problem with the things that we decided to talk about (troops, and a formal treaty with Vietnam) than with the measures Kennedy fully endorsed. Certainly putting troops into Vietnam would increase our stake in the outcome, rather than merely help protect the stake we already had.

So, surely, would a formal treaty, even if the treaty nominally required U.S. support only in the case of overt invasion. How much so would depend on the nature of the troop commitments and the nature of the treaty. But, as we will see in the next chapter (in reviewing Vice President Johnson's visit) Diem turned out to want neither troops nor a treaty for the time being. And so these issues were deferred until the fall.

Aside from questions relating to our commitments to Vietnam, there were also the parallel questions relating to our commitment, if any, to Diem. As noted in the introduction, discussions about Vietnam always had this dual aspect, and this part of the problem was treated with increasing explicitness as time went on (and as the Administration got to know Diem better). In the CIP, it was treated essentially by implication. In the Gilpatric/Lansdale draft of April 26, it was also handled that way: no explicit statement of a change in our relations with Diem was offered, although by implication it was there.

Where the CIP (by implication) saw our increased aid as contingent on Diem's performance, the April 26 program left out any suggestion of a *quid pro quo.* To the contrary, it simply states that "those portions of the plan which are agreed to by the G.V.N. will be implemented as rapidly as possible."

And where the CIP saw Diem's government as our best hope "at the present time" this note of limited commitment to Diem is dropped in the April 26 draft. Instead we have a bland statement that we will "assist the GVN *under President Diem* to develop within the country the widest consensus of public support for a government dedicated to resisting communist domination." [emphasis added]

The May 3 State draft and the May 6 final draft dealt with this issue much as they had with the questions of military commitments: that is, these did not so much conspicuously weaken the proposals of the Gilpatric/Lansdale version, as to qualify and elaborate on them in ways that in effect (again, we cannot make a statement on intent) left the President a ready option to reconsider his position. State explicitly asserted that we were changing our policy on Diem, and spelled out some reasons for doing so.

Here are some extracts from the May 6 final draft; (the language is essentially the same in the May 3 draft).

> . . . we must continue to work through the present Vietnamese government despite its acknowledged weakness. No other remotely feasible alternative exists at this point in time which does not involve an unacceptable degree of risk. . . . Diem is not now fully confident of United States support. This confidence has been undermined partly by our vigorous efforts to get him to mend his ways, and partly by the equivocal attitude he is convinced we took at the time of the November 11, 1960, attempted coup. It is essential that President Diem's full confidence in and communication with the United States be restored promptly . . . Given Diem's personality and character and the abrasive nature of our recent relationships, success or failure in this regard will depend very heavily on Ambassador Nolting's ability to get on the same wavelength with Diem . . .
>
> The chief threat to the viability of President Diem's administration is, without a doubt, the fact of communist insurgency and the government's inability to protect its own people. Thus military measures must have the highest priority. There is, nevertheless, strong discontent with the government among not only the elite but among peasants, labor, and business. Criticism focuses on the dynastic aspects of the Diem rule, on its clandes-

tine political apparatus, and on the methods through which the President exercises his leadership. This is aggravated by Communist attempts to discredit the President and weaken his government's authority. All this is made the easier because of a communications void existing between the government and the people. For many months United States efforts have been directed toward persuading Diem to adopt political, social, and economic changes designed to correct this serious defect. Many of these changes are included in the Counterinsurgency Plan. Our success has been only partial. There are those who consider that Diem will not succeed in the battle to win men's minds in Vietnam.

Thus in giving priority emphasis to the need for internal security, we must not relax in our efforts to persuade Diem of the need for political social and economic progress. If his efforts are inadequate in this field our overall objective could be seriously endangered and we might once more find ourselves in the position of shoring a leader who had lost the support of his people.

Although the paper expresses the hope that through "very astute dealings" ("a combination of positive inducements plus points at which discreet pressure can be exercised") Diem could be successfully worked with, the net effect of the State draft is hardly enthusiastic. The paper tells the President that his Task Force "believes" that the policy will work. But it is a large order: for the aim had been referred to as nothing less than "a major alteration in the present government structure or in its objectives."

In effect, the silence on Diem in the Gilpatric/Lansdale draft was replaced by a detailed statement which, in the course of reaffirming the need to take prompt steps to show confidence in Diem, nevertheless leaves the strong impression that we really did not have much confidence in him at all. Support for Diem became tactical: based explicitly on the hope that he might reform, and implicitly on the fact that trying to overthrow him would be terribly risky in the aftermath of Laos, even if the U.S. had someone to overthrow him with. Further, although the paper explicitly conceded first priority to military needs, there was a strong argument that military efforts alone will not be enough.

It was apparently this equivocal attitude toward Diem (aside from any personal considerations) that led to Lansdale's prediction that State could never "win this battle." Thus in the main paper of the May 6 draft the general political objective was stated as:

> Develop political and economic conditions which will create a solid and widespread support among the key political groups and the general population for a Vietnam which has the will to resist Communist encroachment and which in turn stems from a stake in a freer and more democratic society.

Lansdale, in a pencilled comment to Gilpatric, complained:

> The elected President of Vietnam is ignored in this statement as the base to build upon in countering the communists. This will have the U.S. pitted against Diem as first priority, the communists as second.

Nevertheless, it seems that the May program went a very long way in Lansdale's preferred direction: although the U.S. was expanding its contribution to the

Vietnamese effort it was no longer asking for any *quid pro quo*. The U.S. envisioned "discreet pressure" but certainly not, for then anyway, any hint of withholding aid. The U.S. flatly asserted that it saw no "remotely acceptable alternative to Diem," for the time being, any way. The U.S. thought it vital that Diem do better, but increasing his confidence in the U.S. had top priority. The strongest guidance given the new Ambassador was to "get on Diem's wavelength."

More of this tentative adoption of the Lansdale approach can be seen in the discussion of Vice President Johnson's trip (from the May 6 draft):

> The Vice President's visit will provide the added incentive needed to give the GVN the motivation and confidence it needs to carry on the struggle. We believe that meetings between the Vice President and President Diem will act as a catalytic agent to produce broad agreement on the need for accelerated joint Vietnamese-U.S. actions to resist Communist encroachment in SEA. These meetings will also serve to get across to President Diem our confidence in him as a man of great stature and as one of the strong figures in SEA on whom we are placing our reliance. At the same time, these conferences should impress Diem with the degree of importance we attach to certain political and economic reforms in Vietnam which are an essential element in frustrating Communist encroachments. Recognizing the difficulties we have had in the past in persuading Diem to take effective action on such reforms, as specific an understanding as possible should be solicited from Diem on this point.

It was this sort of guidance (plus, perhaps, a memo from Lansdale describing President Diem in terms that bear comparison with those Jack Valenti would later use in connection with another President) that accounts for Johnson's famous reference to Diem as the Churchill of Asia.

In sum, what emerges from the final version of the report is a sense that the U.S. had decided to take a crack at the Lansdale approach of trying to win Diem over with a strong display of personal confidence in him. What does not emerge is any strong sense that the Administration believed this new approach really had much hope of working, but undoubtedly this pessimistic reading is influenced by the hindsight now available. The drafters of the paper very probably saw themselves as hedging against the possible failure of the policy, rather than implying that it probably would not work.

If we go beyond the paperwork, and ask what judgments might be made about the intent of the senior decision-makers, and particularly the President, it seems that here, even more than in connection with the military commitments discussed earlier, the Administration adopted a course which, whether in hindsight the wisest available or not, probably seemed to have no practical alternative.

Presumably the top level of the Administration believed there was at least some chance that the new policy toward Diem might produce useful results.

But even to the extent this prospect seemed dim, there were political advantages (or at least political risks) avoided in giving this plan a try, and there must not have seemed (as even now there does not seem) to have been much cost in doing so.

Finally, whatever the President thought of the prospects and political advantages of this approach to Diem, it might have been hard at that time to see any drastically different alternative anyway. After all, the heart of the Laos embarrassment was that the U.S was (with some face-saving cover) dropping an anti-communist leader who had come into power with the indispensable assistance of the U.S. This dropping of Phoumi in Laos in favor of support for the neutralist government Phoumi had overthrown with U.S. encouragement and assistance remained an essential part of whatever outcome developed in Laos. In the wake of this embarrassment, the U.S. was now trying to reassure other governments in Southeast Asia. Was it possible to carry out this reassurance while threatening Diem, another anti-communist leader totally dependent on U.S. support, with withdrawal of our support (our only available form of pressure) unless he reformed himself according to U.S. prescription? Was this a prudent time to risk a coup in South Vietnam, which was the widely predicted effect of any show of lack of confidence in Diem?

It is obviously impossible for us to strike a balance among these reasons (or perhaps some others) why the decisions were made the way they were. More interesting, though, is that it seems to have been unnecessary for even the decision-maker himself to strike such a balance. For it seems that whatever his view, the policy of trying to reassure Diem (rather than pressure him, or dissociating from him) seemed like a sensible tactic for the moment, and very possible the only sensible tactic for that particular moment.

IV. FROM MAY TO SEPTEMBER

At the end of September, Admiral Harry Felt, Commander-in-Chief of U.S. forces in the Pacific, stopped off in Saigon on his way to a SEATO meeting in Bangkok. Felt, Ambassador Nolting, and several of their senior aides met with Diem at Independence Palace, on the evening of the 29th. According to Nolting's cable the following day:

> In course of long discussion . . . Diem pointed the question. He asked for a bilateral defense treaty with the U.S. This rather large and unexpected request seemed to have been dragged in by the heels at the end of a far-ranging discussion, but we discovered upon questioning that it was seriously intended . . .

Although the available record does not explicitly say so, this request presumably triggered the intensive attention to Vietnam planning that began early in October (Nolting's cable arrived October 1) and led to the decision on the 11th to send the Taylor Mission.

The balance of this chapter reviews the major developments between the Presidential decisions on the Task Force Report (May 11) and the arrival of Nolting's cable on the treaty request (October 1).

A. THE JOHNSON MISSION

The available record tells us almost nothing about the Vice President's visit to Saigon beyond what is described in the public memoirs. We know from Nolting's cables that Johnson brought up the possibility of U.S. troops in Vietnam and of a bilateral treaty after Diem (in an after-dinner conversation) began to talk about the problems that communist gains in Laos would create for him. We know that Diem replied that he wanted U.S. combat troops only in the event of open invasion and that he also did not show interest in a treaty.

But we do not know what, if anything, Johnson was authorized to say if Diem had reacted affirmatively. And this could have ranged anywhere from attempting to discourage Diem if he did show interest, to offering some specific proposal and timetable. No strong inference can be drawn from the fact that Johnson, rather than Diem, raised the issue. Even if the President had decided against making troop commitments to Vietnam at that time, there would have been nothing outrageous about instructing Johnson to refer to such a possibility once Diem began to talk about his concerns due to Laos. After all, the whole point of the Johnson mission was to reassure Diem and other Asian leaders, that the U.S. could, despite Laos, be counted on in Asia. Simply reading the American newspapers would have told Diem that at least as of May 5, the Administration was seriously considering sending American troops to Vietnam, and that Johnson was expected to discuss this with Diem. A quite reasonable tactical judgment would have been that nothing would have been more likely to make Diem ask for U.S. troops than for Johnson to remain eerily silent on this issue.

Consequently, on the record available, we can do no more than guess what would have happened if Diem reacted affirmatively at the time of Johnson's visit. The most reasonable guess is probably that the Taylor Mission, or something equivalent, would have been undertaken in the spring, rather than in the fall, and nothing very much would have been different in the long run. But that is only a reasonable guess.

For the rest, here are some extracts from a report Johnson wrote after his return. Essentially, Johnson argued for prompt moves by the U.S. to show support for non-communist governments in Southeast Asia. He had in mind expanded conventional military and economic aid, and perhaps a new treaty to replace SEATO. But despite the shock of U.S. willingness to accept a coalition government in Laos, Johnson reported that U.S. troops were neither desired nor required. And although this might not always be the case, Johnson recommended that the U.S. "must remain master of this decision."

The Impact of Laos

There is no mistaking the deep—and long lasting—impact of recent developments in Laos.

Country to country, the degree differs but Laos has created doubt and concern about intentions of the United States throughout Southeast Asia. No amount of success at Geneva can, of itself, erase this. The independent Asians do not wish to have their own status resolved in like manner in Geneva.

Leaders such as Diem, Chiang, Sarit and Ayub more or less accept that we are making "the best of a bad bargain" at Geneva. Their charity extends no farther.

The Impact of the Mission

Beyond question, your judgement about the timing of our mission was correct. Each leader—except Nehru—publicly congratulated you on the "timing" of this mission. Chiang said—and all others privately concurred—that the mission had the effect of "stabilizing" the situation in the Southeast Asian nations.

What happened, I believe, was this: the leaders visited want—as long as they can—to remain as friends or allies of the United States. The public, or, more precisely, the political, reaction to Laos had drastically weakened the ability to maintain any strongly pro-US orientation. Neutralism in Thailand, collapse in Vietnam, anti-American election demagoguery in the Philippines were all developing prior to our visit. The show of strength and sincerity—partly because you had sent the Vice President and partly, to a greater extent than you may believe, because you had sent your sister—gave the friendly leaders something to "hang their hats on" for a while longer.

Our mission arrested the decline of confidence in the United States. It did not—in my judgment—restore any confidence already lost. The leaders were as explicit, as courteous and courtly as men could be in making it clear that deeds must follow words—soon.

We didn't buy time—we were given it.

If these men I saw at your request were bankers, I would know—without bothering to ask—that there would be no further extensions on my note.

*   *   †   ⚜

The Importance of Follow-Through

I cannot stress too strongly the extreme importance of following up this mission with other measures, other actions, and other efforts. At the moment—because of Laos—these nations are hypersensitive to the possibility of American hypocrisy toward Asia. Considering the Vienna talks with Khrushchev—which, to the Asian mind, emphasize Western rather than Asian concerns—and considering the negative line of various domestic American editorials about this mission, I strongly believe it is of first importance that this trip bear fruit immediately.

Personal Conclusions from the Mission

I took to Southeast Asia some basic convictions about the problems faced there. I have come away from the mission there—and to India and Pakistan —with many of those convictions sharpened and deepened by what I saw and learned. I have also reached certain other conclusions which I believe may be of value as guidance for those responsible in formulating policies. These conclusions are as follows:

1. The battle against Communism must be joined in Southeast Asia with strength and determination to achieve sucess there—or the United States, inevitably, must surrender the Pacific and take up our defenses on our own shores. Asian Communism is compromised and contained by the maintenance of free nations on the subcontinent. Without this inhibitory influence, the island outposts—Philippines, Japan, Taiwan—have no security and the vast Pacific becomes a Red Sea.
2. The struggle is far from lost in Southeast Asia and it is by no means inevitable that it must be lost. In each country it is possible to build a sound structure capable of withstanding and turning the Communist surge. The will to resist—while now the target of subversive attack—is there. The key to what is done by Asians in defense of Southeast Asian freedom is confidence in the United States.
3. There is no alternative to United States leadership in Southeast Asia. Leadership in individual countries—or the regional leadership and cooperation so appealing to Asians—rests on the knowledge and faith in United States power, will and understanding.

4. SEATO is not now and probably never will be the answer because of British and French unwillingness to support decisive action. Asian distrust of the British and French is outspoken. Success at Geneva would prolong SEATO's role. Failure at Geneva would terminate SEATO's meaningfulness. In the latter event, we must be ready with a new approach to collective security in the area.

We should consider an alliance of all the free nations of the Pacific and Asia who are willing to join forces in defense of their freedom. Such an organization should:

  a) have a clear-cut command authority
  b) also devote attention to measures and programs of social justice, housing, land reform, etc.

5. Asian leaders—at this time—do not want American troops involved in Southeast Asia other than on training missions. American combat troop involvement is not only not required, it is not desirable. Possibly Americans—fail to appreciate fully the subtlety that recently-colonial peoples would not look with favor upon governments which invited or accepted the return this soon of Western troops. To the extent that fear of ground troop involvement dominates our political responses to Asia in Congress or elsewhere, it seems most desirable to me to allay those paralyzing fears in confidence, on the strength of the individual statements made by leaders consulted on this trip. This does not minimize or disregard the probability that open attack would bring calls for U.S. combat troops. But the present probability of open attack seems scant, and we might gain much needed flexibility in our policies if the spectre of combat troop commitment could be lessened domestically.

6. Any help—economic as well as military—we give less developed nations to secure and maintain their freedom must be a part of a mutual effort. These nations cannot be saved by United States help alone. To the extent the Southeast Asian nations are prepared to take the necessary measures to make our aid effective, we can be—and must be—unstinting in our assistance. It would be useful to enunciate more clearly than we have— for the guidance of these young and unsophisticated nations—what we expect or require of them.

7. In large measure, the greatest danger Southeast Asia offers to nations like the United States is not the momentary threat of Communism itself, rather that danger stems from hunger, ignorance, poverty and disease. We must—whatever strategies we evolve—keep these enemies the point of our attack, and make imaginative use of our scientific and technological capability in such enterprises.

8. Vietnam and Thailand are the immediate—and most important—trouble spots, critical to the U.S. These areas require the attention of our very best talents—under the very closest Washington direction—on matters economic, military and political.

The basic decision in Southeast Asia is here. We must decide whether to help these countries to the best of our ability or throw in the towel in the area and pull back our defenses to San Francisco and [a] "Fortress America" concept. More important, we would say to the world in this case that we don't live up to treaties and don't stand by our friends. This is not my concept. I recommend that we move forward promptly with a major effort to help these countries defend themselves. I consider the key here is to get our best MAAG people to control, plan, direct and exact results from our military aid program. In Vietnam and Thailand, we must move forward together.

a. In Vietnam, Diem is a complex figure beset by many problems. He has admirable qualities, but he is remote from the people, is surrounded by persons less admirable and capable than he. The country can be saved—if we move quickly and wisely. We must decide whether to support Diem— or let Vietnam fall. We must have coordination of purpose in our country team, diplomatic and military. The Saigon Embassy, USIS, MAAG and related operations leave much to be desired. They should be brought up to maximum efficiency. The most important thing is imaginative, creative, American management of our military aid program. The Vietnamese and our MAAG estimate that $50 million of U.S. military and economic assistance will be needed if we decide to support Vietnam. This is the best information available to us at the present time and if it is confirmed by the best Washington military judgment it should be supported. Since you proposed and Diem agreed to a joint economic mission, it should be appointed and proceed forthwith.

b. In Thailand, the Thais and our own MAAG estimate probably as much is needed as in Vietnam—about $50 million of military and economic assistance. Again, should our best military judgment concur, I believe we should support such a program. Sarit is more strongly and staunchly pro-Western than many of his people. He is and must be deeply concerned at the consequence to his country of a communist-controlled Laos. If Sarit is to stand firm against neutralism, he must have—soon—concrete evidence to show his people of United States military and economic support. He believes that his armed forces should be increased to 150,000. His Defense Minister is coming to Washington to discuss aid matters.

*   *   *   *

To recapitulate, these are the main impressions I have brought back from my trip.

The fundamental decision required of the United States—and time is of the greatest importance—is whether we are to attempt to meet the challenge of Communist expansion now in Southeast Asia by a major effort in support of the forces of freedom in the area or throw in the towel. This decision must be made in a full realization of the very heavy and continuing costs involved in terms of money, of effort and of United States prestige. It must be made with the knowledge that at some point we may be faced with the further decision of whether we commit major United States forces to the area or cut our losses and withdraw should our other efforts fail. We must remain master in this decision. What we do in Southeast Asia should be part of a rational program to meet the threat we face in the region as a whole. It should include a clear-cut pattern of specific contributions to be expected by each partner according to his ability and resources. I recommend we proceed with a clear-cut and strong program of action.

B.   DIEM'S JUNE LETTER

During his visit Johnson, on behalf of Kennedy, invited Diem to prepare a set of proposals on South Vietnamese military needs for consideration by Washington. In a letter May 15, Diem told Kennedy that the definitive study would be ready in a few weeks. (He appreciated this invitation, Diem told Kennedy, "particularly because we have not become accustomed to being asked for our own views on our needs.)"

On June 9, Diem signed the promised letter. It was carried to Washington by a key Diem aide (Nguyen Dinh Thuan) and delivered on the 14th. (Thuan played a key role on the Vietnamese side throughout 1961. He was the man Durbrow, in the cable quoted in full earlier, suspected was the only cabinet member Diem had told about the CIP. In a memo to Gilpatric, Lansdale described him as Diem's "Secretary of Security, Defense, Interior, etc.")

In the letter, Diem proposed an increase in the RVNAF to 270,000 men, or to double the 150,000 strength authorized at the start of 1961, and 100,000 men more than envisioned under the CIP. That was a large request: for up until the end of April, the U.S. and South Vietnamese were still haggling over the go-ahead for a 20,000-man increase. Further, Diem made it clear that he saw this force requirement as a semi-permanent increase in South Vietnamese strength, which would continue to be needed even should he eliminate the Viet Cong.

Here are some extracts from Diem's letter:

> [The] situation . . . has become very much more perilous following the events in Laos, the more and more equivocal attitude of Cambodia and the intensification of the activities of aggression of international communism which wants to take the maximum advantage to accelerate the conquest of Southeast Asia. It is apparent that one of the major obstacles to the communist expansion on this area of the globe is Free Vietnam because with your firm support, we are resolved to oppose it with all our energies. Consequently, now and henceforth, we constitute the first target for the communists to overthrow at any cost. The enormous accumulation of Russian war material in North Vietnam is aimed, in the judgment of foreign observers, more at South Vietnam than at Laos. We clearly realize this dangerous situation but I want to reiterate to you here, in my personal name and in the name of the entire Vietnamese people, our indomitable will to win.
>
> On the second of May, my council of generals met to evaluate the current situation and to determine the needs of the Republic of Vietnam to meet this situation. Their objective evaluation shows that the military situation at present is to the advantage of the communists and that most of the Vietnamese Armed Forces are already committed to internal security and the protection of our 12 million inhabitants. For many months the communist-inspired fratricidal war has taken nearly one thousand casualties a month on both sides. Documents obtained in a recent operation, along route No. 9 which runs from Laos to Vietnam, contain definite proof that 2,860 armed agents have infiltrated among us in the course of the last four months.* It is certain that this number rises each day. However, the Viet-

---

* Diem's number implies an infiltration rate about 4 times as high as that estimated by U.S. intelligence in 1961, and twice as high as the hindsight revised 1961 estimates now in use.

namese people are showing the world that they are willing to fight and die for their freedom, notwithstanding the temptations to neutralism and its false promises of peace being drummed into their ears daily by the communists.

In the light of this situation, the council of generals concluded that additional forces numbering slightly over 100,000 more than our new force level of 170,000 will be required to encounter the ominous threat of communist domination . . .

After considering the recommendations of our generals and consulting with our American military advisors, we now conclude that to provide even minimum initial resistance to the threat, two new divisions of approximately 10,000 strength each are required to be activated at the earliest possible date. Our lightly held defensive positions along the demilitarized zone at our Northern border is even today being outflanked by communist forces which have defeated the Royal Laotian Army garrisons in Tchepone and other cities in Southern Laos. Our ARVN forces are so thoroughly committed to internal anti-guerrilla operations that we have no effective forces with which to counter this threat from Southern Laos. Thus, we need immediately one division for the First Army Corps and one for the Second Army Corps to provide at least some token resistance to the sizeable forces the communists are capable of bringing to bear against our Laotian frontier. Failing this, we would have no recourse but to withdraw our forces southward from the demilitarized zone and sacrifice progressively greater areas of our country to the communists. These divisions should be mobilized and equipped, together with initial logistic support units, immediately after completion of activation of the presently contemplated increase of 20,000 which you have offered to support.

Following the activation of these units, which should begin in about five months, we must carry on the program of activation of additional units until over a period of two years we will have achieved a force of 14 infantry divisions, an expanded airborne brigade of approximately division strength and accompanying (support?) . . . The mission of this total 270,000 man force remains the same, namely, to overcome the insurgency which has risen to the scale of a bloody, communist-inspired civil war within our borders and to provide initial resistance to overt, external aggression until free world forces under the SEATO agreement can come to our aid. The question naturally arises as to how long we shall have to carry the burden of so sizeable a military force. Unfortunately, I can see no early prospects for the reduction of such a force once it has been established; for even though we may be successful in liquidating the insurgency within our borders, communist pressure in Southeast Asia and the external military threat to our country must be expected to increase, I fear, before it diminishes. This means that we must be prepared to maintain a strong defensive military posture for at least the foreseeable future in order that we may not become one of the so-called "soft spots" which traditionally have attracted communist aggression. We shall therefore continue to need material support to maintain this force whose requirements far exceed the capacity of our economy to support. . . .

To accomplish this 100,000 man expansion of our military forces, which is perfectly feasible from a manpower viewpoint, will require a great intensification of our training programs in order to produce, in the minimum of time, those qualified combat leaders and technical specialists needed to fill the new units and to provide to them the technical and logistic support required to insure their complete effectiveness. For this purpose a considerable expansion of the United States Military Advisory Group is an essential requirement. Such an expansion, in the form of selected elements of the American Armed Forces to establish training centers for the Vietnamese Armed Forces, would serve the dual purpose of providing an expression of the United States' determination to halt the tide of communist aggression and of preparing our forces in the minimum of time.

While the Government and people of Vietnam are prepared to carry the heavy manpower burden required to save our country, we well know that we cannot afford to pay, equip, train and maintain such forces as I have described. To make this effort possible, we would need to have assurances that this needed material support would be provided.

The record is unclear on the immediate response to this letter. In particular, we have no record of the conversations Thuan had in Washington when he delivered the requests. The issue of the RVNAF increases somehow became part of the business of an economic mission then about to leave for Vietnam (the Staley Mission, discussed in the following section). The request for "selected elements of the American Armed Forces," raised in the next-to-last quoted paragraph, is left thoroughly obscure in the records we have—to the point where we are not at all sure either what Diem meant by it or how the Administration reacted to it. But, as will be seen in the section below on "U.S. Troops," nothing came of it.

C. THE STALEY MISSION

One of the continuing negotiating items through most of 1961 was the extent to which the South Vietnamese should finance their own effort. The U.S. view was that the South Vietnamese were not doing enough. The result was American pressure on Diem to undertake what was called tax "reform." Diem was most reluctant to move. It is pretty clear that a large part of Diem's reluctance to move flowed from the same (well-founded) sense of personal insecurity that made him avoid establishing a clear military chain of command. On the latter issue, the risk of weakening the war effort obviously struck him as less dangerous than the risk of making a coup easier by concentrating military authority in his generals instead of dividing it between the generals and the 38 province chiefs. Similarly, for a ruler so unsure of his hold on the country, a serious effort at imposing austerity looked more risky than holding out for the Americans to provide a few more millions out of their vast resources. But Diem, of course, was hardly likely to admit such reasons to the Americans, assuming he admitted them to himself. Consequently, on these issues (as on many others) the record is a long story of tediously extracted promises, excuses for inaction, and American complaints about Diem's administrative style.

On the economic issue, the substance of the argument was this:

The deficit between what Diem raised in taxes and what his budget required was made up by the U.S. through a commercial import program. The regime sold the goods provided by the U.S. to South Vietnamese businessmen, and used the piasters thus acquired mainly to meet the local currency costs (mostly food and pay) for the armed forces. U.S. dissatisfaction with the South Vietnamese effort showed clearly in the decision to ask the South Vietnamese themselves to provide the local currency costs for the 20,000 man force increase proposed in the CIP, although the U.S. had been paying these costs (through the import program) for the balance of the forces. The South Vietnamese insisted, for the outset, that they could not raise the piasters required.

The basic question of whether the South Vietnamese were bearing a reasonable share of the burden devolved into a number of technical issues, such as the effect of the program on inflation in South Vietnam, and the piaster/dollar exchange rate. The Gilpatric/Lansdale draft of the Task Force Report proposed that Diem be flatly assured that the U.S. would make up any deficit in the Vietnamese budget. But State objected from the start to giving any such assurance. Instead a joint commission of U.S. and South Vietnamese economic experts was proposed to work out a joint program dealing with these economic issues. This was one of the proposals Vice President Johnson carried with him on his mission. Diem accepted the proposal. And the U.S. team, headed by Eugene Staley (president of the Stanford Research Institute) was dispatched to South Vietnam in mid-June.

By the time the Staley Mission left, though, Diem had written the letter just quoted asking for U.S. support for a large further increase in his forces. Staley's group, with its Vietnamese counterpart, found themselves serving as the vehicle for the discussions on force levels. The report they issued is mostly about military issues, on which the economists stated they simply reflected instructions passed on by their respective governments. Here are some excerpts on the military issues (in addition, the report of course contained a discussion, rather vague as it turned out, of the economic issues which were nominally its purpose, and it also contained a good deal of very fine, vigorous language on the need for "crash programs" of economic and social developing).

> Viet Nam is today under attack in a bitter, total struggle which involves its survival as a free nation. Its enemy, the Viet Cong, is ruthless, resourceful, and elusive. This enemy is supplied, reinforced, and centrally directed by the international Communist apparatus operating through Hanoi. To defeat it requires the mobilization of the entire economic, military psychological, and social resources of the country and vigorous support from the United States.
>
> The intensified program which we recommend our two countries adopt as a basis for mutual actions over the next several years is designed not just to hold the line but to achieve a real breakthrough. Our joint efforts must surpass the critical threshold of the enemy's resistance, thereby puting an end to his destructive attacks, and at the same time we must make a decisive impact on the economic, social, and ideological front.
>
> The turn of events in Laos has created further serious problems with regard to the maintenance of the GVN as a free and sovereign non-Communist nation. In particular, the uncovering of the Laotian-Viet Nam border to DRV or DRV-supported forces creates a serious threat of increased covert infiltration of personnel, supplies, and equipment to the Viet Cong. With such increased support, the Viet Cong undoubtedly hope to seize firm military control of a geographic area and announce the establishment therein of a "rebel" government for South Viet Nam which would then be recognized by and receive military support from the DRV, Communist China, and Soviet Russia. (Example: The present situation in Laos.)
>
> The joint VN-US group does not consider itself competent to make specific recommendations as to desired force levels for the defense of Viet Nam. They have, however, after consultation with their respective mili-

tary authorities, adopted for economic planning purposes certain estimated strength figures for the GVN armed forces under two alternative assumptions. *Alternative A* assumes that the Communist-led insurgency effort remains at approximately its present level of intensity and the Government of Laos maintains sufficient independence from the Communist Bloc to deny authority for the transit of DVN or Communist Chinese troops across its borders. *Alternative B* assumes that the Viet Cong are able to significantly increase their insurgency campaign within Viet Nam and that the situation in Laos continues to deteriorate to the point where the Communists gain *de facto* control of that country.

Alternative A called for a build-up of Diem's forces to 200,000 (vs. 170,000 then authorized. Alternative B called for continuing the build-up to 270,000. On this basis, Kennedy agreed to provide support for the increase to 200,000. The 200,000-man approval was supposed to be contingent on South Vietnamese agreement to a plan for using the forces. The question of a further increase to 270,000 was deferred, since it did not need to be faced until the lower figure was being approached, sometime late in 1962.

A consequence of the Staley Mission was the South Vietnamese troop levels needed little attention in the fall review: the U.S. simply decided to support the increase to 200,000 even though the agreed plan for using the forces did not yet exist (as in May the U.S. had agreed to support the increase to 170,000 which also, it will be recalled, was supposed to have been contingent on such a plan).

A few points about the Staley Mission seem useful to keep in mind in reviewing the fall process:

1. It is another reminder of the prevailing (although not universal) overoptimism of U.S. appraisals of the Vietnam problem.

2. One of the follow-on actions to the report was supposed to be a Vietnamese announcement of a program of social reform. Producing this piece of paper (and in the end it was not much more than a piece of paper) took months. It was experiences such as this that gave questions about the viability of the Diem regime greater prominence in the fall review than they had received during April and May.

3. The U.S. was still continuing to deal with Diem most gently. Nothing more was asked of Diem as a *quid pro quo* than that he finally work up a plan for the counterinsurgency. The President explicitly accepted the assumptions of the Joint Plan worked out by the Staley Mission and their Vietnamese counterparts.

This is from the formal record of decision:

Joint Program of Action
With the Government of
Vietnam (Staley Report)

August 4, 1961

The President agrees with the three basic tenets on which the recommendations contained in the Joint Action Program are based, namely:

a. Security requirements must, for the present, be given first priority.

b. Military operations will not achieve lasting results unless economic and social programs are continued and accelerated.

c. It is in our joint interest to accelerate measures to achieve a self-sustaining economy and a free and peaceful society in Viet-Nam.

Similar language was used at the time of the May decisions. So it is not new. It is only that, in the light of Diem's inactivity, the phrases implying that non-military efforts are also important had come to sound a little hollow.

D. U.S. COMBAT TROOPS

From the time of the Laos Annex to the original Gilpatric/Lansdale draft of the Task Force Report (April 28). The record shows persistent activity on some level or other on the issue of sending U.S. combat troops to Vietnam.

At the time of the Task Force review, it will be recalled, Defense recommended sending two 1600-man combat units to Vietnam to set up two training centers for the Vietnamese in the highlands. In later drafts of the Task Force report, this proposal was broadened to consider sending American troops for wider purposes, short of direct combat against the Viet Cong. But the proposal was downgraded to a subject for study and was no longer a definite recommendation.

Here is a summary of the items (on the issue of U.S. combat troops) in the record available to this study following Kennedy's decisions on the Task Force Report (May 11).

On May 12 Vice President Johnson discussed the question with Diem, as described in an earlier section. This seems to have resolved the issue (negatively) so far as Johnson was concerned, and possibly as far as President Kennedy was concerned. But if it did, the President's view was not very emphatically passed on to subordinate members of the Administration. For a week later, Lansdale sent a memo to Gilpatrick noting that Diem did not want U.S. combat units as such, but that he might accept these units if they had a mission of training South Vietnamese forces:

> Ambassador Nolting [said] that President Diem would welcome as many U.S. military personnel as needed for training and advising Vietnamese forces [MAAG Chief] General McGarr, who was also present at this discussion [between Johnson and Diem], reported that while President Diem would not want U.S. combat forces for the purpose of fighting Communists in South Vietnam, he would accept deployment of U.S. combat forces as trainers for the Vietnamese forces at any time.

This language leaves it unclear whether McGarr was merely stating his opinion (which supported his own desire to bring in U.S. combat units), or reporting what he understood Diem to have said.

> (About the same day of Lansdale's memo—May 18—the JCS had restated its recommendation of May 10 that combat troops should be sent to Vietnam; and McGarr, from Saigon, had recommended sending a 16,000 man force, or if Diem would not accept that, a 10,000 man force with the nominal mission of establishing training centers for the Viet-

namese. The similar recommendation made in the Task Force drafts had
suggested 3200 men for the force.)

In any event, Lansdale's memo makes it quite clear that he (along with
McGarr and the JCS) were primarily interested in getting U.S. combat units
into Vietnam, with the training mission a possible device for getting Diem to
accept them. After a discussion of JCS and CINCPAC planning and of alternative locations for the troops, Lansdale comments:

> . . . any of the above locations have good areas for training of Viet-
> namese forces, if this were to be a mission of the U.S. forces.

In the available papers, no one at this time talked about using American
units to directly fight the Viet Cong. Rather it was mainly in terms of relieving
Vietnamese units to undertake offensive action. We can only guess what people
were really thinking. As the training-the-Vietnamese rationale seems essentially
a device for getting Diem to accept the units, the non-combatant role for U.S.
troops may have been (and probably was in the minds of at least some of the
planners) mainly a device for calming those members of the Administration
who were reluctant to involve American units in fighting the Viet Cong. Certainly in hindsight, it seems most unrealistic to suppose that American combat
units could have been stationed in a center of Viet Cong activity (a number of
papers postulate the insurgents were attempting to establish a "liberated area"
in the high plateau, which was the principal local discussed) without themselves becoming involved in the fighting.

Lansdale concluded his memo by reminding Gilpatric that Diem was sending
Thuan ("Secretary of Security, Defense, Interior, etc.") to Washington to
deliver his letter on Vietnam's "definitive military needs." Lansdale recommended that Gilpatric take up the question of whether Diem would accept U.S.
troops with Thuan. "With concrete information, you will then have a firm
position for further decisions."

But apparently someone did not want to wait for Thuan. For on May 27,
Nolting reported that he had brought up the question of what Diem meant
in his conversation with Johnson directly with Diem, and that Diem did not then
want U.S. combat units "for this or any other reason."

Nevertheless, on June 9, Diem signed the letter to Kennedy that, as quoted
above, asked for:

> . . . selected elements of the American Armed Forces to establish train-
> ing centers for the Vietnamese Armed Forces, . . .

a move which Diem stated:

> . . . would serve the dual purpose of providing an expression of the
> United States' determination to halt the tide of communist aggression and
> of preparing our forces in the minimum of time.

This certainly sounded very much like the recommendation of the Task Force
draft, or McGarr's later expanded version of that proposal; particularly since
Diem explicitly stated that he had McGarr's advice in drafting the proposals. But
where the American proposals were for training whole South Vietnamese
divisions, Diem said the training centers would be for combat leaders and tech-

nical specialists. Consequently, it seems that Diem did not have the same thing in mind in referring to "selected elements of the American Armed Forces" as did McGarr and others interested in bringing in American combat units. It may be that Diem agreed to put in this request that sounded like what McGarr wanted as a concession to the Americans in return for support of the large increase in the RVNAF he was asking.

Presumably this was clarified during the discussions Thuan had after delivering the letter. But, as noted earlier, we have no record of the conversations. In any event, nothing came of the proposal.

(A summary of Diem's letter, cabled to the American mission in Saigon the day after the letter was received in Washington, did not use the phrase "selected elements of the American Armed Forces." Instead it said that Diem asked for an increase of "American personnel" to establish the training centers. The crucial issue, of course, was whether Americans would be sent to Vietnam in the form of organized combat units, capable of, if not explicitly intended, for conducting combat operations. We do not know whether the wording of the summary reflected Thuan's clarification of the proposal when he arrived in Washington, or a high level Administration decision to interpret Diem's letter as not asking for combat units, or merely sloppy drafting of the cable.)

It seems clear that either Diem (despite the language of the letter he signed) really did not want American units, or that Kennedy (despite the activity of his subordinates) did not want to send those units, or both.

Sorenson, in his memoir, says that in May Kennedy decided against sending combat units despite the recommendations he received at the time of the Task Force Report. But his account of the Task Force is in error on a number of details, and so it is hard to know how much to credit his recollection.

But there is a final item apparently from this period that seems to support Sorenson. It is a handwritten undated note on a piece of scratch paper from Rostow to McNamara. It looks like a note passed at a meeting. From its location in the file, it was probably written about June 5, that is, a few days before Thuan arrived with Diem's letter. It reads:

Bob:

We must think of the kind of forces and missions for Thailand now, Vietnam later.

We need a guerrilla *deterrence* operation in Thailand's northeast.

We shall need forces to support a counter-guerrilla war in Vietnam:

> aircraft
> helicopters
> communications men
> special forces
> militia teachers
> etc.
>
> WWR

Two things are striking about this note: first, it is a quite exact description of the sort of military assistance Kennedy finally dispatched to Vietnam (i.e., combat support and advisors but not American units capable of independent combat against the guerrillas). Second, it certainly suggests that despite what

Lansdale, McGarr, and others were doing, those close to the President were not at this time thinking about sending American combat units to Vietnam (or any American forces, for even the units Rostow lists are for "later" in contrast to "Thailand now"). Nevertheless on July 20, McGarr again raised the question of combat units for training with Diem, and reported again that he did not want them.

In general, we seem to be seeing here a pattern that first began to emerge in the handling of the Task Force Report and which will be even more strikingly evident in the President's handling of the Taylor Report.

Someone or other is frequently promoting the idea of sending U.S. combat units. Kennedy never makes a clear-cut decision but some way or other action is always deferred on any move that would probably lead to engagements on the ground between American units and the Viet Cong.

We have no unambiguous basis for judging just what had really happened in each case. But we do see a similar pattern at least twice and possibly three different times: in May, perhaps again in June (depending on details of Thuan's talks in Washington not available to this study), and as we will report shortly, again in November. In each case, the record seems to be moving toward a decision to send troops, or at least to a Presidential decision that, in principal, troops should be sent if Diem can be persuaded to accept them. But no such decision is ever reached. The record never shows the President himself as the controlling figure. In June, there does not seem to be any record of what happened, at least in the files available to this study. In May and, as we will see, in November, the President conveniently receives a revised draft of the recommendations which no longer requires him to commit himself.

No reliable inference can be drawn from this about how Kennedy would have behaved in 1965 and beyond had he lived. (One of those who had advised retaining freedom of action on the issue of sending U.S. combat troops was Lyndon Johnson.) It does not prove that Kennedy behaved soundly in 1961. Many people will think so; but others will argue that the most difficult problem of recent years might have been avoided if the U.S. had made a hard commitment on the ground in South Vietnam in 1961.

E.   THE TREATY REQUEST

As to Diem, we have, of course, even less in the way of a record from which to judge what he really thought he was doing. But it is not hard to understand why he should be reluctant to accept U.S. combat troops. His stated reason was always that sending U.S. combat units would signal the end of the Geneva Accords. But this explanation explains little. Diem thought the Geneva Accords were betrayal of Vietnam in 1954, and a farce, freely violated by the communists, later. Consequently, he would be concerned about their demise only if North Vietnam could use this as a pretext for an overt invasion. But North Vietnam had long had a suitable pretext for an invasion in Diem's refusal to discuss the elections called for under the Geneva Accords. Diem's shield was the threat of U.S. intervention, not the Geneva Accords, and it is mighty hard to see how this shield could be weakened by putting American troops on the ground in South Vietnam.

But there were other reasons for Diem to be wary of U.S. troops. For one thing, not even Diem's severest critics questioned his commitment to Vietnamese nationalism. The idea of inviting foreign troops back into Vietnam must surely have been distasteful even once he decided it was unavoidable. Further, the presence of American troops in Vietnam had a very ambivalent effect on the risk to Diem of a military coup. To the extent American troops increased the sense of security, they would lessen the likelihood of a coup, which the military rationalized mainly on the grounds that they could not win the war under Diem. But the larger the American military presence in the country, the more Diem would have to worry about American ability and temptation to encourage a coup if Diem incurred American displeasure.

The net impact of these conflicting effects would depend on the security situation in Vietnam. If Diem felt strong, he would probably not want American troops; if he felt weak, he might see no choice but to risk inviting the Americans in. Even at the time of the Taylor mission, we will see Diem is most erratic on this issue.

Against this background, it is easy to understand why Diem, when the situation got worse in September, should have "pointed the question" at whether the U.S. would give him a treaty, rather than whether the U.S. would send in troops. As far as we can see, he was mostly concerned about what the latest VC attacks were doing to confidence in his regime, rather than any fear that the VC, still estimated at fewer than 20,000 strong, were going to defeat the quarter million regulars and auxiliaries in his own forces. What he probably wanted was an unambiguous public commitment that the Americans would not let Vietnam fall. For this would meet his immediate concern about confidence in his regime, perhaps even more effectively than the dispatch of American troops, and without the disadvantages that would come with accepting American troops. For Diem, a clear-cut treaty probably seemed the best possible combination of maximizing the American commitment while minimizing American leverage. And that, of course, would help explain why the Administration was not terribly attracted to such a proposal.

F. THE SITUATION IN SEPTEMBER

So far as the available record shows, there was no sense of imminent crisis in the official reporting to Washington as fall of 1961 began. An NIE published in mid-August concluded that Diem faced a "prolonged and difficult struggle" against the insurgency, and noted that "the French with their memories of the Indochina that was and the British with their experience in Malaya tend to be pessimistic regarding GVN prospects for combating the insurgency." But the NIE also reported that Diem's army had been performing better in 1961 than in 1960. Warning of possible trouble looked months, rather than weeks, ahead. The danger foreseen was a coup: "if the fight against the Viet Cong goes poorly during the next year or the South Vietnamese Army suffers heavy casualties, the chances of a military coup would substantially increase."

The judgment of the NIE on the effects of such a coup was entirely negative:

> If there is a serious disruption of GVN leadership as a result of Diem's death or as the result of a military coup, any momentum of GVN's counter-insurgency efforts had achieved will be halted or reversed, at least for a time. The confusion and suspicion attending a coup effort could provide the communists with an opportunity to seize control of the government.

There is no mention of any offsetting hope for a coup leading to more effective prosecution of the war. The overall impression left by the NIE is that Diem is not a very effective leader, but that he is getting along well enough to make the risks of a coup look more dangerous than the risks of the war being unwinnable under his leadership. In particular, a coup (or Diem's death) were seen as the only thing that could bring a quick collapse of the Saigon regime, as opposed to the loss over time of a "prolonged and difficult" struggle.

MAAG Chief McGarr, in a report dated September 1, spoke of the "enhanced sense of urgency and offensive spirit now present within both the RVNAF and the Government of Vietnam . . ." Under the heading "Outlook for Next Year," he reported:

> With the increased effectiveness of the Armed Forces beginning to be demonstrated by the recent operations in the Delta Region and the manifest intent of the U.S. to continue and even step up its vital support of the Vietnamese in their struggle against Communism, there is a spirit of renewed confidence beginning to permeate the people, the GVN, and the Armed Forces.

The political reporting from Saigon was less optimistic. Generally, these reports argued that Diem was not doing much to strengthen his support. But there was no disagreement with McGarr's fairly optimistic assessment of the military situation and no sense of crisis.

Through unofficial channels, though, the White House was receiving a far bleaker view of the situation. Schlesinger reports:

> "The situation gets worse almost week by week," Theodore H. White wrote us in August. ". . . The guerrillas now control almost all the southern delta—so much so that I could find no American who would drive me outside Saigon in his car even by day without military convoy." He reported a "political breakdown of formidable proportions: . . . what perplexes hell out of me is that the Commies, on their side, seem to be able to find people willing to die for their cause . . . I find it discouraging to spend a night in a Saigon night-club full of young fellows of 20 and 25 dancing and jitterbugging (they are called 'la jeunesse cowboy') while twenty miles away their Communist contemporaries are terrorizing the countryside." An old China hand, White was reminded of Chungking in the Second World War, complete with Madame Nhu in the role of Madame Chiang Kai-shek. "If a defeat in South Vietnam is to be considered our defeat, if we *are* responsible for holding that area, then we must have authority to act. And that means intervention in Vietnam politics . . . If we do decide so to intervene, have we the proper personnel, the proper instruments, the proper clarity of objectives to intervene successfully?"

It did not take long to confirm White's pessimism, although this must have made the dilemma of what to do about it seem all the more acute. In September, the number of VC attacks jumped to nearly triple the level (about 450 vs. 150) that had prevailed for some months previously. The most spectacular attack, which seems to have had a shattering effect in Saigon, was the seizure of Phuoc Thanh, a provincial capital only 55 miles from Saigon. The insurgents held the town a good part of the day, publicly beheaded Diem's province chief, and departed before government troops arrived. The official reporting to Washington by the end of the month pictured the situation as stagnating, if not dangerously deteriorating, although there continued to be no sense of the imminent crisis that Theodore White foresaw.

Here is an end-of-month report that Nolting sent just prior to the meeting at which Diem asked for the treaty:

Status report on political items as of Sept. 28:

General: Governmental and civil situation at end of month much same as at beginning. While neither of these gave open signs of deterioration, Diem government did not significantly improve its political position among people or substantially further national unity. On positive side several fifty-man district level reconstruction teams were sent to each of 4 provinces, and there was commendable amount country-side travel by ministers. On other hand, report was received of high-level bickering over powers and authority of new central intelligence organization, and Diem expressed dissatisfaction with pace of field command's planning of counter-insurgency operations, but he has still not delegated sufficient authority to field command. All in all we unable report that Sept. saw progress toward attainment task force goals of creating viable and increasingly democratic society. Some such "shot in arm" as proposed joint communique seems desirable.

Series large scale VC attacks in various areas central Vietnam during month highlighted increased VC infiltrations through Laos and underscored urgency of free world policy toward Laos which would bring this situation under control. These VC actions plus temporary VC seizure of provincial capital of Phuoc Thanh demonstrated that tide not yet turned in guerrilla war . . .

The "shot in the arm" Nolting referred to was the communique on social reforms that was agreed to some weeks earlier at the time of the Staley Mission; it would finally be issued, in a watered down form, early in January. The contrast between White's and Nolting's reporting is sharp: White obviously would not have seen the issuing of a communique as a significant "shot in the arm," or commented on the VC show of strength in such mild terms as demonstrating "that tide not yet turned." Consequently, although Diem's request for a treaty [Doc. 91] (a day after this cable was sent) surprised Nolting, its effect at the White House was presumably to confirm the warning that had already been received through White.

The State Department's view of the situation seems also to have been graver than that of the Embassy in Saigon. We have a situation summary on Southeast Asia that refers to Nolting's cable but not to Diem's treaty request, and which consequently must have been distributed about October 1. On the political situation in South Vietnam, the summary quotes Nolting's "no progress" comments. But the military situation is described more bleakly than Nolting did.

SOUTH VIET-NAM—MILITARY

1. Although GVN military capabilities have increased, Viet Cong capabilities are increasing at more rapid rate and Viet Cong attacks have increased in size.

2. Viet Cong "regular" forces have increased from about 7,000 at beginning of year to approximately 17,000.

3. Viet Cong have moved from stage of small hands to large units. During September Viet Cong mounted three attacks with over 1,000 men

in each. Viet Cong strategy may be directed at "liberating" an area in which a "government" could be installed.

4. Although vast majority of Viet Cong troops are of local origin, the infiltration of Viet Cong cadres from North Viet-Nam via Laos, the de-militarized zone, and by sea appears to be increasing. However, there is little evidence of major supplies from outside sources, most arms apparently being captured or stolen from GVN forces or from the French during the Indo-China war.

On Laos, the situation summary showed no such pessimism. But, overall the absence of bad news from Laos only added to the worry about South Vietnam. For the paper reported:

There probably have been some Viet Minh withdrawals from northern Laos but Viet Minh movement into Southern Laos bordering on South Vietnam has increased. Thus it appears enemy may be accepting stalemate for time being within Laos and giving priority to stepping up offensive action against South Vietnam.

Two final items are worth bearing in mind in trying to see the Vietnamese problem as it might have appeared to the White House in the fall of 1961. First, this warning of the effect of U.S. policy in Vietnam, from the August 15 NIE quoted earlier:

International Attitudes. In providing the GVN a maximum of encour-agement and extensive support in its struggle against the Communists, the US will inevitably become identified with the GVN's success or failure. The US will be under heavy pressure from other members of the non-Communist world, many of whom view the Vietnam struggle in differing terms. For example, the neighboring countries, such as Thailand, Cam-bodia, Burma, Indonesia, the Philippines, and Nationalist China, have all to some extent viewed developments in Laos as a gauge of US willingness and ability to help an anti-Communist Asian government stand against a Communist "national liberation" campaign. They will almost certainly look upon the struggle for Vietnam as a critical test of such US willing-ness and ability. All of them, including the neutrals, would probably suffer demoralization and loss of confidence in their prospects for maintaining their independence if the Communists were to gain control of South Viet-nam. This loss of confidence might even extend to India.

Second, a couple of newspaper quotes may serve as a reminder of the extent to which the Kennedy Administration had been under a constant sense of foreign policy crisis throughout its first year, with every evidence of more to come. In late September, in a review piece on Congressional appraisals of Kennedy's first year, Russell Baker comments that not even Congress seems much inter-ested in debate about Kennedy's effectiveness in pushing through legislation:

What makes it particularly irrelevant this autumn is that Congress itself has been far more concerned ever since January with the President's per-formance as guardian of the national security than with how he came out as chief warrior for a legislative program.

From Laos to Cuba to Vienna to Berlin to the Soviet nuclear testing site at Semipalatinsk to New York's East River, crisis after crisis has fallen across the White House with a rapidity and gravity that has absorbed Mr. Kennedy's energy since his inauguration and reduced the Congressional program to secondary importance.

And a couple of days later, James Reston, describing the imminent risk of a nuclear crisis over Berlin, reported:

> Specifically, Khrushchev told one of Mr. Kennedy's political emissaries that once Krushchev signs a separate peace treaty with the Communist East Germans, not only all of the West's rights in Berlin will cease, but all traffic to Berlin will cease until the West negotiates new rights of access with the East German regime.
>
> Khrushchev was questioned minutely on this key point. His reply was unequivocal: Not one truck, or barge, or train, or plane would leave from West Germany for West Berlin after the separate peace treaty until the new arrangements with the East Germans were negotiated.
>
> Now, this is not precisely the same as Mr. Gromyko's bland assurances. This is blockade, and blockade is an act of war. Washington has made clear that it is not going to get stirred up if the East Germans merely replace the Russians on the borders between East and West Germany and approve the flow of adequate supplies. But Mr. Khrushchev did not support this procedure, and went on to threaten that any effort to break his blockade by force would lead to war.

Since Khrushchev had repeatedly pledged to sign the East German treaty by the end of the year, the showdown was not far off.

V. THE FALL DECISIONS–I

A. THE DECISION TO SEND TAYLOR

As of early October, there were several proposals for more active intervention in Southeast Asia on the table. One was the JCS-favored plan to intervene on the ground in Laos to seize and hold major portions of the country, principally to protect the borders of South Vietnam and Thailand. A second plan (referred to in a staff paper as the "Rostow proposal") would have put a SEATO force of about 25,000 men into Vietnam to try to mount a guard on the Vietnam/Laos border between the DMZ and Cambodia. Finally, there were various schemes, dating from the Task Force review, for putting a U.S. force into the highlands, or at DaNang with or without a nominal mission of training South Vietnamese troops.

Except for the Rostow proposal all these plans pre-dated the spurt of Viet Cong activity in September and Diem's subsequent request for a treaty. The record does not tell when and why the Rostow proposal was drawn up. It was probably a direct response to Diem's request, but it may have been simply a part of the on-going Laos contingency planning. In any event, Rostow's proposal was submitted to the JCS for Comment October 5. On the 9th, the JCS responded with a counter-proposal for a substantial (initially about 20,000 men, but expected to grow) commitment of U.S. forces in Vietnam, centered on Pleiku in the highlands.

In hindsight, the JCS reasoning in rejecting the Rostow proposal looks unchallengeable. The JCS stated:

> *a.* SEATO forces will be deployed over a border of several hundred miles, and will be attacked piecemeal or by-passed at the Viet Cong's own choice.
> *b.* It may reduce but cannot stop infiltration of Viet Cong personnel and material.
> *c.* It deploys SEATO forces in the weakest defense points should DRV or CHICOM forces intervene.
> *d.* It compounds the problems of communications and logistical support.

The Chiefs also argued against an alternative border proposal to put the SEATO force along the 17th parallel. Their first preference, very emphatically, was to go into Laos:

> As stated in your [Gilpatric's] memorandum, the proposed concept set forth must be analyzed in the total context of the defense of Southeast Asia. Any concept which deals with the defense of Southeast Asia that does not include all or a substantial portion of Laos is, from a military standpoint, unsound. To concede the majority of northern and central Laos would leave three-quarters of the border of Thailand exposed and thus invite an expansion of communist military action. To concede southern Laos would open the flanks of both Thailand and South Vietnam as well as expose Cambodia. Any attempt to combat insurgency in South Vietnam, while holding areas in Laos essential to the defense of Thailand and South Vietnam and, at the same time, putting troops in Thailand, would require an effort on the part of the United States alone on the order of magnitude of at least three divisions plus supporting units. This would require an additional two divisions from the United States.
>
> What is needed is not the spreading out of our forces throughout Southeast Asia, but rather a concentrated effort in Laos where a firm stand can be taken saving all or substantially all of Laos which would, at the same time, protect Thailand and protect the borders of South Vietnam.

But, if the Laos plan was "politically unacceptable at this time," the Chiefs "provided" (but did not explicitly recommend) "a possible limited interim course of action" which could . . .

> provide a degree of assistance to the Government of South Vietnam to regain control of its own territory, and could free certain South Vietnamese forces for offensive actions against the Viet Cong. While the Joint Chiefs of Staff agree that implementation of this limited course of action would not provide for the defense of Thailand or Laos, nor contribute substantially or permanently to solution of the overall problem of defense of Southeast Asia, they consider the Plan preferable to either of the two military possibilities described in referenced memorandum.

The following day, there appeared a new paper called "Concept of Intervention in Vietnam." The paper, according to a pencilled note on the available copy, was drafted mainly by Alexis Johnson, who was then a Deputy Under Secretary of State. We know from a note William Bundy (then principal Deputy to Paul Nitze, who was then Assistant Secretary of Defense, ISA) sent to McNamara that a "talking paper" by Johnson was to be discussed at a meeting that included, at least, Rusk and McNamara on the afternoon of the 10th. But we do not know whether the draft we have available is the "talking paper" or a revision put together later in the day, after the meeting.

The proposal ("an effort to arrest and hopefully reverse the deteriorating situation in Vietnam") was a blend of Rostow's border force and the Chief's "possible limited interim course of action." Johnson's paper listed both the Rostow mission of the force (attempt to close the border) and that of the Chiefs (win control of the central highlands); otherwise the paper followed the JCS plan. What probably happened, considering the haste with which the paper must have been drafted, was that Johnson simply blended the two proposals together and assumed the fine points could be worked out later. For if the paper is somewhat confusing on the immediate military proposal, it is clear on the long-run thinking that underlays the proposal. And this long-run thinking made the immediate military mission relatively inconsequential, since as with the earlier combat-troops-for-training proposals, it was pretty clear that the main idea was to get some American combat troops into Vietnam, with the nominal excuse for doing so quite secondary.

The plan was described under the heading "Initial Phase." A subsequent section, titled "Anticipated Later Phases" states:

> This initial action cannot be taken without accepting as our real and ultimate objective the defeat of the Viet Cong, and making Vietnam secure in the hands of an anti-Communist government. Thus supplemental military action must be envisaged at the earliest stage that is politically feasible. The ultimate force requirements cannot be estimated with any precision. JCS are now considering. Three divisions would be a guess . . .

Earlier the paper, in a similar vein, had remarked:

> While a satisfactory political settlement in Laos would considerably reduce Viet Minh infiltration through Laos into South Vietnam, it would not entirely climinate it. While such a reduction would materially assist the GVN in meeting the Viet Cong threat, there is no assurance that, even under these circumstances, the GVN will in the foreseeable future be able to defeat the Viet Cong. Under these circumstances, although the need of South Vietnam for outside assistance such as proposed in this plan would probably still be very strong, it would be much more difficult to find a political base upon which to execute this plan.

This judgment was probably influenced by a special NIE issued October 5th, which stated that 80-90% of the estimated 17,000 VC had been locally recruited, and that there was little evidence that the VC relied on external supplies.

The relation of this paper to Diem's request for treaty can only be guessed at. The paper never mentions Diem, or any South Vietnamese request for further assistance. But the paper supplemented one published about a week or so earlier (probably prior to Diem's request) titled "Limited Holding Actions in Southeast Asia." This earlier paper discussed various steps short of major troop deployments.

The impression is that both papers were part of contingency planning (short of major intervention in Laos) for saving something in Southeast Asia should the Laos negotiations continue to drag on with no satisfactory resolution. Thus although the timing of the Vietnam paper was surely influenced and probably triggered by Diem's request for a treaty, it looks essentially like a suggestion (but not a formal recommendation) to the President that if he is unwilling to intervene to try to save Laos, he should at least take strong and unambiguous action to make sure that Vietnam would not also be lost. In this interpretation it is easy to make sense of the emphasis on a deteriorating situation in Vietnam, and the implied warning that it might be best to set this plan in motion before a settlement is reached in Laos, when it seemed relatively easy to provide a politically plausible basis for the action.

(In a recent column, Joseph Alsop quoted Averill Harriman as telling him that Kennedy had told Harriman to get whatever settlement he could on Laos, but that the U.S. really intended to make its stand in Vietnam.)

At the end of the Vietnam paper there is a list of "Specific Actions to be Taken Now" which goes no further [on Vietnam] than to list:

> Use of U.S. naval aircraft and ships to assist GVN in interdiction of sea traffic, to assist self defense of GVN. This is to some extent camouflagable.
>
> If necessity arises, use of U.S. military aircraft for logistic support, including troop lift within Laos and South Vietnam.

Further, there is a long list of pros and cons, with no judgment stated on the balance.

This (and other statements to be cited below) suggests, again, that the paper was prepared for a discussion on Southeast Asia planning in the NSC, rather than in response to a request for a set of recommendations.

Three other points need to be mentioned:

1. The paper, although nominally presenting a SEATO plan, explicitly assumes that "planning would have to be on the basis of proceeding with whichever SEATO Allies would participate."

2. The paper warns (in the balance of the paragraph quoted earlier) that the ultimate force requirements would "much depend" on the capabilities and leadership of the SEATO forces . . . and above all on whether the effort leads to much more better fighting by Diem's forces. They alone can win in the end.

3. Very clearly foreshadowing the Taylor mission (and perhaps indicating a White House hand in the drafting) the paper states:

> The viability of this plan would be dependent on the degree to which it could and would also result in the GVN accelerating political and military action in its own defense. A judgment on this can only be reached after thorough exploration on the spot with the country team and the GVN.

Finally, here is the list of pros and cons presented (but not evaluated) in the paper.

Cons

1. The plan would not in itself solve the underlying problem of ridding SVN of communist guerrillas.

2. It would not seal off the borders of SVN except for the limited area of operations.

3. It breaks the Geneva Accords and puts responsibility on the U.S. for rationalizing the action before the U.N. and the world.

4. It raises questions of U.S. troop relationships with the Vietnamese peasants, montagnards, GVN and its army.

5. The use of SEATO forces in SVN distorts Plan Five [for major intervention in Laos] although these forces are not a net subtraction.

6. The risk of being regarded as interlopers à la the French must be considered.

7. Communist change of tactics back to small-scale operations might leave this force in a stagnant position.

Pros

1. The effect on GVN morale of SEATO engagement in their struggle could be most heartening.

2. It could prevent the Viet Cong move to the next stage of battalion-size, formal organization to challenge the ARVN.

3. The relatively sophisticated SEATO arms, air power, communications and intelligence might spark a real transformation in ARVN tactics and action.

4. Capitalizing on U.S. intelligence sources now unavailable to the GVN could lead to effective attacks on Viet Cong nerve centers of command and communications.

5. The SEATO force commitment could be used to get from Diem a package of actions McGarr feels are needed to step up the GVN effort [mainly the familiar items of clarifying the chain of command and establishing an overall plan].

6. Introducing SEATO forces would give us for the first time some bargaining position with the Russians for a settlement in Vietnam.

7. If we go into South Vietnam now with SEATO, the costs would be much less than if we wait and go in later, or lose SVN.

The available record shows three other papers prepared prior to the NSC meeting, October 11, at which this paper was considered:

1. A special NIE commented on the plan in terms that were a lot less than encouraging:

> In the situation assumed, we believe that the DRV would seek at first to test the seriousness and effectiveness of the SEATO effort by subjecting the SEATO forces and their lines of communication to harassment, ambush, and guerrilla attack. The Communists would probably estimate that by using their Viet Cong apparatus in South Vietnam, and by committing experienced guerrilla forces from North Vietnam in guerrilla operations in territory long familiar to them, and by exploiting the opportunities offered by the sizable junk traffic in coastal waters, they could severely harass the SEATO land forces and penetrate the SEATO blockade. The Communists would expect worthwhile political and psychological rewards from successful harassment and guerrilla operations against SEATO forces, including lowered GVN morale and increased tensions among the SEATO members.
>
> While seeking to test the SEATO forces, the DRV would probably not relax its Viet Cong campaign against the GVN to any significant extent. Meanwhile, Communist strength in south Laos would probably be increased by forces from North Vietnam to guard against an effort to partition Laos or an attack against the Pathet Lao forces. The Soviet airlift

would probably be increased with a heavier flow of military supply into south Laos, and the Communists would probably intensify their efforts to establish a secure route for motor traffic into the south. The establishment of a coalition government in Laos under Souvanna Phouma probably would not significantly reduce Communist infiltration of men and equipment from North to South Vietnam through Laos.

If the Seato action appeared to be proving effective in reducing the present scale of infiltration the Communist probably would increase their use of the mountain trail system through Cambodia. This is a longer and more difficult route but its use could keep at least minimum support flowing to the Viet Cong. At the same time, in order to reduce the apparent success of the SEATO action, they could intensify small unit attacks, assassinations, and local terrorism in South Vietnam; they could also commit more DRV irregular personnel for the harassment of the SEATO forces. In any event, the SEATO commitment in South Vietnam would probably have to be continued over a prolonged period. It might be part of Communist tactics to play upon possible SEATO weariness over maintaining substantial forces and accepting losses, in South Vietnam over a long period of time . . .

The reaction to the assumed SEATO action among concerned non-Communist governments would vary widely. The Asian members of SEATO would find renewed confidence in the organization and the US, if the plan were to go well. If, on the other hand, the SEATO action were to become costly, prolonged, or to involve heavy casualties, the Asian members would soon become disenchanted and look to the US to "do something" to lessen the burden and to solve the problem. The UK and France would be likely to oppose the assumed SEATO action, and their reluctance to participate could be overcome only with great difficulty, if at all.

In this instance, and as we will see, later, the Intelligence Community's estimates of the likely results of U.S. moves are conspicuously more pessimistic (and more realistic) than the other staff papers presented to the President. This SNIE was based on an assumption that the SEATO force would total about 25,000 men. It is hard to imagine a more sharp contrast than between this paper, which foresees no serious impact on the insurgency from proposed intervention, and Supplemental Note 2, to be quoted next.

2. "Supplemental Note 2" to the paper, issued the day of the NSC meeting, contained, among other comments, a JCS estimate of the size of the American force needed "to clean up the Viet Cong threat." It reads:

> *Wider Military Implications.* As the basic paper indicates, the likelihood of massive DRV and Chicom intervention cannot be estimated with precision. The SNIE covers only the initial phase when action might be limited to 20-25,000 men. At later stages, when the JCS estimate that 40,000 US forces will be needed to clean up the Viet Cong threat, the chances of such massive intervention might well become substantial, with the Soviets finding it a good opportunity to tie down major US forces in a long action, perhaps as part of a multi-prong action involving Berlin and such additional areas as Korea and Iran.
>
> Because of this possibility of major Bloc intervention, the maximum possible force needs must be frankly faced. Assuming present estimates of about 40,000 US forces for the stated military objective in South Vietnam,

plus 128,000 US forces for meeting North Vietnam and Chicom intervention, the drain on US-based reserve forces could be on the order of 3 or 4 divisions and other forces as well. The impact on naval capabilities for blockade plans (to meet Berlin) would also be major. In light of present Berlin contingency plans, and combat attrition, including scarce items of equipment, the initiation of the Vietnam action in itself should dictate a step up in the present mobilization, possibly of major proportions.

3. Finally, there is the following memo from William Bundy (then acting Assistant Secretary of Defense, ISA) to McNamara. It is of interest because it is the only piece of paper available for this period that gives anyone's candid recommendations to his boss, as opposed to the more formal staff papers:

> Even if the decision at tomorrow's meeting is only preliminary—to explore with Diem and the British, Australians, and New Zealanders would be my guess—it is clearly of the greatest possible importance. Above all, action must proceed fast.
>
> For what one man's feel is worth, mine—based on very close touch with Indochina in the 1954 war and civil war afterwards till Diem took hold —is that it *is* really now or never if we are to arrest the gains being made by the Viet Cong. Walt Rostow made the point yesterday that the Viet Cong are about to move, by every indication, from the small unit basis to a moderate battalion-size basis. Intelligence also suggests that they may try to set up a "provisional government" like Xieng Khuang (though less legitimate appearing) in the very Kontum area into which the present initial plan would move SEATO forces. If the Viet Cong movement "blooms" in this way, it will almost certainly attract all the back-the-winner sentiment that understandably prevails in such cases and that beat the French in early 1954 and came within an ace of beating Diem in early 1955.
>
> An early and hard-hitting operation has a good chance (70% would be my guess) of *arresting* things and giving Diem a chance to do better and clean up. Even if we follow up hard, on the lines the JCS are working out after yesterday's meeting, however, the chances are not much better that we will in fact be able to *clean up* the situation. It all depends on Diem's effectiveness, which is very problematical. The 30% chance is that we would wind up like the French in 1954; white men can't win this kind of fight.
>
> On a 70-30 basis, I would myself favor going in. But if we let, say, a month go by before we move, the odds will slide (both short-term shock effect and long-term chance) down to 60–40, 50–50 and so on. Laos under a Souvanna Phouma deal is more likely than not to go sour, and will more and more make things difficult in South Viet-Nam, which again underscores the element of time.

Minutes of the NSC meeting of October 11 were not available for this study. But we have the following Gilpatric memorandum for the record. (The JUNGLE JIM squadron—12 planes—was an Air Force unit specially trained for counterinsurgency welfare. Short of engaging in combat itself, presumably it would be used to train Vietnamese pilots):

> At this morning's meeting with the President the following course of action was agreed upon with relation to South Vietnam:

1. The Defense Department is authorized to send the Air Force's Jungle Jim Squadron into Vietnam to serve under the MAAG as a training mission and not for combat at the present time.

2. General Maxwell Taylor accompanied by Dr. Rostow from the White House, General Lansdale, a representative of JCS, Mr. Cottrell from State and probably someone from ISA will leave for Vietnam over the weekend on a Presidential mission (to be announced by the President at this afternoon's press conference as an economic survey) to look into the feasibility from both political and military standpoints of the following:

(a) the plan for military intervention discussed at this morning's meeting on the basis of the Vietnam task force paper entitled "Concept for Intervention in Vietnam";

(b) an alternative plan for stationing in Vietnam fewer U.S. combat forces than those called for under the plan referred to in (a) above and with a more limited objective than dealing with the Viet Cong; in other words, such a small force would probably go in at Tourane [DaNang] and possibly another southern port principally for the purpose of establishing a U.S. "presence" in Vietnam;

(c) Other alternatives in lieu of putting any U.S. combat forces in Vietnam, *i.e.* stepping up U.S. assistance and training of Vietnam units, furnishing of more U.S. equipment, particularly helicopters and other light aircraft, trucks and other ground transport, etc.

3. During the two or three weeks that will be required for the completion of General Taylor's mission, State will push ahead with the following political actions:

(a) protest to the ICC on the step-up in North Vietnamese support of Viet Cong activities,

(b) tabling at the UN a white paper based on Mr. William Jordan's report concerning Communist violations of the Geneva Accords, and

(c) consultation with our SEATO allies, principally the British and Australians, regarding SEATO actions in support of the deteriorating situation in Vietnam.

That afternoon, the President announced the Taylor Mission, but he did not make the hardly credible claim that he was sending his personal military advisor to Vietnam to do an economic survey. He made a general announcement, and was non-committal when asked whether Taylor was going to consider the need for combat troops (there had been leaked stories in the newspapers a few days earlier that the Administration was considering such a move.) Nevertheless, the newspaper stories the next day flatly asserted that the President had said Taylor was going to study the need for U.S. combat troops, which was, of course, true, although not exactly what the President had said.

B. THE NEWSPAPERS AND THE CABLES

The day after Kennedy's announcement of the Taylor mission, Reuters sent this dispatch from Saigon·

Saigon, Vietnam, Oct. 12 [Reuters]—South Vietnamese military sources welcomed today President Kennedy's decision to send his military adviser, General Taylor, here this week.

Sources close to President Ngo Dinh Diem said he did not feel there was a need here yet for troops of the United States or Southeast Asia Treaty Organization.

The sources said the South Vietnamese President was convinced that Vietnam's Army increased in size and better equipped by increased United States aid can defeat the Communists.

But a day later, the public position of the Vietnamese had shifted noticeably. From a *New York Times* dispatch from Saigon:

One question receiving considerable attention here in the light of the Taylor mission is the desirability of sending United States troops to South Vietnam.

The prospect of United States troop involvement is understood to have advanced a step here in the sense that the South Vietnamese Government is reported to be willing to consider such involvement which it had formerly rejected.

However, it is understood that South Vietnamese deliberations still fall far short of the stage wherein Saigon would be ready to request United States forces.

But in private discussions with the U.S. ambassador, Diem had turned around completely. From Nolting's cable [Doc. 93]:

Following major requests:

(1) An additional squadron of AD-6 fighter bombers (in lieu of programmed T-28's) and delivery as soon as possible.
(2) The sending of US civilian contract pilots for helicopters and transport plans (C-47s), for "non-combat" operations.
(3) US combat unit or uints to be introduced into SVN as "combat-trainer units". Proposed use would be to station a part of this force in northern part of SVN near 17th parallel to free ARVN forces presently there for anti-guerrilla combat in high plateau. Thuan also suggested possibility stationing some US forces in several provincial seats in highlands of central Vietnam.
(4) US reaction to proposal to request govt Nationalist China to send one division of combat troops for operations in southwest provinces.

*   *   *

When Thuan raised question of US combat-trainer units, I asked specifically whether this was President's considered request, mentioning his oft-repeated views re US combat forces here. Thuan confirmed that this was considered request from President; confirmed that Diem's views had changed in light of worsening situation. Idea was to have "symbolic" US strength near 17th parallel, which would serve to prevent attack there and free up GVN forces now stationed there for combat operations; Thuan said President Diem also thought similar purpose could be achieved by stationing US combat units in several provincial seats in highlands, thus freeing ARVN guard forces there. I told him this represented major request coming on heels of President Diem's request for bilateral security treaty with United States. I asked whether this request was in lieu of the security treaty. Thuan first said that it represented a first step, which would be quicker than a treaty, and that time was of essence. After some discussion of the pro's and con's of a possible defense treaty (effect on SEATO, ICC, ratification procedures, etc.), Thuan said he felt that proposal for stationing token US forces in SVN would satisfy GVN and would serve the purpose better than a mutual defense treaty. (He had evidently not thought through this nor discussed it with Diem.)

*   *   *

Nolting then indicated he reacted skeptically to Diem's suggestion of bringing in Chiang's forces, and comments to Washington that he thought "this was a trial balloon only." He concluded the cable:

> The above questions will undoubtedly be raised with Gen Taylor. While it is obvious that GVN is losing no opportunity to ask for additional support as result our greater interest and concern this area, situation here, both militarily and psychologically, has moved in my judgment to point where serious and prompt consideration should be given to these requests.

This cable arrived in Washington the night of October 13. The following day an unidentified source provided the *New York Times* with a detailed explanation of what the Taylor Mission was to do. From the way the *Times* handled the story it is plain that it came from a source authorized to speak for the President, and probably from the President himself. The gist of the story was that Taylor was going to Saigon to look into all sorts of things, one of which, near the bottom of the list, was the question of U.S. troops at some time in the indefinite future. Along with a lot of more immediate questions about intelligence and such, Taylor was expected to ". . . recommend long-range programs, including possible military actions, but stressing broad economic and social measures." Furthermore, the *Times* was told,

> Military leaders at the Pentagon, no less than General Taylor himself are understood to be reluctant to send organized U.S. combat units into Southeast Asia. Pentagon plans for this area stress the importance of countering Communist guerrillas with troops from the affected countries, perhaps trained and equipped by the U.S., but not supplanted by U.S. troops.

In the light of the recommendations quoted throughout this paper, and particularly of the staff papers just described that led up to the Taylor Mission, most of this was simply untrue. It is just about inconceivable that this story could have been given out except at the direction of the President, or by him personally. It appears, consequently, the President was less than delighted by Diem's request for troops. He may have suspected, quite reasonably, that Diem's request was prompted by the stories out of Washington that Taylor was coming to discuss troops; or he may have wished to put a quick stop to expectations (and leaks) that troops were about to be sent, or both. This does not mean the President had already decided not to send combat units. Presumably he had not. But he apparently did not want to have his hands tied.

The *Times* story had the apparently desired effect. Speculation about combat troops almost disappeared from news stories, and Diem never again raised the question of combat troops: the initiative from now on came from Taylor and Nolting, and their recommendations were very closely held.

C. CINCPAC RECOMMENDS "NOT NOW"

On the way to Saigon, Taylor stopped off in Hawaii to talk to Admiral Felt at CINCPAC. Felt did not give Taylor a flat recommendation on combat troops at the time. But a couple of days later he cabled Washington a list of pros and cons:

A. Pro

(1) Presence of U.S. forces in SVN, particularly if deployed to important defensive areas such as plateau region, would mean to Communists that overt aggression against SVN will involve US forces from the outset. This eliminates possibility of sudden victory by overt aggression in SVN before US could react. This would settle the question for SVN, and SE Asians as a whole, as to whether we would come to their help. Further, agreement by SEATO to principle of force introduction would strengthen SEATO in world eyes.

(2) Presence of strong U.S. combat forces will influence greatly South Vietnamese will to eliminate the Viet Cong.

(3) If we use U.S. engineers with U.S. military protection to finish Dakto-Ban Net-Attapeu Road in order to enable US to operate near plateau border area, a military corridor of sorts will cut an important part of VC pipeline from north.

(4) U.S. forces will make available larger number ARVN forces for employment against VC. RVNAF tasks accomplished by U.S. forces will decrease proportionately certain RVNAF deficiencies, particularly in logistics, communications, and air support.

(5) U.S. forces in SVN would tend to strengthen Diem's government against pro-Red coup, but would not necessarily preclude non-Communist coup attempts.

(6) Dividends would accrue from fact our troops could provide variety training for ARVN forces, broadening base now provided by MAAG.

B. Con

(1) Would stir up big fuss throughout Asia about reintroduction of forces of white colonialism into SE Asia. Little question that a propaganda issue will be made of this in all world forums including UN.

(2) Action could trigger intensification of Commie aggression against SE Asia. This may not be all-out overt aggression, but could consist, for example, of the DRV moving full blown combat units through the mountain passes into southern Laos under excuse that we initiated invasion of SE Asia and they are protecting the flank of North Vietnam.

(3) Politically, presence of U.S. forces could hasten Commies to establish so called "representative government" in South Vietnam.

(4) Aside from offering Viet Cong a political target, US troops would constitute provocative military one, inducing VC to attack/harass it in manner/degree where issue might ultimately force American units active military campaign, or suffer defensive alternative of being pot-shot at to point of embarrassment.

(5) Presence of US troops could induce Commies to resort to related actions such as introduction of Red Air Force elements in North Vietnam and accelerate modernization of DRV military forces.

(6) This would probably mean garrisoning a U.S. division in SE Asia for an extended period of time in same sense as Army divisions in Korea. However, circumstances differ from Korea. For example, nature of VC warfare such that US units cannot remain long in isolation from conflict realities. Ultimately, they likely to be forced into varying forms of military engagement with VC if only for security against attacks ranging from assassination/sabotage to tactical harassment. In short, we should accept fact that likelihood our troops becoming combat engaged increases in proportion to duration of their stay.

2. A summary of the above appears to me to add up in favor of our not introducing U.S. combat forces until we have exhausted other means for helping Diem.

D. TAYLOR IN SAIGON

The Taylor Mission arrived in Saigon on the 18th. They had barely arrived when Diem went before his National Assembly to declare that the increasing gravity of the Viet Cong threat now required a formal proclamation of a State of Emergency. Diem then went off to meet with the Americans, and after such a spectacular opening shot must have then astonished his visitors by indicating that he did not want American combat troops after all. What he wanted, he said, was the treaty, American support for larger GVN forces, and a list of combat support items that nicely paralleled those Rostow listed in the note to McNamara quoted earlier. It was Taylor (according to Nolting's cable 516, 20 October) who brought up the question of American combat troops.

Taylor said he understood there had been recent discussions of introduction of American or SEATO forces into Viet-Nam and asked why change had occurred in earlier GVN attitude. Diem succinctly replied because of Laos situation. Noting it will take time to build up GVN forces he pointed to enemy's reinforcements through infiltration and increased activities in central Viet-Nam and expressed belief that enemy is trying to escalate proportionally to increase in GVN forces so that GVN will not gain advantage. He asked specifically for tactical aviation, helicopter companies, coastal patrol forces and logistic support (ground transport).

Diem indicated he thought there would be no particular adverse psychological effect internally from introducing American forces since in his view Vietnamese people regard Communist attack on Viet-Nam as international problem. Rostow inquired whether internal and external political aspects such move could be helped if it were shown clearly to world that this is international problem. Diem gave no direct comment on this suggestion. He indicated two main aspects of this problem: (1) Vietnamese people are worried about absence formal commitment by US to Viet-Nam. They fear that if situation deteriorates Viet-Nam might be abandoned by US. If troops are introduced without a formal commitment they can be withdrawn at any time and thus formal commitment is even more important in psychological sense. (2) Contingency plan should be prepared re use American forces in Viet-Nam at any time this may become necessary. In this connection Diem seemed to be talking about combat forces. While it was not completely clear what Diem has in mind at present time he seemed to be saying that he wants bilateral defense treaty and preparation of plans for use American forces (whatever is appropriate) but under questioning he did not repeat his earlier idea relayed to me by Thuan that he wanted combat forces.

Here, as earlier, we get no explicit statement on Washington's attitude toward a treaty. Further, no strong conclusion can be drawn from the fact that Taylor took the initiative in raising the issue of troops, since it might have been awkward not to mention the issue at all after Thuan's presentation to Nolting a few days previous.

But on the 23rd, we find this in a cable from MAAG Chief McGarr:

> Serious flood in Mekong delta area . . . (worse since 1937) raises possibility that flood relief could be justification for moving in US military personnel for humanitarian purposes with subsequent retention if desirable. Gen. Taylor and Ambassador evaluating feasibility and desirability.

Taylor met with Diem and Thuan again the following day, the 24th. Taylor provided the Vietnamese a written summary of items he described as "personal ideas to which I was seeking their reaction." Item E was headed "Introduction of U.S. Combat troops." It proposed "a flood relief task force, largely military in composition, to work with GVN over an extended period of rehabilitation of areas. Such a force might contain engineer, medical, signal, and transportation elements as well as combat troops for the protection of relief operations." Diem now seems to have changed his mind again on combat troops. Here is the cable:

> 1. The essential conclusions which we have reached at the end of a week of briefings, consultations, and field trips follow:
>
> A. There is a critical political-military situation in SVN brought on by western policy in Laos and by the continued build-up of the VC and their recent successful attacks. These circumstances coupled with the major flood disaster in the southwestern provinces have combined to create a deep and pervasive crisis of confidence and a serious loss in national morale.
>
> B. In the field, the military operations against the VC are ineffective because of the absence of reliable intelligence on the enemy, an unclear and unresponsive channel of command responsibility in the Armed Forces, and the tactical immobility of the VN ground forces. This immobility leads to a system of passive, fragmented defense conceding the initiative to the enemy and leaving him free to pick the targets of attack. The harassed population exposed to these attacks turn to the government for better protection and the latter responds by assigning more static missions to the Army units, thus adding to their immobility. In the end, the Army is allowed neither to train nor to fight but awaits enemy attacks in relative inaction.
>
> C. The situation in the Saigon is volatile but, while morale is down and complaints against the government are rife, there is not hard evidence of a likely coup against Diem. He still has no visible rival or replacement.
>
> 2. To cope with the foregoing situation, we are considering recommending a number of possible forms of GVN-US cooperation to reverse the present downward trend, stimulate an offensive spirit and buildup

morale. In company with Ambassador Nolting, Dr. Rostow and Mr. Mendenhall, I discussed some of these Oct 24 with Diem and Thuan, advancing them as personal ideas to which I was seeking their informal reaction. The following outline, distributed in French translation at the start of the interview, indicates the scope of the discussion.

A. Improvement of intelligence on V.C.: the available intelligence on V.C. insurgency is inadequate both for *tactical* requirements and for basis of judgment of situation at governmental levels. A joint GVN-US effort should be able to improve organization, techniques and end product to mutual advantage both parties.

B. Joint survey of security situation at provincial level: The current situation can best be appraised at provincial level where the basic intelligence is found, the incidents occur, and the defenses are tested. The problems vary from province to province and hence require local analysis on the spot. Such a survey should result in better understanding of such important matters as quality of basic intelligence on V.C., needs of civil guard and self defense corps, command relationships between provincial and Army officials and conditions under which assumption of offensive might be possible.

C. Improvement of Army mobility: it appears that size of ARVN can not be much increased before end 1962; to make it more effective and allowing it to cope with increasing number of V.C., it must be given greater mobility. Such mobility can come from two sources. (1) moving Army from static missions and (2) making available to it improved means of transport, notably helicopters and light aircraft. Both methods should be considered.

D. Blocking infiltration into high plateau: increase in enemy forces in high plateau requires special measures for defense and for counter-guerrilla actions. It is suggested that a carefully tailored "frontier ranger force" be organized from existing ranger units and introduced into the difficult terrain along the Laos/Vietnam frontier for attack and defense against the Viet Cong. This force should be trained and equipped for extended service on the frontier and for operations against the communications lines of the VC who have infiltrated into the high plateau and adjacent areas.

E. Introduction of U.S. Military Forces: GVN is faced with major civil problem arising from flood devastation in western provinces. The allies should offer help to GVN according to their means. In the case of U.S., two ways of rendering help should be considered. One is of emergency type, such as offer of U.S. military helicopters for reconnaissance of conditions of flooded areas and for emergency delivery medical supplies and like. A more significant contribution might be a flood relief task force, largely military in composition, to work with GVN over an extended period for rehabilitation of area. Such a force might contain engineer, medical, signal, and transportation elements as well as combat troops for the protection of relief operations. Obviously, such a military source would also provide U.S. military presence in Viet Nam and would constitute military reserve in case of heightened military crisis.

F. Actions to emphasize national emergency and beginning of a new phase in the war: we should consider jointly all possible measures to emphasize turning point has been reached in dealing with Communist aggression. Possible actions might include appeal to United Nations, an assessment by GVN of governmental changes to cope with crisis and exchange of letters between the two heads of State expressing their partnership in a common cause.

3. Dien's reaction on all points was favorable. He expressed satisfaction with idea of introducing U.S. forces in connection with flood relief activities, observing that even the opposition elements in this crisis had joined with the majority in supporting need for presence of U.S. forces. In the course of the meeting, nothing was formally proposed or agreed but the consensus was that the points considered might form agenda for a program of increased GVN-US cooperation offering promise of overcoming many of the current difficulties of GVN. There were no exact figures discussed with regard to such matters as troop strengths, equipment, or flood relief . . .

*   *   *

5. Because of the importance of acting rapidly once we have made up our minds, I will cable my recommendations to Washington enroute home.

Simultaneously with this cable, Taylor sent a second "eyes only" for the President, Chairman of the JCS, Director of CIA, McNamara, and Rusk and Alexis Johnson at State. The cable is a little confusing; for although it sets out to comment on "U.S. military forces" it concerns only the flood Task Force, not mentioning the various other types of military forces (helicopter companies, etc.) which were envisioned. The same slight confusion appears in the "eyes only for the President" cable on this issue to be quoted shortly. The impression Taylor's choice of language leaves is that the support forces (helicopter companies, expanded MAAG, etc.) he was recommending were essentially already agreed to by the President before Taylor left Washington, and consequently his detailed justification went only to the kind of forces on which a decision was yet to be made—that is, ground forces liable to become involved in direct engagements with the Viet Cong.

Here is the cable from Saigon, followed by the two "Eyes only for the President" from the Philippines which sum up his "fundamental conclusions."

FROM SAIGON

WHITE HOUSE EYES ONLY FOR THE PRESIDENT
STATE EYES ONLY FOR RUSK AND UNDER SECRETARY JOHNSON
DEFENSE EYES ONLY SECRETARY McNAMARA
JCS EYES ONLY GENERAL LEMNITZER
FROM GENERAL TAYLOR

*   *   *

With regard to the critical question of introducing U.S. military forces into VN:

My view is that we should put in a task force consisting largely of logistical troops for the purpose of participating in flood relief and at the same time of providing a U.S. military presence in VN capable of assuring Diem of our readiness to join him in a military showdown with the Viet Cong or

Viet Minh. To relate the introduction of these troops to the needs of flood relief seems to me to offer considerable advantages in VN and abroad. It gives a specific humanitarian task as the prime reason for the coming of our troops and avoids any suggestion that we are taking over responsibility for the security of the country. As the task is a specific one, we can extricate our troops when it is done if we so desire. Alternatively, we can phase them into other activities if we wish to remain longer.

The strength of the force I have in mind on the order of 6-8000 troops. Its initial composition should be worked out here after study of the possible requirements and conditions for its use and subsequent modifications made with experience.

In addition to the logistical component, it will be necessary to include some combat troops for the protection of logistical operations and the defense of the area occupied by U.S. forces. Any troops coming to VN may expect to take casualties.

Needless to say, this kind of task force will exercise little direct influence on the campaign against the V.C. It will, however, give a much needed shot in the arm to national morale, particularly if combined with other actions showing that a more effective working relationship in the common cause has been established between the GVN and the U.S.

FROM THE PHILIPPINES

EYES ONLY FOR THE PRESIDENT FROM GENERAL TAYLOR

1. Transmitted herewith are a summary of the fundamental conclusions of my group and my personal recommendations in response to the letter of the President to me dated 13 October 1961. * * * * * * *

2. It is concluded that:

a. Communist strategy aims to gain control of Southeast Asia by methods of subversion and guerrilla war which by-pass conventional U.S. and indigenous strength on the ground. The interim Communist goal—en route to total take-over—appears to be a neutral Southeast Asia, detached from U.S. protection. This strategy is well on the way to success in Vietnam.

b. In Vietnam (and Southeast Asia) there is a double crisis in confidence: doubt that U.S. is determined to save Southeast Asia; doubt that Diem's methods can frustrate and defeat Communist purposes and methods. The Vietnamese (and Southeast Asians) will undoubtedly draw—rightly or wrongly—definitive conclusions in coming weeks and months concerning the probable outcome and will adjust their behavior accordingly. What the U.S. does or fails to do will be decisive to the end result.

c. Aside from the morale factor, the Vietnamese Government is caught in interlocking circles of bad tactics and bad administrative arrangements which pin their forces on the defensive in ways which permit a relatively small Viet-Cong force (about one-tenth the size of the GVN regulars) to create conditions of frustration and terror certain to lead to a political crisis, if a positive turning point is not soon achieved. The following recommendations are designed to achieve that favorable turn, to avoid a further deterioration in the situation in South Vietnam, and eventually to contain and eliminate the threat to its independence.

3. It is recommended:

General

a. That upon request from the Government of Vietnam (GVN) to come to its aid in resisting the increasing aggressions of the Viet-Cong and in repairing the ravages of the Delta flood which, in combination, threaten the lives of its citizens and the security of the country, the U.S. Government offer to join the GV in a massive joint effort as a part of a total mobilization of GVN resources to cope with both the Viet-Cong (VC) and the ravages of the flood. The U.S. representatives will participate actively in this effort, particularly in the fields of government administration, military plans and operations, intelligence, and flood relief, going beyond the advisory role which they have observed in the past.

Specific

b. That in support of the foregoing broad commitment to a joint effort with Diem, the following specific measures be undertaken:

(1) The U.S. Government will be prepared to provide individual administrators for insertion into the governmental machinery of South Vietnam in types and numbers to be worked out with President Diem.

(2) A joint effort will be made to improve the military-political intelligence system beginning at the provincial level and extending upward through the government and armed forces to the Central Intelligence Organization.

(3) The U.S. Government will engage in a joint survey of the conditions in the provinces to assess the social, political, intelligence, and military factors bearing on the prosecution of the counter-insurgency in order to reach a common estimate of these factors and a common determination of how to deal with them. As this survey will consume time, it should not hold back the immediate actions which are clearly needed regardless of its outcome.

(4) A joint effort will be made to free the Army for mobile, offensive operations. This effort will be based upon improving the training and equipping of the Civil Guard and the Self-Defense Corps, relieving the regular Army of static missions, raising the level of the mobility of Army Forces by the provision of considerably more helicopters and light aviation, and organizing a Border Ranger Force for a long-term campaign on the Laotian border against the Viet-Cong infiltrators. The U.S. Government will support this effort with equipment and with military units and personnel to do those tasks which the Armed Forces of Vietnam cannot perform in time. Such tasks include air reconnaissance and photography, airlift (beyond the present capacity of SVN forces), special intelligence, and air-ground support techniques.

(5) The U.S. Government will assist the GVN in effective surveillance and control over the coastal waters and inland waterways, furnishing such advisors, operating personnel and small craft as may be necessary for quick and effective operations.

(6) The MAAG, Vietnam, will be reorganized and increased in size as may be necessary by the implementation of these recommendations.

(7) The U.S. Government will offer to introduce into South Vietnam a military Task Force to operate under U.S. control for the following purposes:

(a) Provide a U.S. military presence capable of raising national morale and of showing to Southeast Asia the seriousness of the U.S. intent to resist a Communist take-over.

(b) Conduct logistical operations in support of military and flood relief operations.

(c) Conduct such combat operations as are necessary for self-defense and for the security of the area in which they are stationed.

(d) Provide an emergency reserve to back up the Armed Forces of the GVN in the case of a heightened military crisis.

(e) Act as an advance party of such additional forces as may be introduced if CINCPAC or SEATO contingency plans are invoked.

(8) The U.S. Government will review its economic aid program to take into account the needs of flood relief and to give priority to those projects in support of the expanded counterinsurgency program.

FROM THE PHILIPPINES

EYES ONLY FOR THE PRESIDENT FROM GENERAL TAYLOR

This message is for the purpose of presenting my reasons for recommending the introduction of a U.S. military force into South Vietnam (SVN). I have reached the conclusion that this is an essential action if we are to reverse the present downward trend of events in spite of a full recognition of the following disadvantages:

a. The strategic reserve of U.S. forces is presently so weak that we can ill afford any detachment of forces to a peripheral area of the Communist bloc where they will be pinned down for an uncertain duration.

b. Although U.S. prestige is already engaged in SVN, it will become more so by the sending of troops.

c. If the first contingent is not enough to accomplish the necessary results, it will be difficult to resist the pressure to reinforce. If the ultimate result sought is the closing of the frontiers and the clean-up of the insurgents within SVN, there is no limit to our possible commitment (unless we attack the source in Hanoi).

d. The introduction of U.S. forces may increase tensions and risk escalation into a major war in Asia.

On the other side of the argument, there can be no action so convincing of U.S. seriousness of purpose and hence so reassuring to the people and Government of SVN and to our other friends and allies in SEA as the introduction of U.S. forces into SVN. The views of indigenous and U.S. officials consulted on our trip were unanimous on this point. I have just seen Saigon 545 to State and suggest that it be read in connection with this message.

The size of the U.S. force introduced need not be great to provide the military presence necessary to produce the desired effect on national morale in SVN and on international opinion. A bare token, however, will not suffice; it must have a significant value. The kinds of tasks which it might undertake which would have a significant value are suggested in BAGU5 (previous cable, 3.b.(7)). They are:

(a) Provide a US military presence capable of raising national morale and of showing to Southeast Asia the seriousness of the US intent to resist a Communist take-over.

(b) Conduct logistical operations in support of military and flood relief operations.

(c) Conduct such combat operations as are necessary for self-defense and for the security of the area in which they are stationed.

(d) Provide an emergency reserve to back up the Armed Forces of the GVN in the case of a heightened military crisis.

(e) Act as an advance party of such additional forces as may be introduced if CINCPAC or SEATO contingency plans are invoked.

It is noteworthy that this force is not proposed to clear the jungles and forests of Viet Cong guerrillas. That should be the primary task of the Armed Forces of Vietnam for which they should be specifically organized, trained, and stiffened with ample U.S. advisors down to combat battalion levels. However, the U.S. troops may be called upon to engage in combat to protect themselves, their working parties, and the area in which they live. As a general reserve, they might be thrown into action (with U.S. agreement) against large, formed guerrilla bands which have abandoned the forests for attacks on major targets. But in general, our forces should not engage in small-scale guerrilla operations in the jungle.

As an area for the operations of U.S. troops, SVN is not an excessively difficult or unpleasant place to operate. While the border areas are rugged and heavily forested, the terrain is comparable to parts of Korea where U.S. troops learned to live and work without too much effort. However, these border areas, for reasons stated above, are not the places to engage our forces. In the High Plateau and in the coastal plain where U.S. troops would probably be stationed, these jungle-forest conditions do not exist to any great extent. The most unpleasant feature in the coastal areas would be the heat and, in the Delta, the mud left behind by the flood. The High Plateau offers no particular obstacle to the stationing of U.S. troops.

The extent to which the Task Force would engage in flood relief activities in the Delta will depend upon further study of the problem there. As reported in Saigon 537, I see considerable advantages in playing up this aspect of the Task Force mission. I am presently inclined to favor a dual mission, initially help to the flood area and subsequently use in any other area of SVN where its resources can be used effectively to give tangible support in the struggle against the Viet Cong. However, the possibility of emphasizing the humanitarian mission will wane if we wait long in moving in our forces or in linking our stated purpose with the emergency conditions created by the flood.

The risks of backing into a major Asian war by way of SVN are present but are not impressive. NVN is extremely vulnerable to conventional bombing, a weakness which should be exploited diplomatically in convincing Hanoi to lay off SVN. Both the DRV and the Chicoms would face severe logistical difficulties in trying to maintain strong forces in the field in SEA, difficulties which we share but by no means to the same degree. There is no case for fearing a mass onslaught of Communist manpower into SVN and its neighboring states, particularly if our airpower is allowed a free hand against logistical targets. Finally, the starvation conditions in China should discourage Communist leaders there from being militarily venturesome for some time to come.

By the foregoing line of reasoning, I have reached the conclusion that the introduction of a U.S. military Task Force without delay offers definitely more advantage than it creates risks and difficulties. In fact, I do not believe that our program to save SVN will succeed without it. If the concept is approved, the exact size and composition of the force should be determined by the Secretary of Defense in consultation with the JCS, the Chief MAAG, and CINCPAC. My own feeling is that the initial size should not exceed about 8000, of which a preponderant number would be in logistical-type units. After acquiring experience in operating in SVN, this initial force will require reorganization and adjustment to the local scene.

As CINCPAC will point out, any forces committed to SVN will need to be replaced by additional forces to his area from the strategic reserve in the U.S. Also, any troops to SVN are in addition to those which may be required to execute SEATO Plan 5 in Laos. Both facts should be taken into account in current considerations of the FY 1963 budget which bear upon the permanent increase which should be made in the U.S. military establishment to maintain our strategic position for the long pull.

These cables, it will be noticed, are rather sharply focused on the insurgency as a problem reducible to fairly conventional military technique and tactics. Together with the cables from Saigon, the impression is given that the major needs are getting the Army to take the offensive, building up a much better intelligence setup, and persuading Diem to loosen up Administrative impediments to effective use of his forces.

E. The Taylor Report

A report of the Taylor Mission was published November 3, in the form of a black loose-leaf notebook containing a letter of transmittal of more than routine significance, a 25-page "Evaluation and Conclusions," then a series of memoranda by members of the mission. Of these, the most important, of course, were the Taylor cables, which, being "Eyes only for the President," were deleted from all but one or a very few copies of the report. There is no separate paper from Rostow, and his views presumably are reflected in the unsigned summary paper.

The impression the "Evaluation" paper gives is more easily summarized than its details. For the impression is clearly one of urgency combined with optimism. Essentially, it says South Vietnam is in serious trouble; major interests of the

United States are at stake; but if the U.S. promptly and energetically takes up the challenge, a victory can be had without a U.S. take-over of the war.

For example:

> Despite the intellectuals who sit on the side lines and complain; despite serious dissidence among the Montagnards, the sects, and certain old Viet Minh areas; despite the apathy and fear of the Viet-Cong in the country-side, the atmosphere in South Vietnam is, on balance, one of frustrated energy rather than passive acceptance of inevitable defeat.
>
> It cannot be emphasized too strongly, however, that time has nearly run out for converting these assets into the bases for victory. Diem himself—and all concerned with the fate of the country—are looking to American guidance and aid to achieve a turning point in Vietnam's affairs. From all quarters in Southeast Asia the message on Vietnam is the same: vigorous American action is needed to buy time for Vietnam to mobilize and organize its real assets; but the time for such a turn around has nearly run out. And if Vietnam goes, it will be exceedingly difficult if not impossible to hold Southeast Asia. What will be lost is not merely a crucial piece of real estate, but the faith that the U.S. has the will and the capacity to deal with the Communist offensive in that area.

The report, drawing on the appendices, includes a wide range of proposals. [Doc. 94] But the major emphasis, very emphatically, is on two ideas: First, there must be a firm, unambiguous military commitment to remove doubts about U.S. resolve arising out of the Laos negotiations; second, there is great emphasis on the idea that the Diem regime's own evident weaknesses—from "the famous problem of Diem as administrator" to the Army's lack of offensive spirit—could be cured if enough dedicated Americans, civilian and military, became involved in South Vietnam to show the South Vietnamese, at all levels, how to get on and win the war. The much-urged military Task Force, for example, was mainly to serve the first purpose, but partly also to serve the second: "the presence of American military forces in the [flood] area should also give us an opportunity to work intensively with the civil guards and with other local military elements and to explore the possibility of suffusing them with an offensive spirit and tactics."

Here are a few extracts which give the flavor of the discussion:

> "It is evident that morale in Vietnam will rapidly crumble—and in Southeast Asia only slightly less quickly—if the sequence of expectations set in motion by Vice President Johnson's visit and climaxed by General Taylor's mission are not soon followed by a *hard U.S. commitment to the ground* in Vietnam. [Emphasis added]

The elements required for buying time and assuming the offensive in Vietnam are, in the view of this mission, the following:

> 1. A quick U.S. response to the present crisis which would demonstrate by deeds—not merely words—the American commitment seriously to help save Vietnam rather than to disengage in the most convenient manner possible. To be persuasive this commitment must include the sending to Vietnam of some U.S. military forces.

2. A shift in the American relation to the Vietnamese effort from advice to limited partnership. The present character and scale of the war in South Vietnam decree that only the Vietnamese can defeat the Viet Cong; but at all levels Americans must, as friends and partners—not as arms-length advisors—show them how the job might be done—not tell them or do it for them.

*   *   *

"Perhaps the most striking aspect of this mission's effort is the unanimity of view—individually arrived at by the specialists involved—that what is now required is a shift from U.S. advice to limited partnership and working collaboration with the Vietnamese. The present war cannot be won by direct U.S. action; it must be won by the Vietnamese. But there is a general conviction among us that the Vietnamese performance in every domain can be substantially improved if Americans are prepared to work side by side with the Vietnamese on the key problems. Moreover, there is evidence that Diem is, in principle, prepared for this step, and that most —not all—elements in his establishment are eagerly awaiting it.

Here is a section titled "Reforming Diem's Administrative Method":

The famous problem of Diem as an administrator and politician could be resolved in a number of ways:

—By his removal in favor of a military dictatorship which would give dominance to the military chain of command.

—By his removal in favor of a figure of more dilute power (e.g., Vice President Nguyen Ngoc Tho) who would delegate authority to act to both military and civil leaders.

—By bringing about a series of *de facto* administrative changes via persuasion at high levels; collaboration with Diem's aides who want improved administration; and by a U.S. operating presence at many working levels, using the U.S. presence (e.g., control over the helicopter squadrons) for forcing the Vietnamese to get their house in order in one area after another.

We have opted for the third choice, on the basis of both merit and feasibility.

Our reasons for these: First, it would be dangerous for us to engineer a coup under present tense circumstances, since it is by no means certain that we could control its consequences and potentialities for Communist exploitation. Second, we are convinced that a part of the complaint about Diem's administrative methods conceals a lack of first-rate executives who can get things done. In the endless debate between Diem and his subordinates (Diem complaining of limited executive material; his subordinates, of Diem's bottleneck methods) both have hold of a piece of the truth.

The proposed strategy of limited partnership is designed both to force clear delegation of authority in key areas and to beef up Vietnamese administration until they can surface and develop the men to take over.

This is a difficult course to adopt. We can anticipate some friction and reluctance until it is proved that Americans can be helpful partners and that the techniques will not undermine Diem's political position. Shifts in U.S. attitudes and methods of administration as well as Vietnamese are required. But we are confident that it is the right way to proceed at this stage; and, as noted earlier, there is reason for confidence if the right men are sent to do the right jobs.

On many points the tone, and sometimes the substance, of the appendices by the lesser members of the Mission (with the exception of one by Lansdale) are in sharp contrast to the summary paper.

William Jorden of State begins a discussion of "the present situation" by reporting:

> One after another, Vietnamese officials, military men and ordinary citizens spoke to me of the situation in their country as "grave" and "deteriorating." They are distressed at the evidence of growing Viet Cong successes. They have lost confidence in President Diem and in his leadership. Men who only one or two months ago would have hesitated to say anything critical of Diem, now explode in angry denunciation of the man, his family, and his methods.

And after a page of details, Jorden sums up with:

> Intrigue, nepotism and even corruption might be accepted, for a time, if combined with efficiency and visible progress. When they accompany administrative paralysis and steady deterioration, they become intolerable.

But the summary paper, under the heading of "The Assets of South Vietnam," lists:

> With all his weaknesses, Diem has extraordinary ability, stubbornness, and guts.
>
> Despite their acute frustration, the men of the Armed Forces and the administration respect Diem to a degree which gives their grumbling (and perhaps some plotting) a somewhat half-hearted character; and they are willing—by and large—to work for him, if he gives them a chance to do their jobs.

The military annex contains this summary comment on the South Vietnamese Army:

> The performance of the ARVN is disappointing and generally is characterized by a lack of aggressiveness and at most levels is devoid of a sense or urgency. The Army is short of able young trained leaders, both in the officer and NCO ranks. The basic soldier, as a result, is poorly trained, inadequately oriented, lacking in desire to close with the enemy and for the most part unaware of the serious inroads communist guerrillas are making in his country.

But the main paper, again in the summary of South Vietnamese assets, reports that the South Vietnamese regulars are "of better quality than the Viet Cong Guerrillas."

The point is not that the summary flatly contradicts the appendices. For example, the statement about the superior quality of ARVN, compared to the Viet Cong, is qualified with the remark "if it can bring the Communists to engagement," and can be explained to mean only that the more heavily armed ARVN could defeat a VC force in a set-piece battle. But the persistence tendency of the summary is to put Saigon's weaknesses in the best light, and avoid anything that might suggest that perhaps the U.S. should consider limiting, rather than increasing, its commitments to the Diem regime, or alternatively face up to a need to openly take over the war.

In contrast, the appendices contemplate (if they do not always recommend) the more drastic alternatives. The military appendix argues (in a paraphrase of the JCS position quoted earlier) that the U.S. ought to move into Southeast Asia, preferably Laos, in force. The appendix by Sterling Cottrell of State (chairman of the Vietnam Task Force) suggests an opposite view:

> Since it is an open question whether the GVN can succeed even with U.S. assistance, it would be a mistake for the U.S. to commit itself irrevocably to the defeat of the communists in SVN.

And Cottrell, in the only explicit statement in the available record on why the U.S. would not want to give Diem the treaty he had asked for, states:

> The Communist operation starts from the lowest social level—the villages. The battle must be joined and won at this point. If not, the Communists will ultimately control all but the relatively few areas of strong military concentrations. Foreign military forces cannot themselves win the battle at the village level. Therefore, the primary responsibility for saving the country must rest with the GVN.
>
> For the above reason, the U.S. should assist the GVN. This rules out any treaty or pact which either shifts ultimate responsibility to the U.S., or engages any full U.S. commitment to eliminate the Viet Cong threat.

(And a treaty which did not apply to the Viet Cong threat would hardly be a very reassuring thing to Saigon; while one that did would face an uncertain future when it came to the Senate for ratification.)

Yet, Jorden and Cottrell had nothing much to recommend that was particularly different from what was recommended in the summary. The effect of their papers is to throw doubt on the prospects for success of the intervention proposed. But their recommendations come out about the same way, so that if their papers seem more realistic in hindsight than the main paper, they also seem more confused.

Cottrell, after recommending that the U.S. avoid committing itself irrevocably to winning in South Vietnam, goes on to recommend:

> The world should continue to be impressed that this situation of overt DRV aggression, below the level of conventional warfare, must be stopped in the best interest of every free nation.

The idea that, if worse comes to worst, the U.S. could probably save its position in Vietnam by bombing the north, seems to underlie a good deal of the optimism that pervades the summary paper. And even Cottrell, in the last of his recommendations, states:

> If the combined U.S./GVN efforts are insufficient to reverse the trend, we should then move to the "Rostow Plan" of applying graduated measures on the DRV with weapons of our own choosing.

Taylor, in his personal recommendations to the President (the cables from Baguio quoted earlier), spoke of the "extreme vulnerability of North Vietnam to conventional bombing."

The summary paper, in its contrast between the current war and the war the French lost, states:

> Finally, the Communists now not only have something to gain—the South—but a base to lose—the North—if war should come.

Bombing was not viewed as the answer to all problems. If things did not go well, the report saw a possible requirement for a substantial commitment of U.S. ground troops. In a section on South Vietnamese reserves, there is the comment that

> . . . it is an evident requirement that the United States review quick action contingency plans to move into Vietnam, should the scale of the Vietnam [Viet Cong?] offensive radically increase at a time when Vietnamese reserves are inadequate to cope with it. Such action might be designed to take over the responsibility for the security of certain relatively quiet areas, if the battle remained at the guerrilla level, or to fight the Communists if open war were attempted.

And the concluding paragraphs of the summary state that:

> One of the major issues raised by this report is the need to develop the reserve strength in the U.S. establishment required to cover action in Southeast Asia up to the nuclear threshold in that area, as it is now envisaged. The call up of additional support forces may be required.
>
> In our view, nothing is more calculated to sober the enemy and to discourage escalation in the face of the limited initiatives proposed here than the knowledge that the United States has prepared itself soundly to deal with aggression in Southeast Asia at any level.

But these warnings were directed to an unexpectedly strong Viet Cong showing during the period of buildup of ARVN, and more still to deterring the likelihood of a Communist resumption of their offensive in Laos, or of an overt invasion of South Vietnam. The Vietnam contingencies, in particular, were not viewed as likely. But the possibility of bombing the North was viewed otherwise. The clearest statements are in General Taylor's letter of transmittal:

> While we feel that the program recommended represents those measures which should be taken in our present knowledge of the situation in Southeast Asia, I would not suggest that it is the final word. Future needs beyond this program will depend upon the kind of settlement we obtain in Laos and the manner in which Hanoi decides to adjust its conduct to that settlement. If the Hanoi decision is to continue the irregular war declared of South Vietnam in 1959 with continued infiltration and covert support of guerrilla bands in the territory of our ally, we will then have to decide whether to accept as legitimate the continued guidance, training, and support of a guerrilla war across an international boundary, while the attacked react only inside their borders. Can we admit the establishment of the common law that the party attacked and his friends are denied the right to strike the source of aggression, after the fact of external aggression is clearly established? It is our view that our government should undertake with the Vietnamese the measures outlined herein, but should then consider and face the broader question beyond.

We cannot refrain from expressing, having seen the situation on the ground, our common sense of outrage at the burden which this kind of aggression imposes on a new country, only seven years old, with a difficult historical heritage to overcome, confronting the inevitable problems of political, social, and economic transition to modernization. It is easy and cheap to destroy such a country whereas it is difficult undisturbed to build a nation coming out of a complex past without carrying the burden of a guerrilla war.

We were similarly struck in Thailand with the injustice of subjecting this promising nation in transition to the heavy military burdens it faces in fulfilling its role in SEATO security planning along with the guerrilla challenge beginning to form up on its northeast frontier.

It is my judgment and that of my colleagues that the United States must decide how it will cope with Krushchev's "wars of liberation" which are really para-wars of guerrilla aggression. This is a new and dangerous Communist technique which bypasses our traditional political and military responses. While the final answer lies beyond the scope of this report, it is clear to me that the time may come in our relations to Southeast Asia when we must declare our intention to attack the source of guerrilla aggression in North Vietnam and impose on the Hanoi Government a price for participating in the current war which is commensurate with the damage being inflicted on its neighbors to the south.

F. SOME CABLES FROM SAIGON

To a current reader, and very likely to the officials in Washington who had access to the full Taylor Mission Report (including Taylor's personal recommendations), there really seem to be three reports, not one.

1. Taylor's own cables read like, as of course they were, a soldier's crisp, direct analysis of the military problem facing the Saigon government. With regard to the Diem regime, the emphasis is on a need to build up intelligence capabilities, clear up administrative drags on efficient action, and take the offensive in seeking out and destroying VC units.

2. The main paper in the Report (the "Evaluations and Conclusions") incorporates General Taylor's views on the military problems. But, it is much broader, giving primary emphasis to the military problem, but also some attention to what we now call the "other war," and even more to conveying an essentially optimistic picture of the opportunities for a vigorous American effort to provide the South Vietnamese government and army with the elan and style needed to win. This paper was presumably drafted mainly by Rostow, with contributions from other members of the party.

It is consistent with Rostow's emphasis before and since on the Viet Cong problem as a pretty straight-forward case of external aggression. There is no indication of the doubts expressed in the Alexis Johnson "Concept of Intervention in Vietnam" paper that Diem might not be able to defeat the Viet Cong even if infiltration were largely cut off. At one point, for example, the paper tells its readers:

It must be remembered that the 1959 political decision in Hanoi to launch the guerrilla and political campaign of 1960-61 arose because of Diem's increasing success in stabilizing his rule and moving his country forward in the several preceding years.

On the very next page (perhaps reflecting the vagaries of committee papers) the paper does not itself "remember" this description of conditions when the war started. For it states:

> The military frustration of the past two months has . . . made acute, throughout his administration, dissatisfaction with Diem's method of rule, with his lack of identification with his people, and with his strategy which has been endemic for some years.

But that seems only a momentary lapse from the general line of the paper, which is fairly reflected in the recommendation that we tell Moscow to:

> use its influence with Ho Chi Minh to call his dogs off, mind his business, and feed his people.

3. Finally, there were the appendices by the military and especially the State representatives on the Mission which, as indicated by the extracts given in the previous section, paint a much darker picture than the reader gets from the main paper. Even when, as is frequently the case, their recommendations are not much different from the main paper, the tone is one of trying to make the best of a bad situation, rather than of seizing an opportunity.

Because of these distinctions between the different parts of the Report, two people reading the full Report could come away with far different impressions of what sort of problem the U.S. was facing in Vietnam, depending on which parts of the Report seemed to them to ring truest. Presumably, officials' judgments here were influenced by their reading of the series of cables that arrived during and just after the Taylor visit, many of which touch on critical points of the report.

Here are some samples.

The day Taylor left, Nolting sent a cable describing the immediate mood in Saigon in pretty desperate terms. All parts of the Taylor Report, including the main paper, did the same. The distinctions in describing the situation were in how deep-rooted the immediate malaise was seen. The main effect of this cable from Nolting was presumably to add weight to the warning of the Report that something dramatic had to be done if the U.S. were not ready to risk a collapse in Saigon within a few months. As the Taylor Report stressed and the cable implies, the very fact of the Taylor Mission would have a very negative impact if nothing came out of it.

> There has been noticeable rise in Saigon's political temperature during past week. Taylor visit, though reassuring in some respects, has been interpreted by many persons as demonstrating critical stage which VC insurgency has reached . . . Following deterioration of general security conditions over past two months cancellation October 26 national day celebrations to devote resources to flood relief and terse, dramatic declaration national emergency caught an unprepared public by surprise and contributed additional unsettling elements to growing atmosphere of uneasiness . . .

This growing public disquietude accompanied by increasing dissatisfaction with Diem's methods of administration on part senior GVN officials. There is considerable cabinet level criticism and growing though still inchoate determination force organizational reforms on President. Similar attitude seems be developing in ARVN upper levels. Though trend of thinking these groups taking parallel courses, there nothing indicate at this moment that collaboration between them taking place. Beginnings of this would, of course, be serious indicator something brewing.

At same time CAS also has from Vietnamese government sources reports (C-3) of movement of certain platoon to company-size VC units (totalling perhaps 200-500 men toward Saigon to profit from any disturbances or confusion which may occur. Knowledge these reports within GVN apparently tending deter disaffected officials from developing radical pace at this moment.

Situation here thus one of insecurity, uneasiness and emergent instability. A genuine and important military victory over VC would do more than anything else to redress balance and allay for moment high-level mutterings of need for change. On other hand, further deterioration of situation over next few weeks or months or new VC success similar Phuoc Hhanh incident might well bring situation to head.

From MAAG Chief McGarr, Washington received an account of Taylor's meeting with "Big Minh," then Chief of Staff, later Head of State for a while after Diem was overthrown. It is interesting because it was one of the very few reports from Saigon in the available record suggesting that the Diem regime might be in need of more than administrative reforms. Minh complains that the Vietnamese army was "losing the support of the people" as indicated by a "marked decrease in the amount of information given by the population." He warned, further, that "GVN should discontinue favoring certain religions . . ." But McGarr stressed the administrative problems, particularly the need for an "overall plan." His reaction explicitly concerns what he saw as the "military" aspects of Minh's complaints. But Ambassador Nolting's cables and the main paper of the Report show a very similar tendency to take note of political problems, but put almost all the emphasis on the need for better military tactics and more efficient administrative arrangements.

. . . Big Minh was pessimistic and clearly and frankly outlined his personal feeling that the military was not being properly supported. He said not only Viet Cong grown alarmingly, but that Vietnamese armed forces were losing support of the people. As example, he pointed out marked decrease in amount of information given by population. Minh said GVN should discontinue favoring certain religions, and correct present system of selecting province chiefs. At this point Minh was extremely caustic in commenting on lack of ability, military and administrative, of certain province chiefs. Minh was bitter about province chief's role in military chain of command saying that although Gen. McGarr had fought for and won on the single . . . command which had worked for few months, old habits were now returning. Also, on urging from Gen. McGarr he had gone on offensive, but province chiefs had not cooperated to extent necessary. He discussed his inability to get cooperation from GVN agencies on developing overall plans for conduct of counterinsurgency. Minh also discussed need to bring sects back into fold as these are anti-communist.

Although above not new Minh seemed particularly discouraged . . .
When analyzed, most of Minh's comments in military field are occasioned
by lack of overall coordination and cooperation. This re-emphasizes absolute necessity for overall plan which would clearly delineate responsibility and create a team effort . . .

Nolting concerned himself, of course, with the civil as well as military arrangements, but with much the same stress on organizational and administrative
formalities. A striking example was when Nolting reported that Diem was willing to consider (in response to American urging of top level administrative reforms) creating a National Executive Council patterned after the U.S. National
Security Council. Nolting was favorably impressed. His cable notes no concern
that under Diem's proposal, Diem's brother Nhu would be chairman of the
NEC, although a year earlier (and of course even more urgently a year or so
later) getting Nhu, and his wife, out of the picture entirely had been seen as
the best real hope of saving the Diem regime.

The report Nolting sent on Taylor's final meeting with Diem also contains
some interesting material. It leaves the impression that Diem was still not really
anxious to get American troops deeply involved in his country, despite his
favorable reaction at the meeting of the 24th, which, in turn, was a reversal of
his reaction at the meeting on the 19th. Because of this, the impression left by
the whole record is that Taylor came to the conclusion that some sort of ground
troop commitment was needed mainly because of what he heard from Diem's
colleagues and his military people, rather than from Diem himself.

According to Nolting's cabled account, Diem, although raising half a dozen
issues relating to increased American military aid, did not mention the flood
task force, or anything else that might imply a special interest in getting some
sort of ground troops commitment. As seemed the case earlier, it was the
Americans who pressed the idea of getting American military people involved
in combat. In the only exchange Nolting reported touching on this issue, he
said:

> 1. Diem stressed importance of reinforcement of aviation: particularly
> helicopters. Taylor and I [Nolting] used this opportunity to make clear to
> Diem that we envisaged helicopters piloted by Americans and constituting
> American units under American commanders which would cooperate with
> Vietnamese military commands.

(At a meeting with McGarr November 9, Diem again raised the helicopter
question, this time taking the initiative in saying he needed American pilots, but
he did not mention the flood task force, or anything else that might imply a request for ground troops.)

On the question of better performance by Diem's regime, we have this exchange, which does not seem likely to have prepared Diem for the fairly substantial *quid pro quo* which turned out to be part of the package proposed by
Washington:

> . . . 3. Taylor told Diem it would be useful if he and I could develop
> specifics with respect to political-psychological point in paper which Taylor
> presented to Diem October 24. Taylor pointed out this would be very
> useful to him in Washington because he will be faced with question that,
> if program he proposes is adopted, what will be chances of early success.

In response Thuan's question asking for exact meaning of this point in Taylor's paper, latter said there has been loss of confidence among both Vietnamese and American people about situation in Vietnam and we need to determine together what measures can be taken to restore confidence. Rostow commented that secret of turning point is offensive action. Diem stated complete psychological mobilization required so that everything can be done to raise potential GVN forces and damage enemy's potential. He referred to GVN efforts in past to collaborate more closely with US in military planning and said these efforts had run up against wall of secrecy surrounding US and SEATO military plans . . .

Finally, there was this exchange, which does not appear to provide much support for the high hopes expressed in the Taylor Report that Diem was anxious for U.S. guidance and "in principle" ready to grant a role for Americans in his administration and army.

. . . 4. Taylor referred to Diem's comments in earlier talk about shortage of capable personnel and suggested US might assist by lending personnel. Diem replied that US could help in this respect in training field. Thuan then brought up dilemma facing GVN re instructors at Thui Duc Reserve Officers' School . . .

VI.   THE FALL DECISIONS—II

A.   CONTEXT

Taylor's formal report, as noted, was dated November 3, a day after the Mission came back to Washington. (A good deal of it had been written during the stopover at Baguio, in the Philippines, when Taylor's personal cables to the President had also been written and sent.) The submission of Taylor's Report was followed by prominent news stories the next morning flatly stating (but without attribution to a source) that the President "remains strongly opposed to the dispatch of American combat troops to South Vietnam" and strongly implying that General Taylor had not recommended such a commitment. Apparently, only a few people, aside from Taylor, Rostow and a handful of very senior officials, realized that this was not exactly accurate—for the summary paper of the Report had not been very explicit on just what was meant by "a hard commitment to the ground." Thus only those who knew about the "Eyes Only" cables would know just what Taylor was recommending.

Diem himself had given one of his rare on-the-record interviews to the *New York Times* correspondent in Saigon while Taylor was on his way home, and he too gave the impression that the further American aid he expected would not include ground troops.

Consequently, the general outline of the American aid that would be sent following the Taylor Mission was common knowledge for over a week before any formal decision was made. The decisions, when they were announced stirred very little fuss, and (considering the retrospective importance) not even much interest. The Taylor Mission had received much less attention in the press than several other crises at the UN, in the Congo, on nuclear testing, and most of all in Berlin, where there had just been a symbolic confrontation of Soviet and American tanks. The Administration was so concerned about public reaction to Soviet aggressiveness and apparent American inability to deal with it that a campaign was begun (as usual in matters of this sort, reported in the *Times* without specific attribution) to "counter-attack against what unnamed 'high officials' called a 'rising mood of national frustration.'" The Administration's message, the *Times* reported, was that a "mature foreign policy" rather than "belligerence of defeatism" was what was needed. What is interesting about such a message is what the necessity to send it reveals about the mood of the times.

In this sort of context, there was no real debate about whether the U.S. ought to do anything reasonable it could to prevent Vietnam from going the way of Laos. There is no hint of a suggestion otherwise in the classified record, and there was no real public debate on this point. What was seen as an issue was whether the limits of reasonable U.S. aid extended to the point of sending American troops to fight the Viet Cong. But even this was subdued. There had been, as noted before, the leaked stories playing down the prospects that combat troops would be sent, and then, immediately on Taylor's return, the unattributed but obviously authoritative stories that Kennedy was opposed to sending troops and Taylor was not recommending them.

In a most important sense, this situation distorts the story told in this account. For this account inevitably devotes a great deal of space to the decision that was not made—that of sending ground troops—and very little space to the important decisions that *were* made. There is simply nothing much to say about these latter decisions: except that they were apparently taken for granted at the time. Even today, with all the hindsight available, it is very hard to imagine Kennedy or any other President responding to the situation faced in 1961 by doing significantly less about Vietnam than he did. The only choices seen then, as indeed even today the only choices seem to have been, whether to do more. And it is on how that question was resolved, inevitably, that any account of the period will be focused.

The Administration faced (contrary to the impression given to the public both before and after the decisions) two major issues when Taylor returned.

1. What conditions, if any, would be attached to new American aid? The Taylor Report implicitly recommended none. But the leaked stories in the press following Taylor's return showed that some in the Administration inclined to a much harder line on Diem than the summary paper of the report. For example, a *Times* dispatch of November 5, from its Pentagon correspondent, reported that Diem would be expected to "undertake major economic, social, and military reforms to provide a basis for increased U.S. support."

2. Would the limited commitment of ground forces recommended by Taylor be undertaken? The news stories suggested they would, although this would be apparent only to those who had seen Taylor's "Eyes Only" cables. The story appearing the day after the report was submitted, despite the flat statements against the use of combat troops, also stated that Taylor had recommended "the dispatch of more specialists in anti-guerrilla warfare to train Vietnamese troops, communications and transportation specialists, *and army engineers to help the Vietnamese government combat its flood problems.*" The November 5 story was more explicit. It is noted that officials seemed to rule out the use of U.S. combat forces, "the move considered here a few weeks ago." But "at the same time it appears that Army engineers, perhaps in unusually large numbers, may be sent to help on flood control work and other civil projects *and to fight if necessary.*" This last phrase was explicitly (and correctly) linked to the fact that

the area in which the floods had taken place (the Delta) was precisely the area of greatest Viet Cong strength.

A final question of great importance did not have to be resolved during this review: for although the Taylor Report had stressed the idea of eventually bombing the north, no immediate decision or commitment on this was recommended.

On the first of these issues (the *quid pro quo* for U.S. aid) our record tells us that demands were made on Diem, as we will see when we come to the actual decision. The newspaper stories strongly suggest that the decision to ask for a *quid pro quo* was made, at the latest, immediately following the return of the Taylor Mission. But the record does not show anything about the reasoning behind this effort to pressure Diem to agree to reforms as a condition for increased U.S. aid, nor of what the point of it was. It certainly conflicted with the main drive of the Taylor Mission Report. The report not only suggested no such thing, but put a great deal of stress on a cordial, intimate relationship with the Diem regime. Pressure for reform (especially when publicly made, as they essentially were in the leaked stories) was hardly likely to promote cordiality. Durbrow's experience earlier in the year had shown that pressure would have the opposite result.

Consequently, the President's handling of this issue had the effect of undermining from the start what appeared to have been a major premise of the strategy recommended to the President: that Diem was "in principle" prepared for what plainly amounted to a "limited partnership," with the U.S. in running his country and his Army.

The advantages, from the American view, of the President's decision to place demands on Diem were presumably that it might (contrary to realistic expectations) actually push Diem in the right direction; and that if this did not work, it would somewhat limit the American commitment to Diem. The limit would come by making clear that the U.S. saw a good deal of the problem as Diem's own responsibility, and not just a simple matter of external aggression. The balance of this judgment would turn substantially on whether whoever was making the decision judged that the "limited partnership" idea was really much more realistic than the trying to pressure Diem, and on whether he wanted to limit the U.S. commitment, rather than make it unambiguous. Further, the cables from Saigon had clearly shown that many South Vietnamese were *hoping* the Americans would put pressure on Diem, so that although such tactics would prejudice relations with Diem, they would not necessarily harm relations with others of influence in the country, in particular his generals.

Finally, although Kennedy's decisions here were contrary to the implications of the summary paper in the Taylor Report, they were not particularly inconsistent with the appendices by the State representatives. For these, as noted, took a far less rosy view of Diem's prospects than appeared in the summary.

On the second issue—the U.S. combat military task force—the available record tells us only the positions of Taylor and of the Defense Department. We are not sure what the position of State was—although Sorenson claims that all the President's senior advisors had recommended going ahead with sending some ground troops.

Even Taylor's position is slightly ambiguous. It is conceivable that he argued for the Task Force mainly because he thought that the numbers of U.S. personnel that might be sent as advisors, pilots, and other specialists would not add up to a large enough increment to have much of a psychological impact on South Vietnamese morale. But his choice of language indicates that a mere question of numbers was not the real issue. Rather Taylor's argument seems to have been that specifically ground forces (not necessarily all or even mainly infantrymen, but ground soldiers who would be out in the countryside where they could be shot at and shoot back) were what was needed. Combat engineers to work in the VC-infested flood area in the Delta would meet that need. Helicopter pilots and mechanics and advisors, who might accompany Vietnamese operations, but could not undertake ground operations on their own apparently would not. There is only one easily imagined reason for seeing this as a crucial distinction. And that would be if a critical object of the stepped up American program was to be exactly what Taylor said it should be in his final cable from Saigon: ". . . assuring Diem of our readiness to join him in a military showdown with the Viet Cong . . ."

Thus the flood task force was essentially different from the balance of the military program. It did not fill an urgent need for military specialists or expertise not adequately available within Vietnam; it was an implicit commitment to deny the Viet Cong a victory even if major American ground forces should be required.

Taylor clearly did not see the need for large U.S. ground involvement as at all probable. ("The risks of backing into a major Asian war because SVN are present but are not impressive," in large part because "NVN is extremely vulnerable to conventional bombing.") At another point, Taylor warns the President, "If the first contingent is not enough, . . . it will be difficult to resist the pressure to reinforce. If the ultimate result sought is the closing of the frontiers and the cleanup of the insurgents within SVN, there is no limit to our possible commitment (unless we attack the source in Hanoi.)"

We have a good record of the DOD staff work, which preceded the President's decision on this issue, but only a bit from State and none from the White House. Rusk, in a cable from Japan on November 1, contributed this note of caution (which also bears on the previous discussion of demands on Diem for a *quid pro quo* for increased American aid):

> Since General Taylor may give first full report prior my return, believe special attention should be given to critical question whether Diem is prepared take necessary measures to give us something worth supporting. If Diem unwilling trust military commanders to get job done and take steps to consolidate non-communist elements into serious national effort, difficult to see how handful American troops can have decisive influence. While attaching greatest possible importance to security in SEA, I would be reluctant to see U.S. make major additional commitment American prestige to a losing horse.
>
> Suggest Department carefully review all Southeast Asia measures we expect from Diem if our assistance forces us to assume de facto direction South Vietnamese affairs.

But the view of the U.S. Mission in Saigon contained no such doubts, nor did most Vietnamese, according to this cable Nolting sent while Taylor was enroute home:

> Our conversations over past ten days with Vietnamese in various walks of life show virtually unanimous desire for introduction U.S. forces into Viet-Nam. This based on unsolicited remarks from cabinet ministers, National Assembly Deputies, University professors, students, shop-keepers,

and oppositionists. Dr. Tran Dinh De, level-headed Minister of Health, told Embassy officer Oct. 29 that while GVN could continue resist communists for while longer if US troops not introduced, it could not win alone against commies. National Assembly members, according to Lai Tu, leader Personalist Community, unanimously in favor entry US forces. Diem told us while General Taylor was here that he had consulted National Assembly Committee on this question and had received favorable response. Even an oppositionist like Ex-Foreign Minister Tran Van Do has told us US forces are needed and is apparently so strongly convinced of this that he did not suggest any conditions precedent about political changes by Diem. Am-Consul Hue reports that opinion among intellectuals and government officials in that city is also almost unanimously in favor of introduction of American combat troops. MAAG believes on basis private conversations and general attitude Vietnamese military personnel toward us that Vietnamese armed forces would likewise welcome introduction US forces.

General Vietnamese desire for introduction US forces arises from serious morale decline among populace during recent weeks because of deterioration in security and horrible death through torture and mutilation to which Col Nam subjected. Expanded VC infiltration has brought fully home to Vietnamese the fact that US has not intervened militarily in Laos to come to rescue of anti-communists. Now that they see Viet-Nam approaching its own crucial period, paramount question in their minds is whether it will back down when chips are down. Vietnamese thus want US forces introduced in order to demonstrate US determination to stick it out with them against Communists. They do not want to be victims of political settlement with communists. This is especially true of those publicly identified as anti-communist like Dean Vu Quoc Thue who collaborated with Dr. Eugene Staley on Joint Experts Report.

Most Vietnamese whose thoughts on this subject have been developed are not thinking in terms of US troops to fight guerrillas but rather of a reassuring presence of US forces in Viet-Nam. These persons undoubtedly feel, however, that if war in Viet-Nam continues to move toward overt conventional aggression as opposed to its guerrilla character, combat role for US troops could eventually arise.

The special commitment involved in committing even a small force of ground troops was generally recognized. We have notes on an ISA staff paper, for example, which ranked the various types of increased U.S. military aid in ascending order of commitment, and of course, placed the flood task force at the top. According to the notes,

Any combat elements, such as in the task force, would come under attack and would need to defend themselves, committing U.S. prestige deeply. U.S. troops would then be fighting in South Vietnam and could not withdraw under fire. Thus, the introduction of U.S. troops in South Vietnam would be a decisive act and must be sent to achieve a completely decisive mission. This mission would probably require, over time, increased numbers of U.S. troops; DRV intervention would probably increase until a large number of U.S. troops were required, three or more divisions.

This assessment differed from that in General Taylor's cables only in not stressing the hope that a U.S. willingness to bomb the north would deter North Vietnamese escalation of its own commitment.

A special NIE prepared at this time reached essentially the same conclusions.

This SNIE, incidentally, is the only staff paper found in the available record which treats communist reactions primarily in terms of the separate national interests of Hanoi, Moscow, and Peiping, rather than primarily in terms of an overall communist strategy for which Hanoi, is acting as an agent. In particular, the Gilpatric Task Force Report, it will be recalled, began with references to a communist 'master plan' for taking over Southeast Asia. The Taylor Mission Report, similarly, began with a section on "Communist Strategy in Southeast Asia" and opening:

> At the present time, the Communists are pursuing a clear and systematic strategy in Southeast Asia. It is a strategy of extending Communist power and influence in ways which bypass U.S. nuclear strength, U.S. conventional naval, air, and ground forces, and the conventional strength of indigenous forces in the area. Their strategy is rooted in the fact that international law and practice does not yet recognize the mounting of guerrilla war across borders as aggression justifying counterattack at the source.

The November 5 SNIE presumably indicates the principal courses of action that were under formal review at the time:

> The courses of action here considered were given to the intelligence community for the purposes of this estimate and were not intended to represent the full range of possible courses of action. The given courses of action are:
>
> A. The introduction of a US airlift into and within South Vietnam, increased logistics support, and an increase in MAAG strength to provide US advisers down to battalion level;
>
> B. The introduction into South Vietnam of a US force of about 8,000-10,000 troops, mostly engineers with some combat support, in response to an appeal from President Diem for assistance in flood relief;
>
> C. The introduction into the area of a US combat force of 25,000 to 40,000 to engage with South Vietnamese forces in ground, air, and naval operations against the Viet Cong; and
>
> D. An announcement by the US of its determination to hold South Vietnam and a warning, either private or public, that North Vietnamese support of the Viet Cong must cease or the US would launch air attacks against North Vietnam. This action would be taken in conjunction with Course A, B, or C.

These proposed courses of action correspond to those outlined for consideration by the Taylor Mission, with the exception that the flood task force proposed by Taylor has been substituted for the former "intermediate" solution of stationing a token U.S. force at DaNang, and that an opinion is asked on the prospects of threats to bomb the north, again reflecting the Taylor Mission Report.

The gist of the SNIE was that North Vietnamese would respond to an increased U.S. commitment with an offsetting increase in infiltrated support for the Viet Cong. Thus, the main difference in the estimated communist reaction to Courses A, B, and C was that each would be stronger than its predecessor. On the prospects for bombing the north, the SNIE implies that threats to bomb would not cause Hanoi to stop its support for the Viet Cong, and that actual attacks on the North would bring a strong response from Moscow and Peiping, who would "regard the defense of North Vietnam against such an attack as imperative."

B. FINAL RECOMMENDATIONS

On November 8, McNamara sent the following memorandum on behalf of himself, Gilpatric, and the JCS:

MEMORANDUM FOR THE PRESIDENT

The basic issue framed by the Taylor Report is whether the U.S. shall:
a. Commit itself to the clear objective of preventing the fall of South Vietnam to Communism, and
b. Support this commitment by necessary immediate military actions and preparations for possible later actions.
The Joint Chiefs, Mr. Gilpatric, and I have reached the following conclusions:
1. The fall of South Vietnam to Communism would lead to the fairly rapid extension of Communist control, or complete accommodation to Communism, in the rest of mainland Southeast Asia and in Indonesia. The strategic implications worldwide, particularly in the Orient, would be extremely serious.
2. The chances are against, probably sharply against, preventing that fall by any measures short of the introduction of U.S. forces on a substantial scale. We accept General Taylor's judgment that the various measures proposed by him short of this are useful but will not in themselves do the job of restoring confidence and setting Diem on the way to winning his fight.
3. The introduction of a U.S. force of the magnitude of an initial 8,000 men in a flood relief context will be of great help to Diem. However, it will not convince the other side (whether the shots are called from Moscow, Peiping, or Hanoi) that we mean business. Moreover, it probably will not tip the scales decisively. We would be almost certain to get increasingly mired down in an inconclusive struggle.
4. The other side can be convinced we mean business only if we accompany the initial force introduction by a clear commitment to the full objective stated above, accompanied by a warning through some channel to Hanoi that continued support of the Viet Cong will lead to punitive retaliation against North Vietnam.
5. If we act in this way, the ultimate possible extent of our military commitment must be faced. The struggle may be prolonged and Hanoi and Peiping may intervene overtly. In view of the logistic difficulties faced by the other side, I believe we can assume that the maximum U.S. forces required on the ground in Southeast Asia will not exceed 6 divisions, or about 205,000 men (CINCPAC Plan 32-59, Phase IV). Our military posture is, or with the addition of more National Guard or regular Army divisions, can be made, adequate to furnish these forces without serious interference with our present Berlin plans.

6. To accept the stated objective is of course a most serious decision. Military force is not the only element of what must be a most carefully co-ordinated set of actions. Success will depend on factors many of which are not within our control—notably the conduct of Diem himself and other leaders in the area. Laos will remain a major problem. The domestic political implications of accepting the objective are also grave, although it is our feeling that the country will respond better to a firm initial position than to courses of action that lead us in only gradually, and that in the meantime are sure to involve casualties. The over-all effect on Moscow and Peiping will need careful weighing and may well be mixed; however, permitting South Vietnam to fall can only strengthen and encourage them greatly.

7. In sum:

a. We do not believe major units of U.S. forces should be introduced in South Vietnam unless we are willing to make an affirmative decision on the issue stated at the start of this memorandum.

b. We are inclined to recommend that we do commit the U.S. to the clear objective of preventing the fall of South Vietnam to Communism and that we support this commitment by the necessary military actions.

c. If such a commitment is agreed upon, we support the recommendations of General Taylor as the first steps toward its fulfillment.

Sgd: Robert S. McNamara

A number of things are striking about this memorandum, including of course the judgment that the "maximum" U.S. ground forces required, even in the case of overt intervention by not only North Vietnam, but China as well, would "not exceed" 205,000 men. This estimate of the requirement to deal with a large scale overt invasion is consistent with the Chief's earlier estimate that the addition of 40,000 U.S. troops to the South Vietnamese forces would be sufficient to "clean up" the Viet Cong.

But the strongest message to the President in the memorandum (growing out of points 3, 4, and 7c) was surely that if he agreed to sending the military task force, he should be prepared for follow-up recommendations for re-enforcements and to threaten Hanoi with bombing. Unless the SNIE was wholly wrong, threats to bomb Hanoi would not turn off the war, and Hanoi would increase its infiltration in response to U.S. commitments of troops. Even should Hanoi not react with counter-escalation, the President knew that the Chiefs, at least, were already on record as desiring a prompt build-up to 40,000 ground troops. In short, the President was being told that the issue was not whether to send an 8,000-man task force, but whether or not to embark on a course that, without some extraordinary good luck, would lead to combat involvement in Southeast Asia on a very substantial scale. On the other hand, he was being warned that anything less than sending the task force was very likely to fail to prevent the fall of Vietnam, since "the odds are against, probably sharply against, preventing that fall by any means short of the introduction of U.S. forces on a substantial scale" (of which the task force would be the first increment).

Although the Chief's position here is clear, because their views are on record in other memoranda, McNamara's own position remains a little ambiguous. For the paper does not flatly recommend going ahead; it only states he and his colleagues are "inclined" to recommend going ahead. Three days later McNamara joined Rusk in a quite different recommendation, and one obviously more to the President's liking (and, in the nature of such things, quite possibly drawn up to the President's specifications).

As with the May revision of the Gilpatric Report, this paper combines an escalation of the rhetoric with a toning down of the actions the President is asked to take. Since the NSAM formalizing the President's decisions was taken essentially verbatim from this paper, the complete text is reprinted here. (The NSAM consisted of the Recommendations section of this memorandum, except that Point 1 of the recommendations was deleted.)

Of particular importance in this second memorandum to the President was Section 4, with its explicit sorting of U.S. military aid into Category A, support forces, which were to be sent promptly; and Category B, "larger organized units with actual or potential direct military missions" on which no immediate decision was recommended. There is no explicit reference in the paper to the flood relief task force; it simply does not appear in the list of recommended actions, presumably on the grounds that it goes in Category B. Category B forces, the paper notes, "involve a certain dilemma: if there is a strong South Vietnamese effort, they may not be needed; if there is not such an effort, United States forces could not accomplish their mission in the midst of an apathetic or hostile population."

If McNamara's earlier memorandum is read carefully, the same sort of warning is found, although it sounds much more perfunctory. But that such warnings were included shows a striking contrast with the last go-around in May. Then, the original Defense version of the Gilpatric Task Force Report contained no hint of such a qualification, and there was only a quite vague warning in the State revisions. Part of the reason, undoubtedly, was the 6 month's additional experience in dealing with Diem. A larger part, though, almost certainly flowed from the fact that the insurgency had by now shown enough strength so that there was now in everyone's minds the possibility that the U.S. might someday face the choice of giving up on Vietnam or taking over a major part of the war.

These warnings (that even a major U.S. commitment to the ground war would not assure success) were obviously in some conflict with the recommendations both papers made for a clear-cut U.S. commitment to save South Vietnam. The contrast is all the sharper in the joint Rusk/McNamara memorandum, where the warning is so forcefully given.

Here is the Rusk/McNamara memorandum.

November 11, 1961

MEMORANDUM FOR THE PRESIDENT

Subject: *South Viet-Nam*

1. *United States National Interests in South Viet-Nam.*

The deteriorating situation in South Viet-Nam requires attention to the nature and scope of United States national interests in that country. The loss of South Viet-Nam to Communism would involve the transfer of a nation of 20 million people from the free world to the Communist bloc. The loss of South Viet-Nam would make pointless any further discussion about the importance of Southeast Asia to the free world; we would have to face the near certainty that the remainder of Southeast Asia and Indonesia would move to a complete accommodation with Communism, if not formal incorporation within the Communist bloc. The United States, as a member of SEATO, has commitments with respect to South Viet-Nam under the Protocol to the SEATO Treaty. Additionally, in a formal statement at the conclusion session of the 1954 Geneva Conference, the United States representative stated that the United States "would view any renewal of the aggression . . . with grave concern and seriously threatening international peace and security."

The loss of South Viet-Nam to Communism would not only destroy SEATO but would undermine the credibility of American commitments elsewhere. Further, loss of South Viet-Nam would stimulate bitter domestic controversies in the United States and would be seized upon by extreme elements to divide the country and harass the Administration.

2. The Problem of Saving South Viet-Nam.

It seems, on the face of it, absurd to think that a nation of 20 million people can be subverted by 15–20 thousand active guerrillas if the Government and people of that country do not wish to be subverted. South Viet-Nam is not, however, a highly organized society with an effective governing apparatus and a population accustomed to carrying civic responsibility. Public apathy is encouraged by the inability of most citizens to act directly as well as by the tactics of terror employed by the guerrillas throughout the countryside. Inept administration and the absence of a strong non-Communist political coalition have made it difficult to bring available resources to bear upon the guerrilla problem and to make the most effective use of available external aid. Under the best of conditions the threat posed by the presence of 15-20 thousand guerrillas, well disciplined under well-trained cadres, would be difficult to meet.

3. The United States' Objective in South Viet-Nam.

The United States should commit itself to the clear objective of preventing the fall of South Viet-Nam to Communism. The basic means for accomplishing this objective must be to put the Government of South Viet-Nam into a position to win its own war against the guerrillas. We must insist that that Government itself take the measures necessary for that purpose in exchange for large-scale United States assistance in the military, economic and political fields. At the same time we must recognize that it will probably not be possible for the GVN to win this war as long as the flow of men and supplies from North Viet-Nam continues unchecked and the guerrillas enjoy a safe sanctuary in neighboring territory.

We should be prepared to introduce United States combat forces if that should become necessary for success. Dependent upon the circumstances, it may also be necessary for United States forces to strike at the source of the aggression in North Viet-Nam.

4. *The Use of United States Forces in South Viet-Nam.*

The commitment of United States forces to South Viet-Nam involves two different categories: (A) Units of modest size required for the direct support of South Viet-Namese military effort, such as communications, helicopter and other forms of airlift, reconnaissance aircraft, naval patrols, intelligence units, etc., and (B) larger organized units with actual or potential direct military missions. *Category (A) should be introduced as speedily as possible.* Category (B) units pose a more serious problem in that they are much more significant from the point of view of domestic and international political factors and greatly increase the probabilities of Communist bloc escalation. Further, the employment of United States comat forces (in the absence of Communist bloc escalation) involves a certain dilemma: if there is a strong South-Vietnamese effort, they may not be needed; if there is not such an effort, United States forces could not accomplish their mission in the midst of an apathetic or hostile population. Under present circumstances, therefore, the question of injecting United States and SEATO combat forces should in large part be considered as a contribution to the morale of the South Viet-Namese in their own effort to do the principal job themselves.

5. *Probable Extent of the Commitment of United States Forces.*

If we commit Category (B) forces to South Viet-Nam the ultimate possible extent of our military commitment in Southeast Asia must be faced. The struggle may be prolonged, and Hanoi and Peiping may overtly intervene. It is the view of the Secretary of Defense and the Joint Chiefs of Staff that, in the light of the logistic difficulties faced by the other side, we can assume that the maximum United States forces required on the ground in Southeast Asia would not exceed six divisions, or about 205,000 men (CINCPAC Plan 32/59 PHASE IV). This would be in addition to local forces and such SEATO forces as may be engaged. It is also the view of the Secretary of Defense and the Joint Chiefs of Staff that our military posture is, or, with the addition of more National Guard or regular Army divisions, can be made, adequate to furnish these forces and support them in action without serious interference with our present Berlin plans.

6. *Relation to Laos.*

It must be understood that the introduction of American combat forces into Viet-Nam prior to a Laotian settlement would run a considerable risk of stimulating a Communist breach of the cease fire and a resumption of hostilities in Laos. This could present us with a choice between the use of combat forces in Laos or an abandonment of that country to full Communist control. At the present time, there is at least a chance that a settlement can be reached in Laos on the basis of a weak and unsatisfactory Souvanna Phouma Government. The prospective agreement on Laos includes a provision that Laos will not be used as a transit area or as a base for interfering in the affairs of other countries such as South Viet-Nam. After a Laotian settlement, the introduction of United States forces into Viet-Nam could serve to stabilize the position both in Viet-Nam and in Laos by registering our determination to see to it that the Laotian settlement was as far as the United States would be willing to see Communist influence in Southeast Asia develop.

7. *The Need for Multilateral Action.*

From the political point of view, both domestic and international, it would seem important to involve forces from other nations alongside of United States Category (B) forces in Viet-Nam. It should be difficult to explain to our own people why no effort had been made to invoke SEATO or why the United States undertook to carry this burden unilaterally. Our position would be greatly strengthened if the introduction of forces could be taken as a SEATO action, accompanied by units of other SEATO countries, with a full SEATO report to the United Nations of the purposes of the action itself.

Apart from the armed forces, there would be political advantage in enlisting the interest of other nations, including neutrals, in the security and well-being of South Viet-Nam. This might be done by seeking such assistance as Malayan police officials (recently offered Diem by the Tunku) and by technical assistance personnel in other fields, either bilaterally or through international organizations.

8. *Initial Diplomatic Action by the United States.*

If the recommendations, below, are approved, the United States should consult intensively with other SEATO governments to obtain their full support of the course of action contemplated. At the appropriate stage, a direct approach should be made by the United States to Moscow, through normal or special channels, pointing out that we cannot accept the movement of cadres, arms and other supplies into South Viet-Nam in support of the guerrillas. We should also discuss the problem with neutral governments in the general area and get them to face up to their own interests in the security of South Viet-Nam; these governments will be concerned about (a) the introduction of United States combat forces and (b) the withdrawal of United States support from Southeast Asia; their concern, therefore, might be usefully expressed either to Communist bloc countries or in political support for what may prove necessary in South Viet-Nam itself.

RECOMMENDATIONS

In the light of the foregoing, the Secretary of State and the Secretary of Defense recommend that:

1. We now take the decision to commit ourselves to the objective of preventing the fall of South Viet-Nam to Communism and that, in doing so, we recognize that the introduction of United States and other SEATO forces may be necessary to achieve this objective. (However, if it is necessary to commit outside forces to achieve the foregoing objective our decision to introduce United States forces should not be contingent upon unanimous SEATO agreement thereto.)

2. The Department of Defense be prepared with plans for the use of

United States forces in South Viet-Nam under one or more of the following purposes:

(a) Use of a significant number of United States forces to signify United States determination to defend South Viet-Nam and to boost South Viet-Nam morale.

(b) Use of substantial United States forces to assist in suppressing Viet Cong insurgency short of engaging in detailed counter-guerrilla operations but including relevant operations in North Viet-Nam.

(c) Use of United States forces to deal with the situation if there is organized Communist military intervention.

3. We immediately undertake the following actions in support of the GVN:

(a) Provide increased air lift to the GVN forces, including helicopters, light aviation, and transport aircraft, manned to the extent necessary by United States uniformed personnel and under United States operational control.

(b) Provide such additional equipment and United States uniformed personnel as may be necessary for air reconnaissance, photography, instruction in and execution of air-ground support techniques, and for special intelligence.

(c) Provide the GVN with small craft, including such United States uniformed advisers and operating personnel as may be necessary for quick and effective operations in effecting surveillance and control over coastal waters and inland waterways.

(d) Provide expedited training and equipping of the civil guard and the self-defense corps with the objective of relieving the regular Army of static missions and freeing it for mobile offensive operations.

(e) Provide such personnel and equipment as may be necessary to improve the military-political intelligence system beginning at the provincial level and extending upward through the Government and the armed forces to the Central Intelligence Organization.

(f) Provide such new terms of reference, reorganization and additional personnel for United States military forces as are required for increased United States participation in the direction and control of GVN military operations and to carry out the other increased responsibilities which accrue to MAAG under these recommendations.

(g) Provide such increased economic aid as may be required to permit the GVN to pursue a vigorous flood relief and rehabilitation program, to supply material in support of the security effort, and to give priority to projects in support of this expanded counter-insurgency program. (This could include increases in military pay, a full suppy of a wide range of materials such as food, medical supplies, transportation equipment, communications equipment, and any other items where material help could assist the GVN in winning the war against the Viet Cong.)

(h) Encourage and support (including financial support) a request by the GVN to the FAO or any other appropriate international organization for multilateral assistance in the relief and rehabilitation of the flood area.

(i) Provide individual administrators and advisers for insertion into the Governmental machinery of South Viet-Nam in types and numbers to be agreed upon by the two Governments.

(j) Provide personnel for a joint survey with the GVN of conditions in each of the provinces to assess the social, political, intelligence, and military factors bearing on the prosecution of the counter-insurgency program in order to reach a common estimate of these factors and a common determination of how to deal with them.

4. Ambassador Nolting be instructed to make an immediate approach to President Diem to the effect that the Government of the United States is prepared to join the Government of Viet-Nam in a sharply increased joint effort to cope with the Viet Cong threat and the ravages of the flood as set forth under 3., above, if, on its part, the Government of Viet-Nam is prepared to carry out an effective and total mobilization of its own resources, both material and human, for the same end. Before setting in motion the United States proposals listed above, the United States Government would appreciate confirmation of their acceptability to the GVN, and an expression from the GVN of the undertakings it is prepared to make to insure the success of this joint effort. On the part of the United States, it would be expected that these GVN undertakings could include, in accordance with the detailed recommendations of [line missing]

(a) Prompt and appropriate legislative and administrative action to put the nation on a wartime footing to mobilize its entire resources. (This would include a decentralization and broadening of the Government so as to realize the full potential of all non-Communist elements in the country willing to contribute to the common struggle.)

(b) The establishment of appropriate Governmental wartime agencies with adequate authority to perform their functions effectively.

(c) Overhaul of the military establishment and command structure so as to create an effective military organization for the prosecution of the war.

5. Very shortly before the arrival in South Viet-Nam of the first increments of United States military personnel and equipment proposed under 3., above, that would exceed the Geneva Accord ceilings, publish the "Jorden report" as a United States "white paper," transmitting it as simultaneously as possible to the Governments of all countries with which we have diplomatic relations, including the Communist states.

6. Simultaneous with the publication of the "Jorden report," release an exchange of letters between Diem and the President.

(a) Diem's letter would include reference to the DRV violations of Geneva Accords as set forth in the October 24 GVN letter to the ICC and other documents; pertinent references to GVN statements with respect to its intent to observe the Geneva Accords; reference to its need for flood relief and rehabilitation; reference to previous United States aid and the compliance hitherto by both countries with the Geneva Accords; reference to the USG statement at the time the Geneva Accords were signed; the necessity now of exceeding some provisions of the Accords in view of the DRV violations thereof; the lack of aggressive intent with respect to the DRV: GVN intent to return to strict compliance with the Geneva Accords as soon as the DRV violations ceased; and request for additional United States assistance in framework foregoing policy. The letter should also set forth in appropriate general terms steps Diem has taken and is taking to reform Governmental structure.

(b) The President's reply would be responsive to Diem's request for additional assistance and acknowledge and agree to Diem's statements on the intent promptly to return to strict compliance with the Geneva Accords as soon as DRV violations have ceased.

7. Simultaneous with steps 5 and 6, above, make a private approach to the Soviet Union that would include: our determination to prevent the fall of South Viet-Nam to Communism by whatever means is necessary; our concern over dangers to peace presented by the aggressive DRV policy with respect to South Viet-Nam; our intent to return to full compliance with the Geneva Accords as soon as the DRV does so; the distinction we draw between Laos and South Viet-Nam; and our expectation that the Soviet Union will exercise its influence on the CHICOMS and the DRV.

8. A special diplomatic approach made to the United Kingdom in its role as co-Chairman of the Geneva Conference requesting that the United Kingdom seek the support of the Soviet co-Chairman for a cessation of DRV aggression against South Viet-Nam.

9. A special diplomatic approach also to be made to India, both in its role as Chairman of the ICC and as a power having relations with Peiping and Hanoi. This approach should be made immediately prior to public release of the "Jorden report" and the exchange of letters between Diem and the President.

10. Immediately prior to the release of the "Jorden report" and the exchange of letters between Diem and the President, special diplomatic approaches also to be made to Canada, as well as Burma, Indonesia, Cambodia, Ceylon, the UAR, and Yugoslavia. SEATO, NATO, and OAS members should be informed through those organizations, with selected members also informed individually. The possibility of some special approach to Poland as a member of the ICC should also be considered.

When we reach this memorandum in the record, the decision seems essentially sealed. Kennedy, by every indication in the press at the time and according to the recollections of all the memoirs, was, at the least, very reluctant to send American ground forces to Vietnam, and quite possibly every bit as "strongly opposed" as the leaked news stories depicted him. He now had a joint recommendation from his Secretary of State and Secretary of Defense telling him just what he surely wanted to hear: that a decision on combat forces could be deferred. Consequently, Kennedy's decision on this point can hardly be considered in doubt beyond November 11, although a formal NSC meeting on the question was not held until the 15th. On the question of demands on Diem, again there is no reason to suspect the issue was in doubt any later, at most, than the 11th. The only questions which are in doubt are the extent to which the Rusk/McNamara memorandum simply happened to come to the President in such convenient form, or whether the President arranged it so; and if so, how far this formal paper differed from the real recommendations of the President's senior advisors. The record available gives no basis for even guessing about this. As noted earlier, even McNamara, who is on record with a previous, quite different memorandum, cannot be flatly said to have changed his mind (or been overruled). There is too much room for uncertainty about what he was really up to when he signed the memorandum.

In any event, Kennedy essentially adopted the Rusk/McNamara set of recommendations, although the record is not entirely clear on when he did so. There was an NSC meeting November 5; but although at least the Chairman of the JCS was there, the record shows that even after this meeting there was some uncertainty (or perhaps reluctance) in the JCS about whether the decision had been made. The record shows that McNamara phoned General Lemnitzer to assure him that this was the case. But the cables transmitting the decision to Saigon were dated November 14, the day before the NSC meeting. The formal decision paper (NSAM 111) was not signed until November 22nd. As noted earlier, the NSAM is essentially the recommendations section of the Rusk/McNamara paper, but with the initial recommendation (committing the U.S. to save Vietnam) deleted.

The NSAM was headed "First Phase of Vietnam Program," which, of course, implied that a further decision to send combat troops was in prospect. Both Sorenson and Hilsman claim this was really a ruse by the President, who had no intention of going ahead with combat troops but did not choose to argue the point with his advisors.

Schlesinger, apparently writing from diary notes, says the President talked to him about the combat troops recommendations at the time, describing the proposed first increment as like an alcoholic's first drink:

> The Taylor-Rostow report was a careful and thoughtful document, and the President read it with interest. He was impressed by its description of the situation as serious but not hopeless and attracted by the idea of stiffening the Diem regime through an infusion of American advisers. He did not, however, like the proposal of a direct American military commitment. "They want a force of American troops," he told me early in November. "They say it's necessary in order to restore confidence and maintain morale. But it will be just like Berlin. The troops will march in; the bands will play; the crowds will cheer; and in four days everyone will have forgotten. Then we will be told we have to send in more troops. It's like taking a drink. The effect wears off, and you have to take another." The war in Vietnam, he added, could be won only so long as it was their war. If it were ever converted into a white man's war, we would lose as the French had lost a decade earlier.

Whether, in fact, Kennedy had such a firm position in mind at the time cannot be surmised, though, from the official record itself. It is easy to believe that he did, for as Sorenson points out, Kennedy had strong views on the difficulties of foreign troops putting down an insurgency dating from his bleak, but correct, appraisals of French prospects in Vietnam as early as 1951, and again in Algeria in the late 1950's. And he was hardly alone in such sentiments, as shown in columns of the period by Reston and Lippman, and in a private communication from Galbraith to be quoted shortly.

But, Kennedy did not need to have such a firm position in mind to make the decisions he did. There was a case to be made for deferring the combat troops decision even if the President accepted the view that U.S. troops commitments were almost certainly needed in Vietnam and that putting them in sooner would be better than waiting. There was, in particular, the arguments in the Rusk/McNamara memorandum that putting combat troops into Vietnam just then would upset the Laos negotiations, and the unstated but obvious argument that the U.S. perhaps ought to hold back on the combat troop commitment to gain leverage on Diem.

General Taylor's advice, as shown in the record, gave a different ground for delaying. Taylor argued that the ground troop commitment was essentially for its psychological, not military, impact. Taylor's judgment was that it was "very doubtful" that anything short of a prompt commitment of ground troops would restore South Vietnamese morale. But such a commitment would obviously be a costly stop. The President was thoroughly forewarned that such a move would lead both to continual pressure to send more troops and to political difficulties at home that would inevitably flow from the significant casualties that had to be expected to accompany a ground troop commitment. The risk of delaying the ground troop commitment might easily have been judged not worth the certain costs that would accompany it. And of course, in hindsight, we know that the limited program approved by the President was sufficient to put off any imminent collapse of the Diem regime. Consequently, Kennedy's decisions do not tell us just what his view was, and indeed he did not need to have a firmly settled view to make the decision, which after all, was only to put off, not to foreclose a decision to send ground troops. He had only to decide that, on balance, the risks of deferring the troop decisions were no worse than the costs of making it, and he could have reached that judgment by any number of routes. The reasons stated in the various papers may or may not accurately reflect the President's state of mind. The only thing we can be sure of is that they conveyed his judgment of the tactically most suitable rationale to put in writing. The most detailed record we have of this rationale and explanation of is the following cable to Nolting:

. . . . Review of Taylor Report has resulted in following basic decisions:

1. Must essentially be a GVN task to contain and reduce the VC threat at present level of capability. Means organizing to go on offensive. We are prepared to contemplate further assistance after joint assessment establishes needs and possibilities of aid more precisely.

2. No amount of extra aid can be substitute for GVN taking measures to permit them to assume offensive and strengthen the administrative and political bases of government.

3. Do not propose to introduce into GVN and US combat troops now, but propose a phase of intense public and diplomatic activity to focus on infiltration from North. Shall decide later on course of action should infiltration not be radically reduced.

4. On flood, decide best course to treat as primarily civil problem, and occasion should be used to draw in as many nationals of other countries as can be used in GVN flood plan. Have been encouraged this course on advice of Desai of Indian Foreign Office who observed a good thing if some Indians and Burmese involved constructively in SVN and subject to VC attack. We prepared to put maximum pressure on FAO. Do not exclude ad hoc US military aid in flood area.

5. Diplomatically position that the violations to be documented in Jor-

den report and strong references to DRV attack against SVN in DM's letter to Kennedy, need not confirm to the world and Communists that Geneva accords are being disregarded by our increased aid. Need not accuse ourselves publicly, make Communist job easier. GVN should be advised to counter charges by leveling charges against DRV and insisting that if ICC investigates in SVN must equally investigate in NVN. Appreciate approach will make ICC task difficult but will explain position to Canadians and Indians to get their support.

6. A crucial element in USG willingness to move forward is concrete demonstration by Diem that he is now prepared to work in an orderly way on his subordinates and broaden the political base of his regime.

7. Package should be presented as first steps in a partnership in which US is prepared to do more as joint study of facts and GVN performance makes increased US aid possible and productive.

8. Still possible Laotian settlement can be reached pertaining our minimum objective of independent Laos on the basis of a neutral coalition, (although weak and unsatisfactory), headed by Souvanna. Would include provision Laos not be used as transit area or base for interference in SVN. Therefore must keep in mind impact of action in SVN or prospects for acceptable Laos settlement.

9. Introduction of US or Seato forces into SVN before Laotian settlement might wreck changes for agreement, lead to break up of Geneva conference, break Laos cease fire by communists with resumption of hostilities.

10. Decision to introduce US combat forces in GVN would have to be taken in light of GVN effort, including support from people, Laotian situation, Berlin crisis, readiness of allies or sharply increased tension with Bloc, and enormous responsibilities which would have to be borne by US in event of escalation SEA or other areas.

11. Hope measures outlined in instructions will galvanize and supplement GVN effort, making decision on use of US combat forces unnecessary and no need for decision in effect to shift primary responsibility for defense of SVN to USG.

12. We are fully cognizant of extent to which decisions if implemented through Diem's acceptance will sharply increase the commitment of our prestige struggle to save SVN.

13. Very strictly for your own information, DOD has been instructed to prepare plans for the use of US combat forces in SVN under various contingencies, including stepped up infiltration as well as organized inventory (sic) [military] intervention. However objective of our policy is to do all possible to accomplish purpose without use of US combat forces.

An accompanying cable also provided this additional comment on troops question:

. . . 4. It is anticipated that one of the first questions President Diem will raise with you after your presentation of the above joint proposals will be that of introducing U.S. combat troops. You are authorized to remind him that the actions we already have in mind involve a substantial number of U.S. military personnel for operational duties in Viet-Nam and that we believe that these forces performing crucial missions can greatly increase the capacity of GVN forces to win their war against the Viet

Cong. You can also tell him that we believe that the missions being undertaken by our forces, under present circumstances, are more suitable for white foreign troops than garrison duty or missions involving the seeking out of Viet Cong personnel submerged in the Viet-Nam population. You can assure him that the USG at highest levels will be in daily contact with the situation in Viet-Nam and will be in constant touch with him about requirements of the situation. . . .

C.   *AFTERMATH*

The President's decisions were apparently sent to Nolting on the 14th, in a cable that is taken essentially verbatim from the description of the Rusk/ McNamara memorandum (paragraphs 3 and 4) of the program the U.S. was offering and the response expected from Diem. But the cable added some new language, putting still more emphasis on pressuring Diem:

> . . . It is most important that Diem come forth with changes which will be recognized as having real substance and meaning. Rightly or wrongly, his regime is widely criticized abroad and in the U.S., and if we are to give our substantial support we must be able to point to real administrative political and social reforms and a real effort to widen its base that will give maximum confidence to the American people, as well as to world opinion that our efforts are not directed towards the support of an unpopular or ineffective regime, but rather towards supporting the combined efforts of all the non-Communist people of the GVN against a Communist take-over. You should make this quite clear, and indicate that the U.S. contribution to the proposed joint effort depends heavily upon his response to this point.
>
> You should inform Diem that, in our minds, the concept of the joint undertaking envisages a much closer relationship than the present one of acting in an advisory capacity only. We would expect to share in the decision-making process in the political, economic and military fields as they affect the security situation.

Overall, then, what Kennedy ended up doing was to offer Diem a good deal less than he was expecting, and nevertheless to couple this offer with demands on Diem for which, on the basis of the available record, we can only assume he was totally unprepared. Nolting's first cable, though, reported Diem listened quietly and "took our proposals rather better than I expected."

Here are some extracts:

> . . . As anticipated [by Washington], his first question was re introduction US combat troops. I replied along line para 4 reftel. . . .
> Diem said that he presumed I realized that our proposals involved the question of the responsibility of the Government of Viet Nam. Viet Nam, he said, did not want to be a protectorate.
> I said that this was well understood; we for our part did not wish to make it one. Diem also pointed out that GVN was constantly in process of making reforms but major action could not be taken without thorough consideration and without having always in mind that there was a war to be won. Object was to restore order, not to create disorder. I said I recog-

nized that this was a delicate judgment, in my opinion, as a friend of his country and of him, his greater risk was to stand pat, or act too cautiously . . .

On the whole, I am not discouraged at Diem's reaction. In fact, he took our proposals rather better than I had expected. He has promised to call me as soon as he has been able to reflect upon our proposals and, until we have heard his considered reaction, I think it would be idle to speculate on outcome . . .

On the 20th, Nolting met with Thuan, who among other things said the U.S. offer had set Diem to wondering "whether U.S. getting ready to back out on Vietnam . . . as we had done in Laos." Nolting hoped Thuan's bleak report was only a bargaining tactic.

Thuan said that Diem had not yet discussed fully with him US proposals presented last Friday; but had given him impression of being "very sad and very disappointed." Thuan said Diem had said he now hesitates to put proposals before even his cabinet ministers, fearing that they would be disappointed and lose heart. He had intended to discuss US proposals with both cabinet and selected members of assembly who had been consulted re advisability of US forces at time of Taylor Mission, but now thought contrast between his earlier question and our proposals too striking. Thuan conveyed impression that Diem is brooding over US proposals and has made no move yet to develop specific ideas on actions GVN expected to take. Thuan said President's attitude seemed to be that US asking great concessions of GVN in realm its sovereignty, in exchange for little additional help; that this is great disappointment after discussions with General Taylor involving, in particular, concept of Delta Task Force; that Diem seemed to wonder whether US was getting ready to back out on Viet Nam, as he suggested, we had done in Laos.

There followed a long discussion in which Thuan described all the difficulties that would be involved in doing what the U.S. was asking, including the risk of looking like a U.S. puppet.

There is nothing in our record to indicate any U.S. reconsideration of the decision against sending the military task force. Thus, if Diem and Thuan's response was a bargaining tactic to get the task force, it failed. On the other hand, if Diem was using disappointment over the failure to send the task force as a bargaining counter to get the U.S. to relent on its demands for reforms, then he got just what he wanted. But what amounted to a complete U.S. reversal on these demands also may have been influenced by the advice Kennedy received from John Kenneth Galbraith at this time. Kennedy had asked Galbraith to stop by Saigon on his return to India. Galbraith did so, and after three days cabled back, among other things, the advice that it was a waste of effort to bargain with Diem.

On the 20th, the day of Thuan's meeting with Nolting, Galbraith cabled the President:

There is scarcely the slightest practical chance that the administrative and political reforms now being pressed upon Diem will result in real change . . . there is no solution that does not involve a change in government.

On the insurgency, though, Galbraith was optimistic, provided Diem was replaced:

> While situation is indubitably bad military aspects seem to me out of perspective. A comparatively well-equipped army with paramilitary formations number a quarter million men is facing a maximum of 15-18,000 lightly armed men. If this were equality, the United States would hardly be safe against the Sioux. I know the theories about this kind of warfare. . . . Given even a moderately effective government and putting the relative military power into perspective, I can't help thinking the insurgency might very soon be settled.

The following day, Galbraith, now in New Delhi, sent a more detailed appraisal, covering essentially the same ground. Here are some extracts.

> . . . The Viet Cong insurrection is still growing in effect. The outbreak on the Northern Highlands is matched by a potentially even more damaging impact on the economy and especially on the movement of rice to Saigon.
>
> In the absence of knowledge of the admixture of terror and economic and social evangelism we had best assume that it is employing both. We must not forever be guided by those who misunderstand the dynamics of revolution and imagine that because the communists do not appeal to us they are abhorrent to everyone.
>
> In our enthusiasm to prove outside intervention before world opinion we have unquestionably exaggerated the role of material assistance especially in the main area of insurrection in the far South. That leaders and radio guidance come in we know. But the amount of ammunition and weaponry that a man can carry on his back for several hundred kilometers over jungle trails was not increased appreciably by Marx. No major conflict can depend on such logistic support.
>
> A maximum of 18,000 lightly armed men are involved in the insurrection. These are GVN estimates and the factor of exaggeration is unquestionably considerable. Ten thousand is more probable. What we have in opposition involves a heavy theological dispute. Diem it is said is a great but defamed leader. It is also said he has lost touch with the masses, is in political disrepute and otherwise no good. This debate can be bypassed by agreed points. It is agreed that administratively Diem is exceedingly bad. He holds far too much power in his own hands, employs his army badly, has no intelligence organization worthy of the name, has arbitrary or incompetent subordinates in the provinces and some achievements notwithstanding, has a poor economic policy. He has also effectively resisted improvement for a long while in face of heavy deterioration. This is enough. Whether his political posture is nepotic, despotic, out of touch with the villagers and hence damaging or whether this damage is the figment of Saigon intellectuals does not bear on our immediate policy and may be by-passed at least in part.
>
> The SVN Army numbers 170,000 and with paramilitary units of the civil guard and home defense forces a quarter of a million. Were this well deployed on behalf of an effective government it should be obvious that the Viet Cong would have no chance of success or takeover. Washington is currently having an intellectual orgasm on the unbeatability of

guerrilla war. Were guerrillas effective in a ratio of one to fifteen or twenty-five, it is obvious that no government would be safe. The Viet Cong, it should be noted, is strongest in the Southern Delta which is not jungle but open rice paddy.

The fundamental difficulties in countering the insurgency, apart from absence of intelligence, are two-fold. First is the poor command, deployment, training, morale and other weaknesses of the army and paramilitary forces. And second while they can operate—sweep—through any part of the country and clear out any visible insurgents, they cannot guarantee security afterwards. The Viet Cong comes back and puts the arm on all who have collaborated. This fact is very important in relation to requests from American manpower. Our forces would conduct the round-up operations which the RVN Army can already do. We couldn't conceivably send enough men to provide safety for the villages as a substitute for an effectively trained civil guard and home defense force and, perhaps, a politically cooperative community.

The key and inescapable point, then, is the ineffectuality (abetted debatably by the unpopularity) of the Diem government. This is the strategic factor. Nor can anyone accept the statement of those who have been either too long or too little in Asia that his is the inevitable posture of the Asian mandarin. For one thing it isn't true, but were it so the only possible conclusion would be that there is no future for mandarins. The communists don't favor them.

I come now to a lesser miscalculation, the alleged weakening emphasis of the Mekong flood. Floods in this part of the world are an old trap for western non-agriculturists. They are judged by what the Ohio does to its towns. Now as the flood waters recede it is already evident that this flood conforms to the Asian pattern, one repeated every year in India. The mud villages will soon grow again. Some upland rice was drowned because the water rose too rapidly. Nearer the coast the pressure on the brackish water will probably bring an offsetting improvement. Next year's crop will be much better for the silt.

I come now to policy, first the box we are in partly as the result of recent moves and second how we get out without a takeover. We have just proposed to help Diem in various ways in return for a promise of administrative and political reforms. Since the administrative (and possibly political) ineffectuality are the strategic factors for success the ability to get reforms is decisive. With them the new aid and gadgetry will be useful. Without them the helicopters, planes and adviser's won't make appreciable difference.

In my completely considered view, as stated yesterday, Diem will not reform either administratively or politically in any effective way. That is because he cannot. It is politically naive to expect it. He senses that he cannot let power go because he would be thrown out. He may disguise this even from himself with the statement that he lacks effective subordinates but the circumstance remains unchanged. He probably senses that his greatest danger is from the army. Hence the reform that will bring effective use of his manpower, though the most urgent may be the most improbable.

The political reforms are even more unlikely but the issue is academic. Once the image of a politician is fixed, whether among opposition intellectuals or peasants, it is not changed . . . Diem's image would not be changed by his taking in other non-communists, initiating some social reforms or otherwise meeting the requirements of our demarche.

However having started on this hopeless game we have no alternative, but to play it out for a minimum time. Those who think there is hope of reform will have to be persuaded.

*   *   *

It is a cliche that there is no alternative to Diem's regime. This is politically naive. Where one man has dominated the scene for good or ill there never seems to be. No one considered Truman an alternative to Roosevelt. There is none for Nehru. There was none I imagine for Rhee. This is an optical illusion arising from the fact that the eye is fixed on the visible figures. It is a better rule that nothing succeeds like successors.

We should not be alarmed by the Army as an alternative. It would buy time and get a fresh dynamic. It is not ideal; civilian rule is ordinarily more durable and more saleable to the world. But a change and a new start is of the essence and in considering opinion we may note that Diem's flavor is not markedly good in Asia.

A time of crisis in our policy on South Vietnam will come when it becomes evident that the reforms we have asked have not come off and that our presently preferred aid is not accomplishing anything. Troops will be urged to back up Diem. It will be sufficiently clear that I think this must be resisted. Our soldiers would not deal with the vital weakness. They could perpetuate it. They would enable Diem to continue to concentrate on protecting his own position at the expense of countering the insurgency. Last spring, following the Vice President's promise of more aid, proposals for increased and reform taxes which were well advanced were promptly dropped. The parallel on administrative and political reform could be close.

It will be said that we need troops for a show of strength and determination in the area. Since the troops will not deal with fundamental faults—since there can't be enough of them to give security to the countryside—their failure to provide security could create a worse crisis of confidence. You will be aware of my general reluctance to move in troops. On the other hand I would note that it is those of us who have worked in the political vineyard and who have committed our hearts most strongly to the political fortunes of the New Frontier who worry most about its bright promise being sunk under the rice fields. Dulles in 1954 saw the dangers in this area. Dean Acheson knew he could not invest men in Chiang.

*   *   *

My overall feeling is that despite the error implicit in this last move and the supposition that Diem can be reformed, the situation is not hopeless. It is only hopeless if we marry our course to that of a man who must spend more time protecting his own position and excluding those who threaten it than in fighting the insurgency. Diem's calculation instinctive or deliberate is evident. He has already been deposed once and not by the Communists. He can see his clear and present danger as well as anyone.

Two things are particularly worth noting about Galbraith's advice: the first, to the extent it had an influence on Kennedy, it counselled him to avoid sending troops, but also not to take seriously the *quid pro quo* with Diem because

Diem was not going to do anything anyway. Consequently, Galbraith, with a limitlessly bleak view of the prospects for success under Diem, really had no quarrel with those who argued against putting pressure on Diem and for trying to win his confidence. He had no argument, because he thought both approaches (pressure and no pressure) were equally hopeless. And indeed, both had been tried during the year—the pressure approach in the CIP negotiations; the "get on his wave length" approach following the Task Force review —and both produced an identical lack of results.

Second, Galbraith's analysis of the situation really has a good deal in common with that of the Taylor Mission. Obviously, he thought we must be rid of Diem, and he apparently thought it was a mistake to put this move off by making new aid offers to Diem rather than letting word get around that we would be prepared to offer more support to Vietnam if Diem should be removed. But at this time, even people like Galbraith (and Schlesinger, as is clear from his memoir) saw no alternative to continuing to support Vietnam, although not to continuing to support Diem personally. Galbraith was, if anything, more optimistic about the chances of putting down the insurgency (given a change in Saigon) than was the Taylor Report. For his optimism was not at all contingent on any hopes of the efficacy of bombing threats against the north. For all we know, he may have been right in supposing any "moderately effective" Saigon government could do all right against the insurgents; but we now know all too well how over-optimistic was his fairly confident expectation that a military replacement of the Diem regime would be at least moderately effective.

To return to the negotiations in Saigon, in late November, we now had the following situation:

1. It was clear that Diem was, to say the least, disappointed with the bargain Kennedy had proposed.
2. Kennedy was obviously aware that he had offered Diem less than Diem expected, and demanded much more in return.
3. Both supporters of Diem, like Lansdale and Kenneth Young, and his severest critics, like Galbraith, were agreed that it was futile to try to force Diem to reform. Kennedy had already had his own experiences with such efforts earlier in the year.
4. Presumably, although we have nothing to show it in the available record, there was some unrest within the Administration about the limited offer that was being made, the demands being pressed, and the delay it was all causing. To put off an agreement too long raised the dual threat of an awkward public squabble and renewed pressure on the President to send the task force after all.

It is hard to think of any realistic counter-arguments to the case for settling the dispute and get on with either trying to do better in the war, or get rid of Diem.

The next phase was a brief flurry of anti-American stories in the government-controlled Saigon press. The U.S. was accused, among other things, of trying to use Vietnam as a "pawn of capitalist imperialism." Nolting went to Diem to complain about the damage that such stories would do to U.S.-Vietnamese relations. But Diem disclaimed responsibility, and suggested they were an understandable reaction of the South Vietnamese to what they had learned about the U.S. proposals from U.S. press reports. Nolting's final comment in his report on this meeting was a suggestion that the U.S. concentrate on "efficiency in

GVN rather than on more nebulous and particularly offensive to Diem concept of political reform." The impression given by the cable is that Nolting felt on the defensive, which was probably the case since the package Washington had proposed must have been disappointing to him as well as to Diem.

It did not take long for Washington to back away from any hard demands on Diem. A sentence from the original guidance telegram stated "we would expect to share in the decision-making process in the political, economic and military fields as they affected the security situation" . . . as opposed to the previous arrangement of "acting in an advisory capacity only." Alexis Johnson and Rostow drafted a cable on December 7 that "clarified" this and a number of other points to which Diem had strongly objected, in this case to explain that,

> . . . what we have in mind is that, in operations directly related to the security situation, partnership will be so close that one party will not take decisions or actions affecting the other without full and frank prior consultations. . . .

This was quite a comedown from the idea that American involvement in the Vietnamese government should be so intimate that the government could be reformed "from the bottom up" despite Diem. Once the U.S. backed away from any tough interpretation of its proposals, agreement was fairly easily reached with Diem, and one of the usual fine sounding statements of agreed principles and measures was drawn up.

On one seemingly modest request from Diem, Washington was curiously firm. Diem repeatedly, both while the Taylor Mission was in Saigon, and after its return, asked for Lansdale to be sent. (Our record shows four such requests, one directly by Diem to Taylor; a second from Thuan; and in a memorandum to McNamara William Bundy referred to two further requests relayed through McGarr.) Cottrell, the senior State representative on the Taylor Mission, strongly endorsed sending Lansdale, and the main paper of the Taylor Report seemed to endorse the idea. William Bundy was in favor of sending Lansdale, and Lansdale wanted to go. But nothing happened. Lansdale never got to Vietnam until Cabot Lodge brought him out later in 1965.

The first contingents of helicopters arrived in Saigon December 11 (having been put to sea several weeks earlier). On the following day a *New York Times* dispatch from Saigon began:

> Two United States Army helicopter companies arrived here today. The helicopters, to be flown and serviced by United States troops, are the first direct military support by the United States for South Vietnam's war against Communist guerrilla forces.
>
> The craft will be assigned to the South Vietnamese Army in the field, but they will remain under United States Army control and operation.
>
> At least 33 H-21C twin-rotor helicopters, their pilots and ground crews, an estimated total of 400 men, arrived aboard the Military Sea Transportation Service aircraft ferry Core.

The *Times* story ended by describing the force as "the first fruits" of the Taylor Mission, with more to come. The *Times* did not find the story important enough to put it on the front page.

A day later, the *Times* published a story about the ICC reaction to the arrival of the helicopters. It began:

> The International Control Commission for Vietnam was reported today to be considering whether to continue functioning here in the face of an increase in United States assistance to South Vietnam's struggle against Communist guerrillas.
>
> The Commission, made up of representatives of India, Canada, and Poland, has been holding emergency sessions since the arrival here yesterday of a United States vessel loaded with at least 33 helicopters and operating and maintenance crews.

A few paragraphs later, the dispatch noted that:

> With the arrival yesterday of the Core, a former escort carrier, bearing the helicopters, four single-engine training planes and about 400 men, the United States military personnel here now are believed to total about 1,500. Many more are expected.

Again, the *Times* ran the story on an inside page.

Finally, on the 15th, a formal exchange of letters between Presidents Diem and Kennedy was published, announcing in general terms a stepped-up U.S. aid program for Vietnam.

2. The Strategic Hamlet Program 1961–1963

Summary and Analysis

A specific strategy by which the U.S. and GVN would attempt to end the insurgency in South Vietnam had never been agreed upon at the time that the U.S. decided, late in 1961, to increase materially its assistance to GVN and to expand its advisory effort into one which would implement a "limited partnership." By early 1962, however, there was apparent consensus among the principal participants that the Strategic Hamlet Program, as it came to be called, represented the unifying concept for a strategy designed to pacify rural Vietnam (the Viet Cong's chosen battleground) and to develop support among the peasants for the central government.

The Strategic Hamlet Program was much broader than the construction of strategic hamlets *per se*. It envisioned sequential phases which, beginning with clearing the insurgents from an area and protecting the rural populace, progressed through the establishment of GVN infrastructure and thence to the provision of services which would lead the peasants to identify with their government. The strategic hamlet program was, in short, an attempt to translate the newly articulated theory of counter-insurgency into operational reality. The objective was political though the means to its realization were a mixture of military, social, psychological, economic and political measures.

The effect of these sequential steps to pacification was to make it very difficult to make intermediate assessments of progress. One could not really be sure how one was doing until one was done. Physical security by itself (the so-called "clear and hold" initial step) was a necessary condition for pacification, not a sufficient one. The establishment of governmental functions was not, by itself, necessarily conducive to a successful effort; the quality of those functions and their responsiveness to locally felt needs was critical. This inherent difficulty in assessing progress did not simply mean that it was difficult to identify problems and to make improvements as one went along—which it was. It also meant that it was quite possible to conclude that the program as a whole was progressing well (or badly) according to evidence relating only to a single phase or a part of a phase.

A related problem arose from the uniqueness of this program in American experience—pacification by proxy. The theory of sequential phases could be variously interpreted. This is not the problem of the three blind men describing the elephant; it is the problem of men with different perspectives each moulding his own conception of a proper body to the same skeleton. If the final product were to have some semblance of coherence and mutual satisfaction it was necessary that the shapers came to agreement on substance and operational procedure, not just that they agree on the proper skeleton upon which to work.

The problem with the apparent consensus which emerged early in 1962 was that the principal participants did view it with different perspectives and expectations. On the U.S. side, military advisors had a set of preferences which affected their approach to the Strategic Hamlet Program. They wanted to make RVNAF more mobile, more aggressive, and better organized to take the offensive against the Viet Cong. They were, consequently, extremely leery of proposals which might lead it to be tied down in strategic defenses ("holding" after "clearing" had been completed) or diverted too much to military civic action undertakings.

The American political leadership, insofar as a generalization may be attempted, may be said to have been most concerned with the later phases of the program—those in which GVN services were provided, local governments established, and the economy bolstered. Military clearing operations were, to them, a distasteful, expensive, but necessary precondition to the really critical and important phases of the effort.

Both of these U.S. groups had perspectives different from those of the Diem administration. In the U.S. view the insurgents were only one of Diem's enemies; he himself was the other. In this view the process of pacification could proceed successfully only if Diem reformed his own government. It was precisely to achieve these goals simultaneously that the U.S. agreed to enter a "limited partnership" with GVN in the counter-insurgent effort. The Strategic Hamlet Program became the operational symbol of this effort.

President Diem—unsurprisingly—had a very different view. His need, as he saw it, was to get the U.S. committed to South Vietnam (and to his administration) without surrendering his independence. He knew that his nation would fall without U.S. support; he feared that his government would fall if he either appeared to toady to U.S. wishes or allowed any single group too much potential power—particularly coercive power. The Strategic Hamlet Program offered a vehicle by which he could direct the counterinsurgent effort as he thought it should be directed and without giving up either his prerogatives to the U.S. or his mantle to his restless generals.

The program, in the form of a plan for pacification of the Delta, was formally proposed to Diem in November 1961 by R. G. K. Thompson, head of the newly arrived British Advisory Mission. U.S. military advisors favored at that time an ARVN penetration of the VC redoubt in War Zone D prior to any operations aimed specifically at pacification. But U.S. political desires to start some local operation which could achieve concrete gains combined with Diem's preference for a pacification effort in an area of strategic importance led to the initial effort in March 1962, "Operation SUNRISE," in Binh Duong Province north of Saigon. This was a heavily VC-infiltrated area rather than one of minimal penetration, as Thompson had urged. But planning—as distinct from operations—continued on the Delta plan and strategic hamlets were constructed in a variegated, uncoordinated pattern throughout the spring and early summer. The U.S. had little or no influence over these activities; the primary impetus was traceable directly to the President's brother and political counselor, Ngo Dinh Nhu.

In August 1962, GVN produced its long awaited national pacification plan with four priority areas and specified priorities within each area. At the same time, however, it indicated that over 2,500 strategic hamlets had already been completed and that work was already underway on more than 2,500 more. Although it was not until October 1962, that GVN explicitly announced the Strategic Hamlet Program to be the unifying concept of its pacification and counterinsurgent effort it was clear earlier that the program had assumed this central position.

Three important implications of this early progress (or, more precisely, reported progress) are also clear in retrospect. These implications seem not to have impressed themselves acutely upon U.S. observers at the time. First, the program was truly one of GVN initiative rather than one embodying priorities and time phasing recommended by the U.S. Diem was running with his own ball in programmatic terms, no matter who articulated the theory of the approach. The geographic dispersion of hamlets already reported to be completed indicated that there was, in fact, a conscious effort to implement this phase almost simultaneously throughout the entire nation rather than to build slowly as Diem's foreign advisors (both U.S. and British) recommended.

Finally, the physical aspects of Diem's program were similar if not identical to earlier population resettlement and control efforts practiced by the French and by Diem. The long history of these efforts was marked by consistency in results as well as in techniques: all failed dismally because they ran into resentment if not active resistance on the part of the peasants at whose control and safety, then loyalty, they were aimed. U.S. desires to begin an effective process of pacification had fastened onto security as a necessary precondition and slighted the historic record of rural resistance to resettlement. President Diem and his brother, for their part, had decided to emphasize control of the rural population as the precondition to winning loyalty. The record is inconclusive with respect to their weighing the record of the past but it appears that they, too, paid it scant attention. Thus the early operational efforts indicated a danger of peasant resistance, on one hand, and of divergent approaches between, in the initial steps, the U.S. (focused on security measures) and Diem (concerned more with control measures). Since the physical actions to achieve security and those to impose control are in many respects the same, there was generated yet another area in which assessments of progress would be inconclusive and difficult to make.

U.S. attention, once an apparent consensus had been forged concentrated on program management efforts in two categories: to convince GVN to proceed at a more measured, coherent pace with a qualitative improvement in the physical construction of strategic hamlets; and to schedule material assistance (fortification materials, etc.) and training for local defense forces to match the rate of desired hamlet construction.

U.S. assessments, at the same time, concentrated on the physical aspects of the program and on VC activity in areas where strategic hamlets had been constructed. Assessments tended to be favorable from a security (or control) viewpoint and uneven with respect to political development. The general conclusion was almost always one of cautious optimism when security (control) was emphasized, one of hopeful pessimism when political follow-up was stressed. The impression in Washington was typically slanted toward the more optimistic appraisals if for no other reason than that hamlet construction and security arrangements were the first chronological steps in the long process to pacification. Was it not, after all, "progress" to have moved from doing nothing to doing something even though the something was being done imperfectly?

These U.S. assessments changed only marginally throughout the life of the program. By the time, in 1963, that the hopeful pessimist voices were clearer, it was also much clearer that the Ngo brothers had made the Strategic Hamlet Program into one closely identified with their regime and with Diem's rather esoterically phrased "personalist revolution." Fears grew that Diem was attempting to impose loyalty from the top through control rather than to build it from the bottom by deeds. These fears were not limited to the Strategic Hamlet Program, however; they extended to urban as well as rural phases of South Vietnamese life and were subsumed, as the Buddhist question moved to the fore, by the general issue of the viability of Diem's regime.

President Diem grew increasingly unwilling to meet U.S. demands for reform. He believed that to do so would cause his government to fail. U.S. observers held that failure to do so would cause the nation, not just the government to fall. In the event the government fell and the nation's counterinsurgent program took a definite turn for the worse, but the nation did not fall. The Strategic Hamlet Program did. Closely identified with the Ngo brothers, it was almost bound to suffer their fortunes; when they died it died, too. The new government of generals, presumably realizing the extent of peasant displeasure with resettlement and control measures, did nothing to save it.

A number of contributory reasons can be cited for the failure of the Strategic Hamlet Program. Over-expansion of construction and poor quality of defenses forms one category. This reason concentrates only on the initial phase of the program, however. While valid, it does little to explain why the entire program collapsed rather than only some hamlets within it. Rural antagonisms which identified the program with its sponsors in the central government are more suggestive of the basis for the complete collapse as Diem and Nhu departed the scene. The reasons why they departed are traceable in part to the different expectations which combined in the apparent consensus at the program's beginning: to Diem's insistence on material assistance and independence, to U.S. willingness to provide assistance only if its advice was heeded, and to the failure to resolve this question either by persuasion or leverage.

Having said this, it does not automatically follow that the program would have succeeded even if Diem had met U.S. demands for change. To point to the causes of failure is one thing; to assume that changes of style would have led to success is quite another. It may well be that the program was doomed from the outset because of peasant resistance to measures which changed the pattern of rural life—whether aimed at security or control. It might have been possible, on the other hand, for a well-executed program eventually to have achieved some measure of success. The early demise of the program does not permit a conclusive evaluation. The weight of evidence suggests that the Strategic Hamlet Program was fatally flawed in its conception by the unintended consequence of alienating many of those whose loyalty it aimed to win.

This inconclusive finding, in turn, suggests that the sequential phases embodied in the doctrine of counterinsurgency may slight some very important problem areas. The evidence is not sufficient for an indictment; still less is one able to validate the counterinsurgent doctrine with reference to a program that failed. The only verdict that may be given at this time with respect to the validity of the doctrine is that used by Scots courts—"case not proved."

End of Summary and Analysis

CHRONOLOGY

1953–1959   French and GVN early attempts at population resettlement into defended communities to create secure zones.

1959   Rural Community Development Centers (Agroville) Program initiated by GVN.

Late 1960   USMAAG *Counterinsurgency Plan Vietnam* completed.

Early 1961   Agroville Program modified by construction of "Agro-Hamlets" to meet peasant objections.

May 1961   Vice President Johnson's visit to RVN.

July 1961   Staley Group report on increased economic aid and increase in RVNAF strength.

15 Sep 1961 USMAAG *Geographically Phased National Level Operation Plan for Counterinsurgency.*

18 Oct 1961 General Taylor arrives in RVN; President Diem declares national emergency.

27 Oct 1961 R. G. K. Thompson submits to President Diem his *Appreciation of Vietnam, November 1961–1962.*

3 Nov 1961   General Taylor submits his report and recommendations to President Kennedy.

13 Nov 1961 R. G. K. Thompson submits his draft plan for pacification of the Delta to President Diem.

15 Nov 1961 NSC drafts NSAM 111. Cable to Ambassador Nolting, instructing him to meet with Diem, lays out proposed U.S. assistance and expected GVN effort.

22 Nov 1961 NSAM 111.

15 Dec 1961 First Secretary of Defense Conference, Honolulu.

2 Feb 1962   Roger Hilsman's *A Strategic Concept for South Vietnam.*

3 Feb 1962   Diem creates Inter-Ministerial Committee on Strategic Hamlets.

19 Mar 1962 Diem approves Thompson's "Delta Plan" for execution.

22 Mar 1962 "Operation SUNRISE" commences in Binh Duong Province.

8 Aug 1962   GVN National Strategic Hamlet Construction Plan.

28 Oct 1962 GVN devotes entire issue of *The Times of Vietnam* to "The Year of the Strategic Hamlet."

8 May 1962   Buddhist controversy erupts when GVN troops fire on demonstrators in Hue.

24 Aug 1963 State to Lodge, Message 243, says that U.S. can no longer tolerate Nhu's continuation in power.

10 Sept 1963 General Krulak and Mr. Mendenhall give contradictory reports on progress of war to NSC.

2 Oct 1963   Secretary McNamara reports to President Kennedy following his visit to RVN with General Taylor.

1 Nov 1963   Coup d'etat by group of generals against President Diem.

I. INTRODUCTION

A. SCOPE AND TERMINOLOGY

The Strategic Hamlet Program in the Republic of Vietnam (RVN)—articulated and carried forward from late 1961 until late 1963—has created some confusion because of terminology. One source of confusion stems from the similarity between the physical aspects of the program and earlier fortified communities of one kind or another. Another source of confusion rises because of the loose usage of "hamlet" as compared to "village" and because of the practice of referring to these communities as "defended," "secure," and "fortified" as well as "strategic." But the greatest source of confusion lies in the distinction between a strategic hamlet *per se* and the strategic hamlet *program*.

The hamlet is the smallest organized community in rural South Vietnam. Several hamlets (typically 3-5) comprise a village. During the strategic hamlet program both hamlets and villages were fortified. The distinction is unimportant for the present analysis, except as it bears on the defensibility of the community protected. The several adjectives coupled with hamlet or village were occasionally used to differentiate communities according to the extent of their defenses or the initial presumed loyalty of their inhabitants. More often no such distinction was made; the terms were used interchangeably. Where a distinction exists, the following account explains it.

The phrase Strategic Hamlet Program when used to represent the program is much broader than the phrase applied to the hamlets themselves. The program, as explained below, envisioned a process of pacification of which the construction of strategic hamlets was but part of one phase, albeit a very important part. This paper examines the program, not just the hamlets.

B. ANTECEDENTS

Population relocation into defended villages was by no means a recent development in Southeast Asia. Parts of South Vietnam had experience with the physical aspects of fortified communities going back many years. As the intellectual godfather of the Strategic Hamlet Program has put it, the concept's use as one of the measures to defeat communist insurgency ", . . has only meant that the lessons of the past had to be relearnt."

The administration of President Diem had relearned these lessons much earlier than late 1961. There was, in fact, no need to relearn them because they had never been forgotten. The French had made resettlement and the development of "secure zones" an important element in their effort near the end of the war with the Viet Minh. The government of newly-created South Vietnam, headed since 1954 by President Diem, had continued resettlement schemes to accommodate displaced persons, to control suspected rural populations, and to safeguard loyal peasants in the threatened areas. None of these efforts involving resettlement had succeeded. Each had inspired antagonism among the peasants who were moved from their ancestral lands and away from family burial plots.

Diem's actions in late 1961 were thus inescapably tied to earlier actions by proximity in time, place, and the personal experiences of many peasants. Chief among the earlier programs was that of the so-called Agrovilles or "Rural Community Development Centers," launched in 1959. The Agrovilles, groupments of 300-500 families, were designed to afford the peasantry the social benefits of city life (schools and services), to increase their physical security, and to control certain key locations by denying them to the communists. They were designed to improve simultaneously the security and well-being of their inhabitants and the government's control over the rural population and rural areas.

The Agroville program was generally unsuccessful. The peasants had many complaints about it ranging from clumsy, dishonest administration to the physical hardship of being too far from their fields and the psychological wrench of being separated from ancestral homes and burial plots. By 1960, President Diem had slowed the program in response to peasant complaints and the Viet Cong's ability to exploit this dissatisfaction.

The transition from Agrovilles to strategic hamlets in 1961 was marked by the so-called "Agro-hamlet" which attempted to meet some of the peasants' objections:

> The smaller 100 family Agro-hamlet was located more closely to lands tilled by the occupants. Construction was carried out at a slower pace filled to the peasant's planting and harvesting schedule. . . By the end of 1961, the Agro-hamlet had become the prototype of a vast civil defense scheme known as strategic hamlets, *Ap Chien Luoc.*

It was inevitable, given this lineage, that the strategic hamlet program be regarded by the peasants as old wine in newly-labelled bottles. The successes and failures of the past were bound to condition its acceptance and by late 1961 the Diem government was having more failures than successes.

C. THE SITUATION IN LATE 1961

By late 1961, if not earlier, it had become clear in both Saigon and Washington that the yellow star of the Viet Cong was in the ascendancy. Following the 1960 North Vietnamese announcement of the twin goals of ousting President Diem and reunifying Vietnam under communist rule, the Viet Cong began sharply to increase its guerrilla, subversive, and political warfare. Viet Cong regular forces, now estimated to have grown to 25,000, had been organized into larger formations and employed with increasing frequency. The terrorist-guerrilla organization had grown to an estimated 17,000 by November 1961. During the first half of 1961, terrorists and guerrillas had assassinated over 500 local officials and civilians, kidnapped more than 1,000, and killed almost 1,500 RVNAF personnel. The VC continued to hold the initiative in the country-side, controlling major portions of the populace and drawing an increasingly tight cinch around Saigon. The operative question was not whether the Diem government as it was then moving could defeat the insurgents, but whether it could save itself.

Much of this deterioration of the situation in RVN was attributable, in U.S. eyes, to the manner in which President Diem had organized his government. The struggle—whether viewed as one to gain loyalty or simply to assert control—was focused in and around the villages and hamlets in the countryside. It was precisely in those areas that the bilineal GVN organization (ARVN and civilian province chiefs) most lacked the capability for concerted and cohesive action. The Army of the Republic of Vietnam (ARVN) was developing a potentially effective institutional framework under U.S. tutelage, but that effectiveness against the VC, Diem realized, could potentially be transferred into effectiveness against himself. The abortive coup of late 1960 had made Diem even more reluctant than he had earlier been to permit power (especially coercive power) to be gathered into one set of hands other than his own. Still, the establishment of an effective military chain of command which could operate where necessary in the countryside remained the prime objective of U.S. military advisors.

A unitary chain of command had recently been ordered into effect within

ARVN, but this had not solved the operational problems, for military operations were inescapably conducted in areas under the control of an independent political organization with its own military forces and influence on operations of all kinds—military, paramilitary, and civic action. The province chiefs, personally selected by President Diem and presumably loyal to him, controlled politically the territory in dispute with the VC and within which ARVN must operate. They also controlled territorial forces comprising the Civil Guard (CG) and Self Defense Corps (SDC).

For President Diem's purposes this bilineal organization offered an opportunity to counterbalance the power (and coup potential) of the generals by the power of the province chiefs. It was a device for survival. But the natural byproduct of this duality, in terms of the effectiveness of actions against the VC, was poor coordination and imperfect cooperation in intelligence collection and production, in planning, and in operational execution in the countryside, where the battles were fought—both the "battle for men's minds" and the more easily understood battles for control of the hamlets, villages, districts, and provinces.

The U.S. and GVN were agreed that in order to defeat the insurgency it was necessary that the rural populace identify with at least the local representatives of the central government. They were agreed, too, that some measure of physical security must be provided the rural population if this end were to be achieved. Both agreed that the GVN must be the principal agent to carry out the actions which would bring the insurgency to an end.

The high level U.S.-GVN discussions held during President Kennedy's first year in office focused on what the U.S. could provide GVN to assist the latter's counterinsurgency efforts and on what GVN should do organizationally to make its efforts more effective. A subsidiary and related discussion revolved around the U.S. advisory organization to parallel the GVN reorganization. The problem of how additional resources in some improved organizational framework were to be applied *operationally* was fragmented into many sub-issues ranging from securing the border to building social infrastructure.

The story of the Strategic Hamlet Program, as it came to be called, is one in which an operational concept specifying a sequence of concrete steps was introduced by an articulate advocate, nominally accepted by all of the principal actors, and advanced to a position of apparent centrality in which it became *the* operational blueprint for ending the insurgency. But it is also the story of an apparent consensus built on differing, sometimes competing, expectations and of an effort which was, in retrospect, doomed by the failure to resolve in one context the problem it was designed to alleviate in another—the problem of GVN stability.

II. THE FORMULATION OF THE STRATEGIC HAMLET PROGRAM

A. U.S.-GVN CONSULTATIONS

Beginning in May 1961, the U.S. and GVN conducted a series of high level conferences to fashion responses to the insurgent challenge. The first of these was the visit to Saigon by the Vice President, Lyndon B. Johnson. The Vice President's consultations were designed to reinforce the U.S. commitment to RVN and to improve the image of President Diem's government.

In a communique issued jointly in Saigon, it was agreed that the RVNAF was to be increased to 150,000 men, that the U.S. would support the entire Civil

Guard with military assistance funds, that Vietnamese and U.S. military specialists would be used to support village-level health and public works activities, and that the two governments would "discuss

[material missing]

> the reserve forces if possible as they come up to defend; and to dramatize the inability of the GVN to govern or to build, by the assassination of officials and the sabotage of public works.

The purpose of this military strategy, Taylor asserted, was apparently not to capture the nation by force. Rather, in concert with non-military means, it was to produce a political crisis which would topple the government and bring to power a group willing to contemplate the unification of Vietnam on Hanoi's terms.

It was in the U.S. interest, Taylor reasoned, to act vigorously—with advice as well as aid—in order to buy the necessary time for Vietnam to mobilize and to organize its real assets so that the Vietnamese themselves might "turn the tide" and assume the offensive. But U.S. aid and U.S. advice on where to use it were not enough. The Diem Government itself had to be reformed in order to permit it to mobilize the nation. Diem had, in Taylor's assessment, allowed two vicious circles to develop which vitiated government effectiveness. In the first of these circles poor military intelligence led to a defensive stance designed primarily to guard against attacks, which in turn meant that most of the military forces came under the control of the province chiefs whose responsibility it was to protect the populace and installations. This control by province chiefs meant that reserves could not, because of tangled lines of command and control, be moved and controlled quickly enough to be effective. The effect of high losses in unsuccessful defensive battles served further to dry up the basic sources of intelligence.

The second vicious circle stemmed from Diem's instinctive attempts to centralize power in his own hands while fragmenting it beneath him. His excessive mistrust of many intellectuals and younger Vietnamese, individuals badly needed to give his administration vitality, served only to alienate them and led them to stand aside from constructive participation—thereby further increasing Diem's mistrust. This administrative style fed back, too, into the military equation and through it, created another potentially explosive political-military problem:

> The inability to mobilize intelligence effectively for operational purposes directly flows from this fact [Diem's administrative practice] as do the generally poor relations between the Province Chiefs and the military commanders, the former being Diem's reliable agents, the latter a power base he fears. The consequent frustration of Diem's military commanders— a frustration well-known to Diem and heightened by the November 1960 coup—leads him to actions which further complicate his problem; e.g., his unwillingness to delegate military operations clearly to his generals.

General Taylor's recommended actions for the U.S. were designed to demonstrate U.S. commitment in order to strengthen Diem's stand and, to broaden U.S. participation in the hope of bringing about necessary reforms in Diem's regime. The President's emissary rejected the alternatives of a military takeover which would make the generals dominant in all fields. He rejected, too, the alternative of replacing Diem with a weaker figure who would be willing to delegate authority to both military and civil leaders. The first course would emphasize the solution to only one set of problems while slighting others; the second would permit action, but not coordinated action.

B. "LIMITED PARTNERSHIP"

In order to move in a coordinated way on the intermingled military, political, economic, and social problems facing South Vietnam, General Taylor recommended that the U.S. initiate a "limited partnership" which would stop short of direct U.S. action but would also, through persuasion at many levels judiciously mixed with U.S. leverage, ". . . force the Vietnamese to get their house in order in one area after another." Increased material assistance from the U.S. would be accompanied with increased U.S. participation at all levels of government in which the American advisors must ". . . as friends and partners—not as arms-length advisors—show them how the job might be done —not tell them or do it for them." If strongly motivated, tactful Americans were assigned primarily outside Saigon, thus avoiding the establishment of large headquarters not actually engaged in operational tasks, Taylor thought that this increased U.S. participation would not be "counter-productive"; e.g., lend substance to claims of U.S. imperialism and dominance of the Diem Government.

Thus, Taylor consciously opted for a U.S. course of action in which the major thrust of effort would be to induce Diem to do the things that the U.S. thought should be done: to draw the disaffected into the national effort and to organize and equip so that effective action would be possible. General Taylor did not argue explicitly that success would follow automatically if Diem's practices could be reformed and his operational capabilities upgraded, but he implied this outcome. The question of an overall strategy to defeat the insurgency came very close to being regarded as a problem in the organization and management of resources. Since GVN had no national plan, efforts were concentrated on inducing them to produce one. There was much less concern about the substance of the non-existent GVN plan. It was almost as though there had to be something to endorse or to criticize before substantive issues could be treated as relevant.

C. U.S.-PROPOSED NATIONAL PLANS

This priority of business is reflected in the U.S. plans which were proposed to GVN for adoption by the latter. In late 1960 the U.S. Country Team in Saigon produced an agreed "Counterinsurgency Plan for Viet-Nam" (CIP). The plan was an attempt to specify roles and relationships within GVN in the counterinsurgency effort, to persuade Diem to abandon his bilineal chain of command in favor of a single command line with integrated effort at all levels within the government, and to create the governmental machinery for coordinated national planning. It was recognized that these recommendations were not palatable to President Diem, but reorganization along the lines specified was regarded as essential to successful accomplishment of the counterinsurgent effort.

The CIP was an indictment of GVN failure to organize effectively and to produce coordinated national plans. It advanced no operational concepts for adoption by GVN. This obvious omission was corrected in the "Geographically

Phased National Level Operation Plan for Counterinsurgency" which MAAG Vietnam published on 15 September 1961. Not only did this plan specify the areas of primary interest for pacification operations—as its title indicates—it also set forth a conceptual outline of the three sequential phases of actions which must be undertaken. In the first, "preparatory phase," the intelligence effort was to be concentrated in the priority target areas, surveys were to be made to pinpoint needed economic and political reforms, plans were to be drawn up, and military and political cadres were to be trained for the specific objective area. The second, or "military phase," would be devoted to clearing the objective area with regular forces, then handing local security responsibility over to the Civil Guard (CG) and to establishing GVN presence. In the final, "security phase," the Self Defense Corps (SDC) would assume the civil action-local security mission, the populace was to be "reoriented," political control was to pass to civilian hands, and economic and social programs were to be initiated to consolidate government control. Military units would be withdrawn as security was achieved and the target area would be "secured" by the loyalty of its inhabitants—a loyalty attributable to GVN's successful responses to the felt needs of the inhabitants.

First priority in this plan (1962 operations) was to go to six provinces around Saigon and to the Kontum area. Second priority (1963) would be given to expansion southward into the Delta and southward in the Central Highlands from Kontum. Third priority (1964) would continue the spread of GVN control in the highlands and shift the emphasis in the south to the provinces north and east of Saigon. Before any of these priority actions were undertaken, however, it was proposed to conduct an ARVN sweep in War Zone D, in the jungles northeast of Saigon, to reduce the danger to the capital and to increase ARVN's self-confidence.

The geographically phased plan complemented the earlier CIP. Together, these two U.S. efforts constituted an outline blueprint for action. It is, of course, arguable that this was the best conceivable blueprint, but it was at least a comprehensive basis for refinement—for arguments for different priorities or a changed "series of events" in the process of pacification.

D. INITIAL VIETNAMESE REACTIONS

This is not how matters proceeded, in the event. Ambassador Durbrow, General McGarr, and others urged acceptance of the CIP upon President Diem, but with only partial success. Diem stoutly resisted the adoption of a single, integrated chain of operational command, showed no enthusiasm for detailed prior planning, continued his practice of centralized decision-making (sometimes tantamount to decision pigeonholing), and continued to play off the province chiefs against the generals. Some aspects of the CIP were accepted, but the basic organizational issues remained unresolved and the strategic approach unresolved by default.

The unsuccessful U.S. attempts to secure organizational reforms within the Diem government had assumed psychological primacy by the time of General Taylor's October 1961 mission to Saigon. The American position was essentially that *no* operational plan could succeed unless GVN were reorganized to permit effective implementation. It was reorganization that Taylor emphasized, as detailed above. But General Taylor did bring up the need for some coordinated operational plan in his talks with President Diem. Diem's response is described in a cable to Washington by Ambassador Nolting:

Taylor several times stressed importance of overall plan—military, political, economic, psychological, etc.—for dealing with guerrillas. Diem tended avoid clear response this suggestion but finally indicated that he has a new strategic plan of his own. Since it was not very clear in spite efforts to draw him out what this plan is, Taylor asked him to let us have a copy in writing.

E. THOMPSON'S COUNTERPROPOSALS

President Diem may have been whistling in the dark about a new plan of his own. It is likely, however, that he was already conversant with the ideas of a new high level advisor who had been in Saigon for several weeks and whose approach to prosecuting the war he would soon endorse officially as his own. The advisor was RGK Thompson, a British civil servant who had come from the position of Permanent Secretary of Defense in Malaya. Thompson's British Advisory Mission was in Saigon in response to Diem's request for experienced third country nationals to assist him in his counterinsurgent operations. There had been some initial U.S. objection to British "advice without responsibility," but fears had been temporarily allayed when it was agreed that Thompson's charter would be limited to civic action matters.

Thompson provided Diem his initial "appreciation" (or, in U.S. terminology, "estimate of the situation") in October 1961. His assessment was well received by the President, who asked him to follow it up with a specific plan. Thompson's response, an outline plan for the pacification of the Delta area, was given to the President on 13 November. Thus, Thompson was in the process of articulating one potentially comprehensive strategic approach at the same time that the U.S. was deeply involved in fashioning a major new phase in U.S.-GVN relations in which major new U.S. aid would be tied to Diem's acceptance of specified reforms and, inferentially, to his willingness to pursue some agreed, coordinated strategy. Thompson's plan was, in short, a potential rival to the American-advanced plans represented by the CIP and the geographically phased MAAG plan of September 1961.

In order to assess the similarities and differences between the U.S. plans and that advanced by the British Advisory Mission, it is necessary to summarize Thompson's argument and proposals. Like Taylor (with whom he talked and to whom he gave a copy of his initial "appreciation" at the latter's request), Thompson saw the VC objective to be one of political denouement by combined military and political action rather than a military takeover of the entire nation. Like McGarr and the other U.S. military advisors, he recognized the probability and danger of VC attempts to control the unpopulated areas and to use them both as a base from which to project an image of political strength and as secure areas from which (in the case of War Zone D., northeast of Saigon) to threaten the capital. But unlike the U.S. military advisors, Thompson viewed the primary threat to be to the political stabiliy of the populated rural areas. Consequently, he regarded McGarr's proposed initial operation in War Zone D to be a step in the wrong direction.

The main government target, Thompson argued, should not be simply the destruction of VC forces. Rather, it should be to offer an attractive and constructive alternative to communist appeals. This could only be done by emphasizing national reconstruction and development in the populated rural areas. To do so would require extensive and stringent security measures, to be sure, but these measures required primarily police rather than regular military forces.

The police could establish a close rapport with the populace; the army could not. The army should have the mission to keep the VC off balance by mobile action in order to prevent insurgent attacks on the limited areas in which GVN would concentrate its initial pacification efforts.

This line of argument was more fully developed in Thompson's draft plan for the pacification of the Delta area, given to President Diem on 11 November. The objective of the plan was to win loyalties rather than to kill insurgents. For that reason Thompson selected a populous area with relatively little VC main force activity. The thrust of his proposal was that "clear and hold" operations should replace "search and destroy" sweeps. ARVN might be used to protect the villages while the villages were organizing to protect themselves and mobile ARVN forces must be available to reinforce local defense units, but the process should be abandoned of "sweeping" through an area—and then leaving it. The peasants must be given the assurance of physical security so that economic and social improvements, the real object of the plan, could proceed without interruption.

The means by which the villagers would be protected was the "strategic hamlet," a lightly guarded village because it was—by definition—in a relatively low risk area. More heavily defended centers, called "defended hamlets" and involving more relocation, would be employed in areas under more VC influence, particularly along the Cambodian border.

To control this effort in the Delta, Thompson recommended that the ARVN III Corps Headquarters be reinforced with paramilitary and civil components, relieved of its responsibility for the area around and north of Saigon, and function under the immediate supervision of the National Security Countil—presided over by President Diem. The province chiefs, already under Diem's personal direction, would be responsible on all emergency matters to the reinforced III Corps Headquarters (to be called the Combined Headquarters), but continue as before with respect to routine administration.

Thompson presented this Delta plan as a program of wide potential:

> . . . It should lead by stages to a reorganization of the government machinery for directing and coordinating all action against the communists and to the production of an *overall strategic operational plan for the country as a whole* defining responsibilities, tasks and priorities. At the same time it will lead to the establishment of a static security framework which can be developed eventually into a National Police force into which can be incorporated a single security intelligence organization for the direction and coordination of all intelligence activities against the communists. I agree with Your Excellency that it would be too disruptive at the present moment to try to achieve these immediately and that they should be developed gradually. Using a medical analogy, the remedy should be clinical rather than surgical.

III.   DEVELOPING A CONSENSUS AMONG THE ADVISORS

A.   *INITIAL REACTION OF U.S. MILITARY ADVISORS*

It is not difficult to imagine the shocked reaction to Thompson's proposals, especially in U.S. military circles. In fact, one need not imagine them; General

McGarr has recorded a detailed rejoinder to Thompson's proposals. He was, to begin with, upset about the lack of prior coordination:

> Following Mr. Thompson's medical analogy . . . we have the case of a doctor called in for consultation on a clinical case, actually performing an amputation without consulting the resident physician—and without being required to assume the overall responsibility for the patient.

General McGarr's unhappiness with Thompson was not simply a case of injured feelings. He had four related categories of disagreements with the plan proposed by the British Advisory Mission. First, Thompson's recommended command arrangements, if adopted, would demolish the prospect of a unitary chain of command within ARVN, an objective toward which McGarr had been working for over a year. Additionally, the Thompson proposals would leave Diem as the ultimate manager of an operation dealing with only a portion (the Delta) of RVN. The elimination of practices such as this had been an explicit objective of the entire U.S. advisory effort for a long time.

Second, the proposed priority in the Delta clashed with McGarr's priorities which placed War Zone D first, the area around Saigon second, and the Delta third. There was a lack of unanimity among the U.S. advisors about the relative importance of the War Zone D operation but the military in particular, were looking for an important operation to help the (hopefully) revitalized ARVN demonstrate its offensive spirit and mobile capabilities. This desire gave rise to the third and fourth objections—or fears.

The "static security framework" in the villages to which Thompson referred struck General McGarr as an unwarranted downgrading of the need for a sizeable conventional military force to play an important role in pacification. Thompson's stated desire to emphasize police forces in lieu of regular military forces was regarded by the U.S. military advisory chief as unrealistic—a transferral of Malayan experience to a locale in which the existing tools of policy were very different.

Related to this objection was a final set of disagreements. Thompson had wanted to go slowly and to let a new GVN organization grow from the effort. The U.S. military advisory chief also wanted to go slowly—but not *that* slowly. Not only would the Viet Cong not wait, it was simply unsound policy not to use the tools at hand. It would not do to reduce the ARVN and increase police forces while the VC continued their successes. It was necessary, in sum, to act in a limited area but to act quickly. Thompson's recommendations did not look to quick action, emphasized the wrong area, were designed to emphasize the wrong operational agency, and proposed unacceptable command lines.

It is important to note that in spite of these explicit disagreements there were broad areas of apparent agreement between Thompson and his U.S. counterparts. (*Apparent,* because the "areas of agreement" concealed differences, too.) The U.S MAAG was amenable to the development of strategic hamlets, General McGarr claimed. Indeed, MAAG's long, diffuse doctrinal "handbook" for advisors in the field did devote three pages—without any particular emphasis— to the "secure village concept." MAAG did not stress the centrality of strategic hamlets *per se,* but neither did Thompson. Strategic hamlets were to Thompson a way station enroute to his real objective—winning the loyalty of the rural peasants. This was apparently compatible with the sequential steps to pacification outlined in MAAG's own Geographically Phased Counterinsurgency Plan. If the competing approaches of the U.S. and British advisors had not been made compatible, there was, at least, some agreed ground from which to launch the effort to make them compatible.

B.   REACTIONS IN WASHINGTON

That such ground existed was fortunate, for Thompson's evolutionary plan was not only finding a warm reception at the Presidential Palace, it was also winning an attentive ear in Washington. As already mentioned, Thompson talked with General Taylor during the latter's October 1961 mission to Saigon and provided Taylor a copy of the initial British "appreciation." Copies of the Thompson memorandum on the Delta were also forwarded to Taylor at the latter's request. Then in January 1962, Thompson, again responding to Taylor's request, sent the latter a long letter outlining his views. In less than a month, General Taylor could present to President Kennedy a plan entitled "A Strategic Concept for South Vietnam" by Roger Hilsman which was an unabashed restatement of most of Thompson's major points and toward which President Kennedy had, not incidentally, already expressed a favorable disposition.

Hilsman's "strategic concept" avowedly flowed from three basic principles: that the problem in Vietnam presented by the VC was political rather than military in its essence; that an effective counterinsurgency plan must provide the people and villages with protection and physical security; and that counter guerrilla forces must adopt the same tactics as those used by the guerrilla himself.

To translate these principles into operational reality, Hilsman called for "strategic villages" and "defended villages" à la Thompson, with first priority to the most populous areas; i.e., the Delta and in the vicinity of Hue. ARVN would, much as in Thompson's proposal, secure the initial effort, when necessary, and be employed to keep the VC off balance in those areas already under Viet Cong control. The plan envisaged a three-phase process by which GVN control would progressively be expanded from the least heavily VC-penetrated provinces with large populations (phase I), into the more heavily penetrated population centers (phase II), and finally into the areas along the Laotian and Cambodian borders (phase III). Hilsman eschewed use of the "oil spot" analogy but the process and rationale he put forth were the same. His plan moved "strategic villages" to a place of prominence greater than that in Thompson's Delta plan and far in excess of the offhanded acceptance which had thus far been afforded them by U.S. military advisors. Strategic hamlets were not the *heart* of the Hilsman plan—civic action was that—but they were the *symbol,* the easily recognizable, easily grasped initial step by which GVN could begin, following Hilsman's second principle, to "provide the people and the villages with protection and physical security."

C.   THE ADVISORS REACH AGREEMENT

Thompson's basic ideas were gaining wide dissemination at the highest level within the U.S. government in early 1962. What of his relations with the U.S. MAAG in Saigon? These had been significantly improved as the result of a meeting between Thompson, Ambassador Nolting, and British Ambassador Hohler. Thompson agreed to revise his paper so as to remove the objection to his proposed command arrangements. Ambassador Nolting reported that Thompson was now working "closely and amicably" with MAAG. This took care of one of McGarr's objections. Thompson had apparently decided, too, to allow the issue to drop for the time being of police primacy in pacification *vis-à-vis* ARVN. It was not, after all, a change that could be made quickly; President Diem was convinced that some start was needed to save his administration. That had been his reason, after all, in reluctantly inviting increased American participation in the war.

Secretary McNamara played an important role in disposing of still another issue in dispute—that of where to begin. In mid-December 1961, after President Kennedy had decided to adopt essentially all of General Taylor's November recommendations except the introduction of major U.S. forces in Vietnam, Secretary McNamara met in Honolulu with the U.S. principals in Vietnam to discuss future plans. A central question was that of what could be done in the short term future. The Secretary of Defense made it clear that RVN had "number one priority." McNamara urged concentration on one province: "I'll guarantee it (the money and equipment) provided you have a plan based on one province. Take one place, sweep it and hold it in a plan." Or, put another way, let us demonstrate that in some place, in some way, we can achieve demonstrable gains.

General McGarr, immediately upon his return to Saigon, wrote to Secretary Thuan and passed on this proposal:

> I would like to suggest that you may wish to set aside one specific area, say a province, and use it as a "test area," in establishing this type "pacification infrastructure." My thinking is that all the various elements of this anti-VC groundwork be designated immediately by your government and trained as a team or teams for the actual reoccupation and holding of the designated communist infiltrated area when it has been cleared by RVNAF military action.

Such teams would embrace, McGarr suggested, police, intelligence, financial, psychological, agricultural, medical, civic action, and civil political functions.

IV. THE ADVISORS "SELL" DIEM (OR VICE VERSA)

A. WHERE TO BEGIN?

GVN did indeed have a province in mind. It was not a Delta province, however. Nor was it a province relatively secure from VC infiltration. Quite to the contrary, Binh Duong Province, extending north and northwest of Saigon, had been heavily infiltrated. Its main communications axis (National Highway 13, extending northward from Saigon into Cambodia) sliced directly between War Zone D and War Zone C. The province was crossed by important routes of communications, liaison, and supply between two insurgent redoubts. Hardly the logical place to begin, one might say, but "logic" was being driven by events and desires more than by abstract reasoning.

One desire was the widely held wish to do something concrete and productive as a symbol of U.S. determination and GVN vitality. Another desire was GVN's wish to commit the Americans to support of Diem's government on terms which would be *in fact* acceptable to that government and would—equally important —*appear* to be U.S. support for GVN-initiated actions. If one were Vietnamese one might reason that Binh Duong was an area of unquestionable strategic importance—and one in which GVN had already initiated some pacification efforts. If the Americans wish to concentrate in one province and if they are willing to underwrite the effort with resources, why not begin in an important strategic area where work is already underway?

GVN had initiated, in August 1961, a "Rural Reconstruction Campaign" in the Eastern Region of South Vietnam to secure the provinces of Tay Ninh, Binh Duong, and Phuoc Tuy. Most of the effort prior to December 1961 had been concentrated in the Cu Chi District of Binh Duong. Xom Hue Hamlet of Tan An Hoi was, during December, in the process of being fortified as a strategic hamlet. General McGarr was under the impression that "considerable progress" had already been made in these three provinces in the establishment of the GVN village level activities so necessary to winning popular support.

In mid-January General McGarr met (just prior to his departure for Honolulu) with President Diem and Secretary Thuan to discuss pacification plans. As McGarr told Secretary McNamara, Diem stressed that the MAAG-endorsed military operation in War Zone D might merely close the string on an empty bag. Such a failure would be detrimental to ARVN morale. Besides, the President observed echoing Thompson, "sweeps" solved nothing; the problem was to hold an area and to separate the VC from the rest of the populace. Diem preferred a concentrated effort in Binh Duong, a heavily infiltrated province, close to Saigon, of great strategic importance, and in which only 10 of 46 villages were under GVN control—but in which the groundwork for a sound government infrastructure had already been laid.

The discussions at the Secretary of Defense's Conference in Honolulu turned on whether or not the War Zone D operation offered more hope for a concrete gain than a "single province" pacification scheme. McNamara concluded that it did not. General McGarr dissented mildly from the selection of Binh Duong. He would have favored Phuoc Tuy (where U.S. troops were scheduled to land *if* a decision were ever made to commit them.) But Binh Duong was GVN's plan and the "limited partners" finally agreed to back Diem's preferred attempt. Thus, the U.S. came to a roundabout decision to support as a "test" of what would later be called the "strategic hamlet program" an operation about whose details they knew little, in an area that all recognized to be difficult, because it allegedly represented a long-sought example of GVN initiative in planning and civil-military preparation. Much of the public image of the strategic hamlet program was to be established by this operation, as it turned out. Its name was "Operation Sunrise." But it was not—U.S. desires to the contrary—the only strategic hamlet effort to be carried forward during this period. It was only one of several—and several grew very quickly into many.

B. CONCURRENT GVN ACTIVITY

It has already been suggested that President Diem responded with some enthusiasm to the early proposals from Thompson's British Advisory Mission. In mid-February 1962, President Diem approved orally Thompson's "Delta Pacification Plan" and said he would like to see it executed without delay. Earlier, on 3 February, he had created by presidential decree the Inter-Ministerial Committee for Strategic Hamlets (IMCSH), comprising the heads of various ministries (Defense, Interior, Education, Civic Action, Rural Affairs, etc.). The IMCSH was, as its membership indicates, a coordinating body designed to give national direction and guidance to the program. Its importance is not in its work—for it apparently did very little—but as an indicator of Diem's early 1962 thinking of strategic hamlets as a *national* program and of the central role which his brother, Ngo Dinh Nhu, would play in this program.

Nhu was the real driving force behind GVN's uneven but discernible movement toward adoption of the strategic hamlet theme as a unifying concept in its pacification efforts. In the early period under discussion he masked his central role, however. He was not announced as the Chairman of the IMCSH (nobody was), but the committee was responsible to him. He did not, however, lead it actively. As two American observers remarked at the time, "Nhu seems to have consulted the committee seldom and to have shared his policy-making power with it even less frequently."

C. EARLY SIGNS OF GVN EXPECTATIONS

But although brother Nhu was behind the scenes in late 1961 and early 1962, an occasional fleeting glimpse of his thinking and the direction in which he was heading has still managed to show through. A CIA report from Saigon summarized Nhu's instructions to a dozen province chiefs from the Delta in a meeting held on 14 December 1961. Primary emphasis was to be placed on the strategic hamlet program, Nhu said, and this program was to be coupled with a "social revolution" against "Viet-Nam's three enemies: divisive forces, low standard of living, and communism." The CIA Task Force—Vietnam observed, in forwarding this report, that Nhu's "social revolution and strategic hamlets appear to be fuzzy concepts with little value in the fight against the Communists."

No doubt these concepts seemed fuzzy at the end of 1961. But within another twelve months, as events would prove, they would be widely recognized as the twin spearheads of GVN's counterinsurgent effort, fuzzy or not. The strategic hamlet program would have broad support within the U.S. government and financial resources to underpin that support. The "social revolution" to which Nhu referred in December 1961 would be surfaced as Diem's "personalism" drive. The important thing for the present analysis is that all of the expectations of the several participant groups—both U.S. and GVN—were identifiable by very early 1962 at the latest, and that the concept of the strategic hamlet program in the broad sense had been fully adumbrated. The skeleton—the rationale—was complete; the body—operational programs—had not yet taken form. Each group could, however, work toward construction of a slightly different body (and for differing reasons) and claim with some plausibility to be working from the same skeleton.

V. DIFFERING PERSPECTIVES AND EXPECTATIONS

Three somewhat different views may be categorized which are of interest to the present inquiry: those of the U.S. military advisors, of the U.S. political leadership, and of the Diem government's leaders. Such generalizations are admittedly risky and easily overdrawn; there were, of course, differences between the perceptions and expectations of, say, the U.S. military advisors. For example, those farthest from Saigon tended to be less patient—with Diem and in expecting results—than were those closer to the area of operations. Still, discernible differences of outlook and expectations may be said to represent the prevailing views in each of these three groups.

A.   U.S. MILITARY ADVISORS

The U.S. military advisors mistrusted arguments which stressed the Vietnamese struggle as essentially political rather than military. They were quite willing to concede that the struggle was multi-dimensional but they feared instinctively any line of reasoning which might appear to argue that military considerations were relatively unimportant in Vietnam. So, too, they were wary of schemes which might lead ARVN to perpetuate its defensive tactical stance. Both dangers were present in the strategic hamlet program. The same military advisors were more forceful than others in stressing the need for the Diem regime to rationalize its command arrangements and to plan comprehensively and in detail from the highest to lowest levels. Their operational interest concentrated on making ARVN not just more mobile but more aggressive. Their creed, developed through years of experience and training (or vicarious experience) was to "close with and destroy the enemy." One could expect them, then, to be more than willing to turn over the job of static defense to the CDC and CG at the earliest opportunity, to keep a weather eye out for opportunities to engage major VC formations in decisive battle, and to chafe under the painfully slow evolutionary process which was implicit even in their own 1961 geographically phased plan.

B.   U.S. POLITICAL LEADERSHIP

The U.S. political leadership, and to varying degrees the leaders in the Saigon Embassy and in USOM, were more attuned to the political problems—both with respect to GVN-U.S. relations and to the problem of winning broad support among the Vietnamese for the Diem administration. This made members of this group inherently more sympathetic to proposals such as the Thompson plan for the Delta than they were, for instance, to increasing ARVN's size and capabilities. They found compelling the logic of analyses such as Hilsman's which cut to the political root rather than treating only the military symptoms. One suspects—though documentation would never be found to support it— that they were attracted by an argument which did suggest some hope for "demilitarizing" the war, de-emphasizing U.S. operational participation, and increasing GVN's ability to solve its own internal problems using primarily its own human resources.

C.   PRESIDENT DIEM

Ngo Dinh Diem's perspective and expectations were the most different of all. U.S. groups differed in degree; Diem's expectations were different in kind. He wanted, first of all, to obtain unequivocal U.S. support, not just to his nation but to his administration. It was essential, in his eyes, that this support not compromise his authority or Vietnamese sovereignty. He did not want to give credence to communist claims that he was a puppet of the U.S., on one hand, or concentrate the coercive instruments of power in the hand of potential antagonists, on the other.

A revealing assessment of Diem's frame of mind is provided by Ambassador Nolting. Diem invited increased U.S. aid and U.S. participation because he feared that, especially with an impending settlement in Laos, South Vietnam would come under increasing communist pressures. If Diem's government could not win over these pressures—and Diem feared it could not—it had only the choice of going down fighting or of being overthrown by a coup. Thus, in requesting additional U.S. help, Diem had "adopted an expedient which runs against his own convictions, and he is apparently willing to accept the attendant diminution of his own stature as an independent and self-reliant national leader."

But when Ambassador Nolting presented to Diem the U.S. *quid pro quo* for its "limited partnership," this apparent acceptance of decreased stature and independence suddenly seemed less apparent. Then, as Nolting reported, President Diem feared the reaction even among his own cabinet aides. Secretary Thuan, in whom Diem did confide, said that the President was brooding over the fact that the U.S. was asking great concessions of GVN in the realm of its sovereignty in exchange for little additional help. Diem argued that U.S. influence over his government, once it was known, would play directly into the communists' hands. The first priority task, he added, was to give the people security, not to make the government more popular. To try it the other way around was to place the cart before the horse.

Diem saw himself caught in a dilemma in which he was doomed if he did not get outside assistance and doomed if he got it only at the price of surrendering his independence. To him the trick was to get the U.S. committed without surrendering his independence. One possible solution lay in getting U.S. material aid for a program that would be almost wholly GVN-implemented: The strategic hamlet program offered a convenient vehicle for this purpose and one which was also appealing for other reasons, It put achieving security before winning loyalty—in an operational context in which it was difficult to differentiate between *security for* the rural populace and *control of* that populace, since many of the actions to achieve one were almost identical to the acts to realize the other.

D. THE CENTRAL ISSUE

The U.S., for its part, was asking Diem to forego independence by accepting the wisdom of the American recommendations for reform. The central question was whether he would—or could—do so. Among those who responded to this question in the negative, J. Kenneth Galbraith was most trenchant:

> In my completely considered view . . . Diem will not reform either administratively or politically in any effective way. That is because he cannot. It is politically naive to expect it. He senses that he cannot let power go because he would be thrown out.

The U.S. decided that Diem could make meaningful reforms and that he would do so—or at least it decided that it was likely enough that he would do so and that support for his administration constituted the best available policy alternative.

E. THE PROBLEM OF ASSESSMENT

The differences in perspectives and expectations outlined above are important in their own right. They loom even larger, however, when one considers the difficulty of assessing progress in the program about to be undertaken.

These groups were about to embark upon a long, arduous joint voyage. Their only chart had never been to sea. This was the newly-articulated and imperfectly understood doctrine of counterinsurgency which stressed the interaction and interdependence of political, military, social, and psychological factors. It posited the necessity for certain actions to follow immediately and *successfully* behind others in order for the process of pacification to succeed. Above all— and this point cannot be overstressed—while this doctrine recognized the need for both the carrot and the stick (for coercive control and appealing programs) it made gaining broad popular acceptance the single ultimate criterion of success. Neither kill ratios nor construction rates nor the frequency of incidents was conclusive, yet these were all indicators applicable to phases within the larger process. The gains of doing well in one phase, however, could be wiped out by inactivity or mistakes in a subsequent phase. It was, in short, very difficult to know how well one was doing until one was done.

VI. THE NATIONAL PLAN EMERGES

A. *AWARENESS OF THE UNIFYING POTENTIAL*

Before examining the quality of execution of the operational programs for which some detailed record is available it will be useful to outline the process by which the strategic hamlet program became—by late 1962—a comprehensive national program embodying the major effort of GVN in pacification.

"Operation Sunrise" in Binh Duong Province was launched on 22 March 1962 in what was initially called the "Ben Cat Project." The Delta project, however, languished in a "planning stage" until May, when it first became known that Diem was considering incorporating it into the Strategic Hamlet Program. By August the IMCSH proposed a priority plan for the construction of strategic hamlets on a nation-wide basis. Later the same month, the U.S. Inter-Agency Committee for Province Rehabilitation concurred in this plan (with minor reservations) as a basis for planning and utilization of U.S. assistance. By October, the Diem government had made the Strategic Hamlet Program the explicit focus and unifying concept of its pacification effort. The government-controlled *Times of Viet Nam* devoted an entire issue to "1962: The Year of Strategic Hamlets." Ngo Dinh Nhu was unveiled as the "architect and prime mover" of the program which was the Vietnamese answer to communist strategy. As Nhu proclaimed: "Strategic hamlets seek to assure the security of the people in order that the success of the political, social, and military revolution might be assured by the enthusiastic movement of solidarity and self-sufficiency." President Diem had earlier put the same thought to an American visitor in clearer words:

> The importance of the strategic hamlets goes beyond the concept of hamlet self defense. They are a means to institute basic democracy in Vietnam. Through the Strategic Hamlet Program, the government intends to give back to the hamlet the right of self-government with its own charter and system of community law. This will realize the ideas of the constitution on a local scale which the people can understand.

By this time, too, influential American circles regarded the Strategic Hamlet Program as the shorthand designation for a process which represented a sensible and sound GVN effort. Roger Hilsman had said so in February to President Kennedy, and found the latter highly receptive. He continued to say so. As he advised Assistant Secretary of State Averell Harriman in late 1962, "The government of Vietnam has finally developed, and is now acting upon, an effective strategic concept." [Doc. 119] Even so lukewarm an enthusiast as the CJCS, General Lyman L. Lemnitzer could report that ". . . the Strategic Hamlet Program promises solid benefits, and may well be the vital key to success of the pacification program."

The public record also shows early support from high U.S. officials for the Strategic Hamlet Program and recognition of its central role in GVN's pacification campaign. Speaking in late April 1962, Under Secretary of State George W. Ball, commented favorably in the progressive development of strategic hamlets throughout RVN as a method of combating insurgency and as a means of bringing the entire nation "under control of the government." Secretary McNamara told members of the press, upon his return to Washington from a Pacific meeting in July 1962, that the Strategic Hamlet Program was the "backbone of President Diem's program for countering subversion directed against his state."

It is reasonable to conclude from the evidence that official U.S. awareness kept abreast of Diem's progressive adoption of the Strategic Hamlet Program as the "unifying concept" in his counterinsurgent effort. The same officials were constantly bombarded by a series of reports from a variety of sources describing the progress of the hamlet program and assessing its efficacy.

B. "OPERATION SUNRISE"

The first operational effort in which the U.S. had a hand, "Operation Sunrise," got under way in Binh Duong Province on 22 March 1962 when work commenced on Ben Tuong, the first of five hamlets to be constructed for relocated peasants in the Ben Cat District in and around the Lai Khe rubber plantation. Phase I of the operation—the military clearing phase—was conducted by forces of the 5th ARVN Division reinforced by ranger companies, a reconnaissance company, two reinforced CG companies, and a psychological warfare company. The Viet Cong simply melted into the jungles.

With the Viet Cong out of the way—at least for the time being—the relocation and construction of the new hamlet commenced. The new program got off to a bad start. The government was able to persuade only seventy families to volunteer for resettlement. The 135 other families in the half dozen settlements were herded forcibly from their homes. Little of the $300,000 in local currency provided by USOM had reached the peasants; the money was being withheld until the resettled families indicated they would not bolt the new hamlet. Some of them came with most of their meager belongings. Others had little but the clothes on their backs. Their old dwellings—and many of their possessions—were burned behind them. Only 120 males of an age to bear arms were found among the more than 200 families—indicating very clearly that a large number had gone over to the VC, whether by choice or as a result of intimidation.

C. OTHER EARLY PROGRAMS

Progress in Binh Duong continued at a steady pace, beset by difficulties. By midsummer 2900 persons had been regrouped into three strategic hamlets. Elsewhere, the pace quickened. Although the Delta Plan, as a coordinated effort, had not been implemented by the summer of 1962, Secretary McNamara found in May an aggressive effort under way without U.S. help near Ca Mao:

> Here the commander of the 31st Infantry Regiment had gone into an area 95% controlled by the VC, declared martial law, and resettled 11,000 people (some under duress) in 9 strategic hamlets, while fighting the VC wherever he found them. Since inception of the program, none of his villages have been attacked, and the freedom from VC taxation (extortion) is proving most appealing to the people. It is the commander's hope (doubtless optimistic) that he will be able to turn the whole area over to the civil guard and self defense corps within 6 months.

These resettlement efforts in areas which had been under VC domination were not the extent of the early hamlet "program," however. Many existing hamlets and villages were "fortified" in one degree or another early in 1962 following no discernible pattern. This appears to have been the natural product of the varied response to Nhu's injunction to emphasize strategic hamlets. In April, the GVN Ministry of the Interior informed the U.S. that 1300 such hamlets were already completed. "Operation Sunrise" had by this time been broadened to embrace efforts in several provinces. Several other Strategic Hamlet Programs were begun: "Operation Hai Yen II" (Sea Swallow) in Phu Yen Province with a goal of 281 hamlets, 157 of which were reported as completed within two months: "Operation Dang Tien" (Let's go) in Binh Dinh Province with a goal of 328 strategic hamlets in its first year; and "Operation Phuong Hoang" (Royal Phoenix) in Quang Nai Province with a goal of 125 strategic hamlets by the end of 1962.

D.   AT LAST—A NATIONAL PLAN

The GVN drew all of the partialistic programs together in its August 1962 national priority plan mentioned earlier. The nation was divided into four priority zones. First priority was assigned to the eleven provinces around Saigon. This included essentially the area of the Thompson Delta plan plus the original area of "Operation Sunrise" plus Gia Dinh Province. Priorities within each zone were further specified. Within the zone of first national priority, for example, the provinces of Vinh Long, Long An, and Phuoc Try were assigned the highest priority; Binh Duong—where operations were already in progress—was given priority three. By the end of the summer of 1962 GVN claimed that 3,225 of the planned 11,316 hamlets had already been completed and that over 33 percent of the nation's total population was already living in completed hamlets.

October 1962, when Diem made the Strategic Hamlet Program the avowed focus of his counterinsurgent campaign, marks the second watershed in the development and implementation of the program. The first such watershed had been the consensus, on the potential value of such a program, which had been developed at the end of 1961 and early 1962. There would be no others until the program died with Diem.

E.   EFFECT ON U.S. PERCEPTIONS

The effect of the GVN's concentration on strategic hamlets was to make U.S. assessments focus on several sub-aspects of the problem. Attention tended to be directed toward how well hamlets were being fortified and whether or not

TABLE 1

GVN REPORT ON STATUS OF STRATEGIC HAMLETS

As of 30 September 1962 *

Area	Strategic Hamlets Planned	Strategic Hamlets Completed	Strategic Hamlets Under Construction	Population in Completed Hamlets
SOUTHERN:				
Saigon	433	105	115	261,470
Eastern Provinces	1,595	291	501	423,060
Western Provinces	4,728	1,236	702	1,874,790
SUB-TOTAL	6,756	1,632	1,318	2,559,320
CENTRAL:				
Central Lowlands	3,630	1,490	682	1,654,470
High Plateau	930	103	217	108,244
SUB-TOTAL	4,560	1,593	899	1,762,714
GRAND TOTAL	11,316	3,225	2,217	4,322,034

—Percentage of planned hamlets completed 28.49%
—Percentage of total population in completed hamlets 33.39%

* Adapted from *The Times of Vietnam,* 28 October 1962, p. 17.

the implementation phase was well managed; i.e., whether peasants were paid for their labor, reimbursed for their losses, and given adequate opportunity to attend their crops. Conversely, attention was directed away from the difficult-to-assess question of whether the follow-up actions to hamlet security were taking place—the actions which would convert the peasantry from apathy (if not opposition) to identification with their central government.

This focusing on details which diverted attention from the ultimate objective took the form of reports, primarily statistical, which set forth the construction rate for strategic hamlets, the incident rate of VC activities, and the geographical areas in which GVN control was and was not in the ascendancy. These "specifics" were coupled to generalized assessments which almost invariably pointed to shortcomings in GVN's execution of the program. The shortcomings, however, were treated as problems in efficient management and operational organization; the ineluctability of increased control (or security) leading somehow to popular identification by a process akin to the economic assumption of "flotation to stability through development" went unchallenged as a basic assumption. Critics pointed to needed improvements; the question of whether or not these could be accomplished, or why, almost never was raised.

"Operation Sunrise," for example, was criticized in some detail by the US MAAG. Much better planning and coordination was needed in order to relocate effectively: Aerial surveys were necessary to pinpoint the number of families to be relocated; unanticipated expenditures needed to be provided for; preparation of sites should begin before the peasants were moved; and GVN resource commitments should be carefully checked by U.S. advisors at all levels. There was no discussion of the vulnerability of the strategic hamlets to VC infiltration (as against VC attacks) or of the subsequent steps to winning support. That was not, one may assume, the military's prime concern.

Political observers who examined this follow-on aspect were cautiously optimistic:

> The strategic hamlet program is the heart of our effort and deserves top priority. While it has not—and probably will not—bring democracy to rural Vietnam, it provides truly *local* administration for the first time. Coupled with measures to increase rice production and farmer income, these local administrations can work a revolution in rural Vietnam.

The same tone was reflected in Michael Forrestal's report to President Kennedy in February 1963 following his visit to Vietnam with Roger Hilsman [Doc. 120]. The visitors found Ambassador Nolting and his deputy, William C. Trueheart, optimistic about the results which the program might achieve once the materials for it, then just beginning to come in, reached full volume.

The Department of Defense was devoting considerable effort to insuring that these materials did reach Vietnam in, the quantities needed and in timely fashion. Secretary McNamara had been stuck with this problem during his May 1962 visit to "Operation Sunrise." He saw especially a need to program SDC, CG, and Youth Corps training so that it would match the role of hamlet building and to insure the provision of proper communications for warning purposes. A substantial amount of the MAAG-DoD effort subsequently went into programming. The Agency for International Development had agreed to fund the "Strategic Hamlet Kits" (building materials, barbed wire and stakes, light weapons, ammunition, and communication equipment), but in August 1962 it demurred, stating that supporting assistance funds in the MAP were inadequate for the purpose. Secretary McNamara agreed to undertake the financing for 1500 kits (13 million) but asked if the additional 3500 kits requested were really necessary and, if so, on what delivery schedule. The target levels and delivery dates underwent more or less continuous revision from then until the question became irrelevant in late 1963. A separate but related effort went into expediting the procurement, delivery, and installation of radios in the strategic hamlets so that each would have the capability to sound the alarm and request the employment of mobile reserves when attacked.

F.   DIFFERENCES BEGIN TO EMERGE

All of these "program management" activities were based on the unstated assumption that the strategic hamlet program would lead to effective pacification if only Diem would make it work. As it turned out, there was some disagreement between what the U.S. considered needed to be done and what President Diem knew very well he was doing. He was using the Strategic Hamlet Program to carry forward his "personalist philosophy." As brother Nhu visibly took the reins controlling the program and began to solidify control over the Youth Corps it became increasingly clear that Diem was emphasizing government *control* of the peasantry at the expense (at least in U.S. eyes) of *pacification*.

As awareness in Washington increased that strategic hamlets could serve several purposes, there developed also a divergent interpretation of whether or not the GVN was "winning the war." When General Krulak, SACSA, and

Joseph Mendenhall, an ex-counselor in Saigon then at State, visited RVN in September 1963, President Kennedy wryly asked upon receiving their conflicting reports, "You two did visit the same country, didn't you?" The answer is that they had, but the general stressed that the *military* war was going well while the diplomat asserted that the *political* war was being lost. The argument was not, it should be stressed, one between the generals and the diplomats; experienced diplomats disagreed fundamentally with Mendenhall. The disagreement was between those who pointed to signs of progress and those who held up examples of poor planning, corruption, and alienation of the peasants whose loyalty was the object of the exercise. Criticisms—frequently accompanied by counterbalancing assertions that "limited progress" was being achieved—mentioned corvee labor, GVN failures to reimburse the farmers for losses due to resettlement, the dishonesty of some officials, and Diem's stress on exhortations rather than on the provision of desirable social services.

Those who emphasized that the program was showing real progress— usually with a caveat or two that there was considerable room for improvement —stressed statistical evidence to portray the exponential increase in strategic hamlet construction (Table 2), the declining trend in Viet Cong-initiated incidents (Table 3), the rise in VC defections (Table 4), and the slow but steady increase in GVN control of rural areas (Table 5).

The JCS observation with respect to the establishment of strategic hamlets, for instance, was that since fewer than two tenths of one percent (0.2%) of them had been overrun by the VC, "The Vietnamese people must surely be finding in them a measure of the tranquility which they seek."

RGK Thompson later claimed that the very absence of attacks was an indicator that the VC had succeeded in infiltrating the hamlets. The point is not Thompson's prescience but the difficulty of reasoned assessment to which this analysis has already pointed. The U.S. course, in the face of these cautiously optimistic and hopefully pessimistic reports, was to continue its established program of material support coupled with attempts to influence Diem to make desired changes.

VII. THE PATH TO THE END

A. DIEM'S POSITION HARDENS

The obvious U.S. alternatives, by mid-1963, remained the same as they were in late 1961: (1) to induce changes within the Strategic Hamlet Program (among other) by convincing Diem to make such changes; (2) to allow Diem to run things his own way and hope for the best; and (3) to find an alternative to President Diem. The U.S. continued to pursue the first course; Diem insisted increasingly on the second. Finally, due to pressures from areas other than the Strategic Hamlet Program, the U.S. pursued the third alternative. The Strategic Hamlet Program, in the event, died with its sponsors.

Far from becoming more reasonable, in U.S. eyes, President Diem by mid-1963 had become more intractable. He insisted, for example, that the U.S. cease to have an operational voice in the Strategic Hamlet Program. The multiplication of U.S. advisors at many levels, he claimed, was the source of friction and dissension. The remedy was to remove the advisors. The essence of Diem's position was that Taylor's "limited partnership" would not work.

Other U.S. missions visited Vietnam to assess the conduct of the war. The

TABLE 2

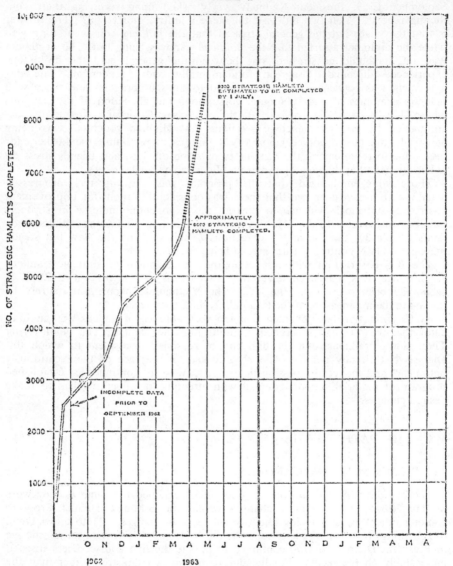

TABLE 3

VIET CONG INITIATED INCIDENTS BROKEN DOWN INTO CATEGORIES (ATTACKS, TERRORISM, SABOTAGE, PROPAGANDA)

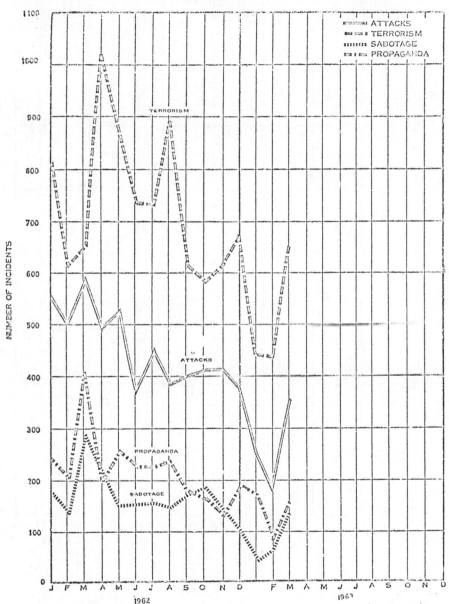

TABLE 4
VIET CONG DEFECTIONS

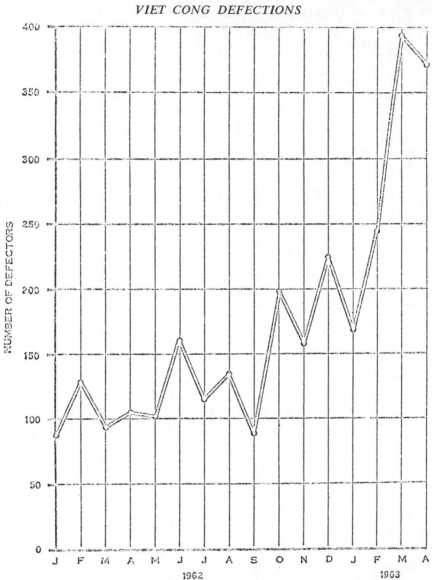

TABLE 5

COMPARISON OF CONTROL: GOVERNMENT OF VIETNAM AND VIET CONG JULY, OCTOBER AND DECEMBER 1962, AND APRIL 1963

	Government of Vietnam Effective Control	Government of Vietnam in Ascendancy	Neither in Control	Viet Cong in Ascendancy	Viet Cong Effective Control
Situation as of 1 July 1962					
Number of Villages	850	710	34	422	454
Rural Population	5,000,000	3,622,000	137,000	1,702,000	1,157,000
% of Rural Population	47%	29%	1%	14%	9%
Situation as of 1 Oct 1962					
Number of Villages	929	613	148	329	437
Rural Population	6,071,000	3,246,000	717,000	1,275,000	1,008,000
% of Rural Population	49%	27%	6%	10%	8%
Situation as of 1 Dec 1962					
Number of Villages	951	666	120	348	445
Rural Population	6,300,000	3,331,000	643,000	1,143,000	926,000
% of Rural Population	51%	27%	5%	9%	8%
Situation as of 1 April 63					
Number of Villages	935	731	139	348	390
Rural Population	6,724,000	3,356,000	609,000	962,000	857,000
% of Rural Population	54%	27%	5%	7%	7%
Changes Jul 62 to April 63					
Number of Villages	+76	+21	+105	−74	−64
Rural Population	+924,000	−266,000	+472,000	−740,000	−300,000
% of Rural Population	+7%	−2%	+4%	−7%	−2%

NOTE: In order to present a better picture of control of rural Vietnam, 1,600,000 population of autonomous cities of Saigon, Danang, Hue, and Dalat under GVN control was not used in this study, (populations are estimates).

result was much the same as reported by Krulak and Mendenhall. This was essentially the findings of the McNamara-Taylor mission in September: the military campaign is progressing, political disaffection is growing; U.S. leverage is questionable. [Doc. 142]

B. THE PROGRAM DIES WITH THE NGOS

The rest may be summarized: the U.S. attempted to insist on a program with more emphasis on broad appeal rather than control; Diem, finding himself increasingly embroiled in the Buddhist controversy, increased repressive measures; a coup toppled the Diem regime on 1 November; the deposed President and his brother Nhu, "architect of the Strategic Hamlet Program," were killed. The Strategic Hamlet Program—or at least the program under that name which they had made the unifying theme of their counterinsurgent effort— died with them. The inhabitants who had wanted to leave the hamlets did so in the absence of an effective government. The VC took advantage of the con- fusion to attack and overrun others. Some offered little or no resistance. The ruling junta attempted to resuscitate the program as "New Life Hamlets" early in 1964, but the failures of the past provided a poor psychological basis upon which to base hopes for the future.

VIII.   AN INCONCLUSIVE SUMMARY

The dominant U.S. view has been that the Strategic Hamlet Program failed because of over-expansion and the establishment of hamlets in basically in- secure areas. That there was overexpansion and the establishment of many poorly defended hamlets is not questioned. This contributed, beyond doubt, to the failure of the program. But this view finesses the problem of the process for which the strategic hamlets were but the tangible symbol. The present analysis has sought to emphasize both the essentially political nature of the objective of the Strategic Hamlet Program and the political nature of the context in which the process evolved—of expectations, bargaining, and attempts to exert influence on other participants in policy formulation and implementation. In this context it is the U.S. inability to exert leverage on President Diem (or Diem's inability to reform) that emerges as the principal cause of failure.

Yet, both of these attempts to pinpoint the reasons why the strategic hamlet program did not succeed fail to get at another whole issue: the validity of that body of writings which one may call the theory and doctrine of counterinsur- gency. Neither the military nor the political aspects of this doctrine can be up- held (*or* proved false) by an examination of the Strategic Hamlet Program. Quite aside from whether or not Diem was able to broaden the program's appeal to the peasantry, what would have occurred had he made a determined and sustained effort to do so? Would this have led in some more-or-less direct way to stability or to even greater dissatisfaction? We simply do not know. The question is as unanswerable as whether the appetite grows with the eating or is satisfied by it. The contention here is that claims of mismanagement are not sufficient to conclude that better management would necessarily have produced the desired results.

In the military sphere the unanswerable questions are different. It is said that the military phase of the Strategic Hamlet Program progressed reasonably well in many areas; the failure was in the political end of the process. But did the military actions succeed? Might failures to develop adequate intelligence and to weed out VC infrastructure in these hamlets not as easily be attributable to the fact that the inhabitants knew they were not really safe from VC intimidation and reprisals? Does the analogy to an "oil spot" have operational meaning when small bands can carry out hit and run raids or when many small bands can concentrate in one location and achieve surprise? Where is the key to this vicious circle—or is there a key?

In conclusion, while the abortive Strategic Hamlet Program of 1961–1963 may teach one something, the available record does not permit one to conclude either that the program fell because of the failure of a given phase or that other phases were, in fact, adequate to the challenge. One may say that the program was doomed by poor execution and by the inability of the Ngo family to reform coupled with the inability of the U.S. to induce them to reform. The evidence does not warrant one to proceed further.

3.   Phased Withdrawal of U.S. Forces, 1962–1964

Summary

A formal planning and budgetary process for the phased withdrawal of U.S. forces from Vietnam was begun amid the euphoria and optimism of July 1962, and was ended in the pessimism of March 1964. Initially, the specific objectives were: (1) to draw down U.S. military personnel then engaged in advisory, training, and support efforts from a FY 64 peak of 12,000 to a FY 68 bottoming out of 1,500 (just HQ, MAAG); and (2) to reduce MAP from a FY 64 peak of $180 million to a FY 69 base of $40.8 million. South Vietnamese forces were to be trained to perform all the functions then being carried out by U.S. personnel. What the U.S.G. was actually trying to accomplish during this period can be described in either or both of two ways: (1) a real desire and attempt to extricate the U.S. from direct military involvement in the war and to make it a war which the GVN would have to learn to win, and (2) straightforward contingency planning and the use of a political-managerial technique to slow down pressures for greater U.S. inputs. A blend of the wish embodied in the first explanation and the hard-headedness of the second seems plausible.

Needless to say, the phase-out never came to pass. The Diem coup with the resulting political instability and deterioration of the military situation soon were to lead U.S. decision-makers to set aside this planning process. An ostensible cut-back of 1000 men did take place in December 1963, but this was essentially an accounting exercise—and the U.S. force level prior to the reduction had already reached 16,732 in October 1963. By December 1964, U.S. strength had risen to 23,000 and further deployments were on the way.

What, then, did the whole phased-withdrawal exercise accomplish? It may have impeded demands for more men an dmoney, but this is doubtful. If the optimistic reports on the situation in SVN were to be believed, and they apparently were, little more would have been requested. It may have frightened the GVN, but it did not induce Diem or his successors to reform the political apparatus or make RVNAF fight harder. It may have contributed, however, to public charges about the Administration's credibility and over-optimism about the end of the conflict. Despite the carefully worded White House announcement of the phase-out policy on October 2, 1963, tentative Johnson Administration judgments came to be regarded by the public as firm predictions. While this announcement made clear that the U.S. effort would continue "until the insurgency has been suppressed or until the national security forces of the GVN are capable of suppressing it," the public tended to focus on the prognosis which followed—"Secretary McNamara and General Taylor reported their judgment that the major part of the U.S. military task can be completed by the end of 1965. . . ." In August 1964, Mr. McNamara further explained the policy: "We have said—as a matter of fact, I say today—as our training missions are completed, we will bring back the training forces."

Quite apart from what was actually accomplished by the phase-out policy and the costs in terms of domestic political perceptions of Administration statements on Vietnam, there are some important lessons to be learned from this exercise. What was the U.S. rationale behind the policy? Was it sound, feasible, and consistent with statements of national objectives? By what policy and programmatic means were we trying to bring about the desired results? Were these, in fact, the most appropriate and effective vehicles? How did the intelligence and reporting system in Vietnam help or hinder policy formulation? Why was not the Diem coup in its darkening aftermath grasped as the opportunity to reexamine policy and unambiguously to decide to phase out, or to do whatever was deemed necessary?

The rationale behind the phased withdrawal policy was by and large internally consistent and sensible.

> —To put Vietnam in the perspective of other U.S. world interests. Vietnam, at this time, was not the focal point of attention in Washington; Berlin and Cuba were. Part of this exercise was to make clear that U.S. interests in Europe and in the western hemisphere came first. Even in terms of Southeast Asia itself, Laos, not Vietnam, was the central concern. So, the phase-out policy made the kind of sense that goes along with the structuring of priorities.
> —To avoid an open-ended Asian mainland land war. Even though violated by U.S. involvement in the Korean war, this was a central tenet of U.S. national security policy and domestic politics. The notion of the bottomless Asian pit, the difference in outlook about a human life, were well understood.
> —To plan for the contingency that events might force withdrawal upon us. Seen in this light, the planning process was prudential preparation.
> —To treat the insurgency as fundamentally a Vietnamese matter, best solved by the Vietnamese themselves. Most U.S. decision-makers had well-developed doubts about the efficacy of using "white faced" soldiers to fight Asians. This view was invariably coupled publicly and privately with statements like this one made by Secretary McNamara: "I personally believe that this is a war that the Vietnamese must fight . . . I don't believe we can take on that combat task for them. I do believe we can carry out training. We can provide advice and logistical assistance."
> —To increase the pressure on the GVN to make the necessary reforms and to make RVNAF fight harder by making the extent and future of U.S. support a little more tenuous. This was explicitly stated in State's instructions to Ambassador Lodge on how to handle the White House statement of October, 1963: "Actions are designed to indicate to Diem Government our displeasure at its political policies and activities and to create significant uncertainty in that government and in key Vietnamese groups as to future intentions of United States." In other words, phased withdrawal was thought of as a bargaining counter with the GVN.
> —To put the lid on inevitable bureaucratic and political pressures for increased U.S. involvement and inputs into Vietnam. It was to be expected and anticipated that those intimately involved in the Vietnam problem would be wanting more U.S. resources to handle that problem. Pressures for greater effort, it was reasoned, eventually would come into play unless counteracted. What Secretary McNamara did was to force all theater justifications for force build-ups into tension with long-term phase-down plans. On 21 December, 1963, in a memo to the President after the Deim coup,

Mr. McNamara urged holding the line: "U.S. resources and personnel cannot usefully be substantially increased. . . ."

—To deal with international and domestic criticism and pressures. While Vietnam was not a front burner item, there were those who already had begun to question and offer non-consensus alternatives. During 1963, for example, both General de Gaulle and Senator Mansfield were strongly urging the neutralization of Vietnam.

It is difficult to sort out the relative importance of these varying rationales; all were important. Paramount, perhaps, were the desires to limit U.S. involvement, and to put pressure on the GVN for greater efforts. And, the rationales were all consistent with one another. But they did not appear as being wholly consistent with other statements of our national objectives in Southeast Asia. For example, on July 17, 1963, President Kennedy said: "We are not going to withdraw from [bringing about a stable government there, carrying on a struggle to maintain its national independence]. In my opinion, for us to withdraw from that effort would mean a collapse not only of South Vietnam, but Southeast Asia." He added: "We can think of Vietnam as a piece of strategic real estate. It's on the corner of mainland Asia, across the East-West trade routes, and in a position that would make it an excellent base for further Communist aggression against the rest of free Asia." In a September 9, 1963 interview, the President stated: "I believe ['the domino theory']. I think that the struggle is close enough. China is so large, looms up high just beyond the frontiers, that if South Vietnam went, it would not only give them an improved geographic position for a guerrilla assault on Malaya, but would also give the impression that the wave of the future in Southeast Asia was China and the Communists." One could argue that such an unequivocally strong statement of strategic importance would not be consistent with any sort of phase-out proposal short of a clear-cut victory over the communists. Despite the caveats about it being essentially a South Vietnamese struggle, President Kennedy's statements were very strong. And, insofar as the U.S. was interested in greater leverage on the GVN, these statements tended to reduce U.S. bargaining power because of the explicit and vital nature of the commitment.

The rationales behind the phased withdrawal policy were incorporated into a formal programming and planning process that began in July 1962 and ended on 27 March 1964. It was at the Honolulu Conference on 23 July 1962, the same day that the 14-nation neutralization declaration on Laos was formally signed, that the Secretary of Defense on guidance from the President put the planning machine in motion. Noting that "tremendous progress" had been made in South Vietnam and that it might be difficult to retain public support for U.S. operations in Vietnam indefinitely, Mr. McNamara directed that a comprehensive long range program be developed for building up SVN military capability and for phasing-out the U.S. role. He asked that the planners assume that it would require approximately three years, that is, the end of 1965, for the RVNAF to be trained to the point that it could cope with the VC. On 26 July, the JCS formally directed CINCPAC to develop a Comprehensive Plan for South Vietnam (CPSVN) in accordance with the Secretary's directives. Thus began an intricate, involved and sometimes arbitrary bargaining process, involving mainly MACV, the Joint Staff, and ISA. There were two main pegs that persisted throughout this process: MAP planning for the support and build-up of RVNAF, and draw-downs on U.S. advisory and training personnel.

The first COMUSMACV CPSVN was floated on 19 January 1963. It envisioned MAP for FY 1963-1964 at a total of $405 million. The total for FY 1965–1968 was $673 million. The RVNAF force level was to peak in FY 64 at 458,000 men. U.S. personnel in SVN were to drop from a high of 12.2 thousand in FY 65 to 5.9 thousand in FY 66, bottoming out in FY 68 at 1.5 thousand (Hq MAAG). No sooner was this first CPSVN cranked into the policy machinery than it conflicted with similar OSD/ISA planning. This conflict between ISA/OSD guidance and COMUSMACV/Joint Staff planning was to be continued throughout the life of the CPSVN.

Secretary McNamara opposed General Harkins version of the plan for a variety of reasons: (1) it programmed too many RVNAF than were trainable and supportable; (2) it involved weaponry that was too sophisticated; (3) it did not fully take account of the fact that if the insurgency came into control in FY 65 as anticipated, the U.S. MAP investment thereafter should be held at no more than $50 million per year; (4) the U.S. phaseout was too slow, and the RVNAF training had to be speeded up. In other words, Mr. McNamara wanted both a more rapid U.S. withdrawal of personnel, and a faster reduction in U.S. military/economic support.

The Secretary's views prevailed. The embodiment of Mr. McNamara's desire to quicken the pace of phase-out *planning* was embodied first in a Model M plan prepared by the JCS and later in what came to be called the Accelerated Model Plan of the CPSVN. The Accelerated Plan provided for a rapid phase-out of the bulk of U.S. military personnel. It also provided for building up GVN forces at a faster pace, but at a more reduced scale. MAP costs for FY 1965-1969 totaled $399.4 million, or nearly $300 million lower than the original projection.

All of this planning began to take on a kind of absurd quality as the situation in Vietnam deteriorated drastically and visibly. Strangely, as a result of the public White House promise in October and the power of the wheels set in motion, the U.S. did effect a 1000 man withdrawal in December of 1963. All the planning for phase-out, however, was either ignored or caught up in the new thinking of January to March 1964 that preceded NSAM 288. The thrust of this document was that greater U.S. support was needed in SVN. Mr. McNamara identified these measures as those that "will involve a limited increase in U.S. personnel and in direct Defense Department costs." He added: "More significantly they involve significant increases in Military Assistance Program costs. . . . ," plus "additional U.S. economic aid to support the increased GVN budget." On 27 March 1964, CINCPAC was instructed not to take any further action on the Accelerated Plan. Quickly, requests for more U.S. personnel poured into Washington. The planning process was over, but not forgotten. Secretary McNamara stated in his August 1964 testimony on the Tonkin Gulf crisis that even today "if our training missions are completed, we will bring back the training forces."

While the phase-out policy was overtaken by the sinking after-effects of the Diem coup, it is important to understand that the vehicles chosen to effect that policy—MAP planning, RVNAF and U.S. force levels—were the right ones. They were programmatic and, therefore, concrete and visible. No better way could have been found to convince those in our own government and the leaders of the GVN that we were serious about limiting the U.S. commitment and throwing the burden onto the South Vietnamese themselves. The public announcement of the policy, on October 2, 1963, after the McNamara-Taylor trip to Vietnam was also a wise choice. Even though this announcement may have contributed to the so-called "credibility gap," publication was a necessity.

Without it, the formal and classified planning process would have seemed to be nothing more than a drill.

While the choice of means was appropriate for getting a handle on the problem, it proceeded from some basic unrealities. First, only the most Micawberesque predictions could have led decision-makers in Washington to believe that the fight against the guerrillas would have clearly turned the corner by FY 65. Other nations' experience in internal warfare pointed plainly in the other direction. With more propitious circumstances, e.g. isolation from sanctuaries, the Philippine and Malayan insurgencies each took the better part of a dozen years to bring to an end.

Second, there was an unrealistic contradiction within the CPSVN itself. As directed by Secretary McNamara, U.S. MAP was to decrease as RVNAF increased. In practical terms, MAP costs should have been programmed to increase as the South Vietnamese Army increased, and as they themselves began to bear most of the burden. The desire to keep MAP costs down after FY 65 could, at best, be perceived as a budgeting or program gimmick not a serious policy.

Three, the political situation in South Vietnam itself should have prompted more realistic contingency plans against failure of the Vietnamese, in order to give the U.S. some options other than what appeared as precipitous withdrawal. The intelligence and reporting systems for Vietnam during this period must bear a principal responsibility for the unfounded optimism of U.S. policy. Except for some very tenuous caveats, the picture was repeatedly painted in terms of progress and success.

In the July 1962 Honolulu Conference the tone was set. Secretary McNamara asked COMUSMACV how long it would take before the VC could be expected to be eliminated as a significant force. In reply, COMUSMACV estimated about one year from the time RVNAF and other forces became fully operational and began to press the VC in all areas. Mr. McNamara was told and believed that there had been "tremendous progress" in the past six months. This theme was re-echoed in April of 1963 by COMUSMACV and by the intelligence community through an NIE. All the statistics and evaluations pointed to GVN improvement. While noting general progress, the NIE stated that the situation remains flexible. Even as late as July 1963 a rosy picture was being painted by DIA and SACSA. The first suggestion of a contrary evaluation within the bureaucracy came from INR. Noting disquieting statistical trends since July, an unpopular INR memo stated that the "pattern showed steady decline over a period of more than three months duration." It was greeted with a storm of disagreement, and in the end was disregarded.

The first, more balanced evaluation came with the McNamara-Taylor trip report late in September and October, 1963. While it called the political situation "deeply serious," even this report was basically optimistic about the situation, and saw little danger of the political crisis affecting the prosecution of the war.

Not until after the Diem coup, the assassination of President Kennedy, and the December Vietnam trip of Secretary McNamara was the Vietnam situation accurately assessed. In Secretary McNamara's December memo to the President, after his trip, he wrote: "The situation is very disturbing. Current trends, unless reversed in the next 2-3 months, will lead to a neutralization at best and more likely to a communist-controlled state." One of the most serious deficiencies he found was a "grave reporting weakness on the U.S. side." Mr. McNamara's judgment, apparently, was not predominant. He noted in the concluding paragraph of his memo that he "may be overly pessimistic, inasmuch as the ambassador, COMUSMACV, and General Minh were not discouraged and look forward to significant improvements in January."

By 6 March 1964 when another major Secretary of Defense Conference convened at CINCPAC Headquarters, the consensus was that the military situation was definitely deteriorating. The issue was no longer whether there was or was not satisfactory progress; the question was how much of a setback had there been and what was needed to make up for it. Mr. McNamara observed that attention should now be focused on near term objectives of providing for necessary greater U.S. support. It was finally agreed that the insurgency could be expected to go beyond 1965.

The intelligence and reporting problem during this period cannot be explained away. In behalf of the evaluators and assessors, it can be argued that their reporting up until the Diem coup had some basis in fact. The situation may not have been too bad until December 1963. Honest and trained men in Vietnam looking at the problems were reporting what they believed reality to be. In retrospect, they were not only wrong, but more importantly, they were influential. The Washington decision-makers could not help but be guided by these continued reports of progress.

Phased withdrawal was a good policy that was being reasonably well executed. In the way of our Vietnam involvement, it was overtaken by events. Not borne of deep conviction in the necessity for a U.S. withdrawal or in the necessity of forcing the GVN to truly carry the load, it was bound to be submerged in the rush of events. A policy more determined might have used the pretext and the fact of the Diem coup and its aftermath as reason to push for the continuation of withdrawal. Instead, the instability and fear of collapse resulting from the Diem coup brought the U.S. to a decision for greater commitment.

End of Summary

CHRONOLOGY

23 Jul 62   *Geneva Accords on Laos*
              14-Nation declaration on the neutrality of Laos.

23 Jul 62   *Sixth Secretary of Defense Conference, Honolulu*
              Called to examine present and future developments in South Vietnam—which looked good. Mr. McNamara initiated immediate planning for the phase-out of U.S. military involvement by 1965 and development of a program to build a GVN military capability strong enough to take over full defense responsibilities by 1965.

26 Jul 62   *JCS Message to CINCPAC*
              CINCPAC was formally instructed to develop a "Comprehensive Plan for South Vietnam" (CPSVN) in line with instructions given at Honolulu.

14 Aug 62   *CINCPAC Message to MACV*
              MACV was directed to draw up a CPSVN designed to ensure GVN military and para-military strength commensurate with its sovereign responsibilities. The CPSVN was to assume the insurgency would be under control in three years, that extensive US support would be available during the three-year period; that those items essential to development of full RVNAF capability would be (largely) available through the military assistance program (MAP).

Oct–Nov.	*GVN National Campaign Plan developed*
1962	In addition to the CPSVN, MACV prepared an outline for an integrated, nationwide offensive military campaign to destroy the insurgency and restore GVN control in South Vietnam. The concept was adopted by the GVN in November.
26 Nov 62	*Military Reorganization Decreed*
	Diem ordered realignment of military chain of command, reorganization of RVNAF, establishment of four CTZ's and a Joint Operations Center to centralize control over current military operations. (JOC became operational on 20 December 1962.)
7 Dec 62	*First Draft of CPSVN Completed*
	CINCPAC disapproved first draft because of high costs and inadequate training provisions.
19 Jan 63	*MACV Letter to CINCPAC, 3010 Ser 0021*
	MACV submitted a revised CPSVN. Extended through FY 1968 and concurred in by the Ambassador, it called for GVN military forces to peak at 458,000 in FY 1964 (RVNAF strength would be 230,900 in FY 1964); cost projected over six years would total $978 million.
22 Jan 63	*OSD(ISA) Message to CINCPAC*
	MAP-Vietnam dollar guide lines issued. Ceilings considerably different from and lower than those in CPSVN.
25 Jan 63	*CINCPAC Letter to JCS, 1010, Ser 0079*
	Approved the CPSVN, supported and justified the higher MAP costs projected by it.
7 Mar 63	*JCSM 190–63*
	JCS recommended SecDef approve the CPSVN; supporting the higher MAP costs, JCS proposed CPSVN be the basis for revision of FY 1964 MAP and development of FY 1965–69 programs.
20 Mar 63	*USMACV "Summary of Highlights, 9 Feb 62–7 Feb 63"*
	Reported continuing, growing RVNAF effectiveness, increased GVN strength economically and politically. The strategic hamlet program looked especially good. MACV forecast winning the military phase in 1963—barring "greatly increased" VC reinforcement and resupply.
17 Apr 63	*NIE 53–63*
	Although "fragile," the situation in SVN did not appear serious; general progress was reported in most areas.
6 May 63	*Seventh SecDef Honolulu Conference*
	Called to [word illegible] the CPSVN. Largely because of prevailing optimism over Vietnam, Mr. McNamara found the CPSVN assistance too costly, the planned withdrawal of U.S. forces too slow and RVNAF development misdirected.
9 May 63	*Buddhist Crisis Begins*
	GVN forces fired on worshipers celebrating Buddha's birthday (several killed, more wounded) for no good cause. Long standing antipathy toward GVN quickly turned into active opposition.

8 May 63   *Two SecDef Memoranda for ASD/ISA*
First: Directed joint ISA/JCS development of plans to replace US forces with GVN troops as soon as possible and to plan the withdrawal of 1,000 US troops by the end of 1963.
Second: Requested the Office, Director of Military Assistance, ISA, "completely rework" the MAP program recommended in the CPSVN and submit new guidelines by 1 September. The Secretary felt CPSVN totals were too high (e.g., expenditures proposed for FY's 1965–68 could be cut by $270 Million in his view).

9 May 63   *JCS Message 9820 to CINCPAC*
Directed CINCPAC to revise the CPSVN and program the withdrawal of 1,000 men by the end of 1963. Force reduction was to be by US units (not individuals); units were to be replaced by specially trained RVNAF units. Withdrawal plans were to be contingent upon continued progress in the counterinsurgency campaign.

11 May 63   *CINCPAC Letter to JCS, 3010 Ser 00447–63*
CINCPAC recommended some changes, then approved MACV's revision of the CPSVN and the MACV plan for withdrawal of 1,000 men. As instructed, those 1,000 men were drawn from logistic and service support slots; actual operations would be unaffected by their absence.

17 May 63   *ASD/ISA Memorandum for the Secretary*
ISA's proposed MAP Vietnam program based on the Secretary's instructions was rejected as still too high.

29 May 63   *OSD/ISA Message to CINCPAC*
CINCPAC was directed to develop three alternative MAP plans for FYs 1965–69 based on these levels:
$585 M (CPSVN recommendation)
$450 M (Compromise)
$365 M (SecDef goal)
MAP for FY 1964 had been set at $180 M.

16 Jun 63   *GVN-Buddhist Truce (State Airgram A-781 to Embassy Saigon, 10 June)*
Reflected temporary and tenuous abatement of GVN-Buddhist hostilities which flared up in May. The truce was repudiated almost immediately by both sides. Buddhist alienation from the GVN polarized; hostilities spread.

17 Jul 63   *DIA Intelligence Summary*
Reported the military situation was unaffected by the political crisis; GVN prospects for continued counterinsurgency progress were "certainly better" than in 1962; VC activity was reduced but VC capability essentially unimpaired.

18 Jul 63   *CINCPAC-proposed MAP program submitted to JCS*
CINCPAC suggested military assistance programs at the three levels set by the JCS but recommended adoption of a fourth Plan developed by CINCPAC. "Plan J" totalled $450.9 M over the five-year period.

4 Aug 63   DIA *Intelligence Bulletin*
Rather suddenly, Viet Cong offensive actions were reported high
for the third consecutive week; the implication was that the VC
were capitalizing on the political crisis and might step up the
insurgency.

14 Aug 63   SACSA *Memorandum for the Secretary*
Discounted the importance of increased VC activity; the comparative magnitude of attacks was low; developments did not yet
seem salient or lasting.

20 Aug 63   *Diem declared martial law; ordered attacks on Buddhist pagodas*
This decree plus repressive measures against the Buddhists shattered hopes of reconciliation, and irrevocably isolated the Diem
government.

20 Aug 63   JCSM629–63
CINCPAC/MACV proposed plan for 1,000-man withdrawal in
three to four increments for planning purposes only; recommended
final decision on withdrawal be delayed until October.

21 Aug 63   *Director,* DIA *Memorandum for SecDef*
Estimated that Diem's acts will have "serious repercussions"
throughout SVN: foresaw more coup and counter-coup activity.
But reported military operations were so far unaffected by these
events.

27 Aug 63   JCSM 640–63
JCS added yet a fifth "Model M" Plan to CINCPAC's four alternative MAP levels. Providing for higher force levels termed necessary
by the JCS, the Model M total was close to $400 M. JCS recom-
mended the Model M Plan be approved.

30 Aug 63   OSD/ISA *Memorandum for the Secretary*
Recommended approval of JCSM 629–63. But noted many "units"
to be withdrawn were ad hoc creations of expendable support
personnel, cautioned that public reaction to "phony" withdrawal
would be damaging: suggested actual strength and authorized
ceiling levels be publicized and monitored.

3 Sep 63   SecDef *Memorandum to* CJCS
Approved JCSM–629–63. Advised JCS against creating special
units as a means to cut back unnecessary personnel; requested the
projected US strength figures through 1963.

5 Sep 63   ASD/ISA *Memoradum to the Secretary*
Concurred in JCS recommendation with minor reservations that
the Model M Plan for military assistance to SVN be approved.

6 Sep 63   SecDef *Memorandum for* CJCS
Approved Model M Plan as the basis for FY 65–69 MAP
planning; advised that US materiel turned over to RVNAF must
be charged to and absorbed by the authorized Model M Plan
ceilings.

11 Sep 63   CJCS *Memorandum for SecDef*
Forwarded the military strength figures (August thru December)

to SecDef; advised that the 1,000-man withdrawal would be counted against the peak October strength (16,732). First increment was scheduled for withdrawal in November, the rest in December.

21 Sep 63   *Presidential Memorandum for the SecDef*
Directed McNamara and Taylor (CJCS) to personally assess the critical situation in SVN—both political and military; to determine what GVN action was required for change and what the US should do to produce such action.

27 Sep 63   *ASD/ISA (ODMA) "MAP Vietnam: Manpower and Financial Summary"*
Approved MAP totals reflected the Model M Plan:

FY 1964	:	$180.6 M
FY 1965–69:		$211.6 M
Total:		$392.2 M

The GVN force levels proposed were substantially below those of the January CPSVN (from a peak strength in FY 1964 of 442,500, levels were to fall to 120,200 in FY 1969).

26 Sep–   *SecDef CJCS Mission to South Vietnam*
2 Oct 63   Positive detailed evidence presented in numerous briefings indicated conditions were good and would improve. Hence, the Secretary ordered acceleration of the planned U.S. force phase-out.

2 Oct 63   *McNamara–Taylor Briefing for the President, and later, the NSC*
Concluded the military campaign has made great progress and continues to progress, but warned that further Diem–Nhu repression could change the "present favorable military trends."

3 Oct 63   *McNamara–Taylor met with President and NSC*
The President approved the military recommendations made by the Secretary and Chairman:

—that MACV and Diem review changes necessary to complete the military campaign in I, II, and III Corps by the end of 1964, in IV Corps by 1965:
—that a training program be established to enable RVNAF to take over military functions from the US by the end of 1965 when the bulk of US personnel could be withdrawn:
—that DOD informally announce plans to withdraw 1,000 men by the end of 1963.

no further reductions in US strength would be made until requirements of the 1964 campaign were clear.

11 Oct 63   *NSAM 263*
Approved the military recommendations contained in the McNamara–Taylor Report; directed no formal announcement be made of implementation of plans to withdraw 1,000 men by the end of 1963.

22 Oct 63   *State Department INR Memo RFE-90*
Assessed trends since July 1963 as evidence of an unfavorable

shift in military balance. (This was one of the first indications that all was not as rosy as MACV *et al* had led McNamara and Taylor to believe.)

1 Nov 63   *Diem Government Overthrown*
The feared political chaos, civil war and collapse of the war did not materialize immediately; US Government was uncertain as to what the new circumstances meant. General Minh headed the junta responsible for the coup.

20 Nov 63   *All-agency Conference on Vietnam, Honolulu*
Ambassador Lodge assessed prospects as hopeful; recommended US continue the policy of eventual military withdrawal from SVN; said announced 1,000-man withdrawal was having salutary effects. MACV agreed. In this light, officials agreed that the Accelerated Plan (speed-up of force withdrawal by six months directed by McNamara in October) should be maintained. McNamara wanted MAP spending held close to OSD's $175.5 million ceiling (because of acceleration, a FY 64 MAP of $187.7 million looked possible).

22 Nov 63   *President Kennedy Assassinated*
One result: US Government policies in general were maintained for the sake of continuity, to allow the new administration time to settle and adjust. This tendency to reinforce existing policies arbitrarily, just to keep them going, extended the phase-out, withdrawal and MAP concepts—probably for too long.

23 Nov 63   *SecDef Memorandum for the President*
Calling GVN political stability vital to the war and calling attention to GVN financial straits, the Secretary said the US must be prepared to increase aid to Saigon. Funding well above current MAP plans was envisaged.

26 Nov 63   *NSAM 273*
President Johnson approved recommendations to continue current policy toward Vietnam put forward at the 20 November Honolulu meeting: reaffirmed US objectives on withdrawal.

3 Dec 63   [material missing]
Region/ISA Memorandum for the ASD/ISA [words missing]
nam developments, for a "fresh new look" at the problem, second echelon leaders outlined a broad interdepartmental "Review of the South Vietnam Situation." This systematic effort did not culminate in high level national reassessment of specific policy re-orientation.

5 Dec 63   *CINCPAC Message to JCS*
Submitted the Accelerated Model Plan version of CPSVN. From a total of 15,200 in FY 1964, US military strength in Vietnam would drop to 11,500 in FY 1965 (*vice* 13,100 recommended by the Model M Plan), to about 3,200 in FY 1966 and 2,600 in FY 1967. GVN force levels were a bit lower but GVN force build-up a bit faster than recommended by the Model M Plan. MAP costs for FYs 1965–1969 totalled $399.4 million (*vice* $392.2 million under Model M Plan).

11 Dec 63 *CM 1079–63 for SecDef*
The adjusted year-end strength figure was 15,394. Although 1,000 men were technically withdrawn, no actual reduction of US strength was achieved. The December figure was *not* 1,000 less than the peak October level.

13 Dec 63 *Director, DIA Memorandum for the Secretary*
Reported the VC had improved combat effectiveness and force posture during 1963, that VC capability was unimpaired. (Quite a different picture had been painted by SACSA in late October: "An Overview of the Vietnam War, 1960–1963," personally directed to the Secretary, was a glowing account of steady military progress.)

30 Jan 64 *Second Coup in Saigon*
General Minh's military regime was replaced by a junta headed by General Khanh.

10, 11, 14, *Deputy Director, CIA Memoranda for SecDef, SecState, et al*
19 Feb 64 Suspicious of progress reports, CIA sent a special group to "look at" South Vietnam. Its independent evaluation revealed a serious and steadily deteriorating GVN situation. Vietcong gains and, significantly, the quality and quantity of VC arms had increased. The Strategic Hamlet Program was "at virtual standstill." The insurgency tide seemed to be "going against GVN" in all four Corps.

6 Mar 64 *Eighth SecDef Conference on Vietnam, Honolulu*
Participants agreed that the military situation was definitely deteriorating, that insurgency would probably continue beyond 1965, that the US must immediately determine what had to be done to make up for the setback(s).

9–16 *McNamara/Taylor Trip to Vietnam*
Mar 64 Personally confirmed the gravity of the Vietnam situation.

16 Mar 64 *SecDef Memorandum for the President: "Report on Trip to Vietnam"*
Mr. McNamara reported the situation was "unquestionably" worse than in September. (RVNAF desertion rates were up: GVN military position was weak and the Vietcong, with increased NVN support, was strong.) Concluding that more US support was necessary, the Secretary made twelve recommendations. These included:

> —More economic assistance, military training, equipment and advisory assistance, as needed.
> —Continued high-level US overflights of GVN borders; authorization for "hot pursuit" and ground operations in Laos.
> —Prepare to initiate—on 72 hours' notice—Laos and Cambodia border control operations and retaliatory actions against North Vietnam.
> —Make plans to initiate—on 30 days' notice—a "program of Graduated Overt Military Pressures" against North Vietnam.

Mr. McNamara called the policy of reducing existing US personnel where South Vietnamese could assume their functions "still sound" but said no major reductions could be expected in the near future. He felt US training personnel could be substantially reduced before the end of 1965.

| 17 Mar 64 | *NSAM 299* |

The President approved the twelve recommendations presented by Mr. McNamara and directed all agencies concerned to carry them out promptly.

[material missing]

forces was superseded by the policy of providing South Vietnam assistance and support as long as required to bring aggression and terrorism under control (as per NSAM 288).

| 6 May 64 | *CINCPAC Message to MACV* |

Indicated growing US military commitment: this 1500-man augmentation raised the total authorized level to 17,000.

| 1–2 Jun 64 | *Special Meeting on Southeast Asia, Honolulu* |

Called in part to examine the GVN National Campaign Plan—which was failing. The conferees agreed to increase RVNAF effectiveness by extending and intensifying the US advisory effort as MACV recommended.

| 25 Jun 64 | *MACV Message 325390 to JCS* |

Formal MACV request for 900 additional advisory personnel. His justification for advisors at the battalion level and for more advisors at district and sector levels was included. Also, 80 USN advisors were requested to establish a Junk Force and other maritime counterinsurgency measures.

| 4 Jul 64 | *CINCPAC Message to JCS* |

CINCPAC recommended approval of the MACV proposal for intensification of US advisory efforts.

| 15 Jul 64 | *Saigon EMBTEL 108* |

Ambassador Taylor reported that revised VC strength estimates now put the enemy force between 28,000 and 34,000. No cause for alarm, he said the new estimate did demonstrate the magnitude of the problem and the need to raise the level of US/GVN efforts. Taylor thought a US strength increase to 21,000 by the end of the year would be sufficient.

| 16 Jul 64 | *MACV Message 6180 to CINCPAC* |

MACV requested 3,200 personnel to support the expansion (by 900) of US advisory efforts—or 4,200 more men over the next nine months.

| 17 Jul 64 | *EMBTEL* |

Ambassador Taylor concurred in MACV's proposed increase, recommended prompt approval and action.

| 21 Jul 64 | *State 205 to Saigon* |

Reported Presidential approval (at the 21 July NSC meeting) of the MACV deployment package.

Dec 64   *Further increases*
Total US strength was 23,000: further deployments were on the way.

I. 1962

A. EARLY 1962

From mid-1962 to early 1964 the U.S. government went through a formal planning process, ostensibly designed to disengage the U.S. from direct and large-scale military involvement in Vietnam. In retrospect, this experience falls into place as a more or less isolated episode of secondary importance; eventually abortive, it had little impact on the evolution of the Vietnam war. It does, however, serve as a vehicle for understanding one long phase of the war and the U.S. role in it.

The genesis lay in a conjuncture of circumstances during the first half of 1962 that prompted the U.S. to shift its Vietnam perspective from the hitherto restricted one of largely tactical responses to current, localized, and situational requirements, to fitting these to more strategic and purposeful long-range courses of action. The expanded perspective was programmatic in outlook, and oriented toward specific goals—end the insurgency and withdraw militarily from Vietnam.

At the outset, the motivation for the idea of phased withdrawal of U.S. forces was threefold: in part, the belief that developments in Vietnam itself were going well; in part, doubt over the efficacy of using U.S. forces in an internal war; and in part, the demands of other crises in the world that were more important to Washington than Vietnam. In the course of materializing into policy and assuming form as plans, these premises were transformed into conclusions, desiderata institutionalized as objectives, and wish took on the character and force of imperative.

For example, in March 1962, Secretary McNamara testified before Congress that he was "optimistic" over prospects for U.S. success in aiding Vietnam, and "encouraged at the progress the South Vietnamese are making." He expressed conviction that the U.S. would attain its objectives there. But he emphasized that the U.S. strategy was to avoid participating directly in the war while seeking an early military conclusion:

> I would say definitely we are approaching it from the point of view of trying to clean it up, and terminating subversion, covert aggression, and combat operations. . . .
>
> . . . We are wise to carry on the operations against the Communists in that area by assisting native forces rather than by using U.S. forces for combat.
>
> Not only does that release U.S. forces for use elsewhere in the world or for stationing in the United States, but also it is probably the most effective way to combat the Communist subversion and covert aggression. To introduce white forces—U.S. forces—in large numbers there today, while it might have an initial favorable military impact would almost certainly lead to adverse political and in the long run adverse military operations. And therefore, we think the program we are carrying out is the

most effective one and certainly it is directed toward termination of operations as rapidly as possible.

In late spring of 1962, the military situation in South Vietnam showed hopeful signs of at last having turned a corner. The various programs under way, initiated the previous fall as a result of decisions in NSAM No. 111, appeared to be bearing out the basic soundness of the new approach. Assessments and evaluations being reported from the field indicated a pattern of progress on a broad front, and their consistency through time reinforced the impression. By midyear the prospects looked bright. Continuing favorable developments now held forth the promise of eventual success, and to many the end of the insurgency seemed in sight. This optimism was not without the recognition that there were unsolved political problems and serious soft spots in certain areas of the military effort. But U.S. leadership, both on the scene in Vietnam as well as in Washington, was confident and cautiously optimistic. In some quarters, even a measure of euphoria obtained.

At the same time, events outside Vietnam, some of them ostensibly unrelated, were asserting a direct and immediate relevance for U.S. policy and strategy in Vietnam. As competing priorities, they far overshadowed Vietnam. In the larger scheme of things, an indefinite military commitment in Southeast Asia was being relegated perforce to a parenthetical diversion the nation could then ill afford. More central issues in Berlin, Cuba, and in Laos were at stake, perhaps even to the extent of survival.

Looming foremost was the Berlin problem. Fraught with grave overtones of potential nuclear confrontation with the USSR, it reached crisis proportions in the spring of 1962 over the air corridor issue, and after a temporary lull, flared anew in early summer. By the first of July it was again as tense as ever. U.S. reserves had been recalled to active duty, additional forces were deployed to Europe, and domestic Civil Defense activities, including shelter construction programs, were accelerated.

The burgeoning Cuba problem too was taking on a pressing urgency by virtue of both its proximity and growing magnitude. The Castro aspects alone were becoming more than a vexing localized embarrassment. Given the volatile Caribbean political climate, Cuban inspired mischief could raise tensions to the flash point momentarily. Moreover, by early summer of 1962 increasing evidence of Soviet machinations to exploit Cuba militarily was rapidly adding an alarming strategic dimension. Though the nature and full significance of these latter developments would not be revealed until the climactic Cuban Missile Crisis a few months later, the U.S. was already apprehensive of serious danger on its very doorstep. Official interpretive evaluations at the time saw an intimate causal nexus between Berlin and Cuba.

Finally, another set of factors altering the strategic configuration in Southeast Asia and affecting the U.S. position there also came to a head in mid-summer of 1962. These were developments regarding Laos, which impinged upon and helped reshape the U.S. relationship toward Vietnam. In the fall of 1961 and through the spring of 1962 the U.S., its objectives frustrated in Laos, had decided to salvage as much as possible by settling for neutralization. After lengthy and complex diplomatic maneuvering, this was essentially achieved by early summer. On 23 July 1962 the 14-nation declaration and protocol on the neutrality of Laos was signed formally, ending the 15-month Geneva Conference on Laos. The outcome had at once the effect of extricating the U.S. from one insoluble dilemma and serving as a stark object lesson for another. The

Laos settlement now both allowed the U.S. a free hand to concentrate on Vietnam and provided the incentive and determination to bring to a close its military commitment there as well—but this time successfully.

It was in this spirit and context that the U.S. decided to pursue actively the policy objective of divesting itself of direct military involvement of U.S. personnel in the Vietnam insurgency. The aim was to create militarily favorable conditions so that further U.S. military involvement would no longer be needed. To this end, two prerequisites had to be satisfied: bringing the insurgency effectively under control; and simultaneously, developing a militarily viable South Vietnam capable of carrying its own defense burden without U.S. military help. In phase with the progress toward both these goals, there then could be proportionate reductions in U.S. forces.

B. THE SECRETARY OF DEFENSE HONOLULU DECISIONS OF JULY 1962

In July 1962, as the prospect of the neutralization of Laos by the Geneva Conference became imminent, policy attention deliberately turned toward the remaining Vietnam problem. At the behest of the President, the Secretary of Defense undertook to reexamine the situation there and address himself to its future—with a view to assuring that it be brought to a successful conclusion within a reasonable time. Accordingly, he called a full-dress conference on Vietnam at CINCPAC Headquarters in Hawaii. On 23 July, the same day that the 14-nation neutralization declaration on Laos was formally signed in Geneva, the Sixth Secretary of Defense Conference convened in Honolulu.

The series of briefings and progress reports presented at the conference depicted a generally favorable situation. Things were steadily improving and promised to continue. Most programs underway were moving forward, as the statistical indicators clearly demonstrated. Those directly related to prosecution of the counterinsurgency effort showed measurable advances being made toward winning the war. Programs for expanding and improving RVNAF capability were likewise coming along well, and in most cases were ahead of schedule. Confidence and optimism prevailed.

Impressed, Mr. McNamara acknowledged that the "tremendous progress" in the past six months was gratifying. He noted, however, that these achievements had been the result of short-term ad hoc actions on a crash basis. What was needed now was to conceive a long-range concerted program of systematic measures for training and equipping the RVNAF and for phasing out major U.S. advisory and logistic support activities. The Secretary then asked how long a period it would take before the VC could be expected to be eliminated as a significant force. COMUSMACV, in reply to the direct question, estimated about one year from the time the RVNAF, the Civil Guard, and the Self-Defense Corps became fully operational and began to press the VC in all areas.

The Secretary said that a conservative view had to be taken and to assume it would take three years instead of one, that is, by the latter part of 1965. He observed that it might be difficult to retain public support for U.S. operations in Vietnam indefinitely. Political pressures would build up as losses continued. Therefore, he concluded, planning must be undertaken now and a program devised to phase out U.S. military involvement. He, therefore, directed that a comprehensive long-range program be developed for building up South Vietnamese military capability for taking over defense responsibilities and phasing out the U.S. role, assuming that it would require approximately three years (end 1965) for the RVNAF to be trained to the point that they could cope with the VC. The program was to include training requirements, equipment requirements, U.S. advisory requirements, and U.S. units.

For the record, the formulation of the decisions made and the directives for action to be taken resulting from the Conference was as follows:

> *a.* Prepare plans for the gradual scaling down of USMACV during the next 3-year period, eliminating U.S. units and detachments as Vietnamese were trained to perform their functions.
>
> *b.* Prepare programs with the objective of giving South Vietnam an adequate military capability without the need for special U.S. military assistance, to include (1) a long-range training program to establish an officer corps able to manage GVN military operations, and (2) a long-range program and requirements to provide the necessary materiel to make possible a turnover to RVNAF three years from July 1962.

The U.S. Military Assistance Advisory Group, Vietnam, had been augmented in 1961 by aviation, communications, and intelligence units, as well as by Special Forces and other advisers. The Secretary of Defense plainly intended that plans be devised for terminating the mission of the augmenting units.

Three days later on 26 July, the JCS formally directed CINCPAC to develop a Comprehensive Plan for South Vietnam (CPSVN) in accordance with the Secretary's decisions of 23 July. CINCPAC, in turn, so instructed COMUSMACV on 14 August, at the same time furnishing additional guidance and terms of reference elaborating on the original SecDef decisions at Honolulu and the JCS directive. The stated objective of the CPSVN was given as:

> Develop a capability within military and para-military forces of the GVN by the end of CY 65 that will help the GVN to achieve the strength necessary to exercise permanent and continued sovereignty over that part of Vietnam which lies below the demarcation line without the need for continued U.S. special military assistance.

Development of the plan was to be based on the following assumptions:

> *a.* The insurgency will be under control at the end of three years (end of CY 65).
>
> *b.* Extensive U.S. support will continue to be required during the three year period, both to bring the insurgency under control and to prepare GVN forces for early take-over of U.S. activities.
>
> *c.* Previous MAP funding ceilings for SVN are not applicable. Program those items essential to do this job.

C. NATIONAL CAMPAIGN PLAN

Planning, in two complementary modes, got underway, immediately. Concurrently with development of the unilateral U.S. CPSVN, USMACV planners prepared a concept and proposed outline of a GVN National Campaign Plan (NCP) for launching an integrated nation-wide campaign of offensive military operations to eliminate the insurgency and restore the country to GVN control. A central purpose was to reorganize and redispose the VNAF and streamline the chain of command, in order to improve responsiveness, coordination, and general effectiveness of the military effort against the VC. Greater authority would be centralized in the Vietnamese Joint General Staff (JGS); Corps Tactical Zones (CTZs) would be increased from three to four; and each CTZ would have its own direct air and naval support.

Over and above organizational considerations, the NCP provided for systematic intensification of aggressive operations in all CTZs to keep the VC off balance, while simultaneously conducting clear and hold operations in support of the expanding Strategic Hamlet Program. Priority of military tasks was first to concentrate on areas north of Saigon, then gradually shift toward the south to Saigon and the Delta.

The proposed NCP was submitted to the GVN in October and a month later was adopted in concept and outline. On 26 November, President Diem promulgated the necessary implementing decrees and directives to effect the reorganization of the SVN armed forces and realign the chain of command. An integrated Joint Operations Center (JOC) was also established and became operational on 20 December, with representation from JGS and its counterpart in USMACV to centralize control over current operations. The following January the draft of a detailed implementing plan for the NCP itself was completed and subsequently approved.

II.   1963

A.   COMPREHENSIVE PLAN FOR SOUTH VIETNAM

Meanwhile, the first cut at the CPSVN was also completed by the MACV planners. It was forwarded to CINCPAC on 7 December, but CINCPAC, upon reviewing the proposed plan, considered it infeasible because of the high costs involved and the marginal capacity of the RVNAF to train the necessary personnel in the required skills within the time frame specified. As a result of CINCPAC's reaction to the initial version, the CPSVN was revised and resubmitted by COMUSMACV on 19 January 1963. The new CPSVN covered the period FY 1963–1968. In transmitting it, COMUSMACV recommended that future Military Assistance Programs (MAPs) be keyed therefore to the CPSVN. He also indicated that the CPSVN had been coordinated with the Ambassador, who concurred in it.

Force levels laid out in the CPSVN provided for total personnel increases reaching a peak of 458,000 (regular and para-military) in FY 64, with RVNAF manning strength raised from 215,000 to a peak of 230,000 in the same FY period and remaining on that plateau thereafter. Order of magnitude costs (in $ millions) of the CPSVN would come to:

FY 63	FY 64	FY 65	FY 66	FY 67	FY 68	Total
187	218	153	138	169	113	978

CINCPAC approved the CPSVN as submitted and sent it on to the JCS. However, in the interim, OSD had issued dollar guidelines for MAP planning for Vietnam. The ceilings indicated therein were significantly at variance with the costing figures employed by MACV in developing the CPSVN. When CINCPAC forwarded the plan, therefore, he went to considerable lengths to explain the discrepancies and to support and justify the higher costs. Comparison of the DOD dollar guidelines with the CPSVN, projected through FY 69, showed a net difference of approximately 66 million dollars, with the preponderance of the increase occurring in FY 64. Most of this difference was accounted for by additional Packing-Crating-Handling-Transportation (PCHT) costs associated with the CPSVN but not accommodated in the DOD guideline figures.

The body of the CPSVN laid out the costs in relation to the DOD dollar guidelines, as follows:

CPSVN—DOD DOLLAR GUIDELINES COST COMPARISON ($ millions)

	FY 64	FY 65	FY 66	FY 67	FY 68	FY 69	Total
CPSVN *	218	153	138	169	113	110	901
DOD Guidelines	160	165	160	150	140	122	897
Difference	+58	−12	−22	+19	−27	−12	+4
PORT Added	+11	+11	+11	+11	+10	+8	+62
Difference	+69	−1	−11	+30	−17	−4	+66

* Excludes PCHT.

The rationale offered was that, in order to prosecute the counter-insurgency to a successful conclusion, while at the same time building up GVN capability to allow early withdrawal of U.S. forces, the major costs of the program had to be compressed into the FY 63–65 time frame, with a particular increase in FY 64 and another following U.S. withdrawal in FY 67. But clearly most of the greater cost throughout the period reflected PCHT.

The pattern of force levels for all South Vietnamese forces that the CPSVN provided for, including the separate non-MAP funded Civilian Irregular Defense Group, is shown in Figure 1. [Figure 1 missing.]

Since the ultimate objective of the CPSVN was early withdrawal of U.S. special military assistance, the plan provided for phasing out U.S. advisory forces. The affected major commands of USMACV that would largely not be required after FY 66 were:

1. The U.S. Marine Element which provided helicopter transportation support.
2. The 2d Air Division which provided the USAF portion of the special military assistance support performed in SVN. This support included "Farmgate" (Fighter), "Mule Train" (Transportation), and "Able Mable" (Reconnaissance). It also provided USAF administration and logistical support for USAF personnel and equipment engaged in special military assistance to SVN.
3. U.S. Army Support Group Vietnam (USASGV) which provided the U.S. Army portion of the special military assistance support for SVN (except that performed by MAAG and Headquarters MACV), including helicopter and fixed wing air transportation, signal communications, and special forces. It also provided U.S. administrative and logistical support for assigned and attached personnel and equipment engaged in the special military assistance.
4. Headquarters Support Activity Saigon (HSAS) which provided administrative support to the U.S. Headquarters and other U.S. government sponsored agencies and activities located in Saigon.
5. MAAG Vietnam would have its strength reduced by one-half after FY 65. Only 1,500 MAAG personnel were to remain in country after FY 68.

The target schedule for U.S. force withdrawal, as then forecast, is contained in Figure 2.

FIGURE 2

CPSVN - Forecast of Phase-Out of U.S. Forces
(*thousands*)

Organization	FY 63	FY 64	FY 65	FY 66	FY 67	FY 68
HQ USMACV	.3	.4	.4	.1	.0	.0
HQ MAAG	3.0	3.0	3.0	1.7	1.6	1.5
2D Air DIV	2.2	2.3	2.3	1.1	.0	.0
USASG (V)	5.1	5.5	5.5	2.7	.0	.0
USMC Helicopter Unit	.5	.5	.5	.0	.0	.0
HSAS	.5	.5	.5	.3	.0	.0
TOTAL	11.6	12.2	12.2	5.9	1.6	1.5

On 7 March 1963, the JCS accepted the MACV CPSVN in toto and forwarded it to the Secretary of Defense. They recommended approval, and proposed that it be the basis for both revising the FY 64 MAP and development of the FY 65-69 MAPs. They requested an early decision on the CPSVN because the greatest increase would occur in the FY 64 MAP. The JCS fully supported the higher costs of the CPSVN above the DOD dollar guidelines.

In OSD, the proposed CPSVN underwent staffing review in ISA MA Plans and elsewhere. Draft responses to the JCS were prepared and then withdrawn. Secretary McNamara was not satisfied with either the high funding levels or the adequacy of the plan regarding exactly how the RVN forces were to take over from the U.S. to effect the desired phase-out of the U.S. military commitment. In mid-April he decided to withhold action pending full review of the CPSVN at another Honolulu conference which he expressly scheduled for that purpose for 6 May. Meantime, the various OSD agencies concerned were instructed to prepare detailed analyses and background studies for him.

The main focus of interest of the Secretary of Defense was on the policy objective behind the CPSVN, namely, to reduce systematically the scale of U.S. involvement until phased out completely. However, the beginnings of a counter-current were already evident. New demands for increases all around were to overwhelm the phasing out objective. Ad hoc requirements for more U.S. forces were being generated piecemeal, each in its own right sufficiently reasonable and so honored. This current, counter-current dynamic can be illustrated well by Mr. McNamara's decisions of late March. As part of the Secretary's policy of demanding strict accounting and tight control on authorized U.S. in-country strength ceilings, he asked for the latest reading on projected U.S. military strength to be reached in Vietnam. He was reassured by the Chairman, JCS, that the estimated peak would not exceed 15,640 personnel. Yet, on this very same day, the Secretary approved a substantial force augmentation, requested earlier, for FARMGATE and airlift support, involving 111 additional aircraft and a total of approximately 1475 additional personnel. Other similar special requirements and ad hoc approvals soon were to follow.

Assessments of continuing favorable developments in the improving Vietnam situation in the spring of 1963 seemed to warrant more than ever going ahead with the planned phase out. The general tenor of appraisals at the USMACV level were that the RVNAF had regained the initiative from the VC and that the GVN position had improved militarily, economically, and politically. Evaluations expressed in the "Summary of Highlights" covering the first year of MACV's existence cited in detail the record of the increasing scale, frequency, and effectiveness of RVNAF operations, while those of the VC were declining. Casualty ratios favored RVNAF by more than two to one, and the balance of weapons captured vs weapons lost had also shifted to the GVN side. Cited as perhaps the most significant progress was the Strategic Hamlet Program. The future looked even brighter, e.g., ". . . barring greatly increased resupply and reinforcement of the Viet Cong by infiltration, the military phase of the war can be virtually won in 1963."

Other evaluations, though more conservative, still tended to corroborate this optimism. NIE 53-63, issued 17 April 1963, found no particular deterioration or serious problems in the military situation in South Vietnam; on the contrary, it saw some noticeable improvements and general progress over the past year. The worst that it could say was that the situation "remains fragile."

B. SECRETARY OF DEFENSE HONOLULU DECISIONS OF MAY 1963

At the 6 May Honolulu Conference, briefing reports again confirmed gratifying progress in the military situation. Addressing the CPSVN, Mr. McNamara questioned the need for more Vietnamese forces in FY 68 (224.4 thousand) than the present level of 215 thousand. His reasoning was that a poor nation of 12 million like Vietnam could not support that many men under arms. Qualitatively, furthermore, the planned evolution of VNAF seemed overambitious in terms of sophisticated weaponry such as fighter aircraft. In sum, the Secretary felt the CPSVN assumed an unrealistically high force level for the SVN military establishment and assigned it equipment that was both unduly complicated to operate and expensive to procure and maintain.

Based on these considerations, the Secretary of Defense concluded that, if the insurgency came under control in FY 65 as anticipated, the U.S. MAP investment in SVN thereafter should not be more than at the rate of about $50 million per year. In his view, thus, the $573 million MAP proposed in the CPSVN for the period FY 65 through FY 68 was at least $270 million higher than an acceptable program.

With regard to phasing out U.S. forces, the Secretary of Defense stated that the pace contemplated in the CPSVN was too slow. He wanted it revised to accomplish a more rapid withdrawal by accelerating training programs in order to speed up replacement of U.S. units by GVN units as fast as possible. While recognizing that the build-up of RVNAF was inherently a slow process, he stressed that in the instance of some U.S. units which had been in SVN since 1961, it would be possible more rapidly to transfer functions to Vietnamese. Specifically toward this end, he decided that 1,000 U.S. military personnel should be withdrawn from South Vietnam by the end of CY 63 and directed that concrete plans be so drawn up.

On returning to Washington the Secretary of Defense instructed the ASD(ISA) on 8 May to develop, in coordination with the Joint Staff, a plan for replacing U.S. forces currently deployed in Vietnam with indigenous SVN forces as rapidly as possible, and particularly, to prepare a plan for withdrawing 1,000 U.S. troops before the end of 1965. In another memorandum the same day to the ASD(ISA) regarding the MAP, he noted that "the plan needs to be completely reworked." He therefore instructed ISA also to develop a new, lower

MAP for Vietnam for the period FY 65 through 69, requesting that the ISA recommendations be submitted by the first of September.

A day later, on 9 May, the JCS formally directed CINCPAC to take the necessary actions resulting from the Honolulu Conference and revise the CPSVN. Guidance and terms of reference were provided reflecting the Secretary of Defense reactions and specifying the decisions reached. Singled out especially was the requirement for U.S. force withdrawal. The JCS directive read:

> As a matter or urgency a plan for the withdrawal of about 1,000 U.S. troops before the end of the year should be developed based upon the assumption that the progress of the counterinsurgency campaign would warrant such a move. Plans should be based upon withdrawal of US units (as opposed to individuals) by replacing them with selected and specially trained RVNAF units.

COMUSMACV in turn was tasked to draft the revised CPSVN and prepare a plan for the 1000-man reduction. CINCPAC, after some changes and revisions, concurred in the proposed plans and forwarded them to the JCS on 11 May. The revised outline CPSVN now provided for the following SVN force levels (in thousands):

	FY 64	FY 65	FY 66	FY 67	FY 68	FY 69
Total Military and Para-military	447.4	445.5	362.9	317.1	268.8	214.7

MAP levels provided for were as follows (in $ millions):

FY 64	FY 65	FY 66	FY 67	FY 68	FY 69	Grand Total
178.9	149.0	130.3	120.4	100.5	85.0	764.1

The proposed plan for withdrawal of the first increment of U.S. forces, in compliance with instructions, emphasized units rather than individuals, but the list of so-called "units" scheduled to be included were all smaller than company size. All Services were represented. The criteria employed, also based on earlier guidance, were to select most of the personnel from service support and logistics skills most easily spared and whose release would have least effect on operations. The total came to 1,003 U.S. military personnel to be withdrawn from South Vietnam by the end of December 1963.

C. MAP PLANNING

ISA meanwhile developed tentative dollar guidelines for MAP planning for Vietnam. The first cut, based on the Secretary of Defense's own suggested total for the FY 65–69 period, was rejected by the Secretary of Defense as too high and returned, with various desired reductions entered by the Secretary of Defense. Reconciling the MAP with the CPSVN proved to be a difficult problem. As CPSVN succeeded, it was logical that MAP would have to increase; yet CPSVN tried to cut back MAP as well. For instance, the contemplated phaseout of U.S. artillery-spotter aircraft squadrons entailed an add-on to MAP to accommodate the squadron's equipment and maintenance after transferral to the Vietnamese.

[Material missing]

therefore would have to be absorbed within the authorized Model Plan ceilings.

Nonetheless, there were still further refinements made. As finally published, the approved MAP reflecting the Model M Plan version of the CPSVN provided for the following SVN active military strength levels (in thousands):

	FY 64	*FY 65*	*FY 66*	*FY 67*	*FY 68*	*FY 69*
ARVN	207.5	201.3	177.5	124.5	104.8	103.9
Total (All Services regular and para-military)	442.5	437.0	340.2	142.1	122.2	120.2

Costing levels were as follows (in $ millions):

FY 64	*FY 65*	*FY 66*	*FY 67*	*FY 68*	*FY 69*	*Total*
180.6	153.0	107.7	46.2	44.6	40.7	392.2

This final product represented a radical reduction in both force levels and financial investment after FY 66, consistent with the Administration's original policy goal of ending the war and the U.S. military involvement by December 1965.

D.   1000-MAN WITHDRAWAL PLAN

Meanwhile, planning for the 1000-man withdrawal directed by the Secretary of Defense on 6 May was split off from the CPSVN proper and the MAP, and was being treated as a separate entity. On 20 August, the JCS, concurring in the proposed plan developed by COMUSMACV and CINCPAC, forwarded it to the Secretary of Defense. They recommended approval at this time for planning purposes only; final decision was to depend upon circumstances as they developed. The JCS also seconded CINCPAC's added proposal to withdraw the 1000 troops in three or four increments, rather than all at one time. The reasons given were that this would be more practical and efficient for the U.S., would minimize the impact on on-going military operational activities within South Vietnam, and would afford the opportunity for "news prominence and coverage over an extended period of time."

ISA, with certain reservations, recommended approval of the withdrawal plan submitted by JCS. ISA pointed out to the Secretary of Defense that the plan as it stood would not draw all of the 1000 troops from U.S. units that were to be relieved by adequately trained SVN units, as had been intended. Many of the so-called "units" designated therein actually were not bona fide existing units but were specially formed "service support units" made up of random individuals most easily spared throughout USMACV. ISA cautioned that the arbitrary creation of such ad hoc "units" solely for the purpose of the withdrawal might backfire in press reaction. ISA also recommended, in order to show credibly that the final year-end U.S. in-country strength had dropped by 1000 from peak strength, that U.S. military strength figures in Vietnam be made public, and that the actual strength as well as the authorized ceilings at any given time be carefully monitored to insure that the desired reductions were indeed achieved.

A few days later the Secretary of Defense approved the 1000-man withdrawal plan forwarded in JCSM-629-63 as recommended. He agreed, however, with ISA and advised the JCS against creating special units if their only purpose was to be a holding unit as a vehicle for withdrawal of individuals. He also requested that he be provided with a projection of U.S. military strength in South Vietnam, by month, for the period September through December 1963.

The following week the Chairman, JCS, responded to the Secretary of Defense's request and furnished the following projection of end-of-month U.S. military strengths in South Vietnam:

August	16,201
September	16,483
October	16,732
November	16,456
December	15,732

It was noted that the planned 1000-man withdrawal would represent a reduction based on the October peak strength. The first increment of 276 personnel would be withdrawn during November and the remaining increments in December. This, as it turned out, was destined to be changed somewhat before the withdrawal was executed.

E. THE BUDDHIST CRISIS

While the CPSVN-MAP and withdrawal planning were going on, significant developments altering the character of the entire situation to which the planning effort was addressed—in fact threatening to invalidate the very premises from which the planning sprung—were occurring within South Vietnam. The Buddhist crisis was rocking the foundations of what precarious political stability the Diem government enjoyed and there was growing concern about its effect on the prosecution of the war against the VC and on improvements of RVNAF.

A series of incidents beginning early in May revealed the deep divisions between militant Buddhist factions, who purported to speak for the bulk of the South Vietnamese population, and the Government. Lack of popular support for the Diem regime had now turned to open opposition. As passions flared and Buddhist activism was met with increasingly severe countermeasures, violence spread and grew more serious. A tenuous truce was reached briefly between Buddhist leaders and the GVN on 10 June (formally signed on 16 June) in a mutual effort to reduce tensions—but proved short-lived. Almost immediately the actions of both sides repudiated the agreements.

The U.S. began to be apprehensive about the possible consequences of the Diem government falling as the result of a coup. By early July, the crisis was recognized as serious at the highest levels of the U.S. Government.

Through mid-July assessments remained reasonably reassuring. There was little evidence of impact on the military sector. In fact, indications pointed to the military situation continuing to improve. DIA reported on 17 July that the general level of VC-initiated actions during the first six months of 1963 was considerably lower than for the same period the year before. Battalion and company-size attacks were at about half the 1962 level. It was noted, however, that despite reduced activity, VC capability remained essentially unimpaired. Regarding the progress of South Vietnamese counterinsurgency efforts, the DIA evaluation was cautiously optimistic: though there was still a long way to go, GVN prospects "are certainly better than they were one year ago."

Quite abruptly, a disturbing element began to emerge. Little more than two weeks later, the DIA Intelligence Bulletin of 4 August reported a significant increase in the level of VC offensive actions. Moreover, the rate was high for the third week in a row since mid-July. The clear implication was that the VC at last were taking advantage of the opportunity presented by the Buddhist crisis. It had been expected—and feared—that they would seek to hasten political collapse and exploit whatever military vulnerabilities there were. The U.S.

was thus justifiably concerned lest the recent revived VC aggressiveness be the opening phase of a stepped up insurgency. Within ten days of this DIA report, however, a reevaluation of the significance to be attached to the increased rate of enemy actions allayed fears somewhat. On 14 August, SACSA, reporting to the Secretary of Defense, discounted the upsurge in VC activity over the past month. Its magnitude, comparatively, was below the average of the preceding year and fell far short of the previous high. In this perspective, SACSA saw no cause to read undue implications into developments that were as yet neither particularly salient nor of long duration.

The political crisis meanwhile took a turn for the worse. President Diem, in an attempt to regain control, declared martial law on 20 August. The decree was accompanied by forcible entry into pagodas and mass arrests of Buddhist leaders and laity, and was immediately followed by a series of preemptory repressive measures. Any hope of reconciliation was now shattered, and the Diem government was irrevocably isolated.

The Director, DIA, in a special report to the Secretary of Defense, expressed concern that the declaration of martial law "will have serious repercussions throughout the country." He foresaw further coup or counter-coup activity in the making, though for the time being the military had effectively assumed full control. So far, he saw little military effect on the war effort; relatively few troops had been withdrawn from normal missions. At an August 31 review of the problem for Vice President Johnson, Secretary of State Rusk and Secretary McNamara agreed that U.S. planning had to be based on two principles—that the U.S. would not pull out of Vietnam until the war were won, and that it would not participate in a coup d'etat against Diem.

For the next month, as the precarious political situation balanced on the brink of imminent disaster, U.S. anxieties mounted. The Administration was confronted by a dilemma. It was helpless to ameliorate conditions as long as Diem remained in power—nor did it want to approve and support such a regime. Yet at the same time, it was equally helpless to encourage a change of government—there was no feasible replacement anywhere on the South Vietnamese political horizon. The upshot was an ambivalent policy of watchful waiting toward the GVN, while the main preoccupation and focus of attention was on the conduct of the South Vietnamese military forces and the progress of the counterinsurgency programs. These still remained the first order of business.

F.   MCNAMARA-TAYLOR MISSION TO SOUTH VIETNAM, OCTOBER 1963

By the middle of September, the President was deeply concerned over the critical political situation, but more importantly, over its effect on the war. A decision juncture had been reached. At issue was the U.S. military commitment in South Vietnam; a redirection of U.S. policy and objectives might be required. On 21 September, the President directed the Secretary of Defense, in company with the Chairman, JCS, to proceed to South Vietnam for a personal examination of the military aspects of the situation. The President gave as the purpose of the trip ". . . my desire to have the best possible on-the-spot appraisal of the military and para-military effort to defeat the Viet Cong." He stated that there had been, at least until recently, "heartening results," but that political deterioration since May had raised serious questions about the continued effectiveness of these efforts and the prospects for success. The President, therefore, needed an assessment of the present situation, and if the McNamara-Taylor prognosis were not hopeful, they were to recommend needed actions by the SVN and steps the U.S. should take to bring about those actions. [Doc. 139]

The Secretary of Defense and the CJCS, accompanied by a team of civilian and military assistants to help in the survey, arrived in South Vietnam on 26 September and returned to Washington on 2 October. During their visit, detailed data were compiled for them, presentations prepared, extensive briefings given, conferences convened, and consultations held. Emerging from the investigations and appraisals was a body of positive evidence indicating that conditions were good and prospects improving. In fact, in the course of these reassurances, the Secretary of Defense decided to order a speed up of the planned program for release of U.S. forces. In guidance furnished at the time, he directed that the projected schedules for force reduction provided for in the currently approved Model M Plan version of the CPSVN be accelerated by approximately six months. Accordingly, necessary planning revisions were undertaken immediately on a priority basis.

In contrast to the generally favorable military situation, however, there were grave misgivings about the political state of affairs. Earlier, a draft text of a proposed letter from the President of the United States to President Diem of the RVN had been forwarded by cable to the Secretary of Defense and the Ambassador, with a request for their reaction and comments. President Kennedy himself thought the letter too extreme, and would reluctantly resort to it only if the situation was found so serious that such direct US Presidential pressure was necessary. The text of the proposed letter was characterized by harsh, blunt candor. In effect it laid down an ultimatum: unless the GVN changed the repressive policies, methods, and actions practiced by some individual officials and gained for itself a broad base of popular political support, the United States might have to consider disassociating itself from the Diem Government, and further US support of Vietnam might become impossible. The Secretary of Defense and the Ambassador promptly responded with a strong recommendation against transmitting the proposed letter. Both agreed that the situation was indeed very serious, but that it was not likely to be influenced by such a letter to Diem.

The proposed Presidential letter was not sent. Instead, many of the points were conveyed in conversations with Diem, and, just before the departure of the McNamara-Taylor Mission from Vietnam, another letter to President Diem was composed and sent in its place. The new version was not only much softer in tone and more circumspect but went out over the signature of General Taylor as Chairman, Joint Chiefs of Staff. The letter was dated 1 October 1963, but was delivered on 2 October, with the approval of the Secretary of Defense and with the concurrence of the US Ambassador to Vietnam (Lodge).

In this letter the CJCS offered his personal, professional comments on the military situation, in response to Diem's earlier expressed interest in receiving them. After acknowledging the encouraging military progress over the preceding two years, the CJCS stated, "It was not until the recent political disturbances beginning in May and continuing through August and beyond that I personally had any doubt as to the ultimate success of our campaign against the Viet Cong." He then added:

> Now, as Secretary McNamara has told you, a serious doubt hangs over
> our hopes for the future. Can we win together in the face of the reaction

to the measures taken by your Government against the Buddhists and the students? As a military man I would say that we can win providing there are no further political setbacks. The military indicators are still generally favorable and can be made more so by actions readily within the power of your Government. If you will allow me, I would mention a few of the military actions which I believe necessary for this improvement.

The Chairman noted that though the military situation in I, II, and III Corps areas was generally good, some of the hard-core war zones of the Viet Cong remained virtually untouched. There were not enough offensive actions against the enemy in the field and, in his opinion, the full potential of the military units was not being exploited, for ". . . only a ruthless, tireless offensive can win the war."

The principal military problems, he pointed out, were now in the Delta, and the time had come to concentrate efforts there. An overhaul of the Strategic Hamlet Program was needed. For it to succeed, there must be a related clear-and-hold campaign by the combat units of IV Corps, and the tactics should be oriented to the waterways that were a natural characteristic of the region. Furthermore, infantry line units would have to operate at full strength, without diversion of combat power to rear echelon functions. The CJCS suggested that this latter problem was the case in ARVN generally, which President Diem might want to examine closely.

Finally he summed up what was intended as the statement of the US position:

> In closing, Mr. President, may I give you my most important overall impression? Up to now, the battle against the Viet Cong has seemed endless; no one has been willing to set a date for its successful conclusion. After talking to scores of officers, Vietnamese and American, I am convinced that the Viet Cong insurgency in the north and center can be reduced to little more than sporadic incidents by the end of 1964. The Delta will take longer but should be completed by the end of 1965. But for these predictions to be valid, certain conditions must be met. Your Government should be prepared to energize all agencies, military and civil, to a higher output of activity than up to now. Ineffective commanders and province officials must be replaced as soon as identified. Finally, there should be a restoration of domestic tranquility on the homefront if political tensions are to be allayed and external criticism is to abate. Conditions are needed for the creation of an atmosphere conducive to an effective campaign directed at the objective, vital to both of us, of defeating the Viet Cong and of restoring peace to your community.

The results of the survey conducted by the McNamara-Taylor mission were consolidated into a lengthy, formal report to the President containing specific findings, general evaluations, and recommendations. The substance of the report was presented in an hour-long, oral briefing to the President immediately upon the return of the mission on the morning of 2 October. Attending the briefing were the Under Secretary of State, the Under Secretary of State for Political Affairs, the Director of the CIA, and the Special Assistant to the President for National Security Affairs. Following the personal report, the President called a special meeting of the full National Security Council, which was held from six to seven that same evening.

The McNamara-Taylor Report generally was optimistic about the military situation and saw little direct effect of the political crisis on the prosecution of the war. Their conclusions, inter alia, were that despite serious political tensions and the increasing unpopularity of the Diem-Nhu regime, "The military campaign has made great progress and continues to progress." GVN military officers, though hostile to the government and its repressive policies, continued to perform their military duties in the larger cause of fighting the Viet Cong enemy. This reassuring evaluation, however, was caveated to the effect that ". . . further repressive actions by Diem and Nhu could change the present favorable military trends."

Specific findings in their appraisal of the military situation bore out the general evaluation. In the body of the report they stated:

> With allowances for all uncertainties, it is our firm conclusion that the GVN military program has made great progress in the last year and a half, and that the progress has continued at a fairly steady rate in the past six months even through the period of greatest political unrest in Saigon. The tactics and techniques employed by the Vietnamese under U.S. monitorship are sound and give promise of ultimate victory.

Especially noteworthy, in their view, was the progress clearly being achieved in the northern areas (I and II) Corps. Their appraisal of the progress of the Strategic Hamlet Program was also largely favorable. In both connections, they cited the effectiveness of the U.S. military advisory and support effort.

Included among their military recommendations were:

a. General Harkins [COMUSMACV] review with Diem the military changes necessary to complete the military campaign in the Northern and Central areas (I, II, III Corps) by the end of 1964, and in the Delta (IV Corps) by the end of 1965.

b. A program be established to train Vietnamese so that essential functions now performed by U.S. military personnel can be carried out by Vietnamese by the end of 1965. It should be possible to withdraw the bulk of U.S. personnel by that time.

c. In accordance with the program to train progressively Vietnamese to take over military functions, the Defense Department should announce in the near future presently prepared plans to withdraw 1000 U.S. military personnel by the end of 1963. This action should be explained in low key as an initial step in a long-term program to replace U.S. personnel with trained Vietnamese without impairment of the war effort.

Germane to the above recommendations, however, it was stated elsewhere in the report, "No further reductions should be made until the requirements of the 1964 campaign become firm."

Following the NSC meeting of 2 October, the White House issued a formal purlic announcement of the major policy aspects of the McNamara-Taylor Mission Report. The White House statement is reproduced below.

U.S. POLICY ON VIET-NAM: WHITE HOUSE STATEMENT, OCTOBER 2, 1963

Secretary [of Defense Robert S.] McNamara and General [Maxwell D.] Taylor reported to the President this morning and to the National Security Council this afternoon. Their report included a number of classified findings and recommendations which will be the subject of further review and action. Their basic presentation was endorsed by all members of the Security Council and the following statement of United States policy was approved by the President on the basis of recommendations received from them and from Ambassador [Henry Cabot] Lodge.

1. The security of South Viet-Nam is a major interest of the United States as other free nations. We will adhere to our policy of working with the people and Government of South Viet-Nam to deny this country to communism and to suppress the externally stimulated and supported insurgency of the Viet Cong as promptly as possible. Effective performance in this undertaking is the central objective of our policy in South Viet-Nam.

2. The military program in South Viet-Nam has made progress and is sound in principle, though improvements are being energetically sought.

3. Major U.S. assistance in support of this military effort is needed only until the insurgency has been suppressed or until the national security forces of the Government of South Viet-Nam are capable of suppressing it.

Secretary McNamara and General Taylor reported their judgment that the major part of the U.S. military task can be completed by the end of 1965, although there may be a continuing requirement for a limited number of U.S. training personnel. They reported that by the end of this year, the U.S. program for training Vietnamese should have progressed to the point where 1,000 U.S. military personnel assigned to South Viet-Nam can be withdrawn.

4. The political situation in South Viet-Nam remains deeply serious. The United States had made clear its continuing opposition to any repressive actions in South Viet-Nam. While such actions have not yet significantly affected the military effort, they could do so in the future.

5. It remains the policy of the United States, in South Viet-Nam as in other parts of the world, to support the efforts of the people of that country to defeat aggression and to build a peaceful and free society.

Considerable emphasis was given to the White House statement, and to the McNamara-Taylor Mission generally, in news media. Played up particularly was the U.S. force withdrawal, especially the prospective 1000-man reduction.

Three days later, on 5 October, in another meeting with the President, followed by another NSC meeting, the McNamara-Taylor recommendations themselves were addressed. The President "approved the military recommendations contained in the report." The President also directed, in line with their suggestion, that no formal announcement be made of the implementation of plans to withdraw 1000 U.S. military personnel from South Vietnam by the end of 1963.

The effect of the McNamara-Taylor mission, thus, was to revalidate the existing U.S. policy position regarding Vietnam. Reaffirmed were the military objectives, courses of action, and programs essentially as they were laid out by the Secretary of Defense at the Honolulu Conference over a year earlier on 23 July 1962. The underlying premises and soundness of the rationale seemed more cogent than ever. In fact, a new impetus was thereby given to pursing the same goals with even greater thrust and purpose. Such an outcome could have been forecast, as noted earlier, when Mr. McNamara set in motion another CPSVN planning cycle to revise the Model M Plan and develop an accelerated plan to withdraw U.S. forces.

Part of the motivation behind the stress placed on U.S. force withdrawal, and particularly the seemingly arbitrary desire to effect the 1000-man reduction by the end of 1963, apparently was as a signal to influence both the North Vietnamese and the South Vietnamese and set the stage for possible later steps that would help bring the insurgency to an end. With regard to the SVN, the demonstration of determination to pull out U.S. forces was intended to induce the South Vietnamese to increase the effectiveness of their military effort. State's instructions to Ambassador Lodge resulting from NSC action on the McNamara-Taylor mission indicated that:

> Actions are designed to indicate to Diem Government our displeasure at its political policies and activities and to create significant uncertainty in that government and in key Vietnamese groups as to future intentions of United States. At same time, actions are designed to have at most slight impact on military or counterinsurgency effort against Viet Cong, at least in short term. . . .

With respect to Hanoi, it might present an opportunity for a demarche—exploiting withdrawal of U.S. forces from South Vietnam by a specified date as exchange for North Vietnam's abandoning its aggression against South Vietnam. But events were already conspiring otherwise, and would soon frustrate such expectations and intentions as developed. The internal SVN situation was about to undergo rapid transformation.

By late October, there was increasing skepticism in some quarters about the military situation in South Vietnam. Indeed, it was beginning to be suspected that reports of progress by U.S. military sources actually cloaked a situation that was not only bleak, but deteriorating. A State Department intelligence evaluation of 22 October showed markedly pessimistic statistical trends since July 1963, in most areas of enemy-friendly relative progress measurement, indicating an unfavorable shift in the military balance. What was disquieting was that the pattern showed steady decline over a period of more than three months' duration.

Circulation of the INR evaluation occasioned controversy and no little recrimination. Substantive differences degenerated into a procedural issue. The outcome was a personal memorandum from the Secretary of State to the Secretary of Defense on 8 November, amounting to an apology for the incident. The Secretary of State stated in regard to INR's RFE-90 of 22 October:

> . . . . It is not the policy of the State Department to issue military appraisals without seeking the views of the Defense Department. I have requested that any memoranda given inter-departmental circulation which include military appraisals be coordinated with your Department.

G. *THE NOVEMBER COUP AND OVERTHROW OF DIEM*

On 1 November, the political situation fell apart. The long-anticipated coup occurred. The Diem regime was overthrown, and both Diem and Nhu were assassinated. A military junta of politically inexperienced generals took over the government as their successors.

The significance of the great change, for good or ill, was not readily apparent. Over the next three weeks the feared political chaos, civil war, and collapse of the war effort following a coup did not seem to be materializing. For the United

States, the important question was what did the new circumstances mean militarily for existing policy and plans oriented to bringing the insurgency under control and to phasing out US force commitments.

On 20 November, at the President's direction, a special all-agencies conference on Vietnam was convened in Honolulu for a "full-scale review" in depth of all aspects of the situation and to reassess U.S. plans and policies in the political, military, economic and information fields since the change of government. Attending were some 45 senior U.S. officials, military and civilian, including: the Secretary of State, Secretary of Defense, Special Assistant to the President for National Security Affairs, Chairman, JCS, Director of CIA, CINCPAC, ambassador to Vietnam, and COMUSMACV. Ambassador Lodge assessed the prospects for Vietnam as hopeful. In his estimation the new government was not without promise. Vietnamese military leadership appeared to be united and determined to step up the war effort. The Ambassador advocated continuing to pursue the goal of setting dates for phasing out U.S. activities and turning them over to the Vietnamese, and he volunteered that the announced withdrawal of 1000 troops by the end of 1963 was already having a salutary effect. COMUSMACV agreed with the Ambassador that the conduct of the war against the VC was coming along satisfactorily. Admitting that the VC-incidents rate shot up 300 to 400 percent after the coup, he noted that since 6 November, however, it had dropped down to "normal" and remained so to the present. Military operational statistics now generally showed a more or less favorable balance. In short, the briefings and assessments received at the conference constituted "an encouraging outlook for the principal objective of joint U.S.-Vietnamese policy in South Vietnam—the successful prosecution of the war against the Viet Cong communists." Moreover, "excellent working relations between U.S. officials and the members of the new Vietnamese government" had been established. All plans for the U.S. phasing out were to go ahead as scheduled.

In this light the U.S. military plans and programs for Vietnam were addressed. The revision of the Model M Plan of the CPSVN, ordered by the Secretary of Defense during his last visit to Vietnam in October was progressing apace and the finished Accelerated Plan was expected to be forwarded shortly. It would cost $6.4 million more than the Model Plan, however. Indications were that the FY 64 MAP would also cost more because of the acceleration—to a total now of $187.5 million. The Secretary of Defense made it clear that he felt that the proposed CINCPAC MAP could be cut back and directed that the program be reviewed to refine it and cut costs to stay as close as possible to the OSD ceiling of $175.5 million. He was equally emphatic, however, that while he would not tolerate fat or inefficiency in the program he was prepared to provide whatever funds might be required under MAP to support the GVN. In fact, he observed that the GVN was already running into "tremendous financial deficits," and opined that neither AID nor MAP had budgeted enough to provide for the emergencies which were likely to arise during 1964.

H.   ASSASSINATION OF PRESIDENT KENNEDY

On 22 November 1963, President Kennedy was assassinated. The consequences were to set an institutional freeze on the direction and momentum of U.S. Vietnam policy. Universally operative was a desire to avoid change of any kind during the critical interregnum period of the new Johnson Administration. Both the President and the governmental establishment consciously strove for continuity, with respect to Vietnam no less than in other areas. In Vietnam this continuity meant that the phase-out concept, the CPSVN withrdawal plan, and the MAP programs probably survived beyond the point they might have otherwise.

The immediate Johnson stamp on the Kennedy policy came on 26 November. At a NSC meeting convened to consider the results of the 20 November Honolulu Conference, the President "reaffirmed that U.S. objectives with respect to withdrawal of U.S. military personnel remain as stated in the White House statement of October 2, 1963." The only hint that something might be different from on-going plans came in a Secretary of Defense memo for the President three days prior to this NSC meeting. In that memo, Mr. McNamara said that the new South Vietnamese government was confronted by serious financial problems, and that the U.S. must be prepared to raise planned MAP levels.

In early December, the President began to have, if not second thoughts, at least a sense of uneasiness about Vietnam. In discussions with his advisors, he set in motion what he hoped would be a major policy review, fully staffed in depth, by Administration principals. The President wanted "a fresh new look taken" at the whole problem. In preparation for such a basic reappraisal, an interdepartmental meeting of second-echelon principals accordingly convened on 3 December and laid out a broad outline of basic topics to be addressed and staff papers to be developed by various departments and agencies. This attempt at a systematic and comprehensive reexamination, however, did not culminate in a fundamental national reassessment.

I. ACCELERATED MODEL PLAN OF THE CPSVN

With no indication of policy change in the offing, U.S. military planning thus went forward with hardly a break in stride. On 5 December CINCPAC submitted the Accelerated Model Plan to the JCS. It was the revision to the Model M Plan version of the CPSVN that the Secretary of Defense had ordered during his early October visit to Vietnam. The Accelerated Plan provided for more rapid phase-out of the bulk of U.S. military personnel and units and a decrease in the residual strength remaining thereafter. It also provided for building up GVN forces at a faster pace but on a more reduced scale, then cutting back from peak sooner and leveling out somewhat lower. MAP costs for the FY 1965–69 period would be little higher than the $392.2 million under the Model M Plan, coming to $399.4 million in the Acelerated Plan.

J. THE 1000-MAN WITHDRAWAL OF DECEMBER 1963

During the month of December, the planned 1000-man reduction was executed. It proved essentially an accounting exercise. Technically, more than a thousand U.S. personnel did leave, but many of these were part of the normal turnover cycle, inasmuch as rotation policy alone, not to mention medical evacuation or administrative reasons, resulted in an average rate of well over a thousand returnees per month. Though the replacement pipeline was slowed somewhat, year-end total in-country strength nevertheless was close to 16,000. This did not even represent a decline of 1000 from the October peak of 16,732.

That the avowed goal of 1000 would not be reached had in fact been anticipated and acknowledged before mid-December. Despite close monitoring of authorized ceilings and actual strengths, the force level kept rising. On 11 December, for example, the estimate of projected year-end U.S. strength in Vietnam had to be revised upward to reflect additional deployments approved since September. The adjusted figure now came to 15,894, a net increase of 162 over the earlier estimate. This new strength ceiling was what would be left after the 1000-man withdrawal then in progress was completed.

III.   1964

A.   THE VIETNAM SITUATION WORSENS

In December conflicting estimates of the situation in Vietnam indicated that the bright hopes and predictions of the past were increasingly less than realistic. A McNamara memo to the President written following a trip to Vietnam of 21 December, was laden with gloom. [Doc. 156] He wrote: "The situation is very disturbing. Current trends, unless reversed in the next 2-3 months, will lead to neutralization at best and more likely to a communist-controlled state." He went on to note that "the new government is the greatest source of concern," and that "it is indecisive and drifting." The Country Team, he added, "lacks leadership, and has been poorly informed." One of the most serious deficiencies he found was a "grave reporting weakness" on the U.S. side. "Viet Cong progress has been great during the period since the coup, with my best guess being that the situation has in fact been deteriorating in the countryside since July to a far greater extent than we realize because of our undue dependence on distorted Vietnamese reporting." Mr. McNamara clearly concluded that none of these conditions could be reversed by the influx of more American personnel, nor did he even mention that the U.S could continue to withdraw troops at all or as scheduled. His proposal was to hold the line: "U.S. resources and personnel," he said, "cannot usefully be substantially increased. . . ." although he did announce his intention to increase staffs "to sizes that will give us a reliable, independent U.S. appraisal of the status of operations." In his concluding paragraph, however, the Secretary of Defense admitted that his own estimate "may be overly pessimistic," inasmuch as the Ambassador, COMUSMACV, and General Minh were not discouraged and looked forward to significant improvements in January. [Doc. 156]

Vestiges of optimism still persisted in one degree or another in some quarters. The earlier sense of confidence that had been established was deep-rooted and not easily shaken. A retrospective evaluation of the Vietnam situation ostensibly covering the period 1960 through 1963, prepared by SACSA (General Krulak) is indicative. Although intended as a broad overview (and so called), and though actually cut off as of sometime in October 1963, it was forwarded in late October or November directly to the Secretary of Defense. The SACSA report presented nothing less than a glowing account of steady progress across the board in the military situation. Significantly, it contained no hint that the rate of progress possibly might have temporarily slowed somewhat in the second half of 1963, despite the fact that it expressly treated events as late as October. Yet by this time, other evaluations giving a quite different picture were already asserting themselves. Near the close of 1963 the Director, DIA, reported to the Secretary of Defense that year-end review and reassessment of the enemy situation revealed VC capabilities had not been impaired over the past year. On the contrary, the VC had in many regards improved in combat effectiveness and now enjoyed a generally improved force posture for insurgency.

Hopeful bias alone does not explain the endurance of past firmly rooted optimism—such as the SACSA overview. The difference between those who stressed the positive and those who saw decline was, in part, the product of viewing the situation in greater or shorter time frames. Those who applied a macroscopic perspective, believed—and not without certain logic—that current unfavorable reports were, at worse, a temporary lapse in the larger curve of progress over the years. Those who took spot checks tended to be more impressed by the immediate situation, and at this time, the immediate situation was critical. The feelings of this latter group were buttressed when on 30 January another coup, this time largely bloodless, ousted the ruling Minh government. It was a factional power struggle in which one military group replaced another, this time with General Khanh emerging as Premier. The latest development held forth little promise of giving the country the political stability so desperately needed in the midst of a war for survival. The event would prove only symptomatic as part of a sequence of similar government upheavals that were to follow.

In the U.S., the coincidence of domestic tragedy and patent instability in Vietnam evoked a chorus urging a Laos-like resolution of the Vietnam conflict. In late August, 1963, President de Gaulle had issued a policy statement on Vietnam which was subsequently officially interpreted as a proposal for "independence and neutrality" for Vietnam—meaning eventual U.S. withdrawal. In the aftermath of the assassinations, speculation turned increasingly to this solution. For example, Senator Mansfield wrote to President Johnson to propose a division of Vietnam between the GVN and the Viet Cong, coupled with a U.S. withdrawal. In early January, 1964, Secretary McNamara furnished the President the following counters to Senator Mansfield's arguments:

1. *We should certainly stress that the war is essentially a Vietnamese responsibility,* and this we have repeatedly done, particularly in our announced policy on U.S. troop withdrawal. At the same time we cannot disengage U.S. prestige to any significant degree. . . .

2. *The security situation is serious, but we can still win,* even on present ground rules. . . .

3. . . . . *Any deal either to divide the present territory of South Vietnam or to "neutralize" South Vietnam would inevitably mean a new government in Saigon that would in short order become Communist-dominated.*

4. *The consequences of a Communist-dominated South Vietnam are extremely serious* both for the rest of Southeast Asia and for the U.S. position in the rest of Asia and indeed in other key areas of the world. . . .

5. Thus, the stakes in preserving an anti-Communist South Vietnam are so high that, in our judgment, we must go on bending every effort to win. . . . And, I am confident that the American people are by and large in favor of a policy of firmness and strength in such situations.

Secretary McNamara in his testimony before Congress on the fiscal year 1965 budget in early February, 1964, declined to link the previously planned U.S. withdrawals with either "pessimism" or "optimism" regarding events in Vietnam, saying simply that the withdrawals had all along been conditioned upon Vietnamese capability to assume full responsibility from the U.S. trainers, and that there would be a "substantial reduction in our force as we train them." Further:

Last fall . . . I wasn't as optimistic perhaps about the course of the war as I was about being able to bring back our personnel in certain numbers by the end of last year and also in increments *between then and the end of 1965.*

I still am hopeful of doing that. We did, of course, bring back 1,000 men toward the latter part of last year. I am hopeful we can bring back additional numbers of men *later this year and certainly next year.* I say this because I personally believe that this is a war that the Vietnamese must fight . . . I don't believe we can take on that combat task for them. I do believe we can carry out training. We can provide advice and logistical assistance.

But after all, the training, by the very nature of the work, comes to an end at a certain point. We will have started this expanded training and carried it out for a period of 4 years, by the end of next year. We started at the end of 1961. The end of next year will have been 4 years later and certainly we should have completed the majority of the training task by that time. This, in General Taylor's view and mine, is what we should be able to do. If we do, we should bring our men back.

I don't believe we should leave our men there to substitute for Vietnamese men who are qualified to carry out the task, and this is really the heart of our proposal. I think it was a sound proposal then and I think so now. . . .

Unsureness about the actual state of affairs in Washington spread eventually to the highest levels of government, and prompted the dispatching to South Vietnam in early February of a CIA "Special CAS Group" for an independent evaluation of the military situation. A series of four reports, dated 10, 11, 14 and 18 February 1964, were produced, each transmitted by the Deputy Director, CIA, to the Secretary of Defense, Secretary of State, and others as soon as it came out. Instead of finding progress, these reported a serious and steadily deteriorating situation. Cited were VC gains in the past several months, and particularly noted was that VC arms were increasing in quantity and quality. As for the Strategic Hamlet Program, they found it "at present at virutal standstill." The Special CAS Group's concluding appraisal was pessimistic: "Tide of insurgency in all four corps areas appears to be going against GVN." COMUSMACV (who had no prior knowledge of the Special CAS Group's reports) took issue with the Group's findings, contesting less the date used than the conclusions, especially the "personal" evaluational opinions as to degree of deterioration. He suggested that in the future such reports be first coordinated before being dispatched.

On 6 March a major Secretary of Defense Conference again convened at CINCPAC headquarters for a broad reassessment. The consensus was that the military situation was definitely deteriorating. No longer was the issue whether it was progressing satisfactorily or not. The question now was how much of a setback had there been and what was needed to make up for it. An opinion shared by many was that the insurgency could be expected to go beyond 1965. This general reorientation of perspective was reflected in the Secretary of Defense's observation that attention should be focused on the near-term objectives of providing the greater U.S. support that would be necessary, and suspending for the time being consideration of longer-range concerns such as 5-year MAP projections. The visit to Vietnam on 8 March corroborated the gravity of the immediate problems at hand.

Following his return from Vietnam, Mr. McNamara, on 16 March, submitted to the President a formal report. In it the Secretary of Defense acknowledged, "The situation has unquestionably been growing worse, at least since September." RVNAF desertion rates were increasing, and the GVN military position generally was weakening noticeably. The VC position, on the other hand, showed signs of improving. He referred pointedly to the increase in North Vietnamese support. The conclusion was that greater U.S. support was needed.

In describing what was required to improve the situation in South Vietnam, Mr. McNamara identified measures that "will involve a limited increase in U.S. personnel and in direct Defense Department costs. More significantly they involve significant increases in Military Assistance Program costs. . . .," plus "additional U.S. economic aid to support the increased GVN budget." The estimated additional annual MAP costs would come to between $30 and $40 million each year, plus a one-time additional cost of $20 million for military equipment. In the recommendation section of the report, the Secretary listed the following 12 items:

1. To make it clear that we are prepared to furnish assistance and support to South Vietnam for as long as it takes to bring the insurgency under control.
2. To make it clear that we fully support the Khanh government and are opposed to any further coups.
3. To support a Program for National Mobilization (including a national service law) to put South Vietnam on a war footing.
4. To assist the Vietnamese to increase the armed forces (regular plus paramilitary) by at least 50,000 men.
5. To assist the Vietnamese to create a greatly enlarged Civil Administrative Corps for work at province, district and hamlet levels.
6. To assist the Vietnamese to improve and reorganize the para-military forces and to increase their compensation.
7. To assist the Vietnamese to create an offensive guerrilla force.
8. To provide the Vietnamese Air Force 25 A-1H aircraft in exchange for the present T-28s.
9. To provide the Vietnamese army additional M-113 armored personnel carriers (withdrawing the M-114s there), additional river boats, and approximately $5-10 million of other additional material.
10. To announce publicly the Fertilizer Program and to expand it with a view within two years to trebling the amount of fertilizer made available.
11. To authorize continued high-level U.S. overflights of South Vietnam's borders and to authorize "hot pursuit" and South Vietnamese ground operations over the Laotian line for the purpose of border control. More ambitious operations into Laos involving units beyond battalion size should be authorized only with the approval of Souvanna Phouma. Operations across the Cambodian border should depend on the state of relations with Cambodia.
12. To prepare immediately to be in a position on 72 hours' notice to initiate the full range of Laotian and Cambodian "Border Control" actions (beyond those authorized in paragraph 11 above) and the "Retaliatory Action" against North Vietnam, and to be in a position on 30 days' notice to initiate the program of "Graduated Overt Military Pressure" against North Vietnam.

As for the future of the phased-withdrawal plans, the Secretary of Defense's report contained the following:

> The U.S. policy of reducing existing personnel where South Vietnamese are in a position to assume the functions is still sound. Its application will

not lead to any major reductions in the near future, but adherence to this policy as such has a sound effect in portraying to the U.S. and the world that we continue to regard the war as a conflict the South Vietnamese must win and take ultimate responsibility for. Substantial reductions in the numbers of U.S. military training personnel should be possible before the end of 1965. However, the U.S. should continue to reiterate that it will provide all the assistance and advice required to do the job regardless of how long it takes. [Doc. 158]

By formal decision at the NSC session of 17 March, the President approved the Secretary of Defense report of 16 March 1964 and directed all agencies to carry out the 12 recommendations contained therein. A White House statement, reproduced below, was issued the same day.

March 17, 1964

IMMEDIATE RELEASE

Office of the White House Press Secretary

THE WHITE HOUSE

Secretary McNamara and General Taylor, following their initial oral report of Friday, today reported fully to President Johnson and the members of the National Security Council. The report covered the situation in South Vietnam, the measures being taken by General Khanh and his government, and the need for United States assistance to supplement and support these measures. There was also discussion of the continuing support and direction of the Viet Cong insurgency from North Vietnam.

At the close of the meeting the President accepted the report and its principal recommendations, which had the support of the National Security Council and Ambassador Lodge.

Comparing the situation to last October, when Secretary McNamara and General Taylor last reported fully on it, there have unquestionably been setbacks. The Viet Cong have taken maximum advantage of two changes of government, and of more long-standing difficulties, including a serious weakness and over-extension which had developed in the basically sound hamlet program. The supply of arms and cadres from the north has continued; careful and sophisticated control of Viet Cong operations has been apparent; and evidence that such control is centered in Hanoi is clear and unmistakable.

To meet the situation, General Khanh and his government are acting vigorously and effectively. They have produced a sound central plan for the prosecution of the war, recognizing to a far greater degree than before the crucial role of economic and social, as well as military, action to ensure that areas cleared of the Viet Cong survive and prosper in freedom.

To carry out this plan, General Khanh requires the full enlistment of the people of South Vietnam, partly to augment the strength of his anti-guerrilla forces, but particularly to provide the administrators, health workers, teachers and others who must follow up in cleared areas. To meet this need, and to provide a more equitable and common basis of service, General Khanh has informed us that he proposes in the near future to put into effect a National Mobilization Plan that will provide conditions and terms of service in appropriate jobs for all able-bodied South Vietnamese between certain ages.

In addition, steps are required to bring up to required levels the pay and status of the paramilitary forces and to create a highly trained guerrilla force that can beat the Viet Cong on its own ground. Finally, limited but significant additional equipment is proposed for the air forces, the river navy, and the mobile forces.

In short, where the South Vietnamese Government now has the power to clear any part of its territory, General Khanh's new program is designed to clear and to hold, step by step and province by province.

This program will involve substantial increases in cost to the South Vietnamese economy, which in turn depends heavily on United States economic aid. Additional, though less substantial, military assistance funds are also needed, and increased United States training activity both on the civil and military side. The policy should continue of withdrawing United States personnel where their roles can be assumed by South Vietnamese and of sending additional men if they are needed. It will remain the policy of the United States to furnish assistance and support to South Vietnam for as long as it is required to bring Communist aggression and terrorism under control.

Secretary McNamara and General Taylor reported their overall conclusion that with continued vigorous leadership from General Khanh and his government, and the carrying out of these steps, the situation can be significantly improved in the coming months.

B. DEMISE OF THE CPSVN

Before the month of March was over the CPSVN, as well as the MAP planning that had been such an integral part of it, finally received the coup de grace. Sacrificed to the U.S. desire "to make it clear that we fully support" the GVN, they were formally terminated, for the record, on 27 March in the OSD message reproduced below:

FROM: OSD WASH DC   DEF 963208   Date: 27 March 1964
        (Col. W. J. Yates)
TO: CINCPAC
REFS: a. CINCPAC Mar 64
        b. DEF 959615 DTG Mar 64

1. As indicated in ref. b., ceiling for Vietnam FY 66 MAP is $143.0 million against $143.1 million for FY 65. Requirements above these program levels should be identified as separate packages.

2. Submission of five-year programs FY 66-70 for Vietnam is suspended until further notice. Your best estimates of FY 66 requirements are necessary inasmuch line detail as feasible by 1 Jul 64 in order that (a) the Military Departments can review for pricing, lead time, availabilities, and prepare for procurement action and (b) requirements can be processed

within DoD, State/AID and BoB for budget/Congressional Presentation purposes.

3. Previous guidance re Model Plan projection for phasedown of U.S. forces and GVN forces is superseded. Policy is as announced by White House 17 Mar 64: Quote The policy should continue of withdrawing U.S. personnel where their roles can be assumed by South Vietnamese and of sending additional men if they are needed. It will remain the policy of the U.S. to furnish assistance and support of South Vietnam for as long as is required to bring Communist aggression and terrorism under control. Unquote.

4. No further action required or being taken here relative to accelerated model plan.

Thus ended de jure the policy of phase out and withdrawal and all the plans and programs oriented to it. Shortly, they would be cancelled out de facto.

C. BUILD-UP OF THE U.S. FORCE COMMITMENT

Soon the whole evolutionary direction of the U.S. military commitment began to change. Rather than diminishing, the magnitude rose thereafter. In early May the approved U.S. military strength ceiling for South Vietnam was raised by more than 1500 so that total in-country authorization came to over 17,000. Further increases were in sight. As the military situation in Vietnam failed to show signs of ameliorating, pressures began to develop in late spring for an even more significant increase in U.S. forces.

A special meeting on Southeast Asia was called at PACOM Headquarters in Honolulu for 1-2 June because of the unsatisfactory progress in execution of the National Pacification Plan. There, COMUSMACV proposed extending and intensifying the U.S. advisory effort in order to improve the operational effectiveness of the VNAF performance generally. The idea was discussed and supported in principle, and a staff working paper outlining the concept was prepared by the conferees. Near the end of June, COMUSMACV submitted to JCS (info CINCPAC, DOD, State, White House) his formal proposal recommending enlargement of the advisory assistance program. He reiterated, and offered further justification for, the need to augment the current advisory detachments at the battalion level and to extend the advisory effort at both the district and sector levels. His detailed breakout of primary personnel requirements came to a total of 9000 more advisors as the net in-country increase, but conceded that additional administrative and logistic support requirements would be substantial and would be submitted separately. Also, approximately 80 additional U.S. Navy advisors would be requested, in connection with recommendations made earlier in the "Bucklew Report" for a Junk Force and other measures to counter infiltration by sea. CINCPAC indicated concurrence and recommended approval of the proposal on 4 July.

In the middle of July, the new U.S. Ambassador to Vietnam, General Maxwell Taylor, sent an evaluation of the military situation to the Secretary of State, Secretary of Defense, and JCS that lent strong support to COMUSMACV's proposal. The Ambassador advised that formal estimates of regular VC strength in South Vietnam had been revised and now were raised to between 28,000 and 34,000. He explained that this did not reflect a sudden dramatic increase, but had been suspected for the past two or three years, though confirmatory evidence had become available only in the last few months. There was thus no occasion for alarm, but the new estimate emphasized the growing magnitude of the problem and the need to increase the level of U.S./GVN efforts. Therefore, additional requirements were being formulated, including U.S. military personnel requirements, to support U.S. plans during the ensuing months to cope with the new understanding of the realities of the situation. He forecast an increase in U.S. military strength to around 21,000 over the next six-month period to meet projected needs.

Immediately the size of the estimated force requirements connected with the proposed expansion of the advisory effort began to climb. On 16 July COMUSMACV submitted the support requirements associated with the program. For the next year he would need, over and above the original 900 additional advisors requested, more than 3200 other personnel, for a total gross military strength increase of about 4200. The Ambassador in Saigon concurred in COMUSMACV's proposed increase in U.S. military strength by 4200 over the next nine months, bringing the total in-country to nearly 22,000, and he urged prompt action. The Secretary of State also recommended approval, as did CINCPAC and JCS, and on 20 July, at the JCS-SecDef meeting, overall support was given to the COMUSMACV requested deployment package. The following day, at the NSC meeting of 21 July, the President gave it final approval, though that action was not included in the NSAM issued the next day.

As eventually refined, the total force increment actually came to over 4900 U.S. personnel. In addition, other requirements not directly related to the advisory effort itself were being generated and met independently. By the close of 1964 the year-end U.S. in-country strength figure had climbed to approximately 23,000 personnel and further authorized deployments were under way or in preparation.

The actual effect of "phased withdrawals" was minimal. Though 1,000 spaces among the personnel authorized MACV were eliminated in 1963, add-ons overtook cut-backs. As an example, U.S. Army strength in Vietnam—the bulk of the advisory effort—was allocated as follows:

PERCENTAGE OF U.S. ARMY STRENGTH IN VIETNAM

	Total Army Strength	Hq & Spt Units	Aviation Units	Communication Units	Special Forces	Other Advisers
Nov 63	10,000	17	35	15	6	27
Mar 64	10,000	19	34	13	7	27
Nov 64	14,000	28	30	12	8	22

D. POSTSCRIPT TO WITHDRAWAL PLANNING

The official termination of formal planning towards withdrawal by no means ended its attraction as one issue in the growing public debate over Vietnam policy. In August, 1964, the Tonkin Gulf crisis brought Congressmen back in perplexity to Secretary McNamara's statements on withdrawals, and elicited the following exchange:

> . . . [Secretary McNamara, you] have again always indicated that you hoped that by the end of this year there would have been a substantial reduction . . . Where we had a planned reduction of the number of troops,

and what appeared to be a withdrawal of the United States from the area, then this attack comes, which would put us firmly in the area, or at least change our mind. The whole thing, to me, is completely, at least, not understanding.

SECRETARY McNAMARA: The period, December 1961, through the summer of 1963 was a period of great progress within South Vietnam, in countering the effort of the Viet Cong to overthrow that government. However, starting in May, 1963, you will recall, a series of religious riots developed, controversy within the country developed, leading eventually upon November 2nd to the overthrow of the Diem government. Prior to that time in September, 1963, General Taylor and I had advised and visited that country. At that time, the progress of the counter insurgency effort was so great it appeared that we would be able to withdraw much of our training force by the end of 1965, and not 1964, and we would—we so stated upon our return. But following that—and I should also mention that in that same statement, we made in September, 1963, we pointed out the very serious nature of the political difficulties that were building up in South Vietnam, because of the conflict between the Buddhists and the Catholics, and the government.

In any event, as I say, in November, 1963, the government was overthrown. There was another change of government January 30th, and this completely changed the outlook and the political instability that followed the two coups has given the Viet Cong an opportunity to take advantage of the political and military weakness. They have taken advantage of it. It is now necessary to add further U.S. military assistance to counter that Viet Cong offensive. . . .

We have never made the statement since September, 1963, that we believed we could bring the bulk of the training forces out by the end of 1965, because the actions in November and January made it quite clear that would not be possible.

We have said—as a matter of fact, I say today—as our training missions are completed, we will bring back the training forces. I think this is only good sense, and good judgment. We have certain training missions that I hope we can complete this year, and others next year, and the forces associated with those missions should be brought back.

We have forces there training the Vietnamese to fly spotter aircraft, for artillery spotting purposes. I am very hopeful that we can bring the U.S. forces out as the Vietnamese acquire that capability.

On the other hand, the Vietnamese quite clearly need additional assistance in training for counter guerilla operations, because of the increased guerrilla activities of the Viet Cong, and we are sending additional special forces to Vietnam for that purpose.

There will be a flow in both directions, but I am certain in the next several months the net flow will be strongly toward South Vietnam.

After Tonkin Gulf, the policy objective of gradual disengagement from Vietnam was no longer relevant. The hope, as well as the concept of phase out and withdrawal, dwindled, since such withdrawal was now seen as tantamount to surrendering SVN to Hanoi. The issue for the future would no longer be withdrawals, but what additional U.S. forces would be required to stem the tide—and how fast they would have to be thrown into the breach.

4.   The Overthrow of Ngo Dinh Diem, May–November, 1963

Summary and Analysis

The Diem coup was one of those critical events in the history of U.S. policy that could have altered our commitment. The choices were there: (1) continue to plod along in a limited fashion with Diem—despite his and Nhu's growing unpopularity; (2) encourage or tacitly support the overthrow of Diem, taking the risk that the GVN might crumble and/or acommodate to the VC; and (3) grasp the opportunity—with the obvious risks—of the political instability in South Vietnam to disengage. The first option was rejected because of the belief that we could not win with Diem-Nhu. The third was very seriously considered a policy alternative because of the assumption that an independent, noncommunist SVN was too important a strategic interest to abandon—and because the situation was not sufficiently drastic to call into question so basic an assumption. The second course was chosen mainly for the reasons the first was rejected—Vietnam was thought too important; we wanted to win; and the rebellious generals seemed to offer that prospect.

In making the choice to do nothing to prevent the coup and to tacitly support it, the U.S. inadvertently deepened its involvement. The inadvertence is the key factor. It was a situation without good alternatives. While Diem's government offered some semblance of stability and authority, its repressive actions against the Buddhists had permanently alientated popular support, with a high probability of victory for the Viet Cong. As efficient as the military coup leaders appeared, they were without a manageable base of political support. When they came to power and when the lid was taken off the Diem-Nhu reporting system, the GVN position was revealed as weak and deteriorating. And, by virtue of its interference in internal Vietnamese affairs, the U.S. had assumed a significant responsibility for the new regime, a responsibility which heightened our commitment and deepened our involvement.

The catalytic event that precipitated the protracted crisis which ended in the downfall of the Diem regime was a badly handled Buddhist religious protest in Hué on May 8, 1963. In and of itself the incident was hardly something to shake the foundations of power of most modern rulers, but the manner in which Diem responded to it, and the subsequent protests which it generated, was precisely the one most likely to aggravate not alleviate the situation. At stake, of course, was far more than a religious issue. The Buddhist protest had a profoundly political character from the beginning. It sprang and fed upon the feelings of political frustration and repression Diem's autocratic rule had engendered.

The beginning of the end for Diem can, then, be traced through events to the regime's violent suppression of a Buddhist protest demonstration in Hué on Buddha's birthday, May 8, in which nine people were killed and another fourteen injured. Although Buddhists had theretofore been wholly quiescent politically, in subsequent weeks, a full-blown Buddhist "struggle" movement demonstrated a sophisticated command of public protest techniques by a cohesive and disciplined organization, somewhat belying the notion that the movement was an outraged, spontaneous response to religious repression and discrimination. Nonetheless, by June it was clear that the regime was confronted not with a dissident religious minority, but with a grave crisis of public confidence. The Buddhist protest had become a vehicle for mobilizing the widespread popular resentment of an arbitrary and often oppressive rule. It had become the focal point of political opposition to Diem. Under strong U.S. pressure and in the face of an outraged world opinion, the regime reached ostensible agreement with the Buddhists on June 16. But the agreement merely papered over the crisis, without any serious concessions by Diem. This intransigence was reinforced by Diem's brother, Ngo Dinh Nhu, and his wife, who bitterly attacked the Buddhists throughout the summer. By mid-August the crisis was reaching a breaking point.

The Buddhists' demonstrations and protest created a crisis for American policy as well. The U.S. policy of support for South Vietnam's struggle against the Hanoi-supported Viet Cong insurgency was founded on unequivocal support of Diem, whom the U.S. had long regarded as the only national leader capable of unifying his people for their internal war. When the Buddhist protest revealed widespread public disaffection, the U.S. made repeated attempts to persuade Diem to redress the Buddhist grievances, to repair his public image, and to win back public support. But the Ngos were unwilling to bend. Diem, in true mandarin style, was preoccupied with questions of face and survival—not popular support. He did not understand the profound changes his country had experienced under stress, nor did he understand the requirement for popular support that the new sense of nationalism had created. The U.S. Ambassador, Frederick Nolting, had conducted a low-key diplomacy toward Diem, designed to bring him to the American way of thinking through reason and persuasion. He approached the regime during the first weeks of the Buddhist crisis in the same manner, but got no results. When he left on vacation at the end of May, his DCM, William Trueheart, abandoned the soft sell for a tough line. He took U.S. views to Diem not as expressions of opinion, but as demands for action. Diem, however, remained as obdurate and evasive as ever. Not even the U.S. threat to dissociate itself from GVN actions in the Buddhist crisis brought movement.

In late June, with Nolting still on leave, President Kennedy announced the appointment of Henry Cabot Lodge as Ambassador to Vietnam to replace Nolting in September. In the policy deliberations then taking place in Washington, consideration was being given for the first time to what effect a coup against Diem would have. But Nolting returned, first to Washington and then to Saigon, to argue that the only alternative to Diem was chaos. The U.S. military too, convinced that the war effort was going well, felt that nothing should be done to upset the apple cart. So Nolting was given another chance to talk Diem into conciliating the Buddhists. The Ambassador worked assiduously at the task through July and the first part of August, but Diem would agree only to gestures and half-measures that could not stop the grave deterioration of the political situation. Nolting left Vietnam permanently in mid-August with vague assurances from Diem that he would seek to improve the climate of relations with the Buddhists. Less than a week later, Nolting was betrayed by Nhu's dramatic August 21 midnight raids on Buddhist pagodas throughout Vietnam.

One of the important lessons of the American involvement in South Vietnam in support of Diem was that a policy of unreserved commitment to a particular leadership placed us in a weak and manipulable position on important internal issues. The view that there were "no alternatives" to Diem greatly limited the extent of our influence over the regime and ruled out over the years a number of kinds of leverage that we might usefully have employed or threatened to employ. Furthermore, it placed the U.S. in the unfortunate role of suitor to a fickle lover. Aware of our fundamental commitment to him, Diem could with relative impunity ignore our wishes. It reversed the real power relationship between the two countries. Coupled with Diem's persistent and ruthless elimination of all potential political opposition, it left us with rather stark alternatives indeed when a crisis on which we could not allow delay and equivocation finally occurred. For better or worse, the August 12 pagoda raids decided the issue for us.

The raids, themselves, were carefully timed by Nhu to be carried out when the U.S. was without an Ambassador, and only after a decree placing the country under military martial law had been issued. They were conducted by combat police and special forces units taking orders directly from Nhu, not through the Army chain of command. The sweeping attacks resulted in the wounding of about 30 monks, the arrest of over 1,400 Buddhists and the closing of the pagodas (after they had been damaged and looted in the raids). In their brutality and their blunt repudiation of Diem's solemn word to Nolting, they were a direct, impudent slap in the face for the U.S. Nhu expected that in crushing the Buddhists he could confront the new U.S. Ambassador with a *fait accompli* in which the U.S. would complainingly acquiesce, as we had in so many of the regime's actions which we opposed. Moreover, he attempted to fix blame for the raids on the senior Army generals. Getting word of the attacks in Honolulu, where he was conferring with Nolting and Hilsman, Lodge flew directly to Saigon. He immediately let it be known that the U.S. completely dissociated itself from the raids and could not tolerate such behavior. In Washington the morning after, while much confusion reigned about who was responsible for the raids, a statement repudiating them was promptly released. Only after several days did the U.S. finally establish Nhu's culpability in the attacks and publicly exonerate the Army.

On August 23, the first contact with a U.S. representative was made by generals who had begun to plan a coup against Diem. The generals wanted a clear indication of where the U.S. stood. State in its subsequently controversial reply, drafted and cleared on a weekend when several of the principal Presidential advisors were absent from Washington, affirmed that Nhu's continuation in a power position within the regime was intolerable (words missing) and did not, "then, we must face the possibility that Diem himself cannot be preserved." This message was to be communicated to the generals, and Diem was to be warned that Nhu must go. Lodge agreed with the approach to the generals, but felt it was futile to present Diem with an ultimatum he would only ignore and one that might tip off the palace to the coup plans. Lodge proceeded to inform only the generals. They were told that the U.S. could no longer support a regime which included Nhu, but that keeping Diem was entirely up to them. This was communicated to the generals on August 27. The President and some of his advisors, however, had begun to have second thoughts abought switching horses so suddenly, and with so little information on whether the coup could succeed, and if it did, what kind of government it would bring to power. As it turned out, Washington's anxiety was for naught, the plot was premature, and after several uncertain days, its demise was finally recognized on August 31.

Thus by the end of August, we found ourselves without a leadership to support and without a policy to follow in our relations with the GVN. In this context a month-long policy review took place in Washington and in Vietnam. It was fundamentally a search for alternatives. In both places the issue was joined between those who saw no realistic alternatives to Diem and felt that his policies were having only a marginal effect on the war effort, which they wanted to get on with by renewing our support and communication with Diem; and those who felt that the war against the VC would not possibly be won with Diem in power and preferred therefore to push for a coup of some kind. The first view was primarily supported by the military and the CIA both in Saigon and in Washington, while the latter was held by the U.S. Mission, the State Department and members of the White House staff. In the end, a third alternative was selected, namely to use pressure on Diem to get him to remove Nhu from the scene and to end his repressive policies. Through September, however, the debate continued with growing intensity. Tactical considerations, such as another Lodge approach to Diem about removing the Nhus and the effect of Senator Church's resolution calling for an aid suspension, focused the discussion at times, but the issue of whether to renew our support for Diem remained. The decision hinged on the assessment of how seriously the political deterioration was affecting the war effort.

In the course of these policy debates, several participants pursued the logical but painful conclusion that if the war could not be won with Diem, and if his removal would lead to political chaos and also jeopardize the war effort, then the war was probably unwinnable. If that were the case, the argument went, then the U.S. should really be facing a more basic decision on either an orderly disengagement from an irretrievable situation, or a major escalation of the U.S. involvement, including the use of U.S. combat troops. These prophetic minority voices were, however, raising an unpleasant prospect that the Administration was unprepared to face at that time. In hindsight, however, it is clear that this was one of the times in the history of our Vietnam involvement when we were making fundamental choices. The option to disengage honorably at that time now appears an attractively low-cost one. But for the Kennedy Administration then, the costs no doubt appeared much higher. In any event, it proved to be unwilling to accept the implications of predictions for a bleak future. The Administration hewed to the belief that if the U.S. be but willing to exercise its power, it could ultimately always have its way in world affairs.

Nonetheless, in view of the widely divergent views of the principals in Saigon, the Administration sought independent judgments with two successive fact-finding missions. The first of these whirlwind inspections, by General Victor Krulak, JCS SACSA, and a State Department Vietnam expert, Joseph Mendenhall, from September 7–10, resulted in diametrically opposing reports to the President on the conditions and situation and was, as a result, futile. The Krulak-Mendenhall divergence was significant because it typifies the deficient analysis of both the U.S. civilian and military missions in Vietnam with respect to the overall political situation in the country. The U.S. civilian observers, for their part, failed to fully appreciate the impact Diem had had in preventing the emergence of any other political forces. The Buddhists, while a cohesive and effective minority protest movement, lacked a program or the means to achieve power. The labor unions were entirely urban-based and appealed to only a small segment of the population. The clandestine political parties were small, urban, and usually elitist. The religious sects had a narrow appeal and were based on ethnic minorities. Only the Viet Cong had any real support and influence on a broad base in the countryside. The only real alternative source of political power was the Army since it had a large, disciplined organization spanning the country, with an independent communications and transportation system and a strong superiority to any other group in coercive power. In its reports on the Army, however, General Harkins and the U.S. military had failed to appreciate the deeply corrosive effect on internal allegiance and discipline in the Army that Diem's loyalty based promotion and assignment policies had had. They did not foresee that in the wake of a coup senior officers would lack the cohesiveness to hang together and that the temptations of power would promote a devisive internal competition among ambitious men at the expense of the war against the Viet Cong.

Two weeks after the fruitless Krulak-Mendenhall mission, with the Washington discussions still stalemated, it was the turn of Secretary McNamara and General Taylor, the Chairman of the JCS, to assess the problem. They left for Vietnam on September 23 with the Presidential instruction to appraise the condition of the war effort and the impact on it of the Buddhist political turmoil and to recommend a course of action for the GVN and the U.S. They returned to Washington on October 2. Their report was a somewhat contradictory compromise between the views of the civilian and military staffs. It affirmed that the war was being won, and that it would be successfully concluded in the first three corps areas by the end of 1964, and in the Delta by 1965, thereby permitting the withdrawal of American advisors, although it noted that the political tensions were starting to have an adverse effect on it. But, more importantly, it recommended a series of measures to coerce Diem into compliance with American wishes that included a selective suspension of U.S. economic aid, an end to aid for the special forces units used in the August 21 raids unless they were subordinated to the Joint General Staff, and the continuation of Lodge's cool official aloofness from the regime. It recommended the public announcement of the U.S. intention to withdraw 1,000 troops by the end of the year, but suggested that the aid suspensions not be announced in order to give Diem a chance to respond without a public loss of face. It concluded by recommending against active U.S. encouragement of a coup, in spite of the fact that an aid suspension was the one step the generals had asked for in August as a sign of U.S. condemnation of Diem and support for a change of government. The report was quickly adopted by Kennedy in the NSC and a brief, and subsequently much rued, statement was released to the press on October 2, announcing the planned withdrawal of 1,000 troops by year's end.

The McNamara-Taylor mission, like the Krulak-Mendenhall mission before it and the Honolulu Conference in November after the coup, points up the great difficulty encountered by high level fact-finding missions and conferences in getting at the "facts" of a complex policy problem like Vietnam in a short time. It is hard to believe that hasty visits by harried high level officials with overloaded itineraries really add much in the way of additional data or lucid insight. And because they become a focal point of worldwide press coverage, they often raise public expectations or anxieties that may only create additional problems for the President. There were many such high level conferences over Vietnam.

Of the recommendations of the McNamara-Taylor mission, the proposal for a selective suspension of economic aid, in particular the suspension of the commercial import program, was the most significant both in terms of its effect, and as an example of the adroit use or denial of American assistance to achieve our foreign policy objectives. In this instance economic sanctions, in the form of selected aid suspensions in those programs to which the regime would be most sensitive but that would have no immediate adverse effect on the war effort, were used constructively to influence events rather than negatively to punish those who had violated our wishes, our usual reaction to coups in Latin America. The proposal itself had been under consideration since the abortive coup plot of August. At that time, Lodge had been authorized to suspend aid if he thought it would enhance the likelihood of the success of a coup. Later in September he was again given specific control over the delay or suspension of any of the pending aid programs. On both occasions, however, he had expressed doubt about the utility of such a step. In fact, renewal of the commercial import program had been pending since early in September, so that the adoption of the McNamara-Taylor proposal merely formalized the existing situation into policy. As might have been expected (although the record leaves ambiguous whether this was a conscious aim of the Administration), the Vietnamese generals interpreted the suspension as a green light to proceed with a coup.

While this policy was being applied in October, Lodge shunned all contact with the regime that did not come at Diem's initiative. He wanted it clearly understood that they must come to him prepared to adopt our advice before he would recommend to Washington a change in U.S. policy. Lodge performed with great skill, but inevitably frictions developed within the Mission as different viewpoints and proposals came forward. In particular, Lodge's disagreements and disputes with General Harkins during October when the coup plot was maturing and later were to be of considerable embarrassment to Washington when they leaked to the press. Lodge had carefully cultivated the press, and when the stories of friction appeared, it was invariably Harkins or Richardson or someone else who was the villian.

No sooner had the McNamara-Taylor mission returned to Washington and reported its recommendations than the generals reopened contact with the Mission indicating that once again they were preparing to strike against the regime. Washington's immediate reaction on October 5 was to reiterate the decision of the NSC on the McNamara-Taylor report, i.e., no U.S. encouragement of a coup. Lodge was instructed, however, to maintain contact with the generals and to monitor their plans as they emerged. These periodic contacts continued and by October 25, Lodge had come to believe that Diem was unlikely to respond to our pressure and that we should therefore not thwart the coup forces. Harkins disagreed, believing that we still had not given Diem a real chance to rid himself of Nhu and that we should present him with such an ultimatum and test his response before going ahead with a coup. He, furthermore, had reservations about the strength of the coup forces when compared with those likely to remain loyal to the regime. All this left Washington anxious and doubtful. Lodge was cautioned to seek fuller information on the coup plot, including a line-up of forces and the proposed plan of action. The U.S. could not base its policy on support for a coup attempt that did not offer a strong prospect of success. Lodge was counseled to consider ways of delaying or preventing the coup if he doubted its prospects for success. By this juncture, however, Lodge felt committed and, furthermore, felt the matter was no longer in our hands. The generals were taking the action on their own initiative and we could only prevent it now by denouncing them to Diem. While this debate was still going on, the generals struck.

Shortly after Ambassador Lodge and Admiral Felt had called on Diem on November 1, the generals made their move, culminating a summer and fall of complex intrigue. The coup was led by General Minh, the most respected of the senior generals, together with Generals Don, Kim and Khiem. They convoked a meeting of all but a few senior officers at JGS headquarters at noon on the day of the coup, announced their plans and got the support of their compatriots. The coup itself was executed with skill and swiftness. They had devoted special attention to ensuring that the major potentially loyal forces were isolated and their leaders neutralized at the outset of the operation. By the late afternoon of November 1, only the palace guard remained to defend the two brothers. At 4:30 p.m., Diem called Lodge to ask where the U.S. stood. Lodge was noncommital and confined himself to concern for Diem's physical safety. The conversation ended inconclusively. The generals made repeated calls to the palace offering the brothers safe conduct out of the country if they surrendered, but the two held out hope until the very end. Sometime that evening they secretly slipped out of the palace through an underground escape passage and went to a hide-away in Cholon. There they were captured the following morning after their whereabouts was learned when the palace fell. Shortly the two brothers were murdered in the back of an armored personnel carrier en route to JGS headquarters.

Having successfully carried off their coup, the generals began to make arrangements for a civilian government. Vice President Tho was named to head a largely civilian cabinet, but General Minh became President and Chairman of the shadow Military Revolutionary Council. After having delayed an appropriate period, the U.S. recognized the new government on November 8. As the euphoria of the first days of liberation from the heavy hand of the Diem regime wore off, however, the real gravity of the economic situation and the lack of expertise in the new government became apparent to both Vietnamese and American officials. The deterioration of the military situation and the strategic hamlet program also came more and more clearly into perspective.

These topics dominated the discussions at the Honolulu Conference on November 20 when Lodge and the country team met with Rusk, McNamara, Taylor, Bell, and Bundy. But the meeting ended inconclusively. After Lodge had conferred with the President a few days later in Washington, the White House tried to pull together some conclusions and offer some guidance for our continuing and now deeper involvement in Vietnam. The instructions contained in NSAM 273, however, did not reflect the truly dire situation as it was to come to light in succeeding weeks. The reappraisals forced by the new information would swiftly make it irrelevant as it was "overtaken by events."

For the military coup d'etat against Ngo Dinh Diem, the U.S. must accept its full share of responsibility. Beginning in August of 1963 we variously authorized, sanctioned and encouraged the coup efforts of the Vietnamese generals and offered full support for a successor government. In October we cut off aid to Diem in a direct rebuff, giving a green light to the generals. We maintained clandestine contact with them throughout the planning and execution of the coup and sought to review their operational plans and proposed new government. Thus, as the nine-year rule of Diem came to a bloody end, our complicity in his overthrow heightened our responsibilities and our commitment in an essentially leaderless Vietnam.

End of Summary and Analysis

CHRONOLOGY

8 May 1963 Hue incident

Government troops fire on a Buddhist protest demonstration, killing nine and wounding fourteen. The incident triggers a nationwide Buddhist protest and a crisis of popular confidence for the Diem regime. GVN maintains the incident was an act of VC terrorism.

10 May 1963   *Manifesto of Buddhist clergy*
A five point demand by the Buddhist clergy is transmitted to the Government. It calls for freedom to fly the Buddhist flag, legal equality with the Catholic Church, an end of arrests, punishment of the perpetrators of the May 8 incident, and indemnification of its victims.

18 May 1963   *Nolting meeting with Diem; Embassy Saigon message 1038*
U.S. Ambassador Nolting meets with Diem and outlines the steps the U.S. wants Diem to take to redress the Buddhist grievances and recapture public confidence. These include an admission of responsibility for the Hue incident, compensation of the victims, and a reaffirmation of religious equality and non-discrimination.

30 May 1963   *Buddhist demonstration*
350 Buddhist monks demonstrate in front of the National Assembly and announce a 48-hour hunger strike.

4 Jun 1963   *Truehart meeting with Thuan*
With Nolting on leave, chargé d'affaires Truehart meets with Secretary of State Thuan, and on instruction from the State Department, warns that U.S. support for the GVN could not be maintained if there were another bloody suppression of Buddhists.

Tho committee appointed
Later that day the Government announces the appointment of an inter-ministerial committee headed by Vice President Tho to resolve the religious issue.

5 Jun 1963   *Tho committee meets Buddhists*
The first meeting between the Tho committee and the Buddhist leadership takes place, after which each side publicly questions the other's good faith in the negotiations.

8 Jun 1963   *Madame Nhu attacks Buddhists*
Madame Nhu, wife of Diem's powerful brother, publicly accuses the Buddhists of being infiltrated with communist agents.

Later on the same day, Truehart protests Mme Nhu's remarks to Diem and threatens to dissociate the U.S. from any future repressive measures against the Buddhists.

11 Jun 1963   *First Buddhist suicide by fire*
At noon in the middle of a downtown intersection, a Buddhist monk, Thich Quang Duc, is immersed in gasoline and sets himself afire. His fiery protest suicide is photographed and is front page material in the world's newspapers. Shock and indignation are universal. Mme Nhu subsequently refers to it as a "barbecue."

12 Jun 1963   *Truehart repeats U.S. dissociation threat*
Truehart sees Diem again to protest his lack of action on the Buddhist problem and says that Quang Duc's suicide has shocked the world. If Diem does not act, the U.S. will be forced to dissociate itself from him.

14 Jun 1963   *Tho committee meets again with Buddhists*
Under U.S. pressure, negotiations between Vice President Tho's committee and the Buddhist leadership reopen in apparent earnest.

16 Jun 1963   *GVN–Buddhist communique*
A joint GVN–Buddhist communique is released as a product of the negotiations that outlines the elements of a settlement, but affixes no responsibility for the May 8 Hue incident.

Late June–
July
Buddhist protest intensifies
Buddhists protest activities intensify as leadership passes from the discredited moderate, older leaders to younger militants. The Saigon press corps is actively cultivated.

27 June 1963 *Kennedy announces Lodge appointment*
President Kennedy, visiting in Ireland, announces the appointment of Henry Cabot Lodge as the new U.S. Ambassador to South Vietnam, effective in September.

3 Jul 1963   *Tho committee absolves regime*
Vice President Tho's committee announces that a preliminary investigation of the May 8 incident has confirmed that the deaths were the result of an act of VC terrorism.

4 Jul 1963   *White House meeting on Vietnamese situation*
At a State Department briefing for the President it is generally agreed that Diem will not voluntarily remove Nhu. A discussion of the likely consequences of a coup reveals divergent views.

5 Jul 1963   *Nolting in Washington*
Having cut short his vacation to return to Washington for consultations, Nolting confers with Under Secretary of State George Ball and voices the fear that an attempt to overthrow Diem would result in a protracted religious civil war that would open the door to the Viet Cong. We should not abandon Diem yet. While in Washington he also sees Secretary McNamara.

10 Jul 1963   *SNIE 53–2–63*
This special intelligence estimate notes coup rumors in Vietnam and warns that a coup would disrupt the war effort and perhaps give the Viet Cong the opportunity for gains they had been hoping for. It concludes, however, that if Diem does nothing to implement the June 16 agreements, Buddhist unrest will continue through the summer and increase the likelihood of a coup attempt.

11 Jul 1963   *Nolting's return to Saigon*
Nolting returns to Vietnam with Washington's blessing to make one last attempt to persuade Diem to conciliate the Buddhists. The hope is to draw on the good will that Nolting has built up in his two years of service.

Nhu squelches coup plotting
At a special meeting for all senior generals, Nhu attacks their loyalty to the regime for not having thwarted the numerous coup

plots that had been reported. The meeting apparently forestalls any immediae threat to the family.

15 Jul 1963   *Embassy Saigon message 85*
Deeply resentful of Truehart's tough pressure tactics, Nolting meets with Diem and attempts to mollify him. He convinces Diem to make a nationwide radio address with concessions to the Buddhists.

19 Jul 1963   *Diem speaks on radio*
Complying with the letter but not the spirit of Nolting's request, Diem delivers a brief cold radio address that makes only very minor concessions to the Buddhists and asks for harmony and support of the Government.

McNamara press conference
At a press conference, Secretary McNamara says the war is progressing well and the Buddhist crisis has not yet affected it.

5 Aug 1963   *Second Buddhist suicide*
A second Buddhist monk commits suicide by burning himself to death in the continuing protest against the Diem regime.

14 Aug 1963 *Nolting-Diem meeting*
In their final meeting before Nolting's departure from Vietnam, Diem promises to make a public statement repudiating Mme Nhu's inflammatory denunciations of the Buddhists. Nolting left the next day.

15 Aug 1963 New York Herald Tribune *article by Marguerite Higgins*
Diem's promised public statement takes the form of an interview with Marguerite Higgins, conservative correspondent of the *New York Herald Tribune*. Diem asserts that conciliation has been his policy toward the Buddhists all along and the family is pleased with Lodge's appointment.

18 Aug 1963 *Generals decide on martial law*
Ten senior Army generals meet and decide that in view of the deteriorating political situation, they will ask Diem for a declaration of martial law to permit them to return monks from outside Saigon to their own provinces and pagodas and thus reduce tensions in the capital.

20 Aug 1963 *Generals propose martial law to Nhu and Diem*
A small group of generals meets first with Nhu and then with Diem to propose that martial law be decreed forthwith. Diem approves the proposal and the decree takes effect at midnight.

21 Aug 1963 *Nhu's forces attack pagodas*
Under the cover of the military martial law, shortly after midnight, forces loyal to Nhu and under his orders attack pagodas throughout Vietnam, arresting monks and sacking the sacred buildings. Over 30 Buddhists are injured and over 1400 arrested. The attack is a shattering repudiation of Diem's promises to Nolting. The Embassy is taken by surprise.

Lodge confers with Nolting and Hilsman
First news of the attacks reaches Lodge in Honolulu where he is conferring with Nolting and Assistant Secretary of State Hilsman. He is dispatched immediately to Vietnam.

Washington reaction
At 9:30 a.m. a stiff statement is released by State deploring the raids as a direct violation of Diem's assurances to the U.S. But first intelligence places the blame for them on the Army, not Nhu.

22 Aug 1963 *Lodge arrives in Saigon*
After a brief stop in Tokyo, Lodge arrives in Saigon at 9:30 p.m. The situation still remains confused.

23 Aug 1963 *CIA Information Report TDCS DB–3/656,252*
General Don, armed forces commander under the martial law decree, has contacted a CAS officer and asked why the U.S. was broadcasting the erroneous story that the Army had conducted the pagoda raids. Nhu's special forces were responsible. The U.S. should make its position known. A separate contact by another general with a member of the mission had brought another inquiry as to the U.S. position. The query is clear. Would we support the Army if it acted against Nhu and/or Diem?

Student demonstrations
Large student protest demonstrations on behalf of the imprisoned Buddhists take place at the faculties of medicine and pharmacy at the University of Saigon. They are a dramatic break with the tradition of student apathy to politics in Vietnam. The regime reacts with massive arrests.

24 Aug 1963 *Embassy Saigon message 316, Lodge to Hilsman*
Lodge lays the blame for the raids at Nhu's feet and states that his influence is significantly increased. But, in view of the loyalty of Saigon area commanders, a coup attempt would be a "shot in the dark."

State message 243, State to Lodge
Subsequently known as the "Aug 24 cable," this controversial message acknowledges Nhu's responsibility for the raids and says that U.S. can no longer tolerate his continuation in power. If Diem is unable or unwilling to remove him, the generals are to be told that the U.S. will be prepared to discontinue economic and military support, accept the obvious implication and will promise assistance to them in any period of interim breakdown of the GVN. Lodge's permission is requested for a VOA broadcast exonerating the Army of responsibility for the Aug 21 raids.

25 Aug 1963 *Embassy Saigon message*
Lodge approves the proposed course of action but sees no reason to approach Diem first. Diem will not remove the Nhus and it would merely tip off the palace to the impending military action.

CAS Saigon message 0292
Lodge, Harkins, and Richardson meet and agree on an approach to the generals with the information in State's 243.

26 Aug 1963 VOA broadcast
Early on this Monday morning, VOA in South Vietnam broadcasts the press stories placing blame for the Aug 21 raids on Nhu and absolving the Army. It also broadcast press speculation that the U.S. is contemplating an aid suspension.

Lodge presents credentials to Diem
Later the same morning, Lodge presents his credentials to Diem, after an early morning meeting with Harkins and Richardson, at which they agree on the details of the approach to the generals.

NSC meeting
The Aug 24 cable of instructions had been drafted, cleared and sent on a weekend with McNamara, McCone, Rusk and the President all out of town. The NSC meeting on Monday morning reveals that these top advisors have reservations about proceeding hastily with a coup when we lack so much basic information about its leadership and chances. Lodge is asked for more details.

27 Aug 1963 CAS agents meet generals
CAS agents Conein and Spera meet with Generals Khiem and Khanh respectively. Khiem tells Conein that other participants are Generals Minh, Kim, Thieu and Le, and that General Don was aware of the plot and approved, but was too exposed to participate.

Embassy Saigon message 364
Lodge gives an optimistic appraisal of the balance of forces for a coup and expresses confidence in the identified leaders.

NSC meeting
At the now daily NSC meeting in Washington, the State Department participants generally favor going ahead with the coup, while the Defense Department, both civilian and military, prefers another try with Diem.

28 Aug 1963 MACV message 1557
Harkins goes on record with doubts about the line-up of forces for the coup and sees no reason for our "rush approval."

State message 269, President to Lodge; and JCS message 3385, Taylor to Harkins
Concerned by the differing views of Lodge and Harkins, as well as the division of opinion in Washington, the President asks the Ambassador and MACV for their separate appraisals.

29 Aug 1963 CAS agents meet Minh
At this meeting, arranged by Minh, he asks for clear evidence that the U.S. will not betray them to Nhu. He is unwilling to discuss the details of his plan. When asked what would constitute a sign of U.S. support, he replies that the U.S. should suspend economic aid to the regime.

Embassy Saigon message 375
Lodge replies to the Presidential query that the U.S. is irrevocably committed to the generals. He recommends showing the CAS

messages to them to establish our good faith and if that is insufficient, he recommends a suspension of economic aid as they requested.

MACV message 1566
Harkins reply to Taylor suggests that one last effort be made with Diem in the form of an ultimatum demanding Nhu's removal. Such a move he feels will strengthen the hand of the generals, not imperil them.

NSC meeting
Another inconclusive meeting is held with the division of opinion on a U.S. course of action still strong. The result is to leave policy making in Lodge's hands.

State message 272
Lodge is authorized to have Harkins show the CAS messages to the generals in exchange for a look at their detailed plans. He is further authorized to suspend U.S. aid at his discretion.

31 Aug 1963 *MACV message 1583; Embassy Saigon message 391; and CAS Saigon message 0499*
Harkins meets with Khiem who tells him that Minh has called off the coup. Military was unable to achieve a favorable balance of forces in the Saigon area and doubts about whether the U.S. had leaked their plans to Nhu were the deciding factors. A future attempt is not ruled out.

NSC meeting; MGen Victor C. Krulak, Memo for the Record, Vietnam Meeting at the State Dept.
With the demise of the coup plot confirmed, the NSC (without the President) meets to try to chart a new policy for Vietnam. The discussion reveals the divergence between the military desire to get on with the war and repair relations with Diem, and the State Department view that continued support for Diem will eventually mean a loss of the war as more and more of the South Vietnamese are alienated from it. No decisions are taken.

2 Sep 1963 *Kennedy TV interview*
The President, in a TV interview with CBS News' Walter Cronkite, expresses his disappointment with Diem's handling of the Buddhist crisis and concern that a greater effort is needed by the GVN to win popular support. This can be done, he feels, "with change in policy and perhaps with personnel . . ."

Lodge meets with Nhu
Avoiding any contact with Diem, Lodge nonetheless meets with Nhu who announces his intention to quit the Government as a sign of the progress of the campaign against the VC. Mme Nhu and Archbishop Thuc, another of Diem's brothers, are to leave the country on extended trips shortly.

6 Sep 1963 *NSC meeting*
The NSC decides to instruct Lodge to reopen "tough" negotiations with Diem and to start by clarifying to him the U.S. position. Robert Kennedy speculates that if the war can be won neither

with Diem nor in the event of a disruptive coup, we should perhaps be considering a U.S. disengagement. Secretary McNamara
proposes a fact-finding trip by General Krulak, and State suggests including Joseph Mendenhall, a senior FSO with Vietnam
experience. They leave later the same day.

7 Sep 1963   *Archbishop Thuc leaves Vietnam*
With the intercession of the Vatican and the Papal Delegate in
Saigon, Archbishop Thuc leaves the country for Rome on an
extended visit.

8 Sep 1963   *AID Director Bell TV interview*
In a televised interview, AID Director Bell expresses concern
that Congress might cut aid to South Vietnam if the Diem Government does not change its repressive policies.

9 Sep 1963   *Mme Nhu leaves Vietnam*
Mme Nhu departs from Saigon to attend the World Parliamen-
tarians Conference in Belgrade and then to take an extended
trip through Europe and possibly the U.S.

Kennedy TV interview
Appearing on the inaugural program of the NBC Huntley–Brinkley News, the President says he does not believe an aid cut-off
would be helpful in achieving American purposes in Vietnam at
present.

10 Sep 1963   *NSC meeting*
Krulak and Mendenhall return from Vietnam after a whirlwind
four day trip and make their report to the NSC. With them are
John Mecklin, USIS Director in Saigon, and Rufus Phillips,
USOM's Director of Rural Programs. Krulak's report stresses
that the war is being won and, while there is some dissatisfaction
in the military with Diem, no one would risk his neck to remove
him. A continuation of present policies under Diem will yield
victory. Mendenhall presents a completely contradictory view of
the situation. A breakdown of civil administration was possible
and a religious civil war could not be excluded if Diem was not
replaced. The war certainly could not be won with Diem. Phillips
and Mecklin support Mendenhall with variations. Nolting agrees
with Krulak. All the disagreement prompts the President to ask
the two emissaries, "You two did visit the same country, didn't
you?"

11 Sep 1963   *Embassy Saigon message 478*
Lodge reverses himself in suggesting a complete study of kinds
of economic aid suspension that might be used to topple the
regime.

White House meeting
White House decides to hold economic aid renewal in abeyance
pending a complete examination of how it might be used to pressure Diem.

12 Sep 1963   *Senator Church's Resolution*
With White House approval, Senator Church introduces a resolu-

tion in the Senate condemning the South Vietnamese Government for its repressive handling of the Buddhist problem and calling for an end to U.S. aid unless the repressions are abandoned.

14 Sep 1963   *State message 411*
Lodge is informed that approval of the $18.5 million commercial import program is deferred until basic policy decisions on Vietnam have been made.

16 Sep 1963   *Martial law ends*
Martial law is ended throughout the country.

17 Sep 1963   *NSC meeting*
Two alternative proposals for dealing with Diem are considered. The first would use an escalatory set of pressures to get him to do our bidding. The second would involve acquiescence in recent GVN actions, recognition that Diem and Nhu are inseparable, and an attempt to salvage as much as possible from a bad situation. A decision is taken to adopt the first as policy, and also to send Secretary McNamara and General Taylor on a fact-gathering mission.

21 Sep 1963   *White House press release*
The forthcoming McNamara–Taylor mission is announced to the press by the White House.

White House instructions to McNamara–Taylor
The White House instructions for the mission ask the two men to (1) appraise the status of the military effort; (2) assess the impact on the war effort of the Buddhist crisis; (3) recommend a course of action for the GVN to redress the problem and for the US. to get them to do it; and (4) examine how our aid can further no. 3.

23 Sep 1963   *McNamara–Taylor mission departs*
The McNamara–Taylor party leaves Washington for its ten day trip to Vietnam.

25 Sep 1963   *Opening meeting of McNamara–Taylor with country team*
The disagreement between Harkins and Lodge about the situation in-country and the progress of the war surfaces immediately in this first conference. McNamara spends several subsequent days touring various parts of Vietnam to appraise the war first hand and talk with U.S. and Vietnamese officers.

27 Sep 1963   *National Assembly elections*
As announced earlier, and at the end of a pro forma one week campaign, the GVN holds nation-wide elections for the National Assembly with predictably high turnouts and majorities for Government candidates.

Embassy Saigon messages 602 and 608
Aware that McNamara and Taylor are tasked to recommend uses of the aid program to pressure Diem, both Lodge and Brent, the USOM Director, go on record against them.

29 Sep 1963   *McNamara, Taylor and Lodge see Diem*
In their protocol call on Diem, and after his two-hour monologue, McNamara is able to pointedly stress that the political unrest and Government repressive measures against the Buddhists were undermining the U.S. war effort. Diem seems unimpressed, but does ask Taylor for his appraisal, as a military man, of the progress of the war.

30 Sep 1963   *McNamara, Taylor and Lodge meet Vice President Tho*
Tho stresses to the two visitors the gravity of the political deterioration and the negative effect it was having on war. He questions the success of the strategic hamlet program. Later that day, the McNamara–Taylor party leaves South Vietnam for Honolulu.

2 Oct 1963   *SecDef Memo for the President: Report of the McNamara–Taylor mission*
After a day in Honolulu to prepare a report, McNamara and Taylor return to Washington and present their findings and recommendations to a morning NSC meeting. Their long report represents a compromise between the military and the civilian views. It confirms the progress of the war, but warns of the dangers inherent in the current political turmoil and recommends pressures against Diem to bring changes. Militarily, it calls for greater GVN effort, especially in the Delta and in clear and hold operations, and a consolidation of the strategic hamlet program. It proposes the announcement of the plans to withdraw 1,000 American troops by year's end. To put political pressure on Diem to institute the reforms we want, it recommends a selective aid suspension, an end of support for the special forces responsible for the pagoda raids, and a continuation of Lodge's aloofness from the regime. It recommends against a coup, but qualifies this by suggesting that an alternative leadership be identified and cultivated. The recommendations are promptly approved by the President.

White House press release
A statement following the meeting is released as recommended by McNamara and Taylor that reiterates the U.S. commitment to the struggle against the VC, announces the 1,000 man troop withdrawal, and dissociates the U.S. from Diem's repressive policies. It does not, however, announce the aid suspensions.

CAS Saigon message 1385
CAS agent Conein "accidentally" meets General Don at Tan Son Nhut. Don asks him to come to Nha Trang that evening. With Embassy approval Conein keeps the appointment. Don states that there is an active plot among the generals for a coup, and that General Minh wants to see Conein on Oct 5 to discuss details. The key to the plan, according to Don, is the conversion of III Corps Commander, General Dinh.

5 Oct 1963   *NSC meeting*
The President approves detailed recommendations of the McNamara–Taylor mission for transmission to Lodge.

CAP message 63560
". . . President today approved recommendation that no initiative should now be taken to give any active covert encouragement to a coup. There should, however, be urgent covert effort . . . to identify and build contacts with possible alternative leadership as and when it appears."

CAS Saigon message 1445
With Lodge's approval, and probably before receipt of foregoing message, Conein meets with General Minh. Minh says he must know the U.S. position on a coup in the near future. The GVN's loss of popular support is endangering the whole war effort. Three possible plans are mentioned, one involving assassination. Conein is noncommital.

CAS Saigon message 34026
Lodge recommends that when Conein is contacted again, he be authorized to say that the U.S. will not thwart a coup, that we are willing to review plans, and that we will continue support to a successor regime.

Richardson recalled
His identity having been compromised in recent press stories about internal policy struggles in the U.S. mission, CIA Chief of Station, John Richardson, is recalled to Washington.

6 Oct 1963 *CAP message 63560*
Washington clarifies its views on a coup by stating that the U.S. will not thwart such a move if it offers prospects of a more effective fight against the VC. Security and deniability of all contacts is paramount.

7 Oct 1963 *National Assembly convenes*
The newly elected National Assembly convenes to hear Diem's State of the Union address. Diem speaks mainly of Vietnam's past progress under his rule, playing down the current political crisis and making only scant reference to U.S. aid.

Mme Nhu arrives in U.S.
Mme Nhu arrives in the U.S. from Europe for a three-week speaking tour. She immediately launches into vituperative attacks on the U.S. and its role in Vietnam.

8 Oct 1963 *UN General Assembly vote*
The UN General Assembly, after a strong debate with many voices denouncing Diem's anti-Buddhist policy, votes to send a fact-finding team to Saigon to investigate the charges of repression.

10 Oct 1963 *CAS officer meets Minh*
A CAS officer reportedly meets with Minh and conveys the U.S. position that it will neither encourage nor thwart a coup attempt, but would hope to be informed about it.

17 Oct 1963 *GVN informed of aid cut-off to special forces*
Acting for the Ambassador, General Stillwell, MACV J–3, in-

forms Secretary Thuan that U.S. aid for the special forces units responsible for the Aug 21 raids is being suspended until they are transferred to the field and placed under JGS command.

22 Oct 1963   *Department of State, INR Research Memo RFE90*
The State Department publishes a controversial research memorandum which takes issue with the Pentagon's optimistic reading of the statistical indicators on the progress of the war. The memo states that certain definitely negative and ominous trends can be identified.

Harkins sees Don
General Harkins sees General Don, and in a conversation whose interpretation is subsequently disputed, tells him that U.S. officers should not be approached about a coup as it distracts them from their job, fighting the VC. Don takes it as U.S. discouragement of a coup.

23 Oct 1963   *CAS agent meets Don*
General Don renews contact with Conein to ask for clarification of U.S. policy after Harkins' statement to him of the previous day. Conein repeats Washington guidance, which relieves Don. Conein asks for proof of the existence of the coup and its plan; Don promises to provide politi-
[material missing]

24 Oct 1963   *Diem invites Lodge to Dalat*
Diem extends an invitation to Lodge and his wife to spend Sunday, Oct 27, with him at his villa in Dalat. Lodge is pleased, Diem has come to him.

1st CAS agent meeting with Don
Conein meets with Don in the morning and the latter reports that Harkins had corrected his previous remarks and apologized for any misunderstanding. The coup is set to take place before Nov 2 and he will meet Conein later that day to review the plans.

2nd CAS agent meeting with Don
In the evening, Don tells Conein that the coup committee voted not to reveal any plans because of concern about security leaks. He promises to turn over to Conein for Lodge's Eyes Only the operation plan two days before the coup occurs.

UN fact-finding team arrives in Saigon
The UN fact-finding team arrives in Saigon and begins its investigation.

25 Oct 1963   *CAS Saigon message 1964*
Lodge argues that the time has come to go ahead with a coup and we should not thwart the maturing plot. He takes strong exception to Harkins reservations about the determination and ability of the plotters to carry off the coup.

CAP message 63590
Bundy, replying for the White House, is concerned about the

dangers of U.S. support for a coup that fails. We must be in a position to judge the prospects for the coup plan and discourage any effort with likelihood of failure.

26 Oct 1963   *Vietnamese National Day*
Diem reviews the troops in the National Day parade before scant crowds with Lodge and all other diplomatic personnel in attendance. The coup had originally been scheduled for this day.

27 Oct 1963   *Lodge–Diem meeting*
As planned, Lodge travels to Dalat with Diem and engages in a day-long conversation that produces little results. Diem makes his standard complaints against the U.S., and whenever Lodge asks what he is planning to do about specific U.S. requests, he changes the subject. At one point, he does inquire, however, about resumption of the commercial import program. Lodge asks what movement he will make on our requests. Diem changes the subject. Lodge's feelings of frustration confirm his conviction that we cannot work with Diem.

Buddhist suicide
A seventh Buddhist monk commits suicide by fire.

28 Oct 1963   *Don contacts Lodge*
At the airport in the morning prior to departing for the dedication of an atomic energy facility in Dalat, General Don approaches Lodge and asks if Conein is authorized to speak for the U.S. Lodge says yes. Don then affirms the need for the coup to be completely Vietnamese. Lodge agrees, but when he asks about timing, Don replies that the generals are not yet ready.

CAS agent meets Don
That evening Conein meets Don again and the latter says that the plans may be available for Lodge only four hours before the coup. Lodge should not change his plans to go to Washington on Oct 31 as this would tip off the palace. Some details of the organization of the coup committee are discussed.

29 Oct 1963   *CINCPAC alerts task force*
CINCPAC alerts a naval and air task force to stand off Vietnam for possible evacuation of American dependents and civilians if required.

NSC meeting
A decision is made at the NSC meeting to have Lodge fully inform Harkins on the coup plotting and arrangements, since if Lodge leaves, Harkins will be in charge. Concern is also registered at the differing views of the two men toward a coup.

Special forces transferred from Saigon
In the first preparatory act of the coup, General Dinh orders Colonel Tung's special forces out of Saigon for maneuvers. It is unclear whether the action came as a part of the generals' coup or Nhu's psuedo coup.

30 Oct 1963   *MACV messages 2028, 2033, and 2034*
Belatedly apprised of the continuing contacts with the generals and the U.S. role in the coup plotting, General Harkins dispatches three angry cables to Taylor in which he disagrees with Lodge's interpretation of the U.S. policy. He understands it to be no active covert encouragement. He opposes personally a coup and doesn't think the generals have the forces to pull one off.

CAS Washington message 79109
The White House is now genuinely concerned at the Saigon dispute and tells Lodge it believes we still have the power to call off the coup if we choose to.

CAS Saigon message 2063
Lodge replies to Washington that he is powerless to stop the coup, the matter is entirely in Vietnamese hands. Harkins does not concur.

CAS Washington message 79407
To clear the air and redefine U.S. policy, Washington sent another cable to Lodge. The U.S. cannot accept as a policy position that it has no power to prevent the coup. If the coup does not have high prospects of success, Lodge should intercede with the generals to have it delayed or called off. More detailed information on the plans is urgently requested. Specific instructions to guide U.S. action during a coup are issued. They prescribe strict noninvolvement and somewhat less strict neutrality.

31 Oct 1963   *Lodge defers departure*
Lodge, who had been scheduled to leave for Washington for high-level conferences, defers his departure because of the tense atmosphere and the apparent immenence of the coup.

1 Nov 1963   *Lodge and Felt meet with Diem*
10:00 a.m.   Admiral Felt, who is visiting, and Lodge call on Diem, who reiterates many of the points he made to McNamara a month earlier. At the end of the meeting, Diem takes Lodge aside and indicates he is ready to talk about what the U.S. wants him to do. Felt leaves Saigon after the meeting.

Late   *Coup units begin to deploy*
morning   The first coup units begin to deploy in and around Saigon.

12:00 a.m.   *Officers meet at JGS*
The coup committee has convened a meeting of all senior Vietnamese officers except Generals Dinh and Cao at JGS. There they are informed of the coup and asked to support it. All except Colonel Tung do. Their pledges of support are taped. Tung is taken into custody later to be executed. The CNO was killed en route by an escort. A CAS officer is invited to the JGS and maintains telephone contact with the Embassy throughout the coup.

1:45 p.m.   *U.S. notified*
General Don calls General Stillwell, J–3 to General Harkins, and informs him that the coup is under way.

2:00 p.m. *Key installations taken*
About his time coup forces are seizing the key installations in Saigon, including the post office, police headquarters, radio stations, airport, naval headquarters, etc. They were also deploying for attacks on the palace and the palace guard barracks and to block any counter-attack from outside the city.

4:00 p.m. *First skirmishes, Diem told to surrender*
By about this time the first skirmish was taking place at the palace and guard barracks. Failing to reach General Dinh, Diem and Nhu realize the coup is serious. The generals called shortly after this and told the two brothers to surrender. They refused.

4:30 p.m. *Coup broadcast, Diem calls Lodge*
The generals go on radio, announce the coup and demand the resignation of Diem and Nhu. At the same time, Diem is calling Lodge. He asks Lodge where the U.S. stands. Lodge replies that the U.S. cannot yet have a view. He expresses concern for Diem's safety, and the conversation ends there.

5:00 p.m. *Generals again call Diem to demand surrender*
Repeated calls are now made to the palace to get Diem to surrender. All the generals try. Colonel Tung is put on the phone and tells Diem he is a captive. Tung is then taken outside and executed. Diem and Nhu now frantically call all unit commanders but can find none loyal. Outside sporadic firing continues.

8:00 p.m. *Diem and Nhu flee*
Sometime in the early evening, probably about eight o'clock, the two brothers escape from the palace through one of the secret underground passages constructed for just such emergencies. They are met by a Chinese friend who takes them to a previously prepared hideaway in Cholon. There they spend the night in telephone contact with the palace.

9:00 p.m. *Palace bombarded*
At about nine o'clock, the attackers launch an artillery and armored barrage on the palace and its defenders which lasts through the night.

2 Nov 1963 *Assault on the palace begins*
3:30 a.m. The tank and infantry assault on the Gia Long palace begins.

6:20 a.m. *Diem calls generals to surrender*
Diem calls General Don from the Cholon hideout to surrender, but does not tell his location.

6:30 a.m. *Palace falls*
Realizing the hopelessness of the situation, Diem issues a cease fire order to the palace guard and the palace falls to the insurgents. Colonel Thao, the commander of the attacking forces, learns of Diem's whereabouts and with JGS permission goes to arrest him.

6:45 a.m. *Diem and Nhu again escape*
Arriving at the Cholon house, Thao calls JGS and is overheard by the brothers who escape to a nearby Catholic church.

6:50 a.m.   *Diem and Nhu are captured*
Diem again calls General Don and surrenders, this time unconditionally. He and Nhu are taken prisoner shortly thereafter and
are murdered in the back of an armored personnel carrier en
route to JGS.

afternoon   *Vice President Tho confers on new government*
Vice President Tho enters into intensive conferences and negotiations with the coup committee on the composition of a new
interim government which he will head.

3 Nov 1963   *Lodge meets with Generals Don and Kim*
Generals Don and Kim call on Lodge at the Embassy and apolo-
gize for the absence of Minh who is closeted with Tho working
on the composition of the new government. A two-tiered government is expected. A military committee chaired by General Minh
will supervise a largely civilian cabinet under Tho's Prime Minis-
tership. Lodge promises the immediate restoration of aid programs
and assures the generals of forthcoming U.S. recognition.

4 Nov 1963   *Lodge meets with General Minh*
On instructions from Washington, Lodge meets with Minh and
Don and urges them to make a clarifying statement on the deaths
of Diem and Nhu to allay anxieties about the new leaders. Minh
promises to do so and to announce the new government soon.

5 Nov 1963   *New government announced*
The new government is announced with Minh as President and
Chief of the Military Committee. Tho is Premier, Minister of
Economy and Minister of Finance. Don is Minister of Defense
and Dinh is Minister of Security. Most other posts are filled by
civilians, but there is a noticeable absence of well-known opponents to Diem. A later announcement suspends the 1956 constitution, and outlines the structure and functions of the new interim
government.

6 Nov 1963   *Composition of the Military Revolutionary Council announced*
Saigon Radio announces the composition of the new Military
Revolutionary Council with Minh as Chairman and including all
important generals except Khanh.

7 Nov 1963   *NLF makes post-coup policy statement*
In a post-coup policy statement, the NLF lists eight demands of
the new regime, all but one of which the Minh-Tho Government
was going to do anyway.

Brent meets with Tho on U.S. aid
USOM Director Brent meets with Tho who indicated that all
economic aid questions would be handled directly by his office. It
was further agreed that a high-level Vietnamese commission would
work with a similar group in the U.S. mission to establish economic and aid policies and levels.

8 Nov 1963   *U.S. recognizes new government*
Lodge calls on the new Foreign Minister, Pham Dang Lam, and

presents a note of U.S. recognition. The new government will be heavily dependent on the U.S. in all areas.

9 Nov 1963   *Embassy Saigon message 986*
In the weekly progress report, the mission notes the greatly increased VC activity in the week following the coup. The return of coup units to the field will reverse this trend, it is hoped.

12 Nov 1963 *CINCPAC message to JCS 120604Z 63*
CINCPAC takes note that the statistical indicators for the war (VC attacks, weapons loss ratio, VC defections) show deterioration dating back to the summer.

17 Nov 1963 *NLF releases stronger set of demands*
Its first set of demands having been effectively preempted by the new Minh Government, the NLF release a new and stronger set of demands including that the U.S. influence be eliminated, the fighting be halted and that a coalition government be established. For the first time the NLF states that reunification of Vietnam is an objective.

20 Nov 1963 *Honolulu Conference*
The entire country team meets with Rusk, McNamara, Taylor, Bundy, and Bell to review the current situation. Lodge voices optimism about the new government, but notes the inexperience of the new leaders. We should not press them too hard. We should secondly pledge aid to them in at least the amounts we were giving it to Diem. Brent notes the economic naivety of the generals and indicates the need for greater U.S. technical assistance to the government. Harkins' assessment is guardedly optimistic, taking note of the higher than average VC activity in the week after the coup. The determination of the new leaders impressed him, but he was concerned about the disruptions that wholesale replacements of province and district chiefs might have.

Press release after Honolulu Conference
The press release gives few details but does reiterate the U.S. intention to withdraw 1,000 troops by the end of the year.

22 Nov 1963 *Lodge confers with the President*
Having flown to Washington the day after the conference, Lodge meets with the President and presumably continues the kind of report given in Honolulu.

23 Nov 1963 *NSAM 273*
Drawing together the results of the Honolulu Conference and Lodge's meeting with the President, NSAM 273 reaffirms the U.S. commitment to defeat the VC in South Vietnam. It reiterates the plan to withdraw 1,000 troops by year's end and to end the war in the first three corps areas by the end of 1964 and in the Delta by the end of 1965. U.S. support for the new regime is confirmed and aid in at least the amounts given to Diem is guaranteed. The Delta is to be the area of concentration for all military, political, economic and social efforts. And clandestine operations against the North and into Laos are authorized.

I. INTRODUCTION

In the spring of 1963, the regime of Ngo Dinh Diem seemed to exhibit no more signs of advanced decay or imminent demise than might have been discerned since 1958 or 1959. Only in hindsight can certain developments be identified as salient. Of these, certainly the steadily increasing influence of the Nhus was the most ominous. Nhu came more and more to dominate Diem in the last year of the Diem rule. But as his power increased, Nhu's grip on reality seems to have slipped and he was reported in that last year to have been smoking opium and to have been mentally ill. Meanwhile, Mme. Nhu was developing a power obsession of her own. The catastrophic effect of their influence during the ensuing crisis, however, was impossible to have predicted. As one perceptive observer noted, the Ngo family "had come to power with a well-developed persecution complex and had subsequently developed a positive mania for survival."

Another source of concern should have been the regime's self-imposed isolation from the populace. It had left the peasants apathetic, a cause for real concern in a struggle with the zealous, doctrinaire Viet Cong; but, more importantly, it had alienated large portions of the restive urban population who felt most directly the impact of the regime's arbitrary rule. The regime, in fact, had no real base of political support and relied on the loyalty of a handful of key military commanders to keep it in power by forestalling any overthrow. The loyalty of these men was bought with promotions and favors. Graft and corruption should also have drawn concern, even if governmental dishonesty was endemic in Asia, and probably not disproportionate at that time in South Vietnam.

It was not, however, the strains that these problems had placed on the Vietnamese political structure that were ultimately decisive. The fundamental weakness of the Diem regime was the curious rigidity and political insensitivity of its mandarin style in the face of a dramatic crisis of popular confidence.

With regard to the war, the consensus of the U.S. military mission and the U.S. intelligence community in the spring of 1963 was that the military situation in South Vietnam was steadily improving and the war was beginning to be won. A National Intelligence Estimate in April 1963 concluded that the infusion of U.S. advisors had begun to have the desired effect of strengthening the ARVN and increasing its aggressiveness. [Doc. 121] The Viet Cong retained good strength, but could be contained by the ARVN if they did not receive a great increase in external support. Statistical indices showed a decline in Viet Cong attacks from the previous year, increased ARVN offensive activity, and improvement in the weapons loss ratio. Continuing problems were Diem's loyalty-based officer promotion policy, ARVN desertions and AWOL's, poor intelligence, and low grade NCO's and company grade officers. Nonetheless, the overall outlook was sanguine. Particular reason for encouragement was the adoption in February 1963 of the National Campaign Plan urged by the U.S. The hopeful prospects were summarized for Secretary McNamara in a briefing paper for the Honolulu Conference of May 6:

> The over-all situation in Vietnam is improving. In the military sector of the counterinsurgency, we are winning. Evidences of improvement are clearly visible, as the combined impact of the programs which involve a long lead time begin to have effect on the Viet Cong.

Even as seasoned an observer of insurgency as Sir Robert Thompson, Chief of the British Advisory Mission, was able to report that, "Now, in March 1963, I can say, and in this I am supported by all members of the mission, that the Government is beginning to win the shooting war against the Viet Cong."

One reason for the optimism of these appraisals was the vigor with which the government, under the direction of Nhu, was pushing the Strategic Hamlet Program. Nhu had been initially cool to the idea, but once he established the U.S. willingness to fund the program, he focused on it as the principal vehicle of the counterinsurgency campaign and as an excellent means of extending the oligarchy's control into the countryside. In April the GVN claimed it had completed 5,000 strategic hamlets and had another 2,000 under construction. There was already official U.S. misgiving, however, about the quality of many of the hamlets and about overextension of the country's limited human resources in the program's frantic rate of expansion. Nevertheless, field reports seemed to support the success of the program which was seen as the key to the struggle against the Viet Cong.

U.S.–GVN relations in the spring of 1963 were beginning to show signs of accumulating stress. As the U.S. commitment and involvement deepened, frictions between American advisors and Vietnamese counterparts at all levels increased. Diem, under the influence of Nhu, complained about the quantity and zeal of U.S. advisors. They were creating a colonial impression among the people, he said. Diem chose to dramatize his complaint by delaying agreement on the commitment of South Vietnamese funds for joint counterinsurgency projects. The issue was eventually resolved, but the sensitivity to the growing U.S. presence remained and as the long crisis summer wore on, it gradually became a deep-seated suspicion of U.S. motives.

The report of the Mansfield mission, published in March, further exacerbated relations between the two countries. Diem and Nhu were particularly incensed by its praise of Cambodian neutralism and criticism of their regime. Coup rumors began to circulate again that spring, and the prevailing palace state of mind hearkened back to suspicions of U.S. complicity in the abortive 1960 coup. Mme. Nhu's ascorbic public criticism of the United States was a further source of friction. By May 1963, these problems in U.S.–GVN relations were already substantial enough to preoccupy officials of both governments. Within a matter of weeks, however, events thrust them into the background of a far more serious crisis.

II.   THE BUDDHIST CRISIS: MAY 8–AUGUST 21

A. THE CRISIS ERUPTS

The incident in Hue on May 8, 1963, that precipitated what came to be called the Buddhist crisis, and that started the chain of events that ultimately led to the overthrow of the Diem regime and the murder of the Ngo brothers, happened both inadvertently and unexpectedly. No one then foresaw that it would generate a national opposition movement capable of rallying virtually all non-communist dissidence in South Vietnam. More importantly, no one then appreciated the degree of alienation of Vietnam's people from their government, nor the extent of the political decay within the regime, a regime no longer capable of coping with popular discontent.

The religious origins of the incident are traceable to the massive flight of

Catholic refugees from North Vietnam after the French defeat in 1954. An estimated one million Catholics fled the North and resettled in the South. Diem, animated, no doubt, by religious as well as humanitarian sympathy, and with an eye to recruiting political support from his coreligionists, accorded these Catholic refugees preferential treatment in land redistribution, relief and assistance, commercial and export-import licenses, government employment, and other GVN largess. Because Diem could rely on their loyalty, they came to fill almost all important civilian and military positions. As an institution, the Catholic Church enjoyed a special legal status. The Catholic primate, Ngo Dinh Thuc, was Diem's brother and advisor. But prior to 1962, there had been no outright discrimination against Buddhists. However, among South Vietnam's 3–4 million practicing Buddhists and the 80% of the population who were nominal Buddhists, the regime's favoritism, authoritarianism, and discrimination created a smoldering resentment.

In April 1963, the government ordered provincial officials to enforce a long-standing but generally ignored ban on the public display of religious flags. The order came just after the officially encouraged celebrations in Hue commemorating the 25th anniversary of the ordination of Ngo Dinh Thuc, the Archbishop of Hue, during which Papal flags had been prominently flown. The order also came, as it happened, just prior to Buddha's birthday (May 8)—a major Buddhist festival. Hue, an old provincial capital of Vietnam, was the only real center of Buddhist learning and scholarship in Vietnam and its university had long been a center of left-wing dissidence. Not surprisingly, then, the Buddhists in Hue defiantly flew their flags in spite of the order and, when the local administration appeared to have backed down on the ban, were emboldened to hold a previously scheduled mass meeting on May 8 to commemorate Buddha's birthday. Seeing the demonstration as a challenge to family prestige (Hue was also the capital of the political fief of another Diem brother, Ngo Dinh Can) and to government authority, local officials tried to disperse the crowds. When preliminary efforts produced no results, the Catholic deputy province chief ordered his troops to fire. In the ensuing melee, nine persons were killed, including some children, and fourteen were injured. Armored vehicles allegedly crushed some of the victims. The Diem government subsequently put out a story that a Viet Cong agent had thrown a grenade into the crowd and that the victims had been crushed in a stampede. It steadfastly refused to admit responsibility even when neutral observers produced films showing government troops firing on the crowd.

Diem's mandarin character would not permit him to handle this crisis with the kind of flexibility and finesse it required. He was incapable of publicly acknowledging responsibility for the tragedy and seeking to conciliate the angry Buddhists. He was convinced that such a public loss of face would undermine his authority to rule, oblivious to the fact that no modern ruler can long ignore massive popular disaffection whatever his own particular personal virtues may be. So the government clung tenaciously to its version of what had occurred.

The following day in Hue over 10,000 people demonstrated in protest of the killings. It was the first of the long series of protest activities with which the Buddhists were to pressure the regime in the next four months. The Buddhists rapidly organized themselves, and on May 10, a manifesto of the Buddhist clergy was transmitted to the government demanding freedom to fly their flag, legal equality with the Catholic Church, an end of arrests and freedom to practice their beliefs, and indemnification of the victims of the May 8th incident with punishment for its perpetrators. These five demands were officially presented to President Diem on May 15, and the Buddhists held their first press conference after the meeting. Publicized hunger strikes and meetings continued throughout May, but Diem continued to drag his feet on placating the dissenters or settling issues. On May 30, about 350 Buddhist monks demonstrated in front of the National Assembly in Saigon, and a 48-hour hunger strike was announced. On June 3, a demonstration in Hue was broken up with tear gas and several people were burned, prompting charges that the troops had used mustard gas. On June 4, the government announced the appointment of an interministerial committee headed by Vice President Tho to resolve the religious issue, but by this time such gestures were probably too late. Large portions of the urban population had rallied to the Buddhist protest, recognizing in it the beginnings of genuine political opposition to Diem. On June 8, Mme. Nhu exacerbated the problem by announcing that the Buddhists were infiltrated by communists.

Throughout the early days of the crisis, the U.S. press had closely covered the events and brought them to the attention of the world. On June 11, the press was tipped off to be at a downtown intersection at noon. Expecting another protest demonstration, they were horrified to witness the first burning suicide by a Buddhist monk. Thich Quang Duc's fiery death shocked the world and electrified South Vietnam.

Negotiations had been taking place between Vice President Tho's committee and the Buddhists since June 5, with considerable acrimonious public questioning of good faith by both sides. After the suicide, the U.S. intensified its already considerable pressure on the government to mollify the Buddhists, and to bring the deteriorating political situation under control. Finally, on June 16, a joint GVN–Buddhist communique was released outlining the elements of a settlement, but affixing no responsibility for the May 8 incident. Violent suppression by the GVN of rioting the next day, however, abrogated the spirit of the agreement. The Nhus, for their part, immediately undertook to sabotage the agreement by secretly calling on the GVN-sponsored youth organizations to denounce it. By late June, it was apparent that the agreement was not meant as a genuine gesture of conciliation by Diem, but was only an effort to appease the U.S. and paper over a steadily widening fissure in internal politics.

The evident lack of faith on the part of the government in the June 16 agreement discredited the conciliatory policy of moderation that the older Buddhist leadership had followed until that time. In late June, leadership of the Buddhist movement passed to a younger, more radical set of monks, with more far-reaching political objectives. They made intelligent and skillful political use of a rising tide of popular support. Carefully planned mass meetings and demonstrations were accompanied with an aggressive press campaign of opposition to the regime. Seizing on the importance of American news media, they cultivated U.S. newsmen, tipped them off to demonstrations and rallies, and carefully timed their activities to get maximum press coverage. Not surprisingly, the Ngo family reacted with ever more severe suppression to the Buddhist activists, and with acrimonious criticism and even threats to the American newsmen.

Early in July, Vice President Tho's committee announced that a preliminary investigation of the May 8 incident had confirmed that the deaths were the result of an act of Viet Cong terrorism. Outraged, the Buddhists denounced the findings and intensified their protest activities. On July 19, under U.S. pressure, Diem made a brief two-minute radio address, ostensibly an expression of conciliation to the Buddhists, but so written and coldly delivered as to destroy in advance any effect its announced minor concessions might have had.

Within the regime, Nhu and his wife were severely criticizing Diem for caving in under Buddhist pressure. Mme. Nhu publicly ridiculed the Buddhist suicide as a "barbecue," accused the Buddhist leaders of being infiltrated with communists, and construed the protest movement as Viet Cong inspired. Both Nhu and his wife worked publicly and privately to undermine Diem's feeble efforts at compromise with the Buddhists, and rumors that Nhu was considering a coup against his brother began to circulate in July.

A U.S. Special National Intelligence Estimate on July 10 concluded with the perceptive prediction that if the Diem regime did nothing to implement the June 16 agreement and to appease the Buddhists, the likelihood of a summer of demonstrations was great, with the strong possibility of a non-communist coup attempt. [Doc. 21] By mid-August a week before Nhu launched general raids on Buddhist pagodas in Saigon and elsewhere, the CIA had begun to note malaise in the bureaucracy and the army:

> Since the Buddhist dispute with the Diem government erupted on 8 May, there have been a series of reports indicating not only intensified plotting and grumbling among Diem's traditional non-Communist critics, but renewed restiveness and growing disaffection in official civilian and military circles over Diem's handling of the dispute.

This estimate went on to detail numerous rumors of coup plots in existence since at least late June. But Nhu, in a bold move designed to frighten coup plotters, and to throw them off guard, had called in the senior generals on July 11, reprimanded them for not having taken action to squelch revolt, and questioned their loyalty to the regime. Nhu's move seemed to have temporarily set back all plans for an overthrow. CIA also reported rumors that Nhu himself was planning a "false coup" to draw out and then crush the Buddhists.

In August, Buddhist militancy reached new intensity; monks burned themselves to death on the 5th, 15th, and 18th. The taut political atmosphere in Saigon in mid-August should have suggested to U.S. observers that a showdown was on the way. When the showdown came, however, in the August 21 raids on the pagodas, the U.S. mission was apparently caught almost completely off guard.

B.   THE U.S. "NO ALTERNATIVES TO DIEM" POLICY

The explanation of how the U.S. mission became detached from the realities of the political situation in Saigon in August 1963, is among the most ironic and tragic of our entire involvement in Vietnam. In dealing with Diem over the years, the U.S. had tried two radically different but ultimately equally unsuccessful approaches. Under Ambassador Elbridge Durbrow from the late '50s until 1961, we had used tough pressure tactics to bring Diem to implement programs and ideas we felt necessary to win the war against the Viet Cong. But Diem soon learned that the U.S. was committed to him as the only Vietnamese leader capable of rallying his country to defeat the communists. Armed with this knowledge he could defer action or ignore the Ambassador with relative impunity. He became adept at playing the role of offended lover. Thus by 1961, Durbrow was cut off from the palace, with little information about what was going on and even less influence over events. Under Frederick Nolting as U.S. Ambassador, the U.S. pursued a very different tactic. Forewarned not to allow himself to be isolated, Nolting set out through the patient cultivation of Diem's friendship and trust to secure a role for himself as Diem's close and confidential advisor. But there had been no basic change in the American belief that there was no alternative to Diem, and Diem must have quickly sensed this, for he continued to respond primarily to family interest, at best only listening impatiently to Nolting's carefully put complaints, secure in the knowledge that ultimately the U.S. would not abandon him no matter what he did. Both tactics failed because of American commitment. No amount of pressure or suasion was likely to be effective in getting Diem to adopt ideas or policies which he did not find to his liking, since we had communicated our unwillingness to consider the ultimate sanction—withdrawal of support for his regime. We had ensnared ourselves in a powerless, no alternatives policy.

The denouement of this policy, the ultimate failure of all our efforts to coerce, cajole and coax Diem to be something other than the mandarin that he was, came in the midnight attack on the pagodas on August 21. And it created a fundamental dilemma for U.S. policy with respect to Diem. On the one hand, withdrawal of support for his regime was the only lever likely to force Diem to redress the Buddhist grievances and to make the political reforms prerequisite for popular support in the common fight against the Viet Cong. On the other hand, withdrawal of U.S. support for Diem would be signal U.S. approval for an anti-Diem coup, with all its potential for political instability and erosion of the war effort. We found ourselves in this predicament not entirely unexpectedly.

In May 1963, though it had failed to anticipate the Buddhist upheaval, the U.S. mission nevertheless quickly recognized the gravity of the threat to Diem and reported it to Washington. Nolting met with Diem on May 18 and outlined the steps he felt were necessary to retrieve the situation. These included a government acknowledgment of responsibility for the Hue incident, an offer to compensate the families of the victims, and a reaffirmation of religious equality and nondiscrimination. As an alternative, he suggested an investigatory commission. Diem's noncommittal response led the Ambassador to think that Diem really believed the Viet Cong had caused the deaths and that the Buddhists had provoked the incident. Diem felt the U.S. was over-reacting to the events. Thus, at a critical time Nolting, in spite of his two years of careful groundwork, was unable to exercise any real influence over Diem. Nolting left on a well-deserved holiday and home leave shortly after this frustrating meeting.

By the end of May, Washington had become concerned at Diem's failure to act, and at the widening Buddhist protest. The Chargé d'Affaires, William Truehart, was instructed to press the GVN for action. Working with Secretary of State for Defense Thuan, Truehart tried to move the government toward negotiations with the Buddhists. After the demonstrations in Hue on June 3, the State Department instructed Truehart to tell Diem or Thuan that the U.S. also had a stake in an amicable settlement with the Buddhists. On the following day, Truehart met with Thuan and told him that U.S. support of South Vietnam could not be maintained if there was bloody repressive action in Hue. This seemed to get action. Later that day, Truehart was informed that Nolting's second suggestion had been adopted and a high-level commission had been named to settle the problem. The commission, headed by Vice President Tho, met belatedly with the Buddhists on June 5.

On June 8, Truehart had an interview with Diem to protest Mme. Nhu's public criticism of the Buddhists, which was poisoning the atmosphere for a settlement. When Diem refused to disavow her statements, Truehart threatened a U.S. "dissociation" from any future repressive measures to suppress demonstrations. Truehart left the meeting with the impression that Diem was more preoccupied with security measures than with negotiations. Nolting's low-key policy had by now been abandoned, both in Washington and in Saigon, in favor of a new tough line.

The situation was dramatically altered by the first Buddhist suicide on June 11. Alarmed, the State Department authorized Truehart to tell Diem that unless drastic action was taken to meet the Buddhist demands promptly, the U.S. would be forced to state publicly its dissociation from the GVN on the Buddhist issue. Truehart made his demarche on June 12. Diem replied that any such U.S. announcement would have a disastrous effect on the GVN-Buddhist negotiations. The negotiations finally got under way in earnest June 14 and the joint communique was issued June 16.

Truehart made repeated calls on Diem in late June and early July, urging him in the strongest language to take some action indicating the government's intention to abide in good faith by the June 16 agreement. His effort's were unavailing. Diem was either noncommittal, or talked in generalities about the difficulties of the problem.

On June 27, President Kennedy named Henry Cabot Lodge to replace Ambassador Nolting effective in September. After a brief stop in Washington, Nolting was hurried back to Saigon on July 11 to make one last effort to get Diem to conciliate the Buddhists. Nolting, evidently resenting the pressure tactics used by Truehart, met immediately with Diem and tried to mollify him. He succeeded only in convincing Diem to make the shallow gesture of the July 19 radio speech. Otherwise, Diem merely persisted in appeals for public harmony and support of the government, without any real attempt to deal with the Buddhist grievances.

Nolting spent his last month in Vietnam trying to repair U.S.–GVN relations and to move Diem to resolve the Buddhist crisis, but his attempts were continually undercut by the Nhus both publicly and privately. They had grown increasingly belligerent about the Buddhists during the summer, and by August spoke often of "crushing" them. Washington asked Nolting to protest such inflammatory remarks, and began to suspect Diem's capacity to conciliate the Buddhists in the face of Nhu sabotage. Nolting was instructed to suggest to Diem that Mme. Nhu be removed from the scene. Nolting asked Diem for a public declaration repudiating her remarks but after initially agreeing, Diem then demurred and postponed it. Finally, as a parting gesture to Nolting, he agreed on August 14 to make a statement. It came in the form of an interview with Marguerite Higgins of the *New York Herald Tribune.* Diem asserted that conciliation had been his policy all along and that it was "irreversible." He further said, in direct contradiction of a previous remark by Mme. Nhu, that the family was pleased with Lodge's appointment. Washington was apparently satisfied by this statement, which Diem viewed merely as a going-away present for Nolting. Less than a week later, Nolting's two years of careful work and an American policy would be in a shambles, betrayed by Nhu's midnight raid on the pagodas.

Underlying the prevailing U.S. view that there was no alternative to Diem was the belief that the disruptive effect of a coup on the war effort, and the disorganization that would follow such a coup, could only benefit the VC, perhaps decisively. Military estimates and reports emanating from MACV through the summer of 1963 continued to reflect an optimistic outlook, indicating good reason to continue our support of Diem even in the face of his inept handling of the Buddhist crisis. In retrospect, it can be seen that by July the GVN position in the war had begun to seriously deteriorate. At the time, however, this weakening was not yet apparent. The then prevailing view also held that the Buddhist crisis had not yet detracted from the war effort, although its potential to do so was recognized. Secretary McNamara on July 19 told a press conference that the war was progressing well and that the Buddhist crisis had thus far not affected it. The intelligence community, however, had already begun to note depressing effects of the crisis on military and civilian morale.

Meanwhile, the U.S. press corps was reporting a far different view of both the war and the Buddhist crisis, one which was, in retrospect, nearer the reality. In particular, they were reporting serious failures in the Delta in both military operations and the Strategic Hamlet Program. Typical of this reporting was an August 15 story in the *New York Times* by David Halberstam presenting a very negative appraisal of the war in the Delta. Such reports were vehemently refuted within the Administration, most notably by General Krulak, the JCS Special Assistant for Counterinsurgency. At the lower echelons in the field, however, there were many U.S. advisors who did not share Krulak's sanguine view of the war's progress.

Within the Administration, no real low-risk alternative to Diem had ever been identified, and we had continued our support for his troublesome regime because Diem was regarded as the only Vietnamese figure capable of rallying national support in the struggle against the Viet Cong. The Buddhist crisis shattered our illusions about him, and increased the domestic U.S. political price to Kennedy of supporting Diem. But the only other option for us seemed a coup, with highly uncertain prospects for post-coup political stability. At a briefing for the President on July 4, the possibilities and prospects for a coup were discussed. [Doc. 123] It was the consensus that the Nhus could not be removed, but that there would surely be coup attempts in the next four months. Nolting's reported view, with which then Assistant Secretary of State, Roger Hilsman, did not entirely agree, was that a coup would most likely produce a civil war. Hilsman felt that the likelihood of general chaos in the wake of a coup was less than it had been the preceding year. (Notes on this briefing, reproduced in the Appendix, provide the first documentary evidence of highest level consideration of the ramifications of a coup.)

In a meeting at State the following day, July 5, Ambassador Nolting, who had cut short his vacation to return to Washington in the wake of the Buddhist crisis, told Under Secretary of State George Ball:

> In his view if a revolution occurred in Viet-Nam which grew out of the Buddhist situation, the country would be split between feuding factions and the Americans would have to withdraw and the country might be lost to the Communists. This led to the question of how much pressure we could exert on Diem. Mr. Nolting replied that if we repudiated him on this issue his government would fall. The Ambassador believed that Diem would live up to the agreement (June 16) unless he believed that he was dealing with a political attempt to cause his overthrow. [Doc. 124]

Earlier in the same interview he had said:

> . . . that although interference by the Nhus was serious, he believed that the GVN would be able to come through this one slowly. As to tactics, the more Diem was prodded the slower he went. While Nhu was troublesome he was chiefly responsible for gains which had been made in the provincial pacification program. [Doc. 124]

Nolting, no doubt, expressed similar views when he met with Secretary McNamara before returning to Saigon.

In spite of the mounting political pressure on the President in Congress and in the press because of the Buddhist repressions, the Administration decided to send Nolting back for another try at getting Diem to settle the dispute with the Buddhists. Anxiety in Washington mounted as the summer wore on, and Nolting's efforts with Diem produced evident progress. By the time of the August 21 raids, Washington's patience with Diem was all but exhausted.

III.   LODGE vs. DIEM: AUGUST 20–OCTOBER 2

A.   THE PAGODA RAIDS AND REPERCUSSIONS

Shortly after midnight on August 21, six days after Nolting's frustrated departure, Nhu, shattering any remaining illusions about the GVN's conciliatory approach to the Buddhists, and betraying Diem's parting pledge to Nolting, staged a general assault on Buddhist pagodas. In Saigon, Hue, and other coastal cities, the regime's private shock troops—the U.S.-trained Special Forces—and the combat police invaded the pagodas and arrested hundreds of Buddhist monks, effectively destroying an American policy and marking the beginning of the end of the Diem regime.

On August 18, ten senior generals had met and decided that they would ask Diem for a declaration of martial law to permit them to return Buddhist monks from outside Saigon to their own provinces and pagodas, hopefully reducing tensions in the capital. Among those in attendance at the meeting were General Ton That Dinh, military governor of Saigon and commander of III Corps surrounding it, and General Huynh Van Cao, IV Corps commander, both of whom owed their positions to their loyalty to the regime. Either or both of them probably reported the outcome of this meeting to Diem and Nhu.

In any case, Nhu had decided to eliminate the Buddhist opposition, and to confront the U.S. with a fait accompli on Lodge's arrival; he assumed the U.S. would protestingly acquiesce, as it always had in the past. On the afternoon of the 20th, Nhu met with a small group of generals, including Don, Khiem, and Dinh who presented the martial law proposal to him. Nhu, his own plans for the raids now far advanced, told them to take their proposal to Diem. At a meeting later that evening, Diem acquiesced in the generals' plan and at midnight the decree was published under the signature of General Don, Chief of the Joint General Staff. Meanwhile, unbeknown to the generals, Nhu had already alerted Colonel Tung's Special Forces and the combat police. Once the facade of martial law was in place, so the army would be blamed for the raids, Nhu gave the word and the crackdown began. To further implicate the army, some of the combat police wore paratroop uniforms. Pagodas were ransacked in all the major South Vietnamese cities, and over 1400 Buddhists, primarily monks, were arrested. In the raid on Xa Loi pagoda in Saigon about thirty monks were wounded or injured, and several were subsequently listed as missing; exact casualties were never established. Diem had approved the martial law decree without consulting his cabinet, but it was never established whether he knew of and approved Nhu's plans for the pagoda raids. Significantly, he never subsequently sought to dissociate himself from Nhu or the raids.

While the martial law decree gave General Don command of all troops, in fact, General Dinh and Colonel Tung took their orders directly from the palace. Thus, when the raids came, General Don was at JGS unaware. In a long discussion on August 23 with a CAS officer, he suggested that the martial law decree was only phase one of a larger Generals' plot. They were thrown off balance, however, by the raids and by General Dinh's rapid assumption of local control of martial law in Saigon.

In planning the raids, Nhu had been extremely careful not to have word leak to the U.S. mission (although the Buddhists and the U.S. press corps had been tipped off by their own informants). On the morning after the attack, Richardson, the CIA chief and the senior American civilian in Saigon, emphatically denied to Halberstam any foreknowledge of the plan. To further isolate the U.S. from an accurate assessment during the operation, Nhu had the telephone lines to the Embassy and the homes of all senior U.S. personnel cut shortly after the raids got under way. His efforts had the desired effect. It was several days before the U.S. mission in Saigon and officials in Washington could piece together what happened. In Washington, Harriman and Michael Forrestal, a member of McGeorge Bundy's staff at the White House, drafted a stiff public statement that was released by the State Department at 9:30 the following morning. It deplored the raids as "a direct violation by the Vietnamese Government of assurances that it was pursuing a policy of reconciliation with the Buddhists." But the first U.S. intelligence reports, based on information from Nhu, accepted army responsibility for the raids, and treated their coincidence with the martial law decree as, in effect, a military coup. In an August 21 memorandum for the Secretary of Defense, the Director of DIA, General Carroll, wrote, "Although the military moves are based on an alleged presidential proclamation, the military leaders have, in effect, assumed full control."

When the raids occurred, Lodge, Nolting, and Roger Hilsman, the Assistant Secretary of State for the Far East, had been conferring in Honolulu. Lodge was immediately instructed to proceed to Saigon. After a brief stop in Tokyo, Lodge touched down in Saigon at 9:30 p.m. on August 22, in an atmosphere charged with tension and official U.S. confusion. Awaiting him was a cable from Hilsman asking for a clarification of the situation. Had the military taken over and retained Diem as a figurehead; had Diem strengthened his own position by calling in the military; or were the Nhus really calling the shots? Within twenty-four hours, Lodge had sent a preliminary reply: there had been no coup, but there seemed also to be no diminution in the roles of the Nhus, although the power roles within the regime were unclear.

That same day, the first military feelers had been put out from the Vietnamese generals to determine what the U.S. reaction would be to a military coup. General Don, the commander of the armed forces under the martial law decree, had a long, rambling conversation with a CAS officer. He first outlined the true role the army had played in the events of August 20–21 and then inquired why the U.S. had blamed the army for the raids on the pagodas:

General Don has heard personally that the military is being blamed by Vietnamese public for the attack on the pagodas. He said that the US Govt is at fault for this misconception because VOA announced that the military took action against the pagodas. Don queried why VOA did not admit that Colonel Tung's Special Forces and the Police carried out the action. Don believes this would help the military at this point. Don stated that the USA should now make its position known.

In a conversation the same day with Rufus Phillips of USOM, General Kim, deputy to General Don, bitterly attacked Nhu, charging him with responsibility for the raids, and deploring his dominant role in the government. He said that unless the popular impression that the army was responsible for the raids were corrected, the army would be handicapped in its fight against the VC. He stated that a firm U.S. stand for the removal of the Nhus would unify the army and permit it to act against them. These two direct and obviously reinforcing requests for U.S. support for military action aimed at Nhu's ouster marked the formal beginning of the U.S. involvement in the protracted plotting against the Diem regime. Two senior civilians in the government, Diem's chef de cabinet, Vo Van Hai, and Secretary of State, Nguyen Dinh Thuan, were simultaneously telling U.S. contacts that Nhu's elimination from the government was vital and that the U.S. should take a strong stand against him.

On August 24, Lodge cabled his appraisal of the situation to Washington, based on these conversations. "Nhu," he reported, "probably with full support of Diem, had a large hand in planning of action against Buddhists, if he did not fully master-mind it. His influence has also been significantly increased." Nhu had simply taken advantage of the concern of certain generals, possibly not fully informing the regular army of the planned action. Nonetheless, none of the important Saigon area troop commanders (Don, Dinh, and Tung) were presently disaffected with the regime. Furthermore, absence of clear-cut military leadership and troop strength in Saigon for a move against the Nhus would make U.S. support of such an action a "shot in the dark."

For the State Department, the problem of clarifying the public record about the raids and affixing responsibility for them had become acute by August 24. The press reports emanating from Saigon had from the outset blamed Nhu for the raids, but VOA, with a large audience in Vietnam, continued to report the official U.S. position that the army was culpable. The accumulating evidence against Nhu and the likelihood of severe damage to army morale if VOA did not broadcast a clarification seemed to call for retractions.

The second issue for Washington was Nhu. The generals had asked, in effect, for a green light to move against him, but Lodge had cautioned against it. Hilsman reports that as he, Harriman, Forrestal, and Ball deliberated over the drafting of a reply on that Saturday morning, the statement of Thuan to Phillips that "under no circumstance should the United States acquiesce in what the Nhus had done," was given great weight. Admiral Felt telephoned Washington from CINCPAC to support a strong U.S. stand against the Nhus. The unanswered question, of course, was whether the Nhus could be removed without also sacrificing Diem, and if not, whether the resulting political instability would not have an even more detrimental effect on the war effort than maintaining Diem.

The August 24 cable of instructions to Lodge resulting from these deliberations outlined an important, and subsequently controversial, new policy approach for the U.S. in South Vietnam. Its opening paragraphs crisply set forth the new American view:

> It is now clear that whether military proposed martial law or whether Nhu tricked them into it, Nhu took advantage of its imposition to smash pagodas with police and Tung's Special Forces loyal to him, thus placing onus on military in eyes of world and Vietnamese people. Also clear that Nhu has maneuvered himself into commanding position.
>
> US Government cannot tolerate situation in which power lies in Nhu's

hands. Diem must be given chance to rid himself of Nhu and his coterie and replace them with best military and political personalities available.

If, in spite of all your efforts, Diem remains obdurate and refuses, then we must face the possibility that Diem himself cannot be preserved. [Doc. 126]

Lodge was instructed to tell the GVN the U.S. could not accept the actions against the Buddhists and that prompt dramatic steps to redress the situation must be taken. The key military leaders were to be privately informed that,

> . . . US would find it impossible to continue support GVN militarily and economically unless above steps are taken immediately which we recognize requires removal of Nhus from the scene. We wish give Diem reasonable opportunity to remove Nhus, but if he remains obdurate, then we are prepared to accept the obvious implication that we can no longer support Diem. You may also tell appropriate military commanders we will give them direct support in any interim period of breakdown central government mechanism. [Doc. 126]

Finally, the message recognized the need to publicly exonerate the army from the raids and asked Lodge to approve a VOA broadcast to that effect. Lodge was requested, as well, to survey urgently for alternative leadership.

Clearance of the draft message was complicated by the coincident week-end absence from Washington of most of the top level members of the Administration. The President was in Hyannis Port; Rusk was in New York; and McNamara and McCone were away on vacation. Both the President and the Secretary of State were reached, however, and approved the draft. Deputy Secretary of Defense Roswell Gilpatric approved for Defense, and General Taylor for the JCS. Schlesinger, in his account of the incident, suggests that the cable was hasty and ill-considered, and that the President immediately began to back away from it.

Lodge replied the following day endorsing the strong position but proposing to forego a futile approach to Diem and to state our position instead only to the generals, thus throwing all our weight behind a coup. The cable stated:

> Believe that chances of Diem's meeting our demands are virtually nil. At the same time, by making them we give Nhu chance to forestall or block action by military. Risk, we believe, is not worth taking, with Nhu in control combat forces Saigon. Therefore, propose we go straight to Generals with our demands, without informing Diem. Would tell them we prepared have Diem without Nhus but it is in effect up to them whether to keep him. [Doc. 127]

Hilsman asserts that the cable also reflected Lodge's view that since our disapproval of GVN action was well known, it was not fitting for the U.S. to go to Diem, it was Diem who should come to us.

In a separate CAS cable the same day, Richardson, the CIA Chief of Station in Saigon, reported that at a meeting with Lodge and Harkins it had been agreed that Diem would not remove Nhu and that therefore, assuming State's cable of instructions on 24 August [Doc. 126] represented Washington's basic policy, the consensus was that contact should be immediately made with generals such as Minh and Khanh to assess the degree of unity and determination of senior officers. Minh was considered the best possible interim leader, with Vice President Tho as the most attractive candidate for President among the civilians. The cable concluded with the view that a junta would probably operate behind the scenes in the event of a successful coup, and that the U.S. should leave the specific tactics of a coup up to the generals. There is a hiatus in the available cable traffic at this point, but Hilsman indicates that Washington decided on Sunday, August 25, to defer a direct approach to Diem until more was known about the situation.

In Lodge's reply, he had also apparently approved the proposed VOA broadcast to exonerate the army. Hilsman briefed the press on the basis of a previously approved draft statement on August 25. The statement expressed strong U.S. disapproval of the raids, which were attributed to Nhu. In reporting the story, the press speculated that such a strong statement probably indicated that measures such as aid suspension were being considered. VOA had been instructed to broadcast only the substances of the U.S. statement as provided in the press guidance and nothing more. The instructions somehow got mislaid; and on Monday morning, August 26, just several hours before Lodge was to present his credentials to Diem, VOA broadcast in full a UPI story which flatly asserted that "the US may sharply reduce its aid to Vietnam unless President Diem gets rid of secret police officials responsible for the attacks." Lodge was understandably upset, and sent a testy cable rhetorically inquiring whether he really was in charge of tactics as he had been given to understand. Rusk sent a personal cable of apology to Lodge, and VOA promptly broadcast a denial of U.S. intent to cut aid, but the initial damage had been done.

The Vietnamese reaction to the attack on the pagodas during this time had been dramatic. In the United States, Mme. Nhu's father and mother, respectively the Vietnamese Ambassador to the U.S. and the Vietnamese observer at the UN, had both resigned, making bitter public statements denouncing the raids. In South Vietnam, the Foreign Minister, Vo Van Mau, had resigned and shaved his head like a Buddhist monk in protest. On August 23, students at the faculties of medicine and pharmacy at the University of Saigon turned out to stage mass demonstrations on behalf of the Buddhists. The GVN reacted in the only way it seemed to know, with massive arrests. But the demonstrations continued, and when the university was closed, the protest was taken up by high school and junior high school students. These were dramatic evidences indeed of the degree of disaffection with the regime, since most of these students were from the middle class families that formed the bureaucracy and the army leadership. Students in Vietnam had no substantial record of political activism as was the case with their counterparts in other parts of Asia, like Korea. Furthermore, some of the Buddhist leadership had survived the raids and gone underground and were soon passing out leaflets on the streets again. On the day of the raids, two monks had taken refuge in the USOM building next door to Xa Loi pagoda. The following day, three others, including the militant young leader Tich Tri Quang, took refuge in the U.S. Embassy, where they were warmly received by Lodge and remained until the successful November coup.

B.   MIS-COUP

Rumors of coup plotting had been a standard part of the Saigon scene under Diem from the very beginning. And there had been several attempts. In 1957, an assassin fired at Diem at an up-country fair. In November 1960, he had narrowly escaped being overthrown by a military coup by negotiating with the dissident officers until loyal reinforcements could be moved into Saigon to restore his control. And in 1962, two disgruntled Air Force pilots had unsuccessfully bombed and strafed the Gia Long Palace. So, when rumors of coup plotting began to gain currency again in the spring of 1963, they were monitored by the U.S. intelligence community, but not given extraordinary prominence or credence. By mid-summer, however, with the Buddhist crisis in full bloom, more serious consideration was given to the growing number of reports identifying plotters and schemes. One plot, identified in late June, was led by Dr. Tran Kim Tuyen, Diem's Director of Political and Social Studies (national intelligence). It involved elements of the Civic Action Ministry, the Information Ministry, the Secret Police, and some junior army officers. A separate plot involving other elements of the army was reported, and on July 8 General Don indicated to a CAS officer that there was support among all but a couple of generals for a coup. Nhu's July 11 meeting with the generals, however, seemed to disorient their efforts temporarily. In an August 14 memorandum, the CIA acknowledged some military support for a coup, but doubted that anyone would risk it unless a deterioration of the political situation threatened a Viet Cong victory. The pagoda attack was just such a deterioration and it precipitated the generals' first approach to the U.S. on August 23 about a coup.

With State's instructions of 24 August as guidance, Lodge met with Harkins, Truehart, Mecklin, and Richardson on the morning of August 26 before presenting his credentials to Diem. They decided that the official U.S. hand should not show—i.e., Harkins should not talk to the generals. It was agreed that Lt. Colonel Conein of the CIA would contact General Khiem, and Mr. Spera (also of CIA) would contact General Khanh, II Corps commander in Pleiku, conveying the following points to each:

a. Solidification of further elaboration of action aspects of present thinking and planning. What should be done?

b. We in agreement Nhus must go.

c. Question of retaining Diem or not up to them.

d. Bonzes and other arrestees must be released immediately and five-point agreement of 16 June be fully carried out.

e. We will provide direct support during any interim period of breakdown of central government mechanism.

f. We cannot be of any help during initial action of assuming power of the state. Entirely their own action, win or lose. Don't expect to be bailed out.

g. If Nhus do not go and if Buddhists' situation is not redressed as indicated, we would find it impossible continue military and economic support.

h. It is hoped bloodshed can be avoided or reduced to absolute minimum.

i. It is hoped that during process and after, developments conducted in such manner as to retain and increase the necessary relations between Vietnamese and Americans which will allow for progress of country and successful prosecution of the war.

Conein met with Khiem on August 27, and after conveying his message learned that Minh was the leader of the cabal, which included also Generals Kim, Khanh, Thieu, and Le. Don was aware of the plot and approved, but was too exposed to participate. General Minh was under surveillance, and had asked not to be contacted by the U.S. Khiem recognized the need to neutralize General Cao, the IV Corps commander, General Dinh, the III Corps and Saigon Area commander, and Colonel Tung. A separate CAS report indicated that General Kim had charge of plans for the provisional successor government which would include both civilians and military, with Minh as President.

Meanwhile, back in Washington, by the time the NSC met on Monday morning, August 26, misgivings about supporting a coup—the policy outlined in State's August 24 message—had developed. Hilsman's account credits McNamara, Taylor, and McCone with second thoughts. Whatever the outcome of Monday's meeting, another was held the next day, after which Lodge was cabled for more details about the coup plans, and an assessment of their chances of success. Reflecting the reservations in Washington, the message asked what effect delaying the coup would have.

Replying the following day, Lodge gave a favorable assessment of coup prospects; expressed confidence in the generals who were to lead it, especially Minh, Khanh, and Kim; and argued, "that chances of success would be diminished by delay." A cable from Harkins to Taylor on the same day is the first documentary indication of Harkins' reservations about supporting the coup attempt. Cryptically, Harkins indicated that he would offer his full support to the Ambassador in implementing State's instructions, but noted that, "Reference b. (CINCPAC 2504562 Aug 1963) *advises* me that reference a. (State 243) embodies CINCPAC opinion and *that my support had been volunteered.*" He would have preferred one last attempt to persuade Diem to dispense with Nhu. Furthermore, the line-up of forces did not indicate a clear-cut advantage for the coup plotters. Therefore, he stated, "In my opinion as things stand now I don't believe there is sufficient reason for a crash approval on our part at this time." He also had concluded that the coup would not take place until we gave the word. In a separate message, Richardson, however, described the situation as having "reached the point of no return." [Doc. 129] Further, he concluded, "Unless the generals are neutralized before being able to launch their operation, we believe they will act and that they have good chance to win." [Doc. 129]

In Washington, State and Defense were divided on the issue. Nolting, who was regularly attending the daily NSC meetings at the President's request, sided with the Pentagon in the view that prospects for the coup were not good, and that another effort should be made with Diem. Hilsman, Harriman, and Ball were convinced the U.S. had to get on with the coup, since Diem offered no prospect of complying the U.S. wishes. The discussions in the NSC, reportedly, were increasingly heated and testy. The division of opinion between Harkins and Lodge concerned the President and upon receipt of their respective messages on August 28, he cabled each of them separately for their "independent judgment" about the prospects for a coup and their personal advice on the course the U.S. should pursue. The President was at pains to reiterate his great confidence in both men, and to assure them that differences of opinion in Washington would not prevent the U.S. government from acting as a unit under his direction. In a separate message, State asked Lodge to indicate the latest point at which the operation could be suspended, and with what consequences; since U.S. prestige would be engaged in the venture, the message stated, once the coup were under way, it had to succeed. Lodge was also asked what actions the U.S. might take to promote the coup.

On August 29, Colonel Conein and Mr. Spera met with Generals Khiem and Minh. Minh bluntly said that the generals had to be cautious until they had clear evidence that the U.S. would not betray them to Nhu. They were unwilling to discuss their plans, and when asked what would constitute a sign of U.S.

support, replied that the U.S. should stop economic aid to the regime. In a subsequent separate contact with Rufus Phillips, General Kim asked for verification that the Minh-Conein meeting had Lodge's approval. After checking with Lodge, Phillips assured Kim who then asked for a meeting to discuss planning on the next day. Lodge then authorized CAS to assist in tactical planning.

Stressing the generals' reported lack of confidence in U.S. support, Lodge's reply to Washington asked Presidential permission for Harkins to show CAS messages to the generals to prove our commitment. If that failed, he reluctantly recommended suspension of economic aid as they requested. Typical of the Ambassador's all-out support for the coup is the following summary he gave of the U.S. position:

> We are launched on a course from which there is no respectable turning back: The overthrow of the Diem Government. There is no turning back in part because US prestige is already publicly committed to this end in large measure and will become more so as facts leak out. In a more fundamental sense, there is no turning back because there is no possibility, in my view, that the war can be won under a Diem administration, still less that Diem or any member of the family can govern the country in a way to gain the support of the people who count, i.e., the educated class in and out of government service, civil and military—not to mention the American people. [Doc. 132]

Harkins, on the other hand, felt that there was still time to make one last approach to Diem, without endangering the plotters, since their plans did not appear fully mature yet. Diem should be handed an ultimatum that the Nhus must go. This, he felt, would strengthen the hand of the generals whose opposition, like ours, was to the Nhus, not Diem. If Diem did not act, there would then be time to back a move by the generals.

These views were all reviewed at the noon meeting of the NSC on August 29. At the meeting, McNamara backed Harkins' view in favor of a final approach to Diem, but the issue was not decided. Rusk took up the question in a subsequent cable to Lodge, asking Lodge's opinion about an approach to Diem, possibly by the generals at a time when they would be ready to act, in which they would insist on the removal of the Nhus, and threaten withdrawal of U.S. support. [Doc. 131] A separate State cable to Lodge and Harkins authorized the latter to show CAS cables to the generals to prove our support. Harkins was instructed to insist on knowing the personnel involved in the coup, and the forces available, and to ask to review the detailed plans, without, however, directly involving himself in the coup planning. Lodge was authorized to suspend aid to Diem, "at a time and under conditions of your choice."

In his response to Rusk's cable, Lodge stoutly opposed any further contact with Diem, even to present an ultimatum. Agreeing that removal of the Nhus was the prime objective, Lodge argued, "This surely cannot be done by working through Diem. In fact, Diem will oppose it. He wishes he had more Nhus, not less. The best chance of doing it is by the generals taking over the government lock, stock and barrel. After this has been done, it can then be decided whether to put Diem back in again or go on without him." [Doc. 134] What genuinely concerned Lodge at that point was the lack of action by the generals, but he was reluctant to use the aid suspension as a lever.

Throughout this period, another CAS officer had been in contact with a

Colonel Thao, an inspector of strategic hamlets, who was the leader of an independent junior officer-civilian plot. On August 30, he told the CAS officer that he was in touch with the generals, and would support any move they might make, but that for the moment the plans of his group had stopped because the risk of failure was too great.

With Lodge's anxiety at the generals' failure to act increasing daily, General Harkins met with General Khiem on August 31. He was told that Minh had called off the coup for the time being because of the inability to achieve a favorable balance of forces in the Saigon area, and because of continuing anxiety among the generals about Richardson's close identification with the Nhus. Both Richardson and Lodge confirmed the end of this coup attempt on the same day. Apparently unable to win over General Dinh, the Saigon III Corps area commander, Minh had decided not to risk an indecisive, protracted blood bath with only a slim likelihood of success. Three factors appear to have been important in Minh's decision to abort the coup: (1) the failure to win over Dinh, leaving the coup forces at a tactical disadvantage in the Saigon area; (2) continuing doubts about the firmness of the U.S. commitment to Diem's overthrow and the related concern that the U.S. had wittingly or unwittingly tipped off Nhu to the plot; and (3) uncertainty about the cohesion of the coup group and the firmness of plans. Lodge concluded somewhat bitterly, ". . . there is neither the will nor the organization among the generals to accomplish anything." He did not, however, rule out a future attempt.

C.   TOWARD A NEW POLICY

Having at long last decided to seek an alternative to the Diem regime by sanctioning a coup, only to have the attempt fail, the U.S. found itself at the end of August 1963 without a policy and with most of its bridges burned. In both Saigon and Washington, the reappraisal and the search for alternatives began anew. In the cable acknowledging the demise of the coup plot on August 31, Lodge suggested that:

> Perhaps an arrangement could be worked out whereby the following could be made to happen: Madame Nhu to leave the country, Mr. Nhu's functions to be limited entirely to strategic hamlets; the office of Prime Minister to be created and Mr. Thuan to become Prime Minister; Archbishop Thuc to leave the country. In addition, the students and Buddhists would be liberated; Decree Law 10 would be repealed; the pagodas would be repaired and conciliatory gestures would be made. All of this, if agreed to, might be announced by President in Washington.

These suggestions became the basis of discussion of a "where do we go from here" NSC meeting on the same day.

In the absence of the President, Secretary Rusk chaired the meeting at the State Department, and called for consideration of the Lodge proposals, but said he felt it was unrealistic to start off by asserting that Nhu must go. Secretary McNamara urged that we "establish quickly and firmly our line of communication between Lodge, Harkins and the GVN." He pointed out that "at the moment our channels of communication are essentially broken" and that "they should be reinstituted at all costs." These considerations were soon submerged, however, in a broader discussion of the negative impact of the regime's actions on the war effort. Hilsman, supported by State's Kattenburg of the Vietnam

Working Group, argued that we should not continue our support of a Nhu-dominated regime because its repressive policies would eventually have a disastrous effect on the war, even if the statistics did not yet reveal their negative impact. Hilsman and Kattenburg pointed to the growing disaffection and restiveness of middle level bureaucrats and military officers as a factor which would steadily erode the military effort. Unconvinced, both Secretary McNamara and General Taylor asked for evidence of this development.

Kattenburg offered his estimate that we would be thrown out of the country in six months if the regime remained in power and that the question the meeting should be considering was "the decision to get out honorably." Taylor and Nolting immediately took exception to these views and Secretary Rusk remarked that they were "largely speculative." He continued, "that it would be far better for us to start on the firm basis of two things—that we will not pull out of Vietnam until the war is won, and that we will not run a coup." Secretary McNamara and Vice President Johnson supported Rusk's views, the Vice President saying he had never really seen an alternative to Diem. The meeting ended inconclusively; the only decision taken was to ask for Lodge's advice. [Doc. 135]

As the only documented meeting during this period of major policy deliberation, the August 31 meeting is significant for the viewpoints it reveals. Rambling inability to focus the problem, indeed to reach common agreement on the nature of the problem, reflects disorientation in the aftermath of the initial failure. More importantly, however, the meeting is the first recorded occasion in which someone followed to its logical conclusion the negative analysis of the situation—i.e., that the war could not be won with the Diem regime, yet its removal would leave such political instability as to foreclose success in the war: for the first time, it was recognized that the U.S. should be considering methods of honorably disengaging itself from an irretrievable situation. The other alternative, not fully appreciated until the year following, was a much greater U.S. involvement in and assumption of responsibility for the war. At this point, however, the negative analysis of the impact of the political situation on the war effort was not shared by McNamara, Taylor, Krulak, nor seemingly by Rusk.

But discussions were overtaken by events. On the following Monday, September 2, the President, appearing on the initial broadcast of the CBS Evening News, was interviewed by Walter Cronkite:

> *Mr. Cronkite*: "Mr. President, the only hot war we've got running at the moment is of course the one in Viet-Nam, and we have our difficulties here, quite obviously."
>
> *President Kennedy*: "I don't think that unless a greater effort is made by the Government to win popular support that the war can be won out there. In the final analysis, it is their war. They are the ones who have to win it or lose it. We can help them, we can give them equipment, we can send our men out there as advisers, but they have to win it—the people of Viet-Nam—against the Communists. We are prepared to continue to assist them, but I don't think that the war can be won unless the people support the effort, and, in my opinion, in the last two months the Government has gotten out of touch with the people.
>
> "The repressions against the Buddhists, we felt, were very unwise. Now all we can do is to make it very clear that we don't think this is the way to win. It is my hope that this will become increasingly obvious to the Gov-

ernment, that they will take steps to try to bring back popular support for this very essential struggle."

Mr. Cronkite: "Do you think this Government has time to regain the support of the people?"

President Kennedy: "I do. With changes in policy and perhaps with personnel, I think it can. If it doesn't make those changes, I would think that the chances of winning it would not be very good."

Confronted by the necessity of public comment, the President had spoken boldly and forthrightly. The President's call for changes of policy and personnel patently conveyed the message that the Buddhist repressions must end, and the Nhus must go. Later in the same interview, however, the President had said, ". . . I don't agree with those who say we should withdraw. That would be a great mistake." As Hilsman summarized it later,

> We had embarked on a policy that avoided the extremes both of withdrawing from Vietnam or of actually taking part in direct action to change the Government. The policy was one of trying to discriminate by continuing to support those Vietnamese who were struggling against the Communists but maintaining the tension of our disapproval of Diem's and Nhu's repressive policies.

It was, in effect, the policy Lodge had proposed.

Meanwhile in Saigon, Lodge had gone ahead with his proposals. He continued to avoid any official contact with Diem, but on September 2 he had his second meeting with Nhu (the first on August 27 was an inconclusive statement of positions on each side) in company with the Italian Ambassador and the Papal Delegate. Nhu, perhaps encouraged by a collateral intercession of the French Ambassador, announced he intended to resign from the government for good and retire to Dalat. A GVN announcement would state that the progress of the program against the Viet Cong permitted his departure. Mme. Nhu was to leave Vietnam for a trip to Yugoslavia, Italy, and possibly the U.S. The Papal Delegate would arrange for Archbishop Thuc to leave the country. Some measures to ease Buddhist tensions would be taken and, as a public relations gesture, a prime minister would be appointed. These were all proposals which Lodge had initially advanced. But as the days passed, nothing happened and Lodge grew impatient. Contributing to his concern were the frequent and often contradictory rumors that Nhu was secretly dealing with Hanoi and/or the VC through the French and the Polish Ambassadors, both of whose governments favored a neutralist solution between North and South Vietnam.

For the remainder of the week, the Italian Ambassador and the Papal Delegate urged Nhu to act on his promises to Lodge. On Friday, September 6, after they had stressed the urgency for action created by Senator Church's rumored aid-suspension resolution, Nhu went into a tirade and said he would not consider leaving the country. He did, however, say he would "formally" resign. On the following day, the Papal Delegate, who had condemned Archbishop Thuc's activity to the Vatican and received the Pope's support, got Thuc out of the country. Mme. Nhu left the country for Europe on September 9. The arrests of students by the regime, however, continued and stories of torture and atrocities began to circulate.

In Washington, the NSC met on September 6 and renewed the discussion of reopening "tough negotiations" with Diem. Lodge, of course, opposed this while continuing his dialogue with Nhu. But others at the meeting (presumably including McNamara on the basis of his views at the August 31 meeting) urged that Lodge be instructed to make another approach to Diem. Lodge was accordingly instructed to clarify for Diem the U.S. position and explain the difficult position his policy placed us in with respect to U.S. and world opinion.

Perhaps the most important discussion at the meeting was that engendered by Robert Kennedy over the fundamental purpose of the U.S. involvement. According to Hilsman, Robert Kennedy said:

> As he understood it we were there to help the people resisting a Communist take-over. The first question was whether a Communist take-over could be successfully resisted with any government. If it could not, now was the time to get out of Vietnam entirely, rather than waiting. If the answer was that it could, but not with a Diem–Nhu government as it was now constituted, we owed it to the people resisting Communism in Vietnam to give Lodge enough sanctions to bring changes that would permit successful resistance. But the basic question of whether a Communist take-over could be successfully resisted with any government had not been answered, and he was not sure that anyone had enough information to answer it.

Kennedy's trenchant analysis, however, did not generate a searching reappraisal of U.S. policy. It did stimulate further efforts to get more information on the situation. McNamara proposed sending General Krulak on an immediate fact-finding trip. It was agreed that a senior Foreign Service Officer with Vietnam experience, Joseph Mendenhall, would accompany him, and that they would bring John Mecklin, the USIS director, and Rufus Phillips, the director of rural programs for USOM, back with them to report. Krulak and Mendenhall left later that day. State, for its part, sent Saigon a long comprehensive cable of questions on Vietnamese attitudes at all levels of society.

The purpose of the Krulak–Mendenhall mission was to assess, in Krulak's words, "the effect of recent events upon the attitudes of the Vietnamese in general, and upon the war effort against the Viet Cong." In a whirlwind four-day trip, the two men visited throughout Vietnam and returned to Washington to report. Krulak went to ten different locations in all four corps areas and spoke with the Ambassador, General Harkins and his staff, 87 U.S. advisors, and 22 Vietnamese officers. Mendenhall went to Saigon, Hue, Da Nang, and several other provincial cities and talked primarily to old Vietnamese friends. Not surprisingly, their estimates of the situation were almost completely opposite.

The NSC convened on the morning of September 10, immediately after their return, to hear their reports. Krulak gave a very optimistic appraisal of the progress of the war and discounted the effect of the political crisis on the army. The following, in his own words, were his general conclusions:

> The shooting war is still going ahead at an impressive pace. It has been affected adversely by the political crisis, but the impact is not great.
> There is a lot of war left to fight, particularly in the Delta, where the Viet Cong remain strong.
> Vietnamese officers of all ranks are well aware of the Buddhist issue. Most have viewed it in detachment and have not permitted religious differences significantly to affect their internal military relationship.
> Vietnamese military commanders, at the various echelons, are obedient and could be expected to execute any order they view as lawful.

The U.S./Vietnamese military relationship has not been damaged by the political crisis, in any significant degree.

There is some dissatisfaction, among Vietnamese officers, with the national administration. It is focused far more on Ngo Dinh Nhu than on President Diem. Nhu's departure would be hailed, but few officers would extend their necks to bring it about.

Excluding the very serious political and military factors external to Vietnam, the Viet Cong war will be won if the current U.S. military and sociological programs are pursued, irrespective of the grave defects in the ruling regime.

Improvements in the quality of the Vietnamese Government are not going to be brought about by leverage applied through the military. They do not have much, and will probably not use what they have.

This sanguine view of the situation was forcefully disputed by Mendenhall. He argued that the disaffection with the regime had reached the point where a breakdown of civil government was threatened, and the possibility of a religious civil war could not be excluded. The war could not be won with the present regime, he concluded. The polar opposition of these two reports prompted Kennedy's now famous query, "You two did visit the same country, didn't you?"

The critical failure of both reports was to understand the fundamental political role that the army was coming to play in Vietnam. It was the only potential force with sufficient power to constitute an alternative to Diem. Diem and Nhu fully understood this fact, and had coped with it by usurping the prerogative of senior officer promotion, and basing those promotions on loyalty to the palace. This had sown deep seeds of distrust among the senior military men, and fragmented their potential power. Krulak failed to see that once the internal political situation deteriorated to the point where massive disaffection with the regime threatened a communist victory, the generals would unite and plunge into politics out of common necessity. But more importantly, neither Krulak nor Mendenhall seemed to anticipate that, if the army achieved power, the divisive effect of Diem's preferential promotion politices would surface in an internal army power struggle. Nor did they fully understand the negative effect on the war effort this preoccupation with politics among the generals would have.

Nolting took issue with Mendenhall's appraisal, noting that Mendenhall had been pessimistic about prospects in Vietnam for several years. But John Mecklin, the USIS director, corroborated Mendenhall's view, and pushed it even further, saying that the U.S. should apply direct pressure, such as suspension of non-military aid, to bring about a change of government. In Mecklin's words:

> This would unavoidably be dangerous. There was no way to be sure how events would develop. It was possible, for example, that the Vietnamese forces might fragment into warring factions, or that the new government would be so incompetent and/or unstable that the effort against the Viet Cong would collapse. The US should therefore resolve now to introduce American combat forces if necessary to present a Communist triumph midst the debris of the Diem regime.

Mecklin appreciated the potential for instability inherent in any army successor regime that Krulak and Mendenhall had not seen. But he, nevertheless, concluded that we should proceed to bring about a change of government, accept the consequences, and contemplate the introduction of U.S. combat troops to stave off a Viet Cong victory.

The meeting went on to hear Rufus Phillips' dour report on the situation in the Delta, and his doubts about the validity of Krulak's optimistic outlook on the military situation. Phillips argued that this was primarily a political contest for the allegiance of people, not a military war, and that the Diem regime was losing it. The Strategic Hamlet Program was a shambles in the field, especially in the Delta. The meeting ended on this note and no decisions were made.

One course of action being given increasing consideration in these meetings, as well as in Saigon and on Capitol Hill, was a suspension of non-military aid to Diem. After the erroneous VOA announcement of aid suspension on August 26, Lodge had been authorized on August 29, as already noted, to suspend aid at his discretion if it would facilitate the coup. Lodge had been reluctant to do so. The question had been raised again in a joint State/AID cable to Lodge on September 3 which listed the items currently up for approval or renewal. Lodge was informed that all approval for non-military aid would be temporarily held up but that no suspension was to be announced, since such a policy decision was still pending. Lodge took advantage of this by having the mission, and especially USOM, reply to all GVN inquiries about the status of the aid renewals or approvals that President Diem would have to talk to Lodge about it. Meanwhile, the U.S. Senate began to put pressure on the Administration to do something about Diem. Hilsman was badgered by the Senate Subcommittee on the Far East, and there were threats of further cuts in the AID bill if something wasn't done. Senator Church informed the Administration he intended to introduce soon a resolution condemning Diem's represssions against the Buddhists and calling for an end of aid to South Vietnam unless they were abandoned. He agreed to delay its introduction temporarily so as not to embarrass the Administration.

The idea of a selective aid suspension to goad Diem into action was actively discussed at State during the Krulak–Mendenhall mission, and later John Mecklin had specifically suggested it to the NSC. On September 8, AID Director David Bell warned in a TV interview that the Congress might cut aid to South Vietnam if the Diem government did not change its policies. On Monday, September 9, however, the President, in a TV interview for the new Huntley–Brinkley News, said, "I don't think we think that (a reduction of U.S. aid to South Vietnam) would be helpful at this time." On September 11, the day after the President received the Krulak–Mendenhall reports, Lodge reversed his previous position, and in a long cable proposed that detailed consideration be given to ways in which non-military aid suspension might be used as a sanction to topple the government. He had concluded we could not get satisfaction from Diem, and had to face up to the unpleasant task of forcing events. This view was reinforced the next day in a long series of cables replying to State's September 7 request for a comprehensive evaluation of South Vietnamese attitudes.

Lodge's proposal, and a proposal by Hilsman for a combined set of public and private measures to bring pressure on Diem, formed the basis of a White House meeting on September 11. On the following day, Senator Church was given the green light and introduced his resolution. On September 14, Lodge was informed that approval of the $18.5 million remainder of the commercial import program (the principal piastre support, anti-inflation aid device) was deferred until basic U.S. policy decisions had been made. The decision on aid suspension was now absorbed into the broader consideration of a set of coordinated measures to put pressure on the GVN.

Throughout September, the division of opinion within the U.S. mission in Saigon had grown sharper and sharper. Harkins, Richardson, and to a lesser extent Brent (Director of USOM), did not believe that the Diem government's bungling of the Buddhist crisis and loss of popular support were threatening the war effort, or that the crisis was as serious as Lodge, Mecklin, Mendenhall, *et al.,* portrayed it. In any case, the situation was not so irretrievable as to require a U.S. abandonment of Diem in a risky venture at coup-making towards an unknown alternative. The opposite view was held by Lodge, Truehart, Mecklin, Phillips, and the majority of the junior officers in the mission. By mid-September, the debate had reached a shrill and acrimonious level, as the following excerpt from a Harkins' cable to Taylor indicates:

> As everyone else seems to be talking, writing and confusing the issue here in Vietnam, it behooves me to also get into the act: From most of the reports and articles I read, one would say Vietnam and our programs here are falling apart at the seams. Well, I just thoroughly disagree.

The situation was of such concern that CIA dispatched a special officer to reach an independent evaluation. His conclusion was that we had hastily expended our capability to overthrow the regime, that an aid suspension would not guarantee a constructive result, and that to prevent further political fragmentation we should adopt a "business as usual" policy to buy time. Amidst all this internal U.S. dissension, the GVN announced on September 14 that martial law would end on September 16 and that National Assembly elections would be held September 27.

In Washington, the NSC convened again September 17 to consider two alternative proposals for dealing with Diem prepared by Hilsman. The first, which Hilsman and others at State favored, was the "pressures and persuasion track," and involved an escalatory ladder of measures both public and private, including selective aid suspension, to coerce Diem into getting rid of Nhu and taking steps to restore the political situation. The alternative proposal, the "reconciliation with a rehabilitated GVN track," involved a public posture of acquiescence in recent GVN actions, recognition that Diem and Nhu were inseparable, and a decision to salvage as much as possible from a bad situation. This, of course, would have involved a reopening of the dialogue with Diem, to which Lodge was opposed. Both proposals assumed that for the moment a coup was out of the question.

There are no available records of what transpired in the meeting, but two decisions were clearly made. The first was, in effect, to adopt Hilsman's "pressures and persuasion" proposal. The guidance cable to Lodge after the meeting, however, came from the White House. It stated that,

> We see no good opportunity for action to remove present government in immediate future; therefore, as your most recent message suggests, we must, for the present, apply such pressures as are available to secure whatever modest improvements on the scene may be possible . . . Such a course, moreover, is consistent with more drastic effort as and when means became available. [Doc. 136]

Lodge was to press for a reduction of Nhu's authority and his departure from Saigon, at least temporarily. The cable included a long list of other measures for the GVN to take to redress the political situation and gave Lodge complete control over the aid program to enhance his bargaining position.

> This authorization specifically includes aid actions currently held in abeyance and you are authorized to set those in train or hold them up further in your discretion. We leave entirely in your hands decisions on the degree of privacy or publicity you wish to give to this process. [Doc. 136]

There is no evidence on the degree of consensus of the principals in this decision.

Lodge replied to the new policy guidance on September 19 in a generally negative vein. The proposals for specific actions by the GVN had all been previously suggested to Diem without any results, and Lodge was not optimistic about their adoption now. He specifically felt that he should not be required to make a futile overture to Diem. The Ambassador's aloofness was beginning to cause official concern at the palace, and he felt he should press views on the Ngo family only when they initiated the contact. He did not think a public relations effort was likely to have any effect on the regime, whose appreciation of questions of public support was virtually nil. Withholding aid was another delicate matter that did not offer great prospects of success. Lodge was particularly concerned that such action would impede the war effort or damage the economy, but have no real effect on the regime. No doubt recalling the generals' previous request for an aid suspension as a sign of U.S. support, Lodge expressed his view that any suspension of aid should be timed to coincide with another coup attempt and should be used to facilitate it. He was troubled by the opinion expressed by both General Minh and Secretary Thuan privately within the previous two days that the war was going very badly and the VC were winning. In general, he felt that a patient "let them come to me" tactic was more likely to have results, unless a real coup possibility emerged, which he felt we should back.

D. THE McNAMARA–TAYLOR MISSION

The second decision to come out of the September 17 NSC meeting was to adopt a suggestion of Secretary McNamara for another fact-finding mission, this time by himself and General Taylor, Chairman of the JCS. [Doc. 137]

Lodge reacted immediately to the proposed McNamara–Taylor mission, pointing out to the President that such a visit would require a call on Diem that would be construed by the regime as a return to business as usual. Since he had been consciously pursuing a policy of official aloofness, he wondered whether such a high level visit was desirable. Furthermore, it coincided with the proposed National Assembly elections on September 27, and could not but be construed as an indication of the lack of importance we attached to them. But the President was insistent, and Lodge acquiesced, suggesting that the public announcement state that Lodge had requested the visit. [Doc. 138] After an exchange of alternative phraseology, it was agreed that the release would say that the President had decided to send the mission after consultation with Lodge. It was so announced on September 21.

The President's instructions to McNamara described the purpose of the mission in the following terms:

I am asking you to go because of my desire to have the best possible on-the-spot appraisal of the military and paramilitary effort to defeat the Viet Cong. . . . The events in South Vietnam since May have now raised serious questions both about the present prospects for success against the Viet Cong and still more about the future effectiveness of this effort unless there can be important political improvement in the country. It is in this context that I now need your appraisal of the situation. If the prognosis in your judgment is not hopeful, I would like your views on what action must be taken by the South Vietnamese Government and what stops our Government should take to lead the Vietnamese to that action.
. . . I will also expect you to examine with Ambassador Lodge ways and means of fashioning all forms of our assistance to South Vietnam so that it will support our foreign policy objectives more precisely. [Doc. 139]

The purpose, thus, was fourfold: (1) appraise the war effort; (2) assess the impact on that effort of recent political developments; (3) recommend a course of action for the GVN and for the U.S.; and (4) examine with Lodge ways of tailoring our aid to achieve our foreign policy objectives. In a statement to the press at Andrews Air Force Base just before leaving for Vietnam on September 23, Secretary McNamara said that the purpose of the trip was, ". . . to determine whether that military effort has been adversely affected by the unrest of the past several weeks."

Both Schlesinger and Hilsman, however, contend that Kennedy sent McNamara and Taylor to Vietnam to convince them of the negative effect on the war effort that the protracted political crisis was having, and of the necessity of applying sanctions to the Diem regime to bring about change. According to this argument, the President felt he could not afford a major policy rift in the Administration over applying sanctions, especially the opposition of the powerful JCS, and concluded that only McNamara, if convinced, could bring the military along.

Whatever the exact purpose of the trip, the party left Washington on September 23 and returned ten days later, on October 2, after an exhausting trip and a comprehensive review of the situation.

The divergent views of the members of the U.S. mission about the relative progress of the war, and the effect on it of the political crisis, were exposed immediately in the opening session that McNamara and Taylor held in Saigon with the country team on September 25. General Harkins and the MACV staff generally presented a favorable picture of the war, emphasizing the progress of the strategic hamlet program, and the generally improved ARVN position, in spite of recent rises in VC initiated incidents and declines in ARVN operations related to the political turmoil. McNamara and Taylor prodded the briefers with questions trying to get comparative indicators of the situation over the previous two years. McNamara in particular pressed for details about the Delta. Lodge's and Mecklin's reading of recent events, and their estimate of war progress, differed sharply from that of General Harkins. Lodge stressed the more political and intangible aspects of the conflict and cast doubt on the "hardness" of the statistical data from MACV. With the Mission's division of opinion exposed and the issues joined, McNamara left to tour the country.

His subsequent itinerary took him throughout the country interviewing

Americans and Vietnamese both at headquarters, and in the field. In Saigon, in the last few days of the visit, he was given extensive briefings by the civilian side of the Mission and, since he stayed with Lodge, had ample opportunity for discussions with the Ambassador.

On September 29, McNamara, Taylor, Harkins, and Lodge called on Diem, after having previously decided against delivery of a stiff letter from Kennedy. After a two-hour monologue by Diem, McNamara was finally able to stress the U.S. concern that political unrest was undermining the war effort. He stressed the problem that repressions were creating for President Kennedy because of aroused public opinion. But he did not ask for the removal of the Nhus, a matter Washington had left to his and Lodge's discretion. All this seems to have had little impact on Diem, however. Diem had asked Taylor for his appraisal of the war, and with the approval of McNamara, a long letter from Taylor was delivered to Diem on October 2. The letter pointedly outlined the major military problems in the Delta, warned of the danger to the war effort of the political crisis, and listed many of the specific steps needed to improve the military effort that subsequently appeared in the report to the President. The letter summed up with a terse, tough statement of the U.S. view:

> In closing, Mr. President, may I give you my most important over-all impression? Up to now, the battle against the Viet Cong has seemed endless; no one has been willing to set a date for its successful conclusion. After talking to scores of officers, Vietnamese and American, I am convinced that the Viet Cong insurgency in the north and center can be reduced to little more than sporadic incidents by the end of 1964. The Delta will take longer but should be completed by the end of 1965. But for these predictions to be valid, certain conditions must be met. Your Government should be prepared to energize all agencies, military and civil, to a higher output of activity than up to now. Ineffective commanders and province officials must be replaced as soon as identified. Finally, there should be a restoration of domestic tranquility on the home front if political tensions are to be allayed and external criticism is to abate. Conditions are needed for the creation of an atmosphere conducive to an effective campaign directed at the objective, vital to both of us, of defeating the Viet Cong and of restoring peace to your community.

On September 30, their last day in Vietnam, McNamara and Taylor, together with Lodge, met with Vice President Tho. Tho said that the U.S., after Taylors report in 1961, had responded to the Vietnam situation promptly and efficiently, but that recently we had failed to use our strength and influence intelligently to prevent the current political deterioration. But he had no methods to suggest. Later he sharply questioned the success of the Strategic Hamlet Program, and said that increased Viet Cong strength had to be attributed to widespread peasant disaffection with the government. These views, from the man most often mentioned in U.S. circles as an alternative to Diem, coming at the end of the visit as they did, must have had an important influence on McNamara's conclusions. Later that day the party left Vietnam to return home.

During the briefings for McNamara, Lodge had raised again his doubts about the efficacy of aid suspension as a lever against Diem, but had also expressed his concern that the foreign aid bill would be penalized in Congress for Diem's repressions. Lodge reiterated in his cables to Washington during the visit his belief that an aid suspension could boomerang and alienate the population as well as the regime. Aware, no doubt, that an aid suspension was a potential recommendation of the mission, Brent went on record against it, too. Both views were important because McNamara and Taylor had been specifically charged by the President with examining ways to make our aid serve our foreign policy goals, and their briefing papers included a program-by-program consideration of the impact of aid suspension prepared by AID–Washington.

After a one-day stop in Honolulu to prepare their report, McNamara and Taylor arrived back in Washington on October 2 and promptly met with the President and the NSC. Their report concluded that the "military campaign has made great progress and continues to progress." But it warned that the serious political tensions in Saigon and the increasing unpopularity of Diem and Nhu could abet the then limited restiveness of some ARVN officers and erode the favorable military trends. They reported no evidence of a successful coup in the making, and felt that U.S. pressure would probably only further harden the regime's attitudes. Nevertheless, "unless such pressures are exerted, they (Diem-Nhu) are almost certain to continue past patterns of behavior." [Doc. 142]

The report's military recommendations were that General Harkins should review the war effort with Diem with a view toward its successful conclusion in I, II, and III Corps by the end of 1964 and in the Delta by the end of 1965. This would necessitate: (a) a shift in military emphasis and strength to the Delta; (b) an increase tempo of military activity throughout the country; (c) an emphasis on "clear and hold operations"; (d) a consolidation of the Strategic Hamlet Program with the emphasis on security; and (e) the fleshing out of combat units and better training and arms for the hamlet militia. It was further proposed that an announcement be made of the planned withdrawal of 1,000 U.S. troops by the end of 1963 in connection with a program to train Vietnamese to replace Americans in *all* essential functions by 1965.

To bring political pressure on the Diem regime to end its repressive policies, the following measures were recommended: (a) a continued withholding of funds in the commodity import program, but without formal announcement; (b) suspension of approval of AID loans for the Saigon-Cholon Waterworks and the Saigon Electric Power Project; (c) suspension of support for Colonel Tung's forces unless they were transferred to the field and placed under JGS authority; (d) maintenance of purely "correct" relations between the Ambassador and Diem (General Harkins' contract with the regime not to be suspended, however). In subsequent evaluations of the success of these sanctions, the report stated:

> . . . the situation must be closely watched to see what steps Diem is taking to reduce repressive practices and to improve the effectiveness of the military effort. We should set no fixed criteria, but recognize that we would have to decide in 2–4 months, whether to move to more drastic action or try to carry on with Diem even if he had not taken significant steps.

Finally, the report recommended against our actively encouraging a coup, although it recommended seeking "urgently to identify and build contacts with an alternative leadership if and when it appears."

The report is a curiously contradictory document. It was, no doubt, a compromise between General Harkins' view of the war's progress as supported by General Taylor, and Secretary McNamara's growing conviction of the gravity of the political crisis and its dire potential for the war effort. Its recommendations for aid suspensions and the announcement of U.S. troop withdrawals were obviously designed as measures, short of a withdrawal of U.S. support, that would create doubt within the Diem regime about U.S. intentions and incentives for policy changes. The fact that these sanctions would be seen by the generals as a signal of our willingness to accept alternative leadership—i.e., a coup—does not seem to have figured in the recommendation, however, because elsewhere the report specifically rules out U.S. encouragement of "a change of government." This is an important lapse in view of the generals' clear statement in August that they would regard an aid suspension as a coup signal.

Nevertheless, the recommendations of the Mission met with swift approval at the NSC on October 2, and later that day Secretary McNamara made the Presidentially approved statement to the press that included the announcement of the 1,000 man troop withdrawal by the end of the year. The statement reiterated the U.S. commitment to the struggle against insurgency and aggression in South Vietnam, noted the progress of the war, announced the troop withdrawal, and dissociated the U.S. from the GVN's repressive policies. It avoided, however, any reference to economic aid suspensions or other sanctions against the regime, thereby giving Diem a chance to come around without a public loss of face.

On October 5, the President approved the specific military recommendations of the McNamara-Taylor report, "but directed that no formal announcement be made of the *implementation* of plans to withdraw 1,000 U.S. military personnel by the end of 1963." [Doc. 146] The details of how the new policy would be applied were spelled out in a long cable to Lodge following this meeting. The purpose of the new course of action was described at the beginning of the message:

> Actions are designed to indicate to Diem Government our displeasure at its political policies and activities and to create significant uncertainty in that government and in key Vietnamese groups as to future intensions of United States. At same time, actions are designed to have at most slight impact on military or counterinsurgency effort against Viet Cong, at least in short term.
>
> The recommendations on negotiations are concerned with what U.S. is after, i.e., GVN action to increase effectiveness of its military effort; to ensure popular support to win war; and to eliminate strains on U.S. Government and public confidence. The negotiating posture is designed not to lay down specific hard and fast demands or to set a deadline, but to produce movement in Vietnamese Government along these lines. In this way we can test and probe effectiveness of any actions the GVN actually takes and, at the same time, maintain sufficient flexibility to permit U.S. to resume full support of Diem regime at any time U.S. Government deems it appropriate.

The cable goes on to acknowledge that the proposed sanctions can only be applied for 2–4 months before they begin to adversely affect the military effort, and therefore when that begins to happen recognizes that, ". . . further major decisions will be required."

The specific actions to be taken included: (1) suspension of the commodity import program without public announcement; (2) selective suspension of PL 480, on an item-by-item, sometimes monthly, basis, after referral to Washington for review; (3) suspension of the loans for the Saigon–Cholon Waterworks and the Saigon Electric Power Project; (4) notification to the GVN that financial support of Colonel Tung's forces would be contingent on their commitment to field operations under JGS control, again without public announcement. Lodge was instructed to maintain his policy of "cool correctness in order to make Diem come to you," but to be prepared to re-establish contact later if it did not work. Specifically he was to seek improvements in the GVN military effort, as outlined in the McNamara–Taylor report; in the GVN's internal policies that would restore popular confidence; and in the GVN's international (particularly American) public image and its attitudes and actions toward the U.S. Once again, however, the discussion of this new program of pressures did not allude to their impact on the military nor how a coup initiative by the generals, stemming from such measures, should be dealt with.

Thus, the Kennedy Administration, after a long month of searching deliberations had made a far-reaching decision on American policy toward South Vietnam. It had chosen to take the difficult and risky path of positive pressures against an ally to obtain from him compliance with our policies. To our good fortune, that policy was to be implemented by an Ambassador who not only supported it, but was uniquely equipped by background and temperament to make it succeed.

IV.   THE COUP MATURES—OCTOBER 2–NOVEMBER 1

A.   THE SOUTH VIETNAMESE SITUATION IN OCTOBER

Through the month of September the GVN resorted to police state tactics ever more frequently. The regime, now more than ever under Nhu's dominance, lifted martial law September 16, but repressions against the Buddhist clergy continued unabated. Students, down to the grade school level, were arrested and detained for the most minor of protests. Civil servants came under pressure to avoid contact with Americans, and to demonstrate their loyalty to the ruling family. Regime-inspired rumors of impending mob attacks on U.S. facilities, and assassination lists of prominent Americans circulated regularly. Then, on October 5, at noon in the central market place, another Buddhist monk burned himself to death, the first self-immolation since the pagoda raids.

In this tense atmosphere, elections for the National Assembly were held on September 27 after a *pro forma* one-week campaign. Predictably, GVN candidates won overwhelming victories. The new assembly convened on October 7 to hear President Diem's state of the union message. Diem spoke mainly of South Vietnam's past and present progress, playing down the internal political crisis, and made only scant reference to U.S. assistance. As might have been expected, he threw the blame for the Buddhist crisis on the Communists, foreign adventurers, and the Western press.

On the same day, Mme. Nhu arrived in the U.S. after a month in Europe to begin a three-week speaking tour. She immediately launched into shrill denunciations of the Buddhists and of U.S. policy that progressively alienated U.S. public opinion. She was followed around the country by her father, the former Ambassador to the United States, however, who acted as a one-man truth squad revealing the inaccuracies and distortions of her statements. The Administration's dignified and temperate reaction further discredited her attacks. On October 8, the UN General Assembly voted to send a fact-finding team to South Vietnam to investigate the changes of repressions against Buddhists.

B. THE NEW AMERICAN POLICY

Lodge's immediate reaction to the new policy approach was enthusiastic, "an excellent instruction outlining a course of action which should yield constructive results." With the exception of the aid suspension, his views, in essence, had prevailed with both McNamara and the President, the standard public kudos to military progress notwithstanding. His plan was to allow the suspension of the commodity import program, the largest and most important of the economic sanctions, to become evident without making any mention of it, and, by maintaining his aloofness from official contact, force the regime to come to him. On October 7, however, Lodge expressed some doubts about the real value of the political concessions itemized in State's instructions if our real goal was removal of Nhu, an objective of questionable feasibility under the current circumstances. In view of Nhu's increasing hostility to the U.S. presence and influence, Lodge felt a request from the regime for a U.S. withdrawal was a distinct possibility.

That same day, the regime's reaction to the aid cut-off hit the streets with banner headlines in its mouthpiece, the *Times of Vietnam*: "USOM Freezes Economic Aid Program." The article accused the U.S. of subverting the war effort, and asserted that the cut-off had been decided in mid-September. Such fantastic pressure for petty reforms would jeopardize the entire revolutionary program of the government, it concluded. Lodge made no comment on the story.

In mid-October, Lodge was requested to provide Washington with a weekly evaluation of the effects, both positive and negative, of the new policy. Lodge's October 16 reply summarized the situation as follows: "So far we appear to be getting virtually no effect from our actions under DEPTEL 534, but we would not have expected effects this early." Other reports indicated that the regime was preparing to take a number of belt-tightening measures, including reductions in civil service salaries; that Chinese businessmen and bankers had begun to get jittery about currency stability; and that the government was planning to draw down its foreign exchange reserves to sustain import levels in the face of the U.S. cut-off of CIP funds. A CIA memorandum concluded that the GVN reaction to the new U.S. policy, particularly the violent anti-U.S. campaign in the *Times of Vietnam* and the surveillance and harassment of Americans and their employees, indicated that Diem and Nhu were preparing for a long fight and were unmoved by the new policy.

Under Lodge's instructions, General Stillwell (MACV—J-3) met with Secretary Thuan on October 17 and informed him of the impending cut-off of funds for the Special Forces, both MAP and CIA, unless the three CIA-funded companies under Colonel Tung's command were placed under JGS control and transferred to the field. Thuan said he would take the matter up with Diem immediately. Harkins informed Diem directly of this action in a letter on October 18. General Don and Colonel Tung were also personally advised of the action, but again no public announcement was made. On October 26 it was learned that Tung and JGS were working on plans to transfer his Special Forces to the Central Highlands. By then, however, coup plans were well advanced and the significance of this transfer must be understood therein.

Militarily, in October while the GVN had taken some minor steps in line with the McNamara–Taylor recommendations (such as agreeing to realign III and IV Corps boundaries to give added emphasis to the Delta war), the combat situation continued to worsen. The tempo of VC attacks, particularly in the Delta, increased; the weapons-loss ratio and casualty ratios deteriorated; and GVN "missing in action" increased. In Washington, further doubt was cast on the optimism of previous reports by a controversial State Department research study of October 22. The memorandum took issue with encouraging conclusions about the progress of the military campaign derived from statistical trends, pointing out important unfavorable trends revealed by the same statistical data. In Saigon, MACV continued unsuccessfully to press Diem to take further steps to strengthen the war effort.

Meanwhile, the U.S. Mission had been feeling the impact of the new policy in internal strains of its own. Hilsman reports that Lodge decided early in October that the recall of John Richardson, the CIA chief in Saigon, would be a useful additional pressure against Nhu because they had been closely identified during Nolting's ambassadorship, and because Richardson was known to favor a more conciliatory approach to the regime. While there are no cables in the available files to confirm it, Hilsman maintains that Lodge sent a private message to the President and CIA Director McCone requesting Richardson's transfer. The President agreed, McCone acquiesced, and Richardson was returned to Washington on October 5. Whatever other motives may have been involved, Richardson had, in fact, been the specific object of an attack in the U.S. press on October 2 that had accused him of insubordination and had compromised his identity. It is not surprising under such circumstances that he should have been transferred. Whatever the case, the press interpreted his recall as a slap at the regime, as Hilsman suggests Lodge wanted.

This was only an incident in the continuing series of stories by U.S. correspondents on divisions within the mission. Lodge's relations with the press, however, remained excellent throughout his tour. He consciously cultivated the U.S. press corps with private luncheons, "backgrounders," and occasional leaks, and it paid off for him personally. But the press sharply attacked those in the mission, like Richardson and Harkins, with whom they disagreed about U.S. policy. Washington registered its concern that these stories, whatever their origin, were damaging to the official posture of unity the U.S. Government was trying to maintain in the implementation of a difficult policy toward South Vietnam. But the stories continued, even after the coup.

In his weekly evaluation of the impact of the new U.S. policy on October 23, Lodge was not encouraged by the results to date. "Diem/Nhu give every appearance of sitting tight and reacting to U.S. pressure with counter pressure and implying through public statements that they can go it alone." Nevertheless, there were several straws in the wind. Secretary Thuan had reported that Diem was worried and that he had instructed Thuan to ask Lodge if Washington had reached any decisions on commercial imports. Lodge also felt that the regime was being more careful about repressive actions. Furthermore, experienced observers felt the U.S. policy was creating favorable conditions for a coup, although Lodge did not see anyone seriously considering it. The day after this message was sent, Lodge and his wife were invited by Diem to spend the next Sunday (the day after the National Day celebration) with him at his villa in

Dalat, after visiting an agricultural station and a strategic hamlet. Lodge promptly accepted. Diem had made the first move.

Washington instructed Lodge to use the occasion of the trip with Diem to test for movement by the GVN on any of the U.S. demands. Lodge was to take advantage of any subject of interest that Diem brought up to determine both the willingness of the government to make concessions and the effect of our selective sanctions. If Diem did not provide such conversational opportunities, Lodge was to assume the initiative. In particular, he was to inquire about changes in the military campaign that had been recommended by the McNamara–Taylor mission and subsequently pressed by General Harkins; he was to suggest that Diem be cooperative to the UN investigatory team that had arrived in the country on October 24, and allow them full access to information and people; and he was to inquire whether Diem did not think it time to end the bitter anti-American campaign of the *Times of Vietnam* and the Nhus.

Lodge's Sunday with Diem on October 27, the day after the National Day celebration, was frustrating in almost all respects. Diem did bring up several issues of interest, but gave no indication that he had changed his position or his attitude about the Buddhists or the U.S. He did inquire about the suspension of the commercial import program to which Lodge inquired in reply about the release of Buddhists and students from jail, the reopening of the schools, and the elimination of anti-Buddhist discrimination. Diem offered excuses and complaints as usual. Taking the initiative, Lodge complained to Diem of the public opinion pressure that his policies were placing the President under in the U.S. He complained about the physical attacks on U.S. newsmen and about Mme Nhu's inflammatory remarks in the U.S. as examples of the kind of thing Diem could prevent that would enhance his public image in the U.S. and the world. Lodge describes the end of the conversation in this manner:

> When it was evident that the conversation was practically over, I said: "Mr. President, every single specific suggestion which I have made, you have rejected. Isn't there some one thing you may think of that is within your capabilities to do and that would favorably impress U.S. opinion?" As on other previous occasions when I asked him similar questions, he gave me a blank look and changed the subject.

While Lodge saw no movement on the basis of the conversation, he nonetheless suggested that consideration be given in Washington to what we would consider adequate response on Diem's part for a resumption of the commercial import program. The following day, after Lodge had related the disappointing results of the conversation to Secretary Thuan over luncheon, the latter observed that the U.S. really wasn't asking much and that perhaps the conversation with Diem had been a beginning. In retrospect, the comment is ironic, for with the coup only five days away, the October 27 conversation was in reality a pathetic ending not a hopeful beginning.

At one level, attention now turned to Lodge's scheduled trip to Washington October 31. The exact purpose of the trip remains a mystery. On October 30, he sent a cable to Washington with some suggestions of steps by the GVN that Washington might consider adequate for resuming the commercial import program under various conditions, steps which he hoped to discuss when he arrived. However, earlier in October, Lodge had sent a private note to McGeorge Bundy, asking that the President make him available for a trip to Vietnam to discuss with Lodge a matter which Lodge did not feel free to enter into through any electronic communication channel. The following cryptic reference suggests that whatever the mysterious subject lodge had in mind, it was the purpose for the planned trip to Washington at the end of October:

> Regarding my wire, I appreciate your willingness to send Bundy. Would not have brought this up if I did not have a proposal which I think contains new ideas and which might just change the situation here for the better. It cannot be properly handled by telegram or letter and requires a chance for me to have a dialogue with Rusk and/or Harriman and/or Bundy. I wired Bundy because I cannot leave here immediately, but I could come for one working day to Washington after Vietnamese National Day on October 26 and dedication of Vietnamese Atomic Energy Plant on October 28, returning here immediately thereafter, and would be glad to do it.

In order to shorten Lodge's absence from Saigon and to add flexibility to his departure timing, the President dispatched a military aircraft to Saigon and left it at his disposal. But as the October 31 date arrived, it coincided with the momentary anticipation of a move by the generals. Lodge, no doubt preferred to remain in control of U.S. actions during a coup rather than see Harkins take over, as Washington's instructions for his absence stipulated, and so, he postponed his own departure.

C.   RENEWED COUP PLOTTING

While Diem's reaction to the tough new American policy was hostile, the senior South Vietnamese generals, predictably, interpreted the new policy as a green light for a coup. Plotting was reactivated almost immediately, if indeed it had ever been completely dormant.

On October 2, the day the McNamara–Taylor mission reported to the President, General Don "accidentally" encountered Lt Colonel Conein, the CIA contact man in the August plot, at Tan Son Nhut airport and asked him to meet him that night in Nha Trang. Truehart approved the contact, instructing Conein to neither encourage nor discourage a coup but only to get information. At the meeting, General Don said that General Minh wanted to meet with Concin at 8:00 a.m. on October 5 at JGS headquarters at which time Minh would be able to go into the details of the generals' plan. Don emphatically stated that there was a plan, and that essential to it was the conversion of General Dinh, III Corps commander, to the cause.

So, with Lodge's approval, Conein met General Minh on October 5. Getting straight to the point, "General Minh stated that he must know American Government's position with respect to a change in the Government of Vietnam within the very near future." The government's loss of popular support was endangering the whole war effort, which was deteriorating rapidly. He did not except any U.S. support, but needed assurances the U.S. would not thwart the attempt. Also involved, he said, were Generals Don, Khiem and Kim. Of three possible and not mutually exclusive plans mentioned by Minh, two involved military action against loyal units in Saigon, and one was an assassination plot against brothers Nhu and Can, but not Diem. Conein remained noncommittal about both U.S. support and the various plans. Minh then expressed doubt about General Khiem whom he suspected of having played a double role in

August, but indicated that the generals would have to act soon to forestall abortive attempts by lower echelon officers. Minh hoped to meet with Conein in the near future to go over the detailed plan of operations. Conein was again noncommittal and Minh said he understood.

Lodge, with Harkins' concurrence, recommended that when Minh, about whom he was now dubious after his August experience, approached Conein again, he be told: (1) that the U.S. would not thwart his plans; (2) that we would be willing to review his plans, except those for assassinations; and (3) "that U.S. aid will be continued to Vietnam under government which gives promise of gaining support of people and winning the war against the Communists." In pressing Minh for details of the planned composition of a successor regime, Lodge felt we should stress the need for a "good proportion of well qualified civilian leaders in key positions."

A message emanating from an NSC meeting was sent to Lodge on the same day and appears to have been dispatched before the arrival of the CAS report on the Conein-Minh meeting and Lodge's comment. In it the President specifically instructed Lodge to avoid encouraging a coup. The message stated:

> . . . President today approved recommendation that no initiative should now be taken to give any active covert encouragement to a coup. There should, however, be urgent covert effort with closest security under broad guidance of Ambassador to identify and build contacts with possible alternative leadership as and when it appears. Essential that this effort be totally secure and fully deniable and separated entirely from normal political analysis and reporting and other activities of country team. We repeat that this effort is not repeat not to be aimed at active promotion of coup but only at surveillance and readiness. In order to provide plausibility to denial suggest you and no one else in Embassy issue these instruction orally to Acting Station Chief and hold him responsible to you alone for making appropriate contacts and reporting to you alone. [Doc. 143]

Responding the next day, October 6, to the report of the Conein-Minh meeting, Washington referred to the preceding day's cable, but, prompted by Lodge's suggestion, added:

> While we do not wish to stimulate coup, we also do not wish to leave impression that U.S. would thwart a change of government or deny economic and military assistance to a new regime if it appeared capable of increasing effectiveness of military effort, ensuring popular support to win war and improving working relations with U.S. We would like to be informed on what is being contemplated but we should avoid being drawn into reviewing or advising on operational plans or any other act which might tend to identify U.S. too closely with change in government. [Doc. 145]

Washington was, further, greatly concerned about the security and deniability of any further contacts and suggested to Lodge that someone could be brought in from outside Vietnam for follow-up contacts if he thought it necessary. Lodge apparently did not.

An important apparent lacuna in the available message traffic occurs at this point. By Shaplen's account, a CAS officer met with Minh on October 10 and conveyed the substance of the U.S. position. Whether or not the date is accurate, it is probable that some such contact took place by mid-October. On October 20 a Colonel Khuong at JGS contacted an American counterpart and reported a coup plot involving Minh, Khiem, Kim, and a fourth unidentified general, plus a number of colonels. He was seeking assurances of U.S. support following a coup.

There were no further reported contacts with the generals until October 23 when Conein again met with Don at the latter's initiative. In a state of agitation, Don stated that the coup had been scheduled to take advantage of the October 26 National Holiday, but that on October 22 Harkins had called on him to report the Khuong contact and to discourage a coup. Don further indicated that the palace had learned of Khuong's overtures, implying that Harkins was responsible, and had taken action to ensure that the vital 5th and 7th Divisions would be away from Saigon. Don demanded to know what the U.S. attitude was toward a coup. Conein reiterated the Washington guidance. Apparently relieved, Don asked Conein to assure Lodge that Khuong was not a member of the coup committee and would be punished. He indicated that the generals had avoided contacting Lodge directly at a party on October 18 because of the presence of members of Harkins' staff. Conein then asked for proof of the existence of the coup group and its plan. Don said that if they could meet the following day, he would give Conein, EYES ONLY for Lodge, the political organization plan.

In a subsequent conversation with Harkins on the matter, Lodge reported that Harkins confirmed his demarche to Don on October 22, and after they had reviewed CAP 74228, said he had misunderstood the policy and hoped he had not upset any delicate arrangements. Harkins added that he would inform Don that his previous statements did not reflect U.S. Government policy.

By Harkins' account, he had not violated Washington's guidance in his conversation with Don. He was merely trying to discourage Vietnamese officers from approaching U.S. counterparts about coup plots which only detracted from the war effort. Furthermore, Don had at no time mentioned coup planning to him. He concluded by commenting about the renewed plotting by the generals that:

> Though I am not trying to thwart a change in government, I think we should take a good hard look at the group's proposals to see if we think it would be capable of increasing the effectiveness of the military effort. There are so many coup groups making noises that unless elements of all are included I'm afraid there will be a continuous effort to upset whoever gains control for sometime out and this to me will interfere with the war effort.

This incident once again highlighted the differing outlooks of the Ambassador and MACV and underscored the lack of close coordination between them. Unfortunately, it did not lead to any improvement in the situation. The close identification of Harkins with Diem made the Vietnamese generals mistrust him. Lodge, responsive to their great sensitivity about security, tended to restrict information about the contacts and coup plans to himself.

In response to this contact by Don, Washington reflected mainly concern that he might be acting as an agent of the palace to lead us down the garden path. As he had indicated, Don contacted Conein on the morning of the 24th, but not with the promised plans. He reported that the previous evening Harkins had spoken to him, correcting his earlier statements about the nondesirability of a change of government. Don further said he had a scheduled meeting with Lodge that evening (which Lodge denied) and that plans were now far advanced for a coup sometime before November 2. He asked Conein to meet him later that afternoon to discuss the details of the plan. In a separate cable disputing some of Lodges interpretative description of his statement to Don, Harkins stated that he had repulsed Don's suggestion that they meet again to discuss the coup plans. "I told Don that I would not discuss coups that were not my business though I had heard rumors of many. Taylor replied immediately, stating, "View here is that your actions in disengaging from the coup discussion were correct and that you should continue to avoid any involvement."

At Conein's meeting with Don on the evening of the 24th, the latter indicated he had misunderstood General Harkins and had not seen Lodge. He said that the coup committee had refused to release any plans because of its anxiety about breaches of security. He did promise to turn over to Conein for Lodge's review detailed plans of the operation and the proposed successor government two days before the coup, which he reiterated would take place before November 2.

At this juncture, the nature of the dialogue between Lodge and the White House began to change. On October 25, Lodge sent McGeorge Bundy a long cable taking exception to Harkins' reservations about a coup and arguing for a policy of "not thwarting." No successor government could bungle the war as badly as Diem had, he argued, and, furthermore, for us to prevent a change of government would be "assuming an undue responsibility for keeping the incumbents in office." In his reply, Bundy expressed the White House anxiety about reaping the blame for an unsuccessful coup.

> We are particularly concerned about hazard that an unsuccessful coup, however carefully we avoid direct engagement, will be laid at our door by public opinion almost everywhere. Therefore, while sharing your view that we should not be in position of thwarting coup, we would like to have option of judging and warning on any plan with poor prospects of success. We recognize that this is a large order, but President wants you to know of our concern. [Doc. 153]

The discussion of these issues dominated the cable traffic between Lodge and the White House up to the day of the coup, with Washington concerned about detailed plans and prospects for success and Lodge stressing the irrevocability of our involvement.

There were no further contacts with the coup group until the day after the fruitless Lodge–Diem conversations. That Monday, October 28, Lodge and Diem were leaving Saigon for Dalat to dedicate the Vietnamese Atomic Energy Plant. At the airport before their departure, General Don daringly took Lodge aside and asked if Conein was authorized to speak for him. Lodge assured Don that he was. Don said that the coup must be thoroughly Vietnamese and that the U.S. must not interfere. Lodge agreed, adding that the U.S. wanted no satellites but would not thwart a coup. When Lodge asked about the timing of the coup, Don replied that the generals were not yet ready.

Later that evening Conein met Don by prearrangement at the latter's initiative. When Conein called Don's attention to Lodge's scheduled trip to Washington on October 31, indicating that it was important for him to review the coup plans before his departure, Don replied that the plans might not be available until four hours in advance, but urged that the Ambassador not change his plans as this might be a tip-off. Don said that nothing would happen in the next 48 hours, but the implication was that the coup would pre-empt Lodge's departure. When pressed for details of the planning, Don indicated that within the committee, Minh had charge of the military plans for the operation, Kim was doing the political planning, and he, Don, was the liaison with the Americans. They had surrounded General Dinh with coup supporters and he would be neutralized. Generals Tri and Khanh were both involved in the planning. General Khiem was being circumspect because he was under palace suspicion. Minor details of the plan and a list of units supporting the coup were also discussed.

Simultaneous separate contacts had confirmed that several important opposition civilians were in contact with the generals, including Phan Huy Quat, Bui Diem, and Tran Trung Dung, and that they expected to play a role in the post-coup government, which reportedly would be headed by Vice President Tho. In a cable dispatched that same day summarizing the situation, Lodge expressed some concern at the possibility of a premature coup by junior officers, but generally expressed confidence in the generals while regretting their reluctance for security reasons to provide details of their plans. He concluded in these words:

> In summary, it would appear that a coup attempt by the Generals' group is imminent; that whether this coup fails or succeeds, the USG must be prepared to accept the fact that we will be blamed, however unjustifiably; and finally, that no positive action by the USG can prevent a coup attempt short of informing Diem and Nhu with all the opprobrium that such an action would entail. Note too Don's statement we will only have four hours notice. This rules out my checking with you between time I learn of coup and time that it starts. It means US will not be able significantly to influence course of events.

Lodge's view was clear. We were committed and it was too late for second thoughts. Moreover, when the balloon went up he did not expect to have time to consult Washington. He expected, and probably preferred, to guide events himself.

In view of the deteriorating situation, instructions were given to Admiral Felt, CINCPAC, to have a task force stand off the Vietnamese coast for the possible evacuation of American dependents and civilians if events required. This was a re-enactment of a similar alert during the abortive August coup.

In Washington, McNamara and the JCS had become concerned about the differing views of Lodge and Harkins as to the correct U.S. course of action. More importantly, they were alarmed at the apparent breakdown of communication and coordination between the Ambassador and MACV. The cable traffic tended "to form a picture of a relationship which lacks the depth and continuity required by the complex circumstances in Saigon." Harkins' suggestions for improving their rapport were invited. After the NSC meeting on October 29, the White House was also concerned and instructed Lodge to show Harkins the relevant cables and be sure he was fully aware of the coup arrangements, since during Lodge's absence in Washington Harkins would have overall responsibility for the U.S. [Doc. 150]

These two cables triggered a flurry of strong opposing reactions from Lodge and Harkins. Harkins, belatedly apprised of the recent Conein-Don contacts and of Lodge's evaluations and recommendations, took bitter exception to the Ambassador's conclusions in three separate cables on October 30. He particularly resented Lodge's independent, gloomy assessments of how the war was going, which were at direct odds with his own views, views which he had provided Lodge for inclusion in his weekly reports to Washington. [Doc. 151] As to U.S. policy toward a coup, he was irate at having been excluded by Lodge from information and consultation about the continuing contacts with the generals. [Doc. 152] The heart of the issue, however, was a disagreement about what was, in fact, U.S. policy toward a coup as defined by the Washington guidance cables. Harkins outlined the disagreement in a separate October 30 cable to Taylor:

> There is a basic difference apparently between the Ambassador's thinking and mine on the interpretation of the guidance contained in CAP 63560 dated 6 October (see Appendix) and the additional thoughts, I repeat, thoughts expressed in CAS Washington 74228 dated 9 October (Appendix). I interpret CAP 63560 as our basic guidance and that CAS 74228 being additional thoughts did not change the basic guidance in that no initiative should now be taken to give any active covert encouragement to a coup. The Ambassador feels that 74228 does change 63560 and that a change of government is desired and feels as stated in CAS Saigon 1964 (Appendix) that the only way to bring about such a change is by a coup.
>
> I'm not opposed to a change in government, no indeed, but I'm inclined to feel that at this time the change should be in methods of governing rather than complete change of personnel. I have seen no batting order proposed by any of the coup groups. I think we should take a hard look at any proposed list before we make any decisions. In my contacts here I have seen no one with the strength of character of Diem, at least in fighting communists. Certainly there are no Generals qualified to take over in my opinion.
>
> I am not a Diem man *per se*. I certainly see the faults in his character. I am here to back 14 million SVN people in their leader at this time.
>
>   *   *   *
>
> I would suggest we not try to change horses too quickly. That we continue to take persuasive actions that will make the horses change their course and methods of action. That we win the military effort as quickly as possible, then let them make any and all the changes they want.
>
> After all, rightly or wrongly, we have backed Diem for eight long hard years. To me it seems incongruous now to get him down, kick him around, and get rid of him. The US has been his mother superior and father confessor since he's been in office and he has leaned on us heavily. [Docs. 151 & 152]

The first Washington message to Lodge on October 30 revealed that White House anxiety about the possible failure of a coup attempt, already evident on October 25 in CAP 63590 (see Appendix), had increased. The CIA's evaluation of the balance of forces cast doubt on whether the coup group could pull off a decisive action. With these concerns in mind, Washington could not accept Lodge's judgment "that no positive action by the USG can prevent a coup attempt . . ." The White House view was that:

. . . our attitude to coup group can still have decisive effects on its decisions. We believe that what we say to coup group can produce delay of coup and that betrayal of coup plans to Diem is not repeat not our only way of stopping coup.

In a long reply (in which Harkins did not concur), Lodge was at pains to point out his powerlessness to prevent what was fundamentally a Vietnamese affair, short of revealing it to the palace.

We must, of course, get best possible estimate of chance of coup's success and this estimate must color our thinking, but do not think we have the power to delay or discourage a coup. Don has made it clear many times that this is a Vietnamese affair. It is theoretically possible for us to turn over the information which has been given to us in confidence to Diem and this would undoubtedly stop the coup and would make traitors out of us. For practical purposes therefore I would say that we have very little influence on what is essentially a Vietnamese affair. In addition, this would place the heads of the Generals, their civilian supporters, and lower military officers on the spot, thereby sacrificing a significant portion of the civilian and military leadership needed to carry the war against the VC to its successful conclusion. After our efforts not to discourage a coup and this change of heart, we would foreclose any possibility of change of the GVN for the better.

*   *   *

As regards your paragraph 10 (question of determination and force of character of coup leaders), I do not know what more proof can be offered than the fact these men are obviously prepared to risk their lives and that they want nothing for themselves. If I am any judge of human nature, Don's face expressed sincerity and determination on the morning that I spoke to him. Heartily agree that a miscalculation could jeopardize position in Southeast Asia. We also run tremendous risks by doing nothing. [Doc. 154]

Whether Lodge seriously believed this or merely used it as an argumentative excuse for not entertaining the possibility of intervention to delay or stop an unviable attempt is not clear. His defense of the plotters and his support for their goal in this telegraphic dialogue with Washington, however, clearly show his emotional bias in favor of a coup. Elsewhere in the cable Lodge objected to the designation of Harkins as the Chief of Mission in the event of a coup during his absence.

The tone and content of these parallel messages from Harkins and Lodge only heightened White House anxiety and, no doubt, raised concern about the objectivity of these two principal U.S. observers of the critical Vietnamese situation. In an effort to clear the air, explicitly redefine and restate the policy guidance, and clarify the assignment of roles and responsibilities within the Mission, the White House sent still another cable to Saigon later on October 30. Taking pointed issue with Lodge's view, the message stated:

We do not accept as a basis for US policy that we have no power to delay or discourage a coup. In your paragraph 12 you say that if you were convinced that the coup was going to fail you would of course do everything you could to persuade coup leaders to stop or delay any operation which, in your best judgement, does not clearly give high prospect of success. We have never considered any betrayal of generals to Diem, and our 79109 explicitly rejected that course. We recognize the danger of appearing hostile to generals, but we believe that our own position should be on as firm ground as possible, hence we cannot limit ourselves to proposition implied in your message that only conviction of certain failure justifies intervention. We believe that your standard for intervention should be that stated above.

Therefore, if you should conclude that there is not clearly a high prospect of success, you should communicate this doubt to generals in a way calculated to persuade them to desist at least until chances are better. In such a communication you should use the weight of US best advice and explicitly reject any implication that we oppose the effort of the generals because of preference for present regime. We recognize need to bear in mind generals' interpretation of US role in 1960 coup attempt and your agent should maintain clear distinction between strong and honest advice given as a friend and any opposition to their objectives. [Doc. 155]

Lodge was also urgently requested to obtain more detailed information about the composition of the forces the coup leaders expected to have at their disposal so that we could better assess their prospects.

With regard to Lodge's absence, the instructions placed Truehart in charge unless a coup occurred, in which case Harkins would be Chief of Mission. The desirability of having Lodge on the scene in the event of a coup, however, was stressed and he was encouraged to delay his departure if he thought the coup was imminent. The following four-point standing instructions for U.S. posture in the event of a coup were also given:

a. US authorities will reject appeals for direct intervention from either side, and US-controlled aircraft and other resources will not be committed between the battle lines or in support of either side, without authorization from Washington.

b. In event of indecisive contest, US authorities may in their discretion agree to perform any acts agreeable to both sides, such as removal of key personalities or relay of information. In such actions, however, US authorities will strenuously avoid appearance of pressure on either side. It is not in the interest of USG to be or appear to be either instrument of existing government or instrument of coup.

c. In the event of imminent or actual failure of coup, US authorities may afford asylum in their discretion to those to whom there is any express or implied obligation of this sort. We believe, however, that in such a case it would be in our interest and probably in interest of those seeking asylum that they seek protection of other Embassies in addition to our own. This point should be made strongly if need arises.

d. But once a coup under responsible leadership has begun, and within these restrictions, it is in the interest of the US government that it should succeed.

With respect to instruction d., however, no specific actions to support or guarantee the success of a coup were authorized. This message was the last guidance Lodge received from Washington before the coup began.

V. THE COUP AND ITS AFTERMATH—NOVEMBER 1–23

A. THE COUP

The atmosphere of Byzantine intrigue in Saigon in the fall of 1963 made it virtually impossible to keep track of all the plots against the regime. In one of his last messages to Washington before the coup, Lodge identified ten individual dissident groups in addition to the generals' group. These various plots were highly fluid in composition and quixotic in character, quickly appearing, disappearing and/or merging with other groups. There were, however, two groups that came into existence in the summer and retained their identity with some mutation until near the end. The first, chronologically, was variously identified as the Tuyen or Thao group after its successive leaders. It was conceived sometime in June by Dr. Tran Kim Tuyen, the Director of Political Studies (national intelligence) under Diem, and involved elements of the Ministries of Civic Action and Information and certain elements of the Army. When Dr. Tuyen was sent out of the country in September, the group was more or less merged with a separate group of middle level officers headed by Lt. Colonel Phamh Goc Thao. Several dates were established by this group for a coup during the summer and fall, but each time critical military units were temporarily transferred by either the palace or the JGS, under General Don, each of whom was somewhat aware of the group's plans and was interested in frustrating them. In the end, it concerted efforts with the generals as the only alternative with prospects of success.

The second group was, of course, composed of the senior generals of the Vietnamese Army. Plotting by this group also began in earnest in June. Initially, its leader was identified as General Khiem and later General Don, but the de facto leader throughout was, no doubt, General Minh who commanded by far the greatest respect and allegiance within the officer corps. The four principal members of the group were Generals Minh, Don, Khiem, and Kim, all of whom were stationed in Saigon without troop command, the latter three at JGS and General Minh as a palace military advisor. Generals Tri and Khanh, I and II Corps commanders respectively, were secondary members of the generals' group, but were also in touch with the Thao group. The abortive attempt by the generals to launch a coup in August has already been described in detail. Important lessons seem to have been learned by these men from that experience, for when they again began to set their plans and make arrangements it was with great attention to detail and with an explicit division of labor.

Among the plotters, General Minh had the overall direction of the coup activities, although the group acted in committee fashion with the members apparently voting at several points on particular actions. He was also responsible for the military operation of the coup itself. General Don was the liaison with the Americans and responsible for wooing General Dinh. General Kim handled planning for the post-coup government and the relations with the civilian groups that were expected to be called on to support the coup. General Khiem was to play a critical role at the end of October as the liaison man with the Thao coup group in working out the details of their support and integration into the actual execution of the coup.

As already noted, the fundamental problem of the plotters was their lack of troop command in the immediate Saigon area. The Ngo family's longstanding fear of military coups, as previously discussed, had been the main factor in all military command assignments and promotion policy. Nowhere was loyalty a more important prerequisite for command than in Saigon, the surrounding III Corps, and the nearby IV Corps, with its headquarters only 40 miles away down Highway 4. In addition to the sizable special forces units in Saigon under Colonel Tung and the various national police and paramilitary units that also took their orders directly from the palace, Diem had appointed the vain, ambitious, and supposedly loyal General Dinh as Commander of III Corps (whose 5th Division was stationed at nearby Bien Hoa) and the Saigon Military District. Furthermore, the IV Corps was commanded by General Cao, who had saved Diem during the 1960 coup by bringing his loyal 7th Division troops up from My Tho. It was on this formidable line-up of forces that the family had staked its survival; and not without reason, as the frustrated coup of August demonstrated.

Saigon, however, was not entirely without dissident elements. With the exception of their commanders, the Marine battalion, the airborne battalion, and the Air Force were all sympathetic to a coup. But the plotters knew that a favorable balance of forces could not be achieved or maintained without either the conversion or neutralization of Generals Dinh and Cao.

During the August pagoda raids, Dinh had been given overall command of the crackdown, although Tung had taken his instructions as always directly from Nhu in carrying out the attacks. Thereafter, Dinh, who was a notorious braggart, boasted that he had saved the country from the Buddhists, Communists, and "foreign adventurers." Carried away with himself, he held a news conference on August 27 in which he was harried and finally humiliated by antagonistic American journalists. The plotting generals decided that they would play on his vanity and egoism to win him over to their side. With his pride injured at the hands of the newsmen, Dinh was easy prey to Don's suggestion that Nhu had played him for a fool, but that he really was a national hero, and that the regime was indebted to him. Don suggested that Dinh go to Diem with a plan to increase military participation in the government, specifically that he, Dinh, be named Minister of Interior. Don rightly expected that Diem would be outraged at such a brazen request, and would reprimand Dinh, further wounding his pride and alienating him from the regime. Diem reacted as expected, and ordered Dinh to take a "vacation" in Dalat for a while. Don at this point began his long effort to woo Dinh to the plotters side against Diem. Dinh, however, lacked self-confidence and vacillated although he does not appear to have played a double roll by revealing the existence of the plot to the palace. While the elaborate stratagems for seducing Dinh were taking place, the plotters had carefully surrounded him with supporters of the coup, including his deputy, Colonel Co, whom they felt they could rely on to neutralize him if he showed signs of rallying to the family once the balloon was up. By the end of the third week in October, the plotters felt reasonably confident that the problem of Dinh had been resolved: he would, as an opportunist, rally to the coup if he felt it was going to succeed; if he did not, he would be eliminated.

At the same time, plans had been under way to neutralize General Cao, the IV Corps commander, since he would certainly betray the plotters to the palace if he got word of the plans, or bring his troops to Diem's aid if the coup started while he was still in control of them. To do this, Colonel Co, Dinh's deputy, was sent to the Delta to win the support of the subordinate commanders in IV Corps. In the ultimate plan, Co would be sent with JGS orders to take command of the 7th Division in My Tho on the day before the coup began; he would order all boats to the Saigon side of the Mekong River; and, thus, act as a blocking force to General Cao who, stranded in Can Tho on the far side of the Mekong, was then be arrested by dissident officers in his own command. Co apparently was successful in getting the support of the great majority of the subordinate officers, but one loyal officer heard of the plans and immediately tipped off Nhu.

Diem and Nhu called in Dinh and revealed what they had learned, attempting to force his hand. Dinh reacted with feigned shock and suggested that Co be executed immediately. This convinced Nhu that Dinh was not involved. They preferred to keep Co alive to get more information from him. Nhu then revealed his own elaborate scheme for a pseudo-coup that would pre-empt the plotters and squelch their plans. His two-part plan was to start with the transfer of Colonel Tung's special forces out of Saigon on maneuvers. The phony coup would then take place with Diem and Nhu escaping to their hideaway at Cap St Jacques. After several days of hooliganism including the murder of several prominent Vietnamese and some Americans, the loyal 5th Division under Dinh and the 7th under Cao would counterattack the city and Diem and Nhu would return as triumphant heroes, more secure than ever. Dinh was the key to Nhu's plan.

Dinh's role becomes confused at this point. He apparently was uncertain about the relative balance of forces and decided to cooperate with both sides until he could decide which he felt was going to gain the upper hand, although he was probably still leaning toward the palace. In any case, if he was trusted by the Nhus, he certainly was not by the generals because they confided in him none of their detailed plans for the operation, and Nhu's plan, in which he would have played the key role, never came to fruition. It was pre-empted by the real coup the generals had been plotting.

By the last week in October, timing had become critical. The Thao group apparently had intended to act on October 24, but were dissuaded by Don and Khiem who argued that they had too few forces to guarantee success. It was at this juncture that Khiem brought the Thao group into the plans and worked out joint arrangements with them for the execution of the coup. Shaplen says that the generals' coup was originally planned for November 4. This conflicts, however, with what Don had told Conein on October 24, namely that it would occur before November 2. By Shaplen's account, Dinh revealed the planned date of the coup to Nhu who instructed him to urge that it be advanced to November 1. Nhu still thought somehow he could carry off his plan by abandoning the phony coup, by letting the real substitute for it in the hope that it would be thrown off balance by the advanced date, and by relying on Dinh's loyal troops as supplemented by Cao's to tip the scale in the family's favor once the chips were down. In allowing the generals to make their move, the principal rebels would all be compromised and Nhu could then act to crush all major dissidence. Whatever the reason, whether by Nhu's intrigue or by their own timetable, the generals set the coup for November 1.

While they had left a worried U.S. officialdom with only sketchy ideas of the planned operation, the generals had themselves devoted great attention to all details of their move. When the hour came for execution, the plan was implemented with hardly a hitch, and the fate of the regime was sealed in the first hours of the coup.

On October 29, the first preparatory action for a coup was taken. General Dinh ordered Colonel Tung to move his special forces out of the capital for maneuvers, but whether he was acting as the agent of the generals or the palace is still unclear. Simultaneously, the chief of intelligence, who had been a member of the Thao plot and was now participating in the generals' plan, passed phony intelligence of a VC build-up outside Saigon to Diem and Nhu to get them to divert loyal units that could have been used to thwart a coup.

The day of the coup itself began improbably with an official U.S. call on Diem. Admiral Felt, CINCPAC, had been visiting General Harkins to review the situation and prior to his departure at noon, he and Lodge paid a courtesy call on the President. Diem's monologue was little different from what he had said to McNamara and Taylor the month before. As they were leaving, however, he called Lodge aside and they talked privately for twenty minutes. Diem, in a tragically unwitting example of too little too late, indicated that he wanted to talk to Lodge about what it was the U.S. wanted him to do. The atmosphere of this meeting must have been strained in the extreme in view of Lodge's awareness of the imminence of the coup. After the meeting, Felt went straight to the airport and held a press conference, with a nervous General Don at his side, before departing at noon unaware of the drama that was already unfolding.

While Lodge and Felt had been at the palace, coup units had already begun to deploy in and around Saigon. At the same time, nearly all the generals and top officers had been convened for a noon meeting at JGS headquarters at Tan Son Nhut. There the coup committee informed them that the coup had begun and asked for their support. Pledges of support were recorded on tape by all those present who supported the action. They were to be used later over the radio and would implicate the entire senior officer corps of the Army in the event the coup failed. In this way the plotters were able to enlist the support of several wavering officers. The only senior officers not present were Generals Dinh and Cao, who were not informed of the meeting to prevent their revealing the coup prematurely to the palace or taking counter action. Also not present was the South Vietnamese Chief of Naval Operations, who had been assassinated by a trigger-happy escort enroute. Several officers suspected of being loyal to Diem were taken into immediate custody at JGS, including Colonel Tung, and the commanders of the Air Force, the airborne brigade, the Marines, the Civil Guard, and the police force. A CAS officer, presumably Lt Colonel Conein, was also invited to come to JGS and was authorized to maintain telephone contact with the Embassy during the coup. He provided reliable reporting throughout the next two days.

At 1:45 p.m., Don called General Stilwell, Harkins' J–3, and informed him that all the generals were assembled at JGS and that the coup had begun. At the same time, coup forces were seizing the post office with its telecommunications facilities, the police headquarters, the radio stations, the airport, and the naval headquarters, and were deploying in positions to assault the special forces headquarters near Tan Son Nhut, the palace, and the barracks of the palace guard. Other units had been deployed in blocking positions to defend against any loyal counterattack from units outside Saigon. These actions were swift and met with little resistance. The units involved included the Marine and airborne units under the leadership of junior officers, the Air Force under junior officers, and units from the 5th Division under orders from Dinh, who had thrown in his lot when he became aware of the unanimity of the senior officers and their apparent likelihood of success. Later in the day, armor and troops from the 7th Division at My Tho, under the insurgent leadership of Colonel Co, arrived for the assault on the palace.

As is always the case in this kind of crisis, the quantity of cables quickly overwhelmed the communications system, and the incompleteness of the reports meant that no clear picture of what was happening could be pieced together until later. As in all such situations, the Embassy became an island linked to outside events only by tenuous reports from telephone contacts.

In the early afternoon, Colonel Tung, who had been arrested on the morning of November 1, was forced to call his special forces and tell them to surrender to the coup forces. Not long thereafter, the adjacent special forces headquarters fell to the coup units after a brief skirmish. When this occurred, the palace was reduced for its defense to the palace guard, since the remainder of the special forces were outside the city and effectively cut off from it, and all other unit commanders had come under the command of officers involved in the coup. General Cao, the IV Corps commander, pledged his support to the coup in the late afternoon, although it is not clear whether this was opportunistic or whether he thought the coup was really Phase I of Nhu's plan. Not trusting him, however, the generals placed him under guard. At 4:30 p.m., the generals went on the radio to announce the coup and demand the resignation of Diem and Nhu. This was followed by a continuing broadcast of the pledges of support of the senior officers that had been recorded that morning. Meanwhile, Air Force transports were dropping prepared leaflets announcing the coup, and calling on the populace to support it.

At the beginning, Diem and Nhu were apparently fooled by the coup, or had completely miscalculated the extent of its support. At the first indications of coup actions, Nhu reportedly assured an alarmed official that it was all part of a palace plan. When word reached the palace that all key points had fallen, Nhu tried to contact General Dinh. When he could not reach him, he realized that he had been outfoxed and that the coup was genuine. By this time, fighting was going on between the coup forces and the palace guard at the palace and the nearby guard barracks. When the generals called the two brothers and asked them to surrender, promising them safe conduct out of the country, Diem replied by asking them to come to the palace for "consultations," an obvious attempt to repeat the 1960 tactic of delaying the coup long enough for loyal troops to reach the city. The generals, however, were not bargaining—they were demanding.

At 4:30 p.m., Diem called Lodge to ask where he stood and the following conversation ensued:

> *Diem:* Some units have made a rebellion and I want to know what is the attitude of the US?
>
> *Lodge:* I do not feel well enough informed to be able to tell you. I have heard the shooting, but am not acquainted with all the facts. Also it is 4:30 a.m. in Washington and the US Government cannot possibly have a view.
>
> *Diem:* But you must have some general ideas. After all, I am a Chief of State. I have tried to do my duty. I want to do now what duty and good sense require. I believe in duty above all.
>
> *Lodge:* You have certainly done your duty. As I told you only this morning, I admire your courage and your great contributions to your country. No one can take away from you the credit for all you have done. Now I am worried about your physical safety. I have a report that those in charge of the current activity offer you and your brother safe conduct out of the country if you resign. Had you heard this?
>
> *Diem:* No. (And then after a pause) You have my telephone number.
>
> *Lodge:* Yes. If I can do anything for your physical safety, please call me.
>
> *Diem:* I am trying to re-establish order.

There is no evidence available as to whether Washington issued further instructions with respect to the personal safety of Diem and Nhu at this time. The above conversation was the last that any American had with DIEM. Lodge, as was his custom, retired that night at about 9:30 p.m.

Shortly after Diem's call to Lodge, the generals called the palace again and put Colonel Tung on the phone. Tung told Nhu he had surrendered. The generals then demanded the immediate surrender of the brothers or they would put the palace under air and ground attack. Each general at JGS, in turn, was put on the phone to assure Diem of safe conduct if he would resign, but Nhu apparently dissuaded him. General Minh himself made a separate telephone call to Diem in a final attempt to get him to surrender, but Diem hung up. The two brothers now began frantically calling unit commanders throughout the country on their private communications system to get them to come to their aid. In most cases they could not get through, and when they did they were told to surrender by officers who now supported the coup. When they could get no help from the regular military, they made a vain effort to enlist the support of paramilitary units and their Republic Youth groups. Sometime in the early evening, probably by eight o'clock, they recognized the hopelessness of the situation and escaped from the palace, unbeknown to its defenders, through one of the secret underground exits connected to the sewer system. They were met by a Chinese friend who took them to his home in Cholon where they had previously set up a communications channel to the palace for just such an emergency. There they spent their last night.

In the face of the brothers' intransigent refusal to surrender and confident that they were now in control of the entire country and that their plans had succeeded, the generals began assembling forces and preparing for the siege of the palace. At about nine o'clock, they opened an artillery barrage of the palace and its defenders. Since the palace was being defended by some tanks, an infantry assault with tank support was required to capture it. This began about 3:30 a.m. on November 2, and lasted until about 6:30 a.m., when the palace fell, after Diem had issued a cease-fire order to the palace guard from his Cholon hideaway.

Throughout the night the brothers had remained in contact with both their loyal supporters at the palace, and periodically with the insurgents. The latter did not learn that the brothers had fled until the rebel forces under Colonel Thao invaded the palace. At 6:20 a.m., Diem called JGS and spoke personally with General Don, offering to surrender in exchange for a guarantee of safe conduct to the airport and departure from Vietnam. Minh agreed to these terms, but Diem did not reveal his whereabouts, still apparently unable to grasp the new realities. Colonel Thao learned of the location of the hideaway from a captured officer of the palace guard and received permission from Minh to go there and get the brothers. When he arrived at the house, he telephoned again to headquarters to report his location and was overheard by the brothers on another extension. They escaped to a nearby Catholic church, where once again Diem called General Don at 6:50 a.m. and surrendered unconditionally. He and Nhu were taken prisoner shortly thereafter by General Mai Huu Xuan, a long time enemy, who according to most accounts ordered or permitted their murder in the back of an armored personnel carrier enroute to JGS headquarters.

The State Department reacted to news of the coup in terms of the recognition problem with respect to the new government. Rusk felt that a delay would be useful to the generals in not appearing to be U.S. agents or stooges and would assist us in our public stance of noncomplicity. He further discouraged any large delegation of the generals from calling on Lodge as if they were "reporting in." A subsequent message stressed the need to underscore publicly the fact that this was not so much a coup as an expression of national will, a fact revealed by the near unanimous support of important military and civilian leaders. It further stressed the importance of Vice President Tho to a quick return to constitutional government and the need, therefore, for the generals to include him in any interim regime. Lodge replied affirmatively to these views, indicating his opinion that we should encourage other friendly countries to recognize the new government first with the assurance that the U.S. would follow suit shortly. Further, we should show our friendly support for the regime and without fanfare resume payments in the commercial import program.

The news of the brutal and seemingly pointless murder of Diem and Nhu, however, was received in Washington with shock and dismay. President Kennedy was reportedly personally stunned at the news, particularly in view of the heavy U.S. involvement in encouraging the coup leaders. Apparently, we had put full confidence in the coup committee's offers of safe conduct to the brothers and, reluctant to intercede on behalf of Diem and Nhu for fear of appearing to offer support to them or of reneging on our pledges of non-interference to the generals, we had not appreciated the degree of hatred of the Ngo family among the generals, nor their fear that if the brothers survived the coup they would somehow, sometime stage a comeback. In their first meeting with Lodge after the coup, however, the generals denied that the assassination had been ordered, and promised to make public their offer of safe conduct to Diem if he would resign.

While the callousness of the murders of Diem and Nhu, their previous repressiveness notwithstanding, horrified the world, the success of the coup and the deaths of the hated brothers were greeted with popular jubilation in South Vietnam. Spontaneous street demonstrations by students in a holiday mood ended in the burning of the offices of the *Times of Vietnam* and the destruction of a statue modeled after Mme. Nhu. The tension released set off celebrations rivaled only by the annual Tet New Year festivities. Americans were greeted and received with great enthusiasm, and Lodge was widely regarded as the hero of the whole train of events. Vietnamese were heard to remark that if an election for president were held Lodge would win by a landslide.

Thus, the nine-year rule of Ngo Dinh Diem came to a sudden, bloody, and permanent end, and U.S. policy in Vietnam plunged into the unknown, our complicity in the coup only heightening our responsibilities and our commitment in this struggling, leaderless land. We could be certain only that whatever new leadership emerged would be fragile, untried, and untested.

B.　ESTABLISHMENT OF AN INTERIM REGIME

Even before the initiation of the coup, the coup committee through General Kim had been in touch with civilian political oppositionists and to some extent with members of Diem's government. Once the success of the coup was certain, negotiations with these civilians by the generals' committee began in earnest. On the night of November 1 and the following day, all ministers of Diem's government were told to submit their resignations and did so, some on U.S. advice. No reprisals were taken against them. Indeed, Vice President Tho entered into intensive negotiations with General Minh on November 2 on the composition of the interim government. He apparently understood the eagerness of the generals to have him head a new government to provide continuity, and he used this knowledge to bargain with them about the composition of the cabinet. He was not to be their pliant tool.

While these conferences were taking place, the coup committee, or "Revolutionary Committee" as it was now calling itself, distributed leaflets and press releases announcing the dissolution of the National Assembly and the abolition of the Diem-Nhu government based on the constitution of 1956, and proclaiming the support of the committee for such democratic principles as free elections, unhampered political opposition, freedom of press, freedom of religion, and an end to discrimination. They were at pains to explain that the purpose of the coup was to bolster the fight against the Communists which they pledge themselves to pursue with renewed vigor and determination.

On the afternoon of November 3, the second day after the coup, Generals Don and Kim called on Lodge at the Embassy, explaining that General Minh was tied up in conversations with Vice President Tho on the new government. The conversation was long and touched on many topics. It began with mutual expressions of satisfaction at the success of the coup, and continued with Lodge's assurance of forthcoming U.S. recognition for their new government. The generals explained that they had decided on a two-tiered government structure with a military committee presided over by General Minh overseeing a regular cabinet that would be mostly civilian with Tho as prime minister. Lodge promised to see to the immediate restoration of certain of the aid programs and the speedy resumption of the others when the government was in place. They then dealt with a host of immediate problems including the return of the Nhu children to their mother and the disposition of the rest of the Ngo family, press censorship, the release of Tri Quang from the Embassy, curfew, reprisals against former ministers, etc. The generals confirmed the psychological importance of the commodity import suspension to the success of their plans. Lodge was elated, both at the efficiency and success of the coup, and the seriousness and determination of the generals to deal with the pressing problems and get on with the war.

The following day, on instructions from Washington, Lodge, in company with Lt Colonel Conein, met with Generals Minh and Don. Washington had been anxious for Lodge to urgently convey to the generals the need to make a clarifying statement about the deaths of the brothers and to take steps to insure humane treatment of other members of the family. The generals were responsive to Lodge's urgings and promised to see that action was taken on the U.S. requests. Minh said that the composition of the new government would be announced shortly. In describing the meeting later, Lodge offered a prophetic description of Minh: "Minh seemed tired and somewhat frazzled; obviously a good, well-intentioned man. Will he be strong enough to get on top of things?" Lodge closed the cable by taking exception to State's excessive pre-occupation with the negative public relations problems of the coup and decrying its failure to note the brilliance with which the coup was planned and executed.

The promised announcement of the new government came on the morning of November 5. It was very much as General Kim had described it to Lodge on November 3. Minh was named President and Chief of the Military Committee; Tho was listed as Premier, Minister of Economy, and Minister of Finance; Don was named Minister of Defense; and General Dinh was named to the Ministry of Security (Interior). Only one other general was included in the cabinet of fifteen which was composed primarily of bureaucrats and civilians with no previous experience. Political figures, either opposed to Diem or not, were conspicuously absent from the cabinet, a fact which would impair the new government's securing the roots in popular support it would need in the long run. The announcement of the new cabinet was followed by the release of "Provisional Constitutional Act No. 1," signed by General Minh, formally suspending the 1956 constitution and outlining the structure and functions of the interim government. On November 6, Saigon radio announced the composition of the Executive Committee of the Military Revolutionary Council. Minh was Chairman, Don and Dinh were Deputy Chairmen, and nine other senior generals, including Kim, Khiem, "little" Minh, Chieu, and Thieu were members. Significantly, General Khanh was not.

On October 5, the new Foreign Minister had sent a note to the Embassy informing the Ambassador officially of the change of government, and expressing the hope that relations between the two countries would be continued and strengthened. State approved Lodge's proposed reply of recognition the following day, November 6, and, under the pressure of other governments and the press, announced its intention to recognize on November 7 in Washington. The note of recognition was delivered on November 8, when Lodge called on the new Foreign Minister, Pham Dang Lam. Lam, emphasizing his own insufficiencies for the job he had been given, asked for Lodge's advice which Lodge was apparently not reluctant to give on a variety of topics. The primary impression left was that the new government would be heavily dependent on U.S. advice and support, not only for the war effort, but also in the practical problems of running the country.

In the first three weeks of November 1963, three problems preoccupied most Americans and Vietnamese in the new political and military situation created by the coup. The first of these was getting the new government started, developing the relations between the new Vietnamese officials and their American counterparts, and most importantly shaking down the power relationships within the new regime. The first two aspects of this problem would be self-resolving and were largely a matter of time. With respect to the latter, it was clear from the outset that General Minh was the dominant figure in the new government and was so regarded by nearly all the military men. Tho, however, had exhibited considerable independence during the negotiations over the cabinet, reflecting his confidence that the generals felt they needed him. The open question, then, was what degree of freedom of action the new cabinet under Tho would have, or alternatively, how deeply the military council intended to involve itself in running the country. This issue was not resolved in the public statements and communiques of the new regime and ambiguity on the subject was clearly reflected in the lack of decisiveness and vigor of the new ministers and in their general uncertainty as to their authority. While the exact reasons for not including any politicians in the cabinet are not known, it is reasonable to assume that neither Tho nor the military were anxious to see potential political rivals, with power deriving from popular support, in positions to challenge the authority of the new leaders. Whatever the case, it was the irresolution of the power relationship within the new government that was one of the factors contributing to the next round of coup-making in January 1964.

The second urgent problem of these first weeks in November was the rapidly deteriorating economic situation in Vietnam. The situation had been serious in September, and a large deficit for the 1964 budget had already been forecast. The suspension of the commercial import payments and selected PL 480 had aggravated the situation during September and October. Furthermore, all negotiations on the 1964 budget levels and U.S. support had been suspended and were now seriously behind schedule. Aware of the urgency of the problem, State, on November 2, had asked for Lodge's recommendations on the resumption of aid and had urged him to identify the people responsible for economic planning in the new government so that negotiations could begin immediately. Concern was also expressed at the lack of expertise in this area among the generals and Lodge was advised to encourage them to make maximum use of economists in the previous government who were familiar with the problems. Lodge proposed in response that the government be asked to name a high level commission of economic experts to work with a similar group from the U.S. Mission. This suggestion had been agreed to in principle the previous day by Tho, through whose office all economic aid matters were to be channeled. Lodge also believed that our aid should be increased as an indication of our support for the new government. But beyond these preliminary discussions, no real progress was made on the economic problems before the Honolulu Conference on November 20.

The third problem that worried Americans was the heightened level of Viet Cong activity in the wake of the coup and the military dislocations caused by it. Related, but of even more importance, was the new information that came to light after the coup and in the atmosphere of free discussion that it generated showing that the military situation was far worse than we had believed. The overall statistical indicators had now begun to show deterioration dating back to the summer. The incidence of VC attacks was up over the first six months of 1963, the weapons loss ratio had worsened and the rate of VC defections was 'way down. In the immediate wake of the coup, VC activity had jumped dramatically as MACV had feared it would and there was great concern to return units participating in the coup to the field quickly to forestall any major Communist offensive. Cause for more fundamental concern, however, were the first rumors and indications that under Diem there had been regular and substantial falsification in the military reporting system and in reporting on the strategic hamlets that had badly distorted the real military situation in Vietnam to make it appear less serious than it was. This, it turned out, was the main reason for the previous discrepancies in MACV and U.S. mission evaluations of the war. In the first flush of self-satisfaction after the coup, Lodge had predicted that the change of regime would shorten the war because of the improved morale of the ARVN troops. But as time wore on, the accumulating evidence of the gravity of the military situation displaced these sanguine prognoses.

The only comforting note in the intelligence was the apparent discomfiture of the National Liberation Front. Throughout the summer and fall, the NLF had seemingly been unable to capitalize on the Buddhist or student struggle movements. In fact, its principal response to the Diem-Buddhist clash had been increasingly vituperative attacks on the U.S. Not until November 7th did the NLF issue a post-Diem policy statement, consisting of a list of "eight demands":

(1) Destroy all strategic hamlets . . . and other disguised camps.
(2) Release all political detainees. . . .
(3) Promulgate without delay democratic freedom. . . .
(4) Root out all vestiges of the fascist and militarist dictatorial regime.
(5) Stop all persecution and repression and raiding operations.
(6) Dissolve all nepotist organizations. . . .
(7) Immediately stop forcible conscription. . . .
(8) Cancel all kinds of unjustified taxes.

The Duong Van Minh government could claim that it was in the process of meeting all of these "demands" except one—halting the draft—so that the NLF was effectively pre-empted. On November 17, the NLF Central Committee issued another series of demands:

(1) Eliminate the vestiges of the Diem regime.
(2) Establish democratic freedom.
(3) Eliminate American influence.
(4) Make social and economic reforms.
(5) Halt the fighting.
(6) Establish a coalition government.

The demands were accompanied by a statement affirming the reunification of Vietnam as a goal of the NLF, the first such statement in over two years. Douglas Pike's analysis was unable to resolve the reasons for the inaction of the NLF throughout the crisis:

Had the NLF leadership wished to do so, it could have used its impressive struggle machine to launch in the name of the Buddha a nation-wide struggle movement that conceivably could have ended with its long-pursued General Uprising . . . Knowledgeable Vietnamese attributed its refusal to act an unwillingness to involve itself in an alien struggle movement. The NLF and the communists, ran the argument, avoid activities over which they do not exercise total control. . . . The Buddhist leadership made it clear it did not seek NLF help since it wished at all costs to avoid the Communist stigma. Another popular explanation for the NLF's "sit-tight" policy during the Buddhist troubles was that the NLF was going to allow the bourgeois revolutionary forces to succeed in toppling Diem, after which it would capture the Revolution as the Kerensky Government was captured in the Russian Revolution. No such effort, however, was made by the NLF. A slanderous but widely bandied explanation among Vietnamese at the time was that the NLF did not want Diem removed, that he and his brothers and sister-in-law were far more valuable to the NLF in office than out. In truth, the NLF posture during this period remains something of a mystery.

C. THE HONOLULU CONFERENCE AND NSAM 273

Having postponed his planned October 31 visit to Washington because of the imminence of the coup, Lodge apparently suggested, in response to a State query, that it be rescheduled for November 10. Rusk proposed a further postponement to insure time for Lodge to establish working relations with the new government and to take advantage of his own planned trip to Tokyo later in the month. Accordingly, a meeting with Rusk, Bundy, Bell, McNamara, and Taylor in Honolulu was scheduled on November 20 for the entire country team. Lodge was invited to proceed on to Washington after the meeting if he felt he needed to talk with the President.

In preparation for the conference, State dispatched a long series of specific questions to Lodge on possible methods of broadening the political base of support of the new government and increasing the effectiveness of the war effort. This was additional to the comprehensive review of the situation, including an evaluation of progress on the McNamara-Taylor recommendations, that the military was expected to provide and the in-depth assessment of the new regime and its prospects by the country team. Lodge replied even before arriving at the conference that the proposed discussions would require detailed information about the functioning of the new rulers which it was far too early to obtain.

In a broad overview of the new political situation in Vietnam at the plenary session in Honolulu, Lodge voiced his optimism about the actions taken thus far by the new government to consolidate its popular support. In particular, he noted the efforts to eliminate forced labor in the strategic hamlets, to curtail arbitrary arrests, to deal with extortion and corruption, to enlist the support of the Hoa Hao and Cao Dai sects, and to consolidate and strengthen the strategic hamlet program. But, he left no doubt that the new leadership was inexperienced and fragile. For this reason, he urged the conferees not to press too much on the government too soon, either in the way of military and economic programs, nor steps to democratize and constitutionalize the country. His second major point was the psychological and political, as well as economic, need for U.S. aid to the new government in at least the amount of our aid to Diem, and preferably more. He recognized the domestic political problems in the U.S. with Congress, but he argued that anything less would be a severe blow to the new rulers who were still getting their bearings. USOM Director Brent supported these latter views, but registered his concern about the naiveté of the new leaders in the face of an extremely grave economic situation. In response to a direct question from Rusk as to whether an increase in dollars would shorten the war, Lodge demurred somewhat and replied that what was required was greater motivation. McNamara immediately disagreed, saying that his understanding of the piaster deficit problem was that it was endangering all the programs, and that both AID and MAP were in need of increased funding. Concurring in this view, AID Administrator Bell agreed to review the entire AID program.

General Harkins' assessment of the military situation took note of the upsurge of Viet Cong activity in the week following the coup, but in general remained optimistic, although more guardedly than in the past. The sharp increase in VC attacks after the coup seemed to have been haphazard, and not part of a well coordinated country-wide response to the uncertain political situation. And in the week just ended, activity had returned to more normal levels. Moreover, he did not show concern about the seeming long term deterioration in the statistical indicators. While he was favorably impressed with the determination of the new leaders to prosecute the war and make needed changes, he was worried about the sweeping replacemnt of division and corps commanders and province chiefs. The discontinuities and disruptions created by wholesale replacement of province chiefs could have a serious negative effect on the whole counterinsurgency program. On the positive side, he noted the strengthened chain of command under General Don as both Defense Minister and Chief of Staff. McNamara pointedly questioned both Harkins and the other military briefers about conditions in the Delta and seemed skeptical of the official optimism, although he was equally disinclined to accept undocumented negative judgments.

The conference ended inconclusively with respect to the military problem. It did, however, underscore U.S. support for the new regime and focus U.S. official concern on the urgency and gravity of the economic problem confronting the new government. An uninformative press release after the conference took note of U.S. support for the new government in facing the difficult political and economic problems in South Vietnam, and pointedly reiterated the plan to withdraw 1,000 U.S. troops by the end of the year with 300 to leave on December 3.

Lodge flew to Washington the following day and conferred with President Johnson. Based on that meeting and the report of the discussions at Honolulu, a National Security Action Memorandum was drafted to give guidance and direction to our efforts to improve the conduct of the war under the new South Vietnamese leadership. It described the purpose of the American involvement in Vietnam as, "to assist the people and Government of that country to win their contest against the externally directed and supported Communist conspiracy." It defined contribution to that purpose as the test of all U.S. actions in Vietnam. It reiterated the objectives of withdrawing 1,000 U.S. troops by the end of 1963 and ending the insurgency in I, II, and III Corps by the end of 1964, and in the Delta by the end of 1965. U.S. support for the new regime was confirmed and all U.S. efforts were directed to assist it to consolidate itself and expand its popular support. In view of the series of press stories during November about the disagreements between Harkins and Lodge, the President requested "full unity of support for established US policy" both in Saigon and in Washington. NSAM 273 directed the concentration of U.S. and Vietnamese military, political, economic and social efforts to improve the counterinsurgency campaign in the Mekong Delta. It further directed that economic and military aid to the new regime should be maintained at the same levels as during Diem's rule. And in conclusion, plans were requested for clandestine operations by the GVN against the North and also for operations up to 50 kilometers into Laos; and, as a justification for such measures, State was directed to develop a strong, documented case "to demonstrate to the world the degree to which the Viet Cong is controlled, sustained and supplied from Hanoi, through Laos and other channels."

As a policy document, NSAM 273 was to be extremely short lived. In the jargon of the bureaucracy, it was simply overtaken by events. The gravity of the military situation in South Vietnam was only hinted at in NSAM 273 and in the discussions in Honolulu. Its full dimensions would rapidly come to light in the remaining weeks of 1963 and force high level reappraisals by year's end. But probably more important, the deterioration of the Vietnamese position in the countryside and the rapid collapse of the strategic hamlet program were to confront the fragile new political structure in South Vietnam with difficulties it could not surmount and to set off rivalries that would fulfill all the dire predictions of political instability made by men as diverse as John Mecklin and Fritz Nolting before Diem's fall.

5. US–GVN Relations, 1964–1967

Summary and Analysis

1964–JUNE 1965

In 1964 the U.S. tried to make GVN strong, effective, and stable, and it failed. When the U.S. offered more aid, GVN accepted it without improving; they promised to mobilize, but failed to speed up the slow buildup of their forces. When the U.S. offered a firmer commitment to encourage them, including possible later bombing of North Vietnam, the GVN tried to pressure us to do it sooner. When the U.S. endorsed Khanh, he overplayed his hand, provoked mob violence, and had to back down to a weaker position than before. When Taylor lectured them and threatened them, the ruling generals of GVN defied him, and allied themselves with the street rioters. After several changes of government in Vietnam, the U.S. could set no higher goal than GVN stability. During this period, the USG was already starting to think about doing the job ourselves if our Vietnamese ally did not perform.

At first the U.S. thought that the power of the Vietnamese generals would make GVN strong and effective. In fact, the U.S. preference, at this time, was for military leadership in the GVN. However, the generals proved to be less than perfectly united. They found they had to bow to the power of student and Buddhist street mobs, and they lacked the will and the ability to compel the civil government to perform. Yet, the U.S. saw no alternative but to back them—to put up with Vietnamese hypersensitivity, their easy compliance combined with non-performance, and their occasional defiance. Moreover, MACV was even less ready to pressure the generals than was the Embassy and the Embassy less willing than Washington. MACV controlled the resources that mattered most to the South Vietnamese.

Pacification lagged, and the military picture steadily worsened. Planning of pressures against the North became more urgent, and the prospect of increasing U.S. inputs to all phases of the war loomed larger. The U.S. was more and more abandoning the hope that the Vietnamese could win the war by themselves. At the same time, the U.S. was preparing itself internally (NSAM 288 with the objective of an "independent non-communist Vietnam") and readying the American people (the Tonkin Gulf Resolution) for deeper commitments.

The period saw six major changes of government. At the end of January, 1964, Khanh seized power from the Minh government. In August, after his attempt to formalize military control, mob violence forced him to give way and to join a Triumvirate. It presided over formation of the civilian High National Council, which wrote a Constitution and elected the civilian President Suu and Prime Minister Huong to replace the Triumvirate. In December the military dissolved the High National Council, and in January 1965 they dismissed Huong, replacing him by Khanh as caretaker. In February, they appointed a new civilian government, with Suu still President and with Quat as Prime Minister. In June, Ky took over. Besides all this, coup groups seized Saigon twice before being faced down each time.

During the first few months of this period the U.S. abandoned the plan for the phased withdrawal of most of our military assistance personnel, and stopped believing that the main-force war would come to a successful end by the close of 1965. With the start of planning pressures against the North, the U.S. first hoped that repeated preliminary signals to Hanoi would bring a response before bombing began; and we hoped that the promise of U.S. force commitments would strengthen Vietnamese unity and resolve. Both hopes proved vain, and we started bombing North Vietnam systematically without getting anything from either Hanoi or GVN. Then the bombing itself failed to stop Hanoi's intervention. Seeing no other choice, the U.S. poured troops into the country.

Throughout 1964, the U.S. pursued the objective of a strong, effective GVN like the Holy Grail. Increasingly, we felt we had to reassure our Saigon ally about the U.S. resolve, and hoped that a firm U.S. commitment through extending advisors and through bombing would improve GVN performance. Recurrently, we looked to the military as the one coherent, anti-communist force in the country. We leaned on them and on their strong-man, who for most of the period was Khanh, at first hoping that he or Minh would play the role that Magsaysay did in the Philippines. We were interested in legitimacy and democratic forms only as a long-run deferrable proposition; although more and more we recognized the need for broad political support—especially after the Buddhist crisis in August, 1964, had proved its importance.

As early as the Honolulu Conference in June, 1964, we worried about the possible emergence of a hostile government or anarchy; and the South Vietnamese played effectively on our fears. We lectured them repeatedly on the importance of national unity, both in periods of political calm and in crises. When the mobs in the streets faced down the generals, we then clung to the position that no one should rock the boat.

Yet, well beyond our control, General Khanh was a central figure in most of these changes. He took over in a coup in January, 1964, and played one role after another, for over twelve turbulent months. Then when a coup attempt failed against a newly installed government in February, 1965, the generals turned on Khanh and exiled him. Only the final coup, in which Ky took over, saw Khanh absent from the scene.

Withall, the military improved their hold on GVN machinery. The high turnover of district and province officials around the time of the Khanh coup put ARVN officers everywhere; and the corps commanders gradually consolidated their power throughout 1964. This tendency reached a climax and received a temporary setback in the rebellion that followed the August constitution. As a result of the successful Buddhist opposition, cabinet changes and the charter of the government in Saigon required Buddhist acquiescence.

These problems were aggravated by the clear and growing lack of legitimacy of GVN. The generals led by Minh, who overthrew Diem, gained an aura of respectability by this act because Diem had so completely alienated the people. Whatever their "respectability" may have been worth went down the drain, however, when Khanh seized power and then later maneuvered Minh out of the country. Khanh's position as a brash usurper gave him little room for maneuver among Saigon's complex political currents, although for a time the U.S. counted on his "raw power." With subsequent shifts in the form and composition of government, the expediency and lack of legitimacy of GVN grew more conspicuous and more debilitating.

Leverage

U.S. attempts to strengthen the GVN's will to govern and to pacify the countryside failed. Moreover, the attempts, conceived in haste, often backfired. In contrast to the steady discussion of alternatives among Washington agencies, the Embassy, and MACV on the subject of pressures on the North, the idea of pressures on GVN seldom surfaced. When it did surface, it was either brushed aside or rushed into. Leverage planning failed to receive even that quality and quantity of attention that pressures against North Vietnam planning did.

As a general rule, Washington was more interested in putting pressure on GVN than was the Embassy, with the notable exception of Taylor's initiatives in December, and MACV was the least interested of all. But these differences were less notable than was the almost universal consensus (most of the time) that the Vietnamese were too sensitive for such pressures to work, and that we had to accept the GVN's non-performance as the best available.

Starting with Rusk's conversation with Khanh at the end of May, 1964, and ending with Taylor's initiative in early December, the U.S. tried to use the prospect of U.S. force commitment as an inducement to the Vietnamese to do better. However, Taylor said that if this inducement were to fail, the U.S. should go ahead with its pressures against the North anyway. Taking this position meant that the attempted inducement was bluff. There is every sign, both in their non-performance and in their December-January defiance, that the GVN sized it up that way and called the bluff.

Our attempted leverage included both inducements and threats at one time and another; and neither worked out well. Rusk's May, 1964, conversation with Khanh, the intensification of pressures planning following the Honolulu Conference in June, and the shift of the Chairman, JCS to the post of Ambassador to SVN, all showed U.S. commitment. We hoped these measures and talks would directly contribute to GVN morale and effectiveness. However, they were followed by the July press leaks and by direct pressure to bomb North immediately. The July public endorsement of Khanh was intended to reassure all concerned of our support, and so to strengthen GVN. Then, the Gulf of Tonkin incidents were followed promptly by Khanh's Constitution, which backfired against him and against us, weakening rather than strengthening GVN.

Taylor's bill of particulars against GVN in December was followed immediately by attacks on GVN by the Buddhists, and then shortly by the military, bringing down the government. Taylor's stern lecture to the Young Turks at this time met only with their defiance. They agreed to a compromise solution to the crisis when Taylor held up the GVN Defense Budget, and then reversed themselves after he released it. The first Flaming Dart raids, opening the deliberate U.S. bombing campaign against the North, were followed shortly by another coup attempt.

There was no disagreement among Washington, the Embassy, and MACV that U.S. commitments should be used to improve GVN's morale and performance. In contrast, however, they often disagreed about putting pressure on GVN. In January, 1964, State showed far more interest than did Lodge in using the AID negotiations to press GVN for more effort; in the upshot we gave them an AID increase with no strings attached. This disagreement continued for several months. McNamara leaned consistently toward giving GVN whatever it needed; only later did he begin to mention increasing our influence. But McNamara and JCS did prod Lodge into asking GVN why they were not progressing well. In May, 1964, Sullivan proposed direct entry of U.S. personnel into the Vietnamese chain of command; his idea was watered down considerably in the State Department, and disappeared at the Honolulu Conference because of opposition by Lodge and Westmoreland. Other proposals agreed to at the conference, relating to new actions and improved programs by GVN, interested State far more than they did the Embassy and MACV, as revealed in the follow-up.

By and large the same contrasts prevailed when Taylor was the Ambassador, although in December he was far more willing to press GVN than Lodge ever was. Even then, at the peak of the crisis, Taylor expressly rejected sanctions. MACV generally rejected sanctions also, and seemed less willing to apply leverage in day-to-day matters than were U.S. civilians in the field. MACV studies on GVN ineffectiveness usually proposed more studies and never proposed pressure on GVN.

If U.S. force commitments and the record of GVN non-performance reflect the failure of leverage, what does the record tell us about how leverage could be made to work? Regrettably, the record tells us nothing about that; it merely shows that everything we tried went wrong. As noted, attempts at leverage or pressure on GVN were seldom thought through and studied carefully. One searches in vain for studies, memoranda, or widespread discussion of alternative techniques for leverage and of what our experience shows about how they might work. Pressures against the North, whose results have disappointed us, were a model of planning, foresight, and detailed consideration, compared to the subject of pressures on GVN. Yet GVN's failure was the heart of our policy problem throughout the period, as many feel it still is.

The Embassy's Lack of Political Contact

The shifts of political loyalties, coups, rebellions, and major changes of public figures often caught the Embassy by surprise. It had no effective system, either through overt or covert contacts, for finding out what was going on. CAS people talked to a few official contacts, who told them things the Vietnamese wanted the U.S. to believe; but CAS had and has no mandate or mission to perform systematic intelligence and espionage in friendly countries, and so lacks the resources to gather and evaluate the large amounts of information required on political forces, corruption, connections, and so on. Moreover, there is no sign that the Embassy understood events after the fact, or saw the connection between what we did and what the Vietnamese did next. It appears that the U.S. had few people experienced at maneuvering and manipulating among oriental politicians.

In the following cases the Embassy was in the dark. (1) We had no information on the degree of truth of Khanh's charges against the four "pro-neutralist" generals plus Minh, and we knew about his coup a day in advance only because he sounded us out on it. (2) During the months of maneuvering between Khanh and Minh after the coup, we had no way to evaluate the coup rumors that always went around, and that peaked around moments of crisis like the trial of the four generals in May. (3) Khanh's complaints of Vietnamese war-weariness starting in late May, in retrospect a transparent tactic to pressure the U.S. to bomb North, took in the USG completely; we eagerly went ahead and planned to bomb "to improve their unity and resolve." (4) Khanh's defiant leaks on cross-border operations in July surprised and perplexed the Embassy; Taylor described them as an attempt to improve his own people's morale, not as an attempt to stampede us. (5) When Khanh asked for our public endorsement and then talked about "reorganization," we failed to see the connection. When he tried to reorganize Minh out of the government, Taylor made no move to save Minh until after street rioting had broken up the whole plan. (6) The September 13 coup attempt surprised everybody. (7) The HNC decision to make Suu President and Huong Prime Minister surprised and angered us. (8) Taylor's December plan to strengthen GVN by lecturing to it about its failures provoked a completely unexpected reaction; both Buddhists and the military turned against the GVN. Taylor's subsequent stern lecture to the Young Turks likewise produced the opposite of the desired result. (9) The generals' January, 1965, moves to renege on the agreed crisis settlement and to dismiss Huong surprised us. (10) The February 19 coup attempt surprised everybody. (11) We did not know what to think of the alleged coup attempt in May, 1965.

In some noteworthy cases we did better. (1) Taylor correctly foresaw that Khanh's August constitution would cause trouble. (2) Westmoreland detected Ky's budding coup attempt in November and, with Embassy authority, squelched it. (3) Taylor foresaw (and tacitly accepted) the Ky coup.

The MACV Role

The MACV organization played an important, mostly hidden, role in US/GVN relations. At every level from Saigon to the districts, the advisory structure was the most pervasive instrument of intergovernmental contact. ARVN officers were accustomed to being spoon-fed military advice; so when military dominance of GVN brought these same officers to high positions in government, the advisor relationship conferred a latent diplomatic role upon MACV. Advisors were used as channels of communications on political matters and became the most reliable sources of information on impending coups. (On occasions such as the Rhade uprising and Ky's first attempt at a coup, senior MACV officers openly became diplomatic emissaries.)

We have less record than we would like of COMUSMACV's influence. He reported regularly to his military seniors only on strictly military matters. Detailed reports of his routine, daily dealings with counterparts were not required of MACV as they were of the Embassy.

From time to time COMUSMACV revealed his own independent objectives. He sought protection of the ARVN officer corps from political machinations and from unfavorable press stories in order to preserve their solidarity and morale; he pressed zealously for early introduction of U.S. ground forces and for their rapid build-up; he opposed encadrement and combined command with ARVN; he resisted exclusion of the military from pacification; he rejected sanctions against ARVN; he objected to the initial constraints on the use of American forces and wanted to be free to operate independently of ARVN.

General Westmoreland's strong position usually assured that his view prevailed. Extension of advisors, increased MAP resources, and the introduction of U.S. ground forces enhanced his relative position. His freedom from detailed reporting of daily contacts was itself an element of strength. When he received unwanted advice and directives, he set up studies (as in the Civic Action Program) to stall for time; when he lacked authority to operate freely, he planned ahead with the Vietnamese (as in the use of U.S. forces for independent offensive operations) and then presented the matter to Washington as a virtual *fait accompli.*

Vietnamese Non-Performance and Sensitivity

Throughout this period the GVN failed to perform in almost every constructive respect. Pacification lagged, when not visibly retreating, even though the GVN was always willing to issue decrees, set up organizations we suggested, and so on. Khanh's promise to mobilize came to nothing. The VC defeated ARVN in bigger and bigger battles, until the military assessment of the situation permitted Westmoreland to call for over 200,000 U.S. troops.

Moreover, on issues purportedly relating to sovereignty or "face," the Vietnamese were and are quite sensitive, and the U.S. was consistently afraid to inflame this sensitivity. Both sides avoided many delicate topics. A prime example is the matter of the lack of a bilateral treaty. The U.S. operated, and still operates, under a Pentalateral protocol signed by the French and Bao Dai under the U.S. military assistance program to France before 1954. It gave U.S. advisers and officials virtual diplomatic status, which was reasonable back when there were less than two hundred of them in all Indochina. But it now applies to all U.S. personnel, and no one has wanted to stir things up.

The sensitivity problem cropped up often. For a time early in 1964, the GVN backed off from an agreement to extend U.S. advisors to district level, and when the GVN did approve, they insisted that the advice be strictly military and that the advisors be labelled "subsector." In like manner, the III Marine Expeditionary Force became the III Marine Amphibious Force, because the French had called their Indochina force "expeditionary." But the GVN, and especially the military, agreed readily to new U.S. troop commitments.

The Vietnamese would often greet a U.S. representative, in moments of tension, with false or exaggerated stories of U.S. dealings, such as a complaint in January, 1964, about U.S. training and CIA contacts with the Cao Dai and Hoa Hao. In contrast, on cabinet appointments they often asked the Ambassador's opinion, and he customarily leaned over backward to avoid giving specific recommendations. Shared sensitivity, closely related to the lack of a treaty governing status of U.S. forces, prevented any move toward joint command and U.S. control of all military operations in Vietnam; both Westmoreland and the Vietnamese preferred to operate separately. The Embassy looked the other way from repressive police measures and political arrests unless these led to embarrassing press stories. When the Ambassador would raise this type of issue with the GVN, it proved always to be touchy.

Vietnamese sensitivity sometimes led to open displays of anti-Americanism. These happened on three main occasions: (1) when Khanh grumbled about being a puppet after the go-North leaks in July, 1964; (2) in the open rupture between Khanh and Taylor in December-January; and (3) in the January riots when rioters overran USIS buildings in Saigon and Hue.

Vietnamese Compliance More in Form Than in Substance

The Vietnamese nevertheless showed a ready willingness throughout the period to declare new policies, sign decrees, and engage in joint studies at our request. But as noted above, that did not mean we got the substance of what we wanted on such matters. The most important case of this kind was Khanh's ready agreement in March to "mobilize" South Vietnam. He promptly made a token announcement; and while students and other potential draft-eligibles waited anxiously to learn what he meant (as did we, he delayed several weeks before any further announcement. Starting in May, he began announcing specifics and signing decrees, and kept the idea live for several months. However, strength of the RVNAF rose less in 1964 than it did in 1963*, and the talk of non-military mobilization came to nothing.

The military and the more militant civilians, on whom the U.S. counted most heavily and regularly supported, turned out to have far more enthusiasm for going North and for other external adventures than they did for getting on with the job of effective government and pacification. They promised much on this latter score, but could not or would not deliver. Knowing that we had no one else to turn to, they continued their old habits and often openly did what they pleased about important matters. The go-North problem was particularly troublesome because the militants rejected the permanent division of Vietnam at the 17th parallel, upheld in practice by the U.S.

The following are interesting instances, among many, of their superficial compliance. They agreed readily to use U.S advisers at the ministerial level (the brain trust), although there is no sign that the brain-trusters accomplished anything. Indeed, on all ten suggestions that accompanied President Johnson's 1964 New Year's Message to Minh, only the one on amnesty found them hesitant to express their full agreement. They regularly agreed on budgetary limits to keep inflation from getting out of hand, but never satisfied us on specifics through 1964 or the first half of 1965. They repeatedly agreed to relieve ineffective, corrupt commanders and officials, but delayed endlessly on doing it and generally promoted those whom they relieved. At Westmoreland's request, Khanh created the Hop Tac plan for pacification around Saigon; but it foundered, and eventually the Vietnamese killed it. When Lodge left Vietnam in June, 1964, he sealed his tour with a general agreement with Khanh on concept, scope, and organization of the pacification efforts; obtaining such agreements presented absolutely no problem. In December, 1964, the JGS issued a directive containing every MACV suggestion on how RVNAF should help pacification.

In July, 1964, Khanh created a National Security Council similar to ours, and it met regularly with the top group of Embassy people to talk agreeably about pacification and manpower problems. MACV set up joint inspection teams and joint studies with JGS people several times a year. The only thing of this class that had any visible follow-through was the joint planning group on bombing North and on other cross-border operations. Two battalions specifically declared ineffective by MACV suffered no penalty or improvement.

The militants' predilection for external adventures began to show in May, 1964, after the Embassy started pressing Khanh about his March agreements

---

* The end-year figures are as follows:

South Vietnam	1962	1963	1964
Infantry-type Battalions	107	123	133
RVNAF Strength ('000)	397	514	571
Total Armed Strength ('000) (Included CIDG, police, etc.)	526	612	692

Source: OSD SEA Statistical Summary, Tables 1 and 2.

with McNamara. Khanh responded within a few days by saying he wanted to declare war, bomb the North with U.S. participation, bring 10,000 U.S. Army Special Forces troops into South Vietnam, "get rid of the politicians," and put Saigon strictly on a war footing. Lodge tried to cool him off, but Khanh brought up a less extreme version again with Rusk at the end of the month, saying that his government could not win without action outside South Vietnam. When Lodge returned from the Honolulu Conference in early June, Khanh responded to discussions of ARVN strength by trying to draw Lodge out on actions against the North. Then, when we did not move fast enough to suit him and Ky, they started a press campaign on the subject, and pressed Taylor more insistently. Finally, in December, when Taylor told GVN all the many ways they should improve to justify further U.S. involvement, their immediate reply included the comment that the U.S. program said nothing about Viet Cong use of Cambodia.

The press leaks about going North were the first major instance of their defiantly going ahead as they pleased against our wishes. Khanh's August constitution was a less flagrant case, because Taylor's words of caution were comparatively diffident. (Moreover, in the following August-September turbulence, Khanh let himself become clearly dependent on the Embassy when he talked to the Buddhist leaders.) In the December crisis the Young Turks defied Taylor at every turn following their dissolution of the HNC; and after a temporary agreement in January double-crossed Taylor, dismissed Huong, and took control of the formation of a new government. They guessed correctly that we saw no choice but to go along.

JUNE 1965—FALL 1967

By the summer of 1965, the war in Vietnam had dramatically changed its complexion from the previous two years. More and more, with U.S. combat forces pouring into SVN and Rolling Thunder underway, it looked like the U.S. against the DRV. The war was no longer being fought with U.S. advice and aid alone; there was now a massive U.S. presence. While official documents still repeated the credo that it was, in the last analysis, a struggle for the GVN to win or lose, the focus of U.S. concern shifted. As the U.S. role increased and then predominated, the need for GVN effectiveness in the now and short-run received less attention. The U.S. would take care of the war now—defeat the enemy main forces and destroy Hanoi's will to persist—then, the GVN could and would reform and resuscitate itself. Only after the immediate security threat to the GVN was blunted and forced to subside did we expect our South Vietnamese ally to improve its performance on all fronts. Until then and in order to get to that point, the U.S. would concentrate on what it could do.

This view—a massive U.S. effort in the short-run leading to and enabling a GVN effort in the long-run—set the tone and content of U.S.-GVN relations. In policy terms, it meant caution in the use of U.S. leverage. There seemed to be no compelling requirement to be tough with Saigon; it would only prematurely rock the boat. To press for efficiency would be likely, it was reasoned, to generate instability. Our objective became simple: if we could not expect more GVN efficiency, we could at least get a more stable and legitimate GVN. Nation-building was the key phrase. This required a constitution and free elections. Moreover, if we could not have the reality, we would start with appearances. U.S. influence was successfully directed at developing a democratic GVN in form. Beginning in September 1966, a series of free elections were held, first for a Constituent Assembly and later for village officials, the Presidency, House and Senate.

U.S.-GVN relations from June of 1965 to 1968, then, have to be understood in terms of the new parameters of the war. Before this date, our overriding objective had to be and was governmental stability. After the Diem coup, the GVN underwent six changes in leadership in the space of one and a half years. From June 1965 on, there was relative stability. Ky and Thieu, while challenged, proved strong enough to keep their power and position. In putting down the Struggle Movement (following General Thi's dismissal by Ky) in the first half of 1966, and then delivering on the September, 1966 election, GVN effectively discredited the militant Buddhist leadership and for the time being ended its threat to political stablility. Concern about possible neutralism or anarchy, which had been important in U.S. thinking in 1964 and early 1965, subsided accordingly. The uneasy agreement between Thieu and Ky to run on the same ticket, resulting partly from U.S. pressure for military unity, and the subsequent transition to legitimacy, gave the U.S. a sense of relief and satisfaction, although no one suggested that GVN had yet built a broad political base or had solved its effectiveness problems. This GVN stability made possible the increased attention to pacification and nation-building.

The pacification parameter had changed as well. From 1961 to June of 1965, the U.S. flooded SVN with the advisory resources of men and money to keep the GVN afloat and RVNAF fighting. This input lacked a clear plan. After June 1965, we made a concerted effort to organize pacification. We exacted an agreement from the GVN in the fall of 1966 to shift half of its ground forces into pacification—although U.S. forces carried a share of this burden and attempted to show RVNAF how to do it. We tried to centralize pacification programs by creating a new GVN structure to control and allocate resources. This was made manifest by the establishment of a separate Ministry for Revolutionary Development. U.S. moves by stages to the unified civil-military CORDS organization in Vietnam paralleled this super-ministry for pacification. And, pacification statistics showed steady increase of GVN control in the countryside, reversing the downward trend of previous years—but, U.S. dissatisfaction with GVN performance also increased nonetheless.

Beyond and more important than all this were the U.S. efforts themselves. By the close of 1965, 170,000 U.S. combat forces were in SVN. By the end of 1967, this figure was almost half a million. By mid-1965, U.S. air strikes against North Vietnam had extended in geographic coverage up to 20°30′, and approved targets had widened beyond LOC's. Total sorties rose to about 900 per week. By 1968, we were bombing throughout the North, with very few though important targets still being prohibited. Total sorties per week reached about 4,000.

It was in this context that U.S.-GVN relations took shape.

Leverage

Having suffered several backfires in the attempts to require or encourage GVN effectiveness in 1964, the Embassy and Washington generally preferred to let well enough alone in 1965 through 1967. The U.S. limited itself to only a few demands, and usually avoided direct confrontations at the top levels of government-to-government contact.

The U.S. had one repetition of its old backfire problem following the Honolulu Conference of February 1966. President Johnson embraced Ky publicly and endorsed his government; Ky then felt strong enough to move against General Thi, who had been making trouble generally and was almost openly waiting for his chance to take over the GVN. Ky eventually succeeded in removing Thi and getting him out of the country, but at the cost of returning to a degree of chaos in May that was in some ways worse than any suffered in 1964 under Khanh. At the height of the crisis, the U.S. went so far as to use force and the threat of force against both sides to keep the confrontation between GVN and the Struggle Movement within bounds. There was no sign of ill effects from our boldness in this instance.

Whatever interest there was in putting pressure on the top levels of GVN was stronger in Washington than in the Embassy, and stronger in the Embassy than in MACV, as it had been in the past. But the past failures of such pressures made everyone gunshy. At one point, Washington felt so strongly about the high GVN dollar balances that it sent out its own representative to negotiate with GVN, and he freely threatened to cut down U.S. dollar aid. However, neither Washington nor the Embassy suggested doing anything so drastic as holding up aid payments and projects until a satisfactory agreement could be reached. Confident that the threats were empty, GVN dug in its heels and gave us nothing but more promises.

Although the U.S. played down pressure or leverage on the top level of GVN, the idea of leverage at lower levels enjoyed a resurgence. Interest in the subject reached a low point in June 1965, when we abandoned the "troika signoff," which had given U.S. province representatives veto control over the use of AID direct-support commodities. For four months starting October 1, 1965, MACV experimented with giving its sector advisors a petty cash fund for urgent projects; however, MACV then dropped the idea. In April 1966, Lodge urged restoration of these types of leverage, and the idea kept coming up thereafter. Two major studies, one in Saigon in 1966 and one in Washington in 1967, came down strongly for regular procedures to use our material support to put pressure on lower echelons of GVN. They particularly emphasized signoff systems and the like, including U.S. distribution of MAP support within Vietnam. But the fear that such methods would prove counter-productive, either by provoking resistance or by making Vietnamese officials more dependent on our people and less able to perform on their own, prevented adoption of the proposals.

In at least three instances, AID cut off its support to a province in order to pressure the province chief. In September 1965, AID accused the province chief of Binh Tuy of misuse of AID funds, and had to withdraw its personnel from the province and cut off support to it after threats on their lives. The incident got into the papers and embarrassed both GVN and the Embassy; after several weeks GVN moved the accused officer to another job, and AID resumed its program in the province. In June 1966, AID cut off shipments to Kontum province for four days to force the province chief to account for the end uses of AID commodities. In August 1967, CORDS cut off shipments to Bien Hoa province for eleven weeks for similar reasons.

In contrast, MACV scrupulously avoided withholding MAP support from military units, regardless of circumstances. The single case of record of taking away MAP support involved two fishing boats owned by the Vietnam Navy that were found ineligible for such support. In his reaction to the PROVN Report in May 1966, in his directives to advisers around the time of the Chinh-Hunnicutt affair in the fall of 1966, and in his reaction to Washington inquiries in May 1967, COMUSMACV consistently brushed aside criticism of ARVN and told both his superiors and his subordinates to lay off. Whatever interest in leverage there was at lower levels in the field received no backing from COMUSMACV. In March 1966, a decision to transfer MAP for Vietnam to service funding had no effect on leverage because MACV continued to put material support in Vietnamese hands as soon as it entered the country.

Although AID tried some leverage in this period, and although the Ambassador, the Mission, and officials tuned to U.S. domestic pressures urged U.S. leverage for GVN reforms, there is still no documented study of GVN's failures, of the reasons for it, and of the ways that leverage of different types might help improve GVN permanently. The basic problem of concern is GVN's overall failure to do its civil and military jobs. Leverage in the hands of U.S. personnel might assure that GVN would do particular things we want; but we have no information on what kind of leverage, if any, would reform GVN. From 1964 onwards, high U.S. officials, including McGeorge Bundy and Secretary McNamara, have said at one time and another that thorough reform of GVN is necessary; but no one has found or even seriously proposed a way to do it. Encadrement proposals, prominent before June 1965, still received occasional mention; but these proposed to make up for GVN's deficiencies by substituting U.S. control for GVN control, and do not purport to reform GVN itself. If this problem has a solution, we have yet to find it.

The Embassy's Lack of Political Contact

The turbulent events of 1964 and early 1965 had shown that the Embassy had no effective system, either through overt or covert contacts, for finding out what was going on. Nothing was done subsequently to correct this problem. CAS people talked to a few official contacts, who told them things the Vietnamese wanted the U.S. to believe; but the CIA had and has no mandate or mission to perform systematic intelligence and espionage in friendly countries, and so lacks the resources to gather and evaluate the large amounts of information required on political forces, corruption, connections, and so on.

General Thi began sounding out his U.S. contacts on whether the U.S. appreciated his superior qualities as a potential leader of Vietnam as early as August 1965; and in other ways we had plenty of warning that there would be trouble. However, we showed no feel for cause and effect. President Johnson's embrace of Ky at Honolulu in February, 1966, could only have had a divisive effect when Ky commanded so little solid support within his own country. On the one hand, civilians and the military had flouted U.S. wishes so often in the past that express U.S. support scarcely counted for much; but on the other hand Ky's weakness and Thi's known ambitions tempted Ky to get whatever mileage he could out of our support. In the subsequent turbulence, all parties again flouted U.S. wishes freely, stopping short only when the U.S. used force and the credible threat of force to oppose them. The maneuverings of the various political groups seemed to surprise the Embassy repeatedly. The same problems arose in the GVN cabinet split and crisis just before the Manila Conference in October 1966. The blandly naive language of the "Blueprint for Vietnam" in late 1967, unmodified by any back channel elaboration, offered no hope of any foreseeable improvement.

The MACV Role

The MACV organization played an important, mostly hidden, role in U.S.-GVN relations. At every level from Saigon to the districts, the advisory structure was the most pervasive instrument of intergovernmental contact. ARVN officers were accustomed to being spoon-fed military advice; so when military dominance of GVN brought these same officers to high positions in government, the advisor relationship conferred a latent diplomatic role upon MACV. Advisors were used as channels of communications on political and pacification matters. (On occasions such as the attempts to get Thi to meet Ky or to leave the country, senior MACV officers openly became diplomatic emissaries.)

We have less record than we would like of COMUSMACV's influence. He reported regularly to his military seniors only on strictly military matters. Detailed reports of his routine, daily dealings with counterparts were not required of MACV as they were of the Embassy.

From time to time, COMUSMACV revealed his own independent objectives. He sought protection of the ARVN officer corps from unfavorable press stories in order to preserve their solidarity and morale; he pressed zealously for the rapid build-up of U.S. ground forces; he opposed encadrement and combined command with ARVN; he rejected sanctions against ARVN; he objected to the initial constraints on the use of American forces and wanted to be free to operate independently of ARVN.

General Westmoreland's strong position usually assured that his view prevailed. Extension of advisors, increased MAP resources, and the build-up of U.S. ground forces enhanced his relative position. By October 1966, MACV had numerical superiority of forces over Regular RVNAF; by late 1967, MACV had over 400 square miles of bases. His freedom from detailed reporting of daily contacts was itself an element of strength. When he received unwanted advice and directives, he set up studies, and, after a time, proceeded as usual. This tendency was most notable in the case of leverage, already noted, and combined command. Likewise, MACV successfully resisted taking over the bulk of Saigon Port operations, despite pressure from Washington, and delayed for about a year the move to take division commanders out of the pacification chain of command. Another instance of MACV independence showed up when Rusk and Lodge wanted to keep U.S. men and equipment out of the confrontation between GVN and the Struggle Movement in I Corps, but they failed to tell MACV about it. On April 5, MACV went ahead and airlifted two battalions of Vietnamese Rangers to Danang; after that Lodge put a stop to it.

Vietnamese Non-Performance and Sensitivity

Although population control statistics began to improve in 1966 and continued to do so in the first half of 1967, and although this seemed partly associated with the creation of the Ministry of Revolutionary Development and with the emphasis on its programs, few suggested that this progress could be held if U.S. forces withdrew. The drumbeat of criticism from field personnel, and the documented cases of non-performance on high-level matters, made it clear that there was no real improvement in GVN performance. Corruption and inaction showed no signs of improvement; province chiefs and military commanders singled out by U.S. advisers as urgently needing removal were simply shuffled around, if moved at all, and often promoted. Increasing traffic in the Port of Saigon led to acute congestion problems, which GVN failed to clear up or materially improve.

Moreover, on issues purportedly relating to sovereignty or "face," the Vietnamese continued to be quite sensitive, and the U.S. was afraid to inflame this sensitivity. Both sides avoided many delicate topics. A prime example is the lack of a bilateral treaty. The U.S. presence has always been based on the Pentalateral Protocol of 1950, signed by France, the Bao Dai government, Laos, Cambodia and the U.S., which gave U.S. advisers and officials virtual diplomatic status—an arrangement reasonable back when there were less than two hundred of them in all Indochina, but of dubious applicability to the hundreds of thousands now there. This matter has cropped up from time to time, as in the case of American civilians being tried for currency violations in Vietnamese courts, where they were subject to extortion. Both governments cooperated in smoothing things over after a momentary disagreement over jurisdiction, and have avoided stirring things up.

Shared sensitivity (and legitimate concern for an independent RVNAF role), closely related to the lack of a bilateral treaty, prevented any move toward joint command and U.S. control of all military operations in Vietnam. Both Westmoreland and the Vietnamese preferred to operate either separately or in loosely coordinated joint operations. The Embassy looked the other way from repressive police measures and political arrests unless these led to embarrassing press stories; and when the Ambassador would raise this type of issue with the GVN, it proved always to be touchy. Especially under Lodge, the Embassy tried to protect GVN from the press and to help it build a favorable image.

Vietnamese sensitivity sometimes led to open displays of anti-Americanism. These displays reached a climax in the Struggle Movement crisis in the first half of 1966, when the Buddhists openly accused the U.S. of helping GVN crush them, and they sacked and burned the U.S. Consulate in Hue. Moreover, newspapers reflecting officials views would occasionally publish stories expressing fear of a U.S. sellout in negotiations, anger at U.S. intervention in Vietnamese affairs (as happened during the Chinh-Hunnicutt affair), and other anti-American themes.

Vietnamese Compliance More in Form Than in Substance

The Vietnamese, nevertheless, showed a ready willingness to declare new policies, sign decrees, and engage in joint studies at our request. But as noted, that scarcely means that we got what we wanted on such matters. Ky was always willing to issue decrees purporting to clear up the port problem, and to make public declarations against corruption. On economic policy, Ky and Hanh gave us one agreement after another promising to control inflation and to run down their dollar balances. The relations of their military with MACV showed the same pattern.

The Vietnamese military, on whom the U.S. counted most heavily, continued as in earlier periods to have far more enthusiasm for external adventures than they did for getting on with the job of effective government and pacification. They promised much on this latter score, but delivered little. Knowing that we had no one else to turn to, they continued their old habits and often openly did what they pleased about important matters, such as the airlift of troops to Danang in May, 1966.

Examples of superficial compliance are almost too numerous to mention. The Honolulu Conference of February 1966, produced over sixty agreed points between the two governments on all areas of mutual interest; getting any follow-up proved to be like pulling teeth, and then the follow-up we got was nothing more as a rule than more promises. Likewise, at the Manila Conference much the same thing happened, where GVN agreed to programs for social revolution, economic progress, and so on. However, at our insistence they did go ahead with the constitution and elections, and they shifted half of ARVN into pacification. How much substantive improvement these moves will produce still remains to be seen.

GVN taste for foreign adventure showed up in small, irritating ways. In July

1965, Thi planned unauthorized operations in the DMZ, but we stopped him. In 1967, we discovered that GVN had brought in Chinese Nationalists disguised as Nungs, to engage in operations in Laos; also, they sent a group to put an airfield on an island 170 miles south of Hainan, apparently without consulting MACV.

Conclusion

Increasingly throughout 1967, GVN legitimacy and performance became a domestic political issue in the U.S. as well as a source of concern for policymakers. No matter what issue was raised, the central importance of the GVN remained. If we wanted to pacify more, we had to turn to the Vietnamese themselves. If we desired to push for a negotiated settlement, we had to seriously weigh the possibilities of SVN collapse. In the last analysis, it was and is a war which only GVN legitimacy and effectiveness can win.

End of Summary and Analysis

CHRONOLOGY

1 Jan 64   *State to Saigon 1000 30 Dec 63*
President's New Year's message to Minh contains reassurance; advice also rendered. Brain trust approved.

10 Jan 64   *Lodge to State 1287 10 Jan*
Lodge and Minh discuss President's advice agree they're doing fine except on anmesty. GVN backs away from previously agreed extension of advisors to districts.

30 Jan 64   *Saigon to State 1433 30 Jan*
Khanh seizes power, arrests four top generals of MRC, but lets Minh continue as President at USG urging.

13 Feb 64   *Memorandum to Secretary of State*
Rostow recommends enforcing NVN compliance with 1962 Geneva agreement.

21 Feb 64   *COMUSMACV to CINCPAC Feb 64*
GVN accepts advisors in 13 districts of the Delta.

21 Feb 64   *Saigon to AID 2334 21 Feb*
GVN asks USG for rice standby commitment, for the first time.

8 Mar 64   *SD PM 16 Mar Sec. III; and Memorandum of Conversation at JGS Hqtrs. 12 Mar*
Secretary McNamara arrives in Saigon for several days of talks, including talks with GVN. Goes away pessimistic, recommends more AID and larger RVNAF, plus unqualified backing for Khanh. Khanh promises mobilization.

17 Mar 64   *NSAM 288*
President approves Secretary of Defense recommendations, directs their execution.

20 Mar 64   *White House Press Release*
White House announces Khanh's mobilization plan.

4 Apr 64	*State to Saigon 1602 4 Apr* Mobilization decree, dissolution of Council of Notables, promise of eventual Constituent Assembly and civil government.
10 Apr 64	*Saigon to State 1964 11 Apr* Beginning of AID and related economic negotiations for fiscal 1965.
29 Apr 64	*Saigon to State 2089 30 Apr* Khanh renews request for brain trust; Lodge euphoric.
30 Apr 64	*Saigon to State 2091 30 Apr* USOM and GVN badger each other on pacification and economic delays.
4 May 64	*Saigon to State 2108 4 May* Khanh wants to bomb NVN, have 10,000 US troops, and set up all-military government in SVN. Lodge says no, no, yes.
13 May 64	*Saigon to State 2203 14 May* McNamara sees Khanh in Saigon; they reach agreement on desirability of progress.
13–27 May 64	*Saigon to State DTG 271200Z May* Forrestal of White House staff "negotiates" AID with GVN, gives GVN AID increases.
25 May 64	*Memorandum to President* McGeorge Bundy recommends force against NVN as the only path to success.
27 May 64	*State to Saigon 1251 18 Feb.* Sullivan distributes proposal for semi-encadrement of GVN as a necessary step for progress.
28–29 May 64	*Saigon to State 2332 and 2338 28 May* MRC censures four "neutralist plot" generals that had been arrested in Khanh coup. Keeps Minh, as urged by Lodge.
30 May 64	*CINCPAC to State 37 2 Jun* Rusk sees Khanh, leaves nothing to the imagination on possible US all-the-way commitment, stresses need for GVN unity.
2–3 Jun 64	*Memo for the Record, Special Meeting on SE Asia. CINCPAC 000211 DTG 8 Jun and Memo for Secretary (State) "Highlights of Honolulu Conference" from W. P. Bundy DTG 3 Jun* Honolulu Conference. Conferees (include Rusk, McNamara, Lodge, Taylor and Westmoreland) agree on increased advisory effort, agree to refine plans for pressures on NVN.
4 Jun 64	*Saigon to State 2405 4 Jun* Lodge hints to Khanh that USG will prepare US public opinion for actions against NVN.
29 Jun 64	*COMUSMACV Command History 1964, p. 69* AID sets up sector adviser fund, with troika signoff to bypass GVN-Saigon.

30 Jun 64   *COMUSMACV 011057Z Jul*
US and GVN agree to joint planning for cross-border operations in Laos.

8 Jul 64   *Saigon to State 56 8 Jul*
Ambassador Taylor presents his credentials to Khanh.

9 Jul 64   *Saigon to State 65 9 Jul*
Ambassador Taylor hears the complaints of civilian cabinet members.

17 Jul 64   *Saigon to State 124 17 Jul*
USOM starts periodic meetings with GVN's National Security Council.

19 Jul 64   *Saigon to State 185 23 Jul*
Khanh and Ky lobby publicly for cross-border operations and air strikes into Laos and NVN.

23 Jul 64   *Saigon to State 185 23 Jul*
Khanh presses Taylor for action, keeps up the lobbying.

24 Jul 64   *Saigon to State 203 24 Jul*
Khanh asks Taylor if he (Khanh) should resign; Taylor says no. Khanh asks for publicly stated US backing and gets it.

25 Jul 64   *Saigon to State 232 27 Jul*
Khanh promises to quit lobbying, reacts favorably to proposed joint planning for air strikes on NVN, and says he plans GVN reorganization.

2–4 Aug 64   *Shaplen,* Lost Revolution, *p. 269*
Gulf of Tonkin incidents, US retaliation.

7 Aug 64   *Shaplen,* Lost Revolution, *p. 270*
Khanh proclaims state of emergency, with press censorship.

8 Aug 64   *COMUSMACV to CINCPAC DTG 080715Z Aug*
Westy and Khanh discuss joint planning, agree not to discuss combined command.

12 Aug 64   *Saigon to State 393 12 Aug*
Khanh's "reorganization" is a new constitution with military openly on top, and with Khanh President. Taylor sceptical, counsels caution.

16 Aug 64   *Saigon to State 415 15 Aug*
Khanh gets MRC approval of constitution after hurried USOM drafting assistance.

18 Aug 64   *Shaplen,* Lost Revolution, *pp. 270–71*
Ambassador Taylor firmly recommends plans for gradual pressures North to start 1 January contingent on improved GVN performance, or not contingent if things get bad enough. Suggests the package include Marines at Danang.

21–27 Aug 64   *Shaplen,* Lost Revolution, *pp. 272–74*
Student demonstrations followed by general rioting.

24 Aug 64	*Saigon to State 542 24 Aug* Taylor advises Khanh to move fast on new cabinet.
25 Aug 64	*Shaplen,* Lost Revolution, *pp. 274–75* One o'clock A.M. Taylor advises Khanh to make some concessions but keep constitution. Khanh does and riots continue. Khanh "resigns." Riots continue.
27 Aug 64	*Shaplen,* Lost Revolution, *pp. 275–78* MRC revokes constitution, keeps Khanh now as member of temporary triumvirate (including Minh and Khiem). New HNC to be appointed.
29 Aug 64	*State to Saigon 555 29 Aug* Paratroopers with bayonets restore order in Saigon.
6 Sep 64	*Saigon to State 785 8 Sep* Taylor takes off on a trip to Washington. Recommends pressures on NVN to begin 1 December.
10 Sep 64	*NSAM 314 10 Sep* Says strengthen GVN.
13 Sep 64	*Shaplen,* Lost Revolution, *pp. 287–290; Saigon to State 836 13 Sep; Saigon to State 878 16 Sep* Abortive coup attempt temporarily captures Saigon. Ky and Thieu back Khanh, defeat coup forces.
20 Sep 64	*Shaplen,* Lost Revolution, *p. 290; Saigon to State 923 22 Sep; 936 23 Sep 937, 952, and 954 24 Sep; 985 29 Sep; and 1046 7 Oct. COMUSMACV to CINCPAC DTG 031137Z Oct* Rhade tribesmen in 4 CIDG camps rebel against GVN.
24 Sep 64	*Saigon to State 938 24 Sep* The new HNC begins deliberations to write a constitution.
30 Sep 64	*NYTimes Articles* W. Bundy predicts publicly that bombing NVN would cut down the threat to GVN in a matter of months.
27 Oct 64	*Saigon to State 1292 27 Oct; State to Saigon 944 29 Oct. Shaplen* Lost Revolution, *pp. 290–9* HNC finishes on time, surprises by naming Suu President, not Minh.
30 Oct 64	*Shaplen,* Lost Revolution, *p. 293; State to Saigon 978 1 Nov; CINCPAC to JCS DTG 020400Z Nov; Saigon to State 1382 2 Nov* Mortar attack on Bien Hoa airbase. State rejects Taylor's recommendation of immediate reprisal raid on NVN.
11 Nov 64	*Saigon to State 1452 and 1460 10 Nov* MRC publishes military reorganization without MACV review; MACV protests and MRC withdraws it for changes.
26 Nov 64	*COMUSMACV to CINCPAC DTG 0260945Z Nov* Westmoreland slaps Ky down just before apparent coup attempt. Taylor is in Washington.

7 Dec 64   *Embassy to State Airgram A-468 15 Dec*
Taylor, just back from Washington with fresh guidance, presents GVN with a candid statement of its failures and couples demands for progress in stated areas to promises of US escalation.

8–20 Dec 64   *Shaplen,* Lost Revolution, *pp. 294–95*
Student and Buddhist demonstrations against Huong government and growing crisis.

20 Dec 64   *Saigon to State 1869, 1870, and 1874 20 Dec; MACV to CINC-PAC rec'd NMCC 200816Z Dec*
Khanh and Generals disregard Taylor's protests, dissolve HNC and arrest opposition; "Young Turks" (Ky, Thieu, Thi and Cang) consolidate their dominance by creating a small Armed Forces Council (AFC) as the top governing body. Taylor reads them the riot act.

21 Dec 64   *Saigon to State 1881 21 Dec*
Taylor asks Khanh to resign and leave the country.

23 Dec 64   *Saigon to State 1914 23 Dec; 1929 and 1930 24 Dec*
Young Turks attack Taylor publicly, and privately seek his recall.

24 Dec 64   *Shaplen,* Lost Revolution, *pp. 295–97*
Taylor tells press that Khanh has outstayed his usefulness.

25 Dec 64   *COMUSMACV Command History 1965, p. 229*
Vietnamese JGS issues Directive A-B 139, at MACV request, on how RVNAF should be employed to improve pacification program.

7 Jan 65   *Saigon to State 2081 7 Jan 2089 8 Jan 2102 9 Jan*
AFC Generals decide to give way by restoring civilian government under a new name (i.e. without HNC) leaving Suu-Huong combination in.

9 Jan 65   *Shaplen,* Lost Revolution, *pp. 297–98*
With Taylor's reluctant concurrence, the AFC announces the 7 January decision.

11 Jan 65   *Saigon to State 2112 and 2120 11 Jan*
US and GVN publicly patch up relations. Young Turks will enter cabinet.

12 Jan 65   *Shaplen,* Lost Revolution, *pp. 298–99*
New demonstrations begin, demanding Huong's resignation.

14 Jan 65   *Saigon to State 2155 14 Jan*
Khanh shows Taylor a new cabinet list; Taylor tries to slow him down.

18 Jan 65   *Saigon to State 2176 18 Jan*
Khanh gives Taylor completed cabinet list and schedules installation for the next day.

19 Jan 65   *COMUSMACV to CINCPAC DTG 191235Z Jan*
Khanh tries to reassure Westmoreland on military repercussions of tying up some generals in the cabinet; then Khanh suddenly "postpones" cabinet installation.

19–24 Jan 65 *Shaplen,* Lost Revolution, *pp. 298–99*
Buddhist demonstrations build up, including sacking of USIS buildings in Saigon and Hue. Buddhist merchants respond to campaign to boycott Americans. Buddhists demand military take-over.

25 Jan 65 *Saigon to State 2276 and 2283 25 Jan*
Khanh tells Deputy Ambassador Alex Johnson that Huong and Suu want to resign and let the military take over. Johnson says no.

27 Jan 65 *Shaplen,* Lost Revolution, *pp. 299–302; Saigon to State 2322 27 Jan; State to Saigon 1542 27 Jan and 1565 29 Jan*
AFC topples Suu-Huong government, openly puts Khanh back in charge. JCS approves COMUSMACV request to use US jet aircraft in a strike role in-country in emergencies, subject to Embassy approval in each instance.

3–4 Feb 65 *Saigon to State 2399 4 Feb*
McGeorge Bundy visits Saigon, has tea with Khanh and the generals.

7–12 Feb 65 *Shaplen,* Lost Revolution, *pp. 305–6 State to Saigon 1438 6 Feb; Saigon to State 2426 7 Feb 2495 11 Feb*
Flaming Dart bombings in North Vietnam. All US dependents ordered to leave Vietnam.

7 Feb 65 *Memorandum to the President*
McGeorge Bundy says the military are the backbone of the country, that the Buddhists should be constructive, and that Vietnam needs a social revolution.

16 Feb 65 *Saigon to State 2617 16 Feb*
After two false starts, AFC selects Quat to form a new cabinet.

18 Feb 65 *Shaplen,* Lost Revolution, *pp. 306–7*
Quat cabinet installed; Buddhists acquiesce.

19 Feb 65 *Shaplen,* Lost Revolution, *pp. 307–12*
New coup groups seizes Saigon, then bows to superior AFC force.

20 Feb 65 *Shaplen,* Lost Revolution, *pp. 307–12*
AFC votes Khanh out.

24 Feb 65 *Saigon to State 2685 20 Feb; 2698 22 Feb; 2720 23 Feb; 2731 24 Feb; and COMUSMACV to CINCPAC DTG 241600Z Feb*
Khanh goes abroad; Rolling Thunder rolls.

27 Feb 65 *Saigon to State 2787 27 Feb*
USOM resumes action level meetings with GVN; both sides agreed to prepare proposals for accelerating pacification and to go forward together with effective execution.

28 Feb 65 *Saigon to State 2800 1 Mar*
State issues White Paper on Vietnam.

6 Mar 65 *COMUSMACV Command History, 1965, p. 132*
MACV gives budget guidelines to RVN Ministry of Defense.

8 Mar 65 *Saigon to State 2991 8 Mar*
Quat discusses sensitive combined-command issue with Taylor.

8–9 Mar 65	*Saigon to State 2908 1 Mar* Two battalions of Marines land at Danang.
24 Mar 65	*Saigon to State 2065 24Mar* Ambassador Taylor formulates a 41-point program for stability and pacification.
26 Mar 65	*COMUSMACV Commander's Estimate of the Situation 26 Mar* Westmoreland issues Commander's Estimate of the Situation, which treads lightly on combined-command issue.
1–2 Apr 65	*NSAM 328 6 Apr* Taylor (in Washington) talks to President and NSC, who approve Taylor's 41-point program and General Johnson's 21 recommendations.
15 Apr 65	*Saigon to State 3419 17 Apr* Taylor objects to proposed Peers mission.
15 Apr 65	*DOD 9164 15 Apr* The 7-point message from State/Defense tells Saigon to encadre RVNAF/GVN and to expect additional US forces, with new missions.
17 Apr 65	*Saigon to State 3421, 3422 and 3423 17 Apr* Taylor objects to 7-point message, and Westmoreland objects to encadrement.
19–20 Apr 65	*ASD McNaughton's Minutes of Honolulu Meeting 23 Apr* Honolulu Conference meets to resolve disagreements on 7-point message. Conferees agree on force increase and medcap, scuttle encadrement, and agree on studies of combined command.
5 May 65	*Saigon to State 3097 and 3100 26 Mar; and 2140 31 Mar* AFC dissolves itself.
20–21 May 65	*Saigon to State 3878 25 May* Abortive coup attempt alleged by GVN, though not firmly confirmed by US observers.
May 22– 12 June 65	*Shaplen,* Lost Revolution, *pp. 342–45* Suu-Quat disagreement on cabinet changes.
27 May 65	*Joint State/ Defense 80466 27 May* State/Defense message agrees to defer approaching GVN on combined command.
12 Jun 65	*COMUSMACV MAC J-3, 19912 to CINCPAC DTG 120828Z Jun* Westmoreland presses for commitment of US forces to offensive operations, has already planned it hand-in-hand with our Vietnamese ally.
12 Jun 65	*Shaplen,* Lost Revolution, *pp. 345–46. Saigon to State 4065 4 Jun, 4119 9 Jun, 4156 11 Jun, 4190 14 Jun, 4312 21 Jun* Generals fire Suu and Quat, create National Leadership Council of ten Generals chaired by Thieu, and make Ky Prime Minister. Taylor reluctantly acquiesces to Ky's appointment.

22 Jun 65	*Memorandum from Vincent Puritano to James P. Grant 25 Sep 65, "Joint Provincial Sign-off Authority," with attachment* Troika sign-off abandoned.
1 Jul 65	*SD PM 1 Jul 65 Sec 8B* SecDef Memorandum to the President recommends more aid for Vietnam.
1 Jul 65	*Saigon to State 14, 2 Jul* Taylor writes a letter to Ky asking him to support constructive USOM/GVN consultations on economic matters and the port.
8 Jul 65	*COMUSMACV to CINCPAC DTG 080020Z Jul* MACV and RVNAF agree on coordination and cooperation, and do not discuss combined command.
20 Jul 65	*SD PM 20 Jul para. 8B* SecDef Memorandum to the President recommends U.S. veto on major GVN commanders and on GVN statements about going North.
28 Jul 65	*Saigon to State 266, 25 Jul* USOM and GVN agree on AID package with no leverage.
15–26 Aug 65	*Saigon to State 626, 26 Aug* Lodge replaces Taylor, takes charge of the Embassy. Ky tells Lodge the U.S. forces should hold strategic points so that RVNAF can concentrate on pacification, and says that the Chieu Hoi Program is a waste of money.
28 Aug 65	*Saigon to State 671, 28 Aug* Thi tells Lodge he can govern better than Ky can.
22 Sep 65	*COMUSMACV Command History 1965, p. 240* COMUSMACV presents proposals for revitalization of Hop Tac to USOM.
1 Oct 65	*COMUSMACV Command History 1965, p. 240* MACV begins four-month experiment with sector and subsector advisor funds.
3 Nov 65	*SecDef DPM* McNamara urges more active role for U.S. advisors.
15 Dec 65	*COMUSMACV Command History 1965, p. 241* JGS Directive AB 140 gives GVN military plan to support 1966 Rural Construction program.
24 Dec 65	*State to Saigon 1855 31 Dec* Beginning of 37 day bombing pause and peace offensive.
6–8 Feb 66	*State to Saigon 2252 4 Feb "Vietnam: Honolulu Conference-Summary of Goals and Status of Activity," 30 Mar* Honolulu Conference to press GVN for action on pacification and on political and economic reforms. Thieu and Ky obligingly agreed to U.S. demands. Vice-President Humphrey flies with them back to Saigon.

10 Mar 66   *Kahin and Lewis,* The U.S. in Vietnam, *p. 244 and passim; Saigon to State 3260 and 3265 9 Mar*
Ky persuades military leadership to approve his plan to exile I Corps Commander, General Thi. Thi resigns.

12 Mar 66   *Kahin and Lewis,* The U.S. in Vietnam, *p. 245; and Saigon 3333 14 Mar*
Annamese Buddhists and students begin demonstration in Danang and Hue.

16 Mar 66   *Saigon to State 3381 17 Mar*
Thi permitted to return to Danang to quiet demonstrations.

March 1966   *COMUSMACV Command History 1966, p. 510 CINCUSARPAC 240312Z May*
PROVN Study completed.

3 Apr 66   *COMUSMACV Command History 1966, p. 824*
Ky declares Danang to be in Communist hands.

5 Apr 66   *COMUSMACV Command History 1966, p. 824; MACV to CINCPAC DTG 051125Z Apr; Saigon to State 2986 5 Apr*
MACV airlifts two ARVN Ranger battalions to Danang. 1st ARVN division commander declares for the Struggle Movement; U.S. advisors withdrawn.

6 Apr 66   *COMUSMACV Command History 1966, p. 824*
Non-essential U.S. civilians removed from Hue.

8 Apr 66   *COMUSMACV Command History 1966, p. 824*
GVN flies two additional Ranger battalions to Danang after MACV refused to do so.

9 Apr 66   *COMUSMACV Command History 1966, p. 824*
U.S. protest to Struggle Movement leaders induces them to pull back howitzers. Two hundred U.S. and third country civilians evacuated from Danang.

12 Apr 66   *COMUSMACV Command History 1966, p. 324; Kahin and Lewis* The U.S. in Vietnam, *p. 256*
GVN withdraws its Ranger battalions from Danang. Relative quiet returns.

14 Apr 66   *COMUSMACV Command History 1966, p. 324; Kahin and Lewis* The U.S. in Vietnam, *p. 256*
The Directorate promises elections for a constituent assembly with 3–5 months. Buddhists and others call off demonstrations.

4 May 66   *Kahin and Lewis,* The U.S. in Vietnam, *p. 256; Saigon to State 4368 4 May and 4605 15 May*
Ky publicly reneges on promises to hold August elections, says perhaps they will be possible by October. Lodge absent on long trip to Washington. Porter follows State guidance closely.

15 May 66   *State to Saigon 3448, 3449, 3450 and 3451 15 May*
GVN airlifts troops to Danang and Hue to quell new disorders. U.S. withholds airlift protests GVN failure to consult, withdraws advisors from both sides.

16 May 66	*Saigon to State 4627 and 4635 16 May* USMC General Walt threatens to use U.S. jets to shoot down any VNAF aircraft used against dissident ARVN units. The threat succeeds.
21 May 66	*State to Saigon 3575 21 May* Lodge returns, tells Ky to be conciliatory, use force with restraint. He does around Saigon pogodas, but naked force in Hue produces self-immolations. U.S. evacuates its consulate and other facilities there.
27 May 66	*Saigon to State 4837 21 May 4849 and 4878 23 May, 4943 and 4963 25 May, 4966 26 May, 5037 27 May, 5073 28 May, 5178 1 Jun, and 1947 7 Jul; Kahin and Lewis ibid.* Ky and Thi meet; latter offered unspecified ARVN job.
31 May 66	*Saigon to State 5163 and 5178 1 Jun* Ky meets leaders of the Buddhist Institute, offers civilian participation in an enlarged Directorate. They appear conciliatory and agree to appointment of General Lam as Commander of I Corps.
1 Jun 66	*NYTimes Article* Student mob burns U.S. consulate and consular residence in Hue. Struggle Movement fills the streets with Buddhist altars.
5 Jun 66	*NYTimes Article* Electoral Law Commission presents its proposals.
18 Jun 66	*NYTimes Article* Piaster devalued to official rate of 80.
18 Jun 66	*Kahin and Lewis The U.S. in Vietnam, p. 257* Anniversary of Thieu-Ky government proclaimed a GVN holiday; one-day general strike called by the Buddhists.
19 Jun 66	*Kahin and Lewis, The U.S. in Vietnam, pp. 258–59* Directorate schedules elections for the Constituent Assembly for 11 September.
22 Jun 66	*Kahin and Lewis, The U.S. in Vietnam, p. 257.* Conditions quiet in I Corps; GVN steadily regaining control.
8–9 Jun 66	*NYTimes Article* Secretary McNamara visits Honolulu for talks with CINCPAC.
31 Jul 66	*State to Saigon 1694 29 Jul 2564 3 Aug* Thi goes into exile.
13–14 Aug 66	*NYTimes Article* General Westmoreland reports to the President at his Texas ranch.
24 Aug 66	*"Roles and Missions" Study 24 Aug* "Roles and Missions" Study to the Embassy.
11 Sep 66	*NYTimes Article* Constituent Assembly elections.
4 Oct 66	*Saigon to State 7616 4 Oct, 7732 and 7752 5 Oct, 6043 7 Oct, 8681 17 Oct, 8749 18 Oct, 8833 19 Oct, 8839 20 Oct. State to Saigon 66781 14 Oct and 68339 18 Oct*

GVN cabinet crisis brews as six civilian ministers, the only Southern members threaten to resign.

5 Oct 66   *COMUSMACV Command History 1966, p. 526*
JGS chairs a high level joint conference to develop a schedule of action to implement road development.

6 Oct 66   *State to Saigon 49294 16 Sep 49399 17 Sep Saigon to State 6997 27 Sep State to Saigon 58092 30 Sep 61330 6 Oct 58280 2 Oct*
Hanh and Komer reach vague and general agreement on GVN budget and financial matters.

10–13 Oct 66   *NYTimes Article*
Secretary McNamara, accompanied by newly appointed Under Secretary of State Katzenback visits Saigon. Saigon Port congestion grows worse.

14 Oct 66   *SecDef Memorandum to the President*
In PM McNamara urges shift of ARVN to pacification, change of US responsibility to MACV, "drastic" reform of GVN.

19 Oct 66   *Saigon to State 7616 4 Oct, 7732 and 7752 5 Oct, 8681 17 Oct, 8749 18 Oct, 8833 19 Oct, and 8839 20 Oct, State to Saigon 66781 14 Oct, 68339 18 Oct*
Cabinet crisis patched up at least until after Manila Conference.

24–25 Oct 66   *NYTimes Article Texts of Communique and Declarations Signed at Close of Manila Conference 26 Oct*
Manila conference of the seven nations aiding South Vietnam. Basic problem is still to get GVN commitment to action on non-military measures.

1 Nov 66   *Saigon to State 10312 7 Nov, 11958 29 Nov*
Promised GVN National Reconciliation proclamation fails to appear; instead only vague reference in a speech on other subjects. Ky promised a NR speech and proclamation in "early December."

2 Nov 66   *Saigon to State 9963 3 Nov*
Komer and Porter in Saigon reach agreement with GVN on foreign exchange.

2 Nov 66   *Saigon to State 7815 6 Oct and 8161 1 Oct*
Ky promises a tough decree on port management.

18 Nov 66   *Saigon to State 11249 18 Nov 11431 21 Nov State to Saigon 93314 28 Nov*
General Quang, deposed IV Corps Commander, appointed to head the new cabinet portfolio "Planning and Development." Concern continues in Washington over AID diversions.

21 Nov 66   *COMUSMACV msg 50331 21 Nov*
In a policy statement, COMUSMACV tells advisors that deficiencies of non-compliance are to be resolved within RVNAF channels.

29 Nov 66   *MACV Commanders Conference 20 Nov*
Washington reminds the Mission that GVN has not yet delivered on its Manila promises about NR, pacification, and land reform; suggests Lodge press Ky.

2 Dec 66
Saigon to State 12321 2 Dec
Saigon declines to suggest formation of a joint inspectorate general to follow up AID diversions.

December 1966
Saigon to State 14009 22 Dec, 12733 7 Dec, 12908 and 12950 9 Dec, 13046 10 Dec, 14009 and 13023 22 Dec, 14112 23 Dec, 14230 26 Dec
Further GVN-USOM negotiations on the dollar balance problem.

8 Dec 66
COMUSMACV to CINCPAC 080245Z Dec
Ceremonial signing of the 1967 Combined Campaign Plan by COMUSMACV and Chief, JGS.

December 1966
Saigon to State 15569 13 Jan 67
Saigon Port congestion grows worse during GVN port commander's "great barge" experiment. State authorizes drastic action which Saigon declines to use.

21 Dec 66
COMUSMACV History 1966 pp. 471–72
Chinh-Hunnicutt affair terminated with transfer of the U.S. adviser outside the theatre and issuance of a memorandum by the division commander stating that the past must be forgotten.

January 1967
NYTimes Article
U Thant advances proposals for peace. President promises careful evaluation. Ky forsees negotiations nearing. Lodge predicts sensational military gains in 1967.

2 Jan 67
Saigon to State 14725 2 Jan
U.S. Mission estimates GVN inflationary budget gap at 14–20 billion piasters.

7 Jan 67
NYTimes Article
Ky signs law providing for spring elections in 1000 villages and 4000 hamlets.

13 Jan 67
Saigon to State 15569 13 Jan
Saigon resists Washington suggestion for complete MACV takeover of Saigon port.

20 Jan 67
Saigon to State 16037 20 Jan
GVN issues Cy 1967 budget of 75 billion piasters without prior consultation with U.S.

23 Jan 67
State to Saigon 123223 21 Jan
Renewed economic negotiations forseen with Hanh in Washington.

24 Jan 67
NYTimes Article
JGS Chief of Staff Vien appointed to replace corrupt Defense Minister Co, who is informed on visit to Taiwan not to return.

20 Feb 67
Saigon to State 18646 22 Feb
GVN agrees to work on an interim memorandum of understanding to include implementation of the previous November's foreign exchange agreements. Komer threatens to reduce CIP; Hanh hints at a raise in the piaster rate.

24 Feb 67
NYTimes Article State to Saigon 140250 19 Feb Saigon to State 18303 18 Feb
Ky postpones U.S. visit to assure free and fair elections.

10 Mar 67   *Saigon to State 19902 9 Mar, 20053 10 Mar, 20201 13 Mar, State to Saigon 153512 11 Mar*
U.S. announces military jurisdiction over American civilians, thus skirts the problems of corrupt GVN justice and status of forces.

17 Mar 67   *State to Saigon 157064 17 Mar*
Another "Interim Agreement" reached with GVN on foreign exchange.

19 Mar 67   *NYTimes Article*
Constituent Assembly unanimously approves new constitution. Next day it is unanimously approved by the military junta and a copy presented to President Johnson at Guam meetings between top level GVN-US leadership.

20–21 Mar 67   *NYTimes Article Joint Communique Guam Meetings 21 Mar*
Guam meetings between top level GVN-US leadership. President Johnson introduces the new U.S. team in Saigon; Bunker to be Ambassador, Locke his deputy, Komer the new pacification czar within the MACV framework.

6 Apr 67   *NYTimes Article*
General Abrams appointed Deputy to COMUSMACV.

18 Apr 67   *Saigon to State 23376 18 Apr*
GVN issues a National Reconciliation proclamation that proves to be a mirage; it emphasizes solidarity vice reconciliation.

25 Apr 67   *NYTimes Article Saigon to State 23749 23 Apr*
Lodge completes his stint, leaves Saigon.

27 Apr 67   *NYTimes Article*
General Westmoreland confers with LBJ in Washington, addresses Congress the next day.

7 May 67   *COMUSMACV MAC J 341 15064 to CINCPAC 071035Z May*
General Westmoreland reports on his command project to improve RVNAF performance, offers $7800 saving in cut-off of MAP support to two VNN fishing boats as sign of progress. ARVN evaluation only partially completed.

12 May 67   *NYTimes Article Saigon to State 25554 12 May*
Premier Ky announces he will seek the Presidency. Thieu-Ky rivalry intensifies.

20 Jun 67   *Saigon to State 28409 20 Jun*
Thieu and Ky invited to informal luncheon hosted by Bunker at which unity of the Armed Forces is discussed.

22 Jun 67   *State to Saigon 213380 22 Jun*
Mission estimates rate of inflation in SVN to be 45–50% per year.

29–30 Jun 67   *Saigon to State 29258 30Jun*
The Armed Forces Council of 50–60 officers holds two day continuous session from which emerges the Thieu-Ky ticket.

7–8 Jul 67   *NYTimes Article OSD(SA) Memorandum 25 Jul, "SecDef VN Trip Briefings"*
Secretary McNamara makes his 9th visit to SVN.

I. AFTERMATH OF THE DIEM COUP

First Half of 1964

A. THE INHERITANCE FROM 1963

The top ruling body of the Government of Vietnam at the end of 1963 was a Military Revolutionary Council of twelve generals, under the chairmanship of the affable and popular but weak General Duong Van "Big" Minh. The Council governed through an all-civilian cabinet headed by Premier Tho, having forbade all military officers to engage in politics. A Council of Notables served as a pseudo-parliament, with a purely advisory role; it included well-known Vietnamese politicians, but could not claim support of a broad popular base or the main political forces in Vietnam. While Premier Tho's previous connection with the Diem government was now a political liability, there was a shortage of national figures who were not tarred with this brush one way or another.

On the U.S. side, General Harkins, COMUSMACV, who had long been known to be pro-Diem, was clearly on his way out, although his departure was to be delayed until the middle of 1964. Ambassador Lodge had replaced Nolting just before the Diem coup, and was held in that cautious respect appropriate to the widespread belief among Vietnamese that he had engineered it.

In the last weeks of 1963, the U.S. government reassessed the progress of the counterinsurgency effort and the policy options. Plans for phased withdrawal of 1,000 U.S. advisers by end-1963 went through the motions by concentrating rotations home in December and letting strength rebound in the subsequent two months. A realistic appraisal by Secretary McNamara showed that the VC were continuing to gain steadily, especially in the Delta. U.S. policy continued to be to provide U.S. resources and personnel to the extent necessary.

The tone of USG internal documents and of its dealings with GVN was that of a benevolent big brother anxious to see little brother make good on his own— but with the benefit of extensive advice. U.S. pressure induced the GVN to break up the palace guard and to move coup-protection Ranger units out into the countryside, though it turned out that other units stayed near Saigon for this purpose. A proposal to put all ammunition stocks in Vietnam under U.S. control surfaced in November, only to sink without a trace. There was gentle pressure to persuade the GVN to allow USOM economics staffs to share the offices of their counterparts, and to let them get involved extensively in GVN budgeting. The USIS and Ambassador Lodge tried to persuade General Minh to travel around the countryside to build a following and convince the people that the government cared about them, but with little success. The overall USG appraisal was that the GVN was weak and drifting at the top level, failing to set firm national policies and to issue detailed instructions, and that at lower levels it was in complete turmoil because of the turnover of personnel following the coup and because of the lack of firm national leadership.

Whether to push the GVN harder was a subject of disagreement between State and Ambassador Lodge. The State view was that the GVN must *prove* its resolution to adopt economic, social and political measures to support the effort against the VC, and must move toward self-support. Moreover, State said:

> We will obscure the actual need for GVN adjustments if we yield too easily at this stage to GVN pressure for more commercial import aid.

In contrast, Lodge said it was essential

> to provide some increase in overall level of economic aid . . . It is in my view politically unacceptable and psychologically impossible to tell Big Minh that he is going to get less than Diem.

Besides wanting to go easy on the GVN on aid leverage, he opposed pressure for early elections. Lodge's position is clear from the Honolulu Conference (November 1963) Report, which stated:

> The Ambassador . . . considers it essential that the U.S. not press the new government unduly. He stated that they are in a most delicate state, and are not ready for a system which replaces governments by elective process rather than by violence; that this is beyond their horizon at this time and we should not seek to recreate in Vietnam our image of the democratic ideal.

Early in January, 1964, Lodge restated this view in a cable:

> It is obvious that [the Vietnamese generals] are all we have got and that we must try as hard to make them into successful politicians as we are trying to make them into successful military men.

Behind these differences within the USG and between the USG and the GVN lay a certain lack of confidence in future behavior. Some in the U.S. were concerned that the GVN might drift toward a "neutralism" like that of Laos. At the same time, the GVN feared the U.S. would negotiate behind its back or force it to accept an unfavorable settlement. These concerns made it appropriate for the President to issue his New Year's greeting to the GVN:

> As we enter the New Year of 1964, I want to wish you, your revolutionary government, and your people full success in the long and arduous war which you are waging so tenaciously and bravely against the Viet Cong forces directed and supported by the Communist regime in Hanoi . . . Our aims are, I know, identical with yours: to enable your government to protect its people from the acts of terror perpetrated by Communist in-

surgents from the North. As the forces of your government become increasingly capable of dealing with this aggression, American military personnel in South Viet-Nam can be progressively withdrawn.

The United States Government shares the view of your government that "neutralization" of South Viet-Nam is unacceptable. As long as the Communist regime in North Viet-Nam persists in its aggressive policy, neutralization of South Viet-Nam would only be another name for a Communist take-over. Peace will return to your country just as soon as the authorities in Hanoi cease and desist from their terrorist aggression.

In keeping with the attitude of concern but not alarm about the GVN's conduct of the war, SecState's cable transmitting the President's message directed Lodge to offer the following eleven points of confidential advice on behalf of the President:

1. It is vitally important to act now to reverse the trend of the war as rapidly as possible.

2. We trust that personnel changes are now virtually complete and that both military commanders and province chiefs can now get down to the job at hand.

3. We hope that General Minh can designate a Chief of the Joint General Staff and a commander of the III Corps who will have no other responsibilities and can devote themselves exclusively to these mammoth tasks.

4. We assume that, as General Don promised Secretary McNamara, the GVN will make available sufficient troops in the six key provinces in the III Corps to give its forces the necessary numerical superiority.

5. We have been glad to learn of the stress which General Minh places on small-unit actions, particularly in the Mekong Delta. We hope that equal stress will be placed on night actions, both for ambushing Viet Cong and for relieving villages under attack. To win the support of the population it needs to be emphatically demonstrated that the Viet Cong are being beaten precisely at their own game.

6. We consider it extremely important that the necessary civil-military coordinating machinery for clear-and-hold operations, followed by an effective program to give the villages protection and security, be established in Saigon.

7. It is likewise extremely important that program directives be issued at an early stage by the central government to lower echelons for proper implementation of all aspects of the program for giving villagers protection.

8. We also urge early revitalization of the amnesty program.

9. We are encouraged by the exploratory talks which the Vietnamese Government has held with Cambodian Government officials for improving relations between the two countries. We hope that both Governments can proceed to actual negotiations for the settlement of their bilateral problems.

10. We accept with pleasure General Minh's invitation to set up an American brain-trust to work with his government and we are prepared to furnish any personnel needed for this purpose.

11. General Minh can also be sure that he has the complete support of the United States Government as *the* leader of Viet-Nam. We believe he can magnetically rally the Vietnamese people if he will really try to do so. He should be told leadership is an essential political ingredient of victory such as was the case with Magsaysay in the Philippines.

In this overall context the U.S. had already moved discreetly toward greater involvement in Vietnamese administration at lower levels. Late in 1963, the USG and GVN agreed on a "Decentralization of Action" package. Using AID *de facto* control of AID commodities to the province level (even though they passed to Vietnamese ownership at the dock), U.S. advisers could assure that no AID commodities came out to the province without their consent. They could and did extend this control to cover releases of these commodities from province warehouses. U.S. officials controlled the distribution of AID commodities because they controlled all Saigon warehouses set aside for these commodities, even though the warehouses, like the commodities, belonged to the Vietnamese.

Among the many problems that were to keep recurring was that of freedom of the press. Following an initial honeymoon period after the coup, trouble broke out between GVN and the U.S. press corps. This reached a climax with the temporary barring of the *New York Times* from Vietnamese distribution channels when it ran a story reporting dissension among the Vietnamese Generals. In general, Lodge sided with GVN on this issue, as shown in his reported views at the November, 1963, Honolulu Conference:

> The U.S. press should be induced to leave the new government alone. They have exerted great influence on events in Vietnam in the past, and can be expected to do so again. Extensive press criticism, at this juncture, could be disastrous.

On January 1, 1964, there were 15,914 U.S. military personnel in South Vietnam. Fewer than 2,000 of these were advisors to RVNAF, but the advisor structure extended down to ARVN line battalions, and advisors accompanied combat units on operations. The MAP budget for South Vietnam in FY 1964 was $175 million, although it was expected that an additional $12.5 million would be required before the end of the year.

In summary, the USG's decisions near the end of 1963 started modest changes in our Vietnam programs. Program levels held even, and earlier hopes of immediate phasedown faded. The USG moved toward more involvement in Vietnamese day-to-day administration, particularly at the province level. The move was gentle, and stopped far short of a takeover; nothing of the sort was contemplated at that time. The USG was sceptical of GVN's leadership and administration at all levels, and continued to offer extensive and detailed advice, but had no drastic policy changes in mind.

B.   THE FIRST MINH GOVERNMENT GOES DOWN, JANUARY, 1964

The year began with increasing Vietnamese criticism of the Minh government. It had done little to gain popularity in the country, and felt the sting of accusations of discrimination from both Buddhists and Catholics. Buddhists attacked Prime Minister Tho, who was Vice President under Diem. Catholics accused the GVN of having gone too far to placate the Buddhists in reaction to repressions under Diem. There were also accusations of secret negotiations with the French to neutralize South Vietnam.

A spate of news stories about U.S. advisor disgust over ARVN's timid attitude toward combat provoked a cable from State to Saigon asking the Ambassador to prevent such stories in the future. (This standard phrase meant to tell the advisors to stop talking to the press.) Thus the Department aligned itself with Lodge's view of bad press stories, which emphasized news silence rather than corrective action.

The Lodge idea of making politicians out of the members of the Military Revolutionary Council translated into a plan for them to send out carefully watched political action teams. (He also suggested ways for the generals to improve their speech-making style.) For example, he proposed there should be three teams of eight men each in each district of Long An Province. He pressed the MRC to produce a program along these lines with priority attention to security. "The workers would be technically government employees, but most of the work they will do would be what we would call political work." On the U.S. role, he said, "U.S. personnel should inspect, without looking as though they were doing it, and see to it that a very high standard is set."

When discussing general objectives, Lodge and his team got on smoothly with GVN. In a meeting with all the top members of General Minh's government early in January to discuss the eleven points transmitted with President Johnson's New Year's greeting, they persuaded Lodge that they were moving effectively on all points except number 8, relating to amnesty. This one evoked little enthusiasm, but they said they had it under study. The USOM team that discussed economic policy matters with GVN economists with the objective of limiting the GVN budget deficit and drawing down its dollar balances found them willing to talk frankly and to examine alternatives freely. GVN was also willing to set up joint working committees to analyze the budget, the import program, and agricultural policy. However, the U.S. team found that getting jointly agreed bench mark data and a clear line of authority for policy actions "may yet prove difficult."

Moreover, a snag developed on the previously agreed plan to extend U.S. advisors to district level. In a one hour meeting January 10 between Ambassador Lodge and General Minh and other top Vietnamese officers and officials, General Kim stressed the extreme undesirability of Americans going into districts and villages. It would play into the hands of the VC and make the Vietnamese officials look like lackeys. There would be a colonial flavor to the whole pacification effort. Minh added that even in the worst and clumsiest days of the French they never went into the villages or districts. Others present went on to add that they thought the USIS should carry out its work strictly hand-in-hand with the province chief. When Lodge pointed out that most of the USIS teams were Vietnamese, Minh said, "Yes, but they are considered the same as Vietnamese who worked for the Japanese and the same as the Vietnamese who drive for Americans and break traffic laws." General Minh went on to complain about the U.S. hand in the training of Cao Dai and Hoa Hao. This was bad because they then became American type soldiers, not Vietnamese soldiers. Later in the discussion, General Minh complained that the ICA had made direct contacts with the above groups. "We simply cannot govern this country if this kind of conduct continues," he said.

In reply to the report of this meeting, the Joint Chiefs of Staff cabled CINCPAC on January 14:

> SecDef seriously concerned regarding . . . General Don's earlier agreement on district level advisors as well as Minh's assertion that no advisors are desired beyond the regimental level. The Secretary considers, and JCS

agree, that this would be an unacceptable rearward step. State is preparing a response . . . in which SecDef and JCS will have a hand.

The State guidance to Lodge on January 17 said:

> . . . We deem it essential to retain advisors down to sector and bat-talion level as we now have them, and consider establishment of subsector advisors as highly desirable improvement from our viewpoint. Such advisors are best assurance that the U.S. material we supply is used to full advantage. Beyond this, we cannot give adequate justification for our great involvement in Vietnam . . . if we are to be denied access to the facts.

However, State indicated a willingness to limit subsector advisors to an experimental program in a few districts, as suggested by Col. Thang, with a review of the question to follow a few weeks later. State suggested that General Minh's erroneous statement regarding U.S. training of Cao Dai and Hoa Hao deserved prompt refutation. "It is suggested Harkins accompany you to meetings where military matters may come up."

In contrast to their reticence about extending U.S. advisors to lower levels, Minh's government had volunteered the idea in December of a group of high-level U.S. advisors to work with the top levels of the GVN. The State Department replied enthusiastically:

> In elaboration of the brain trust concept suggested by General Minh and accepted by President Johnson (DepTel 1000), our view is that high-level advisors may be essential key to ingredient most sorely lacking in GVN: Efficiency and urgency of action. Minh's invitation to establish brain trust and readiness to accept U.S. advice and cooperate . . . should be seized upon . . . We have in mind advisors working directly with VN officials on day-to-day implementation of agreed policy lines. They would of course be completely responsible to you for policy guidance and would in no sense supplant your policy role with top GVN officials nor would they infringe direct and comprehensive military advisory role of COMUS-MACV . . . We recognize such advisors must operate behind the scenes and that their persistent prodding must be done with great tact. . . .

The guidance continued that the department specifically had in mind the assignment of three experienced full-time advisors (and senior assistants) to work with top levels of GVN. One senior FSO would work with Minh and Tho on broad program implementation, one ranking AID official would be with GVN counterinsurgency and economic officials, one high-ranking military would work with the Minister of Defense and JGS. Both advisors and assistants would have office space in a GVN building close to the office they would advise. Authority was given to discuss this with GVN. Lodge was told to ask them whom they would like for these positions.

Meanwhile, political tension increased. Then on January 28, General Nguyen Khanh told his U.S. advisor and friend, Col. Jasper Wilson, that a group of generals, including Minh and Don, were plotting with the French to stage a pro-neutralist "coup" by January 31. He asked whether the U.S. would support him in staging a counter-coup which would assure a stepped-up GVN effort against the Viet Cong. There is no record of an official U.S. reply before Khanh resolved to act. The evening of January 29, Khanh told Wilson he would take over the GVN at 4 a.m. the next morning. Lodge informed State, which directed him to keep a hands-off attitude and to make it clear that the USG had nothing to do with the coup. It also directed Lodge to try to keep "Big Minh" in the government, at least as a figurehead. The next morning, right on schedule, Khanh took over.

C. THE USG ACCEPTS KHANH AND OPENS THE BIDDING AGAINST THE NORTH, FEBRUARY, 1964

Keeping Minh was to prove difficult. Khanh wanted to try four arrested generals for conspiring with the French to neutralize SVN; and not only were these officers Minh's close friends, but Khanh said Minh was a party to the plot also. The affair was to drag on into September, adding to the political uncertainties and thus to the paralysis of government.

To improve government stability, Khanh broadened his government to make the cabinet more representative of all the political and religious groups, and expanded the MRC to include 17 generals and 32 other officers. (By the end of March the MRC had 53 members.) Partly at USOM urging, General Minh travelled around the country and reportedly gained popularity. The Council of Notables continued in its advisory role.

Following the coup, the USG reopened the question of extending U.S. advisors into the districts. On February 7, 1964, the State Department told Saigon:

> Inasmuch as recently displaced government evidently took no definitive position on extension U.S. advisory structure to subsector level . . . we believe [the] Ambassador and General Harkins should raise this subject at early date with General Khanh. It might be useful to point out to Khanh that in addition reasons cited in our 1072, proposed extension U.S. advisory structure would represent expansion U.S. commitment to support GVN in war against VC.

State anticipated that Khanh might object but believed the possible harm would be more than counterbalanced by improved effectiveness of GVN operations in countryside:

> . . . if Khanh will not accept subsector advisors on scale originally envisaged he should be urged to agree at least to their establishment on experimental basis in few districts in order to lay basis for determining whether there is any substantial ill effect in political sense from their presence.

Two weeks later COMUSMACV reported Vietnamese acceptance of district advisors in 13 districts of central Delta provinces. MACV J–3 had casually arranged it with General Khiem, apparently without any new top-level U.S./GVN discussion.

Khan's government was as receptive at first to top-level U.S. advice as it was to advisors at lower levels, although the "brain trust" idea dropped between the cracks. General Khanh made two requests for U.S. recommendations of Vietnamese persons to be members of his cabinet. Ambassador Lodge furnished a list from which a panel could be picked, but refused to make specific recommendations for particular positions.

However, there was still no sign of effective GVN action, with or without U.S. advice. In mid-February JCS recommended a concentrated "counterinsurgency offensive" in Long An province to restore GVN control and to make that a model for other critical provinces. Deputy Ambassador Nes, in Lodge's absence, objected strongly; for he said such a proposal was based on the false assumptions that:

> (1) Indigenous Communist insurgency with full external support could be defeated by an "offensive" of finite duration.
> (2) GVN had adequate political cohesion, leadership, etc., to launch an offensive.
> (3) The U.S. Mission had sufficient influence and control over GVN to persuade it to do so.

A February 19 report from COMUSMACV tells of continuing delay on pacification because the Dien Huang (or Dong Hien) had to be revalidated by the new government. A new plan was presented to General Khanh on the 17th and was to be called Chien Thang ("struggle for victory").

On February 21, 1964, Ambassador Lodge, Admiral Felt, and General Harkins saw Khanh with a proposal for creating a corps of civil administrators to take over the villages and hamlets as soon as pacification was complete. Khanh replied that he was just about to put into effect a program in the seven key provinces around Saigon which would provide the help of doctors, teachers, and government advisors from Saigon.

The subject of funds for ARVN and para-military pay increases came up because counterpart and PL 480 proceeds were U.S. contributions to the GVN budget. Washington requested additional facts and recommendations on how added U.S. input could best be channeled but advised that an outright U.S. grant would be highly undesirable. USOM and MAAG were told to analyze the situation and develop joint U.S./GVN action to meet the threat of inflation. Saigon replied that their analysis indicated (1) the budget deficits would probably be smaller than originally expected, and (2) the economic consequences were extremely difficult to predict. Economic Minister Oanh shunned any immediate "complex study" of the economic outlook because he was completely tied up with a series of important planning exercises for the government, and Oanh felt the potential cost of the pay raise (700 million piasters in 1964) could be absorbed within the present expenditure levels.

The Embassy reported being informed on February 21 by the Minister of National Economy of a threatened Saigon rice shortage. He requested that the U.S. stand ready to provide 40,000 tons under title II PL 480 for distribution to the Armed Forces. No U.S. commitments were made. Talks were exploratory.

Although the USG recognized the weaknesses of GVN, as noted at the end of Section 1, these merely aroused concern at the highest levels, not alarm. An extreme example of the emphasis of this period is found in W.W. Rostow's memorandum to the Secretary of State dated February 13, 1964. In a context emphasizing the importance of success in Vietnam to U.S. interests everywhere, Rostow wrote only about the role of North Vietnam in the insurgency, relegating South Vietnam's governmental problems (and those of Laos) to a vague clause in one sentence:

> South Vietnam is in danger. The internal position in South Vietnam created by the systematic operations conducted from North Vietnam is

precarious . . . although difficult tasks would still be faced in South Vietnam and Laos if North Vietnamese compliance with the 1962 agreement was enforced, we see no possibility of achieving short-run or long-run stability in the area until it is enforced."

In a cable to the President, Lodge expressed the same view. In addition, he compared the sanctions used against Diem with the sanctions being considered against the North, and thus by implication treated the fall of Diem as the end of the problem of good government in the South. Rightly or wrongly, the USG viewed North Vietnamese support and direction of the insurgency as the overriding problem, not merely in its public posture (as represented by President Johnson's new year's greeting to General Minh, quoted on page 3, above, and by the State White Paper, "Aggression From the North," issued February 27), but also in its internal policy discussions. Rostow's statement says that there is no way to achieve short-run or long-run stability in Southeast Asia without putting a stop to this support and direction, and gives short shrift to GVN reform. To the extent that this view was accepted, it tended to set the face of U.S. policy looking outward across South Vietnam's borders, putting South Vietnamese weaknesses in the background, mainly to be dealt with after the 1962 Agreement is enforced.

When the issue came up of the GVN's internal military and political failures, all agreed that these were serious, but there was seldom any action. Occasional references (e.g., Honolulu, 1964), and conversations with some of the principals, make it clear that the explanation for this lack of action was the fear that the GVN was a house of cards, which would collapse if we pushed too hard. This fear of GVN weakness proved to be a consistent source of *strength* to GVN in its negotiations with the Embassy and with the USG.

D. McNAMARA'S MARCH TRIP AND NSAM 288

For several days beginning on March 8, 1964, Secretary McNamara conferred with GVN leaders and with U.S. officials in Saigon. The trip reinforced his pessimistic views of the previous December. In his trip report to the President, he said:

> C. The situation has unquestionably been growing worse, at least since September:
>
> 1. In terms of government control of the countryside, about 40% of the territory is under Viet Cong control or predominant influence. . . .
> 2. Large groups of the population are now showing signs of apathy and indifference, and there are some signs of frustration within the U.S. contingent:
>
> a. The ARVN and paramilitary desertion rates, and particularly the latter, are high and increasing.
> b. Draft dodging is high while the Viet Cong are recruiting energetically and effectively.
> c. The morale of the hamlet militia and of the Self Defense Corps, on which the security of the hamlets depends, is poor and falling.
>
> 3. In the last 90 days the weakening of the government's position has been particularly noticeable. . . .

4. The political control structure extending from Saigon down into the hamlets dissppeared following the November coup. Of the 41 incumbent province chiefs on November 1, 35 have been replaced (nine provinces had three province chiefs in three months; one province had four). Scores of lesser officials were replaced. Almost all major military commands have changed hands twice since the November coup. The faith of the peasants has been shaken by the disruptions in experienced leadership and the loss of physical security. In many areas, power vacuums have developed causing confusion among the people, and a rising rate of rural disorders.

D. The greatest weakness in the present situation is the uncertain viability of the Khanh government . . . After two coups, as was mentioned above, there has been a sharp drop in morale and organization, and Khanh has not yet been able to build these up satisfactorily. There is a constant threat of assassination or of another coup, which would drop morale and organization nearly to zero. Whether or not French nationals are actively encouraging such a coup, de Gaulle's position and the continuing pessimism and anti-Americanism of the French community in South Vietnam provide constant fuel to neutralist sentiment and the coup possibility. If a coup is set underway, the odds of our detecting and preventing it in the tactical sense are not high.

E. On the positive side, we have found many reasons for encouragement in the performance of the Khanh government to date. Although its top layer is thin, it is highly responsive to U.S. advice, and with a good grasp of the basic elements of rooting out the Viet Cong. Opposition groups are fragmentary, and Khanh has brought in at least token representation from many key groups hitherto left out. He is keenly aware of the danger of assassination or coup and is taking resourceful steps to minimize these risks. All told, these evidences of energy, comprehension, and decision add up to a sufficiently strong chance of Khanh's really taking hold in the next few months for us to devote all possible energy and resources to his support.

A memorandum of the conversation held at Joint General Staff (JGS) headquarters between Secretary McNamara and General Khanh, the Prime Minister, on March 12, shows that the U.S. pressed for a national service act. General Khanh agreeably assured the Secretary that the GVN was prepared to embark on a program of national mobilization. The principal question raised by the Vietnamese was the desirability of raising the Civil Guard to the same relative status as ARVN on such matter as salary, pensions, and survivor benefits at a total additional cost of 1 billion piasters. Mr. McNamara's reply that he thought this highly desirable was obviously interpreted by the Vietnamese as an agreement to underwrite much of the bill.

After considering various options in his reports, McNamara recommended the following basic U.S. posture:

1. The U.S. at all levels must continue to make it emphatically clear that we are prepared to furnish assistance and support for as long as it takes to bring the insurgency under control.

2. The U.S. at all levels should continue to make it clear that we fully support the Khanh government and are totally opposed to any further coups. The ambassador should instruct all elements, including the military

advisors, to report intelligence information of possible coups promptly, with the decision to be made by the ambassador whether to report such information to Khanh. . . .

3. We should support fully the Pacification Plan now announced by Khanh . . . This so-called "oil spot" theory is excellent, and its acceptance is a major step forward. However, it is necessary to push hard to get specific instructions out to the provinces, so that there is real unity of effort at all levels. . . .

Many of the actions described in succeeding paragraphs fit right into the framework of the Plan as announced by Khanh. Wherever possible, we should tie our urging of such actions to Khanh's own formulation of them, so that he will be carrying out a Vietnamese plan and not one imposed by the U.S.

4. To put the whole nation on a war footing . . . a new National Mobilization Plan (to include a National Service Law) should be urgently developed by the Country Team in collaboration with the Khanh Government. . . .

5. The strength of the Armed Forces (regular plus paramilitary) must be increased by at least 50,000 men. . . .

6. A Civil Administrative Corps is urgently required to work in the provincial capitals, the district towns, the villages, and the hamlets . . . The U.S. should work with the GVN urgently to devise the necessary recruiting plans, training facilities, financing methods, and organizational arrangements, and should furnish training personnel at once, under the auspices of the AID Mission. . . .

7. The paramilitary forces are now understrength and lacking in effectiveness. They must be improved and reorganized.

d. Additional U.S. personnel should be assigned to the training of all these paramilitary forces.

e. The National Police require special consideration. Their strength in the provinces should be substantially increased and consideration should be given to including them as part of an overall "Popular Defense Force". . . .

8. An offensive guerrilla force should be created to operate along the border and in areas where VC control is dominant. . . .

He recommended more military equipment for ARVN, which along with the expansion recommendations above, added up to a total cost to the U.S. of some $50-60 million in the first year and $30-40 million thereafter. He reasoned:

There were and are sound reasons for the limits imposed by present policy—the South Vietnamese must win their own fight; U.S. intervention on a larger scale, and/or GVN actions against the North, would disturb key allies and other nations; etc. In any case, it is vital that we continue to take every reasonable measure to assure success in South Vietnam. The policy choice is not an "either/or" between this course of action and possible pressures against the North; the former is essential without regard to our decision with respect to the latter. The latter can, at best, only reinforce the former.

The following are the actions we believe can be taken in order to improve the situation both in the immediate future and over a longer term period. To emphasize that a new phase has begun, the measures to be taken by the Khanh government should be described by some term such as "South Vietnam's Program for National Mobilization."

Two courses of action that Secretary McNamara considered and rejected were destined to come up time and again. With respect to the suggestion that the U.S. furnish an American combat unit to secure Saigon, the Secretary reported "It is the universal opinion of our senior people in Saigon, with which we concur, that this action would now have serious adverse psychological consequences and should not be undertaken."

On U.S. assumption of command, he said:

> . . . the judgments of all senior people in Saigon, with which we concur, is that the possible military advantages of such action would be far outweighted by its adverse psychological impact. It would cut across the whole basic picture of the VN running their own war and lay us wide open to hostile propaganda both within SVN and outside. Moreoover the present responsiveness of the GVN to our advice—although it has not yet reduced military reaction time—makes it less urgent. At the same time MACV is steadily taking actions to bring U.S. and GVN operating staff closer together at all levels, including joint operating rooms at key command levels.

The President met with the National Security Council on March 17 and approved McNamara's recommendations; NSAM 288 of that date directed all agencies to execute the parts applying to them. To underline one point further, State cabled USOM Saigon on March 18 to make sure to report all rumors of coups heard by any U.S. personnel to the Ambassador at once; and it gave the Ambassador full reaction authority. Then the President summarized his view of the main thrust of the new policy, in a cable to Lodge on March 20:

> As we agreed in our previous messages to each other, judgment is reserved for the present on overt military action in view of the consensus from Saigon conversations of McNamara mission with General Khanh and you on judgment that movement against the North at the present would be premature. We here share General Khanh's judgment that the immediate and essential task is to strengthen the southern base. For this reason our planning for action against the North is on a contingency basis at present, and immediate problem in this area is to develop the strongest possible military and political base for possible later action.

Anticipating great things, the White House announced Khanh's "mobilization plan" on March 17, and implied USG support for him:

> To meet the situation, General Khanh and his government are acting vigorously and effectively. They have produced a sound central plan . . . To carry out this plan . . . General Khanh has informed us that he pro-proposes in the near future to put into effect a National Mobilization Plan. . . .
>
> The policy should continue of withdrawing United States personnel where their roles can be assumed by South Vietnamese and of sending additional men if they are needed. It will remain the policy of the United States to furnish assistance and support to South Vietnam for as long as it is required. . . .
>
> Secretary McNamara and General Taylor reported their overall conclusion that with continued vigorous leadership from General Khanh and

his government, and the carrying out of these steps, the situation can be significantly improved in the coming months.

In a speech in Washington on March 26, Secretary McNamara more explicitly supported the Khanh government, and gave the accepted priorities of U.S. policy:

> . . . In early 1963, President Kennedy was able to report to the nation that "the spearpoint of aggression has been blunted in South Vietnam." It was evident that the Government had seized the initiative in most areas from the insurgents. But this progress was interrupted in 1963 by the political crises arising from troubles between the Government and the Buddhists, students, and other non-Communist oppositionists. President Diem lost the confidence and loyalty of his people; there were accusations of maladministration and injustice. There were two changes of government within three months. The fabric of government was torn. The political control structure extending from Saigon down into the hamlets virtually disappeared. Of the 41 incumbent province chiefs on November 1 of last year, 35 were replaced. Nine provinces had three chiefs in three months; one province had four. Scores of lesser officials were replaced. Almost all major military commands changed hands twice. The confidence of the peasants was inevitably shaken by the disruptions in leadership and the loss of physical security . . . Much therefore depends on the new government under General Khanh, for which we have high hopes.
>
> Today the government of General Khanh is vigorously rebuilding the machinery of administration and reshaping plans to carry the war to the Viet Cong. He is an able and energetic leader. He has demonstrated his grasp of the basic elements—political, economic and psychological, as well as military—required to defeat the Viet Cong. He is planning a program of economic and social advances for the welfare of his people. He has brought into support of the government representatives of key groups previously excluded. He and his colleagues have developed plans for systematic liberation of areas now submissive to Viet Cong duress and for mobilization of all available Vietnamese resources in the defense of the homeland.
>
> At the same time, General Khanh has understood the need to improve South Vietnam's relations with its neighbors . . . In short, he has demonstrated the energy, comprehension, and decision required by the difficult circumstances that he faces. . . .
>
> The third option before the President [after withdrawal and neutralization, both rejected] was initiation of military actions outside South Vietnam, particularly against North Vietnam, in order to supplement the counterinsurgency program in South Vietnam.
>
> This course of action—its implications and ways of carrying it out—has been carefully studied.
>
> What ever ultimate course of action may be forced upon us by the other side, it is clear that actions under this option would be only a supplement to, not a substitute for, progress within South Vietnam's own borders.
>
> The fourth course of action was to concentrate on helping the South Vietnamese win the battle in their own country. This, all agree, is essential no matter what else is done. . . .
>
> We have reaffirmed U.S. support for South Vietnam's Government and

pledged economic assistance and military training and logistical support for as long as it takes to bring the insurgency under control.

We will support the Government of South Vietnam in carrying out its Anti-Insurgency Plan. . . .

The next day McNamara formally ended the hope of phased withdrawal, by stopping the lower-echelon joint planning activities that had aimed at replacing U.S. elements in Vietnam by Vietnamese. Although the Vietnamese knew that the "withdrawal" of 1000 men in December 1963 had been a pretense, his action now removed any remaining doubt about our intentions. The message was brief:

Model Plan projection for phasedown of U.S. forces and GVN forces is superseded. Policy is as announced by White House on 17 March 64.

E. OPENING BIDS ON ADVICE, LEVERAGE, AND AID, APRIL–MAY, 1964

Armed with our declaration of support and with the promised further material assistance, General Khanh signed a mobilization decree on April 4; at the time the decree satisfied the USG as meeting McNamara's recommendation on the subject. However, Khanh delayed signing implementing decrees for the mobilization decree indefinitely; and it has never become clear what it would have meant, if implemented. In May, Khanh purportedly broadened the draft to include older and younger men, and announced formation of a new "Civil Defense Corps"; but neither came to anything. On April 4, Khanh also abolished the Council of Notables. This latter step he did on his own, without prior discussion with Lodge. As noted in section 1, Lodge, who always believed in the need and importance of constitutional government in SVN, felt no urgency for creating a democratic form of government, although many in State may have wanted to object to Khanh's actions. Such actions without prior consultation were to become a sore point later on with both State and the Embassy. Thus, what the USG actually got for the recognition and material support it gave Khanh in March was the dissolution of the Council of Notables.

During April, Lodge and State continued to debate how hard to push GVN using AID leverage. Lodge agreed with the general principle that the Commercial Import Program (CIP) should not be increased until increased GVN expenditures quickened the economy and drove imports up. However, he noted that GVN had been given to understand that they could expect at least the $95 million CIP in 1964 that Diem had in 1963, and that McNamara had said in Saigon and Washington that U.S. assistance to Vietnam would increase by about $50 million. These assurances had spurred Oanh, Minister of National Economy, to ask for specific increases in CIP. Lodge thought the time unpropitious for detailed joint planning and for austerity measures as conditions for the last increment of 1964 CIP. Oanh received credit for being too busy with pacification planning and other matters to discuss such matters. Therefore, Lodge proposed to use the planning of the CY 1965 program as the right place to apply leverage.

State reacted sharply, questioning whether the USG should let GVN off the hook on its March commitments that easily. Nevertheless, State acknowledged that "formal negotiations may not be desirable at this time," and settled instead for "constant dialogue to keep GVN aware of U.S. adherence to the new approach and of firm desire to see it implemented." The desired GVN actions included drawdown of foreign exchange reserves, promotion of exports, import austerity, and an anti-inflationary domestic policy.

USOM then talked to Oanh about the commitments on the two sides. USOM felt that Oanh understood that GVN was to move first and be backed up by the USG as needed, but thought that some segments of GVN were dragging their heels to avoid living up to their commitments. USOM estimated a $15-30 million drawdown of GVN foreign exchange reserves in 1964.

In the last week of April, General Khanh asked Lodge for one American expert each in the fields of Finance-Economics, Foreign Affairs, and Press relations to be assigned to him personally and to have offices in "a convenient villa . . . We Vietnamese want the Americans to be responsible with us and not merely as advisors." This request revived the "brain trust" concept discussed with the Minh government around the first of the year. Commenting, Lodge noted that he had opposed pushing Americans into GVN because of Colonialist overtones; they would cause resentment, and a lessening of effort by the GVN, placing the blame on the U.S. Therefore, he had avoided raising the idea with Khanh. However, that Khanh himself now proposed it removed that objection, and Lodge felt that the U.S. should respond because it was an urgent necessity.

Late in the same meeting, Lodge told Khanh of a State Department proposal for civil administrators on a crash basis in partially pacified areas. His quick reply, "Yes . . . if you will accept losses."

Lodge recommended a Civil Administrative advisor to join the three others mentioned above, but he advised against more. He said there was no sense dumping several hundred advisors out there. In view of the "trail blazing" nature of the move, he requested a member of the White House staff, possibly Forrestal, to come out for a conference. Ordinarily, it would be surprising that Lodge would make such a big issue of Khanh's revival of an idea that GVN had already advanced through Lodge and that the President himself had approved. However, his effusive reaction in this case merely underlines his oft-repeated reluctance to push GVN. Lodge presented the first three advisors to Khanh on May 6.

On April 30, Lodge, Westmoreland, and USOM Director Brent met with several top members of GVN to discuss GVN's failure to disburse operating funds to the provinces, sectors and divisions and to correct the manpower shortage in ARVN and the paramilitary units. Lodge argued that the McNamara program was failing, not because U.S. support lagged, but because the necessary piaster support was missing. Moreover, he said, there was no shortage of piasters available to GVN. In reply, Oanh of the GVN said they had inherited a bad system from the French, and that he was now trying to implement new procedures. Khanh replied on the manpower problem that to raise the strength would require an ultimatum to the Corps Commanders, but then he also said that remedial moves were underway and were known to MACV. Khanh countered the budgetary argument by saying that he had still not received money from the U.S. to support increased pay for the paramilitary; Lodge replied that if he went ahead with the increased pay, the U.S. would meet the bill. Overall, the meeting was one of thrust and parry rather than of consultation. This meeting followed prodding from McNamara and JCS in a cable sent April 29.

On May 4, Khanh told Lodge he wanted to declare war, bomb North Vietnam with U.S. bombers, put the country on a war footing, including "getting rid of the so-called politicians and having . . . a government of technicians," and bring in 10,000 U.S. Army special forces to "cover the whole Cambodian-

Laotian frontier." Lodge was non-committal on U.S. forces, but said that the war came first and that democratic forms could wait. However, Khanh publicly called for an election by October of a Constitutional Assembly, apparently to bolster his public support; he had his share of rumors and political infighting.

On May 13, during a trip to Saigon to review progress on the March decisions, McNamara met with Khanh to express his concern over GVN inaction. McNamara's main complaints were that RVNAF was failing to reach authorized strength levels and that budget delays were holding up pacification. He felt that GVN should announce that failure to disburse funds is a crime. He also expressed concern about the replacement of incompetent officers, such as the Commanding General of the ARVN Fifth Division. The meeting went agreeably, and produced the following consensus:

> (1) All present expressed satisfaction at Khanh's having accepted the importance of speeding up disbursements.
>
> (2) The case of the commander of the Fifth Division "presented something of an internal problem, but it would be arranged." (This was the second time around for the Fifth Division case. As the result of a personal request from General Harkins, Khanh had agreed on April 25 to change this same officer "immediately."
>
> (3) Khanh hoped to spend more time on military and pacification matters if only "this political stomach trouble" that took so much of his time could be quieted.

MACV presented McNamara with a proposal to give the province advisors a total of $278,000 in petty cash and "seed money," to be used solely at the U.S. advisors' discretion. This initial proposal suggested putting the money under control of the psychological operations committee. The idea received mixed reactions, and went on the agenda of the Honolulu Conference in June.

M. Forrestal of the White House Staff came with McNamara, and led a negotiating team that met Minister Oanh and his staff to discuss budgetary and economic matters. The U.S. team wanted GVN to keep its budget under strict control; GVN wanted the USG to increase CIP, and to give it an additional $18 million from fiscal 1964 funds. On May 27, when the talks ended, the USG had released the requested $18 million, and committed itself to a fiscal 1965 CIP of $135 million, $40 million more than in fiscal 1964, plus a standby arrangement for an additional $30 million. GVN protested that this commitment was not enough to prevent inflation, and did what it pleased about its own budget; the talks ended with an agreement to disagree.

E.   THE POLITICAL CLIMATE AND PREVAILING VIEWS OF THE WAR, MAY 1964

Khanh's "political stomach trouble" was merely a fresh case of a chronic Vietnamese problem. His troubles with General Minh over the four jailed generals continued, and coup rumors abounded. On May 21, Lodge told him of the harmful effects of such rumors, and suggested he talk tough with his cabinet. When their conversation turned to General Minh, Khanh insisted that Minh could be proved to have conspired with the others and with the French to make Vietnam neutral. Khanh and the MRC planned to try the four generals in Dalat by the 29th of May. State then directed Lodge to try to prevent the trial, and failing that to soften its effects and prevent Minh's deposition. Lodge put this position to Khanh on May 28, asserting the special need for unity in view of possible cross-border problems with Laos; Khanh accepted the point and agreed to soften the blow on the generals. He flew immediately to Dalat, and the next day announced to Lodge an amicable settlement of the problem, with lenient treatment of the generals and new-found complete unity among the members of the ruling MRC. State and Lodge were gratified, and agreed that the thing to do was to press for unity in support of getting on with the war. However, it was soon common knowledge that the "settlement," amounting to censure of the accused officers, satisfied no one; and the problem festered on.

In May the first sign appeared of varying emphasis at the highest levels on particular necessary steps for success against the VC. In a DPM dated May 25, 1964, McGeorge Bundy restated the theme of the Rostow memorandum to SecState of February 13:

> It is recommended that you make a Presidential decision that the U.S. will use selected and carefully graduated military force against North Vietnam . . . on these premises:
> (1) That the U.S. cannot tolerate the loss of Southeast Asia to Communism;
> (2) That without a decision to resort to military action if necessary, the present prospect is not hopeful, in South Vietnam or in Laos.

Of course, Bundy knew of the GVN's weaknesses and on other occasions asserted the need to reform GVN; but here he focussed exclusively on using force against NVN.

In contrast, Chairman Sullivan of the newly-created inter-agency Vietnam Committee said in a proposed memorandum for the President (May, 1964, undated):

> The Vietnamese Government is not operating efficiently enough to reverse the adverse trend in the war with the Viet Cong. The Khanh Government has good intentions; it has announced good general plans and broad programs; but these plans are not being translated into effective action against the Viet Cong on either the military or the civil side. It has, therefore, become urgently necessary to find a means to infuse the efficiency into the governmental system that it now lacks.

To remedy the GVN's lack of efficiency, Sullivan proposed that Americans assume de facto command of GVN's machinery.

> American personnel, who have hitherto served only as advisors, should be integrated into the Vietnamese chain of command, both military and civil. They should become direct operational components of the Vietnamese Governmental structure. For cosmetic purposes American personnel would not assume titles which would show command functions, but would rather be listed as "assistants" to the Vietnamese principals at the various levels of government . . .
> Americans should be integrated to *all* levels of the Vietnamese Government . . . Americans would be integrated into the Central Government to insure that decisions are taken, orders are issued and funds, supplies and personnel are made available for their implementation, and execution actually takes place. At the regional level Americans, both military and

civilian, would also be introduced . . . Americans would likewise be
brought into the government machinery at province and district level to
insure that the counterinsurgency programs are actually executed at the
level where the people live.

Aside from the command aspect which Americans would assume, the
principal other new element in this concept would be the introduction of
American civilians at the district level. Their purpose would be to insure
that programs are put into effect at the village and hamlet level to gain the
support of the people . . .

Personnel at the district level would confront a maximum risk and
casualties are virtually certain. Since the U.S. should take any feasible
measure to assure their security, it is important that Vietnamese units of
the Civil Guard and Self-Defense Corps, which operate at this level, be
encadred with an adequate number of American military personnel to
insure that they will operate effectively.

This DPM also proposed extensive reshuffling of the lines of authority in the
GVN itself, including the elimination of divisions from the Vietnamese military
structure and placing all authority for pacification, military and civilian, in the
hands of the province chiefs under the corps commanders.

The Vietnam Committee watered down this proposal immediately, however.
On May 27, it went to four high-level addressees as a talking paper, with the
second sentence of the above recommendation altered to say, "They should
become more than advisors, but should *not* become an integral part of the
chain of command." (Emphasis added.) Recognizing Vietnamese sensitivities
and the GVN's political vulnerability, the revised paper recommended a gradual,
phased approach. But even the watered-down version was termed "radical" in
the cable putting it on the agenda for the upcoming Honolulu Conference.

In the new advisory program already underway, MACV reported a big
improvement by late May in the experimental districts with U.S. advisors.
People rather than messages moved back and forth. Economic and social
bonds were reported improved. Further extension of advisors to districts was
put on the agenda. In preliminary communications, General Taylor, Chairman
of the JCS, assumed that their mission would be to supervise unit training,
operational performance, and operational planning of para-military units in
the districts; but he also suggested discussion of other ways in which military
personnel could be used to advantage in forwarding the pacification program.

The month ended with a Rusk-Khanh meeting that re-emphasized the accepted priorities of U.S. policy, and unquestionably confirmed to the Vietnamese how far we were thinking of going. First, Rusk emphasized to Khanh
the effect of Vietnamese quarreling on the U.S. and on other potential allies in
the struggle. Second, they discussed immediate extensions of the war, such as
attacking the Laotian corridor, and the various further extensions that might
follow. Third, Khanh pushed hard on the idea, which as noted above had already been discussed in Washington, that he could not win without extending
the war. Finally, Khanh pledged to keep all these matters secret until the U.S.
agreed to overt statement or action.

The language of the cable reporting this meeting is candid and revealing:

1. Solidarity Within South Vietnam
    . . . Secretary [Rusk] stated one of main problems President faces in
justifying to American people whatever course of action may be neces-

sary or indicated as matter of internal solidarity of SVN. Secretary noted that if struggle escalates, only U.S. will have the forces to cope with it.

This basic reality means President has heavy responsibility of making vital decisions and leading American public opinion to accept them. Difficult to do this if SVN appears hopelessly divided and rent by internal quarrels.

. . . Secretary said he was not thinking in terms of displaying solidarity so as to convince Paris that struggle could be won, but rather was thinking in terms of sustaining the faith in the possibilities of ultimate success of our Vietnamese effort among those nations we hoped "would be in the foxholes with us" if escalation became necessary and if enemy forces reacted in strength. For example, UK, Australia, New Zealand. Solidarity and unit of purpose in SVN was keystone of whole effort. Was General Khanh doing all he could to bring about such national unity?

Khanh replied affirmatively, saying he fully aware of importance of unity. His recent handling of the case of the arrested Generals showed this. His clemency showed he was primarily interested in protecting unity of Army. But there were many problems. Underlying structure and heritage of country was such that only Army could lead Nation in unity. Only Army had the requisite organization, cadres, discipline, and sense of purpose. The intellectuals would never be able to adopt a common point of view unless it was imposed by a dictatorship—by a party as the Communists did, or a "family dictatorship" such as Diem's. This situation was made worse because of disproportion between measure of political and civil liberties granted in wartime situation on one hand and lack of background and sense of responsibility of recipients on [the] other . . . He was aware he had perhaps given more freedom than really prudent handling of situation would have dictated, but he had to be mindful oft-proclaimed democratic goals of the Vietnamese revolution. All in all, this disunity would not be fatal because Army itself was united, and no potentially disruptive force could hope to oppose Army and overthrow GVN. (N.B. No reference to religious problems, sects, or labor under this heading.)

2. Need for Action Outside South Vietnam.

. . . Khanh dwelt at length on this, laying out some fairly precise ideas about the kind of action that might be taken.

Basically, he said that despite the pacification plan and some individual successes he and his government were "on the defensive" against the Viet Cong. He said pretty flatly that they could not win unless action was taken outside South Vietnam, and that this needed a firm U.S. decision for such action.

. . . He [Khanh] then said that the "immediate" response should be to clean out the Communists in Eastern Laos, who were the same kind of threat to him, and that we should not get bogged down in negotiations but act.

. . . Secretary then noted we could never predict enemy reaction with certainty. How would SVN people react if NVN and China responded by attacking SVN? Khanh replied this would have even more favorable effect on SVN national unity and faith in victory, and would mobilize usual patriotic reactions in face of more clearcut external threat.

3. Timing of Action Against the North and Necessary Prior Action Within South Vietnam.

Khanh asked if Secretary and Ambassador believed he should proclaim state of war existed during next few days and now that Generals' case was settled. Both advised him to wait at least until after Honolulu Conference and in no case ever to take action on such matter without consulting. He agreed, and remarked that if he proclaimed state of war, NVN would know this was preparatory to some form of escalation and he would never act unilaterally and thereby run risk of tipping America's hand. Although the matter was not specifically mentioned, Khanh appeared to accept as entirely natural that he would not necessarily know in advance if U.S. decided to strike outside VN.

. . . Some question as to how enemy camp will react. At various points in conversation Khanh was obviously seeking some more definite statement of specific American intentions in immediate future. Secretary told him he could say nothing on this because he simply did not know. The Honolulu meeting would produce some firm recommendations to the President and some plans, but ultimately only President could decide. His decision would be influenced by consideration of all implications of escalation: On our forces, on our allies, and perhaps even on mankind itself if nuclear warfare should result. Only U.S. had the means to cope with problems escalation would pose, and only President could make the ultimate decisions.

Nevertheless, Secretary said he wished to emphasize the following:

A. Since 1945 U.S. had taken 165,000 casualties in defense of free world against Communist encroachments, and most of these casualties were in Asia.

B. U.S. would never again get involved in a land war in Asia limited to conventional forces. Our population was 190,000,000. Mainland China had at least 700,000,000. We would not allow ourselves to be bled white fighting them with conventional weapons.

C. This meant that if escalation brought about major Chinese attack, it would also involve use of nuclear arms. Many free world leaders would oppose this. Chiang Kai-Shek had told him fervently he did, and so did U Thant. Many Asians seemed to see an element of racial discrimination in use of nuclear arms; something we would do to Asians but not to Westerners. Khanh replied he certainly had no quarrel with American use of nuclear arms, noted that decisive use of Atomic bombs on Japan had in ending war saved not only American but also Japanese lives. One must use the force one had; if Chinese used masses of Humanity, we would use superior fire power.

D. Regardless what decisions were reached at Honolulu, their implementation would require positioning of our forces. This would take time. Khanh must remember we had other responsibilities in Asia and must be able react anywhere we had forces or commitments. Not by chance was this Conference being held at Honolulu; the combined headquarters of all American forces in Pacific was there.

. . . 6. Comment

As can be seen, the Secretary let Khanh develop his ideas fairly fully and do most of the talking.* Khanh talked firmly and effectively, and responded well to the Secretary's several points. He showed clearly that he was aware of the gravity of the decisions (tho he did seem a touch cavalier about the political problems of hitting eastern Laos at once), and did not seem

---

* Comment: Nevertheless, as can be seen, the Secretary spoke freely.

to want a firm U.S. answer the day after tomorrow. But it seemed clear that he did want it pretty soon, and was now convinced he could not win in South Vietnam without hitting other areas including the North. He was careful to point out that the pacification campaign was making gains and would continue to do so. Still, it was essentially defensive.

On the timing, the Secretary said that any action would be preceded in any event by some period of time for force deployments. (He did not refer to diplomatic steps re Laos, the UN side, the U.S. Congressional problem, or other types of factors.) Khanh understood this, and also accepted the Secretary's point that we would need to consult very closely with Khanh himself, try to bring the British and Australians aboard (the Secretary referred only to these two possible active participants), and generally synchronize and work out the whole plan with great care.

Thus although the USG had pressed GVN on many details of economic policy, administration, and pacification, contacts at the highest level told GVN that if the Vietnamese leaders would only stick together to prosecute the war, and if we compelled the North Vietnamese to cease and desist, everything would be all right. Provided the GVN didn't embarrass the USG too much, there was no limit to how far we would go to support them; and apart from "unity" and a reasonable show of effort, there was no onus on them to deliver the goods. Khanh's claim that he could not win without extending the war, and that the Vietnamese were tired of the long dreary grind of pacification, met no U.S. objection.

G.   THE HONOLULU CONFERENCE AND ITS FOLLOW-UP, JUNE, 1964

The Honolulu Conference met on short notice with an air of urgency; principals included McNamara, Rusk, Lodge, Taylor, and Westmoreland. Presentations of the current situation preceded consideration of additional measures to be taken. Lodge briefed those present on the political status. He said the situation could "jog along," but he thought that some external action would be a big lift to South Vietnamese morale. Lodge's prediction was more optimistic than later events, in August, proved justified; he said "if we bombed Tchepone or attacked the [NVN torpedo] boats and the Vietnamese people knew about it, this would . . . unify their efforts and reduce [their] quarreling." In reply to a question by Rusk, he opposed the idea of a more formal joint USG/GVN organization at the top; McNamara hoped that a more formal organization would evolve. Lodge felt that the USG/GVN relationship was harmonious, and that GVN was responsive to advice. He liked the present methods of dealing with them. Westmoreland called the military picture "tenuous but not hopeless" and added that a few victories were badly needed. Both were more optimistic than was the prevailing Washington view.

All present agreed that the emergence of a hostile government or anarchy would be a major threat to the U.S. position. The fear of this threat undoubtedly helps explain the USG's persistent hesitancy to apply leverage to GVN.

Westmoreland circulated a working paper calling for moderate increases in U.S. personnel, both civilian and military, for eight critical provinces. He reported that the GVN had recently responded to massive advisory pressure by increasing the tempo of their military operations. He felt they would similarly respond to a continuing advisory program oriented toward pacification. Both Lodge and Westmoreland rejected, as both unwise and unacceptable to GVN, any major plan for "inter-larding" or "encadrement" which would move U.S. personnel directly into decision-making roles. Their opposition ended conference consideration of the proposals advanced by the Sullivan memorandum.

In a long draft memorandum, dated June 13, 1964, Sullivan added some further insight into US/GVN relations and into the views of Lodge and Westmoreland about national priorities, beyond what is shown in the CINCPAC record of the Conference.

> In attempting to accomplish many of these programs, we have encountered resistance both from the Vietnamese and from our own U.S. Mission. Ambassador Lodge . . . fears that the increased introduction of Amercans would give a colonial coloration to our presence there and would cause the Vietnamese to depend more and more on our execution of their programs. The Vietnamese . . . have some fear of appearing to be American puppets . . . Finally, there is some indication that they are reluctant to associate themselves too closely with the Americans until they feel more confident of ultimate American intentions.

> At the current moment, there is great doubt and confusion in Vietnam about U.S. determination . . . As a leading Saigon newspaper said on June 12: "We must be vigilant and we must be ready to meet any eventuality so as to avoid the possible shameful sacrifice and dishonor to our country as in the past."

> Given this sort of atmosphere in South Vietnam, it is very difficult to persuade the Vietnamese to commit themselves to sharp military confrontations with the communists if they suspect that something in the way of a negotiated deal is being concocted behind their backs. Consequently, many of the actions which we are pressing on the South Vietnamese are flagging because of this uncertainty . . .

> Both Ambassador Lodge and General Westmoreland, at the Honolulu Conference expressed the opinion that the situation in South Vietnam would "jog along" at the current stalemated pace unless some dramatic "victory" could be introduced to put new steel and confidence into the Vietnamese leadership. General Westmoreland defined "victory" as a determination to take some new vigorous military commitment, such as air strikes against Viet Cong installations in the Laos corridor. Ambassador Lodge defined "victory" as a willingness to make punitive air strikes against North Vietnam. The significant fact about both . . . suggestions was that they looked toward some American decision to undertake a commitment which the Vietnamese would interpret as a willingness to raise the military ante and eschew negotiations begun from a position of weakness.

> While it is almost impossible to establish measurements of Vietnamese morale, we are able to say that there is not at the current moment a single galvanized national purpose, expressed in the government leadership and energizing all elements of the country with a simple sense of confidence.

The selective Westmoreland plan offered hope and was sufficiently general to avoid specific opposition. The conference agreed that Saigon should complete the plan and work urgently on its implementation.

Several more minor decisions were made on unilateral matters. "Czar" powers for information were put in the hands of Zorthian. It was agreed that the DCM should be strengthened with a "truly executive man," and there was to be a clearing-of-decks on the military side in Saigon through reductions in social activities and cut-downs in dependents. None of these measures was expected to affect the dubious prognosis for the next 3-6 months. The best that could be hoped for was a slight gain by the end of the year.

There was serious discussion of military plans and intelligence estimates regarding wider actions outside South Vietnam. Subjects included the conduct of military operations in Laos, a major build-up of forces, and planning of possible air strikes against North Vietnam. The conclusion reached was that the somewhat less pessimistic estimate of the present situation afforded the opportunity to further refine these plans.

The conference concluded that the crucial actions for the immediate future were (1) to prosecute an urgent information effort in the United States toward dispelling the basic doubts of the value of Southeast Asia which were besetting key members of Congress and the public in the budding "great debate," and (2) to start diplomatic efforts with the Thais, Australians, New Zealanders, Philippines, and the French on matters within their cognizance which impinged on our effort in South Vietnam.

Upon his return to Washington, the Secretary of State cabled Saigon a specific listing of the Washington understanding of the ten actions that were to be taken to expand U.S. and Vietnamese activities in the super-critical provinces. The gist of the actions is as follows:

(1) Move in additional VN troops to assure numerical superiority over VC.

(2) Assign control of all troops in province to province chief.

(3) Develop and execute detailed hamlet by hamlet "oil spot" and "clear and hold" operations plans for each of the approximate 40 districts.

(4) Introduce a system of population control (curfews, ID papers, intelligence network).

(5) Increase the province police force.

(6) Expand the information program.

(7) Develop a special economic aid program for each province.

(8) Add additional U.S. personnel
320 military province and district advisors
40 USOF province and district advisors
74 battalion advisors (2 from each of 37 battalions)
___
434

(9) Transfer military personnel to fill existing and future USOM shortages.

(10) Establish joint US/GVN teams to monitor the program at both national and provincial level.

The message concluded by asking Saigon to forward specific proposals to effect these decisions and a time schedule, "earliest." The plan to give province advisors a petty cash fund received so little support that there is no mention of it in either CINCPAC or the State Conference Record.

Upon his return to Saigon on June 4 Ambassador Lodge went straight from the airport to call on General Khanh. While Lodge mentions in his report that the subject of low ARVN strength was raised as a matter to be improved upon, the main thrust of his talk with Khanh was to hint that the USG would in the immediate future be preparing U.S. public opinion for actions against North Vietnam. Khanh was reported to be eager to learn more about the details.

On June 13, Saigon replied to the State request for specific proposals. A MACV study had been completed on point 1 and the RVNAF would be approached. On point 2, it was noted that RF and PF were already under the province chiefs; ARVN would be approached on province command of regulars. A wordy description of "concept" spoke to the remainder of State's ten points. It provoked a long series of specific questions from Washington about the 8 provinces, asking in sort, "How soon can action be initiated?"

On June 25, COMUSMACV sent his request to JCS for an increase of 4,200 U.S. personnel to implement this expanded advisory effort. He viewed these as efforts to "influence the successful planning and execution of the National Pacification Plan." Subsector advisors were to be "a general reinforcement of the pacification effort at district level." Consequently, the MACV terms of reference for subsector advisors were developed to provide that teams would extend the capabilities of USOM and USIS. Guidance was intentionally not specific.

The same day General Westmoreland reported that, with the Ambassador's concurrence, he had called on General Khanh to discuss three military matters: (1) Augmentation of advisors at battalion level and extension of larger advisory teams to most districts; (2) The urgent need to coordinate pacification efforts in the provinces surrounding Saigon; and (3) The necessity of moving a regiment to Long An (the pacification show-case) as soon as possible. General Khanh's reply was very receptive and agreeable on all matters.

On June 26, Lodge sent his last message as Ambassador reporting that he and General Westmoreland had that day met with General Khanh and had reached "general agreement" on the concept, scope, and organization set forth in the Saigon reply of June 13 (referred to above).

Meanwhile the proposal for a province advisors' fund reappeared in a new form, and won quick approval. USOM agreed that AID should spend $200,000 from its contingency funds for direct purchase of piasters, to allocate to sector advisors for small expenditures (usually less than $25 at a time). The funds were to buy local materials and services for projects using AID commodities; and their use was to be coordinated with the Vietnamese Province Chief. By subsequent US/GVN agreement, all uses of these funds and commodities, and requisitions of the commodities from Saigon warehouses, required unanimous approval of a three-man ("troika") Provincial Coordinating Committee consisting of the Province Chief, the U.S. AID Provincial Representative and the MACV Sector Advisor. The troika sign-off had already applied to the commodities, as the means to the U.S. veto on their use mentioned above in Section A. Except for a high-level agreement each year on the size and overall allocation of these resources, Saigon allowed the Provinces full freedom of action in their use. The intent of this arrangement was to permit prompt action on urgent projects, unaffected by the delays in the GVN administration that plagued regular GVN operations. It also interfered with corrupt misuse of the AID commodities and of purchase piasters.

II. AMBASSADOR TAYLOR'S FIRST SEVEN MONTHS: PLANNING FOR "BOMB NORTH" AMID TURBULENCE IN THE SOUTH

A. *AMBASSADOR TAYLOR'S INITIATION, JULY, 1964*

Ambassador Taylor arrived in Saigon amid the start of planning to extend the war outside the borders of South Vietnam. Rusk had discussed the options with Khanh on June 1, and the participants of the Honolulu Conference had mulled them over further. Although there was no formal decision to recommend new operations in Laos or North Vietnam, there was an atmosphere of expectation. A joint State-Defense message on June 27 authorized joint planning with the Vietnamese Joint General Staff for cross border operations in Laos; on June 30, Westmoreland discussed it with General Khiem, who agreed to initiate joint planning.

Taylor came with a letter of support from the President that cleared up any previous doubt about the Ambassador's control over MACV:

> I want you to have this formal expression not only of my confidence but of my desire that you have and exercise full responsibility for the effort of the United States in South Vietnam . . . I wish it clearly understood that this overall responsibility includes the whole military effort in South Vietnam and authorizes the degree of command and control that you consider appropriate.

Either the letter was intended to prevent confusion of authority such as existed among Lodge, Felt, and Harkins, or the expectation of greater militarization of the war made it appropriate to appoint Taylor Ambassador and to give him unchallenged authority.

Taylor met Khanh and presented his credentials on July 8. Khanh promised him "the frank cooperation of a soldier." He said the U.S. should not merely advise, but should participate in making and implementing plans; in this he still held the view he had expressed to Taylor when he, Khanh, was still a Corps Commander. (By referring to Zorthian's contacts with the Minister of Information, Khanh made it clear he had the brain trust idea in mind.) However, he noted that this degree of involvement should be kept secret, because of the criticism it would attract if known. They discussed Minh's trips around the country, and agreed these were useful and constructive. Finally, Taylor stressed the importance of Vietnamese unity and resolve.

The next day Taylor called on the three Vice Premiers, Hoan, Do Mau, and Oanh, and received the civilian point of view. Hoan did most of the talking, saying that civilian politicians like himself wanted the Army to be supported by the people, but that Khanh and the MRC were difficult to work with: The ruling generals control everything. He said the II Corps Commander lived like a playboy, and that the people were outraged; "ever since we came to power we have been telling population we are soon going to have change, but it never comes. The people are becoming impatient." Moreover, he said, something must be done to raise the standard of behavior of the armed forces toward the population. Taylor received these views diplomatically.

For a while there was a serious effort to go through with close meshing of USOM and GVN planning. On July 17 USOM met with Khanh, Hoan, Oanh and others as a group, which Khanh designated the National Security Council. They discussed joint planning and further meshing of US/GVN organizations, putting the stamp of approval on the arrangement in the Ministry of Information. On July 23 Taylor met Khanh and discussed a second meeting of the NSC. Khanh said the Vietnamese had some difficulty in adjusting their ministerial organization to the requirements of meshing with the U.S. mission subdivisions. Taylor responded that reciprocal adjustments were possible. Planning and discussion of cross-border operations continued actively. Offensive guerrilla operations in Laos were a major idea; small operations had already begun into North Vietnam, under OPLAN 34A. In the meeting on July 23, Khanh told

Taylor he wanted to intensify the operations under 34A and to start air strikes against North Vietnam. He said again, as he had to Rusk on June 1, that he didn't like to look forward to the long, indecisive pull of the in-country pacification program, and doubted that the Army and the people would carry on indefinitely.

The events of July 19–23 made it clear that GVN was straining at the leash; it started public lobbying for cross-border operations. On July 19 Air Marshal Ky spilled the beans to reporters on plans for operations into Laos. Khanh committed a similar indiscretion at a "Unification Rally" on the 19th, and these were followed by GVN press releases and editorials in the Saigon press urging a "march to the North." All these leaks directly violated Khanh's promises to Rusk on June 1. Taylor spoke to Khanh sharply about them, and pointed out that they could be interpreted as a campaign to force the USG's hand. Khanh insisted that such a campaign was the furthest thing from his mind; and then confirmed that it was exactly what he had in mind. Following a long, eloquent repetition of his remarks of other occasions on Vietnamese war-weariness, he asked: Why does not the USG recognize that the appearance of North Vietnamese draftees among the prisoners taken in the I Corps meant that the war had entered a new phase and the USG and GVN must respond with new measures? He said Vietnamese spirits had been raised by President Johnson's firm statements earlier in the year (specifically, Los Angeles, January 21), but that following them nothing had happened. The effect was wearing off, and the communists would conclude they were only words. Then Khanh took the offensive and complained to Taylor that U.S. officials were contradicting him in public statements. For example, MACV had denied that there was an invasion of I Corps by DRV units, as Khanh had claimed in a speech at Danang. Zorthian soothed him by saying that MACV merely corrected a misquotation of one of MACV's own officials; Taylor said no U.S. official would knowingly contradict Khanh.

Taylor took all this patiently, as he did an intelligence report that said Khanh was trying to incite the USG to action against North Vietnam. (The report also said that Ky was saying privately that the GVN should go it alone, because the USG was stalling on account of the U.S. election.) USOM conjectured that Goldwater's nomination had precipitated the "go North" movement. Moreover, within two hours after Khanh's long meeting with Taylor, the Ministry of Defense let fly another press release in the teeth of USOM disapproval, when Khanh ordered the Ministry to reject Zorthian's suggested changes. The only explanation offered was that GVN was extremely sensitive about appearing to be a U.S. puppet.

In an analysis of these events, Taylor argued for tolerance and patience with GVN, and showed no hint of a desire to get tough. He noted that political sniping and maneuvering pressed Khanh to do something dramatic to bolster his support. Taylor feared the GVN might get tired and want to negotiate if they could not get the U.S. more involved. He proposed joint contingency planning for bombing North Vietnam as a means to cool GVN off and to reopen communications with them.

In a long conversation on July 24 Khanh discussed his political problems with Taylor and asked him point blank if he should resign. Taylor flatly said no, that the USG still supported him and definitely wanted no further change in GVN. Khanh then asked for a declaration of support and for pressure on the generals to continue to support him; Taylor agreed. (Comment: Much of Khanh's political problem still revolved around Minh, who had long had good relations with Taylor. This relationship may have worried Khanh, and led him to approach Taylor in this way. However, it may have merely been a way to keep up the pressure on USG on the matter of bombing North. A couple of days later Khanh was again grumbling publicly about being a U.S. puppet.)

In response to Taylor's discussion of GVN motives and of ways to make them happy, State authorized him to tell Khanh the USG had considered attacks on North Vietnam that might begin, for example, if the pressure from dissident South Vietnamese factions became too great. He must keep this confidential. It said to tell him that the USG position had not changed, and that it never excluded the possibility of wider action. When Taylor brought this matter to Khanh for discussion, they first agreed on a GVN announcement of an increase in U.S. personnel and discussed the press leaks on going North. Khanh then took the offensive, complaining to Taylor about press stories suggesting the USG was negotiating with the Chinese through the Pakistani Government, behind the back of GVN. Taylor soothed him by saying that the USG was merely letting China know how firm our policy was. When Taylor asked Khanh his views of U.S. policy, Khanh said he wanted pressure on the North, meaning a bombing campaign. Taylor replied with the position that State had authorized on joint planning. Khanh acted pleased and surprised, promised to think it over, and promised to hold it tightly. He also said he wanted to reorganize GVN to strengthen his own position; Taylor asked for specifics, and urged him not to do anything drastic that would stir up trouble.

B. THE TONKIN INCIDENTS AND THE POLICY PROGNOSES, AUGUST, 1964

Within a week, North Vietnamese PT boats attacked the U.S. destroyer Maddox, in admitted retaliation for an attack by South Vietnamese boats on two North Vietnamese islands. Then a disputed further attack of North Vietnamese PT boats on the Maddox and the Turner Joy on August 4 provoked a U.S. retaliatory raid on the main North Vietnamese PT boat base and its support facilities. The raids lifted GVN's spirits, as expected, and encouraged Khanh to clamp down internally. On August 7, he proclaimed a state of emergency, the idea he had been discussing for some time with both Lodge and Taylor. He reimposed censorship and restricted movement; but he left politicians and potential coup-plotters alone. Also on August 7, the U.S. Congress in joint session passed the Gulf of Tonkin Resolution.

On August 8, Westmoreland discussed overall joint planning with Khanh; the question of combined command came up, and Westmoreland mentioned the example of Korea. Both agreed to postpone this issue.

On August 14, State directed Saigon to avoid actions that could be called provocative, like the DESOTO patrols (which the Maddox and the Turner Joy had been doing when attacked) and 34A operations. State noted that the U.S. retaliatory raid's effect on GVN's morale would be temporary, and took a pessimistic view of the USOM reports:

> Mission's monthly report (Saigon 377) expresses hope of significant gains by end of year. But also says Khanh's chances of staying in power are only 50-50, that leadership . . . has symptoms defeatism and hates prospect of slugging it out within country, that there will be mounting pressures for wider action "which, if resisted, will create frictions and irritations which could lead local politicians to serious consideration negotiated solution or local soldiers to military adventure without U.S. consent" . . . Our actions

of last week lifted . . . morale temporarily, but also aroused expectations, and morale could easily sag back again if VC have successes and we do nothing further.

The cable went on to state that an essential element of U.S. policy was to devise the best possible means of action—minimum risks for maximum results in terms of SVN morale and pressure on DRV. In the context of a possible new Geneva conference on Laos, its prognosis was that pressure on the North would be the main vehicle for success:

> Basically solution in both South Vietnam and Laos will require combination military pressure and some form of communication under which Hanoi (and Peiping) eventually accept idea of getting out. Negotiation without continued military action will not achieve our objectives in foreseeable future . . . After, *but only after,* we have established clear pattern pressure hurting DRV and leaving no doubts in South Vietnam of our resolve, we could even accept conference broadened to include Vietnam issue. (Underlining in original.)

On the touchy aspect of US/GVN relations, it simply said:

> *Joint US/GVN planning* already covers possible actions against DRV and the Panhandle. It can be used in itself to maintain morale of GVN leadership, as well as to control and inhibit any unilateral GVN moves.

The Taylor reply to the above message differed only in emphasis.

> . . . Underlying our analysis is the apparent assumption of DepTel 439 (which we believe is correct) that the present in-country pacification plan is not enough in itself to maintain National morale or to offer reasonable hope of eventual success. Something must be added in the coming months.
>
> Statement of the problem—A. The course which U.S. policy in South Vietnam should take during the coming months can be expressed in terms of four objectives. The first and most important objective is to gain time for the Khanh government to develop a certain stability and to give some firm evidence of viability. Since any of the courses of action considered in this cable carry a considerable measure of risk to the U.S., we should be slow to get too deeply involved in them until we have a better feel of the quality of our ally. In particular, if we can avoid it, we should not get involved militarily with North Vietnam and possibly with Red China if our base in South Vietnam is insecure and Khanh's Army is tied down everywhere by the VC insurgency. Hence, it is to our interest to gain sufficient time not only to allow Khanh to prove that he can govern, but also to free Saigon from the VC threat which presently rings it and assure that sufficient GVN ground forces will be available to provide a reasonable measure of defense against any DRV ground reaction which may develop in the execution of our program and thus avoid the possible requirement for a major U.S. ground force commitment.
>
> A second objective in this period is the maintenance of morale in South Vietnam, particularly within the Khanh government. This should not be difficult in the case of the government if we can give Khanh assurance of our readiness to bring added pressure on Hanoi if he provides evidence of ability to do his part. Thirdly, while gaining time for Khanh, we must be able to hold the DRV in check and restrain a further buildup of Viet Cong

strength by way of infiltration from the North. Finally, throughout this period, we should be developing a posture of maximum readiness for a deliberate escalation of pressure against North Vietnam, using January 1, 1965, as a target D-Day. We must always recognize, however, that events may force us to advance D-Day to a considerably earlier date . . .

In approaching the Khanh Government, we should express our willingness to Khanh to engage in planning and eventually to exert intense pressure on North Vietnam, providing certain conditions are met in advance. In the first place before we would agree to go all out against the DRV, he must stabilize his Government and make some progress in cleaning up his operational backyard. Specifically, he must execute the initial phases of the Hop Tac Plan successfully to the extent of pushing the Viet Cong from the doors of Saigon. The overall pacification program, including Hop Tac, should progress sufficiently to allow earmarking at least three division equivalents for the Defense in I Corps if the DRV step up military operations in that area.

Finally, we should reach some fundamental understandings with Khanh and his Government concerning war aims. We must make clear that we will engage in action against North Vietnam only for the purpose of assuring the security and independence of South Vietnam within the territory assigned by the 1954 agreements; that we will not repeat not join in a crusade to unify the North and South; that we will not repeat not even seek to overthrow the Hanoi Regime provided the latter will cease its efforts to take over the South by subversive warfare.

With these understandings reached, we would be ready to set in motion the following:

(1) Resume at once 34A (with emphasis on Marine operations) and Desoto patrols. These could start without awaiting outcome of discussions with Khanh.

(2) Resume U-2 overflights over all NVN.

(3) Initiate air and ground strikes in Laos against infiltration targets as soon as joint plans now being worked out with the Khanh Government are ready . . .

Before proceeding beyond this point, we should raise the level of precautionary military readiness (if not already done) by taking such visible measures as introducing U.S. hawk units to Danang and Saigon, landing a Marine force at Danang for defense of the airfield and beefing up MACV's support base. By this time (assumed to be late fall) we should have some reading on Khanh's performance.

Assuming that his performance has been satisfactory and that Hanoi has failed to respond favorably, it will be time to embark on the final phase of course of action A, a carefully orchestrated bombing attack on NVN, directed primarily at infiltration and other military targets . . .

Pros and cons of course of action—A. If successful, course of action A will accomplish the objectives set forth at the outset as essential to the support of U.S. policy in South Vietnam. I will press the Khanh Government into doing its homework in pacification and will limit the diversion of interest to the out-of-country ventures . . . It gives adequate time for careful preparation estimated at several months, while doing sufficient at once to maintain internal morale. It also provides ample warning to

Hanoi and Peking to allow them to adjust their conduct before becoming over-committed.

On the other hand, course of action A relies heavily upon the durability of the Khanh Government. It assumes that there is little danger of its collapse without notice or of its possible replacement by a weaker or more unreliable successor . . . Also, because of the drawn-out nature of the program, it is exposed to the danger of international political pressure to enter into negotiations before NVN is really hurting from the pressure directed against it.

Statement of the Problem—B. It may well be that the problem of U.S. policy in SVN is more urgent than that depicted in the foregoing statement. It is far from clear at the present moment that the Khanh Government can last until January 1, 1965, although the application of course of action A should have the effect of strengthening the Government internally and of silencing domestic squabbling. If we assume, however, that we do not have the time available which is implicit in course of action A (several months), we would have to restate the problem in the following terms. Our objective avoid the possible consequences of a collapse of National morale. To accomplish these purposes, we would have to open the campaign against the DRV without delay, seeking to force Hanoi as rapidly as possible to desist from aiding the VC and to convince the DRV that it must cooperate in calling off the VC insurgency.

Course of action—B. To meet this statement of the problem, we need an accelerated course of action, seeking to obtain results faster than under course of action A. Such an accelerated program would include the following actions:

Again we must inform Khanh of our intentions, this time expressing a willingness to begin military pressures against Hanoi at once providing that he will undertake to perform as in course of action A. However, U.S. action would not await evidence of performance.

Again we may wish to communicate directly on this subject with Hanoi or awaiting effect of our military actions. The scenario of the ensuing events would be essentially the same as under Course A but the execution would await only the readiness of plans to expedite, relying almost exclusively on U.S. military means.

Pros and cons of Course of Action B. This course of action asks virtually nothing from the Khanh Government, primarily because it is assumed that little can be expected from it. It avoids the consequence of the sudden collapse of the Khanh Government and gets underway with minimum delay the punitive actions against Hanoi. Thus, it lessens the chance of an interruption of the program by an international demand for negotiations by presenting a fait accompli to international critics. However, it increases the likelihood of U.S. involvement in ground action, since Khanh will have almost no available ground forces which can be released from pacification employment to mobile resistance of DRV attacks.

Conclusion: It is concluded that Course of Action A offers the greater promised achievement of U.S. policy objectives in SVN during the coming months. However, we should always bear in mind the fragility of the Khanh Government and be prepared to shift quickly to Course of Action B if the situation requires. In either case, we must be militarily ready for any response which may be initiated by NVN or by CHICOMS.

Miscellaneous: As indicated above, we believe that 34A operations should resume at once at maximum tempo, still on a covert basis; similarly, Desoto patrols should begin advance operating outside 12-mile limit. We concur that a number of VNAF pilots should be trained on B-57's between now and first of year. There should be no change now with regard to policy on evacuation of U.S. dependents.

Recommendations: It is recommended that USG adopt Course of Action A while maintaining readiness to shift to Course of Action B.

C. THE RISE AND FALL OF KHANH'S CONSTITUTION

In a state of euphoria after the U.S. reprisals, Khanh broached the subject of a new constitution with Taylor on August 12; presumably this was what he had in mind on July 27 when he mentioned reorganization (above, p. 328). He proposed three branches of government beneath the MRC. The Assembly would have 90 appointed members and 60 elected; Khanh would be the President (and Minh wouldn't). Taylor urged Khanh to go slowly, and to handle the matter gently. Taylor feared renewed political instability if sweeping government changes were announced; but Khanh said that the country could not progress under the existing government. Taylor expressed his scepticism, but objected no further than to caution Khanh on the need to explain these changes adequately in advance.

On August 14, after an NSC joint planning session, Khanh showed Taylor a rough English translation of his proposed new constitution. Taylor expressed reservations:

> We found it brusque in language and suggested to Khanh that in present form it could raise criticism in U.S. and world press. We stressed to him that internal problems of acceptance in Vietnam were his own affair, and we could only offer observations on the objective issue of international reactions.

Khanh allowed Sullivan and Manful to work briefly with his drafting committee, the same day, but they worked in such haste that they had little influence. Taylor commented:

> We conclude that Khanh and his military colleagues have decided that this sort of change is indispensable. It is of course still not determined what General Minh's view will be. We have considered possibility of seeking legal aid from Washington to review this charter, but feel this would not repeat not be useful because this document departs so widely from U.S. experience and because time is so short, we have decided that our best efforts would be devoted to (1) making wording of document less brusque and more palatable both in VN and abroad, and (2) assisting in proclamation and other sources of public relations nature explaining necessity for this sort of change. Whether we like it or not, this is the constitutional form which the MRC repeat MRC fully intends to impose, and we see no repeat no alternative but to make the best of it.

When Khanh secured MRC approval of the final draft on August 16, they also elected him President, displacing Minh. Khanh had earlier complained to Taylor that he had kept Minh, a big source of trouble to him, only at Lodge's urging, as indeed he had. Inasmuch as Khanh had seized power using charges against four generals and using unproved allegations against Minh, and inasmuch as Minh was still a popular figure, Khanh was bound to regard Minh as a threat to his personal prospects.

For several days following the announcement of the new constitution, a head of steam built up among students and Buddhists. There is no sign that the Embassy did anything to anticipate or head off the coming trouble, other than the previously mentioned words of caution that Khanh disregarded. On August 21, student demonstrations broke out. Violence built up in the streets, organized and orchestrated by the Buddhists and the VC.

Taylor called on Khanh on August 24 in his Dalat retreat to tell him how seriously the Embassy viewed the demonstrations. The discussion revolved around "public information" and completion of arrangements for the new government. Khanh agreed to announce the members of the new government by Thursday, the 27th, and to meet the Buddhist leadership to hear their complaints and to try to enlist their help. He also promised to meet some student demands, to crack down on the demonstrations, and to enforce the old mobilization decrees plus new ones.

State responded to these events with a public announcement of support for Khanh in more direct language than any previously used:

> The United States government fully recognizes the need for national unity in South Vietnam and is, therefore, supporting the Khanh government as the best means of building such unity at the same time that the war effort is being prosecuted. Obviously anything of a divisive nature is neither in the interest of the Vietnamese government nor its people.

That evening Khanh met three top Buddhist leaders in Saigon, after they refused to go to Dalat. Their principal demands, among eight, were the immediate abrogation of the August 16 charter and the holding of free elections by November 1, 1965. Khanh made the mistake of telling them he would have to consult the Americans.

Taylor and others met Khanh at 1:00 a.m. August 25. Observing diplomatic propriety, Taylor said his tentative personal views as an interested third party were that Khanh should not knuckle under to a minority group on such an important issue as the August 16 charter, especially under an ultimatum. Khanh agreed and proposed to issue a more limited proclamation immediately (which he did at 5:00 a.m.) that would meet certain concerns of the Buddhists and students.

Khanh's proclamation promised to revise the constitution, diminish censorship, rectify local abuses of government, and permit orderly demonstrations. The Buddhists and students were not satisfied; they formed a mob outside his office, to which he spoke briefly without further concession. The mob failed to disperse, and the authorities left them alone. Then without advance notice, military headquarters (Khanh) announced that afternoon that Khanh had resigned, that the August 16 charter would be withdrawn, and that the MRC would meet the next day to choose a new Chief of State and would then dissolve itself.

Taylor had made it clear to Minh, Khiem, Lam and Khanh that the U.S. favored retaining Khanh as head of the GVN. Both Tri Quang and Tam Chau, fearing a Dai Viet takeover, supported Khanh. Aligned against Khanh were elements of the military angered by Khanh's "down with military dictatorship" statement made from a truck top and the Dai Viet (including Khiem, Hoan and Minh) angered by his appeasement of the Buddhists.

On August 26 and 27, the MRC met, while violence erupted in the streets of Saigon. The evening of the 27th they announced that a triumvirate consisting of Generals Khanh, Minh, and Khiem would rule as an interim government while they tried to form a new one. Khanh withdrew to Dalat, and Vice-Premier Oanh became acting Prime Minister. Violence continued, and coup rumors became especially active.

On August 29, a State Department official briefed the press, interpreting events. He said Buddhists and students interpreted the August 16 charter as a return to Diemism and repression; in meeting their demands the MRC had worried some Catholics, but balanced things out by creating the triumvirate with all views represented. He said the charter had not been the USG's idea, but that we had been consulted and had urged delay. The demonstrations did not contain appreciable anti-Americanism, he said, nor did they arise from differences between the "go North" feelings of the military and refugee Catholics, on the one hand, and neutralist sentiments of students and Buddhists, on the other. However, the cable reporting the press conference to the Embassy showed concern on both these latter points.

D. GVN ACQUIRES A CIVILIAN FLAVOR, AND THE USG REVIEWS PRIORITIES

On August 29th, Vietnamese paratroopers armed with bayonets restored order in Saigon. Khanh rested in Dalat; Taylor called on him on the 31st to try to persuade him to return to Saigon quickly to prove he was in charge. Westmoreland went to see Khanh the next day to urge him to keep ARVN on the offensive and to press on with Hop Tac and other pacification; in exchange for reassurances, Westmoreland revised a previous position and promised that U.S. advisors through MACV would alert Khanh to unusual troop movements. Westmoreland also obtained reassurances from General Khiem. Rusk suggested a letter from President Johnson urging Khanh to return to Saigon, and then cabled the text of such a letter. A Dai Viet coup attempt was blocked by the junior members of the MRC, who had now become powerful. Several Generals went to Dalat to persuade Khanh to return as Prime Minister, which he promised to do in a few days. Khanh did return to Saigon on September 4. Minh was to be chairman of the triumvirate, and would appoint a new High National Council to represent all elements in the population. The Council was to prepare a new constitution and return the government to civilian leadership within a month or so. Khanh was taking the line that he wanted to get the Army out of politics. When Taylor cautioned Khanh, just before the latter's return to Saigon, that an all-civilian government would be too weak and would tend toward neutralism, Khanh replied that the Army would be vigilant. Taylor again advised Khanh to lay the groundwork better before any more changes in government structure. When the Triumvirate announced the creation of the NHC, they also ended the state of emergency and press censorship, which they had declared on September 6.

On the morning of September 6, as he was leaving for Washington, Taylor sent Rusk a full review of the crisis and of its effects on the Embassy-State military and political appraisal of mid-August. He said that the USG now had to give up on the idea of using a plan for pressures on the North as leverage to get the GVN to press on with pacification, and should go ahead with these pressures in the hope that they would raise Vietnamese morale enough to keep up their war effort:

. . . While we must be disappointed by the political turmoil of recent days, we cannot consider it totally unexpected. The very nature of the social, political and ethnic confusion in this country makes governmental turbulence of this type a factor which we will always have with us.

What has emerged from these recent events is a definition within fairly broad limits of the degree to which perfectability in government can be pushed. It should be remembered that the recent fracas started when Khanh sought to make his broad and cumbersome government more tractable and more effective. His motives were of the best even though his methods were clumsy. But now, after this recent experience at government improvement we must accept the fact that an effective government, much beyond the capacity of that which has existed over the past several months, is unlikely to survive. We now have a better feel for the quality of our ally and for what we can expect from him in terms of ability to govern. Only the emergence of an exceptional leader could improve the situation and no George Washington is in sight.

Consequently, we can and must anticipate for the future an instrument of government which will have definite limits of performance. At the very worst, it will continue to seek a broadened consensus involving and attempting to encompass all or most of the minority of popular front. This amalgam, if it takes form, may be expected in due course to become susceptible to an accommodation with the liberation front, which might eventually lead to a collapse of all political energy behind the pacification effort.

At best, the emerging governmental structure might be capable of maintaining a holding operation against the Viet Cong. This level of effort could, with good luck and strenuous American efforts, be expanded to produce certain limited pacification successes, for example, in the territory covered by the Hop Tac plan. But the willingness and ability of such a government to exert itself or to attempt to execute an all-out National pacification plan would be marginal. It would probably be incapable of galvanizing the people to the heightened level of unity and sacrifice necessary to carry forward the counter-insurgency program to final success. Instead, it would look increasingly to the United States to take the major responsibility for prying the Viet Cong and the North Vietnamese off the backs of the South Vietnamese population. The politicians in Saigon and Hue feel today that the political hassle is their appropriate arena: The conflict with the VC belongs to the Americans.

We may, therefore, expect to find ourselves faced with a choice of (A) passively watching the development of a popular front, knowing that this may in due course require the U.S. to leave Vietnam in failure; or (B) actively assuming increased responsibility for the outcome following a time-schedule consistent with our estimate of the limited viability of any South Vietnamese government.

An examination of our total world responsibilities and the significance of Vietnam in relationship to them clearly rules out the option of accepting course (A). If we leave Vietnam with our tail between our legs, the consequences of this defeat in the rest of Asia, Africa, and Latin America would be disastrous. We therefore would seem to have little choice left except to accept course (B).

Our previous views on the right course of action to follow in South Vietnam are set forth in EMBTEL 465. The discussion in this present cable amounts to a recognition that course of action A repeat A of EMBTEL 465 no longer corresponds with the realities of the situation. Recent events have revealed the weakness of our ally and have convinced us of the improbability of attaining the level of governmental performance desired under course A before embarking on a campaign of pressure against the DRV. We are forced back on course of action B with certain revised views on timing.

He went on to recommend that escalating pressures on the DRV begin around December 1.

Taylor brought with him General Westmoreland's assessment of the military situation; it included a look at the political situation from a completely different viewpoint from Taylor's:

> . . . 1. In preparation for your trip to Washington, I thought it might be useful to give you my assessment of the military situation. In subsequent paragraphs I outline in some detail the rather substantial progress which we have already made and, more importantly, the great potential for additional progress. I also describe military problem areas. These, as you know, are many; but all are susceptible to solution assuming that political stability can be achieved, and that armed forces, particularly the Army, remains intact and unified in its purpose. Under the present circumstances, however, the continued solidarity of the armed forces is in doubt. As all else depends on holding the armed forces together, I address this matter first.

> *The Key Military Issue.*

> 2. It seems to me there are certain conditions which must be met in order to preserve the structure and effectiveness of the RVNAF:

>> A. The officers of the RVNAF must be protected against purge, solely by reason of religious or political affiliation. The Commander in Chief, the officers of the Joint General Staff and commanders down the line, must be given some assurance that their careers and reputations will not be sacrificed, for political expediency to the ambitions or interests of political or religious blocs.
>> B. The Officers' Corps must be assured that its members will not be punished or expelled from the armed forces if they faithfully execute the orders of constituted authority in connection with the maintenance of law and order. They must be assured that their superiors will not accede to the arbitrary demands of pressure groups whose interest it is to destroy the discipline of the armed forces and to render ineffective the forces of law and order.

> 3. If I interpret correctly the events of the past two weeks, neither of these minimum conditions have been met. To the contrary, actions best calculated to destroy the morale, the unity, the pride and confidence of the armed forces have transpired in a manner which leads me to believe that a relative free hand has been given to those who aim to destroy the armed forces. The demands of the Buddhists for the resignation of the Commander in Chief, the Chief of Staff, Commander of II Corps, the

Prefect of Saigon and the Director of National Police, to name a few, appear to be blows directed at the heart of the security forces which stand between the Viet Cong and victory. I cannot believe that it is in the interests of the Nation to accede to these demands. To the contrary, I am persuaded that acceptance is a formula for political and military disaster. While aware that the insurgency cannot be overcome by military means alone, I am equally aware that without a strong military foundation no program will ever achieve victory. I am concerned that the Government of Vietnam has already moved some distance down the wrong road in dealing with its Armed Forces. I do not know whether the Armed Forces will collapse or whether, finding the present course intolerable, they will make a desperate move to regain power. Neither course of action is compatible with the objective we seek.

In Washington, Taylor, Rusk, McNamara and Wheeler reached a consensus that (1) Khanh and GVN were too exhausted to be thinking about moves against the North, (2) GVN needs reassurance, and (3) Khanh is likely to stay in control, but not to get much done on the pacification program. There followed NSAM 314, whose main point was that "first order of business at present is to take actions which will help strengthen the fabric of the GVN."

E. THE HNC GOES TO WORK AMID FURTHER TURBULENCE

Helping strengthen the fabric of GVN proved to be easier said than done.

Another coup attempt on September 13 failed when Ky and Thi, along with other young officers, supported the existing government. The USG opposed the coup, and also opposed overt violence to suppress it; in particular, USG opposed VNAF bombing of Saigon, which was threatened at one point when the coup generals gained control of much of the city. When Khanh and Ky asked for U.S. Marines, the USG refused; State authorized a strong line in favor of the Triumvirate, and against internecine war:

> (A) It is imperative that there not be internecine war within VN Armed
>   Forces.
> (B) The picture of petty bickering among VN leaders has created an
>   appalling impression abroad.
> (C) The U.S. has not provided massive assistance to SVN, in military
>   equipment, economic resources and personnel, in order to subsidize
>   continuing quarrels among SVN leaders . . .
> (G) Emphasize that VN leaders must not take the U.S. for granted.

> 2. In line with above you should make it emphatically clear whenever useful, that we do not believe a Phat/Duc government can effectively govern the country or command the necessary popular support to carry forward the effort against the VC. U.S. support for the GVN is based on the triumvirate and its efforts to bring about a broadly based and effective government satisfactorily reflecting the interests and concerns of all groups.

After the coup failed, the Embassy pressed Khanh to exile the coup leaders quietly; and in the upshot they were acquitted of the charges against them.

A fresh problem blew up on September 20 when Rhade tribesmen in four

CIDG camps advised by U.S. Special Forces revolted against Saigon's authority. It arose from a long-festering mistrust and contempt between the Montagnards, encouraged by the VC, and the lowland Vietnamese. This problem also vexed US/GVN relations, because the U.S. Special Forces advisors generally got along well with the tribesmen, and some may have sympathized with them; and in particular, it added to Khanh's suspicions of U.S. intentions. Two or three Rhades had become officers in ARVN, and Westmoreland suggested using them as intermediaries with the rebelling units; but Khanh turned the idea down flat. He also declined to make concessions to Montagnard discontent. Then Taylor sent General DePuy as his intermediary to tell the Rhades they were off the payroll until they submitted to GVN authority. This move produced a temporary settlement, but trouble continued to boil up for another two or three weeks.

The High National Council began its deliberations on September 24; Taylor took the occasion to comment that Khanh conceded too much to organized pressure groups. Noting that GVN effectiveness and morale had virtually collapsed, he disliked the purely civilian makeup of the Council, and hoped that it would take its time about writing a permanent constitution. GVN set a deadline of October 27 for this exercise. Watching on the sidelines, here as at other times, Taylor opposed unsettling change, and opposed excessive civilian influence because of their presumed factionalism and lack of fervor in prosecuting the war.

F. THE HNC INSTALLS CIVILIAN LEADERSHIP, OCTOBER, 1964

The view that bombing the North was the key to success received a fresh airing, this time in a public revelation of what USG was thinking. Assistant Secretary of State William Bundy said in a speech delivered in Tokyo on September 30 that such bombing would cut down the threat to GVN in a matter of months.

Early in October, Khanh succeeded in exiling General Khiem, a member of the triumvirate, whom he had suspected of instigating the September 13 coup attempt; Khiem became Ambassador to the U.S.

As the HNC deliberated, State sent Taylor its guidance on the USG position during the formation of the new government-to-be:

> 1. We concur that we must . . . avoid any public espousal of charter or people, although we will undoubtedly be charged in any event with considerable responsibility for the selection of the form and personnel of any new government . . . We cannot privately disclaim any preference for individuals or form of government because of our intense interest in seeing a new government having sound organization, able members, and broad basis of popular support. We also want to avoid any private impression that we are dumping Khanh and that as far as we are concerned everything is up for grabs . . .
> 2. As seen from here, evolving political situation in Saigon contains at least two major problems for U.S. EmbTel 1054 strongly suggests HNC is leaning toward parliamentary form of government with all the weaknesses which were so apparent in the French 4th Republic. The second problem, highlighted in EmbTel 983, is to avoid a sharp split between the only real powers in the country, the military, and the civilian HNC. This split could occur over form of government or its personnel. U.S. must try to bring stable government of persons acceptable to both military and civilian.

Then there followed three suggestions on form of government and a paragraph on people.

> 7. Finally, there is a delicate problem, during this transition period, in our relations with General Khanh and his military supporters. The present truth is they hold such power as exists in SVN. Their acceptance is prerequisite to any successful constitution of a new government. Our problem is that we must not abandon one horse before there is another horse which can run the course. I would suggest: That you have full and frank discussion with General Khanh about how he sees the development of the situation so that what we ourselves do is in consonance with the consensus among military and civilian leadership which it is now our highest purpose to build . . . The important thing is that during this period we not find ourselves in a position where there is no one with whom we can work.

Meanwhile, Minh allied himself with the High National Council to put provisions for civilian control in the new constitution opposed by Khanh and the now powerful junior membership of the MRC. Taylor tried to persuade them to resolve their differences quietly, and to make sure a widely acceptable document was cleared all around before publication. Thinking that things were more likely to get worse rather than better, Secretary Rusk suggested that the USG should prefer Khanh and the "Young Turks" to Minh and the HNC:

> Bob McNamara and I have following reaction to political moves you have reported during last week.
> A struggle seems to be developing between Minh and HNC on one hand and Khanh and Young Turk military on the other. Between these two groups it seems to us our best interests are served if Khanh comes out on top . . . Problem is to get government with Khanh in a leading role, ideally as chief executive unless some strong civilian shows up who is not now apparent. At least Khanh should remain as leader of Army with co-equal position to civilians in a government, whose mandate will run for at least 18 months . . . We believe it should be made clear that U.S. does not repeat not support Minh as powerful chief executive.
> This is consensus here and we would much appreciate your comment.

Once again the policy was to limit change and to limit civilian influence. Taylor replied:

> The views which you and Bob McNamara express . . . are very much the same conclusions we have reached and acted upon here.

Minh expected to be the new Chief of State and to name the Prime Minister. Taylor talked to him about the selection problem, saying that he wished to be consulted. Minh asked Taylor's view of Saigon's Mayor Huong and of Minister of the Interior Vien. Taylor diplomatically gave his very high opinion of Vien. State urged Taylor to use his influence freely while he could still influence the shape of the new government.

The High National Council finished on schedule on October 27, and surprised the Embassy by electing its chairman, Phan Khac Suu, an elderly and respected politician, to be the new chief of State. Religious group leaders pressured the HNC into this decision at the last minute. Taylor had hoped and expected Minh would be elected; although the action met Khanh's promise in August that the military would get out of politics. Khanh and his cabinet resigned and went into caretaker status. The HNC stayed on as the legislative body. Taylor tried to make the best of it, but protested to Suu about the failure of the HNC to consult him about Suu's election; Suu responded by discussing the composition of the new cabinet with him, naming Huong as Prime Minister. Taylor also gave Suu the usual polite lecture about the need for strong government. State went along reluctantly with the new government; Khanh and the Young Turks also went along.

G. A QUIET NOVEMBER, 1964

At the end of October, the VC staged a mortar attack on the Bien Hoa air base, destroying several U.S. aircraft and killing four Americans. Taylor urged a reprisal bombing like the one in August following the Tonkin Gulf incidents, but Washington declined to approve. Huong told Taylor he hoped the U.S. would respond, in a meeting to consult on Huong's pending cabinet appointments, but the issue was already decided and Taylor had to discourage the idea.

The new cabinet froze out Minh, no doubt to improve the palatability of the new government to the dominant group in the MRC. Minh then packed up and went abroad on a good will tour; Taylor found the cash cost to the U.S. running high, but recommended paying it. In his overall assessment of the balance of power in the new government, Taylor thought that the MRC had allowed civilians to get power (as promised in August) because the MRC feared mob violence, and thought it expedient to let the civilians make a mess of it so that military rule would again become acceptable. That is, he hoped and expected that a military return to power would become widely acceptable. Taylor thought the overall political prospects were "faintly encouraging." Commenting in reply, State once again emphasized the accepted links between U.S. commitment and GVN morale and efforts:

> A key element in either the immediate program or the long-range course of action will be the nature of our discussions with the GVN. Sullivan has impressed on us the seriousness of SVN doubts as to U.S. intentions . . . More basically, we believe no course of action can succeed unless we are able to stiffen GVN to set its house in order and take every possible measure for political stability and to push forward the pacification program.

These links received a full airing between Taylor and State and between Taylor and Huong. To State, Taylor said:

> We have had a great deal of discussion here as to the minimum level of government required to justify mounting military pressure against the North. I would describe that minimum government as one capable of maintaining law and order in the urban areas, of securing vital military bases from VC attacks, and giving its efforts with those of USG. As Reference B indicates we do not expect such a government for 3 to 4 months . . . perhaps not then if the current attempts to chip away at the Huong government continue. . . . However, if the government falters and gives good reason to believe that it will never attain the desired level of performance, I would favor going against the North anyway. The

purpose of such an attack would be to give pulmotor treatment for a government *in extremis* and to make sure that the DRV does not get off unscathed in any final settlement.

In his conversation with Huong, the latter requested:

> That I obtain a reaffirmation of U.S. policy toward VN. Huong referred to U.S. action in Gulf of Tonkin and the lift in morale VN had received at this display of determination by the U.S. to strike against the North. Subsequently, however, U.S. had appeared to emphasize almost exclusively necessity considering war within SVN itself. I responded that reciprocal responsibilities were involved. On the GVN side it was essential that a stable government be established capable of directing affairs of the Nation and particularly of directing the national pacification effort . . . Should his government demonstrate it was capable of achieving satisfactory degree of government stability and effectiveness a wider range of possibilities would undoubtedly be open for discussion . . . Huong indicated his complete understanding of the situation.

At this time another case of non-consultation blew up. RVNAF reorganization plans had passed back and forth between the MRC and MACV since July. Then, on November 10, the MRC produced a plan that differed materially from the last one MACV had seen, Huong signed it, and it was published on November 11 before MACV could review it. Westmoreland and Taylor both protested to their respective contacts in the strongest terms; the decrees were withdrawn, changed to MACV's satisfaction, and reissued.

On November 26, Westmoreland squelched an apparent coup planned by Ky. He heard of unusual activity at VNAF headquarters and asked Ky to his office. Ky bluntly stated a case for a change of leadership. Westmoreland said:

> After patiently listening to the foregoing, I informed Ky in no uncertain terms that the U.S. government would not support a change of command by other than orderly and legal process. (This statement was cleared in advance with Ambassador Johnson.) Ky was obviously impressed by my statement and said that he would not take action for three months, but if the situation continued to deteriorate he would be constrained to act in national interest.

This episode was the first sign of Young Turk action against the new government, and the first recorded sign of Ky's own ambitions. The U.S. reaction underlined the USG's opposition to sudden change without broad support, even though it was expected that the military would return to power eventually.

H. A LECTURE AND A PROGRAM FOR GVN

NSAM 314, September 10, which had called for actions to strengthen GVN, had set wheels in motion toward spelling out a U.S. program within SVN to complement the contemplated actions against the North. Taylor returned to Washington for consultations at the end of November. In the NSC, he argued that a strong message to GVN about its problems would most likely produce the optimum response. He said a threat by the U.S. to withdraw unless they improve would be too much of a gamble. There was no discussion of intermediate leverage or sanctions between this extreme threat and none at all. The discussion also highlighted the fear that GVN might collapse or be replaced by neutralists who would ask the U.S. to withdraw; all agreed that neutralism could not be accepted, and that the U.S. should minimize this risk by full backing of the existing GVN.

Taylor returned to Saigon with an approved statement and program for GVN that embodied his principal recommendations. Its public aspect was an across the board increase in the approved strengths of all elements of RVNAF and the paramilitary, in support of the Hop Tac pacification plan and its outgrowths that had been in the works since July. Its unannounced aspect included a rationale showing a clear shift of emphasis from the views at the highest levels that had developed in the first half of the year. As presented to GVN, it said:

> It was the clear conclusion of the recent review in Washington of the situation in South Vietnam that the unsatisfactory progress being made in the Pacification Program was the result of two primary causes from which many secondary causes stem. The primary cause has been the governmental instability in Saigon, and the second the continued reinforcement and direction of the Viet Cong by the Government of North Vietnam. It was recognized that to change the downward trend of events, it will be necessary to deal adequately with both of these factors.
>
> However it was the clear view that these factors are not of equal importance. First and above all, there must be a stable, effective Vietnamese Government able to conduct a successful campaign against the Viet Cong even if the aid from North Vietnam for the Viet Cong should end. It was the view that, while the elimination of North Vietnam intervention would raise morale on our side and make it easier for the Government of Vietnam to function, it would not in itself bring an end to Viet Cong insurgency. It would rather be an important contributory factor to the creation of conditions favoring a successful campaign against the Viet Cong within South Vietnam.
>
> Thus, since action against North Vietnam would only be contributory and not central to winning the war against the Viet Cong, it would not be prudent to incur the risks which are inherent in an expansion of hostilities until there were a government in Saigon capable of handling the serious problems inevitably involved in such an expansion, and capable of promptly and fully exploiting the favorable effects which may be anticipated if we are successful in terminating the support and direction of the Viet Cong by North Vietnam.

Then it went to the point:

> . . . In the view of the United States, there is a certain minimum condition to be brought about in South Vietnam before new measures against North Vietnam would be either justified or practicable. At the minimum, the Government in Saigon should be able to speak for and to its people who will need special guidance and leadership throughout the coming critical period. The Government should be capable of maintaining law and order in the principal centers of population, assuring their effective execution by military and police forces completely responsive to its authority. The Government must have at its disposal means to cope

promptly and effectively with enemy reactions which must be expected to result from any change in the pattern of our operations.

To bring about this condition will require a demonstration of far greater national unity against the Communist enemy at this critical time than exists at present. It is a matter of greatest difficulty for the United States Government to require great sacrifices by American citizens on behalf of South Vietnam when reports from Saigon repeatedly give evidence of heedless self-interest and shortsightedness among so many major political groups.

As a quid pro quo, it said:

> . . . While the Government of Vietnam is making progress toward achieving the goals set forth above, the United States Government would be willing to strike harder at infiltration routes in Laos and at sea. With respect to Laos, the United States Government is prepared, in conjunction with the Royal Laos Government, to add United States air power as needed to restrict the use of Laotian territory as a route of infiltration into South Vietnam. With respect to the sea, the United States Government would favor an intensification of those covert maritime operations which have proved their usefulness in harassing the enemy. The United States would regard the combination of these operations in Laos and at sea as constituting Phase I of a measured increase of military pressures directed toward reducing infiltration and warning the Government of North Vietnam of the risks it is running.
>
> . . . If the Government of Vietnam is able to demonstrate its effectiveness and capability of achieving the minimum conditions set forth above, the United States Government is prepared to consider a program of direct military pressure on North Vietnam as Phase II . . .
>
> As contemplated by the United States Government, Phase II would, in general terms, constitute a series of air attacks on North Vietnam progressively mounting in scope and intensity for the purpose of convincing the leaders of North Vietnam that it is to their interest to cease aid to the Viet Cong and respect the independence and security of South Vietnam . . .

In short, the USG offered to add some of its aircraft immediately to the Vietnamese ones already bombing the Laotian corridor, in exchange for a GVN promise of a shift to more energy and effectiveness; then when such energy and effectiveness actually became visible, the USG promised, the USG would begin bombing North Vietnam.

The program included the following areas in which progress would aid pacification and would measure the GVN's effectiveness:

1. and 2. Increasing RVNAF, paramilitary, and police to and above existing authorized strengths.
3. Better performance by civilian and military officials.
4. Speeding up budgetary procedures and spending in the provinces.
5. Strengthening the province chiefs.
6. Strengthening police powers.
7. More vigor in Hop Tac.
8. After a delay, "review cases of political prisoners from previous regimes."

To leave no doubt about what it wanted, the program said:

> Better performance in the prosecution of the war against the Viet Cong needs to be accompanied by actions to convince the people of the interest of their government in their well-being. Better performance in itself is perhaps the most convincing evidence but can be supplemented by such actions as frequent visits by officials and ranking military officers to the provinces for personal orientation and "trouble shooting." The available information media offer a channel of communication with the people which could be strengthened and more efficiently employed. The physical appearance of the cities, particularly of Saigon, shows a let-down in civic pride which, if corrected, would convey a message of governmental effectiveness to their inhabitants. Similarly, in the country an expanded rural development program could carry the government's presence into every reasonably secure village and hamlet.
>
> If governmental performance and popular appeal are significantly improved, there will be little difficulty in establishing confidence in the government. However, this confidence should be expressed, not merely implied. It is particularly important that the military leaders continue to express public confidence in the government and the firm intention to uphold it. While not giving an impression of submitting to pressure, the government might explore honorable ways of conciliating its most important opponents among the minority groups. The United States Government is prepared to help by oral statements of support and by further assistance to show our faith in the future of South Vietnam.

Taylor, Westmoreland, and Johnson met Huong, Deputy Premier Vien, and Khanh on December 7 to present them with the new U.S. program. The Vietnamese group politely suggested that they did not know what the USG meant by a stable effective government able to campaign successfully against the Viet Cong, and able to speak for and to its people. Moreover, they noted that the U.S. program said nothing about Viet Cong use of Cambodia. At the next meeting, on December 9, Taylor gave them the paper "Actions Designed to Strengthen the Government of Vietnam," covering the eight areas of desired progress and measures of GVN effectiveness listed above. The Prime Minister replied that the issue of political prisoners from previous regimes was a very delicate matter; Khanh said there was no problem about military support of the existing government. Taylor cabled President Johnson that the USG proposals:

> have been received with an understanding reasonableness in the light of the current situation but without great enthusiasm since they necessarily omit some of the more dramatic actions which the Vietnamese desire.

The only decisions reached were for joint study and consultation. This was the last time the USG tried to set GVN performance preconditions for U.S. force use and deployments. Its effect, if any, was the opposite of that intended.

I. THE GOVERNMENT'S SUPPORT VANISHES, AND TAYLOR CONFRONTS THE GENERALS

A new threat of crisis boiled up immediately; first, the leading Buddhists declared their opposition to the government and went on a forty-eight hour hunger strike. Huong stood fast, but then the Young Turks picked a fight through a sudden demand that the HNC dismiss nine generals and thirty other officers. (These included some, like Minh and the "Dalat" generals expelled by Khanh, who no longer had jobs but still held their rank and received Army pay.) Taylor backed Huong and the HNC against all comers, and tried to get Buddhists and others to support them. The HNC refused to retire the 39 officers. But the Young Turks, playing for Buddhist support, would not be denied. In the early morning hours of Sunday, December 20, they arrested twenty-two or more officials and politicians, including several members of the HNC, and made dozens of other political arrests. They also created an "Armed Forces Council" over or replacing the MRC, to consolidate their power.

Through Huong and indirect contacts, Taylor found out about the dissolution of the HNC several hours before Khanh announced it at a press conference; and one hour before the conference Khanh spoke to Taylor about it. Taylor protested in the strongest terms, but without effect; Khanh went ahead with the announcement. Taylor and Johnson also met with the Young Turk leaders, Ky, Thieu, Thi, and Cang, and gave them a stern lecture, speaking, as he later put it, "as one soldier to another." As recorded just afterward by the U.S. participants, the meeting went as follows:

> . . . AMBASSADOR TAYLOR: Do all of you understand English? (Vietnamese officers indicated they did, although the understanding of General Thi was known to be weak.) I told you all clearly at General Westmoreland's dinner we Americans were tired of coups. Apparently I wasted my words. Maybe this is because something is wrong with my French because you evidently didn't understand. I made it clear that all the military plans which I know you would like to carry out are dependent on governmental stability. Now you have made a real mess. We cannot carry you forever if you do things like this. Who speaks for this group? Do you have a spokesman?
>
> GENERAL KY: I am not the spokesman for the group but I do speak English. I will explain why the Armed Forces took this action last night.
>
> We understand English very well. We are aware of our responsibilities, we are aware of the sacrifices of our people over twenty years. We know you want stability, but you cannot have stability until you have unity . . . But still there are rumors of coups and doubts among groups. We think these rumors come from the HNC, not as an organization but from some of its members. Both military and civilian leaders regard the presence of these people in the HNC as divisive of the Armed Forces due to their influence.
>
> Recently the Prime Minister showed us a letter he had received from the Chairman of the HNC. This letter told the Prime Minister to beware of the military, and said that maybe the military would want to come back to power. Also the HNC illegally sought to block the retirement of the generals that the Armed Forces Council unanimously recommended be retired in order to improve unity in the Armed Forces.
>
> GENERAL THIEU: The HNC cannot be bosses because of the Constitution. Its members must prove that they want to fight.
>
> GENERAL KY: It looks as though the HNC does not want unity. It does not want to fight the Communists.
>
> It has been rumored that our action of last night was an intrigue of Khanh against Minh, who must be retired. Why do we seek to retire these generals? Because they had their chance and did badly . . .
>
> Yesterday we met, twenty of us, from 1430 to 2030. We reached agree-

ment that we must take some action. We decided to arrest the bad members of the HNC, bad politicians, bad student leaders, and the leaders of the Committee of National Salvation, which is a Communist organization. We must put the trouble-making organizations out of action and ask the Prime Minister and the Chief of State to stay in office.

After we explain to the people why we did this at a press conference, we would like to return to our fighting units. We have no political ambitions. We seek strong, unified, and stable Armed Forces to support the struggle and a stable government. Chief of State Suu agrees with us. General Khanh saw Huong who also agreed.

We did what we thought was good for this country; we tried to have a civilian government clean house. If we have achieved it, fine. We are now ready to go back to our units.

AMBASSADOR TAYLOR: I respect the sincerity of you gentlemen. Now I would like to talk to you about the consequences of what you have done. But first, would any of the other officers wish to speak?

ADMIRAL CANG: It seems that we are being treated as though we were guilty. What we did was good and we did it only for the good of the country.

AMBASSADOR TAYLOR: Now let me tell you how I feel about it, what I think the consequences are: first of all, this is a military coup that has destroyed the government-making process that, to the admiration of the whole world, was set up last fall largely through the statesman-like acts of the Armed Forces.

You cannot go back to your units, General Ky. You military are now back in power. You are up to your necks in politics.

Your statement makes it clear that you have constituted yourselves again substantially as a Military Revolutionary Committee. The dissolution of the HNC was totally illegal. Your decree recognized the Chief of State and the Huong Government but this recognition is something that you could withdraw. This will be interpreted as a return of the military to power . . .

AMBASSADOR TAYLOR: Who commands the Armed Forces? General Khanh?

GENERAL KY: Yes, sir . . .

GENERAL THIEU: In spite of what you say, it should be noted that the Vietnamese Commander-in-Chief is in a special situation. He therefore needs advisors. We do not want to force General Khanh; we advise him. We will do what he orders . . .

AMBASSADOR TAYLOR: Would your officers be willing to come into a government if called upon to do so by Huong? I have been impressed by the high quality of many Vietnamese officers. I am sure that many of the most able men in this country are in uniform. Last fall when the HNC and Huong Government was being formed, I suggested to General Khanh there should be some military participation, but my suggestions were not accepted. It would therefore be natural for some of them now to be called upon to serve in the government. Would you be willing to do so? . . .

GENERAL KY: Nonetheless, I would object to the idea of the military going back into the government right away. People will say it is a military coup.

AMBASSADOR TAYLOR and AMBASSADOR JOHNSON: (Together) People will say it anyway. . . .

AMBASSADOR TAYLOR: You have destroyed the Charter. The Chief of State will still have to prepare for elections. Nobody believes that the Chief of State has either the power or the ability to do this without the HNC or some other advisory body. If I were the Prime Minister, I would simply overlook the destruction of the HNC. But we are preserving the HNC itself. You need a legislative branch and you need this particular step in the formation of a government with National Assembly . . .

AMBASSADOR TAYLOR: It should be noted that Prime Minister Huong has not accepted the dissolution of the HNC . . .

GENERAL THIEU: What kind of concession does Huong want from us?

Ambassador Taylor again noted the need for the HNC function.

GENERAL KY: Perhaps it is better if we now let General Khanh and Prime Minister Huong talk.

GENERAL THIEU: After all, we did not arrest all the members of the HNC. Of nine members we detained only five. These people are not under arrest. They are simply under controlled residence . . .

AMBASSADOR TAYLOR: Our problem now, gentlemen, is to organize our work for the rest of the day. For one thing, the government will have to issue a communique.

GENERAL THIEU: We will still have a press conference this afternoon but only to say why we acted as we did.

AMBASSADOR TAYLOR: I have real troubles on the U.S. side. I don't know whether we will continue to support you after this. Why don't you tell your friends before you act? I regret the need for my blunt talk today but we have lots at stake . . .

AMBASSADOR TAYLOR: And was it really all that necessary to carry out the arrests that very night? Couldn't this have been put off a day or two? . . .

In taking a friendly leave, Ambassador Taylor said: You people have broken a lot of dishes and now we have to see how we can straighten out this mess.

Amid the hustle and bustle of meetings between MACV officers, Embassy officials, and their Vietnamese counterparts, Khanh and the Young Turks, stood fast.

On the next day, December 21, Taylor suggested to Khanh that he resign and leave the country. This meeting brought to a head the Khanh-Taylor personal feud which then became public and continued for the balance of Khanh's tenure. Taylor's report of the meeting said his suggestion that Khanh leave the country came in response to Khanh's asking whether he should leave. But Khanh told a different story to the AFC, who were still smarting from the sharp interchange that Ky, Thieu, Thi and Cang had had with Taylor. Immediately they accused Taylor of interfering in GVN affairs. Commenting afterward, he said:

If the military get away with this irresponsible intervention in government and with flaunting proclaimed U.S. policy, there will be no living with them in the future.

State supported Taylor in taking a strong line to bring the situation under control. It approved a Westmoreland proposal, sent by military channels to State, that Huong get the credit for dismissing Khanh and that MACV should bargain with the Armed Forces Council to offer a quid pro quo for reinstating the HNC. State spelled out the quid pro quo in detail:

> In support of your efforts persuade military to at least partially undo damage [Sunday's] actions, we have also been considering possible leverage we might apply in event you conclude it was necessary.
>
> If dispute continues unresolved, most obvious action might be withholding approval any pending U.S. assistance actions and letting this become known. You are in best position to evaluate whether these would impress generals or conversely hurt Huong's position. In addition, following steps aimed more specifically at military have occurred to us:
>
> 1. Suspend operation Barrel Roll—not certain it would affect generals —might have wrong impact on Hanoi—obviously generals couldn't be told because that would imply commitment to resume if they behave.
> 2. Instruct all or selected Corps or division advisors make known our dissatisfaction, perhaps suspending for time being further contacts with counterparts.
> 3. Stand down FARMGATE.
> 4. Suspend logistical airlift where critical supply shortages do not exist.
>
> On balance, we inclined believe none except possibly 1st and 2nd steps would produce desired results. Obviously any would hamper over-all war effort, especially if continued for very long.
>
> We have also considered and rejected possibility of cutting essentials POL and direct military supplies. Similarly we do not favor suspension or interruption CIP, since it would primarily affect civilian confidence in Huong government.

Although Khanh talked to Taylor about travel arrangements for himself and several other generals on the 22nd, the Young Turks had their backs up (or were convinced they could do what they pleased), and all stood fast. Khanh having rallied the military behind him, attacked Taylor for his undiplomatic actions. He spoke to the nation attacking communism and colonialism, the latter an inference to the domineering position of Taylor. In a message to the President on the 22nd, Taylor commented:

> Generals acting greatly offended by my disapproval of their recent actions privately expressed to four of their number and resent our efforts to strengthen Huong government against their pressures. One unfortunate effect has been to drive them closer to Khanh who has sensed the opportunity to solidify his position.

He feared Khanh would air the quarrel publicly. Rusk cabled support:

> I wish to compliment you on the vigor with which you have pursued this issue of unity since your return from Washington.

But Taylor backed off from the sanctions idea. Possibly still hoping that Khanh would go, he said there was no need for action but that the option should be kept open. In particular, he saw no value in suspending the bombing of Laos.

Also on the 22nd, while talking to Taylor of leaving, Khanh met with the Young Turks and agreed to break openly with Taylor by seeking his recall. State continued to back a tough line with them, and rejected Taylor's suggestion of a diversion in the form of a reprisal bombing on North Vietnam for the Brinks BOQ bombing early in the week.

> Hanoi would hardly read into it any strong or continuing signal in view overall confusion in Saigon . . . There might be suspicion, at least internationally, that BOQ bombing was not in fact done by VC."

Taylor urged Huong to insist on restoration of the HNC and declare the generals insubordinate if they refused. Khanh and the generals attacked Taylor publicly on December 23, as Taylor had feared, charging him with insulting them and abusing his power. Then on December 24, Taylor responded in kind, telling the press his version of the Décember 20 confrontation, and suggesting that Khanh had outstayed his usefulness.

Khanh then threatened privately to declare Taylor *persona non grata;* the Embassy replied that asking Taylor to leave was equivalent to asking the U.S. to leave. The implied threat of U.S. withdrawal was enough to stop the Khanh move, if he was ever serious about it. Taylor then suggested that Alex Johnson and the generals should form an ad hoc joint arbitration committee to resolve the differences between Khanh and Taylor. The idea was evidently novel enough to distract Khanh and the generals or to satisfy their dignity; it disconnected the buttons that had been pushed when Khanh and Taylor each said he wanted the other to leave the country. The ad hoc committee never met, but the proposal generated calm discussion between the Embassy and the generals for several days and allowed them to cool off gracefully.

However, the basic issue of the future of the HNC and of civilian government remained unresolved. Huong consulted with Taylor continuously, and followed some of his advice, but stopped short of taking the strong public stance he urged. On December 31, Taylor said to Washington that the USG might have to accept a military government in Saigon, though he said that Khanh must not head it. He said that plans for "Phase II" (bombing the North) should take into account various possibilities within GVN. Although Taylor had earlier favored the military's return to power, he objected to the means and to the timing of their present action.

J. ONGOING PROGRAMS, SECOND HALF 1964

While the political crises of Ambassador Taylor's first six months in Saigon built up to comic opera proportions, MACV and the country team struggled valiantly to conduct business as usual.

In March, MACV J-1 had completed a comprehensive review of ARVN personnel policies, the Murday Report, and forwarded it to JGS for action. A tally at the end of the year indicated progress on only 16 of 28 specific recommendations. One that received no response was the suggestion that the officer appointment base be expanded. In May, the Secretary of Defense had ordered COMUSMACV to develop, jointly with GVN, procedures for programming pacification operations with time-phased requirements for manpower and money. A joint, combined (MACV-USOM-GVN) committee was established. It had completed a programming document in June. After approval by RVNAF and MACV, joint US-GVN teams visited each Corps to acquaint selected personnel with the documents. As of August 31, fewer than half the provinces had submitted pacification plans; so the teams again visited each province to reinstruct province chiefs and sector advisors. All province reports were finally received by October. In July, the first Senior Advisors Monthly Report (SAME) was submitted. These put MACV in a better position to advise, and in October it sent a detailed letter of deficiencies to CINCRVNAF.

A joint combat effectiveness inspection team started its work, and at year's end the ARVN IG faced the question whether the refresher course at the National Training Center was needed for two battalions declared ineffective by COMUSMACV. In October, U.S. advisors to RVNAF units submitted the first semi-annual report of their personal observations of the treatment and use of MAP equipment. Deficiencies were noted in a letter to JGS. In one instance it was found that ordnance vans were being converted into rolling quarters for generals. After a threat to withdraw the vans, the fault was corrected and the vans were returned to their authorized use.

On October 5, COMUSMACV forwarded to the Embassy the report of a month-long study instigated by the Ambassador on how to revitalize the entire civic action program. It recommended that a USOM-USIS-MACV study group develop a joint, integrated mechanism to guide and coordinate civic action. The groups' recommendations were to provide a basis for discussions with the Vietnamese on how best to channel and revitalize the combined civic action effort.

On the subject of command relationships, JCS looked ahead to the possible deployment of U.S. ground forces and anticipated operational control of RVN forces in combined operations. However, that idea would be dropped later.

Following a Taylor-Khanh agreement to launch "Hop Tac" on October 1, USOM and the Vietnamese NSC met on September 25 to discuss pacification, after which Taylor commented:

> In general, I consider the meeting was satisfactory continuation of our bilateral effort and that top priority is at last being given to Hop Tac operation. Also that general result of meeting focused attention on priority problems. The pay-off will be quality of follow-up.

State suggested decentralization of pacification control to Corps and Province, to bypass the central government; USOM disagreed. MACV contacted all senior RVNAF officers and found them taking a responsible attitude toward continuing the war effort; however, MACV noted that the coup leaders had talked the same way just before the September 13 coup attempt. Therefore MACV was candidly sceptical.

In response, a COMUSMACV memorandum of November 14 entitled "Assumption by US of Operational Control of the Pacification Program in SVN," states his position on the US role and is indicative of his later views on combined command. He recognized that any plan to encourage GVN in its efforts should include measures for developing US approved plans, as well as means for controlling money and people during execution of plans, and he envisaged an arrangement whereby GVN agencies would be provided complete planning guidance. He saw a danger of exerting influence over GVN which might be interpreted as excessive and which might boomerang on US interests. Instead, he suggested, "as a less drastic alternative, the Hop Tac idea might be extended to each of the other three tactical zones."

As discussed more fully in *Re-emphasis on Pacification 1965–67*, Hop Tac (working together) was formally proposed at a high level in the US government by Ambassador Lodge on his way home in July 1964. Ambassador Taylor and General Westmoreland implemented the idea. It tied together the pacification plans of the seven provinces around Saigon to insure security and extend government control. A headquarters for US Hop Tac elements was established in

Saigon. The Vietnamese set up a parallel organization primarily to satisfy the US, for their group had no authority or influence.

Meanwhile, the US/GVN study and planning activity continued and gave the impression of accomplishment. A US/GVN Survey Team reviewed RVNAF structure requirements for supporting the GVN National Pacification Plan. After visits to each corps headquarters, it proposed two alternative force increases, one to achieve progress in priority one Hop Tac areas, the other to attain more overall progress. On November 24, COMUSMACV formally requested approval of the first alternative from CINCPAC while at the same time the US Embassy recommended approval to the State Department. Meetings of USOM/NSC mentioned above (pp. 326 and 332) continued till December 5, after which the crisis of the Ambassador's return and its sequel stopped all pretense of joint pacification planning for several weeks.

But the Joint General Staff accepted all MACV suggestions on how RVNAF should be employed to improve the pacification program and issued its implementing Directive A-B 139 as a Christmas present on December 25, 1964, in mid-crisis.

The USMACV staff reviewed the RVN Defense Budget for 1965 and US Mission approval was received in late 1964. However, on order of the Ambassador, due to the political crisis, MACV withheld the budget from GVN until January 13, 1965.

K. *JANUARY, 1965: PRELUDE TO THE BOMBING*

The first week of January was filled with comings and goings with the issue of the HNC's dissolution still unresolved. The Embassy supported Huong publicly and privately, but stopped short of threatening U.S. withdrawal and admitted indirectly to Huong that the U.S. might be forced to accept military government. Then on January 7, the generals backed off slightly and reached a compromise solution, which they announced January 9 amid rumors of a military takeover. The Armed Forces Council and Khanh agreed to release the HNC prisoners and to continue backing civilian government, referring to their August promises; the civilian GVN would convene a new civilian group to legislate and write a new constitution, preparatory to Assembly elections. Taylor saw the statement before its release, and accepted it as the best available compromise. It was followed by a statement agreed on January 11 to patch up US/GVN relations, at which time Khanh agreed also to put several of the Young Turks in the cabinet. The crisis seemed to be over.

However, the end was not yet in sight. The Buddhists started demonstrating and demanding that Huong resign. On January 14, Taylor reacted to Khanh's proposals on the new cabinet by suggesting that he was moving with unseemly haste. Taylor received a complete cabinet list on January 18, and Khanh conferred with Westmoreland on the effects of cabinet roles for the generals on the 19th. Cabinet installation was scheduled for the 19th. However, at almost the last minute Khanh asked for postponement of the cabinet installation, saying afterward that Huong had defaulted on promises to change some of the civilian ministers. Leading Buddhists went on another hunger strike, and a new crisis built up; in Hue the USIS building was sacked and burned, and the USIS building in Saigon was sacked. On the 24th, they demanded that all Vietnamese businessmen, night clubs, etc., refuse to sell to Americans, and a majority apparently complied. On the 25th, Khanh, having allied himself with the Buddhists, told Deputy Ambassador Johnson that Huong and President Suu wanted to resign and let the military take over, as demanded by the Buddhists. Johnson replied that the Buddhists must not be allowed to veto the government, and that the military must not take over.

Then on January 27, the AFC voted no confidence in the Suu-Huong government and directed Khanh to take charge and resolve the crisis. Taylor's comments to State made it clear that events were entirely out of his control; again he objected to the means and to the timing of the military return to power. When he raised the possibility of non-recognition, State authorized him to use his own judgment but advised him to play along with Khanh for the time being, while scouting around for fresh options. Although Suu was technically ousted, he stayed on at Khanh's request; and Oanh again became acting Prime Minister.

In the midst of the crisis Westmoreland obtained his first authority to use U.S. forces for combat within South Vietnam. Arguing that the VC might go for a spectacular victory during the disorders, he asked for and received authority to use U.S. jet aircraft in a strike role in emergencies, subject to Embassy approval in each instance. This move finessed all previous ideas of using potential U.S. force commitments as leverage to bring the GVN into line; but these ideas had no doubt been abandoned anyhow.

III. THE U.S. ENTERS THE WAR: FLAMING DART TO THE STEADY INFLUX OF U.S. FORCES, JUNE, 1965

A. "PHASE II" BEGINS AND COUPS CONTINUE, FEBRUARY, 1965

While the Embassy stood by doing what little it could to undercut Khanh's personal position, VC attacks on the American advisors' barracks at Pleiku, and on three other installations, provided the pretext for US/VNAF bombing attacks on infiltration staging areas in the southernmost province of North Vietnam, February 7-8. Acting Prime Minister Oanh spoke for GVN during the coordination of the attacks and announcements. (The raids were called reprisals, as was the subsequent raid on February 12 following the attacks on the American barracks at Quihon.) U.S. dependents were ordered to leave SVN.

McGeorge Bundy was in town, and in keeping with the going tactics, stayed at arms length from Khanh, though meeting him and the generals socially. As an aside at this point, Taylor gave one last blow to the idea that cutting off the flow of help from the North would turn the tide of the war against the VC: He remarked that perhaps the smell of victory within six months would now lead Khanh to take over again.

On his return to Washington, McGeorge Bundy wrote a Memorandum to the President, dated February 7, 1965. In evaluating the U.S. team and policy, he stated, "U.S. mission is composed of outstanding men and U.S. policy within Vietnam is mainly right and well directed." However, he proceeded to point out two important differences between his current assessment and that of the mission. Taylor had concluded that: (1) the Khanh government was impossible to work with, and (2) the Buddhists (Khanh's ally in the recent struggle) must be confronted and faced down, using force if necessary. Bundy disagreed on both points, stating that Khanh was still the best hope in sight in terms of pursuing the fight against the communists and that the Buddhists should be accommodated and incorporated rather than confronted.

With respect to the scheduled reprisal actions, he stated, "For immediate purposes, and especially for the initiation of reprisal policy, we believe the government need by no stronger than it is today with General Khanh as the focus of a raw power, while a weak caretaker government goes through the motions. Such a government can execute military decisions and it can give formal political support to joint US-GVN policy. That is about all it can do." He further stated that reprisal actions themselves should produce a favorable reaction which would provide an opportunity for increased U.S. influence in pressing for a more effective government.

He acknowledged the latent anti-American sentiments in the country and their potential explosiveness, as had been evidenced in Hue the preceding week. He noted that these feelings limited the pressure that the U.S. could bring to bear on ambitious forces like Khanh and the Buddhists.

On February 9, Taylor again firmly recommended that the program of continuous graduated attacks on North Vietnam should begin. Nothing but political turmoil had followed his early-December attempt to induce the GVN to do better by promising these attacks as a quid pro quo. Now he disregarded this idea, and spoke only of the hope that the attacks would convince North Vietnam to abide by the Geneva Accords of 1954 and 1962, and would unify and encourage the South Vietnamese. On February 13, State cabled authority to begin the plan of graduated strikes with Vietnamese participation. It directed Taylor to get GVN approval and to get their agreement to appear at the UN if that should prove necessary; the condition of stopping the bombing would be the halting of aid by North Vietnam to the VC.

State's guidance to Taylor on political matters was that the U.S. hand should not be too obvious in the government-shuffling outcome and that the power of the Buddhists and of the military must be reflected in the new government being formed. After two political hopefuls failed to round up enough support, Quat formed a cabinet starting February 16. The AFC chose to keep Suu as Chief of State and appointed a National Legislative Council of twenty members balanced to represent all interests including the military. The Buddhists quietly acquiesced in the new government, installed just in time to be greeted by a coup attempt.

On February 19, a new coup group (consisting of Thao and Phat among other neo-Diem proponents) seized most of Saigon, Tan Son Nhut airfield, and the radio station. In this instance, as in September, 1964, MACV had to intervene to stop Ky's threat of VNAF bombing; this time it would have been the airfield, with several thousand Americans in the area. By midnight the leading members of the AFC had rallied forces and faced down the coup group; and the next day they voted Khanh out. On February 24, Khanh left the country; the Embassy and Saigon settled back in relief. The bombing phase of graduated pressures on the North (Rolling Thunder) began, and the decision to land Marines at Danang was in the works. Taylor now opposed the introduction of U.S. combat forces in SVN—except for base security. His acquiescence in the Marine deployment to Danang was in large part due to Westmoreland's strong recommendation to do so.

B. THE CONTINUING CIVILIAN INTERREGNUM AND FIRST U.S. GROUND FORCES, MARCH–MAY, 1965

For several weeks an unaccustomed calm settled over US/GVN relations. The USG white paper on Vietnam issued February 28 without prior clearance with GVN caused no visible upset. The proposal to land the first two BLT's of

Marines received prompt approval in an amicable atmopshere in the first few days of March, and the III MEF became the III MAF without fanfare. An abortive Buddhist "peace" movement died away, and religious groups generally laid low.

Following a State message expressing renewed concern, the USOM resumed meetings with the Vietnamese Internal Security Council (an enlargement of its old NSC) on February 27 to discuss pacification.

It was agreed that both sides would prepare joint proposals for accelerating pacification and for solving manpower problems and go forward together in program for effective execution of agreed programs.

At a March 13 meeting, General Thang gave a "pessimistic but realistic" account of Binh Dinh Province, and Quat said measures would be taken to prevent the situation from spreading. The USG and GVN reverted to the pattern of a year earlier of urging and advice politely received.

Throughout early 1965, it was evident that Pacification plans were failing. Even Hop Tac was at a standstill. When a stop gap allocation of 3 million piasters per province was made, pending release of regular funds, province chiefs were reluctant to spend the funds. They wanted specific authority and direction from higher authorities.

Planning continued unabated between MACV and GVN. Development of a revised budget began on March 6, 1965, when guidelines for budget preparation were furnished the RVN Ministry of Defense. The proposed revision was duly received from RVN.

On March 24, Ambassador Taylor formulated a 41-point program for stability and pacification in preparation for a trip to Washington. This program, without any hint of leverage on GVN, in fact put pacification on the back burner, while main attention focused on bombing and deployments.

In April 1965, General "Little" Minh, Minister of Armed Forces, directed I, II, and IV Corps commanders to develop Hop Tac plans for their areas. The delay between the COMUSMACV memorandum of the previous December that recommended the extension and the order itself is not explained, but in May the Vietnamese indicated to the U.S. Ambassador their dissatisfaction with the Hop Tac program. The Vietnamese wanted to make Region A of the Hop Tac area part of the Capital Military Region and the remaining regions part of the III Corps Commander's area of responsibility. COMUSMACV told the mission council that the Hop Tac organization should be retained for the foreseeable future because Hop Tac had been unique in providing a forum for military and civil authorities to address common problems.

Quiet consultation continued on the evaluation of Vietnamese counterparts in the provinces, on Third Country Forces, on military and paramilitary pay, and so on. Following Taylor's return from Washington early in April, he presented his pacification ideas (now having the stamp of President Johnson's approval), and discreetly got approval for the deployment of the third of the Marine BLT's. Quat discussed the military leadership frankly with Taylor and Westmoreland, and around the middle of April started considering a move to clip their wings. On May 5, the AFC obligingly dissolved itself, and seemed to give Quat a free hand.

The Honolulu Conference of April 20, which rebuffed the idea of encadrement and U.S. takeover (discussed later), approved additional deployments and U.S. force to about 80,000 men and to introduce Korean and Australian troops.

After several days of hesitation, Quat approved the increases. Pacification, under the new name "Rural Construction," still gave no cause for rejoicing; and GVN resisted Taylor's proposal to install some civilians as province chiefs.

Analysis by members of the U.S. mission council of a RVNAF J-3 paper, "The Organization and Operations of the Pacification System," revealed considerable variance between U.S. and GVN views on:

> (1) The role of the corps commander in pacification.
>
> (2) The relationship of provinces with a proposed Bureau for Pacification Affairs.
>
> (3) The position of Minister of Interior in pacification.

MACV forwarded requirements to increase the number of subsector advisory teams to 180, of which 33 in particularly remote locations would be filled initially by Special Forces teams. It was envisioned that in case of escalation by the VC, these teams would perform appropriate civil affairs functions, provide intelligence, and support allied forces in many ways. Should the VC refrain from extensive overt action, the teams would push vigorous rural construction.

In the last half of May, fresh trouble blew up. After an alleged abortive coup attempt on May 20-21, and disorders in the streets, Quat tried to reshuffle his cabinet, without first clearing it with Suu. Suu objected, and the two disagreed on who had the right to decide; such a misunderstanding was understandable, in view of the lack of any recognized constitution and in view of the chaos of the preceding months. The crisis simmered past the end of May, and Taylor correctly predicted the end of civilian government, with evident relief.

C. FIRST MOVES ON COMMAND AND CONTROL, MARCH AND APRIL, 1965

When the Marines arrived in March, the control measure devised for the employment was the TAOR. Under the overall suzerainty of the VN Corps Commander, the Marines were given a well defined geographical area in which U.S. forces exercised command authority over military forces and for which the U.S. accepted defensive responsibility.

On March 3, Ambassador Taylor cabled his fears that GVN would "shuck off greater responsibility on the USG," and the same day, in another message, he said he had no idea what the GVN attitude to a Marine Landing Force might be.

The first battalion of Marines splashed ashore at Danang about 0900, March 8. The next day a second battalion came in by air.

The trip of Army Chief of Staff Johnson to Saigon in mid-March, 1965, signalled the beginning of consideration and planning for the introduction of significant numbers of ground combat forces. General Johnson observed in closing his report:

> In order for the USG to evaluate his (COMUSMACV's) request properly when submitted, a policy determination must be made in the very near future that will answer the question, what should the VN be expected to do for themselves and how much more the U.S. must contribute directly to the security of VN.

Secretary McNamara answered on the margin of his copy of the report, "Policy is: Anything that will strengthen the position of the GVN will be sent."

On March 8, Taylor talked with Prime Minister Quat about his concept of joint command, a matter which had been raised with General Johnson on the occasion of his visit March 6 (EmbTel 2877). Taylor found Quat's ideas very hazy, but:

> his purpose was very clear. He hopes by some joint command device to bring his maverick generals under the steadying influence of General Westmoreland. Taylor told him he sympathized with motive but had never hit upon a command relationship which offered much hope of accomplishing this end. Although Quat's ideas hard to disentangle, he seems to have in mind a mixed US/ARVN staff element reporting to General Westmoreland and a VN C/Staff. He visualizes the staff element as a clearing house for joint studies which would pass recommendations on to the two senior officers. By implication General Westmoreland would have the power of ultimate decision based upon an unofficial understanding which Quat hopes generals would accept. Quat concedes their acceptance far from certain.

Washington was looking toward combined command arrangements that would recognize that the U.S. was no longer limited to the role of advisors to RVNAF. When asked for his input COMUSMACV replied that gradual transition would be more palatable to GVN and suggested only cooperation in the initial phase, followed by establishment of a small combined coordinating staff headed jointly by himself and CINCRVNAF. The staff's powers would be limited solely to coordinating combined operations.

These comments were sketchy, but indicative, for in Saigon COMUSMACV and his staff were putting together the Commander's Estimate of the Situation, a standard document in the military planning process. Started on March 13, the day after General Johnson left Saigon and issued on March 26, it more clearly revealed the MACV concept of command. While recognizing that there was no longer an effective ARVN chain of command because of the irresponsible game of musical chairs among the top leadership, the estimate cautioned that the Vietnamese generals would accept integrated command only to the extent that the United States contributed troops; and it advised against U.S. commitment to any rigid arrangement *because GVN and RVNAF had not achieved sufficient political and military maturity.* MACV omitted further discussion of the function or authority of such integrated staffs. When command arrangements were covered in the detailed description of the most likely course of action, the intent was clear. U.S. commanders would control American troops except in certain clearly defined zones within which they would also be responsible for "controlling and coordinating" operations of both U.S. and RVN forces. A collateral function envisioned for each U.S. division command was that of Deputy Command Support to the ARVN Corps Commander.

D. THE RISE AND DECLINE OF ENCADREMENT, APRIL, 1965

Ambassador Taylor returned to Washington in late March and was present at the April 1-2 NSC meeting at which General Johnson's 21 recommendations and Taylor's 41 points were approved. Almost as soon as Taylor returned to Saigon wide differences of opinion developed on what should happen next.

The State/Defense "7 point message" of April 15 to Ambassador Taylor and General Westmoreland set the pot boiling, following Westmoreland's urgent request via military channels for more forces. The message directed:

(1) Experimental encadrement of U.S. troops into RVNAF.
(2) The introduction of a brigade force into Bien Hoa/Vung Tau for security and later counterinsurgency.
(3) The introduction of several additional U.S. battalions into coastal enclaves.
(4) Expansion of Vietnamese recruiting, using proven U.S. techniques.
(5) Expansion of the MEDCAP program using mobile dispensaries.
(6) Experimentation in 2 or 3 provinces with a team of U.S civil affairs personnel.
(7) Supplement of low RVNAF pay through provision of a food ration.

Taylor objected to the new forces, to encadrement, and to the whole tone of the 7 point message. He sent two principal messages with these objections, one setting out a reasoned comment on the message and a second, personal to McGeorge Bundy, saying how he really felt about it:

> I am greatly troubled by DOD 15 April 15. First, it shows no consideration for the fact that, as a result of decisions taken in Washington during my visit, this mission is charged with securing implementation by the two month old Quat government of a 21 point military program, a 41 point non-military program, a 16 point Rowan USIS program and a 12 point CIA program. Now this new cable opens up new vistas of further points as if we can win here somehow on a point score. We are going to stall the machine of government if we do not declare a moratorium on new programs for at least six months.
>
> Next, it shows a far greater willingness to get into the ground war than I had discerned in Washington during my recent trip. Although some additional U.S. forces should probably be introduced after we see how the Marines do in counterinsurgency operations, my own attitude is reflected in EmbTel 3384, which I hope was called to the attention of the President.
>
> My greatest concern arises over para 6 reftel which frankly bewilders me. What do the authors of this cable think mission has been doing over the months and years? We have presumably the best qualified personnel the Washington agencies (State, AID, DOD, USIA and CIA) can find working in the provinces seven days a week at precisely the tasks described in para 6. It is proposed to withdraw these people and replace them by Army civil affairs types operating on the pattern of military occupation? If this is the thought, I would regard such a change in policy which will gain wide publicity, as disastrous in its likely effects upon pacification in general and on US/GVN relations in particular.
>
> Mac, can't we be better protected from our friends? I know that everyone wants to help, but there's such a thing as killing with kindness. In particular, we want to stay alive here because we think we're winning—and will continue to win unless helped to death.

Another State/Defense message told the Ambassador to discuss with Quat several possible uses of U.S. combat forces beyond the NSC decisions of April 2. He replied, "I cannot raise these matters with Quat without further guidance . . . I need a clarification of our purpose for the large scale introduction of foreign troops unless the need is clear and explicit."
The plaintive words did not sound convincing to the JCS, for they told Sec-

Def, almost cavalierly, in JCSM 281/65, "JCS is confident the Ambassador will be able to accomplish such measures as are required for an appropriate acceptance of these deployments as approved by the highest authority."

As directed in the 7 point message, study commenced in Saigon on the matter of combined command. The message suggested two approaches: Integration of substantial numbers of U.S. combat personnel (e.g., 50) into each of several ARVN battalions (e.g., 10); or combined operations of three additional U.S. battalions with three or more ARVN battalions. General Westmoreland asked his Deputy to give detailed study to three methods:

(1) Assumption of officer and senior NCO command positions within the ARVN battalion by U.S. personnel.

(2) Assignment of U.S. personnel as staff officers, and in technical and specialists positions, within the ARVN battalion.

(3) Employment of U.S. troops as fire support elements within the ARVN battalion.

These approaches were studied in relation to: Language, security, support, mutual US/GVN acceptance, conditions and capabilities within ARVN units. Problems common to all three were the language barrier, increased exposure of U.S. personnel, difficulty of U.S. personnel adapting to ARVN living conditions, and the greatly expanded support requirement that would be generated. The following conclusions were reached:

Method (1) was not feasible nor desirable owing to the language barrier, as well as to probable non-acceptance by GVN.

Method (2) would not materially improve ARVN capabilities.

Method (3), therefore, was the only concept that would benefit ARVN and not detract from GVN morale. A fire support element of six U.S. officers and 49 enlisted men was suggested for each ARVN battalion.

Because of the difficulties of supply and service support, medical support, leadership in ARVN battalions, and anticipated morale problems amongst those U.S. personnel assigned to ARVN battalions, Deputy COMUSMACV opposed the adoption of the principle of encadrement. He recommended that COMUS-MACV not support it and that if it were directed, it be initially applied to only one battalion.

At the same time, as a result of the Warrenton conference of mid-January, serious consideration was being given in Washington to the use of military government by means of Army civil affairs procedures. A straw in the wind which indicated what the Saigon reaction was to be at the forthcoming Honolulu conference was the response by Ambassador Taylor on April 15 to notification that General Peers was coming to Saigon. "If GVN gets word of these plans to impose U.S. military government framework on their country . . . it will have a very serious impact on our relations. We are rocking the boat at a time when we have it almost on an even keel."

E. HONOLULU CONFERENCE, APRIL 19–20, 1965; ENCADREMENT AND COMBINED COMMAND FADE OUT

At Honolulu General Westmoreland had his way with respect to military encadrement. Notes of the meetings reveal:

> General Westmoreland states that individual encadrement of ARVN units neither required nor feasible.

Instead the plan was to "brigade" U.S. forces with ARVN troops. Consideration of the issue was ended with the understanding that General Westmoreland "will submit a written statement describing the command relationships which will prevail when U.S. forces are engaged in offensive combat actions, alone or with Vietnamese or other forces."

The introduction of U.S. Army Civil Affairs teams into the provincial government structure was also considered at Honolulu. It was decided to experiment in three provinces with U.S. teams designed to provide ample civil as well as military initiative and advice. At least one of the three teams was to be headed by a civilian. Ambassador Taylor was instructed to seek the concurrence of GVN, "recognizing that a large number of questions must be worked out subsequently."

Early in May, General Westmoreland submitted his detailed command concept. It traced the evolution of the relationship between U.S. and ARVN armed forces. Initially, U.S. forces were strictly advisory. In the period from 1960 to 1962 the U.S. had in addition provided military capabilities such as helicopters and tactical air support. The advisory effort was extended to ARVN battalions, and advisors accompanied units into combat. With the large scale commitment of U.S. ground forces in Vietnam, a logical extension of this evolution was the suggested command concept of coordination and cooperation. Operational control of each nation's forces was normally to be exercised by commanders of that nation.

COMUSMACV envisioned that the initial mission of U.S. forces would be security of base areas, a function to be coordinated through senior ARVN commanders. Subsequent deep patrolling and offensive operations by U.S. forces would occur within specified Tactical Areas of Responsibility (TAOR's) with ARVN in separate and clearly defined areas. Eventually, on search and destroy operations, U.S. forces would provide combat support at the request of the senior RVNAF commander. The U.S. commander would move to the RVNAF command post to agree on details, but close and intricate maneuver of units of the two nations' forces was to be avoided.

This Saigon proposal did not settle the matter. SecDef urged formation of a joint command with GVN and the creation of a "small combined coordinating staff to be jointly headed by COMUSMACV and CINCRVNAF" as a useful device at this stage of development of the U.S. force structure.

There were continuing indications from USG representatives in Saigon of a sensitivity to South Vietnamese criticism that the United States acted as though we were fighting all by ourselves. On May 17, Ambassador Taylor felt it wise to relay to Washington a Saigon Post column to that effect.

On May 24, both the Ambassador and COMUSMACV sent lengthy messages to their seniors discussing the matter of combined military command. Ambassador Taylor referenced both the JCS and MACV proposals and said, "I must say we are far from ready to propose to GVN anything like a plan for a more formal combined command authority . . . If USG intends to take the position that U.S. command of GVN forces is a prerequisite to the introduction of more U.S. combat troops, that fact would constitute an additional strong reason for recommending against bringing in the reinforcements."

COMUSMACV also voiced strong opposition to the Washington proposal for combined command. He recalled recent discussion of the subject with General Minh who seemed agreeable at first but then moved perceptibly away from anything suggestive of a combined headquarters. Press reports of the views of General Thieu and Air Marshall Ky, as well as the recent Saigon Post column, were referenced to substantiate that there was no prospect of such a combined staff evolving. Instead, a U.S. Army brigadier general staff. "The positioning and accrediting of Brig. General Collins is as far as we can go."

There appears to have been no strong objection by the Joint Chiefs of Staff. In JCSM 516-65 they reviewed the course of events and recommended augmentation of MACV by seven billets (1 Brigadier General, 3 officers, and 3 enlisted) to provide "the requisite staff assistance on combined and operational planning matters associated with the coordinated operations of U.S., RVN, and third country forces in Vietnam."

A joint State/Defense message to Saigon on May 27 deferred any approach to GVN on combined command until it was politically feasible and directed that no planning discussion be undertaken with RVNAF without Ambassador Taylor's approval.

There were two major battles in late May and early June, Ba Gia and Dong Zoai. Although U.S. troops were available to assist in both instances they were not committed and in both cases RVNAF were defeated.

General Westmoreland continued to press Washington for greater freedom of discretion in the use of U.S. ground forces with RVNAF. A June 12 message recalled the three stages envisioned in his May 8 discussion of combined command. So far, in view of statements in Washington by the Secretary of State and by the White House, movement from stage 2 to 3 had been deferred, but it sounded as though some measure of joint planning was in progress.

> The fact is we have moved some distance down the road toward active commitment of U.S. combat forces and have done so hand-in-hand with our Vietnamese ally. They and we recognize that the time has come when such support is essential to the survival of any government of South Vietnam and the integrity of RVNAF.

The message concluded with a request for modification of the letters of instructions on use of U.S. troops.

A minor note, not unrelated to combined command, was raised in May when Prime Minister Quat *pressed within GVN* for a status of forces agreement. The matter arose because of concern about Vietnamese sovereignty over areas where U.S. forces were stationed. Relations were being governed by the 15 year old Pentalateral agreement, clearly inapplicable to the present situation. U.S. military forces in Vietnam were enjoying virtual diplomatic immunity; so the MACV senior judge advocate developed arguments to demonstrate that raising the issue was not in the interests of either government. They were passed to the SVN source of the information for use at ministerial meetings on the subject. There is no indication that GVN formally discussed status-of-forces with the Embassy.

F. THE KY COUP, JUNE, 1965

After extended negotiations between Quat, Suu, and other leaders failed to end the government crisis that started in late May, on June 9 Quat asked the generals to mediate the dispute. They did. On June 12 they forced Quat to resign and took over the government. After several days of jockeying among themselves, the generals formed a National Leadership Council of ten members and made Ky Prime Minister. Taylor was out of town at the critical time, and the Embassy found out about the main decisions after they were taken. However, Taylor was back in time to object unsuccessfully to Ky's appointment as

Prime Minister before it was announced. Once things had settled down and the USG felt it had no choice but to accept the new government, Taylor cabled State:

> . . . It will serve our best interests to strengthen, support and endorse this government.

IV. THE KY GOVERNMENT'S EARLY MONTHS: THE COUP TO THE EMBRACE AT HONOLULU, FEBRUARY 1966

A. THE KY GOVERNMENT'S INHERITANCE

Nguyen Cao Ky, Commander of the Vietnamese Air Force, joined with other "Young Turks" of the Vietnamese Armed Forces to overthrow the civilian government of Prime Minister Quat on June 12, 1965. Attempts at civilian government had limped along since October, 1964, following riots in August-September that had forced the generals to withdraw Khanh's military-dictatorial constitution and to promise civilian rule. That entire period had been marked by riots, coups, and attempted coups. By June, when Quat and the civilian President Suu found themselves in an impasse, Ambassador Taylor easily acquiesced in the return to direct military rule.

Pacification kept lagging, and the dark military picture forced the U.S. to decide in June to pour U.S. troops into the country as fast as they could be deployed. The pattern of GVN civil and military ineffectiveness had led the U.S. Government to resolve to do it ourselves, and to abandon any hope of forcing or inducing GVN to do the job without us. All concerned knew that the Young Turks now in open control of GVN had repeatedly defied Ambassador Taylor and had gotten away with it. Attempts at top-level leverage on GVN had produced a virtual diplomatic rupture for a few days at the end of 1964 and the beginning of 1965, and the U.S. was in no mood to try it again.

B. THE KY GOVERNMENT AND THE U.S. START THEIR DEALINGS, JUNE–JULY, 1965

With Vietnam's return to overt military government, the political blocs with their private armies, perhaps exhausted, bided their time. Communications improved between the U.S. and GVN to a state of cool correctness, gradually revealing lower-level GVN's intention to go on coasting as it always had and higher-level GVN's intention to serve its own interests.

The day after the coup, COMUSMACV cabled CINCPAC in alarm about the military picture, requesting authority to send U.S. troops on offensive missions. He recalled that ARVN had lost five infantry battalions on the battlefield in the last three weeks, and he stated that the only possible U.S. response was the aggressive employment of U.S. troops together with the Vietnamese general reserve forces:

> To meet this challenge successfully, troops must be maneuvered fully, deployed and redeployed as necessary.

To demonstrate how completely the initiative changes on the subject of combined command, Saigon announced to Washington in mid-June its intention within the next few days to conduct a backgrounder on command relationships. A reply from the Secretary of Defense said,

As basis for Washington review of proposed Westmoreland backgrounder on command relationships and MACV organizational structure, please furnish draft of text he will use . . .

In late June, General Westmoreland was authorized by Washington to "commit U.S. troops to combat, independent of or in conjunction with GVN forces in any situation in which use of such troops is requested by an appropriate GVN commander and when, in COMUSMACV's judgment, their use is necessary to strengthen the relative position of GVN forces."

Premier Ky, obviously wishing to play down an issue sensitive to both governments, told Ambassador Taylor he saw no particular reason for any drastic change from the previous practice of combat support. In any specific situation, he said that command should be worked out in accordance with "good sense and sound military principles." Additional deployments caused no problem, and indeed GVN now asked for more US/FW forces than could be deployed or were approved. But in response to a query, Taylor waved aside any hope of using deployments for leverage. Discussions of combined command avoided joining issue and left matters unchanged.

Although Taylor's initial reaction to Ky was one of apprehension, he was soon impressed by Ky's aggressive performance including his 26 point program. He doubted Ky's ability to implement the program, but concluded that military government was less likely to abandon the war effort and thus should be supported.

Early in 1965, AID had decided to stop buying piasters for U.S.-controlled sector funds, and in June agreed with the GVN to change the province procedures. Effective June 22, 1965, the Vietnamese Province Chief would requisition and release AID commodities on his own authority, and all supporting funds came through regular GVN channels. The new procedures included elaborate reporting steps both when the U.S. advisers concurred and when they nonconcurred with the Province Chief's actions. In practice, the change reduced U.S. adviser's leverage.

On July 1, Secretary McNamara submitted a memorandum to the President reviewing all aspects of Vietnam policy. However, he naturally concentrated on U.S. deployments, and had little to say on GVN's problems. In a section titled, "Initiatives Inside Vietnam," his only significant recommendations were that we should increase our AID to GVN and that Chieu Hoi Program should be improved. However, in another memorandum to the President on July 20, following a trip to Saigon, McNamara suggested that the U.S. Government should lay down some terms for its assistance. GVN was again pressing for more U.S. forces than were available. He mentioned rice policy, plus a "veto on major GVN commanders, statements about invading NVN, and so on."

McNamara's overall evaluation was deeply pessimistic, making clear why he recommended increased U.S. forces at that time:

> *Estimate of the Situation.* The situation in South Vietnam is worse than a year ago (when it was worse than a year before that). After a few months of stalemate, the tempo of the war has quickened. A hard VC push is now on to dismember the nation and to maul the army. The VC main and local forces, reinforced by militia and guerrillas, have the initiative and, with large attacks (some in regimental strength), are hurting ARVN forces badly. The main VC efforts have been in southern I Corps, northern and central II Corps and north of Saigon. The central highlands could well

be lost to the National Liberation Front during this monsoon season. Since June 1, the GVN has been forced to abandon six district capitals; only one has been retaken. U.S. combat troops deployments and US/VNAF strikes against the North have put to rest most South Vietnamese fears that the United States will forsake them, and US/VNAF air strikes in-country have probably shaken VC morale somewhat. Yet the government is able to provide security to fewer and fewer people in less and less territory as terrorism increases. Cities and towns are being isolated as fewer and fewer roads and railroads are being isolated as fewer and fewer roads and railroads are usable and power and communications lines are cut.

The economy is deteriorating—the war is disrupting rubber production, rice distribution, Dalat vegetable production and the coastal fishing industry, causing the loss of jobs and income, displacement of people and frequent breakdown or suspension of vital means of transportation and communication; foreign exchange earnings have fallen; and severe inflation is threatened.

In Saigon Ambassador Taylor gave the GVN the first definite sign of U.S. concern about the effects of U.S. deployments on Saigon port operations and on the Vietnamese economy. In a letter to Prime Minister Ky dated July 1, 1965, he said:

> Your experts and ours are in constant contact on [the budgetary deficit] and have always worked effectively together . . . [They] will need your support in carrying out the anti-inflation measures which they may recommend from time to time . . . The rice procurement and distribution agency which you have in mind is an important measure of . . . a program which should also include the further development of port capacities.

USOM also began talking about devaluing the piaster. These matters were to come to a head a year later. At this time, however, the Embassy treated these matters routinely and applied no pressure to GVN. GVN officials opened the serious bidding in their meeting with Secretary McNamara on July 16, saying that their gold and foreign exchange reserves had suffered the alarming drop from $175 million to $100 million since January, 1964, and requested a big increase in AID. Ambassador Taylor preferred to limit our counter-demands to get quick agreement; he said,

> We would avoid giving the impression of asking for new agreements or imposing conditions for our increase AID . . . We do not want to raise conditions in terms likely to be rejected or to require prolonged debate.

On July 28, the Embassy and GVN settled it. The agreement touched very lightly on GVN obligations and on joint economic planning. It provided for "joint discussions to precede policy decisions . . . for control of inflation," etc.

On July 8, MACV reviewed its relationships with the military leadership. There was no problem; they agreed that operations involving both U.S. and ARVN troops would use the concepts of coordination and cooperation. They did not discuss combined command. However, a flap developed late in July when General Thi was reported to be planning operations in the DMZ. Both Taylor and Westmoreland took it up with GVN, who reassured them; Thi got back on his leash before it was too late. Such operations commenced more than a year later. A candid subsequent statement from Saigon shows the Vietnamese desired to have the best of both worlds. Ambassador Lodge reported to Washington the disparaging reactions of ARVN general officers on the JGS staff to the U.S. Marine victory south of Chu Lai. "I flag this small straw in the wind as pointing up the importance of portraying our operations here as combined with the GVN in nature."

C. *QUIET SAILING THROUGH JANUARY, 1966*

In August, Ky wanted to make a trip to Taiwan, being interested in getting Nationalist Chinese troops into Vietnam. The U.S. Government objected both to the trip and to its objective, but failed to persuade him to give up the trip. Later he brought in some Chinats on the sly. An idea floated in Washington that he or Thieu should visit the United States was dropped without having been brought up with the GVN.

Lodge arrived around the middle of August to replace Taylor. Having avoided the confrontations with GVN of the type that Taylor had, he came with a residue of good will. Because he was considered responsible for Diem's overthrow, the Buddhists were pleased, and the militant Catholics dubious. In that connection, State thought it prudent to direct the Embassy to assure GVN that neither Lodge nor Lansdale, whom he was bringing with him, was going to try to make changes in GVN. On August 26, Ky told Lodge that he thought U.S. forces should "hold strategic points" so that the Vietnamese could concentrate on pacification operations. That is, he wanted the United States to take over the main force war. He also said he thought the Chu Hoi program was a waste of money.

In early August, Ky established a Ministry of Rural Construction (MRC and a Central Rural Construction Council (CRCC). These absorbed functions and personnel from predecessor groups and other ministries for the announced purpose of providing centralized direction to the pacification effort. Nguyen Tat Ung was made Minister of Rural Construction while the Council was chaired by General Co, Minister of War and Defense. Timing and circumstances give no evidence of a strong U.S. hand at work. The U.S. Embassy viewed the new organization as the result of political maneuvering, but also hoped the change would promote inter-ministerial cooperation. The move signalled renewed emphasis of pacification by both GVN and the mission. In late August, Ambassador Lodge announced the appointment of retired General Lansdale as chairman of the U.S. Mission liaison group to the GVN CRCC.

There followed a period of shuffling and reorganization during which Ung was killed in a plane crash. Two weeks later Prime Minister Ky announced that General Thang would succeed to the Ministry. The appointment was for six months only, and Thang retained his position on the JGS. At the same time, General Co was elevated to Deputy Prime Minister for War and Reconstruction in a realignment that made six ministries including Rural Reconstruction subordinate to him.

On August 28, General Thi told Lodge he thought he could do a better job running the government than Ky was doing. He spoke at some length on Ky's political weaknesses, with particular emphasis on his lack of support in I Corps, where Thi was strong. As was his usual practice, Lodge politely brushed aside this approach. (Later Thi proved harder and harder to control until his dismissal in March.)

In mid-September, Lodge went on an inspection trip to Da Nang and Qui Nhon. On his return he waxed eloquent about the benefits of the U.S. presence:

> All reports indicated that the American troops are having a very beneficial effect on VN troops, giving them greater confidence and courage. I am always mindful of the possibility that the American presence will induce the VN to slump back and "Let George do it." But there seems to be no sign of this.
>
> I wish I could describe the feeling of hope which this great American presence on the ground is bringing. There can no longer be the slightest doubt that persistence will bring success, that the aggression will be warded off and that for the first time since the end of WW II, the cause of free men will be on an upward spiral.

Lodge's end-of-month appraisal was that civil and political progress lagged behind the military. He felt there would be a political vacuum that the VC would fill if the U.S. pulled out. Therefore, he was trying to start a program to provide security and to generate indigenous political activity at the hamlet level. He noted with pleasure that Ky was taking the initiative in bringing his pacification plans to Lansdale, to get U.S. reactions before these plans were too firm to change.

By September, a combination of inflation, black-marketeering by U.S. troops and other related problems led both governments to agree on important steps. The U.S. introduced military payment certificates, and the GVN agreed to exchange 118 piasters to the dollar for personal use of troops and U.S. civilians. Official U.S. purchases of piasters continued at the old exchange rate of 35, however.

September brought an evaluation of the three-month three-province pacification experiment during which each was under the unified control of a team chief; one an embassy FSO, one a MACV sector adviser, and one an AID province representative. COMUSMACV judged that test only partially successful; progress achieved was attributed to the "keen spirit of cooperation" by all team members. Because he believed the results inconclusive and in view of the existing military situation, General Westmoreland concluded that the team chief concept should not be implemented. The experiment was officially ended.

The U.S. also became deeply involved in the rice trade. Vietnam changed over from a rice exporter in the years through 1964 to a heavy importer from 1965 onwards. AID provided the imported rice under CIP. In September, 1964, Ambassador Lodge spoke of measures *we* are taking to control the price of rice; inasmuch as AID provided the imports, USOM had a say in the GVN's policies on price control, subsidization, and distribution of rice.

During this period a problem flared up over a corrupt Province Chief. Lt. Colonel Chi, Province Chief of Binh Tuy, was accused of misuse of $250,000 of AID funds. After pressure from AID had merely produced threats against the lives of AID personnel in the province, on September 23 AID withdrew them and suspended AID to the province. Chi was a protege of General Co, the Minister of Defense and Deputy Premier, who himself figured in charges of corruption a year later. On October 5, the story got into the papers, and on the 7th Ky promised publicly to remove Chi. Lodge played no role in starting this episode, and told the Mission Council on October 7 that he did not want it repeated. After a six-weeks delay, Ky did remove Chi on November 25, and gave him a job in the Ministry of Defense. AID to the province resumed.

Advisers in the field kept on complaining about the delays in the Vietnamese system, and pressed for restoration of some resources of their own. On October 1, 1965, MACV began giving its sector and subsector advisers piaster funds they could spend on urgent projects. Each subsector adviser had access to 50,-000 piasters which could be replenished as necessary. Toward the end of 1965 it became obvious that this method was highly successful. Consideration was given to permanent establishment of the revolving fund.

However, after the trial period of about four months MACV abandoned the plan because of strong opposition by General Thang, Minister of Revolutionary Development. He argued that under U.S. urging he had been developing an effective, flexible organization that would take care of urgent projects of the type the sector and subsector advisers wanted to promote; letting them bypass his people would encourage the latter to lapse into their old bad habits and thwart both governments' main objectives.

USOM also had second thoughts about abandoning the sign-off system. Early in October 1965, the Mission Council approved a plan to restore the "troika sign-off" procedure as it had existed prior to June. After the Mission had already reopened the issue with the GVN, the State Department objected, saying that the United States wanted to make the Vietnamese more independent and effective.

After a time the frustrations of the advisors began striking a sympathetic chord at the highest levels. In a draft memorandum to the President dated November 3, 1965, Secretary McNamara stated his own impatience with the GVN and urged a more active role for our advisers at province and district. There is no sign of such high-level interest earlier, except as expressed by decisions to extend the advisory system to lower levels; as just noted State objected to the restoration of troika sign-off on October 16, 1965.

Some uncertainty and disagreement with respect to pacification developed within United States groups in Vietnam. In November, Major General Lansdale, Special Assistant to the Ambassador, asked who on the U.S. side should have the executive role in dealing with the Rural Construction Ministry? Lansdale envisaged that MACV and JUSPAO would be observers only.

COMUSMACV disagreed with the proposed limitation. USMACV was the only structure advising GVN at all levels; so MACV shared responsibility for pacification. Manpower required for cadre teams would impact directly and seriously on MACV efforts to maintain RVNAF strengths. Minister of Rural Construction was Major General Thang who also was Director of Operations, JGS. He looked to MACV for advice and assistance on the whole spectrum of pacification problems.

On December 15 in a memorandum to Major General Lansdale, the Ambassador said,

> I consider the GVN effort in this domain (apart from the military clearing phase) to be primarily civilian . . . Consequently, on the American side it is preferable that the two civilian agencies, USAID and CAS, be the operating support agencies.

The GVN military plan in support of the 1966 Rural Construction plan was given in the JGS Directive AB 140 of December 15, 1965, which had been developed in coordination with MACV and the Ministry of Rural Construction. In November onward, portions of the 1966 GVN defense budget prepared in accordance with U.S. guidelines were received by MACV.

At the time of the Christmas truce, President Johnson launched a peace offensive, including a suspension of bombing in North Vietnam that lasted 37 days. The moves were carefully cleared with GVN and with its Ambassador in Washington, and caused no significant problems. Lodge's appraisal was that the "offensive" achieved all its aims, at no significant cost. However, trouble flared up over a plan to release 20 NVA prisoners across the DMZ; General Thi was not consulted, and said he would not permit it (in his Corps). Things were smoothed over amicably by Tet.

One troublesome area was GVN's hawkishness over such issues as border incidents. Ky kept pressing for action against Cambodian sanctuaries; the U.S. stood firm on the rule of self-defense in emergencies only, which could mean shooting across the border but not maneuvering troops across it. Ky wanted to encourage a Khmer Serai expedition, which would cause a flare-up with the Cambodian Government; State directed Lodge to keep him on a tight leash.

Coup rumors started to circulate around the first of the year; Lodge remarked that just before Tet was a normal season for that. On December 29 Ky told Lodge of an alleged assassination plot directed at Ky, Co, the Buddhist leader Thich Tam Chau, and Lodge. On January 15, VNAF took to the air in nervous reaction to some supposedly suspicious troop movements; Lodge reported more rumors on January 19, and took the opportunity to spell out his position:

> If . . . corridor coup . . . caused directorate members to fall out, consequences could be disastrous . . . A peaceful reshuffle within directorate is a continuing possibility. I would deplore it. We take all rumors and reports of government change very seriously and never miss an opportunity to make clear U.S. support for, and the need for, governmental stability.

Around the middle of January 1966, Ky addressed the Armed Forces Convention. He announced the prospective formation, after Tet, of a "Democracy Building Council" to serve as a constituent assembly and legislature. It would write a new constitution by October, 1966, preparatory to elections in 1967. This was the opening shot in what became a big issue within a few weeks.

D. THE HONOLULU CONFERENCE OF FEBRUARY 6–8, 1966

By late January, it was clear that Lodge's policy of not pushing GVN too hard may have helped keep things amicable but permitted pacification to keep lagging and permitted economic problems to grow serious. With conspicuous haste that caused GVN some loss of face, the U.S. summoned Thieu, Ky, and other GVN officials to Honolulu to express renewed and heightened U.S. concern. The U.S. wanted to re-emphasize pacification, with a corresponding shift of authority from the ARVN line command to the province chiefs; and it wanted strong action to limit inflation, to clear the Saigon Port, and to limit the unfavorable effect of U.S. deployments on the U.S. balance of payments.

For the first time in over a year, the U.S. bargained hard with GVN on issues of these kinds. The GVN agreed to the main U.S. demands on authority for the provinces chiefs. Moreover, it promised fiscal reform, devaluation, port and customs reform, and the use of GVN dollar balances to finance additional imports. The GVN also agreed that an International Monetary Fund team should be invited to give technical advice on these economic programs. Thieu and Ky promised to go ahead with a new constitution, to be drafted by an appointed Advisory Council, and then ratified by popular vote in late 1966; following that, they promised, the GVN would create an elected government rooted in the constitution. The U.S. promised to increase AID imports to $400 million in 1966, plus $150 million in project assistance.

Altogether the two governments exchanged over 60 agreed points and assurances, ranging over free world (third country) assistance, rural construction (pacification), refugees, political development, Montagnards, Chieu Hoi, health, education, agriculture, and economic and financial programs. This package was far more specific than any previous US/GVN agreement. Their public statements after the conference emphasized social justice, the promise of elected government, and the U.S. lack of interest in bases or permanent alliance in South Vietnam.

In a public appearance at the conference, President Johnson embraced Prime Minister Ky, before photographers. Although it caused no loss of face directly, in the eyes of many observers this act added to the impression that Ky was tied to our apron strings. If Lodge sensed this effect, he said nothing about it; characteristically, he said to State that the Honolulu Conference was good psychologically for Vietnam.

Directly after the conference USOM remained seriously concerned with the high and rising black market piaster rate for dollars, which they and the Vietnamese business community regarded as the bellweather of inflation. Moreover, besides its harmful psychological effect, the high rate tempted U.S. personnel into illegal transactions, causing unfavorable publicity. Inasmuch as GVN refused to sell dollars in the black market to push the rate down, Porter requested authorization from Washington to do it on the sly with CAS money.

The thrust of the Honolulu Conference was clearly to stimulate nonmilitary pacification efforts. Upon his return to Saigon, Lodge issued a memorandum reconstituting the Mission Liaison Group under Deputy Ambassador Porter. Though charged by the memorandum with the management and control of all U.S. civilian agency activities supporting Revolutionary Development, Porter saw his responsibility as primarily a coordinating effort. He said he did not intend to get into individual agency activities.

V. A REBELLION, A CONSTITUENT ASSEMBLY, AND THE HARDSHIPS OF NEGOTIATING WITH A "WEAK" GOVERNMENT

A. THE RISE OF THE STRUGGLE MOVEMENT, MARCH, 1966

General Thi, Commander of I Corps, was a thorn in Ky's side as a potential rival. Both private and public disagreements showed there was no love lost between them; and Thi had a considerable base of support in his connections with the Buddhist leadership and in his identification with Annamese sensitivities. These factors also made the other generals of the Military Directorate (formerly National Leadership Council, etc.) suspicious of Thi; they felt better able to cope with Ky.

Armed with President Johnson's public support of him, Ky resolved to exile Thi, and he persuaded his colleagues to go along with the idea in a meeting on March 10. The day before he told Lodge of his intention, saying that Thi had been culpably insubordinate; Lodge replied that he should be sure he could prove the charges, so as to put a good public face on the move, and pave the way carefully. Later in the day Lodge also advised him to make sure he had the votes in the Directorate, saying that for him to lose on the issue and be replaced as Prime Minister would be catastrophic. Ky was sure of himself, although he admitted he could not prove his charges. In a later meeting the same day, Thieu told Lodge Thi "had conducted himself in a way that was not suitable," and was confident Thi could be dismissed without ill effects.

On March 10, when the Directorate voted to fire him, Thi resigned. Ky told Lodge that Thi would go to Da Nang the 11th for the change-of-command ceremony and then leave the country for four months. The same day, Thi told Colonel Sam Wilson that he did not want to leave the country, and that he had been encouraged by the Director of National Police to stay; Wilson suggested that he go gracefully. On the 11th, when the time came for Thi to fly to Da Nang, he was detained at Tan Son Nhut; Ky had got wind of, or suspected, his intentions. Ky then urgently requested Lodge to invite Thi to the United States for a physical examination.

The Annamese Buddhists, led by Tri Quang, who had quietly bided their time for about a year, now entered the action. (Ky later told Lodge that Tri Quang had assented to Thi's dismissal and had then double-crossed him.) They began demonstrations in Da Nang and Hue on March 12, joined by the students, and over the next several days gained control of those cities as the police stood aside. Again Ky used Lodge's good offices to try to persuade Thi to leave the country gracefully; but the 16th, Ky and the Directorate decided to try to use Thi to restore order, and permitted him to return to Da Nang. For a few days things quieted down slightly, but the end was not yet in sight.

State offered Lodge suggestions on how to get things calmed down. First, he might counsel a firm attitude by GVN, saying it would meet with the Buddhists but not under threats, and that it would not permit disorders. Second, GVN might steal the initiative from the Buddhists by making a generous public offer of elections. Whichever course they followed, State wanted them to be sure it would work and would avoid a head-on collision with the Buddhists. In reply, Lodge agreed on the need to avoid a head-on collision; as for the means, he, like State, simply hoped for the best:

> We should not settle on one solution or another. Rather it is possible, if not probable, that, unless uncontrollable mass reaction is brought about, each side will seek to arrange what can be looked upon as widely acceptable.

On March 22, Lodge and Ky had a long discussion of tactics relating to elections and constitution-writing. Elections were scheduled to come up for the largely powerless but symbolic provincial councils (which advised the Province Chiefs on policy matters), and Ky had reportedly toyed with calling off these elections. He was also far behind schedule on the constituent assembly he had publicly promised on January 19 for just after Tet, and as noted had privately promised the U.S. Government at Honolulu. Lodge reported:

> 2. . . . He is eager for advice and when he received it, he said he agreed with it. Now it remains to be seen whether it will be carried out.
> 3. My advice was based on careful reflection and consultation with my associates and was to this effect:
> 4. The GVN should not cancel provincial elections as I had heard re-

ported. He said that this was not exactly the case; that there were two provincial councils, which didn't want elections. I said in that event these councils should be made to say publicly that they didn't want elections so that the onus of not holding these elections would not fall on the Government. A public announcement had been made that the Government was in favor of holding these provincial elections; the offices involved have little actual consequence but are of symbolic significance; Washington had been informed of this fact; and if there was some reason why in one or two provinces they should not be held, then the provinces should make the reason plain.

5. I then advised that he should take the lead and influence opinion, and not be at the mercy of events. I suggested that a list of names for so-called consultative assembly (which I suggested would be better named "preparatory commission") which aims to draft a constitution, should be confirmed by the Generals. When this had been done, I suggested that then Ky should make a very carefully written and persuasive announce-ment which would be done on film for use on television and in the movie theaters. The Vietnamese are great movie-goers and it is a very important medium here. I said that he should not read it on film with his head bob-bing up and down as he looked down at the text, but should have it put on cue card along side the camera and read it as he looks right into the lens.

6. His statement should be written in such a way as not to exclude the possibility of elections later on for a constitutional convention. In other words, this should be deliberately fuzzed and left open by implication. I said I much preferred the phrase "constitutional convention" to the per-nicious French phrase "constitutent assembly." The constitutional conven-tion would meet, adopt the constitution and disband, whereas the con-stituent assembly stays around and makes trouble for an idefinite period.

7. He agreed with all this and seemed to understand it. He said that last night, the Generals had unanimously confirmed the names of the members of the preparatory committee. He would announce all this as I suggested. I wish he would do it quickly.

8. I suggested that impulsive unprepared statements were most dangerous at this time. Experienced politicians often make statements which seem to be "off the cuff," but actually are carefully thought out. His unprepared statements always worry me.

9. He agreed with me that certain Buddhists were unwittingly taking Communist inspired advice, as were the students in Hue who had attacked me . . .

10. He was absolutely sure that the Buddhists were divided among them-selves—an analysis which I share. He agrees with me that Tri Quang simply has not got the powerful psychological factors working for him now that he had in October '63. All the Communist Propaganda in the world can-not alter these facts: That in '63, the Buddhists were discriminated against, and now they are not; that in the latter days of '63 the Buddhists were persecuted whereas now they are not; and that Tri Quang was an under-dog then, and now he is not. Yet Tri Quang is evidently determined.

11. My advice to him was not very drastic and quite simple to do, and yet I believe that if he follows it conscientiously and expeditiously without procrastination that there may be enough of a budding sense of National interest to start moving things along in the right direction.

12. He thanked me more effusively and warmly than he has ever done before and said he was so grateful for my interest in his welfare, physical and political.

13. The situation is not yet out of hand. Ky has had offers from Catholics and Southerners for them to enter the fray on his side and start throwing their weight around, which he so far has been able to prevent them from doing. This is one of the things which I have been fearing. I talked in this vein with the Papal delegate and the Archbishop of Saigon yesterday, and they agreed completely. The leadership of the Southerners is not, I fear, as responsible.

On March 25, Ky followed Lodge's advice more or less closely, and announced the Constitutional Preparatory Commission and said it would finish its work within two months; elections might follow by the end of 1966. However, he insisted that GVN would exclude "Vietcong or corrupt elements" from the elected assembly. The move failed to restore order. On March 26, demonstrators in Hue broke out anti-American banners written in English, and an ugly incident followed in which a Marine tore one down. (After detailed negotiations, an apology was given and accepted.) The radio stations at Da Nang and Hue fell under control of dissident elements.

On March 29, Ky told Lodge that he and the generals wanted to move on Hue and Da Nang with military forces, and said that he could show that an unpublicized Buddhists split had caused the uprising. Lodge concurred in Ky's plan to use forces, but urged him not to try to create an open breach among the Buddhists.

Although Lodge had no objection to using force against the Buddhist movement, both he and Rusk felt that U.S. men and equipment should stay out of it, to avoid heightening anti-American feelings. Rusk told Lodge of his deep concern about Vietnamese internal bickering at a crucial time; he was particularly disturbed by the anti-American propaganda coming from the Hue radio, which was physically defended by the U.S. Marines in that general area. He went on to say,

> We face the fact that we ourselves cannot succeed except in support of the South Vietnamese. Unless they are able to mobilize reasonable solidarity, prospects are grim. I appreciate your frank and realistic reporting and am relying heavily upon your good judgment to exert every effort to get us over the present malaise.

Lodge replied that his influence with the Catholics had kept them out of it, but that his talks with Tri Quang had been unproductive. He estimated that Tri Quang had used the anti-American theme to put pressure on the GVN. (Through an intermediary the Embassy learned that General Thi said that the United States was too committed to leave; this belief may have led Thi and the Buddhists to feel free to use the theme as a weapon against GVN.)

On March 29, the Catholic leaders in whom Lodge had placed his hopes came out against the GVN and demanded a return to civilian rule.

B.   KY'S FIRST ATTEMPT TO SUPPRESS THE STRUGGLE MOVEMENT, APRIL, 1966

Events now happened in rapid succession. Assured of Lodge's sympathy, on April 3 Ky declared that Da Nang was in the hands of Communists. On April

5, despite mild questioning from State, MACV airlifted two battalions of Vietnamese Rangers to Da Nang under personal command of Ky, and they started to seize the city. That same day the 1st ARVN Division Commander declared for the Struggle Movement, with his officers backing him, and U.S. advisers were withdrawn from the Division. On April 6, "non-essential" U.S. civilians withdrew from Hue. On April 8, the GVN flew two more Ranger battalions to Da Nang, using its own airlift after MACV refused to provide any. On April 9, U.S. representatives protested to Struggle Movement leaders about Howitzers under their control positioned within range of the Da Nang airbase; the leaders agreed to pull them back. Two hundred U.S. and third country civilians evacuated Da Nang.

Washington played little role in all this. From time to time it offered mild advice, but Lodge had a free hand. It was his decision to withhold any further U.S. airlift on April 8, although after he acted State agreed by urging him to push GVN toward a political rather than a military solution:

> Accordingly we believe you should not repeat not urge immediate Da Nang operations at present, but rather that entire focus of your efforts at all levels should be to get political process started.

(It was at this time that Lodge wrote his long cable, discussed in the next section below, saying that the U.S. does not have enough influence in Vietnam, and that it should set up a leverage system that bypasses Saigon and works at the Province level.) Lodge accepted the fact of Buddhist power, and wanted to avoid bloodshed, but as always his sympathies were squarely with the military leadership:

> The political crisis which has been gripping VN is now almost one month old. The situation has deteriorated steadily as the Buddhist opposition has increased pressure on the GVN.
>
> Buddhist demands, when stripped of hypocrisy [and,] . . . boil down to a naked grab for power.

Throughout this period we have sought certain fundamental objectives:

> A. To preserve the VN nation, and thus, the present government.
> B. To provide for an orderly political evolution from military to civil government.
> C. To preserve the Armed Forces as an effective shield against VC.
> D. To guard and expand all our political, economic, social and military gains, notably those which flowed from the Honolulu declaration.
> E. To maintain the effectiveness of the Free World forces in VN.

On April 12, GVN found a face-saving formula and withdrew its Ranger battalions from Da Nang to Saigon, and the streets became relatively quiet. On the 14th, the Directorate gave way to the demands for elected civilian government by promising elections for a Constituent Assembly within three to five months. For the time being the Buddhists and other political groups, while making additional demands, called off the demonstrations on condition that Ky honor his promises.

On April 23, Lodge reviewed for State all the leverage available that might be used to help bring the I Corps area under government authority, and rejected using any of it.

> We have considered possibility of using U.S. control over economic and military commodities in I Corps to foster re-establishment of government authority in the areas.
>
> The bulk of USAID-controlled commodities are scheduled for use in rural areas. Comparatively little anti-government activity is carried on by the rural population . . .
>
> The Hue-DaNang area currently is relatively well stocked with basic commodities. There is an estimated four month supply of rice on hand and the countryside is now starting the harvesting of a rice crop . . .
>
> The U.S. currently controls, through the USAID, the following: (A) Warehouses in the part of DaNang containing quantities of construction material and PL-480 foodstuffs . . . (B) Three deep draft vessels and one coastal vessel now in the DaNang harbor with CIP cement, rice, fertilizer, and miscellaneous commercial cargo . . . (C) Nine chartered coastal vessels . . . operated for USAID . . .
>
> With respect to military commodities, RVNAF maintains a 30-60 day supply of expendable combat items while their rice stocks are maintained at a 30-day level. However, under rationing these rice stocks can be extended to 60 days. The RVNAF items which are in short supply throughout Vietnam, as well as in the Hue-DaNang area, include vehicle batteries, brake shoes, and POL. We consider it unwise to interfere with the flow of supplies to RVNAF at this time since it would limit effectiveness of operations against Viet Cong forces . . .
>
> Indeed any U.S. effort to withhold resources which it controls in this area may stimulate excesses by the struggle movement even though an attempt is made to conceal the U.S. role in the imposition of sanctions.

C. VIOLENCE EXPLODES IN MAY, 1966

After promising the elections by August 15, against Lodge's public disagreement, Ky said in a public statement on May 4 that "we will try to hold elections by October." In Lodge's absence, on a long trip to Washington, Porter protested privately to Ky that once he had made a public commitment on election timing he was risking further disorders to appear to shirk it. Nevertheless, Ky added to the flames by a further public statement that he expected to remain in office for another year. New disorders broke out, and DaNang and Hue again fell under overt control of the Struggle Movement. Without consulting the Embassy, the Directorate laid plans for several days and then on May 15 airlifted troops to DaNang and then to Hue.

State first reaction showed unrestrained fury, and sanctioned "rough talk" to stop the fighting:

> This may require rough talk but U.S. cannot accept this insane bickering . . . do your best in next few hours. Intolerable that Ky should . . . move . . . against DaNang without consultation with us. Urgent now to insist that fighting stop.

State did not, at first, sanction the threat of force; for example, it said Gen. Walt should continue to harbor the dissident General Dinh in III MAF Headquarters, and that Walt should tell GVN he "can't foresee the U.S. Government reaction" if GVN forces should break into his Headquarters. Its overall guidance was to use persuasion, withdrawal of advisers, and a public posture of non-intervention, with the following specifics:

1. Announce that the U.S. was not consulted, gave no help. Ky's use of T39 routine, "not material assistance."
2. Furnish no airlift.
3. Withdraw all advisers from I CTZ, including from loyal GVN units, except for any clearly in position to fight VC. Keep U.S. forces out, except *maybe* to fight VC.
4. Inasmuch as withdrawal of civilians and military from DaNang in early April had a sobering effect, State authorized withdrawing them again (including combat forces).
5. Exception to 3: Keep contacts with Thi and 1st Division, and make other like exceptions. (Purpose of withdrawal is to avoid appearance of involvement.)
6. Use contacts to get a compromise that avoids bloodshed.
7. Find out "soonest" the effect on election preparations.
8. Do not throw U.S. weight behind GVN effort.

However, the "rough talk" actually used did reach the point of a clear threat of force. General Walt heard of a possible VNAF attack on dissident ARVN units in their compounds, and threatened to use U.S. jets to shoot down the VNAF aircraft if they did. (The pretext was that U.S. advisers would be threatened if they did, and did not apply to VNAF self-defense against dissident ARVN units closing on DaNang.) If such an attack was planned, the threat succeeded.

Porter followed State's guidance closely; he put it strongly to Ky and Thieu that the failure to consult was unacceptable, withheld airlift from GVN and withdrew advisers from units on both sides, and obtained from Thieu the assurance that the election would be held as promised. He refused to give public backing or opposition to either side, and tried to mediate. State sent several more messages with guidance along the same lines, and directed him to tell both sides of USG's impatience with Vietnamese factionalism:

The American people are becoming fed up with the games they are playing while the Americans are being asked to sustain such major burdens.

On May 17, a U.S. helicopter received small arms fire from a dissident ARVN unit when carrying a GVN officer to parley with them; the helicopter returned the fire, causing several casualties. In a stormy meeting the next day with Corcoran, the U.S. Consul in Hue, Tri Quang accused the U.S. of joining forces with GVN in attacking his people, and threatened violence against U.S. forces and facilities. Corcoran stood firm, saying that U.S. forces would defend themselves. State's guidance the same day, reaffirming the previous guidance, was to limit U.S. assistance to administrative aircraft, and then only when GVN had none available, to reassure Thi and the leaders of the Struggle Movement about U.S. support for free elections, to bring opposite sides (especially Ky and Thi) to face to face discussions, and to intervene as needed to end the squabbling. On May 20, Tri Quang complained to another U.S. official about the administrative aircraft who pointed out to him that the U.S. also provided such aircraft to Thi and other dissident military officers. That same day a dissident leader threatened to attack GVN forces at DaNang, and State directed that he be reminded that the U.S. forces also in DaNang would have to defend themselves. State also authorized the threat of total U.S. withdrawal.

On Lodge's return to Vietnam at this time, he received detailed guidance from State, very similar to that previously given to Porter, for his first meeting with Ky. The guidance re-emphasized the demand for prior consultation by GVN before it made any important move, and directed him to urge GVN to be conciliatory and to use its forces with the utmost restraint:

1. We must have absolute candor from Ky as to his plans, and opportunity to comment before significant actions.
2. Tell him to leave pagodas alone, except for surveillance and encirclement.
3. Keep ARVN out of Saigon demonstrations.
4. Elections vs military role: Sound out.
5. Encourage election progress.
6. Keep GVN in contact with Buddhist leaders.
7. Help Ky meet Thi.
8. Consider further the suggestion of withdrawal from DaNang and Hue.
9. Give us "your judgment as to whether we ought to move forcefully and drastically to assert our power" to end strife.
10. Suggest broadening the Directorate with civilians.

By this time, Ky had begun leaning over backward to consult Porter, and then Lodge, before every move. GVN forces overpowered roadblocks and controlled DaNang, but demonstrators were operating freely from pagodas in Saigon, and the Struggle Movement had absolute control of Hue, where in the next few days they surrounded and blockaded the consulate. In Saigon GVN followed Lodge's advice and neutralized the pagodas by surrounding them without violating them; but in the I Corps he was preparing to occupy Hue forcefully as he had DaNang. The Buddhists began a series of self-immolations. Amid mounting threats, the U.S. evacuated the consulate and its other facilities in Hue.

Lodge was unreservedly sympathetic to Ky, as in April, and viewed the Buddhists as equivalent to card-carrying Communists; but he followed instructions and pressed Ky to be conciliatory. When Ky would blurt out fire-eating statements and whittle down his previous promises on elections, Lodge would patiently urge him to avoid off-the-cuff statements and to limit himself to prepared statements on radio and TV. Lodge and Westmoreland repeatedly pressed Ky and Thi to get together, which they did on May 27; Ky offered Thi and Dinh unspecified Army jobs. State was gratified, but cautious.

D.   KY RESTORES GVN CONTROL IN I CORPS, JUNE, 1966

One of the main subjects of Lodge's conferences in Washington was what the U.S. Government position should be on elections for the Constituent Assembly. Having finished deliberations and drafting after Lodge returned to Saigon, State cabled the principles it thought should guide the Mission's operations on election matters:

A. GENERAL PRINCIPLES OF U.S. ACTION

The U.S. Mission should seek to exert maximum influence toward the achievement of the substantive objectives stated in B. below. At the same time, this must be done with recognition that a key objective is to avoid anti-Americanism becoming a major issue; we shall be accused of interferences in any event, but it is vitally important not to give potential anti-American elements (or the press and outside observers) any clear handle to hit us with.

B. OBJECTIVES

1. Elections should be held as announced by GVN on April 15th, that is by September 15 of this year.
2. The issue of anti-Americanism should be kept out of the election campaign as far as possible.
3. The question as to whether the constitutional assembly will only have the role of drafting the constitution or will have some further function should not be allowed to become an active pre-election issue and the U.S. should take no position on this question.
4. The elections should be conducted so as to produce a constitutional assembly fairly representing the various regions and groups within South Vietnam (except those actively participating with the Viet Cong), including the Army, Montagnards, Khmer minorities, et. al.
5. The elections should be conducted so as to gain a maximum improvement in the image of the GVN in the United States and internationally; this calls for a wide turnout, scrupulously correct conduct of the voting and counting process, as little political limitation on voter eligibility as possible and vigorous efforts to avoid voter intimidation from any quarter. Ideas to be explored are a brief election period ceasefire, international observation of the elections, students participating as poll watchers, etc.
6. The emphasis in the campaign should be on the selection of good men to draft the constitution; political parties are not expected to play a major role although the campaign may provide the occasion for laying foundations for future party organization.
7. Unless new developments change our assessment, major efforts should be devoted not to stimulating the formation of a large nationalist party but rather to the adoption of the concept that these elections bring together all non-communist groups who are pledged, among other things, to their country's independence and the continuing need to defend it with American help. Specifically, efforts should not be made to split the Buddhists or isolate the militant Buddhist faction.
8. The election process should be a vehicle for educating and engaging the population in the democratic process and it should be used to launch political and psychological initiatives with youth groups, students, labor, etc.
9. Restore as far as possible the unity of the Directorate and promote a reconciliation between Generals Ky and Thi. However, discourage efforts by the Directorate to form a government party designed purely to perpetuate the Directorate in power to the exclusion of other significant political groups.

At the end of May things seemed to settle down. McNamara sounded out the Embassy about a trip in early June, but Lodge talked him out of it on the grounds that it might tempt the Buddhists to start demonstrating again. Ky met Buddhist Institute leaders on May 31 and offered civilian participation in an enlarged Directorate. He reported that the Buddhists accepted this along with reassurances about elections, and agreed with Ky's new appointment of General Lam as Commander of I Corps. Lodge was skeptical:

> The above is what Ky said and it stood up to questioning. It sounds too good to be true, and we will await next steps.

The next day, June 1, a mob of students burned the consulate and consular residence in Hue. When GVN forces prepared to move on Hue, the Struggle Movement filled the streets with Buddhist altars, serving as roadblocks the GVN forces hesitated to disturb, while dissident ARVN units deployed in the city.

The directorate's April 14 promise of elections of a Constituent Assembly on August 15 had led to the creation of an Electoral Law Commission, which the Buddhists boycotted as a result of the subsequent disagreements. The Commission presented its proposals on June 5, and they included several features unacceptable to the Directorate, especially those related to the powers and tenure of the Assembly. Ky reacted publicly on June 7, saying that if military-civil unity proceeded smoothly enough over the next few months it would be possible to postpone elections. Demonstrations continued in Saigon, while a combination of negotiations and force gradually brought Hue under GVN control.

On June 15, Ky made it clear that the Assembly would not be permitted to continue and to legislate after drafting a constitution, and that the Military Directorate would continue in power until promulgation of the new constitution and the seating of a subsequently elected Assembly in 1967. (Note that Lodge backed this attitude.) The Buddhist Institute called a general strike in response to the GVN declaration that June 18, the anniversary of the Thieu-Ky government, would be a national holiday. On June 19, the Directorate scheduled the elections for the Constituent Assembly for September 11, 1966. The announcement had a calming effect, and the disorders came under control within a few days. The approved electoral law gave the Directorate ample scope to exclude unwanted candidates, and prevented the Buddhists from putting their symbol, the red lotus, on the ballot. (Again, note Lodge's concurrence.)

On July 31, Thi went into exile.

E.   REVOLUTIONARY DEVELOPMENT, MARCH–JUNE, 1966

To help implement the increased emphasis given pacification at Honolulu, President Johnson in late March appointed Robert Komer as his Special Assistant for "peaceful reconstruction." The creation of a high level focal point for pacification planning and coordinating had the effect of supplanting the interagency Vietnam Coordinating Committee (created in 1964 and originally headed by William Sullivan). Though Komer's charter was more limited than that of the VNCC, his direct access to the President conferred particular importance to this position. To his desk came the MACV and Mission reports on the progress of pacification that struck the same gloomy note month after month. The Status Report of March 30 on the Honolulu agreements said:

> 1. Assure that Province Chief actually retains op con over necessary military forces to support program in his Province. Status: In Long An Prov-

ince two regiments of the 25th Division are under Province control. This is encouraging, but tactical situation elsewhere makes it difficult. MACV plans to augment regular forces by 120 companies in 1966–67 (approximately 47 will go to priority areas.) This augmentation if successful will be major step forward.

2. Areas where the program is underway and four priority areas in particular should be placed under superior Province Chiefs who should not be removed while program is underway without serious cause. Status: Since Honolulu, eight Province Chiefs have been replaced. Most fall within category mentioned by General Co at Honolulu when he said GVN was about to make several changes to strengthen their ability to achieve plans. The Mission continues to emphasize at every level the need for continuity, but in most cases it is dangerous for U.S. to go down the line in support of individual Province Chiefs.

The Mission report on the status of "Revolutionary Development" for April said:

> RD remains behind schedule with progress slow. As reported in March, lack of effective leadership, military as well as governmental, marginal local security, and late availability RD cadre teams, continue to hamper program accomplishments.

The corresponding report for May said:

> Lack of effective low-level leadership and lack of local security continued to have adverse effects on RD program . . . progress primarily reflects consolidation of hamlets and population already under a lesser degree of GVN control rather than direct gains from VC control. There was no appreciable expansion in secured area or reduction in VC-controlled population.

An incident in June highlighted the frustrations of U.S. field representatives, and showed that leverage could work, at least on procedural matters. In Kontum, the Province Chief flatly refused to set up any end-use control procedures (filling out requisitions, etc.) for USAID commodities. This refusal could not be accepted, and AID suspended all commodity shipments to the Province. After four days, the Province Chief gave in, and AID resumed shipments.

Meanwhile, the GVN was going nothing about its Honolulu promises in the areas of administration, economic reform, and dollar balances. There were several U.S. Government reactions to these failures and continuing weaknesses. There was a series of studies and proposals for leverage, and there was rising pressure for renewed direct negotiations with GVN.

An example of the studies was the U.S. Army's "Program for the Pacification and Long-Term Development of South Vietnam," (PROVN).

The PROVN study was completed in March 1966 by a Department of the Army staff team and briefed on May 17 at CINCPAC Headquarters during a visit by COMUSMACV to Hawaii. His comments at that time were that most of the recommendations already had been acted on. He emphasized that particular care should be exercised to avoid conditions which would cause RVN officials to be branded as U.S. puppets.

The study results were presented in the MACV conference room on May 21.

In response to a JCS request, COMUSMACV commented in detail on May 27. He noted that PROVN recommended two major initiatives: (1) creation of an organization to integrate the total U.S. civil-military effort, and (2) exercise of greatly increased U.S. involvement in GVN activities.

COMUSMACV agreed with the first recommendation but felt it was already being accomplished. COMUSMACV agreed that immediate and substantially increased U.S. involvement in GVN activities, in the form of constructive influence and manipulations was essential to achievement of U.S. objectives in Vietnam. He felt there was great danger that the involvement envisioned would become excessive and boomerang on U.S. interests; U.S. manipulations could become an American takeover justified by U.S. compulsion to get the job done.

COMUSMACV saw the advantages in removing ARVN divisions from positions of command over provinces, and attaching some of their units to provinces, but this action would require a major shift of Vietnamese attitudes. Assignment of ARVN units to provinces in the past had had limited success because of restrictions on employment and command jealousies.

Accordingly MACV recommended that PROVN, reduced primarily to a conceptual document, carrying forward the main thrusts and goals of the study, be presented to the National Security Council for use in developing concepts, policies, and actions to improve effectiveness of the American effort in Vietnam.

Subsequently, JCS inquired about Revolutionary Development effectiveness. They asked why RD objectives could not be more effectively achieved with the program under military execution. COMUSMACV's reply repeated the views of the Ambassador's December memorandum to Lansdale and said the program was primarily civilian.

F. LODGE FAVORS DECENTRALIZED LEVERAGE

Embassy officials, meanwhile, continued to press for the restoration of the leverage that was lost with the dropping of the troika sign-off in June, 1965. There is no indication that the issue of sign-off came up at Honolulu, very likely because of disagreement on it between State and Saigon. But in April, Ambassador Lodge went on the record in favor of the sign-off system, and against civil encadrement in the Ministries.

> Experience and study have made it apparent that the United States has not the influence which it should have in Viet Nam and also that [we] could be organized so as to be relatively much more immune from some of the worst effects of changes of government in Saigon.
>
> I refer to influence in the provinces, and lower units of government, and not to our influence at the top of the Government in Saigon, which is just about as good as it can be. The GVN in Saigon sometimes disagrees, often agrees, and is rarely able to get much done . . .
>
> An error was made in giving up our right to withhold funds from USAID projects until we have conducted a successful bargain with the Vietnamese in which they agreed to carry out certain things which we wanted . . .
>
> There are two ways of not solving this problem of contact: (a) One is for a US agency head with big administrative responsibilities to pop over to the ministry to argue briefly and intensely, American-fashion, with the Minister—a system which is almost guaranteed not to produce results.

(b) Nor do I believe the problem is solved by putting American offices in the Vietnamese Ministries. This was the French practice, and it too does not prevent bureaucratic paralysis . . .

We should always be on the lookout for Americans who have the sympathy with and the knack of getting along with these people, and we might find some good material among the young men who are in the provinces. Another idea is to bring about a situation where we are really economic partners of the GVN and not merely the people who pay for the CIP Program without effective participation in the use of the piaster proceeds of that program. At present we have very little say in the disposition of such piaster funds. Somewhere along the line we gave up this very important leverage. In fact, we are now trying to recover joint authority over those funds, but progress is difficult . . . If we had this joint GVN/US authority, we could get at corruption, provided we also had advisers with the Ministries who were really "persona grata."

In the first week of May, Porter put the sector fund idea to Ky, who rebuffed him. Lodge tried to keep the idea alive, but without success.

G. THE MILITARY ADVISORY PROGRAM, MARCH–JULY, 1966

COMUSMACV's concern over declining present for combat strength of ARVN units resulted in a study which showed that as of February 28, only 62% of their authorized strength were mustered for operations. There were two principal reasons: (1) Division and regimental commanders had organized non-TOE units such as strike/recon, recon and security, recruiting teams, and (2) Large numbers of deserters, long-term hospital patients, and KIA had not been removed from rolls. MACV instructed JGS to disband non-TOE units and give increased attention to improving administrative procedures. Senior advisers were told to monitor their counterparts and use their influence to bring present for operations strengths up to at least 450 men (75%) per battalion.

At the same time, MACV had a study made to determine the need for reconnaissance units. When field advisers were asked, all replies were favorable; so JGS was asked to develop the organization for a regimental reconnaissance company.

Training was another problem. One adviser stated, "It is more accurate to describe the training program as non-existent instead of unsatisfactory." Another said, "It appears that the battalion commander desires the deterioration of the training status of the battalion so that higher authority will place the unit in a training center to be retrained." COMUSMACV wrote to the Chief JGS in March on the subject of training, but training progress did not change appreciably through 1966 from the level recorded during the first four months.

There was a question of what to do about units which advisers rated ineffective. The combat effectiveness of the 5th and 25th ARVN Divisions was the subject of a staff study completed April 19. Five courses of action were considered:

(1) Deactivate division headquarters and place subordinate units under province chiefs.

(2) Exchange the divisions with two other divisions from different CTZ's.

(3) Relieve the key leaders at all levels who were marginal or unsatisfactory.

(4) Relieve the divisions of their primary responsibility of fighting VC and leave them to pacification.

(5) By expression of COMUSMACV's concern, encourage intensification of adviser efforts to solve the divisions' underlying problems. If there there were no improvement, withdraw all advisers. If there were still no improvement, withdraw all MAP support.

COMUSMACV vetoed the last proposal and had it removed from the study. His guidance was to avoid sanctions against GVN, to intensify the effort to associate and integrate the 5th and 25th ARVN Divisions with the 1st and 25th U.S. Division, and to consider the possibility of greater U.S. participation in pacification in Hau Nghia and Binh Duong provinces.

In April, a study based on exhaustive analysis of field adviser reports and interviews was presented to RVNAF. It concerned itself with several major problem areas: Leadership, discipline, and personnel management. RVNAF reacted positively and quickly to the recommendations by establishing a committee to develop a leadership program.

In response to COMUSMACV guidance in May, J-5 studied courses of action to produce more dynamic progress in the counterinsurgency effort in RVN. It recommended establishing a Deputy COMUSMACV for RVNAF matters as a way to influence RVNAF more. General Westmoreland said in his endorsement that this step had already been taken with the appointment of Brigadier General Freund as Deputy Assistant to COMUSMACV. At the same time, he directed J-5 to review Brigadier General Freund's Terms of Reference and recommend changes or extensions. The completed J-5 study was forwarded to Chief of Staff Army on July 23, recommending that the Special Assistant to COMUSMACV not be given responsibility for any portion of the U.S. Advisory effort.

Low personnel strength was another critical factor in ARVN effectiveness. Only one of 22 battalions rated combat ineffective or marginally effective in July did not report a shortage of personnel. COMUSMACV advised Chief JGS to form an inspection team at general officer level to inspect the strength situation of ARVN division. The Inspector General, JGS, headed the team and was assisted by COMUSMACV's personal representative. The team began its inspection with the 25th Division.

H. ECONOMIC POLICY AND THE PORT OF SAIGON, APRIL–JUNE, 1966

As noted, this period saw rising pressure for renewed direct negotiations with GVN. When the first phase of the Struggle Movement ended in mid-April, Washington was thoroughly dissatisfied with accumulated delays on the economic program agreed at Honolulu. The USG had gone ahead and delivered on its side of the bargain, but GVN had done nothing. State proposed the threat of sanctions; without apparently going that far, Lodge persuaded GVN to cooperate fully with the IMF team, then on its way, to work out an anti-inflationary and balance-of-payments program.

The IMF team worked through late May and at the end of the month agreed with GVN on a program with the following main points:

(1) The exchange rate for imports, including tariff, would be increased from 60 to 118 piasters to the dollar except for rice, which would be brought in at 80. Purchases of piasters by U.S. troops and civilians, and other "invisibles," would have the 118 rate in both directions.

(2) A new tax on beverages would raise about 1.5 billion piasters in revenue.
(3) The GVN would sell gold to jewelers to push the price down closer into line with black market dollar exchange rate.
(4) The GVN would raise wages and salaries of its employees by 20% immediately, with a further 10% to follow in six months if necessary.

The GVN asked the USG for assurance on the following points:

(1) The GVN/IMF plan would substitute for the fiscal and customs reforms promised at Honolulu.
(2) The USG would liberalize the Commodity Imports Program to cover all importers' requests.
(3) The USG would buy all its piasters for official programs at the exchange rate of 80 (versus the previous 35).
(4) All appropriated Commodity Import Funds not used up would be applied to economic development projects in Vietnam.

The USG raised no problem about points (1) and (3) of the GVN requests, but for obvious reasons could give only vague and non-committal assurances on the amount of AID that Congress would authorize and reprogram. However, it made other concessions to increase total economic aid. The two governments reached prompt agreement on these points, and the piaster was devalued as proposed on June 18, along with the associated fiscal reforms. The GVN's promise to hold down its dollar holdings (given at Honolulu) remained "binding," although the generous AID package of the previous July was now raising GVN's dollar balances at a rate of about $100 million per year.

These decisions overrode a proposal from OSD (Systems Analysis) to get tough with GVN and to get deeper and more enforceable reforms. The DASD (Economics) predicted that the GVN would fail to carry out any reforms other than changing the exchange rate, and proposed to force the GVN to maximize its legal revenues from CIP by threatening to curtail the program. Without reform of the licensing, high market prices for CIP commodities yielded extortionate profits to those merchants who could get licenses, with a presumption of kickbacks to the licensing agencies. The proposed reform was to auction the licenses in the presence of US observers. He also proposed direct US purchases of piasters, in a "grey" market.

Upon settling the devaluation package, the Embassy immediately pressed for drastic changes in Saigon port management; the pile-up of civilian cargoes had grown so much as to add to the already serious congestion. Lodge proposed a complete MACV takeover of the port and warehouses with a Vietnamese general to be appointed as figurehead port director. However, the Mission backed away from the idea of complete takeover for the time being, and settled for MACV handling of AID direct assistance commodities, not including CIP. The agreement reached with GVN at the end of June said:

The United States Military Agency appointed by COMUSMACV . . . shall forthwith assume responsibility and all necessary authority for . . .

A. The receipt and discharge of all AID-financed commodities consigned to CPA.
B. The obtaining of customs clearances and all other clearances . . . for such commodities.

C. The storage and warehousing of such commodities intransit as necessary.
D. The transport of such commodities to such first destinations, including GVN holding areas and/or CPA/ministerial depots as may be designated by USAID/CPA.

I. POLITICAL AFFAIRS IN THE THIRD QUARTER, 1966

This period was comparatively quiet, and transactions between the two governments were routine. Late in June, Ky had brought up with Lodge the idea of a cabinet reshuffle, and Lodge had advised him to go slow. In July, Ky agreed to put it off. In August Ky volunteered to do something about the most corrupt generals in the Directorate, especially Co and Quang. Again, Lodge, who had frankly given up on corruption in the highest places, cautioned him to go slow, and Ky decided to put off any action until after the September elections. Lodge's advice, with State concurrence, concentrated on making sure Ky had definitive evidence of the alleged corruption; Lodge was sure that following this advice would delay things sufficiently. Late in August, Ky received an invitation to talk to a press group in Los Angeles, and Ky tentatively accepted. Both Lodge and State panicked, especially when the group started to set up a debate between Ky and Senator Fulbright; and in the upshot they talked Ky out of going.

GVN launched its transition to legitimate government on September 11, electing the long-promised Constituent Assembly. Although GVN systematically excluded from the elections all persons connected with the Struggle Movement, and although the Buddhists declared a boycott, the electorate turned out in large numbers and the results gratified the Embassy. State had reservations about the exclusion of Struggle Movement people, but Lodge unreservedly backed this exclusion, on the ground that GVN "should not be discouraged from taking moderate measures to prevent elections from being used as a vehicle for a Communist takeover of the country." As the election approached, Washington and the Embassy began to think about what they wanted to see in the new constitution. Lodge's view listed the following minimum essentials for the US best interests:

A. A strong, stable executive.
B. Executive control of the military.
C. Emergency powers, so that the legislature can't hamstring the executive during the war emergency.
D. Appropriate provision for the people's aspirations and rights.
E. Minority group representation.

Lodge also listed lower priority requirements for the new constitution:

A. Relative ease of amendment of the constitution.
B. Removal of either the President or the Legislature should be very difficult.
C. A limited term for the President.
D. Appropriate provision for establishment and improvement of the judiciary.
E. A superior court for constitutional review of laws and decrees.

F. Expansion of the powers of provincial councils and other forms of local government.

State expressed broad agreement with Lodge's views, with reservations about emergency powers and about constitutional provisions to forbid communism and neutralism.

J. THE ROLES AND MISSIONS STUDY

In response to a May 27 directive from Deputy Ambassador Porter, the Director JUSPAO had named Colonel George Jacobson chairman of a study group to define RD strategy and the roles and missions of the various elements. The group submitted its report on August 24, 1966.

The major recommendations of Roles and Missions Study were:

(1) The many elements and echelons charged with destroying VC infrastructure are confusing. The National Police should have the primary mission and responsibility for this goal.

(2) Reforms in basic GVN attitudes are necessary. Many rural residents believe that the US condones corrupt practices. This must be changed.

(3) ARVN forces should be encouraged to increase participation in pacification activities.

(4) PF/RF should be developed into a constabulary-type organization.

(5) PF/RF should be transferred from the Ministry of Security to the Ministry of Revolutionary Development.

(6) CIDG should be stationed only in remote areas.

(7) The Vietnamese Information Service is not effective at local level. It should assume supporting role to propaganda activities of other agencies.

(8) A Directorate of Intelligence should be established to coordinate all intelligence activities.

(9) Reinstitution of the MACV Subsector Advisor Fund is urged.

(10) ARVN Divisions (eventually Corps as well) should be removed from the chain of command in RD affairs. For instance, there were no USAID, JUSPAO, or CAS representatives at ARVN division headquarters.

(11) Because of generally bad behavior of ARVN Ranger units, they should be disbanded with Rangers reassigned as individuals throughout the Army.

(12) The physical and attitudinal consequences of present air and artillery employment policies should be studied.

(13) A logistic system which provides for US government control until delivery of material to end users should be substituted for the present MAP procedures.

(14) The Provincial Committee "signoff" provision should be reinstated for the Revolutionary Development budget.

On September 7 COMUSMACV made the following comments with respect to the Roles and Missions Study:

(1) Action had been taken to increase ARVN participation in RD, but removal of Division from the chain of command in RD activities appeared illogical. If ARVN combat battalions were dispersed to all 43

provinces, the Corps span of control would be ineffective and this arrangement would risk having these units defeated in detail. The proposed placement of battalions under sector commanders was feasible only in some areas—to be considered on an individual basis. The 1967 Combined Campaign Plan would clarify the functions of ARVN. Other things such as the buddy system with US units were the realistic ways of accomplishing the goal.

(2) The recommended disbandment of Ranger Battalions would seriously reduce ARVN combat strength. They should be retained and reorganized under new commanders.

(3) Recruitment of PF personnel for RD would weaken hamlet security.

(4) Although the study recommended giving primary responsibility for intelligence to the National Police, the nature of the problem dictated that all US and GVN military and quasimilitary elements contribute to this important goal.

(5) The idea of a single intelligence director seems sound theoretically, but it is not realistic when DIA and CIA are not amalgamated in Washington.

(6) RD requires both military and civil participation. Continued emphasis on military participation would be given but the major change in the MACV organization suggested by the study did not seem necessary.

One of the year's changes that could have led to implementation of a major recommendation of the Roles and Missions Study, but didn't, was the March decision in Washington to transfer the support of FWMAF and RVNAF from MAP funding to service funding. Studies were made by MACV on how best to implement this change, which became effective in September. It was decided that only the logistic advisory function would be transferred to USARV. Programming budgeting and executing programs remained under MACV. Most important, MAP goods were still put into RVNAF logistic channels, although under the new funding they could have been held in US channels down to the receiving unit.

K. ECONOMIC POLICY AND THE PORT, THIRD QUARTER, 1966

Although in political affairs there was no significant friction between USG and GVN in the Third Quarter, GVN's accumulation of dollar balances and its inaction on economic matters caused growing impatience in USOM and in Washington.

In late July, 1966, Komer and Ambassador Lodge laid the basis for the US position, including a suggestion that from now on USOM should make sure it has the means to monitor and enforce GVN compliance with its commitments.

Komer said:

> Devaluation, port takeover, CIP expansion, RD reorganization if all skillfully meshed—could yet have early impact on VN public and do much in these critical weeks to refurbish GVN image at home and abroad.
>
> So far, however, GVN has failed to move aggressively enough with supplies in country to curb rice and port speculation; has been unwilling to try to develop wage restraint policy in private sector, has dithered on promulgating and carrying out promised regulations re Warehouse removals; has gone about moving expanded CIP goods up country on business as

usual basis; has shuffled about on RD reorganization, and Thang's or Ky's famous report to the nation.

Lodge proposed specific means to monitor GVN, and wished to urge the GVN to fund Revolutionary Development with counterpart piasters, so that USG could assure that the funding was adequate. Komer agreed with these proposals. Porter further proposed:

> We intend using budget review process and counterpart releases on lever-age on GVN CY 67 programs and to seek GVN acceptance of both overall ceiling and commitment to essential revolutionary development programs before we agree to support any part of the budget.
> Note degree our effectiveness dependent on credibility our leverage by GVN, which may not be great.

But Porter opposed a complete takeover of the Saigon port, proposed by Komer.

VI. A SEVEN-NATION CONFERENCE, LEGITIMATE GOVERNMENT, AND HIGH HOPES FOR THE FUTURE, OCTOBER, 1966—SEPTEMBER, 1967

A. THE MANILA CONFERENCE, OCTOBER 1966

In the first week of October, just as planning was beginning for a seven-nation conference at Manila on Southeast Asia, latent mistrust between South-erners and Northerners in Ky's cabinet broke into an open split. A Northerner persuaded Colonel Loan, the Police Director, to arrest one of the Southerners, and although Loan released him on Ky's order a few hours later, six Southerners took it as an affront to all of them and threatened to resign from the cabinet. While conference planning was going forward, the crisis simmered on for al-most three weeks, up to the eve of the conference. Lodge tried to mediate, but the six proved difficult to mollify; he conjectured that they were trying to get all the mileage they could out of the embarrassment the crisis would cause Thieu and Ky if it were not resolved before the conference. It was patched up at the last minute.

In preparing for the conference, Lodge was particularly concerned that Ky or Thieu, if put in the limelight through the opening speech to the conference, should avoid embarrassing the USG:

> One crucial factor must be degree to which you believe they can be per-suaded to make constructive and reasonable speech, avoiding talk of in-vasion of the North or any other subjects that put us openly at variance with each other . . . We hope that the GVN can delegate Tran Van Do and Bai Diem as its drafting representatives so that even before they arrive in Manila we would be a long way toward common agreement on the kinds of language we need.

The USG was also concerned that GVN should announce a broad and attractive program that would put a good face on itself and its prosecution of the war:

> We welcome your news that Tran Van Do and Bai Diem will arrive Ma-nila October 21 . . .

Since this gives us at least a solid day, the 22d, to refine drafts, we are inclined here not repeat not to ask you to work with GVN on detailed submissions . . . Rather and absolutely vital to favorable conference result, we believe you should be working with Ky to get his concurrence on the following list of action areas in which we believe forthcoming statement by GVN is not only wise in itself, but essential to US strong and successful public statement from the conference.

A. Land Reform
B. Constitutional Evolution
C. National Reconciliation
D. Economic Stabilization
E. Improved Local Government
F. Radically Increased Emphasis on RD/Pacification
G. Postwar Planning
H. Corruption
I. Port Congestion
J. GVN Reserves

In each of above categories, basic problem is to get GVN commitment and willingness to state its intentions.

Secretary McNamara put down his views on priorities in a Memorandum to the President on October 14. He noted that the US had not yet found the formula for training and inspiring the Vietnamese. The main thrust of the memorandum concerned shifting ARVN more into pacification and shifting the US pacification responsibility to MACV. But in disucssing GVN's weaknesses, he commented, "drastic reform is needed." He let that one drop without any recommendation.

The conferees met in Manila on October 24-25, 1966, and after due deliberation issued a long communique on policies for Southeast Asia in general and South Vietnam in particular. They backed the defense of South Vietnam against North Vietnamese aggression, and supported the major outlines of US policy. The GVN emphasized its promises of social revolution, economic progress, and political freedom. They concluded with the declaration of intent to withdraw all US and Free World forces under specified conditions:

> 29. In particular, they declared that allied forces are in the Republic of Vietnam because that country is the object of aggression and its Government requested support in the resistance of its people to aggression. They shall be withdrawn, after close consultation, as the other side withdraws its forces to the North, ceases infiltration, and the level of violence thus subsides. Those forces will be withdrawn as soon as possible and not later than six months after the above conditions have been fulfilled.

B. BARGAINING BEGINS ON NATIONAL RECONCILIATION, OCTOBER–DECEMBER, 1966

The USG, having chafed at the lack of action on the Chie Hoi Program, wanted GVN to broaden it to attract high-level defectors by offering them posts comparable to their existing ones in the VC organization. This idea went down poorly with the Vietnamese. Lodge was pressing the idea from the beginning of October, and although they were reluctant, Thieu and Ky finally agreed on October 20 to proclaim the new program, called "National Reconciliation," on November 1, a national holiday. As noted above, Washington wanted and got a public commitment on this subject at Manila.

Then on November 1, the promised proclamation failed to appear; instead, there was a vague reference to it in a speech on other subjects. When the Embassy inquired, Ky said the speech had to be prepared very carefully, and that he had not had time before November 1; he promised he would have the speech and proclamation ready in early December. Lodge found this explanation hard to swallow, but had to accept it. When "early December" arrived, there was a dead silence; and the end of this exercise was not yet in sight.

C. MORE HARD BARGAINING ON ECONOMIC POLICY AND THE PORT, OCTOBER–DECEMBER, 1966

Economic policy negotiations had the same flavor as those relating to National Reconciliation. The USG was dissatisfied, in the third quarter 1966, as noted, on the lack of GVN follow-up on budgetary and foreign exchange promise in June following the IMF agreement. And in the fall, the Saigon Port congestion problem grew serious again; the June agreement had not gone far enough.

At the end of September, Governor Hanh of the RVN National Bank came to Washington to negotiate specifics on economic policy. During the negotiations, Komer cabled Lodge:

> [We are pressing GVN] hard to agree to spend rapidly growing foreign exchange reserves on imports. Otherwise, it will appear and rightly so, that GVN is getting rich at US taxpayer's expense. It is apparent that GVN's chief reluctance on this score is that Thanh/Hanh want to squirrel away reserves for postwar rehabilitation in case US goes away and leaves them.

In the upshot, however, they reached only a vague and general agreement, on October 6, the most specific item being that GVN would limit its inflationary gap to 10 billion piasters in 1967. Dollar balances were deferred to later negotiations.

There was some effort to resolve disagreements on economic matters and the Port just before the Manila Conference, but no progress. Komer went to Saigon after the Conference and, assisting Porter in the negotiations, reached the following agreement with GVN on November 2:

> (1) GVN will use all gold and foreign exchange available to it in excess of $250 million, not including commercial bank working balances, to finance invisibles and imports, including import categories now financed by the US.
> (2) GVN will place at least $120 million of its reserves in US dollar instruments of at least 2 year maturity.
> (3) During US FY 67 USG will make available at least $350 million of grant aid for imports, not including PL 480 Title 1 Commodities. Any portion of the $350 million not required for such imports will be used during the US FY 67 as grant assistance for economic development projects.
> (4) Within the balance of payments accounts, the amounts or categories

to be financed by each of the governments will be determined through joint consultation on a quarterly basis.

The putting of GVN dollar reserves into US two-year or longer-term bonds would technically improve the US balance of payments, though the gain would be more nominal than real. The agreement left plenty of room for further problems and State recognized that each item would probably have to be pressed again.

Following this agreement, the Embassy prepared to negotiate a GVN budgetary ceiling and related matters. The strategy would be to seek agreement on a firm budget ceiling for GVN without committing the USG on its spending in Vietnam. But the Embassy had misgivings about this approach:

> . . . It deprives US of the monetary gap analysis as a hinge on which stabilization agreements can be hung . . . Note that Komer-Hanh memorandum signed in Washington used 10 Billion gap figure as objective.
>
> GVN officials are anxious to resume discussions. Prime Minister now has on his desk proposed GVN CY 67 budget of 100 billion piasters. The differences between that figure and acceptable one is much greater than the differences in US ceiling estimates last discussed here during McNamara's visit.

State cabled its agreement that showing GVN the US plan to limit its own piaster spending would help get GVN to accept tight ceilings itself.

In December, Embassy negotiators tried to pin down GVN on the means to limit its accumulation of dollar balances, talking mainly with Governor Hanh. To evade specific commitment, he repeatedly talked as though he could not determine GVN budget policy (which he had negotiated in Washington two months before) and that he could not as a good banker make the bookkeeping transactions that would be required to permit GVN to run them down by buying imports. The Embassy negotiators then turned to the idea of asking for a GVN contribution of 8 billion piasters to the Free World Forces' operating budget in Vietnam as a cost-sharing arrangement, which would incidentally reduce GVN's receipts of dollars and so help run down the balances. GVN's reply was that that was impossible. After a series of talks that read like haggling in an Arabian marketplace, Porter went to Ky about it and got the following understanding:

> The GVN accepts the principle of contributing to free world forces local expense and will make a contribution of 1 Billion piasters for that purpose at the end of March 1967. The matter of further contribution would be considered at that time. I would send him a letter of understanding on that subject.

The story was much the same on GVN support for AID projects.

The Saigon Port congestion problem led to discussions starting around the 1st of October, which produced nominal, ineffective agreements in the first week. When McNamara went to Saigon to discuss new major troop deployments with MACV, he talked to Ky on October 11, Ky kept talking about infiltration whenever McNamara brought up the subject of the Port. Finally, Ky said he had solved the Port problem by telling the Minister of Finance "to write a decree to get rid of the mafia which was dominating the port."

That did not solve the problem; the Embassy kept pressing. On November 2, Ky promised a tough decree on port management and a deliver-or-get-fired order to the General who had been put in charge of the Port after the June agreement. (Accepting merely this order would permit further delay before any change in the system, of course.) Later on in November, Ky changed port charges and accepted some increase in US military personnel there; but both GVN and MACV strongly resisted any increase in MACV responsibility for the port. The GVN also refused to confiscate goods left unclaimed over 30 days in the port warehouses. Further talks in December got nowhere, although State authorized drastic leverage to move GVN:

> To this end you might also tell Ky that I have gone so far as to propose a two month moratorium on shipment of US financed CIP goods beginning 1 January to permit backlog in transit warehouses and on barges to be removed. You could cite my view as being that if GVN won't clear port, why should US add to congestion by continuing to ship goods?
> I recognize that actual moratorium would be draconian measure and perhaps unrealistic, but citing it . . . might help move Ky.

D. CORRUPTION BECOMES AN ISSUE AT YEAR'S END

The issue of corruption came up in several ways in November and December, 1966. On November 10, Ky told Lodge he was now prepared to relieve General Quang of his command of IV Corps, following up on intentions he first told Lodge about in August. Lodge again urged caution, saying Ky should carefully avoid starting "another General Thi incident." But Lodge was satisfied that by this time Ky had prepared well for the move. He had: on November 18, the Embassy got word that General Quang would head a newly-created Ministry of Planning and Development; the Ministry would deal primarily with postwar planning. The command changed and Quang moved up on November 23. Possibly Ky's idea of how to deal with Quang came from an end-October suggestion from the Embassy for a joint postwar study team, to which Ky had agreed and was to announce jointly with the White House. (Creating the Ministry scrambled the plans for the study team and announcement, so the Embassy had to go to work on a new plan.)

A couple of weeks later, following allegations of corruption in news stories, State cabled the Embassy that the President wanted accelerated efforts both to cope with diversions and to deflate distorted allegations. State was also considering sending a "blue ribbon panel" from Washington to assess the problem of AID misuse. Responding to the stories and to the Washington concern, Ky said he planned a national campaign against corruption. State told the Embassy on November 25 of suggestions in Washington for a joint US/GVN inspectorate general to follow up AID diversions, and asked for a reaction. After a delay due to active truce discussions with the VC, Saigon replied on December 2:

> There is already an interchange of information on the working level between Ky's investigative staff and our responsible poeple in USAID. We doubt GVN would respond positively to idea of joint US/GVN inspectorate to work on AID diversions. This would touch very sensitive areas. While we want to expose and cut diversions to maximum extent possible, we doubt that this rather public way is best suited to achieve GVN cooperation.

On December 3, Lodge and Ky had an "amiable discussion" on corruption, and Ky agreed to study and consider all these suggestions.

E. POLITICAL MATTERS AT YEAR'S END, 1966

Washington and the Saigon Mission watched closely as the Constituent Assembly did its work. Concern arose at word that GVN was providing a complete draft constitution either formally or through sympathetic Deputies, particularly because it provided that ultimate political power would be vested in the Armed Forces Council.

Washington, consistent in its championing of National Reconciliation, urged the Mission to make the USG's views known both to GVN and to key CA members before the matter because a major issue. Lodge spoke with Ky who said he was at that very moment about to leave to talk with Thieu on the matter. Lodge further encouraged Ky to state his views on the constitution to the Chairman of the Drafting Committee and reminded Ky that the American constitutional expert, Professor Flanz, was available to go to Ky at any time to give advice in complete confidence.

General Thieu concluded one of his regular discussions of the military situation with General Westmoreland by making a few pronouncements on political matters. Westmoreland stressed what was to become a persistent American theme, the importance of unity in the GVN leadership. Unabashedly Thieu said that the key question was whether the Army would stay in power and what power they would retain.

F. PACIFICATION AND THE SHIFT OF ARVN

Komer, in Washington, continued to prod the Mission to goad GVN. It seemed time to remind them, he thought, of their Manila promise to give top priority to land reform. Lodge was asked to press Ky for vigorous application of existing laws.

Continuing emphasis on pacification and increased impatience at the lack of progress brought another reorganization of the US Mission effort. To unify and streamline the civilian side, the Office of Civil Operations (OCO) was established in late November under Deputy Ambassador Porter. An OCO Director in Saigon and a single Director of Civil Affairs for each of the four corps became responsible for the Mission's civil support of Vietnamese Revolutionary Development. Within GVN General Thang not only lasted beyond the originally envisaged six months but was elevated to Commissioner-General for Revolutionary Development with supervision over the Ministries of RD, Public Works, Agriculture, and Administration (Interior). These changes seemed to enhance the chances for substantive improvements. Washington wired,

> Why not approach Thang and after telling him about your reorganization and new faces you plan to put in region and then provinces, suggest he essay a shake-up too. . . . As I recall, around Tet GVN issues a new promotion list, which usually also entails some joint shifts. This might provide a good cover.

The reply offered now familiar themes as the reasons for inaction,

> Specifically, if we were to give Thang a list of district chiefs and ask that they be removed, we do not think any significant change would result. In the past this tactic has proved cumbersome, even counterproductive, and

tends to lead either to reshuffling of positions with little or no positive end result or to the Asian deep freeze treatment.

. . . At times we will have to make our views known on particular personalities if we find an intolerable situation in key leadership positions, as we have done in Long An and the ARVN 25th Div. Basically, however, we will seek to avoid too deep an immersion in Vietnamese personalities, which can so easily become a quagmire from which there is no escape and concentrate instead on encouraging the GVN/RVNAF to take the initiative in a situation they know best how to tackle in specific tactical terms.

Meanwhile, efforts went forward to convert half of ARVN to the primary mission of supporting Revolutionary Development. On October 5, the Chief of the Central Training Agency, Major General Vy, chaired the high level joint conference which assigned administrative tasks and developed a schedule of required actions. Subsequently, a joint MACV/JGS team visited a few ARVN division headquarters and found that personnel had not understood the July JGS directives and thus had not undertaken the actions directed.

At about the same time, Revolutionary Development Minister Thang entered one of his recurring periods of pouting because he considered recent American criticism of slowness to imply their evaluation of the program as a failure. He told Ky he was ready to resign if Americans were so critical that they wanted to take it over and run it. Lansdale was able to placate Thang, but ARVN reluctance continued.

The conversion to RD was fraught with criticism on both sides, for the American press continued to suggest that the ARVN shift to pacification meant Americans would bear the brunt of the fighting and take the bulk of the casualties. State considered this line tendentious and urged Lodge and MACV to use "all leverage provided through MAP and advisor program" to shift ARVN to RD.

G.   MILITARY ADVISORY MATTERS AT YEAR'S END, 1966

COMUSMACV backed out of ARVN personnel selection by serving notice in a message to Corps Senior Advisors that only policy matters, not the detailed problems of failure to perform, were to be referred to him.

In reviewing the deficiencies discussed in the Senior Advisor's Monthly Reports, it is noted that many items are correctable in command channels at unit, division, or corps level; yet it is not apparent that such action is being taken aggressively at local and intermediate command levels. Deficiencies involving policy are referable appropriately to this headquarters; deficiencies involving non-compliance with directives, apathy on the part of a command, etc., are to be resolved in RVNAF channels.

The role of the advisor is difficult and often frustrating. It requires military acumen, dedication, selflessness, and perseverance. It is desired that addressees channel the professional abilities of the advisory apparatus into efforts designed to complement tactical advice with improvement in the quality, efficiency, and reliability of the RVNAF structure as a whole.

Shortly afterward the Chinh-Hunnicutt affair erupted. As it unfolded it revealed the near impossibility of eliciting satisfactory performance by means of the existing advisory system. CG 25th Division published an order of the day accusing the Senior Advisor of trying to have the CG removed, of attempting to dismiss other division officers, of bypassing the chain of command, and of destroying the "spirit of cooperation between Americans and Vietnamese."

The MACV command history describes General Chinh as extremely weak, afraid to command. The Senior Advisor was a dynamic, competent officer assigned to improve effectiveness. He pursued his objective in a firm manner.

COMUSMACV felt the incident received distorted press coverage in the US where it was portrayed as a challenge to the entire position of the US advisory effort. He noted that the Vietnamese were sensitive to real or imagined infringements on their sovereignty. Great care had to be exercised to avoid even the appearance of violating their pride; an officer who yielded too readily to US advice was regarded as a puppet. He felt the most effective way to work with the Vietnamese was to discuss matters with them and then allow them to resolve their problems. CG 25th Division did have redeeming qualities. He was considered honest; and for his stand at the coup trials in the early 1960's, when he had accepted punishment while many others were running; he had acquired a sizeable following among ARVN officers. He was, in addition, a boyhood friend of CG III Corps, who was said to recognize the CG's fault but felt that his hands were tied.

Deputy COMUSMACV who enjoyed good rapport with CG 25th ARVN Division, visited General Chinh. In a two-hour meeting, the Vietnamese spoke freely and openly. He displayed genuine and extreme concern and admitted his error in issuing the Order of the Day. He had already apologized to CG III Corps. Deputy COMUSMACV received the impression that the advisor might have been a little too aggressive with the Vietnamese general, who was hypersensitive. Deputy COMUSMACV suggested that a memorandum be published to the division which would mention that the Order of the Day had leaked to the press which had taken it out of context and that there was no intention to disparage the advisory effort. The memorandum was published on December 21. It said the past must be forgotten and that cadre of all ranks should display warm, courteous, and friendly attitudes toward their American counterparts. General Chinh appeared to turn over a new leaf. Colonel Hunnicutt was reassigned to an apparent terminal assignment in the United States.

COMUSMACV addressed a letter to all advisors in December, 1966, to again emphasize the importance of rapport. He said, the key to success or failure was the relationship achieved and maintained by the advisor with his counterpart. The natural tendency of the US professional soldier was toward immediate reaction. He expected the same in others, but it was necessary to temper counterpart relationships with patience and restraint.

General Westmoreland affirmed this view in his remarks at a conference of his senior subordinate commanders.

> In order for ARVN to be successful, a re-education process is necessary, from the generals on down . . . The attitude of the soldiers toward the people frequently is poor. . . . We must do all we can toward to change this . . .
> . . . In conduct of operations in support of Revolutionary Development, we will frequently have units buddy up with ARVN units . . . A word on command relations in these combined operations is appropriate. We have had great success with our cooperative efforts in the past. We should establish a proper relationship from a technical command standpoint. Proper types of missions are general support and direct support. When conducting operations where we have the preponderance of forces committed . . . their association will be in direct support or general sup-

port of our operations. This is good military terminology and quite proper for us here. General Vien agrees in this terminology.

Sometimes ARVN was not receptive to advice. In November, recognizing the validity of a recommendation from the Corps Advisor that an additional battalion be activated in the ARVN 23d Battalion, COMUSMACV suggested this to JGS. Inactivation of a marginally effective battalion in another division was suggested as compensation. Chief JGS, for reasons of his own, declined to authorize the 23d Division to have an additional battalion.

Still, the effort moved forward. Training of RD Mobile Training Teams from each ARVN Division was conducted in December. The actual conversion training of divisions started in early 1967, and a similar program for RF/PF was planned. In fact, planning was viewed as the surest sign of progress. The 1967 Combined Campaign Plan was ceremoniously signed by Generals Westmoreland and Vien on December 8. Its significant innovations were requirements for subordinate commands to prepare supporting plans and for quarterly reviews to maintain the plan's viability.

H. CONSTITUTION-WRITING IN JANUARY, 1967

Progress within the Constituent Assembly and preliminary jockeying over the new constitution were persistent concerns during the first quarter of 1967.

At times the Assembly seemed remarkably independent. It publicly fought against a law which gave the military junta the right to over-rule its decisions. The controversy subsided in January with Junta assurance that it would not use the law. There was considerable discussion within USG circles as to how American influence should be disposed in supporting presidential candidates. Marshall Ky was already making noises about running. Washington cautioned Saigon not to automatically oppose a Ky candidacy. While State would prefer a civilian president, the most important matter was to effect transition to a constitutional government that was strong and unified enough to continue to prosecute the war effort (or negotiate a peaceful settlement),

> . . . and at the same time broadly enough based to attract increasing local and national political strength away from VC.

Ambassador Lodge's reply was, "the continued viability of SVN depends very heavily on the cohesiveness of the military." This had been and remained his evaluation of the political situation.

> . . . Unity of the military is essential to government stability in VN. From the standpoint of stability, this is the Law and the Prophets.
> Movement toward a broadly based, truly popular government is impossible without stability.
> The military is also the chief nation-building group in the country. It has education, skills, experience, and discipline which no other group can offer.

State acquiesced in this argument but continued to hope for a government broadly enough based so that the VC would find avenues to conquest of South Vietnam effectively blocked.

> . . . In our view it is less a question of any civilian candidate controlling

the military and more a question of the military being educated to accept a sharing of power and responsibility with civilians as a necessary elementary political progress. This means a readiness to accept the outcome of a free and open election in which the candidate favored by the directorate may not win.

I.   *FOREIGN EXCHANGE NEGOTIATIONS AND THE GVN BUDGET, JANUARY–MARCH, 1967*

The problem of GVN dollar balances remained a thorn. GVN did nothing to carry out its November agreements. With scarcely concealed impatience, Ambassador Porter offered GVN a tough economic program, in a meeting in the first week of January, 1967, with special emphasis on the dollar balances. Reporting on the meeting, he said:

> We underlined many times the very high level of the US commitment and said that we could not make this commitment unless we had [an] iron-clad guaratee that the GVN would live up [to] the foreign exchange agreement . . . we stated that this was the minimum the US could accept.

Hard bargaining continued, including another Hanh trip to Washington. Preliminary to the Conference, Washington considered several steps which might be taken:

1. Agreement on a piaster/dollar rate of 118 for official US purchases.
2. US use of all counterpart over P-30 billion.
3. Increase of Assistance In Kind from GVN.
4. Possible transfer of some official purchases from the 80 to a 118 exchange rate without changing the official rate.
5. Transfer of DoD contracts to the 118 rate.
6. Tying all 80 rate dollars to US procurement.
7. 100% US use of PL 480 sales.

Saigon's opinion was that for these negotiations there were two main routes:

(1) A switch of counterpart funds from their use to ours, and
(2) A change in the exchange rate.

The first seemed preferable because it was more negotiable. The second might be counter-productive by "simply angering Hanh without moving him." On February 20, GVN merely agreed to work on an "interim memorandum of understanding which would include actions to implement the foreign exchange agreement of last November." When Komer went to Saigon later in February to negotiate, he found it necessary to threaten specifically to reduce the CIP program to force down GVN's dollar balances, noting that once the program was cut Congress would be unlikely to restore the cuts. The negotiations amply demonstrated the truth of Hanh's remark that Orientals only act after much bargaining. As Komer started to walk out the door after a meeting, Hanh hinted at a raise in the official purchase piaster rate from 80 to 118, but made no other concession. (At no time did the USG threaten explicitly to buy piasters in the open market, as Porter and DASD (Economics) had earlier proposed, a procedure that would knock down GVN dollar balances to whatever extent we wanted while using fewer dollars to get the required piasters.) In an exchange of letters early in March, Hanh said he understood the US was willing to establish $50 million development fund in return for their purchase of 300 thousand tons of rice on a 100% US use basis and repayment of $25 million ICA loan. From Komer, now back in Washington, came this reply,

> There is in my view no doubt whatever that Hanh, and for that matter Ky, understood full well that we did not agree to the $50 million GVN Development Fund as part of interim package. Nor do I regard our credibility as enhanced if we now retreat even more on this issue. Finally, I regard the Development Fund as a sweetener so clearly wanted by the GVN that we need not give it away too cheaply.
>
> While in one sense we have little immediate leverage to use on the GVN so long as we do not choose to withhold aid in one form or another, in another sense we clearly have the GVN worried. I believe that, either through a definitive solution this June or more likely via Salami tactics, we can keep GVN reserves from rising too far.

In mid-March Komer reached another "Interim Agreement" with GVN on foreign exchange. It provided that:

(1) The United States would supply at least an additional 100,000 tons of PL 480 rice and a further 300,000 tons of rice under terms providing for 100% USG use of proceeds.

(2) GVN would make available up to $120 million of foreign exchange for financing commodities previously imported under the CIP.

(3) The United States would make available for economic development projects the balance of FY 67 funds unused as a result of the reduction of the CIP program and would proceed to initiate and make grants for several interim projects.

(4) The United States agreed to the establishment by GVN of a $50 million development fund for purchase of US goods and services, such fund to be considered as use of Vietnamese foreign exchange resources under the November 4, 1966 agreement.

(5) GVN would repay US loans totalling $53 million.

Closely related on the economic front was the GVN budget. Estimates of the CY 1967 inflationary gap grew during the quarter from 14 to 20 billion piasters. The United States exercised only spotty influence on their budget, specifically on those items receiving direct American support; and general persuasion was used to hold down the overall limit. Governor Hanh tried to transfer all US counterpart funds to the military budget with the explanation that only the US military could adequately control the South Vietnamese military, but the guessing was that this might also be his way of freeing GVN civilian agencies from any American interference.

Washington efforts to get more information on the GVN budget only brought educated guesses and a reminder that the Mission did not participate in a review of the GVN civil budget as was the practice for the military part. The CY 1967 budget of 75 billion piasters was issued without prior discussion with AID. It was unsatisfactory. USAID had the leverage to negotiate because of counterpart funds and PL 480 receipts, but the major problem was how to provide AID the necessary funding mechanics to implement programs at levels sufficient to meet established requirements.

J. THE SAIGON PORT AGAIN

Severe congestion continued to plague the Port of Saigon. A drop in CIP/GVN cargo discharged in December brought queries from Washington. Saigon replied that the drop was due to the GVN port director's abortive great barge experiment and listed a number of corrective steps taken. In fact all were peripheral to the central problem, the failure of commercial importers to remove their goods from crowded warehouses. Saigon warned,

> Any additional actions . . . would require high-level government to government agreements which in our estimation would not be appropriate at this time.

Highest authorities in Washington remained concerned and pressed for a complete military takeover or at least a comprehensive alternate plan which would demonstrably meet the problem. Saigon held back with the view that progress was being made, that Ky was persuaded of the need to eliminate port congestion and that he was doing his utmost to solve the problem. A US takeover was once again viewed as neither politically possible nor desirable. CINCPAC chimed in to support strongly the Saigon position, and at the end of the quarter Washington was still peppering Saigon with comment:

> We here do not take same relaxed view of barge situation Saigon port as Saigon . . . Highest authorities have been consistently concerned.

At the same time an overlooked aspect of the earlier extension of US control of the port was being bounced back and forth. MACV clearance of AID financed project and procured commodities was estimated to have made AID liable for one billion piasters for port clearance costs previously financed by GVN. Nobody was quite certain how to approach GVN on the matter or how the US should pay the bill within existing dollar and piaster ceilings.

K. MINOR BUT PRICKLY PROBLEMS, JANUARY–MARCH, 1967

The clearance costs problem was an example of several minor matters which arose between the governments, problems that were often difficult to handle because prestige and sovereignty were involved. GVN National Bank Governor Hanh and the Embassy tangled over GVN issuance of instructions to commercial banks operating facilities for US military forces.

The Embassy became concerned because American civilians, tried and punished in GVN courts on the basis of American-supplied evidence, were subjected to extortion. The ticklish part of the problem was how to investigate the practice without jeopardizing those in the midst of buying their way out. Soon there were ill-considered remarks to the press by Brigadier General Loan who said that GVN had sole jurisdiction over civilians. State instructed Saigon to keep mum on the subject. Finally, in March it was publicly announced that the United States would exercise court martial jurisdiction over civilians but "only rarely, in exceptional cases." The US did not question, as a matter of law, the existence of a basis for court martial jurisdiction over civilians and indicated that our policy would be to handle the problem of civilians in other ways. The statement was careful to reaffirm US respect for GVN sovereignty, so as to avoid the issue of a formal status of forces agreement.

Whether GVN could levy requirements for reports and payments upon US contract airlines caused bantam-like stances on each side. GVN demanded that contract flights pay landing charges. Porter replied that was improper and offered GVN notification of flights as a sop. Ky's retort was a demand for copies of contracts and schedules, restrictions on in-country flights and limitation of loads to personnel and equipment strictly military. We rejected those terms and the military nature of the problem probably saved a contract flight from becoming the "example" later in January when one plane-load of Pan American passengers baked in tropical heat for several hours while GVN refused them permission to disembark at Tan Son Nhut.

Premier Ky's implied intention in February to accept an invitation to speak in the United States produced an apprehensive reaction from Washington. Ambassador Lodge cautioned, "We have twice headed him off and to object a third time might create strain." Eventually Ky was able to publicly postpone his visit on the grounds that his presence was needed to insure a free and fair election.

Diversion of MAP material remained a closet skeleton to be rattled periodically. In February, MACV performed estimative gymnastics to suggest that no more than 0.3% of MAP material had been so lost. CINCPAC quickly suggested that valid data did not exist and would be hard to compile. He said that the differences between manifests and the material actually received should be otherwise identified, and his thoughts seemed for the moment to take care of a potentially embarrassing need to explain a $5 million problem without even bothering GVN.

Throughout the quarter there were periodic flurries of talks about negotiations with North Vietnam. U Thant was especially active and these maneuvers caused an uneasiness in US/GVN relations because Saigon was never completely certain what role it would have in such discussions.

L. THE OTHER WAR

Top levels in Washington realized that not much progress was being made in Revolutionary Development and exhorted Saigon to integrated, detailed civil/military planning. COMUSMACV waffled once again on whether ARVN battalions supporting RD should actually be retained under the operational control of the province chief. US Army units continued their work in the densely populated Delta provinces. On one occasion Premier Ky called Colonel Sam Wilson in for his view of progress there as well as to ask for an evaluation of the ARVN 46th Regiment. Wilson was able to say plainly that the unit was poor and that its commander was ineffective and, without a doubt, corrupt. Ky explained that the commander in question was a close friend of the division commander who was a close friend of the corps commander who was a close friend of Ky. That seemed to explain the matter.

The US continued to press national reconciliation upon the Saigon government. Unger and CAS assets worked with the Constituent Assembly to get NR into the constitution. The lack of enthusiasm was alleged to be fear of unilateral US peace action. The present GVN continued, as they had so often before, to agree readily in conversations with us to the principle of national reconciliation; yet any concrete implementation remained illusive even through another top level meeting with the President.

M. GUAM MEETINGS, MARCH 20 AND 21, 1967

President Johnson announced that his purpose in calling the Conference at Guam was to introduce the newly appointed US team to the leaders of GVN. The shift of personnel represented the largest shake-up in US leadership in South Vietnam since August 1965. Ambassador Bunker was designated as the replacement for Lodge, and Locke took Porter's place. In a move to resolve the controversy over military versus civil control of Revolutionary Development, Robert Komer took charge with the rank of Ambassador under the COMU-SMACV organizational structure with czar powers and a strong mandate to produce progress.

Most happily, the Constituent Assembly completed its work on the constitution just in time to permit Premier Ky to present a copy to President Johnson at Guam. As had been the case on the two previous occasions of top US/GVN talks, the communique which resulted from the 2-day meeting lay primary emphasis on political, economic, and social matters. The military picture was presumed to be so encouraging and improving as to need no special attention.

N. ROUTINE MATTERS, APRIL-SEPTEMBER, 1967

Most of the previous problems persisted during this period. By June the rate of inflation was predicted to be 45-50 percent per year, and the piaster gap was to be 17.3 billion greater than projected. Hanh, now GVN Economic Minister, scheduled a September trip to Washington and the list of expected topics read very much the same as agendas for many previous such meetings. Hanh could upon occasion get very excited, as in the case where a suit by a Greek shipping line froze the GVN account in a New York City bank; but despite repeated urging from Washington, nobody in Saigon could get up courage enough to approach GVN on those retroactive port clearing charges.

On April 18, GVN finally issued a National Reconciliation Proclamation which stated that "All citizens who rally to the national cause can be employed by the government in accordance with their ability," but the decree proved to be a mirage. It used the Vietnamese words for solidarity rather than those for reconciliation and the program proceeded in consonance with that distinction. Saigon reminded State that Premier Ky had recently told the Ambassador that meaningful progress on national reconciliation could only come after a constitutional government was established.

On the MACV side, Ambassador Komer was getting organized. In response to a Washington query on land reform he recalled his consistent position but pointed out that it was not an important issue in Vietnam. Far more important was the matter of security in the countryside.

The US continued to deliver material assistance to improve the morale of ARVN troops. A $2.83 million program for 913 ARVN dependent houses was upgraded to provide more modern structures with utilities. USAID helped the RVNAF commissary system for RVNAF and dependents. Although rice was eliminated to avoid lowering its open market price, GVN sought compensating increases in the meat and fish supplied. MACV programmed over $3 million to the RVNAF Quartermaster Corps which supplied field and garrison rations.

But there were continuing signs that ARVN as a fighting force needed propping up. Sporadic efforts at encadrement appeared. The USMC Combined Action Companies in I Corps were well publicized. In April, the US 25th Division completed studies, and transmitted to General Chinh, still CG ARVN 25th Division, the Combined Lighting Concept. It brought together in one outpost a US squad, an ARVN squad, and a PF squad.

In response to Washington inquiries, General Westmoreland reported by message in May, 1967, "A command project was initiated on January 26, 1967, to review the performance of RVNAF units and to identify those considered ineffective and non-productive. Units so identified are being evaluated with a view to withdrawal or reduction of military assistance support unless improvement in these units is possible. The evaluation will be conducted every six months resulting in a final determination each June and December . . .

The methodology for evaluation includes:

(1) Identification of units judged ineffective or nonproductive.
(2) Evaluation of credibility or feasibility of present plans to guarantee increased effectiveness.
(3) Study of unit performance trends during the past six months.
(4) Determination of the availability of plans to train personnel.
(5) Evaluation of command interest at all levels for improvement.

Units will be classified as Improvement Probable, Improvement Doubtful, and Improvement Unlikely. Those in the latter two groups must justify continued military assistance or action will be initiated to reduce FY 68 support.
Current Status: All VNAF and VNMC units are effective and productive. Support to VNN reduced by $7800 which reflects discontinuance of support for two fishing boats which are not configured to support any role assigned to VNN. The evaluation of ARVN is only partially completed.

In July, the MACV staff briefed Secretary McNamara in Saigon and touched again on the subject of encadrement. One concept considered was VATUSA (Vietnamese Augmentation to US Army) whereby two or three Vietnamese would be assigned to each squad in US combat battalions. While this scheme offered the advantages of improving ARVN skills and of utilizing additional RVN troops without further strains on already limited ARVN leadership, the only real gain for the US was viewed to be a possible reduction in US strength. The disadvantages pointed out were the political climate, the language barrier, the danger to US unit security, the administrative and disciplinary difficulties and the probable irritation between VATUSA and regular ARVN unit soldiers. These, it was judged, dictated against its adoption.

A second concept considered was salting ARVN forces with US leadership in command positions. The analysis indicated that for political and psychological reasons, it would probably be best to put two US officers and three US NCO's in an instructor's role with each RF company rather than in a command role. Command would be exercised by the RF company commander but he would be required to follow the directions of the US training team leaders.

The conclusion reached was to continue the "salting" experiment with expansion in view if the initial results were good. There is no evidence that anything became of the experiment.

None of this seriously worried top RVNAF leadership; so they indulged in more interesting international activities. In May, talks started between Lao and GVN military staffs. The occasion was planning for barrier extension westward, but Washington realized at once that there was little the US could do to limit the contacts to that subject. In July, it was discovered that GVN was using

Chinat agents, disguised so as to appear to be South Vietnamese with Nung ancestry, on covert operations. JCS disapproved of the effort despite appeals from COMUSMACV. The Chinats appeared to be the result of a secret bilateral agreement concluded during 1966. In September, MACV reported that GVN had occupied Pattle Island in the Crescent Group about 170 miles south of Hainan with the intention of constructing an airfield there. Because these islands are already claimed by Communist and Nationalist Chinas and the Philippines as well, MACV advised against US cooperation in the adventure.

O. THE GVN PRESIDENTIAL ELECTION

Pre-nomination maneuvering and legitimacy of the Presidential campaign were the subjects which occupied American attention above all else. The first task facing Ambassador Bunker as he arrived on station in April was to oversee the delicate transition of GVN to a government based upon a popular election recognized by the world to be fair.

Premier Ky was already openly acting like a Presidential candidate in April. General Thieu was informed that the generals had endorsed Ky while Thieu was absent from the scene recovering from an appendectomy. That was not sufficient to scare Thieu from the race; so the US Mission became increasingly worried that the Thieu-Ky competition threatened the indispensable unity of the military. Dickering remained behind the scenes until Ky formally announced his candidacy on May 12. This served only to intensify the rivalry. By mid-June, the Thieu-Ky confrontation showed no signs of moving toward satisfactory resolution. Basically, Ambassador Bunker believed in an indirect approach. He did not hesitate to approach Ky and Thieu individually on the broader issues of arbitrary press censorship, questionable tactics being pursued by Ky supporters six weeks before it was legal to campaign, or unity of the Armed Forces. But, on the confrontation between the two candidates, Bunker's ploy was to hold an informal luncheon to which the two principals were invited. In the end they had to work out their own solution. They did. At the end of June the 50-60 officers of the Armed Forces Council met in a 2-day, continuous session at which both Thieu and Ky performed histrionics. The surprising result was that Ky agreed to run for the Vice-Presidency on Thieu's ticket. The Mission sighed in relief and agreed that Bunker's approach had worked. The Ambassador congratulated the candidates, and Thieu obligingly announced that if elected he would appoint a civilian as Premier. Ky agreed. The RVNAF chief of staff had earlier announced that there would be no officially endorsed military candidate; yet the Constituent Assembly conveniently approved a draft article which permitted Thieu and Ky to run without resigning from the Armed Forces. By mid-July, the Assembly had voted acceptance of the Thieu-Ky ticket while disallowing one headed by Big Minh who remained in nearby Bangkok as a potential threat to the younger pair. With only a few hitches, the campaigning proceeded so as to satisfy American observers that it was acceptably fair; and the resultant Thieu-Ky victory was a surprise only in its smaller-than-expected plurality.

P. BLUEPRINT FOR VIETNAM, AUGUST, 1967

State suggested that completion of the election process was a proper occasion upon which to consider several proposals, including increased leverage, for advancing the total American effort in South Vietnam. Bunker also mentioned this when he transmitted the paper, "Blueprint for Viet-Nam." The "Blueprint" ranged widely over all topics and struck a consistently optimistic note:

> Progress in the war has been steady on all fronts. We can defeat the enemy by patient, continued, and concerted effort. The way to do this is for the GVN and its allies (a) to reinforce and accelerate the progress already made; (b) to markedly improve the interdiction of infiltration of North Vietnamese troops and supplies; (c) to upgrade, accelerate, and coordinate the pacification program in the countryside; and (d) to maintain political and economic stability and support the development of the constitutional process.
>
> . . . We still have a long way to go. Much of the country is still in VC hands, the enemy can still shell our bases and commit acts of terrorism in the securest areas, VC units still mount large scale attacks, most of the populace has not actively commited itself to the Government, and a VC intrastructure still exists throughout the country. Nevertheless, the situation has steadily improved since the spring of 1965 . . .
>
> Now, that the initiative is ours and the enemy is beginning to hurt, maximum pressure must be maintained on him by (a) intensifying military activity in the South; (b) developing new methods of interdicting infiltration; (c) bombing all targets in the North connected with the enemy's war effort that do not result in unacceptable risk of uncontrolled escalation; (d) accelerating the program of pacification (including better security more effective attacks on the infrastructure, • stepped up National Reconciliation and Chieu Hoi programs, a greater involvement of the people in solving their own problems at the village and hamlet level; (e) encouraging reforms in the government structure and continued improvement in the armed forces; (f) attacking the problem of corruption; (g) using influence to effect a strong, freely elected government with political stability; and (h taking actions necessary to the continued growth and stability of the economy . . .

In a subsequent message Ambassador Bunker stated more specifically that the United States should use its influence to get GVN to do the following:

> A. Seek broad based popular support.
> (1) Appoint prominent civilians including some leading opposition candidates, in new government.
> (2) Use appointments to insure association of a new government with various religious and political groups.
> (3) Adopt a program and identify it with that of a former national hero, "so as to give the new government an idealistic appeal or philosophy which will compete with that declared by the VC." Bunker suggested Nguyen Hue.
> B. Work on a more continuous, although informal basis with US Mission. Bunker suggests regular weekly or *semi-monthly lunches*.
> C. Adopt a program to include the following:
> (1) Public recognition of the
> (a) Necessity for every Vietnamese to contribute to the war effort.
> (b) Need to change draft laws.
> (2) Reaffirm on-going programs relating to RVNAF, including

(a) MACV program of ARVN improvement through merit promotions and a military inspectorate.

(b) Elimination of corrupt, inefficient leaders.

(c) Expansion of RF/PF and adoption of the MACV recommended system of US advisory teams operating with RF/PF for 6-month period.

(d) Greater integration of US forces or joint operations.

(e) Reorientation of the concept of the Pacification Role of ARVN, RF, and PF in accordance with MACV suggestions—from static support to mobile, area security with night patrolling and a system of inspection and grading to insure implementation.

(3) Make the Province Chief the "key" man in pacification—giving him operational control over all military and paramilitary forces engaged in pacification. He should appoint district chiefs. He should report to Corps commander on military matters and to central government on civil matters. An inspection, training, and rates system should be established.

(4) Centralize all rural development efforts in non-RD hamlets under one coordinated control in some manner as is now done in the Ministry of Revolutionary Development for RD hamlets.

(5 Construct an adequate number of processing and detention centers in provinces and permanent prisons on islands on priority basis together with passing of laws that it is a crime to be a VC civilian cadre.

(6) Pay higher salaries to selected GVN officials, including the military, particularly those officials able to control corruption or in a position to be tempted by corruption.

(7) Reaffirm National Reconciliation and Chieu Hoi programs.

(8) Grant villages the power to enforce land rental laws.

(9) Adopt the whole of the "operation Take-off" pacification program prepared by MACCORDS.

(10) Establish joint council procedures over expenditure of counterpart piasters by reinstituting sign-off by US advisors at province level.

(11) Revitalize the veteran's program.

(12) Increase receipts from domestic taxes and tariffs, and revise monetary policies.

Q. THE LEVERAGE STUDY

On August 31 State transmitted a study by Hans Heymann and Col. Volney Warner on the subject of leverage. It reviewed the rationale for leverage and considered a whole array of possible techniques:

. . . In anticipating the US/GVN relationship in the post-election period, it is generally agreed that the US should find ways to exercise leverage with the Vietnamese government which are more commensurate in degree with the importance of the US effort to South Vietnam's survival and which reflect the climate of growing restiveness in the US . . . In its impatience to get results and make progress, the US has increasingly resorted to unilateral programs and action with inadequate consultation with the Vietnamese. On the other hand, the indiscriminate and careless exercise of US leverage could undermine the self-respect of the Vietnamese government in its own eyes and in the eyes of the South Vietnamese people.

. . . To be effective, US leverage must be exercised in the context of a

relationship of mutual respect and confidence, and in ways commensurate with the objective sought. It must also be backed by credible sanctions.
. . . The various tools of leverage available to us are described below. It is not proposed that all of these tools be used at any given time or that some of them be used at all. However, they represent a selection of arrows that might be placed in the US Mission quiver for use as the Mission Council deems appropriate. It will be particularly important to construct a credible and effective system of US leverage for use as necessary and appropriate in connection with the list of priority program objectives which we shall be seeking to achieve with the newly elected government in the immediate post-election period.

Tools of Leverage

. . . A wide range of possible techniques and forms of influence is available at each level of the American presence in Vietnam. A few of these leverage devices are now in use, mostly at the initiative of individual Americans on the spot, but not as part of an organized framework of influence. Other devices have been instituted in the past, only to be subsequently abandoned because of fear of their misuse, actual misuse, or inadequate understanding of their value.
In the following list we array a range of possible instruments of influence that the US might employ, with some indication of their applicability.

A. Rapport . . .
B. Joint Planning and Evaluation . . .
C. Joint Inspection and Audit . . .
D. Joint Secretariats . . .
E. The JCRR approach: Establishing a joint, autonomous, dually-staffed, foundation-like organization headed by a board of commissioners appointed by the two heads of state, to administer all forms of non-military AID . . .
F. Contingency Funds and Special Resources . . .
G. Control Over Expenditure of Counterpart Piasters . . .
H. Retention of Resources in US Channels . . .
I. Joint Personnel Management—to institute career incentive, selection, and removal policies . . .
J. Joint Command . . .
K. Policy-level Monitoring System—to monitor the exercise of authority of key officials of the GVN . . .
L. Withholding US Support—at levels below Saigon, the authority of US senior advisors to cut off or withdraw US civil and military support from Vietnamese activities or operations within their area of responsibility would constitute powerful leverage . . .

At the Saigon level, a range of extremely tough options is available, encompassing selective withdrawal of US support for Vietnam persuading the GVN that these are in fact available requires the will to use them and the political ability to follow through if our hand is called. Options would include halting further troop deployments, standing down US unit operations, suspending CIP and MAP assistance, and so forth.

Ambassador Komer replied on September 19. He recalled his deep interest in this subject and discussed at length both present and potential techniques.

His views seemed considerably mitigated by his several months in Saigon, for "rapport" and "persuasion with implied pressure" headed the list of what was presently being done. He concluded by saying, "All of the above forms of leverage, and yet others, could be useful at the proper time and in an appropriate way. But they must be applied with discretion, and always in such manner as to keep the GVN foremost in the picture presented to its own people and the world at large . . . The exercise of leverage in a personal manner and hidden from the public view is likely to be most effective, while of the more operational means establishment of combined organization under a JCRR-type concept, to include joint control of resources, would be most desirable. In sum, we're gradually applying more leverage in Pacification, but wish to do so in ways that least risk creating more trouble than constructive results."

R. POSTLOGUE

New plans and new hopes marked the immediate post-election period. The story of US-GVN relations continues, but this narrative must end. In conclusion it seems appropriate to quote from the MACCORDS report covering Bien Hoa province for the period ending December 31, 1967.

1. *Status for the RD Plan:*

The GVN in Bien Hoa Province has not met with any measure of success in furthering the pacification effort during 1967. Those areas that do represent advances (such as road openings or repairs or construction, breaking up of main line VC units, etc.) have all been the result of unilateral US actions. It was perhaps naively thought that these US accomplishments would stand as an inspiring example to the GVN and would prompt them to not only continue their efforts but, further, to expand and intensify the fight. However, during 1967 in Bien Hoa Province, this has not been the case. The GVN at all levels has grown weaker, become more corrupt and, today, displays even less vitality and will than it did one year ago . . .

Advisory Leverage: This subject has been an extremely sensitive and controversial issue in both GVN and US circles. However, as painful as it must be to address, the harsh truth is that given a showdown situation or an intolerable divergence between GVN and US methods, the US advisor will lose. CORDS, Bien Hoa has gone to extraordinary lengths in reporting on both corrupt and incompetent officials and practices. The reason for these efforts has been to illustrate clearly to higher US authorities, the enormity of the problems facing the advisor on the province/District level. CORDS Bien Hoa, as perhaps all other echelons of US advisors, is ultimately powerless to rectify or even significantly alter the GVN intentions and performance. The Vietnamese in the street is firmly convinced that the US totally dominates the GVN and dictates exactly what course shall be followed. However, the bitter and tragic truth is that the US has been kept at such a distance from GVN circles and power that in joint councils or plans our views may be heard, some portions of our logic may be endorsed but with confrontations or matters that represent any truly revolutionary departure from existing GVN practices etc, we are light weights and presently do not possess the leverage or power to carry the day.

ARVN Performance: There are presently two ARVN battalions (3/43 and 2/48) who are directly assigned to support RD in Bien Hoa. With the exception of the 1st Bn, 48th Regt which served in the Phu Hoi Campaign area earlier in the year, ARVN performance has been less than satisfactory. The units have demonstrated the same age-old ills that have collectively led to our present commitment of US forces . . .

GVN Officials Interests: The primary interest of GVN officials in Bien Hoa Province is money. The lucrative US presence with all the various service trades that cater to the soldier, have created a virtual gold mine of wealth which is directly or indirectly syphoned off and pocketed by the officials. Thus, revolutionary development with all the ultimate implications of broadening the governing base of this society, is viewed as some sort of necessary device that needs to be propped up and nominally catered to by the GVN in order to keep US and Free World's interest and faith intact. However, any serious or meaningful gesture in support of a program which ultimately is designed to displace the powers-to-be (or at least force them to become accountable or share in the power) is not forthcoming. Infrastructure is not attacked even though the target is known; budgets are not spent although the funds are available; GVN officials steadfastly refuse to visit their districts or villages or hamlets although it is there that most immediate problems exist. The list of limpid, half-hearted efforts to prosecute the war is endless.

Material Cutoffs and Shortages: In August after several months of negotiation, CORDS, Bien Hoa was forced to cut off further shipment of replenishment stocks into province. The reasons for this action were many but could be reduced to sloppy, shoddy and highly questionable logistical practices and procedures on the part of the GVN. After eleven weeks, the Provincial GVN finally agreed to carry out the reforms and renovations as suggested by CORDS. However, that eleven-week gap in the flow of materials (particularly during a period most noted for its relatively high degree of GVN action) had a significant effect on curbing construction programs and causing even more delays. Then, as soon as this issue was resolved, it was learned that cement and roofing weren't in supply and rationed quotas for the remainder of the year further compounded the damage caused by earlier material shortages.

To compensate, in part, for these factors, CORDS has had to increasingly rely on the resources, skills and capabilities of resident US military units. These units have, without exception, effectively filled the gaps and their efforts have succeeded in reducing the critical road situation that has been worsening throughout the years. Their action in many other areas has been highly commendable and CORDS Bien Hoa (as well as the GVN itself) owes a great deal to these units and their commanders who have unselfishly devoted themselves to furthering pacification. However, for all their efforts, for all the resources either expended or on hand, the disturbing truth in Bien Hoa is that it still remains for the government, with forceful and meaningful direction from above, to begin to assume the responsibility for prosecuting this war and the pacification effort. Thus far, the GVN has not done this and it is the considered opinion of CORDS Bien Hoa that unless major revisions are brought about in the factors raised here, there is only to be a continuation of the same ordeal with the accompanying frustrations, inaction, corruption and incompetence. A continuation of this does not connotate stability or even maintenance of the status quo; it spells regression and an ever widening gap of distrust, distaste and disillusionment between the people and the GVN.

6. The Advisory Build-Up, 1961–1967

Summary and Analysis

The United States decided, shortly after the Geneva Accords and during the period of French withdrawal from Indo-China, to give military assistance and advice to the newly proclaimed Republic of Vietnam. It might as easily have decided not to undertake this effort to prevent South Vietnam from falling to communism.

The Joint Chiefs of Staff were pessimistic. The creation of a Vietnamese Army, they said, might not even lead to internal political stability, much less assure the capability to protect South Vietnam from external aggression. The JCS also believed that the limitations imposed by the Geneva agreements on the number of U.S. military personnel would make it impractical to attempt to train a new Army—particularly given the paucity of experienced leaders which was the legacy of French colonialism. The President's military advisors did not wish to assume the responsibility for failure without the resources and influence which would offer a better chance for success.

THE AMERICAN GAMBLE

The available record does not indicate any rebuttal of the JCS's appraisal of the situation. What it does indicate is that the U.S. decided to gamble with very limited resources because the potential gains seemed well worth a limited risk. "I cannot guarantee that Vietnam will remain free, even with our aid," General J. Lawton Collins reported to the National Security Council, "But I know that without our aid Vietnam will surely be lost to Communism."

Secretary of State John Foster Dulles was instrumental in deciding for political reasons to undertake a modest program of military advice aimed at producing political stability. Once launched, however, the program of advice and assistance came to be dominated by conventional military conceptions. Insuring internal stability is a "lesser included capability" of armed force, the reasoning went; the principal purpose of such a force is to protect the territorial integrity of the nation.

It was such a conventional force that the small USMAAG attempted to produce from 1955 until about 1960. The Army of the Republic of Vietnam (ARVN) was made to "mirror image" the U.S. Army to the extent permitted by differences in equipment and locale. The number of U.S. advisors (approximately doubled by "The Equipment Recovery Mission"—a thinly veiled device to increase the number of Americans in Vietnam) remained stable throughout this period. ARVN developed into a multi-divisional force oriented primarily toward conventional defense. The later transition to a force designed for counterinsurgent warfare was thereby made more difficult.

It seemed for a while that the gamble against long odds had succeeded. The Viet Minh were quiescent; the Republic of Vietnam Armed Forces (RVNAF) were markedly better armed and trained than they were when the U.S. effort began (at which time they were unarmed and untrained), and President Ngo Dinh Diem showed a remarkable ability to put down factions threatening GVN stability and to maintain himself in office.

This period of apparent stability disappeared, however, in the events of 1959/61 as the Viet Minh (relabelled Viet Cong—a contraction for Vietnamese Communist) stepped up terrorism, sabotage, and military action by increasingly large units. By mid-1961, the prospect for South Vietnam's independence was at least as dark as it had been six years earlier.

But the U.S. military advisors in Vietnam had learned—or at least thought they had learned—during this period of gradual disintegration the true nature of the battle in which they were engaged by proxy. This was an unconventional, internal war of counterinsurgency rather than a conventional struggle against an external foe. It was a battle for the "hearts and minds" of the indigenous (and especially the rural) population rather than a contest to win and hold key terrain features. It was an intermeshed political-economic-military war rather than one in which political and economic issues were settled by military victory.

U.S. advisors in Vietnam—and U.S. military and civilian theorists in other places, as well—formulated during this period a rudimentary doctrine of counterinsurgent warfare. In response to Premier Khrushchev's endorsement of "wars of national liberation" they proposed to help free world nations save themselves from communism by a series of sequential actions that dealt with the symptoms of social revolution (the insurgency) as well as its causes (the frustration of expectations for social justice).

Thus, at almost the same time that the U.S. began its advisory buildup in South Vietnam in late 1961, military and civilian practitioners found themselves in possession of a simple, apparently logical, outline sketch of a method by which to counter the communist-captured insurgency. Physical security from the acts of the insurgents was a necessary but not a sufficient condition for success. In addition to security the Vietnamese government had to establish the services which would link it in classic terms of legitimacy to its subjects. We would fight fire with fire and we would fight it with water, too.

THE LIMITED PARTNERSHIP

The decisions made by the Kennedy Administration from mid-1961 onward, culminating in the expansion of the U.S. advisory effort following General Maxwell D. Taylor's mission to Saigon in October, did not simply set out to explain this newly-articulated counterinsurgency theory and doctrine to the GVN. They attempted to induce the GVN to reform itself so that identification with its populace would be possible. Beyond this, they chose to attempt to help the Vietnamese, in Taylor's words, "as friends and partners—not as arms-length advisors—[and] show them how the job might be done—not tell them or do it for them."

The "limited partnership" which General Taylor proposed—and which President Kennedy accepted—was designed to place U.S. advisors at many levels within the RVNAF and GVN structure rather than merely at the top. An earlier proposal, to concentrate on advisors at the top with wide discretionary authority and to count on influence as the product of the demonstrated commitment of a carefully selected handful of men, was rejected in favor of many advisors at many levels, each serving normally only for a twelve month period, and with the advisory manpower furnished through normal personnel selection and assignment processes within the military services.

The expectation among U.S. policymakers—recorded in NSAM 111— was that the GVN and U.S. would mutually agree upon necessary steps to end the insurgency. The U.S., for its part, would underwrite an increase in RVNAF and provide advisors throughout the military structure down to battalion level and in each provincial capital. The GVN would rationalize its lines of authority and begin reform measures to bring it closer to the Vietnamese people. This was, of course, a U.S. expectation, not an agreed *quid pro quo.* Diem was unwilling to permit the U.S. to share in his formulation of plans. He was even afraid to discuss the U.S. expectations candidly with his own cabinet ministers. It is a matter of record that he did not reform his government. ("He will not reform because he cannot," J. Kenneth Galbraith cabled President Kennedy.) What remains in issue is whether he could have done so. If he could not, the U.S. plan to end the insurgency was foredoomed from its inception, for it depended on Vietnamese initiatives to solve a Vietnamese problem.

COMMITMENT AND EXPECTATION

Thus the U.S. overall plan to end the insurgency was on shaky ground on the GVN side. Diem needed the U.S. and the U.S. needed a reformed Diem. As U.S. advisors began deploying to Vietnam for service with tactical units in the field, the gamble of the mid-50's was transferred into a broad commitment. President Kennedy and his advisors were determined to save Vietnam from communism by helping the Vietnamese to save themselves. One side of the dual U.S. thrust (GVN reform) was already in trouble. What of the "friends and partners" who were to share the dangers and tasks of RVNAF in the field? What was expected of them? What advantages would accrue from their presence in Vietnam?

The available record is almost totally devoid of any explication (much less any debate) on these questions. General Taylor's report of his mission to Saigon implies an unambiguous convergence of interests between the advisors and the advised. All that was needed was greater competence. More U.S. advisors at more places working on problems of Vietnamese training and operations could not but have an overall beneficial effect.

It is necessary to surmise the expectations in the policymakers minds of just how this would come about. First, they seem to have expected the increased U.S. advisory presence to lead directly to increased RVNAF competence in technical and tactical areas. Basic military skills—how to move, shoot, and communicate—could be improved and the improvements sustained by a continuing U.S. presence at many operational levels. Second, the U.S. policymakers could receive reports from an omnipresent U.S. "network" which would permit them to become better informed about what was really taking place in Vietnam, not only with respect to VC activity but with reference to ARVN plans, operations, and problems as well. Finally, the U.S. expected to realize increased influence within RVNAF from the presence of advisors. (and it expected, as NSAM 111 made clear, to realize increased influence with GVN in exchange for increasing its visible commitment to South Vietnamese independence.)

Increased influence can, of course, be gained in many ways. U.S. advisors could, by example, promote more aggressive Vietnamese leadership and improved standards of conduct. A well-coordinated advisory network could exert persuasive pressure throughout RVNAF to adopt certain policies or practices.

And the U.S. providers of the material resources could, if they wished, keep a tight hand on the spigot and control the flow. They could exert influence negatively. The U.S. was anxious to avoid this last mentioned approach to increased influence. "Leverage," as it is now commonly known, was a subject rarely discussed, much less practiced. The "limited partnership" finessed the whole issue of sanctions by assuming (or hoping or pretending, one cannot know which) that no problem existed.

PACIFICATION AND STRATEGIC HAMLETS

The process of countering insurgency, most commonly called pacification, received a great amount of attention and publicity at the same time the U.S. was increasing its field advisors with ARVN from a handful to over 3,000. Earlier, in 1960, the USMAAG had pressed upon the GVN a national Counter-insurgency Plan for Vietnam (CIP) which was really an organizational blueprint for reordering the GVN-RVNAF lines of command to permit effective action. The nub of the problem was that the political leaders in rural areas (Province and District Chiefs—almost all military officers) were responsible to Saigon directly while RVNAF had a separate chain of command. In 1961, the MAAG presented its complementary Geographically Phased Plan which specified the relative priority for clearing out the VC, holding, then building GVN at the "rice roots." The object, as the U.S. advisors saw it, was to have a workable national plan upon which to base the entire US-GVN effort.

The Strategic Hamlet Program soon became the unifying vehicle to express the pacification process. The theory was that of physical security first, then government programs to develop popular allegiance. The fact was over-expansion, counter-productive coercion in some areas, widespread mismanagement, and dishonesty. U.S. policymakers were not, however, aware of how badly things were going until they became much worse. Optimism dominated official thinking. No need was perceived for new departures. Throughout the period of the Strategic Hamlet Program—that is, until Diem's regime was toppled in late 1963—the number of U.S. advisors remained relatively stable at its new (1962) plateau.

The expectation that more U.S. advisors would mean better information for U.S. policymakers was not realized. One cannot judge accurately the reasons why U.S. leaders in Vietnam and Washington thought the counterinsurgent effort was making headway, but the fact that it was not is crystal clear in retrospect. The expectation that GVN and U.S. interests were sufficiently parallel to permit greater U.S. influence solely as a result of a larger U.S. presence foundered on the personalities and the felt necessities of the Ngo brothers. The extent to which RVNAF technical-tactical competence was increased during this period remains a subject of disagreement but it was not increased sufficiently to "turn the tide" of the war. That much is indisputable.

ANOTHER ROUND OF INCREASES

After Diem's fall there was a brief period of optimism based on the expectation that the new military regime in Saigon would be more receptive to U.S. advice than its predecessor had been. By the summer of 1964, when the decision was made to expand the advisory effort again, this optimistic hope had foundered on the fact of continued VC victories and instability within the GVN.

NSAM 288 had, in March 1964, stated U.S. objectives in Vietnam in the most unambiguous and sweeping terms. If there had been doubt that the limited risk gamble undertaken by Eisenhower had been transformed into an unlimited commitment under Kennedy, that doubt should have been dispelled internally by NSAM 288's statement of objectives:

> We seek an independent non-Communist South Vietnam. We do not require that it serve as a Western base or as a member of a Western Alliance. South Vietnam must be free, however, to accept outside assistance as required to maintain its security. This assistance should be able to take the form not only of economic and social measures but also police and military help to root out and control insurgent elements.

If we cannot save South Vietnam, the NSAM continued in a classic statement of the "domino theory," all of Southeast Asia will probably fall and all of the Western Pacific and South Asian nations will come under increased pressure. There were at this time several steps which the U.S. could have taken to increase its assistance to the GVN. Carrying the war to Hanoi was one; introducing U.S. combat forces was another. Neither appealed much, however, in terms of helping the South Vietnamese to win *their* war. Both were anathema in the midst of Presidential election year politics. Bombing was discussed and plans laid, but no action taken. Troop commitments were not even discussed— at least in the written record of proposals and decisions. Rather, a number of palliative measures to help the GVN economy and RVNAF were adopted and the advisory effort was expanded.

The 1964 expansion of the advisory effort consisted of the beefing-up of the battalion advisory teams and the establishment of district (sub-sector) teams. Thus, a new dimension of American presence was added and the density of U.S. advisors in operational units was increased. There is nothing in the available record to suggest either a challenge to the old, unstated assumption that more U.S. advisors would lead to increased performance or any change in the assumed expectations of U.S. policymakers had changed. The determination remained to advise rather than to command, to develop Vietnamese leadership rather than to supplant it, and to induce the GVN to take the steps necessary to pacify its own dissident elements.

ADVISORS TEMPORARILY FORGOTTEN

The expansion to district level placed U.S. military advisors throughout almost the entire RVNAF hierarchy (from JGS to battalion, with enough men at the lower level to advise companies on a "when needed" basis) and the political hierarchy as well (sector/province and sub-sector/district). U.S. advisors were not present in large numbers with the old Civil Guard and Self-Defense Corps— now relabelled the Regional Forces and Popular Forces under province and district control respectively—but they advised the military men in political positions who controlled these paramilitary forces.

Still the situation continued to deteriorate. Political instability within the GVN had by 1965 become a perennial rather than a transitory problem. The U.S. had initiated a continuing series of military air war measures to dissuade North Vietnam from support of the war in the South. The results were obviously inadequate; they may even have been opposite to those expected. Then ARVN suffered a series of disastrous defeats late in the spring of 1965 which led knowledgeable observers to fear an imminent GVN collapse. U.S. combat units —a few of which were already in-country with restrictive missions—began to be deployed to South Vietnam in earnest.

When the build-up of U.S. combat forces got underway the build-up of U.S. advisors had already been essentially completed. Being an advisor in the field had been the most challenging assignment a U.S. soldier could seek; being with a U.S. unit in combat now became the aim of most. The advisory effort sank into relative obscurity as the attention of policymakers (and of the press and public) focused on the U.S. force deployments, on building the base complexes from which U.S. military might could project itself into the countryside, and in exploring the new relationships and new opportunities occasioned by the commitment of U.S. land forces to the Asian mainland.

A number of measures which would have changed materially the U.S. advisors relationship to their Vietnamese counterparts were examined briefly in mid-1965. Each was dropped. The encadrement of U.S. and ARVN units was favored by President Johnson. General Westmoreland opposed it—apparently because of language problems and the difficult logistic support problem it would create—and the issue quickly died, except for the experimental Combined Action Platoons (CAPs) formed by the Marines. The subject of a combined U.S.-RVNAF command was brought up. Secretary McNamara was more favorably disposed toward achieving "unity of command" than were his senior military advisors and the U.S. Mission representatives in Saigon. They were keenly aware of GVN sensitivity to any measures which would explicitly finger the increasing Americanization of the war effort. So combined command was shelved, too. The GVN even opposed a joint US-JGS staff to coordinate the war effort. The staff was never formed.

PACIFICATION REEMPHASIZED

As the build-up of U.S. combat forces reached a level permitting offensive forays against the VC (and North Vietnamese Army) forces, there gradually evolved a division of responsibilities between U.S. and Vietnamese forces in which the former were to concentrate on defeating the main forces of the VC/NVA and the latter were to give primary emphasis to the pacification program. Half of ARVN was to operate in support of pacification.

This division of effort threw most U.S. advisors into pacification—with ARVN units as well as in the province and district advisory teams. It also threw the U.S. military advisors into closer contact—and competition and conflict —with the growing number of advisors on civil functions (many of whom were U.S. military men on "loan") representing the CIA, AID, and USIA. The question was raised of the optimal internal U.S. organization to support the Vietnamese pacification program.

The result of a drawn-out, occasionally acrimonious debate on this question was an intermixed civil-military organization embracing the entire pacification effort, headed by a civilian of ambassadorial rank under COMUSMACV's direction. Called Civil Operations and Revolutionary Development Support (CORDS), it replaced a bilinear system in which military advisors were controlled through a military chain of command and all civilian advisors were controlled (at least in theory) through an Office of Civil Operations (OCO). The creation of CORDS was hailed as a victory for the "single manager" concept even though some very substantial U.S. programs were defined as outside the pacification program and, hence, beyond CORDS' competence.

RF/PF ADVISORS

The creation of CORDS affected only the organizational context of U.S. advice to the South Vietnamese. It did nothing to change the relationship between advisor and advised. U.S. expectations continued in the well-worn furrows in which they had travelled from the beginning: better information, more U.S. influence over Vietnamese plans and actions, and improved GVN (including RVNAF) performance were the hoped for products of the advisory effort.

This pattern was repeated in 1967 when an increase of over 2,000 military advisors was proposed by MACV to assist the Regional and Popular Forces— whose security missions were almost exclusively devoted to support of the pacification program. The RF and PF were, at that time, the only RVNAF components without a sizeable U.S. advisory complement. When the question of improving their effectiveness was addressed the old assumption that more U.S. advisors would equate to improved effectiveness again went unchallenged.

The question debated was whether this new dimension of the U.S. advisory effort should be structured to give continuing advice to RF companies and PF platoons or should be constituted on a mobile training basis. The decision was to form mobile teams for both tactical and logistical support training. Advisors were detached from their parent U.S. combat units and detailed to these duties pending the manpower accounting change which would transfer these individuals to MACV advisory control and replace them in U.S. units with newly deployed fillers.

AVOIDED ISSUES

This was the situation when the VC/NVA launched a massive series of attacks against urban population centers and surrounding pacification program forces during the 1968 lunar new year (Tet) offensive. In the confused aftermath of this radical change in VC/NVA strategy the U.S. announced in Washington its intention to give renewed attention to modernizing RVNAF so that a larger share of the war effort could be turned back to the Vietnamese. This policy decision, following as it did an unprecedented six-year period of U.S. attempts to wage counterinsurgent war by proxy, constituted an adequate reason to reexamine the experience of the past and to explore more fully some difficult questions which have been consistently avoided in the desire to assist South Vietnam.

The most basic of these questions is whether the U.S. can in any way serve as a makeweight sufficient to change the continuing unfavorable trend of the war in South Vietnam? Can it, that is, overcome the apparent fact that the Viet Cong have "captured" the Vietnamese nationalist movement while the GVN has become the refuge of Vietnamese who were allied with the French in the battle against the independence of their nation? Attempts to answer this question are complicated, of course, by the difficult issue of Viet Cong allegiance to and control by Communist China. But this is the nature of the situation. The issue of whether the U.S. *can* energize the GVN has been too long submerged by repeated assertions that it *must* do so.

A part of any tentative answer to this fundamental question will turn on the issue of how the U.S. might better promote a more adequate pace of GVN reform and improved RVNAF effectiveness to cope with the VC/NVA threat. (A related question, of course, is whether reform *and* increased effectiveness can proceed simultaneously.) Asking this question would open for examination two aspects of the advisory program that have come to be treated by reflexive response: where are advisors needed and what should be the relationship of the advisor to the advised?

The continuing U.S. unstated assumption has been that more advisors somehow equate to better performance. This can be traced in the successive expansions of the military advisory effort—first to the provinces and down to battalion level within ARVN, then to the districts, and most recently to the paramilitary forces within RVNAF. It may be that large numbers of advisors are, in fact, the best way to influence events but one cannot reach such a conclusion validly without first asking the question.

The relationship of advisor to advised has gone through recurrent changes relative to judging an advisor's performance according to the performance of his counterpart. It has almost never deviated, however, from the belief that the conscious and continuing use of leverage at many levels would undercut Vietnamese sovereignty and stultify the development of Vietnamese leadership. Given the results of this policy over a number of years it is fair to ask whether the stick ought not to be more routinely used in combination with the carrot. Again, the answer is not obvious but it is obvious that there can be no sound answer in the absence of inquiry.

Finally, and closely related to any examination of the leverage issue, there is the question of the adequacy of counterinsurgent theory and doctrine. The progression from physical security through the establishment of socially oriented programs (political and economic) to the objective of earning and winning popular allegiance seems both simple and logical. It may also be simplistic, for its transformation into operational reality bumps head-on into some very difficult questions. Is security a precondition to loyalty, for instance, or must some degree of loyalty be realized as a precondition to intelligence information adequate to make security feasible? This chicken-and-egg argument has been debated for years without leading to any noticeable consensus on guides to operational action.

Seeking answers to any of these questions is a difficult, frustrating business. There exists no "control" by which laboratory comparisons of alternative courses can be made. There is almost surely no hard choice which will not carry with it very real liabilities along with its advantages. But if the lives and effort expended in the U.S. military advisory effort in South Vietnam in the 1960's are to be justified, a substantial portion of that justification will consist of a closer examination of past assumptions in order better to guide future policy.

End of Summary and Analysis

CHRONOLOGY

21 Jul 54   *Geneva Cease-fire Accord*
Ended fighting between Viet Minh and French; divided Vietnam at 17th parallel; limited U.S. military personnel in RVN to current level (342).

22 Sep 54   *Memo, JCS for SecDef, Retention and Development of Forces in Indochina*
U.S. resources could better be used to support countries other than RVN.

11 Oct 54   *Letter, J. F. Dulles (Sec State) to C. E. Wilson (SecDef)*
Only small U.S. training forces to RVN to promote internal stability.

19 Oct 54   *Memo, JCS for SecDef, Development and Training of Indigenous Forces in Indochina*
Opposed U.S. training RVN army. Risk not worth the gamble.

22 Oct 54   *Msg, State to Saigon 1679*
Set in motion "crash program" to improve RVN forces.

26 Oct 54   *Memo, SecDef to JCS*
JCS to prepare long-range program to improve RVN forces.

17 Nov 54   *Memo, JCS for SecDef, Indochina*
Development of effective forces and prevention of communist takeover cannot be prevented without Vietnamese effort that is probably not forthcoming.

20 Jan 55   *Memo, Gen. J. Lawton Collins for SecState, Report on Vietnam for the National Security Council*
Vietnam might be "saved" with U.S. aid; would be "lost" without it.

21 Jan 55   *Memo, JCS for SecDef, Reconsideration of U.S. Military Program in Southeast Asia*
Outlines alternative U.S. courses of action in RVN: present program, advice with leverage, U.S. forces, or withdrawal.

24 Oct 55–   Lt Gen Samuel T. Williams, Chief of MAAG to Vietnam.
31 Aug 60

9 Dec 55   *Memo for SecDef, Raising U.S. Military Personnel Ceiling in MAAG Vietnam*
MAAG needed twice the current 342 personnel to train RVNAF.

16 Dec 55   *Memo, Director CIA from SecState*
TERM also to serve as cover for intelligence gathering.

1959   *Report, The President's Committee to Study the United States Military Assistance Program*
Emphasized need for promoting internal security, coined term "mirror imaging."

7 Jun 59   *Msg, State-Defense-ICA-CAS to Saigon 28*
Forbids advisors to participate in combat.

27 Feb 60   *Msg, Saigon to State 2525*
Abolished TERM but added equal number of spaces to MAAG, Vietnam, increasing it from 342 to 685.

10 Jun 60   *U.S. Army Command & General Staff College, Study on Army Aspects of the Military Assistance Program in Vietnam*

Prepared for Gen. Lionel C. McGarr, described Viet Cong strategy but deprecated ARVN participation in pacification.

1 Sep 60–
5 Mar 62
Lt Gen Lionel C. McGarr, Chief of MAAG to Vietnam.

4 Jan 61
Counter Insurgency Plan for South Vietnam (CIP), enclosure to msg, Saigon to State 276
Blueprint for RVNAF reorganization, containing Gen McGarr's recommendations for integrating ARVN and CG/SDC in a common chain of command to promote internal security.

17 Jan 61
Memo, General Lansdale for SecDef, Vietnam
Proposed extra-bureaucratic advisory effort carried out by specially selected and qualified personnel.

15 Mar 61–
1 Aug 63
Frederick E. Nolting, Ambassador to South Vietnam

28 Mar 61
NIE 50–61, Outlook in Mainland Southeast Asia
Report that VC controlled most of countryside.

12 Apr 61
Memo, Walt W. Rostow to the President
Suggested appointment of Presidential Agent to oversee Vietnam programs in Washington.

19 Apr 61
Memo, Gen. Lansdale to SecDef, Vietnam
Proposed creation of interdepartmental task force on Vietnam.

20 Apr 61
Memo, SecDef for DepSecDef
McNamara asked Gilpatric for program to "prevent communist domination" of Vietnam, in response to Lansdale proposal.

27 Apr 61
Memo, DepSecDef for President, Program of Action for Vietnam
Recommended expanded U.S. effort in Vietnam, MAAG increase of 100, MAAG takeover of CG/SDC, U.S. advisors in field operations creation of Presidential Task Force. Foreshadowed later decision.

1 May 61
Memo, R. L. Gilpatric for Presidential Task Force
Recommended augmenting MAAG by 2 training commands (1600 each) and deploy 400 Special Forces (increasing MAAG from 685 to 2285). Marked shift to conventional approach.

3 May 61
Memo, State Department to members of Task Force on Vietnam
Recommended revision of Gilpatric task force, proposed interdepartmental task force under State leadership.

11 May 61
NSAM 52
Recorded President's decision to increase U.S. forces slightly and re-emphasized U.S. commitment.

15 May 61
Msg. Saigon to State 1743
Recorded Diem's refusal of U.S. combat troops on bilateral treaty.

18 May 61
Memo BG Lansdale for DepSecDef, Vietnam
Recorded Diem's acceptance of U.S. forces for training but not for fighting.

23 May 61   *Memo, Vice President Johnson for President Kennedy*
Report from Johnson's trip to Vietnam that "deeds must replace words."

27 May 61   *Letter from President to each American Ambassador abroad.*
(*See Memo, President for Heads of Executive Departments and Agencies, 29 May 1961, "Responsibilities of Chiefs of American Diplomatic Missions,"* Federal Register, *Vol. 26 Nr 22, 17 Nov 1961, p. 10749 (F.R. Doc. 61–11012*).
Set forth coordinating authority for ambassadors.

9 Jun 61   *Letter, President Diem to President Kennedy*
Proposed 100,000 increase in RVNAF and corresponding expansion of MAAG.

15 Sep 61   *MAAG, Vietnam, Geographically Phased National Level Plan for Counterinsurgency*
Suggested operational sequence of priority areas for coordinated counterinsurgency effort under single chain of command.

1 Oct 61   *Msg, Saigon to State 421*
Diem asked for bilateral defense treaty with U.S.

Oct 61   *JCSM 717–61*
JCS proposal to send 20,000 U.S. combat troops to central highlands.

5 Oct 61   *DF, Distribution Division, DCSPER, DA to Multiple Addressees, Improvement of Personnel Continuity and Effectiveness in Short Tour Overseas Areas.*
OSD decision to increase tour of duty to 30 months with dependents, 18 without, instead of 24 and 12. Never put into effect.

10 Oct 61   *SNIE 10–3–61, Probable Communist Reactions to Certain SEATO Undertakings in South Vietnam*
Examined proposal for U.S. troop intervention.

11 Oct 61   *Study, Concept of Intervention in South Vietnam, n.d., discussed at NSC meeting, 11 Oct 61*
Proposed sending U.S. combat troops.

11 Oct 61   *Memo for Record Roswell Gilpatric*
Recorded decision to send Taylor to Vietnam and outlined alternatives to be considered.

25 Oct 61   *Msg, Saigon to State*
Diem's assurance that he favored deployment of U.S. troops.

25 Oct 61   *Msg, Saigon 537, General Taylor to White House, State, Defense, JCS; Msg, Baguio 005, 1 Nov 61, Eyes Only for the President from General Taylor*
Proposed sending 6–8000 troops under guise of "flood relief."

1 Nov 61   *State Dept, Bureau of Intelligence and Research, RFE-3, 1 Nov 61, Communist Threat Mounts in South Vietnam*
Reported increased VC activity in first half 1961: 500 assassinations, 1000 kidnappings, 1500 RVNAF KIA.

3 Nov 61   Report on General Taylor's Mission to South Vietnam.
Discussed VC strategy and threat and the weaknesses of the Diem regime. Proposed shift in U.S. effort "from advice to limited partnership."

14 Nov 61   Msg, State to Saigon 619
Recorded U.S. expectation of sharing in GVN decision-making.

22 Nov 61   NSAM 111, First Phase of Vietnam Program
Outlines U.S. actions and expected improvements in GVN.

22 Nov 61   Msg, Saigon to State 687; Msg, Saigon to State 708
25 Nov 61   Ambassador Nolting reported that Diem refused to bow to U.S. pressure.

Dec 61   Msg, State to Saigon 693
Dropped insistence on explicit U.S. influence on GVN decisions, but assumed such influence as by-product of close partnership.

16 Jan 62   Hq, CINCPAC, Record of Second Secretary of Defense Conference
Recorded decisions of Honolulu Conference: establish battalion advisory teams, province advisors CG/SDC training.

13 Feb 62–   Gen. Paul D. Harkins, COMUSMACV
1 Aug 64

23 Jul 62   Record of 6th Secretary of Defense Conference
McNamara plan for phased withdrawal of U.S. forces, based on optimistic 1962 expectations.

1 Aug 63–   Henry Cabot Lodge, Ambassador to South Vietnam.
1 Jul 64

2 Oct 63   White House Statement
Announcement by President Kennedy of U.S. hopes for planned phased withdrawal of troops.

1 Nov 63   Diem overthrown by military coup d'etat.

1 Nov 63–   Military Revolutionary Council
16 Aug 64   Duong Van Minh, Chief of State and Chairman, Military Revolutionary Council.

26 Nov 63   NSAM 273
Reaffirmed and continued Kennedy administration policies in Vietnam; placed emphasis on Mekong Delta; maintained military assistance at least as great as to Diem; reiterated plans for troop withdrawal; proposed no new programs nor increased U.S. assistance; authorized operations up to 50 km. within Laos.

7 Mar 64   Briefing Paper, Establishment of Critical District Advisory Teams (C), Briefing Book for McNaughton, Saigon [May 1964]
MACV extended U.S. advisory effort to district level in 13 key districts around Saigon.

17 Mar 64   NSAM 288, Implementation of South Vietnam Programs
The situation in Vietnam had deteriorated and was grave; VC controlled much of country; North Vietnamese support of V.C. had

increased; RVNAF should be increased by 50,000; contingency plans for operations in Laos and Cambodia and overt retaliation against DRV should be developed; however, no major increase of U.S. advisory effort was called for.

17 Apr 64   *Memo, DIA for SecDef, Status of the Vietnamese Hamlet Survey*
Aerial photo reconnaissance revealed far fewer fortified hamlets than province officials claimed.

22 Apr 64   *Memo, DepSecDef for CJCS*
Secretary insisted that he personally approve every manpower space for MACV.

May 64   *Briefing Book, Miscellaneous Messages, Status Reports, and Recommendations for Secretary McNamara, n.d.*
Reported great instability in province governments, decline in GVN controlled population, increase in VC control; important provinces were in "critical condition."

12 May 64   *Draft Memo for the Record, Lt. Col. S. B. Berry, Jr., Mil. Asst. to SecDef, n.d., U.S. Embassy Briefing, Saigon.*
USOM 25% understrength, half this shortage in rural affairs staff.

12–13 May 64   *McNamara trip to Saigon*
Situation appeared critical.

22 May 64   *Msg, JCS to COMUSMACV 6448, Vietnamese Civil Guard and Self-Defense Corps.*
COMUSMACV asked to study encadrement of CG/SDC with U.S. teams similar to White Star teams in Laos. JCS was examining alternative advisor expansions (1,000, 2,000, 3,000).

23 May 64   *Msg, CINCPAC to JCS 230418Z, Vietnamese Civil Guard and Self Defense Corps*
MACV opposed to "flooding" RVN with U.S. personnel; preferred build-up on selective basis, challenged "encadrement."

25 May 64   *Msg, JCS to CINCPAC 6473, Vietnamese Civil Guard and Self Defense Corps*
JCS plan for 6 Mobile Training Teams in each province and training center, 70 advisors to each critical province, increase of 1000 personnel.

27 May 64   *Msg, COMUSMACV to CINCPAC 4259, 270045Z*
Gen. Harkins disputed the value of U.S. conducted training for CG/SDC and of Mobile Training Teams; proposed advisors be used at district level for operations; accepted 1000 man increase.

27 May 64   *Msg, CINCPAC to JCS, 270805Z, Vietnamese CG and SDC*
CINCPAC agreed with COMUSMACV and outlined specific advisory build-up recommended: 956 personnel by end CY 65.

27 May 64   *Msg, White House to Saigon (Personal for Gen. Paul Harkins)*
Gen. Harkins requested to return to U.S.

28 May 64   *Msg, Saigon to State 2338*
USOM desire for gradual, not rapid, build-up; need for effective local administration and security.

30 May 64   *JCSM–464–64, Pilot Program for Provision of Advisory Assistance to Paramilitary Forces in Seven Provinces*
One of two JCS proposals submitted to McNamara outlining pilot program for advisory build-up: teams in 49 districts over 6 month period, 300 advisors.

30 May 64   *JCSM–465–64, U.S. Advisory Assistance to the Vietnamese Civil Guard and Self-Defense Corps.*
Second proposal—Broader advisory increase program: 1000 personnel for all 239 districts over 1–1½ years.

30 May 64   *JCSM–466–64, Provision of U.S. Advisors to Company Level Within Vietnamese Regular Ground Forces*
JCS opposed extending U.S. advisors to company level, because of increased casualties, language problems, ARVN opposition.

1 Jun 64   *Honolulu Conference*

25 Jun 64   *Msg, COMUSMACV to JCS, MAC 7325380, Extension of U.S. Advisory Assistance*
Elaborated decision of Honolulu conference to expand advisory effort to district level, and to increase battalion-level advisory groups to make company level advisory teams available.

1 Jul 64–
31 Jul 65   Maxwell Taylor, Ambassador to South Vietnam.

17 July 64   *Msg, COMUSMACV to CINCPAC, MACJ–316180, Support Requirements for Extension of U.S. Advisory Program.*
COMUSMACV reached 4200 personnel in addition to 926 battalion and district advisors—"the straw that broke the camel's back" of the overburdened support base.

28 Jul 64   *Msg, COMUSMACV to JCS, MACJ1 7044, Personnel Augmentation.*
COMUSMACV requested 4200 personnel by 1 Dec 64 and remainder of 4772 total increase by 1 Feb 65.

Jul 64   *Hop Tac*
Idea for Hop Tac, special combined US/GVN effort to secure critical area round Saigon, proposed by Amb. Lodge at Honolulu Conference.

1 Aug 64–
30 Jun 68   Gen. William C. Westmoreland, commander of MACV.

2 Aug 64   *Tonkin Gulf Incident*
U.S.S. Maddox allegedly attacked by North Vietnamese torpedo boats.

4 Aug 64   *JCSM–665–64, Additional Support in RVN on Accelerated Basis*
McNamara wanted additional men provided more quickly than Westmoreland's plan.

5 Aug 64   *Tonkin Gulf Resolution*
Congress passed joint resolution supporting "all necessary action" to protect U.S. forces and assist Vietnam.

7 Aug 64	*Memo, SecDef for CJCS, Additional Support for Republic of Vietnam* McNamara directed that accelerated deployment be completed by end of September.
11 Aug 64	*Msg, COMUSMACV to CINCPAC, MACJ3 7738, Additional Support for RVN* Westmoreland replied that he could not absorb build-up in time requested by McNamara.
15 Aug 64	*Msg, JCS to CSA, CNO, CSAF et al, JCS 7953, Additional Support in RVN* McNamara cancelled accelerated deployment, services instructed to deploy personnel in accordance with Westmoreland's initial recommendations.
16 Aug 64– 26 Oct 64	*Khanh coup.* Nguyen Khanh, President, Head of State and Chief, Revolutionary Military Council (30 Jan 64 to 26 Oct 64, 27 Jan 65 to 21 Feb 65).
12 Sep 64	*Hop Tac* Hop Tac launched with a sweep through Gia Dinh Province. Mission aborted following day by coup.
4 Nov 64– 11 Jun 65	Phan Klac Suu, Chief of State
Dec 64	Crisis between Amb. Taylor and Gen. Khanh resulted from Taylor's attempt to use U.S. decision to begin bombing DRV as lever to get GVN reform. Taylor abandoned further attempts at leverage.
Dec 64	*"Troika sign-off" for piasters abolished* USOM Director Killen decided to abandon joint sign-off for release of piaster funds for pacification—important leverage tool.
23 Jan 65	McNamara approved RVNAF force increase proposal for MAP support. Now strength authorizations: 275,058 Regular Forces, 137,187 RF and 185,000 PF. (Alternative 1).
7 Feb 65	FLAMING DART reprisal attacks against DRV launched.
22 Feb 65	Gen. Westmoreland recommended sending two Marine Battalion Landing Teams to DaNang for base security.
26 Feb 65	ROLLING THUNDER, sustained bombing of DRV, initiated.
26 Feb 65	Decision to send Marines to DaNang made in Washington.
6 Mar 65	Marines went ashore at DaNang.
16 Mar 65	*JCS message 0936* Gen. H. K. Johnson returned from trip to Vietnam with recommendation for deployment of U.S. combat forces and creation of joint command.
20 Mar 65	Westmoreland requested authorization to implement Alternative 2 RVNAF strength increase (greater than alternative 1 by 15,000).

21 Mar 65   COMUSMACV *message 1566*
Westmoreland opposed any formal merging of commands, preferred informal cooperation.

26 Mar 65   MACV *"Commander's Estimate of the Situation"*
As a strategy alternative, Westmoreland rejected proposal for accelerated RVNAF build-up as insufficient to prevent VC victory.

1–2 Apr 65   Washington strategy conference with Brig Gen De Puy, Amb. Taylor.

6 Apr 65   NSAM *328*
President approved dispatch of two more battalions and an air wing and authorized their employment for active combat missions.

12 Apr 65   MACV *Command History 1965*
McNamara approved JCS recommendation for RVNAF expansion of 17,247 160 additional U.S. advisors approved.

15 Apr 65   *Defense Department message 009164, Joint State/Defense Message*
Defense Department sought to have U.S. Army civil affairs officers introduced in provinces to improve civil administration. Amb. Taylor opposition killed proposal.

15 Apr 65   *Department of State message 2332*
McGeorge Bundy informed Amb. Taylor that President wanted to try "encadrement of U.S. troops with Vietnamese."

15 Apr 65   *DOD message 151233Z*
DOD requested COMUSMACV's opinion about feasibility of encadrement of U.S. officers in ARVN divisions to improve effectiveness.

18 Apr 65   *Honolulu Conference, MACV Command History*
Based on study by Gen. Throckmorton, encadrement proposals were rejected because of language problem, expanded support requirement, and adverse effects on South Vietnamese morale.

Apr 65   MACV *Command History 1965*
Westmoreland suggested joint MACV–JGS staff. Gen. Thieu and Gen. Minh were opposed.

3 May 65   *Hop Tac pacification*
Corps commanders for I, II, IV Corps presented Hop Tac plans for their zones, each to extend "oil blot" pacification from its headquarters city. (By end of 1965 became scheme for National Priority Areas.)

11 May 65   Viet Cong attached and overran Song Be, capital of Phuoc Long Province, and a U.S. advisory compound in the city.

14 May 65   *JCS message 142228Z*
McNamara authorized creation of formal combined command in Vietnam and coordinating MACV–JGS staff.

21 May 65   COMUSMACV *message* Combined Command; JCS *message* *240603Z*

Westmoreland recommended against proposed combined command because of Thieu's and Ky's opposition.

26 May 65   *CINCPAC msg to JCS 3027, 260332Z*
CINCPAC supported COMUSMACV's opposition to combined command because of fears of Vietnamese hostility.

late May 65   VC force ambushed and decimated ARVN 51st Regiment and 2 battalions near Ba Gia, west of Quang Ngai City.

Jun 65   *Origin of CAP*
Several Marines assigned to work with local PF near Phu Bai, I Corps.

7 Jun 65   *MACV message to CINCPAC and JCS 19118*
Moratorium on RVNAF build-up required because trainees needed as fillers in existing units to replace heavy casualties. Westmoreland requested 44 additional U.S. battalions; reported severe ARVN deterioration.

19 Jun 65–   Nguyen Van Thieu, Chief of State and Chairman, National
present   Leadership Council, 20 Jun 65 to 9 Nov 67, elected President 31 Oct 67.

June 65   Viet Cong attacked Special Forces camp at Dong Xoai with more than two regiments.

25 Jun 65   VC Central Highlands offensive began, district headquarters at Tou Morong, Kontum Province, was overrun.

26 Jun 65   *MACV Military Report, 19–26 June*
MACV noted 5 ARVN regiments and 9 battalions combat ineffective.

Jul 65   18 US/FW combat maneuver battalions were in Vietnam.

Jul 65   *MACV Command History, 1965*
11 of 15 ARVN training battalions had to be disorganized to provide fillers for line units due to heavy casualties.

7 Jul 65   Six district capitals had been abandoned or overrun.

20 Jul 65   *SecDef Memorandum for the President*
McNamara urged U.S. to lay down terms for continuing assistance before introduction of more forces; suggested exercise leverage through control of rice policy.

25 Jul 65   *Saigon message 266*
Amb. Taylor did not want to appear to impose conditions for increased aid.

28 Jul 65   President announced expanded U.S. effort and increased troop commitment to Vietnam.

7 Aug 65   *MACV Command History 1965*
CG III MAF designated as Senior Advisor to ARVN I CTZ Commander.

Sep 65   *Lodge Ambassador*
Lodge returned to Vietnam for second term as ambassador. Term of office: 31 Jul 65–Apr 67.

Sep 65	COMUSMACV evaluated 3-month experiment with "single manager" teams in 3 provinces, found it partially successful but scrapped the idea.
1 Oct 65	*MACV Command History, 1965* MACV created separate contingency fund for each subsector advisor for urgent projects, in attempt to overcome delays in Vietnamese pacification system.
16 Oct 65 *18 Oct 65*	*State Dept msg 1039* *Saigon msg 1324* USOM sought to restore troika sign-off but State Dept. opposed this idea. The attempt was abandoned.
21 Oct 65	Commander of HQ Field Force, Vietnam (FFORCEV) designated as II CTZ Senior Advisor. (At insistence of ARVN Corps commanders, who felt they would suffer loss of prestige if advised by less than Senior U.S. officer in corps.)
3 Nov 65	*SecDef Draft Memorandum for the President* McNamara recorded impatience with GVN, recommended giving larger role to advisors at province and district level.
5 Nov 65	*MACV Command History* Westmoreland recommended increased RVNAF force levels for FY 66 and FY 67, to limit of available manpower.
Nov 65	*CAP Program* Agreement between I Corps Commander and CG III MAF permitting integration of Marine squads into PF platoons in DaNang area to form Combined Action Platoon (CAP): Marine Rifle Squad (14) and PF Platoon (32–38).
28 Nov 65	McNamara trip to Saigon, approves RVNAF force increase recommendation.
15 Dec 65	*Lodge memorandum for Gen. Lansdale; MACV Command History* Lodge specified that GVN pacification effort was primarily civilian, consequently on U.S. side the two civilian agencies, USAID and CAS, should be generating support agencies.
8–11 Jan 66	*Warrenton Conference Report* Members of Saigon Mission, Vietnam Coordinating Committee and other senior officials met at Warrenton, Virginia, to review pacification problem. It foreshadowed a redirection of advisory effort toward pacification.
Jan 66	*MACV Analysis of RVNAF for CY 66* At Mission Council meeting, Amb. Lodge expressed concern that the number of U.S. advisors not smother the Vietnamese at all levels.
4 Feb 66	*State to Saigon 2252* U.S. requested Honolulu meeting with Thieu, Ky to express concern about pacification, economic problems, GVN lack of popular support.

6–8 Feb 66   Honolulu Conference
LBJ concern about the "other war," Thieu and Ky made pledges of increased pacification, promised elections. Amb. William Porter was assigned responsibility for civil support of RD.

28 Feb 66   Mission Council Minutes, Feb. 28, 1966
Porter described his understanding of his duties to Mission Council: coordinating effort for all civil aspects of revolutionary development, through the Mission Liaison Group.

Feb 66   MACV subsector pacification contingency fund abandoned after 4-month trial period due to opposition of GVN RD Minister Thang; it would encourage Vietnamese dependence on U.S.

Mar 66   PROVN Study Summary Statement, Mar 66
Program for Pacification and Long Term Development of South Vietnam (PROVN) completed for internal army use. Revealed lack of coordination among U.S. agencies in pacification.

23 Apr 66   Saigon to State 4160, Apr 23, 1966; 4200, Apr 26; 4435, May 7; 5546, June 15
Lodge reviewed prospects for introduction of U.S. leverage in Buddhist "Struggle Movement"; desired to bring dissidents under GVN control, but saw no way to achieve decisive results. Recommended to Washington that a sign-off system be reinstated to reduce corruption and increase U.S. influence at lower levels.

Jul 66   Stepped-up pacification effort: Operation Lam Son, combined RD "Search and Seal" operations with U.S. 1st Infantry Division and ARVN 5th Division in Binh Duong. U.S. 25th Division "adopted" districts in Han Nghia Province.

Jul 66   "Roles and Missions" Study Group began work for Amb. Porter. Completed in August. Recommendation for support for a reemphasis on pacification.

Sep 66   McNamara proposed that responsibility for sole management of pacification be assigned to COMUSMACV, who would have a Deputy to command all pacification activities. AID, CIA, USIA opposed such reorganization; Komer and JCS concurred.

29 Sep 66   Komer, "Memorandum for Secretary McNamara"
Komer stressed that unified management of pacification was needed.

23–25 Oct 66   Manila Conference
At Manila Conference Thieu and Ky formally accepted commitment of ARVN to support RD, and "National Reconciliation" program to attract VC back to government was announced.

Oct 66   McNamara trip to Saigon. Ky agreed to shift in combat missions for U.S. and RVNAF forces: U.S. to conduct large-scale offensive operations, RVNAF to provide security to RD.

7 Nov 66   MACV/JGS Combined Campaign Plan 1967 (AB 142)
Spelled out new division of labor between U.S. and RVNAF. JGS agreed to keep 53 ARVN battalions (50% of ARVN combat units) assigned to support RD.

7 Nov 66   *Memorandum, Amb. Lodge for the Secretary of State, SecDef and Komer; message, Saigon 11125, Nov. 17.*
Lodge defined terms of reference for what was established as the Office of Civil Operations (OCO).

8 Dec 66   *MACV msg 52414 to CINCPAC*
Westmoreland reported to CINCPAC on poor quality and performance of ARVN. First 10 months of 1966, the number of ARVN maneuver battalions with minimally acceptable operational strength fluctuated from 31 to 78 of total of 121 organized units.

17 Dec 66   *W. W. Rostow, Memorandum to Secretary of Defense and Acting Secretary of State, draft NSAM attached*
Pacification listed as third strategic objective and five programs concerned with pacification were outlined, heralding reemphasis on pacification in 1967.

27 Dec 66   *JCS Memorandum for the Secretary of Defense, JCSM–792–66, line-in, line-out revised draft NSAM attached.*
JCS replied to Rostow's draft after consulting CINCPAC; stiffening and making more specific U.S. commitment to war, introducing term "revolutionary development," eliminated references to "national reconciliation" for ex-VC, and watered down commitment to constitutional-electoral efforts underway.

9 Jan 67   *MACV msg 00949*
In Dec 1966 a 12-officer team from each ARVN had undergone training on RD support so that each might instruct its division on the new duties. The division training programs began in Jan 67.

18 Jan 67   *MACV msg 02149 to CINCPAC from MACCORDS*
MACV described new Hamlet Evaluation System (HES) to CINCPAC.

20 Jan 67   *ASD(ISA) John T. McNaughton Memorandum for the Secretary of Defense, Subject: Draft NSAM on "Strategic Guidelines for 1967 in Vietnam;" McNaughton's line-in, line-out revised draft and the JCS revision attached.*
McNaughton draft for Vietnam strategic guidelines incorporated most JCS recommendations, emphasized security, anti-infrastructure and intelligence in support of R/D; pushed "National Reconciliation."

24 Jan 67   *MACV msg 02916, Westmoreland sends*
Westmoreland stated that the effectiveness of RVNAF must be increased and that its image must be improved.

28 Jan 67   *Deputy SecDef Cyrus Vance letter to W. W. Rostow*
Vance sent McNaughton version to Rostow as Defense Department reply to his memorandum. No NSAM was ever promulgated.

Feb 67   *"Pacification Slowdown" Southeast Asia Analysis Report, Feb. 67, OASD(SA) SEA Programs Directorate*
OASD(SA) reported that pacification effort in 1966 had failed.

18 Mar 67　*MACV msg 09101, Westmoreland sends*
Westmoreland cabled CINCPAC requesting an "optimum force" increase of 4⅔ divisions (201,250 men) or as a "minimum essential force," 2⅓ divisions (100,000 men). No major expansion of RVNAF called for: 6,307 more spaces for ARVN, 50,000 more RF/PF.

20–21 Mar 67　*Guam Conference*
President Johnson met with Thieu and Ky in Guam. They presented draft constitution and agreed to a proclamation on National Reconciliation.

Johnson decided to transfer control of pacification to MACV and send Robert Komer to head new operation in Saigon.

25 Mar 67　*Embassy Saigon msg 21226, Eyes Only for the President from Lodge*
Lodge stressed importance of RVNAF for MACV success, praised Abrams as man to oversee RVNAF improvement.

Mar 67　Gen. Creighton Abrams became Westmoreland deputy and assumed responsibility for U.S. advisory effort to RVNAF.

1 Apr 67　New South Vietnamese Constitution promulgated.

24 Apr 67　*R. W. Komer Memorandum for the President*
Komer asserted that decisive contest lay in pacification in the South, rejected Westmoreland's request for additional 200,000 troops, proposed methods to improve RVNAF and pacification, suggested increased pressure on GVN for reforms.

1 May 67　New Ambassador, Ellsworth Bunker, arrived in Saigon.

7 May 67　*MACV msg 15064*
Reported Jan. decision to make a unit by unit effectiveness evaluation and to cut off support for superfluous or below standard units. Resulted in several warnings but no suspension of support. Also reported RVNAF desertions were won for Jan–Feb 1967 from Jan–Feb 1966.

9 May 67　*NSAM 362*
Komer's appointment as single manager for pacification announced internally.

12 May 67　*Embassy Saigon Airgram 622, Subject: Revolutionary Development*
Gloomy account of progress of RD in first three months of 1967.

13 May 67　*Ambassador Bunker statements to the press in Saigon, May 13, 1967*
Announcement of transfer of OCO to MACV, Bunker stressed combined civil-military nature of pacification.

15 May 67　*Embassy Saigon msg. 25839*
First meeting of Komer with Ky. Ky declined to place GVN RD efforts under JGS.

28 May 67   *State Department msg DTG 092304Z; MACV Dir 10–12, 28 May 1967*
MACV issued directive with instructions on new RD organizational arrangements.

May 67   *JCSM–530–67, Subject: Increase in FY 1968 RVNAF Force Level, 28 Sep 67 (a review of the year's actions)*
McNamara imposed a temporary ceiling on RVNAF to prevent further inflation in Vietnam, and to arrest some of the balance of payments flow of U.S.

14 Jun 67   *Amb. R. W. Komer, Memorandum for General W. C. Westmoreland, Subject: Organization for Attack on V.C. Infrastructure*
Komer recommended consolidation, under his direction, of U.S. anti-infrastructure intelligence effort. Desired unified GVN/US, civil/military "management structure targeted on infrastructure." ICEX (Intelligence Coordination and Exploitation) structure was developed.

14 Jun 67   *Embassy Saigon msg 28095, For the President from Bunker*
Bunker described MACV actions underway to improve RVNAF: improving leadership, better pay, improving command structure and equipment of RF/PF training, integrated US/RVNAF operations, reviews.

17 Jun 67   *MACCORDS, Project Takeoff, prepared by the ACofS, CORDS, Headquarters MACV*
Project TAKEOFF contained analysis of reasons for part failure, appraisal of current situation, and recommendations for future emphasis in RD; suggested increased use of U.S. leverage and control.

4 Jul 67   *ASD(SA) Alain Enthoven Memo for the SecDef, Subj: Improvement in RVNAF Force Effectiveness*
Enthoven claimed that primary reason for RVNAF ineffectiveness was the quantity and quality of leadership and recommended that the Secretary query MACV on leadership problems.

13 July 67   *ASD(SA) Alain Enthoven Memorandum for the Record, Subj: Fallout for SecDef Trip to South Vietnam (TS–SENS–EYES ONLY for Dr. Heyman); and OASD(SA) General Purpose Forces, W. K. Brehm, Memo for the Record, Subj: SEA Deployments, Jul 14, 1967*
In Saigon, McNamara gave planning authorization for U.S. augmentation up to 525,000 spaces, and civilianization of 10,000 additional spaces to fulfill Westmoreland's lower force alternative.

14 Aug 67   *ASD(SA) Alain Enthoven Memo for the Secretaries of the Military Departments, the Chairman of the Joint Chiefs of Staff and the Assistant Secretaries of Defense, Subj: Southeast Asia Deployment Program #5*
New U.S. force level of 525,000 promulgated as Deployment Program #5.

30 Aug 67   *DASD(SA) Memo for the SecDef*
Amb. Komer complained that the CORDS advisory element's actual strength was seriously below authorization due to bureaucratic delays.

31 Aug 67   *Dept of State Msg 30023*
Study of leverage by Hans Heymann and Lt Col Volney Warner recommended increased use.

7 Sep 66   *COMUSMACV Memo for Ambassador Lodge*
Westmoreland disagreed with Roles and Missions Study Group recommendation to remove division from chain of command below CTZ level and strengthening role of Province Chief.

15 Sep 67   *JCSM 505–67, Subj: U.S. Forces Deployment Vietnam (Refined Troop List)*
JCS submitted final detailed troop list for Program #5. Contained 2,577 additional advisors and 666 Special Forces to perform advisor-like functions.

16 Sep 67   *Review and Analysis System for RVNAF Progress, MACV–J341*
First published Review and Analysis for RVNAF appeared: long catalogue of RVNAF deficiencies.

19 Sep 67   *Embassy Saigon msg 7113*
Komer replied to recommendation for increased use of U.S. leverage that it must be done discreetly. Proposed comprehensive system of country-wide leverage was never adopted.

28 Sep 67   *JCSM-530-67, Subject: Increase in FY 68 RVNAF Force Level*
JCS forwarded with endorsement the MACV–CINCPAC recommendation on FY 68 RVNAF force increases: total increase of 63,586; 47,839 for RF/PF and 15,747 for regular forces. MACV requested further increase of 78,204 for FY 1969.

7 Oct 67   *SecDef Memo for CJCS, Subject: Increase in FY 68 RVNAF Force Level, and attached OASD(SA) memo for the SecDef, 5 Oct 67*
McNamara approved the requested FY 68 augmentations for RVNAF, against the wishes of Enthoven, who would have authorized only half as many.

26 Oct 67   *"Information on MATs (Mobile Advisory Teams) and MALTs (Mobile Advisory Logistics Teams)," 8 May 1968, working paper prepared by the ACofS MA, MACV*
MACV conference on RF/PF, convened to study problems of RF/PF expansion and to plan for expansion of advisory effort, recommended complete reorientation of advisory concept for RF/PF, establishment of Mobile Advisory Teams to be used on a rotating basis.

15 Dec 67   Westmoreland approved new RF/PF advisory system: MATs and MALTs, to be phased in during 1968.

31 Jan 68   *Tet Offensive*
VC/NVA initiate massive attacks on population centers throughout Vietnam during Lunar New Year (Tet) holiday period.

I. ADVISORY STABILITY, 1954–1960

A. THE U.S. GAMBLE WITH LIMITED RESOURCES

1. *Origins of the U.S. Involvement in RVN*

The U.S. decision to attempt, generally within the strictures imposed by the Geneva Accords, to shore up the Government of South Vietnam (GVN) and to prevent the new nation's fall into communist hands appears in retrospect to have been, in Wellington's phrase, "a close run thing." The prevalent American attitude in 1954 was that the deployment of large U.S. forces to the mainland of Asia should be permitted "never again." Spending on national security was to be pegged at tolerable levels which would not threaten the well-being of the domestic economy, yet communist expansion was to be deterred by the threat of massive retaliation combined with U.S. support for free nations capable of managing their own internal order and insuring that any act of armed aggression would appear as just that—the unambiguous precondition for nuclear retaliation.

2. *Initial Military Reluctance*

The policy solution to this problem in national security strategy has been accurately and exhaustively described in recent literature. It need not be repeated here. The important thing to note is that the attempt to achieve stability in RVN was recognized to be a marginal gamble to retain a small but potentially important piece in the larger jig saw puzzle which was U.S. national security policy. As such, it seemed worth the risk of a moderate outlay of assistance and advice. General J. Lawton Collins stated the case succinctly in his assessment for the National Security Council:

> . . . There is at least an even chance that Vietnam can be saved from Communism if the present programs of its government are fully implemented. . . . I cannot guarantee that Vietnam will remain free, even with our aid. But I know that without our aid Vietnam will surely be lost to Communism.

The gamble consisted in making available to the GVN that material support and advice which would enable it to assure its own viability. Much of the military equipment was already in RVN, the residue of earlier efforts to support the French war against the Viet Minh. The framework for military advice was present, too, in the form of MAAG Indochina which had assisted (and attempted to influence—generally unsuccessfully) the French struggle.

The military establishment was not eager, however, to undertake this effort. The JCS feared that the advisory limit imposed by the Geneva Accords (342 military personnel) was too restrictive to permit a successful training program even if all administrative tasks were performed by civilians and all military personnel freed for advisory duties in training the army of the new nation. Even this would create a situation, the JCS argued, in which the U.S. would have only very limited influence, yet assume the responsibility for failure. The same resource allocations would bring a greater return, in the JCS view, if devoted to the support of military forces in other nations. The Joint Chiefs were agreed that the creation of a Vietnamese Army might not even be adequate to the task of establishing a stable GVN, let alone to protecting that nation from external aggression:

> The Joint Chiefs of Staff further consider that the chaotic internal political situation within Vietnam will hamper the development of loyal and effective security forces in the support of the Diem Government and that it is probable that the development of such forces will not result in political and military stability within South Vietnam. Unless the Vietnamese themselves show an inclination to make the individual and collective sacrifices required to resist communism no amount of external pressure and assistance can long delay a complete Communist victory in South Vietnam.

Their conclusion, "from a military point of view," was that the risk was not worth the gamble:

> . . . [T]he Joint Chiefs of Staff consider that the United States should not participate in the training of Vietnamese forces in Indochina. However, if it is considered that political considerations are overriding, the Joint Chiefs of Staff would agree to the assignment of a training mission to MAAG, Saigon, with safeguards against French interference with the US training effort.

3.   *The Decision to Gamble with Limited Commitment*

Political considerations were indeed overriding. Reasonable fears of failure, claims about the inadequacy of resources, and caveats on the necessity for Vietnamese initiatives are inherently inconclusive arguments when one is speaking of a calculated gamble. Indeed, low value chips for high stakes made the gamble all the more appealing. Secretary of State Dulles' position immediately prevailed: only relatively small military forces were needed; their principal purpose should be to promote internal stability rather than to guard against external aggression; nations acting in concert (under the umbrella of U.S. nuclear superiority) would guard against external aggression. On 22 October 1954 Ambassador Heath and General O'Daniel in Saigon were instructed to "collaborate in setting in motion a crash program designed to bring about an improvement in the loyalty and effectiveness of the Free Vietnamese forces." Four days later the JCS were directed to prepare a "long range program for the reorganization and training of the minimum number of Free Vietnamese forces necessary for internal security." The earlier objections of the JCS were neither refuted nor ignored; they were accepted tacitly as part and parcel of the policy gamble.

4.   *From Internal to Conventional Defense*

The language of this decision to train the Vietnamese National Army (VNA), as it was then called, would indicate that internal (rather than external) security would be the principal purpose of that force. That is not the way it developed, for three reasons. First, basic U.S. national strategy (embodied in NSC 162 and NSC 5602 during the period under examination) and Southeast Asia policy (NSC 5429 and NSC 5612) were both ambiguous on a key point: to what degree were indigenous military forces to be expected to defend against a conventional, "limited war" attack by an aggressor? The continuous, unbroken tendency throughout the 1950s was to desire ever more capability for conventional defense.

Second, U.S. military forces were unprepared by their own experience to assist in the structuring of forces designed for other than conventional warfare. The U.S. advisory experiences that were current in terms of institutionalized memory were those of aid to Greece and Korea where the job had been one of training for technical and tactical competence along conventional lines. It was eminently natural for the U.S. advisory effort to follow in this identifiable path. Indeed, to have expected the advisory effort to have stressed "counter insurgency" early in this period would have been completely unrealistic: the term had not been invented and its concepts had not been either developed or articulated. This natural tendency to develop conventional forces was not only in step with the dominant trend in U.S. military strategy, it was also reinforced by a third factor, the generalized assumption that the ability to promote internal security was automatically provided for in the creation of forces capable to promote external security.

The confluence of all three factors led, in fact, to an attempt to create Vietnamese forces along lines which were later called "mirror images" of conventional U.S. force structures. MAAG Vietnam proposed and led in the creation of the Army of Vietnam (ARVN) in formations comprising divisions, regiments, battalions, and companies organized as closely parallel to U.S. organization as local differences in equipment and support would permit. This was not, for the reasons already indicated, an unreasonable or indefensible development —at least not until about 1959 or 1960—and by that time efforts were underway to transform the focus of ARVN to internal security. These later efforts were faced with the reality of a sizeable army—conventionally organized, trained, and equipped—which had been created under different circumstances and for different purposes. One is forced to wonder, if Vietnamese institutions are as difficult to remould as their American counterparts, whether the later advisory effort was not faced from its inception with an almost insurmountable task.

5. *The Early MAAG and the Equipment Recovery Mission*

The number of U.S. advisors to the fledgling Republic of Vietnam Armed Forces (RVNAF) were, as already indicated, limited by the Geneva Accords. Article 16 of the Accords limited military personnel in Vietnam to the number present at the time the Accords were signed. The magic number was 342. The U.S. MAAG Chief, General O'Daniel, complained that he needed twice this number to train the new RVNAF and to oversee the redistribution of U.S. equipment already in RVN as a result of U.S. support for the French during the war just ended. The eventual outcome, when it was learned informally that the Indian Government would instruct its representative on the ICC to interpose no objection, was the creation of the Temporary Equipment Recovery Mission (TERM) with 350 military personnel. TERM served as the principal manager for the redistribution of equipment, assisted in developing RVNAF's embryonic logistical support system, and provided a convenient cover for a larger intelligence effort.

This combined administrative-advisory force remained stable in size during the period prior to 1961. American military advisors were located physically at only a very few locations in RVN. They were notable by their absence in field units. The U.S. effort was concentrated in training centers and in Saigon. In the former it was largely technical; in the latter it consisted primarily of attempts to persuade GVN to adopt measures recommended by the U.S. advisory group. It was essentially an attempt to give advice from the top. This does not mean that the question of leverage was never considered; it was. Early in our involvement, in January 1955, the JCS laid out available U.S. courses of action in South Vietnam and urged that a decision be made at "the highest level" to indicate which of these should be followed:

a. To continue aid to South Vietnam as currently being developed with the cooperation of the French and Vietnamese.

b. To institute a unilateral program of direct guidance to the Vietnamese government through an "advisor" system. Under this course of action, the amount of U.S. aid should be dependent upon Vietnamese adherence to U.S. direction.

c. In the event the courses of action in *a* and *b* above are not sufficient to insure retention of South Vietnam to the Free World, to deploy self sustaining U.S. forces to South Vietnam either unilaterally, or as a part of a SEACDT [Southeast Asia Common Defense Treaty—a term used prior to SEATO] force.

d. To withdraw all U.S. support from South Vietnam and concentrate on saving the remainder of Southeast Asia.

No such decision was made. Indeed, as explained in the summary and analysis, there is no reason to believe that the need for such a decision was even seriously considered at "the highest level."

MAAG Vietnam was by 1960 still quite small in size, though it loomed ever larger in importance. (It was the only U.S. MAAG commanded by a Lieutenant General; all of the other MAAG Chiefs were officers of lesser rank.) It was essentially city-bound, training center and Saigon-oriented, devoted to technical-tactical training and high level persuasion aimed at influencing RVNAF organization. The personnel limitations imposed upon it resulted in highly centralized advice. But through its efforts and material support this MAAG assisted in the creation of a sizeable (140,000 man) conventional army and of small naval and air forces of approximately 5,000 men each.

The U.S. MAAG was also concerned with the establishment and training of paramilitary forces, but it was not as directly concerned as it was with the creation of conventional forces in ARVN. The Civil Guard (CG) and Self Defense Corps (SDC) were at various times under the control of the Ministry of the Interior or directly under President Diem. In the field they were invariably under the direction of the Province Chiefs. The U.S. civilian advisors who had been called in to give assistance with police and internal security matters tended to favor making these paramilitary forces less military *per se* and more police intelligence-minded. MAAG tended to favor making them more consciously military and territorially oriented in order to free ARVN for mobile, offensive operations rather than tying its forces down in static defense duties. By 1960, when Civil Guard training was passed to MAAG control, neither course of action had been followed consistently but it was highly probable that MAAG's views would henceforth prevail. Thus, questions of local physical security would almost inescapably be decided with reference to the effect they would have on the functions of ARVN, itself created with an eye to external defense. This may be said to be an awkward structure from which to launch an effort aimed primarily at internal security. It was, however, the structure that existed.

B. THE TRANSITION PERIOD: 1959–1961

1. Early Steps Toward Emphasis on Internal Security

By the time of the Draper Committee (The President's Committee to Study the United States Military Assistance Program) in 1958–1959, there was an almost imperceptible but growing U.S. awareness of the requirement to promote internal stability. The committee's papers, for instance, sought to popularize military civic action programs and to link them to politically acceptable precedents—such as the U.S. Army's role in the development of the American West. The very term "mirror imaging" was coined in a Draper Committee staff study. One of the committee's studies questioned even the easy assumption that internal security was a "lesser included capability" of forces structured to promote external security:

> It is seldom that a government considers its military forces to have only a mission of maintaining internal security. Their size, organization, equipment, habitual deployment, and so on, are nearly always related to real or supposed requirements of defense against external attack. They are usually considered capable of performing internal security missions as part of this larger role. However, the requirements of the two missions are different, if overlapping; and tailoring a military force to the task of countering external aggression—i.e., countering another regular military force— entails some sacrifice of capabilities to counter internal aggression. The latter requires widespread deployment, rather than concentration. It requires small, mobile, lightly equipped units of the ranger or commando type. It requires different weapons, command systems, communications, logistics. . . .

2. The McGarr Emphasis on Counterinsurgency

These developments were only harbingers of a dawning awareness, however, not indicative of a fundamental shift in focus which had already occurred. The degree to which ARVN and paramilitary forces should be consciously structured to deal with internal security rather than to protect against external invasion was the subject of a developing debate rather than a settled issue. It fell to Lieutenant General Lionel C. McGarr to head the U.S. MAAG during the confusing period of transition which accompanied this debate. He did not come to Vietnam unaware of the issues; a long study prepared for him by his staff at the Army's Command and General Staff College (his post before coming to Saigon) laid out in some detail the Viet Cong's strategy as adapted from the Viet Minh's struggle with the French:

> This form of warfare permitted the Viet Minh to retain the mobility so essential to jungle and mountain operations, facilitated the gathering of detailed, accurate, and timely intelligence information, kept the level of

violence at a low enough level to preclude the active intervention of another major power, accomplished the slow attrition of the French while permitting the Viet Minh to build the regular forces necessary for the final battles, offset the serious logistics problem by the very primitiveness of transportation methods, and surmounted the manpower shortage by making political and economic operations inseparable from military operations.

One could conclude from this assessment that RVNAF should be restructured to deal with this essentially internal challenge to South Vietnamese stability. In a statement which may reflect the difficulty of reversing institutional thought patterns—at the U.S. Army's principal doctrine formulating institution, in this instance—it was claimed that pacification operations were undesirable because they detracted from training. The suggestion was that the CG and SDC takeover of pacification should be expedited:

> The [South Vietnamese] Army is still required to engage from time to time in major pacification (internal security) operations, pending the development of a higher state of operational effectiveness of the Civil Guard and the Self-Defense Corps. Since units have considerable personnel turnover and are filled out with draftees, who have had only basic and perhaps advanced individual training before arrival in units, the orderly pursuit of a progressive unit training schedule is essential to unit effectiveness. Each commitment to an operational (pacification) mission, though of some training value, in general interrupts the planned training of participating units and delays arrival at a satisfactory state of operational readiness.

3. *The Counterinsurgency Plan for South Viet-Nam*

General McGarr's approach was to give emphasis in his advice to recommendations designed to integrate the activities of ARVN and the CG/SDC. He consistently (and persistently) recommended the establishment of a single chain of military command to guide all three forces. He also pushed for steps which would free ARVN from static security (pacification) missions in favor of offensive operations against the Viet Cong. The vehicle for the first of McGarr's desired reforms was the "Counterinsurgency Plan for Viet-Nam" (CIP), produced in late 1960. The CIP was a blueprint for RVNAF reorganization, not an outline of the strategy to be pursued. Not until September 1961 did MAAG present GVN with a set of operational proposals in the form of a "Geographically Phased National Level Operations Plan for Counterinsurgency."

The CIP marks something of a halfway house between concern with external defense and internal security. Both military tasks were recognized, but internal security assumed primacy for the first time:

> Military force, in the form of increased communist insurgency, is clearly the immediate threat to the stability of Viet-Nam today. South Viet-Nam is unique in that it is the only country in the world which is forced to defend itself against a communist internal subversion action, while at the same time being subject to the militarily supportable threat of a conventional external attack from communist North Viet-Nam. The RVNAF force basis is inadequate to meet both these threats.

The problem is twofold, although at present the counterinsurgency phase is the more dangerous and immediate. In this counterinsurgency fight RVNAF is on the defensive. Approximately 75% of ARVN is committed to pacification missions, about half of these being committed to static guard and security roles. . . . The guerrilla problem has [as a result of fragmented lines of authority] become much more serious than the Civil Guard can manage, thereby requiring a disproportionately large RVNAF commitment, which has further resulted in a serious weakening of the RVNAF capability for defense against internal or overt attack in force.

This last point reflected General McCarr's apparently very real concern that ARVN was becoming incapable to meet internal (as well as external) threats posed by the VC in conventional troop formations. As the VC became stronger and formed larger regular units—as distinct from guerrilla bands—the differences between conventional and unconventional warfare seemed to disappear. The problem, as MAAG viewed it, became one of guarding against a spectrum of dangers by means of a short run emphasis on meeting the internal challenge in both its conventional and unconventional (guerrilla) form. In this view ARVN should become the conventional offensive and mobile defensive force, the CG should be the static force in support of pacification efforts. The two should be under a common chain of command, it was argued in the CIP, as should the logistical organization for their support. Such a common chain of command did not exist in 1960–1961:

> The military chain of command has usually been violated at the expense of unity of effort and command. No adequate operations control or overall planning system presently exists. . . . The President has exercised arbitrary control of operations, by-passing command channels of the JGS [Joint General Staff] and often Corps and Division staff. Resources have been fragmented to provincial control. The above practices appear to have been designed to divide responsibility in order to guard against the possibility of a military coup through placing too much power in the hands of a single subordinate.

Poor organization, then, was seen as the principal roadblock in the way of organizing the military and paramilitary forces of South Vietnam into an effective combination. Only through a single chain of command could ARVN be freed to take the offensive, the CG be built up to cope with local guerrillas, and the GVN place itself in a position to start developing useful intelligence—a field which was judged to have been, thus far, a notable failure.

4. *The Supporting Operational Plan*

The Geographically Phased National Plan laid out the priority areas for this coordinated effort under a single chain of command. A three phase sequence of actions (preparation, military action to clear and secure, and combined action to establish civilian political control and consolidate intelligence and security programs) would take place, sequentially, in each of these priority areas. The process would be repeated in expanding spheres as successive areas became pacified.

Together these two American-generated and proposed plans constituted a comprehensive blueprint for GVN action to end the insurgency. Two things common to each should be noted for the purposes of the present inquiry. The first is the simple fact that each was U.S.-generated and proposed. The proposals addressed President Diem's persistent fears of a coup by asking him to ignore those fears. The second point is that neither had anything to say about U.S. advisors. Each was an attempt to give advice, but neither recommended that the U.S. advisory effort in RVN be expanded in scope, size, or content.

5.   Stability in the Number of U.S. Advisors

The number of military advisors had remained fairly level throughout this transition period (roughly, 1959 to mid-1961). TERM had finally been abolished but an approximately equal number of spaces was added to MAAG Vietnam, increasing it from 342 to 685. The ICC agreed that this increase was consistent with the limitations imposed by the Geneva Accords. MAAG advisors had been authorized down to regimental level but expressly forbidden to participate directly in combat operations or to go near the South Vietnamese national boundary. The U.S. had begun to provide Special Forces teams to GVN in an effort to train Vietnamese ranger companies in anti-guerrilla tactics, but this was regarded as a temporary undertaking. As late as November 1961, the total U.S. military strength in South Vietnam was only about 900 personnel. Discussions and arguments had been underway for some time, however, with a view toward increasing U.S. involvement in South Vietnam. The nature of this debate, which took place largely during 1961 and terminated in the decisions at the end of that year to establish a "limited partnership" with GVN, is important to an account of the U.S. advisory build-up. It was in the shadow of opposing contentions about how to make the U.S. contribution most effective in helping GVN to defeat the insurgents that the advisory build-up was to begin in earnest in late 1961. These opposing views, in turn, were cast against the situational developments already outlined: U.S. military desires to make RVNAF more effective in counterinsurgency by improving the military chain of command, increasing the mobility and effectiveness of ARVN, and upgrading the CG/SDC for the performance of pacification tasks.

II.   THE ADVISORY BUILD-UP, 1961–1967

A.   THE KENNEDY PROGRAMS (1961–1963)

1.   The Context of Decisions

By the end of 1961, the U.S. had decided to double its military advisory effort in South Vietnam by establishing advisory teams at the province (sector) level and within ARVN's battalions. The decision to take this step was one of a large number of decisions designed to "buy time" in RVN so that GVN could mobilize its resources and swing over from the defensive to the offensive. All of the major participants appear to have agreed that the situation in RVN was bad and becoming worse, that additional U.S. actions were needed if South Vietnam was to be saved, and that the issue was of sufficient importance in terms of U.S. interest to justify doing whatever was necessary. The question was what *should* be done, not if anything *could* be done. Defeat was too catastrophic an outcome to bear examination. Moreover, decisions about Vietnam in 1961 were, until the very end of the year, made in the shadow of more pressing emergencies—the Berlin crisis and events in Laos. It is most important to recognize this relative lack of centrality if one is to understand the apparently incomplete process by which decisions on Vietnam were reached. Moreover, the *dimensions* of the Vietnamese problem were clear and agreed to by all. Elusive solutions had to be sought in the interstices, as it were, of the policymakers' limited time.

It is difficult to image any responsible individual or group, for instance, taking exception to the litany of problems ticked off by General Taylor in his report following his important October 1961 mission to South Vietnam:

Lack of intelligence
ARVN's defensive posture
Poor command and control
Poor GVN administrative procedures
Lack of initiative

GVN failure to communicate with and mobilize its people, particularly the intellectuals and the young people. But various individuals and groups would stress the importance of different shortcomings and propose quite different methods of "persuading" GVN to overcome them.

The prevalent military view, as already suggested in the summary explanation of the CIP and the Geographically Phased Plan, was that organizational reform and national planning were prerequisites to effective action. If these could be achieved, the military foresaw a pacification process which would proceed from the provision of physical security in the rural areas through the establishment (or reestablishment) of civilian political administration to a state of political stability. The first nut to crack was that of military security. Political analysts, including those of the Department of State, emphasized the need for the Diem government to liberalize itself, to attract dissident groups at least into a loyal active opposition and away from indifference and disaffection. In this view the heart of the matter was essentially political, rather than military.

In both views, it should be noted, advocates agreed that the GVN must be persuaded to take certain necessary steps. Just how such persuasion was to be achieved was a prime subject for discussion. Who was to persuade whom and in what organizational framework was another such subject. But although these subjects were bound to be discussed, neither was the central issue—by late 1961 the question of whether or not to send U.S. combat forces to South Vietnam had clearly earned that title.

The U.S. determination of what steps to take was driven as much by events as by arguments. By late 1961 the course of events dictated that physical security would take primacy over governmental liberalization, not because the arguments for security were inherently more persuasive but because of the very real fear that there would be no GVN to save if the U.S. did not do something very quickly. During the first half of 1961, terrorists and guerrillas had assassinated over 500 local officials and civilians, kidnapped more than 1,000, and killed almost 1,500 RVNAF personnel. The VC had gained the upper hand in most of the countryside and were drawing an increasingly tight cinch around Saigon. Viet Cong regular forces were now estimated to number 25,000 and were being organized into increasingly large regular formations. The terrorist-guerrilla apparatus had grown to embrace an estimated 17,000. The operative question was not whether the Diem government as it was then moving could defeat the insurgents but whether it could save itself.

The deteriorating situation was one reason why the military security argument quickly gained the ascendancy. Another reason was the military's recognition that, while security was an important precondition, political, economic, and social reforms were necessary to the realization of viability within South Vietnam. Thus, security was recognized as a means to a political end. The process outlined in MAAG's Geographically Phased Plan, described earlier, gave recognition to this fact. This process would shortly become known as the "pacification process," widely accepted throughout important places in the U.S. Government (specifically to include what is usually referred to euphemistically as "the highest level").

2.   *Proposal for Extra-Bureaucratic Advisors*

If the deteriorating situation and the potential breadth of the military's view of the pacification process both augured for at least the short run primacy of security considerations, that still left the question of how best to enhance security and to lay the groundwork for the governmental programs which would, hopefully, begin to operate behind a geographically expanding security screen. These questions were addressed, but in a rather one-sided way. An approach to U.S. advice-giving and the organizational context in which it should proceed was tabled as a radical proposal. First the approach, then the organizational framework were struck down. The U.S. decided to take an opposite advisory approach in a very different organizational context as much because of disagreement with the debated proposals as because of reasoned elaboration of the benefits to be realized from the course which was eventually followed. In the process, the difficult question of U.S. leverage got shunted off to the side. GVN reform was simply stated as an expected *quid pro quo* for increased U.S. aid. What the U.S. should do if no reforms materialized was apparently a subject too unpleasant to be considered.

The radical proposals were first floated in January 1961 by a uniquely qualified professional military officer serving in Secretary McNamara's office: Brigadier General Edward Lansdale. Although an Air Force officer, Lansdale had worked closely in the Philippines with Ramon Magsaysay in the latter's successful campaign against the Huk rebellion and served later as head of the U.S. intelligence mission in South Vietnam in the mid-50's. He knew President Diem well and was trusted by the GVN leader. He had gained some notoriety as the real-life hero of the pseudo-fictional best seller, "The Ugly American." His views on counterinsurgency commanded attention.

Lansdale's proposals lend themselves to summarization, not to comprehensive description. That is, he put forward a proposed attitude of mind which should govern U.S. actions, not a program in the usual sense. The thrust of his argument pertaining to advisors was that the U.S. should select dedicated Americans with empathy for the Vietnamese and send them to advise GVN "with sensitive understanding and wisdom." The course of action he recommended was to get such men on the scene, give them total responsibility to match their total commitment, and free them from the encumbrances of the regular bureaucratic machinery (be it military or civilian) in order that they might operate effectively according to the situation:

> When there is an emergency, the wise thing to do is to pick the best people you have, people who are experienced in dealing with this precise type of emergency, and send them to the spot with orders to remedy the situation. When you get the people in position and free them to work, you

should then back them up in every practical way you can. The real decisions will be made in little daily actions in Vietnam, not in Washington. That's why the best are needed on the spot.

Our U.S. team in Vietnam should have a hard core of experienced Americans who know and really like Asia and the Asians, dedicated people who are willing to risk their lives for the ideals of freedom, and who will try to influence and guide the Vietnamese towards U.S. policy objectives with the warm friendships and affection which our close alliance deserves. We should break the rules of personnel assignment, if necessary, to get such U.S. military and civilians to Vietnam.

Not only should the U.S. depend on advisors who *earn* the trust of their counterparts, Lansdale argued, it should depend on them to get the job done without coercion and threats. Leverage should be the product of persuasion and trust, not the result of control over funds and materiel:

. . . Many of the Vietnamese in the countryside who were right up against the Viet Cong terror were full of patriotic spirit. Those who seemed to be in the hardest circumstances, fighting barefoot with makeshift weapons, had the highest morale. They still can lick the Viet Cong with a little help. There's a lesson here on our giving aid. Maybe we should learn that our funds cannot buy friends or a patriotic spirit by mere materialistic giving. Perhaps we should help those who help themselves, and not have a lot of strings on that help.

If the U.S. could adopt this free-wheeling approach to advice, said Lansdale, it would do well to do it at the action level, to get down and share the risks and discomforts of the ARVN rather than to restrict its advice to paper plans and confrontations in offices:

. . . U.S. military men in Vietnam should be freed to work in the combat areas. Our MAAG has a far greater potential than is now being utilized. U.S. military men are hardly in a postition to be listened to when they are snug in rear areas and give advice to Vietnamese officers who have attended the same U.S. military schools and who are now in a combat in which few Americans are experienced. MAAG personnel from General McGarr on down expressed desire to get more into real field work; let's give them what they want as far as U.S. permission is concerned and let them earn their way into positions of greater influence with the Vietnamese military in the field.

3.   *Back to Normal Channels*

In sum, General Lansdale urged an extra-bureaucratic, uninhibited advisory system consciously built on shared U.S.-Vietnamese goals (validated by shared experience) and based on mutual trust and admiration. It was—he would be the first to admit—the kind of unstructured, unprogrammed, "non-organization" which was antithetical to that which the professional military might be expected to propose and so foreign to the typical views of the State Department, with its traditional anti-operational bias, that diplomats would inevitably regard it as a proposal for power without responsibility. Thus, one contemporary account suggests that Lansdale's approach was eventually rejected because of governmental inertia and bureaucratic in-fighting:

When Lansdale returned to Washington—after he had submitted his report to his own superiors—he was suddenly summoned one afternoon to the White House and, much to his surprise, ushered into a conference room where the President was presiding over a mixed group of high Pentagon, State Department, and National Security Council officials. To his further surprise, President Kennedy, after commending his report, indicated that Lansdale would be sent back to Vietnam in a high capacity. Kennedy's declaration at the meeting obviously raised the hackles of many officials whose agencies had been criticized by Lansdale. The upshot was that nothing further happened about Lansdale's appointment. It is now known that objections to it were raised in the highest levels of the Kennedy administration; in fact, there were threats of resignation. In the sense that some drastic action in Vietnam should have been taken at this time, whether it involved Lansdale or not, this was another vital turning point in the long and tortuous history of America's Vietnamese involvement. There was still a chance to do something to save the Diem regime, depending largely on getting Nhu out of the country. Difficult as it would have been to achieve at this late date, Lansdale might have been able to persuade Diem to do it, because he had remained one of the few Americans Diem had ever trusted. More important, some feasible ideas about how to fight a guerrilla war might have been set in motion, and the miscalculation of what had always been essentially a revolutionary situation might thereupon have been altered.

This account simply does not square with the existence of several cogent objections to Lansdale's proposals for "unfettered quality"—though there most certainly was a fair share of bureaucratic in-fighting as the proposals were studied, expanded, and reshaped. Moreover, it compresses the time frame within which Lansdale's two major theses were struck down. His first proposal, for selected individuals to act as advisors, implied—at the very minimum—continuity of personnel selected by an extra-bureaucratic process. Extra-bureaucratic selection was dead by mid-1961; the issue of continuity was finally settled in favor of year-long tours in December 1962 (and has remained in effect since that time). The issue of a supra-departmental organization was fought out in mid-1961. It succumbed to an organizational principle with very deep roots.

The specific form which Lansdale's supra-departmental organizational proposal advanced was that of a Presidential Agent to manage the U.S. effort in RVN. On 12 April 1961, Walt W. Rostow sent a memorandum to President Kennedy which suggested, among other things, that it was imperative to appoint a "fulltime, first-rate back-stop man in Washington" to oversee the U.S. involvement in RVN. Lansdale was either aware of a meaning not conveyed literally by the memorandum or interpreted it to fit his preferences. In any event, he used this springboard to propose, in a 19 April memorandum to Secretary McNamara and his deputy, Roswell Gilpatric, that the President create an interdepartmental task force on Vietnam to "supervise and coordinate the activities of every U.S. agency carrying out operations . . . in Vietnam to ensure success of the [President's] approved plan." On the following day Secretary McNamara, presumably after discussing the matter with the President, requested Gilpatric to prepare within a week a report for the President, setting forth any actions necessary to "prevent communist domination of that country."

On 27 April Secretary Gilpatric submitted his recommendations. Much of the flavor of the earlier Lansdale pleas for a select, individualistic advisory effort was missing from this product of an interdepartmental committee. The earlier recommendations for an expanded U.S. effort were still there, however. These included an RVNAF force increase of 20,000 with a corresponding increase of 100 MAAG advisors, a MAAG takeover of the entire CG and SDC programs, the employment of U.S. advisors in field operations, the continuation of U.S. Mission efforts to get GVN to carry out reforms, the initiation of covert operations with CIA assistance against lines of communications in Laos and North Vietnam, and a U.S. economic team to help GVN speed up national development. One would be hard pressed to identify any other document which, over six months before the operative decision, so closely foreshadowed the U.S. actions that would be agreed to at the end of 1961.

But beyond these programmatic recommendations (hence, contrary to Lansdale's initial proposals) Gilpatric recommended the creation of a Presidential Task Force to provide "over-all direction, interagency coordination and support" for this program of action. Gilpatric was to be Director of the Task Force; Lansdale its operating head in Vietnam. In order to appear not to fly into the face of Ambassadorial primacy in Saigon the memo was forced into some rather fancy obfuscation:

> The Ambassador as head of the Country Team is assigned the authority and the responsibility to see that the Program is carried out in the field and to determine the timing of the actions. He is authorized to advise the Director of the Task Force of any changes which he believes should be made in the Program.

In carrying out his duties in the field, the operations officer of the Task Force will cooperate with the Ambassador.

This equivocation charged directly against the mainstream of current thought as it related to the question of integrating operations abroad. The "Country Team" concept of the late 1950's, buttressed by a series of increasingly comprehensive Executive Orders on the subject, assigned clear primacy to the Ambassador. The State Department was not long in asserting its claim to leadership in accordance with this prevailing concept. On 3 May it provided a recommended revision of Gilpatric's task force proposal in which it proposed an interdepartmental task force under State Department leadership to coordinate the Washington effort and a counterpart task force in Saigon under Sterling J. Cottrell, then POLAD to CINCPAC. It was this proposal which was incorporated into NSAM 52 later in May.

In retrospect, the Lansdale-Gilpatric proposal to conduct the U.S. participation in the Vietnamese war through a supra-departmental agency—whether by a Presidential Task Force or by some other means—probably never had much of a chance. The Department of Defense had too large an operational role to agree to leadership of such an undertaking by anyone other than one of its own principals. (Thus, Gilpatric was acceptable, but few others would have been; Lansdale almost surely was not acceptable as the operating chief in RVN.) The State Department had at stake both the legacy of theoretic interdepartmental primacy and the oft-expressed hope of giving this theory more meaning abroad. Indeed, it was during this same month (May 1961) that President Kennedy sent his oft-quoted letter to each American Ambassador, reminding the recipient of his coordinating duties even while reaffirming that these did not extent to supervising operational military forces. The effects in South Vietnam, as distinct from some other countries, was to preserve claims for independent authority for each of the major governmental departments involved. The Presidential letter to Ambassador Frederick E. Nolting in Saigon read in part:

> In regard to your personal authority and responsibility, I shall count on you to oversee and coordinate all the activities of the United States Government in the Republic of Vietnam.
>
> You are in charge of the entire United States Diplomatic Mission, and I shall expect you to supervise all of its operations. The Mission includes not only the personnel of the Department of State and the Foreign Service, but also the representatives of all other United States agencies which have programs or activities in the Republic of Vietnam. I shall give you full support and backing in carrying out your assignment.
>
> Needless to say, the representatives of other agencies are expected to communicate directly with their offices here in Washington, and in the event of a decision by you in which they do not concur, they may ask to have the decision reviewed by a higher authority in Washington.
>
> However, it is their responsibility to keep you fully informed of their views and activities and to abide by your decisions unless in some particular instance you and they are notified to the contrary.
>
> If in your judgment individual members of the Mission are not functioning effectively, you should take whatever action you feel may be required, reporting the circumstances, of course, to the Department of State.
>
> In case the departure from the Republic of Vietnam of any individual member of the Mission is indicated in your judgment, I shall expect you to make the decision and see that it is carried into effect. Such instances I am confident will be rare.
>
> Now one word about your relations to the military. As you know, the United States Diplomatic Mission includes Service Attaches, Military Assistance Advisory Groups and other Military components attached to the Mission. It does not, however, include United States military forces operating in the field where such forces are under the command of a United States area military commander. The line of authority to these forces runs from me, to the Secretary of Defense, to the Joint Chiefs of Staff in Washington and to the area commander in the field.
>
> Although this means that the chief of the American Diplomatic Mission is not in the line of military command, nevertheless, as Chief of Mission, you should work closely with the appropriate area military commander to assure the full exchange of information. If it is your opinion that activities by the United States military forces may adversely affect our over-all relations with the people or governments of the Republic of Vietnam you should promptly discuss the matter with the military commander and, if necessary, request a decision by higher authority.

It is reasonable to surmise that in mid-1961 events did not seem pressing enough to cast aside a developed—if imperfect—concept of operational integration in favor of an untried substitute arrangement. In fact, if one wanted firm leadership one would have had less radical alternatives to which to turn. To mention two, Secretarial involvement to a degree tantamount to taking charge of the war (much as Secretary McNamara did in 1962) or the appointment of an Ambassador to RVN with such military preeminence that he need not defer to other military judgments (as, General Taylor in 1964).

The decision to supervise the American effort in a more or less conventional way had a direct bearing on the nature of the advisory buildup then being discussed. It was highly unlikely that General Lansdale's radical advisory proposals would be kindly received under a system managed along conventional lines. Even before the Presidential Task Force idea was abandoned Lansdale's proposals for a select, committed advisory group had been reshaped by interdepartmental committee. Instead of "old Vietnam hands" in key spots, the discussion turned to the use of existing organizations and much larger numbers of advisors:

> Augment the MAAG with two US training commands (comprised of approximately 1600 instructors each) to enable the MAAG to establish in the "high plateau" region of South Vietnam two divisional field training areas to accelerate the U.S. training program for the entire GVN army. . . .
>
> Deploy, as soon as possible, a Special Forces Group (approximately 400 U.S. military personnel) to Nha Trang in order to accelerate GVN Special Forces training.

Under this proposal the size of MAAG Vietnam would be increased from 685 to 2285, not including the Special Forces or training commands mentioned above or the 100 man increase already proposed to advise the 20,000 men which were to be added to RVNAF.

After the shift to thinking in terms of existing military organizations (or, alternatively, of individuals drawn as it were by "requisitions" in normal channels) and the understandable—if not inevitable—demise of the Gilpatric-Lansdale proposal for supra-departmental direction, U.S. thinking about possible steps in Vietnam remained firmly within conventional channels. There were subsequent attempts to reintroduce an alternative advisory scheme and an organizational framework compatible with it but these appear to have not been seriously considered.

President Kennedy did not permit the Gilpatric Task Force recommendations to commit him to action. Rather, he used them in an attempt to demonstrate the U.S. commitment to Vietnam. The proof of this contention is in NSAM 52, which records the President's decisions. Only about 14 personnel were to be assigned, for instance, in U.S. Army civic action mobile training teams to assist ARVN with health, welfare, and public works projects. Although it was decided to deploy the Special Forces group of 400 men to Tourane [Da Nang], this was in support of a CIA-directed effort which could be kept largely covert. Increased aerial surveillance assistance required only 6 U.S. personnel. The establishment of a Combat Development and Test Center in RVN required only 4 additional U.S. personnel. The point is not how much was done but, in retrospect, how firmly the probable lines of future actions had been drawn as a result of what it had been agreed *not* to do.

4. *Planning Begins in Earnest*

The President did, however, issue several "hunting licenses." The Defense Department was directed to examine fully (under the guidance of the State Department's Director of the continuing Task Force on Vietnam) "the size and composition of forces which would be desirable in the case of a possible commitment of U.S. forces to Vietnam." The Ambassador was authorized to sound out Diem on a bilateral defense treaty. President Kennedy also apparently decided to feel out Diem's reaction on the subject of U.S. combat troops in Vietnam. Vice President Johnson left almost immediately to visit

South Vietnam and other Asian nations. He was empowered to bring up the question of troops as well as the treaty.

But discussions are one thing; firm commitments are quite another. The range of alternatives that President Kennedy was willing to *consider* seems clear. What he was willing to *do* was quite another matter. Unless he was most unlike other politicians and unless the many personal accounts of his style are completely erroneous he was willing to do what he believed he *had* to do—and events in mid-1961 did not force action even though the "drill" that the Administration went through was instrumental in defining the probable responses when events did force action.

As it quickly turned out, President Diem wanted neither U.S. troops nor a treaty at that time. He told Vice President Johnson that he wanted troops only in the event of overt invasion and showed no interest in a treaty. Nevertheless, the Vice President, upon his return, was trenchant in his observations that the time for deeds to replace words was fast approaching if the U.S. was to make its declared commitment credible:

> Our mission arrested the decline of confidence in the United States. It did not—in my judgment—restore any confidence already lost. The leaders were as explicit, as courteous and courtly as men could be in making it clear that deeds must follow words—soon.
>
> We didn't buy time—we were given it.
>
> If these men I saw at your request were bankers, I would know—without bothering to ask—that there would be no further extensions on my note.

Diem may not have been quite so disinterested in U.S. troops as he appeared to be. NSAM 52 of 11 May had discussed, inconclusively, the proposed buildup of RVNAF from 170,000 to 200,000 in order to create two new divisions to help seal the Laotian border. When President Diem responded (on 9 June) to Vice President Johnson's invitation to prepare a set of proposals on South Vietnam's military needs, he recommended a quantum jump in strength to 270,000 and suggested a substantial increase in the US MAAG, perhaps even in the form of U.S. units:

> To accomplish this 100,000 man expansion [above the strength recommended in the CIP, which was 20,000 above the existing strength] of our military forces, which is perfectly feasible from a manpower viewpoint, will require a great intensification of our training programs in order to produce, in the minimum of time, those qualified combat leaders and technical specialists needed to fill the new units and to provide to them the technical and logistical support required to insure their complete effectiveness. *For this purpose a considerable expansion of the United States Military Advisory Group is an essential requirement. Such an expansion, in the form of selected elements of the American Armed Forces to establish training centers for the Vietnamese Armed Forces,* would serve the dual purpose of providing an expression of the United States' determination to halt the tide of communist aggression and of preparing our forces in the minimum of time.

The response to this letter is not part of the available record. No doubt the initial reaction was one of surprise. The U.S. was not accustomed to GVN initiatives; it seldom sought them. "We have not become accustomed to being asked for our own views on our needs," Diem remarked in his letter to Kennedy. But Diem's proposal did certainly strike one appealing chord: the joint benefits of training coupled to demonstrated commitment through the deployment of existing troop units. As the situation in South Vietnam continued to deteriorate throughout the summer and early fall the issue of U.S. military *advice* continued to be addressed in terms of U.S. *units.* These could, of course, do even more than had been suggested by President Diem: they could fight as units. Diem's generally consistent position, however, continued to be that he would accept U.S. combat forces, but only to train GVN forces. He had said as much to Vice President Johnson:

> General McGarr, who was also present at this discussion [between Johnson and Diem] reported that while President Diem would not want U.S. combat forces for the purpose of fighting Communists in South Vietnam, he would accept deployment of U.S. combat forces as trainers for the Vietnamese forces at any time.

5. *GVN Asks for Additional U.S. Assistance*

By October the situation within South Vietnam had become sufficiently grim for President Diem to reverse his earlier sentiments and to ask for a bilateral defense treaty with the U.S. His new willingness, coupled with the deteriorating situation, kicked off a new series of proposals within the U.S. Government. Walt Rostow proposed that the U.S. place an internationalized force of about 25,000 men into RVN to perform a border sealing mission. The JCS responded with a counter proposal emphasizing Laos and calling for the deployment of a sizeable (initially 20,000) U.S. contingent to the central highlands. In still another proposal a Special National Intelligence Estimate weighed in with a hard look at this rash of proposals. The President's reaction, on 11 October, was to decide to send General Taylor on a mission to South Vietnam to examine several alternative courses of action:

> (a) The plan for military intervention discussed at this morning's meeting on the basis of the Vietnam task force paper entitled "Concept for Intervention in Vietnam";
> (b) An alternative plan for stationing in Vietnam fewer U.S. combat forces than those called for under the plan referred to in (a) above and with a more limited objective than dealing with the Viet Cong; in other words, such a small force would probably go in at Tourane [Da Nang] and possibly another southern port principally for the purpose of establishing a U.S. "presence" in Vietnam;
> (c) Other alternatives in lieu of putting any U.S. combat forces in Vietnam, i.e. stepping up U.S. assistance and training of Vietnam units, furnishing of more U.S. equipment, particularly helicopters and other light aircraft, trucks and other ground transport, etc.

6. *The Taylor Mission to Saigon*

This range of alternatives suggests, even without "20/20 hindsight," that if *something* was going to be done, and if the President were to decide *not* to send U.S. combat units to Vietnam, there would be an advisory buildup of some kind almost by default. This is close enough to what happened to warrant the risk of oversimplification. It does not do justice to the Taylor Report, of course, but Taylor's mission and his reports have been covered fully elsewhere. For their impact on the advisory effort, and to place this in perspective, it is sufficient to describe only a few salient features. First, the Viet Cong were pursuing, in Taylor's appraisal, a political-military strategy aimed at overthrowing Diem and opening the way to unification of Vietnam on Hanoi's terms. Military action by the insurgents was aimed at this objective rather than at a complete military victory:

> The military strategy being pursued is, evidently, to pin down the ARVN on defensive missions; to create a pervasive sense of insecurity and frustration by hit-and-run raids on self-defense corps and militia [CG] units . . . and to dramatize the inability of the GVN to govern or to build. . . .
> Despite the considerable guerrilla capabilities of the Viet-Cong, Communist strategy now appears, on balance, to aim at an essentially political denouement rather than the total military capture of the country, as in the case of Mao's campaign in China. . . . The enemy objective seems to be to produce a political crisis by a combination of military and non-military means out of which would come a South Vietnamese Souvanna Phouma, willing to contemplate unification on terms acceptable to Hanoi, including disengagement from the U.S.

In order for the Diem government to defeat this insurgency, General Taylor reasoned, the Saigon regime must reform itself. It had allowed two vicious circles to develop which vitiated its effectiveness. In the first, poor military intelligence resulted in a defensive military posture which put most of the forces under provincial control. This, in turn, meant that reserves could not be expeditiously employed. The resultant high losses in unsuccessful defensive battles further dried up the sources of intelligence and completed the circle. The second vicious circle was attributable to Diem's instinctive attempts to centralize power in his own hands while fragmenting it beneath him. His excessive mistrust of criticism and fears of a coup caused large elements of society to stand aside from the struggle while the province chiefs and generals were forced into frustrating struggles, further increasing Diem's fears and his inclination to fractionalize authority. The task, then, was to strengthen Diem while, at the same time, inducing him to reform so as to break both of these vicious circles.

In order to strengthen Diem with a U.S. military presence—very much along the lines of the smaller US deployment discussed at the NSC meeting prior to his trip—Taylor recommended the deployment to South Vietnam of a task force of 6–8,000 troops under the guise of flood relief work. This task force, primarily logistical, would necessarily become involved in some defensive operation and sustain some casualties, but its deployment need not commit the U.S. to a land war on the Asian mainland:

> As the task is a specific one, we can extricate our troops when it is done if we so desire. Alternatively, we can phase them into other activities if we wish to remain longer. . . .
> Needless to say, this kind of task force will exercise little direct influence on the campaign against the VC. It will, however, give a much needed shot in the arm to national morale, particularly *if combined with other actions showing that a more effective working relationship in the common cause has been established between the GVN and the U.S.*

Taylor had already received President Diem's assurances that he favored the deployment of U.S. forces for this purpose.

In conjunction with this U.S. troop deployment, Taylor argued that the U.S. should initiate increased assistance to GVN in a new relationship:

> A shift [should occur] in the American relation to the Vietnamese effort from advice to limited partnership. The present character and scale of the war in South Vietnam decree only that the Vietnamese can defeat the Viet-Cong; but at all levels Americans must, as friends and partners—not as arm's-length advisors—show them how the job might be done—not tell them or do it for them.

General Taylor was most explicit that the purpose of the proposed troop deployments and the new "limited partnership" was to buy time for the Vietnamese so that they could marshall their considerable resources and assume the offensive against the VC. As mentioned above, this would require internal reform in GVN. The limited partnership would contribute to both of these interacting objectives:

> The present war cannot be won by direct US action; it must be won by the Vietnamese. But there is a general conviction among us that the Vietnamese performance in every domain can be substantially improved if Americans are prepared to work side by side with the Vietnamese on the key problems. Moreover, there is evidence that Diem is, in principle, prepared for this step, and that most—not all—elements in his establishment are eagerly awaiting it.

7. *The Kennedy Decisions: NSAM 111*

It is useful to approach the effect of General Taylor's mission on the advisory effort from the simple recollection of what President Kennedy decided *not* to do. He decided not to deploy U.S. combat forces to South Vietnam. This meant —given the U.S. assessment of the importance of RVN and the felt necessity to do something—that the expansion of U.S. assistance was a foregone conclusion. This was the general course of action that would be followed as the ineluctable result of having decided not to do something else which was more dramatic, involved more risk, and was more contentious.

Given the decision not to send troop units, then, the general thrusts of U.S. actions were determined—but the specifics were not. Just how did Taylor's "limited partnership," for instance, propose to influence GVN's attitudes and organization, to develop initiative matched by competence, and to insure that the Vietnamese would assume successfully the responsibility for winning the struggle which it was said only they could win? How was this expanded U.S. effort to be organized? From whence would come the new junior partners of the firm? What would be their preparation, their instructions, their duties?

The first of these two groups of questions is more easily answered than the second; the answer to neither of them is retrospectively very satisfying in terms of suggesting that the U.S. entered into its expanded effort at the beginning of 1962 with its eyes wide open and fully aware of just what it was doing. The available record indicates that the U.S. hopefully assumed that material aid and good intentions would be adequate to the task, that a larger U.S.

presence would spur the Vietnamese to effective action without incurring the stigma of a U.S. "takeover," and that the increase in assistance would be—in and of itself—accepted as an adequate *quid pro quo* for the desired reforms within GVN.

GVN organizational reform would be realized, NASM 111 suggested, by getting Diem to agree to clean up his lines of authority in exchange for the U.S. commitment to the limited partnership. One section of the document is a list of approved U.S. actions; another sets forth the expected improvements to be accomplished by GVN. Ambassador Nolting was instructed to use the substance of these decisions in talks to secure Diem's approval. He found Diem despondent that the U.S. asked so much in return for so little, played into the hands of those who claimed undue American infringement upon Vietnamese sovereignty, and placed him in a position where he feared even to make known to his own cabinet the American expectations. Unless the U.S. were to suspend its increased aid, and at the very time it was just gearing up to provide it, Diem had made it clear at the beginning that he would govern South Vietnam in his way and that the U.S. had no choice but to support him wholeheartedly, get out, or find an acceptable alternative to him. The U.S., in turn, had refused to consider the last two of these alternatives. It was stuck with supporting him, at least for the time being.

8.   *Working Out the Basis for U.S. Advice*

But the U.S. approach was only partially framed to secure Diem's acceptance. There was a parallel suggestion that the existence of U.S. advisors in the field, working hand-in-hand in a counterpart relationship with Vietnamese, would reform GVN from the bottom up. This line of policy was neither spelled out in detail nor thought out in terms of operational implications, risks, and costs. But it clearly existed:

> Through this working association at all levels, the U.S. must bring about *de facto* changes in Diem's method of administration and seek to bring all elements of the Vietnamese Government closer to the Vietnamese people—thus helping break the vicious political circle.
>
> By concurrent actions in the fields of intelligence, command and control, mobility, and training, the U.S. must bring about a situation where an effective reserve is mobilized and brought to bear offensively on clearly established and productive offensive targets—thus helping break the vicious military circle. . . .
>
> Behind this concept of a strategy to turn the tide and to assume the offensive lies a general proposition: when an interacting process is yielding a degenerative situation, *the wisest course of action is to create a positive thrust at as many points as are accessible.*

Thus, the U.S. addressed the critical leverage issue as the expected product of its own willingness to increase its participation in the counterinsurgency effort. It did so, moreover, without any conscious examination of the question beyond stating its expectations. There was no plan to make the provision of additional assistance contingent upon GVN actions, only a statement that GVN actions were expected. There was no willingness, in fact, to consider the conscious exercise of leverage; the situation was too critical, the available time too short, the issue too important.

The effect of this avoidance of hard choices—for good and understandable reasons, but avoidance nonetheless—was to place a very large burden on the benefits to be realized by an expansion of the advisory effort. The language of General Taylor's report is reminiscent of Lansdale's earlier proposals for an unstructured, flexible advisory effort comprising totally committed, carefully selected individuals who would earn the respect and cooperation of the Vietnamese. Lansdale had renewed these proposals at the time the Taylor Report was prepared. But when it was suggested to the GVN that the U.S. would expect to share in decisions the Vietnamese reaction led the U.S. almost immediately to modify this expectation. The original communication on the subject to Ambassador Nolting stated that ". . . we would expect to share in the decision-making process in the political, economic and military fields as they affected the security situation" as compared to the earlier arrangement of "acting in an advisory capacity only." By early December insistence on this point was quickly dropped in favor of a view which suggested that close collaboration would produce automatic unanimity:

> What we have in mind is that, in operations directly related to the security situation, partnership will be so close that one party will not take decisions or actions affecting the other without full and frank prior consultations. . . .

Unless such exchanges invariably resulted in unanimity one of the partners would have to give way to the other or inactivity would result. What line to follow if this occurred seems not to have been examined. This simply would not happen.

The "close partnership" envisaged by General Taylor—and endorsed by President Kennedy—suggested something akin to the "total commitment" which General Lansdale had earlier urged as one criterion in selecting advisors for South Vietnam. This, in turn, implied at the very minimum a period of long exposure to the operational problem (and personalities) with which these advisors would deal. In the event, it was decided to expand both the military and sector (provincial military) advisory efforts without any such long term exposure. These questions were settled in detail when Secretary McNamara met in mid-January 1962 at Honolulu with the principal managers of the U.S. effort. It was decided to establish battalion level military advisory teams within ARVN, each to consist of either 5 (infantry battalion) or 3 (artillery battalion) personnel. Each province (sector) would receive 3 U.S. advisors, one officer and 2 enlisted intelligence specialists. The Civil Guard would be trained in a series of 6 training centers by 120 advisors (20 in each center) plus 12 mobile teams of 3 men each. The SDC would be trained in 30 centers. Secretary McNamara made it clear that he wanted these deployments completed as quickly as possible. He suggested that if an ARVN unit was not prepared to receive its advisors the designated individuals be sent to RVN and placed temporarily with another unit to gain experience. He agreed that temporary duty assignments to Vietnam were generally undesirable and asked the JCS to address the question of optimum tour length for advisors.

The length of time a military member spent in Vietnam at that time varied slightly from service to service, according to whether or not dependents accompanied the serviceman and whether he served in Saigon or in some other part of the country. In October 1961 it was allegedly decided at OSD level—without consulting the services—to make the tour of duty 30 months with dependents and 18 without dependents rather than the 24 and 12 month tours that were then typical. The effect of this decision would have been to increase the field advisors' tours of duty from one year to one and a half years. Each of the assignment branches within the Army opposed this change as one which would be inequitable unless reflected in changed tour length for other "unaccompanied" (by dependent) tours. The order was not put into effect. Thus, there was some background against which to reexamine the time which advisors (among others) should spend in RVN. The decision—again based on considerations of equity in "hardship" assignments, health, and resultant morale issues —was to retain the one year tour in the field.*

9. *U.S. Expectations: The Benefits from More Advisors*

To sum up the decision to expand the advisory effort to battalion and province level, it was one reached without extended study or debate. There was neither opposition to it nor any comprehensive explication of what would be involved and the benefits to be expected. This was due in large part to the fact that it was a decision made almost offhandedly in the shadow of a larger issue, the deployment of U.S. combat forces to RVN. When it was decided not to send the combat forces it was a foregone conclusion that more advisors would be sent. This was consistent with the U.S. desire in late 1961 to demonstrate its commitment to South Vietnam and apparently compatible with the oft-expressed belief that only the South Vietnamese could bring their struggle to a satisfactory conclusion.

But the decision to expand the advisory effort attempted, at the same time, to finesse the question of leverage. GVN was informed that the U.S. expected certain reform measures to be adopted in exchange for increased U.S. assistance. It received no clear signals about withholding U.S. help if these actions were not taken. The U.S. had, in fact, made no decisions along this line; it had avoided addressing the issue because of conflicting desires to act forcefully, yet to avoid Americanizing the war. Thus, the U.S. did not know what it would do if GVN failed to respond as it was hoped that it would. In this sense the U.S. advisors became potential pawns in a leverage game of uncertain intensity with no set rules. This *de facto* position was in continuous potential conflict with the expressed hope that a greater U.S. presence would lead—by example, persuasion, and mutual interest—to increased effectiveness both within ARVN and in the political administration of the provinces governed by U.S.-advised ARVN officers.

Not only did the Kennedy Administration decide to enter in General Taylor's "limited partnership" without a careful examination of the relationships being established, it also apparently did not state or debate precisely what benefits were expected as a result of an increased advisory effort. There was, it appears, a generalized and unchallenged assumption that more Americans in more places addressing Vietnamese training and operations could not but have an overall beneficial effect. The available record reflects no explicit discussion of expected

* It has remained basically unchanged, it should be noted, until the present. An unstructured program of voluntary 6 month extensions was inaugurated throughout Vietnam in 1967, a voluntary extension program begun for "selected officers" in key positions in the same year, and a small program initiated in 1968 by which selected Province Advisors would agree to serve two years in Vietnam, then receive almost one year's training prior to deployment. No officers have departed the U.S. under this last program as of the present writing (mid-1968).

benefits. While oral discussions must have addressed this point at some time, it seems most likely that policymakers agreed tacitly on three overlapping categories of expectations—each susceptible to varying interpretations and degrees of relative importance and emphasis—which were neither clearly stated nor critically examined.

The first, and most obvious, was the expectation that an increased U.S. military presence with tactical units and at training centers would lead to improved technical-tactical competence within ARVN. The assumption which underlay this expectation was that the teaching of basic military skills was probably a sufficient (rather than merely necessary) condition to enable ARVN to begin to operate more effectively—and more energetically and aggressively. Earlier experience in Greece and Korea would have seemed to validate this expectation within reasonable limits.

Second, U.S. policymakers probably expected the increased military advisory effort to result in a more effective informational "network." It must have seemed reasonable to expect that an increased but diffuse U.S. presence would not only enhance information on VC actions and probable plans but also improve U.S. knowledge of ARVN plans and performance.

Finally—and most difficult to pinpoint in terms of what policymaker or policymaking group emphasized which aspects—the U.S. expected to gain additional influence from an increased advisory effort. General Taylor viewed this as the natural product of individuals with parallel interests working hand-in-glove in the field (as distinct from large headquarters). This would enable them to escape the petty differences which grow up in the absence of operational responsibility and permit the U.S. advisors to "lead by example" even though they would not be technically empowered to lead.

Other expectations of increased U.S. influence could take a variety of forms. Improved information, for instance, in a hierarchically ordered U.S. advisory system, would permit the U.S. to push more effectively *any* line of endeavor which it wished GVN to adopt. This potential for improved "salesmanship" was not unrelated to an increased potential for coercive influence. What the U.S. would give in material support it might also withhold selectively. Influence need not be dependent upon example alone.

None of these expectations were, however, articulated fully or spelled out in terms which would provide operational guidelines for the new U.S. advisors who were being deployed to SVN. The expectations of benefits were implicit and generalized. The potential existed for a comprehensive, coordinated U.S. approach to advising but the potential was not the reality.

10.   *Implementing the First Build-Up*

The decision just examined to increase the U.S. advisory effort was preceded by a series of marginal increases in the U.S. military strength in Vietnam. (Actual "in-country" strengths are available for only a few months during the early build-up period so it will frequently be necessary to use authorization figures and to realize that newly authorized spaces were generally not filled until some time had passed after their establishment.) Presidential decisions in April and May 1961, taken in the light of a central concern with Laos rather than Vietnam, increased the authorized size of MAAG Vietnam from 685 to 785. The 100-man increase was divided almost equally between technical advisors and advisors for ARVN's tactical training centers. In October 1961 the authorized strength was increased again, to 972, of which 948 spaces were for U.S. Army personnel; 603 of these 948 spaces were actually filled by the end of November.

The increases in advisory strength which reflected the NSAM 111 decisions were authorized in December 1961 and January 1962. By the end of 1961 MAAG's authorized strength had been more than doubled, to 2067. This number was increased again in January to more than 3000. Included in these increases were the new dimensions of U.S. advice: battalion advisors, province advisors, and an additional 500 Special Forces advisors (making a new total of 805 in the Special Forces program under CIA control).

It has already been noted that Secretary McNamara gave forceful impetus to manning these newly created positions in the shortest possible time. They were, indeed, filled quickly. By April 1962 the total number of Army field advisory personnel in RVN exceeded the authorized number. By this time, too, the authorized total for all services had been stabilized at about 3400. This total was reduced in November to 3150, then remained essentially constant until a new round of increases was inaugurated in mid-1964. Thus, the build-up associated with the Taylor mission consisted of a fourfold increase in U.S. advisory presence (a much larger increase if one counts U.S. support units). After the build-up was completed, in the spring of 1962, the number of advisors remained stable until many months after the fall of the Diem government.

While the total number of advisors remained fairly constant, however, shifts occurred in the distribution of advisory personnel. From completion of the build-up, for instance, until the coup which overthrew Diem, the number of field advisors at corps and division level increased severalfold and the number of province advisors doubled while other field advisory strengths remained about the same. These developments are shown in detail in the tabular summary at the end of this study and summarized in the following table:

SELECTED FIELD ADVISORS

Activity Advised	April 1962	November 1963
Corps	63	380
Divisions	162	446
Regiments	150	134
Battalions	366	417
Provinces	117	235
Schools & Training Centers	212	201
CG/SDC	281	215
Total	1351	2028

11.   The U.S. View: 1962–1963

Six months after Diem fell the U.S. would conclude that these advisory levels were inadequate, but during the Diem area the predominant official attitude was one of sustained optimism. The war was being won, it was maintained, by adherence to the newly articulated theory of counterinsurgency. The U.S. even made tentative plans to begin reducing the American presence in Vietnam.

By the time the U.S. began seriously to consider attempts to exercise leverage against the Ngo family's conduct of affairs Diem's regime was already well down the road to its eventual overthrow.

The Strategic Hamlet Program was the principal operational vehicle by which the recently articulated theory of counterinsurgency was to be translated into reality. In general, the plan was to begin by providing to the rural populace a degree of security sufficient to serve as a precondition for further military and political action. In the military field the peasants' increased security was to be the wedge by which more effective intelligence gathering could take place. The rural population could not be expected to inform on VC whereabouts, it was reasoned, unless it was safe from retaliatory acts by the insurgents. Political action to promote identification between the central government and the rural population was also to take place in the shadow of these improved physical security arrangements. Security was viewed, then, as the precondition to the military and political gains at which General Taylor's mission had aimed its recommendations.

The evolution and demise of the Strategic Hamlet Program is examined in another volume of the present series. It is pertinent to the present study, however, to note the points of stress in this program as they pertained to RVNAF. Most of the new American advisory effort was directed to improving ARVN, in its equipment and mobility capability and in its aggressiveness. The central U.S. expectation was that a greater capability to move quickly could be combined with improved leadership so that ARVN could, on one hand, be capable of responding quickly and in force wherever and whenever the VC chose to concentrate for local superiority and, on the other, be made aggressive enough to beat the Viet Cong at their own game—to "take the night away" from the VC and to use guerrilla techniques to hunt down and defeat the insurgents in their own bailiwicks.

The realization of these expectations was dependent upon several developments, *each* of which had to occur if ARVN was to become capable of turning the tide in the insurgent battle. First, the CG and SDC had to become sufficiently effective to permit ARVN to be used as a mobile reserve for protective purposes rather than as part of the static protection force. Second, ARVN had to be given adequate capability to move quickly, whether in reacting or in seizing the initiative. Finally, both ARVN's leaders and the political leaders to whom they were responsible had to accept and put into operational practice a spirit of aggressiveness to take advantage of the existing static defenses and the newly-gained mobility.

12.   *The Actuality: 1962–1963*

What happened during 1962–1963 is that only the second of these developments actually occurred to any significant degree. The U.S. provided helicopter companies for rapid tactical transport, small arms and automatic weapons for increased firepower, and tactical air and artillery support to assure ARVN firepower superiority over the insurgents. There were complaints—as there have been ever since—that individual weapons were too heavy for the Vietnamese, that one helicopter company for each Corps area was too little, and that supporting air and artillery were an inducement to rely on indiscriminate firepower as a substitute for aggressiveness. But the basic tools were provided.

The other developments did not take place. Training of the CG and SDC was speeded up at Secretary McNamara's insistence in order to get a more effective protective force quickly in being. Even by cutting the course of instruction in half it required the remainder of CY 1962 to give a basic familiarization course to even the bulk of the CG and SDC. GVN was not eager to put weapons into SDC hands, fearing that the weapons might wind up in the possession of the VC. In the event, both forces emerged as something much less effective than had been expected. The strategic hamlets which they were to protect proliferated in quantity in an uncontrolled manner and varied widely in quality. It never really became possible for ARVN to free itself from static defensive duties.

Even if it had become possible for ARVN to be cut loose from static duties it is questionable that it could have risen to U.S. expectations. The period in question is one in which the Ngo family felt itself constrained constantly to play off the military against the provincial officials (who controlled the CG and SDC) in order to forestall attempts at a *coup d'etat.* Military leaders seemed inclined to rely increasingly on firepower as a substitute for aggressive maneuver. Rosy reports from the provinces made it unappealing to sustain casualties engaging an enemy who was said to have already been driven from the area. The all-too-common result was that ARVN did not improve as the U.S. had expected it would. U.S. advisors became frustrated and embittered. Even rare opportunities for decisive engagement on the ground were allowed to pass or were mishandled. The debacle at Ap Bac, in_____, 1962, stands as a landmark of this continued impotence.

The failure of ARVN to develop as expected was, however, not officially recognized until much later. Even then the reasons for this failure were variously interpreted. In mid-1962, after the initial advisory build-up had been completed, the commander of the recently established U.S. Military Assistance Command, Vietnam (MACV), General Paul D. Harkins, estimated that the U.S. task was simply one of training ARVN leaders on a one-time basis and that the VC could be eliminated as a disturbing force within a year after this had been accomplished. (This was a clear instance of the "technical-tactical competence" expectation.) Secretary McNamara—probably wishing also to form prudent contingency plans and to have the capability to exert pressure on the Diem regime—directed that the U.S. plan for a phased withdrawal of U.S. forces over a three year period. This decision and the subsequent plans for its implementation, indicates the extent to which optimistic expectations existed at some high official U.S. levels even while (as we were later to learn) the situation in the countryside continued to deteriorate. This, in turn, helps to explain why the advisory build-up completed in April 1962 was not followed by any additional increases in advisors for more than two years.

The central problem in this regard was that the U.S. had neither a firm grasp on reliable indicators to determine how the war was progressing nor a willingness to accept claims that it was not going well. The second of these tendencies was attributable to the approach which finally emerged from the decisions following the Taylor mission: The U.S. would support Diem unstintingly and expect, in return, meaningful reforms and improvements within GVN. But it was caught in a dilemma when the expected reforms did not take place. To continue to support Diem without reforms meant quite simply that he, not we, would determine the course of the counterinsurgent effort and that the steps he took to assure his continuance in power would continue to take priority over all else. To deny him support in any of a variety of ways would erode his power without a viable alternative in sight. The tendency may not have been precisely to "sink or swim with Ngo Dinh Diem," as Homer Bigart phrased it, but it came very close to this.

The inability to know just how things were going presented an even more difficult problem. The tendency was to use forces retrained or newly equipped, strategic hamlets constructed, and trends in VC activity, as indicators of the progress of the war. But training does not necessarily equal effectiveness, the number of hamlets constructed does not tell one of the loyalty of their populations, and enemy attacks might be a misleading guide. Were GVN making progress in a contested area, for instance, Viet Cong reactions might be expected to increase rather than to diminish in frequency and intensity. Conversely, the insurgents would have no good reason to attack populated areas which they had already succeeded in penetrating and over which they had established effective *de facto* control. Data and observations could be variously interpreted—so variously, in fact, that President Kennedy was led to ask two observers just returned from Vietnam who gave him divergent reports, "You two did visit the same country, didn't you?"

13.   *The Stage Is Set for "Better GVN Receptivity"*

While the U.S. groped for a better way to determine how the counterinsurgent effort was going and debated how (or if) to exercise leverage against Diem, it was overtaken by events. The 1963 Buddhist crisis in RVN was met by increasingly repressive measures by the GVN. These developments finally led the U.S. to reassess its support for Diem and to consider other non-communist alternatives to his leadership. On 1 November 1963 Diem was overthrown by a military *coup d'etat*. The pacification effort organized around the Strategic Hamlet Program died with him; the advisory effort was left untouched in terms of size and scope. To the extent that Diem and his family were the ones preventing ARVN from meeting the expectations of late 1961, it was reasoned, now was the time for the military advisory system to begin to function more effectively. To the extent that ARVN commanders in the field had been unresponsive to U.S. advice because of indifference and opposition in the Gia Long Palace, it was hoped the difficulties of the past might be rectified by the new military regime.

B.   *DISTRICT ADVISORS AND THE BEEF-UP OF BATTALION ADVISORY TEAMS (1964–1965)*

The initial U.S. reaction to the Diem coup was thus one of modest optimism. Even given the U.S. disappointment at the death of the Ngo brothers the fact remained that the new regime in the Saigon saddle was expected to be more responsive to U.S. advice than the previous government had been. It was necessary that GVN programs be redirected into more realistic channels, that the efficiency of operations be increased that additional steps be taken to seal the infiltration routes through Laos, and that the U.S. reaffirm its commitment to GVN in a credible way. The key to success—the pacification process—had already been discovered; the task was one of skillful, sustained execution.

Each of these points was addressed by National Security Action Memorandum 273, approved 26 November 1963. The immediate cause for NSAM 273 was the assassination of President Kennedy four days earlier; newly-installed

President Johnson needed to reaffirm or modify the policy lines pursued by his predecessor. President Johnson quickly chose to reaffirm the Kennedy policies. Emphasis should be placed, the document stated, on the Mekong Delta area, but not only in military terms. Political, economic, social, educational, and informational activities must also be pushed: "We should seek to turn the tide not only of battle but of belief. . . ." Military operations should be initiated, under close political control, up to within fifty kilometers inside of Laos. U.S. assistance programs should be maintained at levels at least equal to those under the Diem government so that the new GVN would not be tempted to regard the U.S. as seeking to disengage.

The same document also revalidated the planned phased withdrawal of U.S. forces announced publicly in broad terms by President Kennedy shortly before his death:

> The objective of the United States with respect to the withdrawal of U.S. military personnel remains as stated in the White House statement of October 2, 1963.

No new programs were proposed or endorsed, no increases in the level or nature of U.S. assistance suggested or foreseen. The emphasis was on persuading the new government in Saigon to do well those things which the fallen government was considered to have done poorly.

1. Optimism Turns to Frustration

This attitude of cautious optimism changed gradually by the early summer of 1964 to one of deepening gloom. No radical shift marked this transition; it was one of a heightened awareness of instability in the central government in Saigon (the Khanh coup and maneuvering for advantage by the generals), of a deteriorating situation in the countryside, and of the discovery that things had been worse to begin with than the U.S. had suspected. Not only did events indicate a Viet Cong ascendancy in the countryside; the U.S. was not even able to determine with assurance just how things stood. The informational returns were inadequate from the existing advisory effort, ARVN had not become an effective fighting force, and the extent of U.S. influence was questionable.

This deterioration of the counterinsurgent effort (including the growing awareness that earlier reports had been unrealistically rosy) was one factor which was to lead to an expansion of the U.S. military advisory effort. A second, and complementary, factor was the increasing conviction in official circles that the struggle in Vietnam was so important that we could not afford to lose it. Although these two factors in juxtaposition created a determination to take whatever steps were necessary to ensure a free non-communist South Vietnam, this commitment operated in the shadow of an equal determination to work through the GVN rather than around it and to avoid radical policy departures during the Presidential elections.

A further buildup in U.S. advisors was not the major product of this determined commitment. Rather, there was in 1964 a growing conviction that only by consciously expanding the war—by "going North" in order to punish and dissuade the DRV from support of the insurgency—could the deteriorating situation be arrested and reversed. Governmental stability in South Vietnam and the reduction, if not the elimination, of pressures from the north came to be regarded as desiderata which would turn upon actions outside RVN rather than within it. The decisions to expand the U.S. advisory effort were overshadowed by plans to carry the war to the DRV.*

2. *NSAM 288*

NSAM 273 had, as described above, limited cross-border operations to an area 50 kilometers within Laos. NSAM 288, published in March 1964, reaffirmed these measures but went considerably further in authorizing contingency preparations to be employed in the event that border control operations proved inadequate:

> To prepare immediately to be in a position on 72 hours' notice to initiate the full range of Laotian and Cambodian "Border Control actions" (beyond those authorized . . . above) and the "Retaliatory Actions" against North Vietnam, and to be in a position on 30 days' notice to initiate the program of "Graduated Overt Military Pressure" against North Vietnam.

This initial official signal to prepare to expand the war was cast against a conviction that U.S. objectives in South Vietnam were critically important:

> We seek an independent non-Communist South Vietnam. We do not require that it serve as a Western base or as a member of a Western Alliance. South Vietnam must be free, however, to accept outside assistance as required to maintain its security. This assistance should be able to take the form not only of economic and social measures but also police and military help to root out and control insurgent elements.
>
> Unless we can achieve this objective in South Vietnam, almost all of Southeast Asia will probably fall under Communist dominance (all of Vietnam, Laos, and Cambodia), accommodate to Communism so as to remove effective U.S. and anti-Communist influence (Burma), or fall under the domination of forces not now explicitly Communist but likely then to become so (Indonesia taking over Malaysia). Thailand might hold for a period with our help, but would be under grave pressure. Even the Philippines would become shaky, and the threat to India to the west, Australia and New Zealand to the south, and Taiwan, Korea, and Japan to the north and east would be greatly increased.
>
> All of these consequences would probably have been true even if the U.S. had not since 1954, and especially since 1961, become so heavily engaged in South Vietnam. However, that fact accentuates the impact of a Communist South Vietnam not only in Asia, but in the rest of the world, where the South Vietnam conflict is regarded as a test case of U.S. capacity to help a nation meet a Communist "war of liberation."
>
> Thus, purely in terms of foreign policy, the stakes are high. . . .
>
> The situation has unquestionably been growing worse, at least since September:
> 1. In terms of government control of the countryside, about 40% of

* The sensitive files of the Secretary of Defense for the period under discussion consist in large part of detailed plans to bring increasing military pressure against DRV under careful political control and under "scenarios" which would ensure adequate domestic and foreign support.

the territory is under Viet Cong control or predominant influence. In 22 of the 43 provinces, the Viet Cong control 50% or more of the land area, including 80% of Phuoc Tuy; 90% of Binh Duong; 75% of Hau Nghia; 90% of Long An; 90% of Kien Tuong; 90% of Dinh Tuong; 90% of Kien Hoa; and 85% of An Xuyen.

2. Large groups of the population are now showing signs of apathy and indifference, and there are some signs of frustration within the U.S. contingent:

a. The ARVN and paramilitary desertion rates and particularly the latter, are high and increasing.

b. Draft dodging is high while the Viet Cong are recruiting energetically and effectively.

c. The morale of the hamlet militia and of the Self Defense Corps, in which the security of the hamlets depends, is poor and falling.

3. In the last 90 days the weakening of the government's position has been particularly noticeable. For example:

a. In Quang Nam province, in the I Corps, the militia in 17 hamlets turned in their weapons.

b. In Binh Duong province (III Corps) the hamlet military were disarmed because of suspected disloyalty.

c. In Binh Dinh province, in the II Corps, 75 hamlets were severely damaged by the Viet Cong (in contrast, during the twelve months ending June 30, 1963, attacks on strategic hamlets were few and none was overrun).

d. In Quang Ngai province, at the northern edge of the II Corps, there were 413 strategic hamlets under government control a year ago. Of that number, 335 have been damaged to varying degrees or fallen into disrepair, and only 275 remain under government control.

e. Security throughout the IV Corps has deteriorated badly. The Viet Cong control virtually all facets of peasant life in the southernmost provinces and the government troops there are reduced to defending the administrative centers. Except in An Giang province (dominated by the Hoa Hao religious sect) armed escort is required for almost all movement in both the southern and northern areas of the IV Corps.

4. The political control structure extending from Saigon down into the hamlets disappeared following the November coup. Of the 41 incumbent province chiefs on November 1, 35 have been replaced (nine provinces had three province chiefs in three months; one province had four). Scores of lesser officials were replaced. Almost all major military commands have changed hands twice since the November coup. The faith of the peasants has been shaken by the disruption in experienced leadership and the loss of physical security. In many areas, power vacuums have developed causing confusion among the people and a rising rate of rural disorders.

5. North Vietnamese support, always significant, has been increasing.

The major new action under consideration to help achieve critically important U.S. objectives in the face of this gloomy recording of recent events was, as already noted, that of carrying the war to North Vietnam. Secretary McNamara, whose memorandum to the President was published *en toto* as NSAM 288, did not foresee the need at that time for a further major buildup of the advisory effort or for U.S. steps to take greater control of the war. Again, the approach already selected was deemed adequate. Only qualitative improvement was needed:

> A. The military tools and concepts of the GVN/US effort are generally sound and adequate. . . . Substantially more can be done in the effective employment of military forces and in the economic and civic action areas. These improvements may require some selective increases in the U.S. presence, but it does not appear likely that major equipment replacement and additions in U.S. personnel are indicated under current policy.
> B. The U.S. policy of reducing existing personnel where South Vietnamese are in a position to assume the functions is still sound. Its application will not lead to any major reductions in the near future, but adherence to this policy as such has a sound effect in portraying to the U.S. and the world that we continue to regard the war as a conflict the South Vietnamese must win and take ultimate responsibility for. Substantial reductions in the numbers of U.S. military training personnel should be possible before the end of 1965. However, the U.S. should continue to reiterate that it will provide all the assistance and advice required to do the job regardless of how long it takes.

Two actions which were explicitly considered and rejected indicated that the U.S. would still adhere to its oft-stated (and sometimes ignored) position that the South Vietnamese must win their own war through their own efforts:

> *Furnishing a U.S. Combat Unit to Secure the Saigon Area.* It is the universal judgment of our senior people in Saigon, with which we concur, that this action would now have serious adverse psychological consequences and should not be undertaken.
> *U.S. Taking Over Command.* It has been suggested that the U.S. move from its present advisory role to a role that would amount in practice to directive command. Again, the judgement of all senior people in Saigon, with which we concur, is that the possible military advantages of such action would be far out-weighed by its adverse psychological impact. It would cut across the whole basic picture of the Vietnamese winning their own war and lay us wide open to hostile propaganda both within South Vietnam and outside. Moreover, the present responsiveness of the GVN to our advice—although it has not yet reduced military reaction time—makes it less urgent. At the same time, MACV is steadily taking actions to bring U.S. and GVN operating staffs closer together at all levels, including joint operating rooms at key command levels.

Thus, it was stated national policy that the critically important struggle in South Vietnam must be won by the South Vietnamese, that the U.S. would do all within its power to help arrest and reverse a deteriorating situation, and that plans should be made to employ graduated overt military pressures against the supporters of the insurrection, the DRV. This was the principal thrust of NSAM 288 even though a sizeable portion of the document was devoted to programmatic steps which GVN and the U.S. should take in order better to mobilize South Vietnam's assets. Specifically, RVNAF needed to be increased in size by at least 50,000 men, reorganized, and provided with selected items of modern equipment. These programs presaged more U.S. advisors because there would be more RVNAF units to advise, but there was no mention of more advisors for given units or advisors to perform new functions.

3. *Increasing Political Instability in the Provinces*

The dark picture painted in NSAM 288 in March had become even darker by May 1964. Secretary McNamara visited Saigon on 12 and 13 May to inquire into progress in the "oilspot" national pacification program. What he learned could scarcely be called encouraging. A follow-on conference was scheduled for 1 June in Honolulu and the planning wheels began to turn—or, more accurately, the wheels began to churn—for there was barely two weeks' time in which to propose and coordinate U.S. actions acceptable to the GVN which might reverse the downward spiral of events, and "going North" was not yet feasible in terms of domestic U.S. politics.

Illustrative statistics (the same which Secretary McNamara saw) give the tone of events in South Vietnam. In an effort to determine exactly how many rural communities even *existed*—much less whose *control* they were under—the Department of Defense had earlier initiated an aerial photographic survey of the rural areas of RVN. Even this expensive undertaking left great factual gaps. In Tay Ninh Province, for example, photointerpreters identified 39 fortified hamlets; U.S. reports from provincial officials claimed that there were 106. The discrepancy was not one to appeal to those who wished to base policy determinations on solid facts.

Other facts were more easily ascertainable. Since the Diem coup, for instance, only 5 of RVN's 42 provinces had not experienced a change in Province Chief. Change is, of course, inescapable in the aftermath of a coup, but by 8 May 15 provinces were under their third chief since 1 November 1964, 7 had their fourth, and 2 provinces were governed by the fifth officer since the Diem government fell. Instability in administration was accompanied by a marked GVN decline in numbers of population controlled and a comparable increase in VC population control. These trends were reflected in the official estimates (themselves suspect of being overly optimistic) of control in the rural villages:

COMPARISON, NUMBER OF RURAL VILLAGES CONTROLLED

	Sep 63	Apr 64
RVN	1682	1485
VC	709	866
Contested	139	187

Of the 14 provinces considered critical in terms of location and population, all were reported by their advisors to be in "critical" condition. The prospects in 10 of these were judged to be "poor." Four provinces were regarded to have "fair" prospects. It was apparent that the U.S. could not depend on eventual actions against DRV to save the day in South Vietnam. By the time such actions were politically feasible there might be nothing to save. It was time to take some further direct action within South Vietnam itself—and to take it quickly. Increasing U.S. advisors was an obvious and available action.

4. *MACV's Gradualistic Approach to Expansion*

As early as December 1963, MACV had studied the desirability of extending the U.S. advisory effort to district level in 13 certain key districts, mostly around

Saigon. No action was taken at that time but the proposal was revived in February and implemented during late March 1964. Each of the original 13 "key districts" was assigned one Captain and one noncommissioned officer. Of the original 26 persons selected for this pilot project, 21 were newly arrived in RVN.

This gradualistic, experimental approach to expanding the advisory effort typified the method preferred both by the military and civilian agencies in Vietnam—although for somewhat different reasons. MACV was concerned with the experience and skill levels it could command among necessarily lower ranks as it expanded deeper into ARVN and the political (staffed by ARVN) hierarchy, about increased support requirements, and about increased casualties. USOM claimed that its operatives could work effectively at the "spigot" end of the aid pipeline only where the local administration was energetic and effective and where some modicum of security had already been provided. USOM had severe recruiting difficulties, too. Secretary McNamara discovered on his 12–13 May visit to Saigon that it was about 25 per cent understrength and that approximately half of this personnel shortage was concentrated in the expanding rural affairs staff.

5. McNamara's Willingness to Approve Expansion

Thus, the general attitude among the U.S. agencies in Saigon was to go slowly, to avoid the danger, as it was frequently expressed, of "strewing Americans all over the countryside." Secretary McNamara apparently had other thoughts after his May visit in Saigon. The available record does not reflect that he directed an expansion of the advisory effort—but the Joint Staff was almost immediately hard at work examining *which* of several levels of increase would be most desirable. The available record leaves little doubt that the Secretary of Defense wanted it made clear that he would approve any reasonable proposals for personnel, materiel, or funds. Those sections of NSAM 288 which dealt with recommendations for South Vietnam had concentrated on programs which would assist GVN to mobilize its resources. By May it was clear that the hoped-for actions had not taken effect. The obvious conclusion—given the importance which the U.S. attached to success in South Vietnam—was that additional steps must be taken to halt the deterioration in the countryside.

6. The Initial Proposals and Responses

The initial recorded exchange among the planners occurred when COMUS-MACV was asked on 22 May 1964 to provide an input to a JCS study then in progress on ". . . encadrement of South Vietnamese Civil Guard and Self Defense Corps with U.S. teams along lines of White Star teams in Laos, with objective of making these units as effective as possible in Vietnamese pacification plan." The message made it clear that the JCS was examining alternative levels of increased advisory effort (1,000, 2,000 and 3,000 personnel), not asking *if* the advisory effort should be increased. The compressed time frame available for prior coordination on a recommended course of action was also clear: COMUSMACV was asked to provide his comments on the draft JCS proposal by the following day (23 May). "Regret circumstances do not permit more time," the message stated.

The reply from Saigon, processed through CINCPAC, adhered to the established MACV preference to undertake new departures only in a selective, experimental way:

> I do not think we should flood RVN with number of personnel you mention. Think better solution is to do [this] on selective basis starting with critical districts and provinces and once we get feel of problem expand to remainder of RVN as experience dictates.

Then, in a significant passage, the reply from the field asked in blunt language just what the intended purpose was for the proposed expansion of the advisory effort. The "White Star Teams" used in Laos, the message noted, had the purpose and effect of establishing U.S. control over foreign forces:

> The question arises as to whether you mean encadrement or increase of "advisory" effort. Do you want to take control or improve the performance of CG and SDC by step-up within current policy?

Although this direct question was never answered, the JCS' initial proposal for encadrement was quietly dropped. The U.S. might wish to be in a position to control elements or all of RVNAF but it would not consciously follow any scheme explicitly aimed at such control. Instead, the JCS countered with a plan for six Mobile Training Teams in each province backed up by a Training Center Team and a small Provincial Training Detachment. This proposal would put an additional 70 U.S. training advisors in each selected province in an effort to improve the level of effectiveness of the paramilitary forces. Its recommendation was that the U.S. military advisory effort should be increased by 1000 personnel, enough to provide this new dimension of advice in the fourteen critical provinces which had experienced so much recent instability.

This JCS proposal for Mobile Training Teams for the RVNAF paramilitary forces was tied to an explicit statement of how best to *organize* this effort without any mention of how much *influence* or *leverage* the U.S. would or could exert through this expanded system. The problem was treated as one in the development of technical proficiency; the issue of the extent of U.S. control was largely ignored—though surely not forgotten:

Concept of US Advisory Effort

a. *General*

(1) An underlying principle in the oil-spot concept is accordance of maximum flexibility to province officials in solving individual province problems which vary widely from province to province. This study recognizes that principle and outlines a plan for assignment of additional US instructor and training resources to the province to provide the training and advice needed to improve the effectiveness of the provincial paramilitary forces.

(2) The shortage of trained personnel is acute in the paramilitary forces because of the nature of the forces themselves. They are recruited at province or district level to perform military tasks in those same regions. While the CG and SDC are considered full-time troops, many of the individuals, in fact, must combine earning their livelihood with military

duties. Movement of these people long distances away from their homes to training centers disrupts their lives, creates morale problems and undoubtedly contributes greatly to the high dessertion rates which have been experienced. It appears appropriate, therefore, to bring the trainers and training facilities to the areas where the paramilitary forces live and operate.

(3) According to US standards, the military training needs of the Vietnamese paramilitary are extremely modest. There is no requirement for elaborated technical schools or complex instructional courses. Instead, *the Vietnamese paramilitary require military schooling at the most basic levels, with emphasis on basic infantry weapons and small unit tactics. Such instruction would be provided by the additional numbers of US military personnel.*

b. *Organization for Advisory Effort.* The training deficiencies and problems of the paramilitary are as many and varied as the number of provinces and districts in which those forces operate. Needs in Quang Ngai, for example, may be extremely different from those in Dinh Tuong. Within the provinces, each district also may have different training needs. The reasonable method of approaching this problem, then, appears to be establishment of highly flexible training detachments operating under supervision at province level, which can provide local mobile training teams, small training centers, and temporary encadrement for the smaller paramilitary units when dictated by a specific situation.

7. *MACV Focuses on Operations Rather Than Training*

COMUSMACV and CINCPAC were asked to comment within two days on this study which had been ". . . considered at the highest levels, where initial reaction has been favorable." Their replies, in which the theater commander supported his nominal subordinate in Saigon, contested the value of U.S.-conducted *training* for RVNAF paramilitary forces, proposed that advisors be used at the district level to assist in *operations,* accepted the 1,000-man magnitude, but stretched out the target date 18 months—thereby proposing a gradualistic approach without candidly saying so. General Harkins devoted most of his reply to the question of training teams:

A. A basic premise of the study is that training at the established centers is at the root of many morale and desertion problems. This premise is incorrect as regards the Civil Guard (Regional Forces). It is in part true with respect to SDC (Popular Forces); but the underlying cause thereof—lack of per diem—is in the process of being removed by the new allowances that are about to be promulgated. This is not to say there are not formidable morale problems (one manifestation of which is desertion) within both categories of forces. These need to be and are being tackled. However, basic point is that they do not stem from the present system of training.

B. Mobile training teams have been organized under special circumstances when units have had prior combat experience and/or as an expedient measure only. Experience has proved that units trained by such teams have subsequently required formal training at an established training center where proper facilities are available. The Civil Guard and Self Defense Corps had many units trained by mobile training teams in 1962 in order to provide an immediate operational force. Almost all of these units have since been retrained in the complete unit poi [program of instruction] because it was determined that the mobile team training was inadequate. The mobile training teams consisted of U.S. personnel and Vietnamese interpreters.

C. While the training requirements of paramilitary forces are relatively modest by U.S. standards, an adequate poi must be backed up by firing ranges, training areas, class rooms, training aids and other facilities. These requirements are met by the regional and popular forces training centers. There are five regional force unit training centers; nine regional force/ popular force leader training centers; and thirty-seven popular force training centers. They are properly distributed geographically; they are staffed with qualified Vietnamese instructors; and can be expanded, with little difficulty to support programmed force increase. Some augmentation of the U.S. advisory element at these several centers is desirable, on a selected basis.

D. The concept of U.S. personnel conducting training for the paramilitary forces on either a training center or MTT basis (and especially the latter) is not realistic.

(1) The Vietnamese have an adequate training base with experienced instructors; the latter are doing a satisfactory job. For the U.S. to assume the instructional effort, vice the Vietnamese, would generate serious morale problems and would probably be unacceptable.

(2) The interpreter support requirements would be prohibitive.

(3) Previous experience (sub-paragraph B above) of using U.S. advisors as instructors was unsuccessful due to the inability to communicate.

2. As indicated above, the current method of training both the regional and popular forces is adequate, although we do have under review the length and content of the training. Where the U.S. can make its best contribution to the paramilitary forces effectiveness is in the area of operations. Our formula, discussed in 23 May telecon on this subject, is to increase greatly the U.S. advisory effort at the district level. Therefore, strongly urge that you support our position that approximately 1000 advisors, in the general proportion of one officer to three NCO's be authorized as district detachments, with the precise composition and deployment of said teams left to the determination of COMUSMACV.

CINCPAC informed the JCS that he agreed with COMUSMACV's arguments and quoted the telecon referred to above to explain the course of action preferred by the military commanders in the field:

1. Our comment is based on CG/SDC reorganization concept of 7 May which includes elimination CG Bn Hq in provinces and establishment 90 man sector Hq in lieu thereof with TAC CP capability, and sub-sector Hq 16 men at each 239 districts. This is expected to be accomplished in two to three months.

2. Recommend use of one team composed of mature company grade officer and other specialist as you suggest (Wpns/Demo, Commo Med) per district.

3. Proposal para 2 represents end requirement for 239 teams, totaling 239 officers, 717 enlisted spec aggregate 956 personnel, by end calendar year 65.

4. MACV current plans call for 1 officer and 1 NCO at 116 districts by June 65. Requisitions have been submitted for 100 of these by end CY 64. Two man detachments now assigned to 13 districts.

5. Assume GVN will agree to use US teams at district which represent reasonable security risk. At present time approx 40 of 239 districts are not sufficiently secure to enable use of US advisors.

8. *The JCS Alternative Programs*

The JCS, given the very few days remaining until Secretary McNamara was to meet in Honolulu with COMUSMACV and Ambassador Lodge, did not attempt to reconcile the time-phasing and eventual size of the proposed advisory effort at district level. Rather, it submitted to the Secretary, just prior to his departure for the conference, two separate memoranda: One laid out a prospective program for district advisors throughout RVN; the other outlined a pilot program at the district level. The purpose of both outline advisory efforts was the same—"improving the effectiveness of these paramilitary units in the Vietnamese pacification plan"—but the rate of advisor buildup differed.

In the proposed "pilot program," for instance, the concept envisaged the phased establishment of teams in 49 districts of seven key provinces during a six-month period. This would require approximately 300 additional advisors. The broader program called for an additional 1,000 advisory personnel, phased over a period of 1–1½ years, to cover all 239 districts by the end of CY 1965. The more comprehensive program estimated that 63 districts (compared to 49 districts in the "pilot program") would be manned by the end of CY 1964. Both were represented as suitable bases for the Secretary's impending discussions in Honolulu. Both were hurriedly drawn up alternative schemes for expanding the advisory effort to district level. Both, moreover, incorporated the arguments of COMUSMACV: concentration on operations rather than training and a time-phased buildup with due attention to existing security conditions and interpreter availability. The point was also made that the total number of additional personnel would necessarily include a support slice of approximately 35%.

One other question of expansion was addressed before the Secretary of Defense's conference in Honolulu in June. The JCS studied the possibility, also in late May, of extending the advisory effort to regular ARVN units at the company level. The JCS agreed with the COMUSMACV and CINCPAC reasoning that such an extension would be undesirable because it would lead to greatly increased U.S. casualties, would be unsupportable in terms of necessary language training (one year to 18 months necessary to provide 500 "bilingual" advisors), and would meet resistance from ARVN commanders faced with strange new relationships and potential loss of face.

9. *MACV's Preferred Approach Accepted*

The prevailing military advice, then, when the Secretary met on 1 June with the principal U.S. managers of the Vietnamese effort, was that it was desirable to expand the advisory effort to district level on a careful basis in order to promote better effectiveness in the paramilitary forces engaged in pacification activities, but that U.S. advisors should not be extended to company level in the regular forces. The available record does not make clear the exact positions and arguments put forward at Honolulu. What is clear is that it was decided, following basically the revised estimates proposed by COMUSMACV, to expand the advisory effort to district level at some rate (to be worked out later in detail) and to increase the size of battalion-level advisory groups by two noncommissioned officers in infantry battalions and cavalry troops and by one commissioned and two noncommissioned officers in artillery battalions. The acknowledged effect of the latter decision was to make company-level advisory teams *available* on an ad hoc basis without *assigning* them on a permanent basis. It is unclear how this scheme solved the previous reservations relative to language training, higher casualties, and Vietnamese sensibilities. A likely explanation is that MACV was after a new commander, General Westmoreland, who was more willing to expand the advisory effort and less inclined to cite the potential disadvantages of a larger American presence. General Harkins had already returned to the United States to receive the Distinguished Service Medal in a ceremony on 24 June and, at the request of President Johnson, remained in the U.S. until he retired.

At any rate, it was a new COMUSMACV who cabled on 25 June his proposals for the buildup discussed at the beginning of the month in Honolulu. In sum, he asked for 900 additional advisors for battalions and districts, suggested a small increase at province level, and noted that "significant" numbers of personnel would be needed for administrative and logistical support of the new advisors. He also suggested, in the emphasized portion of the message quoted below, that many of the district advisory teams could complete their work and be moved to new areas for pacification within a year:

> 1. Augmentation of current US Advisory detachments at the battalion level and further extension of the advisory effort at the district level are necessary now to influence the successful planning and execution of the National Pacification Plan. These additions to the currently authorized advisory detachments have been discussed with and agreed to by GVN, and will enable us to place advisors at the lowest level, as needed, in order to insure that all possible actions are properly coordinated. . . . Extension of US Advisory effort to the districts as an initial step toward intensifying the Pacification Program at the lowest level is essential. This will insure supervision and coordination in the employment of paramilitary forces and a general reinforcement of the pacification effort at district level. Initially, teams of two (2) officers and three (3) enlisted men [one (1) of whom will be a radio operator] be placed in the forty-five (45) districts of the eight (8) priority provinces. In ten of these districts, and in three (3) districts of two other provinces, a limited effort is now being made by district teams of one (1) officer and one (1) enlisted man; these teams will be increased to full strength district teams. In the provinces outside of the eight top priority provinces teams will be placed in another sixty-eight (68) districts. Starting 1 Jan 65 it is envisaged that an additional fifty (50) teams can be placed, and that by 1 Jul 65 teams from the original districts can be placed into the remaining districts in SVN. This extension of US Advisory effort to the district level must be conducted on a phased basis with actual composition and employment as determined by COMUSMACV. Two (2) officers and three (3) enlisted men are considered as average team strengths for planning purposes. . . .

2. *RECAPITULATION OF REQUIREMENTS*

	Capts/Lts	E6	E5/4
123 Inf Bns (Incl 4 Marine)		123	123
29 Arty Bns (Incl 1 Marine)	29		58
14 M113 Troops, Armd CA Sqdns		14	14
45 District Adv Teams (Priority province)	90	90	45
68 District Adv Teams (Other provinces)	136	136	68
TOTAL, adjusted for 13 districts teams now	255	363	308

in place, 900 (242 officers; 658 enlisted).

3. While this message deals only with the increased advisory effort at the battalion and district levels consideration is also being given to increases at sector level, also discussed at Honolulu. Those recommendations which will be submitted separately will not approach the magnitude of the increases recommended in this message for battalion and district levels. . . .

5. Administrative and logistical support personnel and equipment requirements will be studied separately. From our earlier studies it is apparent that requirements will be significant.

6. An increase of approximately eighty (80) US Naval Advisors will also be recommended. Chief US Naval Advisory Group, in coordination with CNO VNN, has identified areas in need of additional advisory effort. I concur in the need and will support recommendation to be submitted separately.

10. *Unresolved Issues: Speed and Discretionary Authority*

The decision to increase the advisory effort in the magnitude and fashion just cited had already been made in effect. It was necessary, however, for the Secretary or Deputy Secretary of Defense personally to approve every manpower space for MACV or MAAG Vietnam—not because such decisions could not be delegated but because the Secretary chose to reserve them to himself. The questions which remained were, first, how much freedom to adjust numbers to situations (a discretionary authority COMUSMACV had consistently requested) would be permitted and, second, the rate at which the agreed expansion would take place. There could have been other questions, of course: should the district advisory effort spread in close geographic relation to the pacification plan or follow some other scheme; should the advisors be conscious agents to increase U.S. leverage or essentially technical-tactical assistants to their counterparts; how deeply involved should advisors become in local political administration? There is no indication that these and other related questions of the advisors' role were brought "up the tape" for examination. The principal issue was simply how quickly they should be brought into South Vietnam and at what level discretionary authority would be granted.

The latter question was settled by default. MACV's proposed Joint Table of Distribution (JTD) of 15 May 1964, replete with errors and omissions and antedating the decision to expand the advisory effort, became the base line for authorizations to expand. Nobody in the game seemed quite able to keep the detailed numbers straight. OSD came quickly to focus on the total authorization for U.S. personnel in Vietnam and, as the papers in the Secretary's files demonstrate, found itself pencilling new numbers in even final draft copies which had undergone several checks and redrafts. The product of this concentration on minutiae at high Washington levels was almost complete freedom of employment in the field. The Washington policymakers asked how many men were authorized in various activities and how many were assigned. There is no evidence that, once the decision was made to establish district advisory teams, these same policymakers probed into priorities of employment or the roles of these advisors.

The rate of the build-up was a much more complicated matter, not because of the additional battalion advisors and the new district advisors but because the numbers represented solely by the additional advisors quickly became a relatively small percentage of the total U.S. build-up—all of which was justified as contributing to the GVN pacification plan and a sizeable portion of which was specifically earmarked to provide administrative and logistical support to the newly arriving advisors. By mid-July COMUSMACV was recommending 4200 personnel in addition to the 926 battalion and district advisors, at least two more helicopter companies, one Caribou company, and numerous major items of equipment as part of the required build-up. The increased advisory effort was identified as the cause of this large increase:

> The increases envisaged . . . will provide for the extension and reinforcement of the advisory effort at the combat unit level and, concurrently, a major extension and reinforcement of the advisory effort at the district level in order to improve and accelerate pacification operations. That extension and augmentation of effort has an immediate impact upon the administrative and logistical support base. In a sense the addition of advisors in this quantity becomes the "straw that broke the camel's back" to an already overburdened support base.

11.   *Secretarial Pressure for a Speed-Up*

The Secretary of Defense and JCS met on 20 July to discuss these requirements. The JCS supported COMUSMACV. Secretary McNamara had no argument with the levels of men and equipment requested; his question was why they could not be provided more quickly than indicated by the time-phasing in General Westmoreland's detailed breakdown. COMUSMACV had asked for almost 4200 personnel by 1 December 1964 and the balance (comprising only Special Forces units) of the 4772 total increase by 1 February 1965. Secretary McNamara asked the JCS to study the feasibility of accelerating the build-up so that it would be completed by 30 September. The JCS replied that the advisory personnel could be made available this quickly but that several support units—particularly aviation units—could not reach South Vietnam by 30 September without causing extreme difficulties and the degradation of tests of the airmobile concept then in progress. The Secretary of Defense directed on 7 August that the accelerated deployment, except for certain critical aviation items and jeeps, be completed by the end of September. He further directed that COMUSMACV be queried as to his ability to absorb these personnel and units by that date.

General Westmoreland's reply stated that he could not reasonably absorb this build-up in the time desired by Secretary McNamara. To do so, he said, would generate an unorderly situation with respect to support facilities and an undesirable hump in personnel rotation. The proposed acceleration would not, moreover, satisfy the desired standards of advisor training or dovetail with the planned expansion of the advisory effort:

> The required training/schooling of Bn/District advisors will be further sacrificed under the proposed compression. A two week in-country orientation is being established to handle the Sep-Oct increments which will not receive CONUS schooling prior to arrival. Any further compression would create a requirement for in-country training which is beyond our capability.
>
> Districts must be able to accept advisors based on their status of pacification. The present scheduling of district advisors is phased with the pacification plan and projected to coincide with its progress. . . .
>
> In summary, the compression of personnel and units would overload our existing facilities and create administrative problems beyond our capacity to handle in an orderly manner. COMUSMACV has discussed with Amb. Taylor who concurs.

12. *MACV's Preference Upheld Again*

Faced with this reply from the individual responsible for managing the U.S. contribution to the advisory and support effort, Secretary McNamara cancelled the accelerated deployment. The military services were instructed to deploy personnel and units to South Vietnam in accordance with General Westmoreland's initial recommendation forwarded to Washington a month earlier, in mid-July.

The effect of this sequence of decisions stretching from mid-May to mid-August 1964 was to increase the advisory effort by over 1000 personnel:

District Advisors:	553
Battalion Advisors:	350
Naval (and Marine) Advisory Group:	82
Air Force Advisory Group:	80
TOTAL	1065

This expansion, and the rate at which it was to proceed, was the product of what may be termed "tacit bargaining" between Washington and Saigon. Washington typically assumed the initiative in proposing increases and in recommending that they be accomplished as quickly as possible. The dominant concern was the fear that the countryside was being lost to the VC and that the impending U.S. moves to exert direct military pressure against DRV might come too late unless the pacification program could be vitalized. U.S. officials in Saigon tended to prefer to expand gradually and to insure that adequate support facilities were in place before additional advisors were deployed to the field. The product of desires driven by political awareness of impending failure, on one hand, and desires driven by managerial awareness of operational conditions, on the other, was an advisory increase almost precisely of the magnitude and rate preferred by the managers in the field.

13. *Events Overtake Implementation of the Expansion*

The really important points to be noted, however, do not concern the relative influence of General Westmoreland, Secretary McNamara, the JCS, or other participants in determining the size and rate of this buildup. Rather, the important points are, first, that the carefully studied decisions did not address some central issues and, second, that events acted to overtake the decisions which were made. The policymakers did not really examine how district and additional battalion advisors would improve the execution of the pacification plan: they simply assumed that a greater U.S. presence would produce beneficial effects. The basis for *operational* advisors for the paramilitary forces was, quite simply, COMUSMACV's reasoned elaboration of the disutility of *training* advisors. There was no complementary assessment of the usefulness of operational advisors. It was necessary to do something in South Vietnam to try to reverse a clearly deteriorating position. The provision of more advisors came very close to being a reflexive response to this situation.

The overall magnitude of the advisory increase bears directly on the second major point, in which events in RVN overtook the new U.S. response. This is particularly true in the instance of the new dimension in the advisory effort, the provision of advisory teams at the district (subsector) level. Thirteen teams of one officer and one noncommissioned officer had been deployed in critical districts, it will be recalled, in March 1964. The final August decisions to make 553 district advisors available in RVN by 1 December was designed to provide for a larger team (2 officers, 3 EM) for each of 113 of the total 239 districts. The MACV plan, then, was to provide U.S. military advisors only to about one-half of the total number of districts in RVN.

By the end of CY 1964 all 113 teams were actually deployed. Their total strength at that time was 532 as against the authorized total strength of 565.* By January 1965 the number of district advisors assigned exceeded the number authorized. These teams were deployed, it will be recalled, in the expectation that by some time in 1965 a substantial number of them would have worked themselves out of a job and be available for reassignment to new areas. This expectation was, to put it mildly, not validated by events.

In February 1965, roughly a month after the limited expansion to district advisors had been completed, the Khanh government was replaced by the Quat regime. Over a year of U.S. effort to bring about political stability within the GVN seemed to have been fruitlessly wasted. The U.S. began the sustained bombing campaign against North Vietnam, ROLLING THUNDER, on 26 February. Shortly thereafter, two Marine Battalion Landing Teams (BLTs) were landed at Da Nang for air base security. These measures presaged a growing U.S. material commitment; the trend was heightened by ARVN's performance later in the spring of 1965.

During May and June ARVN suffered a series of near catastrophic defeats that were instrumental in deciding the Johnson Administration to act on Gen-

* The discrepancy between the 553 *additional* authorization and the *total* district advisor authorization of 565 is accounted for by the transfer of some of the spaces involved in the initial experimental program at district level. 565 is the correct total—113 teams of 5 men each.

eral Westmoreland's recommendation for a greatly expanded U.S. ground combat role in the war. On 11 May, the Viet Cong attacked and overran Song Be, the capital of Phuoc Long Province, and a U.S. advisory compound in the city with more than a regiment of troops. Both the U.S. and Vietnamese took heavy casualties. Before the end of the month, a VC force of undetermined size ambushed and decimated the ARVN 51st Regiment near the small outpost of Ba Gia a few kilometers west of Quang Ngai City in I Corps. The ARVN commander in the area immediately rushed reinforcements to the battle scene only to have them become victims of a second ambush. The battle dragged on for several days, but ended in a total defeat for ARVN. Two battalions were completely decimated, but more importantly, the ARVN senior commanders on the scene had displayed tactical stupidity and cowardice. With a crisis of confidence in leadership clearly developing within the armed forces, the very real possibility of a complete ARVN collapse could not be excluded. COMUS-MACV summarized the situation in his 7 June cable to CINCPAC:

> ARVN forces . . . are already experiencing difficulty in coping with this increased VC capability. Desertion rates are inordinately high. Battle losses have been higher than expected; in fact, four ARVN battalions have been rendered ineffective by VC action in the I and II Corps zones. Therefore, effective fighting strength of many infantry and ranger battalions is unacceptably low. As a result, ARVN troops are beginning to show signs of reluctance to assume the offensive and in some cases their steadfastness under fire is coming into doubt.

If anything, Westmoreland's assessment may have been too generous. The next week the Viet Cong launched an attack on the new Special Forces camp and adjoining district headquarters at Dong Zoai on the northwest corner of War Zone D. ARVN forces were committed piecemeal to the engagement and successively chewed up by more than two regiments of enemy troops. The battle lasted for five days and marked some of the bitterest fighting of the war to that date. The VC summer offensive continued unabated through June and July. On 25 June, the long expected offensive in the central highlands began when a district headquarters at Tou Morong in Kontum Province was overrun, reportedly by an NVA regiment reinforced with local guerrillas. Other remote district capitals came under attack in the following weeks and by 7 July a total of six had been abandoned or overrun.

Casualties soared on both sides; ARVN alone sustained 1,672 in the second week of June. But the important factor was the dangerous degradation of ARVN unit integrity. By the end of May, the heavy fighting had rendered two ARVN regiments and three battalions combat ineffective by MACV ratings. By 26 June, MACV was forced to rate 5 ARVN regiments and 9 separate battalions ineffective. Losses were so high that in July, 11 of 15 ARVN training battalions had to be temporarily disorganized to provide fillers for the line units. It was this major degradation of unit effectiveness that evoked the alarm and sense of crisis in Saigon and Washington and constituted the seemingly incontestable arguments in favor of substantial American forces. ARVN units were defeated in most cases by their own tactical ineptness, cowardice, and lack of leadership rather than by overall weight of numbers or inferiority of firepower. The U.S. advisory effort had sought to strengthen precisely these military intangibles, in addition to equipping, training and generally supporting ARVN troops. These skills and qualities are, of course, difficult to teach or impart, but a successful advisory effort must at some point produce a force capable of engaging the enemy and defeating him when the ratios of strength and firepower are roughly equal.

Far from finding many of its advisory teams finishing their task and moving on to new areas or to new units, the U.S. found itself in mid-1965 beginning the commitment of major ground forces to South Vietnam. The deployment of these forces marked the end of a major phase in "advisory warfare." From this time forward the role of U.S. military and political-military advisors would be determined and practiced in a radically changed environment.

C. U.S. COMBAT FORCES AND THE POSSIBILITY OF NEW RELATIONSHIPS (1965)

1. The Abortive Limited Expansion of ARVN

During the spring of 1965 General Westmoreland's staff prepared a full-blown "Commander's Estimate of the Situation." The estimate, delivered to Washington at the beginning of April, examined three courses of action for dealing with the crisis in South Vietnam. Among these was an accelerated RVNAF build-up.

Even by accelerating the rate of ARVN expansion, COMUSMACV concluded, the ratio of ARVN to VC battalions would decline by the end of 1965 from 1.7:1 to 1.6:1. General Westmoreland rejected this alternative on the grounds that it could not prevent a VC victory. It would take too long to accomplish the build-up and there was little assurance that ARVN performance would match that of a constantly improving enemy. (His lack of confidence in ARVN is further reflected in his argument for U.S. forces, in which he estimated that one U.S. Army battalion is the fighting equivalent of two ARVN battalions and one Marine BLT the equivalent of three ARVN battalions.)

These reservations notwithstanding, Westmoreland had requested authorization on 20 March to implement the Alternative 2 RVNAF strength increases proposed by him the previous November. After the April 1–2 conference in Washington and a review of the "Commander's Estimate," the JCS recommended approval and Secretary McNamara agreed on 12 April to expand RVNAF by an additional 17,247 spaces. An additional 160 U.S. advisors were approved at the same time. In late May, the JCS asked the Secretary of Defense to authorize MAP support for another 2,369 ARVN spaces to fatten out division bases for the eventual creation of a tenth ARVN division out of existing separate regiments. This request was approved on 4 June.

Thus, while it was decided not to continue to depend exclusively on larger Vietnamese forces with U.S. air and naval support, the plan was to conduct a modest expansion of ARVN in conjunction with the deployment of U.S. forces. In the event, even the modest plans went down the drain in the aftermath of the heavy casualties sustained in combat during late May and early June. On 7 June, General Westmoreland informed CINCPAC and the JCS that a moratorium on RVNAF build-up was unavoidable because trainees in the pipeline would have to be used as fillers for existing units.

The U.S. build-up continued during the spring and early summer, particularly as a result of ARVN reverses in combat. By the end of July there were 18 US/FW combat maneuver battalions deployed in South Vietnam. In the same message in which he advised of the halt in ARVN expansion, General Westmoreland had requested a significant increase in the number of U.S. troops for Vietnam (the famed "44-Battalion" request). After more than a month of deliberation, the President finally approved the request sometime in mid-July. His historic announcement of the expanded U.S. effort came on 28 July. Understandably, this momentous expansion of the U.S. involvement in the war completely overshadowed the advisory program and the growth of RVNAF during the remainder of 1965.

2. New Possibilities

But the deployment of U.S. forces to South Vietnam did, however, open up a new range of possible relationships which would not have been possible without the presence of substantial U.S. combat forces. Each of these relationships might conceivably promote one or all of the several purposes which this study has reasoned to be behind the U.S. military advisory effort: the development of improved tactical and technical competence in RVNAF, the generation of better intelligence (both friendly and enemy), and increased U.S. influence.

Two categories of new relationships were considered: the encadrement of U.S. and ARVN units (in several forms) and the establishment of a joint command to conduct the war. Both of these courses were rejected by COMU-SMACV. In their place General Westmoreland attempted to create a Joint US-RVNAF staff to coordinate independent national efforts. The basic arrangement enabling tactical independence—within limits—was the creation of mutually exclusive Tactical Areas of Responsibility (TAORs) for each combat maneuver force.

3. Encadrement Considered and Rejected

Deficiencies in ARVN leadership had long been recognized by U.S. military advisors as one of the key impediments to increased ARVN performance. In April, when the first major input of U.S. combat troops took place, consideration was given to the encadrement of U.S. officers in ARVN units as a way of solving this problem. The proposal was touched off by a DoD request on 15 April for COMUSMACV's opinion about the feasibility of using U.S. cadres to improve effectiveness in the ten ARVN divisions. The same day, McGeorge Bundy sent a personal NODIS message to Ambassador Taylor stating among other things, that "The President has repeatedly emphasized his personal desire for a strong experiment in the encadrement of U.S. troops with the Vietnamese." General Westmoreland turned the issue over to his deputy, General Throckmorton, for a recommendation. Throckmorton's study considered three alternative encadrement possibilities: (1) assumption of officer and senior NCO command positions by U.S. personnel within the designated ARVN battalions; (2) assignment of U.S. personnel as staff officers, and in technical and specialist positions within the battalions; and (3) the employment of U.S. troops as fire support elements within ARVN-commanded battalions. Two critical difficulties applicable to all of these schemes were identified: the language barrier and the expanded support requirement that would be generated for U.S. personnel. Another negative factor was the expected adverse effect of any such step on South Vietnamese morale. These formed the basis for General Throckmorton's recommendation that encadrement be rejected. COMUSMACV endorsed his deputy's recommendation and the general encadrement idea was officially pronounced dead during the 18 April Honolulu Conference. Only three days had elapsed from the birth of the proposal to its burial.

4. *Marine Combined Action Platoons (CAPs)*

But while general encadrement was effectively killed by COMUSMACV a specific, limited experiment in encadrement was begun later in the year almost off-handedly by the U.S. Marines near Phu Bai. Since the Marine units had been assigned TAORs larger than they could secure, innovative commanders sought ways to maximize local security resources. In June, a company commander of the 3d Battalion, 4th Marines near Phu Bai assigned a few Marines to the villages in his tactical area to work with the Popular Forces platoons. Marine leadership, training, and access to powerful fire support brought measurable improvement in the PF units. As a result the Commanding General, 1st ARVN Division, placed six PF platoons under the operational control of the Marine battalion.

By November, the effort had achieved such results that it was brought to the attention of the CG III MAF. Later that month an agreement was reached between the I Corps Commander and the CG III MAF permitting the integration of Marine squads into PF platoons in the Da Nang area to improve their effectiveness and stiffen their combat performance. The basic unit of the new venture was the Combined Action Platoon (CAP) formed by adding a Marine Rifle Squad of 14 men plus a Navy corpsman to a PF platoon (32–38 authorized strength). The PF platoon retained its own organization and the integrated Marines advised the entire unit, living with it, sharing its food, conducting combined patrols, and training counterparts. At the end of 1965, there were seven such Combined Action Platoons, but the success of the experiment in enhancing PF performance and extending security prompted a rapid expansion during the next year. The Marines have continued to press for expansion of this program and to see in it an effective method by which to produce increased performance in PF units. Critics have noted that the Marine advisors quickly become *de facto* leaders of the CAPs and argued that a higher level of current performance is purchased at the cost of stultifying the development of South Vietnamese leadership. No general consensus has developed on the relative merits of this combined organization.

5. *Joint Command Considered and Rejected*

The 1965 commitment of U.S. forces also prompted a high level U.S. debate on the advisability of creating some form of unified combined command. The question was first raised in Washington in mid-March when General H. K. Johnson, Army Chief of Staff, returned from a visit to Vietnam with the recommendation for deployment of U.S. combat forces. The idea had the same conceptual origins as the encadrement proposals, namely that if RVNAF could be commanded by or associated with U.S. troops it might be molded at last into an effective fighting force. In addition, such a unified allied command would have given the senior commander—presumably COMUSMACV—far greater freedom to deploy forces and fight the war in the straight-forward pursuit of unambiguous objectives, rather than restricting him to coordination with Vietnamese counterparts whose motivations at all times were a compromise of political and personal as well as military considerations.

When queried on the matter, General Westmoreland opposed any formal merging of commands, preferring instead the maintenance of informal cooperation and coordination together with a limited combined staff under an

American chief with a Vietnamese deputy. This arrangement would better as- suage the GVN's sensitivities to questions of sovereignty and "neo-colonialism." Full integration of command, General Westmoreland advised, should be deferred until some later time when the influx of U.S. forces might require it and GVN sensibilities might be more disposed to its acceptance. In May, Secretary Mc- Namara authorized the creation of a formal combined authority in Vietnam. But since both Ky and Thieu had just publicly condemned any joint command idea in press interviews, both Ambassador Taylor and General Westmoreland recommended against the proposed action. CINCPAC backed up COMUS- MACV's concern about alienating the South Vietnamese:

> Refs A and B [Saigon message 3855, 24 May; and COMUSMACV mes- sage 17292, 24 May] again point out the formidable disadvantages which obstruct early establishment of any formal combined command authority in South Vietnam. I am fully in accord with the views of the Ambassador and General Westmoreland in this regard.
>
> The long-range nature of the actions directed by Ref C [JCS msg 3159, 14 May] is recognized. At the same time it is apparent that we should anticipate continued public speculation as to the purpose and motive of any consolidation of multi-national forces into a single command if we pursue even the most limited measures. Although a combined command might generate an outward illusion of unity, many divisive influences will remain at work beneath the surface to exacerbate claims of American neo- colonialism and self-assumed leadership.
>
> Conventional operations of Corps-level magnitude, in contrast to counterinsurgency operations, would of course require closer coordination and possibly some form of international command mechanism. Until a combined command is clearly in our best interests we should continue to stimulate RVN resolve to fight a counterinsurgency war which is and must remain their primary responsibility. Premature experimentation with new command arrangements would be counter-productive should it weaken national unity within the RVNAF or promote a feeling of apathy in the countryside.

6.   *TAOR*s, Senior Advisors, and a Combined Staff

These exchanges effectively ended the question of unified command. In the absence of unity of command, General Westmoreland had already accepted the concept of the Tactical Area of Responsibility (TAOR), an expedient coordinat- ing mechanism originally worked out between the local ARVN commanders and the Marines defending the DaNang perimeter. The concept was a practical one for a war in which there are no front lines and in which military units operate throughout the country. Specific geographic areas were assigned to specific units who then had exclusive authority and responsibility to operate within them. Military units could not enter or fire into another unit's TAOR without the permission of its commander. Subsequently, the concept would raise some problems as the requirement for rapid redeployment and the extensive use of air mobility made such formal, fixed arrangements awkward. But in 1965 the TAOR provided a simple and effective solution to the coordination problem raised by units under different commands operating throughout the country. Its adoption may be viewed as an attempt to provide limited, territorial unity of command in the absence of an overall, national unifying mechanism.

General Westmoreland attempted to compensate for this absence of unity (which he had endorsed for non-military reasons) by the creation of a combined coordinating staff at the national level and by making the senior U.S. military commanders also the senior military advisor within their respective areas of concern. In April he decided to raise with the GVN the question of a combined MACV-JGS staff. (He had already extended the tour in RVN of the general officer he had chosen to head this staff.) Such a staff might have permitted the development of agreed operational plans based upon agreed priorities. It would have been a possible intermediate step toward unity of effort. But the GVN (represented by Generals Thieu and "Little" Minh) resisted any suggestion for an integrating mechanism of this kind. The proposal was quietly dropped.

On the U.S. side, where his suggestions had the force of orders, General West-moreland took one step to integrate the U.S. combat and advisory functions. The Commanding General, III Marine Amphibious Force, the senior U.S. officer in the area, was designated on 7 August as the Senior Advisor to the ARVN I CTZ Commander. The former U.S. Senior Advisor became the Deputy Senior Advisor under CG, III MAF, although no further integration of the advisory structure into the U.S. chain of command was attempted. This pattern was soon extended to the other two Corps areas where major U.S. units were operating. The latter changes were made at the insistence of the ARVN Corps Commanders who felt that they would suffer a loss of prestige if they were "advised" by anyone other than the senior U.S. officer in the zone. Thus, on 21 October, the commander of Hq, Field Force, Vietnam (FFORCEV), with operational control of all U.S. units in II Corps, was also named II Corps Senior Advisor. On 1 December, CG, 1st Infantry Division was named III Corps Senior Advisor, following the pattern already established. No such arrangement was made, however, in IV Corps since the U.S. had no major units deployed there. Later, when U.S. force deployments had led to the establishment of another FFORCEV headquarters, each ARVN Corps Commander was advised by a U.S. Lieutenant General with equivalent U.S. responsibilities and a U.S. general officer was appointed Senior Advisor in the Delta area, which had no U.S. combat maneuver units.

7.　*Leverage: The Hidden Issue*

It is relevant to ask why COMUSMACV (backed up without exception by the Ambassador and CINCPAC) uniformly opposed integrative measures designed to provide that which was and is almost an article of faith in the military profession—unity of command. U.S. troops in both World Wars and in Korea had fought under at least nominal command unity. There had been reservations for national integrity, to be sure, but the principle of unified command was both established and generally accepted. Why then did the U.S. military commander in Vietnam recommend against its adoption?

The answer to this question is not to be found by an examination of military factors. The issue, rather, was a political one, as CINCPAC's message quoted above makes clear. The U.S. military leaders feared the exacerbations of US–SVN differences which they thought would accompany an overt Americanization of the war. They wished to increase U.S. influence in the conduct of the war but only as a result of persuasion and example. They tended to eschew the use of leverage. A unified command arrangement would have provided—assuming that a U.S. officer would have been the overall commander—an open and obvious means by which to exercise leverage. The U.S. leaders in Saigon rejected its adoption for this reason.

8. *Withdrawing from Overt Influence*

The rejection of a unified military command is only one example of the tendency in 1965 to renounce leverage oriented mechanisms at the very time that the U.S. was committing major land forces to the war. It was as though the U.S. increased its determination to avoid arrangements which smacked of direct, open leverage at the same time that the inadequacy of earlier, indirect measures was made obvious by the deployment to South Vietnam of U.S. ground combat forces.

This may, in fact, be what happened. Some sporadic earlier attempts at leverage had not borne the desired fruit. Ambassador Taylor had had a disastrous experience in trying to use the U.S. decision to commence bombing North Vietnam as a lever to get GVN reform in December 1964. The net outcome was a violent reaction by General Khanh, who very nearly had Taylor thrown out of the country as *personna non grata*. In the end, it was Khanh who went, but the political turmoil that this produced in the first months of 1965, when the course of the war was taking a dramatic turn against the GVN, convinced Taylor that such attempts should not be made again at the national level.

Concurrently, one of the most direct U.S. tools for influencing policy implementation at lower levels, the joint sign-off for release of piaster funds for pacification, was also being abandoned. The decision was made in December 1964 by the USOM Director, Mr. Killen. Early in 1965, AID stopped buying piasters for the U.S.-controlled sector funds and, in June, agreement was reached with the GVN for province chiefs to begin requisitioning and releasing AID commodities on their own authority. Thus, the "troika sign-off" came to an end. While elaborate arrangements were made for getting reports of U.S. advisor concurrence or non concurrence, the practical effect was to remove the advisor's leverage and restrict his influence. In October, USOM began to have second thoughts on the wisdom of abandoning control of its resources in the field and proposed a restoration of the "troika sign-off." The Mission Council endorsed the plan and had already launched discussions with the GVN when the State Department objected to the idea, insisting that it would undermine our efforts to make the Vietnamese more independent and effective. There the matter died.

In a somewhat related effort to overcome the delays in the Vietnamese pacification system, MACV acceded to its advisors' recommendations and, on 1 October, created a separate contingency fund of 50,000 piasters for each subsector (district) advisor to be used for urgent projects. Sector advisors were also given access to special funds. The program was highly successful and toward the end of the year consideration was given to permanent establishment of such revolving funds. The plan was abandoned, however, after the four-month trial period due to the strong opposition of the GVN Minister for RD, General Thang, who contended that such funds were undermining the legitimate efforts of his organization to meet urgent province needs; it would encourage Vietnamese dependence on the U.S.

But USOM did use successfully a form of direct, selective leverage in the late summer of 1965. The Province Chief of Binh Tuy Province, Lt Colonel Chi, was accused of misusing some $250,000 in AID funds. When USOM pressure on the GVN for his removal produced no results, aid to the province was suspended on 23 September, and USOM field personnel were withdrawn. In spite of Chi's friendship with the Defense Minister and Deputy Premier, General Co, Premier Ky removed him six weeks later. Aid to the province then resumed, but Ambassador Lodge made it clear to the Mission Council that he disapproved of the action and did not want it repeated (particularly the press coverage).

As already indicated, both Ambassadors Taylor (after his near-disastrous experience in December 1964) and Lodge preferred not to force the GVN or attempt to use high-level pressure to reach solutions we felt necessary. The fragility of the political arrangements in Saigon at any point in time seemed to dictate against any U.S. action that might precipitate coups or disruption from elements even less disposed to be cooperative than the current group, whoever they might be. In this view, the successive Ambassadors were strongly supported by the State Department. Thus, while we resented the Ky coup in June, we did nothing to exacerbate our delicate relations with Ky. In July, during Secretary McNamara's visit, the GVN requested a devaluation of the piaster and a hefty increase in aid. Rather than use the request as an opportunity to press the GVN for action on matters of U.S. concern, Ambassador Taylor preferred to restrict our counter-demands in the interest of quick agreement:

> We would avoid giving the impression of asking for new agreements or imposing conditions for our increase AID. . . . We do not want to raise conditions in terms likely to be rejected or to require prolonged debate.

Consequently, agreement was reached between the two governments on 28 July, providing only for "joint discussions to precede policy decisions . . . for control of inflation," and scarcely mentioning GVN obligations.

9. *McNamara's Minority Position on Leverage*

The only consistent supporter of increasing and exercising U.S. leverage with the GVN during 1965 was Secretary McNamara. As previously noted, he was one of the principal proponents of the joint command idea and a supporter of the encadrement proposals. In April, the Defense Department had launched an ill-fated effort to have U.S. Army civil affairs officers introduced in the provinces to assure competent, corruption-free civil administration in the combat zones. Ambassador Taylor's stout opposition had killed the proposal, but the Secretary continued to push for stronger U.S. action with the GVN. After his July visit to Saigon he sent a memorandum to the President urging the U.S. to lay down terms for its continuing assistance before the introduction of more U.S. forces. He suggested that we exercise leverage through our control of rice policy and gain a "veto on major GVN commanders, statements about invading NVN, and so on."

Again in November, McNamara recorded his impatience with the GVN and his belief that we should give a larger and more active role to our advisors at the province and district level. But the overall U.S. approach to the GVN in 1965 was dominated by our felt need for any kind of governmental stability which would provide a base from which to conduct the war. Proposals for taking a tough line were widely regarded as rugs that if pulled out from under the GVN would bring it crashing down, rather than as levers that might bring effective change.

10. *U.S. Proposals for GVN Execution: an Example*

With leverage-oriented arrangements effectively ruled out, U.S. advisors in South Vietnam were left with the alternatives of advising their counterparts only on *how* best to conduct a decided course or of expanding their advice to embrace *what* ought to be undertaken. The tendency was to follow the latter course, to urge upon GVN plans and programs American in concept and design for execution by the South Vietnamese. The Chieu Hoi ("Open Arms" for VC who return voluntarily to GVN control) program was one example of this tendency. The Hop Tac ("cooperation," in Vietnamese) program, to clear and hold the immediate area around Saigon, is another. Hop Tac's significance with respect to U.S. advisory activities resides in the fact that it was the most concerted attempt to apply the "oil blot" concept to rural pacification since the demise of the Strategic Hamlet Program. Its failure can be attributed in large measure to GVN lack of interest in and support for what was widely regarded as an "American" program.

The idea of a special combined US/GVN effort to secure the critical area ringing Saigon was first advanced by Ambassador Lodge in July 1964, at the Honolulu Conference. His concern with the problem went back to late 1963 when the re-appraisals of the war following Diem's overthrow revealed a dangerous deterioration in the III Corps area. A special USOM report on Long An Province had particularly troubled the Ambassador. In July 1964, as he was returning from his first tour in Vietnam, he proposed a special effort in eight provinces (Tay Ninh, Binh Duong, Hau Nghia, Long An, Dinh Tuong, Go Cong, Vinh Long, and Quang Ngia), all but one of which was near Saigon. The proposal was picked up by Ambassador Taylor and the program set in motion during the summer of 1964. The initial objective was to stabilize the situation around Saigon and protect the capital, then extend the zone of security in an ever widening ring around the city. MACV appointed Colonel Jasper J. Wilson to head the effort and by September 1964 a plan had been produced and the Vietnamese reluctantly induced to set up a special council to coordinate the multiple commands operating in the area. The plan created four roughly concentric zones around the capital, each to be successively cleared and secured, working from the "inside of the doughnut out." Conceptually, three phases were involved in each zone: first, search and destroy missions to eliminate main force units; then a clearing phase using primarily squad and platoon size forces in patrols and ambushes; and finally, the securing phase in which ARVN turned over responsibilities for security in a zone to RF/PF and national police and in which heavy emphasis was to be laid on positive rural economic and social development efforts.

Hop Tac was launched on 12 September 1964, with a sweep through Gia Dinh Province to the west and southwest of Saigon by the ARVN 51st Regiment. The mission was aborted the following day, however, by withdrawal of the forces to participate in a coup. Nevertheless, organizational efforts continued and more ARVN forces were concentrated in the Hop Tac area. A special survey of the area by USOM, USIS, and MACV in October revealed that little real progress was being made. In spite of the lack of any visible evidence of genuine momentum, the Ambassador and MACV continued to be encouraged by the modest statistical progress of Hop Tac at a time when nearly every other activity in the country looked blacker and blacker. The 1964 MACV Command

History reflects the official view: "At the end of 1964, Hop Tac was one of the few pacification areas that showed some success and greater promise."

Whether in response to Hop Tac or not, the VC substantially increased their forces in the Hop Tac area in the first six months of 1965. MACV estimated the growth at 65 percent and also noted that the new troops were frequently equipped with Chinese weapons. This growth in enemy strength in turn prompted some redeployment of RVNAF to strengthen capabilities in the Capital Military Region. In February, 1965, just at the time the U.S. was initiating the sustained bombing of North Vietnam and beginning the first Marine combat deployments in the South, COMUSMACV asked the I and IV Corps senior advisors to review current programs and to develop Hop Tac-like plans for their respective areas as a basis for discussion with their counterparts. General Westmoreland hoped to concentrate the available resources of each Corps into its most critical areas at a time when VC activity and successes were continually mounting and enemy control of the country increasing dangerously. Again, the operative concept was to be the oil blot. By April General Westmoreland had convinced Minister of the Armed Forces Minh to ask each of the ARVN Corps Commanders (except III Corps, in whose area Hop Tac was being conducted) to draw up similar plans for their own areas of responsibility.

The U.S. effort was clearly aimed at spurring the practical application of the "oil blot" analogy. The effects, however, were to demonstrate how difficult it was to translate simple counterinsurgent theory into practice, how convoluted and personal were the ARVN lines of influence, and how frustrating it was under these circumstances to exercise influence by persuasion.

In May, the Prime Minister proposed organizational changes in Hop Tac to return much of it to the operational control of the III Corps commander. These changes were rejected by COMUSMACV, but he did agree that the III Corps commander might be named chairman of the Hop Tac Council. In June, before anything could be done on this proposal, a coup with General Ky at its head returned the military to power. By the summer of 1965, Hop Tac was being completely overshadowed by the build-up of U.S. forces.

In September, Lodge returned to Vietnam for his second stint as Ambassador. He immediately asked a U.S. Mission officer for a private assessment of the Hop Tac program. The report frankly described Hop Tac as a failure and stressed as reasons the unrealistic goals of the program, the irrelevance of the concentric circle concept to actual areas of GVN and VC strength, the fact that it was an American plan never really given first priority by the Vietnamese, the area's political vulnerability to fallout from Saigon political changes, and General Ky's lack of support for it. The report recommended letting Hop Tac slowly die. On September 15, the Mission Council deliberated inconclusively on the fate of the program:

> General Westmoreland said that while Hop Tac could be said only to have been about 50% successful, it had undoubtedly averted a VC siege of Saigon. Ambassador Lodge then briefly reviewed the original reasons for the emphasis placed on the area surrounding Saigon and said that they were still valid, primarily because of the heavy density of population. He noted, however, lack of a clear commitment to Hop Tac on the part of the GVN, possibly due to the fact that the Vietnamese consider the program an American scheme. The view was also expressed that the trouble may also lie in US/GVN differences over some fundamental concepts in Hop Tac.

By the end of 1965, the proposal for Hop Tac programs in I, II, and IV Corps had refined itself into the scheme for National Priority Areas that became the focus of attention in 1966. Hop Tac itself, in the Saigon vicinity, continued on into 1966 to be finally phased out at the end of the year and replaced by the III Corps R/D Council and a U.S. military effort to protect the capital known as Operation FAIRFAX.

As a test case for the ever popular oil blot theory of pacification, Hop Tac left much to be desired. It did, however, point up some of the difficulties to be encountered in any attempt to implement this appealingly simple—and perhaps simplistic—concept. The oil blot theory, like all abstract analogies, emphasizes the similarity between phenomena and ignores the differences. The important similarity of the pacification problem to the oil blot is the expressed goal of progressively extending the secure zone until it embraces the entire country. Unlike a blank piece of paper, however, the environment in which pacification must take place is neither neutral nor passive; and unlike the oil blot, the pacification forces are not impervious. Moreover, implicit in the theory is the notion that the secure area, like the oil blot, will expand in all directions simultaneously, at roughly the same speed, and that expansion is irreversible and irrevocable. Further, the analogy fails to take into account unique problems of terrain or variances in government and insurgent strength in different areas. One need not belabor the point; the concept is fine as a theory, but not as a program design. In fairness, it must be said that the idea does focus the need for concentration of resources in priority areas. All this notwithstanding, III Corps was less than the optimum place to test such a program. It contains several longtime Viet Cong strongholds and base areas and is extraordinarily sensitive to political changes in Saigon (28 of 31 district chiefs were replaced during the lifetime of Hop Tac).

The most important reason for the failure of Hop Tac, however, was the lack of South Vietnamese support for it. From its inception to its demise, it was an American idea, plan, and program. While the GVN adopted it, established a high-level council to supervise it, and committed some troops and other resources to it, this was seen as a way of appeasing the Americans. The South Vietnamese never accorded Hop Tac a high priority in their own thinking. Moreover, its low status was further emphasized by the massive U.S. force build-up. As this U.S. build-up became relatively routinized, however, the issue of pacification reasserted itself. When it did so, the primary U.S. concern came to focus on the issue of how best to organize the military, paramilitary, and civilian advisory efforts. Since even the civilian advisors in the field were military personnel on loan in many instances, the account of the military advisory build-up decisions became essentially an account of organizing advice for pacification.

D. ORGANIZATION AS THE KEY TO EFFECTIVENESS IN PACIFICATION (1966–1967)

1. The Basis for Organizational Preoccupation

Several factors contributed to the persistent U.S. preoccupation in 1966 and 1967 with reorganizing the advisory effort in order better to support pacification activities. First, it had been an article of faith for several years within U.S. policymaking circles that only by winning the "other war" of pacification could the U.S. hope to realize its objectives in South Vietnam. Secondly, the pacification struggle was still regarded essentially as a task to be performed by the GVN—as the "main force war" no longer was after the introduction of major U.S. combat forces. Reinforcing this belief was a third factor, the widely held conviction that U.S. forces could best concentrate on the main force war while RVNAF focused on pacification.

Such a U.S.–RVNAF division of effort, it was reasoned, would permit U.S. forces to take advantage of their greater tactical mobility and fire support without endangering civilian life and property, employ RVNAF in a manner calculated to minimize the adverse effects of its persistent inability to generate an offensive-minded *esprit,* and avoid the cultural acclimitization and language difficulties which would face U.S. forces in the pacification role. It seemed, in short, that RVNAF concentration on pacification and U.S. concentration on the main force enemy would constitute the optimal use of available resources.

This division of effort meant that most U.S. military advisors would be directly involved in pacification—at least periodically if not continuously. Advisors to regular ARVN units could expect to spend a considerable portion of their time securing pacification programs. Those advisors whose counterparts had political and administrative responsibilities (e.g., province and district advisors) and paramilitary advisors (RF and PF) could expect pacification to be their major concern.

But while the majority of U.S. military advisors would be engaged in pacification activities they would not be the only U.S. advisory personnel whose responsibilities focused on pacification programs. Advisors from USOM, CAS, and USIS had overlapping and in some instances competing responsibilities. Thus it was logical for the U.S. to attempt to devise an organizational framework which would serve to coordinate adequately the activities of the large and diverse body of advisors and which would be capable to integrate their overlapping functions.

2.   *Unresolved Issues*

At the beginning of 1966, three important issues concerning the pacification effort were unresolved. Each of these issues was tentatively resolved during late 1966 or in 1967—in the sense that decisions were made rather than that these decisions were final. The remainder of 1967 and early 1968 (until the Tet offensive) constituted a period of consolidation and refinement based on limited experimentation. The shock caused by the Tet offensive then brought to the fore new questions of RVNAF effectiveness and of U.S.–RVNAF roles and missions.

The first of the unresolved issues in 1966 was that of which U.S. agency or group should take the lead in coordinating pacification programs. The role which RVNAF should assume in support of pacification was the second unresolved issue. Finally, the extent to which the U.S. should be willing to exert leverage in order to influence pacification activities was also unresolved at the beginning of 1966.

The following account of the decisions addressed to these three issues may seem to suggest that a master list of problems was somehow approached as part of an orderly, comprehensive, logical process. This is not, of course, the way it happened. The policy process was confusing and the policymakers were occasionally confused. Decisions were made in the reflection of both U.S. and South Vietnamese domestic pressures and in the shadow of an on-going war. They were affected by personalities on all sides and involved no small amount of bureaucratic in-fighting. The account that follows attempts to reorder and to explain this evolution, not to recreate it.

3. *Who Shall Lead?*

The "reemphasis on pacification," as another study in this series aptly names it, may conveniently be dated from the Honolulu Conference of February 1966. With the build-up of U.S. combat forces proceeding rapidly and with expectations high that 1966 would see the U.S. take the offensive, policy attention returned to address the "other war" in which the object was to provide rural security followed by steps to improve living levels and establish a link between the GVN and its populace. President Johnson made it clear in his informal remarks to the conferees at Honolulu that he wanted concrete results to follow the splendid phrases of the U.S.–GVN communique:

> Preserve this communique, because it is one we don't want to forget. It will be a kind of bible that we are going to follow. When we come back here 90 days from now, or six months from now, we are going to start out to put into effect the announcements that the President, the Chief of State and the Prime Minister made. . . . You men who are responsible for these departments, you ministers and the staffs associated with them in both governments, bear in mind we are going to give you an examination and the "finals" will be on just what you have done.
> . . . How have you built democracy in the rural areas? How much of it have you built, when and where? Give us dates, times, numbers.
> . . . Larger outputs, more efficient production to improve credit, handicraft, light industry, rural electrification—are those just phrases, high-sounding words, or have you "coonskins on the wall?"

All parties regarded it as necessary for some mechanism to coordinate the U.S. advisory activities which would help the Vietnamese to turn promises into solid accomplishments. But they did not agree on how broad should be the unit of the coordinator. Was he, or his office, to be *primus inter pares* or a single manager? Did effective coordination require policy primacy or operational supervision—or both? Above all, the participants did not agree on which individual or agency should exercise whatever supra-departmental authority was needed.

Ambassador Lodge, who had consistently stressed the centrality of the "other war," began by assigning responsibility for all civil support for Revolutionary Development (read "pacification") to his deputy, Ambassador Porter. The latter described his concept of his duties in traditionalist Foreign Service Officer terms:

> Ambassador Porter described briefly his new responsibilities as he sees them in the pacification/rural development area. He pointed out that the basic idea is to place total responsibility on one senior individual to pull together all of the civil aspects of revolutionary development. *He sees this primarily as a coordinating effort and does not intend to get into the middle of individual agency activities and responsibilities.* As he and his staff perceive areas which require attention and action by a responsible agency, he will call this to the attention of that agency for the purpose of emphasis; he intends to suggest rather than to criticize.

Porter's "coordination by suggestion" approach was not only an example of extremely limited effective authority, it was also restricted explicitly to the civil side of support for pacification. Whether the coordinator-in-chief emerged as a persuader or a director it was clear that his charge had to embrace both military and civil advisors. (In this respect "civil" is more accurate than "civilian", for a sizeable number of the civil advisory duties had devolved upon active duty military officers who were "loaned" to other agencies for this purpose.)

It is not surprising that MACV viewed itself as preeminent in this area. It was, as General Westmoreland rightly claimed, the only U.S. organization advising the GVN at all levels and—in one way or another—in all functions. It was to MACV that General Thang, the Minister of Rural Construction (read "pacification") looked for advice and assistance. It is equally unsurprising that Ambassador Lodge was of a different persuasion, as he explained clearly in a memo setting forth his views to General Lansdale in December 1965:

> I consider the government of Vietnam's effort in this domain (apart from the military clearing phase) to be primarily civilian, economic, social and political in nature and in its aims. Consequently, on the American side, it is preferable that the two civilian agencies most directly concerned, i.e., USAID and CAS, be the operating support agencies upon whom you should rely for the implementation of the necessary programs as they develop. Other sections of the Mission, including MACV, JUSPAO . . . should consider themselves associated with . . . USAID and CAS, but not as agencies directly responsible for operations.
>
> The foregoing is intended to insure that the number of persons and agencies contacting the GVN and particularly the Ministry of Rural Construction, on the subject of pacification and development is reduced, and in fact is limited to yourself or your representative, plus the representatives of the two operating agencies, USAID and CAS.

Operational and coordinative responsibilities remained on this particular wicket throughout most of 1966 while Washington fumed over the slow pace of pacification. These months saw the development of sufficient frustration in Washington to permit the growth and final acceptance of the proposal that all U.S. advice for pacification be placed under MACV. An account of this development is treated more fully in another document in this series and will only be summarized here.

President Johnson's Washington coordinator for pacification, Robert W. Komer, set forth in August 1966 three alternative organizational approaches:

> *Alternative No. 1—Give [Deputy Ambassador] Porter operational control over all pacification activity. . . .*
> *Alternative No. 2—Retain the present separate civil and military command channels but strengthen the management structure of both MACV and the U.S. Mission. . . .*
> *Alternative No. 3—Assign responsibility for pacification, civil and military, to COMUSMACV.*

Mr. Komer's categorization was prescient. Ambassador Lodge's personal preference and the fact that most pacification advisors were military seemed to rule out the first course of action. The second alternative described essentially the organization followed under the Office of Civil Operations (OCO) from November 1966 until June 1967. By this late date the U.S. decided to follow the third of Komer's alternatives.

The first of these reorganizations, that which created OCO, was quite literally forced upon Ambassador Lodge. Particularly in view of the fact that OCO was to be given only a 90–120 day trial to produce identifiable results, he was not eager to undergo the turmoil and lost motion of one major reorganization only as a prelude to yet another reorganization. He wanted to retain as much non-military flavor to the pacification effort as possible—regarding it as complementary to military programs, yet separate from them. Military security activities were, in his view, essentially the negative precondition to pacification activities which were the positive acts leading the GVN to vitalize itself at the same time that it developed real ties to its own people.

4. *CORDS Replaces OCO*

Thus OCO entered the world foredoomed by the combination of too short a prescribed life span and the tendency of some of its unwilling partners to do more than support it tacitly while they maneuvered to get their blue chips into another basket. Secretary McNamara had recommended in October 1966 that MACV take responsibility for pacification. Undersecretary of State Katzenbach had marshalled a strong case against this step at least until embassy leadership of civil operations was given a chance. The upshot was that it was given half a chance—which may have been worse than none at all.

OCO did, however, accomplish the creation and selection of Regional Directors and OCO Province Representatives. One individual was made responsible for all civil operations in each Corps Tactical Zone (CTZ) and in each province. The U.S. military chain of command had already adapted itself to parallel the RVNAF organization, but below Corps level it was more complex. Each division within ARVN was advised by a senior advisor (a colonel) who was given supervisory authority over the military Sector (Province) Advisors within the Divisional Tactical Area (DTA) for which his division had responsibility. Thus, while civil lines of authority went directly from corps level (the region) to province, the military advisory chain added an additional link at division. Sector advisors under this arrangement found themselves working under a military officer whose advisory responsibilities were actually military whereas theirs were only partly (and sometimes only nominally) military.

OCO attempted to have the ARVN divisions removed from pacification responsibilities, but without success. When the Office of Civil Operations and Revolutionary Development Support (CORDS) was established under MACV in mid-1967 as the single manager for all pacification advisors, the issue could not be argued with the same force. For by the time COMUSMACV assumed responsibility for pacification (through a civilian deputy—Ambassador Komer), ARVN had also expanded its role in the pacification effort. The ARVN division, it could be argued, was as much a part of the pacification effort as were the programs supported by the U.S. civil agencies.

But although the argument for removing the Senior Division Advisor from the U.S. chain of command over provincial advisors lost theoretic weight with the creation of CORDS, the new civilian deputy to COMUSMACV secured General Westmoreland's approval to remove the division advisors from the pacification chain of command and to work to get ARVN to take parallel action. This step illustrates the extent to which civil influences were able to operate within this new section of MACV. CORDS was of such size that it became quasi-independent. One would have to carry an issue in dispute all the way to COMUSMACV before it moved outside of CORDS channels.

The comprehensiveness of this reorganization may be seen in the following MACV Directive, reproduced in its entirety, and especially in the schematic diagram laying out the new U.S. command structure for a Corps area:

MACV Dir 10–12

HEADQUARTERS
UNITED STATES MILITARY ASSISTANCE COMMAND,
VIETNAM
APO San Francisco 96222

DIRECTIVE   28 May 1967
NUMBER 10–12   (MACCORDS)

*ORGANIZATIONS AND FUNCTIONS FOR CIVIL OPERATIONS
AND REVOLUTIONARY DEVELOPMENT SUPPORT*

1. *PURPOSE.* To provide for the integration of Civil Operations and Revolutionary Development Support activities within MACV.

2. *GENERAL.*

a. To provide for single manager direction of all US civil/military Revolutionary Development activities in the Republic of Vietnam, responsibility has been assigned to COMUSMACV.

b. The position of Deputy for Civil Operations and Revolutionary Development Support to COMUSMACV is established and carries the personal rank of Ambassador. The Deputy for Civil Operations and Revolutionary Development Support to COMUSMACV assists COMUS-MACV in discharging his responsibilities in the field of military and civilian support to the GVN's Revolutionary Development Program. Specifically, he is charged by COMUSMACV with supervising the formulation and execution of all plans, policies and programs, military and civilian, which support the GVN's Revolutionary Development program and related programs.

c. All activities and functions of the former Office of Civil Operations (OCO) and the MACV Directorate for Revolutionary Development (RD) Support are combined in the office of the Assistant Chief of Staff for Civil Operations and Revolutionary Development Support (CORDS).

d. The Assistant Chief of Staff for Civil Operations and Revolutionary Development Support is assigned functions as follows:

(1) Advises COMUSMACV, MACV staff elements and all US civilian agencies on all aspects of U.S. civil/military support for the Government of Vietnam's RD Program.

(2) In conjunction with Government of Vietnam authorities, develops joint and combined plans, policies, concepts and programs concerning US civil/military support for Revolutionary Development.

(3) Supervises the execution of plans and programs for US civil/-military support of Revolutionary Development.

(4) Provides advice and assistance to the Government of Vietnam,

including the Ministry of Revolutionary Development, the Republic of Vietnam Armed Forces Joint General Staff and other GVN agencies on US civil/military support for Revolutionary Development including US advisory and logistical support.

(5) Develops requirements for military and civil assets (US and GVN) to support Revolutionary Development.

(6) Serves as the contact point with sponsoring agencies for RD programs. Maintains liaison with sponsoring agencies in representing their interests in civil non-RD programs and activities in the field. Maintains direct operational communications with field elements for these programs.

(7) Is responsible for program coordination with the various Mission civil agencies in the planning and implementation of non-RD activities as they impinge upon or affect RD-related activities.

(8) Provides MACV focal point for economic warfare to include population and resources control, and for civic action by US forces.

(9) Evaluates all civil/military RD activities including provision of security for RD by US/FWMA/GVN military forces and reports on progress, status and problems of RD Support.

(10) Acts on all RD Support policy matters pertaining to subordinate echelons.

(11) Directs advisory relationships with GVN on RD and RD-related matters.

3. *Implementation*

a. Integration and consolidation of OCO and RD Support activities will be accomplished at all levels: Headquarters MACV, region/CTZ, province and district.

b. Organization for CORDS will conform generally to the schematic organizational diagram attached at Annex A, allowing for differences in the situations in the various regions/CTZ's, provinces and districts.

c. Additionally, in developing detailed organizations and functions at each level, force commanders/senior advisors will be guided by the following principles:

(1) Region/CTZ.

(a) The OCO regional director will be designated the Deputy for Civil Operations and Revolutionary Development Support to the force commander/senior advisor. As such, he will be charged with supervising the formulation and execution of all military and civilian plans, policies and programs which support the GVN's RD program to include civic action performed by US units.

(b) For all matters relating to RVNAF military support for Revolutionary Development, the deputy senior advisor will operate under the supervision of the Deputy for CORDS.

(c) The Deputy OCO regional director will be designated the Assistant Deputy for Civil Operations and Revolutionary Development Support or the Assistant Chief of Staff, CORDS. In this capacity, he will head an integrated civil/military staff which parallels, as appropriate, the MACV CORDS organization. Further, he will direct headquarters-based RD-related and non-RD technical programs.

(d) Except for psychological operations and intelligence, those elements of the staffs of the force commander/senior advisor and deputy senior advisor engaged primarily in RD Support activities will be integrated into the staff of the Assistant Deputy for Civil Operations and Revolutionary Development Support or the Assistant Chief of Staff, CORDS. At a later date, after on-going studies are completed, further guidance may be issued if needed for the integration of civil and military intelligence and psychological warfare functions which represent special cases.

(2) Province.

(a) At province, an integrated provincial advisory team composed of the current OCO provincial team and MACV sector advisory team will be organized.

(b) The new provincial team will continue to carry out all functions currently performed at province. However, the province representative may organize, with the approval of the Deputy for Revolutionary Development Support at region/CTZ, his personnel and functions as he sees fit.

(c) A single team chief, designated the Senior Provincial Advisor, will be assigned to each province. The senior provincial advisor will be chosen by the Deputy for CORDS and the force commander/senior advisor, with the concurrence of the Deputy CORDS to COMUS-MACV, on the basis of security in the province, civil-military balance in the RD effort and qualifications and experience of the current OCO senior provincial advisor and MACV sector advisor. The individual not selected will serve as the other's deputy as well as being his principal advisor for civil operations or military support as the case may be.

(d) The province senior advisor will receive operational direction from and report through the Deputy for CORDS to the force commander/senior advisor. The military element of the provincial team will receive logistical and administrative support from the division advisory team.

(e) Where RVNAF units are attached to the province chief for direct support of RD, advisors to these units will come under the operational control of the senior province advisor.

(f) The senior province advisor will serve as the Vietnamese province chief's principal advisor. However, technical advice, military or civil, should continue to be given to the province chief or his representative by the most qualified member of the provincial team. In all cases, the senior province advisor must be aware of the advice given and will set the policies to which advice will conform.

(3) District.

(a) At district an integrated district advisory team composed of the current MACV sub-sector team and OCO district representative will be organized.

(b) The new district team will be responsible for civil/military advice to the GVN district organization and for the implementation of all US civil and military support programs at district.

(c) A single team chief, designated Senior District Advisor will be assigned to each district. The senior district advisor will be chosen by the senior province advisor with the concurrence of the Deputy CORDS to the force commander/senior advisor on the basis of security in the district, civil-military balance in the RD effort and qualifications and experience of the current OCO district representative and MACV sub-sector advisor. The individual not selected will serve as the other's deputy as well as being his principal advisor for civil operations or military support as the case may be.

(d) Where no OCO district representative is present, the MACV sub-sector team will become the district Civil Operations and Revolutionary Development staff and the sub-sector advisor will be designated senior district advisor.

(4) The III CTZ organization for Civil Operations and Revolutionary Development Support will conform generally to the schematic organizational diagram attached at Annex B.

(5) For the time being there will be no change in the present IV CTZ organization. Implementing instructions for the IV CTZ organization for Civil Operations and Revolutionary Development Support will be provided at a later date.

(6) Force commanders/senior advisors will revise their organizations and redraft their statements of functions to comply with the guidance set out in this directive. The revisions will be forwarded to this headquarters for approval by 15 Jun 67.

4. *Administrative and Logistics Support*

a. For the time being, there will be no change in administrative and logistics support. Civilian elements of the integrated organization will continue to be supported (funds, personnel, and other requirements) by their respective agencies, i.e., Embassy, AID, JUSPAO, USIA and OSA.

b. It is intended that a continuing effort be undertaken toward logistic and administrative economy through consolidation and cross-servicing of appropriate support activities.

5. *Reference.* State Department MSG 9 May 1967

[see following page]

---

5. *RVNAF's Role in Pacification*

It has already been noted that the U.S. gradually came to espouse a division of effort between U.S. forces and RVNAF in which the former would concentrate on defeating the main forces of the insurgents in the unpopulated areas while RVNAF concentrated on securing pacification operations in the populated areas.

General Westmoreland first informed Washington of his intention to follow this general division of effort in late August 1966. But his emphasis was one of degree, he made clear, rather than of mutually exclusive categories:

. . . Our strategy will be one of a general offensive with maximum practical support to area and population security in further support of Revolutionary Development.

The essential tasks of Revolutionary Development and nation building cannot be accomplished if enemy main forces can gain access to the population centers and destroy our efforts. US, Free World Forces, with their mobility and in coordination with RVNAF, must take the fight to the enemy by attacking his main forces and invading his base areas. Our ability to do this is improving steadily. Maximum emphasis will be given to the use of long range patrols and other means to find the enemy and locate his bases. Forces and bases thus discovered will be subjected to either

492

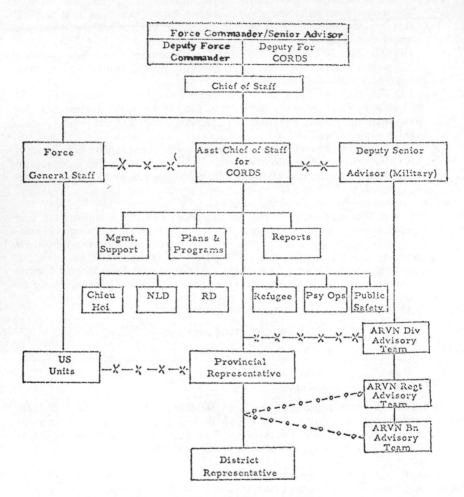

-x-x-x-   Coordination--Military and CORDS matters.
-o-o-o-   Operational Control when unit assigned on
           RD direct support mission.

ground attack or quick reaction B-52 and tactical air strikes. When feasible B-52 strikes will be followed by ground forces to search the area. Sustained ground combat operations will maintain pressure on the enemy.

The growing strength of US/Free World forces will provide the shield that will permit ARVN to shift its weight of effort to an extent not heretofore feasible to direct support of Revolutionary Development. Also, I visualize that a significant number of the US/Free World maneuver battalions will be committed to tactical areas of responsibility (TAOR) missions. These missions encompass base security and at the same time support Revolutionary Development by spreading security radially from the bases to protect more of the population. Saturation patrolling, civic action, and close association with ARVN, regional and popular forces to bolster their combat effectiveness are among the tasks of the ground force elements. At the same time ARVN troops will be available if required to reinforce offensive operations and to serve as reaction forces for outlying security posts and government centers under attack. Our strategy will include opening, constructing and using roads, as well as a start toward opening and reconstructing the national railroad. The priority effort of ARVN forces will be in direct support of the Revolutionary Development program; in many instances, the province chief will exercise operational control over these units. This fact notwithstanding the ARVN division structure must be maintained and it is essential that the division commander enthusiastically support Revolutionary Development. Our highly capable US Division Commanders, who are closely associated with corresponding ARVN commanders, are in a position to influence them to do what is required.

We intend to employ all forces to get the best results measured, among other things, in terms of population secured; territory cleared of enemy influence; VC/NVA bases eliminated; and enemy guerrillas, local forces, and main forces destroyed.

Barring unforeseen change in enemy strategy, I visualize that our strategy for South Vietnam will remain essentially the same throughout 1967.

General Westmoreland had already reached agreement with General Vien, Chief of the Joint General Staff (JGS), to reorient ARVN to pacification support. General Tillson, MACV J-3, had briefed the Mission Council in Saigon on the general plan:

In the 1967 campaign plan, we propose to assign ARVN the primary mission of providing direct support to RD and US/FW Forces the primary mission of destroying VC/NVA main forces and base areas. Agreement has been reached between General Westmoreland and General Vien that, in I, II, and III Corps areas, ARVN will devote at least 50% of its effort directly in support of the RD program. In IV Corps, where there are no US forces, it was agreed that ARVN might have to devote up to 75% of its effort to offensive operations. . . .

General Taylor, now serving as a personal advisor to President Johnson, immediately recognized the importance of this communication. A considered response should be sent to COMUSMACV, he advised the President, lest General Westmoreland regard silence as tacit consent for his proposed strategy. Taylor was enthusiastic about the expressed intent to reemphasize revolutionary development (pacification), seeing in it the best hope for bringing the war to a speedier conclusion. But he was uneasy about future charges that the U.S. had taken over the main war and was sustaining larger numbers of casualties than RVNAF. He was also concerned about involving any U.S. troops in pacification —suggesting that U.S. displacement of GVN leadership would, in the long run, be counterproductive.

Ambassador Lodge, on the other hand, waxed ecstatic over the involvement of U.S. units in pacification work. The crux of the problem, he argued, was security. To promote security U.S. units should be used in a kind of advisory function. They would energize ARVN by example:

> To meet this need we must make more U.S. troops available to help out in pacification operations as we move to concentrate ARVN effort in this work. U.S. forces would be the catalyst; would lead by example; and would work with the Vietnamese on the 'buddy' system. They would be the 10 percent of the total force of men under arms (90 percent of whom would be Vietnamese) which would get the whole thing moving faster.
>
> This has been done on a small scale already by elements of the U.S. Marines, 1st and 25th U.S. Infantry Divisions, and the Koreans. We think it can be made to work and the gains under such a program, while not flashy, would hopefully be solid. Everything depends on whether we can change ARVN habits. Experiments already made indicate that U.S. casualties would be few.

General Taylor's doubts about the benefits of involving U.S. troop units in pacification carried some weight in Washington. State was later to signal Saigon to go slow on U.S. participation:

> We understand General Westmoreland plans use of limited number of US forces in buddy system principle to guide and motivate RD/P. However, we have serious doubts about any further involvement US troops beyond that. . . . We fear this would tempt Vietnamese to leave this work more and more to us and we believe pacification, with its intimate contact with population, more appropriate for Vietnamese forces, who must after all as arm of GVN establish constructive relations with population. *Hence we believe there should be no thought of US taking substantial share of pacification. The urgent need is to begin effectively pressing ARVN.*

6. *The 1967 Combined Campaign Plan*

The upshot of these exchanges, which illustrate the wide acceptance in U.S. quarters of the proposed division of effort between U.S. forces and RVNAF, was that the MACV/JGS Combined Campaign Plan for 1967 (AB 142), published 7 November 1966, reflected "primary missions" for US/FWMAF and RVNAF and implied that few U.S. forces would be committed directly to the pacification effort. The exact number of such forces was not specified; it was left to COMUSMACV's discretion within the restraints already suggested by Washington. The JGS did agree, however, to keep 53 ARVN battalions in support of revolutionary development during 1967. In addition, 230-odd RF companies and over 800 RF platoons were to support the pacification program.

Conceptually, the regular ARVN units were to conduct the more difficult clearing operations and then turn over responsibility for the "securing phase" to the RF/PF outfits. All of this was outlined in considerable detail in the Combined Campaign Plan, with specific assignments to certain kinds of units for each phase of the pacification effort. The pertinent sections of AB 142 follow:

2. (C) ARVN REGULAR FORCES:

Phase   *ARVN Regular Forces*

Clearing   *Tasks in direct support of RD activities:*
     1. Conduct operations to clear VC/NVA main force units from provincial priority areas and other critical areas in accordance with established provincial RD plans.
     2. Conduct, in conjunction with provincial military forces and civil intelligence and police elements, operations to destroy VC guerrillas and infrastructure in specified hamlet or village areas in accordance with established provincial RD plans.

Securing   *Tasks in direct support of RD activities:*
     3. Conduct, in conjunction with provincial military forces and civil intelligence and police elements, operations to destroy VC guerrillas and infrastructure when provincial forces are inadequate for this task.
     4. Provide, in conjunction with provincial military forces and National Police, local area security and security for the population and GVN cadre elements when provincial forces are inadequate for this task.

Developing *Tasks in direct support of RD activities:*
     5. Provide, in conjunction with provincial military forces and National Police, local area security and security for the population and GVN cadre elements when provincial forces are inadequate for this task.

All Phases *Tasks in direct support of RD activities:*
     6. Conduct military PSYOP in support of RD activities with emphasis on operations in support of the Chieu Hoi program.
     7. Conduct, in coordination with sector commanders, military civic action to help win the support of the people for the government with emphasis on the proper behavior and discipline of troops.
     8. Assist sector commanders in the recruiting and training of RF/PF.

     Related tasks:
     9. Conduct offensive search and destroy operations against VC/NVA main forces to prevent their incursion into areas undergoing RD.
     10. Provide elements for reserve/reaction forces in support of military forces in areas undergoing RD.

3. (C) US/FWMAF.

Phase	US/FWMAF

Clearing   *Tasks in direct support of RD activities:*
   1. Conduct combined and unilateral operations to clear VC/
NVA main forces from provincial priority areas and other
critical areas in accordance with established provincial RD
plans.
   2. Conduct combined operations in conjunction with ARVN
and/or provincial military forces and police elements, operations to destroy VC guerrillas and infrastructure in specified
hamlet or village areas in accordance with established provincial RD plans.

All Phases   *Tasks in direct support of RD activities:*
   3. Conduct other combined battalion and smaller unit operations with RVNAF to accomplish specific RD tasks in areas
undergoing clearing, securing, and developing as appropriate.
   4. Conduct, in coordination with sector and subsector commanders, military civic action to help win the support of the
people for the government with emphasis to ensure that credit
is given to the GVN.
   5. Assist sector commanders in the training of RF/PF.

Related tasks:

   6. Conduct combined and unilateral offensive search and
destroy operations against VC/NVA main forces to prevent
their incursion into areas undergoing RD.

4. (C) PROVINCIAL FORCES:

   a. REGIONAL FORCES (RF).

Phase	*Regional Forces*

Clearing   1. Assist, within capabilities, ARVN regular forces and/or
US/FWMAF to clear VC/NVA main force units from provincial priority areas and other critical areas in accordance with
provincial RD plans.
   2. Assist, within capabilities, ARVN regular forces to destroy VC guerrillas and infrastructure.

Securing   3. Conduct, in conjunction with civil intelligence and police
elements, operations to destroy VC guerrillas and infrastructure.
   4. Provide local area security with priority to major communications complexes and other sensitive areas.
   5. Provide local security for the population and GVN civil
cadre elements in hamlet and village areas where PF are inadequate for this task.

Phase   *Regional Forces*

    6. Assist GVN cadre elements to perform economic and social development projects.

    7. Assist National Police in population and resources control and/or to maintain law and order and protect public safety.

    8. Assist in the recruiting and training of PF.

    9. Assist GVN civil cadre elements to organize and train people's self-defense forces.

Developing   10. Continue tasks 4 and 5 until relieved by National Police or other authorized provincial police forces which may be established.

    11. Provide elements for reserve/reaction forces to counter the return of VC/NVA main or irregular forces into areas undergoing developing.

    12. Continue task 6.

    13. Continue task 7 as necessary.

b. POPULAR FORCES (PF)

Phase   *Popular Forces*

Securing   1. Provide local security for the population and GVN civil cadre elements in hamlet and village areas.

    2. Assist RF to provide local area security.

    3. Assist GVN civil cadre elements to perform economic and social development projects.

    4. Assist National Police in population and resources control and/or to maintain law and order and protect public safety.

    5. Assist GVN civil cadre elements to organize and train people's self-defense forces.

Developing   6. Continue tasks 1 and 2 until relieved by National Police or other authorized provincial police forces which may be established.

    7. Continue task 3.

    8. Continue task 4 as necessary.

c. NATIONAL POLICE FORCES.

Phase   *National Police Forces*

Clearing   1. Develop and maintain informant nets and other intelligence nets.

    2. Supply intelligence to military forces.

    3. Participate with military forces in operations to destroy VC guerrillas and infrastructure.

    4. Assume custody of and interrogate VC suspects.

Phase	National Police Forces

Securing   5. Continue tasks 1 through 4 above.
6. Initiate population and resources control.
7. Maintain law and order and protect public safety.
8. Assist, within capabilities, military forces to provide local area security and security for the population and GVN cadre elements.

Developing   9. Maintain population and resources control.
10. Continue tasks 1, 2, 4 and 7 above.
11. Prevent the reorganization of the VC infrastructure.
12. Prevent and control riots and sabotage of public security.
13. Relieve military forces, when capable, and provide local area security and security for the population and GVN cadre elements.

7. *Leverage and Sovereignty*

The decision to effect a division of effort between RVNAF and US/FWMAF suggests how far U.S. policymakers were willing to go (perhaps "determined" would be more accurate) to carve out an area for independent GVN conduct of at least some major phase of the war. It suggests, too, their relative dissatisfaction with RVNAF improvement during the years in which the U.S. advisory effort had been directed toward such improvement. The question remained whether U.S. influence could be brought effectively to bear through example and persuasion or should be back-stopped by more direct measures—by the use of a range of negative measures gathered under the rubric of "leverage."

General Taylor's recommendations at the beginning of the U.S. advisory build-up in 1961, it will be remembered, emphasized a "limited partnership" in which U.S. advisors would actually work alongside their Vietnamese counterparts instead of merely "advising them at arm's length." By means of this closer working relationship in the field rather than just in various headquarters, Taylor had suggested, RVNAF effectiveness would become the product of mutually shared goals pursued through mutually shared experiences. Conscious adoption of an alternative course, the use of leverage, would have changed the relationship from one of nominal "partnership" to one of de facto U.S. leadership—bordering in some instances on U.S. command. This, in turn, would have been a very real infringement of Vietnamese sovereignty and an admission that the GVN could not manage adequately its own affairs. It would have undercut Vietnamese independence in both a legal sense and in terms of GVN competence.

When the Diem regime did not respond as it had been expected (or hoped) it would, and after Diem's government was overturned, the U.S. again refused consciously to adopt leverage procedures to compel improved performance. First with General Minh, then with General Khanh, the hope was that improved receptivity (as compared to the most recent past experience) on the part of the GVN would permit the carrot to work effectively without the stick. The period just ended in mid-1965 when U.S. troops were committed to South Vietnam marked another occasion to examine the putative advantages and disadvantages of the use of leverage.

Generally speaking, Washington policymakers (less so in the State Department), were prone to suggest the use of leverage in the abstract. The U.S. Mission and MACV tended to oppose such proposals. Field advisors were, as a group, most favorably disposed toward the use of leverage. Those whose dealings included establishing a close working relationship with GVN (to include RVNAF) officials found that the threat of leverage was a stumbling block to such a relationship. Some also found that the price of acceptance without leverage was the virtual absence of influence. Robert Shaplen summarized this phenomenon in a pessimistic 1965 evaluation of the U.S. advisory effort:

> The advisory program, while it had been a tribute to the politeness of both parties, had failed in its primary aim of persuading the Vietnamese officers to get their men out into the countryside and to *stay* there, if necessary, day and night, for weeks on end in order to beat the Communists at their own game. This view of the failure of American efforts at persuasion was privately expressed to me by most of the advisers I spoke with during my trip through the vital plateau area, and it was reinforced by what advisers from other battle areas told me. The consensus was that the system was inherently anomalous and unworkable in that it reflected the American predilection for trying to get a difficult and probably impossible job done in what a British friend of mine described as "your typical nice American way."

Having rejected proposals for a combined command (presumably under U.S. leadership) and for the encadrement of U.S. troops with RVNAF units, the U.S. was left—in late 1965—with the continuing and perplexing issue of whether or not to adopt the use of leverage in some comprehensive and planned manner. Earlier decisions had been to avoid the issue by side-stepping it. But the isolated occasions on which its use had been attempted did little to substantiate the argument that cries of neocolonialism were simply the price one had to pay for short run effectiveness. Indeed, some backfires tended to have the opposite effect. Ambassador Taylor, for instance, had had a disastrous experience in trying to use the U.S. decision to commence bombing North Vietnam as a lever to get GVN reform in December 1964. The net outcome was a violent reaction by General Khanh who very nearly had Taylor thrown out of the country as *personna non grata*. In the end, it was Khanh who went, but the political turmoil that this produced in the first months of 1965, when the course of the war was taking a dramatic turn against the GVN, convinced Taylor that such attempts should not be made again at the national level. It was at this time that the "troika sign-off" was abandoned because of claims that it stifled GVN development. Then in late 1965 USOM began to have second thoughts on the wisdom of abandoning control of its resources in the field and proposed a restoration of the troika sign-off. The Mission Council endorsed the plan and had already launched discussions with the GVN when the State Department objected to the idea, insisting that it would undermine U.S. efforts to make the Vietnamese more independent and effective. There the matter died.

In a related effort to overcome delays in the Vietnamese pacification program, MACV acceded to its advisors' recommendations and, in October, created a separate contingency fund of 50,000 piasters for each subsector advisor to be used for urgent projects. Sector advisors were also given access to special funds. The program was highly successful and toward the end of the year consideration was given to permanent establishment of such revolving funds. The plan was abandoned, however, after the four-month trial period due to the strong opposition of the GVN Minister for RD, General Thang, who contended such funds were undermining the legitimate efforts of his organization to meet urgent province needs. They would encourage, he said, Vietnamese dependence on the U.S.

But USOM did experiment successfully with one new form of direct, selective leverage in the late summer of 1965. The Province Chief of Binh Tuy Province, Lt Colonel Chi, was accused of misusing some $250,000 in AID funds. When USOM pressure on the GVN for his removal produced no results, aid to the province was suspended on September 23, and USOM field personnel were withdrawn. In spite of Chi's friendship with the Defense Minister and Deputy Premier (General Co) Premier Ky removed him six weeks later. Aid to the province then resumed, but Ambassador Lodge made it clear to the Mission Council that he disapproved of the action and did not want it repeated (particularly the press coverage).

As already indicated, both Ambassadors Taylor (after his experience in December 1964) and Lodge preferred not to force the GVN or attempt to use high-level pressure to reach solutions we felt necessary. The fragility of the political arrangements in Saigon at any point in time seemed to dictate against any U.S. action that might precipitate coups or disruption from elements even less disposed to be cooperative than the current group, whoever they might be. In this view, the successive Ambassadors were strongly supported by the State Department. The one consistent Washington advocate for an increased use of leverage was Secretary McNamara. But the Secretary of Defense's views did not prevail in this issue as they did in so many others. The overall U.S. approach to advice in South Vietnam continued to be dominated by the felt U.S. need to avoid undercutting governmental stability. U.S. support was figuratively regarded as a rug which if pulled out from under the GVN would cause it to fall, not as a lever whose use might spur increased effectiveness.

8.   *The Inconclusive Debate Over Leverage*

This persistent U.S. avoidance of the planned use of leverage was, until about 1966, paralleled by an equally persistent avoidance of any candid examination of the whole pandora's box which was conjured up by the mere mention of the subject. But during 1966, and continuing into 1967 and beyond, there were repeated attempts by lower echelons within the policymaking apparatus to promote an internal examination. Those who made such proposals were in favor of some kind of authorized, premeditated use of leverage, of course, else they would not have pushed for an examination of this hitherto avoided topic.

When operational groups—as distinct from policymakers who could defer when to implement—urged the adoption of leverage measures the recommendations tended to be summarily struck down. In 1966, for instance, an inquiry by the MACV staff into the poor performance records of the 5th and 25th ARVN Divisions—both stationed near Saigon—concluded that if other measures failed to improve these units, COMUSMACV should withdraw U.S. advisors and Military Assistance Program (MAP) support. General Westmoreland deleted from the study the recommendation for the withdrawal of MAP support. He further directed that sanctions against ARVN be avoided. The U.S. 1st and 25th Infantry Divisions were instructed to assist the two ARVN divisions and to increase their own participation in pacification operations in Binh

Duong and Hau Nghia Provinces. It was clear that the time was not ripe for action; there was no agreed basis upon which action might be taken.

But another Army staff effort, the PROVN Study referred to earlier, set out to rectify this omission. Commissioned in mid-1965 by Army Chief of Staff General Harold K. Johnson, the PROVN group was charged with "developing new sources of action to be taken in South Vietnam by the United States and its allies, which will, in conjunction with current actions, modified as necessary, lead in due time to successful accomplishment of U.S. aims and objectives." After eight months of intensive effort this select group of middle ranking officers produced a comprehensive argument calling for emphasis on the pacification effort. A radical decentralization of U.S. and GVN directive authority was held to be necessary for this purpose. And to make sure that national plans were turned into concrete actions at the operating level, PROVN called for the calculated use of leverage:

> The situation in South Vietnam has seriously deteriorated. 1966 may well be the last chance to ensure eventual success. "Victory" can only be achieved through bringing the individual Vietnamese, typically a rural peasant, to support willingly the GVN. The critical actions are those that occur at the village, district, and provincial levels. This is where the war must be fought; this is where that war and the object which lies beyond it must be won. The following are the most important specific actions required now:

> —Concentrate U.S. operations on the provincial level to include the delegation of command authority over U.S. operations to the Senior U.S. Representative at the provincial level.
> —Reaffirm Rural Construction as the foremost US/GVN combined effort to solidify and extend GVN influence.
> —Authorize more direct U.S. involvement in GVN affairs at those administrative levels adequate to ensure the accomplishment of critical programs.
> —Delegate to the U.S. Ambassador unequivocal authority as the sole manager of all U.S. activities, resources, and personnel in-country.
> —Direct the Ambassador to develop a single integrated plan for achieving U.S. objectives in SVN.

The PROVN Study proposed that leverage be employed at *all* levels within GVN to achieve U.S. objectives. Noting that past uses had been haphazard, it recommended the employment of a "continuum from subtle interpersonal persuasion to withdrawal of U.S. support" following U.S.–GVN agreement on specific programs. The South Vietnamese would, in short, be aware that leverage would be employed if they failed to live up to agreed obligations.

After an initial period during which no discussion of the PROVN Study was permitted outside the Army staff, the study finally received wide distribution. Secretary McNamara was briefed on it, as were the Joint Chiefs of Staff. MACV's comments were also solicited. The carefully worded reply from Saigon stated succinctly the case against the use of leverage.

> MACV is in complete agreement with PROVN position that immediate and substantially increased United States direct involvement in GVN ac-

tivities in form of constructive influence and manipulation is essential to achievement of U.S. objectives in Vietnam. PROVN emphasizes that "leverage must originate in terms of reference established by government agreement," and "leverage, in all its implications, must be understood by the Vietnamese if it is to become an effective tool." The direct involvement and leverage envisioned by PROVN could range from skillful diplomatic pressure to U.S. unilateral execution of critical programs. MACV considers that there is a great danger that the extent of involvement envisioned could become too great. A government sensitive to its image as champion of national sovereignty profoundly affected by the pressure of militant minorities, and unsure of its tenure and legitimacy will resent too great involvement by U.S. Excessive U.S. involvement may defeat objectives of U.S. policy: development of free, independent non-communist nation. PROVN properly recognizes that success can only be attained through support of Vietnamese people, with support coming from the grass roots up. Insensitive U.S. actions can easily defeat efforts to accomplish this. U.S. manipulations could easily become an American takeover justified by U.S. compulsion to "get the job done." Such tendencies must be resisted. It must be realized that there are substantial difficulties and dangers inherent in implementing this or any similar program.

9. *No Decision as a Decision*

Events remained stuck on this fundamental disagreement. The subject of leverage came, during 1967, to be *discussed* more fully, but there was no real authoritative *decision* to employ it or to reject its use under all circumstances. Thus, when CORDS completed its first major study of pacification programs (Project TAKEOFF) in June 1967, it included some candid discussion of the need for some kind of leverage. Entitled "U.S. Influence—The Necessity, Feasibility and Desirability of Asserting Greater Leverage," the analysis proceeded from problem to alternative courses of action:

A. *Necessity of Leverage.*

1. The most crucial problem in achieving the goals and objectives of the RD program is that the programs must be carried out by the Vietnamese. Present US influence on Vietnamese performance is dependent upon our ability to persuade, cajole, suggest, or plead. Political and practican considerations usually have argued against developing any systematic use of the various levers of power at our disposal. The potential reaction of the Vietnamese may become even greater now that they appear to be reasserting themselves and when the question of sovereignty is an increasingly sensitive one.

2. However, the factors of corruption, antique administrative financial procedures and regulations, and widespread lack of leadership probably can be overcome in the short run only if the US increases its influence on Vietnamese performance. The increasing magnitude of corruption and its damage to any program make the need for developing and applying a system of leverage which forces the Vietnamese to take U.S. views into account greater now than ever before. Even the best conceived and executed RD

program will result in failure in terms of gaining the allegiance of the people so long as such extensive corruption prevails.

The study argued that leverage was feasible either at the national level with the GVN leadership in the classic "oriental" style or on a more systematic basis to be applied through the control of resources at all levels down to province and district. The study concluded:

> d. *Courses of Action.* US influence over key decisions must be attained as quickly as possible. We recommend the "oriental" approach. However, should the other alternative of more open exercise of power be selected, the system would have to include US control of resources. As a tactical measure, such control could be associated initially with the introduction of additional resources. The introduction of greater US control and the procedures that would be necessary to ensure an adequate US voice in the decision-making process should be tied to the "New Team" and the new US organization for RD. For that reason, too long a delay would be unfortunate.

Whether or not Komer approved this recommendation, it did not figure in the presentations of pacification given to Secretary McNamara during his 7–8 July visit to Vietnam. The Saigon policymakers were simply not prepared to come down on one agreed line of conduct in this contentious area. This tendency was exhibited later in the summer of 1967 when a long study on leverage produced in Ambassador Komer's old White House staff office by two staff members, Dr. Hans Heymann and LTC Volney Warner, was forwarded from State to Saigon:

> In anticipating the US/GVN relationship in the post-election period, it is generally agreed that the US should find ways to exercise leverage with the Vietnamese government which are more commensurate in degree with the importance of the US effort to South Vietnam's survival and which reflect the climate of growing restiveness in the US. . . . In its impatience to get results and make progress, the US has increasingly resorted to unilateral programs and action with inadequate consultation with the Vietnamese. On the other hand, the indiscriminate and careless exercise of US leverage could undermine the self-respect of the Vietnamese government in its own eyes and in the eyes of the South Vietnamese people.
> To be effective, US leverage must be exercised in the context of a relationship of mutual respect and confidence, and in ways commensurate with the objective sought. It must also be backed by credible sanctions.

Might not the post-election period, State suggested, be a proper time to consider such a new emphasis on the use of leverage. Ambassador Komer, who had been ardent in his advocacy of leverage while working as a Presidential assistant, replied in tempered language which reflected the chastening effect of several months on the firing line in Saigon.

> All of the above forms of leverage, and yet others, could be useful at the proper time and in an appropriate way. But they must be applied with

discretion, and always in such manner as to keep the GVN foremost in the picture presented to its own people and the word at large. . . . The exercise of leverage in a personal manner and hidden from the public view is likely to be most effective, while of the more operational means establishment of combined organization under a JCRR-type concept, to include joint control of resources, would be most desirable. In sum, we're gradually applying more leverage in Pacification, but wish to do so in ways that least risk creating more trouble than constructive results.

What Komer really meant—as his opinions expressed in a time frame later than that embraced by the present inquiry would make clear—was the necessity to reserve the use of leverage for those few occasions in which all else had failed, in which copious records detailing the failure had been accumulated over time, and in which the proven offender could be severed from responsibility after his shortcomings were presented behind the scenes to his superiors. Thus, the GVN would serve as executioner, the U.S. as observer-recorder. Leverage would be a last resort rather than a continuing tool. The product of the intermittent debate on leverage was not so much a decision pro or con as it was a decision to resort to leverage when all else had failed. In this sense it dodged the difficult choices.

10. *Groping Toward Better Information*

One of the programs that came under Komer's jurisdiction after he took over CORDS was the controversial Hamlet Evaluation System (HES). Secretary McNamara had requested, during his October 1966 visit to Vietnam, the development of some ADP system for evaluating the status of rural security on an on-going basis—data which would make possible comparative judgments of progress over time. In November, he sent Mr. George Allen and Colonel Carter Clark to Saigon with a proposal. MACV revised their suggested system and recommended it to the Mission Council which endorsed it on 13 December. MACV described the new system to CINCPAC in January 1967:

> HES provides a fully automated procedure for evaluating hamlet Revolutionary Development progress and establishes a hamlet level data base. Data input for HES is provided by MACV subsector advisors and district representatives, where assigned, who evaluate all hamlets not under VC control. They record their assessments in terms of 18 entries on a hamlet evaluation worksheet utilizing six factors, each with three indicators. Also, eight problem areas are evaluated.

The system operated throughout the year as something of a barometer for the entire pacification effort. It also became one of the focal points of criticism of the excessive reliance on statistical measures of progress, a criticism favored by the press in particular. Nevertheless, it was the most systematic attempt to compare results over time ever used in the assessment of rural security in Vietnam. As such it is a useful indicator. The following tables give summary data from HES for 1967. The first table shows population distribution according to security and development factors. The second table depicts the distribution of hamlets according to different measures of security.

POPULATION DATA

TOTAL SCORE—COUNTRYWIDE THROUGH DECEMBER, 1967

Population in Thousands

	1967 March	June	September	December	Net Change Mar–Dec
Population Weighted Index	2.33	2.42	2.50	2.54	
Secure/Good					
A Hamlets	300.9	489.4	646.8	694.9	394.
B Hamlets	2861.9	3128.7	3489.7	3481.3	619.
C Hamlets	4221.8	4360.5	4044.2	4279.1	57.
Non-Hamlet	3210.1	3277.3	3135.1	3059.4	−150.
Total	10594.7 (63.3%)	11255.9 (65.6%)	11315.8 (66.5%)	11514.7 (67.0%)	920.
Contested/Poor					
D Hamlets	2235.7	1976.2	2087.2	2157.6	−78.
E Hamlets	480.0	402.3	337.2	318.6	−161.
Other Hamlets	.0	152.3	91.7	68.3	68.
Non-Hamlet	274.0	290.8	237.4	243.6	−10.
Total	2989.7 (17.9%)	2821.6 (16.4%)	2753.5 (16.2%)	2808.1 (16.3%)	−181.
VC Controlled					
VC Hamlets	2955.8	2923.2	2809.5	2748.4	−207.
Non-Hamlet	196.4	164.2	134.1	112.5	−83.
Total	3152.2 (18.8%)	3087.4 (18.0%)	2943.6 (17.3%)	2860.9 (16.7%)	−791.
Total Population	16736.6	17164.9	17012.0	17183.7	447.

HAMLET DATA

TOTAL SCORE—COUNTRYWIDE THROUGH DECEMBER, 1967

Number of Hamlets

	1967 March	June	September	December	Net Change Mar–Dec
Secure/Good					
A Hamlets	99	168	213	231	132
B Hamlets	1639	1776	1902	1809	170
C Hamlets	3138	3245	3137	3300	162
Total	4876	5189	5252	5340	466
Contested/Poor					
D Hamlets	2348	2156	2206	2230	− 118
E Hamlets	599	528	483	445	− 154
Other Hamlets	0	686	713	825	875
Total	2947	3370	3402	3500	553
VC Hamlets	4262	3978	3987	3882	− 380
Total Hamlets	12085	12537	12641	12722	637

In February 1968 an analysis of 1967 pacification-R/D results as revealed in the HES was published by OSD Systems Analysis.

> Hamlet Evaluation System (HES) reports for CY 1967 indicate that pacification progressed slowly during the first half of 1967, and lost ground in the second half. Most (60%) of the 1967 gain results from accounting type changes to the HES system, not from pacification progress; hamlet additions and deletions, and revised population estimates accounted for half of the January–June increase and all of the June–December increase. In the area that really counts—VC-D-E hamlets rising to A-B-C ratings—we actually suffered a net loss of 10,100 people between June and December 1967. The enemy's offensive appears to have killed the revolutionary development program, as currently conceived. Recent reports state that to a large extent, the VC now control the country-side.

Written in the pessimistic atmosphere of the 1968 post-Tet period this view may over-emphasize negative factors. Ambassador Komer wrote a stinging dissent that appeared in the next monthly issue of the Systems Analysis Southeast Asia Analysis Report. Statistical analysis aside, pacification clearly failed to make the significant strides that the President had hoped for in 1967. It certainly did not initiate any Revolutionary Development likely to transform the quality of life for the Vietnamese farmer or to alter fundamentally the course of the war.

Concurrently with attempts to improve information on the security programs, MACV exhibited increased interest in 1967 in improving RVNAF effectiveness. Early in the year it was decided to undertake an extensive, unit-by-unit effectiveness evaluation. Units judged to be superfluous or consistently below standard were to be cut off from U.S. support. Decisions on support withdrawal were to be made semi-annually as new evaluations were received. MACV explained to CINCPAC that the review would include:

> . . . all VNAF, VNN, VNMC, ARVN tactical and logistical units, and RF/PF units in the current projected FY 68 force structure. The methodology for the evaluation includes: identification of the credibility and feasibility of current plans of RVNAF officials to guarantee increased effectiveness; study of unit performance trends during the past six months; determination of availability of necessary plans to train personnel in the required skills; and evaluation of the degree of command interest at all levels for improvement of the ineffective or non-productive units. Considering these factors, units are categorized as improvement probable, doubtful, or unlikely. For those units categorized as improvement doubtful or unlikely, justification for continued military assistance will be required or action will be initiated to reduce the FY 68 Military Assistance Program.

The first review (completed in March) cut two marginal navy vessels from the list of U.S. supported units, but only warned JGS of the unacceptable effectiveness of two marginal ranger battalions and an armored cavalry squadron. The June review, while producing recommendations from U.S. advisors that aid be suspended in several cases, again resulted only in warnings and threats. There was no suspension of U.S. support.

11. *RVNAF Effectiveness*

Quantitative efforts to rate RVNAF effectiveness continued in the field, at MACV, and in Washington throughout the year with no clear agreement on what set of statistical indicators best portrayed RVNAF performance and potential. During 1966 MACV had relied on a minimum present for duty strength as a means of evaluating ARVN battalion effectiveness. This method permitted wide fluctuations and was unreliable. The 1967 statistics on RVNAF desertions revealed an improving ability of units to hold their men. MACV soon began to use this trend as an indicator of effectiveness. In May, for instance, COMUS-MACV noted with satisfaction the marked reduction of January and February 1967 desertions compared to desertions in the same period in 1966. The average improvement for this period was about 50 percent:

DESERTIONS/RATES (PER 1000 ASSIGNED)

	January	*February*
1966	9,251/16.0	14,110/24.3
1967	5,900/9.6	5,860/9.6

In the same message, MACV noted with satisfaction recent aggressive actions by the JGS to correct the unacceptably high incidence of desertions, including the singling out of three regiments for special warning on their excessive desertion rate. Year-end statistics compiled by OSD Systems Analysis indicate that the figures quoted by MACV in May erred on the optimistic side somewhat by undercounting RF desertions in both months by about 1,000. Nevertheless, the trend to which MACV was pointing was confirmed during the rest of the year. After rising slightly to 8,127 in March, RVNAF desertion rates leveled off at between about 6,000–7,000 per month for the remainder of 1967. Thus, 1967 produced only 80,912 desertions compared with 117,740 in 1966, an overall reduction of almost one-third. (It also should be noted in passing, that VC/NVA desertions reached a peak in March and thereafter fell off sharply.)

At the Pentagon, Systems Analysis sought measures of RVNAF effectiveness in a comparison between the performances of Vietnamese and American units in selected categories: VC/NVA KIA ratios, battalion days of operations, days of enemy contact, number of operations, weapons loss of ratios, etc. Summarizing the results of some of these statistical studies, Systems Analysis stated in September 1967:

> Per man, Vietnamese forces were about half as effective as U.S. forces in killing VC/NVA during the eleven months (Aug 66 through Jun 67) for which detailed data are available. Effectiveness differs widely among Vietnamese units of the same type and between units in differing parts of the country. Poor leadership is the key reason for inefficiency in most cases.

The MACV staff rebutted many of the premises on which the statistical comparisons had been based and again revealed the difficulty in developing meaningful statistical measures with respect to anything Vietnamese. Their most telling criticism of the Systems Analysis comparison of U.S. and Vietnamese units was the following:

> (a) It is generally accepted that US maneuver battalions have a combat effectiveness ratio of about 3:1 to RVNAF maneuver battalions due to their greater unit firepower and depth of combat support/combat service support forces; RVNAF also lacks the mobility assets available to US units.

(b) Approximately one-third of the RVNAF maneuver battalions are committed to direct support of Revolutionary Development, a mission which constrains the overall potential to find, fix, and fight the enemy forces. In this analysis an RVNAF unit that is 45 percent as effective as US units which have three times the RVNAF combat effectiveness would appear to be doing very well. In fact, anything over 33 percent would reflect superior performance.

But here again one can be misled. One reason that ARVN was given the RD support mission in the first place was its demonstrated inability to engage effectively and destroy the enemy main force. RD was regarded as a residual and semi-passive role more suited to ARVN capabilities. And so the statistical arguments raged, partisans marshalling whatever statistics they could to defend what in most cases were their own preconceived notions

All of this is not to imply that qualitative estimates, diagnoses, prescriptions, and prognosis were lacking in 1967. At the Guam Conference with the President, General Abrams' appointment as the new Deputy COMUSMACV had been announced along with the others already mentioned and his responsibility for overseeing the U.S. advisory effort with RVNAF reemphasized. Upon return to Saigon prior to his own departure Lodge sent a message to the President stressing the importance of RVNAF:

> MACV's success (which means the success of the United States and of all of us) will . . . willy-nilly, be judged not so much on the brilliant performance of the U.S. troops as on its success in getting ARVN, RF and PF quickly to function as a first-class counter terror, counter-guerrilla force.

Lodge concluded with a glowing endorsement of Abrams as the man to see that RVNAF did become an effective force. There is ample evidence that Abrams did work with great energy to do just that.

In mid-June, after Abrams' first quarterly review of RVNAF, Bunker included a report on actions to improve RVNAF in his weekly report to the President:

> A) Improving the leadership and enhancing the personnel effectiveness of the ARVN/RF/PF through such things as improvement in the awarding of commissions and promotions, selection procedures, training of officer candidates, the introduction of an effective personnel management and accounting system, tightening up on discipline, improvement in the treatment of veterans in order to clear the rolls of those incapable of further active duty and an expanded advisory effort to support properly the Revolutionary Development program;
>
> B) To improve motivation and morale through more equitable pay scales, improvement in rations, and revitalization of the dependent housing program;
>
> C) Improvement in the command structure and equipment of the Regional/Popular Forces and a revised motivation and indoctrination program to reflect the role of the PF soldier in Revolutionary Development;
>
> D) A comprehensive training effort to improve intelligence and reconnaissance operations and to improve the combat effectiveness of battalions;

training of ARVN/RF/PF for support of Revolutionary Development particularly in providing security and support to the civil population;

E) Experimentation with various forms of integrated US/RVNAF operations . . . [discussed already];

F) Institution of quarterly reviews at which time progress is measured against objectives, problems discovered and decisions taken. First of these reviews was held last month.

In May, General Abrams established a Program Review and Analysis System for RVNAF Progress. This was essentially an internal MACV effort to examine the problems facing RVNAF in order that MACV might structure its advisory assistance to make the most headway against these problems. The first published review, covering the January–June 1967 period, appeared in September. Like many similar efforts it was a long catalogue of RVNAF deficiencies by U.S. standards. The benefits of these reviews were supposed to be reaped as they were brought to bear during the quarterly RVNAF self-review called for in the Combined Campaign Plan. There is no available information as to how effectively this has worked in practice. This plethora of programs and activities through which we sought either to improve the effectiveness of RVNAF directly or to promote it indirectly by improving the lot and life of the soldier received a full-blown exposition during Secretary McNamara's trip to Saigon in July. With respect to improving RVNAF morale—in addition to the pay scale adjustments, improved rations, and provision of dependent housing—the U.S. has helped the South Vietnamese develop a miniature U.S. style Commissary/PX system.

The leadership problem received very detailed attention by MACV during the course of 1967. Prior to the Secretary's departure for Vietnam, Alain Enthoven, Assistant Secretary of Defense for Systems Analysis, sent McNamara a memo that flatly stated, "There are a number of reasons for the ineffectiveness of many of the RVNAF units, particularly ARVN combat battalions, but the primary one is the quantity and quality of the leadership." After itemizing the contributing factors to this deficiency, he recommended that the Secretary query MACV in detail on leadership problems during his visit. In the briefings for Secretary McNamara in July, fourteen different MACV/JGS actions or programs were cited as ways in which this problem was being addressed. These ranged from better officer career management to regular merit promotion procedures and the publication of leadership materials. One example of the lengths to which we have gone in efforts to remedy the leadership deficit in RVNAF is the replication in South Vietnam of the U.S. elite officer schooling system—a four-year Vietnamese Military Academy, enlarged Command and General Staff College, and, most recently, a National Defense College.

12.   *The Latest Expansion of Advisors*

COMUSMACV faced difficult choices in determining whether he wished to emphasize more U.S. advisors for RVNAF—or advisors for new functions— or to stress a build-up of the number of U.S. combat forces in-country. RVNAF strength had increased by 152% from 1960 to 1966, going up by over 100,000 in the 18 months preceding the beginning of 1967. The table below shows the growth and distribution of RVNAF over the 1965–1967 period. The slight decline in forces from January to April 1967, reflects efforts to weed out absentee personnel still being carried on padded unit rolls.

RVNAF STRENGTHS

	1 Jul 65	1 Jan 66	1 Jul 66	1 Jan 67	30 Apr 67
RVNAF					
ARMY	234,139	267,877	276,473	283,898	283,200
NAVY	9,037	14,559	16,380	17,349	16,000
MARINES	6,842	7,380	6,848	7,049	7,100
AIR FORCE	12,081	12,778	13,895	14,647	15,600
REGIONAL FORCES	107,652	132,221	141,447	149,844	142,018
POPULAR FORCE	149,029	136,398	137,689	150,096	142,491
Sub Total	518,780	571,213	592,732	622,883	606,405
PARA-MILITARY					
National Police	42,700	52,300	54,600	58,300	63,457
CIDG	21,700	28,400	30,400	34,700	31,477
Armed Cmbt Youth	39,000	39,600	22,800	20,000	19,930
Total	625,800	691,500	700,500	735,900	721,269

In March, two days before the Guam Conference was to meet, General Westmoreland sent an important cable to CINCPAC requesting an "optimum force" increase, above and beyond the approved Deployment Program 4, of 4-2/3 U.S. divisions (201,250 personnel spaces), or a "minimum essential force" of an additional 2-1/3 U.S. divisions (84,100 spaces). The optimum force would have raised total U.S. manpower in Vietnam to over 670,000 troops. This request was to kick off (after Guam, where it was not specifically addressed) another prolonged internal administration debate and review of forces in Vietnam which would eventually culminate in Secretary McNamara's July trip to Saigon and the subsequent decision to adopt deployment Program 5, raising total authorized strength to 525,000. COMUSMACV's orientation toward RVNAF's role in the war is clearly revealed in this message:

> Whereas deployment of additional US forces in FY 68 will obviate the requirement for a major expansion of the RVNAF, selective increases will be necessary to optimize combat effectiveness. Regular forces proposed for FY 68 total 328,322, an increase of 6,367 spaces over the FY 67 authorization. As US, Free World and RVNAF operations are expanded, additional areas will be made available for the conduct of Revolutionary Development operations. Based on experience gained thus far, an increase of 50,000 RF/PF spaces will be required to provide a planning figure of 350,000 spaces for this force. The increase will accommodate necessary support of Revolutionary Development and concomitantly, will be compatible with requirements incident to implementation of the constabulary concept.

Without going into detail on the debate and decision on Program 5, from the advisory standpoint the important development was COMUSMACV's view of RVNAF. In March, RVNAF had been regarded almost as a residual, but by September, when the ambitious U.S. force proposals had been rejected in favor of only a modest increase of about 45,000 COMUSMACV reasserted the importance of RVNAF and asked for a major increase in its authorized strength.

Slowly, then, the realization that there was a ceiling on the number of U.S. forces which could be deployed without calling up reserves turned everyone's attention once again to RVNAF.

The one significant increase proposed in the MACV message cited above was the increase of 50,000 in RF/PF. This was not to be immediately forthcoming. In May 1967, Secretary McNamara imposed a temporary ceiling on RVNAF at the level authorized for end FY 66 to prevent further inflation in South Vietnam and to arrest some of the balance of payments imbalance stemming from U.S. Vietnam spending. Subsequently, CINCPAC was authorized to make adjustments among the various components within that limit, thereby permitting augmentation of RF/PF at the expense of ARVN.

The question of additional U.S. troops had refined itself considerably by the time the Secretary went to Saigon in July. Of the two force increase proposals presented by MACV at that time, the first was merely a restatement of the old "minimum essential force" which would have brought total U.S. troops to 571,071 (2-1/3 division force equivalents); the second proposal was a much smaller request for an authorized strength of 535,390 (1-1/3 division force equivalents). Both of these proposals contained a request for 2,577 additional advisors—primarily to support the anticipated expansion of RF/PF and to flesh out the sector and sub-sector advisory teams supporting the pacification effort. The following table shows the breakdown of the 1967 advisory increases, including the request presented to McNamara in July and subsequently approved. The large RF/PF advisory element in this request included spaces for 824 RF Company Advisory Teams of two men each and 119 Company Training Teams of five men each. Before returning to Washington, the Secretary gave planning authorization for a U.S. augmentation not to exceed 525,000 spaces, but fulfilling Westmoreland's lower alternative by civilianizing an additional 10,000 military spaces. A month later, after approval by President Johnson, this new force level was promulgated as Program #5. The final detailed troop list for Program #5 submitted by the JCS on September 15 contained, in addition to the regular advisory spaces already mentioned, a 666-man Special Forces augmentation to perform advisor-like functions with their Vietnamese counterparts.

Even before the Program #5 troop list was completed by MACV and submitted by the JCS, however, Ambassador Komer was complaining that the CORDS advisory element actual strength was seriously below its authorization and that bureaucratic delays had forestalled even the deployment of the 100 priority advisors requested in July. The following day, OSD Systems Analysis advised Secretary McNamara that the shortfall in the actual strength of the overall advisory complement was a longstanding problem. In March, the advisory program had been under-strength 600 men while MACV headquarters exceeded its authorization by 473. In response to Systems Analysis prodding this discrepancy had been partially rectified, but as late as July the advisory staff was still short 237 while MACV had an overage of 130. Systems Analysis further advised the Secretary that while total strength authorizations had been made, MACV's delay in submitting detailed lists of grades and specialties of desired personnel had, in turn, engendered delays at this end in filling the billets. Moreover, the requirement that advisors receive preliminary Stateside background and language training further delayed the actual deployments. Only priority requests could be filled very rapidly, and these necessarily could only constitute a small percentage of the total.

In order to study the problems presented by the anticipated expansion of RF/PF and to plan for the significant expansion of the U.S. advisory effort to

C8311 SUPPLEMENTAL DATA SHEET A
SUBJECT: MACV Recognized Advisory Requirements

22 Oct 67

| | *Auth* | *Required Add-ons* | | | |
STRUCTURE ELEMENT	*Jan 67*	*Feb 67*	*Apr 67*	*Jun 67*	*Total*
Joint General Staff	265	23		8	296
Other National Level	740	30	52	6	828
Naval Advisory Group	517				517
Air Force Advisory Group	493				493
ARVN and RF/PF					
Corps Hq and Support (4)	1,147	29			1,176
Capital Military District	59	7		1	67
Divisions (10) & 24th Special Zone and Support	266	84		11	861
Regiments (31 Infantry)	98	12			110
Battalions (120 Infantry)	613	− 143		120	590
Ranger Command (5 Gps/20 Bn)	130	− 12			118
Regional Force Battalions (12)	31	21			52
Popular Force Training Centers	122	− 13			109
Armored Cavalry Squadrons (10)	107				107
Sector Advisor Teams (Province)	853	56	341	92	1,342
Subsector Advisor Teams (District)	969	137	294	6	1,406
Regional Force Companies				2,243	2,243
Regional Force Camps (Converted from CIDG)		20	12	90	122
Totals	6,910	251	699	2,577	10,437

these forces, MACV convened a conference on RF/PF matters on 26 October for all interested elements of MACV and USARV. The conference recommended a complete reorientation of the advisory concept for RF/PF. Rather than assigning teams to RF companies and PF platoons on a permanent basis, the conferees recommended the establishment of 354 seven-man Mobile Advisory Teams (MATs) to be used on a rotating basis under the direction of the Province Advisor to whom they would be assigned. Further, the conference recommended the deployment of an Engineer Advisor to each province, an S-1 advisor to all provinces without one, increasing the Administrative and Direct Support Logistics (ADSL) companies from three to seven, and creating 7 seven-man Mobile Advisory Logistics Teams (MALTs) to support the RF/PF. Altogether, the conference produced some fifty-odd recommendations from which a 30-point package was forwarded to COMUSMACV.

On 15 December, General Westmoreland gave his approval to the new system which was to be phased in during 1968, the first half by the end of March and the rest by the end of that year. By the end of December 1967, MACV was recommending a further increase of 366 advisors for the FY 1969 program, primarily for district level intelligence slots.

Meanwhile, on September 28, the JCS had forwarded with their endorsement the MACV-CINCPAC recommendation on RVNAF force increases, of which the RF/PF component was the largest. Requested was an increase in FY 68 RVNAF authorized strength from 622,153 to 685,739, a net of 63,586. Of this number, 47,839 were RF/PF spaces, and only 15,747 were for the regular forces (of which ARVN's share was 14,966). To achieve these higher levels, MACV proposed the reduction of the draft age from 20 to 18 and the extension of tours of duty for active RVNAF personnel. The advisory support for these new Vietnamese forces had already been provided for by Program #5. In their concluding paragraph, the JCS took note of a MACV request, to be considered separately, for an FY 1969 RVNAF authorized strength of 763,953, a further increase of 78,204 over the newly proposed FY 1968 level. Of these new troops, 69,000 were to go to RF/PF (including some draftees) and only 9,000 to ARVN. Secretary McNamara approved these requested FY 1968 augmentations for RVNAF against the recommendation of his Systems Analyst, Alain Enthoven, who would have authorized only half of the request pending better justification. But the JCS were informed that a judgment on the proposed FY 1969 increase would be reserved until the military had responded to a series of questions relating to equipment availability, officer supply, costs, and distribution of the new forces between ARVN and RF/PF.

Thus, by the fall of 1967, two factors were pushing U.S. leaders toward increasing the size and role of RVNAF in the war—a step which would increase the importance of the U.S. as advisor rather than combatant: (1) the approaching ceiling on U.S. Forces deployable to Vietnam without mobilization (politically unpalatable in an election year); and (2) a growing U.S. Congressional and public clamor for a larger South Vietnamese contribution to the war and assumption of burdens.

This was essentially the situation that existed when, on 31 January 1968, the VC/NVA launched a series of major attacks on South Vietnamese population centers. This radical change in enemy tactics challenged the efficacy of the division of effort between U.S. forces and RVNAF, shook U.S. public support for the war, and marked the beginning of a new, uncharted phase in the history of U.S. attempts to advise the government and armed forces of the Republic of Vietnam.

7.　Re-Emphasis on Pacification: 1965–1967

Summary

By the summer of 1967, pacification had become a major ingredient of American strategy in Vietnam, growing steadily in importance and the amount of resources devoted to it. The U.S. Mission in Vietnam had been reorganized three times in 15 months and each reorganization had been designed primarily to improve the management of the pacification effort and raise its priority within our overall effort.

Pacification—or as it is sometimes called by Americans, Revolutionary Development (RD)—had staged a comeback in priority from the days in 1964 and 1965 when it was a program with little emphasis, guidance, or support. It has by now almost equalled in priority *for the Americans* the original priority given the Strategic Hamlet program in 1962–1963, although the Vietnamese have not yet convinced many people that they attach the same importance to it as we do.

This study traces the climb in pacification's importance during the last two years, until it reached its present level of importance, with further growth likely.

This study concentrates on American decisions, American discussions, American papers. It will be clear to the reader that, if this version of events is accurate, the Vietnamese played a secondary role in the move to re-emphasize pacification. It is the contention of this paper that this was indeed the case, and that the Americans were the prime movers in the series of events which led to the re-emphasis of pacification. This study does not cover many important events, particularly the progress of the field effort, the CIA-backed PAT/Cadre program, and GVN activity.

The process by which the American government came to increase its support for pacification is disorderly and haphazard. Individuals like Ambassador Lodge and General Walt and Robert Komer, seem in retrospect to have played important roles, but to each participant in a story still unfolding, the sequence may look different. Therefore, it is quite possible that things didn't quite happen the way they are described here, and someone else, whose actions are not adequately described in the files available for this study, was equally important.

Nor was there anything resembling a conspiracy involved. Indeed, the proponents of what is called so loosely in this paper "pacification" were often in such violent disagreement as to what pacification meant that they quarreled publicly among themselves and overlooked their common interests. At other times, people who disagreed strongly on major issues found themselves temporary allies with a common objective.

Moreover, there is the curious problem of the distance between rhetoric and reality. Even during the dark days of 1964–1965, most Americans paid lip service, particularly in official, on the record statements, to the ultimate importance of pacification. But their public affirmation of the cliches about "winning the hearts and minds of the people" were not related to any programs or priorities then in existence in Vietnam, and they can mislead the casual observer.

The resurgence of pacification was dramatically punctuated by three Presidential conferences on Pacific islands with the leaders of the GVN—Honolulu in February, 1966, Manila in October, 1966 (with five other Chiefs of State also present), and Guam in March, 1967. After each conference the relative importance of pacification took another leap upward within the U.S. Government—reflecting a successful effort within the U.S. Government by its American proponents—and the U.S. tied the GVN onto Declarations and Communiques which committed them to greater effort.

In addition, each conference was followed by a major re-organization within the U.S. Mission, designed primarily to improve our management of the pacification effort. After Honolulu, Deputy Ambassador Porter was given broad new authority to run the civilian agencies. After Manila, Porter was directed to reorganize the components of USIA, CIA, and AID internally to create a single Office of Civil Operations (OCO). And after Guam, OCO—redesignated as CORDS—was put under the control of General Westmoreland, who was given a civilian deputy with the personal rank of Ambassador to assist him.

The low priority of pacification in 1965 was the understandable result of a situation in which battles of unprecedented size were taking place in the highlands and along the coast, the air war was moving slowly north towards Hanoi, and the GVN was in a continual state of disarray.

But a series of events and distinct themes were at work which would converge to give pacification a higher priority. They were to meet at the Honolulu conference in February, 1966.

I. THREADS THAT MET AT HONOLULU

A. HOP TAC

The first was the hold-over program from 1964–1965—pacification's one priority even then, the Hop Tac program. It had been suggested first by Lodge on his way home from his first Ambassadorship, and Taylor and Westmoreland had given it recognition as a high priority program. Although Westmoreland judged it repeatedly as a partial success, it appears now to have been a faultily conceived and clumsily executed program. It was conceptually unsound, lacked the support of the Vietnamese, created disagreements within the U.S. Mission which were never resolved, and then faded away. So unsuccessful was it that during its life span the VC were able to organize a regiment—165A—in the Gia Dinh area surrounding Saigon, and thus forced MACV in late 1966 to commit three U.S. infantry battalions to Operation FAIRFAX to protect the capital. No one analyzed Hop Tac before starting FAIRFAX. With the beginning of FAIRFAX, Hop Tac was buried quietly and the United States proceeded to other matters.

B. AMBASSADOR LODGE AND THE "TRUE BELIEVERS"

Henry Cabot Lodge returned as Ambassador in August of 1965, and immediately began to talk of pacification as "the heart of the matter." In telegrams and Mission Council meetings, Lodge told the President, the GVN, and the Mission that pacification deserved a higher priority. Because he saw himself as an advocate before the President for his beliefs rather than as the overall manager of the largest overseas civil-military effort in American history,* Lodge did not try, as Ambassador Maxwell Taylor had done, to devise an integrated and unified strategy that balanced every part of our effort. Instead, he declared, in his first month back in Vietnam (September, 1965), that "the U.S. military was doing so well now that we face a distinct possibility that VC main force units will be neutralized, and VC fortresses destroyed soon," and that therefore we should be ready to give pacification a new push. While his involvement was irregular and inconsistent, Lodge did nonetheless play a key role in giving pacification a boost. His rhetoric, even if vague, encouraged other advocates of pacification to speak up. The man he brought with him, Edward Lansdale, gave by his very presence an implicit boost to pacification.

C. THE III MARINE AMPHIBIOUS FORCE

Meanwhile, to their own amazement, the Marines were discovering that the toughest war for them was the war in the villages behind them near the Da Nang air base, rather than the war against the main force, which had retreated to the hills to build up. In the first 12 months of their deployment, the Marines virtually reversed their emphasis, turning away from the enemy to a grueling and painfully slow effort to pacify the villages of the central coast in their three TAORs. It was a job that Americans were not equipped for, and the Marine effort raised some basic questions about the role of U.S. troops in Vietnam, but nonetheless, the Marines began to try to sell the rest of the U.S. Government on the success and correctness of their still unproved strategy. The result was a major commitment to the pacification strategy by a service of the U.S. Armed Forces, and influence on the other services, particularly the Army.

D. WASHINGTON GRUMBLES ABOUT THE EFFORT

When Lodge was Ambassador, there was widespread concern about the management of the Mission. Lodge was admittedly not a manager. This concern led to a major conference at Warrenton in January of 1966, during which increased emphasis on pacification and better organization within the U.S. Mission were the main topics. Improving the Washington organizational structure was raised, but not addressed candidly in the final report; Washington seemed far readier to tell Saigon how to reorganize than to set their own house in order. But Warrenton symbolizes the growing dissatisfaction in Washington with the Mission as it was.

E. PRESIDENTIAL EMPHASIS ON THE "OTHER WAR" AND PRESS REACTION

Finally, there was the need of the President, for compelling domestic political reasons, to give greater emphasis to "the other war." With the first full years of major troop commitment ending with victory not yet in sight, there was a growing need to point out to the American public and to the world that the United States was doing a great deal in the midst of war to build a new Vietnam. While this emphasis did not necessarily have to also become an emphasis on

---

* No other American Ambassador has ever had responsibility and authority even close to that in Saigon; only military commands have exceeded it in size.

pacification, it did, and thus the President in effect gave pacification his personal support—an act which was acutely felt by Americans in Vietnam.

F. MEANWHILE, BACK AT THE WAR . . .

A summary of the MACV Monthly Evaluations and other reports is contained here, showing how the U.S. command saw its own progress. The summary suggests that MACV foresaw heavy fighting all through 1966, and did not apparently agree with Ambassador Lodge's predictions and hopes that a major pacification effort could be started, but the issue was not analyzed before decisions were made.

II. HONOLULU

A. THE CONFERENCE—FEBRUARY 1966

The details of the working sessions at the Honolulu conference do not appear, in retrospect, to be nearly as important on the future emphasis on pacification as the public statements that came out of Honolulu, particularly the Declaration itself. The discussions and the Declaration are summarized, including the President's final remarks in plenary session.

B. PUBLIC IMPACT . . .

The press reaction to the conference is summarized.

III.   HONOLULU TO MANILA

A. SAIGON: PORTER IN CHARGE

The first reorganization now took place, and Deputy Ambassador Porter was put in direct charge of the civilian agencies. His responsibility and his ability to carry out his responsibility were not equal from the outset, and Porter saw his role in different terms than those in Washington who had given him his difficult task. A major problem was the lack of full support that Porter received from Ambassador Lodge, who had never been fully in favor of the reorganization. Another problem was the lack of a parallel structure in Washington, so that Porter found himself caught between the Washington agencies and their representatives in Saigon, with Komer (see below) as a frequent participant. Nonetheless, Porter accomplished a great deal in the months this arrangement lasted; it just wasn't as much as Washington sought.

B. WASHINGTON: KOMER AS THE BLOWTORCH

In Washington, the President selected a McGeorge Bundy deputy, R. W. Komer, to be his Special Assistant on non-military activities in Vietnam. Komer did not have the same kind of authority over the Washington agencies that Porter, in theory, had over the Saigon extensions. Komer pushed pacification hard, and became the first senior official, with apparently ready access to the President, who put forward the pro-pacification position consistently in high level meetings. His mandate was contained in a loosely worded NSAM, 343, dated March 28, 1966. During the summer of 1966, Komer applied great pressure to both the Mission and the Washington agencies (thus earning from Ambassador Lodge the nickname of "Blowtorch"), with a series of cables and visits to Vietnam, often using the President's name.

C. STUDY GROUPS AND STRATEGISTS: SUMMER 1966

With Porter and Komer in their new roles, a series of Task Forces and Study Groups began to produce papers that gave a better rationale and strategy to pacification. These included the Army study called PROVN, the Priorities Task Force in Saigon, and the Roles and Missions Study Groups in Saigon. At the same time, Westmoreland, whose year end wrapup message on January 1, 1966, had not even mentioned pacification, sent in a new long range strategy which emphasized pacification, to Lodge's pleasure. MACV also produced a new position on revamping ARVN, and briefed the Mission Council on it in August, 1966. The Honolulu emphasis was beginning to produce tangible results on the U.S. side.

D. THE SINGLE MANAGER

Despite the movement described in the above three sections, Washington wanted more, and was not satisfied with the rate of progress. Komer, therefore, in August of 1966 had produced a long paper which offered three possible changes in the management structure of the Mission. They were: (1) put all pacification responsibility and assets, including MACV Advisors, under Porter; (2) reorganize the civilian structure to create a single office of operations, and strengthen MACV internally, but leave the civilians and the military split; (3) give Westmoreland full pacification responsibility. The Mission rejected all these ideas, offering in their stead the proposal that Washington leave Saigon alone for a while, but the pressure for results and better management was too great, and the inadequacies of the Mission too obvious, to leave it alone. Secretary McNamara weighed in at this point with a draft Presidential memorandum proposing that Westmoreland be given responsibility for pacification. Komer and JCS concurred in it, but State, USIA, AID, and CIA nonconcurred. McNamara, Katzenbach, and Komer then went to Saigon to take a look at the situation. When they returned, Katzenbach, new to the State Department and previously uninvolved in the problem, recommended that Porter be told to reorganize the civilians along the lines previously discussed (similar to Komer's Alternative Number 2). The President agreed, discussing it with Lodge and Westmoreland at Honolulu. But he added a vital warning: he would give the civilians only about 90 to 120 days to make the new structure work, and then would reconsider the proposal to transfer responsibility for pacification to MACV.

E. THE MANILA CONFERENCE

The decision had not yet been transmitted to Saigon, but it had been made. At Manila, with six other heads of state in attendance, the discussion turned to other matters. At Manila, in the final Declaration, the GVN announced that they would commit half the armed forces to securing operations in support of pacification/RD. This had previously been discussed, but it was the public commitment that really mattered, and now it was on the record.

IV.   OCO TO CORDS

A.   *OCO ON TRIAL: INTRODUCTION*

The Office of Civil Operations was formed, creating confusion and resentment among the agencies, but also marking an immediate and major step forward. The example of the civilians moving at this pace also created pressure and conflict within MACV, which was for the first time confronted with a strong civilian structure. The GVN indicated that it understood and approved of the new structure.

B.   *OCO ON TRIAL: TOO LITTLE TOO LATE—OR NOT ENOUGH TIME?*

Although it was slower than Washington desired, OCO did get off to a start in December of 1966. Wade Lathram, who had been USAID Deputy Director, was chosen to head up OCO—a choice that was unfortunate, because Lathram, a skilled and cautious bureaucrat, was not the kind of driving and dynamic leader that OCO—in a brink of disaster situation from its inception—needed.

Even worse, Porter was almost immediately diverted from OCO to pay more attention to other matters. While the planners had hoped that Porter would take OCO in hand and give Lathram direct guidance, instead he left Lathram in control of OCO and was forced to turn his attentions to running the Mission, during a long vacation (one month) by Lodge.

The most dramatic action that was taken was the selection of the Regional Directors, a move which even attracted newspaper attention. They included Henry Koren, formerly Porter's deputy; John Paul Vann, the controversial former MACV advisor; and Vince Heymann of the CIA.

Slowly, the OCO then turned to picking its province representatives. All in all, OCO accomplished many things that had never been done before; given time it could no doubt have done much more. But it was plagued from the outset by lack of support from the agencies and their representatives in Saigon, and Washington made higher demands than could be met in Saigon.

C.   *TIME RUNS OUT*

It is not clear when the President made the decision to scrap OCO. He communicated his decision to his field commanders at Guam, but there was a two-month delay before the decision was announced publicly or discussed with the GVN.

D.   *THE CORDS REORGANIZATION*

As Bunker took over the Mission, there was a considerable turnover in key personnel. Bunker asked Lansdale and Zorthian to stay on, but Porter, Habib, Wehrle, all left just as Locke, Komer, Calhoun, Cooper, and General Abrams all arrived.

In the new atmosphere, Komer took the lead, making a series of recommendations which maintained the civilian position within MACV, and Westmoreland accepted them.

An example of Komer's influence was the question of the role of the ARVN divisions in the RD chain of command, and here Westmoreland took Komer's suggestion even though it meant a reversal of the previous MACV position.

E. THE MISSION ASSESSMENT AS CORDS BEGINS

The situation inherited by CORDS was not very promising. Measurements of progress had been irrelevant and misleading, and progress by nearly all standards has been slow or nonexistent. At this point, the study of CORDS and pacification becomes current events.

End of Summary

I. THREADS THAT MET AT HONOLULU

A. HOP TAC

While pacification received a low emphasis during troubled 1964–1965, there was one important exception: the Hop Tac program, designed to put "whatever resources are required" into the area surrounding Saigon to pacify it. The area was chosen by Ambassador Lodge in his last weeks as Ambassador in June, 1964, and Hop Tac deserves study because both its failures and limited achievements had many of the characteristics of our later pacification efforts—and because, like all pacification efforts, there was constant disagreement within the Mission, the press, and the Vietnamese as to how well the program was doing.

Hop Tac—an intensive pacification effort in the provinces ringing Saigon—was formally proposed at a high level strategy session in Honolulu in July of 1964 by Lodge, then on his way home from his first assignment as Ambassador. In a paper presented to Secretaries Rusk and McNamara and incoming Ambassador Taylor at Honolulu (dated June 19, 1964), Lodge wrote:

> A combined GVN–US effort to intensify pacification efforts in critical provinces should be made . . . The eight critical provinces are: Tay Ninh, Binh Duong, Hau Nghia, Long An, Dinh Tuong, Go Cong, Vinh Long, and Quang Ngai. Top priority and maximum effort should be concentrated initially in the strategically important provinces nearest to Saigon, i.e., Long An, Hau Nghia, and Binh Duong. Once real progress has been made in these provinces, the same effort should be made in the five others.

General Taylor and General Westmoreland began Hop Tac, setting up a new and additional headquarters in Saigon which was supposed to tie together the overlapping and quarrelsome commands in the Saigon area. The Vietnamese set up a parallel, "counterpart" organization, although critics of Hop Tac were to point out that the Vietnamese Hop Tac headquarters had virtually no authority or influence, and seemed primarily designed to satisfy the Americans. (Ironically, Hop Tac is the Vietnamese word for "cooperation," which turned out to be just what Hop Tac lacked.)

Hop Tac had a feature previously missing from pacification plans: it sought to tie together the pacification plans of a seven-province area (expanded from Lodge's three provinces to include the adjacent provinces of Phuoc Tuy, Bien Hoa, Phuoc Thanh, and Gia Dinh, which surround Saigon like a doughnut), into a plan in which each province subordinated its own priorities to the concept of building a "giant oil spot" around Saigon. In a phrase which eventually became a joke in the Mission, the American heading the Hop Tac Secretariat at its inception, Colonel Jasper Wilson, briefed senior officials on the creation of "rings of steel" which would grow outward from Saigon until the area from the Cambodian border to the South China Sea was secure. Then, according to the plan, Hop Tac would move into the Delta and North. Colonel Wilson ordered his staff to produce a phased plan in which the area (see map below) to be pacified was divided into four circles around Saigon. Each ring was to be pacified in four months, according to the original plan, which never had any chance of success. But Wilson, under great pressure from his superiors, ordered the plan produced, got his Vietnamese counterparts to translate it, and issued it. The kick-off date for Hop Tac was to be September 12, 1964: the operation, a sweep into the VC-controlled pineapple groves just west and southwest of the city of Saigon—the VC base nearest to the city, which had not been entered by the GVN since the last outpost had been abandoned in 1960.

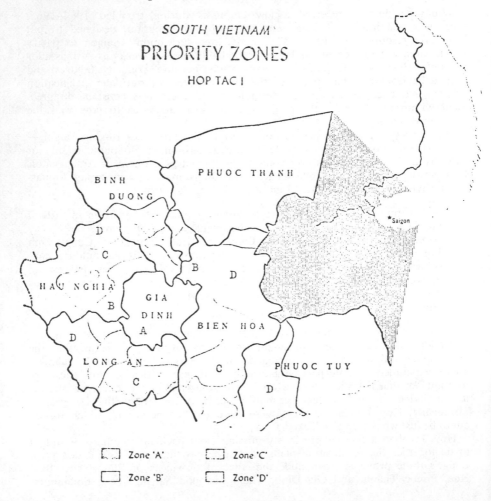

The operation began on schedule, with elements of the 51st Regiment moving toward their objective west of Saigon. During the second day of the operation, the unit ran into a minefield and took numerous casualties. Shortly thereafter, instead of continuing the operation, the unit broke off contact and, to the amazement of its advisors, turned back towards the city of Saigon. When next located it was in the middle of Saigon participating in the abortive *coup d'etat* of September 13, 1964.

From that point on, Hop Tac was a constant source of dispute within the U.S. Mission. Almost to a man, the civilian agencies "supporting" Hop Tac felt that the program was unnecessary, repetitive, and doomed. They claimed that they preferred to work through existing channels, although these, in MACV's view, were inadequate. This view was not stated openly, however, since the Ambassador and General Westmoreland had committed all U.S. agencies to full support. On October 6, 1964, for example, General Taylor sent Washington an EXDIS cable in which he discussed and rejected a suggestion to decentralize the pacification effort, and instead listed several actions that the Mission would take. First among these was a "unanimous recommendation" that the Mission "give full support to Hop Tac Plan, assuring it the necessary priority to give it every chance to succeed . . . When Hop Tac priorities permit, concentrate on selected weak areas." Thus there was a reluctance to criticize the program directly.

Deadlines slipped continually; phase lines were readjusted; the official count of "pacified" hamlets climbed steadily. But a special study of the area made in October, 1964, by representatives of USOM, USIS, and MACV concluded: "Generally speaking, Hop Tac, as a program, does not appear to exist as a unified and meaningful operation."

The official view of Hop Tac was that the new coordinating machinery was doing some good. Thus, during a period in which cables on the general situation were rather gloomy, Ambassador Taylor could tell the President in his weekly NODIS that while "pacification progress throughout the rest of Vietnam was minimal at best, largely because of the political climate . . . Some forward movement occurred in the Hop Tac effort growing out of U.S. Mission discussions with the Prime Minister on September 25. The number of operating checkpoints in the Hop Tac area increased markedly; command areas were strengthened; available troop strength increased." Minor statistical advances, taken out of context, were continually being used in the above manner to prove overall progress.

The MACV Command History for 1964 reflects the official view: "At the end of 1964, Hop Tac was one of the few pacification areas that showed some success and greater promise." But subsequent events in the area do not bear out this view. In February of 1966 for example—18 months after the birth of Hop Tac—when the Hop Tac area was designated as one of the four "National Priority Areas," the briefers were unable to show Ambassadors Lodge and Porter any progress in the preceding year. They could not even produce a plan for the coming year. Originally Hop Tac was focused on cleaning out the nearest VC base areas, but by February of 1966—with the GVN unable to stop the growing VC build-up, the emphasis was "placed on lines of communications, with special attention to be given vital installations including Bien Hoa and Tan Son Nhut air bases and ammunition and gasoline depots." The best the briefers could do, in the final briefing prior to the Honolulu Conference, was to say that they hoped to pacify 72 hamlets in the entire seven-province area, and "consolidate" 144 hamlets in Gia Dinh—which meant the hamlets ringing Saigon, including many which were really part of the city. Lodge and Porter were told that day "there has been a lessening of security in Hau Nghia and Gia Dinh provinces. RF and PF units generally are not up to authorized strengths. The new cadre program should be helpful in solving the problem of continued hamlet security after pacification . . . The 1966 plan is not overly optimistic from a military standpoint." (The memorandum recording of this meeting, made by a member of General Lansdale's staff, shows as the only Ambassadorial guidance after this sobering report: "Maps drawn to depict progress of Rural Construction (Pacification) should show as the goal only that area to be pacified during the year . . . The U.S. Mission manpower committee should look into the use of refugees in the national labor force.")

The Vietnamese were cynical about Hop Tac; it was something, speculation ran, that General Khanh had to do to keep the Americans happy, but it was clearly an American show, clearly run by the United States, and the Viet amese were reluctant to give it meaningful support. It was one of the first major programs with which the United States became publicly identified (since Diem had always kept the United States in as much of a background role as possible —and its shortcomings were in part derived from this fact.

All through Ambassador Taylor's tenure, Hop Tac was something on which he and the Mission Council pinned hope. General Westmoreland thought the program had been reasonably successful, when he told the Mission Council about Hop Tac's first year:

> General Westmoreland said that while Hop Tac could be said only to have been about 50% successful, it had undoubtedly averted a VC siege of Saigon.

This same view was reflected in McGeorge Bundy's comments in a memorandum to the President months earlier in February, 1965, when he said:

> The Hop Tac program of pacification in this area has not been an unqualified success, but it has not been a failure, and it has certainly prevented any strangling seige of Saigon. We did not have a chance to form an independent judgment on Hop Tac, but we did conclude that whatever its precise measure of success, it is of great importance that this operation be pursued with full vigor. This is the current policy of the Mission.

There were others who said that, as a matter of fact, Saigon was almost under seige and that the situation was deteriorating. Westmoreland's own headquarters, for example, sent to Washington in the June Monthly Evaluation from MACV, the following statement which seems to contradict Westmoreland's optimism:

> The sealing off of Saigon from surrounding areas, no matter how incomplete the sealing may be, has had and will continue to have serious economic as well as military effects.

Shortly after he arrived in Vietnam for his second tour, Lodge asked for a private assessment of Hop Tac from an Embassy officer, who reported to him in early September of 1965:

> 1. Hop Tac did not achieve its original goals primarily because they were completely unrealistic and did not take into account the difficulty of

the task. These goals were set quite arbitrarily and with no regard for the available resources and the strength of the enemy.

2. The second reason for the failures of Hop Tac lies in its strategic concept. The idea of concentric circles outward from Saigon to be pacified in successive waves of clearing, securing and developing may be sound in macroscopic terms; when the Hop Tac area is looked at carefully, the viability of this strategy breaks down. The concentric phase lines around Saigon do not adequately take into account existing areas of GVN strength and existing Viet Cong base areas; rather they commit the GVN to a continual expansionary effort on all sides of Saigon simultaneously, an effort which is beyond its capabilities. Above all, they ignore the political structure of the area around Saigon.

3. The U.S. Mission has two broad courses of action available in regard to Hop Tac. First, the Mission Council may feel that the area encompassed by Hop Tac remains the first pacification priority of the U.S. and the GVN. If this is the considered judgment of the Mission Council, then we must seek ways of re-emphasizing, re-invigorating and re-orienting Hop Tac in order to achieve a dramatic and sustained success in pacification.

4. There is an alternative open to the Mission Council. Perhaps it would be politically unwise to attempt to commit the GVN to re-emphasis of Hop Tac at this time. There are several facts which support this view:

   A. The GVN has never considered Hop Tac its own plan and its own number one priority. The staff planning for the plan was done almost entirely by the United States, and then translated into Vietnamese. It is, in the eyes of many Vietnamese, "the plan of the Americans."
   B. It is perhaps the most difficult area in the country in which to attempt pacification. Since it surrounds Saigon (but does not include it), every political tremor in the capital is felt in the neighboring area . . . the High Command has created chains of command in the area which are clearly designed primarily to prevent coups, and only secondarily to pacify the countryside. Another example: in the last 11 months, 24 out of 31 district chiefs and five out of seven province chiefs have been changed.
   C. Prime Minister Ky will never feel that Hop Tac is his plan. If he is seeking a major public triumph, and intends to devote his attention to achieving that triumph, it is unlikely that he will choose Hop Tac, which as mentioned above, is publicly considered an American plan. Moreover, to the extent that any Vietnamese is publicly connected with Hop Tac, it is Nguyen Khanh. For this reason, more than any other, the dangers of re-emphasizing Hop Tac outweigh the possible gains . . .

The situation in the Hop Tac area will not collapse if Hop Tac is not revitalized now. With the available forces, and particularly with the impending arrival of the 1st Infantry Division to take up a position across the southern arc of Zone D, Saigon itself is not going to be threatened any more than it presently is. The threat—which is substantial—comes from the enemy within, and the solution does not lie within the responsibility of the Hop Tac Council: it is a problem for the Saigon police and intelligence communities. This threat, serious as it is, is not directly affected by the presence of the Viet Cong's 506th battalion 20 miles away in Hau Nghia, nor by Zone D. The two problems can be dealt with separately, and solution of the internal security problems of Saigon are not contingent on the success of clearing Hau Nghia and Long An.

In an effort to reconcile these opposing views about Hop Tac, Lodge told the September 15 Mission Council that "the original reasons for the emphasis placed on the area surrounding Saigon . . . were still valid, primarily because of the heavy density of population. Lodge noted, however, lack of a clear commitment to Hop Tac on the part of the GVN, possibly due to the fact that the Vietnamese consider the program an American scheme. The view was also expressed that the trouble may also lie in US/GVN differences over some fundamental concepts in Hop Tac. Finally, Ambassador Lodge said it was essential that all interested American agencies be agreed on concepts and tactics before an approach to the GVN could be made." After this meeting, no significant action was taken, and the matter lapsed.

The importance of Hop Tac is still difficult to assess; it is included here primarily because of its role as the one major pacification program that was tried during the 1964–1965 period when pacification was not receiving its present top-level emphasis. Whether or not it averted a seige of Saigon, as General Westmoreland claimed, is a semantic question: what constitutes a seige in a guerrilla war? Saigon, of course, never was under seige in the classic sense of the word, but it is hard to conceive of it ever being literally cut off as Dien Bien Phu or Mafeking were—this would not be a logical objective to the Viet Cong, who wanted to put pressure on the capital but knew they couldn't seal it off (nor would have wanted to, since they got supplies from it).

What is important is that the failures of Hop Tac were never adequately reported and analyzed prior to embarking on other pacification efforts. Thus, at one point General Westmoreland told each of his Senior Corps Advisors to start a Hop Tac in his area—a strange request since Hop Tac was designed to pull together a multiplicity of commands not duplicated in any other area. Each Corps naturally responded by producing plans which concentrated their pacification assets around the Corps headquarters—Da Nang, and Can Tho or, in the case of II Corps, Qui Nhon. This in turn led naturally to the later National Priority Area program, but had no other value.

With MACV reluctant to close down its Hop Tac Secretariat, with the civilian Americans giving Hop Tac only verbal support, and with the Vietnamese leaving a powerless staff at the headquarters, Hop Tac could well have survived as an appendix to the normal chain of command, as so many outdated structures survive in Vietnam because no one wants to admit their irrelevance. But General Westmoreland saw a way to dispose of Hop Tac cleanly and quietly in the summer of 1966, and he took it. At the Mission Council meeting of July 7, 1966:

> General Westmoreland then turned to the subject of Hop Tac. He summarized the purpose of the Hop Tac concept, which was implemented two years ago, and said that—while it has enjoyed only modest success over the past two years—the situation in the area surrounding Saigon/Cholon would be comparatively worse if we had not had the Hop Tac arrangement. He noted that recent organizational changes have taken place, which have resulted in the Capital Military Region becoming the Capital Military District (as part of the III Corps Tactical Zone) with Saigon remaining as an autonomous city. In view of these changes, there is some question of

the validity of continuing with the original concept. More importantly, III Corps has a Revolutionary Development Council and a Hop Tac Council which results in some duplication of effort. Consequently, the General believes that these two councils should be merged, with the Revolutionary Development Council absorbing the Hop Tac Council. General Westmoreland asked the Mission Council to endorse this proposal for him to carry out. After brief discussion, Ambassador Lodge indicated his approval.

By this time Hop Tac had long lost the "highest priority" which was supposed to justify it, and both the American and the Vietnamese had turned to other matters.

But Hop Tac was not adequately analyzed before embarking on other efforts, and its shortcomings were largely forgotten by the time that the still-deteriorating situation in Gia Dinh led MACV to commit three U.S. Army battalions to the inner area surrounding Saigon—the original first phase of Hop Tac—as part of Operation Fairfax in November of 1966. The Mission, with no institutional memory, forgot—or never learned—the lessons that Hop Tac could have offered.

B. AMBASSADOR LODGE AND THE "TRUE BELIEVERS"

Many senior American officials have paid varying degrees of lip service to the pacification effort since 1962—a fact which makes it extremely hard to determine who really pushed pacification and who didn't. But about Ambassador Lodge, there can be little question. He had repeatedly called pacification "the heart of the matter," and his unfailing belief in the importance of the effort can be clearly shown in his public and private statements and his cables.

His emphasis on pacification resumed the day he returned to Saigon in August 1965, when in his arrival statement he said that the United States supported the "true revolution" of the Vietnamese people. His continual emphasis on the effort seems to have had a definite impact on the mood in Washington and in the Mission, and played a role in the events leading up to the Honolulu Conference in February 1966—where pacification was given (or so it seemed to Americans and Vietnamese alike in Vietnam) the President's blessing.

It is true that Ambassador Taylor also felt that pacification was important and that it would deserve high emphasis; his push on Hop Tac clearly demonstrates this fact. But because Maxwell Taylor saw that it was his responsibility as Ambassador to reconcile competing requirements for limited resources, and develop a single overall strategy for the effort, he never let pacification consume too many resources prematurely. Lodge, on the other hand, did not see himself as an administrator or manager of the U.S. Mission, but as the President's personal representative and advisor in Saigon. Thus, he felt no qualms about advocating a certain course of action—in this case, pacification. There is no record of Ambassador Lodge worrying about the way his latest proposals would affect the balance of the whole effort. He simply did not see himself as responsible for the actions of the operating agencies which represented AID, USIA, and the CIA, let alone DOD, in Vietnam*—not even after receiving a strong letter of authority from President Johnson in July of 1965:

> As you take charge of the American effort in South Vietnam, I want you to have this expression of my confidence, and a reaffirmation of my desire that as Ambassador you exercise full responsibility for the work of

the United States Government in South Vietnam. In general terms this authority is parallel to that set forth in my letter to Ambassador Taylor of July 2, 1964.†

Given his belief in the fundamental importance of the pacification effort, Lodge was ready to push it at any time he could. He did not examine the possibility that certain times were more favorable than others for an effort which needed the full participation of the Vietnamese in order to succeed, and, like many in the government, failed to see that at certain times emphasis on pacification would not only not work but would be harmful to GVN/US relations, and would reduce the chances for a successful joint effort at some more propitious time.

Thus, it is not surprising that one of his last major documents at the end of his first tour as Ambassador proposed Hop Tac—in the face of strong possibilities that the situation was not favorable to it—and that on his return in August 1965 he was advocating more effort in pacification.

Thus, for example, meeting with his senior officers one month after he arrived, Lodge "began the meeting by stating that in his opinion the United States military was doing so well not that 'we face a distinct possibility that VC main force units will be neutralized and that VC fortresses will be destroyed soon. We should be ready to handle the VC in small units. This gives counter-subversion/terrorism or pacification or counterinsurgency—I am not overly concerned with what we call it—a new urgency for all of us here.' "

It is likely that if Lodge had clarified his view of pacification and repeated it continually in public and privately, as he did with anything he believed in, his view would eventually have taken hold in the United States Mission. But the problem of how pacification should work was—and is—a very difficult one. It raises a number of extremely difficult questions on which the United States Government has never reached a unified position.

Sensing that Lodge was receptive to ideas which emphasized pacification but that he had no set views on details, many groups and individuals besieged him with a resurgence of ideas and philosophies on pacification. They were all encouraged by his verbal support or his glowing cables to Washington. The whole atmosphere in the Mission became more favorable towards pacification and pacifiers; Lansdale, Colonel Serong (the Australian who was to organize the Police Field Force with support from Lodge), Sir Robert Thompson (whose Malayan experiences had led him to emphasize the police), Colonel Bohannon (who began as a Lansdale deputy, but whose views took a different line), the Marines (with their pacification efforts and CAP's near Da Nang), the CIA (which produced, with Lodge's strong support, the PAT's-turned RD cadre), USIA and AID (with their small but growing field programs), the Army (which

---

* See for example, Lodge's NODIS to the President, February 1, 1966, in which he said: ". . . I have learned of Zorthian's wire to Marks, which, of course, he has the right to send, since I hold that Zorthian, like U.S. agency chiefs here, has and should have an open channel to his agency. It is a statement of Zorthian's opinion which, of course, was sent without my approval or direction . . ." (The subject was apparently a suggestion that Lodge address the United Nations General Assembly in New York, although Lodge's cable cited does not explicitly state what Zorthian's cable said.)

† The letter to Taylor had said, among other points: "I wish it clearly understood that this overall responsibility includes the whole military effort in South Vietnam and authorizes the degree of command and control that you consider appropriate."

entered the game late but elicited from Lodge on visits to the U.S. 25th Infantry Division and then the 1st Infantry Division, some of his longest and most glowing accounts of pacification in action).

These groups and individuals fought about details, sometimes debating minor points like medieval monks but also disagreeing on rather basic points—such as whether the object was to gain the population's support or to control them by force. (A popular Marine saying, which tried to bridge the gap, went: "Get the people by the balls, and their hearts and minds will follow.") But each group found something that appealed to Lodge, and each in turn gained encouragement from him. The slow change in mood also affected Washington.

In dealing with his role in the re-emphasis of pacification, we must distinguish between Lodge's influence on our overall, or grand, strategy—on which he was ultimately to have considerable impact—and his influence on the operational details of the policy. The latter did not interest him on a continuing basis, and it is thus easy to underestimate his influence. There was, for example, a tendency in Saigon during his Ambassadorship to minimize his importance, since each agency could ignore him when he told them to do something and usually get away with it. But this popular view overlooked Lodge's impact in encouraging all sorts of people to emerge from parts of the USG with renewed hope for pacification. It overlooked the impact of his cables and statements, which added up to a massive endorsement of pacification. In his NODIS weeklies to the President, for example, pacification receives more attention than any other subject.

Alone, Lodge could have done little, if anything, to move the USG around. But his influence seems clear, more so in retrospect than at the time: at a time when frustrations were growing, he was emphasizing a different rhetoric and strategy.

The best way to show his emphasis is simply to quote from the cables and memoranda of the period. Each one shows Lodge, either directly or indirectly, putting forth his general beliefs—sometimes contradictory. They form an important part of the background to Honolulu, where pacification was to get its biggest push to that date:

1. *Lodge at the end of his first tour in Vietnam, defining pacification in his paper proposing Hop Tac:*

The first priority after the military have cleared an area is to bring about the selection of an able man for that area, who will in turn go about creating a basically civilian counter-terrorist organization on the "precinct" level, or equivalent thereof . . . Its prime purpose will be, notably with police help, to create security for the local government and free it from all intimidation by going through the precinct with a fine-toothed comb . . . Once the local government feels safer, it should move energetically to promote public safety for the people; the people should then rally more to the government; and this should create an upward spiral as regards security organization . . . USOM and USIA will support these local "precinct" organizations, will actually work through them, and will seek to make it attractive to be one of those who builds such a counter-terrorism precinct organization . . . The military should take special precautions in their operations not to injure in any way the non-combatants. It must also behave itself so well that the people like the Army . . ."

2. *Lodge's Ten Point Program for Success:*

In each city precinct and each rural hamlet immediately adjacent to a thoroughly pacified city (*i.e.,* the smallest unit from a public safety standpoint) the following program should be undertaken in the following order:

1. Saturate the minds of the people with some socially conscious and attractive ideology, which is susceptible of being carried out.

2. Organize the people politically with a hamlet chief and committee whose actions would be backed by the police or the military using police-type tactics. This committee should have representatives of the political, military, economic and social organizations and should have an executive who directs.

3. With the help of the police or military, conduct a census.

4. Issue identification cards.

5. Issue permits for the movement of goods and people.

6. When necessary, hold a curfew.

7. Thanks to all these methods, go through each hamlet with a fine-tooth comb to apprehend the terrorists.

8. At the first quiet moment, bring in agricultural experts, school teachers, etc.

9. The hamlet should also be organized for its own defense against small Viet Cong attacks.

10. After all these things have been accomplished, hold elections for local office.

COMMENT: Lodge began his second tour as Ambassador where he had left off the year before. The above paper, which he also transmitted to the President in a NODIS message, again represented no official U.S. position. After writing it and giving it to everyone in the Mission, he let the matter drop, and thus the paper did not assume any official character. Since nothing was changed in the procedures of the Mission, and since the old criteria for pacification still applied unchanged, Lodge had, in typical fashion, failed to affect the *operating* Mission.

3. *The Assignment of Lansdale:*

Handpicked group of about ten experienced counter-subversion/counter terrorism workers under direction of Edward G. Lansdale will be going to Saigon to provide Ambassador Lodge with special operating staff in field of political action both at central level and also in connection with rural programs.

COMMENT: From the beginning, there was misunderstanding over Lansdale's role in Lodge's Embassy. The first cable reflects this. The phrase "counter-subversion/counter-terrorism workers," seems to contradict the latter part of the sentence, about "political action." From the start Lodge wanted him to "get pacification going." Thus, less than a month later, Lodge told the President:

I appointed Edward Lansdale, with his complete approval, to be chairman of the U.S. Mission Liaison Group to the newly created Vietnamese governmental body having to do with what we call "pacification," what they call "rural construction," and what means to me *socially conscious practi-*

*cal politics, the by-product of which is effective counter-subversion/
terrorism.* I thought it was important for all concerned for him to have a
definite allocation where he would have the best chance of bringing his
talents to bear. I trust that the hopes of some journalists that he is here in
an adversarial relationship with existing US agencies will be nipped in the
bud by making him the spokesman for the whole US Mission in this
particular regard. (Italics added)

Thus, another action which served to strengthen the pacification priority, although its primary reason probably was to get Lansdale working on something
other than Saigon politics.

4. *Lodge on the Use of U.S. Troops in Pacification:*

The presence of American troops does provide the opportunity for
thorough pacification of the areas in which they are stationed and full advantage should be taken of this opportunity. It is a very big divident from
our investment of men and money. For example, the Third Marine Division has scored impressive successes north, south, and west of Da Nang
. . . If our American troops can emulate this performance (of the proto-
CAC units) of 60 Americans and 150 Vietnamese, we ought to be a tremendous amount of small unit nighttime effective pacification, and we
would be neglecting an opportunity not to use American troops for this
purpose, thereby pacifying the country and transforming the ARVN, making it into a much more vital and effective element of Vietnamese society,
able at some not too remote date to carry on by themselves within outside
help . . . We are already discussing with the Vietnamese the possibility of
singling out areas that look like good prospects, that are potentially pretty
much over on our side, and then pacifying them so as to get a little smell
of across-the-board success in the air . . . I am not ready to say, "What
areas would be chosen for pacification, when should the plan be started,
what objectives would be best," but hope to be able to do so soon. I am
now encouraging General Ky to concentrate GVN efforts and enthusiasm
on pacification so that this can have sustained, wholehearted GVN participation . . . Development of popular electoral processes is part of all our
current planning for counter subversion/terrorism in "rural construction
(pacification)."

COMMENT: Here, for the first time, Lodge addresses a key point: the role
of U.S. troops on pacification. The whole concept of the use of U.S. troops was
being worked out during this period (see following section on Marines), and
Lodge now began to weigh in with qualified support for the Marine approach,
based on an overly optimistic view of the situation.

5. *Lansdale's Weekly Report, October 4, 1965:*

Past week devoted to getting GVN into sound start again on pacification program . . . U.S. Mission Liaison Group shaping up into realistic
instrument for working level teamwork on pacification by all U.S. Missions . . .

COMMENT: Lansdale was responding to the direction given him by Lodge.

6.   *Lodge on the GVN's Attitude Towards Pacification:*

During my talk with General Co, the deputy Prime Minister in charge of six ministries, I was impressed by the amount of sustained analytical thought which he, with his colleagues, had given to how to organize the government for the great new job of pacification which confronts them—*and which is clearly their government's most important single responsibility.*

COMMENT: Lodge had by this time let the GVN know clearly what tune he wanted to hear, and with their usual skill the Vietnamese—even General Co, who turned out to be worthless on pacification—were playing the right song back.

7.   When the chance to win over the people was missed some years ago, a situation came into being in which it was indispensable for the VC large units to be defeated before true community building, with its mixture of political and security measures, would be possible. Otherwise, the VC battalions, emerging from untouchable sanctuaries, would destroy whatever community building had painstakingly been achieved. Now it looks as though the VC know this and has already begun to act on the knowledge, transforming themselves into small units and individual terrorists, and into subversive political operators.

COMMENT: Lodge's sequence of events—destroy the main force enemy first, pacify second—is hard to argue with, but his assessment of VC capabilities and intentions falls short of accuracy.

As a final note to the examination of Lodge's emphasis on pacification, it is worthwhile asking why he has so consistently put such a high priority on the effort—regardless of methodology—to gain control of the villages. The answer may lie in his strong views on the way the war will end in Vietnam. Lodge doubted that there would ever be meaningful negotiations with the Viet Cong. An old hand at negotiating with the communists, Lodge felt that the most likely end to the war was for the enemy to "fadeaway" after a prolonged period of conflict. In his view, therefore, control of the population became the best way to force the fadeaway. Furthermore, in the event that there was some sort of *pro forma* discussions with the communists at some future date, Lodge felt that there were certain minimum conditions of a "satisfactory outcome" which must be met. An examination of his definition of a satisfactory outcome shows the overriding importance of the pacification effort in his mind. The following is from a telegram sent "For the President and the Secretary from Lodge" on October 21, 1965, which Lodge considered one of his most important cables:

What we consider a satisfactory outcome to be would, of course, be a very closely kept secret. It would include the following, not necessarily in this order:

1. The area around Saigon and south of Saigon (all of the Delta) must be pacified. This area includes about 55 to 60% of the population of Vietnam. "Pacified" is defined as the existence of a state of mind among the people that they have a stake in the government as shown by the holding of local elections. It also means a proper local police force. In brief, a pacified area is economically, socially, and politically a part of the RVN.

2. The thickly populated northeastern strip along the coast which includes 25% of the population would be completely pacified.

3. The GVN would retain its present control of all cities and all provincial capitals.

4. All principal roads would be open to the Vietnamese military day and night.

5. Those areas not pacified would not be safe havens for the VC but would be contested by energetic offensive forays to prevent consolidation of a communist base.

6. The VC disarms; and their weapons and explosives are removed from their hands. Their main force units broken up.

7. North Vietnam stops its infiltration.

8. Chieu Hoi rehabilitation would be extended to individual VC who are suitable . . .

9. Hardcore VC to go to North Vietnam.

10. GVN to approve.

COMMENT: This means that we would not be insisting on the complete elimination of the VC although no safe haven would be allocated them. It would mean that we and the GVN would control 80 to 85% of the population and that the VC would be limited to the jungle and mountainous areas where they would go on as bandits, much as their counterparts in Malaya and Luzon—and where the GVN would have the right to pursue them and try to destroy them.

Lodge's formula for a satisfactory outcome is based on the absolute necessity of controlling the villages. In day-to-day terms this meant that, as Ambassador, Lodge had to push pacification as hard as possible. Thus, he was quite pleased with the emphasis that came out of the Honolulu conference in February of 1966.

C. THE III MARINE AMPHIBIOUS FORCE

To what extent the growing Marine emphasis on pacification was a factor during the period before the Honolulu conference is impossible to determine; the timing and evidence would suggest that the impact of the Marine strategy was greatest in the period *after* Honolulu, as they became more sure of the rightness of their approach, and as they garnered more and more publicity for it. Nonetheless, in the first eleven months of their mission in I Corps, the Marines had gotten deeply into the pacification program. The Marines thus became the most vocal advocates within the Armed Forces for emphasizing pacification more, and search and destroy less.

The Marine deployments and mission are covered in earlier decision studies in this series and will thus be treated only briefly here. The emphasis of this section is not on the influence the Marines had on the Honolulu conference, but on the way the Marines gradually moved into their new role, and the difficulties with it. The material here applied, therefore, equally to the pre- and post-Honolulu periods, throughout which the Marine successes, as they reported them, had a growing impact on the thinking of civilian and military alike, in Saigon, CINCPAC, and Washington.

The Marines landed their first troops—two Battalion Landing Teams—in Da Nang in March of 1965. Their original mission, "to secure enclaves in the northern region of Vietnam containing air and communications installations, was simplicity itself." (From "U.S. Marine Corps Civic Action Efforts in Vietnam, March 1965–March 1966, a study done by the USMC Historical Branch, hereafter referred to as *MC History*; from unpaged draft.)

By the time of the Honolulu conference the Marines—by now organized into the III Marine Amphibious Force—had changed their mission considerably, and to a degree then unequalled among other American units was deeply engaged in pacification operations.

A monthly report issued by General Krulak, Commanding General, Fleet Marine Force, Pacific, indicates the evolution of Marine thinking on their mission. Reviewing the first seven months of their deployment in I Corps, the Fleet Marine Force, Pacific, wrote in September, 1965:

> The Mission assigned III MAF was initially confined to airfield security. Subsequently, a limited offensive responsibility was added, which has gradually grown to an essentially unrestrained authority for offensive operations. Finally, and *largely on its own,* III MAF has entered the pacification program, with the bulk of its pacification efforts taking place since June. [Emphasis added]

One month later, after chronicling their successes, the report indicated the major shift in strategic thinking which was taking place at General Walt's headquarters in Da Nang, and at General Krulak's in Hawaii:

> While accomplishing all this the Marines were feeling, with growing impact, a cardinal counterinsurgency principle: that if local forces do not move in promptly behind the offensive effort, then first line forces must be diverted to provide the essential hamlet security, police and stabilization. The alternative is to risk the development of vacua, into which the VC guerrilla can flow. This condition grew during the period. The Popular Forces and police were inadequate in numbers and in quality to do their part of the job, as the Marines did theirs. This operated to complicate the Marines' problem by making the civic action effort more difficult, by permitting harassment of our forces, and by making possible a suicide attack on the Chu Lao and Marble Mountain areas.
>
> The end of the period saw the 676 square mile III MAF area of influence more stable, more prosperous, and far more hopeful, but it saw also an urgent need for efficient regional or local forces to take up their proper burden, so the Marines can maintain the momentum of their search/clear/pacification efforts. It is plain that the most efficient way to bring this about is to give III MAF substantial authority over the RF or PF serving in this area, in order that they may be properly trained and properly led.

This summary, written in the headquarters of the man often regarded as the philosopher of the Marine Corps, shows the Marines in the process of swinging their emphasis around—turning away from the offensive against the enemy waiting in the nearby hills, and towards the people and the VC guerrillas among the people inside their TAOR.

It was a crucial, difficult decision for the men who made it. Significantly, the indications are strong that the decision was made almost entirely inside Marine Corps channels, through a chain of command that bypassed COMUSMACV and the civilian leaders of our government, and ran from General Greene through General Krulak to General Walt. The files do not reveal discussions of the implications, feasibility, cost, and desirability of the Marine strategy among highranking officials in the Embassy, MACV headquarters, the Defense and State Departments. Yet in retrospect it seems clear that the strategy the Marines proposed to follow, a strategy about which they made no secret, was in sharp variance with the strategy of the other U.S. units in the country, with far-ranging political implications that could even affect the ultimate chances for negotiations.

It should be clear that the Marine concept of operations has a different implicit time requirement than a more enemy-oriented search and destroy effort. It is not within the scope of this paper to analyze the different requirements, but it does appear that the Marine strategy, which General Walt sometimes described as the "wringing out of the VC from the land like you wring water out of a sponge," is slow and methodical, requires vast numbers of troops, runs the risk of turning into an occupation even while being called "pacification/ civic action," and involves Americans deeply in the politics and traditions of rural Vietnam. The strategy can succeed, perhaps, but if it is to succeed, it must be undertaken with full awareness by the highest levels of the USG of its potential costs in manpower and time, and the exacting nature of the work. Instead, the documents suggest that the Marines determined their strategy basically on their own, deriving part of it from their own traditions in the "Banana Republics" and China (where Generals Walt, Krulak, Nickerson, and others had served in the 1930's), and partly from an attempt to solve problems of an unprecedented nature which were cropping up inside their TAORs, even on the edge of the great air base at Da Nang.

As it was, the Marine strategy was judged successful, at least by the Marines, long before it had even had a real test. It was applauded by many observers before the VC had begun to react to it, and as such, encouraged imitators while it was still unproven.

The Marine dilemma was how to support the pacification effort without taking it over. They thought they had succeeded in doing this by "self-effacing support for Vietnamese rural construction" after August of 1965, but there is much contradictory evidence on this point. The Marines themselves, according to the classified historical study they recently produced, understood that their pacification work had "to function through local Vietnamese officials. The tendency to produce Marine Corps programs or to work 'democratically' through individuals had to be strictly controlled. Only Vietnamese programs could be tolerated and support of these programs had to take place through Vietnamese governing officials . . ."

But despite their good intentions to work through the existing GVN structure, the Marines found in many cases that the existing structure barely existed, except on paper, and in other cases that the existing structure was too slow and too corrupt for their requirements. And gradually the Marines got more deeply into the politics of rural Vietnam than they had intended, or presumably desired.

Their difficulties were greatest in the area of highest priority, the National Priority Area (as it was to be designated in October 1965) south of Da Nang. In a nine-village complex just south of the air base, the Marines urged upon the GVN successful completion of a special pacification program which had been designed by them in close conjunction with the Quang Nam Deputy Province Chief. The nine villages were divided into two groups, and the first phase, scheduled for completion first in December of 1965, included only five of the villages, with only 23,000 people living in them. By February, 1966, the plan had slipped considerably, and the projected completion date for the first five villages was pushed back to April, 1966. The GVN and the Marines considered their control to extend to over 16,000 of the 23,000 people in the area, but, according to an Embassy evaluation of the area, only 682 were young men between the ages of 17 and 30. It was clear that the Marines were trying to pacify an area in which the young men no longer lived, having either been drafted, joined the VC, or gone to Da Nang to work for the Americans. "The basic problem posed by this lack of manpower must be solved before the area can be expected to participate in its own defense," the Embassy report said. "Until it is solved, the Marines and the ARVN will remain tied to defensive mission involving them with the population. No one in Quang Nam sees any immediate solution to this dilemma." The report concluded with a description of how overinvolved with local politics the Marines were becoming, unintentionally, and said:

> The plan, despite the valiant efforts of the Marines, is in trouble, caused by a confused and fragmented chain of command, a lack of skilled cadre, inability to recruit locally RF and PF—and the open opposition of the VNQDD.

The VNQDD, or Vietnam Quoc Dan Dang, was the political party controlling the provinces of Quang Ngai, Quang Nam, and Quang Tin. The Marines knew little about them, although, according to the study, all the village chiefs in the area were VNQDD members. The VNQDD were not supporting the priority area plan because they had not been consulted in its formulation, and for this reason, and others, the report predicted the failure of the plan, despite the heavy Marine commitment.

Like Hop Tac, it was an unusually difficult situation, but it illustrates the problems that the Marines, and any other U.S. troops that got deeply involved in pacification, confronted in Vietnam.

D. WASHINGTON GRUMBLES ABOUT THE EFFORT

Throughout the period of the buildup in Vietnam, there was a growing chorus of discontent in Washington over the management of the U.S. effort in Vietnam, most of it directed at the civilian agencies—USIA, AID, and the CIA. Unhappiness with the way the Mission ran was to lead to three major reorganizations in the 15-month period from the Honolulu conference to the arrival of Ambassador Ellsworth Bunker. The first reorganization took place immediately after Honolulu, and assigned to the Deputy Ambassador, William J. Porter, specific duties and responsibilities which had previously been dispersed throughout the Mission and handled on an *ad hoc* basis. The second reorganization, which took place in November–December 1966, reorganized the internal components of AID, USIA, and the CIA so that the Deputy Ambassador could control directly a single Office of Civil Operation (OCO), bypassing the agency chiefs. The latest reorganization, which was announced in May 1967, transferred responsibility for OCO from the Deputy Ambassador to COMUSMACV, who in turn was given a civilian Deputy with the rank of Ambassador (R. W. Komer). This section outlines events *leading to the first reorganization* in March 1966, a reorganization which raised the priority of the pacification effort, but left most of the basic problems in the U.S. Mission unsolved. The actual reorganization, and its effects, will be covered below.

Re-Emphasis on Pacification: 1965–1967 537

Efforts to reorganize the Saigon Mission are a recurring theme in recent history. The impetus for reorganization has consistently come from Washington, and the Mission has usually resisted. Its resistance is not hard to understand, since almost every reorganization scheme tended to diminish the authority and autonomy of senior members of the Mission Council such as the JUSPAO Director, the USAID Director, and the CIA Station Chief.

Skeptics have said that whenever things are going poorly, "Americans re-organize." But the opponents of various reorganization schemes have been unable to defend the existing Mission Council system, which must definitely be rated one of Vietnam's casualties. Not since the beginning of the "country team" concept in the 1950's ("Mission Council" being another term for the same structure) had the concept been tested the way it was to be tested in Viet-nam. The pressure of events, the tension, the unprecedented size of the agencies and a host of other factors made the system shaky even under the strong man-ager Maxwell Taylor. Under the man who didn't want to manage, Lodge, it be-gan to crumble. Each agency had its own ideas on what had to be done, its own communication channels with Washington, its own personnel and administrative structure—and starting in 1964–65, each agency began to have its own field personnel operating under separate and parallel chains of command. This latter event was ultimately to prove the one which gave reorganization efforts such force, since it began to become clear to people in Washington and Saigon alike that the Americans in the provinces were not always working on the same team, and that they were receiving conflicting or overlapping instructions from a variety of sources in Saigon and Washington.

Still, while General Taylor was Ambassador, reorganization was not some-thing to be pushed seriously by Washington. With Lodge back in charge, it was a different story. As a matter of fact, so serious were Lodge's managerial deficiencies that even during his first tour, when the U.S. Mission was less than 20,000 men, and the entire civilian component under 1,000, there was talk of reorganization. In a personal message to Lodge on May 26, 1964, the President made the following prophetic statement:

> I have received from [Mike] Forrestal a direct account of your belief that there is need for change and improvement in the civilian side of the country team. We have reached a similar conclusion here, and indeed we believe it is essential for you to have a top-ranking officer who is wholly acceptable to you as chief of staff for country team operations. My own impression is that this should be either a newly appointed civilian of wide governmental experience and high standing, or General Westmoreland. . . .

This message became irrelevant when Lodge suddenly resigned in June of 1964 to assist Governor Scranton's bid for the Republican nomination, but it shows that the President, Lodge, and apparently other people in Washington had deep concern with the structure of the Mission at this early date.

By sending Taylor and Alexis Johnson—then the State Department's highest-ranking Foreign Service Officer—to Saigon in July of 1964, the President in effect put off any Washington-initiated reorganizations for the length of Tay-lor's tour, since no one in Washington could tell the former Chairman of the JCS how to run a mission.

Taylor organized the Mission Council—not a new invention, but a formali-zation of the country team into a body which met once a week, with agendas, minutes, and records of decisions. Taylor was particularly concerned that the

Mission Council should have a "satisfactory meshing with . . . counterpart activities on the GVN side." And while he was Ambassador the U.S. made a determined effort to make the system work without reorganization. In a letter to Elbridge Durbrow, who was once American Ambassador in Saigon himself, Alexis Johnson described the system:

> Max and I dropped the title "Country Team" and set up what we called the "Mission Council" on a formalized basis. In addition to Max and myself, the members were General Westmoreland, Barry Zorthian as JUSPAO (Joint United States Public Affairs Office—this covered both MACV and Embassy info as well as psychological operations in the field and against the DRV), the Director of USOM and the CAS Station Chief. We established an Executive Secretary who was first Bill Sullivan and later Jack Herfurt, who was charged with the preparation of agenda, the recording of decisions, and, most importantly, following up and monitoring of decisions that were taken. We met regularly once a week (with occasional special meetings as required), with paper circulated before hand insofar as possible. One of the responsibilities of the Executive Secretary was to see that issues were worked out beforehand at staff level insofar as possible and the remaining issues clearly defined. . . . It was normally our practice to keep all members of the Council fully informed and to discuss all questions, regardless of their sensitivity. . . . After an informal exchange of views, we took up questions on the agenda, doing our best to obtain the consensus of all members. When in rare cases this was not achieved, the Ambassador of course took the decision. We considered the full range of questions, including such fundamental ones as when and under what circumstances we should bomb the North . . . etc. . . . Below the Mission Council level we established a series of committees in problem areas involving more than one agency of the mission, chaired by the agency of primary interest. These committees were responsible directly to the Mission Council. . . . We persuaded the GVN, on its side, to set up a similar organization that was first called the "Pacification Council" and later the "Rural Construction Council." . . . The GVN Council and the Mission Council met together once a week with an agenda prepared beforehand by the two Executive Secretaries . . . One of my theories, and to a degree I think it was borne out in Saigon, was that the Mission Council and the Joint Council were important not so much for what was in fact decided at the meetings but for the fact that their existence, and the necessity of reporting to them, acted as a spur to the staff people to get things done and to resolve issues at their level. Organization structure of course does not assure brilliant performance, but I do take some satisfaction in feeling that, due to the organizational structure that we established, we established the habit of the Mission elements and the GVN and the Mission, working together in a more effective way.

Whether or not the system described by Ambassador Johnson above really worked the way he says it was supposed to is not the subject of this study. But it appears that within a few months after Lodge returned as Ambassador the people within the USG advocating reorganization as at least a partial solution to the problems of the Mission were once again in full cry.

The relationship of the reorganizers to the pacifiers must be explained. Those who advocated restructuring the Mission for more effective management were not necessarily the same people advocating a higher emphasis for pacification. But usually, since the organization of the Mission was so obviously deficient, both groups of people would end up advocating some kind of change—and even if they disagreed on the nature of the change, the most important fact was that they were generally pushing a similar mood of dissatisfaction with the Mission upon the high-ranking officials with whom they might come in contact. (It should be kept in mind that they were really not groups at all, in the normal sense of the word, but a shifting collection of individuals with varying degrees of loyalty to either their parent agency or their own sense of history; and on each individual issue a different set of allies and antagonists might well exist.)

The efforts of those advocating reorganization began to bear edible fruit in December 1965 and January 1966, when a conference was held at Warrenton, Va., to which the Mission sent an impressive collection of Mission Council members: Deputy Ambassador Porter, USAID Mission Director Mann, JUSPAO Director Zorthian, Political Counsellor Habib, General Lansdale, CIA Station Chief Jorgenson, and Brigadier General Collins, representing Westmoreland. From Washington came the second and third echelons of the bureaucracy: Leonard Unger, Deputy Assistant Secretary of State; Rutherford Poats, Assistant Administrator of AID; Major General Peers, SACSA; Alvin Friedman, ISA; William Colby and Peer da Silva, CIA; Chester Cooper, White House; and Sanford Marlowe, USIA. Other participants included: Major General Hutchins, CINCPAC; Rufus Phillips of Lansdale's group; Charles Zwick and Henry Rowen of BOB; George Lodge, the Ambassador's son; Desmond Fitzgerald, CIA; and Leon Goure, of RAND.

The purpose of the meeting was to "bring together senior representatives of the U.S. Mission, Saigon, the Vietnam Coordinating Committee, Washington, and several other individuals to (a) review the joint GVN–US pacification/rural construction program and seek to promote its more effective operation and (b) address the problem of the increasingly serious shortages and bottlenecks in manpower, materials, and transport in Vietnam and to designate priorities and machinery for resources control and allocation." The major unstated purpose, in addition to those mentioned above, was to discuss the organization of the U.S. Mission in Vietnam.

Warrenton was to turn out to be a prelude to Honolulu, and as such its recomendations never were to become an integral part of the Mission's plans and strategy. But the direction that was developed at Warrenton is significant, because it represents the clear and unmistakable thrust that existed at the time in the "working levels" of both Saigon and Washington. Given the normal time lag before individual thoughts can reach the stage of agreed-upon committee-produced papers, Warrenton, we can assume, reflected the evolution of thinking that had been going on, particularly among the civilians, as the first year of U.S. combat troop and deployment began to end. Indeed, in its catch-all approach to pacification, Warrenton had something for everyone.

The final recommendations from the Warrenton conference were addressed to Secretaries Rusk and McNamara, Admiral Raborn, Mr. Bell, Mr. Marks, and Mr. McGeorge Bundy, from the meeting's co-chairmen, Ambassador Unger and Ambassador Porter. The conclusions included the following points (with comments as required):

   1. There was a consensus that the designation of priority rural construction areas for 1966 was important and that the modest goals set for

these areas were realistic. However, it was emphasized that the contrast between the massive imput of U.S. resources and the modest priority area goals made success in those areas imperative . . .

COMMENT: The National Priority Areas did not meet their 1966 goals.

2. In view of the prime importance to the U.S. of success in the four National Priority Areas, there was discussion of the need for designating U.S. team chiefs to head the U.S. advisory effort in those areas. It was agreed that the U.S. Mission Council would consider this matter promptly and report its conclusions to the VNCC.

COMMENT: The designation of team chiefs for the priority areas did not take place. Here is another example of the Washington effort to reorganize Saigon, with Saigon resisting.

3. There was widespread recognition of the need to provide within the U.S. Mission a single focus of operational control and management over the full range of the pertinent U.S. efforts in order to gear all such U.S. activities and resources effectively into implementation or the rural construction concept. However, some concern was expressed that too drastic organizational changes within the U.S. Mission would create problems with the counterpart GVN organization and would not ensure success of rural construction programs. No agreement was reached on the precise form for organization changes but there was general consensus that the focal point of control and management had to rest just below the Ambassador and that there must be a senior Mission official solely concerned with this subject. Disagreement was registered as to: (1) whether the Deputy Ambassador, assisted by a staff, should serve this function or whether another senior official (perhaps a second Deputy Ambassador) should be appointed; and (2) what extent individual agency personnel, funds, and operations devoted to rural construction could and should be broken out of agency organizations and placed under the direction of the single focal point . . .

COMMENT: Here was the compromise wording on the issue which concerned the participants at Warrenton a great deal. Each representative at Warrenton brought with him a proposed organization chart for the Mission (see below), but no agreement could be reached at that time. In the main body of the memorandum to the principals on January 13, 1966, Unger and Porter wrote:

The optimum organization for the U.S. Mission for its support of the rural construction/pacification program—a senior official with a supporting staff with full-time responsibility in this field was considered necessary. (Coordination is also required with Ambassador Lodge and Mr. Bell on this point.) It would also be desirable for such an official to have in Washington a high-level point of liaison to assure the expeditious discharge here of urgent Vietnam business in this field . . .

When he reported to the Mission Liaison Group on Warrenton two weeks later, on January 27, 1966, Porter sharply downplayed the move for reorganization which was coming from Washington and changed the emphasis. He said:

a. No decision was reached at Warrenton with respect to a U.S. in-country organization for rural construction, although the possibility of a single manager was discussed.

b. *The U.S. Mission will continue to support Rural Construction with the same organizational structure it is now using,* placing particular reliance on the Mission Liaison Group.

c. Officials in Washington were concerned about teamwork among the U.S. agencies in Vietnam but not about ability to do the job. Differences of opinion are expected, and machinery exists to resolve them. Differences due to personalities cannot be tolerated.

d. It is clearly understood in Washington that military operations alone are not enough, and that effective Rural Construction is imperative. The highest levels in the USG are keenly aware of the importance of US/GVN work in Rural Construction . . . [Emphasis added]

Although not much more than a footnote now, the reorganization schemes that were presented at Warrenton deserve brief mention. At Warrenton, the participants were still fishing for ways and means, and their proposals reveal to a limited extent the intent of each agency when faced, three months later, with a new structure in both Saigon and Washington—with Porter in charge in Saigon and Komer in business in the White House.

Chester Cooper, working for McGeorge Bundy in the White House, proposed a second Deputy Ambassador for Pacification, with control over CIA, USAID, JUSPAO, and partial control (not clarified) over MACV's Rural Construction advisors. Cooper also wanted a "Washington representative" in Saigon to expedite resource allocation. He was ambiguous about Lansdale's role. Cooper advocated a unified field chain of command. Poats and Mann submitted a joint Washington–Saigon proposal on behalf of AID (another clear indication of the fact that the real chains of command ran through agency channels, rather than through the Ambassador to Washington). They advocated a complicated arrangement in which a Chief of Staff for Pacification would head up special task forces "drawn from operating agencies but staying in their operational job in their agencies." AID in effect wanted no major change in the Mission, and particularly opposed any change in the multiplicity of chains of command in the provinces. They also advocated a Theater CINC, a resources allocation committee chaired by the AID Mission Director, and a MACV advisory structure that is partially under the Ambassador and partially separate (not clarified).

Zorthian suggested that the Deputy Ambassador coordinate all pacification activities but made it clear that he would make no change in the chains of command. Indeed, he emphasized the direct access of each Mission Council member to the Ambassador, the separateness of each agency's field program.

SACSA proposed a division of MACV into a tactical unit command and a Pacification command. All civilian elements supporting pacification would be under the Deputy for Pacification, who in turn would report to the Ambassador and Deputy Ambassador. The advisory structure would have been split down the middle between tactical unit advisors and province/district advisors.

General Collins suggested no major change in the structure of the Mission, but advocated the information of "Task Groups to deal with specific problems organized on an ad hoc basis from personnel provided by interested agencies. The Deputy Ambassador to be relieved of routine duties and to spend substantially all his time on rural construction duties . . ."

The State Department proposed a "Central Pacification Organization" which would have been not more than a coordinating committee for the existing agencies.

What these reorganization proposals seem to suggest, in light of the ultimate direction that the Mission took, is that when agencies are asked to produce suggestions which may reduce or inhibit their prerogatives, they are unlikely to do so in a manner responsive to the requirements of their politically-appointed chieftains. The prerogatives and privileges of the agencies inevitably come first. One does not reorganize voluntarily; the impetus comes from without. This is also seen in the different attitude that the reorganizers had towards Washington and Saigon. Although the same problem in coordination existed (and still exists) in Washington as in Saigon, the Washington officials always were ready to tell Saigon how to clean up its house, but were slow to suggest self-improvements. At Warrenton, perhaps prodded by the Saigon representatives, they did take note of the matter, although they were reluctant to suggest a clear solution:

> Note was also taken of the inadequacy of present U.S. Government machinery to handle Vietnam problems quickly and decisively. The need for referral of too large a number of problems to the Secretarial level was one of the problems mentioned. While the meeting did not have time to come to any firm conclusions, there was a view that the VNCC because of its coordinating, rather than decision-cum-enforcement powers could not perform this task except in part. If endowing the VNCC or its Chairman with larger powers, and with a staff associated with no one agency, is not a feasible solution, it was considered that the required directing position might have to be set up at a higher level, perhaps related to the National Security Council.

In the Warrenton report, then, all the events of the coming year were foreshadowed, and, reading between the lines, one can now see what was coming. Unfortunately, and obviously, this was not the case at the time—particularly for the Mission in Saigon.

E.   PRESIDENTIAL EMPHASIS ON THE "OTHER WAR" AND PRESS REACTION

At the end of 1965, with the bombing of the north in its tenth month, and our ground forces growing steadily, the Administration was making a determined effort to emphasize those American activities in Vietnam which did not directly involve guns and fighting. This emphasis on what came to be called the "Other War" reached a high point during the conference at Honolulu in February of 1966. The emphasis on the other war did not necessarily have to lead, as it did, to a re-emphasis of pacification; that was a by-product, at least in part, of the renewed support for pacification which had been coming from Ambassador Lodge, the Marines, the CIA (with their cadre), and the advocates of organizational reform (all covered in previous sections). But the two themes merged at Honolulu, and thus, out of the conference, came the first clear statement of Presidential support to pacification.

The need of the Administration to emphasize and publicize the nonmilitary aspects of the war needs little amplification. Few documents show this emphasis in the pre-Honolulu period, since it was so obvious. In an exception, a joint State–USIA message dated October 4, 1965, Washington told the Saigon Mission:

> *There is continuing concern at the highest levels here* regarding need to emphasize our non-military programs in Vietnam and give them maximum possible public exposure both in U.S. and abroad. [Emphasis Added]
>
> We recognize that the Mission is fully cognizant of this problem and already has underway measures to broaden public knowledge and understanding of non-military activities . . . We are also conscious of difficulties involved in enlisting greater press interest in these developments when it finds military actions more dramatic and newsworthy. Nevertheless, we hope will continue to give non-military programs increasing priority . . .

It is useful to recall the situation which existed in February of 1966, when the President went to Honolulu to meet with Ky and Thieu. On January 30, 1966, the bombing of the North began again, after a 37-day pause. There were 197,000 American servicemen in Vietnam by February 1. *The Washington Post*—which supported the Administration—editorialized on February 1:

> It is to be hoped that a new look is being taken at the military tactics in the South so that greater emphasis can be put on the safety of civilians, the rehabilitation of the countryside, the furtherance of economic growth. . . . Efforts behind the lines at economic and social programs must be increased.

Senator Fulbright had launched his public hearings on Vietnam, and on February 4 had subjected David Bell of AID to a nearly four-hour grilling in the committee. That same day, the conference was announced.

The emphasis at Honolulu was clear from before the conference started. In his press conference announcing the meeting, the President said that he would take Secretary Freeman and Secretary Gardner, not previously involved in Vietnam, as well as experts from their staffs. Freeman would go on to Saigon, the President added "to explore and inaugurate certain pacification programs in the fields of health, education, and agriculture." The President then added:

> We are going to emphasize, in every way we can, in line with the very fine pronouncements that the Prime Minister [Ky] has made concerning his desires in the field of education and health and agriculture. We want to be sure that we have our best planning and our maximum effort put into it. But we will, of course, go into the military briefing very thoroughly . . .

Even before the conference began, there were early reactions from the press to this emphasis. The *New York Times* editorialized on February 6:

> Programs in health, education and agriculture of the kind President Johnson evidently has in mind, can make an important contribution. To combat the revolutionary idea the Communists have set loose in Vietnam,

a better idea is needed. Vigorous social reform—and particularly, land reform, which has received little more than lip-service so far—could well be made the price of increased economic aid, which is now to be doubled.

But an effort to seek political "victory" in South Vietnam is likely to prove as fruitless as the long attempt at military "victory." A more limited and realistic objective is essential.

The conference itself, and its repercussions both in Washington and Vietnam, will be discussed in a following section, so there is little need to dwell on the pre-Honolulu period. In Saigon, where the word of the conference barely preceded the departure of the participants, the *New York Times* bureau chief wrote a perceptive article which reflected thinking of many junior and mid-level officials in both the U.S. Mission and the GVN. The theme it stated was not new then, and still has a very familiar ring today:

. . . There are now 230,000 to 250,000 pro-Communist troops in South Vietnam, including the Vietcong guerrillas and about 11 tough regiments of the North Vietnamese Army. That is at least twice as many enemy troops as there were at the start of last year, despite the major United States build-up since then.

This does not mean that the American build-up has been futile: the build-up was all that saved South Vietnam, in the view of most experts. It does mean that no way has yet been found to prevent the enemy from matching an American build-up with a build-up of his own.

About 200,000 American troops are now in South Vietnam along with 550,000 South Vietnamese armed men, of whom about half are well-trained army troops.

American and South Vietnamese military officers have asked for more American troops, requesting a force of about 400,000 men by the end of 1966. Not all of this strength has been promised by President Johnson, but major reinforcements are already in the offing . . .

But while 1966 will be an important year militarily, one in which all generals assume that there will be bloodier fighting, it will also be a year of increased emphasis on the subtle political and social aspects of the struggle.

The Honolulu conference will in fact concentrate largely on economic, social and political problems, according to informed sources.

It is felt in Saigon, however, that the Johnson Administration cannot, even with the best of intentions, guarantee the allegiance of the Vietnamese to their Government merely by pumping more money and technical skill into South Vietnam to give people the "better life" of which officials speak.

At least 20 to 25 per cent of the country's area is so firmly in control of the Vietcong guerrillas that no civic and political programs are possible there at all. Other large areas are so sharply contested that for the time being pacification and rural-improvement workers cannot operate.

Thus, rural-pacification work in 1966 is to be concentrated in one-third or fewer of the rural hamlets that the Government already claims to control. The limitation implies an admission that after five years of war the allies are starting from scratch in this field, and that progress must be slow.

With American enthusiasm, the United States may wish to speed the pace of pacification, but there will be serious obstacles. Most of the sadder but wiser veterans of previous programs in Vietnam seem convinced that pressure from Washington for higher and more seductive statistical goals is a major danger. They counsel "slowly but surely."

As an example, the South Vietnamese Government is trying to turn 23,000 rural-affairs workers, most of them originally trained only in armed propaganda work, into more rounded rural-construction workers.

It then plans to recruit and train 19,000 more workers, for a total of 42,000. In the opinion of some officials, it will be very difficult even to reach this goal, and any great expansion carries a risk of substituting numbers for real training.

The present pacification plan is considered imaginative and sound by experts with long experience in Vietnam, but it is considered certain that the plan could be improved at Honolulu.

Experience has shown that the crucial matter in Vietnam is always execution rather than planning. The scarcest resources in the country are manpower and leadership.

It is generally agreed that it would not be enough, say, for the United States to offer help in improving agriculture in the South Vietnamese countryside. The Americans must also consider, it is felt, whether their suggested plan is one that the South Vietnamese understand and actually— rather than merely politely—approve, and whether the badly strained South Vietnamese administration can execute the plan.

American experts in Saigon also assert that the highly ideological Vietcong movement cannot be offset merely by offers of a "better life" for the peasants.

The Vietcong have a loyal, dedicated and highly disciplined underground political structure that operates in the heart of Saigon itself and in thousands of hamlets. So far the peasants have shown little inclination to inform on this structure and to help the Government activity.

This is the central problem of the South Vietnamese war . . .

F. MEANWHILE, BACK AT THE WAR . . .

The re-emphasis of pacification was, of course, a far more disorderly process than any written review can suggest, and unfortunately must overlook many events and recommendations which were not central to the re-emphasis of pacification. But it is useful and important to review briefly what the Mission was reporting to Washington about the overall effort during 1965, since Saigon's reports should have formed an important part of the background for decision.

This selection should be read not as the "objective" story of what was happening in Vietnam—such an objective study is simply not possible at this time, even if we had access to enemy thinking—but as a reflection of the beliefs of the Americans in Saigon, and as a reflection of what the Mission wanted Washington to believe.

This selection is entirely direct quotations from MACV's Monthly Evaluation Report. Each month this report began with a summary of the month's events, and the following items represent the running evaluation for 1965: [Emphasis Added]

January, 1965: Review of military events in January tend to induce a decidedly more optimistic view than has been seen in recent months. De-

spite adverse influence exerted by national level political disorders and localized Buddhist/student rioting, the military experienced the most successful single month of the counterinsurgency effort . . . *Pacification made little progress this month.* Although some gains were made in the Hop Tac area, effort in the remainder of RVN was hampered by political activity and religious and student disorders . . . *If the RVNAF capability can be underwritten by political stability and durability, a significant turning point in the war could be forthcoming.*

February, 1965: . . . GVN forces continued to make progress in III and IV CTZ, maintained a tenuous balance over the VC in I CTZ, and suffered general regression in II CTZ . . . The indicators of RVNAF operational effort . . . all showed a decline. However, losses on both sides remained high due to the violence of encounters and VC tenacity . . . The long term effect of events in February is impossible to foretell. It is obvious that the complexion of the war has changed. The VC appear to be making a concerted effort to isolate the northern portion of RVN by seizing a salient to the sea in the northern part of II CTZ. Here RVNAF has lost the initiative, at least temporarily. However, *US/GVN strikes against DRV and increased use of U.S. jet aircraft in RVN* has had a salutary effect on both military and civilian morale which may result in a greater national effort and, *hopefully, reverse the downward trend.*

March, 1965: Events in March were encouraging . . . RVNAF ground operations were highlighted by renewed operational effort . . . VC activity was considerably below the norm of the preceding six months and indications were that the enemy was engaged in the re-supply and re-positioning of units possibly in preparation for a new offensive, probably in the II Corps area . . . *In summary, March has given rise to some cautious optimism. The current government appears to be taking control of the situation and, if the present state of popular morale can be sustained and strengthened, the GVN, with continued U.S. support, should be able to counter future VC offenses successfully.*

April, 1965: Friendly forces retained the initiative during April and a review of events reinforces the feeling of optimism generated last month . . . In summary, current trends are highly encouraging and *the GVN may have actually turned the tide at long last.* However, there are some disquieting factors which indicate a need to avoid overconfidence. A test of these trends should be forthcoming in the next few months if the *VC launch their expected counter-offensive* and the period may well be one of the most important of the war.

May, 1965: The encouraging trends of the past few months did not carry through into May and there were some serious setbacks. However, it is hoped that the high morale and improved discipline and leadership which has developed during that period will sustain future GVN efforts . . .

June, 1965: During June the military situation in the RVN continued to worsen despite a few bright spots occasioned by RVNAF successes. In general, however, the VC . . . retained the initiative having launched several well-coordinated, savage attacks in regimental strength . . .

July, 1965: An overall analysis of the military situation at the end of July reveals that GVN forces continued to make progress in IV Corps, maintained a limited edge in I Corps with the increased USMC effort and suffered a general regression in the northern portion of III Corps as well as in the central highlands of II Corps. *The VC monsoon offensive, which was so effective in June, faltered during July as VC casualty figures reached a new high . . .*

August, 1965: An evaluation of the overall military effort in August reveals several encouraging facts. The most pronounced is the steady increase in the number of VC casualties and the number of VC "ralliers" to the GVN . . . In summary, the general increase in offensive operations by GVN, U.S. and Third Country forces and a correlative increase in enemy casualties have kept the VC off balance and prevented his interference with the build-up of U.S. forces. The often spoken of VC "monsoon offensive" has not materialized, and it *now appears that the VC have relinquished the initiative in the conduct of the war.*

September, 1965: As the end of the monsoon season approached, the military situation appears considerably brighter than in May when the VC threatened to defeat the RVNAF. Since May the build-up of Free World Military Assistance Forces, coupled with aggressive combat operations, has thwarted VC plans and has laid the foundation for the eventual defeat of the VC . . .

October, 1965: . . . an increase in magnitude and tempo of engagements as the GVN/FWF maintained the initiative . . . In summary, the military situation during October continued to favor the Allies as the VC experienced heavy casualties from the overwhelming Allied fire power . . .

November, 1965: The increasing tempo of the war was reflected in casualty totals which reached new highs for VC/PAVN and friendly forces . . . While keeping the enemy generally off balance, GVN/FWMAF were able to maintain and, to some degree, to increase the scope and intensity of friendly-initiated operations.

December, 1965: Military activity in December was highlighted by an increase in the number of VC/PAVN attacks on isolated outposts, hamlets, and districts, towns, and the avoidance of contact with large GVN and Free World Forces. *The effectiveness of this strategy was attested by the highest monthly friendly casualty total of the war,* by friendly weapons losses in excess of weapons captured for the first time since July, and by 30% fewer VC casualties than in November . . .

January, 1966: The Free World peace offensive, coupled with TET festivities and the accompanying cease-fire, resulted in a period of restricted military activities for both friendly and enemy forces . . . Despite this decrease in activity, GVN and Free World Forces continued to force inroads into areas long conceded as VC territory . . . [Emphasis Added]

This is not the place for a detailed analysis of the reporting of the war, or of the implications of the above-cited evaluations. But several points do seem to emerge:

1. The reports are far too optimistic from January through April, 1965, and a big switch seems to come in June, 1965, when General Westmoreland had already made his 44-battalion request and warned of disaster if they were not forth-coming. May's report begins to show the change in mood, but its ambiguous evaluation is in sharp contrast to the brief backward look offered in September.
2. Pacification is mentioned in the January evaluation, but fades away to virtually nothing in the months of the build-up.
3. The evaluations do not suggest that the main force threat is in any way

diminishing by the end of 1965. Indeed, they accurately predict larger battles in 1966. They do not suggest, therefore, that the time had come to start emphasizing pacification *at the expense of exerting more pressure directly on the enemy.* The evaluations do not address this question directly, of course, but they do suggest that if any greater emphasis was to be put on pacification, *it could be done only if there was not a corresponding reduction in the attack effort against the VC.* This, in turn, would imply that if pacification was to receive greater emphasis at the beginning of 1966, it would require either more Allied troops or else might lead to a lessening of pressure on the VC.

II. HONOLULU

A. THE CONFERENCE—FEBRUARY 1966

The details of the closed meetings at Honolulu do not appear, in retrospect, to be nearly as important on the future emphasis on pacification as the mere fact that the public statements of all participants carried forward the theme that had been enunciated in the Declaration. This may often be true of conferences; it certainly appears true of this one, which was convened hastily and took place without any preparatory staff work on either side of the Pacific. In addition, the political upheavals in the spring of 1966, which followed the conference closely, contributed to a reduction in the importance of the details of the conference as it related to pacification.

Pacification was discussed frequently during the closed sessions. The first time came during the plenary session, when Ambassador Lodge delivered his statement to the President.

Speaking before a large audience which included General Thieu and Air Vice Marshal Ky, Lodge made a general statement about what he called "the subterranean war," and then discussed the four National Priority Areas which the GVN and the U.S. had established in October 1965:

> I would like to begin by saying that the successes and the sacrifices of the military, both the Vietnamese and the American military, have created a fresh opportunity to win the so-called "subterranean war" . . .
>
> . . . We can beat up North Vietnamese regiments in the high plateau for the next twenty years and it will not end the war—unless we and the Vietnamese are able to build simple but solid political institutions under which a proper police can function and a climate created in which economic and social revolution, in freedom, are possible.
>
> The GVN has organized itself to do this job and you will hear a presentation by General Thang, who is in charge. The American contribution consists of training and equipping of personnel; advice; and material . . .
>
> Four priority areas have been chosen. Three are places of great importance and difficulty. The fourth is largely pacified and is the place where they want to get the economic and social development program going. We think the areas are well chosen. The three tough ones are close to the Vietnamese and American armies which means that the military presence helps pacification. And, as pacification gets going, it improves the base for the military.
>
> In the four priority areas are 192 hamlets, including 238,600 people,

to be secured by the end of 1966. But GVN efforts are not limited to these four priority areas. An effort is underway which aims to raise the percentage of the whole country which is pacified by about 14%; i.e., from the current figure of about 52% to about 66% by the end of the year . . .*

After the statements of Lodge and Westmoreland (who discussed only military matters), the President said:

> I hope that out of this conference we will return with clear views in our own minds as to how we can apply more military pressure and do it better, how we can build democracy in Vietnam and what steps must be taken to do it better, how we can search for peace in the world, honorable and just peace, and do it better.
>
> If we can do the first, namely, develop better methods for defeating the Viet Cong and better methods for developing a democracy, I have no doubt but that the third will be much easier to do because you can bargain much better from strength than you can from weakness.

After a short recess, Secretary Rusk then discussed the reasons why Hanoi was not yet ready to negotiate, and said that if the GVN built "the kind of society which is indestructible," then Hanoi would probably come to the conference table more rapidly. "Anything that can move faster rather than more slowly on our side and your side," he said, "anything that can cause them to realize that an epidemic of confidence is building in the South and that momentum is gathering could hasten the time when Hanoi will decide to stop this aggression."

The President then said: "I hope that every person here from the U.S. side will bear in mind that before I take that plane back, I want to have the best suggestion obtainable as to how we can bring better military pressure on Hanoi and from the pacification side how we can bring a better program to the people of South Vietnam, and finally, third, what other efforts we can make to secure a just and honorable peace. Now, I want to have my little briefcase filled with those three targets—a better military program, a better pacification program that includes everything, and a better peace program."

General Thang then presented the GVN's pacification plans, in a briefing later made public. Thang said:

* On March 4, 1966, Lodge transmitted the text and charts of this briefing to Secretary McNamara and apparently at the same time to the White House, at the request of Jack Valenti. Lodge wrote:

"Dear Bob:

"At the request of Jack Valenti, I have put together a book containing the text and maps used in my presentation at the Honolulu Conference. It is intended to serve as a current indicator of pacification progress being made within the 1966 National Priority Areas . . .

"I think I should call attention to the fact that for Americans, it is natural to set goals and then work to achieve them by a specific date.

"This, however, is not the traditional Vietnamese way. While they have set a goal of 190 hamlets in the four priority areas, my guess would be that by the end of 1966, they may have achieved somewhat more than this, but not necessarily the ones which are listed here. In fact, if they ran into unexpectedly heavy opposition in one place and find a particularly good and unexpected opportunity elsewhere, they probably ought to change the plan . . ."

The objective of the whole people of my country is a unified democratic and strong Vietnam . . . To reach this objective, our National Leadership Committee has promoted three main policies: first, military offenses; second, rural pacification; amd third, democracy.

. . . But it is necessary, Mr. President, to define what this means by pacification. In my opinion, that is a failure of the past government, not to define exactly what we mean by pacification . . .

I think that it is necessary to . . . define pacification as an effort to which aims at improving the standard of living in this area in every respect —political, economic, social.

. . . the prerequisite is security . . . So our concept of pacification is based on four main points:

Point No. 1: The rural pacification operation can only implement restore the public security first, and carrying out a government policy through the real solidarity among the people, the armed forces, and the administration . . .

Point No. 2: Our government should be very clear when it says that it would like to build a new society for a better life in rural areas. That is meaningless to the peasant if you don't develop that in a concrete package.

[At this point, Thang launched into a lengthy explanation of what he meant by a new society. In a vague discussion, he described the social, economic, and political attributes of the new society, all of which were general and idealized statements.]

Point No. 3: The clear and realistic policy of the government contributing to a better life in a new society I just mentioned should be widely known among the population and the cadres . . .

Point No. 4: Rural pacification operations will open lasting peace if the enemy infrastructure is destroyed and permanently followed up, our own infrastructure created and supported by the people . . . All provinces have promised to the government that 75 percent of the following facts maybe can be accomplished by the 1st of January 1967: Pacification of 963 new hamlets; pacification of 1,083 existing hamlets; building of 2251 classrooms; 913 kilometers of roads; 128 bridges; 57 dams; and 119 kilometers of canals . . . While we have selected four areas of priority, the pacification operation has been pushed forward as usual, but with less efforts . . .

Rural pacification will be a long-term operation. We have modest and practical, rather than spectacular, goals for 1966 . . .

After General Thang's remarks, the plenary session records show repeated references to the pacification effort, although there is confusion as to what it means. General Thieu made additional summary remarks on pacification, then Minister Ton gave a briefing on the economic situation, followed by David Bell on the same subject.

The next day, February 8, the working groups presented their findings to the President. First, Secretary Rusk and Foreign Minister Do discussed the session on negotiations. Then General Thang and Secretary Freeman reported on their session on rural construction. The details of the working groups session itself are covered below, but in plenary. Thang emphasized the following points:

Our future should be developed mainly in four priority areas . . . Handicraft should be introduced and developed in those areas also . . . Rural

electrification should be developed and the number of generators increased
in 1967 . . .
Land reform efforts should be pushed forward . . .
We ask that construction material and cement be sent to Vietnam as soon
as possible so our school programs can be developed . . .
The training of officials at hamlet and village levels is vital . . .

Secretary Freeman, who was about to make his first trip to Vietnam, summarized for the Americans:

> Having spent a good deal of time yesterday listening to the very elo-
> quent presentations by the Chairman and the Prime Minister, as well as
> by Minister Ton, this is pretty much what we would call a nuts and bolts
> discussion session.
> One thing that was decided for United States purposes, for purposes of
> phraseology, was that the word "pacification" really did not have the right
> tone. The term "social construction" might better be used . . .
> There was some discussion, considerable, about the selection of prov-
> ince chiefs. It was strongly emphasized that it was important that the men
> be of integrity and ability, and that they be selected and maintained and
> backed up.
> The Prime Minister, General Thieu, and then General Thang both said
> that you [General Thieu] were personally interested in this, and that you
> were going to select them shortly, that they would have a duration of at
> least a year, but would be carefully reviewed and would be changed if they
> didn't do the job, but wouldn't be changed for other reasons, which we
> thought was extremely important and we were gratified to find it out.
> You also explained to us, your associates General Ky and General
> Thang, the change of command, saying in the past they were confused,
> and that they were now clear, so that everyone knew exactly what their
> function would be.
> Then you discussed the training of the cadre . . .
> I want to review the REA question and find out a bit more about why
> that seemed to have some lag.
> Finally, we discussed the possibility of a joint training program for the
> village and hamlet chiefs who presumably would be elected, but that some
> background in the philosophy, purpose and aims of government, and the
> techniques of governing and administration, were felt to be needed by those
> people.

The President then responded to the remarks of Thang and Freeman by urging "all of you connected with our program . . . to give very special attention
to refugee camps and the schools in the refugee camps." He then turned to
Minister Ton and David Bell for a discussion of the economic situation. Then
Secretary Gardner, who had co-chaired a working group on health and education—the distinction between rural construction and the health/education
programs was not clarified—made his remarks. He set out perhaps the most
clearly-defined objectives of the session (except for the economic negotiations), describing the new contract with the AMA for training personnel, the
new goal for provincial medical teams, and the plans for a new medical logistics
system. In large part his goals were more specific than those of the other working group because the USAID Public Health Chief in Saigon, Major General

James Humphries, had already laid groundwork for an excellent program of health services and assistance, and Gardner was able to work from a specific plan.

Gardner went on to discuss education, where his goals and objectives were less clear, and the President asked several detailed questions, concluding by asking General Ky to ask the Ambassador to request an educational team to go to Saigon after the agricultural team headed by Secretary Freeman returned.

The Vietnamese then thanked the Americans for the conference, and in turn some of the senior members of the American delegation—in order, Admiral Sharp, Leonard Marks, General Wheeler, Ambassador Lodge, Ambassador Harriman—made brief statements about the meaning of the conference. The President then made his final statement:

> . . . Preserve this communique, because it is one we don't want to forget. It will be a kind of bible that we are going to follow. When we come back here 90 days from now, or six months from now, we are going to start out and make reference to the announcements that the President, the Chief of State and the Prime Minister made in paragraph 1, and what the leaders and advisors reviewed in paragraph 2 . . . You men who are responsible for these departments, you ministers, and the staffs associated with them in both governments, bear in mind we are going to give you an examination and the finals will be on just what you have done.
>
> In paragraph 5; how have you built democracy in the rural areas? How much of it have you built, when and where? Give us dates, times, numbers.
>
> In paragraph 2; larger outputs, more efficient production to improve credit, handicraft, light industry, rural electrification—are those just phrases, high-sounding words, or have you *coonskins on the wall* . . .
>
> Next is health and education, Mr. Gardner. We don't want to talk about it; we want to do something about it. "The President pledges he will dispatch teams of experts." Well, we better do something besides dispatching. They should get out there. We are going to train health personnel. How many? You don't want to be like the fellow who was playing poker and when he made a big bet they called him and said "what have you got?" He said, "aces" and they asked "how many" and he said "one aces" . . .
>
> Next is refugees. That is just as hot as a pistol in my country. You don't want me to raise a white flag and surrender so we have to do something about that . . .
>
> Growing military effectiveness: we have not gone in because we don't want to overshadow this meeting here with bombs, with mortars, with hand grenades, with "Masher" movements. I don't know who names your operations, but "Masher." I get kind of mashed myself. But we haven't gone into the details of growing military effectiveness for two or three reasons. One, we want to be able to honestly and truthfully say that this has not been a military build-up conference of the world here in Honolulu. We have been talking about building a society following the outlines of the Prime Minister's speech yesterday.
>
> Second, this is not the place, with 100 people sitting around, to build a military effectiveness.
>
> Third, I want to put it off as long as I can, having to make these crucial decisions. I enjoy this agony . . . I don't want to come out of this meeting that we have come up here and added on X divisions and Y battalions or Z regiments or D dollars, because one good story about how many bil-

lions are going to be spent can bring us more inflation that we are talking about in Vietnam. We want to work those out in the quietness of the Cabinet Room after you have made your recommendations, General Wheeler, Admiral Sharp, when you come to us . . . [Emphasis Added]

The President's remarks candidly indicated the type of pressure and the expectations that he had for the effort.

But beyond the high-level interest so clearly demonstrated publicly for the first time at Honolulu, what was accomplished? As mentioned earlier, Honolulu's importance lay in two things: (1) the public support shown for the "other war"; and (2) the sections of the Declaration which committed the GVN to the electoral process. If nothing else was accomplished at Honolulu, that made the conference worthwhile. Thus, it is perhaps petty to criticize the details of the conference. But they do suggest an unfortunate failure to come to grips with any of the basic issues concerning pacification, and, moreover, a skillful performance by the GVN to please their American hosts. Thang's statement to the President after the working session, for example, with its emphasis on rural electrification, handicrafts, and the need for "materials and cement"—none of which were major GVN concerns at that time—can best be explained, in retrospect, by the Vietnamese desire to emphasize those things they felt the Secretary of Agriculture, the co-chairman of the American working group, was most interested in.

Although the inner workings of the conference do not seem to have had much importance on the development of the pacification effort, a record does remain of the "rural construction working group," and it deserves a brief summary. The meeting is useful to examine not because of its ultimate importance, which was marginal, but because it provides us with a record of a type of discussion between Americans and Vietnamese which has been replayed constantly since (and before). To some weary participants, the very words used have seemed to be unchanged since 1962.

A summary cannot, unfortunately, recapture the flavor of confusion which surrounds the memorandum for the record (A-2254, February 15, 1966). The meeting began with a discussion of terminology (see footnote on "revolutionary development") in which it was decided to use the phrase "social construction" in place of pacification in English. Then, according to the memorandum, everyone lapsed back into using the phrase "pacification."

The American representatives then pressed the issue of the role of the province chief, implying strongly that they thought the province chiefs should have more power and autonomy. The Vietnamese, led by General Co, neatly answered this issue, "referring to the establishment of Rural Construction Councils and Division and Corps levels, where such matters as the disposition and use of military forces are arbitrated and decided upon." When Leonard Unger, asked if the military commanders would be committed to providing the necessary military forces for the pacification effort, "General Co again responded, saying that in the past senior commanders tended to pull troops away from Provincial control for search and destroy operations. This is a natural desire on the part of these commanders who tend to feel that this is a more important role for such troops. Now, however, their missions have changed. These senior commanders are now directly involved in the pacification program, are members of the respective Rural Construction Councils . . . In other words, things have changed for the better. Ambassador Unger continued to pursue his point, stressing our concern that vestiges of the past may still remain. General Thang re-entered the discussion, explaining that the GVN now has a new chain of command, clear and clean from Saigon to the Corps to the Division to the Province to the District; there is only one channel in the country and it is a military channel . . . Still on the same subject, Mr. Poats raised the question: What is the primary mission of the Division Commander? Is it pacification? General Thang answered in the affirmative."

The discussion continued along these lines, and the airgram candidly concludes: "Generals Co and Thang were being pressed by rather pointed questions at this juncture and seemed to be trying to indicate that pacification is a primary task, although other military tasks must continue to be performed. It was fairly apparent that troops charged with securing the pacification area are liable still to be withdrawn on a temporary basis to meet situations which ARVN senior commanders judge to be critical."

The meeting then discussed the cadre program; the renewed emphasis on village government; the role of the province chief (at this point General Co made his statement that the GVN would appoint province chiefs for one year minimum period, a decision which was never carried out); the introduction of troops; the cadre (again); the six areas where the effort needed improvement (agriculture, handicraft, land reform, rural electrification, construction materials, and training of local officials); land reform (with Minister Tri presenting his four-month-old plan again, and Poats expressing "concern about the performance to date"); and the general question of pacification goals.

And then, after reporting back to the President in the meeting described earlier, the participants broke up, returning to Saigon and Washington to give "the other war" a new emphasis; to reorganize the Mission in Saigon; to appoint a new Special Assistant to the President in Washington; to start the quest for coonskins (the phrase was in common use in Saigon within a few days); to await the public and press reaction (see following section); and to walk without warning into a major political crisis which almost brought the government down, set back every time-schedule made at Honolulu, forced a postponement of the next scheduled conference from June-July until October, and—through an ironic twist of fate—left the GVN stronger than before, following a remarkably successful election.

B.   IMPACT ON PUBLIC IN U.S., ON U.S. MISSION IN VIETNAM, AND ON VIETNAMESE

"This week the word 'pacification' was on everyone's lips at the Honolulu conference on Vietnam," wrote Charles Mohr in the *New York Times,* February 13, 1966, "and many important members of the Johnson Administration embraced the idea with all the enthusiasm of a horse player with a new betting system. The main purpose of the Honolulu conference was to dramatize this American enthusiasm for the 1966 rural pacification—sometimes called 'rural construction'—program of the Government of South Vietnam and to pledge more American assistance for the program."

Mohr's article may have been slightly exaggerated, but there can be little doubt that the President's pledge on behalf of the U.S. Government to the pacification effort began a new period for the U.S. Government in Vietnam. From Honolulu on it was open and unmistakable U.S. policy to support pacification and the "other war," and those who saw these activities as unimportant or secondary had to submerge their sentiments under a cloud of rhetoric. Despite this fact, of course, many heated discussions still lay ahead of the Mission on program after program, and many major battles remained to be fought. Porter and Komer would fight them, as will be shown later.

This was the great impact of Honolulu—on pacification. But there were other ramifications of the Honolulu conference which overshadowed the emphasis on non-military activities in the months that followed. Because of these events—particularly the political upheavals that rocked Vietnam from March until June—the follow-up conference tentatively planned for June did not take place, and the growth in pacification's importance was probably set back about six months. While this study does not try to cover the concurrent events of the period, it should be emphasized that the most important parts of the Honolulu Declaration were not those dealing with pacification at all, but rather the sections which committed the GVN to "formulate a democratic constitution to the people for discussion and modification; to seek its ratification by secret ballot; to create, on the basis of elections rooted in that constitution, an elected government . . ." With these words, the GVN was openly committed, under U.S. pressure, to a process which they probably did not desire or appreciate. In the months that followed, the words of the Honolulu Declaration were used against General Ky by his Buddhist Struggle Movement opponents, to hoist him on his Honolulu petard; but then, in a remarkable about-face, Ky simultaneously cracked down on the Buddhists and held successful elections for a Constitutional Assembly (September 11, 1966).

The following collection of newspaper items is selected to show that there were differing opinions within the U.S. Mission and among Vietnamese, but that in general the message from Honolulu did get through to the Mission. Since almost every reporter in Saigon had sources within some element of the Mission who were telling him their honest feelings (the Saigon Mission, it was once said by Barry Zorthian, could not keep a secret 24 hours), the stories from Saigon do reflect what the Mission thought in the days just after Honolulu. The editorials and columnists from Washington indicate to what degree the Administration succeeded in convincing the press corps (which is not, of course, the U.S. public) that the emphasis at Honolulu was really on pacification.

EDITORIAL: *The New York Herald Tribune,* February 8:

The meeting presents the prospect of our resuming the war in more favorable circumstances. The meeting of the heads of the American and South Vietnamese governments is a fresh and stronger demonstration of mutual confidence. On this basis they can now proceed to mount measures for dealing with the equally important military and civilian aspects of the war.

The two are intimately related . . . the loyalty and support of the peasants in the interior are essential. President Johnson is bidding for them by offering some of the benefits of his Great Society program to the South Vietnamese. It will not be easy, in time of war, . . . but . . . they must be pursued with the same vigor as we press the war on the battlefield.

EDITORIAL: *The Washington Evening Star,* February 7:

It is particularly significant that the American delegation included HEW Secretary Gardner and Orville Freeman, Secretary of Agriculture. Their presence certainly means that a greater "pacification" effort will be made as the fighting goes on . . ."

COLUMNIST: Marquis Childs, February 9 (from Honolulu)

This conference called by President Johnson is a large blue chip put on the survival value of the wiry, exuberant Air Vice Marshal Nguyen Cao Ky, and the generals who rule with him. It is expected that Ky will not only survive but that with massive economic help from the U.S. the national leadership committee will eventually win the support of the peasant in the countryside . . . Any sensible bookmaker would quote long odds against the bet paying off. But after so many false starts this seems to be the right direction—a determined drive to raise the level of living in the countryside and close the gap of indifference and hostility between the peasant and the sophisticated city dweller . . . Over and over we have been told that only by winning the hearts and minds of the Vietnamese people will we achieve a victory that has meaning beyond the grim choice of pulverization of American occupation into the indefinite future . . . This is the reason teams of American specialists in agriculture, health, and education are going to Vietnam . . .

EDITORIAL: *The New York Herald Tribune,* February 9:

Perhaps the most constructive part of the Honolulu conference was the emphasis it placed on this hitherto badly neglected aspect of the Viet Nam war [Pacification]. It is unfortunate that Chief of State Thieu diverted attention from it by heaping more fuel on the controversy over whether the Viet Cong should or should not sit at a peace conference table . . .

EDITORIAL: *The New York Times,* February 9 and 13:

The Honolulu conference has followed the classic pattern of Summit meetings that are hastily called without thorough preparation in advance; it has left confusion in its wake, with more questions raised than answered . . . The one important area of agreement at Honolulu, apart from continuation of the military efforts, was on an expanded program of "rural construction." The prospective doubling of American economic aid, however, will be futile unless it is accompanied by a veritable social revolution, including vigorous land reform. Premier Ky cast some doubt in his emphasis on moving slowly. His Minister of Rural Pacification envisages action in only 1,900 of South Vietnam's 15,000 hamlets this year.

Vice President Humphrey evidently has his work cut out for him in his follow-up visit to Saigon. Unless some way can be found to give more momentum to this effort, the new economic aid program may go down the same drain as all previous programs of this kind.

It would be a cruel deception for Americans to get the idea that social reforms carried out by the Ky government with American money are going to make any perceptible difference in the near future to the Vietnamese people or to the course of the war.

COLUMNIST: Ted Lewis, *New York Daily News,* February 10 (from Washington):

Why, all of a sudden, has President Johnson begun to come to grips with the "other war" in South Vietnam? . . . Johnson, with his typical oratorical flourishes, has given the impression that he launched something totally new at Honolulu . . . The fact is that for several years this problem of the "other war" has been recognized as vital by the State Department, the Pentagon and even by the White House. But nobody did much about it, except in an offhand way . . .

Johnson is a master of timing. He has definitely gained a political advantage over his Viet policy critics by stressing right now the need of winning over the peasants . . . [Senator Robert] Kennedy complained in a Senate speech just ten days ago that there were 'many indications that we have not yet even begun to develop a program . . . It is absolutely urgent," the Senator said, "that we now act to institute new programs of education, land reform, public health, political participation. . . ."

NEWS ANALYSIS: Richard Critchfield in *The Washington Evening Star*, February 9 (from Saigon):

President Johnson's historic decision at Honolulu backing an American-sponsored brand of social revolution as an alternative to communism in South Vietnam was warmly hailed today by veteran political observers. The Honolulu declaration was viewed as ending postwar era of American foreign policy aimed at stabilizing the status quo in Asia.

The key phrase, in the view of many diplomats here, was the offer of full American "support to measures of social revolution, including land reform based upon the principle of building upward from the hopes and purposes of all the people of Vietnam."

. . . Johnson's decisions to put political remedies on a par with military action are also regarded here as a major personal triumph for Ambassador Henry Cabot Lodge and his top aide, Major General Edward G. Lansdale, the two main advocates of "social revolution" in South Vietnam . . . The Honolulu declaration appears to signify a major shift away from the policy of primarily military support established by President Kennedy in 1961 and closely identified with General Maxwell Taylor, Defense Secretary McNamara, and Secretary of State Rusk . . . The Lodge-Lansdale formula was a striking departure in that it saw the eventual solution not so much in Hanoi's capitulation as in successful pacification in South Vietnam . . . The Honolulu declaration amounts to almost a point by point acceptance of this formula and both its phraseology and philosophy bear Lansdale's unmistakable imprint . . .

EDITORIAL: The *Baltimore Sun*, February 10:

Unless there was more substance to the Honolulu Conference than meets the eye, it could be summed up as much ado—not much ado about nothing but simply much ado . . . It was all spectacular and diverting but so far as we can see the problem of the war is where it was before the burst of activity began . . . It is probably worthwhile to have a reiteration of the social and economic measures needed in South Vietnam . . . It is essential to underscore the political nature of the war, along with the continuing military operations. But these matters were generally understood before the Honolulu meetings. Perhaps events to come will make the purpose of the meeting clearer.

EDITORIAL: *The New York Post*, February 9:

The Hawaii meetings were advertised as the beginning of a vast new movement of economic and social reform in Vietnam, President Johnson, we were told, went to Honolulu to launch the new approach with maximum drama.

Instead, the session inadvertently underscored the lack of interest of the junta in Saigon in anything but military conquest of the Viet Cong, to be carried out by stepped up U.S. armed efforts . . .

NEWS STORY: *AP,* February 10 (from Honolulu):

Vice President Humphrey left for Saigon today with South Vietnam's top leaders to spur action on programs attacking hunger, disease, and ignorance in that war-torn country . . .

NEWS ANALYSIS: Charles Mohr, *The New York Times,* February 10
              (from Saigon):

In the atmosphere of Honolulu, there was much emphasis on form, so much that in some ways it may have obscured substance. The Americans appeared so delighted with Marshal Ky's "style"—with his showing as a politically salable young man with the right instincts rather than as a young warlord—that there seemed to be almost no emphasis on the important differences between the Governments . . . What Marshal Ky told President Johnson was something he had often said before: South Vietnamese society is still riddled with social injustices and political weaknesses; there is not one political party worthy of the name . . . The South Vietnamese leaders believe that they could not survive a "peaceful settlement" that left the VC political structure in place, even if the VC guerrilla units were disbanded. Therefore, the South Vietnamese feel that "rural pacification," of which much was said at Honolulu, is necessary not only to help them achieve military victory but also to prevent a political reversal of that victory . . . As the Vietnamese see pacification, its core is not merely "helping the people to a better life," the aspect on which many American speakers dwelled, it is rather the destruction of the clandestine VC political structure and the creation of an ironlike system of government political control over the population . . .

But the two governments have never been closer than they are in the aftermath of Honolulu, and the atmosphere of good feeling seems genuine . . .

NEWS ANALYSIS: Roscoe Drummond, February 14 (from Washington):

. . . The decisions taken at Honolulu by President Johnson and Premier Ky go to the heart of winning. They were primarily social, economic, and political decisions. They come at a malleable and perhaps decisive turn in the war . . .

NEWS ANALYSIS: Tom Wicker in *The New York Times,* February 13
              (from Saigon):

Vice President Humphrey . . . has left Saigon reverberating with what he said was the "single message" he had come to deliver. The message was that the war in Vietnam was a war to bring social justice and economic and political progress to the Vietnamese people . . . Humphrey said at a news conference here: "Social and economic revolution does not belong to the V.C. Non-communist forces are the ones forwarding the revolution."

The emphasis on social reform could also quiet critics who contend that Washington has concentrated too much on the military problem and not enough on civic action to win the loyalty of the Vietnamese people . . .

NEWS ANALYSIS: Charles Mohr, *The New York Times,* February 13 (from Saigon):

By giving enormous emphasis and publicity to it, an impression was left that pacification is something new. In a sense, there was some truth in this. The men running the program, both Vietnamese and American, are new. And the 1966 plan itself is a new one in many respects.

Pacification is vitally important to success in the guerrilla war in South Vietnam. Without it, purely military success becomes empty even if all the battles are "won."

NEWS ANALYSIS: Joseph Alsop, February 14 (from Saigon):

CART BEFORE HORSE . . . All that really mattered at Honolulu was a Presidential decision to provide the forces needed to keep the pressure on the enemy here in Vietnam. The odds are heavy that the President, who seems to prefer doing good by stealth, actually took this decision behind the electorate smokescreen of talk about other matters. The question remains whether the needed forces will be provided soon enough. One must wait and see.

But at the risk of sounding captious, and for the sake of honesty and realism, it must be noted that there was a big Madison Avenue element in all the talk about "pacification" during the Hawaii meeting and Vice President Humphrey's subsequent visit to Vietnam.

This does not mean that pacification of the Vietnamese countryside is an unimportant and/or secondary problem. On the contrary, it will eventually be all-important and primary. But one need only glance at the list of priority areas marked for pacification now, to see the adman's touch in the present commotion.

There are: An Giang Province, which belongs to the Hoa Hao sect and has been long since pacified by the Hoa Hao; the Hop Tac region near Saigon, where General Harkins experimented unhappily with the so-called oil spot technique; parts of Binh Dinh Province along the north-south highway; and the fringes of the Marine enclave at Da Nang.

Each area differs from the others. In the case of the nine villages on the fringes of the Marines' Da Nang enclave, for instance, pacification is needed to insure airfield security from mortar fire. Most of these villages have been Viet Cong strongholds for over 20 years, and they could be dangerous.

. . . Pacification by the Marines looks very fine . . . But it takes far too many Marines to do the job.

Nonetheless, the real objections to making a big-immediate show of pacification are quite different. The Hop Tac experience tells the story. Here a great effort was made by the Vietnamese authorities with the strong support of General Harkins. A good deal was initially accomplished. Boasts began to be heard. Whereat the enemy sailed forth from the nearest redoubt area, knocked down everything that had been built up, murdered all the villagers who had worked with the government, and left things much worse than they had been before . . . An attempt to make a big immediate show of pacification needs to be warned against, because of the Washington pressure to do just that. A large element of the U.S. Mission was called home a month or so ago. And in effect, these men were commanded to produce a plan for making a show as soon as possible.

Fortunately, they had the courage to point out that the cart was being put before the horse once again. Fortunately, Ambassador Lodge is well aware of the dangers of putting the cart before the horse. The pressure for something showy may continue, but it is likely to be resisted.

If so, the pressure will not be altogether useless. The Vietnamese and the Americans here are getting ready for pacification on a big scale and in an imaginative way, partly because of that pressure.

It is vital to have everything in readiness to do the job of pacification as soon as favorable circumstances arise. But it is also vital to bear in mind that really favorable circumstances cannot arise until the enemy's backbone of regular units is at last very close to the breaking point, if not actually beginning to break.

EDITORIAL: *Christian Science Monitor,* February 11:

If Saigon and Washington fight South Vietnam's economic and social war as vigorously as they fight its military war, the Communist thrust against that country will fail. Yet this is the biggest "if" of the war. Over and over lip-service has been paid to the inescapable need of winning over the peasantry. But time and again this has come to naught.

We are cautiously encouraged by the latest steps being taken. The strong emphasis laid in the Honolulu Declaration on civic reforms is a commitment in the right direction. The sending of Vice-President Humphrey to study South Vietnamese reform programs on the spot is an even stronger earnest of American's intention not to let this program slip back into another do-nothing doldrum . . .

III.   HONOLULU TO MANILA

A.   *SAIGON: PORTER IN CHARGE*

Question. Mr. President, when you were in Los Angeles reporting on the Honolulu Conference, you listed eleven items which you said were discussed, and you said that in all these fields you set targets, concrete targets. Would it be possible to get a list of these concrete targets?

Answer. I don't have any. I think what I had in mind there was saying that we hoped to make certain progress in certain fields and we expect to have another conference after a reasonable length of time, in which we will take the hits, runs, and errors and see what we have achieved and everybody would be answerable, so to speak, as to the progress they have made and whether or not they are nearing their goals . . . I hope to be in Honolulu in the next few months, maybe in the middle of the year, and see what has been done. I thought it was good that we could go there and have the Government and the military leader, General Westmoreland, and the Ambassador and the Deputy Ambassador, meet with the Vice President, the Secretary of Agriculture and technicians, and try to expose to the world for three days what this country is trying to do to feed the hungry, and educate the people, and to improve the life span for people who just live to be 35 now . . . A lot of our folks think it is just a military effort. We don't think it should be that, and we don't want it to be that . . .

As the President returned to Washington from Honolulu, the Vice President, Secretary Freeman, and McGeorge Bundy headed up a large list of high-ranking officials that went on to Saigon. Bundy, about to leave the government, carried with him authority from the President to give the Deputy Ambassador wide authority over all aspects of the rural construction program. On February 12, 1966, the President sent Ambassador Lodge a NODIS telegram, which was designed to pave the way for Bundy's reorganization effort:

> QUOTE. I hope that you share my own satisfaction with the Honolulu Conference. The opportunity to talk face to face with you, General Westmoreland and the Vietnamese leaders has given me a much better appreciation of the problems each of you face, but perhaps even more importantly the opportunities open to us. I was particularly impressed with the apparent determination of Thieu, Ky and the other Vietnamese Ministers to carry forward a social policy of radical and constructive change. However, I full well realize the tremendous job that they and we have in putting this into practice. I intend to see that our organization back here for supporting this is promptly tightened and strengthened and I know that you will want to do the same at your end. I was impressed with Ambassador Porter and it seems to me that he probably has the necessary qualifications to give you the support you will need in this field. While I know that he is already doing so, I suggest that your designation of him as being in total charge, under your supervision, of all aspects of the rural construction program would constitute a clear and visible sign to the Vietnamese and to our own people that the Honolulu Conference really marks a new departure in this vital field of our effort there. We will of course be glad to give prompt support with whatever additional personnel or administrative rearrangement this might require within the Mission or Embassy. Please let me know your own thoughts on this.
>
> I hope that in June we can have a full report showing real progress in our war on social misery in Viet Nam. In the meanwhile, I know that you will not hesitate to let me know how we can be of help. UNQUOTE.

The President has instructed that a copy of this message be given to McGeorge Bundy.

The President also sent General Westmoreland a personal telegram that day, which did not mention the matter of civilian organization. To Westmoreland he wrote:

> QUOTE. I want you to know that I greatly enjoyed the opportunity of talking directly with you at Honolulu and I hope you share my own satisfaction on the outcome of that conference. I was much encouraged by your presentation of the military situation and now have even more pride and confidence in what you and your men are doing. I feel that we are on the right track and you can be sure of my continued support.
>
> I know that you share my own views on the equal importance of the war on social misery, and hope that what we did at Honolulu will help assure that we and the Vietnamese move forward with equal vigor and determination on that front. As I have told Ambassador Lodge and am telling Thieu and Ky, I hope that in June I can have a report of real progress in that field. With continued progress in the military field, we should by that time be able to see ahead more clearly the road to victory over both aggression and misery.
>
> You have my complete confidence and genuine admiration and absolute support. I never forget that I have a lot riding on you. UNQUOTE.

After the mood at the Warrenton Conference, the push for reorganization should have come as no surprise to the higher ranking members of the Mission. Discussions centering around the role of the Deputy Ambassador (and earlier, the DCM) as a manager for the mushrooming Civilian Mission had been going on for a long time, as Lodge and Porter well knew. With Bundy in Saigon to ease the issue, Lodge answered the President on February 15, 1966:

> I do indeed want to "tighten and strengthen the organization for support of the rural construction program at this end," as you tell me you plan to do at yours. And I applaud your determination to treat "rural construction" (for which there should be a better name) * as an end in itself and on a par with the military.
>
> As you say, Ambassador Porter is already putting a great deal of effort into this work. I have never made a formal announcement of this fact because it seemed to me that the arrangement was working pretty well as it was and that public announcement was unnecessary. Also, I felt the U.S. Government was getting really enthusiastic work without thought of self from both Porter and Lansdale under present conditions. I felt public announcements might make Lansdale feel less important without any gain for Porter who does not need or want a sense of importance. I believe that Americans are pulling together here as never before and that there is a spirit here which is worth more than organization charts.
>
> But I can see the merit of the idea that a public designation of Porter as being in total charge of the American aspects of the rural construction program would "constitute a clear and visible sign to the Vietnamese and to our own people that the Honolulu Conference really marks a new departure."
>
> There are pitfalls to be avoided. For example, I assume that if Porter's new allocation means that I am so taken up with U.S. visitors that I am in

---

* Lodge had for some time been troubled by the phrase "rural construction"—the literal translation of the Vietnamese *Xay Dung Nong Thon*—which he felt suggested bricks and cement, rather than the entire program of "revolutionary uplift" which he advocated. Right after the Honolulu meeting, he asked each member of the Mission Council for suggestions on how better to translate the Vietnamese phrase. Out of the suggestions that he received (including Westmoreland's recommendation that we ought to leave the phrase alone, just translating the literal meaning of the Vietnamese as accurately as possible), Lodge chose the phrase "Revolutionary Development." At about the same time, the GVN dropped the word "rural" from the name of the Ministry of Rural Construction (thus, *Xay Dung Nong Thon* was replaced by *Xay Dung*). Lodge and Ky then announced that henceforth the Vietnamese Ministry would be known in English as the Ministry of Revolutionary Development, and the overall program called Revolutionary Development (RD). To this day, the semantic gap remains unbridged: the Vietnamese call it the Ministry of Construction (*Bo Xay Dung*), except when they are talking in English to an American; the Americans call it the MORD. The same applies to the program: moreover, the confusion is often compounded by the fact that in most informal discussions between Americans and Vietnamese, the term most often used is still "pacification." See, for example, the Working Group session at Honolulu, February 7, 1966: "It is perhaps significant that this was the only time in the course of the meeting, i.e., at the outset, that the newly adopted U.S. term was heard. Throughout the remainder of the Working Group discussion, the term pacification was used almost exclusively. In this connection, the Saigon U.S. representatives present at the meeting are inclined to doubt the actual appropriateness of the new term . . .)"

effect separated from "rural construction," then we would take a new look at the whole thing. Much of the most time-consuming job out here is not rural construction but is the handling and educating of U.S. visitors. Although it must be done at the expense of the war effort within Vietnam, it is vitally important. But it was not until the end of January that I was free enough of visitors to start holding meetings of U.S. "rural construction" workers to probe and to prod and to develop the "check-up" maps which I showed you at Honolulu.

I suggest, therefore that I make the following announcement: "I have today designated Deputy Ambassador William Porter to take full charge, under my direction, of all aspects of work of the United States in support of the programs of community building, presently described as rural construction, agreed at the Honolulu Conference. This includes overcoming by police methods the criminal, as distinct from the military aspect of Viet Cong violence; and the training and installation of health, education and agricultural workers and of community organizers. Ambassador Porter will have the support of a small staff drawn from all elements of the U.S. Mission, and he and I will continue to have the help of General Edward Lansdale as senior liaison officer and adviser. Ambassador Porter will continue to serve as my Deputy in the full sense of the word, but he will be relieved as far as possible of all routine duties not connected with the Honolulu program. We are determined that this program for peace and progress shall be carried forward with all the energy and skill of a fully coordinated U.S. Mission effort, always with full recognition that the basic task of nation-building here belongs to the people of Viet Nam and to their government."

I know that you appreciate that this is essentially a Vietnamese program and that what Porter would be supervising would be the American end of it. I recognize the existence of the view that we must in effect impose detailed plans and somehow run the pacification effort ourselves. But I do not share it. Nothing durable can be accomplished that way.

As far as "administrative rearrangement" is concerned, I would like Sam Wilson to take the office now occupied by Porter, with the rank of Minister, and to serve as Mission coordinator. I intend to put Habib in the office now occupied by Chadbourn with the rank of Minister. . . .

As soon as I receive word from you that this is satisfactory, I intend to make the announcement about Porter. The other appointments can be announced later. LODGE

From the beginning, Lodge, who felt that "a public announcement was unnecessary" except as a "clear and visible sign to the Vietnamese and to our own people that the Honolulu conference really marks a new departure," was not overly enthusiastic about the public designation of his deputy as being "in total charge" of something. The documentation is virtually nonexistent on the question of whether Lodge's feelings on this point acted as a constraint on Porter, but it is hard to escape the strong impression that from the outset, Lodge was going along with the new authority for Porter only with reluctance—and that Porter had to keep this in mind whenever he considered putting heavy pressure on an agency.

Porter also had his reservations about his role. Whether these were caused by a feeling that the Ambassador was not going to support him in showdowns with the agencies, or whether his caution came from some more basic feelings, there can be no doubt that he did not, in the period between Honolulu and Manila, perform in his new role as the President and his senior advisors had hoped. And thus once again, at Manila, a reorganization was approved—this time a much broader and far-reaching one.

Porter's intentions were accurately foreshadowed in his first statement to the Mission Council on the subject, February 28, 1966. He sought then to allay the fears which the announcement had raised in the minds of the agency chiefs in Vietnam:

> Ambassador Porter described briefly his new responsibilities as he sees them in the pacification/rural development area. He pointed out that the basic idea is to place total responsibility on one senior individual to pull together all of the civil aspects of revolutionary development. He sees this *primarily as a coordinating effort and does not intend to get into the middle of individual agency activities and responsibilities.* As he and his staff perceive areas which require attention and action by a responsible agency, he will call this to the attention of that agency for the purpose of emphasis; he intends to suggest rather than to criticize . . . Ambassador Porter noted that the non-priority areas are still getting the bulk of the resources, which means that we have not yet really concentrated on the priority areas and which also flags the necessity to bring the priority areas into higher focus. He will have a great interest in the allocation of resources such as manpower; yet he recognizes that under wartime conditions which prevail in Vietnam there will always be some inequity.

It is important to emphasize that the appointment of Porter to his new role did indeed improve the organization of the Mission, and that Porter did accomplish some of the things that Washington had hoped he would—but, under the constraints outlined below, he did not get enough done fast enough to satisfy the growing impatience in Washington with the progress of the effort. This impatience was to lead to the second reorganization and the formation of the Office of Civil Operations (OCO) after the Manila Conference. Although the impatience of Washington was justified, the fact is that under the new and limited mandate Porter had, he did begin the process of pulling together CIA, USAID, and JUSPAO, and forcing them to work more closely together. He also tried to focus General Lansdale's liaison efforts with General Thang more closely on items related to our operational objectives. He presented a new and vastly improved image of the civilian mission to the press, many of whom came to regard him as the most competent high official in the Mission. To one semi-official observer, Henry Kissinger, who visited Vietnam first in October of 1965, and then returned in July, 1966, the situation looked substantially improved:

> The organization of the Embassy has been vastly improved since my last visit. The plethora of competing agencies, each operating their own program on the basis of partly conflicting and largely uncoordinated criteria, has been replaced by an increasingly effective structure under the extremely able leadership of Bill Porter. Porter is on top of his job. It would be idle to pretend that the previous confusion is wholly overcome. He has replaced competition by coordination; he is well on his way to imposing effective direction on the basis of carefully considered criteria. At least the basic structure for progress exists. Where eight months ago I hardly knew where to begin, the problem now is how to translate structure into performance—a difficult but no insuperable task.

Despite Kissinger's hopeful words, there was a growing tendency in Washington to demand more out of the mission than it was then producing. In a paper written in August, 1966, Robert W. Komer, whose role in the re-emphasis of pacification will be discussed in the next section, wrote:

> There is a growing consensus that the US/GVN pacification effort needs to be stepped up, that management of our pacification assets is not yet producing an acceptable rate of return for our heavy support investments, and that pacification operations should be brought more abreast of our developing military effort against the NVA and VC main force. The President has expressed this view, and so has Ambassador Lodge among others.

Why did Porter not live up to the expectations of Washington? While the documentation is weak on this point, the following reasons can be deduced from the available evidence, including discussions with people who worked in both Saigon and Washington:

1. *The Ambassador was not fully backing his Deputy, and Porter was never sure of Lodge's support* in Mission Council meetings, in telegrams, in discussions with the agencies. Many senior officials of the USG, including the President, had told Porter that he had their full support, and that they expected him to manage the Mission. But on a day-to-day basis, Porter had to get along with the Ambassador, who was still (and legitimately so) the boss. The result was a considerable gap between what high officials in Washington considered Porter's mandate, and what Porter felt he would be able to do without antagonizing the the Ambassador.*

2. *The agencies involved—AID, USIA, and CIA—were hostile to the new designation from the outset.* Since every agency paid lip-service to the new role of the Deputy Ambassador, it is difficult to document this fact. But it is virtually self-evident: since every agency was being told that its chief representative in Saigon now worked for the Deputy Ambassador, a career Foreign Service Officer, there was unhappiness with the system, in both Saigon and Washington. Men like the Director of JUSPAO, who had served in Vietnam since January of 1964, and the CIA Station Chief, who retained a completely independent communica-

---

* This problem was foreshadowed in a remarkable way in 1963–1964. After visiting Vietnam in December, 1963, the Secretary of Defense sent President Johnson a memorandum in which he pointed out that the Mission "lacks leadership . . . and is not working to a common plan . . . My impression is that Lodge simply does not know how to conduct a coordinated administration . . . This has of course been stressed to him both by Dean Rusk and myself (and also by John McCone), and I do not think he is consciously rejecting our advice; he has just operated as a loner all his life and cannot readily change now. Lodge's newly-designated deputy, David Nes, was with us and seems a highly competent team player. I have stated the situation frankly to him and he has said he would do all he could to constitute what would in effect be an executive committee operating below the level of the Ambassador." It is fairly well established that Nes, whatever his own ability and shortcomings was unable to establish an "executive committee operating below the level of the Ambassador," and that, as a matter of fact his every attempt to move in the direction indicated by the Secretary further alienated him from the Ambassador. The presumed lesson in the incident was that it is difficult and dangerous to tell one man's deputy that he has to assume broad responsibility and authority if the top man does not want this to happen.

tions channel to Washington, were not going to yield any portion of their autonomy without some quiet grumbling and invisible foot-dragging. To overcome this reluctance was not as easy for Porter as Washington had perhaps hoped, particularly in light of Lodge's attitude.

3. *The Washington organization did not parallel the Saigon structure it was supposed to support, and in fact actually prevented strong and continuous support.* With legitimate legal and traditional responsibilities for programs overseas, each agency in Washington was understandably reluctant to channel their guidance through the Deputy Ambassador, whose authority did not seem to be derived from the normal letter of authority to all Chiefs of Mission sent by President Kennedy in 1961. The agencies, moreover, also had a special problem with regard to Vietnam: Congress was being far more rigorous in its review of the Vietnam program than it was in most other areas. The Moss Subcommittee on Overseas Governmental Operations, for example, was sending investigating teams to Saigon regularly, and issuing well-publicized reports criticizing the AID program across a broad front. The Senatorial group that reviews CIA programs was showing considerable concern with the nature and size of the cadre and counter-terror programs. And beyond that, there was the normal budgetary process, in which each agency generally handles its own requests through an extremely complex and difficult process. Each agency was bound to try to communicate as directly as possible with their representatives in Saigon. Thus, while some major conflicting policies which had previously existed were ironed out through the new system (such as the role of the cadre), many smaller, or second-level matters contained to receive the traditional separate agency approach.

A good example of this was the vital issue of improving village/hamlet government. Although consistently identified as a key element in any successful pacification program, improving the war-torn village structure seemed to escape the Mission organizationally. Responsibility for advice and assistance to the GVN Ministry of Interior (later the Commissariat for Administration), rested with the USAID Public Administration Division, which in turn was at the third level of the USAID, reporting to the USAID Director only through an Assistant Director for Technical Services. Within the Public Administration Division (PAD) itself, to make matters worse, improving village/hamlet government was only one of a large number of activities for which PAD was responsible—and in the eyes of many traditionally-minded professional public administrators, it did not automatically come first.

Other issues of obvious importance—such as budgeting, strengthening the Ministry, improving the National Institute of Administration, sending officials to the U.S. for participant training—all came within the normal PAD program as outlined in the AID Country Assistance Program (CAP) for FY 67, and, moreover, they required more resources, more Americans, more attention at high levels of AID, than the village/hamlet government problem. When Ambassador Porter directed AID, in May of 1966, to begin massive efforts to improve village government, his orders were obeyed *to the extent they could be within the context of previous AID commitments.* The result was a further stretching of the already taut USAID/PAD staff, since no previous commitments or programs were cut back to provide man and/or money for village government.

At the same time, other sections of the Mission which were expected to support the renewed emphasis on local government were not producing as requested. JUSPAO, asked to support the effort with psychological operations, agreed in principle but found its existing list of priorities basically unchanged. The Embassy Political Section, which should have supported the effort at least to the extent of urging through its political contacts that the GVN revitalize the village structure, simply had better things to do. The CIA was also asked to support the effort; with their cadre assets, they were in a crucial position on the matter, particularly since some of the critics of the cadre had stated that the cadre actually undercut village government instead of strengthening it (as they claimed). Again, the CIA gave lip service to the idea, without making any significant change in their training of the cadre at Vung Tau.

In this situation, Ambassador Porter tried several times to get action, each time received enthusiastic, but generalized, words of agreement and support from everyone, and finally turned his attention to other matters; with the crush of business, there was always a more immediate crisis.

B. WASHINGTON: KOMER AS THE BLOWTORCH

The Warrenton conference had discussed not only the reorganization of the Mission in Saigon, but—far more gingerly—the need for a more centralized management of the effort in Washington.

After the Honolulu conference the President decided to take action to change the Washington structure on Vietnam, but not in quite the way suggested at Warrenton. While many people at Warrenton, particularly the State representative, had hoped that the President would designate one man, with an interagency staff, as the overseer of an integrated political-military-diplomatic-economic policy in Vietnam, the President decided to reduce the scope of the job, and give one man responsibility for what was coming to be called "The Other War." Thus, for the very first time, there would be a high-ranking official—a Special Assistant to the President—whose job would be to get the highest possible priority for non-military activities. In effect, the President had assured a place at the decision councils in Washington for someone with built-in pro-pacification, pro-civil side bias. This was Robert W. Komer, whose strenuous efforts in the next few months were to earn him the nickname of "The Blowtorch" (given to him by Ambassador Lodge, according to Komer).

How much authority the President intended to give Komer is not clear. It is quite likely that the issue was deliberately left vague, so as to see what authority and what accomplishments Komer could carve out of an ambiguous NSAM and his ready access to the President.

On March 23, 1966—six weeks after Manila—Joseph Califano, Special Assistant to the President, sent the Secretary of Defense an EYES ONLY draft of the NSAM setting up Komer's authority. In the covering note, Califano said, "We would be particularly interested in whatever suggestions you would have to strengthen Komer's authority." In response, the Defense Department (the actual person making suggestion unidentified in documents) suggested only one minor change, and approved the NSAM.

The other departments also suggested minor changes in other parts of the NSAM, and on March 28, 1966, the President issued it as NSAM 343. It said:

> In the Declaration of Honolulu I renewed our pledge of common commitment with the Government of the Republic of Vietnam to defense

against aggression, to the work of social revolution, to the goal of free self-government, to the attack on hunger, ignorance and disease, and to the unending quest for peace. Before the Honoululu Conference and since, I have stressed repeatedly that the war on human misery and want is as fundamental to the successful resolution of the Vietnam conflict, as our military operations to ward off aggression . . . In my view, it is essential to designate a specific focal point for the direction, coordination and supervision in Washington of U.S. non-military programs relating to Vietnam. I have accordingly designated Mr. Robert W. Komer as Special Assistant to me for carrying out this responsibility.

I have charged him and his deputy, Ambassador William Leonhart, to assure that adequate plans are prepared and coordinated covering all aspects of such programs, and that they are promptly and effectively carried out. The responsibility will include the mobilization of U.S. military resources in support of such programs. He will also assure that the Rural Construction/Pacification program and the programs for combat force employment and military operations are properly coordinated.

His functions will be to ensure and timely support of the U.S. in Saigon on matters within his purview . . .

In addition to working closely with the addressee Cabinet officers he will have direct access to me at all times.

Those CIA activities related solely to intelligence collection are not affected by this NSAM.

Mr. Komer was in business, with a small staff and a mandate, as he saw it, to prod people throughout the government, in both Washington and Saigon. Combined with a personality that journalists called "abrasive," his mandate resulted in more pressure being put on the civilians associated with Vietnam than ever before, and in some understandable frictions.

Komer's significance in the re-emphasis of pacification is important, and must be dealt with briefly, although this section does not relate his story in detail.

First, there was Komer's influence on AID. With little difficulty, he established his ability to guide AID, and began to give them direct instructions on both economic and pacification matters. AID, previously with limited influence in the Mission's pacification policy, found its influence diminished still further.

Of more significance was Komer's emphasis on the RD Cadre program, run by the CIA. Together with Porter, he recommended a premature expansion of the program, in an effort to get the program moving faster. On April 19, 1966, after his first trip to Vietnam, Komer told the President:

> *Cadre Expansion.* While the RD program has some questionable aspects, it seems the most promising approach yet developed. The RD ministry led by General Thang is better than most, and the Vung Tau and Montagnard training centers are producing 5500 trained men for insertion in 59-man teams into 93 villages every 15 weeks.
>
> But Porter sees even this rate as insufficient to keep up with "the growing military capability to sweep the VC out of key areas." He urges rapid expansion via building another training center (which he'd like to get Seabees to build). The aim is roughly to double cadre output from 19,000 to 39,000 trained personnel per year. He thinks this rate could be reached by end CY 1966. I agree with Porter and will press this concept at the Washington end.

Plans were approved, and construction began on the second training center. But by the end of 1966 it was recognized that the attempt to double cadre training would only weaken their quality, which was shaky to begin with. The construction of the second center was abruptly halted. Komer and Porter had miscalculated badly.

Komer also sought to influence the military in both Saigon and Washington to give more attention to the pacification effort.

In cables to Saigon—most of them slugged with his name, and thus known as "Komergrams"—Komer sought to prod the Mission forward on a wide variety of programs. One of his most recurring themes was the Chieu Hoi program* and in time his urgings did contribute to a more successful program, with a high-ranking American official in Ambassador Porter's office working on nothing else, in place of the previous *ad hoc* arrangement between JUSPAO and USAID.

Another recurring theme was refugees, but here he was less successful, particularly since the U.S. Mission was never able to determine whether or not it desired to stimulate more refugees as means of denying the VC manpower. His cables on this complex issue were characterized by an absence of objective, but at least he was addressing frontally questions few other people would raise at all:

> For Porter from Komer: We here deeply concerned by growing number of refugees. Latest reports indicate that as of 31 August, a total of 1,361,288 had been processed . . . Of course, in some ways, increased flow of refugees is a plus. It helps deprive VC of recruiting potential and rice growers, and is partly indicative of growing peasant desire seek security on our side.
>
> Question arises, however, of whether we and GVN adequately set up to deal with increased refugee flow of this magnitude. AID has programmed much larger refugee program for FY 67, but is it enough? . . . Only Mission would have answers, so intent this cable is merely to pose question, solicit bids for increased support if needed, and assure you I would do all possible generate such support.

On another controversial issue, Land Reform, Komer repeatedly pressed the Mission for public signs of progress, but by the time he went out to Saigon as General Westmoreland's deputy in 1967, he—and apparently the President—were still unsatisfied.

But perhaps the most important role Komer played was to keep the general subject of pacification before the President, to encourage Ambassador Lodge to talk pacification up, and to constitute a one-man, full-time, nonstop lobby for pacification within the USG.

After his first trip to Vietnam, for example, Komer reported to the President

* For example: "Porter from Komer: Highest authorities interested in stepping up defection programs. While recognizing limitations Chieu Hoi program and inadequacies GVN administration, program has achieved impressive results and shown high return in terms modest U.S. support costs. Greatly concerned by two recent administrative decisions taken by GVN . . ." Or: "To Porter from Komer: USIA eager help maximize success both Chieu Hoi and RD programs, in which highest authorities vitally interested . . ." Or: "For Mann and Casler from Komer: Would appreciate your following through on coordinated set of action proposals to energize lagging Chieu Hoi program . . . We are concerned about drop-off in returnees since April . . . Bell and Marks concur."

that "while our splendid military effort is going quite well, our civil programs lag behind . . . To achieve the necessary results, we must ourselves give higher priority to (and expand) certain key pacification programs, especially cadres and police—*if necessary at some expense to the military effort.*"

Komer's memorandum constitutes only a small proportion of the information and suggestions reaching the President and his senior advisors on Vietnam, and the intention of this paper is not to suggest that they were in any sense definitive documents which show the direction of U.S. strategy in Vietnam. But it seems clear that Komer was the first senior official in Washington to make a major effort to put pacification near the top of our combined civil-military effort, and that he had a particularly advantageous spot from which to try. He had authorized back-channel communications with the Ambassador and Deputy Ambassador in Saigon, apparent access to the President, and the umbrella of the White House.

His memoranda to the President over his year in Washington showed considerable change in thinking on many issues, but a consistent support for more pacification. A small sample is revealing:

> Key aspects of pacification deserve highest priority—and greater emphasis. Unless we and the GVN can secure and hold the countryside cleared by military operations, we either face an ever larger and quasi-permanent military commitment or risk letting the VC infiltrate again . . . I personally favor more attention to the Delta (IV Corps) region, which contains eight out of Vietnam's 15 million people and is its chief rice bowl . . . Clearly we must dovetail the military's sweep operations and civil pacification. My impression is that, since the military are moving ahead faster than the civil side we need to beef up the latter to get it in phase. There's little point in the military clearing areas the civil side can't pacify. On the other hand, security is the key to pacification; people won't cooperate and the cadre can't function till an area is secure . . .
>
> Somehow the civil side appears reluctant to call on military resources, which are frequently the best and most readily available. I put everyone politely on notice that I would have no such hesitations—provided that the case was demonstrable—and that this was the express request of the Secretary of Defense. [Cited *Supra.*]

In August of 1966, Komer produced the longest of his papers, and the one he considered his most important. Its title was "Giving a New Thrust to Pacification." In addition to discussing the substance of pacification, the paper made some further organizational suggestions, which clearly foreshadowed the second reorganization of the Mission which took place after the Manila conference. It is worth quoting in some length (all italics are part of the original):

> There is a growing consensus that the US/GVN pacification effort needs to be stepped up, that management of our pacification assets is not yet producing an acceptable rate of return for our heavy investments, and that pacification operations should be brought more abreast of our developing military effort against the NVA and VC main force. The President has expressed this view, and so has Ambassador Lodge among others.
>
> I. *What is pacification?* In one sense, "pacification" can be used to encompass the whole of the military, political, and civil effort in Vietnam. But the term needs to be narrowed down for operational purposes, and can be reasonably well separated out as a definable problem area.

If we divide the US/GVN problem into four main components, three of them show encouraging progress. The campaign against the major VC/NVA units is in high gear, the constitutional process seems to be evolving favorably, and we expect to contain inflation while meeting most needs of the civil economy. But there is a fourth problem area, that of securing the countryside and getting the peasant involved in the struggle against the Viet Cong, where we are lagging way behind. It is this problem area which I would term pacification . . .

At the risk of over-simplification, I see management of the pacification problem as involving three main sub-tasks: (1) providing local security in the countryside—essentially a military/police/cadre task; (2) breaking the hold of the VC over the people; and (3) positive programs to win the active support of the rural population.

. . . Few argue that we can assure success in Vietnam without also winning the "village war." Chasing the large units around the boondocks still leaves intact the VC infrastructure, with its local guerrilla capability plus the weapons of terror and intimidation . . . So winning the "village war" which I will loosely call pacification, seems an indispensable ingredient of any high-confidence strategy and a necessary precaution to close the guerrilla option.

. . . Yet another reason for stressing pacification is that the U.S. is supporting a lot of assets in being which are at the moment poorly employed. Even the bulk of ARVN, which increasingly sits back and watches the U.S. take over the more difficult parts of the war against main enemy units and bases, might be more effectively used for this purpose . . . Thus, even if one contends that pacification as I have defined it is not vital to a win strategy, stepping up this effort would add little to present costs and might produce substantial pay offs.

Beyond this, the time is psychologically ripe for greater emphasis on pacification. South Vietnamese confidence is growing as the U.S. turns the tide. New US/FW military forces are arriving to reinforce the campaign against the main force; their presence will release much needed assets to pacification. The GVN, fresh from success against the Buddhist led struggle and confidently facing an election process leading toward a constitution, also has been making the kind of tough decisions—devaluation, turnover of the Saigon port to military management, etc.—that will be needed in pacification, too.

In sum, the assets are available, and the time is ripe for an increased push to win the "village war."

III. *What is Holding Up the Pacification Efforts?* The long history of the Vietnam struggle is replete with efforts to secure the countryside. Most of them, like Diem's strategic hamlet program, proved abortive. . . . Some of the chief difficulties we confront are suggested below:

A. *We had to go after the major VC/NVA units first* . . . It was a matter of first things first . . .

B. *The VC/NVA have been able to select the weakest point in any embryonic GVN pacification effort and destroy it with a lightening attack* . . .

C. *There are inherent difficulties in the pacification process itself* . . .

D. *Lack of high quality assets.* Pacification has also had to take a back seat in the sense that it generally gets only the lowest grade GVN assets—and not enough of these . . .

E. *Last but not least, neither the U.S. nor the GVN have as yet developed an adequate plan, program, or management structure for dealing with pacification* . . .

1. The JCS and MACV are so preoccupied, however justifiably, with operations against the major VC/NVA units that they are not able to pay enough attention to the local security aspects of pacification . . .

2. There is no unified civil/military direction within the GVN . . .

3. A similar divided responsibility prevails on the U.S. side . . .

4. Nor does there yet appear to be a well-understood chain of command from Porter even to the civilians operating in the field . . .

5. There is no integrated civil/military plan for pacification on either the U.S. or GVN side . . .

IV. *How do we step up Pacification?* . . . It demands a multifaceted civil-military response . . .

A. *Provide more adequate, continuous security for the locales in which pacification is taking place.* This is the essential prerequisite. None of our civil programs in the countryside can be expected to be effective unless the area is reasonably secure. Nor, unless the people are protected, and their attitudes likely to change in favor of the GVN . . . To provide security requires the assignment on a long term basis of enough assets to defeat these resident VC companies and battalions, in addition to providing 24-hour security to the people until they are able to assist in providing their own protection. This is primarily the task of RF and PF, supported by the RD cadres and police . . . Some knowledgeable experts contend that even if we improve the . . . RF, PF, police, and cadre, they are together insufficiently to extend local security much beyond existing secured areas. They feel that lacking mobility and heavy firepower, those forces must be thickened with a liberal sprinkling of regular ARVN units working in the area outside the immediate area undergoing pacification. I do not suggest that ARVN regulars gainfully employed in battle against the enemy main forces be so diverted. *I do urge that those ARVN forces not now fully engaged—a substantial fraction of the total be used to contribute directly to improving local security.*

B. *We must devote more effort to breaking the hold of the VC over the people* . . .

C. *Carry out positive revolutionary development programs to win active popular support.* The cliche of winning support by offering the people a better life through a series of interrelated RD programs has great relevance in Vietnam . . .

D. *Establish functioning priorities for pacification* . . .

E. *Better Area Priorities* . . . A greater stress on pacification logically means greater stress on the Delta . . .

F. *Concentrate additional resources on pacification* . . . Arguments made in the past that pacification is a delicate subject to be approached only with care and precision have lost some of their relevance as the intensity of warfare has increased . . . Increase:

> *Police* . . .
> *RD Cadre* . . .
> *Material Support for Pacification* . . .
> *The U.S. Agricultural Effort* . . .
> *Chieu Hoi* . . .
> *Village/Hamlet Administration* . . .

G. *Set more performance goals* . . .

   H. *Rapidly extend the security of key roads* . . .
   I. *Systematize the flow of refugees* . . .
   J. *Get better control over rice* . . .
V. *How can Pacification be Managed More Effectively?*
   A. *Restructuring the GVN* . . .
     —*Place the RD and PF under the RD Military* . . .
     —*Establish a single line of command to the province chiefs* . . .
     —*Remove the Division from the pacification chain of command* . . .
     —*Strengthen the authority of the Province Chiefs* . . .
     —*Appoint civilian chiefs in selected provinces and districts* . . .
   B. *Parallel strengthening of the structure is essential.* U.S. leadership has often sparked major pacification steps by the GVN. The structure for managing pacification advice to the GVN, and direct U.S. military/civilian support, have evolved slowly as the U.S. contributions have grown. Once it was possible to coordinate the U.S. pacification effort through an inter-agency committee for strategic hamlets. Later the Mission Council concept was used extensively. In the wake of the Honolulu Conference, the President appointed Ambassador Porter to take charge of the non-military effort in Vietnam. Several highly qualified people now give Porter the nucleus of a coordination and operations staff. However . . . the U.S. management structure must be strengthened considerably more.

There are three basic alternatives, each building on the present structure, which could provide the needed result. Two of them are based on the principle of a "single manager" over both civilian and military assets by as-signing command responsibility either to Porter or Westmoreland. The third accepts a continued division between the civil and military sides for nu-merous practical reasons, but calls for strengthening the management structure of both.

Alternative No. 1—Give Porter operational control over all U.S. pacification activity . . .

Alternative No. 2—Retain the present separate civil and military command channels but strengthen the management structure of both MACV and the U.S. Mission. This option, recognizing the practical difficulties of putting U.S. civilian and military personnel under a single chief, would be to settle for improved coordination at the Saigon level.

To facilitate improved coordination, however, it would require strengthening the organization for pacification within MACV and the U.S. Mission. MACV disposes of by far the greater number of Americans working on pacification in the field. It has advisory teams spending most of their time on pacification in 200 out of 230 districts and in all 43 prov-inces. These teams—not counting advisors at division, corps and all tactical units down to battalion—number about 2000 men compared with about one-eighth this number from all other U.S. agencies combined.

However, the senior officer in MACV dealing with pacification as his principal function is now a colonel heading the J33 staff division. More-over, with 400,000 U.S. troops soon to be committed, General Westmore-land, his subordinate commanders, and his principal staff officers must spend increasing time on military operations associated with defeating the VC/NVA main formations. Therefore, management of the tremendous advisory resources with MACV inevitably suffers regardless of General Westmoreland's personal effort to give balanced attention to both.

Hence there might be merit in COMUSMACV having a senior deputy to manage pacification within MACV and pacification advice to the JCS, as well as throughout the Vietnamese military chain of command. Key staff sections, such as J33, Polwar Directorate, Senior Advisor for RF/PF, could be controlled by a chief of staff for pacification responsive to the Deputy. Advisory teams at corps and division would receive guidance and orders on pacification from the Deputy. Province and district advisors would receive all orders, except routine administrative instructions, through the pacification channel.

To parallel the MACV organization and provide a single point of liaison on the civil side, Ambassador Porter should have his own field operations office formed by merging USAID Field Operations, JUSPAO Field Services and CAS Covert Action Branch. Control over the people assigned would be removed, as in Alternative No. 1, from their parent agency. All civilian field personnel in the advisory business would also receive their guidance and orders from the Deputy Ambassador.

For this dual civilian-military system to operate effectively, the closest coordination would be required between the offices of the MACV Deputy and the Deputy Ambassador. Since it is difficult and dangerous to separate military and civilian aspects of pacification at the province level, most policy guidance and instructions to the provinces hopefully would be issued jointly and be received by the senior military and civilian advisors who would then develop their plans together.

I would still favor a single civil/military team chief in the province, even though he would have two bosses in Saigon talking to him through different and parallel chains of command. Alternatively, since MACV already has a senior advisor in each province, it would be possible similarly to assign a single civilian as the Vietnamese province chief's point of contact on all non-military matters. All other civilians in the province would be under his control.

Alternative No. 3—Assign responsibility for pacification civil and military, to COMUSMACV. This is not a new suggestion, and has a lot to recommend it. In 1964, General Westmoreland proposed that he be made "executive agent" for pacification. MACV at that time had an even greater preponderance of field advisors than it does today, and was devoting the bulk of its attention to pacification. Since the military still has by far the greatest capacity among U.S. agencies in Vietnam for management and the military advisors outnumber civilians at least 8 to 1 in the field, MACV could readily take on responsibility for all pacification matters.

Turning over the entire pacification management task to COMUSMACV would require him to reorganize his staff to handle simultaneously the very large military operations business involving U.S., Free World and Vietnamese forces and the civil/military aspects of pacification at the same time. The USAID, JUSPAO, and CAS Covert Operations staffs would come under COMUSMACV's control where they would be used as additional "component commands." In this case, *it might be desirable to have a civilian deputy to COMUSMACV for pacification.*

Also appropriate under this concept would be a single U.S. advisory team, under a team chief, at each subordinate echelon. The result would be a single chain of command to the field and coordinated civilian/military pacification planning and operations on the U.S. side. The U.S. Mission would speak to Vietnamese corps and division commanders, province chiefs and district chiefs with a single voice.

In the latter part of this lengthy memorandum, Komer clearly foreshadowed both the formation of OCO after the Manila conference—his Alternative No. 2—and the merger of OCO and MACV into MACCORDS after Guam—his Alternative No. 3. But when he sent the paper to Saigon with his deputy in mid-August, the reaction from Lodge, Porter, and Westmoreland was uniformly negative: they asked him, in effect, to leave them alone since they were satisfied with their present organization.

But Komer had also distributed his paper around Washington, and was lobbying for another change in the structure of the Mission, although he remained, in August, vague as to which of the three alternatives he put forward he personally favored. When other senior officials of government began to voice feelings that additional organizational changes were necessary in the Mission in Saigon, the die was cast.

Another major attribute of Komer was his strong public and private optimism. He produced for any journalist willing to hear him out facts and figures that suggested strongly that the war was not only winnable, but being won at an accelerating pace.

To the President he sounded the same theme:

> After almost a year full-time in Vietnam, and six trips there, I felt able to learn a good deal more from my 11 days in country, 13–23 February. *I return more optimistic than ever before.* The cumulative change since my first visit last April is dramatic, if not yet visibly demonstrable in all respects. Indeed, I'll reaffirm even more vigorously my prognosis of last November (which few shared then) that growing momentum would be achieved in 1967 on almost every front in Vietnam.

Komer believed in the concept of "sheer mass"—that in time we would just overwhelm the Viet Cong:

> Wastefully, expensively, but nonetheless indisputably, we are winning the war in the South. Few of our programs—civil or military—are very efficient, but we are grinding the enemy down by sheer weight and mass. And the cumulative impact of all we have set in motion is beginning to tell. Pacification still lags the most, yet even it is moving forward.
> Indeed, my broad feeling, with due allowance for over-simplification, is that our side now has in presently programmed levels all the men, money and other resources needed to achieve success . . .

In summary, Komer's 13 months in Washington were spent steadily raising the priority of the pacification and other non-military efforts in Vietnam. While he never was in a controlling position within the Washington bureaucracy, he succeeded in making those who were more aware of the "other war" (a term he used continually until Ambassador Bunker announced in May of 1967 that he did not recognize that there was such a thing). While it can be no more than speculation, it would also appear that Komer played an important role in inserting into high-level discussions, including Presidential discussions, the pacification priority. Thus, when General Westmoreland visited the President at the LBJ ranch in August, 1966, Komer put before the President a series of pacification-related subjects to be used during the discussions. This happened again at Manila, where some of the points in final communique were similar to things Komer had been pushing earlier, as outlined in his August memorandum.

C.   STUDY GROUPS AND STRATEGISTS: SUMMER 1966

In the aftermath of Honolulu, task forces and study groups were suddenly assembling, producing papers on priorities, on organization of the Mission, on the role and mission of various forces. They were all manifestations of the new mood that had come over the Mission and Washington on pacification. The advocates of pacification—with their widely differing viewpoints—all saw their chance again to put forward their own concepts to a newly interested bureaucracy, starting with Komer and Porter.

The most important of the numerous studies were:

1. The Program for the Pacification and Long-Term Development of South Vietnam (Short Title: PROVN)—commissioned by the Army Chief of Staff in July of 1965, completed and submitted in March 1966;
2. The Priorities Task Force—formed in Saigon in April 1966 by Deputy Ambassador Porter, completed in July 1966;
3. The Inter-Agency "Roles and Missions" Study Group—formed by Porter in July 1966, completed in August.

While the recommendations of these studies were never accepted *in toto,* they all play key roles in the development of strategic thinking in Washington and Saigon during the latter part of 1966, and they continue to be influential today.

PROVN—As early as the summer of 1965, General Johnson saw the need to select a superior group of officers, and set them to work on a long-term study of the problem in Vietnam. The study was intended for internal Army use, and was for a while after its completion treated with such delicacy that Army officers were forbidden even to discuss its existence outside DOD. This was unfortunate, because in content it was far-ranging and thoughtful, and set a precedent for responsible forward planning and analysis which should be duplicated in other fields.

PROVN was charged with "developing new sources of action to be taken in South Vietnam by the United States and its allies, which will, in conjunction with current actions, modified as necessary, lead in due time to successful accomplishment of U.S. aims and objectives." With this broad mandate, PROVN staff spent eight months questioning returning officers from Vietnam, studying the history of the country, drawing parallels with other countries, analyzing the structure of the U.S. Mission; and making recommendations. In the end, the PROVN team decided that there was "no unified effective pattern" to the then-current efforts in Vietnam, and submitted a broad blueprint for action. Its thesis was simple:

> The situation in South Vietnam has seriously deteriorated. 1966 may well be the last chance to ensure eventual success. "Victory" can only be achieved through bringing the individual Vietnamese, typically a rural peasant, to support willingly the GVN. The critical actions are those that occur at the village, district, and provincial levels. This is where the war must be fought; this is where that war and the object which lies beyond it must be won. The following are the most important specific actions required now:
>
> > Concentrate U.S. operations on the provincial level to include the delegation of command authority over U.S. operations to the Senior U.S. Representative at the provincial level.

Reaffirm Rural Construction as the foremost US/GVN combined effort to solidify and extend GVN influence.

Authorize more direct U.S. involvement in GVN affairs at those administrative levels adequate to ensure the accomplishment of critical programs.

Delegate to the U.S. Ambassador unequivocal authority as the sole manager of all U.S. activities, resources, and personnel in-country.

Direct the Ambassador to develop a single integrated plan for achieving U.S. objectives in SVN.

Reaffirm to the world at large the precise terms of the ultimate U.S. objective as stated in NSAM 288: A free and independent non-communist South Vietnam . . .

Beyond this frank and direct summary, the study had hundreds of recommendations, ranging from the specific and realizable to the vague and hortatory.

In summary, the PROVN was a major step forward in thinking. Although as mentioned above, its value was reduced for a long time by the restrictions placed on its dissemination, the candor with which it addressed matters was probably possible only because it originated within a single service, and thus did not require the concurrences of an inter-agency study.

For example, the PROVN study addressed directly a point of such potential embarrassment to the U.S. Government that it is quite likely an inter-agency group would not have addressed it except perhaps in oblique terms:

A PROVN survey . . . revealed that no two agencies of the U.S. Government viewed our objectives in the same manner. Failure to use that unequivocal statement of our fundamental objective—a free and independent, non-communist South Vietnam—set forth in NSAM 288, hinders effective inter-agency coordination and the integrated application of U.S. support efforts.

As for the study's "highest priority" activities, PROVN recommended:

(1) *Combat Operations*—the bulk of U.S. and FWMA Forces and designated RVNAF units should be directed against enemy base areas and against their lines of communication in SVN, Laos, and Cambodia as required; the remainder of Allied force assets must ensure adequate momentum to activity in priority Rural Construction areas.

(2) *Rural Construction*—in general, the geographic priorities should be, in order, the Delta, the Coastal Lowlands, and the Highlands; currently the highest priority areas are the densely populated and rich resource Delta provinces of An Giang, Vinh Long, Dinh Tuong, Go Cong, and the Hop Tac area surrounding Saigon.

(3) *Economic Stability*—current emphasis must be directed toward curbing inflation and reducing the excessive demands for skilled and semi-skilled labor imposed upon an over-strained economy . . .

On the management of the United States effort—which PROVN found extremely poor—the recommendation was to create a single manager system, with the Ambassador in charge of all assets in Vietnam and the mission of producing a single integrated plan. PROVN suggested major steps in the direction of giving the Ambassador a stronger hold over the military.

Of greatest importance—aside from the reorganizational suggestions—was the PROVN conclusion on the supremacy of Rural Construction activities over everything else:

> Rural Construction must be designated unequivocally as the major US/GVN effort. It will require the commitment of a preponderance of RVNAF and GVN paramilitary forces, together with adequate U.S. support and coordination and assistance. Without question, village and hamlet security must be achieved throughout Vietnam . . . RC is the principal means available to broaden the allied base, provide security, develop political and military leadership, and provide necessary social reform to the people . . .

To this end, PROVN suggested a division of responsibility among the forces:

> The need to sustain security pervades every ramification of RC . . . The various forces capable of providing this environment must be unified . . . at the province level. They must include the ARVN as a major component —as many of its battle-tested units as can possibly be devoted to this mission. These integrated national security forces must be associated and intermingled with the people on a long-term basis. Their capacity to establish and maintain public order and stability must be physically and continuously credible. The key to achieving such security lies in the conduct of effective area saturation tactics, in and around populated areas, which deny VC encroachment opportunities.

Finally, the study advocated a far stronger system of leverage for American advisors in the field—"mechanisms for exerting U.S. influence must be built into the U.S. organization and its methods of operation."

The PROVN study concluded with a massive "Blueprint for National Action" which was never implemented. But the influence of the study was substantial. Within the Army staff, a responsible and select group of officers had recommended top priority for pacification. Even if the Army staff still rejected parts of the study, they were on notice that a study had been produced within the staff which suggested a substantial revision of priorities.

The PROVN study had some major gaps. Proceeding from the unstated assumption that our commitment in Vietnam had no implicit time limits, it proposed a strategy which it admitted would take years—perhaps well into the 1970's—to carry out. It did not examine alternative strategies that might be derived from a shorter time limit on the war. In fact, the report made no mention of one of the most crucial variables in the Vietnam equation—U.S. public support for the Administration.

Further, the report did little to prove that Vietnam was ready for pacification. This "fact" was taken for granted, it seems—a fault common to most American-produced pacification plans. While PROVN did suggest geographic priorities, they were derived not even in part from the area's receptivity to pacification but exclusively from the location and strategic importance of the area. Thus, the same sort of error made in Hop Tac was being repeated in PROVN's suggestions.

MACV analyzed the report in May of 1966, calling it "an excellent over-all approach in developing organization, concepts and policies . . ." In a lengthy analysis of PROVN, MACV cabled:

As seen here, PROVN recommends two major initiatives essential to achieving U.S. objectives in South Vietnam: creation of an organization to integrate total U.S. civil-military effort, and exercise of greatly increased direct U.S. involvement in GVN activities.

MACV has long recognized need for the greatest possible unity of effort to gain U.S. objectives in South Vietnam. MACV agrees with PROVN concept to achieve full integration of effort in attaining U.S. objectives in South Vietnam. Evolution of U.S. organization in Saigon is heading towards this goal. Deputy Ambassador now has charge of revolutionary and economic development programs and MACV is charged with military programs. In addition, special task force has been established by Deputy Ambassador to draft mission-wide statement of strategy, objectives, and priorities. In effect, this task force is engaged in integrated planning which under PROVN concept would be performed by supra-agency staff. PROVN proposal for designation of a single manager with supra-staff is a quantum jump to achieve the necessary degree of military-civil integration. This final step cannot be implemented by evolutions here in Saigon. It would have to be directed and supervised from highest level in Washington.

MACV is in complete agreement with PROVN position that immediate and substantially increased United States direct involvement in GVN activities in form of constructive influence and manipulation is essential to achievement of U.S. objectives in Vietnam. PROVN emphasizes that "leverage must originate in terms of reference established by government agreement," and "leverage, in all its implications, must be understood by the Vietnamese if it is to become an effective tool." The direct involvement and leverage envisioned by PROVN could range from skillful diplomatic pressure to U.S. unilateral execution of critical programs. MACV considers that there is a great danger that the extent of involvement envisioned could become too great. A government sensitive to its image as champion of national sovereignty profoundly affected by the pressure of militant minorities, and unsure of its tenure and legitimacy will resent too great involvement by U.S. Excessive U.S. involvement may defeat objectives of U.S. policy: development of free, independent non-communist nation. PROVN properly recognizes that success can only be attained through support of Vietnamese people, with support coming from the grass roots up. Insensitive U.S. actions can easily defeat efforts to accomplish this. U.S. manipulations could easily become an American takeover justified by U.S. compulsion to "get the job done." Such tendencies must be resisted. It must be realized that there are substantial difficulties and dangers inherent in implementing this or any similar program.

Several important aspects of proven concept require comment, further consideration and resolution or emphasis. Some of the more significant are:

Regarding U.S. organization, MACV considers that any major reorganization such as envisioned by PROVN must be phased and deliberate to avoid confusion and slow-down in ongoing programs . . .

There appears to be an overemphasis on military control in PROVN which may be undesirable. For instance, the study states that all senior U.S. representatives (SUSREPs) initially will be U.S. military officers. This should not necessarily be stated policy. The senior U.S. representative, particularly at province level, should be selected on basis of major tasks to be performed, program emphasis in a particular area and other local considerations. PROVN also limits U.S. single manager involvement in military activities. If single manager concept of a fully integrated civil-military effort is to be successful, military matters, such as roles and missions, force requirements, and deployments must be developed in full coordination and be integrated with civil aspects.

PROVN proposal for enlarged U.S. organization for revolutionary development, particularly at sector and sub-sector levels, will require both military and civilian staff increases. It will necessitate further civilian recruiting and increased military input. Present shortage of qualified civilian personnel who desire duty in Vietnam must be considered. It may fall to the military, as it is now happening to some degree, to provide personnel not only for added military positions, but also for many of civilian functions as well.

Regardless of what U.S. might desire, however, our efforts to bring about new Vietnamese organizational structure must be tempered by continuous evaluation of the pressure such change places on Vietnamese leaders. Our goals cannot be achieved by Vietnamese leaders who are identified as U.S. puppets. The U.S. will must be asserted, but we cannot afford to overwhelm the structure we are attempting to develop.

Accordingly, MACV recommends that PROVN, reduced primarily to a conceptual document, carrying forward the main thrusts and goals of the study, be presented to National Security Council for use in developing concepts, policies, and actions to improve effectiveness of the American effort in Vietnam.

The "Priorities Task Force"—This group was set up at Ambassador Porter's direction in April 1966, following Komer's first trip to Vietnam, during which Komer had strongly urged that the Mission try to establish a set of interagency priorities. The actual work of this task force, which had full interagency representation, was considered disappointing by almost all its "consumers," particularly Komer, since it failed to come up with a final list of priorities from which the Mission and Washington could derive their programs. But it was by far the most ambitious task force the Mission had ever set up, and it provoked considerable thought in the Mission.

Its introductory section was a rather gloomy assessment of the situation. As such, it was at variance with the then current assessment of the situation—but in retrospect, it is of far greater interest than the recommendations themselves!

> After some 15 months of rapidly growing U.S. military and political commitment to offset a major enemy military effort, the RVN has been made secure against the danger of military conquest, but at the same time it has been subjected to a series of stresses which threaten to thwart U.S. policy objectives . . .
> The enemy now has a broad span of capability for interfering with progress toward achievement of U.S. objectives. He can simultaneously operate offensively through employment of guerrilla and organized forces at widely separated points throughout the country, thus tying down friendly forces, while concentrating rehearsed surprise attacks in multi-battalion or even multi-regimental strength. . . . The war will probably increase in intensity over the planning period (two years) though *decisive military victory for either side is not likely*. Guerrilla activity will make much of the

countryside insecure. More of the rural population will be directly affected, and the number of refugees and civilian casualties on both sides seem bound to rise . . .

Reasons for lack of success of the overall pacification program—including all the stages from clear and secure operations to sustaining local government—were varied. First, the primary hindrance to pacification was the low level of area security given active Viet Cong opposition. Second, political instability prevented continuing and coherent GVN direction and support of any pacification program. Third, pacification execution has been almost wholly Vietnamese and can be supported only indirectly by the U.S. This has made it less susceptible to American influence and more subject to political pressures and the weaknesses of Vietnamese administration and motivation. Fourth, no pacification concept since the strategic hamlet program has been sufficiently clear in definition to provide meaningful and consistent operational guidance to those executing the program. Fifth, given the pressure for success and the difficulty of measuring progress the execution of pacification failed to emphasize the political, social and psychological aspects of organizing the people and thus eliciting their active cooperation. The material aspects, being both visible and less difficult to implement, have received too much attention. Sixth, there was an absence of agreed, definitely stated pacification roles and missions not only within the GVN and the U.S. Mission but also between the GVN and the U.S. Mission. This absence caused proliferation of various armed and unarmed elements not clearly related to each other. Seventh, a quantitative and qualitative lack of trained and motivated manpower to carry out pacification existed. In addition, insufficient emphasis has been given to training and orientation of local officials associated with the pacification program. Eighth, lack of a well defined organizational structure in the U.S. Mission created some confusion and conflicting direction of the pacification effort . . .

During 1965, military plans were developed to support revolutionary development; national priority areas were selected where special emphasis would be placed on revolutionary development, and a structure was established by the GVN extending an organizational framework for revolutionary development from national to district levels. Meanwhile, the U.S. Mission has begun action to centralize direction for revolutionary development to ensure coordination of all Mission activities in support of revolutionary development.

A new approach was also taken in 1965 to bring coherence to the use of cadre in the pacification process. Drawing on a concept of armed political action teams, whose relative success locally was at least partly owing to direct U.S. sponsorship and control, a combined cadre team approach was developed. A new organization, the Revolutional Development Cadre, was established, which brought together and replaced a number of disparate cadre organizations. The combined cadre team approach includes armed units and special skills of relating to and assisting the people. The combined teams form the basis of the present pacification program.

While these measures have helped to alleviate some of the problem areas which previously frustrated pacification efforts, some areas of major concern remain: First area security where Revolutionary Development is being initiated is not always adequate because of manpower problems; second, continued existence of various overlapping security forces further reduces effectiveness; third, approved pacification concepts, roles, and missions agreed to by the U.S. and the GVN are lacking; fourth, the effectiveness of the new RD cadre teams remain to be tested and evaluated; fifth, extensive training of local and other officials associated with RD still must be accomplished; sixth, emphasis on rapid expansion and the desire for immediate visible and statistical progress would operate against lasting results; and, seventh, organizational development and functioning on both the GVN and U.S. sides are as yet incomplete.

*   *   *

The situation described above suggests that the course of events in Vietnam during the next two years will be significantly influenced by the following principal current trends.

The war can be expected to increase in intensity, but decisive military victory should not be expected. It will be basically a war of attrition. Troop casualties should increase on both sides, and civilian casualties and refugees as well. The enemy can, if he chooses, increase still further the rate of his semi-covert invasion and the level of combat.

The enemy will continue to build up his forces through infiltration from NVN and recruitment for main force VC units in SVN to achieve a favorable relationship of forces.

At the same time, he will continue to reinforce his capabilities for political action in the urban areas, to exploit anticipated future political disturbances, to increase his terrorist acts in the cities, and to isolate the urban population from the countryside.

GVN control of the countryside is not now being extended through pacification to any significant degree and pacification in the rural areas cannot be expected to proceed at a rapid rate. A new approach to pacification has been developed, but it is too early to judge its effectiveness. In addition, important problems requiring resolution remain . . .

The Vietnamese will continue to face grave problems in creating an effective system of government. Under present conditions we cannot realistically expect a strong GVN to emerge over the planning period, nor can we expect political unity or a broadening of the base of popular support. The increased American presence, rising inflation and an image of considerable corruption are issues which will be increasingly exploited by unfriendly and opportunistic elements. U.S. influence on political events continues to be limited while our responsibility for Vietnam's future is increasing.

The Task Force divided all activities in Vietnam into categories of importance, and assigned them priorities in groups. Unfortunately, the divisions were either too vague to be useful, or else they designated specific activities, such as agriculture, to such a low position that Washington found the selection unacceptable. In its first rank of importance the Task Force placed:

1. Those activities designed to prepare a sound pacification program primarily through strengthening the human resources element of pacification, and through coordinated planning . . .
2. Those activities which draw strength away from the enemy and add to GVN's strength and image of concern for all its citizens . . .
3. Those psychological activities that support the war effort . . .

4. Those activities that persuade the people that RVNAF is wholly on the side of the people and acting in their interests . . .

down through:

16. Those activities which develop the leadership and organization of non-governmental institutions, particularly youth groups . . .

It was scarcely a list from which one could assemble a coherent program. Moreover, the above list of 16 "highest priority" tasks, was followed by a group of ten "high priority" tasks—including strengthening provincial governments, autonomous municipal governments, better budgetary procedures, better refugee programs, minority programs, and so on. These, in turn, were followed by a nine-point list of "high priority programs." Into at least one of the 35 highest, high, or just plain priority activities, one could fit every program and project then being pursued in Vietnam. Furthermore, the proposal seemed to confuse inputs and outputs, placing in the same category "wishes" like "minimizing the adverse impact of and exploiting the opportunities provided by the American presence" (which was only "high priority") with "programs" like "creating a sound base for agricultural development."

The Priorities Task Force recommendations were used, unlike those of PROVN. In the FY 67 Country Assistance Program (CAP), submitted by AID to Congress that fall, the Task Force Strategy statement was used as a foreward, with Ambassador Lodge's approval. Moreover, the concept of priorities outlined in the final paper was applied to the AID program in Vietnam, with each activity being placed in one of the categories of priority. This did not result, however, in the *original objective of reducing* the size of the program and focusing it: instead, the AID program more than doubled in 1967, and a year later people were still complaining about the lack of clear-cut priorities. (As a matter of fact, when Deputy Ambassador Eugene Locke returned to Washington in September of 1967 with a "Blueprint for Vietnam," he was told that it lacked any sense of priorities, and was too much of a "shopping list.")

The "Roles and Missions" Study Group—One of the Priority Task Force recommendations was that the Mission should establish another group to examine the question of the proper role of each military and paramilitary and police and civilian force in the country. This group was set up, under the chairmanship of Colonel George Jacobson in July of 1966, and submitted its final report to the Mission Council on August 24. The group was once again interagency, and it produced a paper of considerable value—indeed, a paper which could well have served as a basic policy document for the Mission and Washington.

The Study Group made 81 recommendations, of which 66 were acceptable to all agencies of the Mission. But even these 66 were not immediately adopted as basic doctrine. Because of inertia and weariness, rather than deliberate sabotage, the recommendations were never treated as basic policy, and simply were carried out or not depending on the drive and desire of the individual officials associated with each individual recommendation.

The report began, as almost all Vietnam studies seem to, with a definition:

Revolutionary Development consists of those military and civil efforts designed to liberate the population of South Vietnam from communist coercion; to restore public security; to initiate economic and political development; to extend effective GVN authority throughout SVN; and to win the willing support of the people to these ends.

From there it developed the most logical and coherent approach to returning an area to GVN control and then gaining its support that had yet been produced by a group in either the Mission or Washington. The report was hailed by Porter, by Komer, and by various mid-level officials. Jacobson himself was to be named Mission Coordinator four months later, a position from which he could present his ideas directly to the Ambassadors.

While, as mentioned above, the recommendations were never issued as Mission policy in a group, many of them found their way into the main stream of the Mission through other means. Some of the more controversial ones—for example: "that Division be removed from the RD Chain of Comand"—remained as potent ideas to be discussed within the government and with the Vietnamese, and to be acted on slowly.

Since the report foreshadowed several major developments in pacification, and since it still has today an intrinsic value of its own, it is worth quoting some of its major points:

> High hopes are now pinned on the RD cadre, as *the* critical element of success in RD. Unfortunately, there is a real danger it is being regarded as a panacea with curative powers it does not, of and by itself, possess. *The introduction of RD Cadre cannot alone achieve success in any of the tasks discussed above.* Even cadre such as may be available in six months . . . cannot compensate for the current failings and limitations of other fundamental elements bearing directly on the RD process.
>
> . . . RD demands for its success *radical* reform within the GVN including its Armed Forces. *This reform must start at the top* . . . These radical changes in the GVN and RVNAF seem most unlikely to occur without a strong, focused and coordinated exertion of U.S. influence at high levels . . .
>
> RECOMMEND:—That FWMAF give increased emphasis to improving the performance and conduct of GVN military forces through combined operations . . .
>
> —That as the increase in FWMAF strength permits, these forces engage with RVNAF in clearing operations in support of RD with the primary objective of improving the associated GVN forces . . .
>
> —That in view of the deployment and capabilities of FWMAF in Vietnam and recognizing the necessity for increased security support to RD, the bulk of ARVN Divisional combat battalions be assigned to Sector commanders with only those Divisional battalions not so assigned to be under the control of Divisions . . .
>
> —That the Division be removed from the RD chain of command . . .
>
> —That Ranger units because of their frequently intolerable conduct toward the populace, be disbanded with individual Rangers reassigned* . . .
>
> —That RF and PF become Provincial and District Constabulary . . .
>
> —That the Constabulary be placed under the Ministry of RD . . .

* This was a recommendation which MACV particularly opposed, arguing that it "would seriously reduce ARVN combat strength." Westmoreland added that he could not countenance the disbanding of units which had just received a Presidential Unit Citation.

—That National Police (Special Branch) assume primary responsibility for the destruction of the VC "infrastructure" . . .

—That Police Field Force be integrated into the Constabulary . . .

—That the Vietnamese Information Service (VIS) terminate its rural information cadre operations and assume a supporting role . . . for RD Cadre, technical cadre, and hamlet officials . . .

And so on. What lay behind each recommendation was an effort to unify the various GVN agencies and ministries working on pacification, streamline their operations, and, at the same time, increase U.S. influence over those operations.

While many items the Study Group recommended have still not been carried out, there has been growing acceptance of the bulk of the recommendations. In its initial reaction to the paper, MACV's Chief of Staff wrote to Ambassador Lodge "that many actions have been taken or are being considered by MACV which support and complement the overall objectives envisioned by the report. There are, however, certain recommendations with which we do not agree."

The most important reservation that MACV had, concerned the allocation of resources for the RD effort:

> We are confronted with a determined, well-organized force operating in regimental and division strength. As long as this situation exists, it is imperative that the regular military forces retain first priority for the available manpower. Once the threat of the enemy's regular forces has diminished and the defeat of external aggression is accomplished, then other programs should have the first priority for recruiting . . .

In addition, MACV opposed the removal of Division from the RD chain of command; suggested a further task force to examine the Constabulary issue in detail; and opposed the suggestion that Special Branch Police—which meant on the American side the CIA—take over the anti-infrastructure effort. (On this latter point, the issue was finally resolved by an ingenious compromise structure under Westmoreland and Komer called ICEX—Intelligence Coordination and Exploitation—in July 1967.) Finally, Westmoreland rejected any internal changes in the MACV structure, as suggested by the Study Group. These had included:

> —the establishment at MACV Division advisory level of a Deputy Senior Advisor for RD, at Corps a Deputy Senior Advisor for RD, and at COMUSMACV level a Deputy COMUSMACV for the entire MACV advisory effort and for RD . . .
>
> —changes in the advisory rating system to emphasize the quality of the advice and the accuracy of reports, rather than the performance of the organization/Vietnamese they advise . . .

USAID reacted favorably to the study. In his memo to Lodge, the Acting USAID Director said that the report "presents an antidote to our having been too indulgent with the GVN in the past to our peril and theirs." Once again, however, as with MACV, USAID added some reservations—and the reservations all fell in areas in which USAID would have the action responsibility if something was to be done. USAID feared that the report recommended steps that would give the Ministry of RD too much strength, reflecting the worry of their Public Safety Division. The Constabulary recommendations, which had far-reaching implications, were given a particularly rough going-over. For example, to protect its own embryonic structure, the Police Field Force USAID made the following comment on the recommendation that the PFF be integrated as units into the Constabulary:

> USAID concurs with the reservation that PFF remain a separate entity with its essential police powers.

The CIA also thought the report was "constructive and helpful," but listed a few "disagreements." Once again, these pertained to those items in which the ICA had a strong vested interest. They opposed strenuously, for example, the suggestion that the MACV subsector advisor—the only American at the district level in almost every district—"be given primary responsibility for monitoring the activities of the cadre." Using the argument that everything possible be done to retain the civilian nature of the cadre, the CIA refused to let the MACV subsector advisors do what they were already doing in many cases.

The CIA and MACV both opposed the suggestion that a single Director of Intelligence be appointed to command civilian and military intelligence structures. The CIA said that this was "unwieldly and unworkable" because "this is not a theater of war."

The Political Section of the Embassy also thought the study was "valuable," but added that "it appears to neglect a number of political considerations." Beyond that, they supported every specific suggestion, while noting how hard it would be to carry some of them out.

JUSPAO shared the fears of USAID that the report would concentrate more power in the hands of the Ministry of RD than it could usefully employ. JUSPAO thought that the Constabulary should be created, therefore, but placed under the Ministry of Defense. JUSPAO also found the removal of the Division from the RD chain of command "hardly feasible or realistic at this juncture"—begging the issue of whether or not the United States should seek this as a valuable objective.

When the exercise was over, there were many in the Mission in Saigon who felt that the Study Group recommendations should have formed a blueprint for action throughout the Mission. They pointed out that almost all the recommendations were concurred in by every agency, and that these could be carried out immediately. The remaining 15 which were still not unanimously accepted could then be discussed and perhaps resolved.

In Washington, at least one high official, R. W. Komer, felt the same way, and urged the Mission to use the recommendations as policy. But somewhere between August 24, when the paper was submitted, and the end of 1966, the paper was relegated to the useful but distinctly secondary role of another "study group," as its name suggests. While everyone was complimentary about the paper, no machinery was set up in Ambassador Porter's office to oversee the implementation of the recommendations. While the agencies said that they agreed with most of the recommendations, the all-important decisions as to how fast and how hard to push forward with each recommendation was left to whichever agency "had the action" on it. This in effect left some crucial decisions—the variables in our effort—outside the Deputy Ambassador's hands. He had no machinery for checking to see what the agencies were doing to carry out the suggestions they said they agreed with. He had virtually no staff to observe how the agencies were actually handling each problem, although it was obvious that success or failure on each item lay to a large extent in the method it was handled. Indeed, Porter had no good way to even find out whether the agencies really did accept the recommendations. He was reliant on a knowledgeable but small staff which could only meddle in the internal matters of other agencies to a limited degree.

It was these shortcomings in the new mandate to Porter that were becoming evident in the late summer of 1966, and pressure began to build in Washington for another reorganization.

The pressure and emphasis on pacification was also producing visible results in MACV. On August 8, 1966, the J-3 of MACV, Major General Tillson, briefed the Mission Council on how MACV intended to "give maximum support to RD." The briefing was general, simplistic, and shallow, but it was a clear indication that General Westmoreland and MACV were beginning to respond to the pressure from outside their command that they should give RD more support. As such, it marked a major step for MACV. Tillson said that "military operations must be used to assure the security necessary for RD to begin. All military operations are designed towards this goal . . ."

He then went on to trace the degree to which criticism of ARVN was justified, and examine the suggestion that ARVN be re-oriented to support RD—something which was to become part of the Manila communique only two months later:

> The ARVN has been at war continuously for a period of over ten years . . . The fact that ARVN today even exists as an organized fighting force is a tribute to its stamina and morale.
>
> Since its inception, ARVN has been oriented, trained, and led towards the task of offensive operations . . . It is difficult, in a short period of time, to redirect the motivation and training of years, *and to offset the long indoctrination that offensive action against the VC is the reason for the existence of the Army* . . .
>
> In the 1967 campaign plan, we propose to assign ARVN the primary mission of providing direct support to RD and US/FW Forces the primary mission of destroying VC/NVA main forces and base areas. Agreement has been reached between General Westmoreland and General Vien that, in I, II and III Corps areas, ARVN will devote at least 50% of its effort directly in support of the RD program. In IV Corps, where there are no U.S. forces, it was agreed that ARVN might have to devote up to 75% of its effort to offensive operations . . .
>
> [General Vien has issued a directive that] flatly states that, while some progress has been made, desired results are still lacking on RD. It emphasizes that RD efforts must be on a par with efforts to destroy the enemy . . . These directives of General Vien resulted from his conversations with General Westmoreland . . . [Emphasis Added]

This was by far the strongest verbal support that MACV had ever given pacification, and it actually contained the kernel which developed into the important passage in the Manila communique that committed the RVNAF to support of RD.

The change in mood in Saigon among the Americans was reflected by Ambassador Lodge in his Weekly NODIS to the President. On August 31, 1966, he began his cable with:

> The biggest recent American event affecting Vietnam was giving pacification the highest priority which it has ever had—making it, in effect, the main purpose of all our activities . . .

The above was brought about in several ways—by word in General Westmoreland's "Concept of Military Operations in South Vietnam" of August 24, and by the deeds of the U.S. 1st and 25th Divisions and the III MAF. There has also been the new MACV proposal to revamp ARVN and turn it into a force better suited to pacification. Also at a special meeting of the Mission Council a stimulating paper was presented by the "Interagency Roles and Mission Study Group" which would take RF and PF, now a part of the Vietnamese Armed Forces, make them into a "constabulary" and call it that. Police Field Force would also be included in the Constabulary under this concept.

A week earlier, Westmoreland had sent forward to CINCPAC and JCS a broad strategy statement for the coming year. He saw the time as "appropriate in light of the fact that we are on the threshold of a new phase in the conflict resulting from recent battlefield successes and from the continuing FWMAF buildup." After reviewing the course of battle since the introduction of U.S. troops, Westmoreland projected his strategy over the period until May 1, 1967, as "a general offensive with maximum practical support to area and population security in further support of RD." He then added:

> The growing strength of US/FW Forces will provide the shield and will permit ARVN to shift its weight of effort to an extent not heretofore feasible to direct support of RD. Also, I visualize that a significant number of US/FW maneuver battalions will be committed to tactical areas of responsibility (TAOR) missions. These missions encompass base security and at the same time support RD by spreading security radially from the bases to protect more of the population . . .
> The priority effort of ARVN forces will be in direct support of the RD program; in many instances the province chief will exercise operational control over these units . . . This fact notwithstanding, the ARVN division structure must be maintained . . .

This long message, with its "new look" emphasis on pacification, was sent apparently not for CINCPAC's routine consideration, as would be the normal case in the military chain of command, but for the edification of high-ranking civilian leaders in Washington. It ended with a comment added by Ambassador Lodge—an unusual procedure in a military message:

> I wish to stress my agreement with the attention paid in this message to the importance of military support for RD. After all, the main purpose of defeating the enemy through offensive operations against the main forces and bases must be to provide the opportunity through RD to get at the heart of the matter, which is the population of SVN.

The new emphasis on RD/pacification was thus coming from many sources in the late summer of 1966. Porter and Komer, pushing the civilians harder than they had ever been pushed before, had not only improved their performance, but also to create pressures inside MACV for greater emphasis on RD. Westmoreland, responding to the pressure, and finding the VC/NVA increasingly reluctant to give battle, was planning a two-pronged strategy for late 1966–early 1967: attack and destroy enemy base areas, and use more forces to protect and build up and expand the GVN population centers.

D. THE SINGLE MANAGER

By the late summer of 1966, as has been shown in detail in the preceding sections, the flaws in the structure of the U.S. Mission had been openly criticized in studies or reports by the U.S. Army Staff (in PROVN), by the Priorities Task Force and by the Roles and Missions Study Group in Saigon, by Robert Komer in repeated memoranda, and by various other visitors and observers. In addition to the written record, there were undoubtedly numerous private comments being made both in Saigon and Washington, some of which were reaching senior officials of the government.

The options before the USG were, in broad outline, fourfold. The Mission could either remain unchanged, or else it could reorganize along one of the three general lines which Komer had outlined in his August 7, 1966 memorandum:

> *Alternative One*—Put Porter in charge of all advisory and pacification activities, including the military;
> *Alternative Two*—Unify the civilian agencies into a single civilian chain of command, and strengthen the military internally—but leave civilian and military separate;
> *Alternative Three*—Assign responsibility for pacification to Westmoreland and MACV, and put the civilians in the field under his command.

The Mission, as usual, argued for leaving the structure the way it was. Their arguments in this direction were unfortunate, because in Washington the mood was certainly in favor of some further changes, and by resisting all suggestions uniformly, the Mission was simply causing friction with Washington and reducing influence on the ultimate decisions.

The issue was joined more rapidly than anyone in Saigon had expected, because in mid-September, 1966, the Secretary of Defense weighed in on the issue in a direct way, producing a Draft Presidential Memorandum which advocated handing over responsibility for pacification to COMUSMACV.

McNamara's draft said:

> Now that a Viet Cong victory in South Vietnam seems to have been thwarted by our emergency actions taken over the past 18 months, renewed attention should be paid to the longer-run aspects of achieving an end to the war and building a viable nation in South Vietnam.
>
> Central to success, both in ending the war and in winning the peace, is the pacification program. Past progress in pacification has been negligible. Many factors have contributed, but one major reason for this lack of progress had been the existence of split responsibility for pacification on the U.S. side. For the sake of efficiency—in clarifying our concept, focusing our energies, and increasing the output we can generate on the part of the Vietnamese—this split responsibility on the U.S. side must be eliminated.
>
> We have considered various alternative methods of consolidating the U.S. pacification effort. The best solution is to place those activities which are primarily part of the pacification program, and all persons engaged in such activities, under COMUSMACV . . . In essence, the reorganization would result in the establishment of a Deputy COMUSMACV for Pacifica-

tion who would be in command of all pacification staffs in Saigon and of all pacification activities in the field.

It is recognized that there are many important aspects of the pacification problem which are not covered in this recommendation, which should be reviewed subsequent to the appointment of the Deputy COMASMACV for Pacification to determine whether they should be part of his task—for example, the psychological warfare campaign, and the Chieu Hoi and refugee programs. Equally important, is the question of how to encourage a similar management realignment of the South Vietnamese side, since pacification is regarded as primarily a Vietnamese task. Also not covered by this recommendation are important related national programs . . . Finally, there is the question of whether any organizational modification in Washington is required by the recommended change in Vietnam.

I recommend that you approve the reorganization described in this memorandum as a first essential step toward giving a new thrust to pacification. Under Secretary Ball, Administrator Gaud, the Joint Chiefs of Staff, Director Helms, Director Marks, and Mr. Komer concur in this recommendation.

This memorandum was apparently never sent to the President, but it was distributed, with a request for comments and concurrence, to Ball (Rusk being out of the country), Gaud, the JCS, Helms, Marks, and Komer. Only Komer and the JCS concurred, with the others producing alternate suggestions. The entire question was handled as an "EYES ONLY" matter.

The positions that were taken were:

State opposed the recommendation. In informal discussions with Komer, Alexis Johnson cited the failure of Hop Tac (which seems irrelevant), the "optics" of militarizing the effort, and the need to check with Lodge as reasons against actions.

AID agreed that the present program had its faults, but resisted the idea of a MACV takeover. Instead, they proposed a complex system of committees and deputies for RD, who would report to a Deputy Ambassador for Pacification.

The *JCS* found that the proposal "provides an excellent rationale for an approach to the problem of appropriately integrating the civil and military effort in the important field of pacification" and concurred in the idea of a Deputy COMUSMACV for RD.

CIA and *USIA* both opposed the reorganization, although their written comments are not in the files.

Komer weighed in with a lengthy rationale supporting the idea. Although he may not have known it at the time, he was talking about the organizational structure he was going to fit into later. After agreeing that the need to get pacification moving was great, and that "the military are much better set up to manage a huge pacification effort," he said that 60–70% of "real job of pacification is providing local security. This can only be done by the military . . ." Komer then raised some additional points:

1. The Ambassador should remain in overall charge.
2. MACV should not assume responsibility for everything, only the high payoff war-related activities.
3. Logistic support should remain a multi-agency responsibility.

As the discussions on the subject continued, Deputy Ambassador Porter arrived in the United States for a combined business-personal trip. When he found out what was being considered, he immediately made strong representations to McNamara, Komer, and Rusk. He also sent a personal cable back to Lodge, alerting him for the first time to what was afoot in Washington:

> Principal topic under discussion here is DOD proposal to bring both U.S. military and U.S. civilian resources needed to advance RD program under direction of Deputy COMUSMACV. This plan will be discussed with you during McNamara visit. It would detach all civilian field operations from direct control of Saigon civilian agencies and would place them under Deputy COMUSMACV for RD. In addition to controlling civilian field resources, latter would also manage U.S. military resources with view to increasing their effectiveness in furthering RD programs. Deputy COMUSMACV would be responsible to Ambassador or Deputy Ambassador through COMUSMACV. This at least is my understanding of proposal which is being strongly pushed here.
>
> I have taken position that this proposal and certain counter proposals put forward by civilian agencies here require careful field study. In its existing form, as I understand it, it does not take into account the fact that militarization of our approach to this important civilian program runs counter to our aim of de-militarizing GVN through constitutional electoral process . . .
>
> I have been stressing here that our military are already heavily loaded with responsibility for achieving military measures required to further civilian RD programs, such as evoking adequate cooperation from RVN . . . I have emphasized need for MACV to grapple with problem of VC guerrilla activity during night, as distinct from main force activity during daytime which we now know can be dealt with. These areas would appear to offer great possibilities for application of military talent and I repeat that in my view question of burdening MACV further with complex programs (cadre, police, etc.) requires careful field study which I would have done promptly, if you agree, by group similar to that which carried out "Roles and Missions" study.

This was the background as Secretary McNamara, Under Secretary Katzenbach, General Wheeler, and Mr. Komer went to Saigon in October. The issue had been deferred, and when the visitors returned, they would make recommendations to the President. Katzenbach, making his first trip as Under Secretary, was requested to look at the problem with a new eye and no prior prejudices.

When they came back from Saigon, Katzenbach and McNamara both sent the President an important memorandum. Katzenbach argued for a strengthening of Ambassador Porter's role, and a deferral of the question of turning the RD effort over to MACV. McNamara concurred, but with a different emphasis. The memorandums were dated October 14 and 15, 1966, less than two weeks before the Manila conference, and the recommendations were accepted by the President. Katzenbach's memorandum was, for a first effort after a short VIP trip, an unusually interesting one. Excerpts:

> . . . I believe decisive, effective RD depends on a clear and precise common understanding of the security as we all recognize to be the foundation of success in the "other war."
>
> To illustrate the divergency of meanings, let me report briefly on a conversation I had with a small group of reporters in Saigon. It quickly de-

generated into a debate, not between the reporters and me, but between Ward Just of the *Washington Post* and Charles Mohr of the *New York Times*.

Just argued heatedly that RD could not begin to be effective unless security were first guaranteed both to the peasants and to RD workers. "An AID man cannot do his job," he said, "while being shot at by the VC."

Mohr responded just as heatedly, that security could not come first—because security from guerrillas is meaningless and impossible until the peasant population is motivated to support the GVN and deprive the guerrillas of havens, secrecy, and resources.

Obviously, the easy answer to this circular chicken-egg debate is to say that both are necessary—military protection and public motivation against the VC. And yet even that answer is incomplete for it defines security only in the American frame of reference . . .

I know of no one who believes we have begun effectively to achieve the goal of gaining the population's active support, despite a series of pacification programs and despite even the budding early efforts of Ambassador Porter's new program.

The Military Aspect. Secretary McNamara, Mr. Komer, Ambassadors Johnson, Lodge, and Porter, Mr. Gaud, I, and all others who have approached the problem are perfectly agreed that the military aspect of RD has been spindly and weak.

*   *   *

This probably is the result of the entirely understandable preoccupation by MACV in recent months with the main force military emergency. However justifiable this has been, a major effect has nonetheless been our failure effectively to press RVNAF to even start meeting their crucial RD responsibilities.

(I know of no one who believes that these should be met principally by American forces—unless we should wish the whole RD effort to collapse once we leave.)

The Civil Aspect. Similarly, the work of civilian agencies has fallen short—largely, but not only because of the failure of RVNAF to provide a military screen behind which to work . . .

Rather than engage in a civil-military debate, I think we should devote our efforts toward trying to devise an administrative structure that capitalizes on the assets each agency can offer to RD.

What should be the elements of an ideal organization?

1. It should have maximum leverage on RVNAF to engage in clear and hold operations in direct support of RDM efforts.

2. It should have a single American "negative," anti-VC channel—that is a single commander for all action against communist guerrilla forces. This commander would calibrate and choose among the various force alternatives —depending on whether he believed the need to be military, para-military, or police.

This command would include complete responsibility for all anti-VC intelligence—that is, concerning all VC suspects either in the infrastructure or in guerrilla units.

3. It should have a single, unified channel for all "positive" pro-people aspects of RD, irrespective of the present lines of command within civilian

agencies, allowing a single commander to calibrate and assign priorities to relevant positive programs on behalf of the peasantry.

This, too, would include the immediate expansion of and control over all "pro-people" intelligence—that is, detailed district-by-district and province-by-province reporting on the particular gains most wanted by the populace (land reform, for example, in one province; or schools in another; or agricultural assistance in another).

4. Sensitivity to political inputs and wise political guidance of the whole process are needed to ensure that military programs support rather than negate efforts to win public support and participation. Failure to assure this —which characterized French efforts in Indochina and Algeria, in contrast to civil-led, successful, British efforts in Malaya and the Filipino campaign against the Huks—means that the very process of gaining security would be weakened and prolonged, at increased cost in Vietnamese and American lives.

Thus, overall civilian command of the RD program is needed for fundamental practical reasons, by no means for considerations of international image alone (though on the latter point, it must be observed that as soon as we put "the other war" under obvious military control, it stops being the *other* war). In particular, it is important not to block or reverse—by the way *we* organize our efforts—the current genuinely hopeful Vietnamese trend toward increased civilian influence and participation in government.

In short, it is not the precise form of organization or the precise choice of flow chart that is important. What *is* important is:

1. An immediate and effective military screen for RD efforts; and

2. Authoritative and compelling administration of the efforts of civilian agencies.

I believe we *can institute* effective administration of the RD program— which Ambassador Lodge has aptly described as the heart of the matter— achieving all of these ideals:

1. Maintain the effect and the appearance of civilian control by immediately assigning overall supervision of all RD activities to Ambassador Porter (and assigning a second deputy to Ambassador Lodge to absorb the substantial other responsibilities now met by Ambassador Porter).

2. That the several civilian lines of command within agencies be consolidated into one. Thus, USAID, JUSPAO, OSA, and the Embassy personnel assigned to RD all would continue under the nominal *administrative* control of their respective agencies but full, unified *operational* control would rest solely with Ambassador Porter.

3. That Ambassador Porter's authority be made clear and full to each constituent agency of the RD team, including:

—relocation of personnel;

—the establishment of priorities irrespective of agency priorities;

—and the apportionment of the funds allocated by each agency to Viet-Nam, bounded only by statutory limitations.

4. That MACV immediately give highest-level command focus and consolidation to its RD concerns and staff, now that it is no longer so completely distracted from RD by the compelling requirements of main force combat. This would be organized around the thesis that the central need is the most effective persuasive power or leverage on RVNAF. This thesis is strengthened substantially by:

—The firm intent, expressed to us in Saigon last week, of President Thieu and Prime Minister Ky to shift ARVN infantry to revolutionary development work starting in January;

—The enhanced powers they intend to give to General Thang, already an able chief of RD for GVN.

5. That the MACV effort embrace at least advisory control over all levels of force—starting with ARVN but also including RF, PF, CIDG, and the para-military operations of the RD cadre, PFF, and PRV.

These steps would greatly strengthen both the military and civil lines of command. They would contribute significantly to the success of RD. *But not even these changes would be decisive without a strong link between them.*

The civil side requires the capacity to influence military movement which no organizational chart can provide. The MACV side requires the political and substantive expertise which a military organization does not—and is not expected to—possess.

Thus the fundamental recommendation I would make is:

6. To appoint, as principal deputy and executive officer to Ambassador Porter, a general of the highest possible ability and stature—of two, three or even four-star rank. To do so would win the following advantages:

a. Compelling indication of the seriousness with which the Administration regards RD.

b. The rank, and stature to insure optimum RD performance from MACV.

c. The rank and stature to afford maximum impact on GVN military leaders and capacity to persuade them properly to prod RVNAF when necessary.

d. Demonstrated command administrative capacities with which to assist Ambassador Porter, while bridging the inevitable institutional difficulties that might well otherwise develop from one arm of MACV's taking orders from a civilian.

e. A solution to the military control image problem, by which the advantages of close military support would be veiled by civilian control.

f. The capacity and position to formulate an effective qualitative plan encompassing both military and civil realities. Previous plans have focused on numbers of provinces, volume of RD cadre trained, and so on. They have put an unrealistic premium on quantitative, "statistical" success. Meaningful criteria, however, must be qualitative. I would envision such a qualitative plan intended to cover at least the next 12 months.

There would be an additional prospective advantage as well. If it should later be found that dual lines of authority—even given this strong link— are not successful, then we could more readily fall back to a unitary, military command structure—with the new RD general taking charge.

He would have the benefit, in that situation, of having been under civilian control and his relationship to RD would already be evident, making the change to military control less abrupt and less susceptible to criticism.

Secretary McNamara's memorandum—sent the day before Katzenbach's— was of greater importance, and stands out as one of the most far-reaching and thoughtful documents in the files. While this study concentrates on pacification, it is necessary to view McNamara's remarks about pacification in this memorandum within the context of the entire paper.

He said that the military situation had gone "somewhat better" than he had anticipated a year earlier, and that "we have by and large blunted the communist military initiative." But he found little cause for hope that the overall situation would turn dramatically in our favor within the next two years. "I see no reasonable way to bring the war to an end soon," he said, and described the enemy strategy as one of "keeping us busy and waiting us out (a strategy of attriting our national will)."

> Pacification is a basic disappointment. We have good grounds to be pleased by the recent elections, by Ky's 16 months in power, and by the faint signs of development of national political institutions and of a legitimate civil government. But none of this has translated itself into political achievements at Province level or below. Pacification has, if anything, gone backward . . .

Thus, the Secretary found us "no better, and if anything worse off—from the point of view of the important war (for the complicity of the people)."

He did not think at that time that major increases in U.S. force levels or bombing programs would make a big difference in the short run. Rather, he suggested a series of actions designed to emphasize to Hanoi that we were setting definite limits on the cost in men and money of the war, while settling down for the long haul—"a posture that makes trying to 'wait us out' less attractive." His strategy was "five-pronged."

First, he suggested that we *stabilize U.S. force levels in Vietnam*, "*barring a dramatic change in the war.*" The limit he proposed was the 470,000 total then under consideration. (CINCPAC had requested 570,000 by end 1967). This limit would "put us in a position where negotiations would be more likely to be productive, but if they were not we could pursue the all-important pacification task with proper attention and resources and without the spectre of apparently endless escalation of U.S. deployments."

Second, he *recommended a barrier near the DMZ* and "across the trails of Laos."

Third, he suggested that we "*stabilize the Rolling Thunder program against the North.*" He thus recommended against the increase in the level of bombing and the broader target systems that the JCS was then requesting. Again, his reason was to "remove the prospect of ever-escalating bombing as a factor complicating our political posture and distracting from the main job of pacification in South Vietnam."

Fourth, he said, we should "*pursue a vigorous pacification program.*"

> The large-unit operations war, which we know best how to fight and where we have had our successes, is largely irrelevant to pacification as long as we do not lose it. By and large, the people in rural areas believe that the GVN when it comes will not stay but that the VC will; that cooperation with the GVN will be punished by the VC; that the GVN is really indifferent to the people's welfare; that the low-level GVN are tools of the local rich; and that the GVN is ridden with corruption.
>
> Success in pacification depends on the interrelated functions of providing physical security, destroying the VC apparatus, motivating the people to cooperate, and establishing responsive local government. An obviously necessary but not sufficient requirement for success of the RD cadre and police is vigorously conducted and adequately prolonged clearing operations by military troops who will "stay" in the area, who behave themselves decently and who show respect for the people.

This elemental requirement of pacification has been missing. In almost no contested area designated for pacification in recent years have ARVN forces actually "cleared and stayed" to a point where cadre teams, if available, could have stayed overnight in hamlets and survived, let alone accomplish their mission . . .

Now that the threat of a communist main-force military victory has been thwarted by our emergency efforts, we must allocate far more attention and a portion of the regular military forces (at least half of ARVN and perhaps a portion of the U.S. forces) to the task of providing an active and permanent security system behind which the RD teams and police can operate and behind which the political struggle with the VC infrastructure can take place.

The U.S. cannot do this pacification security job for the Vietnamese. All we can do is "massage the heart." For one reason, it is known that we do not intend to stay; if our efforts worked at all, it would merely postpone the eventual confrontation of the VC and GVN infrastructures. The GVN must do the job, and I am convinced that drastic reform is needed if the GVN is going to be able to do it.

The first essential reform is in the attitude of GVN officials. They are generally apathetic, and there is corruption high and low. Often appointments, promotions, and draft deferments must be bought; and kickbacks on salaries are common. Cadre at the bottom can be no better than the system above them.

The second needed reform is in the attitude and conduct of the ARVN. The image of the government cannot improve unless and until the ARVN improves markedly. They do not understand the importance (or respectability) of pacification nor the importance to pacification of proper, disciplined conduct. Promotions, assignments and awards are often not made on merit, but rather on the basis of having a diploma, friends, or relatives, or because of bribery. The ARVN is weak in dedication, direction and discipline.

Not enough ARVN are devoted to area and population security, and when the ARVN does attempt to support pacification, their actions do not last long enough; their tactics are bad despite U.S. prodding (no aggressive small-unit saturation patrolling, hamlet searches, quick-reaction contact, or offensive night ambushes); they do not make good use of intelligence; and their leadership and discipline are bad.

Furthermore, it is my conviction that a part of the problem undoubtedly lies in bad management on the American as well as the GVN side. Here split responsibility—or "no responsibility"—has resulted in too little hard pressure on the GVN to do its job and no really solid or realistic planning with respect to the whole effort. We must deal with this management problem now and deal with it effectively.

One solution would be to consolidate all U.S. activities which are primarily part of the civilian pacification program and all persons engaged in such activities, providing a clear assignment of responsibility and a unified command under a civilian relieved of all other duties. (If this task is assigned to Ambassador Porter, another individual must be sent immediately to Saigon to serve as Ambassador Lodge's deputy.) Under this approach, there would be a carefully delineated division of responsibility between the civilian-in-charge and an element of COMUSMACV under a senior officer, who would give the subject of planning for and providing hamlet security the highest priority in attention and resources. Success will depend on the men selected for the jobs on both sides (they must be among the highest rank and most competent administrators in the U.S. Government), on complete cooperation among the U.S. elements, and on the extent to which the South Vietnamese can be shocked out of their present pattern of behavior. The first work of this reorganized U.S. pacification organization should be to produce within 60 days a realistic and detailed plan for the coming year.

From the political and public-relations viewpoint, this solution is preferable—if it works. But we cannot tolerate continued failure. If it fails after a fair trial, the only alternative in my view is to place the entire pacification program—civilian and military—under General Westmoreland. This alternative would result in the establishment of a Deputy COMUSMACV for Pacification who would be in command of all pacification staffs in Saigon and of all pacification staffs and activities in the field; one person in each corps, province and district would be responsible for the U.S. effort.

(It should be noted that progress in pacification, more than anything else, will persuade the enemy to negotiate or withdraw.)

Fifth, the Secretary recommended a renewed effort to get negotiations started, by taking steps "to increase our credibility" with Hanoi, by considering a shift in the pattern of our bombing program considering the possibility of cessation of bombing, by trying to "split the VC off from Hanoi," and by "developing a realistic plan providing a role for the VC in negotiations, postwar life, and government of the nation."

His summation was somber. While repeating his prediction that the next two years would not see a satisfactory conclusion by either large-unit action or negotiations, McNamara advocated pursuing both routes although "we should recognize that success from them is a mere possibility, not a probability."

The solution lies in girding, openly, for a longer war and in taking actions immediately which will in 12 to 18 months give clear evidence that the continuing costs and risks to the American people are acceptably limited, that the formula for success has been found, and that the end of the war is merely a matter of time. All of my recommendations will contribute to this strategy, but the one most difficult to implement is perhaps the most important one—enlivening the pacification program. The odds are less than even for this task, if only because we have failed so consistently since 1961 to make a dent in the problem. But, because the 1967 trend of pacification will, I believe, be the main talisman of ultimate U.S. success or failure in Vietnam, extraordinary imagination and effort should go into changing the stripes of that problem.

The memorandum closed with a comment on the thoughts of Thieu and Ky:

They told me that they do not expect the enemy to negotiate or to modify his program in less than two years. Rather, they expect the enemy to continue to expand and to increase his activity. They expressed agreement with us that the key to success is pacification and that so far pacification has failed. They agree that we need clarification of GVN and U.S. roles and that the bulk of the ARVN should be shifted to pacification. Ky will, between January and July 1967, shift all ARVN infantry divisions to that role. And he is giving Thang, a good Revolutionary Development director, added powers. Thieu and Ky see this as part of a two-year (1967–1968) schedule, in which offensive operations against enemy main force units are continued, carried on primarily by the U.S. and other Free World forces. At the end of the two-year period, they believe the enemy may be willing to negotiate or to retreat from his current course of action.

McNamara's memorandum marked a strong new emphasis on pacification by him, and the ripples that this new emphasis set off were inevitably to spread throughout the USG, changing emphasis and official rhetoric up and down the line. His first reactions were official: comments on his memorandum from George Carver, Helms' Special Assistant for Vietnamese Affairs at the CIA; and from the JCS. Carver agreed with the evaluation of the situation, but objected to some of the recommended actions, particularly the "press for negotiations" items which he felt would be "counter-productive." Carver made the provocative statement that he considered the prognosis "too gloomy." If the odds for enlivening the pacification program are indeed "less than even, present U.S. objectives in Vietnam are not likely to be achieved."

In his memorandum, Carver took issue with McNamara on pacification. Carver felt that "despite the errors and administrative weaknesses of present programs, in the concept of RD we *have* found the right formula, a catalyst that is potentially capable of inspiring the Vietnamese into effective action . . . Serious and systematic effort in this field is really a post-Honolulu Conference development and it would be unrealistic to expect dramatic, readily quantifiable progress in the short span of eight months."

Carver supported the new stress on pacification, adding that he would support "wholeheartedly" a "real reorganizational change under which the civilian director would have a joint staff of sufficient scope to enable him to plan, control, and direct the U.S. effort and have operational control over all—not just civilian—elements engaged in RD . . ." He opposed a "carefully delineated division between the civilian in charge and an element of COMUSMACV under a senior officer."

"A civilian pacification structure cannot be givenen a 'fair trial' unless the civilian director has the necessary authority," Carver said. "Also, the trial will not be fair if major quantifiable results are anticipated in a matter of months."

Carver's vision of pacification rested to a large degree on the idea of gaining the active support of the population. He seemed opposed to the use of troops to merely protect terrain and the people who lived on it, saying, "If an attempt is made to impose pacification on an unengaged populace by GVN or U.S. military forces, that attempt will fail."

He concluded, as he had begun:

> We agree with Secretary McNamara's prognosis that there is little hope for a satisfactory conclusion of the war within the next two years. We do not agree that "the odds are less than even" for enlivening the pacification program. If this were true, the U.S. would be foolish to continue the struggle in Vietnam and should seek to disengage as fast as possible. We think that if we establish adequate management and control on the U.S. side and ensure that the Vietnamese follow through on redirecting their military resources as promised, there are at least fair prospects for substantial progress in pacification over the next two years.

The JCS review of McNamara's memorandum was far more severe. While agreeing that "There is no reason to expect that the war can be brought soon to a successful conclusion," the Chiefs made a strong case, as usual, for increased bombing, no predetermined force ceilings, and stated several times in different ways that the war was going very well indeed—although this same point had been made by McNamara. The Chiefs also disagreed strongly with the move for negotiations which McNamara had suggested. Any bombing pause, they said, would be regarded by Hanoi, by the GVN, and by our Allies, as "renewed evidence of lack of U.S. determination to press the war to a successful conclusion."

On pacification, the JCS "adhered to their conclusion" that "to achieve optimum effectiveness, the pacification program should be transferred to COMUSMACV. However, if for political reasons a civilian type organization should be considered mandatory by the President, they would interpose no objection.

> Nevertheless, they are not sanguine that an effective civilian-type organization can be erected, if at all, except at the expense of costly delays. As to the use of a substantial fraction of ARVN for pacification purposes, the JCS concur. However, they desire to flag that adoption of this concept will undoubtedly elicit charges of a U.S. takeover of combat operations at increased cost in American casualties.

The JCS requested that their views be brought to the attention of the President.

On the record, Secretary McNamara and Under Secretary Katzenbach had been quite frank in telling the American public that they had found pacification lagging during their October trip to Vietnam. Katzenbach said he was "concerned" and, after emerging from the meeting with the President, told the White House press corps that "We have to do a good deal more to get the 'other war' moving and I think we can." Even Komer, who remained more optimistic than McNamara and Katzenbach, was quoted as "acknowledging" that pacification was lagging.

While "military progress has exceeded our expectations," the Defense Secretary said, progress in pacification has "been very slow indeed." His trip also raised fears, for the first time, in Saigon that the military would take over the pacification effort. Thus, at almost the very moment that the President was hearing Katzenbach's recommendation that the civilians be reorganized and given a last chance (see previous action), Ward Just was writing from Saigon:

> McNamara left behind the impression that his visit to South Vietnam last week marked the beginning of the end of civilian supremacy in the American effort . . .
> Sources here were saying today that McNamara, a stickler for detail, was unimpressed with civilian descriptions of progress, or lack of it, in the pacification effort. The American who bears most of the authority for that, Deputy Ambassador William C. Porter, was in the U.S. during the McNamara visit.
> There has always been, as one official here put it, a "military component" to pacification. But it is understood now that that component will be increased and the military will more and more take control of pacification— the task called nation-building.

. . . The other likely outcome of McNamara's four days in Vietnam is that the role of ARVN will change.

Informed sources said that McNamara heard no complaints whatsoever from American military sources regarding the performance of the ARVN, but the fact is that he did. It has been an open secret in Saigon that the role of the ARVN would change next year. Their work would be in pacification, not in striking at main force units . . .

There is now increased certainty that the war effort despite public homage to the "other war" and the "hearts and minds of the people" is more thoroughly military than ever—and more thoroughly American.

In the end, the military is thought to have carried the day not by force or logic or force of wisdom, although their position here can be argued plausibly with both logic and wisdom, but by sheer weight of what one official called the juggernaut . . .

"Westmoreland says do this, do that, and something happens," one informed observer said. "When Lodge says do this, do that, sometimes something happens, and sometimes it doesn't happen."

The men here who wanted to see one ideology beaten by a better one, to see the Vietnamese character (not to mention the countryside) preserved and not submerged by the war, who viewed the struggle as an exercise in counterinsurgency, have now certainly lost . . .

It remains to be seen whether the problems of Vietnam lend themselves to military solutions and whether changing conditions in this war are better handled by colonels than diplomats.

Just's article was wrong, of course, since the decision to give MACV responsibility for pacification had not been made. Indeed, within a few days this fact had also leaked to the press, and stories in the *New York Times*, datelined Saigon, spoke of the "abortive effort" by MACV to take over the effort. But the importance of the stories was not in their accuracy or inaccuracy, but in the fact that they indicated the emotions that had been raised by the subject during and after the McNamara-Katzenbach-Komer visit. In truth, no one in Saigon, not even Lodge and Westmoreland, knew at this time what the final decision was to be. But the subject was up for discussion, and the pressure from Washington had been measurably increased.

With the McNamara and Katzenbach memoranda in hand, the President apparently indicated tentative agreements to give the civilians a short trial period to get pacification moving. Then he left for his Asian tour, which was to climax with the Seven-Nation Conference at Manila. He left behind him instructions to prepare a message to Lodge and Porter and Westmoreland, instructing them in his decision. Since the message was drafted and sent on to the President in Wellington on October 18, before Manila, but not sent on to Lodge and Porter in Saigon until November 4, after Manila, there apparently remained some uncertainty as to his decision, which was not clarified until most of the principals were united briefly in Manila. But this is of marginal importance. The fact was that the President had approved the idea of giving the civilians a final chance.

The Cable Exchange: November, 1966

By October 18, McNamara, Katzenbach, and Komer had an agreed-upon telegram for the President to send Lodge. It was forwarded to Wellington, where the President had begun his Asian tour:

State/Defense and Komer recommend your concurrence in the general plan recommended by both Secretary McNamara and Under Secretary Katzenbach regarding reorganization on the American side of the administration of the Revolutionary Development (RD) program in Viet-Nam. We therefore recommend that you approve our sending the following State-Defense message to Ambassador Lodge:

BEGIN TEXT

Personal For Lodge. You have described the RD program as the heart of the matter in SVN. We agree. Also, you have reported and we agree that progress in the RD program so far has been slight and unsatisfactory. We all agree that progress must be made in this crucial area if the war is to be won in the South and if the North is to be persuaded to negotiate. It is clear to us that some organizational changes are required on the American side to get RD moving—to bring harder pressure on the GVN to do its job and to get solid and realistic planning with respect to the whole effort.

We had considered putting the entire program under COMUSMACV to achieve these ends; and this may ultimately prove to be the best solution. But recognizing certain objections to this approach, we are prepared to try a solution which leaves the civilian functions under civilian management. As we see it, the trial organization would involve the following changes:

1. The several civilian lines of command within U.S. agencies would be consolidated into one. Thus, line responsibility for all personnel assigned to RD civilian functions would rest solely with one high-ranking civilian. (We presume this man would be Ambassador Porter. If so, he would have to be relieved of all other duties, and you would have to have another deputy assigned to absorb the substantial other responsibilities now met by Ambassador Porter.) The authority of this civilian would be made clear and full to each constituent agency of the civilian RD team, including relocation of personnel, the establishment of priorities irrespective of agency priorities, and the apportionment of the funds allocated for RD by each agency to Viet-Nam (bounded only by statutory limitations).

2. To strengthen Porter administratively, it might be well to assign him a competent Principal Deputy and Executive Officer—a military officer of two or three-star rank. If this officer is desired, General Westmoreland can supply him or, if he requests, the officer can be provided from here. This officer would not be to command U.S. military forces or operations or to perform MACV's functions of advising and prodding the ARVN, but would be to provide administrative strength on the civilian side and to serve as a bridge to MACV, ensuring efficient interface between the civilian and military structures.

3. We understand General Westmoreland is already considering a MACV Special Assistant for Pacification or a Deputy for Pacification. We presume that the appointment of such a Special Assistant or Deputy could be timed to coincide with the changes on the civilian side, making possible the highest-level command focus and consolidation to MACV's RD concerns and staff.

4. Careful definition and delineation of responsibilities of the U.S. civilian and U.S. military sides would be necessary in the whole RD establishment in South Viet-Nam to ensure that nothing falls between the stools and that the two efforts fully mesh.

We are most anxious, as we know you are, to make progress in RD. So this new organizational arrangement would be on trial for 90–120 days, at the end of which we would take stock of progress and reconsider whether to assign all responsibility for RD to COMUSMACV.

As mentioned above, this cable was not repeated to Saigon until after the Manila Conference. Presumably, in the intervening period, the President had had a chance to talk directly to Lodge and Westmoreland about the matter, since they were both at Manila (Porter was not). In addition, Komer had gone from Manila back to Saigon for a week's stay, and had given Porter a clear warning that the reorganization was impending. When he left, Komer left behind two members of his staff to assist Porter with the planning for the reorganization, although Porter and Lodge, for some reason not clear today, still seemed doubtful that the reorganization Washington was pressing on them was really necessary, and really desired by the President.

The cable—unchanged from the text cited above—arrived in Vietnam on November 4, 1966. It was slugged "Literally Eyes Only for Ambassador from Secretary, SecDef, and Komer," and because Lodge decided to interpret that slug line literally, the entire process was delayed one week—a sorry spectacle and wholly unnecessary on all counts. When Lodge answered the cable by requesting permission to discuss it with his assistants, there was an understandable suspicion in Washington that he was simply doing so to delay action a little while longer. But on the other hand, the cable had received the highest slug normally available to State Department messages—"Literally Eyes Only"—and Lodge could say truthfully that he was just following instruction.

In any event, Lodge sent his answer to Washington November 6:

> I agree that progress has been "slight and unsatisfactory" and, undoubtedly some organizational changes can be helpful. However, before commenting on that I would like to set out some basic considerations.
>
> Crux of the problem is not defective organization. It is security. Civilian reorganization can affect progress only indirectly, because security will remain outside civilian purview . . .
>
> To meet this need we must make more U.S. troops available to help out in pacification operations as we move to concentrate ARVN effort in this work. U.S. forces would be the catalyst; would lead by example; and would work with the Vietnamese on the "buddy" system. They would be the 10 percent of the total force of men under arms (90 percent of whom would be Vietnamese) which would get the whole thing moving faster.
>
> This has been done on a small scale already by elements of the U.S. Marines, 1st and 25th U.S. Infantry Divisions, and the Koreans. We think it can be made to work and the gains under such a program, while not flashy, would hopefully be solid. Everything depends on whether we can change ARVN habits. Experiments already made indicate that U.S. casualties would be few. While it would take time, it would be clear to everyone at home that time was working for us and it might create a "smell of victory." It would eventually get at Viet Cong recruiting—surely an achievement which would fundamentally affect the course of the war.
>
> I wonder whether the above result could not be achieved if the phrase "offensive operations" were to be redefined so that instead of defining it as meaning "seek out and destroy," which I understand is now the case, it would be defined as "split up the Viet Cong and keep him off balance."

This new definition of the phrase "offensive operations" would mean fewer men for the purely "military" war, fewer U.S. casualties and more pacification.

It would also hasten the revamping of the ARVN, which Ky says is now due to have been completed by normal Vietnamese bureaucratic methods by July 1967 (which seems optimistic to me). What I propose in this telegram would in effect revamp the ARVN by "on-the-job-training." It is the only way that I can think of drastically to accelerate the present pace.

*   *   *

The question of transferring Revolutionary Development civilian functions to COMUSMACV raises questions and I understand you recognize certain objections. I doubt whether it would solve any existing problems, and it would certainly create many new ones. I agree with your second paragraph in which you say civilian functions should be left under civilian management.

I agree that civilian lines of command within U.S. agencies dealing with Revolutionary Development should be consolidated under Ambassador Porter. He should take unto himself the direct operation of the five categories of manpower now in the field. I refer to USAID public safety, USAID province reps; JUSPAO; CIA and the civil functions performed by the military advisers. They would all stay exactly where they are as far as rationing, housing and administration is concerned. Porter would have the operational authority and responsibility.

I am not clear what another Deputy Ambassador would do and advise against such an unnecessary and unwieldy structure. Ambassador Porter does not now absorb "substantial other responsibilities" which distract his attention from revolutionary development. Administrative matters involving the U.S. Mission as a whole are handled by the Mission Coordinator, and political affairs are handled by me with close support from the political counselor. Economic affairs, in which Porter as the man responsible for revolutionary development is intimately and necessarily involved, are well covered by AID and the Economic Counselor. Public affairs not connected with field operations associated with revolutionary development are well in hand and do not take Ambassador Porter's time.

The only "substantial other responsibility" which Porter carries outside of RD, is to take charge in my absence. I see no need, and would find it most inappropriate, for this to be changed.

I think there is great merit in the idea of having a high-ranking military man involved in pacification work. He should be in charge of all the military aspects of pacification—working with ARVN and selecting, expediting, and assigning the U.S. troops who would operate as suggested in para 3 above. He should be an officer with proper knowledge of and talent for the subject and I, of course, think of General Weyand. If the decision is made by all hands to put the military into pacification as suggested in para 3, the decision as to where to place such a general should not be too difficult.

I agree that careful definition and delineation of responsibilities of the U.S. civilian and military sides is necessary. We intend that the two efforts fully mesh.

Clearly there is very little that can be done economically, socially, psychologically, and politically for the "hearts and minds" of men, if these men have knives sticking into their collective bellies. The knife must first be removed. It is not the case—as has so often been said—of which came first, the hen or the egg . . .

*   *   *

This is obviously not reflected in our present organization under which, nonetheless, much has been accomplished. When Mac Bundy told me in February, after the Vice President's visit, of the decision to relieve Porter of all of his duties as Deputy (except that of being Charge d'Affaires in case of my absence) so that he could take charge of the civilian aspects of pacification, I did not at first welcome the idea. I must, however, recognize that under Porter a real asset has been built.

To sum up, therefore, the first priority is more U.S. troops to be allotted to pacification as set forth in paragraph 3; the second priority is better operation and tightening up of the present organization; thirdly, are organizational changes.

Considering that your message was "EYES ONLY," I request authority to discuss it and my comments and plans with the heads of the different Mission agencies involved here. We are all anxious to make progress in RD, and the effort will involve all of us. It requires security and time. Whatever the trial period may be, I suggest we maintain a constant taking stock of progress and of problems. Lodge.

Back came Washington's answer on November 12, giving Lodge permission to discuss the matter and show the cables to Porter, Westmoreland, and "once plans mature, inform members Mission Council." With the civilians in Washington already feeling that their trial period was underway, they sought to get the Mission moving faster to reorganize. The cables became a series of hints and threats and detailed guidance. The difficulty in communication was quite high. Thus, the November 12 cable, drafted by Ambassador Unger and cleared with McNamara, Helms, Gaud, Komer, Marks, Katzenbach, and Rusk, and slugged "for Ambassador from Secretary, SecDef, and Komer," laid out for Lodge and Porter a detailed description of how the new structure should look—although everyone knew that the plans had already been drawn up and were sitting on Lodge and Porter's desks in Saigon—and began with this warning-hint:

Following steps need to be taken promptly if we are, in the time available, to give adequate test to organization which is intended to keep RD civilian functions under civilian management, an objective to which we know you attach considerable important.

The cable went on to outline the organization, and discuss the question of the use of U.S. troops:

. . . We understand General Westmoreland plans use of limited number U.S. forces in buddy system principle to guide and motivate ARVN in RD/P. However, we have serious doubts about any further involvement U.S. troops beyond that in straight pacification operations. We fear this would tempt Vietnamese to leave this work more and more to us and we believe pacification, with its intimate contact with population, more appropriate for Vietnamese forces, who must after all as arm of GVN establish constructive relations with population. Hence we believe there should be no thought of U.S. taking substantial share of pacification. The urgent need is to begin effectively pressing ARVN.

In Saigon, the Mission moved slowly. Three days later, with still no answer from Saigon, the State Department sent out the following very short and curt cable:

> Personal for Lodge and Porter from the Secretary
> Ref State 83699
> REFTEL was discussed today at highest levels, who wished to emphasize that this represents final and considered decision and who expressed hope that indicated measures could be put into effect just as rapidly as possible.

This produced, at last, two long answers from Lodge and Porter, which laid out what the new structure was going to look like, and added some personal comments from Lodge:

> FOR THE SECRETARY, SECDEF AND KOMER
> NODIS
>
> 1. This is in reply to your 83699 as amended by your 85196 concerning which General Westmoreland, Porter and I have had extensive consultation.
> 2. We will, of course, carry out your instructions just as rapidly as possible, and our planning is already far advanced.
> 3. It is very gratifying that you feel as we do on the urgent need to revamp the ARVN, on the importance of putting all civilians in the field under Porter and of having single civilian responsibility in province and corps—measures which we have long advocated. Doubt whether we can change over night habits and organization of ARVN acquired during the last ten years. Unless our success against main force daytime activity is equalled by success against guerrillas during the night, swift improvement cannot be expected to result simply by reorganization on the U.S. civilian side. It is our ability to infuse courage and confidence into all the Vietnamese under arms who are involved in pacification—both military and police—which is at stake.
> 4. As regards your instruction for a military deputy for Porter, General Westmoreland proposes Major General Paul Smith, who is acceptable to Porter. Porter believes General Smith should be attached to civilian agency (State Department—Embassy Saigon) while on this duty, along lines precedents already established. He could wear civilian or military garb as circumstances require.
>
>   *   *   *
>
> 6. General Westmoreland does not wish to have a separate deputy for Revolutionary Development, but has nominated Brigadier General William Knowlton as Special Assistant for Pacification.
>
>   *   *   *
>
> 8. Concerning paragraph 4 (c). Mission directive will state clearly that Deputy Ambassador Porter will be primarily occupied with RD and that other Mission business will be handled by appropriate sections of Mission. There are certain other aspects to consider, however. Porter has assumed charge when I have been absent. Any change in that respect could only derogate from his position in eyes of American community and GVN. He believes, and I concur, that his assumption of charge cannot be "nominal" without risk of downgrading him in local eyes. Additionally, it is essential

that there be a point of decision in Mission, without ambiguity. In practice, Porter intends to leave routine functions of Mission (political, protocol, administrative, personnel, consular, visitors, etc.) to sections normally handling them. He expects, however, to remain closely cognizant of political developments and together with political counselor and CAS chief to consult and decide course of action to take or recommend to department as circumstances dictate. I believe this is reasonable approach and have full confidence in his intention to concentrate on RD.

*   *   *

10. Your paragraph 5. I have always believed that Revolutionary Development/Pacification must be carried out by Vietnamese forces, who, as you say, must establish constructive relations with the population. I have never advocated U.S. forces taking on "substantial" share of this task. I do believe, however, that an American presence in this field amounting to a very small percentage of the total manpower involved could induce ARVN to take the proper attitude by "on the job" training and could give the necessary courage and confidence to the Vietnamese. Lodge

FOR THE SECRETARY, SECDEF AND KOMER
NODIS

1. Herewith I transmit our recommendations carrying out your 83699 and 85196. This is the best we can do in the immediate future and we think it is a forward step. But I believe that you may wish to change it as we advance along this untrod path and learn more about circumstances and people. Our proposal is as follows:

a. The establishment of an office of operations, headed by a Director of Operations. This headquarters office of operations will include the present staff of: (1) USAID/Field Operations; (2) USAID/Public Safety; (3) USAID/Refugees; (4) JUSPAO/Field Services (minus North Viet-Nam branch); (5) CAS/Cadre Operations Division. The Office of Operations will be organized so that the above offices will not necessarily remain intact when they are merged into a single office. For example, I intend to disband USAID/FO's cadre office, and put those people now representing AID on cadre affairs directly under the cadre office. Thus there may be a net saving in manpower.

b. All other divisions of AID and JUSPAO will remain under the control of their respective directors—MacDonald and Zorthian—who will be responsible to Porter, as they are now, for their operations. (I exempt from this the special question of press relations, on which Zorthian will continue to report to me directly.) Thus, for example, MacDonald will continue to oversee to Agriculture, Education, Health, Industry, etc., Divisions, as well as continue, along with the economic counselor Wehrle, to be responsible for the anti-inflation efforts. The Director of USAID will be freed from responsibilities for the field operations, but his job continues to be one of vast importance. I think it will now become more manageable.

*   *   *

d. At province level we will select a single civilian to be in charge of all other U.S. civilians in the province, in same way as MACV senior advisor is responsible for the military involved in the advisory effort in the province. This senior civilian representative will be the U.S. counterpart for civilian affairs to the VN province chief and, together with the MACV senior advisor (sector) and the province chief, will form the provincial coordinating committee. The practice of assaulting the province chief with a multiplicity of advisors, often giving conflicting advice, should cease under this arrangement. The senior civilian representative will write the efficiency reports of the American civilians in the province, regardless of their parent agency, and those reports will be reviewed by Porter's office, which will also control transfers and assignments.

* * *

f. At the more complex region/corps level, we will consider a similar system, with a senior civilian representative responsible for the overall U.S. civilian effort in the corps area. He will work with the MACV senior advisor, and will in effect be my agent (and Bill Porter's) at the corps. I have long believed in the need for a sophisticated politically-minded man in charge of our effort with the politically volatile corps commanders, and this is a step in that direction. Porter and I will be looking carefully for the best men for these four difficult jobs . . .

2. I do not want another deputy Ambassador. I intend to provide office space for Porter in the new chancery (his present office will remain at his disposal even after he moves). There is simply no job for another deputy Ambassador, particularly since the present political counselor works closely with me, reporting directly.

3. There is no doubt that the steps mentioned above are major ones. Clearly I cannot predict now how long they will take to achieve, or how much disruption they will cause in their early stages. For one thing, I feel that a physical relocation of certain offices now spread out across the city is vital, and we are now studying the details of how to do this. Porter will probably need to establish his offices in a building other than the Chancery, in order to give the office of operations a firm guiding hand. He will, however, keep an office close to me, and he will be kept closely informed of policy developments.

* * *

5. I will need your personal support during the period which lies ahead. I am sure that all hands here, regardless of agency affiliation, will support this effort to unify the U.S. team. The same must be true of the agencies that must continue to backstop us in Washington. Personnel recruitment will remain in your hands, and it ultimately determines the caliber of our efforts. Porter will send you separate messages on the question of personnel, so that new guidance and requirements can be put into effect as quickly as possible.

6. We look forward through reorganization to tightening and simplifying contacts, advice and coordination with GVN authorities responsible for RD.

E. *THE MANILA CONFERENCE*

President Johnson arrived in Manila on Ocober 23, 1966, to attend the seven-nation conference of troop contributing countries to the Vietnam war. While the meeting was hectic and short, it did produce a communique which contained some major statements about policy, strategy, and intentions. The three most important points in the communique of October 25 were:

a. The pledge that "allied forces . . . shall be withdrawn, after close consultation, as the other side withdraws its forces to the North, ceases infiltration, and the level of violence thus subsides. Those forces will be withdrawn as soon as possible and not later than six months after the above conditions have been fulfilled."

b. The announcement of a new program, which had been thought up in Washington, for "National Reconciliation." Since the GVN was not in genuine agreement with the idea, but under great pressure from the Americans to commit themselves to it, the communique was quite vague on what difference there was, if any, between the new National Reconciliation program and the old Chieu Hoi program.*

c. The formalization, *in public,* of the move towards getting ARVN more deeply involved with the RD program: "The Vietnamese leaders stated their intent to train and assign a substantial share of the armed forces to clear-and-hold actions in order to provide a shield behind which a new society can be built." This public confirmation of the tentative steps that MACV had been taking was important. Classified documents could not be used as the basis for a far-reaching reform of the ARVN; they would never have received wide enough distribution, nor would they have been fully accepted as doctrine by the doubters within both the RVNAF and MACV. But here was a piece of paper signed by the President and by General Thieu which said in simple language that a new direction and mission was given to the ARVN. After Manila, MACV and the JCS began in seriousness the formation of the mobile training teams which were designed to retrain every RVNAF unit so that it was more aware of the importance of the population.

The reasoning behind the move to commit more troops to the relatively static missions involved in pacification had been laid out in documents and briefings by people as varied as Major General Tillson, in his August briefings of the Mission Council (cited in Section III.C.7) and Robert Komer, in his memorandum to the President. But a key assumption underlying the new emphasis on population control was the growing belief, in late 1966, that the main force war was coming to a gradual end. No other single factor played as great a role in the decision to commit troops to pacification as the belief that they were going to be less and less needed for offensive missions against main force units. The enemy-initiated large unit action statistics showed a sharp drop all through 1966, with a low point of less than two battalion sized or larger enemy initiated actions per month in the last quarter of 1966. There was increasing talk of the "end of the big battalion war," both in the press and in the Mission. Moreover, the first big U.S. push into VC base areas was getting underway, and

* Those Americans who hoped that National Reconciliation would become a major new appeal to VC at middle and higher levels were to be in for a disappointment in the year following Manila. The GVN did not agree with the philosophy behind total forgiveness to the enemy, and continually hedged its statements and invitations to the VC so that they resembled surrender with amnesty rather than "national reconciliation." In fact, the GVN did not make an internal announcement on the National Reconciliation program until Tet, 1967, almost four months after the Manila conference, and three months after the GVN had "promised" the U.S. that it would make the announcement. Then, when the Vietnamese finally did make the announcement, they used the phrase "Doan Ket," which is accurately translated as "National Solidarity," rather than "National Reconciliation." The difference in meaning is, of course, significant, just as the earlier mistranslation of "Xay Dung" into "Revolutionary Development" reflected a divergence of views.

it was possible to believe that when operations like Junction City and Cedar Falls were completed, the VC would have few places left to hide within the boundaries of South Vietnam. Thus, some people were arguing in late 1966 and early 1967 that the number of troops that could be committed to RD was considerably higher than the amount that General Westmoreland was then contemplating; that the "substantial number" of the Manila communique could well be over half of all ARVN. These arguments were usually made orally and tentatively, rather than in formal written papers, since they usually raised the ire of the military. When military opposition to such a large RD commitment stiffened, the suggestions of civilians were often hedged or partially withdrawn. But nonetheless, the fact remains that the undeniable success against the main forces in 1966 was the major justifying factor for those advocating increased commitment of regular units—even some U.S. units—to pacification. At that time, officials were less worried about the possibility of a major resurgence of the enemy than about the possibility of a new guerrilla war phase. The fighting in and near the DMZ during Operations Hastings and Prairie (August-December 1966) had been the heaviest of the war, and had been judged not only as a major defeat for the enemy but as a possible turning point for the enemy, after which he "had begun to shift some of his effort away from conventional, or 'mobile warfare,' toward the more productive (from his standpoint) guerrilla tactics." The Marines considered Hastings and Prairie a foolhardy aberration on the enemy's part, although they noted that the region of the DMZ "is remote, favoring him with interior lines and working to our disadvantage through extension of our own supply lines."

The Marines felt that the enemy attacks at the DMZ had been designed primarily to draw down resources from the Marine pacification efforts near Da Nang, an interesting example of how important they thought their embryonic pacification effort was. But, the Marines added, whenever the enemy probed or patrolled, he was "pursued by Marine infantry and pounded by air, artillery, and naval gunfire. The effort cost him an estimated 5,000 to 6,000 NVA troops killed or disabled and 414 weapons lost . . . and meant a severe loss of prestige, and a further erosion of the morale of his troops."

Thus, the slowdown in large enemy actions, according to the Marine estimate, and signs that the future would see an increase in guerrilla activity—"Major main force and NVA formations have been relatively inactive since September, as far as large unit actions are concerned. However, by the end of December, corresponding increases were already beginning to appear in rates of guerrilla activity."

To what extent other military and civilian leaders accepted the Marine assessment of enemy capability and intentions is not clear from the documents, but the mood of the time was not far removed from the sentiments cited above. The end of the "big war" was coming, and pacification was the next step. It all fueled the proponents of greater pacification efforts by regular troops, and now, after Manila, the debate was already being conducted on terrain favorable for the first time to the pro-pacification advocates.

IV. OCO TO CORDS

A. *OCO ON TRIAL: INTRODUCTION*

With the cable exchange completed, except for a few minor matters, Ambassador Lodge announced the formation of the Office of Civil Operations on

November 26, 1966—one month after the original go-ahead signal had been given in Washington, and three weeks after the cable to Lodge telling him that the President wanted rapid action. While delays of this kind are common in government and do not normally affect events, in this case the delay got OCO off to a visibly slow start despite the fact that the President had clearly indicated to Lodge and Porter that he was putting OCO on trial and would review its accomplishments in a fairly short time.

The reasons for the Mission's slow start revealed again just how far apart Washington and its representatives in Saigon were in their philosophy and approach to the war.

Washington officials consistently underestimated the difficulty of the actions they wanted the Mission to do, and continually expected movement at speeds literally beyond the capability of the Mission. They held these ambitious expectations and exerted pressure accordingly—not primarily because of the situation in the pacification program in South Vietnam (which was fairly static), but because of growing pressure from the public, the press, and Congress for *visible progress* in the war, because of growing American domestic dissatisfaction with the course of the war. If the American public could not *see* progress in Vietnam, the support the Administration had for the war would drop steadily.

In its efforts to show progress some members of the Administration were continually interpreting statistics and events in the most favorable light possible, and its critics—particularly the press—were interpreting the same events in the most unfavorable light possible. Since events in Vietnam were usually open to at least two different interpretations, the gap between the Administration and its critics over the basic question of *How are We Doing?* grew steadily during 1966 and 1967. But beyond the disagreements over facts and statistics, there was a continual effort by Washington officials to prod Saigon forward at a faster pace. Thus, if the Mission had just started a crash program at the highest speed ever achieved by the Mission, Washington officials, particularly Komer, acting (he said) in the President's name, would demand that the Mission redouble its efforts again. Komer, in a reflective moment, called it "creative tension."

The Saigon Mission responded to this pressure with resistance and hostility towards its Washington "backstops." When warned, for example, that the President was giving OCO 90 to 120 days to prove itself, Lodge and Porter both shot back pointed comments to the effect that this was an inadequate time period, and at the end of it results would probably not yet be visible. They were right, of course, but being right was not good enough. They fought the time deadline with too great a vehemence and did not do enough to "prove" OCO's worth. The result was the decision of March 1967 to put OCO under MACV.

The Mission thought that because they were "on the ground" they had a unique understanding of the problems of Vietnam, and that because they were on the ground they were the only accurate judges of the rate at which events needed to move. This point of view did not take into account domestic pressures in the United States; or, worse, it deliberately disregarded them. Thus, the Mission in Vietnam has generally tended to formulate strategy as though the United States will be fighting a slow war in Indochina for decades, while the Washington policymakers and strategists have tended to behave as though time runs out in November of 1968. The mood of the Mission towards Washington is seen more clearly in press leaks than in cables. Thus, for example, the Evans and Novak column, from Saigon, on November 30, 1966, as OCO was being formed and the trial period beginning: "A note of quiet desperation is creeping into the top echelons of the U.S. Mission charged with winning the war in Vietnam. It grows partly out of frustration with what one top Embassy official describes as 'the hot blow torch on our rear ends' that comes from Washington, and, particularly, from the White House in search of ever-new victory proposals . . . Much of this frustration and gloom would vanish if attention in Washington were centered not on impossible trance tables for ending the war next month or next year but on a realistic projection of the modest gain now being made at great and painstaking effort." The difference in mood is reinforced by the climate of Vietnam, which is sluggish and humid, and by the influence of the Vietnamese, who after many years of war are rarely ready to race out and seek instant immortality on the field of battle or in the Ministries.

The one exception to this dangerous generalization has often been the individual American officer, usually military, serving in advisory or combat positions. There, with a 12-month tour standard, the Americans have pushed their Vietnamese counterparts hard, and often encountered great resistance. Indeed, the Americans in Vietnam often think they are already pushing the Vietnamese as hard as is desirable, and that Washington is asking the impossible when they send out instructions to get more out of the Vietnamese.

These were some of the background factors which were playing themselves out in late 1966 and early 1967. While tension between Washington and Saigon had existed before, and is inevitable between headquarters and the field, the pressure had by now reached a level higher than ever before. (It is ironic to note that the same tensions that exist between Washington and Saigon tend to exist between the Americans in Saigon and the Americans in the field. The phrase "Saigon commando" is used continually to castigate the uninformed officials in Saigon. There are too few people serving in Saigon with previous field experience, an unavoidable by-product of the 12-month tour, and this increases the gap.)

So Washington officials talked about the lack of a sense of urgency in the Mission in Vietnam, and the Americans in Saigon talked about the dream world that Washington lived in, and the Americans in the provinces talked about the lack of understanding of the Americans in Saigon who had never seen the real war. Washington was dissatisfied with the progress in Vietnam, and since it could not influence the real obstacle, the Vietnamese, except through the American Mission, it deliberately put extra heat on the Mission. At least one high official involved in this period in Washington felt that it was a necessary and deliberate charade, and that only by overdoing its representations to the Mission could Washington assure that some fraction of its desires got through. More than one high-ranking official in Saigon felt that the only way to handle Washington was to hold out to them promises of progress and generally calm the home front down, or else run the risk of inflaming Washington and bringing still more reorganization down upon the Mission's head.

Rather than try to apportion responsibility for this sorry state of affairs, it would be useful to see the situation as the by-product of tensions produced by the Viet Cong strategy of survival and counter-punching at GVN weak spots, and the GVN's inability to be as good as we dream they should be. The United States could perhaps live with these problems in an age in which communications were not instantaneous, and publicity not so unrelenting.

Beyond this broad philosophical point, however, the fact is that the Mission in Vietnam was badly organized to conduct almost any kind of large and complex operation, let alone a war. Thus Washington was right to reorganize the Mission, and Saigon's reaction to each reorganization inevitably suggested that still more was needed.

Beyond that, the Mission in Vietnam did not have the full confidence of the Washington bureaucracy and Porter still lacked Lodge's full support.

B.   OCO ON TRIAL: TOO LITTLE TOO LATE— OR NOT ENOUGH TIME?

With the formation of OCO in late November the civilian mission began to move at a more rapid pace than it had in the post-Honolulu period. Most of this motion, of course, was internal to the U.S. Mission and could not produce visible results against the VC, an understandable fact when one considers the amount of work that the decision involved.

First, a Director of Civil Operations had to be chosen. Since Washington demanded rapid action, it was decided that the choice had to be someone already in Vietnam and ready to work, which sharply narrowed the list of possible men. The final selection was L. Wade Lathram, who had been the deputy director of USAID. Lathram was to prove to be the wrong man at the wrong time, a methodical and slow worker with strong respect for the very interagency system that he was supposed to supercede. In normal bureaucracies, Lathram could, and had, compiled excellent records, but OCO was demanding extraordinary results, and these required leadership and drive which Lathram did not possess.

It had been anticipated that Porter, a popular Ambassador and a knowledgeable and realistic man, would supply that leadership and drive, and that Lathram would simply run the OCO staff below Porter. But neither Porter nor Lathram saw their roles that way. Once OCO was formed, Porter to an unexpected degree stayed away from the day to day decisions, leaving them to Lathram. And Lathram simply did not have the position nor the stature to stand up to the full members of the Mission Council, whose assets he now partially controlled. (There was continued confusion over what was the responsibility of OCO and what remained under the control of the USAID, CIA and JUSPAO directors, and this confusion was never resolved—and continues today under the CORDS structure.)

Moreover, Porter, who had not wanted a second Deputy Ambassador to come in to relieve him of all non-RD matters, soon found himself tied down in the business of the Embassy. Lodge went on a long leave shortly after the formation of OCO, taking about one month's vacation in Europe and the United States. This left Porter with responsibility for the full gamut of Ambassadorial activities, and he unavoidably became less and less concerned with the progress of OCO, even though it was in its first critical month. He had been given an office in the new OCO building (appropriated from AID), but he rarely used it, staying in the Embassy in another part of Saigon, and showing, in effect, by his failure to use his OCO office often that he could not devote much time to OCO.

The failure, therefore, to isolate Porter from all non-RD matters and provide Lodge with a full time DCM turned out to be a serious error. McNamara had clearly foreseen this in his 15 October memorandum to the President. In retrospect, we can see that Porter should have been given one job or the other, and the vacancy filled—as Washington had suggested. But Washington had just finished cramming an unpleasant action down the Mission's throat, and it was felt that there were limits to how much the Mission should be asked to take, especially since Lodge and Porter were so adamant on the subject. Also, no one could foresee how diverting other matters would become to Porter, or how much he would delegate to Lathram.

The second major decision for OCO was the selection of the Regional Directors—men who would be given full control over all American civilians in their respective regions. Here Porter presented Lathram with three nominees (II Corps was left unfilled until a few weeks later) and the choices appeared to be quite good ones: in I Corps, Porter's former Assistant Deputy Ambassador, Henry Koren; in III Corps, the former MACV Division Senior Advisor, then with AID, John Paul Vann; and in the Delta, the CIA's former support chief, Vince Heymann. These were three respected men, and they came from three different agencies, which emphasized the interagency nature of OCO. In picking Vann, Porter had made a major decision which involved possibly antagonizing both the CIA and MACV, for Vann was without question one of the most controversial Americans in Vietnam. He stood for impatience with the American Mission, deep and often publicly-voiced disgust with the course of the past five years, strong convictions on what needed to be done, driving energy and an encyclopedic knowledge of recent events in Vietnam—and was a burr in the side of the CIA, with which he had frequently tangled, particularly over the cadre program, and MACV, with which he had fought ever since disagreeing publicly with General Harkins in 1963 (a fight which led to his resignation from the Army and was extensively discussed in David Halberstam's book, *The Making of a Quagmire*).

The importance of the appointments was not lost on the Mission or the press. While Lathram's appointment had stirred the bureaucracy but not the press, the regional directors came as a surprise and a major story. In a front-page story in *The Washington Post*, Ward Just described Vann as "one of the legendary Americans in Vietnam," and said that Koren's appointment indicated the great importance the Mission attached to the jobs. Just added that "there were indications that, if OCO did not succeed, the military command would take charge of pacification, or 'Revolutionary Development.' "

Next came the selection of OCO Province Representatives, to be chosen out of the available talent in each province. Here the slowness of the civilians began to tell, and it was not until January that the appointments could be made for every province. Trying to pick men on the basis of their knowledge and ability takes time and requires trips to each province, consultations with other Mission Council members, etc., and the civilians set out to do all this.

Meanwhile, a huge job which no one in Washington could fully appreciate was underway—the physical relocation of offices that Lodge had described as necessary in his November 16 cable. Even in Washington it may be difficult to get furniture and phones moved, except for very high-ranking people; in Saigon a major relocation was more difficult to mount than a military operation. While this was going on, involving literally over one thousand people, work in OCO was even more confused and sporadic than usual.

None of these minor organizational events would be of any importance if it were not for the fact that they were eating away at the meager time allotted to the civilians to prove that OCO should remain independent of MACV. But they did consume time, and this was to prove to be a factor in evaluating OCO.

The documents do not answer the question of whether or not OCO ever really had a chance to survive, or whether it was just allowed to start up by people who had already decided to turn RD over to MACV in a few months. Both possibilities fit the available facts. An educated guess would be that the decision to give Westmoreland control was tentatively made by the President in the late fall of 1966, but that he decided he would gain by allowing the civilians to reorganize first. If OCO proved to be a major success, he could always continue to defer his decision. If OCO fell short of the mark, then it still would be an organization in-being ready to be placed into MACV without further internal changes, and that in itself would be a major gain. Moreover, if the changes came when Lodge and Porter were gone, there would be less difficulties.

If OCO moved too slowly for Washington's satisfaction, it nonetheless accomplished many things which had previously been beyond the Mission's ability:

—Uniting personnel from AID, CIA, and JUSPAO into a single Plans & Evaluations Section, OCO produced the first integrated plans for RD on the U.S. side. These plans were ambitious and far-reaching, and required MACV inputs. The fact that the civilians were asking MACV for inputs to their own planning, rather than the reverse, so startled MACV that MACV, in turn, began more intensive discussions or plans. The planning effort involved several military officers on loan to OCO, a fact which further heightened tension between OCO and MACV. When the plans first formulated were presented to General Westmoreland, he indicated that he was not going to be bound by any plans which reduced his flexibility and ability to respond to military pressure whenever and wherever it occurred; that is, he was reluctant to commit many military assets to permanent RD support activities. But the relentless pressure from OCO, from Komer in Washington, and even from the public attention focused on the issue by Article 11 of the Manila communique ("The Vietnamese leaders stated their intent to train and assign a substantial share of the armed forces to clear-and-hold actions in order to provide a shield behind which a new society can be built") all were working against General Westmoreland, and towards the assignment of ARVN units to RD missions.

—The civilians in the provinces spoke with a single voice for the first time. The province chiefs welcomed the change for this reason, according to most observers. Within the American team in each province, there was now a built-in obligation to consult with each other, instead of the previous situation in which more and more agencies were sending down to the provinces their own men who worked alone on their own projects.

—The very act of physical relocation of the five major branches of OCO into a single building changed attitudes and behavior patterns in the civilian mission. Public Safety and the Special Branch advisors, for example, now were co-located, and began working together closely. Previously, they had both advised the same people through completely separate channels which met only at the top; i.e., when the chief of the Public Safety branch and the deputy CIA station chief had something specific and urgent they had to resolve. On the day-to-day matters, there had actually been a deliberate compartmentalization before OCO was formed.

These examples of gains could be repeated across a broad front. They were first steps in a direction which might ultimately have created a strong civilian mission, given time, better leaders, and more support from Washington. But even without these things, OCO was a definite plus.

The period between December and April was a period in which everyone paid lip service to the idea of supporting OCO, but in reality it was sniped at and attacked almost from the outset by the bureaucracies. In Saigon, Zorthian, and Hart, Directors of JUSPAO and CIA, respectively, made it clear that they wanted to remain very much involved in any decision affecting their respective fields of endeavor. While this was a reasonable point of view, it meant that CIA and even USIA officers in the field often refused to accept any guidance from the OCO representative, and cases began to come to light in which major actions were being initiated by the CIA without any consultation with OCO. (The CIA reasoning and defense rested on the fact that one of Hart's deputies was ostensibly an assistant director of OCO.)

In Washington, there was open skepticism to OCO from almost all quarters, particularly AID, which found itself footing most of the bill. USIA and CIA both indicated that they would continue to deal directly with their field personnel. In theory, everyone in Washington was to participate in the backstopping of the interagency OCO, but in practice, without a single voice in charge, this meant that no one was helping OCO, no one was trying to sell them as a going concern in Washington. Komer's role here was ambiguous; he supported OCO as long as it was in operation, and probably contributed more to its achievements than anyone else in Washington, but at the same time he was already on the record as favoring a military takeover, which was the very thing OCO sought to avoid.

Washington had decreed OCO, and had given Porter great responsibility. Unfortunately, they had failed to give him authority and stature needed to make the agencies work together.

As pointed out before, this might well have been overcome if time had not been so short. The slow methodical way of moving bureaucracies may be more effective than sweeping changes, anyway, if one has time. But in Vietnam no one was being given much time.

Shortly after OCO was formed, Komer's deputy, Ambassador William Leonhart, visited Vietnam, and when he returned, wrote the following penetrating assessment, which was sent to the President, Secretaries Rusk and McNamara, and Mr. Gaud and Mr. Helms:

> Whether Porter's new Office of Civil Operations (OCO) is viewed as a final organizational solution or as an inevitable intermediate step it is achieving a number of useful purposes. It establishes, on the civil side for the first time, unified interagency direction with a chain of command and communication from Saigon to the regions and provinces. It centralizes US-GVN field coordination of civil matters in one US official at each level. It affords a civil-side framework which can work more effectively with US military for politico-military coordination and more integrated pacification planning.
>
> At the time of my visit, OCO's impact had been felt mainly in Saigon. Its headquarters organization was largely completed. Three of the four Regional Directors had been named, all were at work, and one was in full time residence in his region. Regional staffs were being assembled but not yet in place. At province level, teams were being interviewed for the selection of Provincial Representatives. Porter expects them to be designated by January 1. Some slippage is possible, and it may be 90 days or so before the new organization is functioning. I participated in the initial briefings of the province teams I visited, passing along and emphasizing Bob Komer's admonitions against over-bureaucratization of effort and for fast and hard action. These were well-received. Morale was good. All the GVN Province Chiefs with whom I talked thought the new structure a great improvement.

C. TIME RUNS OUT

The decision to turn pacification over to MACV, with an integrated civil-military chain of command, was announced in Saigon on May 11, 1967, by Ambassador Ellsworth Bunker. In his announcement, Bunker said that the decision was entirely his.

But Bunker had been in Vietnam as Ambassador for less than two weeks, and he was therefore clearly acting under strong guidance, if not orders, from Washington. The decision to give MACV responsibility had actually stemmed from the clear and unmistakable fact that the President now considered such a reorganization highly desirable.

It is not clear when the President decided this in his own mind. The documents do not shed any light on this point, and, indeed, they simply fail to discuss the pros and cons of the decision in the early months of 1967, when the subject was a hot one in Washington and Saigon. This all suggests that whatever consideration of the issue was going on was confined strictly to private sessions between principals, and that the staff work previously done on a highly restricted basis was no longer considered necessary by the principals.

It has been suggested that the President had been strongly in favor of the move for months before he finally gave the go-ahead signal, and that he was held back by the strong opposition from Lodge and Porter, from Katzenbach, from the agencies in Washington—and by the fact that it would appear to be a further "militarization" of the effort. This may well be the case; certainly nothing in the record disproves this possibility. But since there is no way that this study can answer the question, it must be left undecided.

Whenever the President made his decision in his own mind, he chose the Guam meeting as the place to discuss with a group of concerned officials outside his own personal staff. In a private meeting on March 20, or 21, 1967, with senior officials from Washington and Saigon, the President indicated that he felt the time had come to turn pacification over to MACV. The President enjoined those in the room at that meeting not to discuss the decision with anyone until it was announced, and he did not inform the GVN.

At the end of the Guam meeting, the President sent Komer back to Saigon with Westmoreland and Lodge, and Komer spent a week there, working out preliminary details of the reorganization. By this time Komer knew that he was to become Deputy to General Westmoreland, although many details remained to be ironed out.

When Komer returned to Washington, with the preliminary plans, a period followed during which no further action on the reorganization was taken. In all, nearly two months went by from the President's statement at Guam to the public announcement, during which only a handful of people in Washington and Saigon knew what was going to happen. The delays were caused by a combination of factors: Bunker's understandable desire to spend some time on personal business before going to Saigon, the President's desire to have Bunker make the final announcement himself after he had reached Saigon, the need to work out final details. Since the President was the man who had pressed everyone else working on Vietnam to greater and greater effort, and since he stood to lose the most from loss of time, it is surprising that he was now willing to see two months lost, with a tired and lame-duck Mission in Vietnam, waiting for the new team in a highly apprehensive state, and confusion at the higher levels. But for reasons which are not readily apparent, the President did not push his new team, and it was not until May 13, 1967, that Bunker made his announcement (which had been drafted by Komer):

> Since being appointed U.S. Ambassador to Vietnam I have been giving a great deal of thought to how to organize most effectively the U.S. Advisory role in support of the Vietnamese government's Revolutionary Development effort. Like my predecessor, I regard RD—often termed pacification—as close to the heart of the matter in Vietnam.

Support of Revolutionary Development has seemed to me and my senior colleagues to be neither exclusively a civilian nor exclusively a military function, but to be essentially civil-military in character. It involves both the provision of continuous local security in the countryside—necessarily a primarily military task and the constructive programs conducted by the Ministry of Revolutionary Development, largely through its 59-member RD teams. The government of Vietnam has recognized the dual civil-military nature of the RD process by assigning responsibility for its execution to the Corps/Region Commanders and by deciding to assign the bulk of the regular ARVN, as well as the Regional and Popular forces, to provide the indispensable security so that RD can proceed in the countryside. As senior American official in Vietnam, I have concluded that the U.S. Advisory and supporting role in Revolutionary Development can be made more effective by unifying its civil and military aspects under a single management concept. Unified management, a single chain of command, and a more closely dovetailed advisory effort will in my opinion greatly improve U.S. support of the vital RD program. Therefore, I am giving General Westmoreland the responsibility for the performance of our U.S. Mission field programs in support of pacification or Revolutionary Development. To assist him in performing this function, I am assigning Mr. Robert Komer to his headquarters to be designated as a deputy to COMUSMACV with personal rank of ambassador.

I have two basic reasons for giving this responsibility to General Westmoreland. In the first place, the indispensable first stage of pacification is providing continuous local security, a function primarily of RVNAF, in which MACV performs a supporting advisory role. In the second place, the greater part of the U.S. Advisory and Logistic assets involved in support of Revolutionary Development belong to MACV. If unified management of U.S. Mission assets in support of the Vietnamese program is desirable, COMUSMACV is the logical choice.

I have directed that a single chain of responsibility for advice and support of the Vietnamese Revolutionary Development program be instituted from Saigon down to district level. Just as Mr. Komer will supervise the U.S. Advisory role at the Saigon level as Deputy To General Westmoreland, so will the present OCO regional directors serve as deputies to U.S. field force commanders.

At the province level, a senior advisor will be designated, either civilian or military, following analysis of the local situation.

While management will thus be unified, the integrity of the Office of Civil Operations will be preserved. It will continue to perform the same functions as before, and will continue to have direct communication on technical matters with its field echelons. The present Revolutionary Development support division of MACV will be integrated into OCO, and its chief will serve as deputy to the Director of OCO. Such a unified civil/military U.S. advisory effort in the vital field of Revolutionary Development is unprecedented. But so too is the situation which we confront. RD is in my view neither civil nor military but a unique merging of both to meet a unique wartime need. Thus my resolution is to have U.S. civilian and military officials work together as one team in order more effectively to support our Vietnamese allies. Many further details will have to be worked out, and various difficulties will doubtless be encountered, but I am confident that this realignment of responsibilities is a sound management step and I count on all U.S. officers and officials concerned to make it work effectively in practice.

Bunker outlined to Washington the line he proposed to take during a question and answer period with the press:

> Besides the above announcement, I intend to stress the following basic points in answer to press questions or in backgrounding: (a) I made this decision not because I think that U.S. civilian support of RD has been unsatisfactory—on the contrary I am pleased with progress to date—but because I think it is essential to bring the U.S. military more fully into the RD advisory effort and to pool our civil/military resources to get optimum results: (b) indeed I regard all official Americans in Vietnam as part of one team, not as part of competing civilian and military establishments: (c) as senior U.S. official in Vietnam, I intend to keep a close eye on all U.S. activities, including pacification—I am not abdicating any of my responsibilities but rather am having the entire U.S. pacification advisory effort report to me through General Westmoreland rather than through two channels as in the past: (d) during 34 years in the business world I have learned that unified management with clear lines of authority is the way to get the most out of large scale and highly diversified programs: (e) since continuous local security, which RVNAF must primarily provide, is the indispensable first stage of the pacification process, the MACV chain of command can obviously be helpful to the RVNAF: and (f) I intend to see that the civilian element of the U.S. effort is not buried under the military—in many instances soldiers will end up working for civilians as well as the reverse—in fact Ambassador Komer will be General Westmoreland's principal assistant for this function while General Knowlton will be deputy to Mr. Lathram of OCO. I intend to keep fully informed personally about all developments in this field and to hold frequent meetings with General Westmoreland and Ambassador Komer for the purpose of formulating policy.

The reaction of the civilians in Vietnam to the announcement of Ambassador Bunker was one of dismay. In the first confused days, before details of the reorganization could be worked out and announced, the press was able to write several articles which probably were accurate reflections of the mood of most civilians:

> Civilian reactions today ranged from the bitter ("We don't think they can do their own job—how can they do ours?") to the resigned ("I'll be a good soldier and go along") to the very optimistic ("We've finally got a civilian in among the generals"). Almost nowhere was there much enthusiasm for what Bunker called "a unique experiment in a unique situation."
> Nor was there jubilation at the American military command. Westmoreland, who wanted to take charge of the pacification program two years ago, is now reported to be deeply skeptical of the possibility of producing the kind of quick results the White House apparently wants.
> "I did not volunteer for the job," he is reported to have said privately this morning, "but now that I've got it, I'll do my best with it."
> . . . Serious officials—both civilian and military—realize there are limi-

tations on how far an officer will go in reporting "negative" information, and how hard a civilian, now his subordinate, will fight for realism.

. . . Officials today sought to mitigate the effect of the announcement by saying that Komer and his staff, physically located in the American Military Command in Saigon, will be in a far better position to influence the course of Pacification than he would among "all the guys with glasses and sack suits" in the Office of Civil Operations.

The Vietnamese reaction to the reorganization was more difficult to gauge. Ward Just, in the same story cited above, said "There was surprisingly little comment today from South Vietnamese, who have seen so many efforts at pacification and so many efforts to attempt to organize and reorganize themselves. One high American who professed to have spoken with the South Vietnamese command reported they are "delighted." But Komer's talk with General Nguyen Duc Thang, the Minister for Construction (RD), did not reveal any delight on Thang's part. Indeed, Thang's first reaction was that the GVN should emulate the U.S. and turn pacification over to the Ministry of Defense— an action which would have run directly counter to the U.S. objective of encouraging civilian government in Vietnam.

There is no telegraphic record of the first series of talks that Komer and Bunker had with Ky, Thieu, Vien, and Thang on the reorganization. Not until a Komer-Ky talk of May 15 does the cable traffic reflect the GVN reaction to the reorganization. By this time, it should be noted, the GVN knew that the U.S. did not want the GVN to follow suit, and it knew all our arguments and could play them back to us with ease:

Ky said that General Thang had suggested that the RD effort be brought under Defense Ministry to conform to the U.S. reorganization. Ky and General Vien had demurred on grounds that such a reorganization on the GVN side would be far more complex than on U.S. side, would disrupt RD process, and would stretch General Vien and MOD too thin. Besides it would not be politically advisable at the very time when there was a hopeful trend toward a more civilianized and representative government. Komer agreed with Ky-Vien reasoning . . .

D. THE CORDS REORGANIZATION

With Bunker's announcement, the Mission began its second massive reorganization in five months. This time, the reorganization was accompanied by one of the periodic turnovers in Mission Council personnel which have characterized the Mission: for some reason, the tours of many high-ranking officers seem to end at roughly the same time, and thus, in 1964, 1965, and again in the spring of 1967, several key members of the Mission Council all left within a few weeks of each other. This time, in addition to Ambassador Lodge, Porter, Habib, and Wehrle all left within a short period of time, and only a high-level decision—announced by Bunker at the same time as the reorganization—kept Zorthian and Lansdale on for extensions. Into the Mission came Bunker, Locke, Komer, General Abrams, the new Deputy COMUSMACV, and Charles Cooper, the new Economic Counselor, and Archibald Calhoun, the new Political Counselor.

Despite the turnover, the reorganization seemed to proceed with comparative ease. Perhaps the fact that OCO had already been formed was critical here, since it meant that instead of MACV dealing with three agencies simultaneously, the first discussions could be restricted primarily to MACV and OCO. Moreover, because OCO was already a going concern, the civilians were better organized than ever before to maintain their own position in dealings with the military.

But above all, it was the decision by Westmoreland and Bunker to let Komer take the lead in the reorganization which was important. Komer now made major decisions on how the new structure would look which were usually backed up by Westmoreland. The result looked much better than many people had dared hope.

The details of the reorganization are not worth detailed discussion here. But one point can illustrate the way CORDS could resolve previously unresolved issues: the question of the role of the ARVN Division in the chain of command.

As noted in an earlier section, study groups had over the years advocated removing the ARVN Divisions from the chain of command on Pacification/RD. But MACV had large advisory teams with the Divisions and these teams controlled both the sector (Province) advisory teams and Regimental advisory teams below them. The structure followed normal military lines, and made good sense to most of the officers in the higher levels of MACV.

The counter-argument was that Division was a purely military instrument and could not adequately control the integrated civilian-military effort that was needed at the Province level. Thus the Roles and Missions Study Group, for example, had recommended that "Division be Removed from the RD Chain of Command . . . that the role of the Province Chief be upgraded . . . that Province Chiefs have operational control (as a minimum) of all military and paramilitary forces assigned to operate exclusively in their sector." The Study Group recognized that "the power structure being what it is in the GVN, major progress toward this goal will not be short range or spectacular." But, they urged, the U.S. should begin to push forward on it.

MACV had nonconcurred in this recommendation. General Westmoreland, in a memorandum to Lodge on September 7, 1966, had said that he did not agree with the idea, and that, if carried out, "the Corps span of control would be too large for effective direction." The suggestion, he added, was "illogical."

This was still the position of MACV when Komer arrived. In his attempts to find a workable civilian-military chain of command, he received two suggestions on the difficult question of the role of the Division advisory teams. The first, and more routine, was to continue the existing MACV system—in which, no matter how good or bad the GVN chain of command may be, the U.S. simply duplicates it on the advisory side. This would mean that all American civilians and military at the Province level would come under the Division-Corps chain of command. The MACV staff assumed that this would happen.

John Paul Vann and a few colleagues had a different suggestion. Vann maintained that the evidence suggested that when the Americans made their desires known clearly to the Vietnamese, without the vagueness and contradictoriness which so often characterized them, then the Vietnamese usually would follow suit after a suitable period of time. Thus, said Vann, if the Americans remove the Division advisory team from the U.S. chain of command, except for tactical matters and logistical support, the GVN may follow, and reduce the power of their politically potent Divisions.

The thesis Vann was putting forward—that the GVN would follow a strong U.S. example—was untested and hotly disputed. Secondly, there was the matter of MACV's stand against downgrading the role of the ARVN Divisions. Few people observing the discussions thought that the Vann suggestion had a chance of success.

But Komer, persuaded by the argument, did overrule many of his staff and make the recommendation to Westmoreland. Westmoreland approved it, and in June, 1967, the new chains of command were announced to the U.S. Mission. After years of arguing, during all of which the trend had been towards stronger ARVN Divisions, the U.S. had suddenly reversed course on its own, without waiting for the Vietnamese to act. The change was so complete that it even extended to that last (and, to career officers, most important) question: who writes the efficiency report. Under the new MACV guidance, the Senior Province Advisor would be rated not by the Division Senior Advisor, but by the Deputy for CORDS and the Corps level—thus confirming the new command arrangements.

While it is still too early to tell if the GVN will completely follow the U.S. lead, the early evidence suggests that the Vann hypothesis was correct, and that following the U.S. action, the GVN has begun to reduce the role of their Divisions in RD. There are now indications that the GVN is seriously considering a plan in which the Divisions would no longer have area responsibility but rather be reduced to support of their forward units, and operational command on large operations of troops.

E. THE MISSION ASSESSMENT AS CORDS BEGINS

The situation that CORDS and Ambassador Komer inherited was not a very promising one. Despite all the lip service and all the "top priorities" assigned RD by the Americans in the preceding 18 months, progress in the field was not only not satisfactory, it was, according to many observers, nonexistent. The question of whether we were inching forward, standing still, or moving backward always seemed to the Mission and Washington to be of great importance, and therefore much effort was spent trying to analyze our "progress."

A strong case can be made for the proposition that we have spent too much time looking for progress in a program in which measurements are irrelevant, inaccurate, and misleading. But, nonetheless, the Mission did try to measure itself, and in May of 1967, as OCO turned into CORDS, produced the following assessment of RD for the first quarter of 1967.

> In truth, there has been little overall progress in RD activities, and the same must be said for the painful process of building a meaningful dialogue between the government and the people. A number of factors have been reported from Region III to account for this unhappy situation, but they might well apply to the rest of the country:
> a. The RD program for 1967 involved many new and different concepts, command arrangements, administrative and procedural functions and allocation of resources. Only recently have the majority of provincial officials involved become aware of the program.
> b. Many Ap Doi Moi (Real New Life Hamlets), through guidance from MORD, were located in fringe security areas. In most of these cases a great

deal of military and jungle clearing operations were necessary. These take time, and, as a result, the deployment of the RD teams often were delayed.

c. The hobbling effect of ineffectual officials has retarded the program.

d. The people have had to develop new working relationships with the RD workers,* the ARVN, and the RF/PF. During this process, there has been a "wait and see" attitude.

If, however, the picture is sombre, it is not unrelieved. The 1967 program may look at this point unencouraging statistically, but its progress is of a different and more important sort. In critical areas, progress has been registered. There has evolved an implicit understanding by many in the GVN that RD is a longer-term progress than hitherto believed, requiring a greater concentration of resources. In fact, there is increasing evidence that programming for 1967 has so concentrated scarce resources in the 11-point Ap Doi Moi that the GVN presence and services are spread very thin indeed in areas of lower priority. The fact that in general each RD team will remain in each hamlet for six months throughout the year, is a fundamental improvement in the program.

As a result of the finer definition of the intent of RD and more interest in its possibilities, the 1967 program has become more vital than its predecessors. This vitality has produced new ideas, an increasing flexibility, which marks important progress in the program. Moreover, what the country has been engaged in is the process of laying a base for development; a long drawn out process which sees little initial reward, but without which nothing of permanence will be achieved. In other words, the first quarter of the year has not been witness to a vital social revolution, but has instead found evidence of a growing understanding of the nature of the revolution to come, and in so doing has taken a further step in the painful process of building a nation.

With the formation of CORDS, this history becomes current events. CORDS is charged now with solving what have previously been unsolvable problems— energizing the GVN to do things which it is not as interested in as we are; winning the hearts and minds of people who do not understand us or speak our language; working under intense pressure for immediate results in a field in which success—if possible at all—may require years. We have concentrated on the history of the United States bureaucracy in this study because that, in retrospect, seems to have been where the push for pacification came from—not the Vietnamese. We have not been able to analyze properly the actual course of the effort in the field, where contradictory assessments of progress have plagued the U.S. In the final section which follows, we try to draw a few lessons from the course of events described in this study.

When completed, CORDS had produced a structure in which, regardless of civil-military tensions that cannot be wished away, all hands were working together under a single chain of command. The structure was massive, so massive that the Vietnamese were in danger of being almost forgotten—and for that there can be no excuse. But at least the Mission was better run and better organized than it had ever been before, and this fact may in time lead to a more

---

* "Workers" was another one of the special words the U.S. began using instead of accurate translations of the Vietnamese. This one was also Lodge's idea, as a more understandable word than "cadre" to describe the members of the 59-man teams.

efficient and successful effort. Without a unified voice in dealing with the Vietnamese, we can never hope to influence the GVN to do the things we believe they must do to save their own country.

Volume II   List of Documents

Southeast Asian nations, creation of an effective armed force, and preservation of a pro-Western orientation. Policies directed toward the achievement of these objectives suffer from the concentration of power in the hands of the President, Ngo Dinh Diem, and a small clique headed by his extremely influential and powerful brother, Ngo Dinh Nhu." Chairman JCS Talking Paper for Briefing President Kennedy, 9 January 1962.

Document 106 (page 659)
The JCS agree that the basic issue of Diem's apprehension about a coup needs to be resolved. "I don't believe there is any finite answer to the question you pose as to how to convince Diem he must delegate authority to subordinates he doesn't fully trust." JCS Memorandum for General Lansdale, CM-491-62, 18 January 1962.

Document 107 (page 660)
The President establishes a Special Group (Counter Insurgency), the functions of which are as follows: (1) to insure proper recognition throughout the U.S. Government that subversive insurgency ("wars of liberation") is a major form of politico-military conflict equal in importance to conventional warfare; (2) to insure that such recognition is reflected in the organization, training, equipment and doctrine of the U.S. armed forces and other U.S. agencies; (3) to continually review the adequacy of U.S. resources to deal with insurgency; and (4) to insure the development of adequate programs aimed at preventing or defeating insurgency. NSAM 124, 18 January 1962.

Document 108 (page 661)
State Department agrees that an increase in the Vietnamese armed forces to the 200,000 man level should be supported provided the following factors are considered: (1) that U.S. military advisors and the Vietnamese authorities continue to set valid tactical and strategic plans; (2) the rate of increase should consider the ability of the Army to absorb and train the additional men and the manpower resources of SVN; (3) that the armed forces should level off at 200,000 and further efforts should be devoted to strengthening the Civil Guard and Self-Defense Corps; and (4) that our training programs for ARVN be based on the concept that the Vietnamese Army will start winning when it has the confidence of the Vietnamese populace. U. Alexis Johnson letter to Mr. Gilpatric, 26 January 1962.

Document 109 (page 662)
Secretary McNamara forwards a JCS Memorandum to the President with the comment, "I am not prepared to endorse the views of the Chiefs until we have had more experience with our present program in SVN." The JCS Memorandum recommends that if, with Diem's full cooperation and the effective employment of SVN armed forces, the VC is not brought under control, then a decision should be made to deploy suitable U.S. military combat forces to SVN sufficient to achieve desired objectives. Secretary of Defense Memorandum for the President, 27 January 1962 (JCSM-33-62, 13 January 1962, attached).

Document 110 (page 666)
The President requests that AID review carefully its role in the support of local police forces for internal security and counter-insurgency purposes, and recommend to him through the Special Group (Counter Insurgency) what new or renewed emphases are desirable. NSAM 132, 19 February 1962.

Document 111   (page 667)
play in counter insurgency programs as well as in the entire range of problems
involved in the modernization of developing countries. The training objectives
The President approves training objectives for personnel who may have a role to
include the study of: the historical background of counter insurgency, departmental tactics and techniques to counter subversive insurgency, instruction in
counter insurgency program planning, specialized preparations for service in
underdeveloped areas. Training of foreign nationals will also be included in the
program. The President desires that current counter insurgency training be examined to ascertain if it meets the above training objectives. NSAM 131, 13
March 1962.

Document 112   (page 669)
The President forwards a memorandum on the subject of VN from Ambassador
Galbraith and requests Department of Defense comments. The Galbraith Memorandum (4 April 62) asserts that the U.S. is backing a weak and ineffectual
government in SVN and that "there is a consequent danger that we shall replace
the French as the colonial force in the area and bleed as the French did." Galbraith urges that U.S. policy keep open the door for political solution, attempt
to involve other countries and world opinion in a settlement, and reduce our
commitment to the present leadership of GVN. In addition to recommended
specific actions, Galbraith suggests the U.S. should resist all steps to commit
American troops to combat action and dissociate itself from programs which are
directed at the villagers, such as the resettlement programs. White House Memorandum for Secretary of Defense, 7 April 1962 (Galbraith Memorandum attached).

Document 113   (page 671)
The JCS comment on Ambassador Galbraith's Memorandum to President Kennedy. The JCS cite the Kennedy letter of 14 December 1961 to President Diem
as a public affirmation of the intention of the U.S. Government to suport President Diem to whatever extent necessary to eliminate the VC threat. In sum, it
is the JCS opinion that the present U.S. policy toward SVN as announced by
the President "be pursued vigorously to a successful conclusion." JCS Memorandum for the Secretary of Defense, JCSM 282–62, 13 April 1962.

Document 114   (page 672)
The President requests contingency planning in the event of a breakdown of the
cease-fire in Laos for action in two major areas: (1) the holding by Thai forces
with U.S. backup of that portion of northern Laos west of the Mekong River;
and (2) the holding and recapture of the panhandle of Laos from Thakhek to
the southern frontier with Thai, Vietnamese or U.S. forces. Kennedy indicates
that he contemplates keeping U.S. forces in Thailand during the period of the
negotiations by the three Princes and the early days of the government of national
union. NSAM 157, 29 May 1962.

Document 115   (page 673)
In an evaluation of the first three months of systematic counter-insurgency,
Hilsman of State's INR reports some progress and reason for modest optimism
although acknowledging the great amount yet to be done. State Department INR
Research Memorandum RFE-27, 18 June 1962.

Document 116 (*page 681*)
The President approves assignments of responsibilities in the development of U.S. and indigenous police, paramilitary, and military resources to various agencies as recommended by the Special Group on Counter Insurgency. Deficiencies revealed in the study pursuant to NSAM 56 include: country internal defense plans, improvement of personnel programs of agencies concerned with unconventional warfare, orientation of personnel, deployment of counter insurgency personnel, support of covert paramilitary operations, increased use of third-country personnel, exploitation of minorities, improvement of indigenous intelligence organizations, and research and development for counter insurgency. NSAM 162, 19 June 1962.

Document 117 (*page 684*)
Memorandum from CIA to Secretary of Defense assessing strategic hamlet program, 13 July 1962.

Document 118 (*page 689*)
The President approves a national counter insurgency doctrine for the use of U.S. departments and agencies concerned with the internal defense of overseas areas threatened by subversive insurgency. NSAM 182, 24 August 1962.

Document 119 (*page 690*)
In a year-end summary of the Vietnamese situation and prognosis, Hilsman (State INR) concludes that at best the rate of deterioration has been decreased. GVN control of the countryside, the Strategic Hamlet Program notwithstanding, has increased only slightly. State Department INR Research Memorandum RFE-59, 3 December 1962.

1963

Document 120 (*page 717*)
Memo for the President from Michael V. Forrestal evaluating situation in Vietnam, February 1963.

Document 121 (*page 725*)
A National Intelligence Estimate states that "Communist progress has been blunted and that the situation is improving. Strengthened South Vietnamese capabilities and effectiveness, and particularly U.S. involvement, are causing the Viet Cong increased difficulty, although there are as yet no persuasive indications that the Communists have been grievously hurt." The VC will continue to wage a war of attrition and there is no threat of overt attack from the North. On the basis of the last year's progress the VC can be contained but it is impossible "to project the future course of the war with any confidence. Decisive campaigns have yet to be fought and no quick and easy end to the war is in sight." NIE 53–63, "Prospects in South Vietnam," 17 April 1963.

Document 122 (*page 726*)
The President approves and directs certain actions outlined in the Department of State Memorandum of 17 June 1963, relative to Laos planning. The President wishes to obtain suggestions for actions in Laos in light of the deteriorating situation and from the British and the French before initiating any action under the Memorandum. Kennedy asks about additional U.S. actions to be taken in Laos before any action directed against NVN. NSAM 249, 25 June 1963.

Document 123   (page 727)
The President is briefed on developments in Indonesia, Laos and VN. Specifically, on SVN, discussions cover the possibility of getting rid of the Nhus (the combined judgment was that it would not be possible), pressure on Diem to take political actions, possible results of a coup, and the replacement of Ambassador Nolting with Ambassador Lodge. Department of State Memorandum of Conversation, 4 July 1963.

Document 124   (page 728)
Memorandum of conversation, Ball, Nolting, Wood, and Springstein on current situation, 5 July 1963.

Document 125   (page 729)
A Special National Intelligence Estimate evaluates the political crisis in South Vietnam arising from the Buddhist protest. It concludes that if Diem does not seek to conciliate the Buddhists new disorders are likely and there will be better than even chances of coup or assassination attempts. U.S.-GVN relations have deteriorated as a function of Diem's distrust of U.S. motives in the Buddhist affair and he may seek to reduce the U.S. presence in Vietnam. The Communists have thus far not exploited the Buddhist crisis and they would not necessarily profit from a non-Communist overthrow. A successor regime with continued U.S. support would have good chances of effectively pursuing the war. SNIE 53-2-63, "The Situation in South Vietnam," 10 July 1963.

Document 126   (page 734)
In a subsequently controversial cable, State informs Lodge that if Diem is unwilling or unable to remove Nhu from the government, that the U.S. will have to prepare for alternatives. Lodge is authorized to inform the Vietnamese generals plotting a coup that if Nhu is not removed we will be prepared to discontinue economic and military aid, to accept a change of government and to offer support in any period of interim breakdown of the central government mechanism. State Department Message to Saigon 243, State to Lodge, 24 August 1963.

Document 127   (page 735)
Lodge's reply to Washington re: Diem, 25 August 1963.

Document 128   (page 735)
CIA cable on contacts with Saigon generals, 26 August 1963.

Document 129   (page 736)
CIA cable on coup prospects in Saigon, 28 August 1963.

Document 130   (page 736)
U.S. policy with respect to a coup is defined in more detail for Lodge and Harkins as a result of an NSC meeting with the President. "The USG will support a coup which has good chance of succeeding but plans no direct involvement of U.S. armed forces. Harkins should state (to the generals) that he is prepared to establish liaison with the coup planners and to review plans, but will not engage directly in joint coup planning." Lodge is authorized to suspend aid if he thinks it will enhance the chances of a successful coup. State Department Message 272, State to Lodge and Harkins, 29 August 1963.

Document 131 (*page 737*)
Rusk raises with Lodge the possibility of a last approach to Diem about removing Nhu before going ahead with the coup. He notes that General Harkins favors such an attempt. Rusk feels that if accompanied by the threat of a real sanction —i.e., the withdrawal of U.S. support—such an approach could be timed to coincide with the readiness of the generals to make their move and might, therefore, offer some promise of getting Diem to act. State Department Message 279, State to Lodge, 29 August 1963.

Document 132 (*page 738*)
Lodge cable to State Department, re: U.S. policy toward a coup, 29 August 1963.

Document 133 (*page 739*)
Lodge response to State on Diem's closeness to brother, 30 August 1963.

Document 134 (*page 740*)
Cable, MAAG Chief to JCS on halt in coup planning, 31 August 1963.

Document 135 (*page 741*)
Vice President Johnson presides over a meeting at the State Department on the subject of SVN. The generals' plot having aborted, Rusk asks what in the situation "leads us to think well of a coup." Further, Rusk feels that it is unrealistic now "to start off by saying that Nhu has to go." McNamara approves Rusk's remarks. Hilsman presents four basic factors bearing on the current situation: (1) the restive mood of the South Vietnamese population; (2) the effect on U.S. programs elsewhere in Asia of the current GVN policy against the Buddhists; (3) the personality and policies of Nhu; and (4) U.S. and world opinion. Vice President has great reservations about a coup because he sees no genuine alternative to Diem. General Krulak Memorandum for the Record, 31 August 1963.

Document 136 (*page 743*)
Lodge is instructed by the White House that since there is no longer any prospect of a coup, pressure must be applied to Diem to get him to adopt an extensive list of reforms. In particular Lodge is authorized to hold up any aid program if he thinks such action will give him useful leverage in dealing with Diem. CAP Message 63516, White House to Lodge, 17 September 1963.

Document 137 (*page 746*)
The President explains to Lodge his urgent need for the McNamara-Taylor assessment of the situation. The visit is not designed to be a reconciliation with Diem, rather he expects McNamara will speak frankly to him about the military consequences of the political crisis. State Department Message 431, The President to Lodge, 18 September 1963.

Document 138 (*page 746*)
Lodge's reply to the White House CAP Message 63516 indicates agreement that a coup is no longer in the offing, but opposes both an approach to Diem on reforms or the use of an aid suspension as a lever. He regards both as likely to be unproductive or worse. Embassy Saigon Message 544, Lodge to State for President Only, 19 September 1963.

Document 139   (page 748)
President Kennedy outlines his reasons for sending McNamara and Taylor to
VN: "I am asking you to go because of my desire to have the best possible on-
the-spot appraisal of the military and paramilitary effort to defeat the VC."
While the results from programs developed after Taylor's Mission in 1961 were
heartening, the serious events in the South since May 1963 have prompted the
President to ask McNamara to make a fresh, first-hand appraisal of the situation.
"In my judgment the question of the progress of the contest in SVN is of the
first importance . . ." President Kennedy Memorandum for Secretary of Defense, 21 September 1963.

Document 140   (page 749)
Pending McNamara's visit and the subsequent review of policy, Lodge is given
the following interim guidance: "(1) The United States intends to continue its
efforts to assist the Vietnamese people in their struggle against the Viet Cong.
(2) Recent events have put in question the possibility of success in these efforts
unless there can be important improvements in the government of South Vietnam. (3) It is the policy of the United States to bring about such improvement." State Department Message 458, Eyes Only for Lodge from Ball, 22 September 1963.

Document 141   (page 749)
Memorandum of conversation (Diem, Thuan, Lodge, McNamara, Taylor, Harkins, Flott), September 29, 1963.

Document 142   (page 751)
The McNamara-Taylor Mission Report concludes that the military campaign
has made great progress, and, while the political crisis in Saigon is serious, "there
is no solid evidence of the possibility of a successful coup . . ." The Report
recommends against promoting a coup and, although it is not clear that U.S.
pressure will move Diem to the moderations and reforms we desire, nevertheless,
as the only course of action with any prospect of producing results, the report
recommends the application of selective economic sanctions, including a suspension of funds for the commodity import program. The Mission further recommends a shift of military emphasis to the Delta and a consolidation of the Strategic
Hamlet Program. In addition, it is recommended that a training program be
established for RVNAF such that the bulk of U.S. personnel may be withdrawn
by the end of 1965. In conjunction with this program, the U.S. should announce
plans to withdraw 1,000 U.S. military personnel by the end of 1963.

Document 143   (page 766)
Lodge is advised that as a result of the policy review just completed, the "President today approved recommendation that no initiative should now be taken to
give any active covert encouragement to a coup." Efforts to build and maintain
contacts with "alternative leadership" is authorized, however. CAP Message
63560, to Lodge via CAS channel, 5 October 1963.

Document 144   (page 767)
Contact has been renewed by the generals with a CAS agent who has been
apprised of the reactivation of plotting. In the meeting, General Minh states that
he must know the U.S. position on a coup. He stresses that a coup is urgently
needed to prevent the loss of the war to the VC. The U.S. contact is noncommittal. CAS Saigon Message 1445, Lodge to State, 5 October 1963.

Document 145 (*page 769*)

Washington reaffirms Lodge's guidance that he is not to promote a coup. Neither, however, is he to thwart one. He should try to obtain as much information as possible from the plotters about their plans on which to base an American judgement about their likelihood of success. CIA Message 74228, 6 October 1963.

Document 146 (*page 769*)

The President approves the detailed military recommendations contained in the McNamara-Taylor Report, but directs that no announcement of the implementation of the 1,000-man withdrawal plan be made. NSAM 263, 11 October 1963.

Document 147 (*page 770*)

A Department of State Research Memorandum contends that the statistical indicators on the war in Vietnam reveal "that the military position of the Vietnam Government may have reverted to the point it had reached six months to a year ago." The analysis angers the JCS and Rusk subsequently apologizes to McNamara. Department of State, INR Research Memorandum RFE-90, 22 October 1963.

Document 148 (*page 780*)

With the coup plotting now far advanced and the U.S. clearly committed to the generals' attempt, Lodge seeks to calm Washington's anxieties about the lack of detailed information on the generals' plans. He is at pains to oppose any thought of thwarting the coup because he thinks the military will create a government with better potential for carrying on the war, and because it would constitute undue meddling in Vietnamese affairs. Embassy Saigon Message 1964, Lodge to McGeorge Bundy, 25 October 1963.

Document 149 (*page 782*)

While thanking Lodge for his views, the White House indicates that short of thwarting a coup we should retain the prerogative of reviewing the plans and discouraging any attempt with poor prospects of success. CAP Message 63590, McGeorge Bundy to Lodge, 25 October 1963.

Document 150 (*page 782*)

The White House instructs Lodge to bring General Harkins completely up to date on the coup plotting, and asks that Harkins, Lodge and the CIA Station Chief provide a combined assessment of the prospects of the plotters. Individual comments are to be sent if desired. With these assessments, a decision can be made telling the generals: (a) we will maintain a hands-off policy, (b) we will positively encourage the coup, or (c) we will discourage it. More detailed military plans should be sought from Minh. CAS Message 79109, McGeorge Bundy to Lodge, 30 October 1963.

Document 151 (*page 784*)

After complaining about Lodge's failure to keep him informed about the coup planning, General Harkins opposes the proposed coup against Diem. He does not see an alternative leadership with Diem's strength of character, especially not among the generals. The war continues to go well. MACV Message 2028, Harkins to Taylor, 30 October 1963.

Document 152   (page 785)
General Harkins takes detailed exception to the interpretations of a deteriorating war effort that Lodge has been transmitting throughout October. He offers an optimistic appraisal of the trend of the war and sees the political crisis as having only a marginal effect on troop morale and military effectiveness. MACV Message 2033, Harkins to Taylor, 30 October 1963.

Document 153   (page 788)
Bundy cable to Lodge voicing White House concern on coup, October 30, 1963.

Document 154   (page 789)
Lodge argues forcefully for the coup. "It is theoretically possible for us to turn over the information which has been given to us in confidence to Diem and this would undoubtedly stop the coup and would make traitors out of us. For practical purposes, therefore, I would say that we have very little influence on what is essentially a Vietnamese affair." In the event the coup fails, he believes we should do what we can to help evacuate the generals' dependents. Lodge believes the generals are all taking enormous risks for the sake of their country and their good faith is not to be questioned. "Heartily agree that a miscalculation could jeopardize position in Southeast Asia. We also run tremendous risks by doing nothing." General Harkins did not concur in the cable. CAS Saigon Message 2063, 30 October 1963.

Document 155   (page 792)
Taking note of the difference of opinion on the advisability of a coup between Lodge and Harkins, the White House specifically informs Lodge that he is to discourage the generals from any attempt that in his judgment has a poor prospect of success. Lodge is given full authority for country team actions in the event of a coup; if he has left for Washington, Harkins will have charge. In the event of a coup, U.S. policy will be: (a) to reject appeals for direct intervention from either side; (b) if the contest is indecisive, U.S. authorities may perform any actions agreed to by both sides; (c) in the event the coup fails, asylum may be offered to anyone to whom we have an obligation; but (d) once the coup has started, it is in our interests to see that it succeeds. CAS Washington Message 79407, 30 October 1963.

[Document 96]

Reprinted from New York *Times*

U.S. Ambassador's '60 Analysis of Threats
to Saigon Regime

Cablegram from Elbridge Durbrow, United States Ambassador in Saigon, to Secretary of State Christian A. Herter, Sept. 16, 1960.

As indicated our 495 and 538 Diem regime confronted by two separate but related dangers. Danger from demonstrations or coup attempt in Saigon could occur earlier; likely to be predominantly non-Communistic in origin but Communists can be expected to endeavor infiltrate and exploit any such attempt. Even more serious danger is gradual Viet Cong extension of control over countryside which, if current Communist progress continues, would mean loss free Viet-nam to Communists. These two dangers are related because Communist successes in rural areas embolden them to extend their activities to Saigon and because non-Communist temptation to engage in demonstrations or coup is partly motivated by sincere desire prevent Communist take-over in Viet-nam.

Essentially [word illegible] sets of measures required to meet these two dangers. For Saigon danger essentially political and psychological measures required. For countryside danger security measures as well as political, psychological and economic measures needed. However both sets measures should be carried out simultaneously and to some extent individual steps will be aimed at both dangers.

Security recommendations have been made in our 539 and other messages, including formation internal security council, centralized intelligence, etc. This message therefore deals with our political and economic recommendations. I realize some measures I am recommending are drastic and would be most [word illegible] for an ambassador to make under normal circumstances. But conditions here are by no means normal. Diem government is in quite serious danger. Therefore, in my opinion prompt and even drastic action is called for. I am well aware that Diem has in past demonstrated astute judgment and has survived other serious crises. Possibly his judgment will prove superior to ours this time, but I believe nevertheless we have no alternative but to give him our best judgment of what we believe is required to preserve his government. While Diem obviously resented my frank talks earlier this year and will probably resent even more suggestions outlined below, he has apparently acted on some of our earlier suggestions and might act on at least some of the following:

1. I would propose have frank and friendly talk with Diem and explain our serious concern about present situation and his political position. I would tell him that, while matters I am raising deal primarily with internal affairs, I would like to talk to him frankly and try to be as helpful as I can be giving him the considered judgment of myself and some of his friends in Washington on appropriate measures to assist him in present serious situation. (Believe it best not indicate talking under instructions.) I would particularly stress desirability of actions to broaden and increase his [word illegible] support prior to 1961 presidential elections required by constitution before end April. I would propose following actions to President:

2. Psychological shock effect is required to take initiative from Communist propagandists as well as non-Communist oppositionists and convince population government taking effective measures to deal with present situation, otherwise we fear matters could get out of hand. To achieve that effect following suggested:

(A) Because of Vice President Tho's knowledge of south where Communist guerrilla infiltration is increasing so rapidly would suggest that he be shifted from ministry national economy to ministry interior. (Diem has already made this suggestion but Vice President most reluctant take job.)

(B) It is important to remove any feeling within armed forces that favoritism and political considerations motivate promotions and assignments. Also vital in order deal effectively with Viet Cong threat that channels of command be followed both down and up. To assist in bringing about these changes in armed forces, I would suggest appointment of full-time minister national defense. (Thuan has indicated Diem has been thinking of giving Thuan defense job.)

(C) Rumors about Mr. and Mrs. Nhu are creating growing dissension within country and seriously damage political position of Diem government. Whether rumors true or false, politically important fact is that more and more people believe them to be true. Therefore, becoming increasingly clear that in interest Diem government some action should be taken. In analogous situation in other countries including U.S. important, useful government personalities have had to be sacrificed for political reasons. I would suggest therefore that President might appoint Nhu to ambassadorship abroad.

(D) Similarly Tran Kim Tuyen, Nhu's henchman and head of secret intelligence service, should be sent abroad in diplomatic capacity because of his growing identification in public mind with alleged secret police methods of repression and control.

(E) One or two cabinet ministers from opposition should be appointed to demonstrate Diem's desire to establish government of national union in fight against VC.

3. Make public announcement of disbandment of Can Lao party or at least its surfacing, with names and positions of all members made known publicly. Purpose this step would be to eliminate atmosphere of fear and suspicion and reduce public belief in favoritism and corruption, all of which party's semicovert status has given rise to.

4. Permit National Assembly wider legislative initiative and area of genuine debate and bestow on it authority to conduct, with appropriate publicity, public investigations of any department of government with right to question any official except President himself. This step would have three-fold purpose: (A) find some mechanism for dispelling through public investigation constantly generated rumors about government and its personalities; (B) provide people with avenue recourse against arbitrary actions by some governmental officials, (C) assuage some of intellectual opposition to government.

5. Require all government officials to declare publicly their property and financial holdings and give National Assembly authority to make public investigation of these declarations in effort dispel rumors of corruption.

6. [Words illegible] of [word illegible] control over content of the Vietnamese publication [word illegible] magazines, radio, so that the [words illegible] to closing the gap between government and [words illegible] ideas from one to the other. To insure that the press would reflect, as well as lead, public opinion without becoming a means of upsetting the entire GVN [word illegible], it should be held responsible to a self-imposed code of ethics or "canon" of press-conduct.

7. [Words illegible] to propaganda campaign about new 3-year development plan in effort convince people that government genuinely aims at [word illegible] their welfare. (This suggestion [word illegible] of course upon assessment of soundness of development plan, which has just reached us.)

8. Adopt following measures for immediate enhancement of peasant support of government: (A) establish mechanism for increasing price peasant will receive for paddy crop beginning to come on market in December, either by direct subsidization or establishment of state purchasing mechanism; (B) institute modest payment for all corvee labor; (C) subsidize agroville families along same lines as land resettlement families until former on feet economically; (D) increase compensation paid to youth corps. If Diem asks how these measures are to be financed I shall suggest through increased taxes or increased deficit financing, and shall note that under certain circumstances reasonable deficit financing becomes a politically necessary measure for governments. I should add that using revenues for these fundamental and worthy purposes would be more effective than spending larger and larger sums on security forces, which, while they are essential and some additional funds for existing security forces may be required, are not complete answer to current problems.

9. Propose suggest to Diem that appropriate steps outlined above be announced dramatically in his annual state of union message to National Assembly in early October. Since Diem usually [word illegible] message in person this would have maximum effect, and I would recommend that it be broadcast live to country.

10. At [words illegible] on occasion fifth anniversary establishment Republic of Vietnam on October 26, it may become highly desirable for President Eisenhower to address a letter of continued support to Diem. Diem has undoubtedly noticed that Eisenhower letter recently delivered to Sihanouk. Not only for this reason, but also because it may become very important for us to give Diem continued reassurance of our support. Presidential letter which could be published here may prove to be very valuable.

Request any additional suggestions department may have and its approval for approach to Diem along lines paras 1 to 9.

We believe U.S. should at this time support Diem as best available Vietnamese leader, but should recognize that overriding U.S. objective is strongly anti-Communist Vietnamese government which can command loyal and enthusiastic support of widest possible segments of Vietnamese people, and is able to carry on effective fight against Communist guerrillas. If Diem's position in country continues deteriorate as result failure adopt proper political, psychological, economic and security measures, it may become necessary for U.S. government to begin consideration alternative courses of action and leaders in order achieve our objective.

[Document 97]

TO: THE PRESIDENT September 29, 1967

FROM: CLARK CLIFFORD

*Memorandum of Conference on January 19, 1961
between President Eisenhower and President-Elect Kennedy
on the Subject of Laos*

The meeting was held in the Cabinet Room with the following men present: President Eisenhower, Secretary of State Christian Herter, Secretary of Defense Thomas Gates, Secretary of Treasury Robert Anderson, and General Wilton B. Persons.

With President-elect Kennedy were the new Secretary of State Dean Rusk, the new Secretary of Defense Robert McNamara, the new Secretary of Treasury Douglas Dillon, and Clark M. Clifford.

An agenda for the meeting had been prepared by Persons and Clifford. The subjects on the agenda had been recommended by the parties present at the conference and were arranged under the headings of "State," "Defense," and "Treasury." The first subject under the heading of "State" was Laos.

President Eisenhower opened the discussion on Laos by stating that the United States was determined to preserve the independence of Laos. It was his opinion that if Laos should fall to the Communists, then it would be just a question of time until South Vietnam, Cambodia, Thailand and Burma would collapse. He felt that the Communists had designs on all of Southeast Asia, and that it would be a tragedy to permit Laos to fall.

President Eisenhower gave a brief review of the various moves and coups that had taken place in Laos involving the Pathet Lao, Souvanna Phouma, Boun Oum, and Kong Le. He said that the evidence was clear that Communist China and North Vietnam were determined to destroy the independence of Laos. He also added that the Russians were sending in substantial supplies in support of the Pathet Lao in an effort to overturn the government.

President Eisenhower said it would be fatal for us to permit Communists to insert themselves in the Laotian government. He recalled that our experience had clearly demonstrated that under such circumstances the Communists always ended up in control. He cited China as an illustration.

At this point, Secretary of State Herter intervened to state that if the present government of Laos were to apply to SEATO for aid under the Pact, Herter was of the positive opinion that the signatories to the SEATO Pact were bound. President Eisenhower agreed with this and in his statement gave the impression that the request for aid had already come from the government of Laos. He corroborated the binding nature of the obligation of the United States under the SEATO Pact.

President Eisenhower stated that the British and the French did not want SEATO to intervene in Laos, and he indicated that they would probably continue to maintain that attitude. President Eisenhower said that if it were not appropriate for SEATO to intervene in Laos, that his next preference would be the International Control Commission. He was sure, however, that the Soviet Union did not want the ICC to go into Laos. President Eisenhower stated that if this country had a choice as to whether the task should be assumed by SEATO or the ICC, that he personally would prefer SEATO.

Secretary Herter stated that we possibly could work out some agreement with the British, if they could be persuaded to recognize the present government in Laos. The chances of accomplishing this, however, appeared to be remote.

Secretary Herter stated, with President Eisenhower's approval, that we should continue every effort to make a political settlement in Laos. He added, however, that if such efforts were fruitless, then the United States must intervene in concert with our allies. If we were unable to persuade our allies, then we must go it alone.

At this point, President Eisenhower said with considerable emotion that Laos was the key to the entire area of Southeast Asia. He said that if we permitted Laos to fall, then we would have to write off all the area. He stated that we must not permit a Communist take-over. He reiterated that we should make every effort to persuade member nations of SEATO or the ICC to accept the burden with us to defend the freedom of Laos.

As he concluded these remarks, President Eisenhower stated it was imperative that Laos be defended. He said that the United States should accept this task with our allies, if we could persuade them, and alone if we could not. He added that "our unilateral intervention would be our last desperate hope" in the event we were unable to prevail upon the other signatories to join us.

At one time it was hoped that perhaps some type of arrangement could be made with Kong Le. This had proved fruitless, however, and President Eisenhower said "he was a lost soul and wholly irretrievable."

Commenting upon President Eisenhower's statement that we would have to go to the support of Laos alone if we could not persuade others to proceed with us, President-elect Kennedy asked the question as to how long it would take to put an American division into Laos. Secretary Gates replied that it would take from twelve to seventeen days but that some of that time could be saved if American forces, then in the Pacific, could be utilized. Secretary Gates added that the American forces were in excellent shape and that modernization of the Army was making good progress.

President-elect Kennedy commented upon the seriousness of the situation in Laos and in Southeast Asia and asked if the situation seemed to be approaching a climax. General Eisenhower stated that the entire proceeding was extremely confused but that it was clear that this country was obligated to support the existing government in Laos.

The discussion of Laos led to some concluding general statements regarding Southeast Asia. It was agreed that Thailand was a valuable ally of the United States, and that one of the dangers of a Communist take-over in Laos would be to expose Thailand's borders. In this regard, it was suggested that the military training under French supervision in Thailand was very poor and that it would be a good idea to get American military instructors there as soon as possible so the level of military capability could be raised.

President Eisenhower said there was some indication that Russia was concerned over Communist pressures in Laos and in Southeast Asia emanating from China and North Vietnam. It was felt that this attitude could possibly lead to some difficulty between Russia and China.

This phase of the discussion was concluded by President Eisenhower in commenting philosophically upon the fact that the morale existing in the democratic forces in Laos appeared to be disappointing. He wondered aloud why, in interventions of this kind, we always seem to find that the morale of the Communist forces was better than that of the democratic forces. His explanation was that the Communist philosophy appeared to produce a sense of dedication on the part of its adherents, while there was not the same sense of dedication on the part of those supporting the free forces. He stated that the entire problem of morale was a serious one and would have to be taken into consideration as we became more deeply involved.

[Document 98]

Reprinted from New York *Times*

Excerpts from "A Program of Action for South Vietnam," 8 May 1961 [Ed. Note: Date questionable], *presented to President Kennedy by an interdepartmental task force comprising representatives from the Departments of State and Defense, the Central Intelligence Agency, the International Cooperation Administration, the United States Information Agency and the Office of the President.*

. . . 2. MILITARY:

a. The following military actions were approved by the President at the NSC meeting of 29 April 1961:

(1) Increase the MAAG as necessary to insure the effective implementation of the military portion of the program including the training of a 20,000-man addition to the present G.V.N. armed forces of 150,000. Initial appraisal of new tasks assigned CHMAAG indicate that approximately 100 additional military personnel will be required immediately in addition to the present complement of 685.

(2) Expand MAAG responsibilities to include authority to provide support and advice to the Self-Defense Corps with a strength of approximately 40,000.

(3) Authorize MAP support for the entire Civil Guard force of 68,000. MAP support is now authorized for 32,000; the remaining 36,000 are not now adequately trained and equipped.

(4) Install as a matter of priority a radar surveillance capability which will enable the G.V.N. to obtain warning of Communist overflights being conducted for intelligence or clandestine air supply purposes. Initially, this capability should be provided from U.S. mobile radar capability.

(5) Provide MAP support for the Vietnamese Junk Force as a means of preventing Viet Cong clandestine supply and infiltration into South Vietnam by water. MAP support, which was not provided in the Counter-Insurgency Plan, will include training of junk crews in Vietnam or at U.S. bases by U.S. Navy personnel.

b. The following additional actions are considered necessary to assist the G.V.N. in meeting the increased security threat resulting from the new situation along the Laos-G.V.N. frontier:

(1) Assist the G.V.N. armed forces to increase their border patrol and insurgency suppression capabilities by establishing an effective border intelligence and patrol system, by instituting regular aerial surveillance over the entire frontier area, and by applying modern technological area-denial techniques to control the roads and trails along Vietnam's borders. A special staff element (approximately 6 U.S. personnel), to concentrate upon solutions to the unique problems of Vietnam's borders, will be activated in MAAG, Vietnam, to assist a similar special unit in the RVNAF which the G.V.N. will be encouraged to establish; these two elements working as an integrated team will help the G.V.N. gain the support of nomadic tribes and other border inhabitants, as well as introduce advanced techniques and equipment to strengthen the security of South Vietnam's frontiers.

(2) Assist the G.V.N. to establish a Combat Development and Test Center in South Vietnam to develop, with the help of modern technology, new techniques for use against the Viet Cong forces. (Approximately 4 U.S. personnel.)

(3) Assist the G.V.N. forces with health, welfare and public work projects by providing U.S. Army civic action mobile training teams, coordinated with the similar civilian effort. (Approximately 14 U.S. personnel.)

(4) Deploy a Special Forces Group (approximately 400 personnel) to Nha Trang in order to accelerate G.V.N. Special Forces training. The first increment, for immediate deployment in Vietnam, should be a Special Forces company (52 personnel).

(5) Instruct JCS, CINCPAC, and MAAG to undertake an assessment of the military utility of a further increase in the G.V.N. forces from 170,000 to

200,000 in order to create two new division equivalents for deployment to the northwest border region. The parallel political and fiscal implications should be assessed. . . .

4. ECONOMIC:

1. Objective: Undertake economic programs having both a short-term immediate impact as well as ones which contribute to the longer range economic viability of the country.

a. Undertake a series of economic projects designed to accompany the counter-insurgency effort, by the following action:

(1) Grant to ICA the authority and funds to move into a rural development-civic action program. Such a program would include short-range, simple, impact projects which would be undertaken by teams working in cooperation with local communities. This might cost roughly $3 to $5 million, mostly in local currency. Directors of field teams should be given authority with respect to the expenditure of funds including use of dollar instruments to purchase local currency on the spot.

b. Assist Vietnam to make the best use of all available economic resources, by the following action:

(1) Having in mind that our chief objective is obtaining a full and enthusiastic support by the G.V.N. in its fight against the Communists, a high level team preferably headed by Assistant Secretary of the Treasury John Leddy, with State and ICA members, should be dispatched to Saigon to work out in conjunction with the Ambassador a plan whereby combined U.S. and Vietnamese financial resources can best be utilized. This group's terms of reference should cover the broad range of fiscal and economic problems. Authority should be given to make concessions necessary to achieve our objectives and to soften the blow of monetary reform. Ambassador Nolting and perhaps the Vice President should notify Diem of the proposed visit of this group stressing that their objective is clearly to maximize the joint effort rather than to force the Vietnamese into inequitable and unpalatable actions.

(2) As a part of the foregoing effort, an assessment should be undertaken of the fiscal and other economic implications of a further force increase from 170,-000 to 200,000 (as noted in the Military section above).

c. Undertake the development of a long-range economic development program as a means of demonstrating U.S. confidence in the economic and political future of the country by the following action:

(1) Authorize Ambassador Nolting to inform the G.V.N. that the U.S. is prepared to discuss a long-range joint five-year development program which would involve contributions and undertakings by both parties. . . .

5. PSYCHOLOGICAL:

a. Assist the G.V.N. to accelerate its public information program to help develop a broad public understanding of the actions required to combat the Communist insurgents and to build public confidence in the G.V.N.'s determination and ability to deal with the Commuinst threat.

b. The U.S. Country Team, in coordination with the G.V.N. Ministry of Defense, should compile and declassify for use of media representatives in South Vietnam and throughout the world, documented facts concerning Communist infiltration and terrorists' activities and the measures being taken by the G.V.N. to counter such attacks.

c. In coordination with CIA and the appropriate G.V.N. Ministry, USIS will increase the flow of information about unfavorable conditions in North Vietnam to media representatives.

d. Develop agricultural pilot-projects throughout the country, with a view toward exploiting their beneficial psychological effects. This project would be accomplished by combined teams of Vietnamese Civic Action personnel, Americans in the Peace Corps, Filipinos in Operation Brotherhood, and other Free World nationals.

e. Exploit as a part of a planned psychological campaign and rehabilitation of Communist Viet Cong prisoners now held in South Vietnam. Testimony of rehabilitated prisoners, stressing the errors of Communism, should be broadcast to Communist-held areas, including North Vietnam, to induce defections. This rehabilitation program would be assisted by a team of U.S. personnel including U.S. Army (Civil Affairs, Psychological Warfare and Counter-Intelligence), USIS, and USOM experts.

f. Provide adequate funds for an impressive U.S. participation in the Saigon Trade Fair of 1962.

6. COVERT ACTIONS:

a. Expand present operations in the field of intelligence, unconventional warfare, and political-psychological activities to support the U.S. objective as stated.

b. Initiate the communications intelligence actions, CIA and ASA personnel increases, and funding which were approved by the President at the NSC meeting of 29 April 1961.

c. Expand the communications intelligence actions by inclusion of 15 additional Army Security Agency personnel to train the Vietnamese Army in tactical COMINT operations. . . .

7. FUNDING:

a. As spelled out in the funding annex, the funding of the counter-insurgency plan and the other actions recommended in this program might necessitate increases in U.S. support of the G.V.N. budget for FY 61 of as much as $58 million, making up to a total of $192 million compared to $155 million for FY 60. The U.S. contribution for the G.V.N. Defense budget in FY 62 as presently estimated would total $161 million plus any deficiency in that budget which the G.V.N. might be unable to finance. The exact amount of U.S. contributions to the G.V.N. Defense budgets for FY 61 and FY 62 are subject to negotiation between the U.S. and the G.V.N.

b. U.S. military assistance to G.V.N., in order to provide the support contemplated by the proposed program would total $140 million, or $71 million more than now programmed for Vietnam in the U.S. current MAP budget for FY 62. . . .

ANNEX 6

Covert Actions

a. Intelligence: Expand current positive and counter-intelligence operations against Communist forces in South Vietnam and against North Vietnam. These include penetration of the Vietnamese Communist mechanism, dispatch of agents to North Vietnam and strengthening Vietnamese internal security services. Authorization should be given, subject to existing procedures, for the use in North Vietnam operations of civilian air crews of American and other nationality, as appropriate, in addition to Vietnamese. Consideration should be given for overflights of North Vietnam for photographic intelligence coverage, using American or Chinese Nationalists crews and equipment as necessary.

b. Communications Intelligence: Expand the current program of interception and direction-finding covering Vietnamese Communist communications activities in South Vietnam, as well as North Vietnam targets. Obtain further USIB authority to conduct these operations on a fully joint basis, permitting the sharing of results of interception, direction finding, traffic analysis and cryptographic analysis by American agencies with the Vietnamese to the extent needed to launch rapid attacks on Vietnamese Communist communications and command installations.

This program should be supplemented by a program, duly coordinated, of training additional Vietnamese Army units in intercept and direction-finding by the U.S. Army Security Agency. Also, U.S. Army Security Agency teams could be sent to Vietnam for direct operations, coordinated in the same manner—Approved by the President at the NSC meeting of 29 April 1961.

c. Unconventional Warfare: Expand present operations of the First Observation Battalion in guerrilla areas of South Vietnam, under joint MAAG-CIA sponsorship and direction. This should be in full operational collaboration with the Vietnamese, using Vietnamese civilians recruited with CIA aid.

In Laos, infiltrate teams under light civilian cover to Southeast Laos to locate and attack Vietnamese Communist bases and lines of communications. These teams should be supported by assault units of 100 to 150 Vietnamese for use on targets beyond capability of teams. Training of teams could be a combined operation by CIA and U.S. Army Special Forces.

In North Vietnam, using the foundation established by intelligence operations, form networks of resistance, covert bases and teams for sabotage and light harassment. A capability should be created by MAAG in the South Vietnamese Army to conduct Ranger raids and similar military actions in North Vietnam as might prove necessary or appropriate. Such actions should try to avoid any outbreak of extensive resistance or insurrection which could not be supported to the extent necessary to stave off repression.

Conduct overflights for dropping of leaflets to harass the Communists and to maintain morale of North Vietnamese population, and increase gray broadcasts to North Vietnam for the same purposes.

d. Internal South Vietnam: Effect operations to penetrate political forces, government, armed services and opposition elements to measure support of government, provide warning of any coup plans and identify individuals with potentiality of providing leadership in event of disappearance of President Diem.

Build up an increase in the population's participation in and loyalty to free government in Vietnam, through improved communication between the government and the people, and by strengthening independent or quasi-independent organizations of political, syndical or professional character. Support covertly the GVN in allied and neutral countries, with special emphasis on bringing out GVN accomplishments, to counteract tendencies toward a "political solution" while the Communists are attacking GVN. Effect, in support, a psychological program in Vietnam and elsewhere exploiting Communist brutality and aggression in North Vietnam.

e. The expanded program outlined above was estimated to require an additional 40 personnel for the CIA station and an increase in the CIA outlay for

Vietnam of approximately $1.5 million for FY 62, partly compensated by the withdrawal of personnel from other areas. The U.S. Army Security Agency actions to supplement communications intelligence will require 78 personnel and approximately $1.2 million in equipment. The personnel and fund augmentations in this paragraph were approved by the President at the NSC meeting of 29 April 1961.

f. In order adequately to train the Vietnamese Army in tactical COMIT operations, the Army Security Agency estimates that an additional 15 personnel are required. This action has been approved by the U.S. Intelligence Board.

[Document 99]

Reprinted from New York *Times*

U.S. Approval, in 1961, of Steps to
Strengthen South Vietnam

National Security Action Memorandum 52, signed by McGeorge Bundy, Presidential adviser on national security, 11 May 1961.

1. The U.S. objective and concept of operations stated in report are approved: to prevent Communist domination of South Vietnam; to create in that country a viable and increasingly democratic society, and to initiate, on an accelerated basis, a series of mutually supporting actions of a military, political, economic, psychological and covert character designed to achieve this objective.

2. The approval given for specific military actions by the President at the National Security Council meeting on April 29, 1961, is confirmed.

3. Additional actions listed at pages 4 and 5 of the Task Force Report are authorized, with the objective of meeting the increased security threat resulting from the new situation along the frontier between Laos and Vietnam. In particular, the President directs an assessment of the military utility of a further increase in G.V.N. forces from 170,000 to 200,000, together with an assessment of the parallel political and fiscal implications.

4. The President directs full examination by the Defense Department, under the guidance of the Director of the continuing Task Force on Vietnam, of the size and composition of forces which would be desirable in the case of a possible commitment of U.S. forces to Vietnam. The diplomatic setting within which this action might be taken should also be examined.

5. The U.S. will seek to increase the confidence of President Diem and his Government in the United States by a series of actions and messages relating to the trip of Vice President Johnson. The U.S. will attempt to strengthen President Diem's popular support within Vietnam by reappraisal and negotiation, under the direction of Ambassador Nolting. Ambassador Nolting is also requested to recommend any necessary reorganization of the Country Team for these purposes.

6. The U.S. will negotiate in appropriate ways to improve Vietnam's relationship with other countries, especially Cambodia, and its standing in word opinion.

7. The Ambassador is authorized to begin negotiations looking toward a new bilateral arrangement with Vietnam, but no firm commitment will be made to such an arrangement without further review by the President.

8. The U.S. will undertake economic programs in Vietnam with a view to both short-term immediate impact and a contribution to the longer-range eco-

nomic viability of the country, and the specific actions proposed on pages 12 and 13 of the Task Force Report are authorized.

9. The U.S. will strengthen its efforts in the psychological field as recommended on pages 14 and 15 of the Task Force Report.

10. The program for covert actions outlined on page 15 of the Task Force Report is approved.

11. These decisions will be supported by appropriate budgetary action, but the President reserves judgment on the levels of funding proposed on pages 15 and 16 of the Task Force Report and in the funding annex.

12. Finally, the President approves the continuation of a special Task Force on Vietnam, established in and directed by the Department of State under Sterling J. Cottrell as Director, and Chalmers B. Wood as Executive Officer.

[Document 100]

Reprinted from New York *Times*

Excerpts from memorandum from Brig. Gen. Edward G. Lansdale, Pentagon expert on guerrilla warfare, to Gen. Maxwell D. Taylor, President Kennedy's military adviser, on "Resources for Unconventional Warfare, S.E. Asia," undated but apparently from July, 1961. Copies were sent to Secretary of Defense Robert S. McNamara, Deputy Secretary of Defense Roswell L. Gilpatric, Secretary of State Dean Rusk, Allen W. Dulles, Director of Central Intelligence, and Gen. C. P. Cabell, Deputy Director of Central Intelligence.

This memo is in response to your desire for early information on unconventional-warfare resources in Southeast Asia. The information was compiled within Defense and CIA.

A. SOUTH VIETNAM

1. Vietnamese

a. First Observation Group

This is a Special Forces type of unit, with the mission of operating in denied (enemy) areas. It currently has some limited operations in North Vietnam and some shallow penetrations into Laos. Most of the unit has been committed to operations against Viet Cong guerillas in South Vietnam.

Strength, as of 6 July, was 340. The First Observation Group had an authorized strength of 305 and now is being increased by 500, for a total of 805, under the 20,000-man force increase. Personnel are volunteers who have been carefully screened by security organizations. Many are from North Vietnam. They have been trained for guerrilla operations, at the Group's training center at Nha Trang. The unit is MAP-supported, as a TO&E unit of the RVNAF (Republic of Vietnam Armed Forces). It receives special equipment and training from CIA and U.S control is by CIA/MAAG.

The Group and its activities are highly classified by the Government of Vietnam. Only a select few senior RVNMAF officers have access to it. Operations require the approval of President Diem, on much the same approval basis as certain U.S. special operations. The unit is separate from normal RVNAF command channels.

The Group was organized in February, 1956, with the initial mission of preparing stay-behind organizations in South Vietnam just below the 17th Parallel, for guerrilla warfare in the event of an overt invasion by North Vietnamese forces. It was given combat missions against Viet Cong guerrillas in South Vietnam last year, when these Communist guerrillas increased their activities. The plan is to relieve the Group from these combat assignments, to ready its full strength for denied area missions, as RVNAF force increases permit relief. It is currently being organized into twenty teams of 15 men each, with two RS-1 radios per team, for future operations.

b. Other RVNAF

MAAG-Vietnam has reported the formation of additional volunteer groups, apart from the First Observation Group, for similar operations to augment the missions of the Group. As of 6 July, the additional volunteers were reported as:

1). 60 Mois (Montagnard tribesmen) recruited, being security screened, to receive Special Forces training.

2). 400 military (RVNAF), to receive Special Forces training. 80 will be formed into small teams, to augment operations of the First Operations Group. 320 will be formed into two Ranger (Airborne) companies.

3). 70 civilians, being organized and trained for stay-behind operations, penetration teams, and communicators.

Other special units of the RVNAF, now committed to operations against the Viet Cong and with Special Forces/Ranger training, are:

9,096 Rangers, in 65 companies.

2,772 more Rangers being activated, part of 20,000-man increase

4,786 Paratroopers

2,300 Marines

673 men in Psychological Warfare Bn.

In addition, cadres from all other combat elements of the RVNAF have received Special Forces/Ranger training.

2. U.S.

a. Defense

1). There are approximately 6 officers and 6 enlisted men from the 1st Special Group on Okinawa currently attached to the MAAG to assist with Ranger-type training.

2). There are three 4-man intelligence training teams present—Combat Intelligence, Counter-Intelligence, Photo-Interpretation and Foreign Operations Intelligence (clandestine collection) in addition to eight officers and two enlisted intelligence advisors on the MAAG staff.

3). There are two Psychological Warfare staff officers on the MAAG staff and a 4-man Civil Affairs mobile training team (3 officers—1 enlisted man) advising the G-5 staff of the Vietnamese Army in the psy/ops-civic action fields.

b. CIA

1). There are 9 CIA officers working with the First Observation Group in addition to one MAAG advisor.

2). CIA also has five officers working with the Vietnamese Military Intelligence Service and one officer working with the covert [one word illegible] of the Army Psychological Warfare Directorate.

B. THAILAND

1. Thai

a. Royal Thai Army Ranger Battalion (Airborne)

A Special Forces type unit, its stated mission is to organize and conduct guerrilla warfare in areas of Thailand overrun by the enemy in case of an open invasion of Thailand. It currently has the mission of supplying the Palace Guard for the Prime Minister.

Based at Lopburi, the Ranger Battalion has a MAP authorized strength of 580. It is organized into a Headquarters and Headquarters company, a Service company, and four Ranger companies. The Battalion has 4 command detachments and 26 operations detachments, trained and organized along the lines of U.S. Special Forces in strength, equipment, and rank structure.

The Ranger Battalion is loosely attached to the 1st Division. In reality, it is an independent unit of the Royal Thai Army, under the direct control of Field Marshal Sarit, the Commander in Chief, and receives preferential treatment.

Each ranger company has been assigned a region of Thailand, in which it is to be prepared to undertake guerrilla warfare in case of enemy occupation. Field training is conducted in these assigned regions, to acquaint the detachments with the people, facilities and terrain.

b. Police Aerial Resupply Unit (PARU)

The PARU has a mission of undertaking clandestine operations in denied areas. 99 PARU personnel have been introduced covertly to assist the Meos in operations in Laos, where their combat performance has been outstanding.

This is a special police unit, supported by CIA (CIA control in the Meo operations has been reported as excellent), with a current strength of 300 being increased to 550 as rapidly as possible. All personnel are specially selected and screened, and have been rated as of high quality. Officers are selected from the ranks.

Training consists of 10 weeks' basic training, 3 weeks' jumping, 3 weeks' jungle operations, 4 weeks' police law and 3 months of refresher training yearly. Forty individuals have been trained as W/T communicators.

All personnel have adequate personal gear to be self-sustaining in the jungle. Weapons are M-1 rifles, M-3 submachine guns and BAR. In addition, personnel are trained to use other automatic weapons, 2.34 rocket launchers, and 60-mm. mortars.

There are presently 13 PARU teams, totaling 99 men, operating with the Meo guerrillas in Laos. Combat reports of these operations have included exceptionally heroic and meritorious actions by PARU personnel. The PARU teams have provided timely intelligence and have worked effectively with local tribes.

c. Thai Border Patrol (BPP)

The mission of the BPP is to counter infiltration and subversion during peacetime, in addition to normal police duties, in the event of an armed invasion of Thailand, the BPP will operate as guerrilla forces in enemy-held areas, in support of regular Thai armed forces.

The BPP has a current strength of 4,500. It was organized in 1955 as a gendarmerie patrol force (name changed to BPP in 1959), composed of 71 active and 23 reserve platoons, from existing police units. It is an element of the Thai National Police, subordinate to the Ministry of the Interior.

Although technically a police organization, the BPP is armed with infantry weapons, including light machine guns, rocket launchers and light mortars. It is trained in small-unit infantry tactics and counter-guerrilla operations. Training is currently being conducted by a 10-man U.S. Army Special Forces team from Okinawa, under ICA auspices.

This unusual police unit was created initially to cope with problems posed by foreign guerrilla elements using Thailand as a safehaven: the Vietminh in eastern Thailand and the Chinese Communists along the Malayan border in the south. There has been some tactical liaison with Burmese Army units.

2. U.S.

a. Defense

1(. A special Forces qualified officers is assigned to advise the RTA Ranger Battalion.

2). A ten-man Special Forces team from the 1st Special Forces Group in Okinawa is currently conducting training for the Thai Border Patrol Police under ICA auspices.

3). There are 5 officers and 1 enlisted man attached to MAAG as advisers to J-2 and the Thai Armed Forces Security Center.

b. CIA

1). 2 advisers with PARU.

2). 3 officers who work with the Border Patrol Police providing advice, guidance and limited training in the collection and processing of intelligence in addition to management of their communications system.

C. LAOS

1. Lao

a. Commandos

According to CINCPAC, there are two special commando companies in the Lao Armed Forces (FAL), with a total strength of 256. These commandos have received Special Forces training.

b. Meo Guerrillas

About 9,000 Meo tribesmen have been equipped for guerrilla operations, which they are now conducting with considerable effectiveness in Communist-dominated territory in Laos. They have been organized into Auto-Defense Choc units of the FAL, of varying sizes. Estimates on how many more of these splendid fighting men could be recruited vary, but a realistic figure would be around 4,000 more, although the total manpower pool is larger.

Political leadership of the Meos is in the hands of Touby Lyfoung, who now operates mostly out of Vientiane. The military leader is Lt-Col Vang Pao, who is the field commander. Command control of Meo operations is exercised by the Chief CIA Vientiane with the advice of Chief MAAG Laos. The same CIA paramilitary and U.S. military teamwork is in existence for advisory activities (9 CIA operations officers, 9 LTAG/Army Special Forces personnel, in addition to the 99 Thai PARU under CIA control) and aerial resupply.

As Meo village are over-run by Communist forces and as men leave food-raising duties to serve as guerrillas, a problem is growing over the care and feeding of non-combat Meos. CIA has given some rice and clothing to relieve this problem. Consideration needs to be given to organized relief, a mission of an ICA nature, to the handling of Meo refugees and their rehabilitation.

c. National Directorate of Coordination

This is the Intelligence arm of the RLG. Its operations are mainly in the Vientiane area at present. It has an armed unit consisting of two battalions and is under the command of Lt-Col Siho, a FAL officer. In addition to intelligence operations this force has a capability for sabotage, kidnapping, commando-type raids, etc.

d. There is also a local veteran's organization and a grass-roots political organization in Laos, both of which are subject to CIA direction and control and are capable of carrying out propaganda, sabotage and harassment operations. Both are located (in varying degrees of strength and reliability) throughout Laos.

2. U.S.

a. Defense

1). There are 154 Special Forces personnel (12 teams) from the 7th Special Forces Group at Fort Bragg, N. C., attached to the MAAG and providing tactical advice to FAL commanders and conducting basic training when the situation permits.

2). A 10-man intelligence training team is assisting the FAL in establishing a military intelligence system.

3). An 8-man psychological warfare team is assisting the FAL with psy war operations and operation of its radio transmitters.

b. CIA

1). Nine CIA officers are working in the field with the Meo guerrillas, backstopped by two additional officers in Vientiane.

2). Three CIA officers plus 2–3 Vietnamese are working with the National Directorate of Coordination.

D. OTHERS

1. Asian

a. Eastern Construction Company [Filipinos]

This is a private, Filipino-run public service organization, similar to an employment agency, with an almost untapped potential for unconventional warfare (which was its original mission). It now furnishes about 500 trained, experienced Filipino technicians to the Governments of Vietnam and Laos, under the auspices of MAAGs (MAP) and USOMs (CIA activities). Most of these Filipinos are currently augmenting U.S. military logistics programs with the Vietnamese Army and Lao Army. They instruct local military personnel in ordnance, quartermaster, etc., maintenance, storage, and supply procedures. MAAG Chiefs in both Vietnam and Laos have rated this service as highly effective. CIA has influence and some continuing interest with individuals.

The head of Eastern Construction is "Frisco" Johnny San Juan, former National Commander, Philippines Veterans Legion, and former close staff assistant to President Magsaysay of the Philippines (serving as Presidential Complaints and Action Commissioner directly under the President). Its cadre are mostly either former guerrillas against the Japanese in WW II or former Philippine Army personnel. Most of the cadre had extensive combat experience against the Communist Huk guerrillas in the Philippines. This cadre can be expanded into a wide range of counter-Communist activities, having sufficient stature in the Philippines to be able to draw on a very large segment of its trained, experienced, and well-motivated manpower pool.

Eastern Construction was started in 1954 as Freedom Company of the Philippines, a non-profit organization, with President Magsaysay as its honorary president. Its charter stated plainly that it was "to serve the cause of freedom." It actually was a mechanism to permit the deployment of Filipino personnel in other Asian countries, for unconventional operations, under cover of a public service organization having a contract with the host government. Philippine Armed Forces and government personnel were "sheep-dipped" and served abroad. Its personnel helped write the Constitution of the Republic of Vietnam, trained Vietnam's Presidential Guard Battalion, and were instrumental in founding and organizing the Vietnamese Veterans Legion.

When U.S. personnel instrumental in the organization and operational use of Freedom Company departed from the Asian area, direct U.S. support of the organization (on a clandestine basis) was largely terminated. The Filipino leaders in it then decided to carry on its mission privately, as a commercial undertaking. They changed the name to Eastern Construction Company. The organization survived some months of very hard times financially. Its leaders remain as a highly-motivated, experienced, anti-Communist "hard core."

b. *Operation Brotherhood* (*Filipino*)

There is another private Filipino public-service organization, capable of considerable expansion in socio-economic-medical operations to support counter-guerilla actions. It is now operating teams in Laos, under ICA auspices. It has a measure of CIA control.

Operation Brotherhood (OB) was started in 1954 by the International Jaycees, under the inspiration and guidance of Oscar Arellano, a Filipino architect who was Vice President for Asia of the International Jaycees. The concept was to provide medical service to refugees and provincial farmers in South Vietnam, as part of the 1955 pacification and refugee program. Initially Filipino teams, later other Asian and European teams, served in OB in Vietnam. Their work was closely coordinated with Vietnamese Army operations which cleaned up Vietminh stay-behinds and started stabilizing rural areas. . . .

c. *The Security Training Center* (*STC*)

This is a counter-subversion, counter-guerrilla and psychological warfare school overtly operated by the Philippine Government and covertly sponsored by the U.S. Government through CIA as the instrument of the Country Team. It is located at Fort McKinley on the outskirts of Manila. Its stated mission is: "To counter the forces of subversion in Southeast Asia through more adequate training of security personnel, greater cooperation, better understanding and maximum initiative among the countries of the area." . . .

The training capability of the STC includes a staff of approximately 12 instructors in the subjects of unconventional and counter-guerrilla warfare. . . .

d. *CAT. Civil Air Transport* (*Chinese Nationalist*)

CAT is a commercial air line engaged in scheduled and non-scheduled air operations throughout the Far East, with headquarters and large maintenance facilities located in Taiwan. CAT, a CIA proprietary, provides air logistical support under commercial cover to most CIA and other U.S. Government agencies' requirements. CAT supports covert and clandestine air operations by providing trained and experienced personnel, procurement of supplies and equipment through overt commercial channels, and the maintenance of a fairly large inventory of transport and other type aircraft under both Chinat and U.S. registry.

CAT has demonstrated its capability on numerous occasions to meet all types of contingency or long-term covert air requirements in support of U.S. objectives. During the past ten years, it has had some notable achievements, including support of the Chinese Nationalist withdrawal from the mainland, air drop support to the French at Dien Bien Phu, complete logistical and tactical air support for the Indonesian operation, air lifts of refugees from North Vietnam, more than 200 overflights of Mainland China and Tibet, and extensive air support in Laos during the current crisis. . . .

2. U.S.

b. CIA

1). Okinawa—Support Base

Okinawa Station is in itself a paramilitary support asset and, in critical situations calling for extensive support of UW activity in the Far East, could be devoted in its entirety to this mission. Located at Camp Chinen, it comprises a self-contained base under Army cover with facilities of all types necessary to the storage, testing, packaging, procurement and delivery of supplies—ranging from weapons and explosives to medical and clothing. Because of its being a controlled area, it can accommodate admirably the holding of black bodies in singletons or small groups, as well as small groups of trainees. . . .

4). Saipan Training Station.

CIA maintains a field training station on the island of Saipan located approximately 160 miles northeast of Guam in the Marianas Islands. The installation is under Navy cover and is known as the Naval Technical Training Unit. The primary mission of the Saipan Training Station is to provide physical facilities and competent instructor personnel to fulfill a variety of training requirements including intelligence tradecraft, communications, counter-intelligence and psychological warfare techniques. Training is performed in support of CIA activities conducted throughout the Far East area.

In addition to the facilities described above, CIA maintains a small ship of approximately 500 tons' displacement and 140 feet in length. This vessel is used presently to provide surface transportation between Guam and Saipan. It has an American Captain and First Mate and a Philippine crew, and is operated under the cover of a commercial corporation with home offices in Baltimore, Maryland. Both the ship and the corporation have a potentially wider paramilitary application both in the Far East area and elsewhere.

[Document 101]

Reprinted from New York *Times*

Cablegram from the United States Embassy in Saigon to the State Department, 1 Oct. 1961. A copy of the message was sent to the commander in chief of Pacific forces.

Discussion with Felt and party, McGarr, Nolting yesterday Diem asked for bilateral defense treaty. Large and unexplained request. Serious. Put forward as result of Diem's fear of outcome of Laos situation, SVN vulnerability to increased infiltration, feelings that SEATO action would be inhibited by UK and France in the case of SVN as in Laos.

Nolting told Diem question had important angle and effect on SEATO. Major repeated to Thuan and believe he understands better than Diem some of thorny problems.

Fuller report of conversation with Diem will follow but would like to get quick preliminary reaction from Washington on this request.

Our reaction is that the request should be seriously and carefully treated to prevent feeling that U.S. is not serious in intention to support SVN. But see major issues including overriding Article 19, Geneva Accords, possible ratification problems as well as effect on SEATO.

Diem's request arises from feeling that U.S. policy on Laos will expose his flank in infiltration and lead to large-scale hostilities in SVN. So seeking a stronger commitment than he thinks he has now through SEATO. Changing U.S. policy on Laos, especially SEATO decision to use force if necessary to protect SVN and Thailand, would relieve pressure for bilateral treaty.

[Document 102]

CM-390-61
12 October 1961

MEMORANDUM FOR GENERAL TAYLOR

SUBJECT: Counterinsurgency Operations in South Vietnam

1. You will recall that I recently had occasion to look into allegations that the United States is overtraining the Vietnamese Army for a Korea-type war with little or nothing being done to meet the terrorist problem in Vietnam. My inquiries have highlighted the following main points:

a. The success of the counter-terrorist police organization in Malaya has had considerable impact.

b. The concept of using local police force to combat local insurgency is politically and diplomatically attractive.

2. I fully agree that we should make maximum use of those aspects of the British counterinsurgency experience in Malaya which are pertinent to the situation in Vietnam. You will recognize, however, that there are major differences between the situations in Malaya and South Vietnam:

a. Malayan borders were far more controllable in that Thailand cooperated in refusing the Communists an operational safe haven.

b. The racial characteristics of the Chinese insurgents in Malaya made identification and segregation a relatively simple matter as compared to the situation in Vietnam where the Viet Cong cannot be distinguished from the loyal citizen.

c. The scarcity of food in Malaya versus the relative plenty in South Vietnam made the denial of food to the Communist guerrillas a far more important and readily usable weapon in Malaya.

d. Most importantly, in Malaya the British were in actual command, with all of the obvious advantages this entails, and used highly trained Commonwealth troops.

e. Finally, it took the British nearly 12 years to defeat an insurgency which was less strong than the one in South Vietnam.

3. Furthermore, as you well know, the success of the counterinsurgency operations in Malaya is not unique. Major terrorist activities have been defeated in both the Philippines and Burma, and in neither place was the police organization used as the framework for coordination and control. In the Philippines, for example, the military framework used was highly successful.

4. Closely associated with the allegation that the MAAG is "overtraining"

the Vietnamese Army is the concern frequently expressed over the length of time required to train military officers and NCO's. No one knows better than you do that well-trained officers and NCO's are not produced in brief training programs. I am sure you will want to discuss this in detail with General McGarr when you visit Saigon. It is most important to note that the heaviest casualties in the Vietnam insurgency have been suffered by the Civil Guard previously trained as police. Almost without exception, the Viet Cong have attacked the untrained Civil Guard rather than the better trained Army units. This has resulted in a heavy loss of weapons and equipment to the Viet Cong. Untrained Civil Guard units have, in fact, been an important source of weapons and supplies for the Viet Cong, and their known vulnerability has been an invitation for the Viet Cong to attack. General McGarr believes that reversion of the Civil Guard to police control would set back the counterinsurgency operation in South Vietnam by at least a year.

5. With respect to training the Vietnamese Army for the "wrong war," it seems clear that in recent months the insurgency in South Vietnam has developed far beyond the capacity of police control. All of the Vietnamese Army successes this past summer have met Viet Cong opposition in organized battalion strength. Even larger Communist units were involved in the recent Viet Cong successes north of Kontum. This change in the situation has not been fully understood by many U.S. officials.

6. In this regard, there is some concern that the Thompson Mission may try to sell the Malayan concept of police control without making a sufficiently careful evaluation of conditions in South Vietnam. Additionally, there are some indications that the British, for political reasons, wish to increase their influence in this area and are using the Thompson Mission as a vehicle. Consequently, your forthcoming trip to South Vietnam is most timely. Despite repeated urging, the Government of South Vietnam has not yet written an overall national plan for counter-insurgency. The question of police or military organization for combatting Viet Cong insurgency should be laid to rest in that plan. Your evaluation of this matter could have an important effect on the Governments of both South Vietnam and the United States.

> L. L. Lemnitzer
> Chairman
> Joint Chiefs of Staff

[Document 103]

Reprinted from New York *Times*

Cablegram from United States Embassy in Saigon to the State Department 13 Oct. 1961, on requests by Nguyen Dinh Thuan, Defense Minister of South Vietnam. Copies of this message were sent to Commander in Chief of Pacific forces and to the United States Embassies in Bangkok, Thailand, and Taipei, Taiwan.

Thuan in meeting October 13 made the following requests:
1. Extra squadron of AD-6 in lieu of proposed T-28's and delivery ASAP.
2. U.S. Civilian contract pilots for helicopters and C-47's for "non-combat" operations.
3. U.S. combat units or units to be introduced into SVN as "combat-trainer

units." Part to be stationed in North near 17th Parallel to free ARVN forces there for anti-guerrilla aftion in high plateau. Also perhaps in several provincial seats in the highlands of Central Vietnam.

4. U.S. reaction to proposal to request Nationalist China to send one division of combat troops for operations in the Southwest.

Thuan referred to captured diary of VM officer killed in Central SVN, containing information on VM plans and techniques. Being analyzed, translated and would pass on. Said Diem in light of situation in Laos, infiltration into SVN, and JFK's interest as shown by sending Taylor, requested U.S. to urgently consider requests.

On U.S. combat trainer units, Nolting asked whether Diem's considered request, in view of repeated views opposed. Thuan so confirmed, Diem's views changed in light of worsening situation. Wanted a symbolic U.S. strength near 17th to prevent attacks there, free own forces there. Similar purpose station U.S. units in several provincial seats in central highlands, freeing ARVN ground forces there. Nolting said major requests on heels of Diem request for bilateral treaty. Nolting asked if in lieu of treaty. Thuan said first step quicker than treaty and time was of the essence. Thuan said token forces would satisfy SVN and would be better than treaty (had evidently not thought through nor discussed with Diem).

Discussed ICC angle. Nolting mentioned value SVN previously attached to ICC presence. Thuan agreed, felt case could be made for introduction of U.S. units for guard duty not combat unless attacked. Could be put in such a way to preserve ICC in SVN. Nolting said doubted if compatible but could be explored (McGarr and I call attention to two points: in view of proposed units, training function more a cover than reality; if send U.S. units should be sufficient strength, since VC attack likely).

On Chinat force, Thuan said Chiang had earlier given some indication (not too precise I gathered) of willingness. Thuan said GVN did not want to follow-up without getting U.S. reaction. Idea to use about 10,000 men in southwest as far from 17th as possible. Also intended to draft eligibles of Chinese origin into forces. Thuan thought perhaps Chinats could be introduced covertly, but on analyses gave this up. Nolting said he thought Chinats would want something out of deal, maybe political lift from introducing Chinat forces on Asia mainland (Nolting thinks trial balloon only).

Questions will undoubtedly be raised with Taylor. Obvious GVN losing no opportunity to ask for more support as a result of our greater interest and concern. But situation militarily and psychologically has moved to a point where serious and prompt consideration should be given.

(Note: Will be meeting on this in Admiral Heinz's office, 1330, 16 October to get reply out today. Applicable CINCPAC 140333, 140346)

[Document 104]

Reprinted from New York *Times*

Excerpts from General Taylor's report, 3 Nov. 1961, on his mission to South Vietnam for President Kennedy.

. . . LIMITED PARTNERSHIP

. . . Following are the specific categories where the introduction of U.S. working advisors or working military units are suggested . . . an asterisk indicating where such operations are, to some degree, under way.

—A high-level government advisor or advisors. General Lansdale has been requested by Diem; and it may be wise to envisage a limited number of Americans—acceptable to Diem as well as to us—in key ministries. . . .

—A Joint U.S.-Vietnamese Military Survey, down to the provincial level, in each of three corps areas, to make recommendations with respect to intelligence, command and control, more economical and effective passive defense, the build-up of a reserve for offensive purposes, military-province-chief relations, etc. . . .

—Joint planning of offensive operations, including border control operations.* . . .

—Intimate liaison with the Vietnamese Central Intelligence Organizations (C.I.O.) with each of the seven intelligence [rest of sentence illegible].

—Jungle Jim. . . .

—Counter infiltration operations in Laos.* . . .

—Increased covert offensive operations in North as well as in Laos and South Vietnam.* . . .

—The introduction, under MAAG operational control, of three helicopter squadrons—one for each corps area—and the provision of more light aircraft, as the need may be established. . . .

—A radical increase in U.S. trainers at every level from the staff colleges, where teachers are short—to the Civil Guard and Self-Defense Corps, where a sharp expansion in competence may prove the key to mobilizing a reserve for offensive operations. . . .

—The introduction of engineering and logistical elements within the proposed U.S. military task force to work in the flood area within the Vietnamese plan, on both emergency and longer term reconstruction tasks. . . .

—A radical increase in U.S. special force teams in Vietnam: to work with the Vietnamese Ranger Force proposed for the border area . . . ; to assist in unit training, including training of Clandestine Action Service. . . .

—Increase the MAAG support for the Vietnamese Navy.* . . .

—Introduction of U.S. Naval and/or Coast Guard personnel to assist in coastal and river surveillance and control, until Vietnamese naval capabilities can be improved. . . .

—Reconsideration of the role of air power, leading to more effective utilization of assets now available, including release from political control of the 14 D-6 aircraft, institution of close-support techniques, and better employment of available weapons. . . .

To execute this program of limited partnership requires a change in the charter, the spirit, and the organization of the MAAG in South Vietnam. It must be shifted from an advisory group to something nearer—but not quite—an operational headquarters in a theater of war. . . . The U.S. should become a limited partner in the war, avoiding formalized advice on the one hand, trying to run the war, on the other. Such a transition from advice to partnership has been made in recent months, on a smaller scale, by the MAAG in Laos.

Among the many consequences of this shift would be the rapid build-up of an intelligence capability both to identify operational targets for the Vietnamese and to assist Washington in making a sensitive and reliable assessment of the progress of the war. The basis for such a unit already exists in Saigon in the Intelligence Evaluation Center. It must be quickly expanded. . . .

In Washington, as well, intelligence and back-up operations must be put on a quasi-wartime footing. . . .

CONTINGENCIES

The U.S. action proposed in this report—involving as it does the overt lifting of the MAAG ceiling, substantial encadrement and the introduction of limited U.S. forces—requires that the United States also prepare for contingencies that might arise from the enemy's reaction. The initiative proposed here should not be undertaken unless we are prepared to deal with any escalation the communists might choose to impose. Specifically we must be prepared to act swiftly under these three circumstances: an attempt to seize and to hold the Pleiku-Kontum area; a political crisis in which the communists might attempt to use their forces around Saigon to capture the city in the midst of local confusion; an undertaking of overt major hostilities by North Vietnam.

As noted earlier, the present contingency plans of CINCPAC must embrace the possibility both of a resumption of the communist offensive in Laos and these Vietnamese contingency situations. Taken together, the contingencies in Southeast Asia which we would presently choose to meet without the use of nuclear weapons appear to require somewhat more balanced ground, naval, and air strength in reserve in the U.S. than we now have available, so long as we maintain the allocation of the six divisions for the Berlin crisis.

Therefore, one of the major issues raised by this report is the need to develop the reserve strength in the U.S. establishment required to cover action in Southeast Asia up to the nuclear threshold in that area, as it is now envisaged. The call up of additional support forces may be required.

In our view, nothing is more calculated to sober the enemy and to discourage escalation in the face of the limited initiatives proposed here than the knowledge that the United States has prepared itself soundly to deal with aggression in Southeast Asia at any level.

[Document 105]

Talking Paper for the Chairman, JCS, for meeting with the President of the United States 9 January 1962

Subject: Current US Military Actions in South Vietnam

Background—Today Communist China and North Vietnam are suffering from the effects of failure of their communes to produce adequate amounts of food to feed their peoples. Recently, large quantities of wheat were purchased by Red China from Canada and Australia to overcome this failure. Southeast Asia, primarily South Vietnam and Thailand, is a food surplus area in normal times. Because of this and the standard Marxist-Leninist concept of peripheral aggression and pressure, the main communist threat in the Western Pacific appears to be directed at Southeast Asia. Of principal concern for the purpose of this briefing is the situation in South Vietnam, the US national objectives there and the military actions that have been implemented since October in support of our objectives.

The Current Situation in South Vietnam

The Viet Cong have heavily infiltrated, organized and now effectively control the colored areas on this chart.

To achieve their purposes the Viet Cong have divided the country into two major geographical areas, Intersector V with headquarters in the high plateau region north and west of Kontum, and the Nambo sector in the south with headquarters northeast of Saigon. Each major area is subdivided into interprovincial commands—four in Intersector V and three in Nambo, with a special zone for Saigon. Each interprovincial area is further organized into provinces which are further subdivided into districts, villages, and hamlets.

Methods of VC Operation

The 16,500-man Viet Cong military establishment is divided into two operational groups—regular and regional-local forces. Regular battalions and companies, numbering about 8,500 personnel, constitute the offensive element of the "Liberation Army" and operate throughout their respective interprovincial zone.

The 8,000 regional and local forces, which correspond functionally to the Self Defense Forces of SVN, are essentially security troops recruited and organized on district levels for limited operations and to provide security for command headquarters, conferences, and political rallies. Regional units are also used to provide semi-trained personnel as replacements in regular battalions and as fillers for newly activated units. Under regional unit control guerrilla platoons made up of daytime farmers sabotage, terrorize, assassinate, kidnap, disseminate propaganda, and attempt to subvert their neighbors.

Availability of weapons appears to be a continuing problem for Viet Cong forces, particularly in regional units in which less than half of the men are armed. The primary source of arms for all VC forces appears to be those captured from South Vietnamese security forces.

Most officers and key NCOs, as well as political and propaganda specialists, are former South Vietnamese who went north with the Communists in 1955, or who have since been recruited and sent to North Vietnam. These southerners are given special training and are then infiltrated back into South Vietnam through Laos (or by junks) to cadre regular and regional forces.

Training of regional troops and the activation of new regular battalions have been stepped up since the first of the year. In recent anti-guerrilla operations South Vietnamese troops uncovered several major Viet Cong training areas, one of which had barracks space for more than a battalion, 200 dummy rifles and tons of food.

In Communist-controlled areas, the Viet Cong have ordered villagers to dig trenches and prepare combat villages. The Viet Cong are collecting money from the peasants and plantation owners to finance the war against the government, and have implemented a rice tax to build up supplies for future operations. Pitched battles are avoided wherever possible, unless they are essential to a given plan, or the military advantages are at least four to one. The campaign to assassinate all who try to implement the Government of Vietnam's policies in the countryside is being intensified.

All indications point to the Viet Cong maintaining the current high level of guerrilla action in the south, and increasing activity in the high plateau area in efforts to build the decreed semi-permanent bases.

Routes of Infiltration and Supply

Prisoner of war interrogation recently conducted by the South Vietnamese Intelligence Service has shed additional light on the means employed by Communist North Vietnam to assist the Viet Cong in the latter's military and psychological campaigns against the Government of South Vietnam.

North Vietnam maintains a training camp for Special Troops in the vicinity of Vinh, where pro-Viet Cong South Vietnamese receive an 18-month military course interspersed with intensive Communist political indoctrination. Two 600-man battalions already have completed training, and another two battalions began training in May 1961. Personnel are assigned to units within the battalion according to their respective regions of origin in South Vietnam.

Upon completion of training, Viet Cong volunteers reenter South Vietnam by taking a circuitous route through territory in neighboring Laos controlled by Communist Pathet Lao forces.

In addition to land infiltration, some Viet Cong guerrillas and cadres are infiltrated by sea using junks and small craft to land at various points on the long South Vietnam coastline. It is estimated that no more than 20% of the total infiltrees use the sea route.

Relative Strengths

The current strength of the Viet Cong is 16,500 with the possible infiltration of 1,000 per month. The increase in strength by infiltration is offset by the estimated Viet Cong casualties which average over 1,000 a month according to South Vietnam official figures. A recent refinement in intelligence reporting indicates that the official estimate of Viet Cong strength may be raised to about 20,000 in the near future.

The current actual strength of the South Vietnamese forces are as follows:

Army	163,696
Navy	4,207
Air Force	5,314
Marines	3,135

In addition paramilitary forces total 65,000 in the Civil Guard and 45,000 Self Defense Corps.

The regular Army forces are organized and assigned to three corps areas with major command headquarters and units located as shown on the chart.

Current US Military Actions

The President on 22 November 1961 authorized the Secretary of State to instruct the US Ambassador to Vietnam to inform President Diem that the US Government was prepared to join the GVN in a sharply increased effort to avoid a further deterioration of the situation in SVN. On its part the US would immediately

a. Provide increased airlift to the GVN in the form of helicopters, light aviation and transport aircraft.

b. Provide required equipment and US personnel for aerial reconnaissance, instruction in and execution of air-ground support and special intelligence.

c. Augment the Vietnamese Navy operationally with small craft.

d. Provide expedited training and equipping of the Civil Guard and Self-Defense Corps.

e. Provide necessary equipment and personnel to improve the military-political intelligence system.

f. Provide such new terms of reference, reorganization, and additional personnel for US military forces as are required for increased US military assistance.

Discussion—As a result of the decision to accelerate US support of the GVN, the following US military units are in place or enroute as shown on this chart: (Overlay No. 1)

a. Two Army Light Helicopter Companies are operating in support of the RVNAF from Tan Son Nhut and Qui Nhon. The third company is enroute to Da Nang with an ETA of 15 January and an operational readiness date of 1 February. This will provide one company of 20 H-21 and two H-13 in support of each of three RVNAF Corps areas.

b. The US Army has alerted the 18th Fixed Wing Aircraft Company equipped with 16 U1A (Otter) aircraft to be ready for deployment by 15 January.

c. The 346th USAF Troop Carrier Squadron with 16 C-123 aircraft has four aircraft at Clark and four operating from Tan Son Nhut. The remaining eight aircraft are in the Pacific Theatre enroute to Clark with an ETA of 10 January. This unit will rotate aircraft into SVN from Clark to support RVNAF operations as required.

d. Four RP-101 aircraft and a small photo processing element operated by the USAF are in place at Den Muang Airfield, Thailand, fulfilling aerial photo requirements in SVN.

e. The USAF JUNGLE JIM unit at Bien Hoa with eight T-23, four RB-26 and four SC-47 aircraft, is instructing the Vietnamese Air Force in combat air support tactics and techniques. The Pacific Air Force is deploying personnel and equipment to SVN to establish a joint US/GVN Tactical Air Control System (TACS). This system will permit positive control of all air operations and rapid response to requests for air-ground support.

f. The 3rd Radio Reconnaissance Unit at Tan Son Nhut is being augmented. The additional 279 personnel will be on board by 14 January.

g. Six C-123 spray equipped aircraft for support of defoliant operations have received diplomatic clearance to enter SVN.

h. US Navy Mine Division 73 with a tender and five mine sweepers is operating from Tourane Harbor in conjunction with the Vietnamese Navy conducting maritime surveillance patrols south of the 17th parallel.

i. Air surveillance flights 30 miles seaward from the SVN coast (17th parallel) to 50 miles beyond the Paracel Islands are conducted every other day by Seventh Fleet patrol aircraft.

In addition to deployment of organized US military units to SVN and increased personnel strength for the MAAG, accelerated delivery of MAP equipment has already begun. Nine additional L-20 light observation aircraft are enroute to SVN for use by the Vietnamese Air Force. Also, 15 T-28C aircraft have been delivered to augment the Vietnamese air-ground support capability. These were provided on an interim, loan basis until 30 T-28B (NOMAD) with a greater ordnance delivery capability could complete modification and be delivered to SVN, early in March. Department of the Army is also providing an additional 12 H-34 helicopters from active Army units to the USAF on a reimbursable basis for accelerated MAP delivery to the RVNAF early in March.

[words missing]

Advisory Group in Vietnam was 841, present strength is 1204 and projected strength as of 30 June 1962 is 2394. The total personnel strength of US units and elements, other than the MAAG, was 1442 as of 2 January 1962 and projected strength as of 30 June 1962 is 3182. The total US personnel in South Vietnam is now 2646 and projected strength as of 30 June 1962 is 5576.

The MAAG is extending its advisory teams to battalion level within the RVNAF MA Military establishment and beginning to participate more directly in advising Vietnamese unit commanders in the planning and execution of military operations plans. Since delivery of MAP equipment has been accelerated and RVNAF military operations are increasing, the MAAG training activities have been expanded. This training includes operations, planning, logistics, intelligence, communications and electronics as they apply to each service within the RVNAF. They are also accelerating the training of the Vietnamese Civil Guard and Self-Defense Corps.

Shown on the chart are the approved and funded construction projects in South Vietnam. These include:

a. Improvement of the Pleiku Airfield.

b. Improvements at Tan Son Nhut Airfield which included installations of:

  (1) Pierced steel planking parking apron.

  (2) POL hydrant system.

  (3) POL pipeline to Nha Be.

  (4) Ammunition storange facility

  (5) Concrete parking apron

[line missing]

d. Improvement of the Bien Hoa Airfield.

—Communications and electronics improvements include the following:

a. An improved intelligence communications network. Net control station to be located in Saigon and to extend down to battalion and provincial level.

b. An improved Gate Way Station communications facilities at Saigon.

c. Three mobile navigational aid packages in the Pacific Theatre are approved for deployment to SVN as directed by CINCPAC.

The Future Outlook

The foremost national objective today of the Diem government in South Vietnam is survival against the incursions of Communist forces; cadred, supplied, and directed from North Vietnam. Secondary, but nonetheless extremely important objectives include: (1) improvement of the national economy with emphasis on agrarian reform; (2) enhancement of South Vietnam's economic, cultural, and prestige position among Southeast Asian nations; (3) the creation of an armed force capable of defending the country from potential invaders; (4) and the preservation of a pro-Western orientation.

Policies directed toward the achievement of these objectives suffer from the concentration of power in the hands of the President, Ngo Dinh Diem, and a small clique headed by his extremely influential and powerful brother. Ngo Dinh Nhu. Continued receipt of US military, economic and technical aid, application of Catholic philosophies, and the repulsion of the Viet Cong guerrillas are additional major policy considerations.

Planned courses of action include: (1) the building up of the armed forces with US aid and assistance; (2) defeat of the Viet Cong forces; and (3) the implementation of a series of reforms and measures to correct imbalances in the power hier- [words illegible]

Certainly some of the projects we are implementing are outright R&D efforts such as the defoliation project and bear all the earmarks of gimmicks that cannot and will not win the war in South Vietnam. However, the commitment of US units to support the RVNAF and additional personnel to train, equip and advise them in conjunction with increased economic and administrative aid, should make it obvious to the Vietnamese and the rest of the world that the United States is committed to preventing Communist domination of South Vietnam and Southeast Asia.

All of the recent actions we have taken may still not be sufficient to stiffen the will of the government and the people of SVN sufficiently to resist Communist pressure and win the war without the US committing combat forces. Whether we will have to take this decision within the coming year depends to a great [conclusion missing].

[Document 106]

THE JOINT CHIEFS OF STAFF
Washington 25, D.C.

CM-491-62
JAN 18 1962

MEMORANDUM FOR GENERAL LANSDALE

Subject: *Vietnamese Command Problem*

1. As you point out in your memorandum of 27 December 1961, it is quite clear that Diem's apprehension about a coup is the basis for his reluctance to authorize his military field commander to implement the task force concept that was an important part of the over-all plan of operations against the Viet Cong. I fully agree that this basic issue needs to be resolved.

2. You are well aware that Chief MAAG, Vietnam, in accordance with his assigned mission, has operated principally as an adviser and trainer rather than as a commander. As such he has suggested and counseled, dropping ideas which the Vietnamese could pick up and incorporate in their own plans. This method "saved face" for them, and has been the accepted method of overcoming simultaneously the inexperience and the pride of the Vietnamese officers. Now a strong case can be made for increased direct participation by US personnel in the planning and supervision of Vietnamese counterinsurgency operations. Inherent in such increased direct participation should be some assurance of US support for Diem personally. Convincing Diem of this personal support remains a principal task of the senior US representatives in Vietnam. The increased US military stake in Vietnam should be of great assistance in this task.

3. In my view, however, some of the decisions made during the 16 December SecDef meeting at CINCPAC Headquarters offer a greater hope for progress in Vietnam. It was agreed that, while we should continue to press for acceptance of an over-all plan or concept of operations, we must place immediate emphasis on smaller, more specific, and more readily-accomplished operations. Such a techinque is more likely to be acceptable to Diem. At the same time, successful small operations will provide the impetus for larger scale offensive operations.

4. I don't believe there is any finite answer to the question you pose as to how we convince Diem he must delegate authority to subordinates he doesn't fully trust. We discussed this subject at considerable length at Monday's (15 January 1962) conference in Honolulu. The Ambassador, General McGarr and other top level officers of the Embassy and MAAG recognize the nature of the problem and the importance of reaching a satisfactory solution thereto. If it was not for the heavy responsibilities you are now assigned which would preclude your going to Saigon, I believe that one of the best ways to deal with this prob-

lem would be to implement the earlier recommendation to send one Brigadier General Lansdale out to Saigon to be personal adviser and confidant to Diem.

> *L. L. Lemnitzer*
> Chairman
> Joint Chiefs of Staff

cc: Secretary McNamara
     Deputy Secretary Gilpatric
     Admiral Heinz

[Document 107]

January 18, 1962

NATIONAL SECURITY ACTION MEMORANDUM NO. 124

TO: The Secretary of State
               The Secretary of Defense
               The Attorney General
               The Chairman, Joint Chiefs of Staff
               The Administrator, Agency for International Development
               The Director, United States Information Agency
               The Military Representative of the President
               Director of Central Intelligence

SUBJECT: Establishment of the Special Group (Counter-Insurgency)

To assure unity of effort and the use of all available resources with maximum effectiveness in preventing and resisting subversive insurgency and related forms of indirect aggression in friendly countries, a Special Group (Counter-insurgency) is established consisting of the following members:

> Military Representatives of the President, Chairman
> The Attorney General
> Deputy Under Secretary of State for Political Affairs
> Deputy Secretary of Defense
> Chairman, Joint Chiefs of Staff
> Director of Central Intelligence
> Special Assistant to the President for National Security
>   Affairs
> Administrator, Agency for International Development
> Director, United States Information Agency

On invitation:

> Other department and agency representatives, as deemed
>   necessary

The functions of the Special Group (C.I.) will be as follows:

    a. To insure proper recognition throughout the U.S. Government that subversive insurgency ("wars of liberation") is a major form of politico-military conflict equal in importance to conventional warfare.

b. To insure that such recognition is reflected in the organization, training, equipment and doctrine of the U.S. Armed Forces and other U.S. agencies abroad and in the political, economic, intelligence, military aid and informational programs conducted abroad by State, Defense, AID, USIA and CIA. Particular attention will be paid the special training of personnel prior to assignment to MAAG's and to Embassy staffs in countries where counter-insurgency problems exist or may arise.

c. To keep under review the adequacy of U.S. resources to deal with actual or potential situations of insurgency or indirect aggression, making timely recommendation of measures to apply, increase or adjust these resources to meet anticipated requirements.

d. To insure the development of adequate interdepartmental programs aimed at preventing or defeating subversive insurgency and indirect aggression in countries and regions specifically assigned to the Special Group (C. I.) by the President, and to resolve any interdepartmental problems which might impede their implementation.

In performing the above functions, the members of the Special Group (C.I.) will act on behalf of their respective departments and agencies, and will depend for staff support upon their own staffs, and upon such country or regional interdepartmental task forces (normally chaired by a State Department Assistant Secretary) as may be established. The Group will confine itself to establishing broad lines of counter-insurgency policy, subject to my direction and decision as appropriate, insuring a coordinated and unified approach to regional or country programs, and verifying progress in implementation thereof. It will also undertake promptly to make decisions on interdepartmental issues arising out of such programs.

The critical areas initially assigned to the Special Group (C. I.) pursuant to paragraph *d* of this memorandum are set forth in the attached annex.

ANNEX TO NATIONAL SECURITY ACTION MEMORANDUM NO. 124

Hereby assign to the cognizance of the Special Group (Counter-Insurgency) the following countries:

> Laos
> South Viet-Nam
> Thailand

[Document 108]

January 26, 1962

The Honorable
    Roswell Gilpatric,
        Deputy Secretary of Defense.

Dear Mr. Gilpatric:

I have received your letter of December 28 to the Secretary on the question of an increase in the Vietnamese armed forces to the 200,000 man level. The matter was discussed with our Task Force while Ambassador Nolting was here on consultation.

In view of the gravity of the situation in Viet-Nam and of the importance of not interrupting the accelerated rate of our assistance to Viet-Nam, we agree that an increase to about 200,000 should be supported provided the following factors are given careful consideration:

1. That the U.S. military advisers and the Vietnamese authorities continue the joint effort to build up a set of valid tactical and strategic plans. We suggest that the locus of this effort should be in Viet-Nam in order to obtain full Vietnamese cooperation and to meet the speed requirements of a guerrilla war where a large number of incidents are constantly occurring. We would envisage strategic plans made in Saigon giving priority to areas to be cleared and held and setting forth general methods to be used. We believe these should be accomplished by numerous small tactical actions planned and executed by American and Vietnamese officers on the spot to meet the local situation at the moment.

2. The rate of increase to approximately 200,000 men should take into consideration:

   a. The ability of the army to absorb and train these men without unduly weakening its fighting ability.
   b. Viet-Nam must husband its manpower resources carefully. A minimum number of trained civilians must be left at their posts in order to at least partially satisfy the rising expectations of Viet-Nam's citizens.

3. That the armed forces might best level off at about 200,000 with future emphasis to be devoted to strengthening and enlarging the Civil Guard and Self Defense Corps. Their job would be to hold ground that had been recovered.

4. That henceforth our training programs for ARVN be based primarily on the concept that the Vietnamese army will start winning on the day when it has obtained the confidence of the Vietnamese peasants. As a specific example I suggest that we immediately seek Vietnamese implementation of a policy of promptly giving a small reward in rice, salt or money (commodities in which the Viet Cong are in short supply) to every person who gives information to the army. Similarly, villages which show determination to resist the Viet Cong should receive the promptest possible support.

I would be glad to receive any comments you may have with respect to the foregoing.

Sincerely yours,

s/U. Alexis Johnson
Deputy Under Secretary
for Political Affairs

[Document 109]

27 January 1962

MEMORANDUM FOR THE PRESIDENT

The Joint Chiefs of Staff have asked that the attached memorandum, stating their views concerning the strategic importance may be required if the situation continues to deteriorate, be brought to your attention. The memorandum requires no action by you at this time. I am not prepared to endorse the experience with our present program in South Vietnam.

Robert S. McNamara

cc: Sec. Rusk

THE JOINT CHIEFS OF STAFF JCSM-33-62
Washington 25, D.C. 13 Jan 1962

MEMORANDUM FOR THE SECRETARY OF DEFENSE

Subject: The Strategic Importance of the Southeast Asia Mainland

1. The United States has clearly stated and demonstrated that one of its unalterable objectives is the prevention of South Vietnam falling to communist aggression and the subsequent loss of the remainder of the Southeast Asian mainland. The military objective, therefore, must be to take expeditiously all actions necessary to defeat communist aggression in South Vietnam. The immediate strategic importance of Southeast Asia lies in the political value that can accrue to the Free World through a successful stand in that area. Of equal importance is the psychological impact that a firm position by the United States will have on the countries of the world—both free and communist. On the negative side, a United States political and/or military withdrawal from the Southeast Asian area would have an adverse psychological impact of even greater proportion, and one from which recovery would be both difficult and costly.

2. It must be recognized that the fall of South Vietnam to communist control would mean the eventual communist domination of all of the Southeast Asian mainland. There is little doubt that the next major target would be Thailand. Cadres are now being established in that country and "land reform" or "capitalist dictatorship" ploys may prove fertile exploitation fields for the communists. Thailand is bordered by a "pink" Burma and a vacillating Cambodia, either of which will easily fall under communist pressure. Thailand would almost certainly then seek closer accommodation with the Sino-Soviet Bloc. SEATO would probably cease to exist. The only determined opposition to a communist drive would then be Malaya and Singapore. While the people of Malaya have the will to fight and might have the backing of the United Kingdom, the country itself would be isolated and hard pressed. The communist element in Singapore is strong. Short of direct military intervention by the United States, it is questionable whether Malaya and Singapore could be prevented from eventually coming under communist domination or control.

3. *Military Considerations.* (The Appendix contains a more detailed appraisal of these military considerations.)

a. *Early Eventualities*—Loss of the Southeast Asian Mainland would have an adverse impact on our military strategy and would markedly reduce our ability in limited war by denying us air, land and sea bases, by forcing greater intelligence effort with lesser results, by complicating military lines of communication and by the introduction of more formidable enemy forces in the area. Air access and access to 5300 miles of mainland coastline would be lost to us, our Allies and neutral India would be outflanked, the last significant United Kingdom military strength in Asia would be eliminated with the loss of Singapore and Malaya and US military influence in that area, short of war, would be difficult to exert.

b. *Possible Eventualities*—Of equal importance to the immediate losses are the eventualities which could follow the loss of the Southeast Asian mainland. All of the Indonesian archipelago could come under the domination and control of the USSR and would become a communist base posing a threat against Australia and New Zealand. The Sino-Soviet Bloc would have control of the eastern access to the Indian Ocean. The Philippines and Japan could be pressured to assume at best, a neutralist role, thus eliminating two of our major bases of defense in the Western Pacific. Our lines of defense then would be pulled north to Korea, Okinawa and Taiwan resulting in the subsequent overtaxing of our lines of communications in a limited war. India's ability to remain neutral would be jeopardized and, as the Bloc meets success, its concurrent stepped-up activities to move into and control Africa can be expected.

4. *Political Considerations.* The Joint Chiefs of Staff wish to reaffirm their position that the United States must prevent the loss of South Vietnam to either communist insurgency or aggression, must prevent the communist control or domination of the Southeast Asia mainland and must extend its influence in that area in such a manner as to negate the possibility of any future communist encroachment. It is recognized that the military and political effort of Communist China in South Vietnam and the political and psychological thrust by the USSR into the Indonesian archipelago are not brushfire tactics nor merely a campaign for control of the mainland area. More important, it is part of a major campaign to extend communist control beyond the periphery of the Sino-Soviet Bloc and overseas to both island and continental areas in the Free World, through a most natural and comparatively soft outlet, the Southeast Asian Peninsula. It is, in fact, a planned phase in the communist timetable for world domination. Whereas, control of Cuba has opened for the Sino-Soviet Bloc more ready access to countries of South and Central America, control of Southeast Asia will open access to the remainder of Asia and to Africa and Australia.

5. In consideration of the formidable threat to the Free World which is represented in the current actions in South Vietnam, the need for US and GVN success in that area cannot be overemphasized. In this connection, reference is made to the staff level document entitled "Summary of Suggested Courses of Action" prepared for General Taylor for reference in his mission to South Vietnam. On 21 October 1961, this document circulated comments and recommendations on 20 courses of action that could be taken in South Vietnam short of the direct utilization of US combat forces. The Joint Chiefs of Staff note that, in keeping with the President's decision that we must advise and support South Vietnam but not at this time engage unilaterally in combat, all of the courses of action recommended with few exceptions have either been implemented or authorized for implementation. In this connection, it is noted that the Vietnamese Government has specifically requested further assistance from the United States.

6. Reference is also made to the agreement made between the Government of Vietnam and the United States on 4 December 1961 wherein the Government of Vietnam agreed to take several major steps to increase its efficiency.

7. In response to President Diem's request for assistance and the agreement between the governments, men, money, materials and advice are being provided to South Vietnam. Unfortunately, our contributions are not being properly employed by the South Vietnamese Government and major portions of the agreement have either not been carried out or are being delayed by Diem.

8. For a combined US/Vietnam effort to be successful, there must be combined participation in the decision making process. To date efforts made on both the military and diplomatic level have failed to motivate Diem to agree to act forthrightly on our advice and properly utilize the resources placed at his disposal. He has been slow to accept the plans and proposals of Admiral Felt and General McGarr and he has in many instances disregarded the advice of Am-

bassador Nolting. The reason for Diem's negative reaction to proposals to save South Vietnam while he maintains a positive position that it must be saved may be found in CINCPAC's appraisal of his character—an uncompromising inflexibility and his doubts concerning the judgment, ability and individual loyalty of his military leaders. Recent intelligence reports of coup d'etat plotting involving senior Vietnamese military officers and the possibility that high Vietnamese officers have approached US officials tend to confirm Diem's doubts concerning the loyalty of some of his military leaders.

9. In this regard, should a successful coup overturn Diem, we might discover that many of Diem's difficult characteristics are national rather than personal. The Vietnamese are tough, tenacious, agile, proud, and extraordinarily self confident. Their recent political tradition is one of the multiplicity of parties and groups inclining toward conspiratorial and violent methods. The disappearance of a strong leader who can dampen and control these tendencies could well mean reversion to a condition of political chaos exploitable by the strongly led and well disciplined communists. If Diem goes, we can be sure of losing his strengths but we cannot be sure of remedying his weaknesses. Achievement of US objectives could be more difficult without Diem than with him. Therefore, it must be made clear to Diem that the United States is prepared and willing to bolster his regime and discourage internal factions which may seek to overthrow him.

10. In consideration of the foregoing, the Joint Chiefs of Staff believe that there is an immediate requirement for making a strong approach to Diem on a Government-to-Government level. If we are to effectively assist South Vietnam, we must convince Diem that (a) there is no alternative to the establishment of a sound basis upon which both he and the United States Government can work and (b) he has an urgent requirement for advice, as well as assistance, in military, political and economic matters.

11. Accordingly, it is recommended that you propose to the President and to the Secretary of State that:

> a. Upon his return to Saigon, Ambassador Nolting meet with President Diem and advise him that, since the United States considers it essential and fundamental that South Vietnam not fall to communist forces:
>
> > (1) The United States is prepared and willing to bolster his regime and discourage internal factions which may seek to overthrow him.
> >
> > (2) Suitable military plans have been developed and jointly approved. Diem must permit his military commanders to implement these approved plans to defeat the Viet Cong.
> >
> > (3) There must be established an adequate basis for the reception and utilization of US advice and assistance by all appropriate echelons of the GVN.
> >
> > (4) There must be no further procrastination.
> >
> > (5) Should it be found impossible to establish such a satisfactory basis for cooperation, the United States foresees failure of our joint efforts to save Vietnam from communist conquest.

12. Vigorous prosecution of the campaign with present and planned assets could reverse the current trend. If, with Diem's full [words missing] forces, the Viet Cong is not brought under control, the Joint Chiefs of Staff see no alternative to the introduction of US military combat forces along with those of the free Asian nations that can be persuaded to participate.

13. Three salient factors are of the greatest importance if the eventual introduction of US forces is required.

a. Any war in the Southeast Asian Mainland will be a peninsula and island-type of campaign—a mode of warfare in which all elements of the Armed Forces of the United States have gained a wealth of experience and in which we have excelled both in World War II and Korea.

b. Study of the problem clearly indicates that the communists are limited in the forces they can sustain in war in that area because of natural logistic and transportation problems.

c. Our present world military posture is such that we now have effective forces capable of implementing existing contingency plans for Southeast Asia without affecting to an unacceptable degree our capability to conduct planned operations in Europe relating to Berlin or otherwise.

14. The Joint Chiefs of Staff recommend that in any consideration of further action which may be required because of possible unacceptable results obtained despite Diem's full cooperation and the effective employment of South Vietnam armed forces, you again consider the recommendation provided you by JCSM-320-61, dated 10 May 1961, that a decision be made to deploy US forces to South Vietnam sufficient to accomplish the following:

a. Provide a visible deterrent to potential North Vietnam and/or Chinese Communist action;

b. Release Vietnamese forces from advanced and static defense positions to permit their future commitment to counterinsurgency actions;

c. Assist in training the Vietnamese forces;

d. Provide a nucleus for the support of any additional US or SEATO military operations in Southeast Asia; and

e. Indicate the firmness of our intent to all Asian nations.

We are of the opinion that failure to do so under such circumstances will merely extend the date when such action must be taken and will make our ultimate task proportionately more difficult.

For the Joint Chiefs of Staff:

L. L. Lemnitzer
Chairman
Joint Chiefs of Staff

[Document 110]

THE WHITE HOUSE
Washington

February 19, 1962

NATIONAL SECURITY ACTION MEMORANDUM NO. 132

TO: The Honorable Fowler Hamilton
             The Administrator
             Agency for International Development

SUBJECT: Support of Local Police Forces for Internal Security
             and Counter-Insurgency Purposes

As you know, I desire the appropriate agencies of this Government to give utmost attention and emphasis to programs designed to counter Communist indirect aggression, which I regard as a grave threat during the 1960s. I have already written the Secretary of Defense "to move to a new level of increased activity across the board" in the counter-insurgency field.

Police assistance programs, including those under the aegis of your agency, are also a crucial element in our response to this challenge. I understand that there has been some tendency toward de-emphasizing them under the new aid criteria developed by your agency. I recognize that such programs may seem marginal in terms of focusing our energies on those key sectors which will contribute most to sustained economic growth. But I regard them as justified on a different though related basis, i.e., that of contributing to internal security and resisting Communist-supported insurgency.

I am further aware that police programs, as a relatively minor facet of the functions of the aid agency, may have tended to receive little emphasis as a result. Therefore, I would like you to consider various ways and means of giving the police program greater autonomy within AID, if this seems necessary in order to protect it from neglect. I fully recognize that police programs must be looked at on a case-by-case basis and that in some instances they can indeed be cut back or eliminated. I simply wish to insure that before doing so we have taken fully into account the importance of the counter-insurgency objective as I view it.

In sum, I should like AID to review carefully its role in the support of local police forces for internal security and counter-insurgency purposes, and to recommend to me through the Special Group (Counter-Insurgency) what new or renewed emphases are desirable.

(signed) *John F. Kennedy*

Information Copy to:
    The Secretary of State
    The Secretary of Defense
    The Attorney General
    Director of Central Intelligence
    Director, Bureau of the Budget
    Director, Peace Corps
    General Maxwell D. Taylor

[Document 111]

THE WHITE HOUSE
Washington

March 13, 1962

NATIONAL SECURITY ACTION MEMORANDUM NO. 131

TO: The Secretary of State
            The Secretary of Defense
            The Attorney General
            The Chairman, Join Chiefs of Staff
            The Director of Central Intelligence
            The Administrator, Agency for International Development
            The Director, United States Information Agency

SUBJECT: Training Objectives for Counter-Insurgency

1. The President has approved the following training objectives for officer grade personnel of the departments and agencies indicated above who may

have a role to play in counter-insurgency programs as well as in the entire range of problems involved in the modernization of developing countries.

a. *The Historical Background of Counter-Insurgency*

Personnel of all grades will be required to study the history of subversive insurgency movements, past and present, in order to familiarize themselves with the nature of the problems and characteristics of Communist tactics and techniques as related to this particular aspect of Communist operations. This kind of background historical study will be offered throughout the school systems of the responsible departments and agencies, beginning at the junior level of instruction and carrying forward to the senior level.

b. *Study of Departmental Tactics and Techniques to Counter Subversive Insurgency*

Junior and middle grade officers will receive instructions in the tactics and techniques of their particular departments which have an application in combating subversive insurgency. This level of instruction will be found in the schools of the Armed Services at the company/field officer level. In the case of the Central Intelligence Agency, this kind of instruction will be offered at appropriate training installations. The State Department will be responsible for organizing appropriate courses in this instructional area for its own officers and for representatives of the Agency for International Development and the United States Information Agency. Schools of this category will make available spaces in agreed numbers for the cross-training of other U.S. agencies with a counter-insurgency responsibility.

c. *Instruction in Counter-Insurgency Program Planning*

Middle grade and senior officers will be offered special training to prepare them for command, staff, country team and departmental positions involved in the planning and conduct of counter-insurgency programs. At this level the students will be made aware of the possible contributions of all departments, and of the need to combine the departmental assets into effective programs. This type of instruction will be given at the Staff College-War College level in the Armed Services. The State Department will organize such courses as may be necessary at the Foreign Service Institute for officials of State, Agency for International Development and United States Information Agency. All schools of this category will make available spaces in agreed numbers for the cross-training of other U.S. agencies with a counter-insurgency responsibility.

d. *Specialized Preparations for Service in Underdeveloped Areas*

There is an unfulfilled need to offer instruction on the entire range of problems faced by the United States in dealing with developing countries, including special area counter-insurgency problems, to middle and senior grade officers (both military and civilian) who are about to occupy important posts in underdeveloped countries. A school will accordingly be developed at the national level to meet this need, to teach general (including counter-insurgency) policy and doctrine with respect to under-developed areas, to offer studies on problems of the underdeveloped world keyed to areas to which the students are being sent, and to engage in research projects designed to improve the U.S. capability for guiding underdeveloped countries through the modernization barrier and for countering subversive insurgency. In addition, this school would undertake to assist other more specialized U.S. Government institutions engaged in underdeveloped area problems (i.e., those conducted by the Foreign Service Institute, Agency for International Development, the Joint Chiefs of Staff and the Services, including the Military Assistance Institute and the Central Intelligence Agency) to develop curricula on the nontechnical aspects of their courses of instruction.

e. *Training of Foreign Nationals*

It is in the interest of the United States to provide counter-insurgency training to selected foreign nationals, both in the United States and in their own countries. The emphasis should be placed on those countries with an actual or potential counter-insurgency problem. This training will be given in the following places:

(1) In facilities operated by the Department of Defense and the Central Intelligence Agency which are available to foreigners.

(2) In special facilities operated by the Department of Defense and the Agency for International Development in Panama for the benefit of foreign nationals.

(3) U.S. MAAGs/missions and USOMs in countries with counter-insurgency programs.

2. It is desired that the Special Group (Counter-Insurgency) explore ways of organizing a school of the type described in paragraph 1 d above as a matter of urgency and develop appropriate recommendations. The Special Group (Counter-Insurgency) should also examine the possibility of setting up interim courses at the Foreign Service Institute and/or at the National War College to fill the gap during consideration of a new school.

3. It is desired that the addressees examine the counter-insurgency training which is currently offered in their departments and agencies, and to report by June 1, 1962 upon the adequacy with which it meets the training objectives above. If any deficiencies are determined to exist, the responsible department or agency will report its plan for correcting them.

/s/ *McGeorge Bundy*

[Document 112]

THE WHITE HOUSE
Washington

April 7, 1962

The Honorable
   Robert S. McNamara
      Secretary of Defense
         Washington, D.C.

Dear Mr. Secretary:

The President has asked me to transmit to you for your comments the enclosed memorandum on the subject of Viet-Nam to the President from Ambassador J. K. Galbraith dated April 4, 1962.

Sincerely

Michael V. Forrestal

Encl: Memo to Pres. from Amb. Galbraith

April 4, 1962

MEMORANDUM FOR THE PRESIDENT

Subject: Viet-Nam

The following considerations influence our thinking on Viet-Nam:

1. We have a growing military commitment. This could expand step by step into a major, long-drawn out indecisive military involvement.

2. We are backing a weak and, on the record, ineffectual government and a leader who as a politician may be beyond the point of no return.

3. There is consequent danger we shall replace the French as the colonial force in the area and bleed as the French did.

4. The political effects of some of the measures which pacification requires or is believed to require, including the concentration of population, relocation of villages, and the burning of old villages, may be damaging to those and especially to Westerners associated with it.

5. We fear that at some point in the involvement there will be a major political outburst about the new Korea and the new war into which the Democrats as so often before have precipitated us.

6. It seems at least possible that the Soviets are not particularly desirous of trouble in this part of the world and that our military reaction with the need to fall back on Chinese protection may be causing concern in Hanoi.

In the light of the foregoing we urge the following:

1. That it be our policy to keep open the door for political solution. We should welcome as a solution any broadly based non-Communist government that is free from external interference. It should have the requisites for internal law and order. We should not require that it be militarily identified with the United States.

2. We shall find it useful in achieving this result if we seize any good opportunity to involve other countries and world opinion in settlement and its guarantee. This is a useful exposure and pressure on the Communist bloc countries and a useful antidote for the argument that this is a private American military adventure.

3. We should measurably reduce our commitment to the particular present leadership of the government of South Viet-Nam.

To accomplish the foregoing, we recommend the following specific steps:

1. In the next fortnight or so the ICC will present a report which we are confidentially advised will accuse North Viet-Nam of subversion and the Government of Viet-Nam in conjunction with the United States of not notifying the introduction of men and materiel as prescribed by the Geneva accords. We should respond by asking the co-chairmen to initiate steps to re-establish compliance with the Geneva accords. Pending specific recommendations, which might at some stage include a conference of signatories, we should demand a suspension of Viet Cong activity and agree to a standstill on an introduction of men and materiel.

2. Additionally, Governor Harriman should be instructed to approach the Russians to express our concern about the increasingly dangerous situation

that the Viet Cong is forcing in Southeast Asia. They should be told of our determination not to let the Viet Cong overthrow the present government while at the same time to look without relish on the dangers that this military build-up is causing in the area. The Soviets should be asked to ascertain whether Hanoi can and will call off the Viet Cong activity in return for phased American withdrawal, liberalization in the trade relations between the two parts of the country and general and non-specific agreement to talk about reunification after some period of tranquillity.

3. Alternatively, the Indians should be asked to make such an approach to Hanoi under the same terms of reference.

4. It must be recognized that our long-run position cannot involve an unconditional commitment to Diem. Our support is to non-Communist and progressively democratic government not to individuals. We cannot ourselves replace Diem. But we should be clear in our mind that almost any non-Communist change would probably be beneficial and this should be the guiding rule for our diplomatic representation in the area.

In the meantime policy should *continue* to be guided by the following:

1. We should resist all steps which commit American troops to combat action and impress upon all concerned the importance of keeping American forces out of actual combat commitment.

2. We should disassociate ourselves from action, however necessary, which seems to be directed at the villagers, such as the new concentration program. If the action is one that is peculiarly identified with Americans, such as defoliation, it should not be undertaken in the absence of most compelling reasons. Americans in their various roles should be as invisible as the situation permits.

[Document 113]

JSCM-282-62
13 APR 1962

MEMORANDUM FOR THE SECRETARY OF DEFENSE

Subject: US Policy Toward Vietnam

1. Reference is made to a memorandum by the Assistant Secretary of Defense (ISA) dated 10 April 1962, requesting comments on a memorandum to the President by the Honorable J. K. Galbraith, US Ambassador to India, wherein he proposes changes to the present US policy toward Vietnam and the government of President Diem.

2. The burden of Mr. Galbraith's proposals appears to be that present US policy toward Vietnam should be revised in order to seek a political solution to the problem of communist penetration in the area. The effect of these proposals is to put the United States in a position of initiating negotiations with the communists to seek disengagement from what is by now a well-known commitment to take a forthright stand against Communism in Southeast Asia.

3. The President of the United States and the Secretary of Defense both have recently and publicly affirmed the intention of the US Government to support the government of President Diem and the people of South Vietnam to whatever extent may be necessary to eliminate the Viet Cong threat. In his letter of 14 December 1961 to President Diem, President Kennedy said:

> Your (President Diem's) letter underlines what our own information has convincingly shown—that the campaign of force and terror now being waged against your people and your Government is supported and directed

from the outside by the authorities at Hanoi. They have thus violated the provisions of the Geneva Accords designed to ensure peace in Vietnam and to which they bound themselves in 1954.

At that time, the United States, although not a party to the Accords, declared that it would view any renewal of the aggression in violation of the agreements with grave concern and as seriously threatening international peace and security. We continue to maintain that view.

In accordance with that declaration, and in response to your request, we are prepared to help the Republic of Vietnam to protect its people and to preserve its independence.

4. The various measures approved for implementation by the United States in support of our objectives in South Vietnam have not yet been underway long enough to demonstrate their full effectiveness. Any reversal of US policy could have disastrous effects, not only upon our relationship with South Vietnam, but with the rest of our Asian and other allies as well.

5. The problems raised by Mr. Galbraith with regard to our present policy have been considered in the coordinated development of that policy. The Joint Chiefs of Staff are aware of the deficiencies of the present government of South Vietnam. However, the President's policy of supporting the Diem regime while applying pressure for reform appears to be the only practicable alternative at this time. In this regard, the views of the Joint Chiefs of Staff as expressed in JCSM-33-62 are reaffirmed.

6. It is the opinion of the Joint Chiefs of Staff that the present US policy toward South Vietnam, as announced by the President, should be pursued vigorously to a successful conclusion.

For the Joint Chiefs of Staff:

L. L. Lemnitzer
Chairman
Joint Chiefs of Staff

[Document 114]

May 29, 1962

NATIONAL SECURITY ACTION MEMORANDUM NO. 157

TO: The Secretary of State
               The Secretary of Defense
               The Director of Central Intelligence
               Chairman, Joint Chiefs of Staff

SUBJECT: Presidential Meeting on Laos, May 24, 1962

The President has approved the following Record of Actions for the subject meetings:
At the meeting on the situation in Laos held in the Cabinet Room at 4:30 p.m. today, the President requested contingency planning in the event of a breakdown of the cease fire in Laos for action in two major areas:

(a) the investing and holding by Thai forces with U.S. backup of Sayabouri Province (being that portion of northern Laos to the west of the Mekong River); and

(b) the holding and recapture of the panhandle of Laos from Thakhek to the southern frontier with Thai, Vietnamese or U.S. forces.

In connection with the above contingency plans, the President desired an estimate of the military value of the Mekong River in Sayabouri Province as a defensive barrier in relation to the cost of taking and holding it.

The President also asked that the above planning be undertaken unilaterally by the United States without discussion at this time with the Thais or the Lao.

The President also indicated that he contemplated keeping U.S. forces in Thailand during the period of the 3-Prince negotiations and the early days of the government of national union, i.e. as long as they serve a necessary purpose.

The President observed that a cable would have to go in answer to Bangkok's 1844.

McGeorge Bundy

[Document 115]

DEPARTMENT OF STATE
Bureau of Intelligence and Research

Research Memorandum
RFE-27, June 18, 1962

TO: FE—Governor Harriman

FROM: INR—Roger Hilsman

SUBJECT: Progress Report on South Vietnam

In this report, an expansion of an earlier informal paper, we summarize the major goals and accomplishments of the present counter-insurgency effort against Communist armed and subversive forces in the Republic of Vietnam (South Vietnam). A brief assessment of the general situation is also included. It should be emphasized, however, that this report is not a complete appraisal; it does not, for example, discuss Communist strength, capabilities, and achievement in recent months nor compare these with those of the Vietnamese Government. It should also be noted that this report does not follow the usual format of a Research Memorandum.

I. *WHAT ARE WE TRYING TO DO?*

A. Devise an integrated and systematic military-political-economic strategic counterinsurgency concept and plan to eliminate the Vietnamese Communist armed-subversive force, the Viet Cong.
B. Orient the Vietnamese Government's military and security forces increasingly toward counter-guerrilla or unconventional warfare tactics.
C. Broaden the effective participation of Vietnamese Government officials in the formulation and execution of government policy.
D. Identify the populace with the Vietnamese Government's struggle against the Viet Cong.

II. *PROGRESS: WHERE ARE WE?*

A. *The importance of an integrated and systematic military-political-economic strategic counterinsurgency concept and plan has been recognized; the plan is being implemented.*

1. *Progress*

a. *Delta Pacification Plan*

(1) president Ngo Dinh Diem approved a systematic counter-insurgency plan on March 19, 1962, which contains the bulk of the British Advisory Mission's (headed by Mr. R. G. K. Thompson) recommendations and those security concepts developed by the US. The counterinsurgency plan is to be implemented in 10 provinces around Saigon in the Mekong River delta region (the so-called "Delta Pacification Plan"). Col. Hoang Van Lac, a former province chief apparently regarded highly by Diem, is responsible for executing the plan, operating under the authority of Nguyen Dinh Thuan, Secretary of State for the Presidency, and Ngo Dinh Nhu, Diem's brother and principal political adviser.

(2) "Operation Sunrise" in Binh Duong province just north of Saigon, favored by Diem for special tactical purposes, constitutes the initial effort in a systematic, province-by-province pacification campaign. "Operation Sunrise" is headed by Brig. Gen. Van Thanh Cao, the administrator of the Southeastern Provincial Region. Three strategic hamlets have been constructed in Binh Duong province as a result of this operation and, as of mid-May 1962, more than 2,700 persons had been relocated in these hamlets. (Two additional hamlets are in the planning or early construction stage.) They are well defended and supported by Civic Action teams living with the peasantry and assisting them in a variety of ways. Reports tend to be optimistic as to the ultimate success of these hamlets.

b. *Other Pacification Programs*

On May 8, 1962, the second systematic operation to pacify a specific area was started in Phu Yen province in central Vietnam. It is known as "Operation Sea Swallow" and is similar to "Operation Sunrise" in methods and objectives.

(1) More than 80 strategic hamlets are to be constructed before the end of 1962; a large number are already in the process of final construction.

(2) As of May 18, 1962, there were more than 600 Civic Action personnel in Phu Yen province formed into more than 70 teams; another 11 teams were to be formed within two weeks. As in "Operation Sunrise" these [words missing]

c. *Strategic Villages and Hamlets*

(1) The strategic village-hamlet concept has taken hold within the Vietnamese Government and is now priority national policy.

(2) President Diem signed a decree on February 3, 1962, creating a special "Interministerial Committee for Strategic Hamlets" to coordinate the program on a countrywide basis. The committee is officially chaired by its Secretary General, Secretary of State for Interior Bui Van Luong, but actually operates under Ngo Dinh Nhu.

(3) Estimates on the number of strategic villages and hamlets vary. As of December 1961, the Vietnamese Department of Interior reportedly tabulated almost 800 such villages and hamlets although in February 1962 the US Embassy estimated that possibly there were only 150–200 such settlements scattered in more than half of Vietnam's 39 provinces, principally north of Saigon. In April

1962, the Secretary of State for Interior informed a US Mission inter-agency group, the Province Pacification Committee, that there were 1,300 strategic hamlets already in place.

(4) On June 6, 1962, about 500 officials from all provinces completed a special training course on strategic villages and hamlets. Training reportedly emphasized the Civic Action aspects of the strategic village-hamlet program as well as the responsibilities of the officials involved.

d. *Civic Action*

(1) The Vietnamese Department of Civic Action was reorganized in January 1962, creating (i) a central Civic Action Service in Saigon by combining related and heretofore separate services within the Department and (ii) an integrated Civic Action office in each province and district.

(2) As of January 1962 a Civic Action chief and deputy chief reportedly had been assigned to every province in Vietnam.

(3) The Civic Action teams working in strategic villages and hamlets, particularly in support of "Operation Sunrise" and "Operation Sea Swallow," are excellently oriented and are doing a good job.

(4) USOM has established a committee to provide on a priority basis direct US assistance (and to coordinate such assistance) to Civic Action operations through the relevant Vietnamese Government agencies.

(5) The Vietnamese Department of Defense is also organizing its own Civic Action program.

e. *Internal Security and Police Services*

(1) The importance of the counterinsurgency role of the rural internal security services is reflected in the US Mission's recommendation that the Civil Guard be increased to 90,000 by FY 1962 and the Self Defense Corps to 80,000 by FY 1963.

(2) As of the end of April 1962, 89 Civil Guard companies or almost 12,000 personnel and 276 Self Defense Corps platoons or about 10,500 personnel had been trained. The goal is reportedly to train a total of some 49,000 Civil Guard and 60,000 Self Defense Corps personnel by the end of 1962.

(3) The Vietnamese Government, with the help of USOM, has taken steps to extend the police system to rural areas in view of the gap created by the paramilitarization of the security services. AID is seeking to hire 20 additional police advisers for rural areas. (The present USOM advisory police complement in Vietnam is just over 20 personnel most of whom operate principally in urban areas.) US aid for the police program for FY 1962 is US$3.5 million (of which US$2.3 million is for commodities), in addition to about US$4 million in unused aid.

(4) As of the end of May 1962, almost 2.8 million of the estimated 7 million persons of the age of 18 years or over have been issued identity cards. As a result of this effort, over 2,000 military deserters and 52 Viet Cong agents have been apprehended and about 4,000 irregularities in the previous identity card program have been uncovered.

f. *Village Radio System*

(1) As of the end of May 1962, more than 530 USOM-distributed communication radios had been installed in villages and other places in the provinces

of Gia Dinh, An Xuyan, Binh Duong, Dinh Thuong, Kien Giang, Kien Phong, Tay Ninh, and Phuoc Tuy. Since the rate of installation is now about 300 radios per month, USOM expects to have more than 1,000 village radios installed by the end of July 1962. Another 1,000 sets scheduled to be installed soon thereafter, thus equipping more than 2,000 villages with radio communication facilities.

(2) The public safety role of village radios was demonstrated on March 20, 1962, when a joint USOM-Vietnamese radio installation team was attacked by Viet Cong guerrillas. The security escort engaged the Viet Cong while the team proceeded to install the village radio and then notified district headquarters and nearby villages. Assistance was despatched and resulted in an ambush of the Viet Cong as they were fleeing toward another village which had been alerted.

g. Utilization of US Assistance

(1) Effective utilization and integration of US non-military assistance to Vietnam was strengthened by AID action in March 1962 establishing first, second, and third priorities on the basis of the immediate impact of aid projects on the counterinsurgency effort: first priority projects are those with impact during the next 12 months, including, for example, Rural Development, Public Safety (especially radio sets), and Health Services; second priority projects are those with impact during the next 1 to 3 years, including, for example, Agricultural Credit and Cooperatives and Highway and Bridge Construction; and third priority projects are those with long-term economic and social significance.

(2) The US Mission has established a number of inter-agency groups, such as the Province Pacification Committee, for the purpose of coordinating and expediting assistance to Vietnamese Government projects in rural areas.

(3) In anticipation of future needs, the US Mission is also taking measures to stockpile commodities (for example, pharmaceuticals, pesticides, barb wire, fence posts, fertilizer, etc.) which would be released on short notice for immediate despatch to the countryside.

2. Critique

a. Although the bulk of the British Advisory Mission's recommendations have been incorporated into the "Delta Pacification Plan," the enabling presidential decree omits the Mission's proposals on "prompt payment of compensation for damage to property or loss of life," on "complete coordination of all civil and military action," on a "clear chain of command," and on "direction and coordination of the information services and psy-war units."

b. US and British officials in Vietnam have voiced serious concern over (i) President Diem's delay in approving the organizational and implementing machinery for the "Delta" plan and (ii) a possible subordination of the "Delta" plan to the strategic village-hamlet program. It has been very recently reported, however, that President Diem has approved a merger of the "Delta" and the strategic village-hamlet organizational machinery and has agreed to give the 10 provinces specified in the "Delta" plan first priority, subject to modification as required by developments in the security situation.

c. Although the Vietnamese Government is giving the strategic village-hamlet program high priority, there is reliable evidence that the program suffers seriously from inadequate direction, coordination, and material assistance by the central government and from misunderstanding among officials at the provincial and local levels. Province chiefs have tended to draw up unrealistically high quotas (generally in order to please the authorities in Saigon), and the lack of sufficient resources provided by the government at the local level has in certain instances resulted in poorly constructed and poorly defended settlements and in financial levies on the peasant. Moreover, the construction of these settlements has not followed any particular pattern or plan based on priorities. In his reported recent merger of the "Delta" plan and the strategic village-hamlet program, however, President Diem has indicated that priorities would be established.

d. Although the mission of the Vietnamese Department of Civic Action is being oriented increasingly toward supporting strategic villages and hamlets, it appears that there is still considerable emphasis on informational and intelligence activities. This has reduced the effectiveness of Civic Action operations and has been somewhat detrimental to the favorable reputation built up in the past by Civic Action personnel. The Civic Action Department also suffers from weak leadership and internal power rivalries.

e. The principal problems of the Civil Guard and Self Defense Corps pertain to tactical utilization which is discussed below, under B. However, there is also some question as to whether these services are being trained and equipped adequately and as rapidly as necessary.

f. Village radios will substantially improve the defense of the countryside and the reaction capability of the Vietnamese military and security forces. However, no effort has yet been made to improve radio communications at the hamlet level where the battle with the Viet Cong is actually joined.

g. Two of the principal weaknesses in the effective utilization of US aid are insufficient awareness on the part of central authorities in the Vietnamese Government of the need to establish project priorities and the general inability of these authorities to act quickly to despatch aid in support of projects in the countryside. The distribution of US aid must be approved in most cases by President Diem personally, frequently resulting in delays and in administrative bottle-necks. Moreover, Diem continues to exhibit considerable sensitivity to attempts by US officials to distribute aid directly to the countryside without clearance from the central government. Recently, for example, the Vietnamese Government turned down a USOM proposal aimed at increasing the impact of US aid at the local level by establishing a special fund for direct financing of provincial projects.

B. *The Vietnamese armed and security forces are being oriented toward counter-guerrilla or unconventional warfare tactics.*

1. *Progress*

a. *Air Support*

(1) Helicopter operations have decreased the reaction time and increased the mobility of army and security units.

(2) During May 16–23, 1962, Vietnamese Air Force and US helicopter units flew at least 347 sorties: 46 were offensive sorties; 216 sorties lifted 1,511 troops and 24,000 pounds of cargo of which 12,000 pounds were air-dropped; and 85 sorties were for air evacuation, observation, training, and other missions.

b. *Tactical Utilization of Army and Security Forces*

(1) The Vietnamese Army is getting out and fighting more than ever before. During March 20–28, 1962, the armed forces launched more than 23 operations of at least company size throughout the country. During April 12–May 3, 1962, more than 11 operations were launched, each operation involving more than a battalion; some of these operations continued beyond May 3.

(2) Army units are becoming more conscious of the necessity of following through during attacks in order to prevent the Viet Cong from disengaging.

(3) Civil Guard and Self Defense Corps units apparently are being employed increasingly with army units. During April 12–May 3, 1962, for example, Civil Guard and Self Defense Corps units were combined with army units in at least 3 operations. There have also been reports of Civil Guard units receiving helicopter support.

(4) There are reports of effective utilization of artillery bombardment. In early March 1962, for example, a combined Army ranger, Civil Guard, and Self Defense Corps force engaged the Viet Cong in Kien Hoa province. Artillery was introduced only after the Viet Cong attempted to withdraw, harassing their escape routes and inflicting substantial casualties.

(5) Army ranger units are being deployed in the highlands area, recognizing the equal priority of this area with the Mekong River delta region where the pacification program has been initiated. As of February 1962, there was a total of 18 ranger companies in the I and II Army Corps Areas.

(6) It is estimated that some 3,000–5,000 *Montagnard* tribesmen have been recruited and are being trained and armed by the Vietnamese Army against the Viet Cong in the highlands area. In addition, there are some irregular *Montagnard units.*

2. *Critique*

a. Despite the increasing utilization of Civil Guard and Self Defense Corps units jointly with army forces, the former continue to be employed excessively on independent offensive missions. The principal stumbling block to the rectification of this problem is the province chief under whose authority the security services operate.

b. Despite the increasing deployment of ranger units in the highlands area, there is no evidence that these units are being used to any appreciable degree for patrolling the Vietnamese-Lao frontier.

c. The principal deficiency in the utilization of air support is not tactical but rather is related to the availability and reliability of intelligence on the Viet Cong.

C. *The participation of Vietnamese Government civilian and military officials in the formulation and execution of government policy has been broadened somewhat.*

1. *Progress*

a. Military commanders in the field are playing a greater role than in the past in the actual formulation and execution of operational plans. For example, much of the planning of "Operation Sunrise" and "Operation Sea Swallow" has been carried out by Vietnamese Army division commanders and their staffs.

b. Col. Lac has been delegated limited but real authority for executing the "Delta Pacification Plan" and for his recent and concurrent responsibilities in the strategic village-hamlet program.

c. There has been limited use of the National Internal Security Council established in December 1961.

d. The Director of the Central Intelligence Organization, Colonel Nguyen Van Y, has been delegated real though limited authority both with regard to his intelligence responsibilities and his concurrent role as head of the regular police services, the National *Surete* and the Municipal Police.

e. There is evidence that the authority of certain cabinet members has been increased, notably Secretary of State for the Presidency Thuan and Secretary of State for Interior Luong.

f. The Vietnamese Government has also taken various measures to improve morale among rank-and-file military and security personnel. In January 1962, the family allowance rates for Army and Civil Guard privates, privates first class, and corporals (as well as the combat pay rates for Army personnel in these ranks) were increased, and Army conscripts became eligible to receive a private's pay after completing four months rather than one year in service.

2. *Critique*

Ineffectiveness in administration at the national level, in carrying out the control functions of the government, and in extending services to the country-side continues to represent the Vietnamese Government's main weakness. In large measure, this is due to the limited authority President Diem delegates to his subordinates. Diem continues to make virtually all major decisions and even many minor ones, to rely largely on his inner circle of official and unofficial advisors rather than on his cabinet officers and the formal channels of military and civil command in formulating and executing policy, and to interfere personally in purely and often minor operational matters. Discontent within the government bureaucracy and the military establishment with these tactics by Diem and his lieutenants does not appear to have decreased substantially during the past year. The prospects that Diem may change his method of operation are not favorable.

D. *Popular identification of the Vietnamese people with the struggle against the Viet Cong appears to have increased somewhat.*

1. *Progress*

a. President Diem's frequent travels to the countryside may have improved somewhat the popular image of the central government. During July–December 1961, for example, Diem made 18 known trips outside Saigon and visited 19 different provinces (9 in the central and northern provinces and 10 in the Mekong delta provinces).

b. There is evidence that villagers are passing an increasing amount of information on the Viet Cong to government officials. One striking example is the Viet Cong attack on an Army post in An Hoa in Quang Ngai province on April 6, 1962. (The Viet Cong used about 300 men, well armed with recoilless rifles and machine guns.) As a result of an earlier warning by villagers of a possible attack, the Army unit was on alert and, when the attack came, repulsed the Viet Cong with serious losses.

c. It appears that defections from the Viet Cong may be increasing. It has been estimated that only around 400 Viet Cong surrendered to government forces during all of 1961. Since the first of 1962, however, US military sources have been reporting statistics on Viet Cong surrenders on a weekly basis, and it is estimated that during February 13–April 30, more than 207 Viet Cong surrendered. (These and other statistics on the Viet Cong are derived from various official Vietnamese sources and must be treated with caution since the Vietnam Government is prone to exaggerate them.)

d. President Diem signed a decree on December 18, 1961, providing for the establishment of provincial councils, ultimately to be elected by popular ballot but for the time being to be appointed by the central government. (Youth representatives on village councils have been elected since early 1961.)

e. According to the chiefs of Kontum and Pleiku provinces some 35,000 *Montagnards* have been resettled from Viet Cong-infested to relatively secure areas in these two provinces since January 1962 as a result of coordinated measures by Vietnamese military and civilian officials. These measures have been aimed at reducing the Viet Cong's access to tribal elements for recruits, labor, intelligence, and supplies.

2. Critique

a. Despite favorable developments, there has been no major break-through in improving the popular image of the government, particularly in the countryside. In the short run, the success of this effort will depend largely on the degree of physical security provided the peasantry, but in the long run the key to success will be the ability of the government to walk the thin line of meaningful and sustained assistance to the villagers without obvious efforts to direct, regiment, or control them.

b. There is growing concern among Vietnamese field personnel in Kontum, Pleiku, and other provinces that the Vietnamese Government is not moving fast enough to provide adequate assistance to the *Montagnard* resettlement program and, as a result, that the Viet Cong may succeed in subverting resettlement efforts. According to one report almost 70,000 of an estimated 105,000 *Montagnard* refugees have not yet been resettled.

III. SUMMARY ASSESSMENT

A. It is about three months since the current phase of a major systematic counterinsurgency effort began in Vietnam, and too short a time to expect any substantial weakening of the Communist position. Moreover, final victory is likely to take some years and to be brought about more by a steady erosion of Communist strength than by dramatic military successes.

B. In the military-security sector, US materiel, training, and advice, supplemented by tactical support by US units, have produced an improvement in armed operations against the Viet Cong. US military operational reports reflect improved tactics, shortened reaction times, and more effective use of communications and intelligence. It is too early to say that the Viet Cong guerrilla-terrorist onslaught is being checked, but it can be said that it is now meeting more effective resistance and having to cope with increased aggressiveness by the Vietnamese military and security forces. Nonetheless, the Viet Cong continue to increase their armed strength and capability and, on balance, to erode government authority in the countryside.

C. There has not been a corresponding improvement in other sectors of the total counterinsurgency effort. Serious problems remain in the civil and military command structures and in the exercise of command responsibility. Diem continues to prefer personalized rule through a very small group of trusted official and unofficial advisers and traditional methods in matters affecting domestic political opposition. Civil government effectiveness is also impeded by shortages in experienced personnel, particularly at lower levels, and aggravated by confusion and suspicion at most levels of the bureaucracy. More effective direction and coordination and realistic implementation are needed, for example, for such crucially important programs as the "Delta" plan, strategic villages and hamlets, and Civic Action, and greater authority must be delegated to upper echelon civil and military officials in order to make better use of Vietnamese Government resources. Similarly, while there are encouraging signs of popular support for the government, there has been no major break-through in identifying the people with the struggle against the Viet Cong.

D. We conclude that:

1. there is no evidence to support certain allegations of substantial deterioration in the political and military situations in Vietnam;

2. on the contrary, there is evidence of heartening progress in bolstering the fighting effectiveness of the military and security forces;

3. however, there is still to be done in strengthening the overall capacity of the Vietnamese Government to pursue its total counter-insurgency effort, not only in the military-security sector but particularly in the political-administrative sector;

4. a judgment on ultimate success in the campaign against the Communist "war of national liberation" in Vietnam is premature; but

5. we do think that the chances are good, provided there is continuing progress by the Vietnamese Government along the lines of its present strategy.

[Document 116] June 19, 1962

NATIONAL SECURITY ACTION MEMORANDUM NO. 162

TO: The Secretary of State
               The Secretary of Defense
               The Attorney General
               The Director of Central Intelligence
               The Director, United States Information Agency

SUBJECT: Development of U.S. and Indigenous Police,
                  Paramilitary and Military Resources

The President has approved the following statement and proposed assignments of responsibilities to various agencies as recommended by the Special Group (Counterinsurgency):

The study of U.S. and indigenous paramilitary resources pursuant to NSAM 56 reflects gratifying progress in the development of an adequate U.S. capability to support both the training and active operations of indigenous paramilitary forces. Certain deficiencies, however, were clearly revealed. The deficiencies, to which all efforts and shortcomings to date are related, should be the basis upon which internal defense requirements are established for each country to be assisted.

1.   *Country Internal Defense Plans*

With one or two exceptions, there exist no outline plans to unify and orchestrate U.S. internal defense programs and activities in friendly countries facing a threat of subversive insurgency, or which provide strategic guidance for assisting such countries to maintain internal security. The Department of State has prepared a list identifying the countries facing a threat of subversive insurgency and will direct the formulation of outline plans for internal defense (Country Internal Defense Plans) by the Country Team in each such country which encompass the total U.S.-supported internal defense field. *These plans will include the military, police, intelligence and psychological measures comprising a well rounded internal defense plan and will be consistent with the military, economic, political and social measures constituting the overall country plan.* Such plans should be completed and in the hands of the Department of State by September 1, 1962, available for review by the Special Group (Counterinsurgency). From that time on, in accordance with the provisions of NSAM 124, the Special Group will keep these country internal defense plans under periodic review, and insure prompt resolution of interdepartmental problems arising in connection with their implementation.

2.   *Improvement of Personnel Programs of Agencies Concerned with Unconventional Warfare*

A study will be made by the Armed Forces and appropriate civil agencies concerned with unconventional warfare activities of how to improve their personnel programs. Particular attention will be directed to the following:

(a) Personnel programming for officers and men, including establishment of career programs which protect the special skills and professional qualifications of personnel assigned to unconventional warfare duties.
(b) Ability to perform efficiently in foreign areas in conditions of stress and danger for prolonged periods.
(c) Morale factors such as family housing, tours of duty, hardship allowances, hazardous duty pay, special recognition such as rewards.

3.   *Orientation of Personnel*

As part of the current effort to train more personnel in the problems confronting underdeveloped societies, both civil and military agencies of the Government will assign, where feasible and subject to the availability of funds and personnel, middle-grade and senior officers to temporary duty for orientation purposes in selected countries experiencing internal security problems.

4.   *Deployment of Counterinsurgency Personnel*

In order to insure a timely deployment of qualified counterinsurgency specialists to impending crisis areas, CIA and AID will take action to insure that adequate qualified personnel with paramilitary skills are available. Periodic reports of progress to achieve this objective will be submitted to the Special Group (Counterinsurgency) by CIA and AID.

5. *Support of Covert Paramilitary Operations*

More Special Forces personnel will be assigned to support CIA covert paramilitary operations where acute insurgency situations exist. The Department of Defense has taken steps to expedite these assignments. In addition the Department of Defense will increase its capability to fund, support, and conduct wholly or partly covert paramilitary operations under the criteria of NSAM 57 which distinguishes responsibilities of the Department of Defense and CIA:

> Where such an operation is to be wholly covert or disavowable, it may be assigned to CIA, provided that it is within the normal capabilities of the agency. Any large paramilitary operation wholly or partly covert which requires significant numbers of militarily trained personnel, amounts of military equipment which exceed normal CIA-controlled stocks and/or military experience of a kind and level peculiar to the Armed Services is properly the primary responsibility of the Department of Defense with the CIA in a supporting role.

This cooperation will be intensified and the President will be given periodic reports on the progress of these efforts.

6. *Increased Use of Third Country Personnel*

The Department of Defense, in collaboration with the Department of State and the Central Intelligence Agency, will undertake a study to determine on a selective basis the feasibility of the concept of the increased use of third-country personnel in paramilitary operations. Particular attention will be given to the following:

> (a) The whole range of this concept from the current limited use of Thai and Filipino technicians in Laos to the creation of simply equipped regional forces for use in remote jungle, hill and desert country. Such forces would be composed of foreign volunteers supported and controlled by the U.S.
> (b) The feasibility of using third-country military or paramilitary forces to operate under their own or other national auspices in crisis areas.

7. *Exploitation of Minorities*

In view of the success which has resulted from CIA/US Army Special Forces efforts with tribal groups in Southeast Asia, continuing efforts will be made to determine the most feasible method of achieving similar results in other critical areas. On a selective basis, CIA and the Department of Defense will make studies of specific groups where there is reason to believe there exists an exploitable minority paramilitary capability.

8. *Improvement of Indigenous Intelligence Organizations*

Recent experience shows that most underdeveloped countries need more efficient intelligence coordination and dissemination systems to counter subversive insurgency. Therefore, the CIA will expand its present training and support efforts to achieve needed improvements in indigenous intelligence organizations and that other U.S. agencies contribute to this CIA coordinated program.

9. *Research and Development for Counterinsurgency*

The Department of Defense and the Central Intelligence Agency will carry in their research and development programs a special section devoted to the requirements of counterinsurgency. The Special Group (Counterinsurgency) will follow up on this action and receive reports from time to time with regard to progress in developing modern equipment suitable to meet the requirements of counterinsurgency.

McGeorge Bundy

[Document 117]

CENTRAL INTELLIGENCE AGENCY
Washington 25. D.C.

OFFICE OF THE DIRECTOR

13 July 1962

MEMORANDUM FOR: The Secretary of Defense

1. Following up the conversation that you had with Mr. McCone on 6 July, he asked our Chief of Station in Saigon for an overall analysis of the situation in South Vietnam, with specific emphasis on the Strategic Hamlet Program, the Montagnard situation, and capabilities of the Armed Forces.

2. Attached herewith is a copy of report from our Chief of Station. Copies have also been furnished to Secretary Gilpatric, General Lemnitzer, General Taylor, Mr. Alexis Johnson, and Mr. Sterling Cottrell, of the SEA Task Force.

Marshall S. Carter
Lieutenant General, USA
Acting Director

Part I.

1. In assessing strategic hamlet program, think it important make distinction between program as generalized national rallying symbol and as specific tactic counterinsurgency campaign. In former sense strategic hamlet program has grown in recent months into government's major ideological and institutional tool in attempting generate popular consensus in support efforts to defeat enemy. This clear in President's double seven message on eighth anniversary his accession to power. He proclaimed this the year of strategic hamlets, describing their establishment as constituting "three-fold political, social and military revolution adapted to under-developed countries. Strategic hamlets bring the solution to

our triple struggle against underdevelopment, disunity and Communism." Diem defines strategic hamlet as "militant democracy in underdeveloped countries. . . . the gaining of liberty, of habeas corpus and social justice by all the people, liberating them from grip of all determinisms."

2. These concepts not new, having been frequently expressed by Ngo Dinh Nhu during past year in his efforts articulate strategic hamlet concept and bring it into sharper focus. It encouraging, however, that President saw fit embrace these ideas and make them main theme double seven message. Hitherto some indication President not entirely sold on program. Nhu and other government spokesmen have been at pains make clear that strategic hamlet program is in mainstream of "personalist" philosophy which they consider South Vietnam's alternative to Communism on one hand and Western-type liberalism on other. Whatever merits this philosophy, it has suffered from diffuseness and lack discernible application day to day problems. By tying it to strategic hamlets concept it possible they have finally found much needed focus, which may serve to arouse certain amount of support among those intellectuals not irreparably alienated from Diem regime.

3. Nhu and other supporters strategic hamlet program seem quite aware need descend from plain of philosophy in order make program attractive to peasants who are main target. In recent conversation held by the CIA Station Chief with Nhu, Nhu stated heretofore appeal VC had for peasants was in terms private and immediate interests peasants, with latter persuaded or deluded into believing Communists could best look to their material needs. Main purpose strategic hamlet program to counter this appeal by proving to peasants that GVN can help organize defenses against VC while at same time giving them tangible benefits which will convince them they have stake in support of GVN and defeat of enemy. Extent government can actuate promise of "triple revolution" in countryside may in long run be most important result strategic hamlet program, outweighing immediate tactical advantage.

4. As tactic counterinsurgency program, should be emphasized strategic hamlets constitute only one of number of different approaches being developed to pacify countryside, even though there general tendency, even among Vietnamese, to lump all approaches together under general term strategic hamlet. Under current GVN planning strategic hamlets per se are preventive mechanism aimed at arresting erosion government control and presence in countryside. Strategic hamlets are being constructed in what Nhu calls "A" areas, i.e., areas where VC threat least serious and where government can organize village defenses most quickly and with least expenditure overextended conventional military capability. In these hamlets peasants generally must look after own defense. In "B" areas, where VC strength greater, although some strategic hamlets being built, projected major emphasis will be on construction defended hamlets, as in case Operation Sunrise in Binh Duong Province. In "B" areas provision made, in theory at least, for outside defense help from CG/SDC and in some cases from ARVN elements. In "C" areas, which deep in territory controlled by VC, concept is to establish large settlements reminiscent Diem's earlier agrovilles, into which even VC would be herded and kept pending "reeducation" and improvement security situation. This kind of resettlement must largely await future, and is in our mind most debatable feature current GVN plans. Fourth type of hamlet defense setup now envisaged by Nhu is string of kibbutz-type posts to which young, highly motivated families would be sent to live on permanent basis in areas adjacent VC strongholds.

5. Techniques used strategic hamlet program. Operation Sunrise, other pro-

grams increasingly being incorporated into overall province pacification programs, of which Operation Hai Yen II in Phu Yen is prototype. Two more plans, for Binh Dinh and Quang Ngai Provinces in central Vietnam, currently in mill and outlook for several more next few months.

6. As of 30 June, there were approximately 2000 strategic hamlets already completed. This represents increase of 1300 since January 1962, indicating monthly construction rate of something over 200. GVN sources claim 7000 are scheduled for completion by end of year. Qualitatively, there is a considerable variation, some being virtual fortresses and others having only token size fences or other defensive devices which could be easily breached by Viet Cong. In past much has depended on degree energy, initiative and resources of province chief, as well as his understanding of what Nhu and other national leaders wanted in terms strategic hamlets. It is hoped some standardization effort will ensue as program becomes more clearly defined, especially through strategic hamlets cadre school, second course of which began 2 July.

7. Geographically, strategic hamlets are widely distributed. As of 30 June, about 950 had been constructed in III Corps, of which over 300 built in single province of Vinh Binh; 858 in II Corps, with highs in Darlac and Binh Dinh with 173 and 164 respectively; and 195 in I Corps, with high of 85 in Quang Nam. Low rate in I Corps may in part reflect Ngo Dinh Can's often reported coolness toward strategic hamlets concept. There have been indications recently, however, that Can has reached at least tacit understanding with brother Nhu exchanging greater support for strategic hamlets for fuller Saigon support Can's cherished Force Populaire program.

8. Generally, present strategic hamlets constructed safer areas away from main concentrations Viet Cong strength. This does not mean, however, that they not within striking distance Viet Cong elements sufficiently strong to attack isolated hamlets with serious effect. To date, there have been only few scattered instances Viet Cong attacks on strategic hamlets, but we expect pace to step up considerably, particularly at end of rainy season. That strategic hamlet program is bothering Viet Cong is well documented in form virulent propaganda attacks by Radio Hanoi and National Liberation Front outlets, in addition captured documents and agent reports, which indicate problem of how to cope with strategic hamlets now one of main Viet Cong preoccupations. This spring there were several instances of Viet Cong attacks on larger agrovilles and land development centers, which may suggest some confusion in Viet Cong minds—as well as western—as to distinction between strategic hamlets and other defended installations.

9. At this stage development strategic hamlet program, one major weakness is hit-and-miss construction with insufficient integration hamlet defenses into overall district and provincial security plans. Hamlets thus vary considerably in vulnerability to Viet Cong attack. Local observers rightly state that until country considerably more saturated with strategic hamlets, many of those already in being will be exposed to Viet Cong destruction. In our view, best way use strategic hamlets as tactic in counterinsurgency program is, when possible, to make their phased construction integral part broader pacification programs extending, where practicable, to province-wide scope. This one of more attractive aspects Hai Yen II in Phu Yen, where construction strategic hamlets

carefully phased with other aspects of plan such as availability civic action teams, emplacement village defenders, and gradual displacement of Viet Cong back toward mountains.

10. As to overall popular reaction to strategic hamlet program, must confess that, as in many other aspects situation in South Vietnam, it extremely difficult come up with firm generalizations. Peasant reaction varies from district to district and province to province depending on how question handled by respective authorities. In certain cases where peasants have been directly harassed or attacked by Viet Cong, they often welcome or seek self-defense. In other instances peasants reportedly feel some initial resentment at changes enforced in way of life imposed by program, as well as at exactions of money and labor. In some cases, at least, initial coolness largely disappears as advantages of program become manifest. One of most encouraging developments is trend toward election hamlet councils. Another hopeful sign is the idea USOM now considering under which certain part its funds for direct piaster aid to provinces would be set aside for small economic projects originated by hamlet councils in consultation with district and provincial-level officials. USOM's concept is that such program would help sustain momentum of strategic hamlet idea after initial impetus for construction defenses had been dissipated.

11. In sum, we believe strategic hamlet program definitely moving forward both as organizing principle around which whole GVN counterinsurgency program has fair chance of being sold to people and as specific tactic in preventing spread Viet Cong influence among people. But strategic hamlets in themselves not sufficient to carry day against still strong and determined enemy. Until they supplemented by broader pacification programs involving wide variety of counterinsurgency measures, they remain vulnerable Viet Cong countermeasures.

II. Montagnard Situation.

12. A mixed US-GVN team currently making systematic survey 18 provinces in which montagnards live. Until survey completed and results made available, cannot provide full statistical exposition of problem. In first four provinces visited (Darlac, Tuyen Duc, Lam Dong, and Ninh Thuan) some 18,000 out of total montagnard population of about 165,000 have moved away from their normal living areas in past few months.

On basis these provinces and some subsequently visited, team has reached conclusion that there has been extensive relocation Montagnards during past six months stemming from combination of factors, including fear Viet Cong, resentment enemy confiscation of much of food supply, and new found respect for power GVN has manifested bombing attacks and use helicopters. In some instances, however, movement has been at invitation GVN in accordance with long-term plans resettle tribesmen. Thus movement 4,500 of 11,000 Montagnards in Tuyen Duc made at invitation provincial officials to areas prepared in advance. With exception Tuyen Duc Province (Dalat), where 10,000 refugees, many of whom seem in need immediate provision food and other essentials, most provinces visited to date not considered have emergency situations in terms Montagnards needs. Becoming increasingly apparent, however, that GVN and U.S. faced with long term problem looking after uprooted

Montagnards, either by making settlement in present locations palatable to them or preferably in creating conditions security necessary inspire them return to original locales. Whatever inspiration their movement toward GVN-controlled centers, GVN faced with opportunity and challenge forge new and better relationships with tribal people. Failure do so could conceivably mean loss entire plateau and mountain areas to Communists. As soon as we have results of survey now being undertaken, a summary of salient points will be provided.

13. Station has for some time felt GVN and U.S. agencies moving too slowly in meeting challenge of Montagnard problem, but hopes that when current survey completed situation will clarify and more expeditious action will be possible. USOM now negotiating project agreement with Lt. Colonel Cao, Chief GVN agency responsible Montagnard affairs, providing for allocation 500 million piastres directly to province chiefs for use mutually approved projects. Rationale this approach is to give greater flexibility in dealing with varying problems in connection with Montagnards in different provinces.

III. SVN Armed Forces Capabilities.

14. South Vietnam's armed forces, with about 175,000 men, have demonstrated their willingness stand up and fight enemy, and given proper tactical circumstances, have on occasion inflicted severe defeats on Viet Cong. No question RVNAF's capabilities fight at least conventional warfare have increased measurably as result long period training by MAAG. Still not convinced, however, that regular forces properly geared fight kind of war needed defeat Viet Cong, or that commanders, either by training or temperament, possess sufficient tactical flexibility and imagination seek out elusive enemy and destroy him.

15. One of major weaknesses to date has in our view been RVNAF tendency organize too large-scale operations which serve to tip off enemy giving him opportunity melt into countryside. Even when some element surprise achieved, ARVN sweep forces seem inadequately prepared with detailed tactical planning to make thorough job of it. These operations, on other hand, do serve keep Viet Cong off balance and tend prevent them from concentrating forces. In recent weeks, moreover, ARVN sweep forces have been systematically destroying VC installations and rice and ammo stocks, which inevitably will begin have serious effect on enemy supply position. Nevertheless, we feel RVNAF capabilities could be used with much more telling effect if smaller-scale operations conducted.

16. Where RVNAF have had greatest success is in blundering into sizeable concentrations Viet Cong and in responding calls for help from besieged civil guard and SDC posts. In this connection USOM-supported village radio installation program very important, as well as availability of helicopters in reserve to enable RVNAF respond rapidly to targets opportunity. When spread of strategic hamlets forces VC into larger attacking units, ARVN's capability of locating and attacking VC is expected to improve. British advisor Thompson recently pointed out, however, that it took three years after beginning of emergency in Malaya before British and Malayans really began operate effectively against Commie terrorists in various aspects of counterinsurgency program. Turning point comes when increasing numbers of villagers begin to volunteer information against Communists.

17. Vietnamese Airforce appears slowly be working its way out of political cloud it came under as result palace bombing incident last February. According

air attache, performance in flying pre-planned interdiction missions and responding to calls for close-in air support improving considerably. One of main reasons for this is increasing effectiveness joint US-GVN Operations Center (JOC) in developing targets and in scheduling missions. Ambassador has frequently expressed concern whether targets being selected with proper care, fearing adverse political impact of bombing non-VC installations and concentrations of people. We share this concern but feel only remedy is steady refinement criteria for target selection utilized by JOC.

End of message

[Document 118]

August 24, 1962

NATIONAL SECURITY ACTION MEMORANDUM NO. 182

TO: The Secretary of State
                     The Secretary of Defense
                     The Attorney General
                     The Chairman, Joint Chiefs of Staff
                     The Director of Central Intelligence
                     The Administrator, Agency for International
                        Development
                     The Director, U.S. Information Agency
                     The Military Representative of the President

SUBJECT: Counterinsurgency Doctrine

The President has approved the document entitled "U.S. Overseas Internal Defense Policy," which sets forth a national counterinsurgency doctrine for the use of U.S. departments and agencies concerned with the internal defense of overseas areas threatened by subversive insurgency, and has directed its promulgation to serve as basic policy guidance to diplomatic missions, consular personnel, and military commands abroad; to government departments and agencies at home; and to the government educational system. The addressees of this NSAM will take action to insure that the policies set forth in the document are reflected in departmental and agency operations and in such additional instructions and guidance as may be required to assure uniformity of effort. They will also initiate the formulation of the internal doctrine, tactics, and techniques appropriate to their own department or agency, based upon "U.S. Overseas Defense Policy." These studies when completed will be reviewed by the Special Group (CI). The Department of State in consultation with the other addressees of this memorandum is assigned the task of keeping the "U.S. Overseas Internal Defense Policy" up to date, making such modification as changes in policy or practical experience may require, and publishing revised editions as necessary.

McGeorge Bundy

[Document 119]

DEPARTMENT OF STATE

Bureau of Intelligence and Research

Research Memorandum

RFE-59, December 3, 1962

TO: The Secretary

THROUGH: S/S

FROM: INR—Roger Hilsman

SUBJECT: *The Situation and Short-Term Prospects in South Vietnam**

This appraisal covers the Communist insurgency and the internal political situation in South Vietnam during the past year and focusses particularly on the direction and effectiveness of the Vietnamese-US counterinsurgency effort. It was prepared as a contribution to the forthcoming NIE 53-62, Prospects in South Vietnam.

ABSTRACT

President Ngo Dinh Diem and other leading Vietnamese as well as many US officials in South Vietnam apparently believe that the tide is now turning in the struggle against Vietnamese Communist (Viet Cong) insurgency and subversion. This degree of optimism is premature. At best, it appears that the rate of deterioration has decelerated with improvement, principally in the security sector, reflecting substantially increased US assistance and GVN implementation of a broad counterinsurgency program.

The GVN has given priority to implementing a basic strategic concept featuring the strategic hamlet and systematic pacification programs. It has paid more attention to political, economic, and social counterinsurgency measures and their coordination with purely military measures. Vietnamese military and security forces—now enlarged and of higher quality—are significantly more offensive-minded and their counterguerrilla tactical capabilities are greatly improved. Effective GVN control of the countryside has been extended slightly. In some areas where security has improved peasant attitudes toward the government appear also to have improved.

As a result, the Viet Cong has had to modify its tactics and perhaps set back its timetable. But the "national liberation war" has not abated nor has the Viet Cong been weakened. On the contrary, the Viet Cong has expanded the size and enhanced the capability and organization of its guerrilla force—now estimated at about 23,000 in elite fighting personnel, plus some 100,000 irregulars and sympathizers. It still controls about 20 percent of the villages and about 9 percent of the rural population, and has varying degrees of influence among an additional 47 percent of the villages. Viet Cong control and communication lines to the peasant have not been

* This report is based on information available through November 12, 1962.

seriously weakened and the guerrillas have thus been able to maintain good intelligence and a high degree of initiative, mobility, and striking power. Viet Cong influence has almost certainly improved in urban areas not only through subversion and terrorism but also because of its propaganda appeal to the increasingly frustrated non-Communist anti-Diem elements.

The internal political situation is considerably more difficult to assess. Diem has strengthened his control of the bureaucracy and the military establishment. He has delegated a little more authority than in the past, and has become increasingly aware of the importance of the peasantry to the counterinsurgency effort. Nevertheless, although there are fewer reports of discontent with Diem's leadership within official circles and the civilian elite, there are still many indications of continuing serious concern, particularly with Diem's direction of the counterinsurgency effort. There are also reports that important military and civil officials continue to participate in coup plots. Oppositionists, critics, and dissenters outside the government appear to be increasingly susceptible to neutralist, pro-Communist, and possibly anti-US sentiments. They are apparently placing increased reliance on clandestine activities.

The Viet Cong is obviously prepared for a long struggle and can be expected to maintain the present pace and diversity of its insurgent-subversive effort. During the next month or so, it may step up its military effort in reaction to the growing GVN-US response. Hanoi can also be expected to increase its efforts to legitimatize its "National Front for the Liberation of South Vietnam" (NFLSV) and to prepare further groundwork for a "liberation government" in South Vietnam. On present evidence, the Communists are not actively moving toward neutralization of South Vietnam in the Laos pattern, although they could seek to do so later. Elimination, even significant reduction, of the Communist insurgency will almost certainly require several years. In either case, a considerably greater effort by the GVN, as well as continuing US assistance, is crucial. If there is continuing improvement in security conditions, Diem should be able to alleviate concern and boost morale within the bureaucracy and the military establishment. But the GVN will not be able to consolidate its military successes into permanent political gains and to evoke the positive support of the peasantry unless it gives more emphasis to non-military aspects of the counterinsurgency program, integrates the strategic hamlet program with an expanded systematic pacification program, and appreciably modifies military tactics (particularly those relating to large-unit actions and tactical use of airpower and artillery). Failure to do so might increase militant opposition among the peasants and their positive identification with the Viet Cong.

A coup could occur at any time, but would be more likely if the fight against the Communists goes badly, if the Viet Cong launches a series of successful and dramatic military operations, or if Vietnamese army casualties increase appreciably over a protracted period. The coup most likely to succeed would be one with non-Communist leadership and support, involving middle and top echelon military and civilian officials. For a time at least, the serious disruption of government leadership resulting from a coup would probably halt and possibly reverse the momentum of the government's counterinsurgency effort. The role of the US can be extremely important in restoring this momentum and in averting widespread fighting and a serious internal power struggle.

TABLE OF CONTENTS

I. The Nature of the Communist Threat to South Vietnam

    A. Strategy and Objectives

    B. Viet Cong Organization and Capabilities

        1. General

        2. Military Strength and Effectiveness

        3. Viet Cong Logistic Support

            a. Local Support

            b. External Support

        4. Political Capabilities

            a. The Communist Position in the Countryside

            b. The Urban Sector

II. The Vietnam Government's Counterinsurgency Effort

    A. Background: Gradual Response

    B. Formulation and Implementation of Basic Strategic Concept

        1. Strategic Hamlet Program

        2. Systematic Military-Political Pacification Operations

    C. Military Operations and Effectiveness

III. The Political Situation

    A. Background: Rapid Deterioration

    B. The Current Situation

        1. Political Attitudes of Diem and His Family

        2. Diem and the Bureaucracy

        3. Diem's Position in the Countryside

        4. Diem's Position in Urban Centers

IV. Economic Trends

V. Outlook

    A. Communist Actions

    B. GVN Counterinsurgency Effort

    C. The US Role

    D. Political Situation

I. THE NATURE OF THE COMMUNIST THREAT TO SOUTH VIETNAM

The Communist threat to the Republic of Vietnam (South Vietnam) consists of three interrelated elements. Within South Vietnam, but under the direction of the Democratic Republic of Vietnam (DRV), an expanding campaign of guerrilla warfare and terrorism and an intensive political psychological subversion effort are carried out by an apparatus commonly known as the Viet Cong,*

* Viet Cong is the popular term used by the South Vietnamese to refer to Vietnamese Communists, singularly or collectively. For all practical purposes, the Viet Cong apparatus is an extension of the North Vietnamese Communist Party (*Dang Lao Dong Viet Nam* or merely *Lao Dong*), which also operates in Laos, Cambodia, and other countries with important Vietnamese minority groups.

left behind by the DRV after it withdrew most of its military forces to the north in 1954 and since reinforced by local recruitment and infiltration from the DRV. Externally, the DRV holds over South Vietnam the tacit threat of invasion by the numerically superior North Vietnamese military forces.

In part because the Government of the Republic of Vietnam (GVN) focussed its defense efforts too much upon the implicit external threat and too little upon the internal threat, not only was it unable to counter effectively the developing Communist movement but also its authority and internal stability in the period from late 1959 until early 1962 were increasingly weakened by Viet Cong insurgent and subversive activities. Since the early part of 1962 however, the rate of deterioration appears to have decelerated as a result of substantially increased US assistance to South Vietnam and expanding GVN implementation of its broad military-political counterinsurgency program. The apparent improvement is principally in the security sector, but with some resultant effects on the political situation. Many US advisers in South Vietnam, as well as President Ngo Dinh Diem and other top GVN officials, are more optimistic and believe that the deteriorating trends in effect have been checked and that the tide is now being turned in favor of the GVN. Whether this optimism is justified may well be determined by developments during the next few months.

A. STRATEGY AND OBJECTIVES

In South Vietnam, the Communists are clearly embarked on a "national liberation war" of insurgency and subversion from within rather on overt aggression. It is probably the Communist view that this strategy greatly reduces the risk of direct US military intervention and, at the same time, provides good prospects of success at relatively little cost. In addition, it permits the Communist Bloc to claim continued adherence to the 1954 Geneva Agreements. This strategy was most recently reaffirmed by the Third National Congress of the North Vietnamese Communist Party in Hanoi in September 1960 and the Moscow conference of all Communist parties held the following November and December.

The immediate Communist objectives are to demoralize the South Vietnamese public and the military and security forces, weaken and eventually supplant government authority in the countryside, and discredit and ultimately precipitate the overthrow of President Diem's government. Simultaneously, the Communists are attempting to gain broad popular support for their effort, including the creation of a "united front" with non-Communist elements, and gradually to strengthen and transform their guerrilla forces into regular forces capable of undertaking a general offensive.

The DRV is the implementing agency for Communist activity in South Vietnam. It exercises close control over the Viet Cong guerrillas and over the "National Front for the Liberation of South Vietnam" (NFLSV), the political instrument of the Viet Cong. However, while Hanoi is probably allowed considerable freedom of action, Moscow and Peiping probably would have overriding influence over any major decision critically affecting the situation in South Vietnam, as for example, international negotiations on South Vietnam, cessation of Communist guerrilla operations, and escalation to conventional warfare or overt introduction of North Vietnamese army units. In any event, important Communist policies for South Vietnam are probably coordinated with Moscow and Peiping and the latter scrutinize developments in South Vietnam carefully with an eye to their own interests. Both Moscow and Peiping also furnish strong propaganda support for the Communist effort in South Vietnam and, in addition, the USSR carries on supporting diplomacy, largely in its capacity as a Geneva Conference Co-chairman. There is little evidence of material support of the Viet Cong guerrillas by Moscow or Peiping.

There are no apparent major policy differences between Hanoi, Moscow, and Peiping regarding South Vietnam. During the first six months of 1962, it appeared that Moscow differed somewhat with Peiping's and Hanoi's propaganda for an international conference to settle the South Vietnam situation; this difference presumably continues to exist although little has been said by the Bloc on a conference since mid-1962. There also may be underlying intra-Bloc differences on the subject of neutralization of South Vietnam or reunification. In any event, even though Moscow might prefer neutralization, all would work to communize a neutral South Vietnam if one were established. Moscow has also generally exerted a restraining influence over Communist willingness to take risks.

The sharp increase of the US military presence in South Vietnam and the events of recent months in Laos apparently have not weakened Communist resolve to take over South Vietnam. However, these events have clearly caused some modification of Viet Cong guerrilla tactics and may have caused the Communists to revise their timetable. Nevertheless, the Communists probably continue to look primarily to the long run in South Vietnam and to remain confident of eventual victory.

B.   VIET CONG ORGANIZATION AND CAPABILITIES

1. *General.* Available intelligence indicates that two parallel structures, military and political, exist at all organizational levels of the Viet Cong apparatus in South Vietnam. At the top of the organization are two bodies, the Nambo Regional Committee (NRC) and the Interzone V Regional Committee (IVRC), equal in status and each apparently responsible directly to Hanoi. The NRC directs and is responsible for all operations in the southern provinces, or roughly the former Cochinchina region, while the IVRC directs and is responsible for all operations in the central and northern provinces. These committees consist of several staffs responsible for military and political activities. The organization of the two regional committees appears to be duplicated among intermediate and lower level committees responsible for operations at the interprovincial (i.e., area covering more than one province), provincial, district, and village levels. Information is not available on the size of the political component of the Viet Cong apparatus, but it must be assumed that the regular and irregular guerrilla forces also serve as penetration, espionage, sabotage, propaganda, and terrorist agents.

Viet Cong capabilities have increased considerably during the past three years. In 1959 a relatively small but effective military-political apparatus operating largely in the Mekong River delta provinces, the Viet Cong has since grown into a formidable force operating throughout the countryside and even in many urban centers, including Saigon, the capital. In addition to increasing its numerical strength, the Viet Cong has significantly improved its military and political organization and its tactical, weapons, and subversive capabilities.

2. *Military Strength and Effectiveness.* Communist assets for guerrilla action in South Vietnam are considerable. In spite of an apparently increasing casualty rate, Viet Cong hard-core personnel has grown from an estimated 4,000 in April 1960 to about 23,000 in October 1962. These forces are distributed principally in the southern provinces, the former Cochinchina

region which includes the Mekong River delta area and where most of the fighting occurs. They are well-trained and well-armed (utilizing such weapons as light machine-guns and mortars and even 57 mm. recoilless rifles). The units into which these forces are organized range up to battalion and include the key personnel infiltrated from North Vietnam. These units in effect constitute the elite fighting elements of the Viet Cong force and operate at the interprovincial, provincial, and district levels. There has been no hard evidence that the Viet Cong has yet formed regimental-size units or that they have an anti-aircraft capability, other than the small arms which they are using with increasing effectiveness against helicopters.

In addition to this elite force, the Viet Cong has an auxiliary armed force roughly estimated at 100,000 and distributed throughout the country. This force operates essentially at the village and hamlet levels and consists largely of part-time or full-time armed cadres and sympathizers. Its functions are probably varied, but there is considerable evidence that it serves as a local defense force, provides logistic support (food and intelligence, for example), and constitutes the reserve from which personnel are drawn as replacements for the elite force or to help activate new units. The auxiliaries appear to be partially trained and partially armed, frequently utilizing nothing more than spears, scimitars, and a variety of small weapons manufactured in home workshops or "arms factories." However, these limited capabilities apparently are partly offset by the ability of the auxiliaries, many of whom cannot easily be identified by the GVN, to pass themselves off as innocent peasants.

By relying on small-unit actions and tactics of surprise, constant movement, concentration for attack, and dispersal upon withdrawal, the Viet Cong guerrillas have achieved considerable effectiveness. They ambush, carry out company-size attacks against army and security units, and have the capability to strike in battalion force against several targets simultaneously. According to official GVN statistics, the Viet Cong since 1960 has killed more than 9,500 and wounded at least 13,300 military and security personnel. In addition, the GVN estimates that at least 8,700 local officials and civilians have been assassinated or kidnapped since 1960.*

The Viet Cong appears to be well-informed particularly on the plans and movements of government forces sent on large counterguerrilla operations. Morale is probably also good and desertions or defections to the GVN forces, although reportedly increasing, are relatively few. In recent months, however, shortages of food and the increased aggressiveness of GVN forces are believed to have adversely affected the morale and capability of some Viet Cong forces in the central provinces.

3. *Viet Cong Logistic Support*

a. *Local Support*. The Viet Cong relies principally on local resources to sustain its operations. Both the character of this support and the means by which it is acquired vary considerably. It is obtained voluntarily, by propaganda and promises of material or political benefit, by threats and intimidation, and finally

---

* The statistics on Viet Cong and GVN casualties are incomplete and not entirely reliable partly because the GVN probably understates its own casualties and overstates those of the Viet Cong. Since the latter part of 1961, casualty estimates have improved largely because of the increased US presence in South Vietnam. Despite reservations regarding their accuracy, these figures are helpful as one indicator of the magnitude of the fighting in South Vietnam.

by outright force. It includes, among other things, personnel, arms, food, funds, and intelligence.

Most of the Viet Cong guerrillas and agents are recruited locally, with a large percentage coming from the youth. Most of their weapons are either captured or stolen from GVN military and security forces, are manufactured in home workshops or "arm factories" in Viet Cong concentration areas, or are activated from stocks cached since the end of the Indochina war. A considerable portion of Viet Cong funds apparently comes from fees levied on buses and other means of transportation, from taxes on the wealthy and on business enterprises (such as rubber plantations), and from ransoms paid for persons kidnapped. The Viet Cong is entirely dependent upon the local populace and the countryside for food which is obtained through purchase, pilferage, capture of stocks, taxation (in the form of rice), and even actual cultivation of crops by sympathizers and part-time guerrillas. Finally, the ability of Viet Cong guerrillas and agents to disperse, regroup, and indeed retain their presence intact, even after GVN military clearing operations have been completed, is considerably enhanced by the concealment afforded them, voluntarily or otherwise, by the local population.

In addition, the Viet Cong guerrillas and subversive agents rely heavily on the villagers for information and supplementation of intelligence gained from espionage and from penetration of GVN military and civilian services. Intelligence supplied by the villagers is largely of a tactical nature and deals, for example, with the location and movement of local GVN military and security forces and the defenses of individual army and security posts, villages, and hamlets.

b. *External Support.* The Viet Cong insurgent-subversive movement in South Vietnam is directed, inspired, and organized by the DRV. Logistical support from North Vietnam, however, appears to be limited, and existing evidence indicates that there is no large-scale infiltration of men and equipment. On the other hand, infiltration almost certainly occurs on a sporadic if not continuing basis and apparently increases from time to time, as was probably the case during May and June 1962.

Infiltrators are believed to consist largely of well-trained cadres (military personnel, key political and subversive agents, technicians, and couriers) rather than units. However, in recent months there have been two reliable reports confirming the infiltration of two Viet Cong groups (200 and 400 men respectively) from southern Laos. There is considerable evidence that infiltrators in general are largely South Vietnamese (Cochinchinese and Annamites), regrouped and retrained in North Vietnam since the end of the Indochina war and familiar with the people and terrain of South Vietnam. They carry in their own weapons and, in some instances, a limited amount of additional small and even large weapons, technical equipment, medical supplies, and funds. The infiltrators apparently are distributed among existing Viet Cong units, thus increasing the number of hard-core personnel and thereby the capability of these units, or become the nuclei of new units.

Since the latter part of 1960, the principal infiltration routes have been through the corridor of southern Laos controlled by Laotian and North Vietnamese Communist forces. However, infiltration continues through eastern Cambodia, across the Demilitarized Zone at the 17th parallel, and by junk landings along South Vietnam's long coastline. In addition, Viet Cong guerrillas are believed to use the border areas of both southern Laos and eastern Cambodia to a limited extent for safe haven purposes during their hit-and-run attacks or when pursued by GVN forces.

4. *Political Capabilities*

a. *The Communist Position in the Countryside.* There have long been major gaps in our knowledge of rural conditions in South Vietnam. In view of the over-riding importance that the Viet Cong attaches to the countryside in its strategy, these gaps have now assumed critical proportions. Although our knowledge of rural conditions is improving, principally because of the substantially increased US presence in South Vietnam, any assessment of Communist political strength outside urban areas remains questionable and at best tentative.

The Viet Cong appears to have had considerable success in reducing or sup-planting government authority in the countryside. By the latter part of 1961, US officials estimated that probably more than one half of the entire rural region south and southwest of Saigon, as well as several areas just to the north and in the central and northern provinces, were under effective Viet Cong control by night, with the government generally capable of maintaining its authority only by day. Many other areas were under varying degrees of Viet Cong influence.

According to a more recent and apparently more refined study, US officials estimated in mid-1962 that of South Vietnam's some 2,500 villages, which con-tain around 85 percent of the total population, 20 percent were effectively con-trolled by the Viet Cong. Although the Viet Cong-controlled villages were inhabited by an estimated 9 percent of the rural population, the total area repre-sented by these villages encompassed a much larger proportion of the countryside. In contrast, the GVN effectively controlled about 47 percent of the village population, and 33 percent of the villages, largely located, however, in the en-virons of major towns and provincial capitals and in the more heavily populated areas along main lines of communication. In the remaining 47 percent of the villages and 44 percent of the village population, neither the GVN nor the Viet Cong exercised effective control, even though GVN influence seemed greater in most of these villages.

The accelerated GVN counterinsurgency effort, principally the strategic ham-let program and the increasing aggressiveness of the military and security forces, reportedly has enlarged somewhat the number of villages and peasants under effective GVN control. However, this improvement has presumably occurred principally in areas formerly contacted by the GVN and the Viet Cong since the rural area and populace estimated as under effective Viet Cong control has been reduced by only 17 villages with a population of 150,000.

Partly by the sheer strength of its presence and partly because of the pro-longed absence of strong government military and security forces, the Viet Cong has been able to transform some rural areas—such as portions of the Ca Mau peninsula, the swampy *Plaine des Janos,* and the highlands in the north—into major concentration or base areas which are dangerously close to becoming "liberated" areas. Here, the Viet Cong has virtually a free hand in levying and collecting taxes, directing the cultivation of rice and other farm products, and controlling their distribution, propagandizing the populace, conscripting cadres, and even setting up overt political organizations and provisional local govern-ment units.

The political capability and strength of the Viet Cong in the countryside is inextricably associated with and strongly dependent upon its military presence and power. The threat or the use of force, as demonstrated by the high rate of assassinations and kidnappings of local officials and even ordinary peasants, is a continual reminder of the penalty of noncooperation with the local Viet Cong. Moreover, by successful military operations against the GVN, the Viet Cong is able to demonstrate its superiority and its determination and ability to remain. In turn, the political apathy of the peasant—i.e., his traditional and overriding sensitivity and attachment to local, village, and indeed family matters and his minimal awareness of national or even regional issues and developments—has made him prone to seek an accommodation with whatever force seems for the moment capable of exercising authority.

The Viet Cong also uses non-violent, positive means to appeal to the peasantry. Although their tactics vary and depend partly on prevailing local conditions, they have, for example, purchased rather than seized rice and food stuffs in many cases, have taxed the wealthy with effective publicity, and reportedly even distributed land to landless peasants. Even their terrorist acts from time to time have been against harsh, disliked, or corrupt officials. These acts are held out as proof of the Viet Cong's ability to improve the peasant's economic and political lot. Their appeal is enhanced by the peasant's basic distrust of government officials engendered partly by their excessive and harsh implementation of government programs and by the average Vietnamese bureaucrat's belief that he does not serve but is to be served by the people.

Viet Cong propaganda to the peasant, therefore, is both positive and negative. It extols Viet Cong achievements and power, credits the Communist forces under Ho Chi Minh with expelling the French from Vietnam and keeping the north free of "foreign control," holds out economic and political inducements, derides GVN capabilities, and points to the excessive, oppressive, and corrupt character of GVN demands and practices, as for example, military conscription and forced labor in the creation of strategic hamlets. Viet Cong propaganda also exploits the Vietnamese peasant's credulity and animistic beliefs, spreading bizarre stories intended to limit popular participation in government programs.

Viet Cong penetration efforts have been directed largely against local government services and Army, Civil Guard, and Self Defense Corps field units. While the extent of this penetration is difficult to determine accurately, there have been increasing reports in recent months of successful Viet Cong penetration of Self Defense Corps units and strategic hamlets. Moreover, the apparent advance knowledge of some GVN military operations and the generally high rate of Army desertions is probably partly due to Viet Cong penetration of Army field posts and training centers.

b. *The Urban Sector.* Communist activities in urban areas are limited largely to propaganda, penetration, and terrorism. The immediate objective of these activities is to encourage dissent and opposition to President Diem and the US presence in South Vietnam and to foment neutralist sentiments among intellectuals, professionals, disgruntled politicians and government officials, and labor and youth groups. In this manner, the Viet Cong hopes to create a common ground with actual and potential non-Communist opposition elements, legitimize its insurgent-subversive effort, and ultimately precipitate Diem's overthrow. The Viet Cong has stepped up this effort since 1961, particularly with the creation of its "National Front for the Liberation of South Vietnam" (NFLSV) which also seeks to gain international support for the Communist position.

As reflected by Radio Hanoi which also relays NFLSV statements, the paramount Viet Cong propaganda theme is the dictatorial family rule imposed by the Diem government and its subservience to US "foreign imperialist intervention" which are combining to "oppress" and "murder" the South Vietnamese people and block reunification. This Viet Cong propaganda campaign, coupled with recent political developments in Laos (which some Communist propaganda has implied provides an acceptable model for "settlement" of the South Vietnamese conflict) and with Diem's persistent reluctance to tolerate any appreciable non-Communist opposition, has already contributed to an increase in neutralist sentiment among urban circles. Moreover, some oppositionists, including a few leaders of the once-powerful *Cao Dai* and *Hoa Hao* religious sects, are reportedly cooperating with the Viet Cong to the point of being committed to participating in an eventual Communist-led anti-Diem coup attempt.

Viet Cong capabilities for leading a successful coup are limited, however. Its own forces, even if combined with any remnant armed bands of the *Cao Dai* and *Hoa Hao* religious sects, do not appear strong enough to overthrow the government by military means. Nor is there any evidence that the Viet Cong has any support in the middle or top levels of the GVN bureaucracy or its military and security establishments. Although the Viet Cong might well be able to exploit the confusion and instability resulting from Diem's overthrow, it does not yet have the ties with the non-Communist opposition to Diem that would enable it to lead a successful coup.

There is no reliable evidence of Viet Cong penetration of the middle or top echelons of the GVN bureaucracy and defense establishment. There is believed to be penetration of the lower echelons, and it is clear that the GVN security and intelligence services do not now have the capability to prevent such penetration. A GVN police interrogation report in early 1962 revealed that there was a large Viet Cong subversive network in the Saigon post office and that an employee of the post office was possibly using the telegraphic system for clandestine communication with North Vietnam.

The Viet Cong has also progressively improved its terrorist capability in Saigon and other urban centers. There have been increasing reports that the Viet Cong has enlarged its terrorist corps in Saigon and that the principal targets of these attacks are to be Americans. Evidence of this capability is the increasing number of grenade bombings in Saigon. For example, there were three bombing incidents against Americans in May 1962 and three bombing incidents in connection with Independence Day celebrations on October 26, 1962.

II.   THE VIETNAM GOVERNMENT'S COUNTERINSURGENCY EFFORT

A.   BACKGROUND: GRADUAL RESPONSE

In contrast to the rapid acceleration of the Communist insurgent and subversive effort, the GVN response until this year was gradual and relatively uncoordinated and generally did not reflect the sense of urgency acknowledged by Vietnamese officials themselves. It was not until the early part of 1961 that a comprehensive counterinsurgency plan was drawn up, with the help of US officials, and several months elapsed before general implementation began. Moreover, the GVN leadership continued to view the situation as one created and supported largely by external forces with little popular appeal and saw their problem as essentially a military one requiring overriding emphasis on purely military measures.

Even these military measures, however, were weakened principally by the GVN leadership's reluctance to abandon static defense concepts and permit more offensive actions, for which it had sufficient forces—a reluctance that reflected both fear of overt DRV aggression and internal political considerations. In addition, the GVN military and security forces themselves, despite their experience in combatting guerrillas during the Indochina war and thereafter, were inadequately trained, equipped, and organized to wage a sustained and large-scale counterguerrilla effort.

The turning period in the GVN response occurred in late 1961 and early 1962 and resulted largely from substantially increased US aid, repeated US reaffirmations of political support for President Diem, and persistent US recommendations, including those developed by special US missions to South Vietnam. Accordingly the GVN has diversified its response by giving increasing emphasis to political counterinsurgency measures. It has improved the coordination of these measures with purely military operations, given priority to implementing a basic strategic concept for eliminating the insurgents, significantly increased the counter-guerrilla tactical capability of its military and security services, and departed appreciably from static defense concepts, thereby greatly aiding the development of increasingly offensive-minded and aggressive military and security forces. By the early part of 1962, the GVN had begun to act upon the recognition that the crisis situation in South Vietnam was an internal and political problem, requiring largely political measures to eliminate Communist appeal, support, and control among the peasants.

B.   FORMULATION AND IMPLEMENTATION OF BASIC STRATEGIC CONCEPT

As a result of persistent US recommendations, the GVN has developed a basic strategic concept for the implementation of its diverse counterinsurgency measures. The two principal features of this concept are the strategic hamlet program and a closely integrated and coordinated military-political approach directed toward isolating the Viet Cong and regaining control of the countryside on a systematic, area-by-area basis.

1. *Strategic Hamlet Program.* The strategic hamlet program embodies principally the recommendations of the British Advisory Mission, headed by R. G. K. Thompson, a key figure in the campaign against Communist insurgency in Malaya. It also reflects US innovations and the experience and concepts developed by the GVN in similar earlier projects. Briefly, the program involves regrouping hamlets into fortified and more readily defendable settlements and undertaking in these settlements political, social, and economic measures designed to weed out Viet Cong agents and sympathizers, reestablish and improve local government administration, improve the general popular image of the GVN, and increase the peasantry's identification with the government's fight against the Viet Cong. The program is initiated in relatively secure areas and is then expanded into less secure areas. The majority of the hamlets provide most of their own resources, although the US is supplying some of the equipment and necessary construction materials and it is expected that this aid will increase substantially.

The strategic hamlet program is now priority national policy. President Diem has created a special interministerial committee to implement and coordinate the program on a countrywide basis. The committee is headed by Diem's brother, Ngo Dinh Nhu, and delegates its responsibilities to regional committees under each of the army division commanders. Increasing efforts have been made to regularize the procedure for implementing the program, educate the responsible local officials and the peasants on procedures and objectives, speed up the distribution of US material assistance, and train the necessary specialized personnel. The GVN has reported that, as of mid-October 1962, more than 3,000 strategic hamlets had been completed and more than another 2,000 were under construction; more than one-half of these are in the southern provinces, including the Mekong River delta area.

The completed strategic hamlets vary widely in the quality of their physical defenses, the effectiveness of the defense, internal security, and administrative systems and the degree to which necessary political, social, and economic measures have been implemented. Among the most effectively organized hamlets are those in areas where integrated and systematic military-political pacification operations have been undertaken, such as "Operation Sunrise" in Binh Duong province and "Operation Sea Swallow" in Phu Yen province. In these and other hamlets, fortifications and the defense forces are adequate for repulsing guerrilla attacks, radio communication has been provided, hamlet administrative officials have been elected or selected by the inhabitants rather than appointed by the village or district chiefs, and Civic Action teams have been active in improving the health, educational, and general living standards of the people. In many other hamlets, however, fortifications are extremely inadequate or virtually non-existent, defense forces are greatly under-strength and inadequately armed, there are no radio communications or Civic Action teams, and hamlet officials continue to be appointed. Moreover, despite improving peasant morale in many hamlets, particularly as the benefits of security against Viet Cong intimidation and taxation become evident, there are continuing reports that GVN officials have exacted too heavily from local resources and have not compensated the peasants for the material and labor required to build the hamlets, that the peasant's ability to earn a living has declined because of the time he is required to spend on construction, and that the government has been more concerned with controlling the hamlet population than with providing services and improving living conditions.

It is still too early for accurate evaluation of the strategic hamlet program. On balance, the program appears successful and probably has contributed to the reported slight increase in the number of persons and villages that have come under effective government control. The fact that the strategic hamlets have become a major target for Viet Cong armed attacks is in itself an indicator of the importance of the program to the GVN's counterinsurgency effort, if not a measure of its success. Most of the deficiencies of the strategic hamlet program appear to be the result of implementation and, to some extent, are to be expected during the early stages. Many provinces and district chiefs continue to be relatively uninformed or confused as to procedure and objectives or are over-zealous in their attempt to impress their superiors and thus have established unrealistic goals. Moreover, some GVN leaders, including President Diem and Ngo Dinh Nhu, tend to place exaggerated importance on the program, viewing it almost as a universal panacea to the Communist insurgency rather than as merely a measure for cutting off the Viet Cong from the peasantry. Accordingly, the strategic hamlet program has not been effectively integrated with the basic military-political pacification effort to eliminate the Viet Cong gradually and systematically, principally because of the much more rapid implementation of the strategic hamlet program. As a result, the necessary basis for the continuing defense of the strategic hamlets does not exist in many of the areas where they have been established.

2. *Systematic Military-Political Pacification Operations.* After considerable delay, and with the advice of the British Advisory Mission and U.S. officials, the GVN has developed the general outlines of an integrated military-political approach for pacifying the country on a systematic, gradual, and province-by-

province basis. The approach involves large-scale and continuing military operations to clear and hold a given province. As the province is cleared, strategic hamlets are established with Civic Action teams moving into the hamlets to direct construction and help establish administrative, informational, health, educational, security, and other services. In March 1962, President Diem approved a "Delta Pacification Plan," calling for the pacification of 11 provinces around Saigon and in the Mekong River delta area and embodying most of the recommendations of the British Advisory Mission and other security concepts developed by the US. In August 1962, the GVN divided the country into four priority areas for purposes of pacification.

Implementation of the integrated pacification approach began in March 1962, and since then four operations have been initiated: "Operation Sunrise" in Binh Duong province (and portions of surrounding provinces), "Operation Sea Swallow" in Phu Yen province, "Operation Let's Go" in Binh Dinh province, and "Operation Royal Phoenix" in Quang Ngai province. Plans for another operation in Vinh Long province, "Operation West Wind," are being drawn up. In addition to continuing military operations, over 160 strategic hamlets, the great majority in Phu Yen province, have already been constructed and more than an additional 1,000 hamlets are planned for completion by mid-1963 or shortly thereafter.

The results of the systematic, integrated military-political pacification approach are encouraging. However, its limited application to relatively few provinces has not yet appreciably altered the balance between the government and the Viet Cong in the countryside. Moreover, there is evidence that the GVN has some doubt as to the feasibility of this approach as the principal basis of its counterinsurgency effort. For example, in addition to the heavy reliance on the strategic hamlet program, there are reports that President Diem feels that his military forces now have sufficient strength and capability to make quick, large-scale military strikes simultaneously in and behind various areas of Viet Cong concentration with the hope of dispersing and ultimately isolating the guerrilla forces into small and easily eliminated pockets.

C. MILITARY OPERATIONS AND EFFECTIVENESS

The GVN military and security forces have significantly stepped up their offensive operations against the Viet Cong insurgents, particularly since the early part of 1962. In large measure, this has been the direct result of US agreement to support a substantial increase in the size of the GVN military and security establishments. Since the latter part of 1961, the GVN has increased its military forces from about 160,000 to around 200,000 and its security forces, the Civil Guard and Self Defense Corps, from just over 90,000 to almost 155,000. This has enabled the GVN to satisfy its requirements for defending transportation facilities and what it considers key areas, including the 17th parallel, while it attempts to seek out and eliminate the Viet Cong. During the period October 1-25, for example, the GVN military and security forces launched 19 large offensive operations, involving units with equivalent strengths ranging from two battalions to several regiments, in addition to small-unit offensive actions and defensive engagements.

The general effectiveness of GVN military operations has also improved as a result of President Diem's apparent increasing awareness that he must rely on his military establishment to formulate the execute military strategy and plans. In close cooperation with US military advisers, GVN army division commanders and their subordinates are participating increasingly in formulating and executing offensive missions against the Viet Cong. However, it appears that Diem's willingness to delegate this responsibility is due partly to his appointment of division commanders whom he believes to be loyal to him and his family. This reliance essentially on colonels to direct the fighting reinforces continuing reports that Diem and Ngo Dinh Nhu still mistrust most of the generals and even have doubts as to their military competence. In any event, Diem and Nhu continue to play dominant roles in the development of general military strategy and must approve plans for major operations and frequently will initiate or modify them.

As a result of the substantial increase in US military assistance and accelerated training programs by US military personnel in South Vietnam, who now number almost 11,000, the GVN military and security forces have rapidly developed considerable counterguerrilla capability. These forces are substantially better armed with weapons and equipment suitable to counterguerrilla warfare. They are now ambushing and patrolling more than ever before, are engaging the Viet Cong increasingly in small unit actions, and are following through their attacks in order to keep the Viet Cong from disengaging. Probably of greater importance, however, is the considerably improved tactical mobility of the GVN forces. These forces are now able to strike more quickly and in greater strength than ever before during defensive, relief, or offensive operations. The single most important reason for this accelerated tactical mobility is the increasing utilization of air power, principally US helicopter support. Although better intelligence and communications, particularly the installation of radios in most villages, and improvements in the tactical organization of the GVN military establishment, have also contributed significantly.

The improvement in GVN tactical intelligence is due partly to administrative and organizational reforms but principally to the success of US officials in impressing the South Vietnamese with the necessity for more effective interrogation of Viet Cong prisoners and to the apparent increase in the willingness of the peasants, at least in areas where security has improved, to inform on the Viet Cong. On balance, however, GVN intelligence continues to be seriously weakened by the shortage of trained personnel, ineffective prisoner interrogation techniques, overlapping responsibilities among several agencies and interagency rivalries, and the continuing reluctance of the peasantry to inform on the Viet Cong for fear of reprisal, particularly in insecure areas or where the GVN presence is regarded as temporary.

Despite this improvement in counterguerrilla tactics, GVN military forces continue to rely more on large operations or clearing sweeps than on small-unit actions, employ Civil Guard and Self Defense Corps units excessively in independent offensive missions, and, during large operations, deploy combat units, particularly artillery and airforce, according to conventional tactical methods. As a result, the Civil Guard and Self Defense Corps are incurring heavy casualties and Viet Cong guerrillas generally have advance knowledge of major GVN operations, especially when artillery or air power is used to "soften up" the enemy, and are able to disperse or avoid engagement.

The increased US support and presence, the greater role played by GVN military officials in formulating and directing military operations, and more successes against the Viet Cong than ever before have apparently improved morale among members of the middle and upper echelons of the GVN military establishment. The state of morale at the lower level, however, is more difficult to determine. Desertions, particularly among recruits and recalled reservists, appear to be running very high for a wide variety of reasons, and some GVN officials continue to claim serious difficulty in meeting conscription quotas. During the first seven months of 1962, for example, a total of 17,287 personnel were dropped from the rosters of the Army, Navy, Airforce, Civil Guard, and Self Defense Corps as deserters or as personnel absent without official leave. On the other hand, some GVN officials have recently claimed that voluntary candidates have for the first time oversubscribed the quota at the army officers' training school at Thu Duc.

III. THE POLITICAL SITUATION

A. *BACKGROUND: RAPID DETERIORATION*

During 1960 and 1961, the internal political situation in South Vietnam deteriorated rapidly, breaking the relative stability and general surface calm that had prevailed since President Diem consolidated his authority in 1955-56. Criticism of Diem increased substantially throughout all sectors of Vietnamese society but was more urgently articulated within the government and bureaucracy, including the armed forces. A wide range of civilian and military officials, including Vice President Nguyen Ngoc Tho and other members of the cabinet, privately questioned Diem's handling of the internal security problem and his ability to rally and lead the people against the Viet Cong during what they regarded as the most critical period since the end of the Indochina war. Their concern with the Communist threat, however, was almost inseparably entwined with an accumulation of grievances principally over Diem's failure to delegate responsibility, the excessive power exercised by Diem's family, and the use of secret security services and semicovert political organizations to scrutinize the attitudes of the bureaucracy.

Open deprecation of Diem also increased sharply among intellectuals, professionals, and disgruntled ex-politicians in urban areas, particularly in Saigon, the focal point of non-Communist political opposition to Diem since 1956, and to a lesser extent among labor and business elements. They repeatedly and, on occasion, vociferously demanded that Diem liberalize and reform his government, lift restrictions on civil liberties, eliminate corruption in government, and permit an opposition to operate. These demands were supported, as in the past, by a disparate group of anti-Diem Vietnamese expatriates in Paris who have long advocated Diem's removal.

Unrest also increased among the peasantry principally because of the government's inability to assure adequate protection from the Viet Cong but partly because of the cumulative reaction to the excessively arbitrary and severe behavior of local security and administrative officials. Possibly underlying this unrest also was the character of the GVN's economic development activities which, however limited, were oriented more toward developing an urban industrial base than toward improving the economic lot of the peasant.

Vietnamese confidence in the Diem government was obviously seriously shaken and morale within the bureaucracy, particularly the military establishment, declined greatly. In November 1960 a small group of middle level paratroop officers staged a near-successful coup in Saigon. Although the abortive coup obviously made Diem take serious stock of the prospects for political survival, it also strengthened his confidence in the correctness of his political views and increased his suspicion of many of his subordinates and the oppositionists outside the government.

During this period also, Diem's view of US policies toward South Vietnam underwent considerable change. For the first time since he consolidated his position, Diem appeared to question seriously US political support of his leadership and US commitments to defend South Vietnam from Communist encroachment. His apparent concern, although partly reflecting his disagreement with US actions in Laos, was due largely to earlier persistent US representations on internal issues which he regarded as pressing him unduly to reform and liberalize his regime. This concern was further aggravated by his belief, partly instilled by members of his family, that the US was in some way involved in the abortive coup.

During the immediate post-coup period, Diem took a number of measures to strengthen his controls over the bureaucracy. He and Ngo Dinh Nhu made it publicly and privately clear that future coup attempts or even public criticism of the government would be dealt with severely. The *Can Lao,* the government's semicovert political control organization, and the secret police were ordered to maintain close surveillance over critics within the bureaucracy and the military establishment and over the oppositionists outside the government, and officials were apparently instructed that passing information to or even having social relations with Americans would lead to serious consequences. As a result, there was a sharp decline in the heretofore large number of reports on coup plotting and criticism of Diem and his family. In the meantime, Diem reportedly organized a countercoup group from among the most loyal members of the *Can Lao,* the bureaucracy, and the military and security services. Ostensibly to impress the US with his willingness to reform the government, he later reorganized his cabinet, taking the opportunity to remove cabinet officials he believed to be critical of his leadership.

During the last half of 1961, the political situation became somewhat less disturbed, despite the continuing rapid deterioration of security conditions. The predominant factor in this development was external: strong US public manifestations of support for Diem, including the visits of Vice President Johnson and General Maxwell Taylor, and the substantial increase in US assistance to South Vietnam. Other contributing factors were the slightly greater participation that Diem now appeared to permit his military advisers in the conduct of the fighting, the favorable psychological effect on the middle and lower military echelons of a few large offensive operations, and Diem's initiation of some modest political reforms. However, there was no conclusive reversal of deteriorating trends as was made clearly evident when Diem's palace was bombed by two GVN airforce pilots in February 1962.

B. THE CURRENT SITUATION

The political situation in South Vietnam is now probably more complex and more difficult to analyze than at any time since 1954. On the one hand, the sense that political reform is urgently needed appears to have subsided significantly, at least on the surface, and indeed a relative calm seems again to have descended over the bureaucracy. There has been a significant decline in reports of serious discontent, and of criticism by GVN officials of Diem's leadership and his family. Reports of the concern of officials with inefficiency, corruption, and morale in the government have likewise declined significantly since the early part of 1962, as have reports on coup plotting. Some US officials believe that morale within the bureaucracy and the military services has improved appreciably, largely because of the improved capabilities of the armed forces and several large successful operations against the Viet Cong; that some heretofore strong oppositionists are now seeking to identify themselves with the government and contribute positively to the war effort; and that peasant loyalty is shifting toward the government, particularly in areas where the government is making its presence increasingly felt. Finally, Diem and his principal lieutenants have very recently shown considerable confidence and optimism that the tide has been turned against the Viet Cong and have even stated that a general offensive is about to be launched.

On the other hand, the indicators of serious internal political instability remain, however diminished in apparent intensity, and are as varied as the indicators of political stability. There are reports from officials from various levels of the administration, including Vice President Tho and Generals Duong Van Minh and Le Van Kim, that Diem continues to run the war himself or through his inner circle of confidants, that corruption within the government continues unabated (as evident in the recent national lottery scandal), that there is no political consolidation of military successes against the Viet Cong in the countryside, that indiscriminate bombing in the countryside is forcing innocent or wavering peasants toward the Viet Cong, and that coup plotting persists and only the fear of Communist exploitation and the belief that the US would not tolerate a coup keep it from materializing. As recently as late October 1962, Gen. Ton That Dinh, commander of Army Corps II and generally considered one of the most loyal although opportunistic of Diem's generals, stated that he was highly dissatisfied with the regime, that Diem and Nhu tolerate corruption in high places, and that he was planning to precipitate a coup in early February 1963.

1. *Political Attitudes of Diem and His Family.* Diem and his family remain firmly convinced of the wisdom of their political outlook and of their method of governing their country. They are basically impatient with democratic processes. They consider democracy a useful goal but its methods they regard as wasteful and as dangerous to political stability and public safety in a country such as South Vietnam. They contend therefore that the Vietnamese people, with their national survival at stake, must submit to a collective discipline until they develop a greater national consciousness and a better sense of civic responsibility. While willing to rule within the framework of constitutional and representative government, they are firm in their convictions that government is effective and dynamic only when its power is closely held and exercised by a small, highly dedicated, and uncompromising element at the very top through a machinery founded more on personal relationships and loyalty than on formal or institutional chains of command. Where representative government and civil liberties come in conflict with the highly centralized authority, the latter generally prevails. Finally, Diem and his family continue to believe strongly, almost fanatically, that their leadership is crucial if not indispensable to the survival of their country in the present crisis.

Some slight modifications have slowly appeared in these attitudes during the past year, partly because Diem and his family are increasingly aware that the Communist threat to South Vietnam is largely internal, and partly because of the magnitude and complexity of the US assistance program and its increasing orientation toward the needs of the countryside. More than ever before, they have been made aware that government must not only be served but must also serve, that the peasant and his active participation rather than his passive obedience may well be crucial for final victory over the Viet Cong, and that a little more sharing of power at the top would probably improve administrative efficiency rather than lead to their ouster.

At the same time, however, Diem and especially Nhu have gone to great lengths to convince US officials that this has always been their basic approach to government and to elaborate on what it means for the peasant. Nhu has repeatedly stated that the strategic hamlet program, for example, will create a social, economic, and political revolution in the countryside, which will uproot vested economic interests, implant democracy and efficient and benevolent administration at the local level, and raise the peasant to a new social status. There is no evidence, however, either in recent developments or in the records of past performance, particularly Nhu's, that such are their real objectives and expectations.

Probably the most significant change is in Diem's attitude toward the US. He has apparently become substantially persuaded that US defense commitments to South Vietnam are firm, despite his continued disagreement with the US on the Laotian problem. His earlier suspicions that the US was looking for a successor in South Vietnam and that the US was implicated in the abortive 1960 coup have been considerably relieved. On the other hand, Diem has remained firm against any US pressure on matters that he interprets as vital to his own and his government's best interests and is convinced that in the final analysis he can have absolute confidence only in himself and in his family.

2. *Diem and the Bureaucracy.* Diem probably has somewhat strengthened his control of the administration. For example, he has reorganized a number of his agencies, has removed a number of critical and potentially disloyal officials and by various means neutralized the influence of some others, such as Vice President Tho and Gen. Duong Van Minh, and has improved his means of surveillance of the bureaucracy through such techniques as the creation in the military establishment of a system of "political commissars" known as the Political Welfare Division. He has attempted to reinforce further his control of the military establishment by the appointment of personally loyal colonels as division commanders, some of whom have demonstrated from time to time that they regard their responsibility as principally to Diem rather than to their corps commanders.

On balance, however, it appears that the general efficiency of the administration has improved slightly, partly because of the appointment of more competent officials to several key positions, partly because of some increase in the authority delegated by Diem, and partly because of the enlarged US presence in South Vietnam. For example, Secretary of State for the Presidency Nguyen Dinh Thuan appears to be exercising greater authority than before, as is Secretary of State for Interior Bui Van Luong who, like the head of the new Central Intelligence Organization, Col. Nguyen Van Y, and Secretary of State for Public Health Tran Dinh Do, is among the newly-appointed and more competent members of Diem's entourage in Saigon. At Diem's initiative, the National Assembly recently passed an amendment to the constitution enabling it to call upon members of Diem's cabinet to give testimony on pending legislation.

Diem also has become increasingly aware of the need to revive and accelerate training programs for his civil service and has been somewhat more selective in his appointment of middle echelon officials and province chiefs. As a result of the increased number of US advisers, particularly at this level of the government, some of these officials have also shown a somewhat greater willingness to act on their own initiative and to attempt to improve their general effectiveness in such matters as military planning and operations, information and propaganda, intelligence, and Civic Action. Finally, there has been greater consultation and coordination of activities between GVN and US officials in Saigon which in turn has tended to reduce delays in the formulation and implementation of policies.

Nevertheless, participation by the central elements of the administration in Saigon in the formulation and direction of policies, as well as initiative and constructive criticism upward from its middle and lower echelons, continue to be restricted seriously. Diem and his family continue to operate the government largely on the basis of personal relationships rather than through the regular or formal channels of command. They have remained steadfast against any US pressure to broaden government participation at the top, and have been keenly alert and highly sensitive to the possibility that the role of US advisers in the field or at the middle and lower echelons of the administration may weaken their authority outside Saigon.

3. *Diem's Position in the Countryside.* Diem has never had widespread popular appeal and support, even during his period of greatest achievement, 1955–58. An austere and disciplined introvert, he is incapable of demagoguery and has never made a great effort—to the extent that Prince Sihanouk of Cambodia and Ho Chi Minh of North Vietnam, for example, have done so—to inspire among the South Vietnamese people a national consciousness centered and moulded around him personally. While he has enacted measures that have helped the peasants, he has not attempted to identify himself intimately with the peasants. Relatively few peasants have ever seen Diem or heard him speak, and there are probably many others who are not aware that he is head of the government. For the great majority of peasants, the district chief is probably the highest government official with whom there has been any notable degree of contact.

Diem undoubtedly has become increasingly aware of the serious need to improve the public image of himself, his family, and his government. He now travels extensively in the countryside, and his manner of talking with the peasant has become more relaxed and sympathetic than before; during the last half of 1961, for example, Diem made 18 known trips outside Saigon and visited 19 provinces, 9 in the central and northern parts of the country and 10 in the south. Both Diem and Nhu have from time to time attended the inauguration of relatively small rural projects. With US assistance, the GVN is expanding its information and Civic Action programs at the village level and has become more conscious of the need to conduct these activities along lines understood and appreciated by the peasant. Finally, there are reports that a number of the villages and hamlets which have been given arms have resisted the Viet Cong, instead of surrendering their weapons as some GVN officials had expected they would do.

There seems to be some feeling among GVN and US officials operating at the local level that the popular appeal of and support for Diem and his government in the countryside is improving, particularly in areas where security has improved and the government's power is increasing. However, they warn against any undue optimism, particularly since they believe social and economic advances are still not keeping pace with military successes, and that the positive identification of the peasantry with the government is still a long way off. While over a 100,000 *Montagnard* or mountain tribespeople have fled Viet Cong-controlled areas and are being temporarily housed and fed by the GVN, their flight apparently was due principally to Viet Cong excesses and the general intensification of the fighting in the highlands rather than to any positive measures taken by the GVN to appeal to the tribespeople. The extensive use of artillery and aerial bombardment and other apparently excessive and indiscriminate measures by GVN military and security forces in attempting to eliminate the Viet Cong have undoubtedly killed many innocent peasants and made many others more willing than before to cooperate with the Viet Cong, particularly in areas where the government has conducted extensive military operations, but has failed to follow up by providing the means for permanent security.

4. *Diem's Position in Urban Centers.* Diem's legitimacy as South Vietnam's national leader may be, at best, a vague and impersonal concept in the countryside. It is seriously questioned, however, among many elements of the urban society, principally among professionals, intellectuals, and former politicians in Saigon. As in the recent past, this questioning largely continues to take the form of dissent and private criticism rather than openly organized opposition. Within this educated and politically sensitive sector of the Vietnamese society, there is a wide variety of political sentiments, including varying degrees of Vietnamese nationalism, neutralism, communism, pro-US and anti-US, and pro-French and anti-French. The common themes among these critics and active opponents of Diem continue to be related to his system and manner of rule.

Reports of open criticism and opposition to Diem among the Saigon civilian elite, already on the decline by early 1961, have decreased further during this year. Little has been heard, for example, of Dr. Pham Quang Dan's Republican Party of Vietnam (Dan himself has been in prison since the 1960 coup attempt), of GVN-created or GVN-controlled "opposition" groups, or of the once vociferous critics of Diem, such as the 18 intellectuals and ex-politicians who signed a public protest petition to Diem in 1960. The probable causes for this decline in reports are varied: GVN repression and increased fear of repression; the increased realization that there is little the oppositionists can do legally to change conditions, particularly in view of reaffirmed US support for Diem; and increased concern over the possibility of Communist exploitation of any coup attempt.

This relative surface silence might be regarded as an indicator of improvement in Diem's position with the urban public if it were not for the increasing number of reports of clandestine activities by his non-Communist critics and opponents. Factional leaders of such old and once important political groups as the *Dai Viets* and the Nationalist Party of Vietnam (VNQDD) reportedly are seeking ways to get their members secretly installed in the government. (There is evidence of some collusion between elements of one of these groups and the two pilots who bombed Diem's palace in February 1962.) Other opposition elements, including factions of the *Cao Dai* religious sect and the *Hoa Hao* Social Democratic Party, are reportedly preparing plans for a future coup, either in cooperation with other non-Communist groups or with the Viet Cong. It also appears that expatriate groups in France, such as the Democratic Party of Vietnam, are attempting to expand their covert activities in Saigon.

While it appears that Diem has not improved his standing among urban groups, there is no evidence that the anti-Diem intellectual-elite elements in Saigon have been able to overcome their chronic disunity and sectarianism or to increase their very small followings. On the other hand, Diem's persisting disdain of most of these oppositionists and his refusal to bring into the government even some of their least reprehensible members have contributed to a growing neutralist sentiment among them and, by forcing many of them under cover, have made it extremely difficult to estimate their real strength and disruptive potential. In addition to the growing appeal of neutralism among them, their pro-US orientation may also be rapidly declining.

IV. ECONOMIC TRENDS

There has been little inflationary pressure in South Vietnam as yet. Prices have been stable and the money supply has been nearly constant for over a year. For example, in August 1962, total money supply, made up of demand deposits in the banks and currency in circulation, was only fractionally above what it had been in March 1961. Further, prices have been generally stable and the cost of living in the cities has risen only very slowly.

The stability in money supply and prices that has been such a marked feature of the Vietnamese economy has been the direct result of very conservative GVN policies with respect to prices, wages, and fiscal management. So long as the immediate problem in South Vietnam was reconstruction, i.e., the restoration of production to pre-World War II levels, it was possible to obtain substantial increases in output at relatively small cost, and conservative price-wage and fiscal policies were not only useful but also to some extent necessary. Although GVN policies have been more conservative in nature than was really required (for example, budget surpluses from 1954 to 1959 amounted to a total of 2.7 billion piasters), they have kept the specter of inflation from adding yet another element of instability to the scene.

Since the reconstruction phase ended in about 1959, GVN economic policy has preserved the status quo in the countryside, including the traditional disparity between rural and urban living standards, and has not stimulated economic development. There are some indications, in fact, that there has recently been net disinvestment in agriculture. Given the security situation in the countryside and the current depressed state of trade there, revised policies directed toward increasing rural income and production would be an essential element in persuading the peasants to cast their lot with the government and not with the Viet Cong.

Two encouraging developments have occurred in the economic field in South Vietnam in the last several months. First, the Second Five-Year Plan was endorsed by the National Assembly in June and approved by President Diem. The Plan calls for the investment of 45 billion piasters over the period 1962-1966 and emphasizes the development of agriculture, public works, and industry. On June 30 the National Assembly appropriated an initial 1.2 billion piasters to finance the piaster costs of several projects, none of them in the agricultural sector.

Second, President Diem, in his state of the nation message to the National Assembly on October 1, emphasized that agriculture is the economic base of South Vietnam and must have priority in development. He also said that private investment must be encouraged and provided the rationale for deficit financing by pointing out that a developing nation normally experiences a budgetary deficit. Diem referred to the necessity of raising the living standards of the rural population and said that the present guaranteed minimum wage would be reexamined because of the rise in the cost of living. Although measures to implement new economic policies may not be presented to the National Assembly until its next regular session in April 1963, Diem's statements indicate a new awareness that the trend of declining income among the lowest income groups must be reversed. This awareness is encouraging but, unless the additional income generated by deficit financing is largely directed to the countryside and to the lower income urban groups, the price rises resulting from deficit financing will merely widen the income gap which already exists and further alienate the peasants from the GVN. Moreover, the additional income must be directed to the rural areas in such a way as to encourage agricultural production. Stable and attractive prices for farm products are the best and perhaps only means to accomplish this.

Viet Cong activities in South Vietnam can be expected to have a depressing effect on agricultural production, although the major determinants will continue to be price, the weather, and agricultural techniques, including the use of fertilizer, and improved seed. These latter factors however, are less important with respect to rubber production, which provides South Vietnam's largest single export. For the eight months through August 1962, rubber production on major plantations declined by some 2,500 metric tons as compared to 1961. A fungus disease affecting the rubber trees was partially responsible for the decline, but an important additional cause was clandestine tapping by the Viet Cong and general insecurity which interfered with legitimate tapping on the estates and extension of the planted area. Also, the government's urgent financial needs arising from the emergency have prevented it since 1960 from making anything more than token payments in support of its rubber replanting program. Given the vulnerability of the estates, there is little prospect for an improvement in the rubber situation until security improves generally.

It can also be expected that Viet Cong harassment will continue to interfere with the transport system, especially the railroads. The resumption of night passenger operations between Saigon and Hue on September 15 was apparently not based on any improvement in security but on the hope that the Viet Cong would not sabotage trains carrying passengers. The resumption may have also been due to the fact that additional revenues are urgently needed in view of the 10 million piaster monthly deficit on railway operations.

If President Diem's statements on October 1 are followed by the necessary measures to stimulate development of the agricultural sector in South Vietnam, which accounts for the employment of 80% of the population, important steps will have been taken not only to provide the peasantry with the motivation to side with the government but also to direct economic development along the lines most promising for the economic future of South Vietnam. This will be particularly the case if the GVN's economic development program also emphasizes industries utilizing domestically produced raw materials, particularly agricultural ones, as well as those that provide import substitutes but are based solely on imported raw materials.

In short, the GVN is showing a new awareness of the necessity of directing its attention to programs which will directly benefit the rural population. It has not as yet put into effect any concrete measures to carry out its program. Its actions in the next six months to a year will indicate how deep its new-found conviction is.

V. OUTLOOK

A. COMMUNIST ACTIONS

There seems little prospect that the Viet Cong will be able to achieve a take-over of South Vietnam by armed force during the next year. The Communists are obviously prepared for a long struggle. Even though the strengthened GVN response and increased US assistance have apparently necessitated some modification of plans, it is not likely that the Communists will diminish there diversified campaign of guerrilla warfare, terrorism, and subversion. They can be expected to make every effort to maintain, consolidate, and expand their control of the countryside; increase their overall armed strength, the number of organized fighting units, and the percentage of hard-core personnel in those units; improve their weapons capability particularly against helicopters; and increase their attacks against strategic hamlets. Acts of terrorism, particularly against Americans, and sabotage, particularly of trains and important installations, may well increase to unprecedented proportions in an effort to tie down more GVN military and security forces and thus relieve the pressure against the Viet Cong.

Hanoi can also be expected to continue to infiltrate personnel and material into South Vietnam and has the capability to step up infiltration, as the situation warrants, with relatively little danger of detection and no great difficulty. The DRV's capability is further enhanced by the nature of the border terrain and the limited border-control capabilities of the South Vietnamese, Lao, and Cambodian governments. However, because of tactical and strategic military and political considerations, Hanoi will probably continue to infiltrate elements primarily from the pool of regrouped South Vietnamese rather than from the Vietnamese Communist forces in Laos most of whom are believed to be North Vietnamese or Tonkinese.

It is entirely possible that the Viet Cong will step up its armed operations during the next month or so with the advent of the dry season, in the belief that further military escalation is necessary in order to counter the growing response and effectiveness of the GVN forces and US support. There are a number of indicators that support this expectation: numberous earlier intelligence reports of Viet Cong regroupment and consolidation of forces; a slight increase in the number of armed incidents during roughly the last week of October; and two Viet Cong battalion-size attacks in the Mekong River delta area in late October and early November 1962, the first since July 1962. Further military escalation during the next several months might involve the formation of regimental-size units, including the transformation of some guerrilla units into conventional units with heavier weapons; selected and simultaneous large attacks against one or more targets, including military installations and towns; establishment of "liberated areas" in South Vietnam; the creation of reserve bases in Communist-held areas in southern Laos; and increased infiltration, particularly if Communist forces in southern Laos can provide adequate protection along infiltration routes. (It does not appear likely that inspection by the International Control Commission in Laos will seriously impede Communist infiltration.) However, Hanoi will probably not resort to overt military invasion.

The Viet Cong and Hanoi probably will step up significantly their political and propaganda activities. Inside South Vietnam, the Viet Cong will make increased efforts to penetrate the strategic hamlets and army and security units, recoup its psychological losses with the *Montagnards,* and in general subvert the GVN's effort to win the support of the peasants. In urban areas, the Viet Cong will rely on terrorism to demoralize the citizenry and on increased propaganda and subversion to inspire anti-Diem demonstrations and coup plots, encourage neutralist sentiment, and, in general, gain support for its "united front" tactics among non-Communist oppositionists and youth and labor groups.

Outside South Vietnam, Hanoi will probably increase its diplomatic and propaganda efforts to gain support particularly among neutral nations for the

"National Front for the Liberation of South Vietnam" (NFLSV). It may have some success in establishing "unofficial" relations between the NFLSV and Laotian and Cambodian leaders, in gaining support for the NFLSV among Vietnamese minorities in Laos, Cambodia, and Thailand, and in persuading prominent Vietnamese expatriates in France to support a change of government in South Vietnam. In addition to advocating the reunification of Vietnam, Hanoi and the NFLSV can be expected to continue propaganda support for the neutralization of South Vietnam. However, the extent to which neutralization is emphasized will depend on the course of the war in South Vietnam and the degree to which the concept is found to appeal to the elements in and outside South Vietnam, as well as on developments in the Bloc itself.

The pattern of events relating to the creation and development of the NFLSV, as well as the pattern of Communist political tactics and strategy in similar situations in other countries in the past, indicates that Hanoi and the Viet Cong are preparing the groundwork for transformation of the NFLSV into a shadow or "liberation government" in South Vietnam. However, it is extremely difficult to predict when, whether, or under what conditions this will occur. Hanoi might find it politically advantageous to create a shadow government under any one of the following circumstances: during a period of internal political crisis in South Vietnam following a successful or near-successful coup attempt; during a period when there has been a series of major and dramatic Viet Cong military successes; during a period of serious military or diplomatic reverses for the US in the Far East; or at a time when several neutralist countries had given assurances of diplomatic recognition of a new 'government" in South Vietnam. Under any circumstances, however, the decision would be considerably influenced by Moscow and Peiping and their estimate of the general international situation.

B. GVN COUNTERINSURGENCY EFFORT

The elimination and even the significant reduction of the Communist insurgency in South Vietnam will almost certainly require several years. However, in addition to continuing US assistance, a considerably greater effort by the GVN is crucial. An effective strategic military-political concept for implementing the GVN counterinsurgency plan has been developed and is now being acted upon, and the armed and security forces have been enlarged and improved. GVN success will in large measure depend on the manner and speed with which it continues to implement this concept. Ultimately, however, the effectiveness of its implementation will depend on the willingness of Diem and his family to utilize fully the basic resources available to the GVN. The GVN military leaders are among the best in Southeast Asia and the rank and file have the spirit and willingness to fight; the civilian bureaucratic leadership is strongly anti-Communist, even though its effectiveness continues to be impeded by inadequate delegation of authority; there are as yet no serious trends toward neutralism or toward a political accommodation with Hanoi; and finally, the Vietnamese peasants, however politically apathetic and discontented with the government, are by no means ready to surrender themselves to the Viet Cong, given greater effort by the government to protect them from Communist intimidation and improve their economic and political status.

During the next year, the GVN probably will not be able to halt completely the deteriorating security trends, let alone reverse the tide against the Viet Cong, unless Saigon significantly accelerates and improves its response to the insurgency. Among other things, the government leadership must give much greater emphasis to political, social, and economic measures in support of its military operations, make a substantially greater effort to integrate the strategic hamlet program into a continuing systematic pacification effort, and appreciably improve its counterguerrilla tactics and capabilities, including increased reliance on small-unit actions and restriction of the tactical use of airpower and artillery. Failure to do this will seriously weaken the strategic hamlet program, particularly since the Viet Cong can be expected to step up its efforts against the program during the next year. Such failure will also greatly restrict the ability of the GVN to weaken Viet Cong capabilities, to consolidate its own military successes into permanent political gains, and to evoke, particularly among the peasants, the needed greater sense of stake in the government's fortunes. Indeed, the continuation of such tactical measures as extensive use of airpower and crop destruction, however carefully controlled, may well contribute to the development of militant opposition among the peasants and positive identification with the Viet Cong.

Progress against the insurgents will probably remain difficult to evaluate accurately. There are many indicators on the basis of which progress can be judged; the more meaningful would appear to be the peasants' willingness to inform on the Viet Cong and to defend themselves against Viet Cong attacks, and Viet Cong weapons losses, shortages of food and medicine, and defections. In this respect, a national program by the GVN to encourage Viet Cong defections, with the promise of fair treatment of the defectors is long overdue and could be extremely effective in improving GVN intelligence and weakening Viet Cong morale. GVN statistics on casualties, while helpful as an indicator of the magnitude of the fighting, should continue to be treated with extreme caution partly because they undoubtedly include many casualties among innocent peasants or wavering supporters of the Viet Cong.

C. THE US ROLE

The course of US-GVN relations will be an important element in the struggle against the Viet Cong and in sustaining South Vietnamese morale. The fact that the US is South Vietnam's only source of significant support and assistance is the controlling factor in GVN relations and attitudes toward the US. Despite considerable improvement in relations between the US and the GVN during the past year or so, disagreements and frustrations can be expected to continue over a number of issues, including the implementation of the counterinsurgency plan and GVN relations with Laos and Cambodia.

Diem will almost certainly continue to press for increased aid and remain adamant against any US pressures upon him to delegate appreciably more authority to his cabinet and military advisors or to expand the political base of his government to any significant extent. Moreover, while he has welcomed the increased US presence in South Vietnam and generally approved of the activities of US advisers in the countryside, Diem and his family will continue to maintain a close watch over those activities in the interests of protecting their authority at the local level. Diem and particularly Nhu may also remain extremely reluctant to accept possible US proposals directed toward further integration of the strategic hamlet and systematic pacification programs or directed toward substantially altering the present balance between emphasis on purely military measures to defeat the Viet Cong and emphasis on political, social, and economic measures.

Diem probably still has some lingering suspicion of the extent of US confidence in and support of his leadership. In the event of another coup attempt, Diem would expect quick and strong manifestations of US support and would regard the absence of such manifestations as demonstrating lack of US confidence.

There is considerable evidence that the substantial increase in the US presence in South Vietnam has improved morale at all levels of the GVN administration. Relations between individual US advisers and their GVN counterparts especially at the local level have generally been good and, despite Viet Cong propaganda efforts, have not resulted in any noticeable degree of association of the US presence with the former French presence. Among the probable major considerations are the fact that US personnel, unlike the French in the past, are acting as advisers rather than as directors and implementers of GVN policy, and the apparent willingness of US military personnel to live and operate closely with their GVN counterparts, assisting more by example rather than by persuasion. There is, therefore, cause for optimism over the effectiveness of the US presence in South Vietnam, even though it will come under increasing strain as the counterinsurgency effort develops and as Communist propaganda is increasingly focussed on it.

D. POLITICAL SITUATION

The stability of the government during the next year will continue to depend principally on Diem's handling of the internal security situation. If Diem can demonstrate a continuing improvement in security conditions, he should be able to alleviate concern and boost morale within his bureauracy and military establishment. However, if the fight against the Viet Cong goes badly, if the Viet Cong launches a series of successful and dramatic military operations, or if South Vietnamese army casualties increase appreciably over a protracted period, the chances of a coup attempt against Diem could increase substantially. Moreover, the possibility of a coup attempt at any time cannot be excluded. Many officials and oppositionists feel that, despite the government's military victories and improved military capabilities and initiative, the GVN is not winning the war principally because of Diem's virtual one-man rule and his failure to follow through with the political and economic measures necessary to gain the support of the peasants.

It is more difficult now than at any time since the crisis in South Vietnam began in late 1959 to estimate reliably the elements that would be most likely to precipitate a coup attempt, the prospects for the success of a coup attempt, or the effects of such an attempt on internal stability and on the counterinsurgency effort itself. During the past year or so, the Viet Cong presumably has improved its ability to initiate a coup and might attempt to do so. However, the Viet Cong probably would not be able to carry out a successful coup, and the odds that it could gain control of a successful coup, although somewhat better than last year, appear to be less than even.

The coup most likely to succeed would be one with non-Communist leadership and support, principally involving South Vietnamese military elements and civilian officials and perhaps some oppositionists outside the government. The abortive coup attempt in November 1960 and the palace bombing in February 1962 have undoubtedly demonstrated to coup plotters the necessity for better preparation and broader participation by the military. Any future non-Communist coup group probably would not be as deficient in this respect and its leaders, unlike the leaders of the 1960 coup attempt, can be expected to be better prepared to execute their plan quickly. Although the possibility of a Kong Le-type coup, i.e., a coup led by a junior and relatively unknown officer, cannot be completely discounted, it is more likely that the coup leadership would include some middle and top echelon military officials. While their role is by no means certain, a major polarization of the GVN military leadership into coup and anti-coup groups does not appear likely. Most of them would probably elect to remain uncommitted at the outset of the coup, as they apparently did in November 1960, and would then give their tacit or active support to whatever side appeared to have the best chance of winning. Under these circumstances, a military coup appears to have a better than even chance of succeeding.

Diem's removal—whether by a military coup, assassination, or death from accidental or natural causes—would probably considerably strengthen the power of the military. The odds appear about even between a government led by a military junta or by Vice President Tho, with the army, in the latter case, playing a major if not the predominant role behind the scenes. On the one hand, the military might conclude that a military-led government would be better able to maintain national unity and internal political cohesion and, more importantly, to conduct a determined and effective campaign against the Viet Cong. On the other hand, they might conclude that Tho, who apparently has been on good terms with some of the present top military leaders, would not disagree with their views on the manner of conducting the fight against the Communists and that his constitutional succession would legalize the change in government and possibly avert a serious power struggle. (Although Diem's brothers, Nhu and Can, would probably also be removed by a coup, if Diem left the scene for other reasons his brothers might attempt to retain real political power.) In any event, a government led by the military, by Tho, or by any other civilian approved by the military would probably maintain South Vietnam's pro-US orientation.

If there is a serious disruption of government leadership as a result of a military coup or as a result of Diem's death, any momentum the government's counterinsurgency efforts had achieved would probably be halted and possibly reversed, at least for a time. Moreover, the confusion and suspicion attending the disruption would provide the Viet Cong guerrillas an opportunity to strengthen their position in the countryside and attack some installations in large force, but they would probably fail if they attempted to seize control of the government.

Under most of the foreseeable circumstances involving a coup, the role of the US would be extremely important. Although this is by no means certain, US military and intelligence officials might well have advance notice of an impending coup and might be able to restrain the coup plotters from precipitous action. Even if unable to restrain such action, however, US officials might have greater success in averting widespread fighting and a serious power struggle which would lead to excessive bloodshed and weaken the front against the Viet Cong. The US could also be helpful in achieving agreement among the coup leaders as to who should head the government and in restoring the momentum of the government's counterinsurgency effort.

[Document 120]

MEMORANDUM FOR THE PRESIDENT

A Report on South Vietnam

The war in South Vietnam is clearly going better than it was a year ago. The government claims to have built more than 4,000 Strategic Hamlets, and although many of these are nothing more than a bamboo fence, a certain proportion have enough weapons to keep out at least small Viet Cong patrols and the rudiments of the kind of social and political program needed to enlist the villagers' support.

The program to arm and train the Montagnards, which should go far toward choking off the infiltration routes, has also made progress. There are 29 U.S. Special Forces teams training Montagnards (as well as certain minority groups in the Delta), with eleven more teams on the way. By mid-autumn training camps had been set up in all the provinces bordering Laos, and a system of regular patrolling started that hopefully will one day cover the entire network of trails in the mountain regions. Under this program over 35,000 Montagnards have been trained, armed, and assisted in setting up their village defenses, the eventual goal being one hundred thousand.

In both the mountain regions and the heavily populated lowlands, the areas through which one can travel without escort have been enlarged. In contested areas, the government is beginning to probe out, gradually repairing the roads and bridges cut by the Viet Cong as they go. In some of the moderately populated areas fringing the Delta and the coastal plain, as for example Binh Duong province, isolated villages have been bodily moved to positions along the roads where they can be more easily defended.

As of December 1, the Vietnamese government controlled 951 villages containing about 51% of the rural population—a gain of 92 villages and 500,000 people in six months. The Viet Cong control 445 villages with 8% of the rural population—a loss of 9 villages and 231,000 people in six months.

The impact of previously authorized U.S. aid programs is also beginning to be felt. On the military side, U.S. advisors, helicopters, air support, and arms have given the Vietnamese military new confidence which they are showing by increased aggressiveness. For the first time since the war began in 1959, for example, the government forces began in September to capture more weapons than they lost. From January to August, government forces captured 2,728 weapons but lost 3,661. But in September and October, they captured 908 weapons and lost only 765.

On the Strategic Hamlet and civilian programs, U.S. aid is just coming in. Strategic Hamlet "kits" are now arriving, a U.S. military advisor has been stationed with each province chief, and twenty of the forty-one provinces will soon have a U.S. Rural Development advisor as well. Finally, there is considerably more optimism among Vietnamese officials than there was a year ago, although it is probably based more on the visible flow of U.S. aid than on an objective analysis of actual progress.

The Viet Cong, in sum, are being hurt—they have somewhat less freedom of movement than they had a year ago, they apparently suffer acutely from lack of medicines, and in some very isolated areas they seem to be having trouble getting food.

Qualifications

Even so, the negative side of the ledger is still awesome. The Viet Cong continue to be aggressive and are extremely effective. In the last few weeks, for example, they fought stubbornly and with telling results at Ap Bac, near My Tho. They completely escaped an elaborate trap in Tay Ninh province. They fought their way inside the perimeter of a U.S. Special Forces training camp at Plei Mrong, killing 39 of the trainee defenders and capturing 114 weapons. And they completely overran a strategic hamlet in Phu Yen province that was defended by a civil guard company in addition to the village militia, killing 24 of the defenders and capturing 35 weapons.

Probably even more significant are the figures on Viet Cong strength. Intelligence estimates credit the Viet Cong with actually increasing their regular forces from 18,000 to 23,000 over this past year in spite of having suffered what the government claims were losses of 20,000 killed in action and 4,000 wounded. Part of this increase may result from nothing more than better intelligence, but even so it is ominous that in the face of greatly increased government pressure and U.S. support the Viet Cong can still field 23,000 regular forces and 100,000 militia, supported by unknown thousands of sympathizers.

What these figures suggest is that the Viet Cong are still able to obtain an adequate supply of recruits and the large quantities of food and other supplies they need from the villagers of South Vietnam itself. Infiltration by sea has been effectively blocked since early in 1962. As for infiltration by land, captured documents, POW interrogation, evidence gathered by patrolling, and other intelligence indicates that 3,000 to 4,000 Viet Cong at the most have come over the so-called Ho Chi Minh trails since January, 1962. As to supplies, there seems to be no doubt that the trails have so far been used only for specialized equipment, such as radios; for medicines; and perhaps for a few automatic weapons, although no weapons have yet been captured which could be proved to have been brought in after 1954. Thus the conclusion seems inescapable that the Viet Cong could continue the war effort at the present level, or perhaps increase it, even if the infiltration routes were completely closed.

Villagers' Attitudes

The question that this conclusion raises—and the basic question of the whole war—is again the attitude of the villagers. It is difficult, if not impossible, to assess how the villagers really feel and the only straws in the wind point in different directions. The village defenders in many of the strategic hamlets that have been attacked have resisted bravely. But in an unknown, but probably large number of strategic hamlets, the villagers have merely let the Viet Cong in or supplied what they wanted without reporting the incident to the authorities. There is apparently some resentment against the Viet Cong about the "taxes" they collect and suspicion based on the stories the villagers hear about what is going on in the North. But there may be just as much resentment and suspicion directed towards the government. No one really knows, for example, how many of the 20,000 "Viet Cong" killed last year were only innocent, or at least persuadable villagers, whether the Strategic Hamlet program is providing enough government services to counteract the sacrifices it requires, or how the mute mass of the villagers react to the charges against Diem of dictatorship and nepotism. At the very least, the figures on Viet Cong strength imply a continuing flow of recruits and supplies from these same villages and indicate that a substantial proportion of the population is still cooperating with the enemy, although it is impossible to tell how much of this cooperation stems from fear and how much from conviction. Thus on the vital question of villagers' attitudes, the net impression is one of some encouragement at the progress in building strategic hamlets and the number that resist when attacked, but encouragement overlaid by a shadow of uneasiness.

Conclusion

Our overall judgment, in sum, is that we are probably winning, but certainly more slowly than we had hoped. At the rate it is now going the war will last longer than we would like, cost more in terms of both lives and money than we anticipated, and prolong the period in which a sudden and dramatic event could upset the gains already made.

The question is where improvements can be made—whether in our basic approach to fighting a guerrilla war, or in the implementation of that approach.

The Strategic Concept

We feel that the basis strategic concept developed last year is still valid. As mentioned above, the Viet Cong have gotten trained cadre and specialized equipment from the North, but the vast bulk of both recruits and supplies come from inside South Vietnam itself. Thus the strategic objectives of the war in South Vietnam, as in most guerrilla wars, are basically political—not simply to kill Viet Cong, but to win the people. Although the strategic concept has never been spelled out in any one document, the consensus seems to be that it consists of the following objectives: (1) to create the incentive for resistance in the basic population by providing for a flow upward of information on villagers' needs and a flow downward of government services, and by knitting them into the fabric of community decision-making; (2) to provide the basic population with the means and training for resistance; and (3) to cut the guerrillas' access to the villagers, their true line of communications, by essentially police-type measures for controlling the movement of goods and people. In this context, the military objectives are also threefold: (1) to protect installations vital to the economy and government; (2) to provide rapid reinforcement for villages under heavy attacks; and (3) to keep the *regular* guerrilla units off balance and prevent them from concentrating by aggressive but highly discriminating and selective offensive military operations.

This combination of civilian and military measures is designed to reduce the guerrillas to their die-hard nucleus and isolate them in areas remote from the basic population. Only when this is done does the task finally become one of killing Viet Cong, of simple elimination.

As we say, this concept seems sound. For, even though it is difficult to assess the attitudes of the villager, two assumptions seem reasonable. The first is that the villagers will be prudently cooperative with the Viet Cong if they are not given physical security, both in the military sense of security from attacks on their village and in the police sense of security from individual acts of terror and retaliation. The second is that if the villagers are in fact politically apathetic, as they seem to be, they are likely to remain so or even become pro-Communist if the government does not show concern for their welfare in the way it conducts the war and in the effort it makes to provide at least simple government services. It may be that these measures will not be enough to create popular support for the government and the incentive to resist, but it seems obvious that support could neither be created nor long maintained without them.

Implementing the Concept

Thus it is in the implementation of the strategic concept that there seems to be the greatest room for improvement. Success requires, first, full understanding of the strategy at all levels of the government and armed forces, and, second, the skills and organization for effective coordination of military activities with civilian activities. Some parts of the Vietnamese government do understand the strategy, but in other parts the understanding is imperfect at best. The same is true of the necessary skills and organization. Specific areas in particular need of improvement are listed in the paragraphs below, which discuss both programs and continuing issues and conclude with a proposal as to how the United States might increase its leverage on the Vietnamese government so as to bring the improvements about.

Lack of an Overall Plan

The most serious lack in South Vietnam is that of an overall plan, keyed to the strategic concept described above, through which priorities can be set and the coordination of military and civilian activities accomplished. In spite of U.S. urgings there is still no single country-wide plan worthy of the name but only a variety of regional and provincial plans, some good and some not so good. There are, for example, a number of special plans—the Delta Plan, Operation Sunrise, Operation Sea Swallow, Waves of Love—; several plans developed by the commanders of the Corps and Divisional areas; and an unknown number of plans developed by each of the forty-one province chiefs. Regional and provincial plans are, of course, necessary, but they should be elements of a country-wide plan rather than a substitute for it. As it is, the impression is strong that many of these plans are both inconsistent and competitive.

Strategic Hamlets

One result of the lack of an overall plan is the proliferation of strategic hamlets that are inadequately equipped and defended, or that are built prematurely in exposed areas.

Gaps: The Police Program

The second result is that essential aspects of the strategy are neglected. The police program is an example. An effective police system is vital to guard against Communists remaining inside strategic hamlets, and to man the check points and patrols that are essential in controlling the movements of goods and people. The present police system is clearly inadequate, and although the Public Safety Division of U.S. AID has put forward a proposal for expansion, no action has yet been taken.

Multiple Armies

A third result is what appears to be an extremely uneconomic use of manpower. There is in South Vietnam a confusing multiplicity of separate armies.

In addition to the regular forces (the ARVN), there are under arms the Civil Guard, the Self Defense Corps, the Civilian Irregular Defense Groups (CIDG), the Hamlet Militia, the Montagnard Commandoes, the Force Populaire, the Republican Youth, the Catholic Youth, several independent groups under parish priests, such as Father Hoa's Sea Swallows, and even one small army trained, armed, and commanded by a private businessman to protect his properties in Cap St. Jaques. All these forces add up to almost half a million men under arms, a number which if so organized would come to the astounding total of 51 divisions.

This multiplicity of separate armies results not only in an uneconomic use of manpower, but also difficulties in coordination and confusion as to function. One also suspects that it is a misallocation of manpower as well, with too much emphasis on military activities and not enough on civilian, such as government services to the villages and police work. So many armed men with different loyalties will also create problems in the transition to a peace-time economy if victory is in fact won, as well as the obvious danger that one or another chief will use the forces under his command for political purposes. South Vietnam does not need any more armed men, but it does need to reorganize what it has.

Coordination of Military and Civilian Activities

Still another result of the lack of an overall plan are the difficulties in coordinating military and civilian activities. One example is the proportion of "clear and hold" as opposed to "hit and withdraw" operations. There are no statistics available, but a number of American military advisors feel that the proportion of "clear and hold" operations, in which troops clear an area and then remain to protect the civic action teams and villagers while they build strategic hamlets, is too low in proportion to the "hit and withdraw" operations designed to destroy regular Viet Cong units. The latter type of operation is essential to keep the Viet Cong off balance and to prevent their concentrating for large-scale attacks, but it should be subordinate to the systematic expansion of secure areas.

Amnesty Program

A final result of the lack of an overall plan, or perhaps of imperfect understanding of an effective counter-guerrilla strategy, is the Vietnamese reluctance to embark on a meaningful amnesty program. After much U.S. urging, the Vietnamese have finally developed a plan, but it is far from satisfactory. The basic trouble is revealed by the Vietnamese insistence that what they want is not an "amnesty" policy but a "surrender" policy.

Civil Programs

The inadequacies in the police program, the tendency to build strategic hamlets in exposed places with inadequate arms and equipment, and the reluctance to develop a meaningful amnesty program have already been discussed. Other inadequacies in civilian programs are discussed below.

One continuing problem is the failure of the Vietnamese government to organize its economy on an emergency basis. A resistance to deficit spending and stricter controls has permitted too large a part of the country's internal and external resources to go to non-essential purposes, especially in the Saigon area.

There should be more planning for what the Vietnamese economy will be like after the shooting has ended. There is almost none of this kind of planning now, and some of the things being done today might make sensible planning in the future very difficult. An obvious example is the rise of consumption levels, especially in nonessential imports which Vietnam could not buy without U.S. aid. At some point, and probably soon, the U.S. should undertake a long-range economic study of the country's future development.

Military Operations with Political Aspects

The opinion of some American military advisors that the proportion of "clear and hold" offensive operations is too low in relation to "hit and withdraw" operations designed to keep the Viet Cong off balance has already been mentioned. Another aspect of military operations that may have political consequences is the tactics used in the offensive operations needed to keep the Viet Cong off balance. Some American military advisors feel that the Vietnamese have a bias toward elaborate, set-piece operations. These large-scale operations provide insurance against defeat, but they are expensive, cumbersome, and difficult to keep secret. From the political point of view they have the additional disadvantages for the Vietnamese of maximizing the chances of killing civilians and from the American point of view of requiring a very heavy use of helicopters.

An alternative, and apparently effective way of keeping the regular Viet Cong off balance is long-range patrolling by small units, such as Ranger companies. In this tactic, the patrols, resupplied by air, stay out in the field for extended periods of time, never sleeping two nights in the same place, ambushing, and in general using guerrilla tactics to fight the guerrilla. The remaining forces are kept in reserve for rapid reinforcement and sealing off an area when the patrol encounters resistance. Although American military advisors in South Vietnam have worked hard to overcome Vietnamese reluctance to operate for extended periods in the field and at night, which would permit greater use of this tactic, they have had only partial success. (Paradoxically, President Diem spent a substantial part of his four and a half hour lecture to us praising a province chief who has used the long-range patrol tactic to very good effect recently in Zone D.)

Use of Air Power

On use of air power, and the danger of adverse political effects, our impression is that the controls over air strikes and the procedures for checking intelligence against all possible sources are excellent. In spite of this, however, it is difficult to be sure that air power is being used in a way that minimizes the adverse political effects. U.S. Air Force advisors tell us that the demand for air strikes from the South Vietnamese has gone up enormously. There are now 1,000 strikes per month, and there would be considerably more if the air power were available. During November, thirty-two per cent of these 1,000 strikes were so-called "interdiction"—that is, attacks on installations located in air photos and identified as Viet Cong by intelligence. Fifty-three per cent of the air strikes during November were in direct support—that is, bombing and strafing in advance of an attack on a location intelligence indicated as being occupied by Viet Cong or in response to a request by a ground unit in contact with the enemy. Fifteen percent were other kinds of mission, such as reconnaissance. There is no doubt that the Viet Cong fear air attacks and that some interdiction is necessary and useful. On the other hand, it is impossible to assess how much resentment among persuadable villagers is engendered by the inevitable accidents. In general, the final judgment probably lies in the answer to the questions raised above about the relative emphasis on "clear and hold" and long-range patrolling versus "hit and withdraw" of the more elaborate type. If the proportion is correct between extending control and the necessary offensive operations to keep the Viet Cong off balance, then the killing of civilians is probably at an unavoidable minimum. If the proportion of "hit and withdraw" is too high in relation to "clear and hold," on the other hand, then air power, too, is probably being overused in ways that have adverse political consequences.

Reinforcement of Strategic Hamlets

One final point on the political aspects of military operations concerns quicker reinforcement for strategic hamlets under attack. Some American military advisors feel that more attention should be paid to ways of providing quicker reinforcement for the hamlets, including air support, although in the case of air support there are formidable problems of communications and in providing airfields close enough to threatened villages.

Foreign Policy

In its complete concentration on the civil war and on the means and ideology for winning it, the government of South Vietnam has a naivete in foreign affairs which is dangerous for both Vietnam and for the U.S. There has been massive resistance to U.S. suggestions on policies for cooperation in other problems in the area, i.e. Laos and Cambodia. To some extent this is unavoidable in view of Diem's rather simple view of the Communist threat. But U.S. interests are so heavily involved in the country that our voice should carry more weight.

Vietnamese Domestic Politics

The Diem government is frequently criticized for being a dictatorship. This is true, but we doubt that the lack of parliamentary democracy bothers the villagers of Vietnam or much affects their attitudes toward the war. The real question is whether the concentration of power in the hands of Diem and his family, especially Brother Nhu and his wife, and Diem's reluctance to delegate is alienating the middle and higher level officials on whom the government must depend to carry out its policies. Our judgment is that the United States does not really have as much information on this subject as it should. All that can be said at the moment is that it is the feeling of Americans in contact with these officials that they are encouraged by U.S. aid and apparently getting on with the job. Both the American and British missions, for example, feel that Brother Nhu's energetic support for the Strategic Hamlet program has given it an important push. The only evidence to contradict these judgments that we found was in a conversation with Buu, the head of the Vietnamese labor movement and, paradoxically, one of the co-founders with Diem and Nhu of Diem's political party.

Diem's Press Relations

The American press in South Vietnam now has good relations with the Embassy and MACV and generally are grateful for the help that they have received. But their attitude toward Diem and the government of South Vietnam is the complete opposite, and with much justice. Diem wants only adulation and is completely insensitive to the desires of the foreign press for factual information. He is equally insensitive to his own image, the political consequences of the activities of Madame Nhu and the other members of his family, and his own tendencies of arbitrariness, failure to delegate, and general pettiness. After much effort, Ambassador Nolting persuaded Diem to let the Defense Ministry give regular military briefings. True to form, however, the content of the briefings is deplorable. One of these briefings, for example, the transcript of which we examined, contained little more than a saccharine eulogy of President Diem.

It would be nice if we could say that Diem's image in the foreign press was only his affair, but it seriously affects the U.S. and its ability to help South Vietnam. The American press representatives are bitter and will seize on anything that goes wrong and blow it up as much as possible. The My Tho operation, for example, contained some mistakes, but it was not nearly the botched up disaster that the press made it appear to be.

Action for the United States

By way of summary, then, we feel that the United States should push the Diem government harder on the need for an overall plan, on a reduction in the number of different military organizations, on foreign policy questions in which the United States has an interest, on an effective police program, for a greater emphasis on military operations in extending and securing government control as opposed to large-scale offensives and air interdiction, on a meaningful amnesty program, on planning for the post-war economy, and on a realistic effort to get a more favorable press.

On many of these issues, of course, the United States has already been pressing. Thus in one sense the question is how to increase our leverage in the face of Diem's biases and general resistance to advice.

Actually, the United States is in a much better position to see that its advice is taken than it was a year ago. At that time Diem and officials at the national level were practically the only point of contact the U.S. had with either civil or military programs. Today, however, the U.S. has military advisors not only at the lower levels of the Army but with each province chief and steps are being taken to put U.S. AID advisors in at least 20 of the 41 provinces. It therefore is becoming possible to accomplish much of what we want at the local level without going through the vastly inefficient national bureaucracy. An example is the work of the special forces teams. They work at the village level, and at a number of places have done wonders not only in training and supervising the erection of village defenses but also in medical aid, school construction, and even in agriculture and marketing.

In general, it is our judgment that an effort should be made to increase this influence at the local level even more by putting additional U.S. AID people with province chiefs and, where it is indicated, even at selected places further down in the civilian hierarchy.

In addition, having gotten past the first year of increased U.S. support and demonstrated our sincerity, the time has probably come when we can press our views on Diem more vigorously and occasionally even publicly.

One final recommendation for U.S. action concerns our dealings with the press here in Washington. In our judgment a systematic campaign to get more of the facts into the press and T.V. should be mounted. Although our report, for example, is not rosily optimistic, it certainly contains the factual basis (e.g., the first few paragraphs) for a much more hopeful view than the pessimistic (and factually inaccurate) picture conveyed in the press.

Michael V. Forrestal

[Document 121]

NIE. 53-63

17 April 63

PROSPECTS IN SOUTH VIETNAM

THE PROBLEM

To assess the situation and prospects in South Vietnam, with special emphasis upon the military and political factors most likely to affect the counter-insurgency effort.

CONCLUSIONS

A. We believe that Communist progress has been blunted and that the situation is improving. Strengthened South Vietnamese capabilities and effectiveness, and particularly US involvement, are causing the Viet Cong increased difficulty, although there are as yet no persuasive indications that the Communists have been grievously hurt. (*Paras. 27-28*)

B. We believe the Communists will continue to wage a war of attrition, hoping for some break in the situation which will lead to victory. They evidently hope that a combination of military pressure and political deterioration will in time create favorable circumstances either for delivering a *coup de grâce* or for a political settlement which will enable them to continue the struggle on more favorable terms. We believe it unlikely, especially in view of the open US commitment, that the North Vietnamese regime will either resort to overt military attack or introduce acknowledged North Vietnamese military units into the south in an effort to win a quick victory. (*Paras. 29-31*)

C. Assuming no great increase in external support to the Viet Cong, changes and improvements which have occurred during the past year now indicate that the Viet Cong can be contained militarily and that further progress can be made in expanding the area of government control and in creating greater security in the countryside. However, we do not believe that it is possible at this time to project the future course of the war with any confidence. Decisive campaigns have yet to be fought and no quick and easy end to the war is in sight. Despite South Vietnamese progress, the situation remains fragile. (*Para. 32*)

D. Developments during the last year or two also show some promise of resolving the political weaknesses, particularly that of insecurity in the countryside, upon which the insurgency has fed. However, the government's capacity to embark upon the broader measures required to translate military success into lasting political stability is questionable. (*Paras. 33-35*)

[Document 122]

THE WHITE HOUSE

Washington

June 25, 1963

NATIONAL SECURITY ACTION MEMORANDUM NO. 249

TO: The Secretary of State

The Secretary of Defense

The Director, Central Intelligence Agency

The Chairman, Joint Chiefs of Staff

SUBJECT: Laos Planning

1. At a meeting on June 19, 1963 the President considered the Memorandum addressed to him from the Department of State dated June 17, 1963 ("Memorandum").

2. The President approved Phase 1 of the plan outlined in the Memorandum and authorized that the steps outlined therein might be taken at such time and in such manner as the appropriate officials concerned might direct.

3. The President directed the Department of State to consult with the French and British before initiating any action under the Memorandum. He wished to obtain their suggestions for action in Laos in light of the deteriorating situation there.

4. The President approved Phase 2 of the Memorandum for planning purposes, but directed that none of the steps outlined in Phase 2 be put into final execution until after further consultation with him.

5. The President directed that the steps described in Phase 3 of the Memorandum be further refined and reviewed; and he asked that the question be explored whether additional U.S. actions should be taken in Laos before any action be directed against North Vietnam.

Carl Kaysen

Copies furnished: Governor Harriman

General McKee

Mr. Colby

General Clay

[Document 123]

DEPARTMENT OF STATE

Memorandum of Conversation

FOR THE RECORD

DATE: July 4, 1963

TIME: 11:00 to 11:50 a.m.

PLACE: The White House

SUBJECT: Situation in South Viet-Nam

PARTICIPANTS: The President

Mr. Ball

Mr. Harriman

Mr. McGeorge Bundy

Mr. Hilsman

Mr. Forrestal

The President was briefed on developments in Indonesia, Laos and Viet-Nam. The portion on Viet-Nam follows:

A joint agreement was signed on June 16 in which the Government met the Buddhists' five demands. The Buddhists and the Government then worked together on the funeral arrangements for the *bonze* who burned himself to death so that incidents could be avoided. The funeral came off without trouble.

Since then there have been rumors circulating in Saigon that the Government does not intend to live up to the agreement. These rumors were given credence by an article appearing in the English language "Times" of Viet-Nam, which is dominated by the Nhus. The article contained a veiled attack on the US and on the Buddhists. There was a suggestion that the Monk who burned himself to death was drugged and a provocative challenge to the Buddhists that, if no further demonstrations occurred on July 2, this would amount to an admission by the Buddhists that they were satisfied with the Government's action. (The President injected questions on the possibility of drugging, to which Mr. Hilsman replied that religious fervor was an adequate explanation.)

At this point there was a discussion of the possibility of getting rid of the Nhus in which the combined judgment was that it would not be possible.

Continuing the briefing, Mr. Hilsman said that the Buddhists contained an activist element which undoubtedly favored increasing demands as well as charging the Government with dragging its feet. There was thus an element of truth in Diem's view that the Buddhists might push their demands so far as to make his fall inevitable.

During these events the US had put extremely heavy pressure on Diem to take political actions. Most recently we had urged Diem to make a speech which would include announcements that he intended to meet with Buddhist leaders, permit Buddhist chaplains in the army and so on. If Diem did not make such a speech and there were further demonstrations, the US would be compelled publicly to disassociate itself from the GVN's Buddhist policy. Mr. Hilsman reported that Diem had received this approach with what seemed to be excessive politeness but had said he would consider making such a speech.

Our estimate was that no matter what Diem did there will be coup attempts over the next four months. Whether or not any of these attempts will be successful is impossible to say.

Mr. Hilsman said that everyone agreed that the chances of chaos in the wake of a coup are considerably less than they were a year ago. An encouraging sign relative to this point is that the war between the Vietnamese forces and the Viet Cong has been pursued throughout the Buddhist crisis without noticeable let-up.

At this point Mr. Forrestal reported on General Krulak's views that, even if there were chaos in Saigon, the military units in the field would continue to confront the Communists.

Mr. Hilsman went on to say that Ambassador Nolting believes that the most likely result of a coup attempt that succeeded in killing Diem was civil war. Mr. Hilsman disagreed with this view slightly in that he thought civil war was not the most likely result but that it was certainly a possible result.

The timing of Ambassador Nolting's return and Ambassador Lodge's assumption of duty was then discussed. The President's initial view was that Ambassador Nolting should return immediately and that Ambassador Lodge should assume his duties as soon thereafter as possible. The President volunteered that Ambassador Nolting had done an outstanding job, that it was almost miraculous the way he had succeeded in turning the war around from the disastrously low point in relations between Diem and ourselves that existed when Ambassador Nolting took over. Mr. Hilsman pointed out the personal sacrifices that Ambassador Nolting had been forced to make during this period, and the President said that he hoped a way could be found to commend Ambassador Nolting publicly so as to make clear the fine job he had done and that he hoped an give his children a suitable home in the years immediately ahead.
appropriate position could be found for him in Washington so that he could
The President's decision was to delegate the authority to decide on the timing of Ambassador Nolting's return to the Assistant Secretary for Far Eastern Affairs; that Ambassador Lodge should report to Washington no later than July 15 so that he could take the Counterinsurgency Course simultaneously with the normal briefings for an ambassador; and that Ambassador Lodge should arrive in Saigon as soon as possible following completion of the CI Course on August 14. Arrangements were made for Ambassador Nolting to see the President at 4:00 p.m. on Monday, July 8.

Prepared by R. Hilsman

[Document 124]

MEMORANDUM OF CONVERSATION

July 5, 1963

George Ball, Nolting, Chalmers Wood, George Springstein

Nolting opened with review of the Buddhists situation which he characterizes as serious. He regretted that Diem had not taken it in hand earlier but emphasized that Diem had given his word that the agreement would be carried out. It was Nolting's experience that when Diem gave his word, he followed through although sometimes it was handled in his own way. The ambassador said that although interference by the Nhus was serious, he believed that the GVN would be able to come through this one slowly. As to tactics, the more Diem was prodded, the slower he went. While Nhu was troublesome, he was chiefly responsible for gains which had been made in the provincial pacification program. The Under Secretary asked what would happen if there were a change in government. The ambassador replied that he would give his view which was not completely shared by Mr. Wood. In his view, if a revolution occurred in Vietnam which grew out of the Buddhist situation, the country would be split between feuding factions and the Americans would have to withdraw, and the country might be lost to the Communists. This led to the question of how much pressure we could exert on Diem. Mr. Nolting replied that if we repudiated him on this issue, his government would fall. The ambassador believed that Diem would live up to the agreement unless he believed that he was dealing with the political attempt to cause his overthrow. As to the role of the Catholics in the government, Ambassador Nolting did not believe that Diem gave them preference. Unfortunately, many persons in the government felt that it would help their careers if they became Catholic. It was true that the government had been unwise in the ostentatious manner in which it supported and encouraged the publicizing of Catholic ceremonies, however. In general, Vietnam had been a country in which there was a great degree of religious tolerance. Now the situation seemed out of hand. It was deplorable because we had been winning. . . . Turning the point of Ambassador Lodge, Mr. Nolting commented that the more Lodge was built up as a strong man who was going to tell Diem where to get off, the harder it would be for Lodge to do his job in Vietnam. The Under Secretary suggested that Ambassador Nolting could reassure President Diem on this point.

|Document 125|

SNIE 53-2-63

10 July 63

THE SITUATION

IN SOUTH VIETNAM

SCOPE NOTE

NIE 53-63, "Prospects in South Vietnam," dated 17 April 1963 was particularly concerned with the progress of the counterinsurgency effort, and with the military and political factors most likely to affect that effort. The primary purpose of the present SNIE is to examine the implications of recent developments in South Vietnam for the stability of the country, the viability of the Diem regime, and its relationship with the US.

CONCLUSIONS

A. The Buddhist crisis in South Vietnam has highlighted and intensified a widespread and longstanding dissatisfaction with the Diem regime and its style of government. If—as is likely—Diem fails to carry out truly and promptly the commitments he has made to the Buddhists, disorders will probably flare again and the chances of a coup or assassination attempts against him will become better than even. (*Paras. 4, 14*)

B. The Diem regime's underlying uneasiness about the extent of the US involvement in South Vietnam has been sharpened by the Buddhist affair and the firm line taken by the US. This attitude will almost certainly persist and further pressure to reduce the US presence in the country is likely. (*Paras. 10-12*)

C. Thus far, the Buddhist issue has not been effectively exploited by the Communists, nor does it appear to have had any appreciable effect on the counterinsurgency effort. We do not think Diem is likely to be overthrown by a Communist coup. Nor do we think the Communists would necessarily profit if he were overthrown by some combination of his non-Communist opponents. A non-Communist successor regime might be initially less effective against the Viet Cong, but, given continued support from the US, could provide reasonably effective leadership for the government and the war effort. (*Paras. 7, 15-17*)

DISCUSSION

I. INTRODUCTION

1. The two chief problems which have faced the Government of South Vietnam (GVN) since its birth in 1954 have been: (a) to forge the institutions and loyalties necessary to Vietnam's survival as an independent nation, and (b) to counter the menace of Hanoi's subversive and aggressive designs—pursued since 1960 by a campaign of widespread guerrilla warfare. In attempting to cope with these problems, the GVN has been hampered by its lack of confidence in and its inability to engage the understanding and support of a considerable portion of the Vietnamese people—including large segments of the educated classes and the peasantry. In recent weeks these inadequacies and tensions in the South Vietnamese body politic have been further revealed and intensified.

II. THE BUDDHIST AFFAIR

2. President Diem, his family, and a large proportion of the top leaders of the regime are Roman Catholics, in a population that is 70 to 80 percent Buddhist. The regime has clearly accorded preferential treatment to Catholics in its employment practices and has favored the Catholic Church. But there have been no legal restrictions on religious freedom and, until recently, most Buddhists appeared passive in their response to the privileged institutional position occupied by the Catholic Church. There have, however, been various administrative discriminations against the Buddhists, though these may have resulted as much from thoughtlessness or misplaced zeal on the part of minor officials as from conscious GVN policy. These have obviously created an undercurrent of resentment, as is evidenced by the extent and intensity of the recent outbreaks.

3. In April 1963, the GVN ordered its provincial officials to enforce a longstanding but generally ignored edict regulating the public display of religious flags. As it happened, this order was issued just prior to Buddha's birthday (8 May), a major Buddhist festival, and just after Papal flags had been prominently flown during a series of officially encouraged celebrations commemorating the 25th anniversary of the ordination of Ngo dinh Thuc, Diem's brother, the Arch-

bishop of Hue. A protest demonstration developed in Hue on 8 May, which was dispersed by fire from a Civil Guard unit. In the ensuing melee several persons were killed, including some children. The GVN has blamed the deaths on Viet Cong terrorists despite evidence to the contrary, and its subsequent stiff-necked handling of this incident and its aftermath has sparked a national crisis. The Buddhists, hitherto disorganized and nonprotesting, have shown considerable cohesion and force—enough to elicit a set of "compromise" agreements from President Diem on 16 June. Moreover, the fact that the Buddhist leaders have been able to challenge the government openly without evoking serious government retaliation has presumably given them considerable confidence.

4. For the moment, the Buddhist movement remains under the effective control of moderate bonzes who have refused to accept support from or countenance cooperation with any of Diem's political opponents, Communist or non-Communist, and appear to be trying to insure that the Buddhists live up to their part of the bargain. This leadership gave the GVN a period of grace (which expired about the end of June) in which to show that it was moving in good faith to carry out its undertakings, failing which protests would resume. So far there have been no further demonstrations, but the Buddhist leadership is clearly restive.

5. Despite Buddhist restraint in the political exploitation of the affair, it has obvious political overtones. It has apparently aroused widespread popular indignation and could well become a focal point of general disaffection with the Diem government. It provides an issue on which most of Diem's non-Communist opponents (even including some Catholics) can find common ground of agreement. There is considerable evidence that the issue itself and, even more, the Diem family's handling of it to date has occasioned restiveness at virtually all levels of the GVN's military and civil establishments, both of whose lower and middle echelons are largely staffed by Buddhists. In some cases, civil servants seem to have ignored or tempered GVN instructions, superiors have on occasion evaded their assigned task of propounding the official GVN line to their subordinates, and information on impending government actions has obviously leaked to Buddhist leaders. In any case, recent developments are causing many GVN officials to reexamine their relations with and the limits of their loyalty to the Diem regime; there is accumulating evidence of serious disaffection and coup plotting in high military and civilian circles.

6. The Buddhist affair appears to have given considerable heart to the various non-Communist political opposition splinter groups in and out of South Vietnam. There also appears to be a growing feeling among former supporters of the regime that Diem's position may have been permanently and dangerously impaired. Thus far, however, we have no evidence that the diverse opposition groups have been able to form new or effective alliances with one another.

7. The Buddhist issue would appear to be an obvious windfall for the Communists, but so far there is no evidence that they have been able to exploit it effectively. They may have penetrated the Buddhist clergy to some extent, but are not presently exerting any discernible influence, despite the suggestions to the contrary in GVN pronouncements. To date the Buddhist crisis does not appear to have had any appreciable effect on the continuing counterinsurgency effort, though the morale and efficiency of the GVN's military and civil forces are likely to be impaired if the issue is prolonged.

8. The Buddhist crisis has also hurt the GVN internationally, with potentially important effects upon the future success of US policy towards southeast Asia.

Protests are growing in other predominantly Buddhist countries, with the implication that US action could help resolve the crisis. Cambodia and Ceylon have made representations to the UN and more may be forthcoming. In other countries, including the US, the crisis has given new stimulus to criticism of US policy on the grounds that the US is supporting an oppressive and unrepresentative regime.

9. The future course of the Buddhist affair will be largely determined by the GVN's actions in the near term. It is likely that the issues recently raised can be resolved if the GVN executes its portion of the negotiated bargain. However, politically sophisticated segments of South Vietnamese society, Buddhists included, are mindful of Diem's past practice of often using negotiations as a stall for time and of making promises in order to weather an immediate crisis. The real danger in the present situation is that Diem may be tempted to employ such tactics which have served him well in the past but could prove disastrous if essayed this time. If demonstrations should be resumed, they would probably assume an increasingly political cast, and less moderate Buddhist leadership would be likely to come to the fore. Public order would be threatened. In particular, we cannot be sure how various army or police units would react if ordered to fire on demonstrations headed by Buddhist bonzes.

III.   THE EFFECT OF RECENT DEVELOPMENTS ON US-GVN RELATIONS

10. The GVN has always shown some concern over the implications of US involvement in South Vietnamese affairs and from time to time has felt moved to restrict US activities and presence in South Vietnam. This attitude springs partly from legitimate, if hypersensitive, concern for the appearance as well as the fact of Vietnam's recently acquired sovereignty. To a considerable degree, however, it springs from the Diem government's suspicion of US intentions toward it, and from its belief that the extensive US presence is setting in motion political forces which could eventually threaten Diem's political primacy.

11. The Buddhist affairs erupted at one of these periods of GVN sensitivity, and the strain has been aggravated by subsequent events. The GVN's initial handling of the issue gave the US ground for serious embarrassment and concern which, in turn, produced a succession of forceful US *démarches*. The Diem family has bitterly resented these US actions and may well feel that the Buddhist protests were at least indirectly due to the US presence. Under the circumstances, further pressure to reduce that presence is likely.

12. A key role in this regard will be played by Diem's brother, Ngo dinh Nhu. He has always been Diem's chief political lieutenant, but the years since 1954 have witnessed a steady accretion of Nhu's personal power and authority—an accretion due partly to circumstance and primarily to deliberate effort on Nhu's part. Nhu has political ambitions of his own and almost certainly envisages himself as his brother's successor. For a variety of reasons, Nhu has long privately viewed the US with some hostility and suspicion. American criticism of the GVN has especially irritated Nhu, for he is aware that he and his wife are often its primary targets. Above all, Nhu almost certainly doubts whether the support which the US has given to his brother would be transferred to him.

13. In the negotiations with the Buddhists, Nhu urged his brother to take a firm line and is, by his own statement, wholly out of sympathy with the concessions made. On the basis of past performance, we think it unlikely that he will help to implement the settlement; his influence on Diem will be rather in the

direction of delaying and hedging on commitments, a tendency to which Diem himself is already disposed. This will be the more likely since not only the Nhus and Diem, but also his brothers Archbishop Thuc and Ngo dinh Can, the political boss of the central provinces, obviously continue to doubt the legitimacy of Buddhist complaints and to underestimate the intensity of the crisis.

IV. THE OUTLOOK

14. If the Diem government moves effectively to fulfill its 16 June commitments, much of the resentment aroused by the Buddhist controversy could be allayed. However, even if relations between the GVN and the Buddhists are smoothed over, the general discontent with the Diem regime which the crisis has exacerbated and brought to the fore is likely to persist. Further, if—as is probable—the regime is dilatory, inept, and insincere in handling Buddhist matters, there will probably be renewed demonstrations, and South Vietnam will probably remain in a state of domestic political tension. Under these circumstances, the chances of a non-Communist assassination or coup attempt against Diem will be better than even. We cannot exclude the possibility of an attempted Communist coup, but a Communist attempt will have appreciably less likelihood of success so long as the majority of the government's opponents and critics remain—as they are now—alert to the Communist peril.

15. The chances of a non-Communist coup—and of its success—would become greater in the event renewed GVN/Buddhist confrontation should lead to large-scale demonstrations in Saigon. More or less prolonged riot and general disorder would probably result—with the security forces confused over which side to support. Under such circumstances, a small group, particularly one with prior contingency plans for such an eventuality, might prove able to topple the government. Conversely, a continued or resumed truce between the GVN and the Buddhists would serve to reduce the likelihood of such an overthrow.

16. Any attempt to remove Diem will almost certainly be directed against Nhu as well, but should Nhu survive Diem, we are virtually certain that he would attempt to gain power—in the first instance probably by manipulating the constitutional machinery. We do not believe that Nhu's bid would succeed, despite the personal political base he has sought to build through the Republican Youth (of which he is the overt, uniformed head), the strategic hamlet program (whose directing Interministerial Committee he chairs), and in the army. He and his wife have become too much the living symbols of all that is disliked in the present regime for Nhu's personal political power to long outlive his brother. There might be a struggle with no little violence, but enough of the army would almost certainly move to take charge of the situation, either rallying behind the constitutional successor to install Vice President Tho or backing another non-Communist civil leader or a military junta.

17. A non-Communist successor regime might prove no more effective than Diem in fighting the Viet Cong; indeed at least initially it might well prove considerably less effective, and the counterinsurgency effort would probably be temporarily disrupted. However, there is a reasonably large pool of under-utilized but experienced and trained manpower not only within the military and civilian sectors of the present government but also, to some extent, outside. These elements, given continued support from the US, could provide reasonably effective leadership for the government and the war effort.

[Document 126]

August 24, 1963

STATE 243

STATE TO LODGE

It is now clear that whether military proposed martial law or whether Nhu tricked them into it, Nhu took advantage of its imposition to smash pagodas with police and Tung's Special Forces loyal to him, thus placing onus on military in eyes of world and Vietnamese people. Also clear that Nhu has maneuvered himself into commanding position.

US Government cannot tolerate situation in which power lies in Nhu's hands. Diem must be given chance to rid himself of Nhu and his coterie and replace them with best military and political personalities available.

If, in spite of all of your efforts, Diem remains obdurate and refuses, then we must face the possibility that Diem himself cannot be preserved.

We now believe immediate action must be taken to prevent Nhu from consolidating his position further. Therefore, unless you in consultation with Harkins perceive overriding objections you are authorized to proceed along following lines:

(1) First, we must press on appropriate levels of GVN following line:

 (a) USG cannot accept actions against Buddhists taken by Nhu and his collaborators under cover martial law.
 (b) Prompt dramatic actions redress situation must be taken, including repeal of decree 10, release of arrested monks, nuns, etc.

(2) We must at same time also tell key military leaders that US would find it impossible to continue support GVN militarily and economically unless above steps are taken immediately which we recognize requires removal of Nhus from the scene. We wish give Diem reasonable opportunity to remove Nhus, but if he remains obdurate, then we are prepared to accept the obvious implication that we can no longer support Diem. You may also tell appropriate military commanders we will give them direct support in any interim period of breakdown central government mechanism.

(3) We recognize the necessity of removing taint on military for pagoda raids and placing blame squarely on Nhu. You are authorized to have such statements made in Saigon as you consider desirable to achieve this objective. We are prepared to take same line here and to have Voice of America make statement along lines contained in next numbered telegram whenever you give the word, preferably as soon as possible.

Concurrently, with above, Ambassador and country team should urgently examine all possible alternative leadership and make detailed plans as to how we might bring about Diem's replacement if this should become necessary.

Assume you will consult with General Harkins re any precautions necessary protect American personnel during crisis period.

You will understand that we cannot from Washington give you detailed instructions as to how this operation should proceed, but you will also know we will back you to the hilt on actions you take to achieve our objectives.

Needless to say we have held knowledge of this telegram to minimum essential people and assume you will take similar precautions to prevent premature leaks.

[Document 127]

Reprinted from New York *Times*

Lodge's Reply to Washington

Cablegram from Ambassador Lodge to Secretary of State Dean Rusk and Assistant Secretary of State Roger Hilsman, Aug. 25, 1963.

Believe that chances of Diem's meeting our demands are virtually nil. At same time, by making them we give Nhu chance to forestall or block action by military. Risk, we believe, is not worth taking, with Nhu in control combat forces Saigon.

Therefore, propose we go straight to Generals with our demands, without informing Diem. Would tell them we prepared have Diem without Nhus but it is in effect up to them whether to keep him. Would also insist generals take steps to release Buddhist leaders and carry out June 16 agreement.

Request immediate modification instructions. However, do not propose move until we are satisfied with E and E plans. Harkins concurs. I present credentials President Diem tomorrow 11 A.M.

[Document 128]

Reprinted from New York *Times*

C.I.A. Aide's Cable to Chief on Contact with Saigon Generals

Cablegram from John Richardson, the Central Intelligence Agency's Saigon station chief, to John A. McCone, Director of Central Intelligence, Aug. 26, 1963.

During meeting with Harkins, Truehart, Mecklin and COS on morning 26 Aug Lodge made decision that American official hand should not show. Consequently, Harkins will take no initiative with VNese generals. (Conein to convey points below to Gen. Khiem; Spera to Khanh; if Khiem agrees on Conein talking to Don, he will).

(A) Solicitation of further elaboration of action aspects of present thinking and planning. What should be done?

(B) We in agreement Nhus must go.

(C) Question of retaining Diem or not up to them.

(D) Bonzes and other arrestees must be released immediately and five-point agreement of 16 June fully carried out.

(E) We will provide direct support during any interim period of breakdown central gov mechanism.

(F) We cannot be of any help during initial action of assuming power of state. Entirely their own action, win or lose. Don't expect be bailed out.

(G) If Nhus do not go and if Buddhists situation is not redressed as indicated, we would find it impossible continue military and economic support.

(H) It hoped bloodshed can be avoided or reduced to absolute minimum.

(I) It hoped that during process and after, developments conducted in such manner as to retain and increase the necessary relations between VNese and Americans which will allow for progress of country and successful prosecution of the war.

[Document 129]

Reprinted from New York *Times*

C.I.A. Station Chief's Cable on Coup Prospects in Saigon

Cablegram from Mr. Richardson to Mr. McCone, Aug. 28, 1963.

Situation here has reached point of no return. Saigon is armed camp. Current indications are that Ngo family have dug in for last ditch battle. It is our considered estimate that General officers cannot retreat now. Conein's meeting with Gen. Khiem (Saigon 0346) reveals that overwhelming majority of general officers, excepting Dinh and Cao, are united, have conducted prior planning, realize that they must proceed quickly, and understand that they have no alternative but to go forward. Unless the generals are neutralized before being able to launch their operation, we believe they will act and that they have good chance to win. If General Dinh primarily and Tung secondly cannot be neutralized at outset, there may be widespread fighting in Saigon and serious loss of life.

We recognize the crucial stakes are involved and have no doubt that the generals do also. Situation has changed drastically since 21 August. If the Ngo family wins now, they and Vietnam will stagger on to final defeat at the hands of their own people and the VC. Should a generals' revolt occur and be put down, GVN will sharply reduce American presence in SVN. Even if they did not do so, it seems clear that American public opinion and Congress, as well as world opinion, would force withdrawal or reduction of American support for VN under the Ngo administration.

Bloodshed can be avoided if the Ngo family would step down before the coming armed action. . . . It is obviously preferable that the generals conduct this effort without apparent American assistance. Otherwise, for a long time in the future, they will be vulnerable to charges of being American puppets, which they are not in any sense. Nevertheless, we all understand that the effort must succeed and that whatever needs to be done on our part must be done. If this attempt by the generals does not take place or if it fails, we believe it no exaggeration to say that VN runs serious risk of being lost over the course of time.

[Document 130]

August 29, 1963

STATE 272

STATE TO LODGE AND HARKINS

1. Highest level meeting noon today reviewed your 375 and reaffirmed basic course. Specific decisions follow:

2. In response to your recommendation, General Harkins is hereby authorized

to repeat to such Generals as you indicate the messages previously transmitted by CAS officers. He should stress that the USG supports the movement to eliminate the Nhus from the government, but that before arriving at specific understandings with the Generals, General Harkins must know who are involved, resources available to them and overall plan for coup. The USG will support a coup which has good chance of succeeding but plans no direct involvement of U.S. armed forces. Harkins should state that he is prepared to establish liaison with the coup planners and to review plans, but will not engage directly in joint coup planning.

3. Question of last approach to Diem remains undecided and separate personal message from Secretary to you develops our concern and asks your comment.

4. On movement of U.S. forces, we do not expect to make any announcement or leak at present and believe that any later decision to publicize such movements should be closely connected to developing events on your side. We cannot of course prevent unauthorized disclosures or speculation, but we will in any event knock down any reports of evacuation.

5. You are hereby authorized to announce suspension of aid through Diem government at a time and under conditions of your choice. In deciding upon the use of this authority, you should consider importance of timing and managing announcement so as to minimize appearance of collusion with Generals and also to minimize danger of unpredictable and disruptive reaction by existing government. We also assume that you will not in fact use this authority unless you think it essential, and we see it as possible that Harkins' approach and increasing process of cooperation may provide assurance Generals desire. Our own view is that it will be best to hold this authority for use in close conjunction with coup, and not for present encouragement of Generals, but decision is yours.

[Document 131]

STATE 279

STATE TO LODGE   29 Aug 1963

Deeply appreciate your 375 which was a most helpful clarification. We fully understand enormous stakes at issue and the heavy responsibilities which you and Harkins will be carrying in the days ahead and we want to do everything possible from our end to help.

Purpose of this message is to explore further question of possible attempt to separate Diem and the Nhus. In your telegram you appear to treat Diem and the Nhus as a single package whereas we had indicated earlier to the Generals that if the Nhus were removed the question of retaining Diem would be up to them. My own personal assessment is (and this is not an instruction) that the Nhus are by all odds the greater part of the problem in Vietnam, internally, internationally and for American public opinion. Perhaps it is inconceivable that the Nhus could be removed without taking Diem with them or without Diem's abandoning his post. In any event, I would appreciate your comment on whether any distinction can or should be drawn as between Diem and Counsellor and Madame Nhu.

The only point on which you and General Harkins have different views is whether an attempt should be made with Diem to eliminate the Nhus and presumably take other steps to consolidate the country behind a winning effort against the Viet Cong. My own hunch, based in part on the report of Kattenburg's conversations with Diem is that such an approach could not succeed if it were cast purely in terms of persuasion. Unless such a talk included a real sanction such as a threatened withdrawal of our support, it is unlikely that it would be taken completely seriously by a man who may feel that we are inescapably committed to an anti-Communist Vietnam. But if a sanction were used in such a conversation, there would be a high risk that this would be taken by Diem as a sign that action against him and the Nhus was imminent and he might as a minimum move against the Generals or even take some quite fantastic action such as calling on North Vietnam for assistance in expelling the Americans.

It occurs to me, therefore, that if such an approach were to be made it might properly await the time when others were ready to move immediately to constitute a new government. If this be so, the question then arises as to whether an approach to insist upon the expulsion of the Nhus should come from Americans rather than from the Generals themselves. This might be the means by which the Generals could indicate that they were prepared to distinguish between Diem and the Nhus. In any event, were the Generals to take this action it would tend to protect succeeding Vietnam administrations from the charge of being wholly American puppets subjected to whatever anti-American sentiment is inherent in so complex a situation.

I would be glad to have your further thoughts on these points as well as your views on whether further talks with Diem are contemplated to continue your opening discussions with him. You will have received formal instructions on other matters through other messages. Good luck.

[Document 132]

Reprinted from New York *Times*

Lodge Cable to Secretary Rusk on U.S. Policy Toward a Coup

Cablegram from Ambassador Lodge to Secretary Rusk, Aug. 29, 1963.

We are launched on a course from which there is no respectable turning back: the overthrow of the Diem government. There is no turning back in part because U.S. prestige is already publicly committed to this end in large measure and will become more so as the facts leak out. In a more fundamental sense, there is no turning back because there is no possibility, in my view, that the war can be won under a Diem administration, still less that Diem or any member of the family can govern the country in a way to gain the support of the people who count, i.e., the educated class in and out of government service, civil and military—not to mention the American people. In the last few months (and especially days) they have in fact positively alienated these people to an incalculable degree. So that I am personally in full agreement with the policy which I was instructed to carry out by last Sunday's telegram.

2. The chance of bringing off a Generals' coup depends on them to some extent; but it depends at least as much on us.

3. We should proceed to make all-out effort to get Generals to move promptly. To do so we should have authority to do following:

(a) That Gen. Harkins repeat to Generals personally message previously transmitted by CAS officers. This should establish their authenticity. Gen. Harkins should have order on this.

(b) If nevertheless Generals insist on public statement that all U.S. aid to VN through Diem regime has been stopped, we would agree, on express understanding that Generals will have started at same time. (We would seek persuade Generals that it would be better to hold this card for use in event of stalemate. We hope it will not be necessary to do this at all.)

(c) VNese Generals doubt that we have the will power, courage, and determination to see this thing through. They are haunted by the idea that we will run out on them even though we have told them pursuant to instructions, that the game had started.

5. We must press on for many reasons. Some of these are:

(a) Explosiveness of the present situation which may well lead to riots and violence if issue of discontent with regime is not met. Out of this could come a pro-Communist or at best a neutralist set of politicians.

(b) The fact that war cannot be won with the present regime.

(c) Our own reputation for steadfastness and our unwillingness to stultify ourselves.

(d) If proposed action is suspended, I believe a body blow will be dealt to respect for us by VNese Generals. Also, all those who expect U.S. to straighten out this situation will feel let down. Our help to the regime in past years inescapably gives a responsibility which we cannot avoid.

6. I realize that this course involves a very substantial risk of losing VN. It also involves some additional risk to American lives. I would never propose it if I felt there was a reasonable chance of holding VN with Diem.

[Point 7 unavailable.]

8. . . . Gen. Harkins thinks that I should ask Diem to get rid of the Nhus before starting the Generals' action. But I believe that such a step has no chance of getting the desired result and would have the very serious effect of being regarded by the Generals as a sign of American indecision and delay. I believe this is a risk which we should not run. The Generals distrust us too much already. Another point is that Diem would certainly ask for time to consider such a far-reaching request. This would give the ball to Nhu.

9. With the exception of par. 8 above Gen. Harkins concurs in this telegram.

[Document 133]

Reprinted from New York *Times*

Lodge's Response to Rusk on Diem's Closeness to Brother

Cablegram from Ambassador Lodge to Secretary Rusk, Aug. 30, 1963.

I agree that getting the Nhus out is the prime objective and that they are "the greater part . . ."

This surely cannot be done by working through Diem. In fact Diem will oppose it. He wishes he had more Nhus, not less.

The best chance of doing it is by the Generals taking over the government lock, stock and barrel.

After this has been done, it can then be decided whether to put Diem back in again or go on without him. I am rather inclined to put him back, but I would not favor putting heavy pressure on the Generals if they don't want him. My greatest single difficulty in carrying out the instructions of last Sunday is inertia. The days come and go and nothing happens. It is, of course, natural for the Generals to want assurances and the U.S. Government has certainly been prompt in its reactions. But here it is Friday and, while in one way much has been done, there is not yet enough to show for the hours which we have all put in.

If I call on Diem to demand the removal of the Nhus, he will surely not agree. But before turning me down, he will pretend to consider it and involve us in prolonged delays. This will make the Generals suspicious of us and add to the inertia.

Such a call by me would look to the Nhus like an ultimatum and would result in their taking steps to thwart any operation dealing with them.

I agree with you that if a sanction were used, it could provoke an even more fantastic reaction. In fact I greatly dislike the idea of cutting off aid in connection with the Generals' operation and while I thank you for giving me the authority to make an announcement, I hope I will never have to use it.

It is possible, as you suggested . . . for the Generals when, as and if their operation gets rolling to demand the removal of the Nhus before bringing their operation to fruition. But I am afraid they will get talked out of their operation which will then disintegrate, still leaving the Nhus in office.

If the Generals' operation does get rolling, I would not want to stop it until they were in full control. They could then get rid of the Nhus and decide whether they wanted to keep Diem.

It is better for them and for us for them to throw out the Nhus than for us to get involved in it.

I am sure that the best way to handle this matter is by a truly VNese movement even if it puts me rather in the position of pushing a piece of spaghetti.

I am contemplating no further talks with Diem at this time.

[Document 134]

Reprinted from New York *Times*

Cable by U.S. General in Saigon to Taylor on End of August Plot

Cablegram from Gen. Paul D. Harkins, United States commander in Saigon, to Gen. Maxwell D. Taylor, Chairman of the Joint Chiefs of Staff, Aug. 31, 1963.

(saw Khiem: he stated Big Minh had stopped planning at this time, and was working on other methods; others had called off planning also, himself and Khanh, following Minh. He knew Thao was making plans—but that few of military trusted him because of his VC background—and that he might still be working for the VC. The Generals were not ready as they did not have enough forces under their control compared to those under President and now in Saigon. He indicated they, the Generals, did not want to start anything they could not successfully finish.

. . . At a meeting yesterday, Mr. Nhu said he now went along with everything the U.S. wants to do, and even had the backing of Pres. Kennedy. I said this was news to me. Khiem said he wondered if Nhu was again trying to flush out the generals. He intimated the generals do not have too much trust in Nhu and that he's such a friend of Mr. Richardson the generals wonder if Mr. Nhu and Mme. Nhu were on the CIA payroll. . . .

. . . I asked if someone couldn't confront the Nhus with the fact that their absence from the scene was the key to the overall solution. He replied that for anyone to do that would be self-immolation—he also went on to say he doubted if the Nhus and Diem could be split.

. . . So we see we have an "organisation de confusion" with everyone suspicious of everyone else and none desiring to take any positive action as of right now. You can't hurry the East. . . .

[Document 135]

OFFICE OF THE SPECIAL ASSISTANT FOR
COUNTERINSURGENCY AND SPECIAL ACTIVITIES

31 August 1963

MEMORANDUM FOR THE RECORD

Subject: Meeting at the State Department, 1100, 31 August 1963; Subject: Vietnam

Present:

The Vice President	General Carter
Secretary Rusk	Mr. Helms
Secretary McNamara	Mr. Colby
Mr. Gilpatric	Ambassador Nolting
Mr. Bundy	Mr. Hilsman
General Taylor	Mr. Kattenburg
Mr. Murrow	General Krulak

1. Secretary Rusk stated that, in his judgment, we were back to where we were about Wednesday of last week, and this causes him to go back to the original problem and ask what in the situation led us to think well of a coup. Ruling out hatred of the Nhus, he said, there would appear to be three things:

  a. The things that the Nhus had done or supported, which tended to upset the GVN internally.
  b. The things that they had done which had an adverse external effect.
  c. The great pressures of U.S. public opinion.

2. Mr. Rusk then asked if we should not pick up Ambassador Lodge's suggestion in his message of today (Saigon 391) and determine what steps are required to re-gird solidarity in South Vietnam—such as improvement in conditions concerning students and Buddhists and the possible departure of Madame Nhu. He said that we should determine what additional measures are needed to improve the international situation—such as problems affecting Cambodia— and to *improve the Vietnamese position wherein U.S. public opinion is concerned.* He then said that he is reluctant to start off by saying now that Nhu has to go; that it is unrealistic.

3. Mr. McNamara stated that he favored the above proposals of the Secretary of State, with one additional step—that is to establish quickly and firmly our line of communication between Lodge, Harkins and the GVN. He pointed out that at the moment our channels of communication are essentially broken and that they should be reinstituted at all costs.

4. Mr. Rusk added that we must do our best not to permit Diem to decapitate his military command in light of its obviously adverse effect on the prosecution of the war. At this point he asked if anyone present had any doubt in his mind but that the coup was off.

5. Mr. Kattenburg said that he had some remaining doubt; that we have not yet sent the generals a strong enough message; that the BOA statement regard-

ing the withdrawal of aid was most important, but that we repudiated it too soon. He stated further that the group should take note of the fact that General Harkins did not carry out his instructions with respect to communication with the generals. Mr. Rusk interrupted Kattenburg to state that, to the contrary, he believed Harkins' conduct was exactly correct in light of the initial response which he received from General Kheim (they were referring to Harkins' report in MACV 1583).

6. Mr. Hilsman commented that, in his view, the generals are not now going to move unless they are pressed by a revolt from below. In this connection Ambassador Nolting warned that in the uncoordinated Vietnamese structure anything can happen, and that while an organized successful coup is out, there might be small flurries by irresponsible dissidents at any time.

7. Mr. Hilsman undertook to present four basic factors which bear directly on the problem confronting the U.S. now. They are, in his view:

a. The mood of the people, particularly the middle level officers, non-commissioned officers and middle level bureaucrats, who are most restive. Mr. McNamara interrupted to state that he had seen no evidence of this and General Taylor commented that he had seen none either, but would like to see such evidence as Hilsman could produce. Mr. Kattenburg commented that the middle level officers and bureaucrats are uniformly critical of the government, to which Mr. McNamara commented that if this is indeed the fact we should know about it.

b. The second basic factor, as outlined by Hilsman, was what effect will be felt on our programs elsewhere in Asia if we acquiesce to a strong Nhu-dominated government. In this connection, he reported that there is a Korean study now underway on just how much repression the United States will tolerate before pulling out her aid. Mr. McNamara stated that he had not seen this study and would be anxious to have it.

c. The third basic factor is Mr. Nhu, his personality and his policy. Hilsman recalled that Nhu has once already launched an effort aimed at withdrawal of our province advisors and stated that he is sure he is in conversation with the French. He gave, as supporting evidence, the content of an intercepted message, which Mr. Bundy asked to see. Ambassador Nolting expressed the opinion that Nhu will not make a deal with Ho Chi Minh on Ho's terms.

d. The fourth point is the matter of U.S. and world opinion, Hilsman stated that this problem was moving to a political and diplomatic plane. Part of the problem, he said, is the press, which concludes incorrectly that we have the ability to change the things in Vietnam of which they are critical. To this Mr. Murrow added that this problem of press condemnation is now worldwide.

8. Mr. Kattenburg stated that as recently as last Thursday it was the belief of Ambassador Lodge that, if we undertake to live with this repressive regime, with its bayonets at every street corner and its transparent negotiations with puppet bonzes, we are going to be thrown out of the country in six months. He stated that at this juncture it would be better for us to make the decision to get out honorably. He went on to say that, having been acquainted with Diem for ten years, he was deeply disappointed in him, saying that he will not separate from his brother. It was Kattenburg's view that Diem will get very little support from the military and, as time goes on, he will get less and less support and the country will go steadily down hill.

9. General Taylor asked what Kattenburg meant when he said that we would be forced out of Vietnam within six months. Kattenburg replied that in from six months to a year, as the people see we are losing the war, they will gradually go to the other side and we will be obliged to leave. Ambassador Nolting expressed general disagreement with Mr. Kattenburg. He said that the unfavorable activity which motivated Kattenburg's remarks was confined to the city and, while city support of Diem is doubtless less now, it is not greatly so. He said that it is improper to overlook the fact that we have done a tremendous job toward winning the Vietnam war, working with this same imperfect, annoying government.

10. Mr. Kattenburg added that there is one new factor—the population, which was in high hopes of expelling the Nhus after the VOA announcement regarding cessation of aid; now, under the heel of Nhu's military repression, they would quickly lose heart.

11. Secretary Rusk commented that Kattenburg's recital was largely speculative; that it would be far better for us to start on the firm basis of two things —that we will not pull out of Vietnam until the war is won, and that we will not run a coup. Mr. McNamara expressed agreement with this view.

12. Mr. Rusk then said that we should present questions to Lodge which fall within these parameters. He added that he believes we have good proof that we have been winning the war, particularly the contrast between the first six months of 1962 and the first six months of 1963. He then asked the Vice President if he had any contribution to make.

13. The Vice President stated that he agreed with Secretary Rusk's conclusions completely; that he had great reservations himself with respect to a coup, particularly so because he had never really seen a genuine alternative to Diem. He stated that from both a practical and a political viewpoint, it would be a disaster to pull out; that we should stop playing cops and robbers and get back to talking straight to the GVN, and that we should once again go about winning the war. He stated that after our communications with them are genuinely reestablished, it may be necessary for someone to talk rough to them—perhaps General Taylor. He said further that he had been greatly impressed with Ambassador Nolting's views and agreed with Mr. McNamara's conclusions.

14. General Taylor raised the question of whether we should change the disposition of the forces which had been set in motion as a result of the crisis. It was agreed that there should be no change in the existing disposition for the time being.

V. H. Krulak
Major General, USMC

[Document 136]

CAP 63516

WHITE HOUSE TO LODGE   17 September 1963

1. Highest level meeting today has approved broad outline of an action proposals program designed to obtain from GVN, if possible, reforms and changes in personnel necessary to maintain support of Vietnamese and US opinion in war against Viet Cong. This cable reports this program and our thinking for your comment before a final decision. Your comment requested soonest.

2. We see no good opportunity for action to remove present government in immediate future; therefore, as your most recent messages suggest, we must for the present apply such pressures as are available to secure whatever modest improvements on the scene may be possible. We think it likely that such improvements can make a difference, at least in the short run. Such a course, moreover, is consistent with more drastic effort as and when means become available, and we will be in touch on other channels on this problem.

3. We share view in your 523 that best available reinforcement to your bargaining position in this interim period is clear evidence that all U.S. assistance is granted only on your say-so. Separate telegram discusses details of this program, but in this message we specifically authorize you to apply any controls you think helpful for this purpose. You are authorized to delay any delivery of supplies or transfer of funds by any agency until you are satisfied that delivery is in U.S. interest, bearing in mind that it is not our current policy to cut off aid, entirely. In other words, we share your view that it will be helpful for GVN to understand that your personal approval is a necessary part of all U.S. assistance. We think it may be particularly desirable for you to use this authority in limiting or rerouting any and all forms of assistance and support which now go to or through Nhu or individuals like Tung who are associated with him. This authorization specifically includes aid actions currently held in abeyance and you are authorized to set those in train or hold them up further in your discretion. We leave entirely in your hands decisions on the degree of privacy or publicity you wish to give to this process.

4. Subject to your comment and amendment our own list of possible helpful action by government runs as follows in approximate order of importance:

   A. Clear the air—Diem should get everyone back to work and get them to focus on winning the war. He should be broadminded and compassionate in his attitude toward those who have, for understandable reasons, found it difficult under recent circumstances fully to support him. A real spirit of reconciliation could work wonders on the people he leads; a punitive, harsh or autocratic attitude could only lead to further resistance.

   B. Buddhists and students—Let them out and leave them unmolested. This more than anything else would demonstrate the return of a better day and the refocusing on the main job at hand, the war.

   C. Press: The press should be allowed full latitude of expression. Diem will be criticized, but leniency and cooperation with the domestic and foreign press at this time would bring praise for his leadership in due course. While tendentious reporting is irritating, suppression of news leads to much more serious trouble.

   D. Secret and combat police—Confine its role to operations against the VC and abandon operations against non-Communist opposition groups thereby indicating clearly that a period of reconciliation and political stability has returned.

   E. Cabinet changes to inject new untainted blood, remove targets of popular discontent.

   F. Elections—These should be held, should be free, and should be widely observed.

   G. Assembly—Assembly should be convoked soon after the elections. The government should submit its policies to it and should receive its confidence. An assembly resolution would be most useful for external image purposes.

H. Party—Can Lao party should not be covert or semi-covert but a broad association of supporters engaged in a common, winning cause. This could perhaps be best accomplished by [words missing] starting afresh.

I. Repeal or suitable amendment Decree 10.

J. Rehabilitation by ARVN of pagodas.

K. Establishment of Ministry of Religious Affairs.

L. Liberation of passport issuances and currency restrictions enabling all to leave who wish to.

M. Acceptance of Buddhist Inquiry Mission from World Federation to report true facts of situation to world.

5. You may wish to add or subtract from the above list, but need to set psychological tone and image is paramount. Diem has taken positive actions in past of greater or less scope than those listed, but they have had little practical political effect since they were carried out in such a way as to make them hollow or, even if real, unbelievable (e.g., martial law already nominally lifted, Assembly elections scheduled, and puppet bonzes established).

6. Specific "reforms" are apt to have little impact without dramatic, symbolic move which convinces Vietnamese that reforms are real. As practical matter we share your view that this can best be achieved by some visible reduction in influence of Nhus, who are symbol to disaffected of all that they dislike in GVN. This we think would require Nhus departure from Saigon and preferably Vietnam at least for extended vacation. We recognize the strong possibility that these and other pressures may not produce this result, but we are convinced that it is necessary to try.

7. In Washington, in this phase, we would plan to maintain a posture of disapproval of recent GVN actions, but we would not expect to make public our specific requests of Diem. Your comment on public aspects of this phase is particularly needed.

8. We note your reluctance to continue dialogue with Diem until you have more to say, but we continue to believe that discussions with him are at a minimum an important source of intelligence and may conceivably be a means of exerting some persuasive effect even in his present state of mind. If you believe that full control of U.S. assistance provides you with means of resuming dialogue, we hope you will do so. We ourselves can see much virtue in effort to reason even with an unreasonable man when he is on a collision course. We repeat, however, that this is a matter for your judgment.

9. Meanwhile, there is increasing concern here with strictly military aspects of the problem, both in terms of actual progress of operations and of need to make effective case with Congress for continued prosecution of the effort. To meet these needs, President has decided to send Secretary of Defense and General Taylor to Vietnam, arriving early next week. It will be emphasized here that it is a military mission and that all political decisions are being handled through you as President's Senior Representative.

10. We repeat that political program outlined above awaits your comment before final decision. President particularly emphasizes that it is fully open to your criticism and amendment. It is obviously an interim plan and further decisions may become necessary very soon.

[Document 137]

STATE 431

FROM THE PRESIDENT TO LODGE   18 September 1963

I appreciate your prompt comment and I quite understand the problem you see in visit of McNamara and Taylor. At the same time my need for this visit is very great indeed, and I believe we can work out an arrangement which takes care of your basic concerns. Will you let me have your comment on the following as soon as possible:

1. We can make it clear here, and McNamara and Taylor can make it clear in Saigon to the GVN, that this visit is not designed to bring comfort to Diem. My own thought is that in any visit McNamara makes to Diem he will want to speak some home truths on the military consequences of the current difficulties, and also to make it clear that the United States Government is not open to oriental divisive tactics.

2. We can readily set up this visit as one which you and I have decided on together, or even one which is sent in response to your own concern about winning the war in the current situation. For example, we could announce that the purpose of the mission is to consider with you the practical ways and means of carrying out my announced policy that we will support activities which will further the war effort in South Vietnam and avoid supporting activities which do not. The whole cast of the visit will be that of military consultation with you on the execution of the policy which you and I have determined.

3. As our last message said, my own central concern in sending this mission is to make sure that my senior military advisors are equipped with a solid on-the-spot understanding of the situation, as a basis both for their participation in our councils here, and for the Administrations accounting to the Congress on this critically important contest with the Communists. Having grown up in an Ambassador's house, I am well trained in the importance of protecting the effectiveness of the man on-the-spot, and I want to handle this particular visit in a way which contributes to and does not detract from your own responsibilities. But in the tough weeks which I see ahead, I just do not see any substitute for the ammunition I will get from an on-the-spot and authoritative military appraisal.

4. I do not think I can delay announcement of the McNamara mission beyond Saturday, and I will be grateful for a further prompt comment on this message so that we can be firmly together on the best possible handling of the announcement and of the mission itself.

[Document 138]

SAIGON 544

    (Ref White House Msg CAP 63516 atchd at Wash Guidance TAB)

FROM LODGE TO STATE   FOR PRESIDENT ONLY   19 Sep 1963

1. Agree that no good opportunity for action to remove present government in immediate future is apparent and that we should, therefore, do whatever we can as an interim measure pending such an evantuality.

2. Virtually all the topics under paragraph 4, letters A to M, have been taken up with Diem and Nhu at one time or another, most of them by me personally. They think that most of them would either involve destroying the political structure on which they rest or loss of face or both. We, therefore, could *not* realistically hope for more than lip service. Frankly, I see no opportunity at all for substantive changes. Detailed comments on items A to M are contained in separate telegram.

3. There are signs that Diem-Nhu are somewhat bothered by my silence. According to one well placed source, they are guessing and off-balance and "desperately anxious" to know what U.S. posture is to be. They may be preparing some kind of a public relations package, possibly to be opened after the elections. I believe that for me to press Diem on things which are *not* in the cards and to repeat what we have said several times already would be a little shrill and would make us look weak, particularly in view of my talk with Nhu last night at a dinner where I had a golden opportunity to make the main points of your CAP 63516 as reported in 541.

4. Also, I doubt that a public relations package will meet needs of situation which seems particularly grave to me, notably in the light of General Big Minh's opinion expressed very privately yesterday that the Viet Cong are steadily gaining in strength; have more of the population on their side than has the GVN; that arrests are continuing and that the prisons are full; that more and more students are going over to the Viet Cong; that there is great graft and corruption in the Vietnamese administration of our aid; and that the "Heart of the Army is *not* in the war." All this by Vietnamese No. 1 General is now echoed by Secretary of Defense Thuan (See my 542), who wants to leave the country.

5. As regards your paragraph 3 on withholding of aid, I still hope that I may be informed of methods, as requested in my 478, September 11, which will enable us to apply sanctions in a way which will really affect Diem and Nhu without precipitating an economic collapse and without impeding the war effort. We are studying this here and have not yet found a solution. If a way to do this were to be found, it would be one of the greatest discoveries since the enactment of the Marshall Plan in 1947 because, so far as I know, the U.S. had never yet been able to control any of the very unsatisfactory governments through which we have had to work in our many very successful attempts to make these countries strong enough to stand alone.

6. I also believe that whatever sanctions we may discover should be directly tied to a promising coup d'etat and should *not* be applied without such a coup being in prospect. In this connection, I believe that we should pursue contact with Big Minh and urge him along if he looks like acting. I particularly think that the idea of supporting a Vietnamese Army independent of the government should be energetically studied.

7. I will, of course, give instructions that programs which one can be effectively held up should be held up and not released without my approval provided that this can be done without serious harmful effect to the people and to the war effort. Technical assistance and (omission) support to communications support programs may be one way. This would be a fly-speck in the present situation and would have *no* immediate effect, but I hope that U.S. (omission) may get Vietnamese officials into the habit of asking me to release items which are held up and that, over a long period of time, it might create opportunities for us to get little things done.

8. But it is not even within the realm of possibility that such a technique

could lead them to do anything which causes loss of face or weakening of their political organization. In fact, to threaten them with suppression of aid might well defeat our purposes and might make a bad situation very much worse.

9. There should in any event be no publicity whatever about this procedure. If it is possible (omission) a program, I intend to (omission).

10. As regards your paragraph 6 and "dramatic symbolic moves," I really do not think they could understand this even if Thao wanted to, although I have talked about it to Diem, and to Nhu last night (See my 541). They have scant comprehension of what it is to appeal to public opinion as they have really no interest in any other opinion than their own. I have repeatedly brought up the question of Nhu's departure and have stressed that if he would just stay away until after Christmas, it might help get the Appropriation Bill through. This seems like a small thing to us but to them it seems tremendous as they are quite sure that the Army would take over if he even stepped out of the country.

11. Your paragraph 8. I have, of course, no objection to seeing Diem at any time that it would be helpful. But I would rather let him sweat for awhile and not go to see him unless I have something really new to bring up. I would much prefer to wait until I find some part of the AID program to hold up in which he is interested and then have him ask me to come and see him. For example, last night's dinner which I suspect Nhu of stimulating is infinitely better than for me to take the initiative for an appointment and to call at the office. Perhaps my silence had something to do with it.

[Document 139]

September 21, 1963

MEMORANDUM FOR THE SECRETARY OF DEFENSE

It may be useful to put on paper our understanding of the purpose of your visit to South Vietnam. I am asking you to go because of my desire to have the best possible on-the-spot appraisal of the military and paramilitary effort to defeat the Viet Cong. The program developed after General Taylor's mission and carried forward under your close supervision has brought heartening results, at least until recently. The events in South Vietnam since May have now raised serious questions both about the present prospects for success against the Viet Cong and still more about the future effectiveness of this effort unless there can be important political improvement in the country. It is in this context that I now need your appraisal of the situation. If the prognosis in your judgment is not hopeful, I would like your views on what action must be taken by the South Vietnamese Government and what steps our Government should take to lead the Vietnamese to that action.

Ambassador Lodge has joined heartily in supporting this mission and I will rely on you both for the closest exchange of views. It is obvious that the overall political situation and the military and paramilitary effort are closely interconnected in all sorts of ways, and in executing your responsibility for appraisal of the military and paramilitary problem I expect that you will consult fully with Ambassador Lodge on related political and social questions. I will also expect you to examine with Ambassador Lodge ways and means of fashioning all forms of our assistance to South Vietnam so that it will support our foreign policy objectives more precisely.

I am providing you separately with a letter from me to President Diem which

Ambassador Lodge and you should discuss and which the Ambassador should deliver on the occasion of a call on President Diem if after discussion and reference to me I conclude that such a letter is desirable.

In my judgment the question of the progress of the contest in South Vietnam is of the first importance and in executing this mission you should take as much time as is necessary for a thorough examination both in Saigon and in the field.

John F. Kennedy

[Document 140]

STATE 458, 22 September 1963

EYES ONLY FOR AMBASSADOR LODGE FROM BALL

Understand desire for guidance expressed your 577. Pending further review of situation by President which will follow your consultation with McNamara and Taylor we wish to give you following interim guidance:

1. The United States intends to continue its efforts to assist the Vietnamese people in their struggle against the Viet Cong.
2. Recent events have put in question the possibility of success in these efforts unless there can be important improvements in the government of South Vietnam.
3. It is the policy of the United States to bring about such improvements. Further specific guidance on your meeting with Diem being developed here and will be subject further consultation with you. In any event the President believes object of this meeting should be to increase your authority and leverage with Diem government. In meantime CAP 63516 still represents Washington's current thinking on specifics. A possible Presidential letter to Diem is in preparation and will be forwarded for your comments before a decision on delivery.

[Document 141]

Memorandum of Conversation   September 29, 1963

Diem, Thuan, Lodge, McNamara, Taylor Parkins, Flott

. . . The war was going well, thanks in large measure to the strategic hamlets' program. Due to that program the VC enemy was having increasing difficulties in finding food and recruits, and was being steadily forced into increasingly difficult and unrewarding tactical situations. . . . He said that the British had given the Vietnamese government valuable advice at the outset of the program based on British experience in Malaya. He said that for a variety of local reasons, his government had not followed the British advice in all instances. He recalled that the British had advised him to consolidate and hold firmly one area before extending the strategic hamlet program to another. They had also advised him to hold the arterial coastal highway and consolidate the area between it and the seacoast before trying to secure areas further inland. He noted that the British had said that the strategic hamlets' program should be limited at first to the most populus and most productive areas of the country. He remarked in this connection he had made important departures from the

British plan but always for good and valid reasons. Outlining his thoughts on maps he explained that if he had disregarded even for a short time the under-populated and comparatively unproductive highlands, these areas would have become a base for VC attacks and for a VC drive to the sea to cut the highway and split the Republic. He acknowledged their strategic hamlets' program was overextended and that in some areas the VC could attack and overwhelm the poorly garrisoned strategic hamlets. He said that he realized some strategic hamlets were set up before the defense personnel were properly trained or armed, but that on balance both the risks and the losses were acceptable. For example, he said he could push ahead rapidly with the establishment of ten sub-standard strategic hamlets. The VC could attack these and overwhelm, say, two of them, but if two fell eight others would survive and grow stronger. And the area within which the VC could operate with impunity would shrink faster than otherwise would have been the case.

Another reason he gave for making departures from the British plan was that by so doing he could put isolated, strategic hamlets into key crossroads and junction points and force on the VC considerable detours in their supply routes. He said he had taken a calculated risk of opening highways for the areas through which they passed were absolutely secure. He said on the whole he was satisfied with this gamble and that thanks to his willingness to make departures from the plan and accept risks the war effort was further along. . . . He noted the elections held a few days before had been a great success. Many more people voted than ever before, thanks in part to the fact that there were about fifty percent more ballot boxes than at the time of the last election. Communists efforts to disrupt the voting had been a failure, partly as a result of several security operations in which all three security services participated. Again, the vast extension of the strategic hamlets' program made it easier and safer for people to vote than in past years, and he was touched at the interest that even the simplest peasants in exercising their suffrage and participating in the democratic process. In spite of the improve security situation at least two people were killed by VC because they voted, and he showed this loss deeply and personally. The discussion groups in the strategic hamlets had further increased people's interest in government and voting. (Ambassador's comment: This contrasts with well-founded observations. The truck loads of soldiers were carted around in trucks so that they could vote several times in one day.) . . . Diem noted that while the total number of VC had declined in the past year, the number of relatively large units, companies and battalions engaged had risen. He explained this was because of the success of the strategic hamlet's program. In the past the VC could get what they wanted from the village—food and recruits—with a mere handful of men. Now they were in-creasingly forced to mount a company scale attack to get into the village. Furthermore, since the whole rural environment had become much more actively hostile to the VC, they were forced to group in larger units to survive. These larger units, of course, offered better targets to the government forces. The fact that there was a greater use of large units by the VC is one more indi-cation of how well the war was going for the government. It was one more indi-cation that the VC found themselves more and more in a position of being like a foreign expeditionary corps rather than as a force that could exist and move in the population like a fish in the sea. . . .

Secretary McNamara said he was concerned over a number of things: that while the progress of the war was reasonably satisfactory, he was concerned over a number of things. There was the political unrest in Saigon and the evident inability of the government to provide itself with a broad political base. There was the disturbing probability that the war effort would then be damaged by the government's political deficiencies and the attendant loss of popularity. The recent wave of repressions have alarmed public opinion both in Vietnam and in the United States. . . . The Secretary warned Diem that public opinion in the U.S. seriously questioned the wisdom or necessity of the U.S. government's aiding a government that was so unpopular at home, and it seemed increasingly unlikely to forge the kind of national union or purpose that could bring the war to an early and victorious conclusion.

(Comment: Diem offered absolutely no assurances that he would take any steps in responses to the representations made to American visitors. In fact, he said nothing to indicate or acknowledge that he had received even friendly advice. His manner was one of at least outward serenity and of a man who had patiently explained a great deal and who hoped he had thus corrected a number of misapprehensions.)

[Document 142]

THE SECRETARY OF DEFENSE
WASHINGTON

2 October 1963

MEMORANDUM FOR THE PRESIDENT

Subject: Report of McNamara-Taylor Mission to South Vietnam

Your memorandum of 21 September 1963 directed that General Taylor and Secretary McNamara proceed to South Vietnam to appraise the military and para-military effort to defeat the Viet Cong and to consider, in consultation with Ambassador Lodge, related political and social questions. You further directed that, if the prognosis in our judgment was not hopeful, we should present our views of what action must be taken by the South Vietnam Government and what steps our Government should take to lead the Vietnamese to that action.

Accompanied by representatives of the State Department, CIA, and your Staff, we have conducted an intensive program of visits to key operational areas, supplemented by discussions with U.S. officials in all major U.S. Agencies as well as officials of the GVN and third countries.

We have also discussed our findings in detail with Ambassador Lodge, and with General Harkins and Admiral Felt.

The following report is concurred in by the Staff Members of the mission as individuals, subject to the exceptions noted.

I. CONCLUSIONS AND RECOMMENDATIONS

A. CONCLUSIONS

1. The military campaign has made great progress and continues to progress.

2. There are serious political tensions in Saigon (and perhaps elsewhere in South Vietnam) where the Diem-Nhu government is becoming increasingly unpopular.

3. There is no solid evidence of the possibility of a successful coup, although assassination of Diem or Nhu is always a possibility.

4. Although some, and perhaps an increasing number, of GVN military officers are becoming hostile to the government, they are more hostile to the Viet Cong than to the government and at least for the near future they will continue to perform their military duties.

5. Further repressive actions by Diem and Nhu could change the present favorable military trends. On the other hand, a return to more moderate methods of control and administration, unlikely though it may be, would substantially mitigate the political crisis.

6. It is not clear that pressures exerted by the U.S. will move Diem and Nhu toward moderation. Indeed, pressures may increase their obduracy. But unless such pressures are exerted, they are almost certain to continue past patterns of behavior.

B. RECOMMENDATIONS

We recommend that:

1. General Harkins review with Diem the military changes necessary to complete the military campaign in the Northern and Central areas (I, II, and III Corps) by the end of 1964, and in the Delta (IV Corps) by the end of 1965. This review would consider the need for such changes as:

a. A further shift of military emphasis and strength to the Delta (IV Corps).

b. An increase in the military tempo in all corps areas, so that all combat troops are in the Field an average of 20 days out of 30 and static missions are ended.

c. Emphasis on "clear and hold operations" instead of terrain sweeps which have little permanent value.

d. The expansion of personnel in combat units to full authorized strength.

e. The training and arming of hamlet militia at an accelerated rate, especially in the Delta.

f. A consolidation of the strategic hamlet program, especially in the Delta, and action to insure that future strategic hamlets are not built until they can be protected, and until civic action programs can be introduced.

2. A program be established to train Vietnamese so that essential functions now performed by U.S. military personnel can be carried out by Vietnamese by the end of 1965. It should be possible to withdraw the bulk of U.S. personnel by that time.

3. In accordance with the program to train progressively Vietnamese to take over military functions, the Defense Department should announce in the very near future presently prepared plans to withdraw 1000 U.S. military personnel by the end of 1963. This action should be explained in low key as an initial step in a long-term program to replace U.S. personnel with trained Vietnamese without impairment of the war effort.

4. The following actions be taken to impress upon Diem our disapproval of his political program.

a. Continue to withhold commitment of funds in the commodity import program, but avoid a formal announcement. The potential significance of the withholding of commitments for the 1964 military budget should be brought home to the top military officers in working level contacts between USOM and MACV and the Joint General Staff; up to now we have stated $95 million may be used by the Vietnamese as a planning level for the commodity import program for 1964. Henceforth we could make clear that this is uncertain both because of lack of final appropriation action by the Congress *and* because of executive policy.

b. Suspend approval of the pending AID loans for the Saigon-Cholon Waterworks and Saigon Electric Power Project. We should state clearly that we are doing so as a matter of policy.

c. Advice Diem that MAP and CIA support for designated units, now under Colonel Tung's control (mostly held in or near the Saigon area for political reasons) will be cut off unless these units are promptly assigned to the full authority of the Joint General Staff and transferred to the field.

d. Maintain the present purely "correct" relations with the top GVN, and specifically between the Ambassador and Diem. Contact between General Harkins and Diem and Defense Secretary Thuan on military matters should not, however, be suspended, as this remains an important channel of advice. USOM and USIA should also seek to maintain contacts where these are needed to push forward programs in support of the effort in the field, while taking care not to cut across the basic picture of U.S. disapproval and uncertainty of U.S. aid intentions. We should work with the Diem government but not support it.*

As we pursue these courses of action, the situation must be closely watched to see what steps Diem is taking to reduce repressive practices and to improve the effectiveness of the military effort. We should set no fixed criteria, but recognize that we would have to decide in 2-4 months whether to move to more drastic action or try to carry on with Diem even if he had not taken significant steps.

5. At this time, no initiative should be taken to encourage actively a change in government. Our policy should be to seek urgently to identify and build contacts with an alternative leadership if and when it appears.

6. The following statement be approved as current U.S. policy toward South Vietnam and constitute the substance of the government position to be presented both in Congressional testimony and in public statements.

a. The security of South Vietnam remains vital to United States security. For this reason, we adhere to the overriding objective of denying this country to Communism and of suppressing the Viet Cong insurgency as promptly as possible. (By suppressing the insurgency we mean reducing it to proportions manageable by the national security forces of the GVN, unassisted by the presence of U.S. military forces.) We believe the U.S. part of the task can be completed by the end of 1965, the terminal date

---

* Mr. Colby believes that the official "correct" relationship should be supplemented by selected and restricted unofficial and personal relationships with individuals in the GVN, approved by the Ambassador, where persuasion could be fruitful without derogation of the official U.S. posture.

which we are taking as the time objective of our counterinsurgency programs.

b. The military program in Vietnam has made progress and is sound in principle.

c. The political situation in Vietnam remains deeply serious. It has not yet significantly affected the military effort, but could do so at some time in the future. If the result is a GVN ineffective in the conduct of the war, the U.S. will review its attitude toward support for the government. Although we are deeply concerned by repressive practices, effective performance in the conduct of the war should be the determining factor in our relations with the GVN.

d. The U.S. has expressed its disapproval of certain actions of the Diem-Nhu regime and will do so again if required. Our policy is to seek to bring about the abandonment of repression because of its effect on the popular will to resist. Our means consist of expressions of disapproval and the withholding of support from GVN activities that are not clearly contributing to the war effort. We will use these means as required to assure an effective military program.

II. MILITARY SITUATION AND TRENDS

A. THE STANDARDS OF MEASURE

The test of the military situation is whether the GVN is succeeding in widening its area of effective control of the population and the countryside. This is difficult to measure, and cannot be stated simply in terms of the number of stragetic hamlets built or the number of roads that can now be travelled without escort. Nor can the overall situation be gauged solely in terms of the extent of GVN offensive action, relative weapon losses and defections, VC strength figures, or other measures of military performance. All of these factors are important and must be taken into account; however, a great deal of judgment is required in their interpretation.

We have looked at these factors carefully, but we have also given great weight to the evidence of the men on the spot—the U.S. military advisors and the USOM field representatives—as to whether government control is in fact extending and becoming more accepted and solid in the various areas. We have been greatly impressed with the variation of the situation from area to area and from province to province; there is a different war in each area and province, and an example can be found somewhere to support any attitude toward the state of the counterinsurgency campaign. Our task has been to observe the situation as broadly as possible to avoid giving exaggerated importance to any single angle of observation.

B. OVERALL PROGRESS

With allowance for all uncertainties, it is our firm conclusion that the GVN military program has made great progress in the last year and a half, and that this progress has continued at a fairly steady rate in the past six months even through the period of greatest political unrest in Saigon. The tactics and techniques employed by the Vietnamese under U.S. monitorship are sound and give promise of ultimate victory.

Specifically, progress is most clear in the northern areas (I and II Corps); especially noteworthy work has been done in key coastal provinces where VC

strength once threatened to cut the country in half but has now been substantially reduced. In the central area and the highlands (III Corps), progress has been steady though slower, and the situation remains difficult in the provinces to the west and north of Saigon itself.   [Material Missing]
Throughout the northern two-thirds of the country the strategic hamlet program has matured effectively and freedom of rural movement has grown steadily.

The Delta remains the toughest area of all, and now requires top priority in both GVN and U.S. efforts. Approximately 40% of the people live there; the area is rich and has traditionally resisted central authority; it is the center of Viet Cong strength—over one-third of the "hard core" are found there; and the maritime nature of the terrain renders it much the most difficult region to pacify.

A first step has just been taken by the move of a third division to the Delta, but further major actions are needed. They include priority decisions by the GVN in the use of its resources, the consolidation rather than further spread of strategic hamlets in many areas, the elimination of many fixed outposts, better hamlet defenses and more trained hamlet militia. Regular army units should be reserved for use in mobile actions and for clear and hold operations in support of the strategic hamlet program. Though there are unresolved problems in several key provinces close to Saigon, as well as in the southernmost parts where the VC are strongly established, it is clear that the Delta situation has generally improved over the past year, even with the limited resources allocated to it. Despite recent evidences of greater VC effort and better weapons, the Delta campaign can continue to go forward if the essential priority is assigned to Delta requirements.

C. MILITARY INDICATORS

From a more strictly military standpoint, it should be noted that this overall progress is being achieved against a Viet Cong effort that has not yet been seriously reduced in the aggregate, and that is putting up a formidable fight notably in the Delta and key provinces near Saigon. The military indicators are mixed, reflecting greater and more effective GVN effort but also the continued toughness of the fight.

	June	*July*	*August*	*September (estimated)*	*Mo. Ave. Year ago*
No. of government initiated:					
Small operations	851	781	733	906	490
Large operations	125	163	166	141	71
Viet Cong Killed	1896	1918	1685	2034	2000
GVN Killed	413	521	410	525	431
GVN Weapons Lost	590	780	720	802	390
VC Weapons Captured	390	375	430	400	450
Viet Cong Military Defectors	420	310	220	519	90
Viet Cong Initiated Incidents of all Types	1310	1380	1375	1675	1660
Viet Cong Attacks	410	410	385	467	410
Estimated Viet Cong Strength					
HardCore	21000	21000	21000	21000	22000
Irregular	85000	82000	76000	70000	98000

Recent days have been characterized by reports of greater Viet Cong activity, countrywide, coupled with evidence of improved weaponry in their hands. Some U.S. advisors, as well as some Vietnamese, view this increased activity as a logical reaction to the steadily growing strategic hamlet program, which they believe is progressively separating the Viet Cong from the rural population and from their sources of food and reinforcements. Others view it as a delayed effort to capitalize upon the political trouble. All agree that it reflects a continuing capability for offensive action.

D.   THE STRATEGIC HAMLET PROGRAM

In this generally favorable military picture, two main factors have been the strategic hamlet program and the effectiveness of the U.S. advisory and support effort.

We found unanimous agreement that the strategic hamlet program is sound in concept, and generally effective in execution although it has been overextended in some areas of the Delta. The teamwork of U.S. military men and civilians is generally excellent, and on the GVN side a number of the province chiefs who handled the program poorly in its initial phases have been replaced by men who appear to have a better grasp of the central purpose of the program—to bring people under clear GVN control, in a way that really solidifies their support of their government and opposition to the VC. The economic and civic action element of the program (schools, medicine, fertilizer, etc.) has been carried forward on the U.S. side with considerable effectiveness, but has necessarily lagged behind the physical completion of hamlets and in insecure areas has made little progress. Without this element, coupled with effective hamlet defense measures, what are called "strategic hamlets" may be only nominally under GVN control. We were particularly struck by some evidence that a hamlet's readiness to defend itself often bears a direct relation to whether the Province Chief, with U.S. help, has managed to make a convincing start in civic action.

E.   THE U.S. MILITARY ADVISORY AND SUPPORT EFFORT

We may all be proud of the effectiveness of the U.S. military advisory and support effort. With few exceptions, U.S. advisors report excellent relations with their Vietnamese counterparts, whom they characterize as proud and willing soldiers. The stiffening and exemplary effect of U.S. behavior and attitudes has had an impact which is not confined to the war effort, but which extends deeply into the whole Vietnamese way of doing things.

The U.S. advisory effort, however, cannot assure ultimate success. This is a Vietnamese war and the country and the war must, in the end, be run solely by the Vietnamese. It will impair their independence and the development of their initiative if we leave our advisors in place beyond the time they are really needed. In some areas reductions in the U.S. effort and transfer of U.S. responsibilities to the Vietnamese can now be carried out without material impairment of the total war effort. As a start, we believe that a reduction of about 1000 U.S. personnel (for which plans have been in preparation since the spring) can be carried out before the end of 1963. No further reductions should be made until the requirements of the 1964 campaign become firm.

F. CONCLUSION

Acknowledging the progress achieved to date, there still remains the question of when the final military victory can be attained. If, by victory, we mean the reduction of the insurgency to something little more than sporadic banditry in outlying districts, it is the view of the vast majority of military commanders consulted that success may be achieved in the I, II and III Corps area by the end of CY 1964. Victory in the IV Corps will take longer—at least well into 1965. These estimates necessarily assume that the political situation does not significantly impede the effort.

III. ECONOMIC SITUATION AND TRENDS

The current economic situation in South Vietnam is, in the main, satisfactory. The internal price level is reasonably stable. Commercial inventories are high and national bank reserves of foreign exchange stand at approximately $160 million which equals approximately 11 to 12 months. Imports at current rate ($240 million imports less $75 to $80 million exports). The effective rate of exchange of the piastre to the dollar is within the range of reasonable economic value.

Trends are difficult to discuss but the business community was optimistic before the present crises. Rice exports for the current calendar year are projected at approximately $80 million against $8.75 million last year. Total exports are anticipated at $70 million as against $55 million last year. Banking circles point to one bearish factor in the export picture. Rubber, which represents more than half in value of all exports, faces a situation of declining world market prices and some plantations may curtail operations in the next year.

On the domestic side South Vietnam is almost self-sufficient in cotton textiles and is on its way to satisfying its own fertilizer and cement requirements by 1966. At the beginning of the current year banking circles noted a healthy increase in local investments in small enterprises which reflects, in their judgment an increase of confidence in the future that is unusual for recent years. The prospects for next year, under normal circumstances, appear reasonably good. If the Government encourages diversification in agriculture, exports of such products together with the increasing availability of rice should offset the decline in foreign exchange earnings from rubber.

The projected GVN budget for CY 1964 totals P27 billion: tax revenues are estimated at P11 billion, leaving an internal budget deficit of P16 billion. External resources (resulting from U.S. operations but requiring also use of foreign exchange reserves) are estimated to generate an additional P9.5 billion, leaving a P6.5 billion estimated deficit. This deficit might be somewhat reduced by additional tax revenues. To meet the remaining deficit, borrowings from the National Bank would still be required with a resulting increase in the money supply.

The money supply has been increasing rather sharply in the last nine months, although the inflationary effect has been dampened by the recent arrival of large shipments under USOM's commodity import program. This has been accompanied by an increase in import licensing brought about principally by the GVN's adoption at the beginning of this year of an open general licensing system for certain manufactured goods such as trucks, automobiles, fabricated steel and some industrial raw materials. The banks estimate that the open general licensing system will result in a $10 million increase in GVN-financed imports in CY 1963.

In short, while the general economic situation is good, the prospects for holding the line on inflation and the balance of payments do not appear bright for CY 1964 unless the GVN can be persuaded to impose severe restraints.

Effect of the Political Crisis on the Economic Situation

At the present time the current political problems have not had a significant effect on the internal economic situation. French banking sources report a slight increase in the rate of withdrawals from private Vietnamese bank deposits over the last two months; but this increase has only been on the order of 1 to 2 percent.

Commercial inventory stocks seem to be increasing, but this can be explained by the recent increase in arrivals of foreign goods. In any case prices have remained stable with exception of a slight increase in the cost of cement, automobiles and certain industrial equipment.

The value of the piastre has fallen 10% on the Hong Kong market in the last month. Virtually no abnormal flight of capital has yet been observed in banking circles.

The most apparent effect of the crisis of the past several weeks is a slowdown in investment decisions, both in industry and in the limited capital market. Inventors and industrialists are worried about a reduction in U.S aid. They are aware of the suspension in the issuances of procurement authorizations and are therefore concerned about the availability of imported raw materials and spare parts.

Since the Saigon business community has lived through some violent times before this, they have not reacted to events with as much panic as might have been expected. If the U.S. should long suspend import commitments, however, it should be apparent that the private sector of the economy will react in an inflationary manner.

IV.   POLITICAL SITUATION AND TRENDS

Although our observations of the political situation were necessarily less extensive than of the military picture, they were ample to confirm that the existing situation is one of high tension. We reviewed the situation carefully with the relevant U.S. officials and were also impressed by frank interviews with GVN officials and with third country representatives.

In essence, discontent with the Diem/Nhu regime, which had been widespread just below the surface during recent years, has now become a seething problem. The Buddhist and student crises have precipitated these discontents and given them specific issues. But the problem goes deeply into the personalities, objectives, and methods of operation of Diem and Nhu over a long period.

The evidence appears overwhelming that Diem and Nhu operate in close collaboration, and that each needs the other. They undoubtedly regard themselves as carrying out a social and political revolution for the good of their country, using all means—including the strategic hamlet program—to build up a secure base of political strength in the rural areas.

At the same time, the positive and educative sides of their actions, aimed primarily at the countryside, but with extensive countrywide educational efforts as well, have been increasingly matched by negative and repressive measures of control against the urban population. The urban elite or "Establishment"— which includes intellectuals, civilian officials at all levels, and a high proportion of military officers—has never been trusted by Diem and Nhu. Always sensitive to signs of opposition—with some justification from events in 1954–55 and the attempted coups of 1960 and 1962—the regime has turned increasingly to police methods, particularly secret arrests, that have almost all the bad effects of outright totalitarianism even though a good deal of freedom to criticize still remains.

Concurrently, the palace has always manipulated and controlled the government structure to ensure its own control. The degree to which centralized control and intervention have been carried, and the often quixotic nature of its use, have had a steadily growing adverse effect on efficiency and morale.

Both of these adverse characteristics of the regime, and the resentment of them, focus more and more on Nhu. Not merely is he the hatchet man, but his statements on "personalism" and his building up with Madame Nhu of a wide personal apparatus have smacked more and more of outright totalitarianism. A further disturbing feature of Nhu is his flirtation with the idea of negotiating with North Vietnam, whether or not he is serious in this at present. This deeply disturbs responsible Vietnamese and, more basically, suggests a possible basic incompatibility with U.S. objectives.

Nhu's role and scope of action have increased, and he may well have the designs imputed to him of succeeding his brother in due course. Diem is still quite a long way from being a figurehead, and his personal prestige in the country has survived remarkably well. But Diem does depend heavily on Nhu, their central ideas are very close if not identical, and it would be remarkable if Diem dropped Nhu from a commanding position.

Until the Buddhist and student crises, it was probably true that the alienation between Diem and the elite was more a matter of basically divergent views of the right social structure and of Diem and Nhu's handling of individuals in the government than it was a matter of reaction to repressions. However, the crises have now brought the repressions so directly into the lives of many of the elite that more orderly methods, which might previously have kept the loyalty of the needed amount of talent, now probably cannot do so without a convincing degree of restoration of personal security. Yet both more orderly methods and a restoration of personal security cut diametrically across the grain of Diem's and especially Nhu's view of what is necessary to maintain their power and move toward their idea of social revolution.

Thus, the discontent of the elite—reflected chiefly in the progressive loss of responsible men—has now reached the point where it is uncertain that Diem can keep or enlist talent to run the war. The loss of such men as Mau and Tuyen, and the deeply disturbed attitude of such a crucial figure as Thuan, are the strongest evidences of the seriousness of the situation.

This is not to discount groups other than the elite. However, the Buddhists and students cannot in themselves either threaten the regime or do more than focus issues—although of course they seriously damage the regime's standing in the U.S. and elsewhere, with uninhibited press reactions that contribute further to the persecution complex that drives Diem and Nhu into repression. The business community in a passive factor only. Urban labor is simply trying to hold its position, being anti-regime but not to the point of being an independent source of trouble. The rural peasantry appear little affected even by the

Buddhist issue. If these groups can be kept even in an acquiescent state the war could go forward.

As matters stand, political tension in the urban centers is so high that it could boil over at any time into another cycle of riots, repressions, and resignations. This tension would disappear in a very short time if Nhu were removed. Whether it could be reduced to acceptable proportions by measures short of this is a very doubtful question, but it is clear that such measures would have to include both more moderate control methods and a better government climate particularly for civilian officials.

V.   EFFECT OF POLITICAL TENSION

A.   ON MILITARY OPERATIONS

So far this has not significantly affected countryside operations in any area. U.S. personnel in the field testified that a few officer or civilian counterparts showed concern over the Buddhist and student issues, but not to the extent, as yet, of materially affecting their doing their jobs. The rural population has been almost untouched. The pace of GVN operations was sharply cut for a short period at the end of August by transfers of units and general uncertainty, but has now largely renewed its previous intensity. The Delta particularly has been so concerned with the war that it has been virtually unaffected.

Basically, the unifying factors embodied in the hatred of the military for Communism remain very sharp. This hatred is real and pervasive. It transcends domestic policies in the minds of most officers.

However, there are disturbing elements that could change this picture greatly unless the political tension can be reduced. Certain high officers have been heavily preoccupied with coup possibilities. Those who have had relatives directly involved in the regime's repressions are deeply disturbed though not necessarily ready to act against Diem.* Resentment of Nhu exists in top military circles and probably to some extent at middle levels. The fact that the great bulk of military officers—and Province Chiefs—come from urban areas (simply because of educational requirements in many cases) clearly does open up the possibility of progressive loss of morale and effectiveness, as well as coup participation, if the regime does not cease its oppressions against Buddhists, students, and real or supposed opposition individuals.

B.   ON CIVILIAN OFFICIALS

On the civilian official side, which is also relevant to the war effort, the reaction to the regime's actions has been sharper. The Embassy and USOM report unanimously that their normal counterparts have become afraid of associating too closely with Americans, and that there is a general atmosphere of watch-and-wait, just going through the motions of the job but failing to exert what limited initiative and imagination they had previously been ready to exert in face of the constant and power-directed interventions of Nhu. The decline in the contribution of these officials is less serious than any similar decline among

---

* A specific example of this is the Commandant of the Marine Corps in Saigon. His brother, along with many other relatives of military officers and cabinet members, was picked up in the student roundups of early September. Some were tortured, and—as in the case of the Commandant's brother—released only after intercession. However, the Commandant shows no inclination to take action against the Diem government.

the military and province chiefs, but is nonetheless a potentially significant and growing factor if tension persists because these officials play a substantial role in the strategic hamlet program.

In summary, the political tension has not yet significantly affected progress in the field, nor does it seem likely to have major effects in the near future. Beyond that, however, the prognosis must be considered uncertain if political tension persists or mounts.

VI. OVERALL EVALUATION

From the above analysis it is clear that the situation requires a constant effort by the U.S. to obtain a reduction of political tensions and improved performance by the Vietnamese Government. We cannot say with assurance whether the effort against the Viet Cong will ultimately fail in the absence of major political improvements. However, it does seem clear that after another period of repressive action progress may be reduced and indeed reversed. Although the present momentum might conceivably continue to carry the effort forward even if Diem remains in power and political tensions continue, any significant slowing in the rate of progress would surely have a serious effect on U.S. popular support for the U.S. effort.

VII. U.S. LEVERAGES TO OBTAIN DESIRED CHANGES IN THE DIEM REGIME

A. CONDUCT OF U.S. REPRESENTATIVES

U.S. personnel in Saigon might adopt an attitude of coolness toward their Vietnamese counterparts, maintaining only those contacts and communications which are necessary for the actual conduct of operations in the field. To some extent this is the attitude already adopted by the Ambassador himself, but it could be extended to the civilian and military agencies located in Saigon. The effect of such action would be largely psychological.

B. ECONOMIC LEVERAGE

Together, USOM's Commodity Import Program (CIP) and the PL 480 program account for between 60 and 70 percent of imports into Vietnam. The commitment of funds under the CIP has already been suspended. CIP deliveries result in the generation of piastres, most of which go to the support of the defense budget. It is estimated that CIP pipelines will remain relatively large for some five or six months, and within this period there would not be a serious material effect. Even within this period, however, the flow of piastres to support the defense budget will gradually begin to decline and the GVN will be forced to draw down its foreign exchange reserves or curtail its military expenditures.

Within the domestic economy the existing large pipelines would mean that there would be no material reason for inflation to begin in the short term period. However, the psychological effect of growing realization that the CIP program has been suspended might be substantial in 2-4 months. Saigon has a large number of speculative traders, and although there is considerable police effort to control prices, this might not be able to contain a general trend of speculation and hoarding. Once inflation did develop, it could have a serious effect on the GVN budget and the conduct of the war.

Apart from CIP, two major AID projects are up for final approval—the Saigon-Cholon Waterworks ($9 million) and the Saigon Electric Power Project ($4 million). Suspension of these projects would be a possible means of demonstrating to Congress and the world that we disapprove of GVN policies and are not providing additional aid not directly essential to the war effort.

C. PARAMILITARY AND OTHER ASSISTANCE

(1) USOM assistance to the Combat Police and USOM and USIS assistance to the Director General of Information and the ARVN PsyWar Program could be suspended. These projects involve a relatively small amount of local currency but their suspension, particularly in the case of USIS, might adversely affect programs which the U.S. wishes to see progress.

(2) However, there would be merit in a gesture aimed at Colonel Tung, the Special Forces Commander, whose forces in or near Saigon played a conspicuous part in the pagoda affair and are a continuing support for Diem. Colonel Tung commands a mixed complex of forces, some of which are supported by MAP and others presently through CIA. All of those now in or near Saigon were trained either for combat missions or for special operations into North Vietnam and Laos. Purely on grounds of their not being used for their proper missions, the U.S. could inform Diem that we would cut off MAP and CIA support unless they were placed directly under Joint General Staff and were committed to field operations.

The practical effect of the cut-off would probably be small. The equipment cannot be taken out of the hands of the units, and the pay provided to some units could be made up from the GVN budget. Psychologically, however, the significance of the gesture might be greater. At the least it would remove one target of press criticism of the U.S., and would probably also be welcomed by the high military officers in Vietnam, and certainly by the disaffected groups in Saigon.

At the same time, support should continue, but through General Harkins rather than CIA, for border surveillance and other similar field operations that are contributing to the war effort.

We have weighed this cut-off action carefully. It runs a risk that Colonel Tung would refuse to carry out external operations against the Lao corridor and North Vietnam. It might also limit CIA's access to the military. However, U.S. liaison with high military officers could probably be fully maintained through the U.S. military advisors. On balance, we conclude that these possible disadvantages are outweighed by the gains implicit in this action.

(3) Consideration has been given both by USOM and the military (principally the JCS in Washington) to the possibility of redirecting economic and military assistance in such a fashion as to bypass the central government in Saigon. Military studies have shown the technical feasibility, though with great difficulty and cost, of supplying the war effort in the countryside over lines of communications which do not involve Saigon, and it is assumed that the same conclusions would apply to USOM deliveries to the field under the rural strategic hamlet program. However, there is a consensus among U.S. agencies in Saigon that such an effort is not practical in the face of determined opposition by the GVN unless, of course, a situation had developed where the central government was no longer in control of some areas of the country. Nor is it at all clear that such diversion would operate to build up the position of the military or to cut down Nhu's position.

D. PROPAGANDA

Although the capability of USIS to support the United States campaign of pressure against the regime would be small, the Ambassador believes consideration must be given to the content and timing of the United States pronouncements outside the country. He has already suggested the use of the Voice of America in stimulating, in its broadcasts to Vietnamese, discussions of democratic political philosophies. This medium could be used to exploit a wide range of ascending political pressure. In addition, a phased program of United States official pronouncements could be developed for use in conjunction with the other leverages as they are applied. We must recognize the possibility that such actions may incite Diem to strong countermeasures.

E. THE LEVERAGE OF CONDITIONING OUR MILITARY AID ON SATISFACTORY PROGRESS

Coupled with all the above there is the implicit leverage embodied in our constantly making it plain to Diem and others that the long term continuation of military aid is conditioned upon the Vietnamese Government demonstrating a satisfactory level of progress toward defeat of the insurgency.

F. CONCLUSIONS

A program of limited pressures, such as the CIP suspension, will not have large material effects on the GVN or the war effort, at least for 2-4 months. The psychological effects could be greater, and there is some evidence that the suspension is already causing concern to Diem. However, the effect of pressures that can be carried out over an extended period without detriment to the war effort is probably limited with respect to the possibility of Diem making necessary changes.

We have not analyzed with care what the effect might be of a far more intensive level of pressure such as cessation of MAP deliveries or long continued suspension of the commodity import program. If the Diem government should fail to make major improvements, serious consideration would have to be given to this possible course of action, but we believe its effect on the war effort would be so serious—in psychological if not in immediate material terms—that it should not be undertaken at the present time.

VIII. COUP POSSIBILITIES

A. PROSPECTS OF A SPONTANEOUS COUP

The prospects of an early spontaneous replacement of the Diem Regime are not high. The two principal sources of such an attempt, the senior military officers and the students, have both been neutralized by a combination of their own inability and the regime's effective countermeasures of control. The student organizations have been emasculated. The students themselves have displayed more emotion than determination and they are apparently being handled with sufficient police sophistication to avoid an explosion.

The generals appear to have little stomach for the difficult job of secretly arranging the necessary coalescence of force to upset the Regime.

Diem/Nhu are keenly aware of the capability of the generals to take over the country, utilizing the tremendous power now vested in the military forces. They, therefore, concentrate their manipulative talent on the general officers, by transfers, and by controls over key units and their locations. They are aware that these actions may reduce efficiency, but they tolerate it rather than risk the prospect that they be overthrown and their social revolution frustrated. They have established a praetorian guard to guarantee considerable bloodshed if any attack is made. The generals have seen slim hope of surmounting these difficulties without prohibitive risk to themselves, the unity of the Army and the Establishment itself.

Despite these unfavorable prospects for action in the short term, new factors could quickly arise, such as the death of Diem or an unpredictable and even irrational attack launched by a junior officer group, which would call urgently for U.S. support or counteraction. In such a case, the best alternative would appear to be the support of constitutional continuity in the person of the Vice President, behind whom arrangements could be developed for a more permanent replacement after a transitional period.

B. PROSPECTS FOR IMPROVEMENT UNDER AN ALTERNATIVE GOVERNMENT

The prospects that a replacement regime would be an improvement appear to be about 50-50.* Initially, only a strongly authoritarian regime would be able to pull the government together and maintain order. In view of the pre-eminent role of the military in Vietnam today, it is probable that this role would be filled by a military officer, perhaps taking power after the selective process of a junta dispute. Such an authoritarian military regime, perhaps after an initial period of euphoria at the departure of Diem/Nhu, would be apt to entail a resumption of the repression at least of Diem, the corruption of the Vietnamese Establishment before Diem, and an emphasis on conventional military rather than social, economic and political considerations, with at least an equivalent degree of xenophobic nationalism.

These features must be weighed, however, against the possible results of growing dominance or succession by Nhu, which would continue and even magnify the present dissension, unhappiness and unrest.

C. POSSIBLE U.S. ACTIONS

Obviously, clear and explicit U.S. support could make a great difference to the chances of a coup. However, at the present time we lack a clear picture of what acceptable individuals might be brought to the point of action, or what kind of government might emerge. We therefore need an intensive clandestine effort, under the Ambassador's direction, to establish necessary contacts to allow U.S. to continuously appraise coup prospects.

If and when we have a better picture, the choice will still remain difficult whether we would prefer to take our chances on a spontaneous coup (assuming some action by Diem and Nhu would trigger it) or to risk U.S. prestige and having the U.S. hand show with a coup group which appeared likely to be a

---

* Mr. Sullivan (State) believes that a replacement regime which does not suffer from the overriding danger of Nhu's ambition to establish a totalitarian state (the control of which he might easily lose to the Communists in the course of his flirtations) would be inevitably better than the current regime even if the former did have the deficiencies described.

better alternative government. Any regime that was identified from the outset as a U.S. "puppet" would have disadvantages both within South Vietnam and in significant areas of the world, including other underdeveloped nations where the U.S. has a major role.

In any case, whether or not it proves to be wise to promote a coup at a later time, we must be ready for the possibility of a spontaneous coup, and this too requires clandestine contacts on an intensive basis.

IX. ANALYSIS OF ALTERNATIVE POLICIES

Broadly speaking, we believe there are three alternative policies the U.S. could pursue to achieve its political and military objectives:

1. Return to avowed support of the Diem regime and attempt to obtain the necessary improvements through persuasion from a posture of "reconciliation." This would not mean any expression of approval of the repressive actions of the regime, but simply that we would go back in practice to business as usual.

2. Follow a policy of selective pressures: "purely correct" relationships at the top official level, continuing to withhold further actions in the commodity import program, and making clear our disapproval of the regime. A further element in this policy is letting the present impression stand that the U.S. would not be averse to a change of Government—although we would not take any immediate actions to initiate a coup.

3. Start immediately to promote a coup by high ranking military officers. This policy might involve more extended suspensions of aid and sharp denunciations of the regime's actions so timed as to fit with coup prospects and planning.

Our analysis of these alternatives is as follows:

1. Reconciliation.

We believe that this course of action would be ineffective from the standpoint of events in South Vietnam alone, and would also greatly increase our difficulties in justifying the present U.S. support effort both to the Congress and generally to significant third nations. We are most unlikely, after recent events, to get Diem to make the necessary changes; on the contrary, he would almost certainly regard our reconciliation as an evidence that the U.S. would sit still for just about anything he did. The result would probably be not only a continuation of the destructive elements in the Regime's policies but a return to larger scale repressions as and when Diem and Nhu thought they were necessary. The result would probably be sharp deterioration in the military situation in a fairly short period.

2. Selective Pressures.

We have examined numerous possibilities of applying pressures to Diem in order to incline him to the direction of our policies. The most powerful instrument at our disposal is the control of military and economic aid but any consideration of its use reveals the double-edged nature of its effects. Any long term reduction of aid cannot but have an eventual adverse effect on the military campaign since both the military and the economic programs have been consciously designed and justified in terms of their contribution to the war effort. Hence, immediate reductions must be selected carefully and be left in effect only for short periods.

We believe that the present level of pressures is causing, and will cause, Diem some concern, while at the same time not significantly impairing the military effort. We are not hopeful that this level (or indeed any level) of pressure will actually induce Diem to remove Nhu from the picture completely. However, there is a better chance that Diem will at least be deterred from resuming large scale oppressions.

At the same time, there are various factors that set a time limit to pursuing this course of action in its present form. Within 2-4 months we have to make critical decisions with the GVN about its 1964 budget and our economic support level. In addition, there is a significant and growing possibility that even the present limited actions in the economic field—more for psychological than for economic reasons—would start a wave of speculation and inflation that would be difficult to control or bring back into proper shape. As to when we would reverse our present course, the resumption of the full program of economic and military aid should be tied to the actions of the Diem government.

As a foundation for the development of our long-term economic and military aid programs, we believe it may be possible to develop specific military objectives to be achieved on an agreed schedule. The extent to which such objectives are met, in conjunction with an evaluation of the regime's political performance, would determine the level of aid for the following period.

3. Organizing a coup.

For the reasons stated earlier, we believe this course of action should not be undertaken at the present time.

*   *   *

On balance we consider that the most promising course of action to adopt at this time is an application of selective short-term pressures, principally economic, and the conditioning of long-term aid on the satisfactory performance by the Diem government in meeting military and political objectives which in the aggregate equate to the requirements of final victory. The specific actions recommended in Section I of this report are consistent with this policy.

Chairman, Joint Chiefs of Staff   Secretary of Defense

[Document 143]

5 Oct 1963

TO: Lodge

Via CAS Channel   CAP 63560

In conjunction with decisions and recommendations in separate DEPTEL, President today approved recommendation that no initiative should now be taken to give any active covert encouragement to a coup. There should, however, be urgent covert effort with closest security under broad guidance of Ambassador to identify and build contacts with possible alternative leadership as and when it appears. Essential that this effort be totally secure and fully deniable and separated entirely from normal political analysis and reporting and other activities of country team. We repeat that this effort is not repeat not to be aimed at active promotion of coup but only at surveillance and readiness. In order to provide plausibility to denial suggest you and no one else in Embassy issue these instructions orally to Acting Station Chief and hold him responsible to you alone for making appropriate contacts and reporting to you alone.

All reports to Washington on this subject should be on this channel.

[Document 144]

TO STATE FROM LODGE

CAS 1445

1. Lt. Col. Conein met with Gen. Duong Van Minh at Gen. Minh's Headquarters on Le Van Duyet for one hour and ten minutes morning of 5 Oct 63. This meeting was at the initiative of Gen. Minh and has been specifically cleared in advance by Ambassador Lodge. No other persons were present. The conversation was conducted in French.

2. Gen. Minh stated that he must know American Government's position with respect to a change in the Government of Vietnam within the very near future. Gen. Minh added the Generals were aware of the situation is deteriorating rapidly and that action to change the Government must be taken or the war will be lost to the Viet Cong because the Government no longer has the support of the people. Gen. Minh identified among the other Generals participating with him in this plan:

> Maj. Gen. Tran Van Don
> Brig. Gen. Tran Thien Khiem
> Maj. Gen. Tran Van Kim

3. Gen. Minh made it clear that he did not expect any specific American support for an effort on the part of himself and his colleagues to change the Government but he stated he does need American assurances that the USG will not rpt not attempt to thwart this plan.

4. Gen. Minh also stated that he himself has no political ambitions nor do any of the other General Officers except perhaps, he said laughingly, Gen. Ton That Dinh. Gen. Minh insisted that his only purpose is to win the war. He added emphatically that to do this continuation of American Military and Economic Aid at the present level (He said one and one half million dollars per day) is necessary.

5. Gen. Minh outlined three possible plans for the accomplishment of the change of Government:

   a. Assassination of Ngo Dinh Nhu and Ngo Dinh Can keeping President Diem in Office. Gen. Minh said this was the easiest plan to accomplish.

   b. The encirclement of Saigon by various military units particularly the unit at Ben Cat. (Comment: Fifth Division elements commanded by Gen. Dinh).

   c. Direct confrontation between military units involved in the coup and loyalist military units in Saigon. In effect, dividing the city of Saigon into sectors and cleaning it out pocket by pocket. Gen. Minh claims under the circumstances Diem and Nhu could count on the loyalty of 5,500 troops within the city of Saigon.

6. Conein replied to Gen. Minh that he could not answer specific questions as to USG non-interference nor could he give any advice with respect to tactical planning. He added that he could not advise concerning the best of the three plans.

[material missing]

Nam are Ngo Dinh Kau, Ngo Dinh Can and Ngo Trong Hieu. Minh stated that Hieu was formerly a Communist and still has Communist sympathies. When Col. Conein remarked that he had considered Col. Tung as one of the more dangerous individuals, Gen. Minh stated "if I get rid of Nhu, Can and Hieu, Col. Tung will be on his knees before me."

8. Gen. Minh also stated that he was worried as to the role of Gen. Tran Thien Khiem since Khiem may have played a double role in August. Gen. Minh asked that copies of the documents previously passed to Gen. Khiem (plan of Camp Long Thanh and munitions inventory at that camp) be passed to Gen. Minh personally for comparison with papers passed by Khiem to Minh purportedly from CAS.

9. Minh further stated that one of the reasons they are having to act quickly was the fact that many regimental, battalion and company commanders are working on coup plans of their own which could be abortive and a "catastrophe".

10. Minh appeared to understand Conein's position of being unable to comment at the present moment but asked that Conein again meet with Gen. Minh to discuss the specific plan of operations which Gen. Minh hopes to put into action. No specific date was given for this next meeting. Conein was again non-committal in his reply. Gen. Minh once again indicated his understanding and stated that he would arrange to contact Conein in the near future and hoped that Conein would be able to meet with him and give the assurance outlined above.

SAIGON CAS 34026, 5 October 1963

TO STATE FROM LODGE   (REF: CAS SAIGON 1445)

EYES ONLY FOR SECRETARY RUSK FROM LODGE

Reference Big Minh-Conein meeting (Cas Saigon 1445). While neither General Harkins nor I have great faith in Big Minh, we need instructions on his approach. My recommendation, in which General Harkins concurs, is that Conein when next approached by Minh should:

1. Assure him that US will not attempt to thwart his plans.

2. Offer to review his plans, other than assassination plans.

3. Assure Minh that US aid will be continued to Vietnam under Government which gives promise of gaining support of people and winning the war against the Communists. Point out that it is our view that this is most likely to be the case if Government includes good proportion of well qualified civilian leaders in key positions. (Conein should press Minh for details his thinking Re composition future Government). I suggest the above be discussed with Secretary McNamara and General Taylor who contacted Minh in recent visit.

[Document 145]

6 Oct 1963

FROM: CIA

TO: Lodge

74228

Re CAS 1445

1. Believe CAP 63560 gives general guidance requested REFTEL. We have following additional general thoughts which have been discussed with President. While we do not wish to stimulate coup, we also do not wish to leave impression that U.S. would thwart a change of government or deny economic and military assistance to a new regime if it appeared capable of increasing effectiveness of military effort, ensuring popular support to win war and improving working relations with U.S. We would like to be informed on what is being contemplated but we should avoid being drawn into reviewing or advising on operational plans or any other act which might tend to identify U.S. too closely with change in government. We would, however, welcome information which would help us assess character of any alternate leadership.

2. With reference to specific problem of General Minh you should seriously consider having contact take position that in present state his knowledge he is unable present Minh's case to responsible policy officials with any degree of seriousness. In order to get responsible officials even to consider Minh's problem, contact would have to have detailed information clearly indicating that Minh's plans offer a high prospect of success. At present contact sees no such prospect in the information so far provided.

3. You should also consider with Acting Station Chief whether it would be desirable in order to preserve security and deniability in this as well as similar approaches to others whether appropriate arrangements could be made for follow-up contacts by individuals brought in especially from outside Vietnam. As we indicated in CAP 63560 we are most concerned about security problem and we are confining knowledge these sensitive matters in Washington to extremely limited group, high officials in White House, State, Defense and CIA with whom this message cleared.

[Document 146]

October 11, 1963

NATIONAL SECURITY ACTION MEMORANDUM NO. 263

TO: Secretary of State

Secretary of Defense

Chairman of the Joint Chiefs of Staff

SUBJECT: South Vietnam

At a meeting on October 5, 1963, the President considered the recommendations contained in the report of Secretary McNamara and General Taylor on their mission to South Vietnam.

The President approved the military recommendations contained in Section I B (1-3) of the report, but directed that no formal announcement be made of the implementation of plans to withdraw 1,000 U.S. military personnel by the end of 1963.

After discussion of the remaining recommendations of the report, the President approved an instruction to Ambassador Lodge which is set forth in State Department telegram No. 534 to Saigon.

McGeorge Bundy

Copy furnished:

Director of Central Intelligence

Administrator, Agency for International Development

[Document 147]

DEPARTMENT OF STATE

BUREAU OF INTELLIGENCE AND RESEARCH

Research Memorandum

RFE-90, October 22, 1963

TO: The Secretary

THROUGH: S/S

FROM: INR—Thomas L. Hughes

SUBJECT: *Statistics on the War Effort in South Vietnam Show Unfavorable Trends*

This report reviews the more significant statistics on the Communist insurgency in South Vietnam as indicators of trends in the military situation since July 1963.

ABSTRACT

Statistics on the insurgency in South Vietnam, although neither thoroughly trustworthy nor entirely satisfactory as criteria, indicate an unfavorable shift in the military balance. Since July 1963, the trend in Viet Cong casualties, weapons losses, and defections has been downward while the number of Viet Cong armed attacks and other incidents has been upward. Comparison with earlier periods suggests that the military position of the government of Vietnam may have been set back to the point it occupied six months to a year ago. These trends coincide in time with the sharp deterioration of the political situation. At the same time, even without the Buddhist issue and the attending government crisis, it is possible that the Diem regime would have been unable to maintain the favorable trends of previous periods in the face of the accelerated Viet Cong effort.

Statistics as Indicators

Statistics, in general, are only partial and not entirely satisfactory indicators of progress in the total counterinsurgency effort in South Vietnam.* First, some statistics are incomplete, as for example, those relating to Viet Cong attacks against strategic hamlets and desertions within the South Vietnamese military and security services. Second, all statistics are acquired largely if not entirely from official South Vietnamese sources. As such, their validity must, to some degree at least, remain questionable, even though the efforts of the United States military and civilian advisers have improved the quality of this data during the past year or

[words missing]

Third, there are several other important indicators which are extremely difficult, if not impossible, to handle statistically. These include: morale and efficiency within the bureaucracy and the armed services, the degree of locally acquired or volunteered intelligence, popular attitudes toward the Viet Cong and the government, and the status and impact of the government's political, social, and economic activities in support of the strategic hamlet program. Nonetheless, statistics touch on some significant aspects of the military situation and provide a guide at least to trends in the fighting.

Viet Cong Incidents

Statistics show that the Viet Cong have accelerated their military and subversive effort since July 1963. From January 1962 until July 1963, the total number of Viet Cong armed attacks, as well as all other incidents (sabotage, terrorism, and propaganda), dropped consistently. However, since July of this year, total incidents and armed attacks have increased appreciably. If the present trend continues through the end of this year, total incidents will exceed by more than 10% the level for the period July-December 1962. Large Viet Cong attacks (company-size or larger) have also increased appreciably since July of this year, and, if the trend continues, could exceed by almost 30% the level for July-December 1962.

In addition, the Viet Cong during the last half of 1963 have shown increased daring, planning, and coordination in their attacks. This has been evidenced by an attack against a United States helicopter base, and by simultaneous actions against two or more strategic hamlets and even against two district capitals. Until this period, towns had not been attacked since September 1961, when the capital of Phuoc Thanh province was raided by a large Viet Cong force.

* The statistics used in this paper were compiled by the Defense Intelligence Agency (DIA) and by the Office of the Special Assistant for Counterinsurgency and Special Activities (SACSA) in the Department of Defense and are based on field reports submitted by the Military Assistance Command Vietnam (MACV).

Casualties

Although the Viet Cong have incurred relatively heavy losses during some of their more daring recent attacks, their overall casualties since July of this year have not been correspondingly high. If the accelerated Viet Cong effort and losses suffered are maintained at present levels during the rest of this year, casualties will remain about 10% below the level in July-December 1962, the peak period in Viet Cong casualties last year.

In contrast, casualties among the South Vietnamese military and security forces since July of this year are increasing and, at the present rate, could exceed by about 20% the level for the preceding six-month period. This would raise the total casualties for 1963 by some 30% above the 1961 and 1962 levels. Indeed, the ratio of Viet Cong to South Vietnamese forces killed and captured dropped from five-to-one for the last half of 1962 to three-to-one for the period July-September 18, 1963. This ratio would be still less favorable to the government if casualties among such paramilitary groups as the village militia and *Montagnard* scouts were taken into account. Casualty statistics on these groups are not complete and are not shown in this report. During the period August-September 18, 1963, however, their casualties exceeded 500 as compared with the combined total of more than 2,300 casualties among the Army, Civil Guard, and Self Defense Corps for the same period.

Weapons Losses

During 1962, weapons losses among both the Viet Cong and government forces increased progressively, although government losses were somewhat greater than those of the Viet Cong. The increase continued during January-April 1963, but losses on both sides were about even. However, during May-August, Viet Cong weapons losses dropped by more than 10%, while losses among government forces increased by about 15%. If the trend noted during the last three weeks of September should continue throughout the year, the Viet Cong will lose almost 70% fewer weapons than the government. Moreover, a large number of the Viet Cong weapons lost are of the home-made variety while the great bulk of government weapons losses are of standard or modern-type pieces.

Defections and Desertions

Viet Cong military defections increased progressively during 1963 until June, dropping from a high of 414 in May to a low of 107 for about the first three weeks of September. (These Viet Cong are usually members of the insurgent armed forces, although only a small percentage are believed to be hard-core cadres. They generally defect to South Vietnamese military forces who interrogate and screen them and determine their disposition.)

In addition to the military defectors, some 13,700 persons "rallied" to the government from April through August 1963 under a national surrender and amnesty campaign. This campaign, known as "Chieu Hoi," was officially inaugurated on April 19. The South Vietnamese government regards the bulk of these as Viet Cong. United States officials, who do not screen these statistics, believe the vast majority to be refugees and persons who, for one reason or another, have left areas controlled or formerly controlled by the Viet Cong.

I. STATISTICAL TRENDS, 1962–1963

	Jan. 1–June 30, 1962	July 1–Dec. 30, 1962 (and % of change)	Jan. 1–June 30, 1963 (and % of change)	July 1–Sept. 18, 1963 *	% of previous period
1. Viet Cong Incidents (total)	10,481	8,595 (−18%)	6,847 (−20%)	3,777	55%
2. Viet Cong Armed Attacks (total)	3,024	2,441 (−19%)	1,941 (−20%)	1,067	55%
Company-size and larger	156	63 (−40%)	72 (+14%)	34	47%
3. Viet Cong Casualties (total)	13,755	17,338 (+26%)	13,944 (−20%)	6,425	46%
4. GVN Casualties (total)	6,036	6,846 (+13%)	8,056 (+18%)	4,220	52%

	Jan.–April 1962	May–Aug. 1962	Sept.–Dec. 1962	Jan.–April 1963	May–Aug. 1963 (and % of change)	Thru Sept. 18, 1963 (and % of previous period)
5. Viet Cong Weapons Losses	1,202	1,526	1,806	1,917	1,703 (−11%)	335 (20%)
GVN Weapons Losses	1,777	1,834	1,534	1,974	2,260 (+15%)	644 (28%)
6. Viet Cong Defections**	1962 Total: 1,956			1,178	1,307 (+10%)	107 (8%)

* Although only 42% of this period has elapsed, the statistics in this column are already 46%–55% of the total figures for the previous six-month period, as shown in the last column.
** This excludes "Chieu Hoi" returnees which have totalled 13,664 through August 1963 but which have declined sharply since July 1963.

II. CONDENSED FIGURES ON MILITARY ACTIVITY
FROM JANUARY 1, 1962

1. Viet Cong-Initiated Incidents

1962*	Total Attacks	Large-Scale Attacks (Company-size and larger)	Terror-ism	Sabo-tage	Prop	Total Inci-dents
Jan.	549	21	839	180	257	1,825
Feb.	500	20	613	137	210	1,460
Mar.	588	27	660	290	423	1,961
Apr.	497	27	1,024	220	192	1,933
May	528	38	892	154	251	1,825
June	362	23	736	157	222	1,477
July	448	12	735	158	223	1,564
Aug.	378	10	885	146	233	1,642
Sept.	391	10	624	178	182	1,375
Oct.	419	14	583	189	166	1,357
Nov.	421	8	614	144	132	1,311
Dec.	384	9	670	107	185	1,346
Total	5,465	219	8,875	2,060	2,676	19,076

* These figures closely parallel year-end figures furnished by COMUSMACV.

1963

Jan.	252	10	447	49	179	927
Feb.	195	14	433	69	91	788
Mar.	344	11	653	131	154	1,282
Apr.	383	12	688	105	155	1,331
May	357	13	608	93	150	1,208
June	410	12	652	107	142	1,311
July	407	9	698	80	183	1,368
Aug.	319	12	569	93	186	1,167
Sep. 18	341	13	613	115	173	1,242
Total	3,008	106	5,361	842	1,413	10,624

2. Casualties**

Jan. 1962	GVN				Viet Cong			
	KIA	WIA	Cap/ Miss.	Total	KIA	WIA	Cap.	Total
ARVN—Army of Vietnam	116	221	8					
CG—Civil Guard	76	108	43					
SDC—Self-Defense Corps	107	146	65					
Totals	299	475	116	890	1,294	212	390	1,896

** COMUSMACV has reported the following statistics for 1962 on Viet Cong casualties: Killed—20,919; wounded—4,235; captured—5,518; total 30,673.

2. *Casualties* (continued)

| February 1962 | GVN | | | | Viet Cong | | | |
	KIA	WIA	Cap/ Miss.	Total	KIA	WIA	Cap.	Total
ARVN	72	118	7					
CG	68	76	42					
SDC	104	106	75					
Totals	244	300	124	668	1,205	316	353	1,874

March 1962

	KIA	WIA	Cap/ Miss.	Total	KIA	WIA	Cap.	Total
ARVN	97	219	28					
CG	160	223	27					
SDC	266	295	85					
Total	523	737	140	1,400	1,456	551	523	2,530

April 1962

	KIA	WIA	Cap/ Miss.	Total	KIA	WIA	Cap.	Total
ARVN	94	164	1					
CG	108	146	66					
SDC	185	222	84					
Totals	387	532	151	1,070	1,596	292	415	2,303

May 1962

	KIA	WIA	Cap/ Miss.	Total	KIA	WIA	Cap.	Total
ARVN	62	140	2					
CG	131	154	24					
SDC	197	215	68					
Totals	390	509	94	993	1,756	352	524	2,632

July 1962

	KIA	WIA	Cap/ Miss.	Total	KIA	WIA	Cap.	Total
ARVN	84	133	13	230				
CG	91	186	19	296				
SDC	150	294	45	489				
Totals	325	613	77	1,015	1,666	413	441	2,520

July 1962

	KIA	WIA	Cap/ Miss.	Total	KIA	WIA	Cap.	Total
ARVN	86	165	13	264				
CG	62	149	46	257				
SDC	236	372	153	761				
Totals	384	686	212	1,282	1,544	424	542	2,510

Aug. 1962

	KIA	WIA	Cap/ Miss.	Total	KIA	WIA	Cap.	Total
ARVN	67	149	2	218				
CG	103	170	15	288				
SDC	207	307	46	560				
Total	377	626	63	1,066	2,271	367	669	3,307

2. *Casualties* (continued)

	GVN				Viet Cong			
	KIA	WIA	Cap/ Miss.	Total	KIA	WIA	Cap.	Total
Sept. 1962								
ARVN	125	231	2	358				
CG	46	101	3	150				
SDC	248	314	54	616				
Total	419	646	59	1,124	2,218	365	446	3,029
Oct. 1962								
ARVN	77	238	2	317				
CG	63	142	3	208				
SDC	225	239	59	523				
Total	365	619	64	1,048	1,967	286	373	2,626
Nov. 1962								
ARVN	66	233	15	314				
CG	72	156	6	234				
SDC	272	445	71	788				
Total	410	834	92	1,336	1,982	368	561	2,911
Dec. 1962								
ARVN	50	232	1	283				
CG	50	118	7	175				
SDC	194	268	70	532				
Total	294	618	78	990	2,203	289	463	2,955
Totals, 1962	4,417	7,195	1,270	12,882	21,158	4,235	5,700	31,093
Jan. 1963								
ARVN	153	432	10	595				
CG	83	152	12	247				
SDC	217	324	80	621				
Total	453	908	102	1,463	1,754	318	379	2,451
Feb. 1963								
ARVN	82	224	6	312				
CG	87	139	10	236				
SDC	210	293	66	569				
Total	379	656	82	1,117	1,084	303	292	1,679
March 1963								
ARVN	75	306	4	385				
CG	161	259	11	431				
SDC	174	286	51	511				
Total	410	851	66	1,327	1,443	368	205	2,016

2. *Casualties* (continued)

	GVN				Viet Cong			
	KIA	WIA	Cap/ Miss.	Total	KIA	WIA	Cap.	Total
April 1963								
ARVN	192	352	15	559				
CG	91	136	13	240				
SDC	223	390	68	681				
Total	506	878	96	1,480	1,660	256	388	2,304
May 1963								
Total	435	889	94	1,418	1,895	295	695	2,885
June 1963								
ARVN	99	256	2	357				
CG	89	158	6	253				
SDC	201	358	82	641				
Total	389	772	90	1,251	1,862	310	437	2,609
July 1963								
ARVN	178	476	23	677				
CG	103	198	51	352				
SDC	248	397	232	877				
Total	529	1,071	306	1,906	1,918	372	387	2,677
August 1963								
ARVN	92	313	14	419				
CG	68	104	14	186				
SDC	150	218	151	519				
Total	310	635	179	1,124	1,447	206	416	2,069
Sept. 18, 1963								
ARVN	83	251	2	336				
CG	101	221	84	406				
SDC	151	211	86	448				
Total	335	683	172	1,190	1,249	101	329	1,679
Totals, 1963 *	3,746	7,343	1,187	12,276	14,312	2,529	3,528	20,369

* These figures do not include GVN casualties for other paramilitary forces, which are incomplete but which in August and September 1963 totalled 571.

3. Weapon Losses*

	Viet Cong	GVN
1961	2,753	5,982
1962		
Jan.–Apr.	1,202	1,777
May–Aug.	1,526	1,884
Sept.–Dec.	1,806	1,534
Total	4,534	5,195
1963		
January	683	457
February	399	253
March	367	467
April	468	797
May	564	463
June	394	580
July	374	663
August	371	554
Sept. 18	335	644
Total	3,955	4,878

4. Viet Cong Defections**

1962	1,956
1963	
January	168
February	245
March	394
April	371
May	414
June	394
July	308
August	191
Sept. 18	107
Total	2,592

* Many VC weapons lost are of the homemade variety.
** This does not include "defectors" coming in under the "Chieu Hoi" or amnesty program.

III. DESERTIONS IN THE SOUTH VIETNAMESE MILITARY AND SE-
CURITY SERVICES *

Date	RVNF**	Civil Guard and Self Defense Corps	Total	Percent of Combined Strength of RVNAF, Civil Guard, Self Defense Corps***
1962				
January	933	1,553	2,486	.8
February	483	1,082	1,565	.5
March	1,168	2,110	3,278	1.0
April	1,273	1,424	2,697	.8
May	1,344	1,057	2,401	.7
June	1,160	1,638	2,798	.8
July	855	1,997	2,852	.8
August	867	2,105	2,972	.8
September	629	1,269	1,898	.5
October	767	1,505	2,272	.6
November	847	1,711	2,558	.7
December	877	1,270	2,147	.6
Total	11,203	18,721	29,924	Average: .7
1963				
January	865	1,814	2,679	.7
February	723	1,389	2,122	.5
March	656	2,260	2,916	.7
April	853	2,018	2,871	.7
May	999	2,165	3,164	.8
June	877	1,441	2,318	.6
July	686	2,289	2,975	.7
August	830	2,501	3,331	.8
Total	6,489	15,877	22,376	Average: .7

* From January 1962 through May 1963, the above statistics include, in addition, to deserters all other persons who have been absent without official leave ("awol") for any length of time or for any reason. The statistics have not been adjusted to take into account those persons who returned to duty. From June through August 1963, the statistics consist entirely of deserters and exclude "awols," but still have not been adjusted to account for returnees.
** Army, Navy, Marines, and Airforce.
*** From January through December 1962, the combined strength of these services increased from 315,454 to 390,220. From January through August 1963, the increase was from 392,460 to 404,799.

Many of them, however, may well have assisted the Viet Cong in some way voluntarily or under duress. The number of "Chieu Hoi" returnees increased progressively from April 19 to June 1963, when a high of about 3,200 was reached. By August, returnees dropped to a low of about 1,600. Complete statistics are not yet available for September.

Until June 1963, statistics on South Vietnamese desertions included all military and security personnel who had been absent from duty without official leave for any reason or for any length of time. Moreover, there was apparently no attempt to adjust these all-inclusive statistics to account for persons who had returned to duty. Including "awols," the 1962 monthly average of deserters was .7% of the combined strength of the military and security services. On this basis, there was no change in the monthly average during the first five months of 1963. Beginning in June, however, statistics on deserters excluded "awols" although they were still not adjusted to cover returnees. Even so, on the new basis, the monthly average of deserters increased from .6% in June 1963 to .8% in August 1963. Complete statistics are not yet available for September.

Conclusions

On the basis of available statistical trends, there appear to have been a number of significant and unfavorable changes in the military situation in South Vietnam since July of this year. Indeed, virtually all of the indicators noted in this report suggest that the military position of the Vietnam Government may have reverted to the point it had reached six months to a year ago. While it is difficult to relate precisely cause and effect for adverse changes in the military situation in South Vietnam, their occurrence at a time when the political situation has deteriorated must be considered as more than coincidental. At the same time, even without the Buddhist crisis and the more serious political difficulties following in its wake, it is possible that the Diem government would have been unable to maintain the favorable trends of preceding periods in the face of the accelerated Viet Cong effort since July 1963.

[Document 148]

SAIGON 1964, 25 Oct. 63

FROM LODGE TO McG. BUNDY

1. I appreciate the concern expressed by you in ref. a relative to the Gen. Don/Conein relationship, and also the present lack of firm intelligence on the details of the general's plot. I hope that ref. b will assist in clearing up some of the doubts relative to general's plans, and I am hopeful that the detailed plans promised for two days before the coup attempt will clear up any remaining doubts.

2. CAS has been punctilious in carrying out my instructions. I have personally approved each meeting between Gen. Don and Conein who has carried out my orders in each instance explicitly. While I share your concern about the continued involvement of Conein in this matter, a suitable substitute for Conein as the principal contact is not presently available. Conein, as you know, is a friend of some eighteen years' standing with Gen. Don, and General Don has expressed extreme reluctance to deal with anyone else. I do not believe the involvement of another American in close contact with the generals would be productive. We are, however, considering the feasibility of a plan for the introduction of an additional officer as a cut-out between Conein and a designee of Gen. Don for communication purposes only. This officer is completely unwitting of any details of past or present coup activities and will remain so.

3. With reference to Gen. Harkins' comment to Gen. Don which Don reports to have referred to a presidential directive and the proposal for a meeting with

me, this may have served the useful purpose of allaying the General's fears as to our interest. If this were a provocation, the GVN could have assumed and manufactured any variations of the same theme. As a precautionary measure, however, I of course refused to see Gen. Don. As to the lack of information as to General Don's real backing, and the lack of evidence that any real capabilities for action have been developed, ref. b provides only part of the answer. I feel sure that the reluctance of the generals to provide the U.S. with full details of their plans at this time, is a reflection of their own sense of security and a lack of confidence that in the large American community present in Saigon their plans will not be prematurely revealed.

4. The best evidence available to the Embassy, which I grant you is not as complete as we would like it, is that Gen. Don and the other generals involved with him are seriously attempting to effect a change in the government. I do not believe that this is a provocation by Ngo Dinh Nhu, although we shall continue to assess the planning as well as possible. In the event that the coup aborts, or in the event that Nhu has masterminded a provocation, I believe that our involvement to date through Conein is still within the realm of plausible denial. CAS is perfectly prepared to have me disavow Conein at any time it may serve the national interest.

5. I welcome your reaffirming instructions contained in CAS Washington 74228. It is vital that we neither thwart a *coup* nor that we are even in a position where we do not know what is going on.

6. We should not thwart a *coup* for two reasons. First, it seems at least an even bet that the next government would not bungle and stumble as much as the present one has. Secondly, it is extremely unwise in the long range for us to pour cold water on attempts at a coup, particularly when they are just in their beginning stages. We should remember that this is the only way in which the people in Vietnam can possibly get a change of government. Whenever we thwart attempts at a coup, as we have done in the past, we are incurring very long lasting resentments, we are assuming an undue responsibility for keeping the incumbents in office, and in general are setting ourselves in judgment over the affairs of Vietnam. Merely to keep in touch with this situation and a policy merely limited to "not thwarting" are courses both of which entail some risks but these are lesser risks than either thwarting all coups while they are stillborn or our not being informed of what is happening. All the above is totally distinct from not wanting U.S. military advisors to be distracted by matters which are not in their domain, with which I heartily agree. But obviously this does not conflict with a policy of not thwarting. In judging proposed coups, we must consider the effect on the war effort. Certainly a succession of fights for control of the Government of Vietnam would interfere with the war effort. It must also be said that the war effort has been interfered with already by the incompetence of the present government and the uproar which this has casued.

7. Gen. Don's intention to have no religious discrimination in a future government is commendable and I applaud his desire not to be "a vassal" of the U.S. But I do not think his promise of a democratic election is realistic. This country simply is not ready for that procedure. I would add two other requirements. First, that there be no wholesale purges of personnel in the government. Individuals who were particularly reprehensible could be dealt with later by the regular legal process. Then I would be impractical, but I am thinking of a government which might include Tri Quang and which certainly should include men of the stature of Mr. Buu, the labor leader.

8. Copy to Gen. Harkins.

[Document 149]

25 Oct 63

FROM: McGeorge Bundy to Lodge

CAP 63590

Your 1964 most helpful.

We will continue to be grateful for all additional information giving increased clarity to prospects of action by Don or others, and we look forward to discussing with you the whole question of control and cutout on your return, always assuming that one of these D-Days does not turn out to be real. We are particularly concerned about hazard that an unsuccessful coup, however carefully we avoid direct engagement, will be laid at our door by public opinion almost everywhere. Therefore, while sharing your view that we should not be in position of thwarting coup, we would like to have option of judging and warning on any plan with poor prospects of success. We recognize that this is a large order, but President wants you to know of our concern.

[Document 150]

30 Oct 1963

FROM: McGEORGE BUNDY

TO: LODGE

CAS 79109

1. Your 2023, 2040, 2041 and 2043 examined with care at highest levels here. You should promptly discuss this reply and associated messages with Harkins whose responsibilities toward any coup are very heavy especially after you leave (see para. 7 below). They give much clearer picture group's alleged plans and also indicate chances of action with or without our approval now so significant that we should urgently consider our attitude and contingency plans. We note particularly Don's curiosity your departure and his insistence Conein be available from Wednesday night on, which suggests date might be as early as Thursday.

2. Believe our attitude to coup group can still have decisive effect on its decisions. We believe that what we say to coup group can produce delay of coup and that betrayal of coup plans to Diem is not repeat not our only way of stopping coup. We therefore need urgently your combined assessment with Harkins and CAS (including their separate comments if they desire). We concerned that our line-up of forces in Saigon (being cabled in next message) indicates approximately equal balance of forces, with substantial possibility serious and prolonged fighting or even defeat. Either of these could be serious or even disastrous for U.S. interests, so that we must have assurance balance of forces clearly favorable.

3. With your assessment in hand, we might feel that we should convey message to Don, whether or not he gives 4 or 48 hours notice that would (A) continue explicit hands-off policy, (B) positively encourage coup, or (C) discourage.

4. In any case, believe Conein should find earliest opportunity express to Don that we do not find presently revealed plans give clear prospect of quick results. This conversation should call attention important Saigon units still apparently loyal to Diem and raise serious issue as to what means coup group has to deal with them.

5. From operational standpoint, we also deeply concerned Don only spokesman for group and possibility cannot be discounted he may not be in good faith. We badly need some corroborative evidence whether Minh and others directly and completely involved. In view Don's claim he doesn't handle "military planning" could not Conein tell Don that we need better military picture and that Big Minh could communicate this most naturally and easily to Stillwell? We recognize desirability involving MACV to minimum, but believe Stillwell far more desirable this purpose than using Conein both ways.

6. Complexity above actions raises question whether you should adhere to present Thursday schedule. Concur you and other U.S. elements should take no action that could indicate U.S. awareness coup possibility. However, DOD is sending berth-equipped military aircraft that will arrive Saigon Thursday and could take you out thereafter as late as Saturday afternoon in time to meet your presently proposed arrival Washington Sunday. You could explain this being done as convenience and that your Washington arrival is same. A further advantage such aircraft is that it would permit your prompt return from any point en route if necessary. To reduce time in transit, you should use this plane, but we recognize delaying your departure may involve greater risk that you personally would appear involved if any action took place. However, advantages your having extra two days in Saigon may outweigh this and we leave timing of flight to your judgment.

7. Whether you leave Thursday or later, believe it essential that prior your departure there be fullest consultation Harkins and CAS and that there be clear arrangements for handling (A) normal activity, (B) continued coup contacts, (C) action in event a coup starts. We assume you will wish Truehart as charge to be head of country team in normal situation, but highest authority desires it clearly understood that after your departure Harkins should participate in supervision of all coup contacts and that in event a coup begins, he become head of country team and direct representative of President, with Truehart in effect acting as POLAD. On coup contacts we will maintain continuous guidance and will expect equally continuous reporting with prompt account of any important divergences in assessments of Harkins and Smith.

8. If coup should start, question of protecting U.S. nationals at once arises. We can move Marine Battalion into Saigon by air from Okinawa within 24 hours—if available. We are sending instructions to CINCPAC to arrange orderly movement of seaborne Marine Battalion to waters adjacent to South Vietnam in position to close Saigon within approximately 24 hours.

9. We are now examining post-coup contingencies here and request your immediate recommendations on position to be adopted after coup begins, especially with respect to requests for assistance of different sorts from one side or the other also request you forward contingency recommendations for action if coup (A) succeeds, (B) fails, (C) is indecisive.

10. We reiterate burden of proof must be on coup group to show a substantial possibility of quick success; otherwise, we should discourage them from proceeding since a miscalculation could result in jeopardizing U.S. position in Southeast Asia.

[Document 151]

30 October 1963

FROM: Harkins, Saigon

TO: Taylor, Washington, D. C.

NR 2028

Your JCS 4188-63 arrived as I was in the process of drafting one for you along the same lines. I share your concern. I have not as yet seen SAIGON 768. I sent to the Embassy for a copy at 0830 this morning—as of now 1100—the Embassy has not released it. Also CINCPAC 0-300040Z infor JCS came as a surprise to me as I am unaware of any change in local situation which indicates necessity for actions directed. Perhaps I'll find the answer in SAIGON 768. Or perhaps actions directed in CINCPAC 300040Z are precautionary in light of Gen. Don's statement reported in CAS 1925 that a coup would take place in any case not later than 2 November. It might be noted Don also is supposed to have said CAS SAIGON 1956—that though the coup committee would not release the details, the Ambassador would receive the complete plan for study two days prior to the scheduled times for the coup.

I have not been informed by the Ambassador that he has received any such plan. I talked to him yesterday on my return from Bangkok and he offered no additional information. He has agreed to keep me completely informed if anything new turns up.

Incidentally he leaves for Washington tomorrow (31st) afternoon. If the coup is to happen before the second he's hardly going to get two days notice.

One thing I have found out, Don is either lying or playing both ends against the middle. What he told me is diametrically opposed to what he told Col. Conein. He told Conein the coup will be before November 2nd. He told me he was not planning a coup. I sat with Don and Big Minh for 2 hours during the parade last Saturday. No one mentioned coups. To go on:

Both CAS SAIGON 1896 and 1925 were sent first and delivered to me after dispatch. My 1991 was discussed with the Ambassador prior to dispatch. My 1993 was not, basically because I had not seen CAS SAIGON 1925 before dispatch and I just wanted to get the record straight from my side and where my name was involved.

The Ambassador and I are certainly in touch with each other but whether the communications between us are effective is something else. I will say Cabot's methods of operations are entirely different from Amb Noltings as far as reporting in the military is concerned.

Fritz would always clear messages concerning the military with me or my staff prior to dispatch. So would John Richardson if MACV was concerned. This is not so today. Cite CAS 1896 and 1925 for examples. Also you will recall I was not the recipient of several messages you held when you were here.

CINCPAC brought this matter up again when I saw him in Bangkok, this past weekend. He is going to make a check when he returns to see if he holds messages I have not received. Have just received SAIGON 768. I will have to report you are correct in believing that the Ambassador is forwarding military reports and evaluations without consulting me. For his weekly report to the President, at his request, I furnish him a short military statement. For preparation of 768 I made no mention of the Delta. I will answer 768 separately today.

There is a basic difference apparently between the Ambassadors thinking and mine on the interpretation of the guidance contained in CAP 63560 dated 6 October and the additional thoughts, I repeat, thoughts expressed in CAS Washington 74228 dated 9 October. I interpret CAP 63560 as our basic guidance and that CAS 74228 being additional thoughts did not change the basic guidance in that no initiative should now be taken to give any active covert encouragement to a coup. The Ambassador feels that 74228 does change 63560 and that a change of government is desired and feels as stated in CAS SAIGON 1964 that the only way to bring about such a change is by a coup.

I'm not opposed to a change in government, no indeed, but I'm inclined to feel that at this time the change should be in methods of governing rather than complete change of personnel. I have seen no batting order proposed by any of the coup groups. I think we should take a hard look at any proposed list before we make any decisions. In my contacts here I have seen no one with the strength of character of Diem, at least in fighting communists. Clearly there are no Generals qualified to take over in my opinion.

I am not a Diem man per se. I certainly see the faults in his character. I am here to back 140 million SVN people in their fight against communism and it just happens that Diem is their leader at this time. Most of the Generals I have talked to agree they can go along with Diem, all say its the Nhu family they are opposed to.

Perhaps the pressures we have begun to apply will cause Diem and Nhu to change their ways. This is apparently not evident as yet. I'm sure the pressures we have begun to apply if continued will affect the war effort. To date they have not. I am watching this closely and will report when I think they have.

I do not agree with the Ambassadors assessment in 768 that we are just holding our own. The GVN is a way ahead in the I, II and parts of the III corps and making progress in the Delta. Nothing has happened in October to change the assessment you and Secretary McNamara made after your visit here.

I would suggest we not try to change horses too quickly. That we continue to take persuasive actions that will make the horses change their course and methods of action. That we win the military effort as quickly as possible, then let them make any and all the changes they want.

After all, rightly or wrongly, we have backed Diem for eight long hard years. To me it seems incongruous now to get him down, kick him around, and get rid of him. The US has been his mother superior and father confessor since he's been in office and he has leaned on us heavily.

Leaders of other under-developed countries will take a dim view of our assistance if they too were led to believe the same fate lies in store for them.

[Document 152]

30 October 1963

FROM: General Harkins, Saigon

TO: General Taylor, Washington

NR: MAC 2033

1. Admiral Felt not addee this message but will be provided copy upon his arrival Saigon tomorrow.

2. I now hold copy of SAIGON 768 and this amplifies my MAC 2028 which initially responded to your JCS 4188-63.

3. SAIGON 768 was Ambassador Lodge personal report to President in response to DEPTEL 576 which is possible explanation why I had not seen 768 until one week after dispatch and only then when I requested a copy so that I might intelligently respond to your JCS 4188-63 which referred to 768.

4. Upon receipt of DEPTEL 576 Ambassador Lodge requested that I provide him brief suggested inputs for responses to questions 1 and 2 (a) 1 of DEPTEL 576 in that they were principally military in nature. I have done this on weekly basis but have had no knowledge as to whether my suggested brief inputs were utilized in his personal report since as indicated above these were not opened to me.

5. My suggested brief inputs for para 1 which were provided the Ambassador for use as he saw fit in drafting his personal evaluations for the past three weeks follow:

16 OCT: On balance we are gaining in the contest with the VC. There will continue to be minor ups and downs but the general trend has been and continues upward.

23 OCT: While significant changes are, and will be, difficult to identify on a day to day or even weekly comparative basis as regards the contest with the Viet Cong, the general trend continues to be favorable. The tempo of RVN-initiated operations is increasing and recently the tempo of VC-initiated activity has fallen off.

30 OCT: No change from that previously reported. National day affairs this past week tended to bring about a slight reduction in the tempo of RVN initiated actions, however VC initiated actions also waned and on balance the trend continues to be favorable.

6. My suggested brief inputs for paragraph 2 (a) which were provided the Ambassador for use as he saw fit in drafting his personal evaluations for the past three weeks follow:

16 OCT: The government has responded at many points when we have cited need for improvement in the campaign against the VC (shift of boundaries; placement of VNSF activities in corps areas under OPCON of corps comdr; reallocation of forces). Additionally Gen Don and Gen Stilwell, my G-3 have spent the last week in the conduct of a Corps by Corps assessment of the present situation with a view to further desirable reallocation of forces. Based on their recommendations I will make further recommendations to Pres. Diem (for inclusion in ANS to para 2 (a) Ambassador was advised that US/GVN military relations remain good).

23 OCT: Response received from the government in reaction to military areas where we have cited needed improvement has been favorable in some areas, while in other areas no indication of response has been received to date. In no case have they flatly resisted recommended improvements. Favorable indications are the commitment of nearly half of the general reserve to operations, plans for possible further redistribution of forces, and a recognition of the requirement to effect consolidation in the strategic hamlet program.

30 OCT: No specific responses have been received from the government this past week in reaction to military areas where we have cited need for improvement. This is believed due in great part to their preoccupation with National day affairs.

7. Comparison of my 23 October suggested brief inputs quoted above with SAIGON 768 indicates Ambassador Lodge did not see fit to utilize my suggestions to any significant degree. It also apparent that upon further reflection

Ambassador determined that more detailed response was required than he initially felt necessary when he requested brief inputs on principally military items.

8. I believe certain portions SAIGON 768 require specific comment. These follow:

Para F of answer to question 1—View of Vice Pres Tho that there are only 15 to 20 all-around hamlets in the area south of Saigon which are really good is ridiculous and indicates need for him to get out of Saigon and visit country-side so as to really know of progress which is being made. In past two weeks I have visited nine Delta provinces (Tay Ninh, Binh Duong, Hau Nghia, Long An, Kien Phong, Kien Hoa, An Giang, Phong Dinh, Chuong Thein), eight of which are south of Saigon, and I do not find the province chiefs or sector advisors to hold the same views as Vice Pres Tho.

Para H of answer to question 1—I am unable to concur in statement that quote one cannot drive as much around the country as one could two years ago end of quote. I believe it will be some time before, if we ever do, experience mass surrenders of the VC. I am unable to concur in statement that VC is quote in fact, reckoned at a higher figure than it was two years ago end quote. I have not observed the signs that hatred of the government has tended to diminish the Army's vigor, enthusiasm and enterprise. I find it difficult to believe the few rumors one hears regarding Generals being paid off with money and flashy cars. Most cars I see in use by Generals are same they have been using for past two years and few if any qualify as flashy to my mind. I do not concur with the evaluation of the 14 October report of the Delta Subcommittee of the Committee on Province Rehabilitation which states that the VC are gaining. Moreover I take exception to the implication that the report represents official country team agency views and is consequently authoritative in the views it presents. Agency representatives on this sub-committee served as individuals in reporting to the COPROR Committee, incidentally there were wide divergencies even among sub-committee members. COPROR Committee received but did not place its stamp of approval or concurrence on report of its Sub-Committee. COPROR Committee returned the report to its Sub-Committee for rework. Consequently this report has not as yet been submitted to country team nor has it been referred to individual country team agencies for review and/or comment. Any views quoted from this Sub-Committee report therefore have no rpt no validity as expressions of country team or individual agency views.

Para J of answer to question 1—With regard to the quote existing political control over troop movements, which prevents optimum use of the Army end quote. I do not deny that political influences enter into this picture however I feel we have made and are making significant strides in this area and do not concur that time is not working for us—so long as political controls remain as at present.

Para J of answer to question 1—As indicated in paras 5 and 6 above and in other reports I have filed my evaluation is that from the military point of view the trend is definitely in RVN favor consequently I cannot concur that quote we at present are not doing much more than holding our own end quote.

Answer under (a) to question 2—I am correctly quoted here but para 6 above gives full context of my suggested input.

Answer under (c) to question 2—As indicated para 6 above Ambassador was advised that US/GVN military relations remain good.

[Document 153]

[This duplication of Document 150 was noted late in the manufacturing process.]

Cablegram from McGeorge Bundy to Ambassador Lodge, Oct. 30, 1963.

1. Your 2023, 2040, 2041 and 2043 examined with care at highest levels here. You should promptly discuss this reply and associated messages with Harkins whose responsibilities toward any coup are very heavy especially after you leave (see para. 7 below). They give much clearer picture group's alleged plans and also indicate chances of action with or without our approval now so significant that we should urgently consider our attitude and contingency plans. We note particularly Don's curiosity your departure and his insistence Conein be available from Wednesday night on, which suggests date might be as early as Thursday.

2. Believe our attitude to coup group can still have decisive effect on its decisions. We believe that what we say to coup group can produce delay of coup and that betrayal of coup plans to Diem is not repeat not our only way of stopping coup. We therefore need urgently our combined assessment with Harkins and CAS (including their separate comments if they desire). We concerned that our line-up of forces in Saigon (being cabled in next message) indicates approximately equal balance of forces, with substantial possibility serious and prolonged fighting or even defeat. Either of these could be serious or even disastrous for U.S. interests, so that we must have assurance balance of forces clearly favorable.

3. With your assessment in hand, we might feel that we should convey message to Don, whether or not he gives 4 or 48 hours notice that would (A) continue explicit hands-off policy, (B) positively encourage coup, or (C) discourage.

4. In any case, believe Conein should find earliest opportunity express to Don that we do not find presently revealed plans give clear prospect of quick results. This conversation should call attention important Saigon units still apparently loyal to Diem and raise serious issue as to what means coup group has to deal with them.

5. From operational standpoint, we also deeply concerned Don only spokesman for group and possibility cannot be discounted he may not be in good faith. We badly need some corroborative evidence whether Minh, and others directly and completely involved. In view Don's claim he doesn't handle "military planning" could not Conein tell Don that we need better military picture and that Big Minh could communicate this most naturally and easily to Stillwell? We recognize desirability involving MACV to minimum, but believe Stillwell far more desirable this purpose than using Conein both ways.

6. Complexity above actions raises question whether you should adhere to present Thursday schedule. Concur you and other U.S. elements should take no action that could indicate U.S. awareness coup possibility. However, DOD is sending berth-equipped military aircraft that will arrive Saigon Thursday and could take you out thereafter as late as Saturday afternoon in time to meet your presently proposed arrival Washington Sunday. You could explain this being done as convenience and that your Washington arrival is same. A further advantage such aircraft is that it would permit your prompt return from any point en route if necessary. To reduce time in transit, you should use this plane, but we recognize delaying your departure may involve greater risk that you person-

ally would appear involved if any action took place. However, advantages your having extra two days in Saigon may outweigh this and we leave timing of flight to your judgment.

7. Whether you leave Thursday or later, believe it essential that prior your departure there be fullest consultation Harkins and CAS and that there be clear arrangements for handling (A) normal activity, (B) continued coup contacts, (C) action in event a coup starts. We assume you will wish. Truehart as charge to be head of country team in normal situation, but highest authority desires it clearly understood that after your departure Harkins should participate in supervision of all coup contacts and that in event a coup begins, he become head of country team and direct representative of President, with Truehart in effect acting as POLAD. On coup contacts we will maintain continuous guidance and will expect equally continuous reporting with prompt account of any important divergences in assessments of Harkins and Smith.

8. If coup should start, question of protecting U.S. nationals at once arises. We can move Marine Battalion into Saigon by air from Okinawa within 24 hours if—[sic] available. We are sending instructions to CINCPAC to arrange orderly movement of seaborne Marine Battalion to waters adjacent to South Vietnam in position to close Saigon within approximately 24 hours.

9. We are now examing post-coup contingencies here and request your immediate recommendations on position to be adopted after coup begins, especially with respect to requests for assistance of different sorts from one side or the other also request you forward contingency recommendations for action if coup (A) succeeds, (B) fails, (C) is indecisive.

10. We reiterate burden of proof must be on coup group to show a substantial possibility of quick success; otherwise, we should discourage them from proceeding since a miscalculation could result in jeopardizing U.S. position in Southeast Asia.

[Document 154]

30 Oct 1963

FROM: Lodge

TO: State

CAS 2063

1. We must, of course, get best possible estimate of chance of coup's success and this estimate must color our thinking, but do not think we have the power to delay or discourage a coup. Don has made it clear many times that this is a Vietnamese affair. It is theoretically possible for us to turn over the information which has been given to us in confidence to Diem and this would undoubtedly stop the coup and would make traitors out of us. For practical purposes therefore I would say that we have very little influence on what is essentially a Vietnamese affair. In addition, this would place the heads of the Generals, their civilian supporters, and lower military officers on the spot, thereby sacrificing a significant portion of the civilian and military leadership needed to carry the war against the VC to its successful conclusion. After our efforts not to discourage a coup and this change of heart, we would foreclose any possibility of change of the GVN for the better. Diem/Nhu have displayed no intentions to date of a desire to change the traditional methods of control through police

action or take any repeat any actions which would undermine the power position or solidarity of the Ngo family. This, despite our heavy pressures directed DEPTEL 534. If our attempt to thwart this coup were successful, which we doubt, it is our firm estimate that younger officers, small groups of military, would then engage in an abortive action creating chaos ideally suited to VC objectives.

2. While we will attempt a combined assessment in a following message, time has not yet permitted substantive examination of this matter with General Harkins. My general view is that the U.S. is trying to bring this medieval country into the 20th Century and that we have made considerable progress in military and economic ways but to gain victory we must also bring them into the 20th Century politically and that can only be done by either a thoroughgoing change in the behavior of the present government or by another government. The Viet Cong problem is partly military but it is also partly psychological and political.

3. With respect to paragraph 3 Ref., I believe that we should continue our present position of keeping hands off but continue to monitor and press for more detailed information. CAS has been analyzing potential coup forces for some time and it is their estimate that the Generals have probably figured their chances pretty closely and probably also expect that once they begin to move, not only planned units, but other units will join them. We believe that Vietnam's best Generals are involved in directing this effort. If they can't pull it off, it is doubtful other military leadership could do so successfully. It is understandable that the Generals would be reticent to reveal full details of their plan for fear of leaks to the GVN.

4. Re para. 4, Ref., we expect that Conein will meet Don on the night of 30 Oct or early morning 31 Oct. We agree with Para. 4, Ref., that we should continue to press for details and question Don as to his estimate of the relative strengths of opposing forces. We do not believe, however, that we should show any signs of attempting to direct this affair ourselves or of giving the impression of second thoughts on this Vietnamese initiation. In the meantime, we will respond specifically to CAS Washington 79126. Please note that CAS Saigon 2059 corrects CAS Saigon 2023 and two regiments of the 7th Division are included in the coup forces.

5. Apparently Para. 5, Ref., overlooks CAS 1445, 5 Oct 1963 which gave an account of the face to face meeting of General "Big Minh" and Conein at Minh's instigation and through the specific arrangement of Gen Don. Minh specifically identified Gen Don as participating in a plan to change the government. Please note that Minh's remarks parallel in every way the later statements of Gen. Don. We believe that the limitation of contact to Don and Cein is an appropriate security measure consonant with our urging that the smallest number of persons be aware of these details.

6. We do not believe it wise to ask that "Big Minh" pass his plans to Gen. Stilwell. The Vietnamese believe that there are members of the U.S. military who leak to the Government of Vietnam. I do not doubt that this is an unjust suspicion but it is a fact that this suspicion exists and there is no use in pretending that it does not.

7. I much appreciate your furnishing the berth-equipped military aircraft which I trust is a jet. I intend to tell Pan American that a jet has been diverted for my use and therefore I will no longer need their services. This will undoubtedly leak to the newspapers and the GVN may study this move with some suspicion. I will answer any inquiries on this score to the effect that I

am most pleased by this attention and that this is obviously done as a measure to insure my comfort and save my time. To allay suspicions further, I will offer space on the aircraft to MACV for emergency leave cases, etc., and handle this in as routine fashion as possible. I wish to reserve comment as to my actual time of departure until I have some additional information, hopefully tomorrow.

8. Your para. 7 somewhat perplexes me. It does not seem sensible to have the military in charge of a matter which is so profoundly political as a change of government. In fact, I would say to do this would probably be the end of any hope for a change of government here. This is said impersonally as a general proposition, since Gen. Harkins is a splendid General and an old friend of mine to whom I would gladly entrust anything I have. I assume that the Embassy and MACV are able to handle normal activities under A, that CAS can continue coup contacts under B, and as regards C, we must simply do the very best we can in the light of events after the coup has started.

9. We appreciate the steps taken as outlined in para. 8. However, we should remember that the GVN is not totally inept in its foreign soundings and that these moves should be as discreet and security conscious as possible. I would, of course, call for these forces only in case of extreme necessity since my hope coincides with the Generals that this will be an all-Vietnamese affair.

10. We anticipate that at the outset of the coup, unless it moves with lightning swiftness, the GVN will request me or Gen. Harkins to use our influence to call it off. I believe our responsibilities should be that our influence certainly could not be superior to that of the President who is Commander-in-Chief and that if he is unable to call it off, we would certainly be unable to do so and would merely be risking American lives attempting to interfere in this Vietnamese problem. The Government might request aircraft. Helicopters, for the evacuation of key personalities that would have to be studied closely, but we would certainly not commit our planes and pilots between the battle lines of the opposing forces. We should, rather, state that we would be willing to act in this fashion during a truce in which both sides agree to the removal of key personalities. I believe that there would be immediate political problems in attempting to take these personalities to another neighboring country and probably we would be best served in depositing them in Saipan where the absence of press, communications, etc., would allow us some leeway to make a further decision as to their ultimate disposition. If senior Vietnamese personalities and their families requested asylum in the Embassy or other American installations, we would probably have to grant it in light of our previous action with respect to Tri Quang. This will undoubtedly present later problems but hopefully the new government might feel disposed to help us solve this problem. Naturally, asylum would be granted on the same basis as the Buddhists, i.e., physical presence at the Embassy or other location.

11. As to requests from the Generals, they may well have need of funds at the last moment with which to buy off potential opposition. To the extent that these funds can be passed discreetly, I believe we should furnish them, provided we are convinced that the proposed coup is sufficiently well organized to have a good chance of success. If they are successful, they will undoubtedly ask for prompt recognition and some assurance that military and economic aid will continue at normal level. We should be prepared to make these statements if the issue is clear-cut predicating our position on the President's stated desire to continue the war against the VC to final victory. VOA might be an important means of disseminating this message. Should the coup fail, we will have to pick up the pieces as best we can at that time. We have a commitment

to the Generals from the August episode to attempt to help in the evacuation of their dependents. We should try to live up to this if conditions will permit. American complicity will undoubtedly be charged and there might be some acts taken against specific personalities which we should anticipate and make provision against as best we can. Should the coup prove indecisive and a protracted struggle is in progress, we should probably offer our good offices to help resolve the issue in the interest of the war against the VC. This might hold some benefit in terms of concessions by GVN. We will naturally incur some opprobrium from both sides in our role as mediator. However, this opprobrium would probably be less distasteful than a deadlock which would open the door to the VC. We consider such a deadlock as the least likely possibility of the three.

12. As regards your para. 10, I do not know what more proof can be offered than the fact these men are obviously prepared to risk their lives and that they want nothing for themselves. If I am any judge of human nature, Don's face expressed of sincerity and determination on the morning that I spoke to him. Heartily agree that a miscalculation could jeopardize position in Southeast Asia. We also run tremendous risks by doing nothing.

If we were convinced that the coup was going to fail, we would, of course, do everything we could to stop it.

13. Gen. Harkins has read this and does not concur.

[Document 155]

CAS 79407, 30 Oct '63

FROM BUNDY TO LODGE

1. Our reading your thoughtful 2063 leads us to believe a significant difference of shading may exist on one crucial point (see next para.) and on one or two lesser matters easily clarified.

2. We do not accept as a basis for U.S. policy that we have no power to delay or discourage a coup. In your paragraph 12 you say that if you were convinced that the coup was going to fail you would of course do everything you could to stop it. We believe that on this same basis you should take action to persuade coup leaders to stop or delay any operation which, in your best judgment, does not clearly give high prospect of success. We have not considered any betrayal of generals to Diem, and our 79109 explicitly reject that course. We recognize the danger of appearing hostile to generals, but we believe that our own position should be on as firm ground as possible, hence we cannot limit ourselves to proposition implied in your message that only conviction of certain failure justifies intervention. We believe that your standard for intervention should be that stated above.

3. Therefore, if you should conclude that there is not clearly a high prospect of success, you should communicate this doubt to generals in a way calculated to persuade them to desist at least until chances are better. In such a communication you should use the weight of U.S. best advice and explicitly reject any implication that we oppose the effort of the generals because of preference for present regime. We recognize need to bear in mind generals' interpretation of U.S. role in 1960 coup attempt, and your agent should maintain clear distinction between strong and honest advice given as a friend and any opposition to their objectives.

4. We continue to be deeply interested in up-to-the-minute assessment of

prospects and are sending this before reply to our CAS 79126. We want continuous exchange latest assessments on this topic.

5. To clarify our intent, paragraph 7 of our 79109 is rescinded and we restate our desires as follows:

a. While you are in Saigon you will be Chief of Country Team in all circumstances and our only instruction is that we are sure it will help to have Harkins fully informed at all stages and to use advice from both him and Smith in framing guidance for coup contacts and assessment. We continue to be concerned that neither Conein nor any other reporting source is getting the clarity we would like with respect to alignment of forces and level of determination among generals.

b. When you leave Saigon and before there is a coup, Truehart will be Chief of the Country Team. Our only modification of existing procedures is that in this circumstance we wish all instruction to Conein to be conducted in immediate consultation with Harkins and Smith so that all three know what is sold in Conein. Any disagreement among the three on such instruction should be reported to Washington and held for our resolution, when time permits.

c. If you have left and a coup occurs, we believe that emergency situation requires, pending your return, that direction of country team be vested in most senior officer with experience of military decisions, and the officer in our view is Harkins. We do *not* intend that this switch in final responsibility should be publicized in any way, and Harkins will of course be guided in basic posture by our instructions, which follow in paragraph 6. We do not believe that this switch will have the effect suggested in your paragraph 8.

6. This paragraph contains our present standing instructions for U.S. posture in the event of a coup.

a. U.S. authorities will reject appeals for direct intervention from either side, and U.S.-controlled aircraft and other resources will not be committed between the battle lines or in support of either side, without authorization from Washington.

b. In event of indecisive contest, U.S. authorities may in their discretion agree to perform any acts agreeable to both sides, such as removal of key personalities or relay of information. In such actions, however, U.S. authorities will strenuously avoid appearance of pressure on either side. It is not in the interest of USG to be or appear to be either instrument of existing government or instrument of coup.

c. In the event of imminent or actual failure of coup, U.S. authorities may afford asylum in their discretion to those to whom there is any express or implied obligation of this sort. We believe however that in such a case it would be in our interest and probably in interest of those seeking asylum that they seek protection of other Embassies in addition to our own. This point should be made strongly if need arises.

d. But once a coup under responsible leadership has begun, and within these restrictions, it is in the interest of the U.S. Government that it should succeed.

7. We have your message about return to Washington and we suggest that all public comment be kept as low-key and quiet as possible, and we also urge that if possible you keep open the exact time of your departure. We are strongly sensitive to great disadvantage of having you out of Saigon if this should turn out to be a week of decision, and if it can be avoided we would prefer not to see you pinned to a fixed hour of departure now.

Justification of the War—Public Statements
KENNEDY ADMINISTRATION

CONTENTS

Summary

Public Statement 10 (*page 803*)
Johnson-Diem communique expressing U.S. awareness of Communist subversion in Vietnam and U.S. responsibilities and interest in assisting the Saigon Government (13 May 1961).

Public Statement 11 (*page 804*)
Kennedy stresses the subversive threat facing the southern half of the globe (25 May 1961).

Public Statement 12 (*page 804*)
Kennedy enumerates border violations to Southeast Asian nations, denounces the "war of liberation" justification, and stresses the consequences of successful Communist efforts in Laos and Vietnam (25 September 1961).

Public Statement 13 (*page 805*)
Kennedy comments on evidence that guerrilla activity in South Vietnam is originating outside that country (11 October 1961).

Public Statement 14 (*page 805*)
Kennedy acknowledges Hanoi direction of guerrilla effort in violation of Geneva Accords; indicates the U.S. is prepared to assist in the defense of Vietnam independence through increased aid (14 December 1961).

Public Statement 15 (*page 806*)
Kennedy acknowledges a step-up in U.S. effort to resist aggression in Vietnam under the guise of a "war of liberation" (11 January 1962).

Public Statement 16 (*page 806*)
Kennedy's response to a question on the hazards of a coalition government in Laos provides insight into his thinking on military intervention as the other alternative (15 January 1962).

Public Statement 17 (*page 807*)
Kennedy discusses U.S. involvement in Vietnam in general terms; specifics avoided in interest of security (7 February 1962).

Public Statement 18 (*page 807*)
Kennedy reviews the development of U.S. involvement in Vietnam in response to question suggesting a credibility problem (14 February 1962).

Public Statement 19 (*page 809*)
Kennedy gives an excellent assessment of the state of the Communist world (23 March 1962).

Public Statement 20 (*page 810*)
Kennedy emphasizes the need to pursue our established goal of non-Communist Vietnam (11 April 1962).

Public Statement 21 (*page 810*)
Kennedy, commenting on cease-fire violations in Laos, stresses the desirability of a political solution as contrasted to military intervention (9 May 1962).

Public Statement 22 (*page 811*)
Kennedy announces the movement of troops to Thailand as evidence of U.S. concern over the Laotian cease-fire violations (15 May 1962).

Public Statement 23   (page 811)
Kennedy responds to questions on troop deployment to Thailand; cites SEATO obligations as the legal basis (17 May 1962).

Public Statement 24   (page 813)
Kennedy describes Communist threat of infiltration and subversion as he envisioned it (6 June 1962).

Public Statement 25   (page 813)
Kennedy comments on Mansfield's concern about the Administration's Asian policies; suggests he does not think that Mansfield would advocate withdrawing from Vietnam or Thailand (14 June 1962).

Public Statement 26   (page 814)
An official statement calling attention to findings of International Control Commission that North Vietnam was violating the Geneva Accords (16 July 1962).

Public Statement 27   (page 815)
Kennedy cautions that a split in the Communist world is over the means not the end of communizing the world (14 January 1963).

Public Statement 28   (page 816)
Kennedy argues for foreign aid to help eliminate root causes of unrest in developing world (14 January 1963).

Public Statement 29   (page 816)
Kennedy expresses disagreement with recommendation of Mansfield committee to reduce aid to Southeast Asia; refuses to withdraw and turn it over to the Communists (6 March 1963).

Public Statement 30   (page 817)
Deputy Under Secretary for Political Affairs presents important analysis of U.S. interests in Southeast Asia; resources and location emphasized as is the importance of Communist revolutionary momentum; validity of SEATO commitment also cited (8 April 1963).

Public Statement 31   (page 818)
Kennedy points out the interrelationship of Southeast Asian nations in response to question on domino theory (24 April 1963).

Public Statement 32   (page 819)
Kennedy comments on reasons for sending troops to South Vietnam but not to Laos (8 May 1963).

Public Statement 33   (page 819)
Rusk stresses the strategic importance of South Vietnam and the history of our involvement (13 May 1963).

Public Statement 34   (page 821)
Hilsman discusses Communist threat to Asia and the U.S. commitment to combat its spread; explains Viet Cong role in South Vietnam and attempts to place it in perspective to worldwide threat (8 July 1963).

Public Statement 35 (*page 824*)
Kennedy emphasizes the need for U.S. presence in South Vietnam to avoid collapse of the government; vows to stay (17 July 1963).

Public Statement 36 (*page 825*)
Heavner, Deputy Director of Vietnam Working Group, discusses in detail the evolution of U.S. involvement; he looks at South Vietnam as a strategic location, a moral commitment, a fulfillment of SEATO obligations and a test case for "war of liberation" (9 September 1963).

Public Statement 37 (*page 827*)
Kennedy admits Diem's failings but feels it essential that the U.S. remain (25 September 1963).

Public Statement 38 (*page 827*)
Kennedy confirms his belief in "domino theory" and emphasizes need to remain and help government strengthen and reform (9 September 1963).

Public Statement 39 (*page 828*)
Kennedy admits to the presence of 25,000 Americans in South Vietnam with a primary goal of winning the war (12 September 1963).

Public Statement 40 (*page 828*)
Kennedy gives excellent assessment of U.S. role and responsibility to lead the defense of the world's free nations (25 September 1963).

Public Statement 41 (*page 829*)
Kennedy cites U.S. role as leader of Free World (26 September 1963).

Public Statement 42 (*page 830*)
Policy statement reaffirming U.S. intent to fight aggression in Vietnam and elsewhere where independence and freedom are threatened (2 October 1963).

Public Statement 43 (*page 830*)
Kennedy had planned in his Dallas speech to emphasize that work alone cannot defend the Free World from Communist advances; military and economic assistance must be available to back U.S. promises (22 November 1963).

KENNEDY ADMINISTRATION

Summary

The Administration of President Kennedy justified the growing U.S. involvement in Vietnam utilizing much the same rationale that had been employed by the Administrations of President Truman and President Eisenhower. Initially, the situation in Vietnam received less emphasis than the crisis in Laos, although the principles cited for U.S. concern for Laos—the identification of U.S. interests with its independence; SEATO obligations—were couched in terms of collective security for Southeast Asia. Thereafter, as insurgency in Vietnam itself came to the fore, the Administration's public statements stressed the following:

a. The struggle against the worldwide communist offensive had to confront the danger that through "subversion, infiltration, and a host of other tactics . . . our security may be lost piece by piece, country by country, without the firing of a single missile or the crossing of a single border."

b. The "domino principle": the countries of Southeast Asia are interdependent for security, and the independence of each is important to the United States.

c. ICC reports, as well as U.S. and South Vietnamese intelligence, demonstrate that Communist North Vietnam has provided illegally, armed and unarmed personnel, arms, munitions, and other supplies from North Vietnam to insurgents in South Vietnam for the purpose of supporting an organized attempt to overthrow the government there.

d. "Now our great responsibility is to be the chief defender of freedom, in this time of maximum danger. Only the U.S. has the power and the resources and the determination."

e. The United States, although not a party to the Geneva Accords, declared at Geneva in 1954 that it would "view any renewal of the aggression in violation of the agreements with grave concern and as seriously threatening international peace and security." President Kennedy assured President Diem that "in accordance with that declaration, and in response to your request, we are prepared to help the Republic of Vietnam to protect its people and to preserve its independence."

f. The SEATO Pact, by a protocol, extended the protection of the treaty to Vietnam; hence the treaty, in President Kennedy's words, "stated that the United States recognized that aggression by means of armed attack against Vietnam would threaten our own peace and security . . . the attack on the government by the communist forces, with assistance from the north, became of greater and greater concern to the Government of Vietnam and the Government of the United States."

End of Summary

1. *Senator John F. Kennedy, Congressional Record, February 29, 1960, p. 3582:*

*   *   *

"But both before and after 1953 events have demonstrated that our nuclear retaliatory power is not enough. It cannot deter Communist aggression which is too limited to justify atomic war. It cannot protect uncommitted nations against a Communist takeover using local or guerrilla forces. It cannot be used in so-called brush-fire peripheral wars. In short, it cannot prevent the Communists from gradually nibbling at the fringe of the free world's territory and strength, until our security has been steadily eroded in piecemeal fashion—each Red advance being too small to justify massive retaliation, with all its risks.

*   *   *

"In short, we need forces of an entirely different kind to keep the peace against limited aggression, and to fight it, if deterrence fails, without raising the conflict to a disastrous pitch.

"And our capability for conventional war is insufficient to avoid the hopeless dilemma of choosing between launching a nuclear attack and watching aggressors make piecemeal conquests."

2. *Senator John F. Kennedy's statement in Congressional Record, June 14, 1960, p. 11631:*

*   *   *

"We must regain the ability to intervene effectively and swiftly in any limited war anywhere in the world—augmenting, modernizing and providing increased mobility and versatility for the conventional forces and weapons of the Army and Marine Corps. As long as those forces lack the necessary airlift and sealift capacity and versatility of firepower, we cannot protect our commitments around the globe—resist non-nuclear aggressions—or be certain of having enough time to decide on the use of our nuclear power."

*   *   *

3. *Senator John F. Kennedy's statement as quoted in the Washington Daily News, September 22, 1960:*

*   *   *

"The recognition is not really the crux of our foreign policy. The real question is what should be done about the harsh facts that China is a powerful and aggressive nation. The dangerous situation now existing can be remedied only by a strong and successful India, a strong and successful Japan, and some kind of regional group over Southeast Asia which gives these smaller countries the feeling that, in spite of their distaste for a military alliance, they will not be left to be picked off one by one at the whim of the Peiping regime."

4. *Senator John F. Kennedy Interview as Reported in The Washington Post, October 22, 1960:*

*   *   *

Cronkite: ". . . What areas do you see where the United States might take the offensive in a challenge to communism over the next 4 to 8 years?"

Kennedy: ". . . the most vulnerable area, I have felt, has been eastern Europe. I have been critical of the Administration's failure to suggest policies which would make it possible for us to establish, for example, closer relations with Poland, particularly after the '55–'56 period and the Hungarian revolution. We indicated at that time that we were not going to intervene militarily. There was a period there when Poland demonstrated a national independence, and even the Polish Government moved some distance away from the Soviet Union.

". . . Secondly, the relations between Russia and China. They are now engaged in a debate over whether war is the means of communizing the world, or whether they should use subversion and infiltration, economic struggles and all the rest. No one can say what that course of action will be, but I think the next President of the United States should watch it carefully. If those two years should split, it could have great effects throughout the entire world.

"Thirdly, I believe that India represents a great area for affirmative action by the Free World. India started from about the same place that China did. The Chinese Communists have been moving ahead the last 10 years. India . . . has been making some progress, but if India does not succeed with her 450 million people, if she can't make freedom work, then people around the world are going to determine, particularly in the underdeveloped world, that the only way they can develop their resources is through the Communist system."

*   *   *

5. *Kennedy Presidential News Conference as Quoted in the New York Times, March 24, 1961. News Conference of March 23, 1961:*

*   *   *

"My fellow Americans, Laos is far away from America, but the world is small. Its 2,000,000 people live in a country three times the size of Austria. The security of all Southeast Asia will be endangered if Laos loses its neutral independence. Its own safety runs with the safety of us all, in real neutrality observed by all.

"I want to make it clear to the American people and to all of the world that all we want in Laos is peace and not war, a truly neutral government and not a cold war pawn, a settlement concluded at the conference table and not on the battlefield."

*   *   *

Q. "Mr. President, there appears to be some national unawareness of the importance of a free Laos to the security of the United States and to the individual American. Could you spell out your views on that a little further?"

A. "Well, quite obviously geographically Laos borders on Thailand, which is, to which the United States has treaty obligations under the SEATO agreement of 1954, it borders on South Vietnam—it borders on Vietnam—to which the United States has very close ties, and also which is a signatory of the SEATO pact.

"The aggression against Laos itself was referred to in the SEATO agreement, so that given this, the nature of the geography, its location the commitments which the United States and obligations which the United States has assumed towards Laos as well as the surrounding countries—as well as other signatories of the SEATO pact—it's quite obvious that if the Communists were able to move in and dominate this country, it would endanger the security of all, and the peace of all of Southeast Asia.

"And as a member of the United Nations and as a signatory to the SEATO pact, and as a country which is concerned with the strength of the cause of freedom around the world, that quite obviously affects the security of the United States."

6. *President Kennedy's Special Message to Congress on the Defense Budget, March 28, 1961, Public Papers of the Presidents, Kennedy, 1961, p. 229:*

*   *   *

"The strength and deployment of our forces in combination with those of our allies should be sufficiently powerful and mobile to prevent the steady erosion of the Free World through limited wars; and it is this role that should constitute the primary mission of our overseas forces. Non-nuclear wars, and sub-limited or guerrilla warfare, have since 1945 constituted the most active and constant threat to Free World security. Those units of our forces which are stationed overseas, or designed to fight overseas, can be most usefully oriented toward deterring or confining those conflicts which do not justify and must not lead to a general nuclear attack. In the event of a major aggression that could not be repulsed by conventional forces, we must be prepared to take whatever action with whatever weapons are appropriate. But our objective now is to increase our ability to confine our response to non-nuclear weapons, and to lessen the incentive for any limited aggression by making clear what our response will accomplish. In most areas of the world, the main burden of local defense against overt attack, subversion and guerrilla warfare must rest on local populations and forces. But given the great likelihood and seriousness of this threat, we must be prepared to make a substantial contribution in the form of strong, highly mobile forces trained in this type of warfare, some of which must be deployed in forward areas, with a substantial airlift and sealift capacity and prestocked overseas bases.

"In this area of local wars, we must inevitably count on the cooperative efforts of other peoples and nations who share our concern. Indeed, their interests are more often directly engaged in such conflicts. The self-reliant are also those whom it is easiest to help—and for these reasons we must continue and reshape the Military Assistance Program which I have discussed earlier in my special message on foreign aid.

"Strengthened capacity to meet limited and guerrilla warfare—limited military adventures and threats to the security of the Free World that are not large enough to justify the label of 'limited war.' We need a greater ability to deal with guerrilla forces, insurrections, and subversion. Much of our effort to create guerrilla and anti-guerrilla capabilities has in the past been aimed at general war. We must be ready now to deal with any size of force, including small externally supported bands of men; and we must help train local forces to be equally effective."

7. *President Kennedy's Address to American Society of Newspaper Editors, April 20, 1961, Public Papers of the Presidents, Kennedy, 1961, p. 306:*

*　　*　　*

". . . we face a relentless struggle in every corner of the globe that goes far beyond the clash of armies or even nuclear armaments. The armies are there, and in large number. The nuclear armaments are there. But they serve primarily as the shield behind which subversion, infiltration, and a host of other tactics steadily advance, picking off vulnerable areas one by one in situations which do not permit our own armed intervention.

"Power is the hallmark of this offensive—power and discipline and deceit. The legitimate discontent of yearning people is exploited. The legitimate trappings of self-determination are employed. But once in power, all talk of discontent is repressed, all self-determination disappears, and the promise of a revolution of hope is betrayed, as in Cuba, into a reign of terror. Those who on instruction staged automatic 'riots' in the streets of free nations over the efforts of a small group of young Cubans to regain their freedom should recall the long roll call of refugees who cannot now go back—to Hungary, to North Korea, to North Viet-Nam, to East Germany, or to Poland, or to any of the other lands from which a steady stream of refugees pours forth, in eloquent testimony to the cruel oppression now holding sway in their homeland.

"We dare not fail to see the insidious nature of this new and deeper struggle. We dare not fail to grasp the new concepts, the new tools, the new sense of urgency we will need to combat it—whether in Cuba or South Viet-Nam. And we dare not fail to realize that this struggle is taking place every day, without fanfare, in thousands of villages and markets—day and night—and in classrooms all over the globe.

"The message of Cuba, of Laos, of the rising din of Communist voices in Asia and Latin America—these messages are all the same. The complacent, the self-indulgent, the soft societies are about to be swept away with the debris of history. Only the strong, only the industrious, only the determined, only the courageous, only the visionary who determine the real nature of our struggle can possibly survive.

"No greater task faces this country or this administration. No other challenge is more deserving of our every effort and energy. Too long we have fixed our eyes on traditional military needs, on armies prepared to cross borders, on missiles poised for flight. Now it should be clear that this is no longer enough—

that our security may be lost piece by piece, country by country, without the firing of a single missile or the crossing of a single border.

"We intend to profit from this lesson. We intend to re-examine and re-orient our forces of all kinds—our tactics and our institutions here in this community. We intend to intensify our efforts for a struggle in many ways more difficult than war, where disappointment will often accompany us.

"For I am convinced that we in this country and in the free world possess the necessary resource, and the skill, and the added strength that comes from a belief in the freedom of man. And I am equally convinced that history will record the fact that this bitter struggle reached its climax in the late 1950's and the early 1960's. Let me then make clear as the President of the United States that I am determined upon our system's survival and success, regardless of the cost and regardless of the peril!"

8. *President Kennedy's Address, in Chicago to Democratic Party Dinner, April 28, 1961, Public Papers of the Presidents, Kennedy, 1961, p. 340:*

*   *   *

"We live in a hazardous and dangerous time. I do not think it's possible to overstate it. We live in a world which has changed tremendously in our lifetime —history only will secure a full perspective on that change. But here is Africa, which was held by Western European powers for several centuries, now independent—which holds within its countries masses of people, many of them illiterate, who live on average incomes of 50 or 60 or 75 dollars a year, who want a change, who now are the masters of their own house but who lack the means of building a viable economy, who are impressed by the example of the Soviet Union and the Chinese, who—not knowing the meaning of freedom in their own lives—wonder whether the Communist system holds the secret of organizing the resources of the state in order to bring them a better life.

"And what is true of Africa is true of Asia, and what is true of Africa and Asia is true in some degree of Latin America. The Communists move among them, disciplined, organized, subject to an international discipline, promising under their system that all will be well, knowing that if they can win just once, then the iron grip of the totalitarian state goes upon the population—those who resist become refugees, or are shot—and they manage to control the population.

"Tonight, in Viet-nam, where the President was re-elected recently in the last 2 weeks by a majority of 75 to 80 percent, yet a small army of guerrillas, organized and sustained by the Communist Viet Minh in the north, control most of the countryside in the nighttime—in the last 12 months have assassinated over four thousand civil officers, two thousand state employees and two thousand police, believing if they can 'spill the wine,' that then they can win control of the population. And when they have won, they do not intend to give way.

"Now our great responsibility is to be the chief defender of freedom, in this time of maximum danger. Only the United States has the power and the resources and the determination. We have committed ourselves to the defense of dozens of countries stretched around the globe who look to us for independence, who look to us for the defense of their freedom.

"We are prepared to meet our obligations, but we can only defend the freedom of those who are determined to be free themselves. We can assist them —we will bear more than our share of the burden, but we can only help those who are ready to bear their share of the burden themselves.

"The Russians and the Chinese, containing within their borders nearly a billion people, totally mobilized for the advance of the Communist system, operating from narrow, interior lines of communication, pressuring on Southeast Asia with the masses of the Chinese armies potentially ready to move—of the Russians who hold great power potentially in the Middle East and Western Europe—the United States stands as the chief defender of freedom.

"I said in my Inaugural Address that no group of people in any generation since democracy was first developed by the ancient Greeks nearly twenty-four or -five hundred years ago, have ever borne a responsibility as great as ours. And I welcome it—and I welcome it tonight.

"There is no easy answer to the dilemmas that we face. Our great ally is the fact that people do desire to be free, that people will sacrifice everything in their desire to maintain their independence. And as the true nature of the Communist conspiracy becomes better known around the globe, when people come to realize—as they surely will—that the Communist advance does not represent a means of liberation but represents a final enslavement, then I believe that they will rally to the cause to which we have given our support and our commitment.

"I believe that we must build our country well, also. Senator Douglas described what we are attempting to do. The burdens are heavy upon us. We have to make this society an example to the world, strong enough to serve not only as an example but strong enough to maintain the commitments that we have assumed."

*   *   *

9. *President Kennedy's Presidential News Conference, May 5, 1961, Public Papers of the Presidents, Kennedy, 1961, p. 356:*

*   *   *

Q. "There have been reports that you would be prepared to send American forces into South Vietnam if that became necessary to prevent Communist domination of that country. Could you tell us whether that is correct and also anything else you have regarding plans for that country?"

A. "Well, we have had a group working in the Government and we've had a Security Council meeting about the problems which are faced in Vietnam by guerrillas and by the barrage which the present Government is being subjected to. The problem of troops . . . the matter of what we're going to do to assist Vietnam to obtain its independence is . . . a matter still under consideration.'. . ."

*   *   *

10. *Joint Communique Issued at Saigon by the Vice President of the United States and the President of Viet-Nam, May 13, 1961, Department of State Bulletin, June 19, 1961, p. 956:*

"The United States, for its part, is conscious of the determination, energy and sacrifices which the Vietnamese people, under the dedicated leadership of President Ngo Dinh Diem, have brought to the defense of freedom in their land.

"The United States is also conscious of its responsibility and duty, in its own self-interest as well as in the interest of other free peoples, to assist a brave country in the defense of its liberties against unprovoked subversion and Communist terror. It has no other motive than the defense of freedom."

11. *President Kennedy's Special Message to Congress, May 25, 1961, Public Papers of the Presidents, Kennedy, 1961:*

"The great battleground for the defense and expansion of freedom today is the whole southern half of the globe—Asia, Latin America, Africa and the Middle East—the lands of the rising peoples. Their revolution is the greatest in human history. They seek an end to injustice, tyranny, and exploitation. More than an end, they seek a beginning.

"And theirs is a revolution which we would support regardless of the Cold War, and regardless of which political or economic route they should choose to freedom.

"For the adversaries of freedom did not create the revolution; nor did they create the conditions which compel it. But they are seeking to ride the crest of its wave—to capture it for themselves.

"Yet their aggression is more often concealed than open. They have fired no missiles; and their troops are seldom seen. They send arms, agitators, aid, technicians and propaganda to every troubled area. But where fighting is required, it is usually done by others—by guerrillas striking at night, by assassins striking alone—assassins who have taken the lives of four thousand civil officers in the last twelve months in Vietnam alone—by subversives and saboteurs and insurrectionists, who in some cases control whole areas inside of independent nations.

"With these formidable weapons, the adversaries of freedom plan to consolidate their territory—to exploit, to control, and finally to destroy the hopes of the world's newest nations; and they have ambition to do it before the end of this decade. It is a contest of will and purpose as well as force and violence—a battle for minds and souls as well as lives and territory. And in that contest, we cannot stand aside.

"We stand, as we have always stood from our earliest beginnings, for the independence and equality of all nations. This nation was born of revolution and raised in freedom. And we do not intend to leave an open road for despotism.

"There is no single simple policy which meets this challenge. Experience has taught us that no one nation has the power or the wisdom to solve all the problems of the world or manage its revolutionary tides—that extending our commitments does not always increase our security—that any initiative carries with it the risk of a temporary defeat—that nuclear weapons cannot prevent subversion—that no free people can be kept free without will and energy of their own—"

*   *   *

12. *President Kennedy's Address to the United Nations, September 25, 1961, Public Papers of the Presidents, Kennedy, 1961, p. 624:*

*   *   *

"Finally, as President of the United States, I consider it my duty to report to this Assembly on two threats to the peace which are not on your crowded agenda, but which causes us, and most of you, the deepest concern.

"The first threat on which I wish to report is widely misunderstood: the smoldering coals of war in Southeast Asia. South Vietnam is already under attack—sometimes by a single assassin, sometimes by a band of guerrillas, recently by full battalions. The peaceful borders of Burma, Cambodia and India have been repeatedly violated. And the peaceful people of Laos are in danger of losing the independence they gained not so long ago.

"No one can call these 'wars of liberation.' For these are free countries living under governments. Nor are these aggressions any less real because men are knifed in their homes and not shot in the fields of battle.

"The very simple question confronting the world community is whether measures can be devised to protect the small and weak from such tactics. For if they are successful in Laos and South Vietnam, the gates will be opened wide.

"The United States seeks for itself no base, no territory, no special position in this area of any kind. We support a truly neutral and independent Laos, its people free from outside interference, living at peace with themselves and with their neighbors, assured that their territory will not be used for attacks on others, and under a government comparable (as Mr. Khrushchev and I agreed at Vienna) to Cambodia and Burma.

"But now the negotiations over Laos are reaching a crucial stage. The cease-fire is at best precarious. The rainy season is coming to an end. Laotian territory is being used to infiltrate South Vietnam. The world community must recognize —all those who are involved—that this potent threat to Laotian peace and freedom is indivisible from all other threats to their own."

13. *President Kennedy's News Conference, October 11, 1961, Public Papers of the Presidents, Kennedy, 1961, p. 660:*

Troops to Vietnam?

Q: "Mr. President, in reference to your decision to send General Taylor to Vietnam, there may be some interpretation of that decision as implying confirmation of reports that you intend to send American forces to Vietnam or Thailand or Laos. Can you give us your appraisal of the conditions under which you might find it necessary to send troops?"

THE PRESIDENT: "We are going to wait until General Taylor comes back and brings an up-to-date description of the situation, particularly in Vietnam. As you know, in the last two or three months there has been a large increase in the number of the forces that have been involved. There has been evidence that some of these forces have come from beyond the frontiers. General Taylor will give me and the Joint Chiefs of Staff an educated military guess as to what the situation is that the government there faces. Then we can come to conclusions as to what is the best thing to do."

*   *   *

14. *President Kennedy letter to President Diem, December 14, 1961, Department of State Bulletin, January 1, 1962, p. 13:*

"Dear Mr. President: I have received your recent letter in which you described so cogently the dangerous condition caused by North Viet-Nam's efforts to take over your country. The situation in your embattled country is well known to me and to the American people. We have been deeply disturbed by the assault on your country. Our indignation has mounted as the deliberate savagery of the Communist program of assassination, kidnapping and wanton violence became clear.

"Your letter underlines what our own information has convincingly shown —that the campaign of force and terror now being waged against your people and your Government is supported and directed from the outside by the authorities at Hanoi. They have thus violated the provisions of the Geneva Accords designed to ensure peace in Viet-Nam and to which they bound themselves in 1954.

"At that time, the United States, although not a party to the Accords, declared that it 'would view any renewal of the aggression in violation of the agreements with grave concern and as seriously threatening international peace and security.' We continue to maintain that view.

"In accordance with that declaration, and in response to your request, we are prepared to help the Republic of Viet-Nam to protect its people and to preserve its independence. We shall promptly increase our assistance to your defense effort as well as help relieve the destruction of the floods which you describe. I have already given the orders to get these programs underway.

"The United States, like the Republic of Viet-Nam, remains devoted to the cause of peace and our primary purpose is to help your people maintain their independence. If the Communist authorities in North Viet-Nam will stop their campaign to destroy the Republic of Viet-Nam, the measures we are taking to assist your defense efforts will no longer be necessary. We shall seek to persuade the Communists to give up their attempts of force and subversion. In any case, we are confident that the Vietnamese people will preserve their independence and gain the peace and prosperity for which they have sought so hard and so long.

"John F. Kennedy

"His Excellency Ngo Dinh Diem
President and Secretary of State for
    National Defense
The Republic of Viet-Nam
Saigon, Viet-Nam"

15. *President Kennedy's State of the Union Message, January 11, 1962, Public Papers of the Presidents, Kennedy, 1962, p. 12:*

*   *   *

"A satisfactory settlement in Laos would also help to achieve and safeguard the peace in Viet Nam—where the foe is increasing his tactics of terror—where our own efforts have been stepped up—and where the local government has initiated new programs and reforms to broaden the base of resistance. The systematic aggression now bleeding that country is not a 'war of liberation'— for Viet Nam is already free. It is a war of attempted subjugation—and it will be resisted."

16. *President Kennedy's News Conference, January 15, 1962, Public Papers of the Presidents, Kennedy, 1962, p. 18:*

*   *   *

Q. "In the past it would seem that coalition governments lean towards Communist control. Are we then taking a chance in supporting a coalition-type government in Southeast Asia?"

A. "We are taking a chance in all of Southeast Asia and we're taking a chance in other areas.

"Nobody can make any predictions sure for the future really on any matter in which there are powerful interests at stake. I think, however, that we have to consider what our alternatives are and what the prospects for war are in that area if we fail in our present efforts, and the geographic problems which would have to be surmounted in such a military engagement where there is no easy entrance by sea and where the geographic location is extremely—a long way from us and very close to those who might become involved. So that there is no easy sure answer for Laos.

"But it is my judgment that it is in the best interests of our country to work for a neutral and independent Laos. We are attempting to do that and I can assure you that I recognize the risks that are involved. But I also think we should consider the risks if we fail. And particularly of the possibility of escalation of a military struggle in a place of danger. So we're going to attempt to work out this matter in a way which permits us to try."

17. *President Kennedy's News Conference, February 7, 1962, Public Papers of the Presidents, Kennedy, 1962, p. 121:*

The Subterranean War

Q. "Mr. President, there seems to be some doubt, at least on the local level and in the region where this is going on, as to the right of the American people and the rest of the world to know the extent of the battle in South Vietnam. Could you tell us, sir, what the situation is there? How deeply are we involved in what seems to be a growing war and what are the rights of the people to know what our forces are doing?"

THE PRESIDENT: "There is a war going on in South Vietnam, and I think that last week there were over 500 killings, and assassinations and bombings and the casualties are high. As I said last week, it is a subterranean war, a guerrilla war of increasing ferocity. The United States, since the end of the Geneva Accord, setting up the South Vietnamese government as an independent government, has been assisting Vietnam economically to maintain its independence, viability and also sent training groups out there, which have been expanded in recent weeks, as the attacks on the government and the people of South Vietnam have increased.

"We are out there on training and on transportation, and we are assisting in every way we properly can the people of South Vietnam, who with the greatest courage and under danger are attempting to maintain their freedom.

"Now, this is an area where there is a good deal of danger and it is a matter of information. We don't want to have information which is of assistance to the enemy and it is a matter which I think will have to be worked out with the government of Vietnam which bears the primary responsibility."

18. *President Kennedy's News Conference, February 14, 1962, Public Papers of the Presidents, Kennedy, 1962, p. 136:*

Involvement in Vietnam

Q. "Mr. President, the Republican National Committee publication has said that you have been less than candid with the American people as to how deeply we are involved in Vietnam. Could you throw any more light on that?"

THE PRESIDENT: "Yes, as you know, the United States for more than a decade has been assisting the government, the people of Vietnam, to maintain their independence. Way back on Dec. 23, 1950, we signed a military assistance agreement with France and with Indo-China which at that time included Vietnam, Laos and Cambodia. We also signed in December of 1951 an agreement directly with Vietnam.

"Now, in 1954, the Geneva agreements were signed, and while we did not sign those agreements, nevertheless Under Secretary Bedell Smith stated that he would view any renewal of aggression in Vietnam in violation of the aforesaid agreements with grave concern, and as seriously threatening international peace and security. At the time that the SEATO Pact was signed in 1954, Sept. 8, Vietnam was not a signatory, it was a protocol state, and, therefore, this pact which was approved by the Senate with only, I think, two against it, under Article 4, stated that the United States recognized that aggression by means of armed attack against Vietnam would threaten our own peace and security. So since that time the United States has been assisting the government of Vietnam to maintain its independence. It has had a military training mission there and extensive economic assistance.

"As you know, in the last two years the war has increased. The Vice President visited there last spring. The war became more intense every month; in fact, every week. The attack on the government by the Communist forces with assistance from the north became of greater and greater concern to the government of Vietnam and the Government of the United States.

"We sent—I sent General Taylor there to make a review of the situation. The President of Vietnam asked us for additional assistance. We issued, as you remember, a white paper which detailed the support which the Viet Minh in the north were giving to this Communist insurgent movement and we have increased our assistance there. And we are supplying logistic assistance, transportation assistance, training, and we have a number of Americans who are taking part in that effort.

"We have discussed this matter—we discussed it with the leadership of the Republicans and Democrats when we met in early January and informed them of what we were doing in Vietnam. We—Mr. Rusk has discussed it with the House and Senate Foreign Affairs Committee. Mr. McNamara has discussed it with the Armed Services Committee. The leadership on both sides, Republicans and Democrats—we have explained to them our concern about what is happening there, and they have been responsive, I think, to evidence their concern. So that there is a long history of our efforts to prevent Vietnam from falling under control of the Communists. That is what we are now attempting to do. And as the war has increased in scope, our assistance has increased as a result of the request of the government. So that I think we should—as it is a matter of great importance, a matter of great sensitivity—my view has always been that the headquarters of both of our parties should really attempt to leave these matters to be discussed by responsible leaders on both sides. In my opinion, we have had a very strong bi-partisan consensus up to now, and I am hopeful that it will continue in regard to the action that we are taking."

Q. "Mr. President, do you feel that you have told the American people as much as can be told, because of the sensitivity of the subject? Is that right?"

THE PRESIDENT: "I think I have just indicated what our role is. We have increased our assistance to the government, its logistics, and we have not sent combat troops there, although the training missions that we have there have been instructed that if they are fired upon they are, of course, to fire back, to protect themselves, but we have not sent combat troops, in the generally understood sense of the word. We have increased our training mission, and we have increased our logistics support, and we are attempting to prevent a Communist take-over of Vietnam, which is in accordance with a policy which our Government has followed for the last—certainly since 1954, and even before then as I have indicated. We are attempting to make all of the information available that we can, consistent with our security needs in the area. So I feel that we are being as frank as we can be, and I think what I have said to you is a description of our activity there.''

*   *   *

19. *President Kennedy's Speech at University of California, March 23, 1962, Public Papers of the Presidents, Kennedy, 1962, p. 265:*

"The leaders of the Communist world are not only confronted by acute internal problems in each Communist country—the failure of agriculture, the rising discontent of the youth and the intellectuals, the demands of technical and managerial groups for status and security. They are confronted in addition by profound divisions within the Communist world itself—divisions which have already shattered the image of communism as a universal system guaranteed to abolish all social and international conflicts, the most valuable asset which the Communists had for many years.

"Wisdom requires the long view. And the long view shows us that the revolution of national independence is a fundamental fact of our era. This revolution cannot be stopped.

"As new nations emerge from the oblivion of centuries, their first aspiration is to affirm their national identity. Their deepest hope is for a world where, within a framework of international cooperation, every country can solve its own problems according to its own traditions and ideals.

"It is in the interests of the pursuit of knowledge—and it is in our own national interest—that this revolution of national independence succeed. For the Communists rest everything on the idea of a monolithic world—a world where all knowledge has a single pattern, all societies move toward a single model, all problems have a single solution, and all roads lead to a single destination.

"The pursuit of knowledge, on the other hand, rests everything on the opposite idea—on the idea of a world based on diversity, self-determination and freedom. And that is the kind of world to which we Americans, as a nation, are committed by the principles on which this republic was formed.

"As men conduct the pursuit of knowledge, they create a world which freely unites national diversity and international partnership. This emerging world is incompatible with the Communist conception of world order.

"It will irresistibly burst the bonds of Communist organization and Communist ideology. And diversity and independence, far from being opposed to the American conception of world order, represent the very essence of our vision of the future.

"There used to be much talk a few years ago about the inevitable triumph of communism. We hear such talk much less now. No one who examines the modern world can doubt that the great currents of history are carrying the world away from the monolithic idea toward the pluralist idea—away from communism and toward national independence and freedom.

"No one can doubt that the wave of the future is not the conquest of the world by a single dogmatic creed, but the liberation of the diverse energies of free nations and free men. No one can doubt that cooperation in the pursuit of knowledge must lead to freedom of the mind and of the soul.

"The specter of thermonuclear war will hang over mankind; and we must heed the advice of Oliver Wendell Holmes of 'freedom leaning on her spear' until all nations are wise enough to disarm safely and effectively.

*   *   *

"We must seize the vision of a free and diverse world—and shape our policies to speed progress toward a flexible world order.

"This is the unifying spirit of our policies in the world. The purpose of our aid programs must be to help developing countries to move forward as rapidly as possible on the road to genuine national independence.

"Our military policies must assist nations to protect the processes of democratic reform and development against disruption and intervention."

*   *   *

20. *President Kennedy's News Conference, April 11, 1962, Public Papers of the Presidents, Kennedy, 1962, p. 322:*

Viet-Nam

Q: "Sir, what are you going to do about the American soldiers getting killed in Viet-Nam?"

A: ". . . We are attempting to help Viet-Nam maintain its independence and not fall under the domination of the communists . . . But we cannot desist in Viet-Nam . . ."

*   *   *

21. *President Kennedy's News Conference, May 9, 1962, Public Papers of the Presidents, Kennedy, 1962, p. 377:*

The Broken Cease-fire

Q: "Mr. President, last February at a news conference you told us that the cease-fire was becoming frayed in Laos and in the event that it was broken, it could lead to a very serious decision. I wonder, Mr. President, now that the cease-fire has been broken, if efforts should fail to re-establish it, would it cause a re-examination on the part of the United States towards its policy there?"

THE PRESIDENT: "Well, we are concerned about the break in the cease-fire. As you know, the State Department, the Acting Secretary of State, and the Assistant Secretary of State, met today with Ambassador Dobrynin, this afternoon. We have already indicated to one of the co-chairmen, the British government, our great concern about it. Our ambassador in Moscow met with the foreign secretary of the Soviet Union, Mr. Gromyko.

"We do believe, and have said from the beginning, that the negotiations should move much more quickly than they have. The longer this rather frayed cease-fire continues, the more chance we will have of the kind of incidents we have had in the past few days. That is why we were hopeful, after the meetings at Geneva last summer and fall, that the negotiations between the parties involved would take place last fall, and we could organize a government, rather than trying to continue to hold lines which in some cases are exposed, and which are subject to this kind of pressure. So that has been our view.

"So that has been our view, and the longer it goes on, and the longer there is not an agreement on a government, the longer some groups stand out from these kinds of conversations, then the more hazardous the situation becomes.

"Now, on the particular incident, it is a clear breach of the cease-fire. We have indicated and we hope that the Soviet Union, which is committed to a policy based on the statement at Vienna, in regard to Laos, we are hopeful that we can bring about a restoration of the cease-fire. But we have got to use the time to try to move ahead in our political negotiations.

"I agree it is a very hazardous course, but introducing American forces is the other one—let's not think there is some great third course. That also is a hazardous course and we want to attempt to see if we can work out a peaceful solution, which has been our object for many months. I believe that these negotiations should take place quickly. This is not a satisfactory situation today."

*   *   *

22. *White House Statement of the President, May 15, 1962, Public Papers of the Presidents, Kennedy, 1962, p. 396:*

"Following joint consideration by the governments of the United States and Thailand of the situation in Southeast Asia, the Royal Thai Government has invited, and I have today ordered, additional elements of the United States military forces, both ground and air, to proceed to Thailand and to remain there until further orders. These forces are to help ensure the territorial integrity of this peaceful country.

"The dispatch of United States forces to Thailand was considered desirable because of recent attacks in Laos by Communist forces, and the subsequent movement of Communist military units toward the border of Thailand.

"A threat to Thailand is of grave concern to the United States. I have, therefore, ordered certain additional American military forces into Thailand in order that we may be in a position to fulfill speedily our obligations under the Manila Pact of 1954, a defense agreement which was approved overwhelmingly by the U.S. Senate, and to which the Secretary of State and Foreign Minister of Thailand referred in their joint statement of March 6, 1962. We are in consultation with SEATO Governments on the situation.

"I emphasize that this is a defensive act on the part of the United States and wholly consistent with the United Nations Charter which specifically recognizes that nations have an inherent right to take collective measures for self-defense. In the spirit of that Charter, I have directed that the Secretary General of the United Nations be informed of the actions that we are taking.

"There is no change in our policy toward Laos, which continues to be the reestablishment of an effective cease-fire and prompt negotiations for a government of national union."

23. *President Kennedy's News Conference, May 17, 1962, Public Papers of the Presidents, Kennedy, 1962, p. 402:*

No Further Breach in Laos

Q: "Mr. President, could you bring us up to date on the Laotian situation since the dispatch of our troops in Thailand? Specifically, do you feel that we have increased the chances of our getting caught in a Communist shooting war in Southeast Asia?"

THE PRESIDENT: "We are continuing to hope that there will be a national government or national union, which has been our policy, as you know, for a year. We are going to Thailand, at the decision of the Thai government, our own decision to provide for the defense of Thailand. The latest information indicates no further breach of the cease-fire. We also have indications that the three princes will engage in conversation shortly. I hope they will produce a government. That is our object. I have already indicated the great hazards of a shooting war in Asia. In Asia, it is our object to bring about a diplomatic solution which will make the chances of such a war far less likely."

Troops in Thailand

Q: "Mr. President, in light of your answer to this question, sir, could you give us any idea how long the American troops will be needed in Thailand?"

THE PRESIDENT: "I cannot at this time."

Q: "Have you any idea under what conditions they might return?"

THE PRESIDENT: "I cannot at this time. They have only been in there for a very short while, and we can't tell when they will come out. It will depend a good deal on what conditions are in Thailand and the neighboring countries."

Restoring the Cease-fire

Q: "Mr. President, could you tell us, please, what you would consider the restoration of an effective cease-fire? Would this involve the withdrawal of the Communist forces to their position before the attack on Nam Tha, or more or less a quiescence which would permit the talks to go forward on the government?"

THE PRESIDENT: "Obviously, we would prefer as great a withdrawal to the line that was in effect a week or so ago as we could get. I would think, however, that the peace along the line which now may exist, of course, is essential."

Objectives in Laos

Q: "Mr. President, would you review for us the considerations that you had in mind last weekend when you took this rather swift action to move more American troops into Thailand?"

THE PRESIDENT: "Yes. We are concerned about the breach of the cease-fire, the sign of deterioration in Laos, which brought Communist forces to the border of Thailand up in the Mekong River section, up not too far from Nam Tha, and we did not know whether this was an indication of a general breach of the cease-fire which, of course, would immediately imperil Thailand. So in our desire to stabilize the situation, we got in touch with the government, which was already in touch with us, and worked out the proposed course of action."

*   *   *

Legality of Thailand Move

Q: "Mr. President, what was the legal basis for our sending troops to Thailand? Was it a bilateral arrangement that we have with the Thai government, or was it possibly secret arrangements?"

THE PRESIDENT: "No, the actual legal basis was to put us in a position to fulfill our obligations under the SEATO Treaty."

Q: "Mr. President, are the other members of the SEATO Treaty organization doing the same?"

THE PRESIDENT: "They have been asked to do so, and there have been indications of a favorable response from several of them. This is a decision for them. But we have responded and met our obligations."

* * *

The Intentions of Pathet Lao

Q: "Mr. President, back on the subject of Southeast Asia, has there been any indication that the Pathet Lao intended to march against Thailand or against the capital of Laos, and, second, under what conditions would the United States send its troops into Laos?

THE PRESIDENT: "In answer to your first question, I don't know what their intentions may be. I am hopeful their intentions will be to maintain a cease-fire. Obviously, as I have said, the breach of the cease-fire in the case of Nam Tha was a blow to the concept of the cease-fire. That is what initiated our action in the case of Thailand. On the second matter, we have to wait and see. I think it is very important that the princes form a government of national union for the preservation of their own country."

24. *President Kennedy's Address at Graduation Exercises of the U.S. Military Academy, Public Papers of the Presidents, Kennedy, 1962, p. 453:*

"Korea has not been the only battle ground since the end of the Second World War. Men have fought and died in Malaya, in Greece, in the Philippines, in Algeria and Cuba, and Cyprus and almost continuously on the Indo-Chinese Peninsula. No nuclear weapons have been fired. No massive nuclear retaliation has been considered appropriate. This is another type of war, new in its intensity, ancient in its origin—war by guerrillas, subversives, insurgents, assassins, war by ambush instead of by combat; by infiltration, instead of aggression, seeking victory by eroding and exhausting the enemy instead of engaging him. It is a form of warfare uniquely adapted to what has been strangely called 'wars of liberation,' to undermine the efforts of new and poor countries to maintain the freedom that they have finally achieved. It preys on economic unrest and ethnic conflicts. It requires in those situations where we must counter it, and these are the kinds of challenges that will be before us in the next decade if freedom is to be saved, a whole new kind of strategy, a wholly different kind of force, and therefore a new and wholly different kind of military training."

25. *President Kennedy's News Conference, June 14, 1962, Public Papers of the Presidents, Kennedy, 1962, p. 492:*

Mansfield's Criticisms

Q: "Mr. President, Senator Mansfield a few days ago suggested a review of Far Eastern policies because he said they seem to him either marking time, or at least on a collision course.

"Do you think such a review is necessary?"

THE PRESIDENT: "Well, we have been reviewing. As you know, we have been attempting in the case of Laos to work out a policy which would prevent either one of those situations, whether we shall be successful or not, only time will tell.

"I know that we have put large sums of money, and the situation there is still hazardous, what is true there of course is true all around the world. This is a period of great tension and change. But if the United States had not played a part in Southeast Asia for many years, I think the whole map of Southeast Asia would be different.

"I am delighted, as you know, I have the highest regard for Senator Mansfield, and I think that we should constantly review, and I think that he suggested we should make judgments between what is essential to our interest and what is marginal. We have been attempting with great difficulty to carry out a policy with Laos which would permit a neutral and independent government there, and in Senator Mansfield's speech he used the examples of Burma and Cambodia. Those were the examples that were also used at the Vienna meeting by Chairman Khrushchev and myself in which we stated the kind of government that we both said we hoped would emerge in Laos. That is the commitment that was made by the Soviet Union, and by the United States.

"Now we have moved to a different plateau, and we are going to see whether that commitment can be maintained. But on the other hand, I am sure and I know Senator Mansfield would not think we should withdraw, because withdrawal in the case of Vietnam and in the case of Thailand might mean a collapse of the entire area."

26. *U.S. Comments on Report of Control Commission for Viet-Nam, Department of State Bulletin, July 16, 1962, p. 109:*

Department Statement

"The report just issued by the International Control Commission for Viet-Nam demonstrates that the Communist North Vietnamese are engaged in a campaign of aggression and subversion aimed at the violent overthrow of the Government of South Viet-Nam. It indicates clearly that the hostilities in Viet-Nam, which in the first 5 months of this year alone resulted in the death of more than 9,000 people, are planned, caused, and led by the Communist authorities in North Viet-Nam. These are the conclusions of the Commission's Legal Committee:

> . . . there is evidence to show that armed and unarmed personnel, arms, munitions and other supplies have been sent from the Zone in the North to the Zone in the South with the object of supporting, organizing and carrying out hostile activities, including armed attacks, directed against the Armed Forces and Administration of the Zone in the South . . . there is evidence to show that the PAVN [People's Army of Viet-Nam] has allowed the Zone in the North to be used for inciting, encouraging and supporting hostile activities in the Zone in the South, aimed at the overthrow of the Administration in the South.

"The Commission accepted these conclusions of the Legal Committee that there was sufficient evidence to show 'beyond reasonable doubt' that the authorities in Communist North Viet-Nam committed these violations. The Commission also cited the Republic of Viet-Nam for its activities in importing military equipment and personnel above the limits imposed by the 1954 Geneva Accords. The report clearly demonstrates, however, that these actions were taken by South Viet-Nam as part of its effort to defend itself against aggression and subversion from the North. In December of last year President Diem requested increased military assistance from the United States. We have responded to this request.

"President Diem and President Kennedy have both stated that they look forward to the discontinuance of the present level of military assistance when the Communist North Vietnamese halt their campaign to destroy the Republic of Viet-Nam. The report of the International Control Commission takes note of this position. The United States welcomes the Commission's report and recommends it for world attention. We hope that the Commission will continue its efforts to restore peace in Viet-Nam."

27. *President Kennedy's Annual Message to the Congress on the State of the Union, January 14, 1963, Public Papers of the Presidents, Kennedy, 1963, p. 17:*

* * *

"Third, what comfort can we take from the increasing strains and tensions within the Communist bloc? Here hope must be tempered with caution. For the Soviet-Chinese disagreement is over means, not ends. A dispute over how best to bury the free world is no grounds for Western rejoicing.

"Nevertheless, while a strain is not a fracture, it is clear that the forces of diversity are at work inside the Communist camp, despite all the iron disciplines of regimentation and all the iron dogmatisms of ideology. Marx is proven wrong once again: for it is the closed Communist societies, not the free and open societies which carry within themselves the seeds of internal disintegration.

"The disarray of the Communist empire has been heightened by two other formidable forces. One is the historical force of nationalism—and the yearning of all men to be free. The other is the gross inefficiency of their economies. For a closed society is not open to ideas of progress—and a police state finds that it cannot command the grain to grow.

"New nations asked to choose between two competing systems need only compare conditions in East and West Germany, Eastern and Western Europe, North and South Viet-Nam. They need only compare the disillusionment of Communist Cuba with the promise of the Alliance for Progress. And all the world knows that no successful system builds a wall to keep its people in and freedom out—and the wall of shame dividing Berlin is a symbol of Communist failure.

"Finally, what can we do to move from the present pause toward enduring peace? Again I would counsel caution. I foresee no spectacular reversal in Communist methods or goals. But if all these trends and developments can persuade the Soviet Union to walk the path of peace, then let her know that all free nations will journey with her. But until that choice is made, and until the world can develop a reliable system of international security, the free peoples have no choice but to keep their arms nearby.

* * *

"In short, let our adversaries choose. If they choose peaceful competition, they shall have it. If they come to realize that their ambitions cannot succeed—

if they see their 'wars of liberation' and subversion will ultimately fail—if they recognize that there is more security in accepting inspection than in permitting new nations to master the black arts of nuclear war—and if they are willing to turn their energies, as we are, to the great unfinished tasks of our own peoples—then, surely, the areas of agreement can be very wide indeed: a clear understanding about Berlin, stability in Southeast Asia, an end to nuclear testing, new checks on surprise or accidental attack, and, ultimately, general and complete disarmament.

*   *   *

"My friends: I close on a note of hope. We are not lulled by the momentary calm of the sea or the somewhat clearer skies above. We know the turbulence that lies below, and the storms that are beyond the horizon this year. But now the winds of change appear to be blowing more strongly than ever, in the world of communism as well as our own . . ."

*   *   *

28. *President Kennedy's Annual Message to the Congress on the State of the Union, January 14, 1963, Public Papers of the Presidents, Kennedy, 1963, p. 16:*

*   *   *

"Second, what of the developing and non-aligned nations? They were, I believe, shocked by the Soviets' sudden and secret attempt to transform Cuba into a nuclear striking base—and by Communist China's arrogant invasion of India.

"They have been reassured by our prompt assistance to India, by our support through the United Nations of the Congo's unification, by our patient search for disarmament, and by the improvement in our treatment of citizens and visitors, whose skin does not happen to be white. And as the older colonialism recedes, and the neo-colonialism of the Communist powers stands out more starkly than ever, they realize more clearly that the issue in the world struggle is not communism versus capitalism, but coercion versus a free choice.

"They realize that the longing for independence is the same the world over, whether it is the independence of West Berlin or Viet-Nam. They realize that such independence runs athwart all Communist ambitions, but is in keeping with our own—and that our approach to their needs is resilient and resourceful, while the Communists rely on ancient doctrines and old dogmas.

"Nevertheless, it is hard for any nation to focus on an external or subversive threat to its independence when its energies are drained in daily combat with the forces of poverty and despair. It makes little sense for us to assail in speeches and resolutions the horrors of communism, to spend $50 billion a year to prevent its military advance—and then to begrudge spending, largely on American products, less than one-tenth of that amount to help other nations strengthen their independence and cure the social chaos in which communism has always thrived."

29. *President Kennedy's News Conference, March 6, 1963, Public Papers of the Presidents, Kennedy, 1963, p. 243:*

*   *   *

Q: "Mr. President, the Mansfield committee, sent at your suggestion to the Far East and Europe, has recommended a thorough security reassessment in the

Far East and a clamp down, if not a reduction in our aid to that part of the world. Would you have any comment on this, sir?"

THE PRESIDENT: "I don't see how we are going to be able, unless we are going to pull out of Southeast Asia and turn it over to the Communists, how we are going to be able to reduce very much our economic programs and military programs in South Viet-Nam, in Cambodia, in Thailand.

"I think that unless you want to withdraw from the field and decide that it is in the national interest to permit that area to collapse, I would think that it would be impossible to substantially change it particularly, as we are in a very intensive struggle in those areas.

"So I think we ought to judge the economic burden it places upon us as opposed to having the Communists control all of Southeast Asia with the inevitable effect that this would have on the security of India and, therefore, really begin to run perhaps all the way toward the Middle East. So I think that while we would all like to lighten the burden, I don't see any real prospect of the burden being lightened for the U.S. in Southeast Asia in the next year if we are going to do the job and meet what I think are very clear national needs."

30. *U. Alexis Johnson's Address Made Before the Economic Club of Detroit, "The United States and Southeast Asia," April 8, 1963, Department of State Bulletin, April 29, 1963, p. 636:*

* * *

"What is the attraction that Southeast Asia has exerted for centuries on the great powers flanking it on all sides? Why it is desirable, and why is it important? First, it provides a lush climate, fertile soil, rich natural resources, a relatively sparse population in most areas, and room to expand. The countries of Southeast Asia produce rich exportable surpluses such as rice, rubber, teak, corn, tin, spices, oil, and many others. It is especially attractive to Communist China, with its burgeoning population and its food shortages.

"Militarily and strategically, Southeast Asia has great assets. It stands astride of east-west trade routes. It stands in a critical, strategic relationship not only to China and India but to Australia, the western Pacific, and Japan. Bearing in mind the implications of the recent Chinese attack on India, Southeast Asia takes on an additional significance, since its domination by the Communist powers would outflank the Asian subcontinent.

"Although still thinly populated for the most part, the human resources of this area are considerable and growing. Taken together, the peoples of Southeast Asia represent an important segment of the free world and a target of prime importance to Communist imperialism.

"There is a rhythm to the tides of history. Just as the pressures on Southeast Asia have in the past come alternately from China in the north, India in the west, and the maritime powers along the sea, so Southeast Asia is again threatened by a resurgence of pressure from the north. But today the danger from this quarter is multiplied a hundredfold by the virulence of the political doctrine which now rides on the backs of the Chinese people.

"As my colleague Under Secretary Averell Harriman said recently, 'I don't know how you can distinguish between Chinese communism and Chinese imperialism. Chinese communism and all communism is imperialist.'

"Even before World War II, Communist parties of varying strengths existed in all Southeast Asian countries, from Burma to the Philippines. After the war the signal was given for armed Communist-led uprisings, and these occurred in

Burma, Indonesia, Malaya, Indochina, and the Philippines. Even Thailand, the one country in Southeast Asia that had not known colonial rule, was threatened. By 1952 the revolts were crushed in all but Malaya and Indochina. It took the British and the new Malay Federation until 1958 to quell Communist guerrilla forces there. This struggle, incidentally, provided valuable lessons which are now being applied in Viet-Nam. We also might note that, except for Japan, Malaya is now the most prosperous country in Asia.

"The efforts of some powers following World War II to restore colonial rule along the pre-war pattern permitted the Communists more effectively to wave the banner of anticolonialism and, for example, through Ho Chi Minh, at that time largely to capture the nationalist movement in Viet-Nam.

"After the Geneva Agreements of 1954 on Indochina we took the lead in the establishment of the Southeast Asia Treaty Organization, an alliance of the Philippines, Thailand, Pakistan, Australia, New Zealand, France, Great Britain, and ourselves, with the objective of providing security to Southeast Asia through collective military action if the Communists embarked on outright military aggression. The opening of the eighth meeting of ministers of this organization was attended by Secretary Rusk this morning in Paris.

"Whatever may be the criticisms of SEATO, the fact remains that, since its inception, the Communists have not attempted open military action in the area. Instead they have turned to the more subtle tactics of subversion and insurgency, the prime example being the guerrilla warfare in Viet-Nam carried on in the method made classic in China by Mao Tse-tung. Whereas the method employed by the Communists has changed, the objective remains the same—destruction of the independence of the Southeast Asian countries one by one and return to the days when they bore their tribute to Peiping. While the armed struggle is manifest now only in Viet-Nam, it ceased in Laos through the settlement reached just last year at Geneva, after 14 months of negotiation.

Implications of Struggle in Viet-Nam

"I have pointed out that Southeast Asia is not a homogeneous region but rather a geographic expression. By this same token of geographic interrelation, the security of the area is not stronger than that of its component countries. All of us who were at Geneva in 1954 recognized that Communist domination of the Red River Delta of North Viet-Nam would make it much more difficult to defend the remaining areas. This has been true. However, for the Communists to advance any further in the area would render the defense problem very much more difficult, if not well-nigh impossible. This is why the valiant struggle now being waged in South Viet-Nam has implications far beyond the borders of that troubled country.

"Our massive assistance to free Viet-Nam is designed to avoid just such a catastrophe."

*   *   *

31. *President Kennedy's News Conference, April 24, 1963, Public Papers of the Presidents, Kennedy, 1963, p. 343:*

*   *   *

Falling Dominoes

Q: "Mr. President, on Laos again, several years ago we heard a great deal about the 'falling domino' theory in Southeast Asia.

"Do you look upon Laos in terms of that country alone, or is your concern the effect that its loss would have in Thailand, Vietnam, and so on?

"Would you discuss that?"

THE PRESIDENT: "That is correct. The population of Laos is 2 million and it is scattered. It is a very rough country. It is important as a sovereign power. The people desire to be independent, and it is also important because it borders the Mekong River and, quite obviously, if Laos fell into Communist hands it would increase the danger along the northern frontiers of Thailand. It would put additional pressure on Cambodia and would put additional pressure on South Vietnam which in itself would put additional pressure on Malaya.

"So I do accept the view that there is an interrelationship in these countries and that is one of the reasons why we are concerned with maintaining the Geneva Accords as a method of maintaining stability in Southeast Asia. It may be one of the reasons why others do not share that interest."

*   *   *

32. *President Kennedy's News Conference, May 8, 1963, Public Papers of the Presidents, Kennedy, 1963, p. 375:*

*   *   *

Q: "Back on the subject of Vietnam. Could you explain to us, sir, why we have committed ourselves militarily in Vietnam but have not committed ourselves militarily in Laos, depending instead upon this neutralist government?"

A: "Because the situations are different. That's why the remedy has been different. We have had a commitment for a good many years to the integrity of South Vietnam. We are anxious to maintain the neutrality of Laos. It may not be possible to do so and it may be necessary to seek other remedies. But we have adopted what we considered to be, considering the geography, the history, the nature of the threat and the alternate solution—we've adopted for each country what we regarded as the best strategy. And we'll have to wait and see what happens on them."

*   *   *

33. *Secretary Rusk's Address Before the Economic Club of New York, at New York, April 22, 1963, "The Stake in Viet-Nam," Department of State Bulletin, May 13, 1963, p. 727:*

*   *   *

"Viet-Nam is a narrow strip along the South China Sea, nearly as large as California, with a population of some 30 million people—about 16 million in the North and 14 million in the South.

"With Cambodia and Laos, Viet-Nam formed what was formerly known as French Indochina. During the Second World War, the Vichy regime yielded control of French Indochina to the Japanese. In the spring of 1945 the Japanese proclaimed the independence of Viet-Nam. And in August of that year they permitted the Communist-oriented Viet Minh to seize rule.

"In the Indian subcontinent and in Burma and the Philippines, Western countries recognized at war's end that national demands for independence would have to be met promptly. But this was not the case with Indochina. Instead, we ourselves were somewhat at a loss for a policy with regard to that particular part of the world. So our people in charge of war plans in 1944 sent a colonel out there who sent a cable back to the Joint Chiefs of Staff saying 'Request policy guidance on American policy toward Indochina, because we are beginning to get military access to that country and we need direction.'

"Well, there ensued a vast silence which lasted for months. We sent staff officers back to try to find the answer. We sent cables out there, and after about 6 months the reply came and it said, 'When asked by the Joint Chiefs of Staff for a statement of American policy toward Indochina, the President'—that was President Roosevelt—'replied, I don't want to hear any more about Indochina.'

"Well, now the result of no significant Allied policy at that point was that the French did return and take over where they left off at the time of the Japanese occupation, and they encountered therefore a militant resistance movement. For 8 years, with material help from the United States, they sought to pacify the country. At the same time they granted increasing autonomy to non-Communist Vietnamese. But the Viet Minh, reforms in Japan and on Taiwan, was pressed forward—123,000 heads of families became small landowners. A comprehensive system of agricultural credit was set up. Thousands of Vietnamese were moved into the highlands to raise industrial crops. Rubber production rose, and new plantings of better varieties promised still higher production for the future. Sugar production doubled in 1958. South Viet-Nam was soon producing enough rice to resume exports on a rising scale. Various small industries were established. Textile production rose from near zero to near self-sufficiency. Electric power nearly doubled. Per capita national income rose by 20 percent.

"Thousands of new schools were built. Between 1956 and 1960, enrollment in the elementary schools rose from 400,000 to 1,500,000. The expansion of health facilities included new hospitals and 3,500 village health stations. Rail transportation was restored. Roads were repaired and improved, and three new major highways were built.

"The Communists were not completely eliminated—especially along the land and sea frontiers, where they could be supplied—but most of South Viet-Nam became, for a period, safe for travel.

"Although North Viet-Nam inherited most of the industry of Viet-Nam, and although its population is larger, it fell rapidly behind South Viet-Nam in food production, the number of children in school, and in standards of living. While per capita food production rose 20 percent in the South, it fell 10 percent in the North.

"This was competition which the Communists apparently could not endure. Very likely it was one of the reasons why they decided in 1959 to renew their assault on South Viet-Nam. And in 1960 the Lao Dong Party—that is, the Communist Party—ordered the 'liberation' of South Viet-Nam.

"According to Communist propaganda, the war in South Viet-Nam is a civil war, a local uprising. The truth is that it is an aggression organized, directed, and partly supplied from North Viet-Nam. It is conducted by hardened Communist political organizers and guerrilla leaders trained in North Viet-Nam, who, upon their arrival in the South, recruit local assistance. This has been done in a variety of ways, including terror and assassination. Schoolteachers, health workers, malaria eradication teams, local officials loyal to the Republic—these were the first targets of the assassins. But many ordinary villagers who refused to cooperate with the Communist guerrillas likewise have been ruthlessly killed.

Strategic Importance of South Viet-Nam

"This assault on South Viet-Nam was a major Communist enterprise, carefully and elaborately prepared, heavily staffed, and relentlessly pursued. It made headway. In 1961 President Diem appealed for further assistance and President Kennedy responded promptly and affirmatively.

"The strategic importance of South Viet-Nam is plain. It controls the mouth of the Mekong River, the main artery of Southeast Asia. The loss of South Viet-Nam would put the remaining states of Southeast Asia in mortal danger.

"But there are larger reasons why the defense of South Viet-Nam is vital to us and to the whole free world. We cannot be indifferent to the fate of 14 million people who have fought hard against communism—including nearly 1 million who fled their former homes to avoid living under Communist tyranny. Since we went to the aid of Greece and Turkey 16 years ago, it has been the attitude of the United States to assist peoples who resist Communist aggression. We have seen this form of attack fail in Burma, Malaya, and the Philippines. The South Vietnamese are determined to win their battle, and they deserve our help.

"Critics have complained that South Viet-Nam is not a full constitutional democracy and that our aid has been subject to waste and mismanagement. Let us be clear that these criticisms are not merely alibis for inaction. For in passing judgement, let us recall that we are talking about a nation which has been responsible for its own affairs for less than a decade, about a people who have had no peace since 1941 and little experience in direct participation in political affairs. Their four national elections, their thousands of elected hamlet councils, and their forthcoming village council elections show steady movement toward a constitutional system resting upon popular consent."

* * *

34. *Assistant Secretary for Far Eastern Affairs, Roger W. Hilsman, Address Made at 1963 Conference on Cold War Education, Tampa, Florida, June 14, 1963, "The Challenge to Freedom in Asia," Department of State Bulletin, July 8, 1963, p. 44:*

* * *

"As to the nature of the danger, the ideology of communism is a threat to the United States today mainly because it is joined with the population, resources, and military strength of the countries of the Soviet Union and Communist China, because it is joined with two bases of power.

"But the fact that ideology has been joined to these two bases of power should not be misinterpreted: the threat is not just military; it is also political. And of the two, the political threat is probably the more pervasive. This is true because this nation and its allies have made sure that their military defenses are adequate and up to date.

"The political threat is also serious because of the Communists' skill in manipulating all the elements of power—political, economic, and psychological as well as military. They use these instruments with considerable sophistication, playing first one then another according to the opportunities open to them in any given situation. Mao Tse-tung has described this alternation of tactics and instruments as 'talk/fight; talk/fight,' and it describes the technique very well. This sudden alternation between talking and fighting is designed also to induce a maximum amount of confusion, instability, and trouble in the free world. One of the latest examples of their use of this tactic occurred last October in the Chinese Communist attack along the Indian border, followed by their withdrawal beginning a month later.

"The immediate goal of the Communists is, of course, to capture the in-between nations, those smaller and weaker nations which today are struggling against odds to remain independent. If the Communists can capture such free nations, turning them against the United States and making them feel that it is the U.S. which poses the danger or forms an obstacle to their goals, then the Communists could win without using military power. Moreover, the Communists have waged an unremitting attack on the foundations of our way of life, just as they are a threat to freedom elsewhere in the world. Although they argue over differences in emphasis as to how the Communist world should carry out its attacks on free men, their common goal is plain enough: to further the destruction of the values all free men cherish.

"In Asia the greatest danger to independent nations comes from Communist China, with its 700 million people forced into the service of an aggressive Communist Party. We can't ignore that problem, and we don't ignore it. Communist China lies in direct contact with, or very close to, a whole series of free nations ranged in an arc from Afghanistan, India, Pakistan, and Nepal in South Asia; through Burma, Malaya, Thailand, Cambodia, Laos, and Viet-Nam in Southeast Asia; and on up through the Republic of China, on its island base of Taiwan, to Japan and Korea. Indonesia, the Philippines, Australia, and New Zealand are also alive to the threat posed by the Communist Chinese.

"All these free nations must deal with the facts of Communist China and its ambitions. No matter what response each has made, be it nonalignment or alliance with friendly nations, they all are aware that the aim of the Chinese Communists is to gain predominant control in Asia and eventually to secure the establishment of Communist regimes throughout the world. The reaction of each nation is determined by its own material circumstances and, sometimes more importantly, by its own national psychology.

"The United States is determined that communism shall not take over Asia.

"For this reason we do not recognize Communist China and seek in all possible ways to limit the ability of Communist China to implement its threat to obtain hegemony in the Far East. We recognize the Republic of China as the legal government of China and support its position in the United Nations. We are aware that the economic and social progress on Taiwan, carried out by free Chinese, stands in stark contrast to the failures of the mainland Communist government. Also the existence on Taiwan of a well-trained and -equipped force of 600,000 men, dedicated to the fight against communism, must have a restraining effect on any expansionist ambitions of the Communist Chinese. Furthermore the spirit of the people of the Republic of China, and of their leader, President Chiang Kai-shek, who have conducted a 40-year struggle against Communist imperialism, is an inspiration to free peoples everywhere.

"We stand ready to help peoples who want to help themselves to maintain their independence. Sometimes this involves outright alliance, as with the Republic of China, Japan, South Korea, and, through the Southeast Asia Treaty Organization, with the Philippines, Thailand, and Pakistan. If any of these nations is attacked the United States is committed to help defend it. Our contribution to security in the Far East also takes other forms, forms designed to meet threats of varying nature.

"These threats are never simple ones; some are extremely subtle and sophisticated. If we are to meet these threats successfully, certain qualities of mind must be stressed and certain dangers avoided. Governor Bryant, in a recent address, referred to the danger that the 'timid American' poses for our democracy. I think he is quite right. I have often had a similar thought, which I would like to emphasize in what I have to say today.

"What has often occurred to me is that, if the United States is not only going to meet the Communist threat but carry off the difficult task of helping to create a new and stable world in the process, then Americans are going to need very steady nerves.

"By this phrase 'steady nerves,' I mean not only not being timid but two additional qualities: first, the capacity for cold, deliberate analysis in order to know when to act and when to bide one's time; second, the unemotional self-discipline and self-control that enables one to act effectively as a result of that analysis. I mean the kind of self-control that enabled President Kennedy to use United States power with such coolness and skill as he did during the Cuban crisis. In negotiations, also, extraordinary qualities of mind and will are demanded, among which the element of cold calm in dealing with complex situations is increasingly important. President Kennedy was speaking of this in his inaugural address when he said: 'Let us never negotiate out of fear. But let us never fear to negotiate.'

"The quality of 'steady nerves' is needed in both of the fundamental tasks before us. For there are two separate tasks.

"One is the meeting of crises; the other is the slower, but more positive, task of nation building, of helping to build a system of stable, strong, and independent states which have solved the problem of both political and economic development."

*   *   *

"By 1960 the situation had so deteriorated that it seemed possible the Viet Cong would be able to establish a territorial base in South Viet-Nam, the next step in the Mao formula for a successful 'national liberation movement.' At this point, President Kennedy sent General Maxwell Taylor to South Viet-Nam to confer with the Vietnamese Government and to observe the situation for himself. General Taylor reported that the Vietnamese people retained the will to fight communism and that, given more extensive support, had a chance to defeat the Viet Cong.

"While this support has come predominantly from the United States, a number of other countries have provided significant support, moral and material.

"The first requirement of the struggle today is to pull the teeth of the Viet Cong terrorist campaign. This can best be done not so much by killing the terrorists but by depriving them of the opportunity to coerce the farmers into providing supplies and recruits. This can only be done by providing practical protection to the farming population. The technique which has been adopted to achieve this protection is the construction of fortified villages, called strategic hamlets. This technique was used successfully in Malaya against the Communist movement there. The same concept had been applied successfully in the late 1790's by the Manchu dynasty of China against the White Lotus sect, a fanatical group whose use of terror resembled closely the methods of the present-day Viet Cong."

*   *   *

"The struggle in Viet-Nam gains the headlines in today's newspapers. But throughout Asia, new nations, in varying degrees, are facing the challenge of creating progressive, yet stable, societies in a world of uncertainty. American policy aims to provide our experience, our enthusiasm, and, insofar as our resources permit, our material aid to this great enterprise of nation building."

*   *   *

"Thirdly, while we are combating Communist imperialism in all its forms, we must remember that it is not enough to be against something and that in the last analysis success depends upon our ability to build, to construct, to contribute to man's spiritual and material welfare. We are cooperating with many free peoples in great efforts at nation building, while the Communists try to tear down, in order to impose their hold and their system on the world.

"Fourthly, there is a larger need for tolerance in international life. Happily there is a growing understanding among us of the diverse ways by which different peoples seek to obtain happiness and security in a troubled world. In passing I also wish to observe that, remembering our own unfinished business in fulfilling the ideals of the American Constitution, we must be tolerant of the shortcomings we may see in other societies. While we are justifiably proud of our institutions and our freedoms and stand as leaders in the democratic world, our prestige and influence in the world suffer whenever we fall short of our own ideals."

*   *   *

35. *President Kennedy's News Conference, July 17, 1963, Public Papers of the Presidents, Kennedy, 1963, p. 569:*

*   *   *

Q: "Mr. President, there has been a good deal of public concern about the political situation in South Viet-Nam, and I would like to ask you whether the difficulties between the Buddhist population there and the South Vietnamese Government has been an impediment to the effectiveness of American aid in the war against the Viet Cong?"

THE PRESIDENT: "Yes, I think it has. I think it is unfortunate that this dispute has arisen at the very time when the military struggle has been going better than it has been going in many months. I would hope that some solution could be reached for this dispute, which certainly began as a religious dispute, and because we have invested a tremendous amount of effort and it is going quite well.

"I do realize of course, and we all have to realize, that Viet-Nam has been in war for 20 years. The Japanese came in, the war with the French, the civil war which has gone on for 10 years, and this is very difficult for any society to stand. It is a country which has got a good many problems and it is divided, and there is guerrilla activity and murder and all of the rest. Compounding this, however, now is a religious dispute. I would hope this would be settled, because we want to see a stable government there, carrying on a struggle to maintain its national independence.

"We believe strongly in that. We are not going to withdraw from that effort. In my opinion, for us to withdraw from that effort would mean a collapse not only of South Viet-Nam, but Southeast Asia. So we are going to stay there. We hope with the great effort which is being carried by the Vietnamese themselves, and they have been in this field a lot longer than we have, and with a good deal more deaths and casualties, that behind this military shield put up by the Vietnamese people they can reach an agreement on the civil disturbances and also in respect for the rights of others. That's our hope. That's our effort. That—we're bringing our influence to bear. And the decision is finally theirs, but I think that before we render too harsh a judgment on the people, we should realize that they are going through a harder time than we have had to go through."

*   *   *

36. *Deputy Director of Viet-Nam Working Group, Theodore J.C. Heavner, Address Made Before National Sec & Leg Committee at the National Convention of Veterans of Foreign Wars, in Seattle, Washington, August 25, 1963, "The Viet-Nam Situation," Department of State Bulletin, September 9, 1963, p. 392:*

*   *   *

"In the light of long-term trends in Communist and free Asia let me now review the elements of U.S. strategy and policy. Our policy in the Far East can be summed up in these four points:

"1. To stand firmly behind our commitments to the defense of independent nations and to turn back any aggressive thrust from communism;

"2. To contribute as we are able to the prosperity and development of nations which request our assistance as the surest way of helping to build a system of free, viable, and strong nations in Asia;

"3. To recognize the value of initiatives by the Pacific nations themselves to develop their own modes of cooperation and communication, and to stand ready to assist when called upon to do so;

"4. To work patiently for the realization of a Pacific community of nations so prosperous and progressive that its attraction will prove, in the long run, irresistible to those peoples now kept by their rulers from participation in it."

*   *   *

The Guerrilla War in Viet-Nam

"To understand why President Kennedy said in his state of the Union message that 'The spearpoint of aggression has been blunted in South Viet-Nam,' we need to consider the situation in the fall of 1961 and early 1962. The Vietnamese were quite plainly losing their fight against the Communist guerrillas then.

"The Communist guerrillas, 1,500 strong, took and held overnight a provincial capital in September of 1961, and, to underline the fact, they publicly beheaded the Chief of Province there. The flow of rice into Saigon, normally a rice export center, was choked off by the guerrillas to the point where the United States sent P.L. 480 rice to Saigon in early 1962. Enemy attacks in January of last year were running at the rate of more than 120 per week. We even feared that the Communist Viet Cong might soon be able to declare 'a liberated area' somewhere in the highlands.

"Faced with this deteriorating situation, President Diem in December of 1961 sent a letter to President Kennedy in which he outlined the nature of the attack on his government and asked for increased American assistance. The United States considered this request very carefully. Vice President Johnson had visited Viet-Nam in May of 1961, and President Kennedy had sent General [Maxwell

D.] Taylor to Viet-Nam again in the fall of that year. So we were very clear about the nature of the threat.

"We knew that the Viet Cong attack was caused, led, and directed by the Communist authorities in North Viet-Nam. This was a case of Communist aggression, although the Communists made great efforts to conceal the fact, aggression against a friendly people with whom the United States had strong ties. There could be little question about our decision. We promptly agreed to step up our military and economic assistance.

"When we increased our assistance to Viet-Nam we issued a study of the evidence of Communist infiltration into South Viet-Nam and Communist direction of the war against the Government of South Viet-Nam. This was necessary, not just out of a 'decent respect for the opinions of mankind,' but because of the great and continuing Communist effort to portray the Viet Cong as an indigenuous and legitimate popular movement against a repressive government. I think it is worth noting in this connection that the international body specifically established in 1954 at the Geneva conference to oversee and keep the peace in Viet-Nam—the International Control Commission, composed of India, Canada, and Poland—has confirmed the fact that Communist North Viet-Nam is engaged in an attempt to overthrow by violence the Government of South Viet-Nam. After sifting the evidence for almost a year, the International Control Commission in June of 1962 issued a special report which makes it clear that the Viet Cong are the instruments of Hanoi's deliberate attack on South Viet-Nam.

"If we were losing the war in the fall of 1961 and early 1962, where are we today? I think it is fair to say that the tide has now turned and that the Government of Viet-Nam is with our help slowly overcoming the Communist guerrillas. No more provincial capitals have been taken, the Communists have not 'liberated' any part of South Viet-Nam, and Saigon is once again exporting rice. In fact we anticipate that Saigon will export 300,000 tons of rice this year.

*   *   *

The 'Why,' of Our Involvement

"I have described the American role in the Vietnamese war—the 'how' of our involvement. I would like to close by indicating something of the 'why.'

"You can think of Viet-Nam as a piece of strategic real estate. It is on the corner of mainland Asia, across the east-west trade routes, and in a position that would make it an excellent base for further Communist aggression against the rest of free Asia.

"You can think of our involvement in South Viet-Nam in terms of a moral commitment. The Vietnamese, on the frontier of the free world, are fighting not just for themselves but for all men who wish to remain free. I believe the 300–500 casualties they suffer each week is a precious contribution to the security of the whole free world.

"You can think of the American role in South Viet-Nam in terms of our SEATO [Southeast Asia Treaty Organization] commitment. You can regard it as a fulfillment of the implied obligation which we as a nation undertook when we said at the Geneva Conference in 1954 that we would regard any renewal of aggression in violation of the Geneva Agreements with grave concern and as seriously threatening international peace and security.

"You can think of South Viet-Nam as a test case; there is good reason to believe that this is the view of the Communist bloc. In Viet-Nam we are determining whether or not the free world can help a nation defend itself against the subversion and guerrilla warfare which make up the 'war of national liberation' tactics. I think it is fair to say that we have largely stopped the Communist thrust all around the world in conventional and nuclear terms. We are now confronted by a new kind of threat, and we have to a degree invented a new kind of response to meet it. All of the underdeveloped nations of the world are watching the event. If South Viet-Nam falls, their will to resist this kind of aggression will be weakened and the whole fabric of free-world strength and determination damaged thereby.

"Perhaps, in more human terms, you may want to think of our support to Viet-Nam as American help to the nearly 1 million Vietnamese refugees who fled North Viet-Nam in 1954 and 1955 to avoid living under a Communist regime."

37. *President Kennedy's TV Interview, September 25, 1963, Department of State Bulletin, September 30, 1963, p. 499:*

* * *

Mr. Cronkite: "Hasn't every indication from Saigon been that President Diem has no intention of changing his pattern?"

President Kennedy: "If he does not change it, of course, that is his decision. He has been there 10 years, and, as I say, he has carried this burden when he has been counted out on a number of occasions.

"Our best judgment is that he can't be successful on this basis. We hope that he comes to see that; but in the final analysis it is the people and the Government itself who have to win or lose this struggle. All we can do is help, and we are making it very clear. But I don't agree with those who say we should withdraw. That would be a great mistake. I know people don't like Americans to be engaged in this kind of an effort. Forty-seven Americans have been killed in combat with the enemy, but this is a very important struggle even though it is far away.

"We took all this—made this effort to defend Europe. Now Europe is quite secure. We also have to participate—we may not like it—in the defense of Asia."

* * *

38. *President Kennedy's NBC Interview, September 9, 1963, Department of State Bulletin, September 30, 1963, p. 499:*

* * *

Mr. Huntley: "Mr. President, in respect to our difficulties in South Viet-Nam, could it be that our Government tends occasionally to get locked into a policy or an attitude and then finds it difficult to alter or shift that policy?"

THE PRESIDENT: "Yes, that is true. I think in the case of South Viet-Nam we have been dealing with a Government which is in control, has been in control for 10 years. In addition, we have felt for the last 2 years that the struggle against the Communists was going better. Since June, however—the difficulties with the Buddhists—we have been concerned about a deterioration, particularly in the Saigon area, which hasn't been felt greatly in the outlying areas but may spread. So we are faced with the problem of wanting to protect the area against the Communists. On the other hand, we have to deal with the Government there. That produces a kind of ambivalence in our efforts which exposes us to some criticism. We are using our influence to persuade the Government there to take those steps which will win back support. That takes some time, and we must be patient, we must persist."

Mr. Huntley: "Are we likely to reduce our aid to South Viet-Nam now?"

THE PRESIDENT: "I don't think we think that would be helpful at this time. If you reduce your aid, it is possible you could have some effect upon the government structure there. On the other hand, you might have a situation which could bring about a collapse. Strongly in our mind is what happened in the case of China at the end of World War II, where China was lost—a weak government became increasingly unable to control events. We don't want that."

Mr. Brinkley: "Mr. President, have you had any reason to doubt this so-called 'domino theory,' that if South Viet-Nam falls, the rest of Southeast Asia will go behind it?"

THE PRESIDENT: "No, I believe it. I believe it. I think that the struggle is close enough. China is so large, looms so high just beyond the frontiers, that if South Viet-Nam went, it would not only give them an improved geographic position for a guerrilla assault on Malaya but would also give the impression that the wave of the future in Southeast Asia was China and the Communists. So I believe it."

*　　*　　*

39. *President Kennedy's News Conference, September 12, 1963, Public Papers of the Presidents, Kennedy, 1963, p. 673:*

*　　*　　*

Q. "Mr. President, in view of the prevailing confusion, is it possible to state today just what this Government's policy is toward the current government of South Viet-Nam?

THE PRESIDENT: "I think I have stated what my view is and we are for those things and those policies which help win the war there. That is why some 25,000 Americans have traveled 10,000 miles to participate in that struggle. What helps to win the war, we support; what interferes with the war effort, we oppose. I have already made it clear that any action by either government which may handicap the winning of the war is inconsistent with our policy or our objectives. This is the test which I think every agency and official of the United States Government must apply to all of our actions, and we shall be applying that test in various ways in the coming months, although I do not think it desirable to state all of our views at this time. I think they will be made more clear as time goes on.

"But we have a very simple policy in that area, I think. In some ways I think the Vietnamese people and ourselves agree; we want the war to be won, the Communists to be contained, and the Americans to go home. That is our policy. I am sure it is the policy of the people of Viet-Nam. But we are not there to see a war lost, and we will follow the policy which I have indicated today of advancing those causes and issues which help win the war."

*　　*　　*

40. *President Kennedy's Remarks at the Yellowstone County Fairgrounds, Billings, Montana, September 25, 1963, Public Papers of the Presidents, Kennedy, 1963, p. 724:*

*　　*　　*

". . . Countries which we had never heard of before, Viet-Nam, Laos, the Congo, and the others, countries which were distant names in our geographies, have now become matters of the greatest concern, where the interests of the United States are vitally involved, and where we have, for example, in Viet-Nam, over 25,000 of your sons and brothers bearing arms.

"So this is a difficult and complex world. I am sure a citizen in this community and in this country must wonder what we are doing. I think what we are trying to do is comparatively simple, and that is, with our own power and might—and the only country which has that power and might—and, I believe, the long-range determination and perseverance, we are trying to assist the hundred-odd countries which are now independent to maintain their independence. We do that not only because we wish them to be free, but because it serves our own national interest. As long as there are all of these countries separate, free, and independent, and not part of one great monolithic bloc which threatens us, so long we are free and independent.

"When it appeared at the end of the fifties that there would be over a billion people organized in the Communist movement, Russia and China and Eastern Europe working closely together, that represented a danger to us which could turn the balance of power against us. As there has been a division within the bloc, as there has been a fragmentation behind the Iron Curtain, as the long-range interests of geography and nationalism play a part even behind the Iron Curtain, as it does on this side of the Iron Curtain, we have made progress, not toward an easier existence, but, I think, toward a chance for a more secure existence.

"In 1961 the United States and the Soviet Union came face to face over Berlin. The United States called up more than 150,000 troops. At the meeting in Vienna, of 1961, Mr. Khrushchev informed me that he was going to sign a peace treaty in Berlin by the end of the year, and if the United States continued to supply its forces in Berlin it would be regarded as a possible act of war. In 1962 we came face to face with the same great challenge in Cuba, in October. So we have lived, even in the short space of the last 3 years, on two occasions when we were threatened with a direct military confrontation. We wish to lessen that prospect. We know that the struggle between the Communist system and ourselves will go on. We know it will go on in economics, in productivity, in ideology, in Latin America and Africa, in the Middle East and Asia."

*   *   *

41. *President Kennedy's Remarks at the High School Memorial Stadium, Great Falls, Montana, September 26, 1963, Public Papers of the Presidents, Kennedy, 1963, p. 727:*

"I know that there are many of you who sit here and wonder what it is that causes the United States to go so far away, that causes you to wonder why so many of your sons should be stationed so far away from our own territory, who wonder why it is since 1945 that the United States has assisted so many countries. You must wonder when it is all going to end and when we can come back home. Well, it isn't going to end, and this generation of Americans has to make up its mind for our security and for our peace, because what happens in Europe or Latin America or Africa or Asia directly affects the security of the people who live in this city, and particularly those who are coming after.

"I make no apologies for the effort that we make to assist these other countries to maintain their freedom, because I know full well that every time a country, regardless of how far away it may be from our own borders—every time that country passes behind the Iron Curtain the security of the United States is thereby endangered. So all those who suggest we withdraw, all those who suggest we should no longer ship our surplus food abroad or assist other countries, I could not disagree with them more. This country is stronger now than it has ever been. Our chances for peace are stronger than they have been in years. The nuclear test ban which was strongly led in the Senate of the United States by Mike Mansfield and Lee Metcalf is, I believe, a step toward peace and a step toward security, and gives us an additional chance that all of the weapons of Montana will never be fired. That is the object of our policy.

"So we need your support. These are complicated problems which face a citizenry. Most of us grew up in a relative period of isolation, and neutrality, and unalignment which was our policy from the time of George Washington to the Second World War, and suddenly, in an act almost unknown in the history of the world, we were shoved onto the center of the stage. We are the keystone in the arch of freedom. If the United States were to falter, the whole world, in my opinion, would inevitably begin to move toward the Communist bloc.

"It is the United States, this country, your country, which in 15 to 18 years has almost singlehandedly protected the freedom of dozens of countries who, in turn, by being free, protect our freedom. So when you ask why are we in Laos, or Viet-Nam, or the Congo, or why do we support the Alliance for Progress in Latin America, we do so because we believe that our freedom is tied up with theirs, and if we can develop a world in which all the countries are free, then the threat to the security of the United States is lessened. So we have to stay at it. We must not be fatigued."

*   *   *

42. *U.S. Policy on Viet-Nam*: *White House Statement, October 2, 1963, Department of State Bulletin, October 21, 1963, p. 623:*

"1. The security of South Viet-Nam is a major interest of the United States as other free nations. We will adhere to our policy of working with the people and Government of South Viet-Nam to deny this country to communism and to suppress the externally stimulated and supported insurgency of the Viet Cong as promptly as possible. Effective performance in this undertaking is the central objective of our policy in South Viet-Nam."

*   *   *

"5. It remains the policy of the United States in South Viet-Nam as in other parts of the world, to support the efforts of the people of that country to defeat aggression and to build a peaceful and free society."

*   *   *

43. *President Kennedy's Remarks Prepared for Delivery at the Trade Mart in Dallas, November 22, 1963, Public Papers of the Presidents, Kennedy, 1963, p. 890:*

*   *   *

"I want to discuss with you today the status of our strength and our security because this question clearly calls for the most responsible qualities of leadership and the most enlightened products of scholarship. For this Nation's strength and security are not easily or cheaply obtained, nor are they quickly and simply explained. There are many kinds of strength and no one kind will suffice. Overwhelming nuclear strength cannot stop a guerrilla war. Formal pacts of alliance cannot stop internal subversion. Displays of material wealth cannot stop the disillusionment of diplomats subjected to discrimination.

"Above all, words alone are not enough. The United States is a peaceful nation. And where our strength and determination are clear, our words need merely to convey conviction, not belligerence. If we are strong, our strength will speak for itself. If we are weak, words will be of no help.

"I realize that this Nation often tends to identify turning-points in world affairs with the major addresses which preceded them. But it was not the Monroe Doctrine that kept all Europe away from this hemisphere—it was the strength of the British fleet and the width of the Atlantic Ocean. It was not General Marshall's speech at Harvard which kept communism out of Western Europe —it was the strength and stability made possible by our military and economic assistance.

"In this administration also it has been necessary at times to issue specific warnings—warnings that we could not stand by and watch the Communists conquer Laos by force, or intervene in the Congo, or swallow West Berlin, or maintain offensive missiles on Cuba. But while our goals were at least temporarily obtained in these and other instances, our successful defense of freedom was due not to the words we used, but to the strength we stood ready to use on behalf of the principles we stand ready to defend."

*   *   *

"But American military might should not and need not stand alone against the ambitions of international communism. Our security and strength, in the last analysis, directly depend on the security and strength of others, and that is why our military and economic assistance plays such a key role in enabling those who live on the periphery of the Communist world to maintain their independence of choice. Our assistance to these nations can be painful, risky and costly, as is true in Southeast Asia today. But we dare not weary of the task. For our assistance makes possible the stationing of 3-5 million allied troops along the Communist frontier at one-tenth the cost of maintaining a comparable number of American soldiers. A successful Communist breakthrough in these areas, necessitating direct United States intervention, would cost us several times as much as our entire foreign aid program, and might cost us heavily in American lives as well."

*   *   *

Glossary

AAA   Antiaircraft Artillery

ACR   Armored Cavalry Regiment

ABM   Antiballistic Missile

ABN   Airborne

ADP   Automatic Data Processing

AFB   Air Force Base

AID   Agency for International Development

AIROPS   Air Operations

AM   Airmobile

AMB   Ambassador

ANG   Air National Guard

APB   Self-propelled barracks ship

ARL   Landing craft repair ship

ARVN   Army of the Republic of [South] Vietnam

ASA   U.S. Army Security Agency

ASAP   As soon as possible

ASD   Assistant Secretary of Defense

BAR   Browning automatic rifle

BDE   Brigade

BLT   Battalion Landing Team

BN   Battalion

BOB   Bureau of the Budget

B-52   U.S. heavy bomber

B-57   U.S. medium bomber

CAP   Combined Action Platoon

CAS   Saigon Office of the U.S. Central Intelligence Agency

CDC   Combat Development Command

CG   Civil Guard

CHICOM   Chinese Communist

CHMAAG   Chief, Military Assistance Advisory Group

CI   Counterinsurgency

CIA   Central Intelligence Agency

CIDG   Civilian Irregular Detachment Group

CINCPAC   Commander in Chief, Pacific

CIP   Counterinsurgency Plan

CNO VNN   Chief of Naval Operations, Vietnamese Navy

CJCS   Chairman, Joint Chiefs of Staff

CMD   Capital Military District

COMUS   U.S. Commander

COMUSMACV   Commander, U.S. Military Assistance Command, Vietnam

CONARC   Continental Army Command

CONUS   Continental United States

CORDS   Civil Operations and Revolutionary Development Support [pacification]

COS   Chief of Station, CIA

CPR   Chinese Peoples Republic

CPSVN   Comprehensive Plan for South Vietnam

CTZ   Corps tactical zone

CY   Calendar year

DCM   Deputy Chief of Mission

DCPG   Defense Command Planning Group

DEPTEL   [State] Department telegram

DESOTO   Destroyer patrols off North Vietnam

DIA   Defense Intelligence Agency

DMZ   Demilitarized Zone separating North and South Vietnam

DOD   Department of Defense

DPM   Draft Presidential Memorandum [from the Secretary of Defense]

DRV   Democratic Republic of [North] Vietnam

DULTE   Cable identifier, from Secretary of State Dulles to addressee

ECM   Electronic Countermeasures

EXDIS   Exclusive (high level) distribution

FAL and FAR   Royal Armed Forces of Laos

FARMGATE   Clandestine U.S. Air Force unit in Vietnam, 1964

FE and FEA   Bureau of Far Eastern Affairs in the State Department

FEC   French Expeditionary Corps

FLAMING DART   Code name of bombing operations, in reprisal for attacks on U.S. forces

FOA   Foreign Operations Administration

FWMA   Free World Military Assistance

FWMAF   Free World Military Assistance Force

FY   Fiscal Year
FYI   For your information
GRC   Government of the Republic of China (Nationalist China)
GVN   Government of [South] Vietnam
G-3   U.S. Army General Staff, Branch for Plans and Operations
HES   Hamlet Evaluation System
HNC   High National Council
Hop Tac   Program to clear and hold land around Saigon, 1964
IBP   International Balance of Payments
ICA   International Cooperation Administration
ICC   International Control Commission
IDA   Institute for Defense Analyses
IMCSH   Inter-ministerial Committee for Strategic Hamlets
INR   Bureau of Intelligence and Research in the Department of State
ISA   Office of International Security Affairs in the Department of Defense
I Corps   Northern military region of South Vietnam
II Corps   Central military region in South Vietnam
III Corps   Military region in South Vietnam surrounding Saigon
IV Corps   Southern military region in South Vietnam
JCS   Joint Chiefs of Staff
JCSM   Joint Chiefs of Staff Memorandum
JGS   Vietnamese Joint General Staff
JOC   Joint Operations Center
Joint Staff   Staff organization for the Joint Chiefs of Staff
JUSPAO   Joint United States Public Affairs Office, Saigon
J-2   Intelligence Branch, U.S. Army
KANZUS   Korean, Australian, New Zealand, and U.S.
KIA   Killed in action
LANTFLT   Atlantic Fleet
LOC   Lines of communications (roads, bridges, rail)
LST   Tank Landing Ship
LTC   Lt. Col.
MAAG   Military Assistance Advisory Group.
MAB   Marine Amphibious Brigade
MAC   Military Assistance Command
MACCORDS   Military Assistance Command, Civil Operations and Revolutionary Development Support
MAF   Marine Amphibious Force
MAP   Military Assistance Program

MAROPS   Maritime Operations
MEB   Marine Expeditionary Brigade
MEF   Marine Expeditionary Force
MIA   Missing in action
MDAP   Mutual Defense Assistance Program
MOD   Minister of Defense
MORD   Ministry of Revolutionary Development
MRC   Military Revolutionary Committee
MR5   Highland Area
NATO   North Atlantic Treaty Organization
NCO   Non-commissioned officer
NFLSV   National Front for the Liberation of South Vietnam
NIE   National Intelligence Estimate
NLF   National Liberation Front
NODIS   No distribution (beyond addressee)
NSA   National Security Agency (specializes in electronic intelligence, i.e. monitoring radio communications)
NSAM   National Security Action Memorandum (pronounced nas-sam; described presidential decisions under Kennedy and Johnson)
NSC   National Security Council
NVA   North Vietnamese Army
NVN   North Vietnam
OB   Order of battle
OCO   Office of Civil Operations [pacification]
O&M   Operations and Management
Opcon   Operations Control
OPLAN   Operations Plan
Ops   Operations
OSA   Office of the Secretary of the Army
OSD   Office of the Secretary of Defense
PACFLT   Pacific Fleet
PACOM   Pacific Command
PAT   Political Action Team
PAVN   People's Army of [North] Vietnam
PBR   River Patrol Boat
PDJ   Plaine Des Jarres, Laos
PF   Popular Forces
PFF   Police Field Force
PL   Pathet Lao
PNG   Provisional National Government
POL   Petroleum, oil, lubricants
POLAD   Political adviser (usually, State Department representative assigned to a military commander)
PRV   People's Republic of Vietnam

PSYOP   Psychological Operations
qte   Quote
RAS   River Assault Squadron
RCT   Regimental Combat Team
RD   Rural (or Revolutionary) Development
RECCE   Reconnaissance
Reclama   Protest against a cut in budget or program
RF   Regional Forces
RLAF   Royal Laotian Air Force
RLG   Royal Laotian Government
RLT   Regimental Landing Team
ROK   Republic of [South] Korea
Rolling Thunder   Code name for sustained bombing of North Vietnam
rpt   Repeat
RSSZ   Rung Sat Special Zone (east of Saigon)
RT   Rolling Thunder Program
RTA   Royal Thai Army
RVN   Republic of [South] Vietnam
RVNAF   Republic of Vietnam Air Force or Armed Forces
RVNF   Republic of Vietnam Forces
SA   Systems Analysis Office in the Department of Defense
SAC   Strategic Air Command
SACSA   Special Assistant [to the JCS] for Counterinsurgency and Special [covert] Activities
SAM   Surface-to-air missile
SAR   Search and Rescue
SDC   Self Defense Corps
SEA   Southeast Asia
SEACOOR   Southeast Asia Coordinating Committee
SEATO   Southeast Asia Treaty Organization
SecDef   Secretary of Defense
SECTO   Cable identifier, from Secretary of State to addressee
Sitrep   Situation Report
SMM   Saigon Military Mission
SNIE   Special National Intelligence Estimate
SQD   Squadron
STRAF   Strategic Army Force

SVN   South Vietnam
TAOR   Tactical Area of Responsibility
TCS   Tactical Control System
TEDUL   Cable identifier, overseas post to Secretary of State Dulles
TERM   Temporary Equipment Recovery Mission
TF   Task force
TFS   Tactical Fighter Squadron
TO&E   Table of organization and equipment (for a military unit)
TOSEC   Cable identifier, from overseas post to Secretary of State
TRIM   Training Relations and Instruction Mission
TRS   Tactical Reconnaissance Squadron
34A   1964 operations plan covering covert actions against North Vietnam
T-28   U.S. fighter-bomber
UE   Unit equipment allowance
UH-1   Helicopter
UK   United Kingdom
USAF   U.S. Air Force
USARAL   U.S. Army, Alaska
USAREUR   U.S. Army, Europe
USASGV   U.S. Army Support Group, Vietnam
USG   United States Government
USIA   U.S. Information Agency
USIB   U.S. Intelligence Board
USIS   U.S. Information Service
USOM   U.S. Operations Mission (for economic assistance)
VC   Viet Cong
VM   Viet Minh
VN   Vietnam
VNA   Vietnamese National Army
VNAF   [South] Vietnamese Air Force or Armed Forces
VNQDD   Vietnam Quocdandang (pre-independence, nationalistic political party)
VNSF   [South] Vietnamese Special Forces
VOA   Voice of America
WESTPAC   Western Pacific Command
WIA   Wounded in action